Les démonstrations correctes ne sont jamais,
en définitive, qu'une «mise en forme» de l'intuition.

Jean Dieudonné

To Elisabeth,
Annick and Alain,
Pascale, Johan, Elena and Emily

ADVANCED RISK THEORY

Directeur de la collection « Actuariat »
Marc Hallin

Dans la même collection

Les nouveaux produits d'assurance-vie,
Thierry Delvaux et Martine Magnée, 1991

Finance stochastique,
Pierre Devolder, 1993

EDITIONS DE L'UNIVERSITÉ DE BRUXELLES
SWISS ASSOCIATION OF ACTUARIES

ADVANCED RISK THEORY

A SELF-CONTAINED INTRODUCTION

F. ETIENNE DE VYLDER

FOREWORDS BY HANS BÜHLMANN AND HANS U. GERBER

COLLECTION
ACTUARIAT

Avenue Paul Héger 26 - 1000 Bruxelles (Belgique)
D/1996/0171/11
ISBN 2-8004-1142-2
Printed in Belgium

Forewords

Part I

Risk Theory has its roots in the first half of this century. Pioneers such as Harald Cramér and Bruno De Finetti have contributed to it, and ever since then the discipline has become a fascinating combination of applied probability and actuarial science. This monograph extends the tradition in a commendable way.

Professor Fl. De Vylder is a researcher with an international reputation. He contributed substantially to the advancement of risk theory, on the one hand as a cofounder (together with Marc Goovaerts and the late Jean Haezendonck) of the Journal *Insurance: Mathematics and Economics*, and on the other hand through a series of well known papers that were published in the *Astin Bulletin*, the *Scandinavian Actuarial Journal*, *Insurance: Mathematics and Economics*, and the *Bulletin of the Swiss Actuarial Association*.

This monograph includes some very recent results and it is unique in its kind. Rarely researchers take the time to write a book that is at an advanced level and nevertheless largely self-contained, and in this respect the monograph is a noteworthy exception. This will be appreciated by students and colleagues of Professor De Vylder alike. The *Swiss Association of Actuaries* is pleased to be involved in the publication of the monograph.

The monograph contains three parts. Part I is devoted to Ruin Theory, which is at the heart of Risk Theory. It provides a modern and original treatment of the topic. The spectrum of the text extends from elegant applications of martingales to very practical aspects such as the numerical evaluation of the probability of ruin.

Lausanne, March 1996, Hans U. Gerber.

Part II

Practical actuaries have always worried how moments of claims distribution relate to premiums to be charged. Mathematically this leads very often to the problem

Maximize $L(F)$ ~ functional of the claims distribution

given $\alpha_1(F),\ldots,\alpha_p(F)$ ~ moments of F up to order p.

The most famous example is

F with support [a,b],
L ~ expected stop loss premium,
$\alpha_1(F)$ ~ mean of F.

Prof. De Vylder has been one of the first actuaries who has worked in this domain and it is hence very instructive to read this monograph giving all ramifications of the basic problem.

The practical actuary should learn from this text how many of his daily problems can be put into a very general optimization scheme, which often leads to solutions providing better understanding of his practical work. So also the practitioner should make an effort to study the basic ideas of this volume. If he/she succeeds he/she will be an even more successful practitioner.

Zürich, March 28, 1996, Hans Bühlmann.

Part III

Credibility Techniques have become a decisive tool for actuarial work in Non-Life area. In particular in Motor Insurance they provide the theoretical basis for Bonus-Malus Systems but their range of application is much wider. Generally speaking credibility provides the basis for rational assessments of premiums and reserves in all situations where the actuary is confronted with a heterogeneous portfolio of risks.

The technical approach to credibility can be formulated in different ways. Prof. De Vylder has been among the first actuarial pioneers to advance a technique based on Hilbert Space Theory. In this setup credibility estimates become projections on appropriate (translated) subspaces. It is to be noted that this view helps by elegant reasoning to bypass explicit intricate least squares calculations in many cases.

It is a pleasure for me to congratulate Prof. De Vylder on this well written part and to recommend it for reading to all those actuaries who in particular not just want to find the right numbers for their problem but who wish to gain more insight into some of their most fundamental concepts.

Zürich, March 28, 1996, Hans Bühlmann.

Preface

Risk Theory is based on Probability Theory and Statistics, Stochastic Processes, Renewal Theory, Functional Analysis, Optimization Theory and Hilbert Space Theory. The potential user of Risk Theory is any person involved in some risk business. The user by excellence, is the actuary. It is not realistic to require that the non-academic reader is familiar with all the indicated topics.

My own experience is that I put books with too many results or demonstrations based on other publications very quickly aside. With these facts in mind, I started the redaction of this *Advanced Risk Theory, A Self-Contained Introduction*. The mathematical reader will find complete proofs. The more technical demonstrations are presented in Appendices. There, simplified particular cases of great classical results are completely proved.

The book does not suppose any familiarity with continuous-time stochastic processes. All stochastic processes are defined in a deterministic way from stochastic sequences. The exceptions to this rule are two sections dealing with martingales. They can be omitted, without interruption of the understanding of the other matters.

Part I. Ruin Theory

Beyond the classical model, very general risk models, with stochastic premium income process, or with general claim number process, are discussed. Algorithms are indicated for the numerical calculation of ruin probabilities in risk models with barriers, dividends, interests or variable security loadings.

Part II. Optimization Theory

Part II shows how to obtain best upper and lower bounds on functionals T(F) of the distribution F of a risk, under moment or other integral constraints. Examples of functionals T(F) are pure or loaded premiums of not or well reinsured risks, ruin probabilities (Schmitter's problem) and adjustment coefficients.

Part III. Credibility Theory

The great models of Modern Credibility Theory, initiated by Prof. Dr. Hans Bühlmann in his historical 1967 paper (see References) are developed by a uniform projection method in Hilbert space.

A remarkable property of modern credibility estimators is that they do not depend on the involved distributions: they are distribution-free. The credibility estimators depend on parameters and the latter must be estimated from the observable random variables. Large classes of unbiased distribution-free parameter estimators can be defined. Most of them are furnished by classical statistics.

Probably the most original characteristic of this Part III, is the research and determination of optimal parameter estimators. Unfortunately, optimal parameter estimators cannot always be derived in a completely distribution-free way. But a good amount of distribution freedom is preserved. Indeed, the unique assumptions adopted when necessary, are zero-excess assumptions. A zero-excess random variable X is such that $[X-E(X)]^4=3E^2[X-E(X)]^2$. Normal random variables are very particular zero-excess random variables. All estimators can be used if the zero-excess assumptions are not satisfied, but then they may lose some optimality.

Acknowledgments

I appreciate the favor of the *Swiss Association of Actuaries* to include this monograph in their collection and I am proud that my book can figure in the neighbourhood of Professor Straub's *Non-Life Insurance Mathematics*.

I am grateful to Mrs. Michèle Mat, Directeur of the *Editions de l'Université de Bruxelles*, to accept the publication of this book and to Professor Marc Hallin to welcome it in his collection *Actuariat*.

I am honoured by the Forewords of two very old masters. Of course, we actuaries reckon ages in operational time, measured by the volume and deepness of scientific achievements. Professor Hans Bühlmann, father of actuaries of all generations, is the creator of Modern Credibility Theory. His book *Mathematical Methods in Risk Theory* was my first classic. Professor Hans Gerber is responsible for the introduction of martingales in actuarial risk theory. His monograph *An Introduction to Mathematical Risk Theory* still inspires me today.

I have learned so much from so many colleagues and friends that it is impossible to mention them all. I specially admire the art and science of Professor Erwin Straub and Professor Greg Taylor to combine practice and theory. They were often on my mind when I developed practical applications.

I owe very much to Professor Marc Goovaerts. He involved our late friend Professor Jean Haezendonck and myself in great projects which could not have succeeded without his intelligence, courage and tenacity. Thanks to Marc, I could teach some matters of this book at the University of Leuven.

In Canada and specially through the Province of Québec, Professor André Prémont, chair of *L'Ecole d'actuariat de l'Université Laval*, kindly took care of the advertising for this book. Sincerest thanks, André. *Je me souviens*.

Ghent, June 1996, F. Etienne De Vylder

Table of Contents

Part I. Ruin Theory

I. Chapter 1. Basic Analysis, Convolutions and Renewal Equations

I. Chapter 2. Conditional Expectations

I. Chapter 3. Risk Models

I. Chapter 4. Point Processes

I. Chapter 5. Fixed-Time Ruin Probabilities

I. Chapter 6. Finite-Time Ruin Probabilities

I. Chapter 7. Infinite-Time Ruin Probabilities in Classical Risk Model

I. Chapter 9. Infinite-Time Ruin Probabilities in Risk Models with Stochastic Premium Income

I. Chapter 10. Discrete Risk Models

II. Chapter 4. General Optimization Problems

II. Chapter 6. Integral Optimization Problems

II. Chapter 7. Duals of Integral Optimization Problems

II. Chapter 8. Moment Problems by Dual Method

II. Chapter 9. General Optimization Algorithm

II. Chapter 10. Loaded Premium Problems

Part III. Credibility Theory

III. Chapter 1. Projections in Hilbert Space

III. Chapter 2. Elementary Classical Statistical Models

III. Chapter 3. Time-Homogeneous Credibility Theory

III. Chapter 4. Hilbert Spaces of Random Vectors and Random Matrices

III. Chapter 5. Classical Regression Models

III. Chapter 6. Credibility Regression Models

A Guide to Terminology and Notation

The notations $:=$, $=:$, $:\Leftrightarrow$, $\Leftrightarrow:$ are used for definitions. The defined symbol, or property, is on the side of the double point. The symbol $\equiv$ connects identical quantities expressed in different notations, or it indicates that a function has a constant value on some domain.

$$\mathbf{R}:=\,]-\infty,+\infty[,\ \mathbf{R}_+:=[0,\infty[,\ \mathbf{R}_{++}:=\,]0,\infty[,\ \mathbf{R}_- :=\,]-\infty,0],\ \mathbf{R}_{--}:=\,]-\infty,0[$$

$$\mathbf{N}:=\{...,-2,-1,0,1,2,...\},\ \mathbf{N}_+:=\{0,1,2,...\},\ \mathbf{N}_{++}:=\{1,2,...\},\ \mathbf{N}_{--}:=\{...,-2,-1\}$$

We call $\leq$ the **inequality symbol** and $<$ the **strict inequality symbol** and we use a corresponding consistent terminology. Examples:

x is **positive** $:\Leftrightarrow x \geq 0$, x is **strictly negative** $:\Leftrightarrow x < 0$.

The letters i,j,k,m,n denote **positive integers**, i.e. points of $\mathbf{N}_+$ (when nothing is specified) or **integers**, i.e. points of **N** (only when explicitly specified).

[a] is the **integer part** of a , Int(a) is the **integer closest to** a :

$[a]:= n\ (n \leq a < n+1)$, $\mathrm{Int}(a):= n\ (n-0.5 \leq a < n+0.5)$.

The **factorial powers** $\mathbf{a^{[k]}}$ and the **factorial exponents [k]** are defined by the relations

$$a^{[0]}:= 1\ ,\ a^{[k]} := a(a-1)(a-2)...(a-k+1)\ (k\in\mathbf{N}_{++}).$$

The meaning of [ ], integer part or factorial exponent, is always obvious from the context.

$$a\vee b := \max(a,b)\ ,\ a\wedge b := \min(a,b)\ ,\ a_+ := a\vee 0\ ,\ a_- := -(a\wedge 0)\ .$$

Iff is an abbreviation of **if and only if**. In definitions, **iff** is not used, but there the meaning of **if** is **iff** in all cases.

If **Prop(p)** is a proposition depending on p, then **Prop(p) (p∈A)** is an abbreviation of the proposition **p∈A⇒Prop(p)**, i.e. **For all p in A, Prop(p) is true**. It never means that **Prop(p)** is true for some particular p in A.

The set $CA:=\{x\in B/x\notin A\}$ is the **complement of the set A**, with respect to some fixed basic set B. The **indicator function** $\mathbf{1_A}$ **of the set A** is the function defined on B by the relations $1_A:=1$ on A, $1_A:=0$ on CA.

The **indicator function** $\mathbf{1_{Prop}}$ **of the proposition Prop** is defined by

$1_{\mathrm{Prop}} := 1$ if Prop is true , $1_{\mathrm{Prop}} := 0$ if Prop is false.

A **real function** is a function with values in **R** (when nothing is specified) or in $\mathbf{R}\cup\{-\infty,+\infty\}$ (only when explicitly specified).

Let $P_1,...,P_n$ be points (functions, random variables, ...). Then the following combinations may be meaningful: **A linear combination of $P_1,...,P_n$** is an expression

$$a_1P_1 + ... + a_nP_n \qquad (*)$$

with $a_1,...,a_n \in \mathbf{R}$. **A conical combination** is a linear combination (*) with $a_1,...,a_n \in \mathbf{R}_+$. **A convex combination** is a conical combination (*) with $a_1+...+a_n=1$. **An affine combination** is a linear combination (*) with $a_1+...+a_n=1$.

The set A **is closed under some operation**, if that operation is meaningful whenever it is applied to points in A, and if it then furnishes points in A. The set A is a **vector space,** or a **linear space**, if it is closed under the formation of linear combinations. It is a **cone**, or a **conical set**, if it is closed under the formation of conical combinations. It is a **convex set** if it closed under the formation of convex combinations. It is a **plane**, or an **affine set**, if it is closed under the formation of affine combinations.

The real function f defined on the linear (conical, convex, affine) set A, is **linear on** A, if $f(a_1P_1+...+a_nP_n)=a_1f(P_1)+...+a_nf(P_n)$ for all linear (conical, convex, affine) combinations (*) of points $P_1,...,P_n$ in A.

A flexible notation is used for **sequences** and **subsequences**. **A_n (n=1,2,...)** or **(A_1, A_2,...)** or **$A_1,A_2,...$** denote the sequence with elements $A_1,A_2,...$ Subsequences are represented by A_{n_k} , $A_{n(k)}$, $A_{n'}$, $A_{n''}$,...

The notation **$E=E_1+E_2+...$** expresses that E is the union of the sets E_k (k=1,2,...) and that these sets are non-overlapping: $E_i \cap E_j = \varnothing$ ($i \neq j$). Then the sequence $E_1,E_2,...$, finite or not, is **a partition of the set E**.

The set E is **enumerable** (or **denumerable** or **countable**) if its points can be arranged as a finite or infinite sequence $a_1,a_2,...$

The point λ (finite or not) is **a limit point of the real function f(x) as $x \to c$** (where c is finite or not), if a sequence x_n (n=1,2,...) exists such that $x_n \to c$ and $f(x_n) \to \lambda$ as $n \to \infty$. The smallest limit point and the largest limit point (which always exist) are represented by

$$\liminf_{x \to c} f(x) \ , \ \limsup_{x \to c} f(x)$$

resp. **The limit of f(x) as $x \to c$ exists** if only one limit point exists and then the latter point is **the limit**

$$\lim_{x \to c} f(x).$$

Similar definitions and notations are used in case of other types of convergence such as $x \uparrow c$, $x \downarrow c$, and also in discrete cases $k \to -\infty$, $k \to +\infty$. In the case $x \uparrow c$ it is assumed that $x<c$ (some authors use the notation $x \uparrow\uparrow c$ in order to insist on the strict inequality $x<c$). In the case $x \downarrow c$, it is assumed that $x>c$ (the notation $x \downarrow\downarrow c$ is used by some authors).

Comments printed in small characters can be ignored. They provide further technical information.

Part I

Ruin Theory

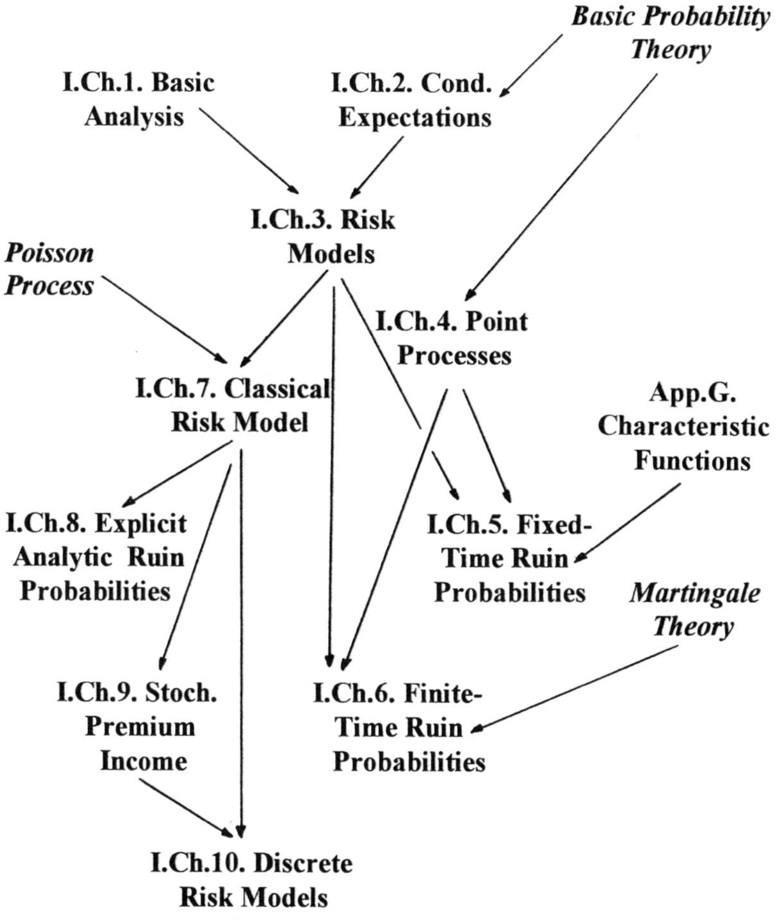

Exceptionally, proofs are based on connexions which are not indicated in the interdependency tables. Then only initial results of the not mentioned Chapters or Appendices are used or the proofs can be omitted without loss of continuity.

Chapter 1

Basic Analysis, Convolutions and Renewal Equations

1.1. Integration

1.1.1. Particular Functions on R

The functions on **R** considered in this book are real finite functions. In the particular cases in which infinite values are admitted, this is specified explicitly. The scalars a,b,...,x,... are supposed to be finite, unless the contrary is mentioned explicitly.

Distribution functions

A **distribution function** is any increasing, right-continuous function defined on **R**. Distribution functions are denoted by capital letters F,G,H,...,U,V,W.

For example, the **identity function** L on **R**, defined by $L(x):=x$ ($x\in\mathbf{R}$) is a distribution function.

Theorem 1

Let F_0, F_1, F_2, ... be positive distribution functions such that the function $F:=\sum_{k\geq 0} F_k$ is finite. Then F is a positive distribution function.

Proof
We prove that F is right-continuous at the point x. Let $\varepsilon>0$. We can take n so large that

$$\sum_{k>n} F_k(x+1) < \varepsilon .$$

because $F(x+1)<\infty$. Let $\delta_0 \in]0,1]$ be such that

$$F_k(x+\delta)-F_k(x) \leq \varepsilon/n \quad (k=0,1,\ldots,n\ ;\ 0\leq\delta\leq\delta_0).$$

This is possible because the functions $F_0,\ldots,F_n$ are right-continuous at the point x. Then, if $0\le\delta\le\delta_0$,

$$F(x+\delta)-F(x) = \sum_{k\le n}[F(x+\delta)-F(x)] + \sum_{k>n}[F(x+\delta)-F(x)]$$

$$\le \sum_{k\le n}[F(x+\delta)-F(x)] + \sum_{k>n} F(x+\delta) + \sum_{k>n} F(x)$$

$$\le \sum_{k\le n}[F(x+\delta)-F(x)] + \sum_{k>n} F(x+1) + \sum_{k>n} F(x+1) \le 3\varepsilon \bullet$$

Functions bounded on bounded intervals

The function f is **bounded on bounded intervals** if, for each bounded interval J, a constant b_J exists, such that $|f|\le b_J$ on J. All distribution functions are bounded on bounded intervals.

The function f, defined by $f(x):=1/x$ $(x\ne0)$, $f(0):=0$, is not bounded on bounded intervals.

Functions of bounded variation

In this book, differences of distribution functions are called **functions of bounded variation**. All functions of bounded variation are bounded on bounded intervals. Conversely, the "familiar" functions, bounded on bounded intervals, are functions of bounded variation.The function f defined by $f(x):= \sin(1/x)$ $(x\ne0)$, $f(0):=0$, is bounded, but it is not of bounded variation, because it oscillates too much at the point 0.

1.1.2. Distribution Functions and Measures

Let F be a distribution function. This is a **point function**, associating a value to points. Now we define a **set function**, attaching a value, called **mass**, to sets in **R**. This latter function is called a **measure**. It may have infinite values, and it is denoted by the same letter F as the original point function. We use the term **distribution** for the measure as well as for the distribution function. From the context, the meanings are always evident. The masses in the intervals are defined as follows:

$$F(]a,b]) := F(b)-F(a) \ , \ F([a\ b]) := F(b)-F(a-),$$

$$F(]a,b[) := F(b-)-F(a) \ , \ F([a,b[) := F(b-)-F(a-).$$

In these relations we may have $a=-\infty$, $b=+\infty$. In particular

$$F(\{a\}) = F([a,a]) = F(a)-F(a-) .$$

Of course,

$$F(x-) := \lim_{\varepsilon\downarrow 0} F(x-\varepsilon).$$

Here, the old-fashioned notation for intervals is convenient:

$$(a+,b+) \equiv]a,b] \ , \ (a-,b+) \equiv [a,b],$$

$$(a+,b-) \equiv]a,b[\ , \ (a-,b-) \equiv [a,b[.$$

Then the relations connecting the point function F and the interval function F can be displayed as

$$F((a\pm,b\pm)) = F(b\pm) - F(a\pm).$$

In such relations, a± can be a– (at all occurrences) or a+ (at all occurrences), and similarly for b±. Indeed, from the right continuity of F results that

$$F(x+) := \lim_{\varepsilon\downarrow 0} F(x+\varepsilon) = F(x).$$

We notice that the distribution functions F and F+c define the same measure. Often, the irrelevant additive constant c is fixed by the condition $F(-\infty)=0$.

The point **a** is an **atom** of the measure F if $F(\{a\})>0$. Hence, **a** is an atom of F iff it is a discontinuity point of the distribution function F, and then the mass at the point **a** equals the jump of the function F at **a**.

Measure theory proves that the set function F, already defined on the intervals in **R**, has a unique extension defined on a very large class of sets in **R**, called **Borel sets**, with the following **σ-additivity property**:

$$F(B_1+B_2+\ldots) = F(B_1)+F(B_2)+\ldots$$

for any sequence, finite or not, of non overlapping Borel sets $B_1,B_2,\ldots$ For the reader not familiar with Borel sets, it is enough to know that all the sets that he will ever encounter are Borel sets.

The Borel sets in $\mathbf{R}^n$ are the sets of the σ-algebra generated by the intervals.

We say that F is **concentrated on the set** B if F places no mass outside B, i.e. if F(**C**B)=0, where **C**B:= **R**–B is the **complement of the set B.**

The distribution resulting from the identity function L is the **Lebesgue measure**. Lebesgue measure is **length**, i.e. the Lebesgue measure of any interval is its usual length: $L((a\pm,b\pm))=b-a$. Here the condition $L(-\infty)=0$ cannot be satisfied by the introduction of an additive constant c.

1.1.3. Integrals

We assume that the reader has some familiarity with integrals such as

$$\int_B f(x)dF(x). \tag{1}$$

The abbreviated notation $\int_B fdF$ is also used for this integral. The set B is the **integration domain**. It may be omitted and then it is understood that B=**R**. The function f is the **integrated function**, or the **integrand** of the integral. The function F is the **distribution of the integral**. The integral (1) is the **integral of f on B with respect to F**.

Practical integral

In the practical cases, f is a rather regular function and B a simple set, say an interval. We assume the following for the moment: $B:=]a,b[$, the function F has a finite number of discontinuity points $d_1<...<d_n$ in B, and F has a continuous derivative on the intervals $]a,d_1[$, $]d_1,d_2[$, ... , $]d_{n-1},d_n[$, $]d_n,b[$. Then integral (1) equals

$$\begin{aligned}\int_{]a,b[} f(x)dF(x) = \int_{]a,d_1[} f(x)F'(x)dx + f(d_1)F(\{d_1\}) \\ + \int_{]d_1,d_2[} f(x)F'(x)dx + f(d_2)F(\{d_2\}) \\ + \dots \\ + \int_{]d_{n-1},d_n[} f(x)F'(x)dx + f(d_n)F(\{d_n\}) \\ + \int_{]d_n,b[} f(x)F'(x)dx,\end{aligned}$$

if the classical integrals in the last member are defined. If the integration domain is $[a,b[$, then the last member must be completed with the term $f(a)F(\{a\})$ if it is different from 0. Similarly, the integrals with integration domain $]a,b]$, $[a,b]$, $]-\infty,b[$, ... are defined.

General integral

The general integral (1) is defined if the following condition a. is satisfied, and if moreover one of the conditions b. or c. is satisfied:

a. F is a distribution function.

b. f is positive, possibly with infinite values. Then the integral (1) may have the value $+\infty$.

c. $$\int_B |f(x)|dF(x) < \infty. \tag{2}$$

The integral (2) exists by b.

The function f is F-integrable on B if condition (2) is satisfied. If $f \geq 0$, and condition (2) is not satisfied, then f is not F-integrable on B, but the integral (1) is nevertheless defined and considered (case b). This is current terminology.

The integration domain B is supposed to be a Borel set and the integrand f a Borel function. A Borel mapping $\mathbf{R}^m \to \mathbf{R}^n$ is a measurable mapping with respect to the Borel σ-algebras on $\mathbf{R}^m$ and on $\mathbf{R}^n$.

Integration with respect to functions of bounded variation

Let $g=F-G$ be a function of bounded variation, F and G distribution functions, and f a Borel function bounded on B. Then

$$\int_B f dg := \int_B f\, dF - \int_B f\, dG.$$

This definition does not depend on the decomposition $F-G$ of g.

1.1.4. Great Theorems

We here recall the **great theorems** of Modern Real Integration Theory. We indicate the useful forms, not the general versions. A general rule is that f can be replaced by g in the integral $\int f dF$ if $F(\{x/f(x) \neq g(x)\})=0$.

The following limits are limits as $n \uparrow \infty$. Convergences of functions are usual pointwise convergences (i.e. convergences at each fixed point x of the domain of the function), if nothing else is specified.

In the following Theorem 2, the functions f and f_n, and the integrals, may have infinite values. The notation $f_n \uparrow f$ implies that $f_1 \leq f_2 \leq \dots$ (with weak inequalities).

Theorem 2 (Monotone Convergence Theorem – Lebesgue)

Let $f_1, f_2, \dots$ be positive functions on B so that $f_n \uparrow f$ on B. Then

$$\int_B f_n\, dF \uparrow \int_B f\, dF \quad \bullet$$

Theorem 3 (Dominated Convergence Theorem – Lebesgue)

Let g be a positive F-integrable function on B, and let f, f_1, f_2,... be functions on B such that $|f_n| \leq g$ on B and $f_n \to f$ on B. Then $\int_B f_n dF \to \int_B f dF$ •

In next Theorem we consider **double integrals** and **repeated integrals**. The not mentioned integration domains are $\mathbf{R}^2$ or $\mathbf{R}$. This is no real restriction, because the function f can be replaced by $f1_B$ where B is any integration domain in $\mathbf{R}^2$, and because the integral of $f1_B$ on $\mathbf{R}^2$ equals the integral of f on B. In case of a positive integrand f, this integrand and the integrals may have infinite values.

Theorem 4 (Fubini)

If f is a positive function on $\mathbf{R}^2$ (case of a positive integrand), or if one of the integrals

$$\iint |f(x,y)| dF(x) dG(y) \ , \ \int[\int |f(x,y)| dF(x)] dG(y) \ , \ \int[\int |f(x,y)| dG(y)] dF(x)$$

is finite (case of an integrable integrand), then

$$\iint f(x,y) dF(x) dG(y) = \int[\int f(x,y) dF(x)] dG(y) = \int[\int f(x,y) dG(y)] dF(x) \quad \bullet$$

The great theorems can be applied to series, i.e. sums $\sum_{n\geq 0} f(n)$ with an infinite number of terms. By definition, this sum is the limit as $n\uparrow\infty$ of the partial sums $\sum_{0\leq k\leq n} f(k)$. If $\sum_{n\geq 0} |f(n)|<\infty$, the sum equals the integral $\int_{[0,\infty[} f(x)dS(x)$, where S is the distribution with mass 1 at the points 0, 1, 2, ... and where the function $f(x)(x\in\mathbf{R}_+)$ is any extension of the function $f(n)(n\in\mathbf{N}_+)$. Then the great theorems can be used in order to justify relations such as

$$\sum_n \int_B f(n,x)dF(x) = \int_B \sum_n f(n,x)dF(x) \ , \ \sum_m \sum_n f(m,n) = \sum_n \sum_m f(m,n).$$

1.1.5. Integration by Parts

Integration by parts on bounded intervals

We use the notation

$$[fg]_a^b := f(b)g(b) - f(a)g(a), \tag{3}$$

where a, b may be a±, b± resp. In the two following Theorems, the old-fashioned notation for the intervals, and even the mixed notation (a±,∞[, are most convenient.

Theorem 5 (Integration by Parts on Bounded Intervals)

Let f and g be functions of bounded variation. Then

$$\int_{(a\pm,b\pm)} f(x)dg(x) = [fg]_{a\pm}^{b\pm} - \int_{(a\pm,b\pm)} g(x-)df(x). \qquad (4)$$

In the last member, g(x–) may be replaced by g(x) if f and g have no common discontinuity points on the integration domain.

Proof
We will demonstrate the relation

$$\int_{]a,b]} F(x)dG(x) = F(b)G(b)-F(a)G(a) - \int_{]a,b]} G(x-)dF(x), \qquad (5)$$

where F and G are distribution functions. This implies the corresponding relation for differences of distribution functions. For the intervals]a,b[, [a,b[, [a,b], the proof is easily adapted.

In $\mathbf{R}^2$, we consider the sets

$$A := \{(x,y) \,/\, a<x\leq b \,,\, a<y\leq b\},$$
$$B := \{(x,y) \,/\, a<x\leq y\leq b\} = \{(x,y) \,/\, a<x\leq b \,,\, x\leq y\leq b\},$$
$$C := \{(x,y) \,/\, a<y<x\leq b\} = \{(x,y) \,/\, a<y<b \,,\, y<x\leq b\}.$$

Then

$$A=B+C \quad , \quad \iint_A dFdG = \iint_B dFdG + \iint_C dFdG.$$

By Fubini,

$$\iint_A dFdG = [F(b)-F(a)][G(b)-G(a)]$$
$$= F(b)G(b)-F(b)G(a)-F(a)G(b)+F(a)G(a),$$
$$\iint_B dFdG = \int_{]a,b]}dF(x)\int_{[x,b]}dG(y) = \int_{]a,b]}[G(b)-G(x-)]dF(x)$$
$$= G(b)[F(b)-F(a)] - \int_{]a,b]} G(x-)dF(x),$$
$$\iint_C dFdG = \int_{]a,b[}dG(y)\int_{]y,b]}dF(x) = \int_{]a,b[} [F(b)-F(y)]dG(y)$$
$$= F(b)[G(b-)-G(a)] - \int_{]a,b[}F(y)dG(y)$$
$$= F(b)[G(b-)-G(a)] - \int_{]a,b]}F(y)dG(y) + F(b)[G(b)-G(b-)].$$

These relations imply (5).

If we replace g(x–) by g(x) in the last member of (4), we commit an error equal to

$$\int_{(a\pm,b\pm)}[g(x)-g(x-)]df(x),$$

where the integrand vanishes, except at the discontinuities of g in (a±,b±). Let d_1, d_2,... be an enumeration of these discontinuities. It exists because the number of discontinuity points of a distribution function is denumerable (App.E. Th.E1). The error equals the sum

$$\sum_k[g(d_k)-g(d_k-)][f(d_k)-f(d_k-)]$$

and this sum is zero if no discontinuity of f is a discontinuity of g •

Integration by parts on unbounded intervals

Theorem 6 (Integration by Parts on Unbounded Intervals)

Let G be a distribution function, G(∞) < ∞. Then

$$\int_{(a\pm,\infty[} F(x)dG(x) = F(a\pm)[G(\infty)-G(a\pm)] + \int_{(a\pm,\infty[} [G(\infty)-G(x-)]dF(x). \quad (6)$$

In the last member of this relation, G(x–) may be replaced by G(x) if F and G have no common discontinuity points on the integration domain.

Proof
We will demonstrate the relation

$$\int_{]a,\infty[} F(x)dG(x) = F(a)[G(\infty)-G(a)] + \int_{]a,\infty[} [G(\infty)-G(x-)]dF(x). \quad (7)$$

Integrating by parts,

$$\int_{]a,b]} F(x)dG(x) = -\int_{]a,b]} F(x)d[G(\infty)-G(x)]$$

$$= -F(b)[G(\infty)-G(b)] + F(a)[G(\infty)-G(a)] + \int_{]a,b]} [G(\infty)-G(x-)]dF(x).$$

We may replace G(x–) by G(x) if F and G have no common discontinuities. Hence,

$$\int_{]a,b]}F(x)dG(x) + F(b)[G(\infty)-G(b)]$$

$$= \int_{]a,b]} [G(\infty)-G(x-)]dF(x) + F(a)[G(\infty)-G(a)], \quad (8)$$

where each term in each member is positive. We consider two cases.

Case $\int_{]a,\infty[} FdG < \infty$. Then

$$F(b)[G(\infty)-G(b)] = \int_{]b,\infty[} F(b)dG(x)$$
$$\leq \int_{]b,\infty[} F(x)dG(x) \downarrow 0 \text{ as } b\uparrow\infty,$$

by dominated convergence. Then (7) results from (8) as $b\uparrow\infty$.

Case $\int_{]a,\infty[} FdG = \infty$. Then it results from (8) that

$$\int_{]a,b]}[G(\infty)-G(x-)]dF(x) \uparrow\infty \text{ as } b\uparrow\infty,$$

whatever happens to the positive term $F(b)[G(\infty)-G(b)]$. Hence, in that case (7) takes the form $\infty=\infty$ •

The foregoing proof shows the following:

When an integration by parts is performed as in the preceding proof, one can always proceed AS IF $F(b)(G(\infty)-G(b))\to 0$ as $b\uparrow\infty$.

It is better and easier to remember this observation than (6).

As a simple illustration, let X be a positive random variable with distribution function F. Then the expectation of X equals

$$E(X) = \int_{[0,\infty[} xdF(x) = \int_{[0,\infty[} (1-F(x))dx.$$

This is exact, even when $E(X)=\infty$. We call

$$\int_{[0,\infty[}(1-F(x))dx$$

the **surface interpretation of the first moment of F**.

1.1.6. Helly-Bray Theorem

We say that **$F_n\to F$, weakly as $n\uparrow\infty$**, if $F_n(x)\to F(x)$ at the continuity points x of F. This **weak convergence** of distribution functions is denoted as: $F_n\to_w F$. See App.G.Th.G2 for a proof of the practical version of the following Theorem. For a general proof, see Loève (1955).

Theorem 7 (Helly-Bray)

Let F, F_1, F_2, ... be distribution functions such that $F_n \rightarrow_w F$ as $n \uparrow \infty$, and let f be a bounded continuous function on R.

a. (Case of bounded integration domain). If $F_n(a\pm) \rightarrow F(a\pm)$ and $F_n(b\pm) \rightarrow F(b\pm)$ as $n \uparrow \infty$, then

$$\int_{(a\pm,b\pm)} f dF_n \rightarrow \int_{(a\pm,b\pm)} f dF \text{ as } n \uparrow \infty.$$

b. (Case of integrand vanishing at $\pm\infty$). If $f(\pm\infty)=0$ and the functions $F_n (n \geq 0)$ are uniformly bounded on R, then

$$\int_R f dF_n \rightarrow \int_R f dF \text{ as } n \uparrow \infty.$$

c. (Case of total mass conservation). If $F_n(R) \rightarrow F(R) < \infty$ as $n \uparrow \infty$, then

$$\int_R f dF_n \rightarrow \int_R f dF \text{ as } n \uparrow \infty \bullet$$

Of course, Theorem 7.a contains four statements akin to the four bounded integration domains [a,b[, [a,b] ,]a,b] ,]a,b[.

In the following less classical version of the Helly-Bray Theorem, no continuity conditions on the integrated function f are present.

Theorem 8

Let F_0, F_1, F_2,... be positive distribution functions such that the function

$$F := \sum_k F_k$$

is a finite function. Then F is a distribution function and

$$\int_R f\, dF = \sum_k \int_R f\, dF_k,$$

if f is positive or F-integrable on R.

Proof

F is a distribution function by Theorem 1. For the function $f := 1_{]a,b]}$, the formula to be proved is exact. Then, by a monotone class argument (see a textbook on measure or on modern probability theory) it is exact for $f := 1_B$ (B Borel set), and then also for any positive Borel function f. This sketches the proof in case $f \geq 0$. If f is F-integrable, not necessarily positive, then the formula to be proved results from the decomposition $f = f_+ - f_-$ of f in its positive and negative parts $\bullet$

1.2. Differentiation

1.2.1. Functions with a Density

The function g is a **density of the function f on the interval J** if

$$f(x) = f(c) + \int_{[c,x]} g(y)dy \quad (c,x \in J;\ c \le x). \tag{9}$$

If J contains its left extremity **a**, then this condition can be replaced by

$$f(x) = f(a) + \int_{[a,x]} g(y)dy \ (x \in J). \tag{10}$$

The function g remains a density of f on J if it is modified on a Lebesgue-null set. Hence, the density, when it exists, is not specified univoquely. Often, the density is specified by a supplementary condition, such as right-continuity.

By Modern Real Analysis, (only used very scarcely in this book), the functions f with a density g on J are the absolutely continuous functions on the compact sub-intervals of J. Then g=f' Lebesgue-a.e. on J.

By Classical Real Analysis, f has the density f' on J if the latter derivative exists and is continuous on J. The densities encountered in the applications are familiar derivatives in almost all cases. Hereafter, the densities are represented by accents.

1.2.2. Density Theorem for Integrals

Theorem 9 (Density Theorem for Integrals)

a. Let the distribution function F have the density F′ on the interval [a,b]. If one of the integrals

$$\int_{]a,b]} f(x)dF(x)\ ,\ \int_{]a,b]} f(x)F'(x)dx$$

exists, then the other exists, and they are equal.

b. Let f be bounded on the interval]a,b], and let g be a function of bounded variation, with a density g′ on [a,b]. Then

$$\int_{]a,b]} f(x)dg(x) = \int_{]a,b]} f(x)g'(x)dx \ \bullet$$

The proof of the Theorem is direct by a monotone class argument, starting with indicator functions $f:=1_{]c,d]}$ ($a\leq c\leq d\leq b$). The Theorem has obvious versions for integrals on unbounded intervals, resulting from $a\downarrow-\infty$ or $b\uparrow+\infty$.

1.3. Convolutions on $\mathbf{R}_+$

1.3.1. Functions on $\mathbf{R}_+$

A **distribution function on $\mathbf{R}_+$** is a distribution function F such that $F\equiv 0$ on $\mathbf{R}_{-}:=]-\infty,+\infty[$. In the rest of this Chapter, we stay on $\mathbf{R}_+$ and we suppose that all considered functions vanish on $\mathbf{R}_{-}$. Functions initially defined on $\mathbf{R}_+$ only, are extended to $\mathbf{R}$ by stating that they equal zero on $\mathbf{R}_{-}$. The constant function c is in fact the function $c1_{[0,\infty[}$. The convenient agreement that all functions vanish on $\mathbf{R}_{-}$ has the following implications:

The distribution F on $\mathbf{R}_+$ places the mass

$$F(\{0\}) = F(0)-F(0-) = F(0)$$

at the origin 0. Hence,

$$\int_{[0,a\pm)} f(x)\,dF(x) = f(0)F(0) + \int_{]0,a\pm)} f(x)dF(x).$$

If g is a function of bounded variation on $\mathbf{R}_+$, then

$$\int_{[0,a\pm)} f(x)\,dg(x) = f(0)g(0) + \int_{]0,a\pm)} f(x)dg(x).$$

In particular **if g is the constant function c, then**

$$\int_{[0,a\pm)} \mathbf{f(x)dc = f(0)c}.$$

1.3.2. Convolution Products on $\mathbf{R}_+$

The **convolution product** $\varphi*f$ is a function defined on $\mathbf{R}_+$, under the following conditions a. and b. :

a. φ is a function on $\mathbf{R}_+$, bounded on bounded intervals.

b. f is a function of bounded variation on $\mathbf{R}_+$.

The definition is:

$$(\varphi*f)(x) := \int_{[0,x]} \varphi(x-y)df(y)\ (x\in\mathbf{R}_+). \tag{11}$$

We assume that the conditions a. and b. are satisfied, whenever convolution products are considered. The following properties are direct:

The value $(\varphi*f)(x)$ of the convolution product $\varphi*f$ at the point $x\in\mathbf{R}_+$, only depends on the restriction of φ and f to the interval [0,x], and not on the values of these functions outside that interval.

If φ_1 and φ_2 are functions on $\mathbf{R}_+$, bounded on bounded intervals, then the linear combination $a_1\varphi_1+a_2\varphi_2$ is a function on $\mathbf{R}_+$, bounded on bounded intervals.

If f_1 and f_2 are functions of bounded variation on $\mathbf{R}_+$, then the linear combination $a_1f_1+a_2f_2$ is a function of bounded variation on $\mathbf{R}_+$.

The convolution product $\varphi*f$ is bilinear, i.e. linear in φ and linear in f:

$$(a_1\varphi_1+a_2\varphi_2)*f = a_1\,\varphi_1*f + a_2\,\varphi_2*f,$$

$$\varphi*(a_1f_1+a_2f_2) = a_1\,\varphi*f_1 + a_2\varphi*f_2.$$

Convolution products by constants are usual products:

$$\varphi*c = c\,\varphi \quad , \quad c*f = c\,f.$$

The convolution product is a usual product at 0 :

$$(\varphi*f)(0) = \varphi(0)f(0).$$

From the following Theorem 11 results that this factorization property also holds at $+\infty$, under particular assumptions.

We denote by I the identity function on $\mathbf{R}_+$: $I(x)=x$ $(x\in\mathbf{R}_+)$ As all other functions, when convolutions are considered, I vanishes on $\mathbf{R}_-$. The function I has the following interesting property:

Convolution products by I are Lebesgue integrals (i.e. integrals with respect to Lebesgue measure):

$$(\varphi*I)(x) = \int_{[0,x]} \varphi(x)dx.$$

Then

$$[f' \text{ is a density of f on } \mathbf{R}_+] \Leftrightarrow [f = f(0) + f'*I], \tag{12}$$

where f(0) is the constant function with value f(0) on $\mathbf{R}_+$.

Theorem 10 (Properties of Convolution Product)

Let φ be a function on R_+ bounded on bounded intervals, f and g functions of bounded variation on R_+, F and G distribution functions on R_+. Then

a. **φ*f is bounded on bounded intervals.**

b. **F*G is a distribution function.**

c. **f*g is a function of bounded variation.**

d.

$$\iint_{\{x+y\le z\}} dF(x)dG(y) = (F*G)(z) \quad (z\in R_+).$$

e. (Commutativity of the Convolution Product)

$$f*g = g*f.$$

f. (Associativity of the Convolution Product)

$$(\varphi*f)*g = \varphi*(f*g).$$

Proof

a. If f=F−G, then

$$\varphi*f = \varphi*F - \varphi*G.$$

Hence, it is sufficient to verify that $\varphi*F$ is bounded on bounded intervals. We prove that $\varphi*F$ is bounded on [0,c]. Let b be such that $|\varphi| \le b$ on [0,c]. Then, for $x\in[0,c]$,

$$|(\varphi*F)(x)| = |\int_{[0,x]} \varphi(x-y)dF(y)| \le \int_{[0,x]} |\varphi(x-y)|dF(y)$$

$$\le \int_{[0,x]} b\, dF(y) = b\, F(x) \le bF(c).$$

b. Let $0\le x<c$. Then

$$(F*G)(x) = \int_{[0,c]} F(x-y)1_{y\le x}\, dG(y).$$

For fixed y, the integrand $F(x-y)1_{y\le x}$ increases with x. Hence (F*G) is an increasing function of x. For fixed y, the integrand is a right-continuous function of x. Let $0\le a<x<c$. By dominated convergence,

$$(F*G)(x) \downarrow \int_{[0,c]} F(a-y)1_{y\le a}\, dG(Y) = (F*G)(a) \text{ for } x\downarrow a.$$

This proves that F*G is right-continuous at the point a.

c. Let $f=F_1-F_2$, $g=G_1-G_2$, where F_1, F_2, G_1, G_2 are distribution functions on $\mathbf{R}_+$.

$$f*g = (F_1-F_2)*(G_1-G_2) = (F_1*G_1+F_2*G_2) - (F_1*G_2+F_2*G_1).$$

By b., the last member is a difference of distribution functions.

d.
$$\{(x,y)/x+y\leq z\} = \{(x,y)/0\leq y\leq z,\ 0\leq x\leq z-y\}.$$

Then by Fubini,

$$\iint_{\{x+y\leq z\}} dF(x)dG(y) = \int_{[0,z]} [\int_{[0,z-y]}dF(x)]\, dG(y)$$
$$= \int_{[0,z]} F(z-y)dG(y) = (F*G)(z).$$

e. By a decomposition such as in the proof of c, it is enough to demonstrate that

$$(F*G)(z)=(G*F)(z)\ (z\in\mathbf{R}_+).$$

The latter relation results from d.

f. By a decomposition such as in the proof of c, it is sufficient to prove that

$$(\varphi*F)*G = \varphi*(F*G).$$

We shall verify that relation for the particular indicator functions $f:=1_{[0,a[}$ $(a\geq 0)$. Then it is also valid for differences of such indicator functions, and then a monotone class argument completes the proof.

Let H be a distribution function on $\mathbf{R}_+$. Then

$$(1_{[0,a[}*H)(x) = \int_{[0,x]} 1_{[0,a[}(x-y)dH(y) = \int_D dH(y),$$

where

$$D := \{y/0\leq y\leq x\ ,\ 0\leq x-y<a\}$$
$$= \{y/0\leq y\leq x,\ x-a<y\leq x\} = [0,x]\cap]x-a,x].$$

Hence,
$$(\varphi*H)(x) = H(x) - H(x-a) \quad (\varphi = 1_{[0,a[}).$$

We apply this result, with H=F and with H=F*G :

$$[(\varphi*F)*G](x) = \int_{[0,x]} (\varphi*F)(x-y)dG(y) = \int_{[0,x]} [F(x-y)-F(x-y-a)]dG(y)$$
$$= \int_{[0,x]} F(x-y)dG(y) - \int_{[0,x]} F(x-a-y)dG(y) = (F*G)(x) -(F*G)(x-a)$$
$$= [\varphi*(F*G)](x) \bullet$$

Theorem 11 (Factorization of Convolution Product at ∞)

a. Let F and G be distribution functions on $\mathbf{R}_+$. Then

$$(F*G)(\infty) = F(\infty)G(\infty). \quad (13)$$

b. Let f be a function on $\mathbf{R}_+$, bounded on bounded intervals, and such that f(∞) exists and is finite. Let G be a bounded distribution function on $\mathbf{R}_+$. Then

$$(f*G)(\infty) = f(\infty)G(\infty). \quad (14)$$

Proof

a. $$(F*G)(x) = \int_{[0,x]} F(x-y)dG(y) = \int F(x-y)1_{[0,x]}\, dG(y).$$

In the last integral, the integrand increases to $F(\infty)$ as $x\uparrow\infty$. By monotone convergence

$$(F*G)(x) \uparrow \int F(\infty)dG(y) = F(\infty)G(\infty).$$

b. The function f is bounded because it is bounded on bounded intervals and because $f(\infty)<\infty$. Hence $|f|<b\in\mathbf{R}_+$. Then $|f(x-y)1_{[0,x]}|<b$ $(x,y\in\mathbf{R}_+)$. The constant function b is G-integrable on $\mathbf{R}_+$ because $G(\infty)<\infty$. Then, by dominated convergence,

$$(f*G)(x) = \int_{\mathbf{R}_+} f(x-y)1_{[0,x]}\, dG(y) \rightarrow \int_{\mathbf{R}_+} f(\infty)dG(y) = f(\infty)G(\infty) \text{ as } x\uparrow\infty \bullet$$

1.3.3. Density Theorem for Convolutions

Theorem 12 (Density Theorem for Convolutions)

Let f be a function on $\mathbf{R}_+$, bounded on bounded intervals, with a density f′ on $\mathbf{R}_+$, bounded on bounded intervals. Let g be a function of bounded variation on $\mathbf{R}_+$ with a density g′ on the interval J=[a,b[or J=[a,∞[(a≥0). Then f*g has the density

$$(f*g)' := f(0)g' + f'*g \quad \text{on } J. \quad (15)$$

Proof

We have to verify that

$$(f*g)(x)-(f*g)(a) = \int_{[a,x]} f(0)g'(y)dy + \int_{[a,x]} (f'*g)(y)dy \quad (x\in J). \quad (16)$$

The last member equals

$$f(0)[g(x)-g(a)] + [\int_{[0,x]} - \int_{[0,a]}](f'*g)(y)dy.$$

Lebesgue integrals are convolution products by I. Then, by (12), and by the commutativity and associativity of the convolution product,

$$\int_{[0,x]} (f'*g)(y)dy = [(f'*g)*I](x) = [(f'*I)*g](x)$$
$$= [[f-f(0)]*g](x) = (f*g)(x) - f(0)g(x),$$
$$\int_{[0,a]} (f'*g)(y)dy = (f*g)(a) - f(0)g(a).$$

This proves that (16) is correct •

The interesting case is $J=\mathbf{R}_+$. Then, if the involved convolutions are defined:

$$(f*g)' = f(0)g' + f'*g \ , \ (g*f)' = g(0)f' + g'*f$$

and we have two expressions for $(f*g)'=(g*f)'$. The density Theorem for integrals shows that they are equal. Indeed,

$$(f'*g)(x) = \int_{[0,x]} f'(x-y)dg(y) = f'(x)g(0) + \int_{]0,x]} f'(x-y)g'(y)dy \ ,$$
$$(g'*f)(x) = g'(x)f(0)+\int_{]0,x]} g'(x-y)f'(y)dy = g'(x)f(0) + \int_{]0,x]} f'(x-y)g'(y)dy.$$

1.3.4. Positive random variables

A **probability distribution function on $\mathbf{R}_+$** is a distribution function F on $\mathbf{R}_+$ with $F(\infty)=1$. Let X be a positive random variable. Its distribution function F defined by

$$F(x) = P(X\leq x), \tag{17}$$

is a probability distribution function on $\mathbf{R}_+$.

Let X and Y be positive random variables with distribution functions F and G resp. Then the distribution function H of the sum X+Y is the convolution product F*G:

$$H(x) = P(X+Y\leq x) = (F*G)(x) \ (x\in\mathbf{R}_+).$$

This relation results from Theorem 10.d.

The random variables are supposed to have **finite values**, unless the contrary is specified explicitly. Exceptionally, positive random variables with possible infinite values are considered. The distribution function F of a positive random variable X with possible infinite values, is still defined by (17).

Then

$$F(\infty) = P(X<\infty) \leq 1,$$

and F is not necessarily a probability distribution function on $\mathbf{R}_+$.

The following is a result of Probability Theory.

Let F_1, F_2, ..., be a sequence, finite or not, of probability distribution functions on $\mathbf{R}_+$. Then a corresponding sequence X_1, X_2,..., of independent random variables exists on some probability space, such that F_k is the distribution function of X_k (k=1,2,...).

If it is assumed only that $F_k(\infty)\leq 1$ (k=1,2,...), then a sequence of independent random variables X_k (k=1,2,...) with possible infinite values, does exist.

Remark

Convolutions on **R** are not used in the following Chapters. The distribution function F of any random variable X, with positive and negative finite values, is still defined by (17), on **R**. Then F is a distribution function, in the sense of 1.1.1, with the properties:

$$0\leq F\leq 1\ ,\ F(-\infty)=0\ ,\ F(+\infty) = 1.$$

Any distribution function F with these properties is called a **probability distribution function on R**.

1.4. Renewal Equations on $\mathbf{R}_+$

1.4.1. Convolution Power Series on $\mathbf{R}_+$

In the rest of this Chapter, the function G is a probability distribution function on $\mathbf{R}_+$ not concentrated at the point 0.

The **convolution powers G^{*k} (k=0,1,2,...)** are defined recursively on $\mathbf{R}_+$ by

$$G^{*0} := 1\quad,\quad G^{*(k+1)} := (G^{*k})*G\quad (k=0,1,2,...).$$

As all other functions in this Chapter, they vanish on $\mathbf{R}_{-}$.

By successive applications of Theorem 10.b, G^{*k} is a distribution function on $\mathbf{R}_+$. Then, by successive applications of Theorem 11.b, G^{*k} is a probability distribution function on $\mathbf{R}_+$.

The **convolution power series in G**, with positive coefficients a_k (k=0,1,2,...), is the function, possibly with infinite values,

$$\sum_{k\geq 0} a_k G^{*k}, \tag{18}$$

on $\mathbf{R}_+$. By Theorem 1, convolution power series with finite values only, are distribution functions on $\mathbf{R}_+$. We consider the particular convolution power series

$$V_{G,q} := \sum_{k\geq 0} q^k G^{*k}, \tag{19}$$

for $0<q\leq 1$. The subscript q is mostly omitted if it equals 1: $V_G \equiv V_{G,1}$.

Lemma

Let G be a probability distribution on $\mathbf{R}_+$, not concentrated at the origin. Then a constant r exists in]0,1[, such that

$$G^{*k}(x) \leq e^x r^k \quad (x\in\mathbf{R}_+;\ k=0,1,2,\ldots).$$

Proof

Let X, X_1, X_2,..., be independent positive random variables with distribution function G. Then $r:=E(e^{-X})<1$, because G is not concentrated at the origin. Then

$$\begin{aligned} G^{*k}(x) &= P(X_1+\ldots+X_k \leq x) = P[\exp(-X_1-\ldots-X_k) \geq \exp(-x)] \\ &\leq e^x\, E[\exp(-X_1-\ldots-X_k)] = e^x (Ee^{-X})^k = e^x r^k \end{aligned}$$

by the general relation

$$P(Y\geq a) \leq E(Y)/a \quad (Y \text{ positive random variable, } a>0) \ \bullet$$

Theorem 13

Let G be a probability distribution function, not concentrated at the point 0. Then $V_{G,q}$ (0<q<1) is a bounded distribution function on $\mathbf{R}_+$ and V_G is an unbounded distribution function on $\mathbf{R}_+$.

Proof

If $0<q<1$, then

$$V_{G,q}(x) = \sum q^k G^{*k}(x) \leq \sum q^k G^{*k}(\infty) = \sum q^k = (1-q)^{-1} < \infty \quad (x\in\mathbf{R}_+).$$

Then $V_{G,q}$ is a bounded distribution function on $\mathbf{R}_+$ by Theorem 1.

If q=1, then by the Lemma,

$$V_G(x) = \sum G^{*k}(x) \le e^x \sum r^k = e^x(1-r)^{-1} < \infty \quad (x \in \mathbf{R}_+),$$

and then again by Theorem 1, V_G is a distribution function on $\mathbf{R}_+$. It is unbounded, because

$$V_\infty(\infty) = \sum_{k\ge0} G^{*k}(\infty) = \sum_{k\ge0} 1 = \infty \quad \bullet$$

1.4.2. Renewal Equations on $\mathbf{R}_+$

A **renewal equation on $\mathbf{R}_+$**, is an equation

$$f = g + q\, f*G, \tag{20}$$

where

a. G is a probability distribution function on $\mathbf{R}_+$ not concentrated at 0.

b. g is a function on $\mathbf{R}_+$, bounded on bounded intervals.

c. q is a constant in]0,1].

d. The unknown function f is a function on $\mathbf{R}_+$, bounded on bounded intervals.

Theorem 14

a. The renewal equation $V=1+qV*G$ on $\mathbf{R}_+$, has the unique solution $V=V_{G,q}$.

b. The renewal equation $f=g+qf*G$ on $\mathbf{R}_+$, has the unique solution $f=g*V_{G,q}$.

Proof
We first verify the announced solutions are indeed solutions.

$$1+qV_{G,q}*G = 1+q\left[\sum_{k\ge0} q^k G^{*k}\right]*G = 1+q\sum_{k\ge0} q^k (G^{*k})*G$$

$$= 1+\sum_{k\ge0} q^{k+1} G^{*(k+1)} = q^0 G^{*0} + \sum_{k\ge0} q^{k+1} G^{*(k+1)}$$

$$= \sum_{k\ge0} q^k G^{*k} = V_{G,q},$$

by monotone convergence for the second equality (because series of positive terms are increasing limits).

From the convolution product of the relation $V_{G,q}=1+qV_{G,q}*G$ by g, results

$$(g*V_{G,q}) = g+q(g*V_{G,q})*G.$$

Only the unicity of the solution of the renewal equation f=g+qf*G needs a proof, because the renewal equation V=1+qV*G is a particular case.

Let f_1 and f_2 be solutions of f=g+qf*G. By definition, they are bounded on bounded intervals. Let $h:=f_1-f_2$. Then,

$$f_1=g+qf_1*G \ , \ f_2=g+qf_2*G,$$

and by difference, h=qh*G. From the latter relation results successively:

$$h=qh*G = q(qh*G)*G = q^2h*G^{*2}$$

$$= q^2(qh*G)*g^{*2} = q^3h*G^3 = \ldots = q^kh*G^{*k}$$

Let x be fixed and let b be such that $|h|\leq b$ on [0,x]. Then

$$|h(x)| = q^k\left|\int_{[0,x]} h(x-y)dG^{*k}(y)\right|$$

$$\leq q^k\int_{[0,x]} |h(x-y)|dG^{*k}(y) \leq q^k\int_{[0,x]} b\ dG^{*k}(y)$$

$$= bq^kG^{*k}(x) \leq bq^ke^xr^k \to 0 \text{ as } k\uparrow\infty,$$

where we used the Lemma of Theorem 13 for the last inequality. Hence, $h(x)=0$, $f_1(x)=f_2(x)$ •

Corollary

The solution f of the renewal equation f=g+qf*G on $\mathbf{R}_+$ is bounded on bounded intervals. It is a function of bounded variation if g is a function of bounded variation. It is a distribution function on $\mathbf{R}_+$ if g is a distribution function on $\mathbf{R}_+$.

Proof
The solution equals $f=g*V_{G,q}$, where $V_{G,q}$ is a distribution function on $\mathbf{R}_+$ by Theorem 13. Then the Corollary results from Theorem 10.a,b,c •

1.4.3. Density Theorem for Renewal Equations

Theorem 15 (Density Theorem for Renewal Equations)

In the renewal equation f=g+qf*G on $\mathbf{R}_+$, let g and G have the density g′ and G′ on $\mathbf{R}_+$, and let these densities be bounded on bounded intervals. Then the solution f has the density f′ on $\mathbf{R}_+$, satisfying the renewal equation on $\mathbf{R}_+$

$$f' = [g'+qf(0)G'] + qf' * G, \tag{21}$$

(resulting from a formal application of the density Theorem for convolutions to the convolution product f*G in f=g+qf*G.)

Proof

By Theorem 13, (21) is a renewal equation with unique solution f′ (not yet a density of f). By the Corollary of Theorem 14, f′ is bounded on bounded intervals. By (12), and by the renewal equation f=g+qf*G at the point 0:

$$g'*I = g-g(0)\,,\ G'*I = G-G(0)\,,\ f(0) = g(0)+qf(0)G(0)\,.$$

From these relations and from the convolution product of (21) by I, results that

$$f'*I = g'*I + qf(0)\,G'*I + q(f'*I)*G =$$

$$[g-g(0)] + qf(0)[G-G(0)] + q(f'*I)*G = g-f(0) + q[f(0)+f'*I]*G.$$

This proves that f(0)+f′*I is a solution of the renewal equation f=g+qf*G, with unique solution f. Hence f=f(0)+f′*I and then f′ is a density of f on $\mathbf{R}_+$ by (12) •

1.5. Renewal Theory on $\mathbf{R}_+$

1.5.1. Renewal Theory Model

Let us consider some physical device (an electric bulb, some component of an engine...) that must be replaced when it fails. Let D_1, D_2, ... be the durations of the successive components. Then the **renewal instants,** or **renewal points**, are the random variables

$$D_1,\ D_1+D_2,\ D_1+D_2+D_3,\ldots$$

We denote by N_x be the number of renewal instants in the interval [0,x], and we define $N^+_x := 1+N_x$.

The random variable N^+_x is the number of renewal points in [0,x], when also 0 is regarded as a renewal point.

$$N^+_x = 1_{0\le x} + 1_{D_1\le x} + 1_{D_1+D_2\le x} + 1_{D_1+D_2+D_3\le x} + \dots$$

$$E(N^+_x) = 1 + P(D_1\le x) + P(D_1+D_2\le x) + P(D_1+D_2+D_3\le x) + \dots \qquad (22)$$

because the expectation of an indicator function equals the probability of the indicated event.

Assumptions

We assume that D_1, D_2,... are positive, independent, not necessarily finite, random variables with the same distribution G_0, not concentrated at the origin. We define

$$q := G_0(\infty)\ ,\ G := G_0/q.$$

Then q is the probability that D_k is finite, and G is a probability distribution function not concentrated at 0. (See 1.3.4).

Under these *Assumptions*,

$$\mathbf{E(N^+_x) = V_{G,q}(x)\ (x\in R_+).} \qquad (23)$$

The expected number of renewal points in [0,∞[equals $(1-q)^{-1}$ if q<1. It is infinite if q=1.

Indeed,

$$E(N^+_x) = \Sigma_{k\ge0}\, G_0{*^k}(x) = \Sigma_{k\ge0}\, q^k G{*^k}(x) = V_{G,q}(x)\ ,\ V_{G,q}(\infty) = \Sigma_{k\ge0}\, q^k,$$

by (22) and (23).The latter sum is $(1-q)^{-1}$ if q <1. It is infinite if q=1.

1.5.2. Renewal Theorems

We continue with the case q=1. Then the variables D_1, D_2,... are finite independent usual random variables, each with distribution function G.

Assumptions

G is a probability distribution on R_+ with strictly positive finite first moment μ, with no mass at 0, and with a bounded density G′ on R_+.

Before we indicate the famous renewal Theorems, we make some heuristic considerations. The expected number of renewal points in $[0,x]$ is $V_G(x)$ by (23). By difference, the expected number of renewal points in interval $]x,x+h]$ is $V_G(x+h)-V_G(x)=V_G(]x,x+h])$. The length of the interval $]x,x+h]$ is h and the expected distance between two successive renewal points is μ. Hence, $h \cong \mu V_G(]x,x+h])$. Precise renewal Theorems are the limit relations

$$\lim_{x\uparrow\infty} V_G(]x,x+h]) = h/\mu \ , \ \lim_{x\uparrow\infty} V_G'(x) = 1/\mu \ .$$

In this Chapter, we shall prove them under the assumption, only dropped in the Appendix A, that $V_G'(\infty)$ exists and is finite.

Theorem 16 (Renewal Theorem for the Density of V_G – Weak Version)

Under the indicated *Assumptions*, V_G has a density V_G' on $\mathbf{R}_+$, satisfying the renewal equation

$$\mathbf{V_G' = G' + V_G'{*}G.} \tag{24}$$

If the limit $V_G'(\infty)$ exists and is finite, then it equals $1/\mu$.

Proof

By Theorem 14.a, $V_G=1+V_G{*}G$. The function 1 has the density 0 on $\mathbf{R}_+$, and G has the density G' on $\mathbf{R}_+$. By Theorem 15, V_G has the density V_G' satisfying renewal equation

$$V_G' = V_G(0)G' + V_G'{*}G. \tag{25}$$

From this relation results (24). Indeed, $V_G(0)=1$ because $G(0)=0$. Hence,

$$V_G'{*}(1-G) = G'. \tag{26}$$

Let

$$H := {}^1\!/\!_\mu\,(1-G){*}I.$$

Then H is a probability distribution function by the surface interpretation of the first moment of G (last paragraph of 1.1.5). From the convolution product of (26) by $(1/\mu)I$ results the relation

$$V_G'{*}H = {}^1\!/\!_\mu\, G'{*}I. \tag{27}$$

By (25) and the Corollary of Theorem 14, the function V_G' is bounded on bounded intervals. We now take (27) at the point x and we let $x\uparrow\infty$.

By Theorem 11.b,

$$V_G'(\infty).H(\infty) = {}^1/_\mu\ (G'*I)(\infty),$$

where $H(\infty)=1$ because H is a probability distribution, and where $(G'*I)(\infty)=1$ because G' is the density of a probability distribution •

Theorem 17 (Key Renewal Theorem – Weak Version)

In the renewal equation $f=g+f*G$, let

$$\int_{R_+} |g(x)|dx < \infty \quad , \quad g(\infty) = 0. \tag{28}$$

Then, under the assumptions of Theorem 16,

$$f(\infty) = {}^1/_\mu \int_{R_+} g(x)dx. \tag{29}$$

Proof

The density V_G' is bounded on $\mathbf{R}_+$ by (24), the Corollary of Theorem 14, and because $V_G'(\infty) \leq \infty$. Then, by Theorem 14.b for q=1, by the density Theorem for integrals and by dominated convergence,

$$\begin{aligned} f(x) &= (g*V_G)(x) = \int_{[0,x]} g(x-y)dV_G(y) \\ &= g(x)V_G(0) + \int_{]0,x]} g(x-y)V_G'(y)dy \\ &= g(x) + \int_{R_+} g(y)V_G'(x-y)1_{]0,x]}dx \\ &\to \int_{R_+} g(y)V_G'(\infty)dy = {}^1/_\mu \int_{R_+} g(y)dy \ \text{ as } x\uparrow\infty \end{aligned}$$ •

Theorem 18 (Renewal Th. for the increments of V_G – Weak Version)

Under the assumptions of Theorem 16,

$$\lim_{x\uparrow\infty} [V_G(x)-V_G(x-h)] = h/\mu \ (h>0). \tag{30}$$

Proof

The Theorem results from the particular function $g:=1_{[0,h[}$ in the preceding Theorem. Indeed, then by Theorem 14.b, if $x>h$,

$$\begin{aligned} f(x) &= (1_{[0,h[}*V_G)(x) = \int_{[0,x]} 1_{[0,h[}(x-y)dV_G(y) \\ &= \int_{]x-h,x]} dV_G(y) = V_G(x)-V_G(x-h) \end{aligned}$$ •

1.5.3 Exponential Transformation

We here consider the renewal equation

$$f=g+q\, f*G \quad (q<1), \tag{31}$$

on $\mathbf{R}_+$. The **exponential transformation** replaces (31), by an equivalent equation with q=1, to which the renewal Theorems could be applied.

An **adjustment coefficient** of the couple (G,q) is a number $\rho\in\mathbf{R}_{++}$, such that

$$q\int_{[0,\infty[} e^{\rho x}\, dG(x) = 1. \tag{32}$$

The adjustment coefficient is unique, when it exist. Indeed, let ρ and ρ′ be two adjustment coefficients, ρ<ρ′. Then

$$\int_{[0,\infty[}(e^{\rho' x}-e^{\rho x})dG(x) = 0.$$

But this is impossible because the first member of this relation is strictly positive. Indeed, the integrand is strictly positive on the interval $]0,\infty[$ and $G(]0,\infty[)>0$ because G is not concentrated at the origin.

Let the couple (G,q) have the adjustment coefficient ρ. The **exponential transformation of the renewal equation** (31) is defined as follows on $\mathbf{R}_+$:

$$f_e(x) := f(x)e^{\rho x} \;,\;\; g_e(x) := g(x)e^{\rho x} \;,\;\; G_e(x) := q\int_{[0,x]}e^{\rho y}dG(y). \tag{33}$$

Then G_e is a probability distribution on $\mathbf{R}_+$ by the very definition of ρ and

$$f_e = g_e + f_e*G_e \;\text{ on } \mathbf{R}_+. \tag{34}$$

Indeed,

$$(f_e*G_e)(x) = \int_{[0,x]} f_e(x-y)dG_e(y) = \int_{[0,x]} f(x-y)e^{\rho(x-y)}qe^{\rho y}dG(y)$$

$$= qe^{\rho x}\int_{[0,x]} f(x-y)dG(y) = e^{\rho x}\, q(f*G)(x)$$

$$= e^{\rho x}[f(x)-g(x)] = f_e(x)-g_e(x) \;\; (x\in\mathbf{R}_+).$$

Chapter 2

Conditional Expectations

2.0. Introduction

One of the most important concepts in Probability Theory is that of **conditional expectation**. Conditional expectations can be defined in the old-fashioned and in the modern way. By a juxtaposition and comparison of the two definitions of the same concept, we can profit from the advantages of both.

The old-fashioned conditional expectation has serious drawbacks. It does not exist in full generality. It needs separate treatments of discrete and continuous random variables. In the continuous case, the existence conditions are cumbersome,... But it also has fantastic merits. It is intuitive. It is constructive and it furnishes explicit expressions ready for classical transformations and numerical calculations.

The modern conditional expectation has great advantages. It exists in full generality. All kinds of conditionings can be considered. It satisfies very simple general rules,... But it has a major inconvenient: it is existential, and it does not furnish a recipe for its practical calculation.

Without scruples, we use **infinitesimal numbers** dx in the old definition, although everybody knows that such things cannot exist in our every-day logic, because they should have, simultaneously, the properties of 0 and of numbers different from 0.

We also use **infinitesimal intervals** dx. The interval dx is an interval of infinitesimal length containing the point x. From the context it is always clear wether dx denotes an infinitesimal number or an infinitesimal set.

The infinitesimals are used in a very free way in the definition of the old-fashioned conditional expectation. This is allowed, in the present situation, because the obtained results will be proved afterwards to be correct via the modern definition. The modern definition is the only one that we have finally adopted.

2.1. Old-Fashioned Conditional Expectation

2.1.1. Continuous Case

Distribution of a random vector

We consider a random triplet (X,Y,Z) of random variables X, Y, Z with values in the intervals I, J, K resp. We suppose that

$$P(X\in dx, Y\in dy, Z\in dz) = f(x,y,z)dxdydz, \tag{1}$$

where f is a positive function on IxJxK such that

$$\iiint_{IxJxK} f(x,y,z) = 1. \tag{2}$$

The right version of (1), without infinitesimals, is

$$P((X,Y,Z)\in B) = \iiint_B f(x,y,z)dxdydz \ (B\subseteq IxJxK). \tag{3}$$

The function f(x,y,z) is the **density** of the triplet (X,Y,Z).

Marginal random vectors and random variables

The distribution of the **random couples** (X,Y), (X,Z), (Y,Z), and the distribution of the **random variables** X, Y, Z result from the distribution of the triplet (X,Y,Z).

Let us first consider a couple, say (X,Y). Then

$$P(X\in dx, Y\in dy) = P(X\in dx, Y\in dy, Z\in K) = [\int_K f(x,y,z)dz]dxdy .$$

This means that the couple (X,Y) has the density

$$f(x,y) := \int_K f(x,y,z)dz \ \ (x\in I, y\in J) \tag{4}$$

on the interval I×J. Obviously, the function f in the right member of (4) is not the same as that one in the left member. A more complete notation such as $f_{X,Y}(x,y)$ could be used for the latter.

In the same way, the couple (X,Z) has the density

$$f(x,z) := \int_J f(x,y,z)dy \ \ (x\in I, z\in K). \tag{5}$$

The function defined by (4) is not the same as that one defined by (5). In fact the notation is unambiguous as only literal values x, y, z, are considered. It should be completed when numerical values are used.

Let us now consider the random variable X of the triplet (X,Y,Z).

$$P(X\in dx) = P(X\in dx, Y\in J, Z\in K) = [\iint_{JxK} f(x,y,z)dydz]dx.$$

Hence, X has the density

$$f(x) := \iint_{JxK} f(x,y,z)dz \ (x\in I).$$

We also can consider X as random variable of the couple (X,Y) and as random variable of the couple (X,Z) :

$$f(x) = \int_J f(x,y)dy \ , \ f(x) = \int_K f(x,z)dz.$$

The compatibility of these expressions results from Fubini.

Conditional random vectors and random variables

The distribution of the **conditional random couples** or **conditional random variables** $(X,Y)_{/Z=z}$, $(X,Z)_{/Y=y}$, $X_{/Y=y,Z=z}$,... where $x\in I$, $y\in J$, $z\in K$, is defined from the distribution of the random triplet (X,Y,Z).

We start with the conditional couple $(X,Y)_{/Z=z}$. The probability of the condition Z=z is zero . We replace this condition by $Z\in dz$, which probability can be treated as different from zero. By the elementary formula for the probability of an event conditioned by another event,

$$P(X\in dx, Y\in dy/Z\in dz) = P(X\in dx, Y\in dy, Z\in dz)/P(Z\in dz)$$
$$= [f(x,y,z)dxdydz]/[f(z)dz].$$

Hence,

$$P(X\in dx, Y\in dy/Z=z) = f(x,y/z)dxdy,$$

where

$$\mathbf{f(x,y/z) := f(x,y,z)/f(z).} \qquad (6)$$

For fixed $z\in K$, the conditional random couple $(X,Y)_{/Z=z}$ has the conditional density f(x,y/z) on the interval $I\times J$ (or on the subset $I\times Jx\{z\}$ of $I\times J\times K$).

The conditional density (6) may be defined arbitrarily when f(z)=0, because (6) is essentially used in the way f(x,y,z)=f(z)f(x,y/z). In a similar way, we conclude the following:

For fixed y in J and z in K, the conditional random variable $X_{/Y=y,Z=z}$ has the density

$$f(x/y,z) := f(x,y,z)/f(y,z) \text{ on } I\times\{y\}\times\{z\}.$$

For fixed y in J, the conditional random variable $X_{/Y=y}$ has the density

$$f(x/y) := f(x,y)/f(y) \quad \text{on} \quad I\times\{y\}.$$

Conditional expectations

The usual unconditional expectation of the random variable α(X,Y), where α is a real function on I×J, equals

$$E[\alpha(X,Y)] = \iint_{I\times J} \alpha(x,y)f(x,y)dxdy.$$

We assume that all displayed integrals and sums exist.

Conditional expectations are defined in the same way. The **conditional expectation of α(X,Y), for Z fixed at z∈K,** is

$$E[\alpha(X,Y)/Z=z] := \iint_{I\times J} \alpha(x,y)f(x,y/z)dxdy.$$

This is a function, say g(z) of z∈K.

The **conditional expectation of α(X,Y), for fixed Z,** is the random variable

$$E[\alpha(X,Y)/Z] := \iint_{I\times J} \alpha(x,y)f(x,y/Z)dxdy = g(Z).$$

This conditional expectation has the following property.

$$E[g(Z)h(Z)] = E[\alpha(X,Y)h(Z)] \quad \text{(h bounded function).} \tag{7}$$

Indeed, the first member of (7) equals

$$\int_K g(z)h(z)f(z)dz = \int_K[\iint_{I\times J} \alpha(x,y)f(x,y/z)dxdy]h(z)f(z)dz\ ,$$

and the last

$$\iiint_{I\times J\times K} \alpha(x,y)h(z)f(x,y,z)dxdydz.$$

By Fubini, these members are equal because f(x,y,z)=f(z)f(x,y/z).

Similarly, the **conditional expectation of $\alpha(X)$ for Y fixed at $y \in J$ and Z at $z \in K$,** is

$$E[\alpha(X)/Y=y,Z=z] := \int_I \alpha(x)f(x/y,z)dx.$$

This is a function g(y,z) of $(y,z) \in J \times K$.

The **conditional expectation of $\alpha(X)$ for fixed Y and Z**, is the random variable

$$E[\alpha(X)/Y,Z] := \int_I \alpha(x)f(x/Y,Z)dx = g(Y,Z).$$

Now

$$E[g(Y,Z)h(Y,Z)] = E[\alpha(X)h(Y,Z)] \text{ (h bounded function),} \quad (8)$$

by Fubini and because f(x,y,z)=f(y,z)f(x/y,z).

Finally, as a last example,

$$E[\alpha(X)/Y=y] := \int_I \alpha(x)f(x/y)dx =: g(y) \quad (y \in K),$$

$$E[\alpha(X)/Y] := \int_I \alpha(x)f(x/Y)dx = g(Y)$$

and now

$$E[g(Y)h(Y)] = E[\alpha(X)h(Y)] \text{ (h bounded function).} \quad (9)$$

2.1.2. Discrete Case

Marginal and conditional random variables

Here we consider, as an example, a couple (M,N) of random variables with values in $\mathbf{N}_+$. Let

$$P(M=m,N=n) =: f(m,n).$$

Here and hereafter, m and n are positive integers. The total probability mass must be equal to 1. Hence, $\sum_m \sum_n f(m,n)=1$. The distribution of M results from the relations

$$P(M=m) = P(M=m, n \in \mathbf{N}_+) = \sum_n f(m,n) =: f(m),$$

and that of N is obtained in a similar way. The distribution of $M_{/N=n}$ results from the relations

$$P(M=m/N=n) = P(M=m,N=n)/P(N=n) = f(m,n)/f(n) =: f(m/n).$$

Conditional expectations

The **conditional expectation of $\alpha(M)$ for N fixed at point n**, is

$$E(\alpha(M)/N=n) := \sum_m \alpha(m)f(m/n) =: g(n).$$

The **conditional expectation of $\alpha(M)$ for fixed N**, is

$$E[\alpha(M)/N] := \sum_m \alpha(m)f(m/N) = g(N).$$

Then

$$E[g(N)h(N)] = E[\alpha(M)h(N)] \quad \text{(h bounded function)}. \tag{10}$$

2.1.3. Mixed Case

Marginal and conditional random variables

Here we consider a random couple (X,N) where X is a continuous random variable with values in $I \subseteq \mathbf{R}_+$ and N a random variable with values in $\mathbf{N}_+$. Now

$$P(X \in dx, N=n) = f(x,n)dx.$$

The point x is always a point in I and the point n a positive integer. Now $\sum_n \int_I f(x,n)dx=1$ and

$$f(x) := \sum_n f(x,n)\ ,\ f(n) := \int_I f(x,n)dx,$$

$$f(x/n) := f(x,n)/f(n)\ ,\ f(n/x) := f(x,n)/f(x).$$

Conditional expectations

$$E(\alpha(X)/N=n) := \int_I \alpha(x)f(x/n)dx =: g(n),$$

$$E(\alpha(X)/N) := \int_I \alpha(x)f(x/N)dx =: g(N),$$

$$E[g(N)h(N))] = E[\alpha(X)h(N)] \quad \text{(h bounded function)}. \tag{11}$$

Similarly,

$$E[\alpha(N)/X=x] := \sum_n \alpha(n)f(n/x) =: g(x),$$

$$E(\alpha(N)/X) := \sum_n \alpha(n)f(n/X) =: g(X),$$

$$E[g(X)h(X)] = E[\alpha(N)h_2(X)] \quad \text{(h bounded function)}. \tag{12}$$

2.2. Modern Conditional Expectation

2.2.1. Expectations

All random variables X,Y,... are supposed to be defined on some fixed probability space. **Almost surely equal random variables are identified**. This agreement does not lead to contradictions, (certainly not in relations in which no more than a denumerable number of random variables do occur). It allows to omit the **a.s.** (almost surely) indication.

The variable X is **integrable** if $E|X|<\infty$. The expectation E(X) of any positive random variable is defined, but it may be infinite. **If the expectation of a positive random variable equals zero, then this random variable is zero.** This must be understood as follows: If $X\geq 0$ and $E(X)=0$, then $X=0$ a.s. and then we can replace X by 0, because almost surely equal random variables are identified. Positive random variables may have the value ∞. The products $0.\infty$ and $\infty.0$ equal 0. **If the expectation of a positive random variable is finite,** (i.e. if the random variable is integrable), **then this random variable is finite**. Here the meaning is: If $X\geq 0$ and $E(X)<\infty$, then $X<\infty$ a.s. and then we can replace X by any finite variable almost surely equal to X, for instance by $X1_{X<\infty}$.

An **n-dimensional random vector Y** is a vector $(Y_1,...,Y_n)$, where $Y_1,...,Y_n$ are random variables. Any random variable is considered being a random vector with a dimension equal to 1.

No other mappings on $\mathbf{R}^m$ or on intervals in $\mathbf{R}^m$, with values in $\mathbf{R}^n$ or in $\mathbf{R}_+\cup\{\infty\}$, are ever considered in this book than Borel mappings. No other subsets of $\mathbf{R}^m$ are ever considered than Borel subsets. "For all functions" , "for all sets", means in fact "for all Borel functions", "for all Borel sets". In particular, the function f occurring (1), is supposed to be a Borel function, and the set B occurring in (3) is supposed to be a Borel set. The functions f, g, h occurring in the next Theorem are Borel functions.

Theorem 1

Let Y be an n-dimensional random vector, f and g functions on $\mathbf{R}^n$. Let f(Y) and g(Y) be both integrable, or both positive, such that

$$E[f(Y)h(Y)] \leq E[g(Y)h(Y)] \text{ (h bounded positive function on } \mathbf{R}^n). \quad (13)$$

Then $f(Y)\leq g(Y)$.

Proof

Let us assume first that f(Y) and g(Y) are integrable. For $h:=1_{g<f}$:

$$E[(f(Y)-g(Y))1_{g(Y)<f(Y)}] \le 0.$$

The left member is the expectation of a positive function, and this expectation is negative. Hence, the function is zero:

$$(f(Y)-g(Y))1_{g(Y)<f(Y)} = 0,$$

i.e. $f(Y) \le g(Y)$. If f(Y) and g(Y) are positive, not necessarily integrable, then we take h equal to

$$h_k := 1_{g<f,g<k} \ (k\in \mathbf{N}_+).$$

Then gh_k is a finite function, and $\varphi_k := fh_k - gh_k$ is a positive function. From the assumptions results that $E(\varphi_k(Y))\le 0$ and this implies that $\varphi_k(Y)=0$:

$$f(Y)1_{g(Y)<f(Y),g(Y)<k} = g(Y)1_{g(Y)<f(Y),g(Y)<k},$$

and for $k\uparrow\infty$,

$$f(Y)1_{g(Y)<f(Y),g(Y)<\infty} = g(Y)1_{g(Y)<f(Y),g(Y)<\infty}.$$

This implies that f(Y)=g(Y) if the conditions g(Y)<f(Y) and g(Y)<∞ are both satisfied. Hence, they cannot both be satisfied, i.e. $f(Y)\le g(Y)$ or $g(Y)=\infty$. In any case $f(Y)\le g(Y)$ •

2.2.2. Conditional Expectations

Let X be a positive (or integrable) random variable and Y an n-dimensional random vector. The **conditional expectation E(X/Y) of X, for fixed Y**, is the unique positive (or integrable) random variable g(Y) such that

$$\mathbf{E[g(Y)h(Y)] = E[Xh(Y)]} \ \textbf{(h bounded positive function on } \mathbf{R^n}\textbf{)}. \quad (14)$$

The unicity of this definition results from the preceding Theorem. Indeed, if $g_1(Y)$ and $g_2(Y)$ satisfy the definition, then

$$E[g_1(Y)h(Y)] = E[Xh(Y)] = E[g_2(Y)h(Y)] \ \text{(h bounded positive)}$$

and then $g_1(Y)\le g_2(Y)$ and $g_2(Y)\le g_1(Y)$ by that Theorem.

In the classical cases, the existence of the conditional expectation results from relations such as (7), (8), (9), (10), (11), (12) and these relations show that **the modern definition and the old-fashioned definition are equivalent** in these cases. This is enough evidence, for the reader not yet familiar with the modern conditional expectation, to admit its existence.

Of course E(X/Y) is the conditional expectation of X with respect to the sub-σ-algebra (of the basic σ-algebra of the probability space on which all random variables are defined) generated by Y. Then the definition via (14) is easily seen to be equivalent to the usual definition (via Radon-Nikodym, or via projections). The topic is discussed in App.F.

In the following Theorem, any random variable occurring before the slash is supposed to be integrable or positive. After the slash, any random vectors may occur. If several vectors occur after the slash, they are supposed to be grouped in a unique vector.The functions α, β, γ are defined on some $\mathbf{R}^m$ and they have values in some $\mathbf{R}^n$. The function f has values in **R**. The convexity of a function is defined at the start of the proof of (22).

Theorem 2 (Properties of Conditional Expectations)

Constants:

$$\mathbf{E(c/Y) = c \ , \ E(Y/c) = E(Y).} \tag{15}$$

Linearity:

$$\mathbf{E(aX+bY/Z) = aE(X/Z)+bE(Y/Z).} \tag{16}$$

Monotone character:

$$\mathbf{E(X/Z) \leq E(Y/Z) \quad (X \leq Y),} \tag{17}$$

$$\mathbf{E(X/Y) \geq 0 \quad (X \geq 0).} \tag{18}$$

Conditionally constant factor :

$$\mathbf{E[Xf(Y)/Y] = f(Y)E(X/Y).} \tag{19}$$

Iterativity :

$$\mathbf{E[E(X/Y)] = E(X).} \tag{20}$$

Contraction :

$$\mathbf{|E(X/Y)| \leq E(|X|/Y) \ , \ E|E(X/Y)| \leq E|X|.} \tag{21}$$

Jensen : If f is positive and convex on the closed interval I and if X is integrable and has all its values in I, then the values of E(X/Y) also lie in I and

$$\mathbf{f[E(X/Y)] \leq E[f(X)/Y].} \tag{22}$$

General iterativity :

$$\mathbf{E[E(X/Y)/\alpha(Y)] = E[X/\alpha(Y)],} \tag{23}$$

$$\mathbf{E[E(X/\alpha(Y))/Y] = E[X/\alpha(Y)],} \tag{24}$$

$$\mathbf{E[E(X/Y)/Y,Z] = E(X/Y),} \tag{25}$$

$$\mathbf{E[E(X/Y,Z)/Y] = E(X/Y).} \tag{26}$$

Equivalent conditionings :

$$\mathbf{E(X/Y) = E(X/Z)\ \ if\ \ Y{=}\beta(Z)\ and\ Z{=}\gamma(Y).} \tag{27}$$

Proof

In this proof, h is always a bounded positive function defined on some $\mathbf{R}^n$.

(15) E(c/Y) is the unique random variable g(Y) such that

$$E[g(Y)h(Y)] = E[c\ h(Y)] \ \ \text{(all h)}.$$

The solution of this equation is g(Y)=c. Similarly, E(Y/c) is the unique random variable g(c) such that

$$E[g(c)h(Y)] = E[E(Y)h(Y)] \ \text{(all h)}.$$

Hence, g(c)=E(Y).

(16) If X,Y are positive, then it is assumed that a,b≥0. Let

$$f(Z) := E(X/Z) \ \ ,\ \ g(Z) := E(Y/Z).$$

Then

$$E[f(Z)h(Z)] = E[Xh(Z)] \ \ ,\ \ E[g(Z)h(Z)] = E[Yh(Z)] \ \ \text{(all h)}.$$

Then

$$E\{[af(Z)+bg(Z)]h(Z)\} = E[(aX+bY)h(Z)] \ \text{(all h)}$$

and then

$$E(aX+bY/Z) = af(Z)+bg(Z)\ .$$

(17) Let

$$X\leq Y \ \ ,\ \ f(Z) := E(X/Z) \ \ ,\ \ g(Z) := E(Y/Z).$$

Then

$$E[f(Z)h(Z)] = E[Xh(Z)] \leq E[Yh(Z)] = E[g(Z)h(Z)] \ \ \text{(all h)}$$

and then

$$f(Z) \leq g(Z)$$

by Theorem 1.

(18) Results from (17) and the assumption 0≤X.

(19) We may assume $X \geq 0$, $f \geq 0$ because we can use the decompositions $X = X_+ - X_-$, $f = f_+ - f_-$ and use the linearity already proved. Let

$$g(Y) := E(X/Y).$$

Then

$$E[g(Y)h(Y)] = E[Xh(Y)] \text{ (all h)}. \tag{28}$$

That relation holds in fact for all $h \geq 0$, not necessarily bounded. Indeed, if h is not bounded, then we replace that function by $h1_{h<k}$ ($k \in \mathbf{N}_+$) in (28) and we let $k \uparrow \infty$. Then, by monotone convergence, we obtain (28) for unbounded h. Hence, in (28), we may replace h by f.h:

$$E[g(Y)f(Y)h(Y)] = E[Xf(Y)h(Y)] \quad \text{(all h)}$$

and then

$$E[Xf(Y)/Y] = g(Y)f(Y).$$

(20) Let

$$g(Y) := E(X/Y).$$

Then

$$E[g(Y)h(Y)] = E[Xh(Y)] \text{ (all h)}.$$

In particular, for $h \equiv 1$, $E[g(Y)] = E(X)$.

(21) If $X \geq 0$, then the first formula (21) is tautological by (18). If X is integrable, then by the linearity already proved,

$$E(X/Y) = E(X_+ - X_-/Y) = E(X_+/Y) - E(X_-/Y),$$

$$|E(X/Y)| = |E(X_+/Y) - E(X_-/Y)| \leq E(X_+/Y) + E(X_-/Y) = E(X_+ + X_-/Y) = E(|X|/Y)$$

The last formula (21) results from the first by the application of E and then by the iterativity already proved.

(22) The function f is **convex** on the interval I. This means that a function λ exists on I such that

$$(x-c)\lambda(c) \leq f(x) - f(c) \quad (x \in I,\ c \in I). \tag{29}$$

We assume that $I = [a, \infty[$ (the argument is similar, or simpler, for other closed intervals). Then $a \leq X$, and by (15) and (17),

$$a \leq E(X/Y) < \infty,$$

where the strict inequality results from the integrabiliy assumption and from (21). Indeed

$$E|E(X/Y)| \leq E|X| < \infty$$

and this implies that E(X/Y) is a finite function. Hence, the values of E(X/Y) also lie in I. In (29) we replace x by X and c by E(X/Y) :

$$[X-E(X/Y)]\lambda[E(X/Y)] \leq f(X)-f[E(X/Y)]. \tag{30}$$

Then it is enough to apply $E\{\cdot/Y\}$ to this relation. Indeed, then the first member of (30) becomes, by the conditionally constant factor property,

$$E\{[X-E(X/Y)]\lambda[E(X/Y)]/Y\} = \lambda[E(X/Y)]\, E\{[X-E(X/Y)]/Y\}$$

$$= \lambda[E(X/Y)]\{E(X/Y)-E[E(X/Y)/Y]\} = \lambda[E(X/Y)]\{E(X/Y)-E(X/Y)\} = 0.$$

Hence,

$$0 \leq E\{f(X)-f[E(X/Y)]/Y\} = E[f(X)/Y]- f[E(X/Y)].$$

(23) We have to verify that

$$E\{E[X/\alpha(Y)]h[\alpha(Y)]\} = E\{E(X/Y)h[\alpha(Y)]\} \quad \text{(all h)}. \tag{31}$$

By the conditionally constant factor property and by iterativity, the first member of (31) equals,

$$E\{E[Xh[\alpha(Y)]/\alpha(Y)]\} = E\{Xh[\alpha(Y)]\}.$$

In the same way, the last member of (31) equals

$$E\{E(Xh[\alpha(Y)]/Y)\} = E(Xh[\alpha(Y)].$$

(24) The conditional expectation $E[X/\alpha(Y)]$ is some function $g[\alpha(Y)]$. Hence the property of the conditionally constant factor applies in the first member.

(25) This is a particular case of (23), because $Y=\alpha(Y,Z)$ if α is defined by $\alpha(x,y):=x$.

(26) This is a particular case of (24).

(27)
$$E[X/Y] = E[X/\beta(Z)] = E\{E[X/Z]/\beta(Z)\}$$

$$= E\{E[X/\gamma(Y)]/Y\} = E[X/\gamma(Y)] = E[X/Z],$$

by the general iterativity relations •

Remarks

a. In (22), the assumption that f is positive can be replaced by the much weaker assumption that f is bounded below. Indeed, if $-c \leq f$, then (22) can be applied to $c+f$.

For $Y \equiv c$ in (22), that relation becomes by (15), $f[E(X)] \leq E[f(X)]$, i.e. **Jensen for usual unconditional expectations**.

b. The relations (23), (24), (25), (26) are instances of a general rule that can be formulated as follows: **Iterated conditional expectations, with comparable conditions, can be reduced to a single conditional expectation in which only the weakest condition is retained.** For instance, in the first member of (25) a conditioning by Y, and another by (Y,Z) occur. These **conditionings are comparable**: the Y information is weaker than the (Y,Z) information. In (23), the $\alpha(Y)$ information is weaker than the Y information.

c. No general formula is available for iterated non comparable conditionings. The intuitive formula $E[E(X/Y)/Z]=E(X/Y,Z)$, stating that it is equivalent to condition successively by Y and Z, or to condition simultaneously by Y and Z, is false in general.

d. Illustrations of (27) are:

$$E(X/Y,Z) = E(X/Z,Y) = E(X/Z,Z+Y) = E(X/Z+Y,Z-Y),$$

where Y and Z are random variables.

e. Let f be a function on the interval I, with positive continuous second order derivative f'' on I. By Taylor,

$$f(x) = f(c) + (x-c)f'(c) + 1/2\,(x-c)^2 f''(\xi) \geq f(c) + (x-c)f'(c) \quad (x,c \in I),$$

where ξ is some number between x and c. Hence, f is convex with $\lambda := f'$ according to the definition based on (29).

Convex functions do not necessarily have second order derivatives everywhere. For instance, the absolute value function $|\cdot|$ is convex on $\mathbf{R}$ but the derivatives $|x|'$, $|x|''$ do not exist at the origin $x=0$. The λ function corresponding to $|\cdot|$ can be defined by the conditions

$$\lambda \equiv -1 \text{ on } \mathbf{R}_- , \quad \lambda(0) = 0 , \quad \lambda \equiv +1 \text{ on } \mathbf{R}_+.$$

Simplified notations

Simplified notations are used for expectations and conditional expectations. Examples:

$$E(X) \equiv EX \ , \ E[f(X)] \equiv Ef(X),$$

$$E[E(X/Y)] \equiv EE(X/Y) \ , \ E\{E[f(X)/Y]\} \equiv EE[f(X)/Y].$$

Theorem 3 (Monotone Convergence for Conditional Expectations)

Let X_k ($k \in N_+$) be a sequence of positive random variables such that $X_k \uparrow X$ as $k \uparrow \infty$. Let Y be a random vector. Then $E(X_k/Y) \uparrow E(X/Y)$.

Proof
Let

$$g_k(Y) := E(X_k/Y).$$

Then

$$E[g_k(Y)h(Y)] = E[X_k h(Y)] \ \text{(h positive bounded function)}. \qquad (32)$$

By (17)

$$g_k(Y) = E(X_k/Y) \leq E(X_{k+1}/Y) = g_{k+1}(Y).$$

Let

$$g := \lim \sup_{k \uparrow \infty} g_k .$$

Then

$$g_k(Y) \uparrow g(Y).$$

As $k \uparrow \infty$ in (32), we obtain

$$E[g(Y)h(Y)] = E[Xh(Y)] \ \text{(h positive bounded function)},$$

by monotone convergence. Then

$$g(Y) = E(X/Y) \ \bullet$$

2.3. Conditional Independence

2.3.1. Definitions

We illustrate the definitions and the Theorems on the **four random variables X, Y, Z, Θ**. All definitions and results (with similar proofs) can be extended to **any number of random vectors $X_1, X_2, \ldots, X_n$, Θ**.

In this section A,B,C,Δ are subsets of **R** and f,g,h are real functions on **R**.

We assume that the reader is familiar with the usual unconditional independence of random variables. However, in order to show the analogy with conditional independence, we recall some definitions and properties.

The random variables X,Y,Z are independent if

$$P(X\in A, Y\in B, Z\in C) = P(X\in A)\ P(Y\in B)\ P(Z\in C) \quad \text{(all A,B,C)}.$$

The random variables X,Y,Z are conditionally independent for fixed Θ, if

$$P(X\in A, Y\in B, Z\in C/\Theta) = P(X\in A/\Theta)\ P(X\in B/\Theta)\ P(X\in C/\Theta) \quad \text{(all A,B,C)}.$$

The **conditional probability of an event**, is the corresponding conditional expectation of the indicator function of that event. For instance, in the last relation,

$$P(X\in A, Y\in B, Z\in C/\Theta) := E(1_{X\in A, Y\in B, Z\in C}/\Theta)\ .$$

In the relations defining the independence and the conditional independence, we can take C=**R**. This shows that **if X,Y,Z are independent, then X and Y are independent. If X,Y,Z are conditionally independent for fixed Θ, then X,Y are conditionally independent for fixed Θ.**

Several Theorems on independence do have a **conditional version**, corresponding to a conditioning by Θ, and an **unconditional version**. By (15), the unconditional version is in fact a particular case of the conditional version, because it corresponds to a conditioning by $\Theta\equiv c$.

2.3.2. Properties

Theorem 4

If X,Y,Z are independent random variables, then f(X),g(Y),h(Z) are independent random variables. If X,Y,Z are conditionally independent random variables for fixed Θ, then f(X),g(Y),h(Z) are conditionally independent for fixed Θ.

Proof
We only consider the statement concerning conditional independency. Let X,Y,Z be conditionally independent for fixed Θ. Then

$$P(f(X)\in A,\ g(Y)\in B,\ h(Z)\in C\ /\Theta) = P(X\in f^{-1}(A),\ Y\in g^{-1}(B),\ Z\in h^{-1}(C)\ /\Theta)$$
$$= P(X\in f^{-1}(A)/\Theta)\ P(Y\in g^{-1}(B)/\Theta)\ P(\ Z\in h^{-1}(C)\ /\Theta)$$
$$= P(f(X)\in A/\Theta)\ P(g(Y)\in B/\Theta)\ P(h(Z)\in C/\Theta)\quad \text{(all A,B,C)}\ \bullet$$

Theorem 5

Let f(X), g(Y), h(Z) be positive or integrable.

If X, Y, Z are independent random variables, then

$$\mathbf{E[f(X)g(Y)h(Z)] = Ef(X).Eg(Y).Eh(Z).} \tag{33}$$

If X, Y, Z are conditionally independent for fixed Θ, then

$$\mathbf{E[f(X)g(Y)h(Z)/\Theta] = E[f(X)/\Theta]E[g(Y)/\Theta]E[h(Z)/\Theta].} \tag{34}$$

Proof

We consider (34). It is enough to verify that relation for the indicator functions

$$f=1_A\ ,\ g=1_B\ ,\ h=1_C, \tag{35}$$

because then the proof can be completed by a monotone class argument, and the decompositions

$$f=f_+-f_-\ ,\ g=g_+-g_-\ ,\ h=h_+-h_-$$

can be used in case of functions of any sign. In case of functions (35),

$$E[f(X)g(Y)h(Z)/\Theta] = E[1_A(X)1_B(Y)1_C(Z)/\Theta] = E(1_{X\in A}1_{Y\in B}1_{Z\in C}/\Theta)$$
$$= P(X\in A, Y\in B, Z\in C/\Theta) = P(X\in A/\Theta)P(X\in B/\Theta)P(X\in C/\Theta)$$
$$= E(1_{X\in A}/\Theta)\ E(1_{Y\in B}/\Theta)\ E(1_{Z\in C}/\Theta) = E[f(X)/\Theta]\ E[g(Y)/\Theta]\ E[h(Z)/\Theta)]\ \bullet$$

Theorem 6

Let X,Y,Z be conditionally independent for fixed Θ. Then, if X is positive or integrable,

$$\mathbf{E(X/Y,Z,\Theta) = E(X/\Theta).} \tag{36}$$

Proof

It is enough to consider the case X positive, because that result can be applied to X_+ and to X_-.

We start with the proof of the relation

$$E[E(X/\Theta)1_{(Y,Z,\Theta)\in B\times C\times\Delta}] = E[X1_{(Y,Z,\Theta)\in B\times C\times\Delta}] \text{ (all } B,C,\Delta). \quad (37)$$

The first member of (37) equals

$E[E(X/\Theta)1_{Y\in B}1_{Z\in C}1_{\Theta\in\Delta}]$

(Iterativity)

$= E\{E[E(X/\Theta)1_{Y\in B}1_{Z\in C}1_{\Theta\in\Delta}/\Theta]\}$

(Conditionally constant factor)

$= E\{E(X/\Theta)1_{\Theta\in\Delta}E[1_{Y\in B}1_{Z\in C}/\Theta]\}$

(Conditional independence)

$= E\{E(X/\Theta)1_{\Theta\in\Delta}E[1_{Y\in B}/\Theta]E[1_{Z\in C}/\Theta]\}$

(Theorem 5)

$= E\{1_{\Theta\in\Delta}E[X1_{Y\in B}1_{Z\in C}/\Theta]\}$

(Conditionally constant factor)

$= E\{E[1_{\Theta\in\Delta}X1_{Y\in B}1_{Z\in C}/\Theta]\}$

(Iterativity)

$= E\{1_{\Theta\in\Delta}X1_{Y\in B}1_{Z\in C}/\Theta\} = E[X1_{(Y,Z,\Theta)\in(B\times C\times\Delta)}]$.

From (37) follows, by a monotone class argument,

$$E[E(X/\Theta)\gamma(Y,Z,\Theta)] = E[X\gamma(Y,Z,\Theta)] \text{ (}\gamma\text{ bounded positive)}. \quad (38)$$

Then (36) follows from (38) by the very definition of the modern conditional expectation •

2.4. Conditional Variances and Covariances

2.4.1. Definitions

Theorem 7 (Schwarz)

Let X and Y be positive random variables. Then

$$\mathbf{E^2(XY) \leq E(X^2)E(Y^2).} \quad (39)$$

Proof

Let us first assume that X and Y are bounded. Let (X′,Y′) be a couple of random variables, independent of the couple (X,Y), with the same distribution. Then

$$0 \leq E(X'Y-XY')^2 = E(X'^2Y^2) + E(X^2Y'^2) - 2E(X'YXY')$$

$$= E(X'^2)E(Y^2) + E(X^2)E(Y'^2) - 2E(XY)E(X'Y')$$

$$= 2E(X^2)E(Y^2) - 2E^2(XY).$$

In the general case, we replace X, Y by the bounded random variables $X1_{X<k}$, $Y1_{Y<k}$ in (39), we let $k\uparrow\infty$ and we use monotone convergence •

Hereafter, **X,Y,Z are square-integrable random variables** of any sign:

$$EX^2 < \infty \ , \ EY^2 < \infty \ , \ EZ^2 < \infty.$$

Then **the product XY is an integrable random variable** by Schwarz. Indeed,

$$E^2|XY| \leq E(X^2)E(Y^2) < \infty .$$

We suppose that the reader is familiar with the usual unconditional variances and covariances, but we recall the definitions and properties, in order to show the analogies with the conditional concepts.

The **covariance of X and Y** is

$$\mathrm{Cov}(X,Y) := E[(X-EX)(Y-EY)]. \tag{40}$$

The **variance of X is**

$$\mathrm{Var}\, X \equiv \mathrm{Var}(X) := \mathrm{Cov}(X,X) .$$

Hereafter, **Θ is a random vector**. We recall that the results of section 2.3 are stated and proved for a random variable Θ, but that they are valid, with identical proofs, when Θ is a random vector.

The **conditional covariance of X and Y for fixed Θ** is the random variable

$$\mathrm{Cov}(X,Y/\Theta) := E[[X-E(X/\Theta)][Y-E(Y/\Theta)]/\Theta].$$

The **conditional variance of X for fixed Θ** is the random variable

$$\mathrm{Var}(X/\Theta) := \mathrm{Cov}(X,X/\Theta).$$

2.4.2. Properties

The following properties are obvious.

Symmetry:

$$\mathrm{Cov}(X,Y) = \mathrm{Cov}(Y,X) \ , \ \mathrm{Cov}(X,Y/\Theta) = \mathrm{Cov}(Y,X/\Theta).$$

Linearity:

$$\mathrm{Cov}(aX+bY,Z) = a\,\mathrm{Cov}(X,Z) + b\,\mathrm{Cov}(Y,Z).$$

$$\mathrm{Cov}(aX+bY,Z/\Theta) = a\,\mathrm{Cov}(X,Z/\Theta) + b\,\mathrm{Cov}(Y,Z/\Theta).$$

Positiveness:

$$\mathrm{Var}(X) \geq 0 \ , \ \mathrm{Var}(X/\Theta) \geq 0.$$

Theorem 8 (Properties of Variances and Covariances)

$$\mathbf{Cov(X,Y) = E(XY) - EX.EY.} \tag{41}$$

$$\mathbf{Var(X) = EX^2 - E^2X.} \tag{42}$$

$$\mathbf{Cov(X,Y/\Theta) = E(XY/\Theta) - E(X/\Theta)\ E(Y/\Theta).} \tag{43}$$

$$\mathbf{Var(X/\Theta) = E(X^2/\Theta) - E^2(X/\Theta).} \tag{44}$$

$$\mathbf{Cov(X,Y) = E\ Cov(X,Y/\Theta) + Cov[E(X/\Theta),E(Y/\Theta)].} \tag{45}$$

$$\mathbf{Var(X) = E\ Var(X/\Theta) + Var\ E(X/\Theta).} \tag{46}$$

$$\mathbf{Cov(c,X) = 0.} \tag{47}$$

If X and Y are independent,

$$\mathbf{Cov(X,Y) = 0.} \tag{48}$$

If X and Y are conditionally independent for fixed Θ,

$$\mathbf{Cov(X,Y/\Theta) = 0.} \tag{49}$$

If f(Θ) is square-integrable,

$$\mathbf{Cov(f(\Theta),X/\Theta) = 0.} \tag{50}$$

Proof

(43) $\mathrm{Cov}(X,Y/\Theta) = E[XY - X\,E(Y/\Theta) - Y\,E(X/\Theta) + E(X/\Theta)\,E(Y/\Theta)/\Theta]$

$$= E[XY/\Theta] - E(Y/\Theta)\,E[X/\Theta] - E(X/\Theta)\,E[Y/\Theta] + E(X/\Theta)E(Y/\Theta)$$

$$= E(XY/\Theta) - E(X/\Theta)\,E(Y/\Theta),$$

by linearity and by the property of the conditionally constant factor.

(45) By (43),

$$\mathrm{E\,Cov}(X,Y/\Theta) = E[E(XY/\Theta) - E(X/\Theta)\,E(Y/\Theta)]$$

$$= E[E(XY/\Theta)] - E[E(X/\Theta)E(Y/\Theta)] = E(XY) - E[E(X/\Theta)E(Y/\Theta)],$$

by linearity and iterativity. By (41) applied to the random variables $E(X/\Theta)$ and $E(Y/\Theta)$, and by the iterativity property,

$$\mathrm{Cov}[E(X/\Theta),E(Y/\Theta)] = E[E(X/\Theta)\,E(Y/\Theta)] - EE(X/\Theta).EE(Y/\Theta)$$

$$= E[E(X/\Theta)\,E(Y/\Theta)] - EX.EY,$$

$$\mathrm{E\,Cov}(X,Y/\Theta)+\mathrm{Cov}[E(X/\Theta),E(Y/\Theta)] = E(XY)-EX.EY = \mathrm{Cov}(X,Y),$$

where the last equality results from (41).

(49) Results from (43), and the conditional independence assumption, by which

$$E(XY/\Theta)= E(X/\Theta)E(Y/\Theta).$$

The verification of the other relations is similar, or simpler •

The relations of the theorems of this chapter are of the utmost importance. We will not refer to them hereafter. The reader must know them by heart, especially if he wants to attack the Credibility Theory of Part III of this book.

Chapter 3

Risk Models

3.0. Introduction

Actuarial risk models deal with **portfolios** of **insurance companies**.

A **portfolio** is any collection of **contracts** or **policies**, considered in a fixed period. This period is necessarily finite in practice, but mostly infinite in the theoretical **risk model** describing the portfolio.

The portfolio could contain all the contracts of the company, and it could be limited to a single policy. More frequently, it is constituted of a rather large collection of contracts of the same nature.

Claims can occur on the contracts. The **claim instant** must be understood as the **instant of settlement of the claim**, rather than its instant of occurrence.

The insurer starts, at time 0, with a positive **working capital**, called the **initial risk reserve**. The initial risk reserve can be considered as the amount that the insurer is willing to risk, in compensation of the profits that he could make.

The insurer collects **premiums** during the lifetime of the portfolio. The amount

(initial risk reserve)
+(amount of premiums earned before t)
−(amount of claims settled before t)

is the **risk reserve at the instant t**. In some models the risk reserve is augmented by the interests that it produces.

The insurer is **ruined**, for the considered portfolio, if at some time he cannot pay the amount of claims occurred in the portfolio.

3.1. Risk Model and Ruin Events

3.1.1. Components of the Risk Model

The components of the risk model, are

a. The **claim process** $(T_1,X_1,T_2,X_2,...)$.

b. The **risk reserve process** R_τ $(\tau \geq 0)$.

T_k is the **instant of settlement** of the claim with amount X_k.

Claim instants process

The **claim instants process** is the sub-process $(T_1,T_2,...)$ of the claim process.We assume that $0<T_1\leq T_2\leq...$ The claim instants process is a particular **point process**. The following Chapter 4 is devoted to point processes.

We denote by N_t the **number of claims in the time-interval [0,t]**.

Claim amounts process

The **claim amounts process** is the sub-process $(X_1,X_2,...)$ of the claim process. We assume that the claim amounts X_k are positive.

We denote by S_t the **claim amount in [0,t]**:

$$S_t = X_1+X_2+...+X_{N_t},$$

Of course, $S_t=0$ if $N_t=0$. The claim amounts S_t are called **total claim amounts**. The claim amounts X_k are **partial claim amounts**.

Risk reserve process

The risk reserve process R_τ $(\tau \geq 0)$ is a stochastic process **defined in a deterministic way from the claim process**:

$$R_\tau := \varphi(\tau,N_\tau,T_1,X_1,...,T_{N_\tau},X_{N_\tau}) \quad (\tau \geq 0).$$

The complete stochastic part of any risk model is its claim process.

All models in the first nine Chapters are continuous-time models, briefly **continuous models**. Discrete models are considered in the last Chapter 10. In the continuous models, the trajectories of the risk reserve process $R(\tau) \equiv R_\tau (\tau \geq 0)$ have the following properties.

a. They all start at the same positive value u, called the **initial risk reserve**: $R(0) = u$.

b. They are right-continuous, bounded on bounded intervals.

c. They are continuous strictly increasing on the intervals $[0, T_1[$ and $[T_k, T_{k+1}[$ $(k=1,2,...)$.

d. $$R(T_k) = R(T_k-) - X_{T_k} \ (k=1,2,...).$$

An example of such a trajectory is represented in Fig.1, page 55.

Premium income process

In most continuous risk models (exceptions are the models of Chapter 9), the risk reserve process is defined via the **premium income process** P_τ $(\tau \geq 0)$. This is a stochastic process **defined in a deterministic way from the claim process**:

$$P_\tau := \gamma(\tau, N_\tau, T_1, X_1, ..., T_{N_\tau}, X_{N_\tau}) \ (\tau \geq 0).$$

P_τ is the **total premium collected in the interval $[0,\tau]$**.

The trajectories of the process P_τ $(\tau \geq 0)$ have the following properties:

a. They all start at the value 0: $P_0 = 0$.

b. They are continuous, strictly increasing, bounded on bounded intervals.

When the premium income process is defined, then the risk reserve R_τ equals

$$R_\tau := u + P_\tau - S_\tau \ (\tau \geq 0),$$

where u is the positive **initial risk reserve**.

The following **general assumptions** and **general notations** are adopted in all continuous risk models.

General assumptions

a. **The claim instants process and the claim amounts process are independent.**

b. **The number N_t of claims in any bounded interval [0,t] is finite. The number of claims in the time-interval [0,∞[is infinite. The expectation EN_t is finite for all t.**

c. **The random variables $X_1, X_2...$ are i.i.d. (Independent Identically Distributed). They have a finite strictly positive expectation.**

General notations

The distribution function of $X \equiv X_1$, i.e the (partial) **claimsize distribution function** is denoted by F. It is a distribution function on $\mathbf{R}_+$, not concentrated at 0.

The **moments of** F, considered in 3.2.1, are denoted by μ_k (k=1,2,...). The first moment $\mu \equiv \mu_1$ is finite. The **concave transform** of F, defined in 3.2.2, is denoted by G. The **adjustment coefficient** of the couple (G,q) (0<q<1), defined in 3.2.3, is denoted by ρ when it exists.

3.1.2. Ruin and Non-Ruin Events

The following events are considered:

Ruin at the fixed time t: $R_t < 0$.

Non-ruin at the fixed time t: $R_t \geq 0$.

Ruin before t: $R_\tau < 0$ for some $\tau \in [0,t]$.

Non-ruin before t: $R_\tau \geq 0$ for all $\tau \in [0,t]$.

Ruin in [0,∞[: $R_\tau < 0$ for some $\tau \in R_+$.

Non-ruin in [0,∞[: $R_\tau \geq 0$ for all $\tau \in R_+$.

These are *measurable events* because the stochastic process $R_\tau(\tau\geq0)$ has right-continuous trajectories.

The following notations are used

$$\Psi(t,u) := P(\text{Ruin before t}),$$

$$U(t,u) := P(\text{Non-ruin before t}) = 1-\Psi(t,u),$$

$$\Psi(u) := P(\text{Ruin in } [0,\infty[),$$

$$U(u) := P(\text{Non-ruin in } [0,\infty[) = 1-\Psi(u).$$

The probabilities $P(R_t\geq0)$ and $P(R_t<0)$ are **fixed-time** ruin and non-ruin probabilities. They depend on the initial risk reserve u. They do not have a specific notation.

The probabilities $\Psi(t,u)$ and $U(t,u)$ are **finite-time** ruin and non-ruin probabilties.

The probabilities $\Psi(u)$ and $U(u)$ are **infinite-time** ruin and non-ruin probabilities.

The ruin and non-ruin probabilities do depend on more parameters than u and t. The other parameters are not indicated because, mostly, they are kept fixed in the discussion. If they vary, they can be mentioned explicitly. For instance, if several claimsize distributions F are considered, notations such as U(u,F) and U(t,u,F) can be adopted.

3.1.3. Model Time and Real Time

The time t used in a continuous-time risk model is the **model time**, or the **operational time**. It rarely coincides with real time t′. Real time is measured in years. In practice, the connection between the times can be found out as follows. Let [0,t′] be a real time-interval. For instance, if t′=1, then [0,t′] is a specific year. Let [0,t] be the corresponding model time-interval. Then t results from the relation

$$EN_t = \lambda'(t'),$$

where $\lambda'(t')$ is the expected number of claims in the real time-interval [0,t′].

When infinite-time ruin probabilities are considered, the connection between real time and model time is irrelevant, because they are simultenaously infinite.

3.1.4. The Classical Risk Model

Assumptions of the classical risk model

a. **The claim instants process is a classical Poisson process with parameter λ.**

b. **The premium income process is the deterministic process**

$$p(\tau) \equiv p_\tau := \mu\lambda\tau(1+\eta) \ (\tau \geq 0),$$

where η is a strictly positive parameter, called the *security loading.*

The number $\mu\lambda(1+\eta)$ is the constant **premium income rate**.

$EN_\tau=\lambda\tau$ and $ES_\tau=\mu\lambda t$ in the classical risk model by next Th.5.b.d. Hence,

$$p_\tau = (1+\eta)\, ES_\tau.$$

This relation furnishes the interpretation of the security loading η.

The assumption on the premium income process seems to be an over-simplification. In fact it is not, when the model is interpreted in the right way. Indeed, any real premium income process is a jump process, but usually the jumps are so small, compared with the claim amounts, that the process can be approximated closely enough by a continuous one. It can be assumed that the dollars, say, flow in in a continuous way. Further, from the interpretation of the model time results that the assumption b. of a constant premium income rate, is in fact the following:

If $\lambda'(t')$ is the expected number of claims in the real-time interval $[0,t']$ and if $P'(t')$ is the premium collected in $[0,t']$, then $P'(t')/\lambda'(t')$ does not depend on t'.

Very often, it is preferable to work in a simple model describing a real situation only approximatively, than in a complicated model describing it rather exactly: If you have to estimate the volume of the earth, you better treat our planet as a perfect sphere, rather than to take all mountains and valleys into account.

A trajectory of the risk reserve process in the classical risk model is represented in Fig.2.

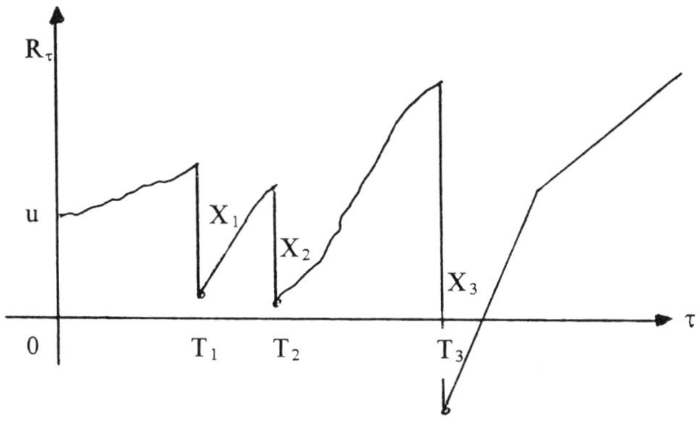

Fig.1. A trajectory of the risk reserve in the general risk model.

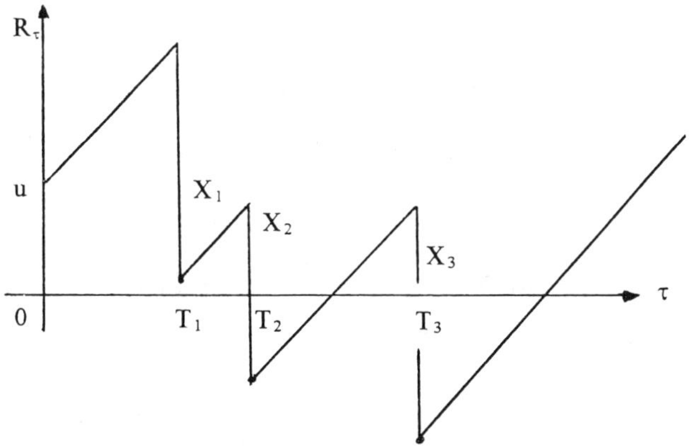

Fig.2. A trajectory of the risk reserve in the classicall risk model.

3.2. Characteristics of Claimsize Distribution

3.2.1. Moments of F

The **moments** of F are

$$\mu_k := EX^k = \int_{[0,\infty[} x^k \, dF(x) \; (k=1,2,\ldots). \quad (1)$$

The moments $\mu_2, \mu_3, \ldots$ may be infinite. From an integration by parts, after the replacement of dF(x) by $-d[1-F(x))]$ results that

$$\mu_k = k \int_{[0,\infty[} [1-F(y)]y^{k-1}\, dy \quad (k=1,2,\ldots), \tag{2}$$

by the discussion following Ch.1.Th.6. For k=1, (2) furnishes the **surface interpretation of the first moment** μ of F:

$$\mu \equiv \mu_1 = \int_{[0,\infty[} [1-F(y)]\, dy. \tag{3}$$

This relation expresses that μ is the surface of the domain delimited by the following lines in the usual Cartesian plane: the graph of F, the vertical axis and the horizontal line with ordinate 1.

3.2.2. Concave Transform G of F.

The **concave transform G of F** is the function defined by

$$G(x) := {}^{1}/_{\mu} \int_{[0,x]} [1-F(y)]dy \quad (x\geq 0). \tag{4}$$

From (4) results that $G(0)=0$ and that G has the density

$$G' = {}^{1}/_{\mu}\,(1-F). \tag{5}$$

By the density Theorem for integrals Ch.1.Th.9, $dG(x)$ can be replaced by ${}^{1}/_{\mu}[1-F(x)]dx$ in integrals with respect to G.

From (3) and (4) results that G is a continuous probability distribution function on $\mathbf{R}_+$. The moments of G are denoted by $\mu_k(G)$ (k=1,2,...).

Theorem 1

a. **The function G is a continuous concave probabibility distribution function on $\mathbf{R}_+$**

b. **The function G′ expressed by (5) is the density and the right-sided derivative of G on $\mathbf{R}_+$.**

c. $$\mu_1(G) = \mu_2/2\mu\,.$$

Proof
We start with b. We already know that G′ is a density of G. In order to show that G′ is the right-sided derivative of G, we consider the fixed point $x \geq 0$. Let $\varepsilon>0$. Then by (4),

$$G(x+\varepsilon)-G(x) = {}^{1}/_{\mu} \int_{[x,x+\varepsilon]} [1-F(y)]dy.$$

The value of the latter integral lies between $\varepsilon[1-F(x+\varepsilon)]$ and $\varepsilon[1-F(x)]$. Then

$${}^{1}/_{\mu}[1-F(x+\varepsilon)] \le {}^{1}/_{\varepsilon}[G(x+\varepsilon)-G(x)] \le {}^{1}/_{\mu}[1-F(x)].$$

As $\varepsilon\downarrow 0$, the common limit of the extreme members is ${}^{1}/_{\mu}[1-F(x)]$ by the right-continuity of F.

From (5) results that G′ is a decreasing function. Then a. results from b. and from the discussion preceding the statement of the Theorem.

For the proof of c, we have by (2) for k=2:

$$\mu_1(G) = \int_{[0,\infty[} x dG(x) = {}^{1}/_{\mu} \int_{[0,\infty[} x[1-F(x)]dx = \mu_{2/2\mu} \quad \bullet$$

3.2.3. Characteristic Function of F

The **characteristic function**, or **Fourier transform**, of F is the complex function φ_F defined on **R**, by

$$\varphi_F(\tau) := E\, e^{i\tau X} = \int_{\mathbf{R}} e^{ix} dF(x) \quad (\tau\in\mathbf{R})$$

If all moments of X are finite, then

$$\varphi_F(\tau) = Ee^{i\tau X} = E \sum_{k\ge 0} (i\tau X)^k/_{k!}$$

$$= \sum_{k\ge 0} (i\tau)^k/_{k!}\, EX^k = \sum_{k\ge 0} (i\tau)^k/_{k!}\, \mu_k$$

under convergence conditions.

If μ_2 exists, the following Theorem can be applied.

Theorem 2

If $\mu_2<\infty$,

$$\boldsymbol{\varphi_F(\tau) = 1 + i\tau\mu_1 - \tau^2/_2\, \mu_2 + \tau^2\, o(\tau) \quad \text{as} \quad \tau\to 0} \quad \bullet \tag{6}$$

This Theorem is a particular case of App.G.Th.G7. $o(\tau)$ represents a function of τ such that $o(\tau)\to 0$ as $\tau\to 0$.

3.2.4. Adjustment Coefficient

The **adjustment coefficient** ρ of the couple (G,q) ($0<q<1$) has been defined by Ch.1.(32). Equivalent definitions are furnished by the following Theorem. Here G is the concave transform of F, defined in 3.2.2.

Theorem 3 (Equivalent Definitions of the Adjustment Coefficient)

Let $\eta>0$, $q:=(1+\eta)^{-1}$. The following relations (7), (8), (9) and (10) are equivalent if $\rho>0$. Each of them defines the adjustment coefficient ρ of the couple (G,q).

$$q \int_{[0,\infty[} e^{\rho x}\, dG(x) = 1, \tag{7}$$

$$\rho \int_{[0,\infty[} (1-G(x))e^{\rho x}\, dx = \eta, \tag{8}$$

$$q \int_{[0,\infty[} (1-F(x))e^{\rho x} dx = \mu, \tag{9}$$

$$\int_{[0,\infty[} e^{\rho x}\, dF(x) = 1+\rho\mu(1+\eta), \tag{10}$$

where $\mu:=\mu_1(F)$.

Proof

In order to show that (7) and (8) are equivalent, it is sufficient to integrate by parts in the first member of (7) after replacement of dG(x) by $-d[1-G(x)]$. Similarly, starting with (10), it is verified that (9) and (10) are equivalent. The equivalence of (7) and (9) results from the fact that G is the concave transform of F •

The adjustment coefficient can exist only if all moments of G and F are finite. Indeed, if ρ exists

$$1 = q \int_{[0,\infty[} e^{\rho x}\, dG(x) = q \int_{[0,\infty[} \sum_{k\geq 0} \rho^k x^k/k!\, dG(x)$$

$$=q \sum_{k\geq 0} \int_{[0,\infty[} \rho^k x^k/k!\, dG(x) = q \sum_{k\geq 0} \rho^k/k!\, \mu_k(G),$$

by (7) and by monotone convergence. Then

$$\mu_k(G) < \infty \ (k=1,2,...).$$

In the same way, starting with (10), the existence of ρ implies that

$$\mu_k < \infty \ (k=1,2,...).$$

3.3. Characteristics of Distribution of Total Claim Amounts

3.3.1. General Risk Models

The **generating function** of the distribution of N_t is the function $\gamma_t(z)$ defined for complex z by

$$\gamma_t(z) := Ez^{N_t} = \sum_{k\geq 0} P(N_t=k)z^k \ (|z|\leq 1).$$

We denote by F_t the **distribution function of the total claim amount** S_t in [0,t]. The distribution function F_t is called a **compound Poisson (binomial, geometric,...) distribution function** if the distribution of N_t is Poisson (binomial, geometric,...).

We denote by φ_t the **characteristic function of the total claim amount** S_t:

$$\varphi_t(\tau) = Ee^{i\tau S_t} \ (\tau\in\mathbf{R}).$$

The following general relations are used in the demonstration of the next Theorem (See Chapter 2).

$$ES = EE(S/N),$$

$$\text{Var } S = E \text{ Var}(S/N) + \text{Var } E(S/N),$$

From the idependence of the partial claim amounts X_k results that

$$\text{Var}(X_1+...+X_n) = \text{Var } X_1 + ... + \text{Var } X_n.$$

The distribution function of the sum $X_1+...+X_n$ equals F^{*n}.

Theorem 4

In the general risk model, for all $t\in\mathbf{R}_+$:

a. $$\mathbf{F_t = \sum_{n\geq 0} P(N_t=n) F^{*n}.}$$

b. $$\mathbf{ES_t = \mu\, EN_t.}$$

c. $$\varphi_t(\tau) = \gamma_t(\varphi_F(\tau)) \quad (\tau\in\mathbf{R}).$$

d. If the partial claim amounts are square-integrable, then

$$\mathbf{Var\ S_t = Var\ X_1.EN_t + \mu^2\ Var\ N_t\ ,\ Var\ X_1 = \mu_2-\mu^2.}$$

Proof

Let $S \equiv S_t$, $N \equiv N_t$, $X \equiv X_1$.

a.
$$F_S(x) = P(X \le x) = P(X_1 + ... + X_N \le x)$$
$$= E\, P(X_1 + ... + X_N \le x \,/\, N) = EF^{*N}(x) = \textstyle\sum_{n \ge 0} P(N=n) F^{*n}(x).$$

b.
$$ES = EE(S/N) = EE(X_1 + ... + X_N \,/\, N) = E(N\mu) = \mu\, EN.$$

c.
$$\varphi_S(\tau) = Ee^{i\tau S} = EE(e^{i\tau S}/N) = E\, E[\exp(i\tau(X_1 + ... + X_N)) \,/\, N]$$
$$= E\, E^N(e^{i\tau X}) = E(\varphi_X(\tau))^N = \gamma_N(\varphi_X(\tau)).$$

d.
$$\text{Var } S = E \text{ Var}(S/N) + \text{Var } E(S/N)$$
$$= E\text{Var}(X_1 + ... + X_N/N) + \text{Var } E(X_1 + ... + X_N/N)$$
$$= E(N \text{ Var } X) + \text{Var}(N\mu) = \text{Var } X.\ EN + \mu^2 \text{ Var } N.$$
$$\text{Var } X = EX^2 - E^2X = \mu_2 - \mu^2 \quad \bullet$$

3.3.2. The Classical Risk Model

Theorem 5

In the classical risk model, for all $t \in R_+$,

a.
$$\gamma_t(z) = e^{-\lambda t} e^{\lambda t z} \quad (|z| \le 1).$$

b.
$$EN_t = \lambda t \ , \ \text{Var } N_t = \lambda t.$$

c.
$$F_t = \textstyle\sum_{n \ge 0} e^{-\lambda t} (\lambda t)^n / n!\ F^{*n}.$$

d.
$$ES_t = \mu \lambda t.$$

e.
$$\varphi_t(\tau) = e^{-\lambda t} \exp[\lambda t \varphi_F(\tau)] \quad (\tau \in R).$$

f. If the partial claim amounts are square-integrable, then
$$\text{Var } S_t = \mu_2 \lambda t.$$

Proof

N_t is a Poisson variable with parameter λt (see Ch.4.Th.5.Cor.d). Then

$$P(N_t = n) = e^{-\lambda t} (\lambda t)^n / n!\ \cdot$$

Then a. results from the relations

$$\gamma_t(z) = Ez^{N_t} = \sum_{n\geq 0} e^{-\lambda t}(\lambda t)^n/_{n!} \,.z^n$$

$$= e^{-\lambda t} \sum_{n\geq 0} (\lambda tz)^n/_{n!} = e^{-\lambda t}e^{\lambda tz}.$$

The expectation and variance of a Poisson variable equal the parameter. Then b. results from this observation. The other propositions follow directly from the foregoing Theorem 4 •

3.4. Limit Distributions

In next Chapter 5, the asymptotic behaviour of the total claim amount S_t, as $t\uparrow\infty$, is studied. It it based on the following general definitions and results.

3.4.1. Weak Convergence and Pointwise Convergence

Let H and H_t ($t\in\mathbf{R}_+$) be distribution functions on **R**. Then **H is the weak limit of the functions H_t as $t\uparrow\infty$**, if

$$\lim_{t\uparrow\infty} H_t(x) = H(x) \quad (x\in\mathbf{R}, x \text{ continuity point of H}). \tag{11}$$

This is indicated as

$$H_t \to H \text{ weakly as } t\uparrow\infty$$

or briefly, as

$$H_t \to_w H \text{ as } t\uparrow\infty.$$

Let Y and Y_t be random variables with distribtion function H and H_t resp. We then say that **Y_t is asymptotically distributed as Y for $t\uparrow\infty$**, if $H_t \to H$ weakly as $t\uparrow\infty$.

When nothing is specified, convergence of functions means usual **pointwise convergence**, i.e. convergence at each point of the domain on which the functions are defined. Sometimes the superfluous adjective "pointwise" is used in order to emphasize the difference with another mode of convergence.

3.4.2. Continuity Theorem for Characteristic Functions

Theorem 6 (Continuity Theorem for Characteristic Functions)

Let H and H_t ($t\in R_+$) be probability distributions on R, such that $H_t \to_w H$ as $t\uparrow\infty$. Then the characterisitic function φ_{H_t} of H_t converges to the characteristic function φ_H of H as $t\uparrow\infty$.

Conversely, let H_t ($t\in R_+$) be probability distributions on R, such that the characteristic function $\varphi_{H_t}\to\varphi$ on R as $t\uparrow\infty$. If φ is continuous at 0, then φ is the characteristic function of some probability distribution function H on R and $H_t \to_w H$ as $t\uparrow\infty$ •

This Theorem is equivalent to App.G.Th.G5.

Let Y and Y_t ($t\in \mathbf{R}_+$) be random variables with distribution function H and H_t resp. Then **Y_t is asymptotically distributed as Y for $t\uparrow\infty$ iff $\lim_{t\uparrow\infty}\varphi_{H_t}=\varphi_H$** by Theorem 6.

3.4.3. Centered and Standardized Random Variables and Distributions

A **centered random variable** is a variable Y such that $E|Y|<\infty$ and $EY=0$. A **standardized random variable Y** is a centered random variable Y such that $EY^2<\infty$ and $Var(Y)=1$. This terminology is also used for the corresponding distribution functions.

For any random variable Y, we denote by Y° and Y^{01} resp. the following centered and standardized random variable

$$Y^\circ := Y-EY \ , \ Y^{01} := (Y-EY)/Var^{1/2}(Y),$$

if it exists.

Let Y_t ($t\in \mathbf{R}_+$) be random variables with distribution function H_t. Then it happens that the standardized random variable Y_t^{01} is asymptotically standardized normal as $t\uparrow\infty$. By Theorem 6, **Y_t^{01} is asymptotically standardized normal as $t\uparrow\infty$ iff**

$$\mathbf{\lim_{t\uparrow\infty} \varphi_{H_t}(\tau) = e^{-\tau^2/2} \ (\tau\in R)}.$$

because the characteristic function of the standardized normal distribution is $\exp(-\tau^2/2)$ (see App.G.G7).

3.5 Martingales

3.5.1. Definitions

The following sections Ch.6.3 and Ch.6.4 are less elementary than the rest of the book. They are based on Continuous-Time Martingale Theory, and ipso facto, on more general conditionings than those considered in Chapter 2. No further results are based on this section 3.5, or on the sections Ch.6.3. or Ch.6.4. They can be omitted by the reader not familiar with martingales.

We here recall very briefly and incompletely some definitions and properties.

A **filtration** $\boldsymbol{F}_\tau$ is a family of random variables increasing with $\tau \in \mathbf{R}_+$. Intuitively, $\boldsymbol{F}_\tau$ is the information available at the instant τ. The filtration that we consider is

$$\boldsymbol{F}_\tau := \{N_\tau, T_1, X_1, T_2, X_2, \ldots, T_{N_\tau}, X_{N_\tau}\}.$$

We recall that the unique stochastic component of all risk models is the claim process $(T_1, X_1, T_2, X_2, \ldots)$. Hence $\boldsymbol{F}_\tau$ informs completely on the evolution of the stochastic process in the **past interval** $[0,\tau]$.

A **submartingale** is a stochastic process Y_τ $(\tau \in \mathbf{R}_+)$, such that Y_τ is integrable and $\boldsymbol{F}_\tau$- measurable, and such that

$$Y_r \leq E(Y_s/\boldsymbol{F}_r) \text{ a.s. } (0 \leq r \leq s). \tag{13}$$

Then, taking expectations,

$$EY_r \leq EY_s \ (0 \leq r \leq s). \tag{14}$$

A **martingale** is a stochastic process Y_τ $(\tau \in \mathbf{R}_+)$, such that Y_τ is integrable and

$$Y_r = E(Y_s/\boldsymbol{F}_r) \text{ a.s. } (0 \leq r \leq s). \tag{15}$$

Then, taking expectations,

$$EY_r = EY_s \ (0 \leq r \leq s). \tag{16}$$

A **stopping time** S is a random variable with values in $\mathbf{R}_+ \cup \{\infty\}$, such that the event $P(S \leq \tau)$ is $\boldsymbol{F}_\tau$-measurable for all $\tau \in \mathbf{R}_+$. Intuitively, S is a stopping time iff the information contained in $\boldsymbol{F}_\tau$ allows to decide whether $S \leq \tau$ or not.

3.5.2. A Basic Theorem.

Remarkable is the following famous Theorem by Doob. We only state a simple version here, used in Ch.6.3 and in Ch.6.4.

Theorem 7 (Doob's Optional Stopping Theorem)

If Y_τ ($\tau \in R_+$) is a submartingale with right-continuous trajectories and S,T are bounded stopping times such that S≤T, then Y_S and Y_T are integrable random variables and

$$EY_S \leq EY_T.$$

If Y_τ ($\tau \in R_+$) is martingale with right-continuous trajectories, and S,T are bounded stopping times such that S≤T, then Y_S and Y_T are integrable random variables and

$$EY_S = EY_T \quad \bullet$$

Hence, (14) or (16) remain valid when the deterministic times r≤s are replaced by bounded stopping times S≤T.

Chapter 4

Point Processes

4.1. General Processes

4.1.1. General Point Processes

A **point process** is a sequence of random variables $(T_1, T_2, \ldots)$, such that $0 \leq T_1 \leq T_2 \leq \ldots$ Hence, T_1, T_2, ... are considered as successive **random points** in $\mathbf{R}_+$.

For any point process, we denote **the number of points** T_k in the bounded interval $[0,t]$ by N_t. Precisely, N_t is the number of subscripts $k=1,2,\ldots$ such that $T_k \leq t$. We consider $T_\infty := \lim_{k\uparrow\infty} T_k$. The random variables N_t and T_∞ may have infinite values.

An **explosion** occurs at the realization ω of the point process if $T_\infty(\omega) < \infty$. (Realizations $\omega = (t_1, t_2, \ldots)$ can be identified with the points of the basic probability space Ω on which the process is defined. Mostly, ω is omitted in th notations). The point process is **explosive** if $P(T_\infty < \infty) > 0$. It is **non-explosive** if $P(T_\infty < \infty) = 0$.

The relation

$$\sum_{k\geq 0} P(N_t = k) = 1$$

is the **norm relation on [0,t]**. It is not necessarily satisfied. The first member of that relation equals $P(N_t < \infty)$.

Lemma

Let $(T_1, T_2, \ldots)$ be a point process. Then

$$\lim_{n\uparrow\infty} P(T_n \leq t) = P(T_\infty \leq t) \quad (t \in \mathbf{R}_+),$$

$$\lim_{t\uparrow\infty} P(T_\infty \leq t) = P(T_\infty < \infty).$$

Proof

$$T_\infty(\omega)\le t \Leftrightarrow [\text{For all } n=1,2,\ldots: T_n(\omega)\le t].$$

Then, because "for all" corresponds to an intersection,

$$P(T_\infty\le t) = P[\cap_{n\ge 1}\{T_n\le t\}] = \lim_{n\uparrow\infty} P(T_n\le t).$$

For the second limit relation, we observe that

$$T_\infty(\omega) <\infty \Leftrightarrow [\text{For some } k=1,2,\ldots: T_\infty(\omega)\le k].$$

Then, because "for some" corresponds to a union,

$$P(T_\infty<\infty) = P[\cup_{k\ge 1} \{T_\infty\le k\}] = \lim_{k\uparrow\infty} P(T_\infty\le k) = \lim_{t\uparrow\infty} P(T_\infty\le t) \bullet$$

Theorem 1 (Non-Explosion Conditions)

Let $(T_1,T_2,\ldots)$ be a point process. The conditions a. to f. are equivalent:

a. The process is non-explosive.

b. $P(T_\infty<\infty) = 0$.

c. For all $t\in R_+$, $P(T_\infty\le t) = 0$.

d. For all $t\in R_+$, $\lim_{n\uparrow\infty} P(T_n\le t) = 0$.

e. For all $t\in R_+$, $P(N_t=\infty) = 0$.

f. For all $t\in R_+$, the norm relation is satisfied on $[0,t]$.

Proof

a⇔b by the definition of non-explosiveness.

$$c \Leftrightarrow [\lim_{t\uparrow\infty} P(T_\infty\le t)=0] \Leftrightarrow P(T_\infty<\infty)=0 \Leftrightarrow b,$$

because $P(T_\infty\le t)$ is an increasing function of t, and by the Lemma.

$$d \Leftrightarrow [\text{For all } t: P(T_\infty\le t)=0] \Leftrightarrow c,$$

by the Lemma. The equivalence c⇔e holds because

$$T_\infty(\omega)\le t \Leftrightarrow N_t(\omega)=\infty,$$

$$P(T_\infty \le t) = P(N_t = \infty).$$

The equivalence e⇔f results from the relation $P(N_t<\infty)+P(N_t=\infty)=1$ •

Explosive claim instants processes are discarded in risk models (Ch.3.3.1. *General assumptions* b). Hence, the detection and proof of the non-explosiveness of the involved point processes is important.

4.1.2. Density of a Random Vector. Compatible Densities

A **density of the random vector** $(Y_1,\ldots,Y_n)$ is a positive function p_n on $\mathbf{R}^n$, such that

$$P[(Y_1,\ldots,Y_n)\in B] = \int_B p_n(y_1,\ldots,y_n)dy_1\ldots dy_n \ (B\subseteq\mathbf{R}^n). \tag{1}$$

Densities wich are equal Lebesgue-a.e, are regarded as identical. Then the density of the random vector $(Y_1,\ldots,Y_n)$ is unique when it exists. This identification of densities allows the suppression of the "Lebesgue-a.e." indication.

For $B=\mathbf{R}^n$ in (1), we obtain the **norm relation**

$$\int_{\mathbf{R}^n} p_n(y_1,\ldots,y_n)dy_1\ldots dy_n = 1 \tag{2}$$

The relation (1) is displayed in infinitesimal form as

$$P(Y_1\in dy_1,\ldots,Y_n\in dy_n) = p_n(y_1,\ldots,y_n)dy_1\ldots dy_n. \tag{3}$$

Relations such as (3) are very convenient in the treatment of point processes presented hereafter. In fact no infinitesimals are involved: the relation (3) must be considered as abbreviation of (1).

A **probability density function on $\mathbf{R}^n$** is any positive function p_n satisfying the norm relation (2). The densities p_n on $\mathbf{R}^n$ and p_{n+1} on $\mathbf{R}^{n+1}$ are **compatible**, if

$$\int_{\mathbf{R}} p_{n+1}(y_1,\ldots,y_n,y_{n+1})dy_{n+1} = p_n(y_1,\ldots,y_n) \ \ [(y_1,\ldots,y_n)\in\mathbf{R}^n] \tag{4}$$

One version of Kolmogoroff's famous extension Theorem is the following Theorem later used in the construction of point processes.

Kolmogorov's Extension Theorem

Let $p_1(\cdot)$, $p_2(\cdot,\cdot)$, $p_3(\cdot,\cdot,\cdot)$, ... be a sequence of probability density functions on R^1, R^2, R^3 ... resp., such that p_n is compatible with p_{n+1} (n=1,2,...). Then a sequence of random variables $(Y_1,Y_2,Y_3,...)$ exists on some probability space, so that p_n is the density of the random vector $(Y_1,...,Y_n)$ (n=1,2,...) •

4.2. Point Processes with Independent Delays

4.2.1. Delays of a Point Process

The **delays** of the point process $(T_1,T_2,...)$ are the positive random variables

$$D_1 := T_1 \ , \ D_2 := T_2 - T_1 \ , \ D_3 = T_3 - T_2 \ , ...$$

We here consider **point processes with independent delays**. In such processes, the sequence

$$(D_1,D_2,...) \tag{5}$$

can be considered as the basic process. The random variables of the point process result from it by the relations

$$T_1 = D_1 \ , \ T_2 = D_1+D_2 \ , \ T_3 = D_1+D_2+D_3 \ , ...$$

We denote the distribution function of D_k (k=1,2,...) by H_k. **Renewal processes** (Ch.1.5) are point processes with i.i.d. delays, i.e. point processes with independent delays and $H_1=H_2=...$

4.2.2. Explosions in Point Processes with Independent Delays

Theorem 2

In a point process with independent delays, the probability of an explosion equals 0 or 1.

Proof

Let $(T_1,T_2,...)$ be a point process with independent delays D_k (k=1,2,...). Then

$$\exp(-T_\infty) = \exp[-(D_1+...+D_k)].\exp[-(D_{k+1}+D_{k+2}+...)],$$

because

$$T_\infty = D_1+D_2+\ldots$$

Then

$$E[\exp(-T_\infty)]$$

$$= E[\exp(-(D_1+\ldots+D_k))].E[\exp(-(D_{k+1}+D_{k+2}+\ldots))],$$

by the independence assumption. As $k\uparrow\infty$, by dominated convergence,

$$E[\exp(-T_\infty)] = E[\exp(-T_\infty)]\, E[\exp(-L)], \tag{6}$$

where

$$L := \lim_{k\uparrow\infty} (D_{k+1}+D_{k+2}+\ldots).$$

But $L(\omega)=\infty$ if $T_\infty(\omega)=\infty$ and $L(\omega)=0$ if $T_\infty(\omega)<\infty$. Hence

$$e^{-L} = 1_{T_\infty<\infty}\ ,\ \ E(e^{-L}) = P(T_\infty<\infty)$$

and (6) becomes

$$E[\exp(-T_\infty)] = E[\exp(-T_\infty)].P(T_\infty<\infty) \tag{7}$$

If the first member of (7) is different from 0, we can simplify and we obtain $P(T_\infty<\infty)=1$. If it equals 0, then $T_\infty=\infty$ a.s. and $P(T_\infty<\infty)=0$ •

Lemma

Let $a_n\in]0,1]$ ($n\in N_{++}$). Then $\Pi_{n\geq1}\, a_n=0$ iff $\sum_{n\geq1}(1-a_n)=\infty$.

Proof

We replace a_n by $1-b_n$ and we prove that

$$\Pi_{n\geq1}(1-b_n) = 0 \tag{8}$$

iff

$$\sum_{n\geq1} b_n = \infty. \tag{9}$$

We consider the relation

$$(1-x) \leq e^{-x}\ \ (x \geq 0),$$

We replace x by $b_1,b_2,\ldots,b_n$ successively. Then we take the product of the relations, and we let $n\uparrow\infty$:

$$\Pi_{n\geq1}(1-b_n) \leq \exp(-\sum_{n\geq1} b_n).$$

Hence (9)⇒(8).

In order to prove the converse implication, we notice that a strictly positive number c exists such that

$$e^{-2x} \leq 1-x \quad (0 \leq x \leq c). \tag{10}$$

If an infinity of numbers b_n is larger than c, then (9) is true. If only a finite number is larger than c, then we may suppose that all numbers b_n are smaller than c, because any finite segment $b_1, b_2, ..., b_k$ may be suppressed in the sequence $b_1, b_2, ...,$ without changing the meaning of (8) or (9). In the latter case, we replace x by $b_1, b_2, ..., b_n$ in (10), we take the product of the relations, and we let $n \uparrow \infty$:

$$\exp(-2\textstyle\sum_{n\geq 1} b_n) \leq \prod_{n\geq 1}(1-b_n).$$

Hence (8)$\Rightarrow$(9) •

Theorem 3 (Explosion Theorem. Independent Delays)

We assume the following :

$(T_1,T_2,...)$ is a point process with independent delays D_1, D_2, ... The distribution function of D_n is H_n and $H_n(0)=0$.

h is a positive decreasing Lebesgue-integrable function on R_+ and h is strictly positive on some interval $[0,\varepsilon]$ where $\varepsilon>0$.

Then the following propositions a. and b. are equivalent.

a. **The process $(T_1,T_2,...)$ is non-explosive.**

b. $$\textstyle\sum_{n\geq 1} \int_{[0,\infty[} [1-H_n(\tau)]h(\tau)d\tau = \infty.$$

Proof

Let

$$d_n := E[\exp(-D_n)].$$

Then

$$E[\exp(-T_n)] = E[\exp(-D_1-...-D_n)] = d_1 d_2 ... d_n.$$

By dominated convergence, as $n \uparrow \infty$,

$$E[\exp(-T_\infty)] = \textstyle\prod_{n\geq 1} d_n =: \Pi_\infty .$$

Hence, the process is non-explosive iff $\Pi_\infty = 0$. Integrating by parts,

$$d_n = \int_{[0,\infty[} e^{-\tau}\, dH_n(\tau) = -\int_{]0,\infty[} e^{-\tau}\, d(1-H_n(\tau)) = 1-\int_{[0,\infty[} (1-H_n(\tau))e^{-\tau}d\tau.$$

By the Lemma, the process is non-explosive iff

$$\sum_{n\geq 0} \int_{[0,\infty[}(1-H_n(\tau))e^{-\tau}\, d\tau = \infty. \tag{11}$$

We prove the equivalence of b. and

$$\sum_{n\geq 0} \int_{[0,\varepsilon]}(1-H_n(\tau))\, d\tau = \infty. \tag{12}$$

If (12) is true, then

$$\sum_{n\geq 0} \int_{[0,\infty[}(1-H_n(\tau))h(\tau)\, d\tau \geq h(\varepsilon)\sum_{n\geq 0} \int_{[0,\varepsilon]}(1-H_n(\tau))\, d\tau = \infty$$

and then b. is true.

Conversely, let us now suppose b. By monotone convergence, (12) can be displayed as

$$\int_{[0,\varepsilon]} \alpha(\tau)d\tau = \infty, \tag{13}$$

and the assumption b. as

$$\int_{[0,\infty[} \alpha(\tau)h(\tau)d\tau = \infty, \tag{14}$$

where

$$\alpha(\tau) := \sum_{n\geq 0} (1-H_n(\tau))$$

is a positive decreasing function on $\mathbf{R}_+$ with values in $[0,\infty]$. If $\alpha(\varepsilon)=\infty$, then $\alpha\equiv\infty$ on $[0,\varepsilon]$, and then (13) is true. Hence, we may assume that $\alpha(\varepsilon)<\infty$. Then

$$\int_{[0,\infty[} \alpha(\tau)h(\tau)d\tau = \int_{[0,\varepsilon]} \alpha(\tau)h(\tau)d\tau + \int_{[\varepsilon,\infty[} \alpha(\tau)h(\tau)d\tau$$
$$\leq \int_{[0,\varepsilon]} \alpha(\tau)h(\tau)d\tau + \alpha(\varepsilon) \int_{[\varepsilon,\infty[} h(\tau)d\tau.$$

The last term is finite, because h is Lebesgue-integrable. By (14), the first member is infinite. Hence, the first term of the last member is infinite, i.e. the relation (13) is true.

This proves the equivalence of b. and (12). In particular, for $h(\tau)=e^{-\tau}$, we obtain that (11) and (12) are equivalent. Hence, the process is non-explosive iff (12) is true, i.e. iff b. is true. This proves the equivalence of a. and b. •

Corollary

Let $(T_1,T_2,\ldots)$ be a point process with independent delays D_1, D_2, ... Let H_n be the distribution function of D_n, $H_n(0)=0$ $(n=1,2,\ldots)$. For any fixed $\varepsilon>0$ and $k>0$, the explosiveness of the process depends only on the restriction of the functions H_k, H_{k+1}, H_{k+3}, ... to the interval $[0,\varepsilon]$.

Proof

The Corollary results from the equivalence of a. and b. in the Theorem. The condition b. remains the same when a finite number of terms is suppressed in the first member. For h, the indicator function $1_{[0,\varepsilon]}$ can be used •

4.3. Densities of Point Processes

4.3.1. Densities p_n of a Point Process

Let $(T_1,T_2,\ldots)$ be a point process. When it exists, we denote by p_n the density of the random vector $(T_1,\ldots T_n)$. We say that **$(T_1,T_2,\ldots)$ is a point process with densities p_n (n=1,2,...)** if p_n exists for all n=1,2,...

The infinitesimal interpretation of the density p_n is

$$p_n(t_1,\ldots t_n)dt_1\ldots dt_n = P(T_1 \in dt_1,\ldots,T_n \in dt_n). \tag{15}$$

The domains $\mathbf{W}_{tn}$ and $\mathbf{W}_n$ are defined by

$$\mathbf{W}_{tn} := \{(t_1,\ldots,t_n) / \ 0 \le t_1 \le \ldots \le t_n \le t\} \ \ (n=0,1,2,\ldots),$$

$$\mathbf{W}_n := \{(t_1,\ldots,t_n) / \ 0 \le t_1 \le \ldots \le t_n < \infty\} \ \ (n=0,1,2,\ldots). \tag{16}$$

The unique point of the domains $\mathbf{W}_{t0}$ and $\mathbf{W}_0$ is the void sequence ( ). The density p_n vanishes outside $\mathbf{W}_n$, because $0 \le T_1 \le \ldots \le T_n < \infty$.

Here, the norm relation (2) becomes

$$\int_{\mathbf{W}_n} p_n(t_1,\ldots t_n)dt_1\ldots dt_n = 1 \ \ (n=1,2,\ldots) \tag{17}$$

and the compatibility relation (4) is

$$\int_{[t_n,\infty[} p_{n+1}(t_1,\ldots,t_n,t_{n+1})dt_{n+1} = p_n(t_1,\ldots,t_n) \ \ [(t_1,\ldots t_n) \in \mathbf{W}_n;\ n=1,2,\ldots]. \tag{18}$$

4.3.2. Densities π_{tn} of a Point Process

Let $(T_1,T_2,\ldots)$ be a point process with densities p_n(n=1,2,...). **The densities π_{tn}** ($t \in \mathbf{R}_+$, n=0,1,2,...) of the process are defined by

$$\pi_{tn}(t_1,\ldots,t_n)$$

$$:= \int_{[t,\infty[} p_{n+1}(t_1,\ldots,t_n,t_{n+1})dt_{n+1} \ [t \in \mathbf{R}_+;\ n=0,1,2,\ldots;\ (t_1,\ldots,t_n) \in \mathbf{W}_{tn}]. \tag{19}$$

By Fubini,

$$P[N_t=n, (T_1,...,T_n)\in B] = P[(T_1,...,T_n)\in B\ ,\ T_{n+1}>t]$$

$$= \int_B[\int_{]t,\infty[}\ p_{n+1}(t_1,...,t_n,t_{n+1})dt_{n+1}]dt_1...dt_n = \int_B \pi_{tn}(t_1,...,t_n)dt_1...dt_n\quad (B\subseteq \mathbf{W}_{tn}).$$

Hence,

$$P[N_t=n, (T_1,...,T_n)\in B]\ = \int_B \pi_{tn}(t_1,...,t_n)dt_1...dt_n\quad (n=0,1,2,...B\subseteq \mathbf{W}_{tn}).\quad (20)$$

In particular, for $B:=\mathbf{W}_{tn}$:

$$P(N_t=n) = \int...\int_{\{0\le t_1\le...\le t_n\le t\}} \pi_{tn}(t_1,...,t_n)dt_1...dt_n\ (n=0,1,2,...).\quad (21)$$

For n=0 in (19),

$$\pi_{t0} = \int_{[t,\infty[}\ p_1(t_1)dt_1 = P(T_1\ge t) = P(T_1>t) = P(N_t=0).$$

The infinitesimal interpretation, of π_{tn}, resulting from $B:= dt_1\times...\times dt_n$ in (20), is

$$\pi_{tn}(t_1,...,t_n)dt_1...dt_n$$
$$= P(N_t=n,\ T_1\in dt_1,\ ...,T_n\in dt_n)\ (n=0,1,2,...;\ 0\le t_1\le...\le t_n\le t).\quad (22)$$

By (19) for $t=t_n$, and by the compatibility relation (18),

$$p_n(t_1,...,t_n) = \pi_{t_n,n}(t_1,...,t_n)\quad (n=1,2,...;\ 0\le t_1\le...\le t_n).\quad (23)$$

4.3.3. Integration by Symmetrization

Theorem 4 (Integration by Symmetrization)

Let g be a symmetric function, positive or Lebesgue-integrable, on the n-dimensional cube $[s,t]^n$ ($n\ge 1$). Then

$$\int_{\{s\le t_1\le...\le t_n\le t\}} g(t_1,...,t_n)dt_1...dt_n = 1/n!\ \int_{[s,t]^n} g(t_1,...,t_n)dt_1...dt_n.\quad (24)$$

Proof

Let n=2. The square $[s,t]^2$ can be partitioned as

$$[s,t]^2 = \{(t_1,t_2)/s\le t_1<t_2\le t\} + \{(t_1,t_2)/s\le t_2<t_1\le t\} + \{(t_1,t_2)/s\le t_1=t_2\le t\}.\quad (25)$$

By the symmetry of g, the Lebesgue-integral of g on each of the two first sets in the last member equals the first member of (24). The integral on the last set of (25) equals 0. This proves the case n=2.

In the general case, $[s,t]^n$ is partitioned in n! sets, corresponding to the n! permutations of $(t_1,...,t_n)$, and a residual set of Lebesgue measure zero. Then the integral of g on each of the first n! sets equals the first member of (24), and the integral on the residual set equals zero •

4.4. Definition of Point Processes by Intensities

4.4.1. Intensities

We consider a point process $(T_1,T_2,...)$. We denote by N_B the number of points T_k in the set $B \subseteq \mathbf{R}_+$, i.e. the number of subscripts k=1,2,... such that $T_k \in B$. In particular, $N_t \equiv N_{[0,t]}$. The event $N_B=n$ is abbreviated as n–B ("n points in B").

Intensity functions are positive functions

$$\lambda_n(\tau/t_1,...,t_{n-1}) \quad (n=1,2,...;\ 0 \leq t_1 \leq ... \leq t_{n-1} \leq \tau < \infty) \tag{26}$$

with the following properties (27) and (28):

Lebesgue-integrability on bounded intervals:

$$\int_{[t_{n-1},t]} \lambda_n(\tau/t_1,...,t_{n-1})d\tau < \infty \quad (n=1,2,...;\ 0 \leq t_1 \leq ... \leq t_n \leq t). \tag{27}$$

Non Lebesgue-integrability on $[t_{n-1},\infty[$:

$$\int_{[t_{n-1},\infty[} \lambda_n(\tau/t_1,...,t_{n-1})d\tau = \infty \quad (n=1,2,...;\ 0 \leq t_1 \leq ... \leq t_n). \tag{28}$$

For n=1, the function (26) is $\lambda_1(\tau)$. **We define t_0:=0**. Then the meaning of (27) and (28) is clear in case n=1.

The infinitesimal interpretation of the intensity (26) is

$$\lambda_n(\tau/t_1,...,t_{n-1})d\tau = P(T_n \in d\tau /\ T_1=t_1,\ ...,\ T_{n-1}=t_{n-1}). \tag{29}$$

Hence, $\lambda_n(\tau/t_1,...,t_{n-1})$ is **the conditional intensity of T_n for fixed $T_1=t_1$, ..., $T_{n-1}=t_{n-1}$.**

4.4.2. Method of Definition of Point Processes

Starting with intensities (26), we define a point process, and we explicit the probability of particular events, in the way here summarized.

0. The densities p_n (n=1,2,...) are discovered in a heuristic way.

1. It is verified that these densities satisfy the compatibility relation (18) and the norm relation (17).

2. Then, by Kolmogorov's extension Theorem, a point process $(T_1,T_2,...)$ with densities p_n (n=1,2,...) exists on some probability space.

3. Then the densities π_{tn} ($t\in\mathbf{R}_+$; n=0,1,2,...) result from (19).

4. Then, by (20), the probability of events in $\mathbf{W}_{tn}$ ($t\in\mathbf{R}_+$; n=0,1,2,...) can be found. In particular cases, the distribution of N_t results from an integration by symmetrization (Theorem 4).

The heuristic step 0 could be omitted, because definitions must not be justified. But it is a most instructive step, explaining the origin of the densities p_n. Without step 0, the source of the densities seems too artificial.

The non-homogeneous Poisson process is treated separately (4.4.3), because it is used as a basis for the definition of the general point process with intensities (4.4.4). Later, the densities of the general process are particularized, furnishing different classes of point processes.

4.4.3. Non-Homogeneous Poisson Process

Here $\lambda(\tau)$ is a function of $\tau\in\mathbf{R}_+$, Lebesgue-integrable on bounded intervals, non Lebesgue-integrable on $[0,\infty[$.

Heuristic step

The goal is the construction of a non-explosive point process with densities, so that

$$P(1-d\tau) \equiv P(N_{d\tau}=1) = \lambda(\tau)d\tau, \tag{30}$$

$N_I,N_J,...N_K$ are independent if I,J,...,K are non-overlapping intervals. (31)

We here assume that this process exists. We start with the discovery of the densities π_{tn}. By (30), (31) and the infinitesimal interpretation of the densities π_{tn},

$$\pi_{tn}(t_1,\ldots,t_n)dt_1\ldots dt_n$$

$$= P\{0\text{–}[0,t_1[\ ,\ 1\text{–}dt_1\ ,\ 0\text{–}]t_1,t_2[\ ,\ 1\text{–}dt_2,\ldots,\ 0\text{–}]t_{n-1},t_n[\ ,\ 1\text{–}dt_n\ ,\ 0\text{–}]t_n,t]\}$$

$$= P\{0\text{–}[0,t_1[\}.P(1\text{–}dt_1).P\{0\text{–}]t_1,t_2[\}\ldots P\{0\text{–}]t_{n-1},t_n[\}.P(1\text{–}dt_n).P\{0\text{–}]t_n,t]\}$$

$$= P\{0\text{–}[0,t_1[\}\lambda(t_1)dt_1P\{0\text{–}]t_1,t_2[\}\ldots P\{0\text{–}]t_{n-1},t_n[\}\lambda(t_n)dt_nP\{0\text{–}]t_n,t]\}$$

$$= P\{0\text{–}[0,t_1[\ ,\ 0\text{–}]t_1,t_2[\ ,\ldots,\ 0\text{–}]t_{n-1},t_n[\ ,\ 0\text{–}]t_n,t]\}\lambda(t_1)dt_1\ldots\lambda(t_n)dt_n$$

$$= P\{0\text{–}[0,t]\}\lambda(t_1)dt_1\ldots\lambda(t_n)dt_n = \pi_{t0}\ \lambda(t_1)dt_1\ldots\lambda(t_n)dt_n.$$

Hence

$$\pi_{tn}(t_1,\ldots,t_n) = \pi_{t0}\ \lambda(t_1)\ldots\lambda(t_n). \qquad (32)$$

Let

$$\Lambda(t) := \int_{[0,t]} \lambda(\tau)d\tau. \qquad (33)$$

Then, by an integration by symmetrization,

$$P(N_t{=}n) = \int\ldots\int_{[0\le t_1\le\ldots\le t_n\le t]} \pi_{tn}(t_1,\ldots,t_n)dt_1\ldots dt_n$$

$$= 1/n!\ \int\ldots\int_{[0,t]^n} \pi_{t0}\ \lambda(t_1)\ldots\lambda(t_n)dt_1\ldots dt_n = 1/n!\ \pi_{t0}\ [\Lambda(t)]^n,$$

and then π_{t0} results from the relation

$$1 = \sum_{n\ge0} P(N_t{=}n) = \pi_{t0} \sum_{n\ge0} 1/n!\ [\Lambda(t)]^n = \pi_{t0}\ e^{\Lambda(t)}.$$

By (32)

$$\pi_{tn}(t_1,\ldots,t_n) = e^{-\Lambda(t)}\ \lambda(t_1)\ldots\lambda(t_n)\ (n=0,1,2,\ldots;\ 0\le t_1\le\ldots\le t_n\le t), \qquad (34)$$

and then by (23)

$$p_n(t_1,\ldots,t_n) = e^{-\Lambda(t_n)}\ \lambda(t_1)\ldots\lambda(t_n)\ (n=0,1,2,\ldots;\ 0\le t_1\le\ldots\le t_n\le t). \qquad (35)$$

Theorem 5 (Definition of Non-Homogeneous Poisson Processes)

Let $\lambda(\tau)$ be a function of $\tau\in R_+$, Lebesgue-integrable on bounded intervals, non Lebesgue-integrable on $[0,\infty[$. Then a point process $(T_1,T_2,\ldots)$ with densities

$$p_n(t_1,\ldots,t_n) = \exp[-\int_{[0,t_n]} \lambda(\tau)d\tau]\ \lambda(t_1)\ldots\lambda(t_n)\ (n=0,1,2,\ldots;\ 0\le t_1\le\ldots\le t_n) \qquad (36)$$

exists. This *non-homogeneous Poisson process with intensity function* $\lambda(.)$ has the following properties:

a. The process is non-explosive.

b. The densities π_{tn} $(n=0,1,2,...;\ 0\le t_1\le...\le t_n\le t)$ of the process are

$$\pi_{tn}(t_1,...,t_n) = \exp[-\textstyle\int_{[0,t]} \lambda(\tau)d\tau]\ \lambda(t_1)...\lambda(t_n). \tag{37}$$

c. Let I, J, ..., K be bounded non-overlapping intervals in [0,∞[. Then the random variables N_I, N_J, ..., N_K are independent.

d. Let I be a bounded interval in [0,∞[. Then

$$P(N_I=n) = \exp[-\textstyle\int_I \lambda(\tau)d\tau]\ 1/n!\ [\int_I \lambda(\tau)d\tau]^n\ (n=0,1,2,...). \tag{38}$$

e. If the function $\lambda(\cdot)$ is continuous, then

$$P(N_{[t,t+\varepsilon]}=1) = \lambda(t)\varepsilon + o(\varepsilon)\ \text{ as } \varepsilon\downarrow 0. \tag{39}$$

Proof

For the existence of the process, it is sufficient, by Kolmogorov's extension Theorem, to verify the compatibility relation (18) and the norm relation (17). In fact, if the compatibility relation holds, then the verification of the norm relation amounts to its verification for n=1, and this is direct. Relation (18) is correct because

$$\begin{aligned}
&\textstyle\int_{[t_n,\infty[} p_{n+1}(t_1,\dots,t_n,t_{n+1})dt_{n+1}\\
&= \textstyle\int_{[t_n,\infty[} \exp[-\int_{[0,t_{n+1}]} \lambda(\tau)d\tau]\ \lambda(t_1)\dots\lambda(t_n)\lambda(t_{n+1})dt_{n+1}\\
&= \lambda(t_1)\dots\lambda(t_n) \textstyle\int_{[t_n,\infty[} \exp[-\int_{[0,t_{n+1}]} \lambda(\tau)d\tau]\lambda(t_{n+1})dt_{n+1}\\
&= -\lambda(t_1)\dots\lambda(t_n) \textstyle\int_{[t_n,\infty[} d\big[\exp[-\int_{[0,t_{n+1}]} \lambda(\tau)d\tau]\big]\\
&= \lambda(t_1)\dots\lambda(t_n) \exp[-\textstyle\int_{[0,t_n]} \lambda(\tau)d\tau] = p_n(t_1,\dots,t_n).
\end{aligned}$$

a. For the non-explosiveness, it is enough to verify the norm relation on [0,t], by Theorem 1. The latter will result from (38) with I:=[0,t]. Indeed, using the notation (33),

$$\textstyle\sum_{n\ge 0} P(N_t=n) = e^{-\Lambda(t)} \sum_{n\ge 0}\ 1/n!\ [\Lambda(t)]^n = e^{-\Lambda(t)}\, e^{\Lambda(t)} = 1.$$

b. The relation (37) results from (19), by the same calculation as that one proving the compatibility relation (18).

c. Let

$$[0,t] = I+J+...+K$$

be a partition of [0,t] in a finite number of successive intervals I,J,...,K.

$$P(N_I=i,N_J=j,...,N_K=k)$$

$$= {}^1\!/_{i!}\ [\Lambda(I)]^i e^{-\Lambda(I)}.{}^1\!/_{j!}\ [\Lambda(J)]^j e^{-\Lambda(J)}...\ {}^1\!/_{k!}\ [\Lambda(k)]^k e^{-\Lambda(k)}, \tag{40}$$

where $\Lambda(I)$ is the Lebesgue-integral of the function $\lambda(\cdot)$ over the interval I. Indeed, by (20) and (37) with n=i+j+...+k, also using the notation (33),

$$P(N_I=i,\ N_J=j,...,N_K=k)$$

$$= e^{-\Lambda(t)}\int...\int_D \lambda(r_1)dr_1...\lambda(r_i)dr_i\ \lambda(s_1)ds_1...\lambda(s_j)ds_j\ ...\ ...\ ...\lambda(t_1)dt_1...\lambda(t_k)dt_k.$$

Here the integration domain D is defined by the relations

$$r_1,...,r_i\in I\ ;\ r_1\leq...\leq r_i\ ;\ s_1,...s_j\in J\ ;\ s_1\leq...\leq s_j\ ;\ ...\ ...\ ...\ ;\ t_1,...t_k\in K\ ;\ t_1\leq...\leq t_k.$$

Then (40) results from successive integrations by symmetrization. In (40), we can successively eliminate anyone of the random variables $N_I,N_J,...,N_K$ by summation over its possible values.This implies that (40) is valid for any finite number of bounded non-overlapping intervals I,J,...,K. In particular,

$$P(N_I=i) = {}^1\!/_{i!}\ [\Lambda(I)]^i e^{-\Lambda(I)}. \tag{41}$$

Then

$$P(N_I=i,\ N_j=j,\ ...,N_K=k) = P(N_I=i)P(N_J=j)...P(N_K=k).$$

d. (38) is (41), in different notations.

e. For $B:=[t,t+\varepsilon]$ and n=1 in (38), this relation becomes

$$P(N_{[t,t+\varepsilon]}=1) = \exp[-\int_{[t,t+\varepsilon]} \lambda(\tau)d\tau].\int_{[t,t+\varepsilon]} \lambda(\tau)d\tau\ \bullet$$

The following Corollary results from the particular function $\lambda(\cdot)\equiv\lambda\in\mathbf{R}_{++}$.

Corollary (Definition of the Homogeneous Poisson Process)

Let $\lambda \in R_{++}$. Then a point process $(T_1,T_2,...)$ with densities

$$p_n(t_1,...,t_n) = e^{-\lambda t_n}\lambda^n \ (n=0,1,2,...;\ 0 \le t_1 \le ... \le t_n). \tag{42}$$

exists. This *Poisson process with intensity λ* has the following properties:

a. The process is non-explosive.

b. The densities π_{tn} of the process are

$$\pi_{tn}(t_1,...,t_n) = e^{-\lambda t}\lambda^n \ (n=0,1,2,...;\ 0 \le t_1 \le ... \le t_n \le t). \tag{43}$$

c. Let I, J, ..., K be bounded non-overlappng intervals in $[0,\infty[$. Then the random variables N_I, N_J, ..., N_K are independent.

d. Let I be an interval in $[0,\infty[$ with length $|I| < \infty$. Then

$$P(N_I=n) = e^{-\lambda|I|}\, 1/n!\ [\lambda|I|]^n. \tag{44}$$

e.

$$P(N_{[t,t+\varepsilon]}=1) = \lambda\varepsilon + o(\varepsilon) \text{ as } \varepsilon \downarrow 0 \ \bullet \tag{45}$$

The intensity λ of the Poisson process is also called the **parameter** of the process.

The following are other names of the Poisson process with constant intensity:

Homogeneous Poisson Process,

Classical Poisson process,

Usual Poisson Process.

They are used in ordor to emphasize that not the more general process defined by Theorem 5 is considered.

4.4.4. General Point Processes Defined by Intensities

We here consider the general intensity functions λ_n (n=1,2,...) defined in 4.4.1. and from them, we define a point process $(T_1,T_2,...)$, in the way summarized in 4.4.2.

Heuristic step

From Theorem 5.d. results that the probability of no point in the interval I equals

$$\exp[-\int_I \lambda(\tau)d\tau] \tag{46}$$

in case of a Poisson process with intensity function $\lambda(.)$. Then by the infinitesimal interpretation (29) of the intensities λ_n,

$$P\{0-[0,t_1[\} = \exp[-\int_{[0,t_1]} \lambda_1(\tau)d\tau],$$

because the active intensity function is λ_1 as long as no point occurs. Then

$$P(T_1 \in dt_1) = P\{0-[0,t_1[,\ T_1 \in dt_1\} = \exp[-\int_{[0,t_1]} \lambda_1(\tau)d\tau]\lambda_1(t_1)dt_1.\ (*)$$

At the occurrence of the first point, λ_2 becomes the active intensity function. Then

$$P\{0-]t_1,t_2[/T_1=t_1\} = \exp[-\int_{[t_1,t_2]} \lambda_2(\tau/t_1)d\tau]$$

and

$$P(T_2 \in t_2/T_1=t_1) = P\{0-]t_1,t_2[,T_2 \in dt_2\ /T_1=t_1\}$$

$$= \exp[-\int_{[t_1,t_2]} \lambda_2(\tau/t_1)d\tau]\lambda_2(t_2/t_1)dt_2.\ (*)$$

In the same way,

$$P(T_3=t_3/T_1=t_1,T_2=t_2) = \exp[-\int_{[t_2,t_3]} \lambda_3(\tau/t_1,t_2)d\tau]\lambda_3(t_3/t_1,t_2)dt_2.\ (*)$$

because λ_3 becomes active at the occurrence of the second point. By (15),

$$p_3(t_1,t_2,t_3)dt_1dt_2dt_3 = P(T_1 \in dt_1,T_2 \in dt_2,T_3 \in dt_3)$$

$$= P(T_1 \in dt_1)P(T_2 \in dt_2/T_1=t_1)P(T_3 \in dt_3/T_1=t_1,T_2=t_2).$$

The last member is the product of the expressions marked with an asterisk. This furnishes p_3. The general density p_n is found in the same way.

Theorem 6 (Definition of General Point Processes with Intensities)

Let $\lambda_n(\tau/t_1,\ldots,t_{n-1})$ $(n=1,2,\ldots;\ 0\le t_1\le\ldots\le t_{n-1})$ be intensity functions (4.4.1). Then a point process $(T_1,T_2,\ldots)$ with densities

$$p_n(t_1,\ldots,t_n) =$$

$$\exp[-\textstyle\int_{[0,t_1]} \lambda_1(\tau)d\tau]\lambda_1(t_1)$$

$$\times \exp[-\textstyle\int_{[t_1,t_2]} \lambda_2(\tau/t_1)d\tau]\lambda_2(t_2/t_1)$$

$$\times \ldots\quad \ldots\quad \ldots\quad \ldots$$

$$\times \exp[-\textstyle\int_{[t_{n-1},t_n]} \lambda_n(\tau/t_1,\ldots,t_{n-1})d\tau]\lambda_n(t_n/t_1,\ldots,t_{n-1}). \tag{47}$$

exists. It is called *the point process with intensity functions λ_n (n=1,2,...)*.

The densities $\pi_{tn}(t_1,\ldots,t_n)$ $(n=0,1,2,\ldots;\ 0\le t_1\le\ldots\le t_n\le t)$ of the process are

$$\pi_{tn}(t_1,\ldots,t_n) = p_n(t_1,\ldots,t_n)\exp[-\textstyle\int_{[t_n,t]} \lambda_{n+1}(\tau/t_1,\ldots,t_n)d\tau], \tag{48}$$

where $p_0:=1$ and $t_0:=1$ if $n=0$.

Proof
For the existence of the process, it is sufficient, by Kolmogorov's extension Theorem, to verify the compatibility relation (18) and the norm relation (17). These verifications, and then (48) for π_{tn} defined by (19), are direct because

$$\exp[-\textstyle\int_{[t,t_{n+1}]} \lambda_{n+1}(\tau/t_1,\ldots,t_n)d\tau]\lambda_{n+1}(t_{n+1}/t_1,\ldots,t_n)dt_{n+1}$$

$$= -d\big[\exp[-\textstyle\int_{[t,t_{n+1}]} \lambda_{n+1}(\tau/t_1,\ldots,t_n)d\tau]\big]\ (0\le t_1\le\ldots\le t_n\le t\le t_{n+1}), \tag{49}$$

where the differential in the last member is a differential in t_{n+1} •

The formula (48) has the following infinitesimal interpretation, say for n=2:

$$\pi_{t2}(t_1,t_2)dt_1dt_2 = P\{T_1\in dt_1,T_2\in dt_2,0-]t_2,t]\}$$

$$= P(T_1\in dt_1,T_2\in dt_2)P\{0-]t_2,t]/T_1=t_1,T_2=t_2\}$$

$$= p_2(t_1,t_2)\exp[-\textstyle\int_{[t_2,t]} \lambda_3(\tau/t_1,t_2)d\tau].$$

The following notations are convenient.

$$p_n(\tau/t_1,\ldots,t_{n-1}) := \exp[-\int_{[t_{n-1},\tau]} \lambda_n(s/t_1,\ldots,t_{n-1})ds]\lambda_n(\tau/t_1,\ldots,t_{n-1}), \quad (50)$$

$$P_n(\tau/t_1,\ldots,t_{n-1}) := 1 - \exp[-\int_{[t_{n-1},\tau]} \lambda_n(s/t_1,\ldots,t_{n-1})ds], \quad (51)$$

for

$$n=1,2,\ldots\ ;\ 0 =: t_0 \leq t_1 \leq \ldots \leq t_{n-1} \leq \tau < \infty.$$

For any fixed $t_1,\ldots,t_{n-1}$, $P_n(\cdot/t_1,\ldots,t_{n-1})$ is a probability distribution function on the interval $[t_{n-1},\infty[$, with density function $p_n(\cdot/t_1,\ldots,t_{n-1})$ on that interval.

Here (47) and (48) become

$$p_n(t_1,t_2,\ldots,t_n) = p_1(t_1)p_2(t_2/t_1)\ldots p_n(t_n/t_1,\ldots,t_{n-1}) \quad (0=:t_0\leq t_1\leq\ldots\leq t_n), \quad (52)$$

$$\pi_{tn}(t_1,\ldots,t_n) = p_n(t_1,\ldots,t_n)[1-P_{n+1}(t/t_1,\ldots,t_n)] \quad (0=:t_0\leq t_1\leq\ldots\leq t_n\leq t). \quad (53)$$

Now the following Theorem clarifies our initial intuition. It says that **P_n is the conditional distribution function of T_n , for fixed $T_1,\ldots,T_{n-1}$.**

Theorem 7 (Interpretation of P_n)

In the point process with intensity functions λ_n (n=1,2,...),

$$\mathbf{P(T_n\leq t /T_1,\ldots,T_{n-1}) = P_n(t/T_1,\ldots,T_{n-1}) \quad (t\in R_+).} \quad (54)$$

Proof

The first member is the conditional expectation

$$E(1_{T_n\leq t} /T_1,\ldots,T_{n-1}).$$

By the modern definition of the conditional expectation, it is enough to verify that

$$E[P_n(t/T_1,\ldots,T_{n-1})f(T_1,\ldots,T_{n-1})] = E[1_{T_n\leq t}\, f(T_1,\ldots,T_{n-1})], \quad (55)$$

where f is positive and bounded. We take n=3 (the verification being similar for any n). The first member of (55) equals

$$\iint_{\{0\leq t_1\leq t_2\leq t\}} P_3(t/t_1,t_2)f(t_1,t_2)p_2(t_1,t_2)dt_1dt_2,$$

because the density of the random vector (T_1,T_2) is $p_2(\cdot,\cdot)$ by Theorem 6, and because $P_3(t/t_1,t_2)=0$ if $t<t_2$.

The density of the random vector (T_1,T_2,T_3) is $p_3(\cdot,\cdot,\cdot)$. Hence, the last member of (55) equals, by Fubini,

$$\iiint_{\{0\le t_1\le t_2\le t_3<\infty\}} 1_{t_3\le t}\, f(t_1,t_2)p_3(t_1,t_2,t_3)dt_1dt_2dt_3$$

$$= \iint_{\{0\le t_1\le t_2\le t\}} \int_{\{t_2\le t_3\le t\}} f(t_1,t_2)p_1(t_1)p_2(t_2/t_1)p_3(t_3/t_1,t_2)dt_1dt_2dt_3$$

$$= \iint_{\{0\le t_1\le t_2\le t\}} f(t_1,t_2)p_1(t_1)p_2(t_2/t_1)dt_1dt_2 \int_{\{t_2\le t_3\le t\}} p_3(t_3/t_1,t_2)dt_3$$

$$= \iint_{\{0\le t_1\le t_2\le t\}} f(t_1,t_2)p_1(t_1)p_2(t_2/t_1)dt_1dt_2.P_3(t/t_1,t_2)$$

$$= \iint_{\{0\le t_1\le t_2\le t\}} f(t_1,t_2)p_2(t_1,t_2)P_3(t/t_1,t_2)\, dt_1dt_2 \quad \bullet$$

Theorem 8 (General Sufficient Condition for Non-Explosiveness)

In the general point process with intensities defined by Theorem 6, let

$$\boldsymbol{\lambda_n(\tau/t_1,...,t_n) \le b_n\, f(\tau)\ \ (n=0,1,2,...;\ 0\le t_1\le...\le t_n\le\tau<\infty),} \tag{56}$$

where f is Lebesgue-integrable on the bounded intervals of R_+ and where $b_1, b_2, ...$ are positive numbers so that

$$\boldsymbol{\lim_{n\uparrow\infty} 1/n!\ b_1b_2...b_nc^n = 0\ \ (c>0).} \tag{57}$$

Then the point process $(T_1,T_2,...)$ is non-explosive.

Proof

By Theorem 1, part a⇔d, it is enough to prove that $P(T_n\le t)\to 0$ as $n\uparrow\infty$. By (47), (56), an integration by symmetrization and by (57),

$$P(T_n\le t) = P(0\le T_1\le...\le T_n\le t) = \int...\int_{\{0\le t_1\le...\le t_n\le t\}} p_n(t_1,...,t_n)dt_1...dt_n$$

$$\le \int...\int_{\{0\le t_1\le...\le t_n\le t\}} \lambda_1(t_1)\lambda_2(t_2/t_1)...\lambda_n(t_n/t_1,...,t_{n-1})dt_1...dt_n$$

$$\le \int...\int_{\{0\le t_1\le...\le t_n\le t\}} b_1f(t_1)b_2f(t_2)...b_nf(t_n)\, dt_1...dt_n$$

$$= b_1b_2...b_n \int...\int_{\{0\le t_1\le...\le t_n\le t\}} f(t_1)f(t_2)...f(t_n)\, dt_1...dt_n$$

$$= b_1b_2...b_n\ 1/n!\ [\int_{[0,t]} f(\tau)d\tau]^n \to 0 \text{ as } n\uparrow\infty \quad \bullet$$

Theorem 8 specifies a very large class of non-explosive point processes. For instance, by Stirling's formula, the condition (57) is satisfied for the numbers $b_n := n^{1-\alpha}$ (n=1,2,...), where $0<\alpha\leq 1$.

Markov intensities are intensity functions λ_n (n=1,2,...) such that for all $n\geq 3$, the functions

$$\lambda_n(\tau/t_{n-1}) \equiv \lambda_n(\tau/t_1,\dots,t_{n-1}) \quad (0\leq t_1\leq\dots\leq t_{n-1}\leq\tau) \tag{58}$$

do not depend on $t_1,\dots,t_{n-2}$. **Regular Markov intensities** are Markov intensities λ_n (n=1,2,...) such that for all $n\geq 3$ and $\tau>0$, the integral

$$\int_{\{r<s<\tau\}} \lambda_n(s/r)ds$$

is a decreasing function of $r\in[0,\tau]$.

Hereafter, a process with intensities λ_n and a process with intensities λ°_n are simultaneously considered. For the latter process, the preceding notations, completed by the superscript °, are used.

The process $(T_1,T_2,\dots)$ is intensity-dominated by the process $(T^\circ_1,T^\circ_2,\dots)$ on the interval [0,t], if

$$\lambda_n(\tau/t_1,\dots,t_{n-1}) \leq \lambda^\circ_n(\tau/t_1,\dots,t_{n-1}) \quad (n=1,2,\dots;\ 0=:t_0\leq t_1\leq\dots\leq t_{n-1}\leq\tau\leq t). \tag{59}$$

The process $(T_1,T_2,\dots)$ is intensity-dominated by the process $(T^\circ_1,T^\circ_2,\dots)$ if it is intensity-dominated by that process on any interval [0,t] ($t\in\mathbf{R}_+$).

Lemma

Let [r,t] be a fixed interval, $g(\tau)$ $(r\leq\tau\leq t)$ and $P(\tau/s)$ $(r\leq s\leq\tau\leq t)$ functions so that

a. **$g(\tau)$ is a continuous decreasing function of $\tau\in[r,t]$ and $g(t)=0$.**

b. **For all $s\in[r,t]$, $P(\tau/s)$ is an increasing function of $\tau\in[s,t]$ and $P(s/s)=0$.**

c. **For all $\tau\in[r,t]$, $P(\tau/s)$ is a decreasing function of $s\in[r,\tau]$.**

Then

$$\int_{]s,t[} g(\tau)d_\tau P(\tau/s)$$

is a decreasing function of $s\in[r,t]$.

Proof

$$\int_{]s,t[} g(\tau)d_\tau P(\tau/s) = \int_{]s,t[} P(\tau/s)d[-g(\tau)]$$

by an integration by parts. The integral in the last member is an integral with respect to the increasing function [−g]. The integrand, and the integration domain decrease when s increases. Hence the integral decreases when s increases •

Theorem 9 (Comparison Theorem for Explosions. General Case)

Let $(T_1,T_2,...)$ and $(T°_1,T°_2,...)$ be the point processes with intensities λ_n (n=1,2,...) and $\lambda°_n$ (n=1,2,...) resp. For fixed t>0, we assume the following:

a. The process $(T_1,T_2,...)$ is intensity-dominated by the process $(T°_1,T°_2,...)$ on the interval [0,t].

b. The intensities $\lambda°_n$ (n=1,2,...) are bounded on bounded sets.

c. The intensities $\lambda°_n$ (n=1,2,...) are regular Markov intensities.

Then

$$P(T_n \le t) \le P(T°_n \le t) \quad (n=1,2,...). \tag{60}$$

and

$$P(T_\infty \le t) \le P(T°_\infty \le t). \tag{61}$$

If a. is satisfied for all t>0, and the process $(T°_1,T°_2,...)$ is non-explosive, then the process $(T_1,T_2,...)$ is non-explosive.

Proof

Hereafter n is a strictly positive integer and only values $0 \le t_1 \le ... \le t_{n-1} \le \tau$ are considered. By a. and (51):

$$P_n(\tau/t_1,...,t_{n-1}) \le P°_n(\tau/t_1,...,t_{n-1}), \tag{62}$$

We will prove (60) for n=4. The general argument, by induction, is clear from that case. By (50), (51) and (52), and because p_4 is the density of the random vector (T_1,T_2,T_3,T_4):

$$P(T_4 \le t) = P(0 \le T_1 \le T_2 \le T_3 \le T_4 \le t)$$

$$= \int_{]0,t[} p_1(t_1)dt_1 \int_{]t_1,t[} p_2(t_2/t_1)dt_2 \int_{]t_2,t[} p_3(t_3/t_1,t_2)dt_3 \int_{]t_3,t[} p_4(t_4/t_1,t_2,t_3)dt_4$$

$$= \int_{]0,t[} d_1P_1(t_1) \int_{]t_1,t[} d_2P_2(t_2/t_1) \int_{]t_2,t[} d_3P_3(t_3/t_1,t_2) \int_{]t_3,t[} d_4P_4(t_4/t_1,t_2,t_3),$$

where d_k indicates a differentiation with respect to t_k. Hence,

$$P(T_4 \le t) = \int_{]0,t[} d_1P_1(t_1) \int_{]t_1,t[} d_2P_2(t_2/t_1) \int_{]t_2,t[} P_4(t/t_1,t_2,t_3)d_3P_3(t_3/t_1,t_2). \quad (63)$$

In case of process $(T°_1, T°_2, ...)$, (63) becomes,

$$P(T°_4 \le t) = \int_{]0,t[} d_1P°_1(t_1) \int_{]t_1,t[} d_2P°_2(t_2/t_1) \int_{]t_2,t[} P°_4(t/t_3)d_3P°_3(t_3/t_2),$$

because $P°_n$ $(n \ge 3)$ does not depend on $t_1,...,t_{n-2}$ by c. Then

$$P(T°_4 \le t) = \int_{]0,t[} d_1P°_1(t_1) \int_{]t_1,t[} d_2P°_2(t_2/t_1) \int_{]t_2,t[} g°_3(t_3)\, d_3P°_3(t_3/t_2)$$

$$= \int_{]0,t[} d_1P°_1(t_1) \int_{]t_1,t[} g°_2(t_2)\, d_2P°_2(t_2/t_1) = \int_{]0,t[} g°_1(t_1)\, d_1P°_1(t_1) =: g°_0.$$

where
$$g°_3(t_3) := P°_4(t/t_3) \quad (t_2 \le t_3 \le t),$$

$$g°_2(t_2) := \int_{]t_2,t[} g°_3(t_3)\, d_3P°_3(t_3/t_2) \quad (t_1 \le t_2 \le t),$$

$$g°_1(t_1) := \int_{]t_1,t[} g°_2(t_2)\, d_2P°_2(t_2/t_1) \quad (0 \le t_1 \le t),$$

$$g°_0 := \int_{]0,t[} g°_1(t_1)\, d_1P°_1(t_1) = P(T°_4 \le t).$$

The functions $g°_3$, $g°_2$, $g°_1$ are continuous on the indicated domain, and

$$g°_3(t) = 0 \ , \ g°_2(t) = 0 \ , \ g°_1(t) = 0.$$

By c, the functions $P°_4(t/t_3)$, $P°_3(t_3/t_2)$, $P°_2(t_2/t_1)$ are decreasing functions of the variable after the slash. The functions $P°_3(t_3/t_2)$, $P°_2(t_2/t_1)$ are increasing functions of the variable before the slash, and $P°_3(t_2/t_2)=0$, $P°_2(t_1/t_1)=0$. By successive applications of the Lemma, the functions $g°_3$, $g°_2$, $g°_1$ are decreasing functions on the indicated domain.

By (63), (62) for n=4, and the definition of $g°_3(t_3)$:

$$P(T_4 \le t) \le \int_{]0,t[} d_1P_1(t_1) \int_{]t_1,t[} d_2P_2(t_2/t_1) \int_{]t_2,t[} g°_3(t_3)\, d_3P_3(t_3/t_1,t_2). \quad (64)$$

The last integral in the last member equals

$$\int_{]t_2,t[} g°_3(t_3)\, d_3P_3(t_3/t_1,t_2) = \int_{]t_2,t[} P_3(t_3/t_1,t_2)\, d[-g°_3(t_3)]$$

$$\le \int_{]t_2,t[} P°_3(t_3/t_2)\, d[-g°_3(t_3)]$$

$$= \int_{]t_2,t[} g°_3(t_3)\, d_3P°_3(t_3/t_2) = g°_2(t_2).$$

These relations result, successively, from an integration by parts, (62) for n=3, an integration by parts, and the definition of $g^\circ_2(t_2)$. Hence,

$$\int_{]t_2,t[} g^\circ_3(t_3)\, d_3P_3(t_3/t_1,t_2) \le g^\circ_2(t_2)$$

and similarly

$$\int_{]t_1,t[} g^\circ_2(t_2)\, d_2P_2(t_2/t_1) \le g^\circ_1(t_1),$$

$$\int_{]0,t[} g^\circ_1(t_1)\, d_1P_1(t_1) \le g^\circ_0.$$

Then by (64),

$$P(T_4 \le t) \le \int_{]0,t[} d_1P_1(t_1) \int_{]t_1,t[} g^\circ_2(t_2)\, d_2P_2(t_2/t_1)$$

$$\le \int_{]0,t[} g^\circ_1(t_1)\, d_1P_1(t_1) \le g^\circ_0 = P(T^\circ_4 \le t).$$

This proves (60). As $n\uparrow\infty$ in (60), we obtain (61), by the Lemma of Theorem 1. As $t\uparrow\infty$ in (61) we obtain $P(T_\infty<\infty) \le P(T^\circ_\infty<\infty)$ by the same Lemma. Then the last part of the Theorem results from Theorem 1, a⇔b •

4.5. Classes of Point Processes Defined by Intensities or by Densities

4.5.1. Processes with Independent Delays

Densities p_{dn} of the delay process

In the following notations p_{dn} and λ_{dn}, the first letter d of "delay" is used as fixed subscript. It cannot be replaced by numerical values.

Theorem 10 (Densities p_{dn} of the Delay Process)

Let $(T_1,T_2,\dots)$ be a point process with densities p_n (n=1,2,...). Then the vector $(D_1,\dots,D_n)$ has the density p_{dn} defined by

$$p_{dn}(\tau_1,\dots\tau_n) := p_n(\tau_1,\tau_1+\tau_2,\dots,\tau_1+\tau_2+\dots+\tau_n) \quad (n=1,2,\dots;\tau_1,\dots,\tau_n\in\mathbf{R}_+). \quad (65)$$

Proof

The formula (65) results from a classical change of random variables. The random variables T_1, ..., T_n and D_1, ..., D_n are connected by the relations of 4.2.1 •

Intensities λ_{dn} of the delays, when the delays are independent.

Theorem 11 (Point Processes with Independent Delays Defined by Intensities λ_{dn})

Let $\lambda_{dn}(.)$ (n=1,2,...) be positive functions on R_+, Lebesgue-integrable on bounded intervals, non Lebesgue-integrable on $[0,\infty[$. Then the point process $(T_1,T_2,...)$ with intensities

$$\lambda_n(\tau/t_1,...,t_{n-1}) := \lambda_{dn}(\tau-t_{n-1}) \quad (n=1,2,...;\ 0=:t_0\leq t_1\leq...\leq t_{n-1}\leq\tau<\infty) \qquad (66)$$

has independent delays D_1, D_2, ... The delay D_n has the density function h_n and the distribution function H_n defined by

$$h_n(t) := \exp[-\textstyle\int_{[0,t]} \lambda_{dn}(\tau)d\tau]\ \lambda_{dn}(t) \quad (n=1,2,...;\ t\in R_+) \qquad (67)$$

$$H_n(t) := 1-\exp[-\textstyle\int_{[0,t]} \lambda_{dn}(\tau)d\tau] \quad (n=1,2,...;\ t\in R_+). \qquad (68)$$

Proof
The function h_n defined by (67) is a probability density function, and H_n is the corresponding distribution function. By (47), (65) and (66), we express the density of the vector $(D_1,...,D_n)$, and we observe that it presents the right factorization.

It is enough to consider the case n=3.

$$\begin{aligned}
p_{d3}(\tau_1,\tau_2,\tau_3) &= \exp[-\textstyle\int_{[0,\tau_1]} \lambda_1(\tau)d\tau]\lambda_1(\tau_1)\\
&\quad\times \exp[-\textstyle\int_{[\tau_1,\tau_1+\tau_2]} \lambda_2(\tau/\tau_1)d\tau]\lambda_2(\tau_1+\tau_2/\tau_1)\\
&\quad\times \exp[-\textstyle\int_{[\tau_1+\tau_2,\tau_1+\tau_2+\tau_3]} \lambda_3(\tau/\tau_1,\tau_1+\tau_2)d\tau]\lambda_3(\tau_1+\tau_2+\tau_3/\ \tau_1,\tau_1+\tau_2)\\
&= \exp[-\textstyle\int_{[0,\tau_1]} \lambda_{d1}(\tau)d\tau]\lambda_{d1}(\tau_1)\\
&\quad\times \exp[-\textstyle\int_{[\tau_1,\tau_1+\tau_2]} \lambda_{d2}(\tau-\tau_1)d\tau]\lambda_{d2}(\tau_2)\\
&\quad\times \exp[-\textstyle\int_{[\tau_1+\tau_2,\tau_1+\tau_2+\tau_3]} \lambda_{d3}(\tau-\tau_1-\tau_2)d\tau]\lambda_{d3}(\tau_3)\\
&= \exp[-\textstyle\int_{[0,\tau_1]} \lambda_{d1}(\tau)d\tau]\lambda_{d1}(\tau_1)\\
&\quad\times \exp[-\textstyle\int_{[0,\tau_2]} \lambda_{d2}(\tau)d\tau]\lambda_{d2}(\tau_2)\\
&\quad\times \exp[-\textstyle\int_{[0,\tau_3]} \lambda_{d3}(\tau)d\tau]\lambda_{d3}(\tau_3) = h_1(\tau_1)h_2(\tau_2)h_3(\tau_3) \quad \bullet
\end{aligned}$$

The point process defined by Theorem 11 is the **point process with independent delays and delay intensities $\lambda_{dn}(\cdot)$ (n=1,2,...)**. The interpretation of the process and of the intensity functions λ_{dn} is the following. For fixed n and $T_{n-1}=t_{n-1}$, let t_{n-1} be the new origin of times, and let us consider the Poisson process with intensity function $\lambda_{dn}(\cdot)$. Then the probability of a first point in $d\tau$ equals $h_n(\tau)d\tau$. Hence:

The point process with independent delays and delay intensities $\lambda_{dn}(\cdot)$ (n=1,2,...) can be viewed as a succession of Poisson processes with intensity functions λ_{d1}, λ_{d2},... At the origin, the intensity function λ_{d1} is active. At the occurrence of the first point, the latter becomes the new origin and the intensity λ_{d2} becomes active, ...

The usual Poisson process is a point process with independent delays. The non-homogeneous Poisson process has not, in general, independent delays. We define

$$\Lambda_{dn}(s,t) = \int_{[s,t]} \lambda_{dn}(\tau)d\tau \quad (n=1,2,...;\ 0\le s\le t). \tag{69}$$

By (67) and (68),

$$h_n(t) = e^{-\Lambda_{dn}(0,t)}\,\lambda_{dn}(t) \quad (n=1,2,...;\ t\ge 0), \tag{70}$$

$$H_n(t) = 1-e^{-\Lambda_{dn}(0,t)} \quad (n=1,2,...;\ t\ge 0). \tag{71}$$

H_n is a probability distribution function on $\mathbf{R}_+$ with density h_n.

Theorem 12 (Comparison Theorem for Explosions. Independent Delays)

We consider two point processes with independent delays, the first with delay intensities $\lambda_{dn}(.)$ (n=1,2,...), the second with delay intensities $\lambda^{\circ}_{dn}(\cdot)$ (n=1,2...). Let $n_0\ge 0$ and $\varepsilon>0$ exist such that

$$\lambda_{dn}(\tau) \le \lambda^{\circ}_{dn}(\tau) \quad (n\ge n_0,\ 0\le\tau\le\varepsilon). \tag{72}$$

If the process with intensities λ°_{dn} is non-explosive, then the process with intensities λ_{dn} is non-explosive.

Proof

By (68) and Theorem 3 with $h:=1_{[0,\varepsilon]}$, the non-explosiveness of the process with intensities λ_{dn} is equivalent to relation

$$\sum_{n\ge 0}\int_{[0,\varepsilon]} \exp[-\int_{[0,t]} \lambda_{dn}(\tau)d\tau]dt = \infty.$$

If we replace λ_{dn} by $\lambda°_{dn}$, we obtain a relation equivalent to the non-explosiveness of the process with intensities $\lambda°_{dn}$. Then the Theorem is obvious from these relations •

Remark

Let $(T_1,T_2,...)$ be a point process with independent delays and delay intensities λ_{dn} (n=1,2,...). By (66), the corresponding intensities λ_n (n=1,2,...) are Markov intensities. They are regular because

$$\int_{\{r\leq s\leq \tau\}} \lambda_n(s/r)ds = \int_{\{r\leq s\leq \tau\}} \lambda_{dn}(s-r)ds = \int_{\{0\leq s\leq \tau-r\}} \lambda_{dn}(s)ds,$$

where the last member is a decreasing function of $r\in[0,\tau]$.

Hence, Theorem 9 can be applied in case of independent delays. but Theorem 12 is better because the delay intensities must only be considered on any arbitrarily small interval $[0,\varepsilon]$ in the latter Theorem.

Theorem 13 (Expression of $P(N_t\leq n)$. Independent Delays)

Let $(T_1,T_2,...)$ be the point process with independent delays and delay intensities $\lambda_{dn}(\cdot)$ (n=1,2,...). Then, for all $t\geq 0$,

$$\mathbf{P(N_t=0) = e^{-\Lambda_{d1}(0,t)},} \tag{73}$$

$$\mathbf{P(N_t\leq n) = \int_{[0,t]} P(N_{t-\tau}\leq n-1)\, e^{-\Lambda_{d,n+1}(0,\tau)}\, \lambda_{d,n+1}(\tau)d\tau + e^{-\Lambda_{d,n+1}(0,t)} \quad (n=1,2,...).} \tag{73}$$

Proof

For the proof of the second relation (73), we observe that

$$N_t(\omega) \leq n \Leftrightarrow T_{n+1}(\omega) > t.$$

Then
$$P(N_t\leq n) = P(T_{n+1}>t) = \int_{[0,\infty[} P(T_{n+1}>t\,,\, D_{n+1}\in d\tau)$$

$$= \int_{[0,t]} P(T_{n+1}>t/D_{n+1}=\tau)P(D_{n+1}\in d\tau) + \int_{]t,\infty[} P(D_{n+1}\in d\tau)$$

$$= \int_{[0,t]} P(T_n+\tau>t)h_{n+1}(\tau)d\tau + \int_{]t,\infty[} h_{n+1}(\tau)d\tau$$

$$= \int_{[0,t]} P(T_n>t-\tau)\, e^{-\Lambda_{d,n+1}(0,\tau)}\, \lambda_{d,n+1}(\tau)d\tau + [1-H_{n+1}(t)]$$

$$= \int_{[0,t]} P(N_{t-\tau}\leq n-1)\, e^{-\Lambda_{d,n+1}(0,\tau)}\, \lambda_{d,n+1}(\tau)d\tau + e^{-\Lambda_{d,n+1}(0,t)}$$ •

4.5.2. Processes with No Location Memory

A **point process with no location memory** is a process, defined by Theorem 6, with intensity functions $\lambda_n(\tau)$ (n=1,2,...; $\tau\in\mathbf{R}_+$) not depending on $t_1,...,t_{n-1}$. Intuitively, such a process may remember, at each instant τ, the number n−1 of points occurred earlier, but it forgets their locations $t_1,...,t_{n-1}$. In this section, a process $(T_1,T_2,...)$ with no location memory is considered. We define

$$\Lambda_n(s,t) := \int_{\{s\le\tau\le t\}} \lambda_n(\tau)d\tau \quad (n=1,2,...;0\le s\le t). \tag{74}$$

Then (50), (52), (53) become

$$p_1(t)= e^{-\Lambda_1(0,t)}\lambda_1(t)\ (0\le t),$$

$$p_n(t/s) = e^{-\Lambda_n(s,t)}\ \lambda_n(t)\quad (n=2,3,...;\ 0\le s\le t), \tag{75}$$

$$p_n(t_1,...,t_n) = p_1(t_1)p_2(t_2/t_1)p_3(t_3/t_2)...p_n(t_n/t_{n-1})\quad (n=1,2,...), \tag{76}$$

$$\pi_{t0} = e^{-\Lambda_1(0,t)}\ (0\le t),$$

$$\pi_{tn}(t_1,...,t_n) = p_n(t_1,...,t_n)e^{-\Lambda_{n+1}(t_n,t)}\ (n=1,2,...), \tag{77}$$

for all $0=:t_0\le t_1\le...\le t_n\le t$.

The process with no location memory has regular Markov intensities. They are regular because the integral $\Lambda_n(s,t)$ defining the regularity is a decreasing function of $s\in[0,t]$. Hence, the general comparison Theorem 9 can be applied if $(T^\circ_1,T^\circ_2,...)$ is a point process with no location memory.

Theorem 14 (Expression for $P(N_t=n)$. No Location Memory)

In the point process $(T_1,T_2,...)$ with no location memory and intensity functions $\lambda_n(\cdot)$ (n=1,2,...),

$$P(N_t=0) = e^{-\Lambda_1(0,t)}\quad (t\ge 0), \tag{78}$$

$$P(N_t=n) = \int_{[0,t]} P(N_\tau=n-1)\ \lambda_n(\tau)\ e^{-\Lambda_{n+1}(\tau,t)}\ d\tau\ (t\ge 0;\ n=1,2,...) \tag{78}$$

and

$$\partial/\partial_t P(N_t=0) = -\lambda_1(t)P(N_t=0)\quad (t\ge 0), \tag{79}$$

$$\partial/\partial_t P(N_t=n) = \lambda_n(t)P(N_t=n-1) - \lambda_{n+1}(t)P(N_t=n)\ (t\ge 0;\ n=1,2,...). \tag{79}$$

Proof

The relations (79) follow from (78) by differentiation. The relations (78) follow from (21) and (77). Indeed, we consider case n=3 (general case is similar). By Fubini,

$$P(N_t=3) = \iiint_{\{0\leq t_1\leq t_2\leq t_3\leq t\}} p_1(t_1)p_2(t_2/t_1)p_3(t_3/t_2)e^{-\Lambda_4(t_3,t\}}\, dt_1dt_2dt_3$$

$$= \int_{\{0\leq t_3\leq t\}} [\iint_{\{0\leq t_1\leq t_2\leq t_3\}} p_1(t_1)p_2(t_2/t_1)e^{-\Lambda_3(t_2,t_3)}\, dt_1dt_2]\, \lambda_3(t_3)\, e^{-\Lambda_4(t_3,t\}}dt_3$$

$$= \int_{\{0\leq t_3\leq t\}} P(N_{t_3}=2)\, \lambda_3(t_3)\, e^{-\Lambda_4(t_3,t\}}dt_3 \quad \bullet$$

Remarks

a. The partial derivatives occurring in the relations (79) exist because $\Lambda_n(s,t)$ is an absolutely continuous function of t. As usual, the "Lebesgue-a.e." indication is omitted.

b. In some cases, the relations (78) allow the successive explicit calculation of the probabilities $P(N_t=n)$ (n=0,1,2,...).

c. The **differential equations** (79), and the **initial conditions**

$$P(N_0=0)=1 \quad , \quad P(N_0=n)=0 \ (n=1,2,...)$$

determine the functions $P(N_t=n)$ (n=0,1,2,...) of $t\in\mathbf{R}_+$. They can be used as verification (and proof) of the correctness of the expressions $P(N_t=n)$.

d. The relations (79) show that **the intensities $\lambda_n(t)$ of the point process with no location memory are determined by the functions $P(N_t=n)$.** By this remark, some rather general processes can be replaced by a process with no location memory, without modification of the $P(N_t=n)$ functions. It is enough to use the original functions in (79) and then to consider the process with no location memory defined by the intensities resulting from (79). Of course, then it must be verified that these functions $\lambda_n(t)$ are intensities indeed.

d. The second formula (78) has the following infinitesimal interpretation:

$$P(N_t=n) = \int_{[0,t]} P(N_t=n\, ,\, T_n\in d\tau)$$

$$= \int_{[0,t]} P\{(n-1)-[0,\tau[\, ,\, 1-d\tau\, ,\, 0-]\tau,t]\}$$

$$= \int_{[0,t]} P\{(n-1)-[0,\tau[\}.P\{1-d\tau\, /\, (n-1)-[0,\tau[\}.P\{0-]\tau,t]\, /\, n-[0,\tau]\}$$

$$= \int_{[0,t]} P(N_\tau=n-1).\lambda_n(\tau)d\tau.\, e^{-\Lambda_{n+1}(\tau,t)}.$$

4.5.3. Homogeneous Point Processes

A **homogeneous point process** is a process, defined by Theorem 6, with constant intensity functions $\lambda_n \in \mathbf{R}_{++}$ (n=1,2,...). (No intensity λ_n can be zero by the non Lebesgue-integrability condition (28)). **Homogeneous point processes are point processes with no location memory.**

The homogeneous point process with intensities λ_n (n=1,2,...) is the same as the point process with independent delays and delay intensities $\lambda_{dn}=\lambda_n$ (n=1,2,...) defined by Theorem 11.

Theorem 15 (Explosion Theorem. Homogeneous Point Processes)

The homogeneous point process $(T_1,T_2,...)$ with intensities λ_n (n=1,2,...) is non-explosive iff

$$\sum_{n\geq 0} 1/\lambda_n = \infty. \tag{80}$$

Proof
By the explosion Theorem 3 for processes with independent delays, with the particular function $h(\tau) := e^{-\tau}$ $(\tau \in \mathbf{R}_+)$, the process is non-explosive iff the sum

$$\sum_{n\geq 1} \int_{[0,\infty[} \exp[-(\lambda_n+1)\tau]d\tau = \sum_{n\geq 1} (\lambda_n+1)^{-1}$$

is infinite. The sums $\sum_{n\geq 1}(\lambda_n)^{-1}$ and $\sum_{n\geq 1}(\lambda_n+1)^{-1}$ are infinite or not at the same time (see 4.6.2.a) •

Theorem 16 (Expression of $P(N_t=n)$ and $P(N_t\leq n)$. Homogeneous Point Processes)

In the homogeneous point process $(T_1,T_2,...)$ with all different intensities λ_n (n=1,2,...),

$$P(N_t=0) = e^{-\lambda_1 t}, \tag{81}$$

$$P(N_t\leq n) = \sum_{1\leq k\leq n+1} \left[\prod_{1\leq i\leq n+1, i\neq k} \lambda_i\right]\left[\prod_{1\leq i\leq n+1, i\neq k} (\lambda_i-\lambda_k)\right]^{-1} e^{-\lambda_k t}, \tag{82}$$

$$P(N_t=n) = \left[\prod_{1\leq i\leq n} \lambda_i\right] \sum_{1\leq k\leq n+1} \left[\prod_{1\leq i\leq n+1, i\neq k} (\lambda_i-\lambda_k)\right]^{-1} e^{-\lambda_k t}, \tag{83}$$

for all n=1,2,... and $t\geq 0$.

Proof
A proof by recurrence of (82) is based on (73) and on the identity

$$\sum_{1\le k\le n+1} [\Pi_{1\le i\le n+1, i\ne k}\, \lambda_i][\Pi_{1\le i\le n+1, i\ne k}\, (\lambda_i - \lambda_k)]^{-1} = 1 \ (n=0,1,2,\ldots).$$

Then (83) results from (82) and the relations

$$P(N_t=0) = P(N_t\le 0),$$

$$P(N_t=n) = P(N_t\le n) - P(N_t\le n-1) \ \ (n=1,2,\ldots) \ \bullet$$

4.5.4. Renewal Point Processes with Delay Intensity Function

The **renewal point process with delay intensity function $\lambda_d(\cdot)$**, is the point process with independent delays and all delay intensity functions $\lambda_{dn}(\cdot)$ (n=1,2,...) equal to $\lambda_d(\cdot)$.

Theorem 17 (Expression of $P(N_t=n)$. Renewal Process with Delay Intensity Function)

Let $(T_1,T_2,\ldots)$ be the renewal point process with delay intensity function $\lambda_d(\cdot)$. Then, for all $t\ge 0$,

$$P(N_t=0) = e^{-\Lambda_d(0,t)}, \tag{84}$$

$$P(N_t=n) = \int_{[0,t]} P(N_{t-\tau}=n-1)\, e^{-\Lambda_d(0,\tau)}\, \lambda_d(\tau)d\tau \ \ (n=1,2,\ldots). \tag{84}$$

Proof
Here the relations (73) become the first relation (84) and the relations

$$P(N_t\le n) = \int_{[0,t]} P(N_{t-\tau}\le n-1)\, e^{-\Lambda_d(0,\tau)}\, \lambda_d(\tau)d\tau + e^{-\Lambda_d(0,t)} \ (n=1,2,\ldots).$$

We replace n by n−1:

$$P(N_t\le n-1) = \int_{[0,t]} P(N_{t-\tau}\le n-2)\, e^{-\Lambda_d(0,\tau)}\, \lambda_d(\tau)d\tau + e^{-\Lambda_d(0,t)} \ (n=1,2,\ldots),$$

where the integral vanishes if n=1. By difference, (84) is obtained $\bullet$

4.5.5. Mixed Processes

Hereafter, point processes depending on some parameter λ are considered. For these processes, the foregoing notations, completed by the subscript λ, are used.

Theorem 18 (Definition of Mixed Point Processes with Densities)

For all λ in the interval I, let $(T_{\lambda 1},T_{\lambda 2},...)$ be the point process with density functions $p_{\lambda n}$ (n=1,2,...) and let U be a probability distribution on I. Then a point process $(T_1,T_2,...)$ with density functions

$$p_n(t_1,...,t_n) = \int_I p_{\lambda n}(t_1,...,t_n)dU(\lambda) \quad (n=1,2,...;\ 0\leq t_1\leq ...\leq t_n>\infty). \tag{85}$$

exists. It is called *the mixture, with mixing distribution* U, *of the processes* $(T_{\lambda 1},T_{\lambda 2},...)$. The densities $\pi_{tn}(t_1,...,t_n)$ $(n=0,1,2,...;\ 0\leq t_1\leq ...\leq t_n\leq t)$ of the process are

$$\pi_{tn}(t_1,...,t_n) = \int_I \pi_{\lambda tn}(t_1,...,t_n)dU(\lambda). \tag{86}$$

If the processes $(T_{\lambda 1},T_{\lambda 2},...)$ $(\lambda\in I)$ are non-explosive, the mixed process $(T_1,T_2,...)$ is non-explosive.

Proof

For the existence of the process, it is sufficient to verify the norm and compatibility relations (17) and (18). The latter are satisfied for the densities $p_{\lambda n}$. Then by an integration with respect to $U(\lambda)$ $(\lambda\in I)$, they are satisfied for the densities p_n, by Fubini. The justification of (86) is similar. Now the starting relations are the relations (19) connecting the densities $p_{\lambda n}$ and $\pi_{\lambda tn}$.

Let us now assume that the λ-processes are non-explosive. Then the norm relation

$$\sum_{n\geq 0} P(N_{\lambda t}=n) = 1.$$

is satisfied for all $\lambda\in I$ and $t\in\mathbf{R}_+$. The probabilities $P(N_{\lambda t}=n)$ in the left member result from (21) with π_{tn} replaced by $\pi_{\lambda tn}$. Then the norm relation for the mixed process results from the integration with respect to $U(\lambda)$ $(\lambda\in I)$, and by Fubini. (Sums are particular integrals. Here everything is positive.) •

Remarks

a. Sometimes, **mixed processes** are called **compound processes**. We reserve the adjective **compound** for distributions of random sums $X_1+...+X_N$ with a random number of terms (see Ch.3.3.1).

b. The interval I and the probability distribution U may be replaced by a set in some $\mathbf{R}^k$ and a probability distribution on that set (or even by an abstract probability space).

c. Processes with densities p_n are processes with intensities λ_n (rather obviously found from infinitesimal interpretations and then defined correctly). In particular, mixed processes with densities are processes with intensities. One basic goal, when point processes with densities or intensites are considered, is the calculation of probabilities via the densities π_{tn}, by relation (20). In case of mixed processes, the densities π_{tn} already result from (86), and then the consideration of the intensities λ_n is not necessary.

4.5.6. Mixed Poisson Processes

The mixed Poisson process, with mixing distribution U on]0,∞[, is the point process $(T_1,T_2,...)$ with density functions p_n, not depending on $t_1,...,t_{n-1}$,

$$p_n(t_n) := \int_{]0,\infty[} e^{-\lambda t_n} \lambda^n \, dU(\lambda) \; (n=1,2,...;0\le t_1\le...\le t_n). \tag{87}$$

A distribution U on]0,∞[is a distribution on [0,∞[, with no mass at 0, i.e. with U(0)=0. By the expression (42) of p_n in the case of the Poisson process with intensity $\lambda>0$, the mixed Poisson process is a particular case of the mixed processes defined by Theorem 17. (Mixed Poisson processes are also called **compound Poisson processes** by some authors. See the foregoing *Remark* a.)

We here justify the restriction U(0)=0. Let us assume that U(0)>0, and that the integration domain in the last member of (87) is replaced by the interval [0,∞[. Then the density of T_1 is the function $p_1(t)=\int_{[0,\infty[} e^{-\lambda t}\lambda dU(\lambda)$ of $t\in\mathbf{R}_+$. Its Lebesgue-integral over [0,∞[must be equal to 1. By the relation $\int_{[0,\infty[}e^{-\lambda t}\lambda dt=1_{\lambda>0}$ and Fubini

$$\int_{[0,\infty[} p_1(t)dt = \int_{[0,\infty[} [\int_{[0,\infty[} [e^{-\lambda t}\,\lambda dt]\, dU(\lambda)$$

$$= \int_{[0,\infty[} 1_{\lambda>0} \, dU(\lambda) = \int_{]0,\infty[} dU(\lambda) = 1-U(0) < 1.$$

Hence, the process cannot be a process **with densities** if U(0)>0.

Point processes are regarded as identical if they have the same finite-dimensional distributions, even when they are defined on different probability spaces. In particular, point processes with densities are identical if they have the same densities p_n (n=1,2,...). Hence, the meaning of d. in next Theorem is that mixed Poisson processes with the same function π_{t0} of t, do have the same densities $p_n(t_n)$ for all n and t_n.

Theorem 19 (Properties of the Mixed Poisson Process)

Let $(T_1,T_2,...)$ be the mixed Poisson Process with mixing distribution U.

a. The density functions π_{tn} $(n=0,1,2,...:0\leq t_1\leq ...\leq t_n\leq t)$ of the process are the constants (for fixed n and t)

$$\pi_{tn} = \int_{[0,\infty[} \lambda^n e^{-\lambda t} dU(\lambda) \quad (n=0,1,2,...;\ t\geq 0). \tag{88}$$

b.

$$P(N_t=n) = \int_{[0,\infty[} 1/n!\ (\lambda t)^n e^{-\lambda t} dU(\lambda) \quad (n=0,1,2,...;\ t\geq 0). \tag{89}$$

c. The process is non-explosive.

d. The process is determined by the function $P(N_t=0) = \pi_{t0}$ of $t\in R_+$.

Proof

a. and c. result from the general Theorem 17. Then b. results from a. by an integration by symmetrization. For the proof of d. we consider (88) for n=0:

$$\pi_{t0} = \int_{[0,\infty[} e^{-\lambda t} dU(\lambda).$$

In the last member, the differentiation with respect to t can be performed as many times as wanted, under the integral symbol (by App.G.Th.G8). Hence

$$(\partial/\partial t)^m \pi_{t0} = \int_{[0,\infty[} (-\lambda)^m e^{-\lambda t} dU(\lambda) = (-1)^m \pi_{tm}.$$

Hence, the functions π_{tm} are determined by the function π_{t0}. Then, by (23), the densities p_n are determined by π_{t0} •

An essential property of the mixed Poisson process with mixing function U is relation (89). Sometimes the point process is defined by this relation. This is an incomplete definition, because different processes may have the same $P(N_t=n)$ probabilities (see *processes 5* and *6* of 4.6.3).

The definition can be completed by the condition that the process has no location memory. Hence, a possible definition (which we do not use) is the following:

The mixed Poisson process, with mixing function U, is the point process with no location memory, and probabilities $P(N_t=n)$ ($t\in R_+$; n=0,1,2,...) defined by (89).

Theorem 20 (Characterization of the Mixed Poisson Process)

Let $(T_1,T_2,...)$ be a non-explosive point process with densities p_n(n=1,2,...). Then $(T_1,T_2,...)$ is a mixed Poisson process iff the densities π_{tn} (n=0,1,...; $0\leq t_1\leq...\leq t_n\leq t$) do not depend on $t_1,...,t_n$.

Proof

One part of the Theorem results from Theorem 18.a. For the other part, we suppose that the densities π_{tn} do not depend on $t_1,...,t_n$.

a. We start with the justification of the formula

$$\textstyle\sum_{n\geq 0} P(N_{[0,s]}=m,\ N_{]s,t]}=n) = P(N_{[0,s]}=m) \quad (m=0,1,2,...). \tag{90}$$

The first member equals

$$P(N_{[0,s]}=m,\ N_{]s,t]}<\infty).$$

Let us assume that it is strictly less than $P(N_{[0,s]}=m)$ for some m. Then

$$P(N_{[0,t]}<\infty) = P(N_{[0,s]}<\infty,\ N_{]s,t]}<\infty) = \textstyle\sum_{m\geq 0} P(N_{[0,s]}=m,\ N_{]s,t]}<\infty)$$

$$< \textstyle\sum_{m\geq 0} P(N_{[0,s]}=m) = P(N_{[0,s]}<\infty) = 1,$$

where the last equality results from the norm relation on [0,s]. But then the norm relation on [0,t] is not satisfied. This contradiction proves (90).

b. The probabilities occurring in (90) can be obtained by integrations by symmetrization (see the justification of relation (40)).

$$P(N_{[0,s]}=m,\ N_{]s,t]}=n) = \pi_{t,n+m}\ {}^{1}/_{m!}\ s^m\ {}^{1}/_{n!}\ (t-s)^n \quad (m,n=0,1,2,...;\ 0\leq s<t), \tag{91}$$

$$P(N_{[0,s]}=m) = \pi_{sm}\ {}^{1}/_{m!}\ s^m \quad (m=0,1,2,...;\ s\geq 0). \tag{92}$$

Hence,

$$\textstyle\sum_{n\geq 0} \pi_{t,n+m}\ {}^{1}/_{m!}\ s^m\ {}^{1}/_{n!}\ (t-s)^n = \pi_{sm}\ {}^{1}/_{m!}\ s^m, \tag{93}$$

$$\pi_{sm} = \textstyle\sum_{n\geq 0} \pi_{t,n+m}\ {}^{1}/_{n!}\ (t-s)^n\ (m=0,1,2,\ldots;\ 0\leq s<t). \tag{94}$$

In particular, for m=0,

$$\pi_{s0} = \textstyle\sum_{n\geq 0} \pi_{tn}\ {}^{1}/_{n!}\ (t-s)^n\ (0\leq s<t). \tag{95}$$

For fixed t, the last member is a power series, convergent for s=0. From general properties of power series results that the differentiations with respect to $s\in]0,t[$ can be performed as many times as wanted, under the sum symbol:

$$(\partial/\partial s)^m\ \pi_{s0} = (-1)^m \textstyle\sum_{n\geq m} \pi_{tn}\ {}^{1}/_{(n-m)!}\ (t-s)^{n-m}$$

$$= (-1)^m \textstyle\sum_{n\geq 0} \pi_{t,m+n}\ {}^{1}/_{n!}\ (t-s)^n.$$

Then, by (94),

$$(\partial/\partial s)^m\ \pi_{s0} = (-1)^m\ \pi_{sm}\ \ (m=0,1,2,\ldots;\ s>0). \tag{96}$$

This relation is correct for all s>0, because for any s, we can take t>s.

c. By (96) π_s (s>0) is a completely monotone function on $]0,\infty[$. Moreover, $\pi_{s0}=P(N_s=0)$ is a bounded function of $s\in\mathbf{R}_+$ and $\pi_{00}=1$. By Bernstein's Theorem (App.J.Th.J4), π_{s0} can be displayed as

$$\pi_{s0} = \textstyle\int_{[0,\infty[} e^{-\lambda s}\ dU(\lambda)\ (s\geq 0). \tag{97}$$

In that relation U is a probability distribution on $[0,\infty[$ because $U(\mathbf{R}_+)=\pi_{00}=1$.

We now show that U(0)=0. As $s\uparrow\infty$:

$$\pi_{s0} = P(N_s=0) = P(T_1>s) = \textstyle\int_{[s,\infty[} p_1(\tau)d\tau \to 0,$$

$$e^{-\lambda s} \to 1_{\lambda=0}\ ,\ \pi_{s0} = \textstyle\int_{[0,\infty[} e^{-\lambda s}\ dU(\lambda) \to \int_{\{0\}} dU(\lambda) = U(0).$$

d. In the last member of (97), differentiations with respect to t may be performed, as many times as wanted, under the integral symbol (App.G. Th.G8). Then by (96),

$$\pi_{sm} = (-1)^m\ (\partial/\partial s)^m\ \pi_{s0} = \textstyle\int_{[0,\infty[} \lambda^m\ e^{-\lambda s}\ dU(\lambda).$$

Finally, for $s=t_n$,

$$p_m(t_1,\ldots,t_n) = \textstyle\int_{[0,\infty[} \lambda^m\ e^{-\lambda t_n}\ dU(\lambda),$$

by (23). This proves that the point process $(T_1,T_2,\ldots)$ is mixed Poisson •

The inverse probabilities relation

A remarkable relation resulting from (91) and (92) is the following **inverse probabilities relation** (98). It is valid in any point process, explosive or not, in which the densities π_{tn} are constants. In particular, it holds in any mixed Poisson process.

The last member does not depend on the densities π_{tn} nor on the mixing distribution U.

$$P(N_s{=}m/N_t{=}n) = n!/(m!(n-m)!)\ (s/t)^m(1 - s/t)^{n-m}\ (0\le s\le t;\ 0\le m\le n). \quad (98)$$

Indeed, the first member of this relation equals

$$P(N_s{=}m,\ N_t{=}n)\ /\ P(N_t{=}n),$$

where the numerator equals

$$P(N_{[0,s]}{=}m,\ N_{]s,t]}{=}n-m)\ = \pi_{tn}\ 1/m!\ s^m\ 1/(n-m)!\ (t-s)^{n-m}$$

and the denominator

$$P(N_{[0,t]}{=}n) = \pi_{tn}\ 1/n!\ t^n.$$

4.6. Miscellaneous Illustrations

4.6.1. General Explosion Theorem for Processes with Intensities

Theorem 21 (Explosion Theorem. Processes with Intensities)

Let $b_n(\cdot)$ (n=1,2,...) be strictly positive functions on R_+ such that

$$\sum_{n\ge 0} 1/b_n(t) = \infty\ (t\in R_+). \quad (99)$$

Let the intensities λ_n (n=1,2,...) of the point process $(T_1,T_2,...)$, defined by Theorem 6, be such that

$$\lambda_n(\tau/t_1,...,t_n) \le b_n(t)\ \ (n=1,2,...;\ 0\le t_1\le ...\le t_n\le \tau\le t). \quad (100)$$

Then the process is non-explosive.

Proof
Let t be fixed for the moment. Let $(T°_1,T°_2,...)$ be the homogeneous point process with intensities

$$\lambda°_n := b_n(t) \ (n=1,2,...).$$

Then the conditions a, b and c of Theorem 9 are satisfied and (61) holds. By (99) and by Theorem 15, the process $(T°_1,T°_2,...)$ is non-explosive. Then $P(T°_\infty \le t)=0$ and by (61), $P(T_\infty \le t)=0$. This holds for all $t \in \mathbf{R}_+$. Then, by the Lemma of Theorem 1,

$$P(T_\infty < \infty) = \lim_{t\uparrow\infty} P(T_\infty \le t) = 0$$

and then the process $(T_1,T_2,...)$ is non-explosive by Theorem 1, a⇔b •

We recall the **factorial powers** notation:

$$a^{[0]} :=1 \ , \ a^{[n]} := a(a-1)(a-2)...(a-n+1) \ (a \in \mathbf{R}, \ n=1,2,...). \qquad (101)$$

Then the **binomial development**

$$1/(1-x)^{1+\alpha} = \sum_{n\ge 0} 1/n! \ (n+\alpha)^{[n]} \ x^n \ (|x|<1, \ \alpha \in \mathbf{R}). \qquad (102)$$

is valid for all values of α. It is the **negative binomial development** if $1+\alpha$ is positive. It is the elementary development, with a finite number of terms in the last member, if $1+\alpha$ is a negative integer.

4.6.2. Classical Series and Integrals

We here recall some simple facts about classical series and integrals. We assume that the numbers a_n, b_n and the functions f, g are strictly positive.

a. **Let $\lim_{n\uparrow\infty} a_n/b_n = c \in \mathbf{R}_{++}$. Then $\sum_{n\ge 0} a_n$ and $\sum_{n\ge 0} b_n$ both are finite or infinite.** Indeed, n° exists such that

$$1/2 \ c \le a_n/b_n \le 2c \ (n \ge n°).$$

Then

$$1/2 \ c \ b_n \le a_n \le 2c \ b_n \ (n \ge n°),$$

$$1/2 \ c \sum_{n\ge n°} b_n \le \sum_{n\ge n°} a_n \le 2c \sum_{n\ge n°} b_n.$$

b. **Let f and g be bounded on the bounded intervals in $[a,\infty[$, and let $\lim_{x\uparrow\infty} f(x)/g(x)=c\in\mathbf{R}_{++}$. Then $\int_{[a,\infty[} f(x)dx$ and $\int_{[a,\infty[} g(x)dx$ both are finite or infinite.** Indeed $a°\geq a$ exists such that

$$1/2\ c \leq f(x)/g(x) \leq 2c(x\geq a°).$$

Then

$$1/2\ c\ g(x) \leq f(x) \leq 2c\ g(x)\ (x\geq a°),$$

$$1/2\ c \int_{[a°,\infty[} g(x)dx \leq \int_{[a°,\infty[} f(x)dx \leq 2c \int_{[a°,\infty[} g(x)dx.$$

c. **Let f and g be bounded on the closed intervals in $]0,b]$, and let $\lim_{x\downarrow 0} f(x)/g(x)=c\in\mathbf{R}_{++}$. Then $\int_{]0,b]} f(x)dx$ and $\int_{]0,b]} g(x)dx$ both are finite or infinite.** Indeed $b°\in]0,b]$ exists such that

$$1/2\ c \leq f(x)/g(x) \leq 2c\ (0<x\leq b°).$$

Then

$$1/2\ cg(x) \leq f(x) \leq 2cg(x)\ (0<x\leq b°),$$

$$1/2\ c \int_{]0,b°]} g(x)dx \leq \int_{]0,b°]} f(x)dx \leq 2c \int_{]0,b°]} g(x)dx.$$

d. **Let f be decreasing on $[n,\infty[$. Then $\int_{[n,\infty[}f(x)dx$ and $\sum_{k\geq n}f(k)$ both are finite or infinite.** Indeed, let f_1 and f_2 be defined on $[n,\infty[$ by

$$f_1(x) := \sum_{k\geq n} f(k+1)1_{k\leq x<k+1}\ ,\ \ f_2(x) := \sum_{k\geq n} f(k)1_{k\leq x<k+1}.$$

Then $f_1(x)\leq f(x)\leq f_2(x)$, and by integration on $[n,\infty[$,

$$\sum_{k>n} f(k) \leq \int_{[n,\infty[} f(x)dx \leq \sum_{k\geq n} f(k).$$

e. **The integral $\int_{[a,\infty[} 1/x^{\alpha}\ dx$ (a>0) is finite if $\alpha>1$, infinite if $\alpha\leq 1$.**

f. **The integral $\int_{]0,b]} 1/x^{\alpha}\ dx$ (b>0) is finite if $\alpha<1$, infinite if $\alpha\geq 1$.**

The integrals in e. and f. can be calculated explicitly, and then e. and f. are direct.

By way of illustration,

$$\int_{[1,\infty[} 1/x\ dx = \infty,$$

by e. Then

$$\sum_{n\geq 1} 1/n = \infty,$$

by d. Then by a,

$$\sum_{n\geq 0} 1/(a+n) = \infty\ (a>0).$$

4.6.3. Particular Point Processes

We here consider particular point processes with intensities. The probabilities $P(N_t=n)$ result from the general formula (21) and integrations by symmetrization. The densities π_{tn} result from (48), or from (77) in case of processes with no location memory. In case of independent delays, the intensities λ_n result from the delay intensities λ_{dn} by (66). The probabilities $P(N_t=n)$ can also be obtained by recurrence from (78) in case of processes with no location memory. Then the correctness of the expressions $P(N_t=n)$ can be proved by substitution in (79). In case of processes with independent delays, the probabilities $P(N_t=n)$ can be obtained via (73), or more simply by (84) in case of renewal processes.

We do not here discuss again the *usual Poisson process* (Corollary of Theorem 5) nor the *non-homogeneous Poisson process* (Theorem 5).

We consider processes with increasing complexity. Some processes are particular cases of processes defined later.

We assume that

$$0 \leq t < \infty \ ; \ n=0,1,2,... \ ; \ 0 =: t_0 \leq t_1 \leq ... \leq t_n \leq \tau \leq t.$$

The product of the terms in a void set equals 1. This means that the product $\Pi_{1\leq k\leq n}\, a_k$ equals 1 if n=0. The sum of the terms in a void set equals 0.

Process 1: **$\lambda_n := n$ (n=1,2,...)**

The process is homogeneous, non-explosive by Th.15, because $\Sigma_n 1/n=\infty$.

$$\pi_{tn}(t_1,...,t_n) = e^{-(n+1)t} \exp(t_1+...+t_n).$$

$$P(N_t=n) = e^{-t}(1-e^{-t})^n.$$

Process 2: **$\lambda_n := a+bn$ (n=1,2,...)** , where $a+b>0$, $b>0$.

The process is homogeneous, non-explosive by Th.15, because $\Sigma_n 1/(a+bn)=\infty$.

$$\pi_{tn}(t_1,\ldots,t_n) = e^{-at-(n+1)bt}\,\Pi_{1\le k\le n}[(a+kb)\exp(bt_k)].$$

$$P(N_t=n) = {}^1\!/_{n!}\ ({}^a\!/_b + n)^{[n]}\, e^{-(a+b)t}\,(1-e^{-bt})^n.$$

Process 3 (Polya): **$\lambda_n(\tau) := (a+bn)/(1+c\tau)$ (n=1,2,...)**, where $a+b\ge 0, b>0, c>0$

This is a process with no location memory. It is non-explosive by Theorem 21 with $b_n(t) := \lambda_n(t)$.

$$\exp[-\textstyle\int_{[s,t]}\lambda_n(\tau)d\tau] = [(1+cs)/(1+ct)]^{a'+b'n},\ \text{where}\ a' := a/c,\ b' := b/c.$$

$$\pi_{tn}(t_1,\ldots,t_n) = (1+ct)^{-a'-(n+1)b'}\,\Pi_{1\le k\le n}[(a+kb)(1+ct_k)^{b'-1}].$$

$$P(N_t=n) = {}^1\!/_{n!}({}^a\!/_b + n)^{[n]}\,(1+ct)^{-a'-b'}[1-(1+ct)^{-b'}]^n.$$

The non-explosiveness results also from the norm relation. The verification of the latter is direct by (102).

By Theorem 19, the **Polya process is a mixed Poisson process iff b=c.** Then the mixing distribution is the gamma with density,

$$U'(\lambda) = {}^1\!/_{\Gamma(\alpha)}\,\beta^\alpha\,\lambda^{\alpha-1}\,e^{-\beta\lambda}\ (\lambda\in\mathbf{R}_+),\ \text{where}\ \beta := {}^1\!/_b,\ \alpha := {}^a\!/_b + 1.$$

(Usually, the Polya process is defined for b=c only).

Process 4: **$\lambda_n(\tau) := 2n\tau$ (n=1,2,...)**

This is a process with no location memory. It is non-explosive by Theorem 21 with $b_n(t) := \lambda_n(t)$.

$$\pi_{tn}(t_1,\ldots,t_n) = n!e^{-(n+1)t^2}\,\Pi_{1\le k\le n}[2t_k\exp(t_k^2)].$$

$$P(N_t=n) = e^{-t^2}(1-e^{-t^2})^n.$$

Process 5: **$\lambda_n(\tau) := \tau/(\tau+2n-1)$ (n=1,2,...)**

This is a non-explosive process with no location memory. By (79)

$$P(N_t=n) = [t^{2n}/(2n)! + t^{2n+1}/(2n+1)!]e^{-t}.$$

Process 6: $\lambda_d(\tau) = \tau/(1+\tau)$

This is a renewal process. Renewal processes are non-explosive. The probabilities

$$P(N_t=n) = [t^{2n}/(2n)! + t^{2n+1}/(2n+1)!]e^{-t}$$

result from (84) by induction. Hence, **the processes 5 and 6 are different processes with the same $P(N_t=n)$ probabilities**.

Hereafter, the explosiveness of some point processes with independent delays is examined. In any case, Theorem 3 is used with $h(\tau) := e^{-\tau}$ ($\tau \in \mathbf{R}_+$), and we define

$$S := \sum_{n\geq 1} \int_{[0,\infty[} [1-H_n(\tau)]e^{-\tau}\, d\tau.$$

Then the non-explosiveness is equivalent to $S=\infty$.

Process 7: $\lambda_{dn}(\tau) := 2n^2\tau$ $(n=1,2,...)$

$$H_n(\tau) = 1-\exp(-n^2\tau^2),$$

$$S = \sum_{n\geq 1} \int_{[0,\infty[} \exp(-n^2\tau^2-\tau)\, d\tau \geq \sum_{n\geq 1} \int_{[0,\infty[} \exp[-(n\tau+1)^2]d\tau$$

$$= \sum_{n\geq 1} 1/n \,.\, \int_{[1,\infty[} \exp(-s^2)ds = \infty.$$

Non-explosive.

Process 8: $\lambda_{dn}(\tau) := 2n^{2+2a}\,\tau$ $(n=1,2,...)$, where $a>0$.

$$H_n(\tau) = 1-\exp(-n^{2+2a}t^2),$$

$$S = \sum_{n\geq 1} \int_{[0,\infty[} \exp(-n^{2+2a}\tau^2-\tau)\, d\tau \leq \sum_{n\geq 1} \int_{[0,\infty[} \exp(-n^{2+2a}\tau^2)\, d\tau$$

$$= \sum_{n\geq 1} 1/(n^{1+a}) \,.\, \int_{[0,\infty[} \exp(-s^2)\, ds < \infty.$$

Explosive.

Process 9: $\lambda_{dn}(\tau) := na\lambda^{a-1}(1+\tau^a)^{-1}$, where $a>0$.

$$H_n(\tau) = 1-(1+\tau^a)^{-1}.$$

By Fubini,

$$S = \int_{[0,\infty[} \sum_{n\geq 1} (1+\tau^a)^{-1}\, e^{-\tau}\, d\tau = \int_{[0,\infty[} (1/\tau^a)e^{-\tau}d\tau.$$

By 4.6.2. c. and f, the latter integral is infinite if $a\geq 1$. Then the process is non-explosive. The integral is finite if $0<a<1$. Then the process is explosive.

Chapter 5

Fixed-Time Ruin Probabilities

5.1. Asymptotic Fixed-Time Ruin Probabilities in Classical Risk Model

5.1.1. Central Tendency in Classical Risk Model

Generally speaking, **central tendency** is the convergence of probability distributions to a normal distribution.

We here follow the classical risk model defined in Ch.3.1.4, and we make the supplementary assumption : $\mu_2<\infty$.

Theorem 1 (Central Limit Theorem in Classical Risk Model)

In the classical risk model, let $\mu_2<\infty$. Then the standardized total claim amount S_t^{01} is asymptotically standardized normal as $t\uparrow\infty$.

Proof

By the final observation of Ch.3.4.3, applied to S_t^{01}, it is enough to prove that the characterisitc function of S_t^{01} tends pointwise to the function $e^{-\tau^2/2}$ as $t\uparrow\infty$.

By Ch.3.Th.2,

$$\varphi_F(\tau) = 1 + i\tau\mu - \tau^2/2\ \mu_2 + \tau^2 o(\tau).$$

By Ch.3.Th.5.d.f,

$$ES_t = \mu\lambda t \quad , \quad \text{Var } S_t = \mu_2\lambda t. \tag{1}$$

Let

$$\sigma_t := \text{Var}^{1/2}\ S_t = (\mu_2\lambda t)^{1/2}. \tag{2}$$

Then

$$S_t^{01} = (S_t - \mu\lambda t)/\sigma_t. \tag{3}$$

By Ch.3.Th.5.e, the characteristic function of S_t^{01} equals

$$E\exp[i\tau(S_t-\mu\lambda t)/\sigma_t] = \exp(-i\tau\mu\lambda t/\sigma_t)\, E\exp[i(\tau/\sigma_t)S_t]$$

$$= \exp(-i\tau\mu\lambda t/\sigma_t)\,\varphi_t(\tau/\sigma_t) = \exp(-i\tau\mu\lambda t/\sigma_t)\, e^{-\lambda t}\exp[\lambda t\varphi_F(\tau/\sigma_t)].$$

Hence, the characteristic function of S_t^{01} equals $\exp[f(\tau,t)]$ where

$$f(\tau,t) := -[i\tau\mu\lambda t\sigma_t^{-1} + \lambda t - \lambda t - i\lambda t\mu\tau\sigma_t^{-1} + \lambda t\mu_2\tau^2\sigma_t^{-2}/2 + \lambda t\tau^2\sigma_t^{-2}o(\tau\sigma_t^{-1})]$$

$$= -[\tau^2/2 + \tau^2\mu_2^{-1}o(\tau(\mu_2\lambda t)^{-1/2})] \to -\tau^2/2 \text{ as } t\uparrow\infty \bullet$$

Hence, if t is large enough, S_t^{01}, and then also S_t, can be treated as normal random variables. In fact, what really matters is that the product λt is large. (See the occurrences of the product λt in the foregoing demonstration).

We hereafter consider a real portfolio, described by the classical risk model. We define the parameter λ of the model to be the expected number of claims in one real year, say the year [0,1]. Then the model year [0,1] coincides with the real year [0,1], by Ch.3.1.3, and very often, the value t=1 is large enough. More concretely: **Very often the expected number of claims in 1 real year is so large that S_1 can be treated as a normal random variable**.

5.1.2. Central Tendency in Practice

Let Z be a normal standardized random variable. Let $\varepsilon>0$ and let z_ε be defined by the relation

$$P(Z > z_\varepsilon) = \varepsilon.$$

Numerical values of z_ε can be found in tables of the normal distribution. Some particular values are

$$z_{0.1} = 1.282$$
$$z_{0.05} = 1.645$$
$$z_{0.01} = 2.326$$
$$z_{0.001} = 3.090$$

We consider a fixed value of t, and we treat S_t as a normal random variable. We are interested in the fixed-time ruin probability at t. This is the fixed-time ruin probability at the end of the real year if t=1.

The fixed-time ruin probability at the instant t equals

$$P(R_t < 0) = P[S_t > u+\mu\lambda t(1+\eta)] = P[\sigma_t S_t^{01}+\mu\lambda t > u+\mu\lambda t(1+\eta)]$$

$$= P[(\mu_2\lambda t)^{1/2}Z+\mu\lambda t > u+\mu\lambda t(1+\eta)] = P[Z > (u+\lambda t\mu\eta)(\lambda t\mu_2)^{-1/2}].$$

Hence

$$P(R_t < 0) \le \varepsilon \Leftrightarrow P[Z > (u+\lambda t\mu\eta)(\lambda t\mu_2)^{-1/2}] \le \varepsilon$$

$$\Leftrightarrow (u+\lambda t\mu\eta)(\lambda t\mu_2)^{-1/2} \ge z_\varepsilon$$

and we have obtained the most important practical equivalence:

$$\mathbf{P(R_t < 0) \le \varepsilon \Leftrightarrow u+\lambda t\mu\eta \ge z_\varepsilon (\lambda t\mu_2)^{1/2}} \qquad (4)$$

This equivalence is used in the following way. At the start, the insurer must fix ε. His decisions are based on the assumption that, in practice, events with a probability less than ε do not occur. The safer he wants to work, the smaller he takes ε.

Suppose that everything is fixed, except the initial risk reserve u. Then the insurer learns from (4) that he must take u larger than

$$z_\varepsilon (\lambda t\mu_2)^{1/2} - \lambda t\mu\eta$$

This value is negative if

$$EN_t = \lambda t \ge z_\varepsilon^2\mu_2(\mu^2\eta^2)^{-1}.$$

In that case, no initial risk reserve is necessary: Large portfolio's can operate safely without any initial risk reserve.

Let us now assume that everything is fixed, except η. Then (4) learns that η must be larger than

$$[z_\varepsilon(\lambda t\mu_2)^{1/2} - u]/(\lambda t\mu)$$

5.1.3. Reinsurances

If no reinsurance is involved, only variations of ε, u and η can be considered. Then (4) indicates how these parameters must be connected. In reinsured portfolio's, also variations of μ and μ_2 are possible.

The risk models, in particular the classical one, apply to reinsurances in which the partial costs are reinsured individually. Let $\alpha(x)$ be a function of $x\in\mathbf{R}_+$ such that $0\leq\alpha(x)\leq x$ ($x\in\mathbf{R}_+$) and let $\beta(x):=x-\alpha(x)$.

We consider a reinsurance treaty in which the first insurer covers the part $\alpha(X_k)$ of each partial cost X_k, and the reinsurer the part $\beta(X_k)$. Then the first insurer can apply the risk model to his sequence of claim amounts $(\alpha(X_1),\alpha(X_2),\ldots)$. The reinsurer uses his sequence $(\beta(X_1),\beta(X_2),\ldots)$.

If the function α depends on parameters, then (4), with the adapted values of μ and μ_2, can be used in order to fix these parameters.

Examples of such reinsurances are the following.

Proportional reinsurance:

$$\alpha(x) = \theta x\ ,\ \beta(x) = (1-\theta)x\quad (x\in\mathbf{R}_+),$$

where θ is a parameter, $0<\theta<1$.

Excess of loss reinsurance:

$$\alpha(x) = \xi\wedge x\ ,\ \beta(x) = (x-\xi)_+\quad (x\in\mathbf{R}_+),$$

where the strictly positive parameter ξ is the **retention limit**.

5.1.4. Statistics

The parameters λ, μ and μ_2 occurring in (4) can be estimated from earlier observations in the considered portfolio, or in similar portfolios. An unbiased estimator of λ is $1/_t\, N_t$. Unbiased estimators of μ and μ_2 are

$$M := (X_1+\ldots+X_{N_t})/N_t, \tag{5}$$

$$M_2 := (X_1^2+\ldots+X_{N_t}^2)/N_t. \tag{6}$$

Of course, here $X_1, \ldots, X_{N_t}$ are **past partial claim amounts**, different from the **future partial claim amounts** $X_1, X_2, \ldots$ of the risk model.

5.1.5. Amount-Homogeneity Assumption

All risk models in this book are based on the **amount-homogeneity assumption** (Ch.3.3.1. *General Assumption c*) stating that the partial claim amounts $X_1,X_2,...$ are i.i.d. In 5.1.7, we justify the equivalence (4) in the case of heterogeneous portfolios.

(Credibility Theory, developed in Part III, deals with heterogeneous portfolios, nevertheless amount-homogeneous in some practical applications. For instance, the bonus-malus systems in automobile insurance are based on claim numbers, not on claim amounts. The subjacent portfolios are of heterogeneous composition because good and bad drivers are involved. They are amount-homogeneous because it is assumed that the partial claims are i.i.d.)

5.1.6. Junction of Independent Portfolios

We here consider two independent amount-homogeneous portfolios and corresponding classical risk models. The general notations, completed by the superscript ^{1} and ^{2} are used for the first and the second portfolio resp. Then

$$ES^1_t = \lambda^1 t\, \mu^1 \quad , \quad Var\, S^1_t = \lambda^1 t\, \mu^1_2,$$

$$ES^2_t = \lambda^2 t\, \mu^2 \quad , \quad Var\, S^2_t = \lambda^2 t\, \mu^2_2.$$

We consider the total claim amount $S_t{:=}S^1_t{+}S^2_t$, in **the junction of the two portfolios**, hereafter called the **large portfolio**. Unless $F^1{=}F^2$, the classical risk model does not apply to the large portfolio because it is not amount-homogeneous. Let

$$\lambda := \lambda^1+\lambda^2 \quad , \quad \mu := 1/\lambda\, (\lambda^1\mu^1+\lambda^2\mu^2) \quad , \quad \mu_2 := 1/\lambda\, (\lambda^1\mu^1_2+\lambda^2\mu^2_2), \qquad (7)$$

$$R_t := u + \mu\lambda t(1+\eta) - S_t. \qquad (8)$$

Then

$$ES_t = \lambda t\, \mu \quad , \quad Var\, S_t = \lambda t\, \mu_2. \qquad (9)$$

The equivalence (4) is only based on the relations (9) and the assumption that S_t is normal. Hence, **if the total claim amount S_t in the large portfolio is a normal random variable, then the equivalence (4) holds**. Of course, if S^1_1 and S^2_1 are normal, then S_1 is normal.

This argument applies to the junction of any number of independent amount-homogeneous portfolios.

5.1.7. Heterogeneous Portfolios

We now assume that the the two portfolios of the foregoing section are already merged, and that we ignore this provenance of the large portfolio. Then μ and μ_2 can still be estimated by (5) and (6). Indeed, then (5) becomes

$$M=[(X^1{}_1+...+X^1{}_{N^1_t})+(X^2{}_1+...X^2{}_{N^2_t})]/N_t, \quad \text{where } N_t=N^1{}_t+N^2{}_t.$$

This is a theoretical formula. The grouping in the square brackets is impossible in practice because we cannot distinguish between the partial claims $X^1{}_k$ in the first portfolio and the partial claims $X^2{}_k$ in the second portfolio. Now

$$M^1 := (X^1{}_1+...+X^1{}_{N^1_t})/N^1{}_t$$

and

$$M^2 := (X^2{}_1+...X^2{}_{N^2_t})/N^2{}_t$$

are unbiased estimators of μ^1 and μ^2 resp.

$$N^1{}_t/N_t \quad \text{and} \quad N^2{}_t/N_t$$

are estimators of

$$(\lambda^1 t)/(\lambda t) = \lambda^1/\lambda \quad \text{and} \quad (\lambda^2 t)/(\lambda t) = \lambda^2/\lambda$$

resp. Then

$$M = (N^1{}_t/N_t)M^1 + (N^2{}_t/N_t)M^2$$

is an estimator of μ. In the same way, M_2 is an estimator of μ_2.

This argument remains valid if any finite number of independent claim-homogeneous portfolios are merged in a large heterogeneous portfolio. Then λ, μ and μ^2 are defined by the obvious extensions of relations (7), and R_t by (8). Then μ=EX and μ_2=EX^2, where X is a partial claim amount selected at random in the portfolio, and **μ and μ_2 can be estimated by (5) and (6)**.

We now have reached the most important practical conclusion: **Also in heterogeneous portfolios with independent partial claim amounts, the fixed-time ruin probability $P(R_t<0)$ results from (4) if S_t can be treated as a normal random variable.** In particular, (4) can be used for all portfolios of some company, merged in a unique large portfolio, when fixed-time ruin probabilities are considered.

It can be admitted that the total claim amount S_t is approximatively normal, in rather general situations. The proof is only furnished by Theorem 1 in case of homogeneous portfolios. The classical central limit Theorem (the sum of n i.i.d. random variables, with finite second order moment, is asymptotically normal as $n\uparrow\infty$), has wide extensions. Similar extended versions of Theorem 1 must exist.

In case of finite- or infinite-time ruin probabilities, the theoretical treatment of heterogeneous portfolios is more difficult. Some actuaries apply the formulas proved in the classical risk model in case of i.i.d. partial claim amounts only, to much more general situations.

5.2. Numerical Fixed-Time Ruin Probabilities in General Risk Models

5.2.1. The Risk Model

We here consider risk models with deterministic premium income process p_τ ($\tau\geq 0$) and risk reserve process defined by

$$R_\tau = u + p_\tau - S_\tau \ (\tau\geq 0),$$

where $u\geq 0$ is the initial risk reserve. We consider the fixed-time ruin probability $P(R_t<0)$. It equals

$$P(R_t<0) = P(S_t>u+p_t) = 1-P(S_t\leq u+p_t) = 1-F_t(u+p_t).$$

Hence, our problem is the determination of the distribution function F_t of the total claim amount S_t. The fixed index t is dropped hereafter. We use the notations

$$X\equiv X_t \ , \ N\equiv N_t \ , \ S\equiv S_t \ , \ F_{tot}\equiv F_t \ , \ p_k := P(N_t=k) \ (k=0,1,2,\ldots).$$

Assumption on the claim instants process:

Real numbers a, b exist such that

$$\mathbf{kp_k = [a+b(k-1)]p_{k-1} \ (k=1,2,\ldots).} \tag{10}$$

We insist on the fact that this is an assumption on the distribution of the random variable N_t, where t is fixed, and that nothing is assumed on the random variables N_τ for $\tau\in[0,t[$. It is not even necessary here, that $N\equiv N_t$ results from some point process defined on $\mathbf{R}_+$. The numbers **a**, **b** may depend on t.

The assumption (10) is satisfied in the following cases.

N *is a Poisson random variable:*

$$p_k = e^{-\lambda}\,\lambda^k/k! \quad (k=0,1,2,\ldots)\,,\ \text{where } \lambda>0. \tag{11}$$

Indeed, then

$$kp_k = e^{-\lambda}\,\lambda^k/(k-1)! = \lambda.e^{-\lambda}\,\lambda^{k-1}/(k-1)! = \lambda p_{k-1} \quad (k\geq 1).$$

Then (10) holds for $a=\lambda$, $b=0$. If the claim instants process is the Poisson process with parameter λ, then the λ in (11) is in fact λt.

N *is a binomial negative random variable:*

$$p_k = q^{1+\alpha}\,(\alpha+k)^{[k]}/k!\ p^k \quad (k\geq 0),\ \text{where } \alpha\geq 0\,,\ 0\leq p\leq 1,\ q=1-p, \tag{12}$$

where the factorial powers notation is used. By (12)

$$kp_k = (\alpha+k)p\ p_{k-1} = [(\alpha+1)p + p(k-1)]p_{k-1} \quad (k\geq 1)$$

and then (10) is satisfied for $a=(\alpha+1)p$, $b=p$.

N *is a geometric random variable:*

$$p_k = qp^k \quad (k\geq 0),\ \text{where } 0\leq p\leq 1,\ q=1-p. \tag{13}$$

This is an important special case of (12) corresponding to $\alpha=0$. Hence, then (10) holds for $a=p$, $b=p$.

N *is a binomial random variable:*

$$p_k = n^{[k]}/k!\ p^k q^{n-k}\ (k\geq 0)\ ,\ \text{where}\ n\in\mathbf{N}_+\ ,\ 0\leq p\leq 1\ ,\ q=1-p. \qquad (14)$$

Then

$$kp_k = (n-k+1)p/q\ p_{k-1} = [(np/q)+(k-1)(-p/q)]p_{k-1}\ \ (k\geq 1)$$

and (10) is true for $a=np/q$, $b=-p/q$. It must be noticed that (14) also holds for $k>n$, because then $n^{[k]}=0$.

5.2.2. Claimsize Distribution Discretization

We now consider the numerical calculation of the distribution function F_{tot} of S. By Ch.3.Th.4.a,

$$F_{tot} = \textstyle\sum_{k\geq 0} p_k\ F^{*k}. \qquad (15)$$

In order to be able to apply the next Theorem 2, the claimsize distribution F must be discretized. Let $\delta>0$. We approximate the distribution F of the partial claim amount X by a distribution $F^{\sim}$ concentrated on the set $\{0,\delta,2\delta,3\delta,\ldots\}$. Then Theorem 2 allows the numerical calculation of the distribution function $F^{\sim}_{tot}$ corresponding to $F^{\sim}$, defined by

$$F^{\sim}_{tot} = \textstyle\sum_{k\geq 0} p_k\ (F^{\sim})^{*k}. \qquad (16)$$

By (15), (16):

$$F \leq F^{\sim} \Rightarrow F_{tot} \leq F^{\sim}_{tot} \quad \text{and} \quad F \leq F^{\sim} \Rightarrow F_{tot} \leq F^{\sim}_{tot}. \qquad (17)$$

If

$$F^{\sim} := F(k\delta)\ \text{on}\ [k\delta,(k+1)\delta[\ \ (k=0,1,2,\ldots),$$

then $F^{\sim}\leq F$ and by (17), $F^{\sim}_{tot}\leq F_{tot}$.

If we define $F^{\sim}$ by the left limit

$$F^{\sim} := F[(k+1)\delta-]\ \ \text{on}\ \ [k\delta,(k+1)\delta[\ \ (k=0,1,2,\ldots),$$

then $F\leq F^{\sim}$ and by (17), $F_{tot}\leq F^{\sim}_{tot}$.

Hence, by the next Theorem, we can calculate upper and lower bounds for the distribution function F_{tot}.

We can also consider the distribution function $F^{\sim}$ defined as follows:

$$F^{\sim} := 1/\delta \int_{[k\delta,(k+1)\delta[} F(x)dx \ \text{ on } \ [k\delta,(k+1)\delta[\ \ (k=0,1,2,...).$$

Here $F^{\sim}$ is the mean value of F on each interval $[k\delta,(k+1)\delta]$. By the surface interpretation of the first moment, F and $F^{\sim}$ have the same first moment in that case. Then $F^{\sim}_{tot}$ can be a good approximation of F_{tot}

We now adopt a **new unit of money**, so that the amounts 0, δ, 2δ, ... become the amounts 0, 1, 2, ... with the new unit. Then the new discretized claimsize distribution is concentrated on $\mathbf{N}_+$, and we are ready for the application of the numerical algorithm of the next Theorem 2.

In order to avoid the introduction of more notations, we assume in that Theorem, that F is already concentrated on $\mathbf{N}_+$.

The following Theorem has been a revolution in the numerical calculation of compound distribution functions F_{tot}. Earlier methods, based on improvements of the normal approximation of Theorem 1, or on Monte-Carlo methods, mainly retain historical interest.

The following proof is based on general properties of power series with positive coefficients. See Ch.8.1.1 and App.H.Th.H2.

5.2.3. Basic Theorem

Theorem 2 (Panjer's Recursions)

We assume that X_1, X_2, ... are positive integer i.i.d. random variables with distribution function F, independent of the positive integer random variable N, and that real numbers a, b exist so that

$$kp_k = [a+b(k-1)]p_{k-1} \ \ (k=1,2,...), \tag{18}$$

where

$$p_k := P(N=k) \ \ (k=0,1,2,...). \tag{19}$$

Then

$$S := X_1+...+X_N, \text{ equal to 0 if } N=0, \tag{20}$$

is a positive integer random variable with distribution function

$$\mathbf{F_{tot} = \sum_{k\geq 0} p_k\, F^{*k}.} \tag{21}$$

Let

$$\mathbf{f_k := P(X_1{=}k)\ ,\ h_k := P(S{=}k)\ \ (k{=}0,1,2,\ldots).} \tag{22}$$

Then

$$\mathbf{h_0 = \sum_{k\geq 0} p_k\, f_0^{\,k},} \tag{23}$$

$$\mathbf{h_k = [k(1-bf_0)]^{-1} \sum_{1\leq j\leq k}[(a-b)\, jf_jh_{k-j} + bk\, f_jh_{k-j}]\ \ (k{=}1,2,\ldots)} \tag{24}$$

and

$$\mathbf{F_{tot}(x) = \sum_{0\leq k\leq x} h_k\ \ (x\in R_+).} \tag{25}$$

Proof

$$h_0 = F_{tot}(0) = \sum_{k\geq 0} p_k\, F^{*k}(0) = \sum_{k\geq 0} p_k\, F^k(0) = \sum_{k\geq 0} p_k\, f_0^{\,k},$$

because convolution products are usual products at 0. This proves relation (23). Relation (25) is valid for any distribution concentrated on $\mathbf{N}_+$. In order to prove (24), we consider the generating function of N, X, S for $s\in[0,1[$:

$$\alpha(s) := E(s^N) = \sum_{k\geq 0} p_k s^k,$$

$$\beta(s) := E(s^X) = \sum_{k\geq 0} f_k s^k,$$

$$\gamma(s) := E(s^S) = \sum_{k\geq 0} h_k s^k.$$

All coefficients p_k, f_k, h_k are positive. In each of the foregoing power series, the sum of the coefficients equals 1. The radius of convergence is 1 at least. If s remains in the interval $[0,1[$, then the values of the power series also remain in that interval (unless p_0 , f_0 or h_0 equal 1; these degenerate cases can be treated separately; we may discard them here). Now

$$\gamma(s) = \alpha(\beta(s)). \tag{26}$$

Indeed, using the properties of conditional expectations,

$$\gamma(s) = Es^S = EE(s^S/N) = EE^Ns^X = E[\beta(s)]^N = \alpha(\beta(s)).$$

Hence,

$$\gamma(s) = \sum_{k\geq 0} p_k\, \beta^k(s). \tag{27}$$

We multiply (18) by $\beta^k(s)$, we sum over $k\geq 1$ and we multiply by $\beta'(s)$:

$$\beta'(s)\sum_{k\geq 1} kp_k\beta^k(s) = a\beta'(s)\sum_{k\geq 1} p_{k-1}\beta^k(s) + b\beta'(s)\sum_{k\geq 1}(k-1)p_{k-1}\beta^k(s). \tag{28}$$

The terms occurring in (28) can be transformed as follows. Taking the derivative of (27) we obtain

$$\gamma'(s) = \sum_{k\geq 1} k\, p_k\, \beta^{k-1}(s).\beta'(s) = \beta'(s) \sum_{k\geq 1} k\, p_k\, \beta^{k-1}(s).$$

because the differentiation of any power series can be performed termwise in the interior of the cercle of convergence. Then

$$\beta'(s)\sum_{k\geq 1} k\, p_k\, \beta^k(s) = \beta(s)\beta'(s)\sum_{k\geq 1} k\, p_k\, \beta^{k-1}(s) = \beta(s)\gamma'(s), \tag{29}$$

$$\beta'(s)\sum_{k\geq 1} p_{k-1}\beta^k(s) = \beta'(s)\sum_{k\geq 0} p_k\beta^{k+1}(s) = \beta'(s)\beta(s)\gamma(s), \tag{30}$$

$$\beta'(s)\sum_{k\geq 1}(k-1)p_{k-1}\beta^k(s) = \beta'(s)\sum_{k\geq 0}kp_k\beta^{k+1}(s)$$

$$= \beta^2(s)\beta'(s)\sum_{k\geq 1}kp_k\beta^{k-1}(s) = \beta^2(s)\gamma'(s). \tag{31}$$

Hence, by (28)

$$\beta(s)\gamma'(s) = a\, \beta'(s)\beta(s)\gamma(s) + b\, \beta^2(s)\gamma'(s)$$

In this relation, we may simplify by $\beta(s)$ because $\beta(s)>0$ $(s>0)$. Hence

$$\gamma'(s) = a\, \beta'(s)\gamma(s) + b\, \beta(s)\gamma'(s). \tag{32}$$

(This relation is valid for $s=0$ because we can let $s\downarrow 0$). By the definition of $\gamma(s)$ and $\beta(s)$, and differentiation,

$$\gamma'(s) = \sum_{k\geq 0} kh_k s^{k-1},\ \beta'(s) = \sum_{k\geq 0} kf_k s^{k-1}. \tag{33}$$

By Fubini,

$$\beta'(s)\gamma(s) = \sum_{j\geq 0} jf_j s^{j-1}\sum_{k\geq 0} h_k s^k = \sum_{n\geq 0}\sum_{j+k=n} jf_j h_k s^{n-1}$$

$$= \sum_{n\geq 0}\sum_{0\leq j\leq n} jf_j h_{n-j} s^{n-1} = \sum_{k\geq 0}\sum_{0\leq j\leq k} jf_j h_{k-j} s^{k-1}, \tag{34}$$

because everything is positive (sums are particular integrals). Then

$$\gamma'(s)\beta(s) = \sum_{k\geq 0}\sum_{0\leq j\leq k} jh_j f_{k-j}\, s^{k-1}, \tag{35}$$

by the permutation of β and γ, and the simultaneous permutation of f and h. We use (33), (34) and (35) in (32), and then, for $k\geq 1$, we take the coefficient of s^{k-1} in each member:

$$kh_k = a\sum_{0\leq j\leq k} jf_j h_{k-j} + b\sum_{0\leq j\leq k} jh_j f_{k-j} = a\sum_{0\leq j\leq k} jf_j h_{k-j} + b\sum_{0\leq j\leq k} (k-j)h_{k-j} f_j,$$

$$kh_k = a\sum_{1\leq j\leq k} jf_j h_{k-j} + b\sum_{1\leq j\leq k} (k-j)h_{k-j} f_j + bkh_k f_0.$$

(24) results from the latter relation •

5.3. Asymptotic Fixed-Time Ruin Probabilities in General Risk Models

5.3.1. Risk Model

We consider a risk model with deterministic premium income process $p_\tau(\tau\geq 0)$ and usual corresponding risk reserve process $R_\tau=u+p_\tau-S_\tau$ $(\tau\geq 0)$, where u is the initial risk reserve. As in section 5.1, we are interested in the asymptotic behaviour of the distribution of the total claim amount S_t as $t\uparrow\infty$. But now the claim instants process is very general. From the distribution function F_t of S_t for t large, results the fixed-time ruin probability $P(R_t<0)=1-F_t(u+p_t)$ (see the beginning of 5.2.1). A large value of t is a value such that the expected number of claims in [0,t] is large.

Assumptions on claim instants process

For all $t\in\mathbf{R}_+$, N_t has a finite second order moment and a strictly positive variance. The standardized random variable N_t^{01} is asymptotically distributed as some random variable Y as $t\uparrow\infty$ and

$$\lambda_t := EN_t\ ,\ s_t := Var^{1/2}N_t\ ,\ r_t := \lambda_t/s_t^2.$$

$$\lambda_t \to \infty\ ,\ r_t \to r \in \mathbf{R}_+\cup\{\infty\}.$$

Assumptions on partial claim amounts

The second moment μ_2 of the distribution F of $X\equiv X_1$ is finite. The variance $\sigma^2 := \mu_2-\mu^2$ is strictly positive.

5.3.2. Basic Theorem

Theorem 3 (Central Limit Theorem in General Risk Model. Haezendonck)

Under the *Assumptions* of 5.3.1, the standardized total claim amount S_t^{01} is asymptotically distributed as the random variable pY+qZ as $t\uparrow\infty$, where Z is a standardized normal random variable, independent of Y, and

$$p := \mu(\mu^2+r\sigma^2)^{-1/2}\ ,\ q := (1-p^2)^{1/2} = \sigma r^{1/2}(\mu^2+r\sigma^2)^{-1/2}.$$

If r=0, then p=1 and q=0. If r=∞, then p=0 and q=1.

Proof

a. We first verify that the characteristic function φ of X can be displayed as

$$\varphi(\tau) = e^{\gamma(\tau)} \quad (\tau \in \mathbf{R}), \tag{36}$$

where

$$\gamma(\tau) := i\tau\mu - \tau^2/2\,\sigma^2 + \tau^2 o(\tau) \text{ as } \tau \to 0. \tag{37}$$

Indeed,

$$1+z = e^{\log(1+z)} = \exp[z - z^2/2 + z^2 o(z)] \text{ as } z \to 0 \text{ (z complex)}.$$

By Ch.3.Th.2,

$$\varphi(\tau) - 1 = i\tau\mu - \tau^2/2\,\mu_2 + \tau^2\, o(\tau) \text{ for } \tau \to 0.$$

Then

$$\varphi(\tau) = 1 + [\varphi(\tau) - 1] = e^{\gamma(\tau)}.$$

Here

$$\gamma(\tau) := [i\tau\mu - \tau^2/2\,\mu_2] - [i\tau\mu]^2/2 + \tau^2 o(\tau).$$

This implies (36) because $\sigma^2 = \mu^2 - \mu_2$. We can display $\gamma(\tau)$ as

$$\gamma(\tau) = -\alpha(\tau) + i\beta(\tau), \tag{38}$$

where

$$\alpha(\tau) := 1/2\,\tau^2\sigma^2 + \tau^2 o(\tau) \text{ and } \beta(\tau) := \tau\mu + \tau^2 o(\tau) \tag{39}$$

are real functions of $\tau \in \mathbf{R}$. The function $\alpha(\tau)$ is positive. Indeed

$$e^{-\alpha(\tau)} = |e^{-\alpha(\tau)+i\beta(\tau)}| = |\varphi(\tau)| = |Ee^{i\tau X}| \le E|e^{i\tau X}| = E\,1 = 1.$$

b. Let φ_t be the characteristic function of S_t. By Ch.3.Th.4,

$$ES_t = \mu\lambda_t\ ,\ \sigma_t^2 := \text{Var } S_t = \sigma^2\lambda_t + \mu^2 s_t^2\ ,\ \varphi_t(\tau) = E\varphi^{N_t}(\tau).$$

Let φ_t^{01} be the characteristic function of S_t^{01}. Then,

$$\varphi_t^{01}(\tau) = E\exp(i\tau S_t^{01}) = E\exp[i\tau(S_t - \mu\lambda_t)\sigma_t^{-1}]$$

$$= \exp(-i\tau\mu\lambda_t\sigma_t^{-1})E\exp[i(\tau\sigma_t^{-1})S_t] = \exp(-i\tau\mu\lambda_t\sigma_t^{-1})\varphi_t(\tau\sigma_t^{-1})$$

$$= \exp(-i\tau\mu\lambda_t\sigma_t^{-1})\,E\varphi^{N_t}(\tau\sigma_t^{-1}).$$

Hence, by (36), and because $N_t = s_t N_t^{01} + \lambda_t$,

$$\varphi_t^{01}(\tau) = \exp(-i\tau\mu\lambda_t\sigma_t^{-1})\, E \exp[\gamma(\tau\sigma_t^{-1})N_t]$$

$$= \exp[-i\tau\mu\lambda_t\sigma_t^{-1} + \lambda_t\gamma(\tau\sigma_t^{-1})]\, E \exp[\gamma(\tau\sigma_t^{-1})s_t N_t^{01}].$$

Then

$$\varphi_t^{01}(\tau) = \xi_t(\tau)\eta_t(\tau), \tag{40}$$

where

$$\xi_t(\tau) := \exp[-i\tau\mu\lambda_t\sigma_t^{-1} + \lambda_t\gamma(\tau\sigma_t^{-1})] \tag{41}$$

and

$$\eta_t(\tau) := E \exp[\gamma(\tau\sigma_t^{-1})s_t N_t^{01}]. \tag{42}$$

We hereafter examine $\xi_t(\tau)$ and $\eta_t(\tau)$ as $t\uparrow\infty$ separately.

The value of $\tau \in R$ is kept fixed in the rest of this proof, and all limits are limits as $t\uparrow\infty$.

c. From the assumptions results that

$$\lambda_t \to \infty \;,\; \sigma_t \to \infty \;,\; \tau\sigma_t^{-1} \to 0 \;,\; o(\tau\sigma_t^{-1}) \to 0, \tag{43}$$

for all functions $o(\cdot)$ occurring in the proof.

$$\sigma_t^{-2}\lambda_t \to r(\mu^2 + r\sigma^2)^{-1} \; (=\sigma^{-2} \text{ if } r=\infty), \tag{44}$$

$$\sigma_t^{-1}s_t \to (\mu^2 + r\sigma^2)^{-1/2}. \tag{45}$$

d. By (37), (41) and (44),

$$\begin{aligned}\xi_t(\tau) &= \exp[-\tau^2/2\; \sigma^2\sigma_t^{-2}\lambda_t + \tau^2\sigma_t^{-2}\lambda_t o(\tau\sigma_t^{-1})]\\ &\to \exp[-1/2\; \tau^2\sigma^2 r(\mu^2 + r\sigma^2)^{-1}] = \exp(-1/2\; \tau^2 q^2).\end{aligned} \tag{46}$$

e. By (38) and (42),

$$\eta_t(\tau) = E[\exp[-\alpha(\tau\sigma_t^{-1})s_t N_t^{01}]\exp[i\beta(\tau\sigma_t^{-1})s_t N_t^{01}]]$$

$$= \eta_{t1}(\tau) - \eta_{t2}(\tau), \tag{47}$$

where

$$\eta_{t1}(\tau) := \mathrm{E}\ \exp[i\beta(\tau\sigma_t^{-1})s_t N_t^{01}], \tag{48}$$

$$\eta_{t2}(\tau) := \mathrm{E}\{[1-\exp[-\alpha(\tau\sigma_t^{-1})s_t N_t^{01}]]\exp[i\beta(\tau\sigma_t^{-1})s_t N_t^{01}]\}. \tag{49}$$

f. Let ω_t be the characteristic function of N_t^{01}, ω the characteristic function of Y. By the continuity Theorem for characteristic functions (Ch.3.Th.6), $\omega_t \to \omega$. Characteristic functions are continuous functions. This implies (by Classical Analysis) that $\omega_t \to \omega$ uniformly on compact sets. From this results that $\omega_t(c_t) \to \omega(c)$ if $c_t \to c \in \mathbf{R}$.

By (48) and (39),

$$\eta_{t1}(\tau) = \omega_t[\beta(\tau\sigma_t^{-1})s_t] = \omega_t[\tau\mu\sigma_t^{-1}s_t + \tau^2\sigma_t^{-2}o(\tau\sigma_t^{-1})].$$

By (43) and (45), the limit of the term in square brackets in the last member equals $\tau\mu(\mu^2+r\sigma^2)^{-1/2} = \tau p$. Then

$$\eta_{t1}(\tau) \to \omega(\tau p). \tag{50}$$

g. We now prove that $\eta_{t2}(\tau) \to 0$. By (49),

$$|\eta_{t2}(\tau)| \le \mathrm{E}|1-\exp[-\alpha(\tau\sigma_t^{-1})s_t N_t^{01}]| =: \delta_t(\tau). \tag{51}$$

Let K_t be the distribution of N_t^{01} and K the distribution of Y. As usual, K_t and K denote the point function as well as the measure (Ch.1.1.2). Then $K_t \to K$ weakly. By (51),

$$\delta_t(\tau) = \int_{\mathbf{R}} f_t(\tau,x)dK_t(x), \tag{52}$$

where

$$f_t(\tau,x) = |1-\exp[-\alpha(\tau\sigma_t^{-1})s_t x]|\,1_{x \ge -\lambda_t/s_t}. \tag{53}$$

The indicator function results from the fact that N_t^{01} is concentrated on the interval $[-\lambda_t/s_t, \infty[$:

$$N_t^{01} = (N_t - \lambda_t)/s_t \ge -\lambda_t/s_t.$$

If $x \ge 0$, then $f_t(\tau,x) \le 1$ because $\alpha(\cdot)$ is positive. For $x \le 0$, the largest value of $f_t(\tau,x)$ is that one corresponding to the value $x = -\lambda_t/s_t$. By (39), this maximum is

$$\exp[\alpha(\tau\sigma_t^{-1})\lambda_t] - 1 = \exp[1/2\ \tau^2\sigma^2\sigma_t^{-2}\lambda_t + \tau^2\sigma_t^{-2}\lambda_t o(\tau\sigma_t^{-1})] - 1.$$

The last member has a finite limit, by (44). Hence, b and t_0 do exist in $\mathbf{R}_{++}$, such that

$$f_t(\tau,x) \le b \ (t\ge t_0,\ x\in\mathbf{R}). \tag{54}$$

(Of course, b and t_0 depend on τ, but τ is fixed in this discussion). By (53), (39), (43) and (44),

$$f_t(\tau,x) = |1 - \exp[1/2\ \tau^2\sigma^2\sigma_t^{-2}s_t x + \tau^2\sigma_t^{-2}s_t x\, o(\tau\sigma_t^{-1})]| \to 0, \tag{55}$$

for fixed $x\in\mathbf{R}$. This limit relation holds, uniformly in $x\in I$, where I is any bounded interval.

Let $\varepsilon>0$. Let I be a bounded interval, so large that

$$K(\mathbf{C}I) \le \varepsilon/b,$$

where $\mathbf{C}I$ is the complement of I with respect to $\mathbf{R}$. Extending I if necessary, we may assume that the extremities of I are continuity points of K. Then $K_t(I)\to K(I)$ and $t_1\ge t_0$ exists, such that

$$|K(\mathbf{C}I)-K_t(\mathbf{C}I)| = |K_t(I)-K(I)| \le \varepsilon/b \ \ (t\ge t_1).$$

Let $t_2\ge t_1$ be such that

$$f_t(\tau,x) \le \varepsilon \ (t\ge t_2,\ x\in I).$$

This is possible by (55), and by the remark on uniform convergence following that relation. Then

$$|\eta_{t2}(\tau)| \le \delta_t(\tau) = \int_I f_t(\tau,x)dK_t(x) + \int_{\mathbf{C}I} f_t(\tau,x)dK_t(x) \le \varepsilon + b\, K_t(\mathbf{C}I)$$

$$\le \varepsilon + b|K_t(\mathbf{C}I)-K(\mathbf{C}I)| + bK(\mathbf{C}I) \le \varepsilon + \varepsilon + \varepsilon \le 3\varepsilon.$$

This proves that $\eta_{t2}\to 0$.

h. Then by (40), (41), (42), (46), (47) and (50),

$$\varphi_t^{01}(\tau) \to \omega(\tau p)\exp(-1/2\ \tau^2 q^2).$$

This is the characteristic function of the random variable pY+qZ. By the continuity Theorem for characteristic functions, S_t^{01} is asymptotically distributed as pY+qZ •

The expression (36) for the characteristic function of X is valid for any random variable X with finite second order moment. In some cases, it is more convenient than the expression furnished by Ch.3.Th.2.

5.3.3. Illustrations

***Example 1:* N_t *is Poisson with parameter* $\lambda_t \to \infty$ *as* $t \uparrow \infty$.**

This case happens if the claim instants process is a non-homogeneous Poisson process with intensity function $\lambda(\cdot)$. Indeed, then by Ch.4.Th.5.d, N_t is a Poisson variable with parameter

$$\lambda_t = \int_{[0,t]} \lambda(\tau)d\tau = EN_t = \text{Var } N_t.$$

The characteristic function of N_t equals

$$\omega_t(\tau) = Ee^{i\tau N_t} = \sum_{k\geq 0} P(N_t{=}k)e^{i\tau k} = \sum_{k\geq 0} 1/k!\; e^{-\lambda_t}\, \lambda_t^{\,k}\, e^{i\tau k}$$

$$= e^{-\lambda_t} \sum_{k\geq 0} 1/k!\; (\lambda_t e^{i\tau})^k = e^{-\lambda_t} \exp(\lambda_t e^{i\tau}).$$

Let ω_t^{01} be the characteristic function of

$$N_t^{01} := (N_t-\lambda_t)/\lambda_t^{1/2} = N_t\lambda_t^{-1/2} - \lambda_t^{1/2}.$$

$$\omega_t^{01}(\tau) = \exp(i\tau N_t^{01}) = \exp(-i\tau\lambda_t^{1/2})\exp[i(\tau\lambda_t^{-1/2})N_t]$$

$$= \exp(-i\tau\lambda_t^{1/2})\omega_t(\tau\lambda_t^{-1/2}) = \exp(-i\tau\lambda_t^{1/2})\exp(-\lambda_t)\exp[\lambda_t\exp(i\tau\lambda_t^{-1/2})]$$

$$= \exp[-i\tau\lambda_t^{1/2} - \lambda_t + \lambda_t(1+i\tau\lambda_t^{-1/2} - 1/2\;\tau^2\lambda_t^{-1} - 1/6\; i\tau^3\lambda_t^{-3/2} + \ldots)]$$

$$= \exp(-1/2\;\tau^2 - 1/6\; i\tau^3\lambda_t^{-1/2} + \ldots) \to e^{-\tau^2/2} \text{ as } t\uparrow\infty.$$

Hence N_t^{01} is asymptotically distributed as a standardized normal random variable as $t\uparrow\infty$. Then Y is a standardized normal random variable in Theorem 3 and then pY+qZ is also a normal random variable. Its expectation equals E(pY+qZ)=0 and its variance

$$\mathrm{Var}(pY+qZ) = p^2\mathrm{Var}(Y)+q^2\mathrm{Var}(Z) = p^2+q^2=1.$$

Hence, pY+qZ is a standardized normal random variable:

If N_t is a Poisson random variable with parameter $\lambda_t \to \infty$ as $t\uparrow\infty$, then S_t^{01} is asymptotically standardized normal as $t\uparrow\infty$.

Example 2:* N_t *is a geometric random variable

Let

$$P(N_t=k) = p_t q_t^k \ (t\geq 0, k\geq 0), \quad 1 \geq p_t \downarrow 0 \text{ as } t\uparrow\infty \ , \ q_t = 1-p_t. \tag{56}$$

The assumptions (56) are satisfied for the following point processes considered in Ch.4.6.3 : *Process 1, Process 2* with a=0, *Process 3* with a=0, *Process 4.*

In order to find the two first moments of N_t, we consider the power series

$$(1-x)^{-1} = \sum_{k\geq 0} x^k \ (|x|<1).$$

Taking the derivative, multiplying by x and repeating these operations, we obtain

$$(1-x)^{-2} = \sum_{k\geq 1} kx^{k-1} \ , \ x(1-x)^{-2} = \sum_{k\geq 1} kx^k, \tag{57}$$

$$(1-x)^{-2} + 2x(1-x)^{-3} = \sum_{k\geq 1} k^2 x^{k-1} \ , \ x(1+x)(1-x)^{-3} = \sum_{k\geq 1} k^2 x^k. \tag{58}$$

From the last relation (57) multiplied by (1−x) results for $x=q_t$,

$$\lambda_t := EN_t = q_t p_t^{-1}.$$

From the last relation (58) multiplied by (1−x) results for $x=q_t$:

$$EN_t^2 = q_t(1+q_t)p_t^{-2}.$$

Then

$$s_t^2 = \mathrm{Var}\, N_t = q_t p_t^{-2} \ , \ r_t := \lambda_t/s_t^2 = p_t \downarrow 0 =: r \ \text{ as } t\uparrow\infty \ .$$

Hence, we will have p=1, q=0 in Theorem 3 and the standardized total claim amount S_t^{01} will have the same asymptotic distribution as the standardized number of claims N_t^{01} as $t\uparrow\infty$. In order to find the latter distribution, we consider the characteristic function of N_t. It equals

$$\omega_t(\tau) := E\exp(i\tau N_t) = \sum_{k\geq 0} p_t q_t^k e^{i\tau k} = \sum_{k\geq 0} p_t(q_t e^{i\tau})^k = p_t(1-q_t e^{i\tau})^{-1}.$$

The standardized random variable N_t^{01} equals

$$N_t^{01} = (N_t - q_t p_t^{-1})/(q_t^{1/2} p_t^{-1}) = p_t q_t^{-1/2} N_t - q_t^{1/2}.$$

The characteristic function of N_t^{01} equals

$$\omega_t^{01}(\tau) := E\exp(i\tau N_t^{01}) = \exp(-i\tau q_t^{1/2})\, E\exp[i(\tau p_t q_t^{-1/2})N_t]$$

$$= \exp(-i\tau q_t^{1/2})\omega_t(\tau p_t q_t^{-1/2}) = p_t \exp(-i\tau q_t^{1/2})[1-q_t\exp(i\tau p_t q_t^{-1/2})]^{-1}$$

$$= p_t \exp(-i\tau q_t^{1/2})[1-q_t(1+i\tau p_t q_t^{-1/2} - 1/2\, \tau^2 p_t^2 q_t^{-1} + \ldots)]^{-1}$$

$$= p_t \exp(-i\tau q_t^{1/2})\, [p_t - i\tau p_t q_t^{1/2} + 1/2\, \tau^2 p_t^2 q_t - \ldots]^{-1}$$

$$= \exp(-i\tau q_t^{1/2})\, [1 - i\tau q_t^{1/2} + 1/2\, \tau^2 p_t q_t - \ldots]^{-1} \to e^{-i\tau}(1-i\tau)^{-1} \text{ as } t\uparrow\infty.$$

The function $(1-i\tau)^{-1}$ is the characteristic function of the exponential distribution

$$1-e^{-x} \quad (x\in\mathbf{R}_+). \tag{59}$$

Let Z_{exp} be a random variable with that distribution function. Then the function $e^{-i\tau}(1-i\tau)^{-1}$ is the characteristic function of $Z_{exp}-1$. Hence, N_t^{01} is asymptotically distributed as $Z_{exp}-1$ as $t\uparrow\infty$. Then, by Theorem 3:

If N_t is a geometric random variable satisfying the relations (56), then S_t^{01} is asymptotically distributed as $Z_{exp}-1$ as $t\uparrow\infty$.

5.3.4. Extended Validity of Basic Theorem

S_t and N_t must not necessarily be strictly interpreted as total claim amount in [0,t] and number of claims in that interval in some risk model. The basic Theorem 3 is a statement about the compound distribution

$$\sum_{k\geq 0} p_{tk} F^{*k}$$

where

$$\sum_{k\geq 0} p_{tk} = 1\ ,\quad p_{tk} \geq 0 \quad (t\in\mathbf{R}_+,\ k\geq 0)$$

and where F is a distribution on **R**. The proof of Theorem 3 does not use the fact that F is concentrated on $\mathbf{R}_+$. Moreover, another parameter as t and another convergence as convergence to $+\infty$ can be considered.

Hence, the foregoing *Example 2* furnishes the following Theorem. It will be useful in connexion with infinite-time ruin probabilities in the classical risk model.

Theorem 4

Let S_p ($0<p<1$) be a random variable with the compound geometric distribution

$$U_p = p \sum_{k\geq 0} q^k G^{*k},$$

where $q=1-p$ and G is a distribution with moments μ_1, μ_2 and variance $\sigma^2=\mu_2-\mu_1^2$. Then the standardized random variable

$$S_p^{01} = (pS_p-q\mu_1)(pq\sigma^2+q\mu_1^2)^{-1/2}$$

is asymptotically distributed as $Z_{exp}-1$ as $p\downarrow 0$, where Z_{exp} is the exponential random variable with distribution function $1-e^{-x}$ ($x\in\mathbf{R}_+$).

Proof
The Theorem results from the discussion preceding its statement. The expression of S_p^{01} results from Ch.3.Th.4 and from the relations of *Example 2* •

If p is small, then the distribution of S_p^{01} can be approximated by the distribution of $Z_{exp}-1$. Hence

$$P(S_p^{01} > y) \approx P(Z_{exp}-1>y) = P(Z_{exp} >1+y) = 1-P(Z_{exp} \leq 1+y) = 1-e^{-1-y} \ (y\in\mathbf{R}).$$

But

$$S_p > x \Leftrightarrow S_p^{01} > (px-q\mu_1)(pq\sigma^2+q\mu_1^2)^{-1/2}.$$

Hence, for small values of p,

$$\mathbf{1-U_p(x) = P(S_p>x) \approx \exp[-1-(px-q\mu_1)(pq\sigma^2+q\mu_1^2)^{-1/2}].} \qquad (60)$$

Chapter 6

Finite-Time Ruin Probabilities

6.1. Multiple Integral Series for U(t,u) in general Risk Models

6.1.1. Risk Model

The *general assumptions* in all continuous risk models are indicated in Ch.3.1.1. The *special assumptions* here adopted, are:

Assumption on premium income process

The premium income process $p_\tau \equiv p(\tau)$ $(\tau \in \mathbf{R}_+)$ is deterministic.

Then the risk reserve process is

$$R_\tau = u + p(\tau) - S_\tau \ (\tau \in \mathbf{R}_+),$$

where u is the initial risk reserve.

Assumptions on claim instants process

The claim instants process is a general point process defined by densities.

Only the densities π_{tn} $(t \geq 0;\ n=0,1,2,...)$ of the claim instants process are used (in all continuous risk models considered in this book). We recall that

$$\pi_{t0} = P(N_t = 0)$$

and that the infinitesimal interpretation of π_{tn} (n=1,2,...) is (see Ch.4.3.2)

$$\pi_{tn}(t_1,...,t_n)dt_1...dt_n = P(N_t=n,\ T_1 \in dt_1,...,T_n \in dt_n) \ \ (0 \leq t_1 \leq ... \leq t_n \leq t).$$

No special assumptions are made on the claim amounts process.

6.1.2. Basic Theorem

From the *General Assumptions* on continuous risk models results that

$$P(N_t=n,\ T_1\in dt_1,\ X_1\in dx_1,\ \ldots,\ T_n\in dt_n,\ X_n\in dx_n)$$

$$= \pi_{tn}(t_1,\ldots,t_n)dt_1\ldots dt_n\ dF(x_1)\ldots dF(x_n)\quad (n=1,2,\ldots;\ 0\le t_1\le\ldots\le t_n\le t;\ x_1,\ldots,x_n\ge 0).$$

The correct meaning, without infinitesimals, of this relation is:

$$P[N_t=n,\ (T_1,X_1,\ldots,T_n,X_n)\in D_n)]$$

$$= \int\ldots\int_{D_n} \pi_{tn}(t_1,\ldots,t_n)dt_1\ldots dt_n\ dF(x_1)\ldots dF(x_n)\quad (D_n\subseteq \mathbf{R}^{2n}),$$

where it is assumed that $\pi_{tn}(t_1,\ldots,t_n)=0$ if the condition $0\le t_1\le\ldots\le t_n\le t$ is not satisfied.

We denote by $U(t,u,n)$ ($t\ge 0$; $u\ge 0$; $n=0,1,2,\ldots$) the probability of exactly n claims in $[0,t]$, and no ruin, corresponding to the initial risk reserve u. Then the following Theorem is obvious.

Theorem 1 (Multiple Integral Series for U(t,u))

Under the *Assumptions* of 6.1.1,

$$\mathbf{U(t,u) = \textstyle\sum_{n\ge 0} U(t,u,n)\quad (u,t\ge 0),} \tag{1}$$

where

$$\mathbf{U(t,u,0) = \pi_{t0},} \tag{2}$$

and

$$\mathbf{U(t,u,n) = \int\ldots\int_{D_n} \pi_{tn}(t_1,\ldots,t_n)dt_1dF(x_1)\ldots dt_ndF(x_n)\quad (n\ge 1),} \tag{3}$$

where D_n is the set of claim instants $t_1,\ldots,t_n$ and claim amounts $x_1,\ldots,x_n$ for which no ruin occurs in $[0,t]$, i.e. D_n is the set of 2n-tuples

$$\mathbf{(t_1,x_1,\ldots,t_n,x_n)}$$

satisfying the relations

$$\mathbf{0 \leq t_1 \leq t_2 \leq ... \leq t_n \leq t,} \tag{4}$$

$$\mathbf{x_1, x_2, ..., x_n \geq 0,} \tag{5}$$

$$\mathbf{x_1 \leq u+p(t_1) \ , \ x_1+x_2 \leq u+p(t_2) \ , ... , \ x_1+x_2+...+x_n \leq u+p(t_n)} \ \bullet \tag{6}$$

Remarks

a. All ruin probabilities, in continuous risk models, considered in this book, will be calculated via relations such as (1) to (6).

By Fubini, these relations can be transformed "à volonté", because everything is positive, and because series are particular integrals. This furnishes **complete, simple, elementary proofs**.

b. An inconvenience of these proofs is their lengthiness. Very often, the long complete proofs do have ***quick versions*** which we mention. The quick proofs are based on properties (mostly intuitively obvious) of the involved stochastic processes, not demonstrated in the book (such as the stationarity and the independence of the increments).

c. Although continuous-time stochastic processes, such as S_τ, P_τ and R_τ ($\tau \in \mathbf{R}_+$) are used, the general theory of these processes is not necessary in this book (except in the following sections 6.3 and 6.4 dealing with martingales).

6.2. Prabhu's Formula in Mixed Poisson Risk Models

6.2.1. Risk Model

The **mixed Poisson risk model** is the continuous model satisfying the *general assumptions* (Ch.3.1.1) and the following *special assumptions*.

Assumptions on the premium income process

The premium income process is the process $c\tau$ ($\tau \geq 0$), where c is any strictly positive constant.

Assumptions on the claim instants process

The claim instants process is a point process defined by densities, with densities π_{tn} ($t\leq 0$; $n=1,2,\ldots$) not depending on $t_1,\ldots,t_n$ ($0\leq t_1\leq\ldots\leq t_n\leq t$).

By Ch.4.Th.20, the claim instants process is a mixed Poisson process.

No special assumptions are made on the claim amounts process.

The classical risk model is a particular mixed Poisson risk model. In the classical model, the next formula (13) is known as the **Prabhu formula**.

6.2.2. Basic Theorem

Let us take $u=0$ and $p(\tau)=c\tau$ ($\tau\in\mathbf{R}_+$) in Theorem 1. Then the relations (4), (5), and (6) are equivalent to the relations

$$x_1,x_2,\ldots,x_n \geq 0 \quad , \quad x_1+x_2+\ldots+x_n \leq ct \tag{7}$$

$$(x_1+x_2+\ldots+x_{n-1}+x_n)/c \leq t_n \leq t \tag{8}$$

$$(x_1+x_2+\ldots+x_{n-1})/c \leq t_{n-1} \leq t_n \tag{8}$$

$$\ldots \quad \ldots \quad \ldots \quad \ldots \quad \ldots$$

$$(x_1+x_2)/c \leq t_2 \leq t_3 \tag{8}$$

$$x_1/c \leq t_1 \leq t_2 \tag{8}$$

Hence, by Fubini,

$$U(t,0,n) = \int\ldots\int_{D7} [\int\ldots\int_{D8} \pi_{tn}(t_1,\ldots,t_n)dt_n\ldots dt_1]dF(x_1)\ldots dF(x_n), \tag{9}$$

where D7 is the domain described by the relations (7) and where, for fixed x_1, x_2, ..., x_n, D8 is the domain described by the relations (8).

In the mixed Poisson model, the densities π_{tn} are constant. Then by Ch.4.(20),

$$P(N_t=n) = \int\ldots\int_{\{0\leq t_1\leq\ldots\leq t_n\leq t\}} \pi_{tn}\, dt_1\ldots dt_n, \tag{10}$$

and, integrating by symmetrization,

$$P(N_t=n) = \pi_{tn}\, t^n/n!\ (n\geq 0). \tag{11}$$

Theorem 2

In the mixed Poisson model, for all t>0:

$$U(t,0,n) = P(N_t=n)\int_{[0,ct]} (1-\tau/ct)\, dF^{*n}(\tau)$$

$$= 1/ct\; P(N_t=n)\int_{[0,ct]} F^{*n}(\tau)d\tau \;(n=0,1,2,...) \qquad (12)$$

and

$$U(t,0) = \int_{[0,ct]} (1-\tau/ct)\, dF_t(\tau) = 1/ct \int_{[0,ct]} F_t(\tau)d\tau, \qquad (13)$$

where

$$F_t := \sum_{n\geq 0} P(N_t=n)\, F^{*n} \qquad (14)$$

is the distribution function of the total claim amount S_t in [0,t].

Proof
The second relation (12) results from an integration by parts, taking into account that the integrals are performed over the closed interval [0,ct], and that $F^{*n}(0-)=0$.

The sum for n=0,1,2,...of the last member of (12) furnishes the last member of (13). The last relation (13) results from an integration by parts. By (1), only the first relation (12) must yet be proved. The case n=0 is trivial. Hence, we may assume that n>0. Here (9) becomes,

$$U(t,0,n) = \pi_{tn} \int...\int_{D7} [\int...\int_{D8} dt_n...dt_1]dF(x_1)...dF(x_n). \qquad (15)$$

We use the abbreviation

$$s_n \equiv (x_1+...+x_n)/c$$

When n=3, for instance, the interior integral of the last member of (15) equals

$$\iiint_{D8} dt_3dt_2dt_1 = \int_{s_3\leq t_3\leq t} dt_3 \int_{s_2\leq t_2\leq t_3} dt_2 \int_{s_1\leq t_1\leq t_2} dt_1. \qquad (16)$$

The last member is a polynomial in s_1, s_2, s_3. Hence, it is a polynomial in x_1, x_2, x_3 (t is fixed). This conclusion is general: the interior integral of the last member of (15) is a polynomial $p(x_1,...,x_n)$ in x_1, ..., x_n. We say that **the polynomials $p(x_1,...,x_n)$ and $q(x_1,...,x_n)$ are equivalent** if

$$\int...\int_{D7} p(x_1,...,x_n)\, dF(x_1)...dF(x_n) = \int...\int_{D7} q(x_1,...,x_n)\, dF(x_1)...dF(x_n),$$

and we denote this equivalence by

$$p(x_1,\dots,x_n) =^\circ q(x_1,\dots,x_n)$$

The trick of the proof consists in the replacement of the interior integral in the last member of (15) by an equivalent polynomial. We notice the following:

a. If $(i_1,\dots,i_n)$ is a permutation of $(1,\dots,n)$, then the polynomials $p(x_1,\dots,x_n)$ and $p(x_{i_1},\dots,x_{i_n})$ are equivalent.

Indeed, the dummy integration variables $x_1,\dots,x_n$ may be permuted. This permutation does not affect the product $dF(x_1)\dots dF(x_n)$ nor the symmetrical domain D7.

b. If $p(x_1,\dots,x_n)$ is symmetrical in $x_1,\dots,x_{k+1}$ $(k+1\le n)$, then

$$(k+1)\ s_k\ p(x_1,\dots,x_n) =^\circ k\ s_{k+1}\ p(x_1,\dots,x_n)\ .$$

Indeed, by a.

$$x_i\ p(x_1,\dots,x_n) =^\circ x_j\ p(x_1,\dots,x_n)\ (i,j=1,\dots,k+1) \tag{17}$$

and the summation over $i=1,\dots,k$ and $j=1,\dots,k+1$ furnishes the required result. The relation (17) is obvious. For instance, for $i=1$, $j=2 \le k+1$,

$$\begin{aligned} x_1\ p(x_1,x_2,x_3,\dots,x_{k+1},\dots,x_n) &=^\circ x_2\ p(x_2,x_1,x_3,\dots,x_{k+1},\dots,x_n) \\ &=^\circ x_2\ p(x_1,x_2,x_3,\dots,x_{k+1},\dots,x_n). \end{aligned}$$

c. The interior integral of (15) is equivalent to the polynomial

$$t^n/n!\ (1- s_n/t)$$

Indeed, we make a repeated use of the equivalence of b. We take n=3. The general argument, by induction, is transparent from this case. By (16),

$$3! \iiint_{D8} dt_3dt_2dt_1 = 3! \int_{s_3\le t_3\le t} dt_3 \int_{s_2\le t_2\le t_3} dt_2 \int_{s_1\le t_1\le t_2} dt_1$$

$$= 3! \int_{s_3\le t_3\le t} dt_3 \int_{s_2\le t_2\le t_3} (t_2-s_1)dt_2$$

$$= 3! \int_{s_3\le t_3\le t} dt_3 \int_{s_2\le t_2\le t_3} t_2dt_2 - 3.2s_1 \int_{s_3\le t_3\le t} dt_3 \int_{s_2\le t_2\le t_3} dt_2$$

$$=^\circ 3! \int_{s_3\le t_3\le t} dt_3 \int_{s_2\le t_2\le t_3} t_2dt_2 - 3.1s_2 \int_{s_3\le t_3\le t} dt_3 \int_{s_2\le t_2\le t_3} dt_2$$

$$= 3\int_{s_3\le t_3\le t} dt_3\int_{s_2\le t_2\le t_3} (2t_2-s_2)dt_2 = 3\int_{s_3\le t_3\le t} dt_3\int_{s_2\le t_2\le t_3} d(t_2^2-s_2t_2) = 3\int_{s_3\le t_3\le t} (t_3^2-s_2t_3)dt_3$$

$$= 3\int_{s_3\le t_3\le t} t_3^2\ dt_3 -3s_2 \int_{s_3\le t_3\le t} t_3\ dt_3 =^\circ 3\int_{s_3\le t_3\le t} t_3^2\ dt_3 -2s_3 \int_{s_3\le t_3\le t} t_3\ dt_3$$

$$= \int_{s_3 \le t_3 \le t} (3t_3^2 - 2s_3 t_3)\, dt_3 = \int_{s_3 \le t_3 \le t} d(t_3^3 - s_3 t_3^2) = t^3 - s_3 t^2 = t^3(1 - s_3/t).$$

By c, (11) and (15),

$$U(t,0,n) = P(N_t = n) \int \ldots \int_{D7} (1 - s_n/t) dF(x_1) \ldots dF(x_n)$$

With the new variable $\tau := cs_n$, the last member equals

$$P(N_t = n) \int_{[0,ct]} (1 - \tau/ct)\, dF^{*n}(\tau)$$

in the convolution notation •

6.3. Martingale of Classical Risk Model

6.3.1. Risk Model

We consider the classical risk model defined in Ch.3.1.4 We assume the existence of the **adjustment coefficient** ρ satisfying the relation

$$Ee^{\rho X} = 1 + \rho\mu(1+\eta). \tag{18}$$

By Ch.3.(10), ρ is the adjustment coefficient of the couple (G,q), where G is the concave transform of the distribution function F of X and $q := 1/(1+\eta)$. The **premium income rate** is denoted by $c := (1+\eta)\mu\lambda$. Then the risk reserve process is

$$R_\tau = u + c\tau - S_\tau \ (\tau \in \mathbf{R}_+),$$

where the initial risk reserve u is positive. The filtration $\boldsymbol{F}_\tau$ $(\tau \in \mathbf{R}_+)$ is defined in Ch.3.5.1.

The **instant of ruin T** is the first claim instant T_k such that $R_{T_k} < 0$ if such an instant exists. If it does not exist then $T = \infty$. The instant of ruin T is a stopping time.

6.3.2. Basic Theorem

Theorem 3 (Classical Martingale. Gerber)

In the classical risk model, the stochastic process $Y_\tau := e^{-\rho R_\tau}$ $(\tau \in \mathbf{R}_+)$ is a martingale if the adjustment coefficient ρ exists.

Proof

We demonstrate that

$$E(e^{\rho S_\tau}) = e^{\rho c \tau} \ (\tau \geq 0). \qquad (19)$$

Indeed,

$$E\, e^{\rho S_\tau} = EE(e^{\rho S_\tau}/N_\tau) = EE[\exp(\rho(X_1+...+X_{N_\tau}))/N_\tau] = EE^{N_\tau} e^{\rho X}$$

$$= \sum_{k\geq 0} e^{-\lambda\tau}(\lambda\tau)^k/k!\ E^k e^{\rho X} = e^{-\lambda\tau} \sum_{k\geq 0} (\lambda\tau\, Ee^{\rho X})/k!$$

$$= e^{-\lambda\tau} \exp(\lambda\tau\, Ee^{\rho X}) = e^{-\lambda\tau}\, e^{\lambda\tau[1+\rho\mu(1+\eta)]} = e^{\lambda\tau\rho\mu(1+\eta)} = e^{\rho c\tau},$$

where we used the definition (18) of the adjustment coefficient ρ. All transformations are allowed by monotone convergence, because everything is positive (and also by Fubini, because series are particular integrals). By (19) $EY_\tau<\infty$, i.e. Y_τ is integrable.

We now verify the martingale relation Ch.3.(15). Let $0\leq r\leq s$. This verification is based on the following relations:

$$E(e^{\rho(S_s-S_r)}/\boldsymbol{F}_r) = E\, e^{\rho(S_s-S_r)} \ \text{a.s.}$$

because the difference S_s-S_r is independent of the story $\boldsymbol{F}_r$ before r.

$$E\, e^{\rho(S_s-S_r)} = E\, e^{\rho S_{s-r}}$$

because the total claim amount in the interval]r,s] has the same distribution as the total claim amount in the interval of the same length [0,s−r]. From

$$R_s = R_r + (R_s-R_r) = R_r + c(s-r) - (S_s-S_r)\,,$$

results

$$E(Y_s/\boldsymbol{F}_r) = E[\exp(-\rho R_s)/\boldsymbol{F}_r] = E[\exp(-\rho R_r - \rho c(s-r) + \rho\,(S_s-S_r))/\boldsymbol{F}_r)$$

$$= \exp(-\rho R_r - \rho c(s-r))\, E(e^{\rho(S_s-S_r)}/\boldsymbol{F}_r)$$

$$= \exp(-\rho R_r - \rho c(s-r))\, E\, e^{\rho(S_s-S_r)}$$

$$= \exp(-\rho R_r - \rho c(s-r))\, E\, e^{\rho S_{s-r}}$$

$$= \exp(-\rho R_r - \rho c(s-r)) \exp(\rho c(s-r)) = e^{-\rho R_r} = Y_r \ \text{a.s.} \ \bullet$$

6.3.3. Classical Exponential Inequality

Theorem 4 (Lundberg's Exponential Inequality)

In the classical risk model

$$\Psi(u) \le e^{-\rho u} \quad (u \ge 0) \tag{20}$$

if the adjustment coefficient ρ exists.

Proof
We consider the martingale Y_τ ($\tau \in \mathbf{R}_+$) of Theorem 3. From the implication

$$T \le t \Rightarrow R_{T\wedge t} < 0$$

results that

$$1_{T\le t} \le \exp(-\rho R_{T\wedge t}).$$

We consider the stopping times 0 and $T\wedge t$. By the preceding inequality and by Doob for martingales (Ch.3.Th.7),

$$\Psi(t,u) = P(T\le t) = E(1_{T\le t}) \le E \exp(-\rho R_{T\wedge t}) = E \exp(-\rho R_0) = E\, e^{-\rho u} = e^{-\rho u}.$$

Hence, for all $t\ge 0$, $\Psi(t,u)\le e^{-\rho u}$. As $t\uparrow\infty$, we obtain (20) •

6.4. Martingales in General Risk Models

6.4.1. Risk Model

The ***special assumptions*** on the risk model are the following.

Assumptions on claim instants process

The claim instants process is defined by intensity functions λ_n so that

$$\lambda_n(\tau/t_1,\dots,t_n) \le b_n(t) \quad (n=1,2,\dots;\ 0\le t_1\le\dots\le t_n\le\tau\le t), \tag{21}$$

for strictly positive functions $b_n(\cdot)$ on $\mathbf{R}_+$ satisfying relation

$$\sum_{n\ge 1} 1/b_n(t) = \infty \quad (t\in\mathbf{R}_+). \tag{22}$$

By Ch.4.Th.21, the claim instants process is non-explosive.

Assumptions on premium income process

In the interval $d\tau$, the insurer collects the premium $(1+\eta)\mu\lambda_1(\tau)d\tau$ if $N_\tau=0$ and the premium $(1+\eta)\mu\lambda_n(\tau/t_1,...,t_{n-1})d\tau$ if

$$N_\tau = n-1 \geq 1 \ , \ T_1 = t_1 \ , ... , \ T_{n-1} = t_{n-1}.$$

This means that the insurer collects a premium proportional to the intensity of the claim instants process in each interval $d\tau$. The premium of the interval $d\tau$ equals the expected claim amount in that interval, multiplied by $(1+\eta)$.

The non-infinitesimal expression of the premium income process is

$$P_\tau = (1+\eta)\mu Q_\tau \ (\tau\in\mathbf{R}_+), \tag{23}$$

where

$$Q_\tau = \int_{[0,T_1]} \lambda_1(\tau)d\tau + \int_{[T_1,T_2]} \lambda_2(\tau/T_1)d\tau + ... + \int_{[T_{N_\tau},\tau]} \lambda_{N_\tau+1}(\tau/T_1,...,T_{N_\tau})d\tau.$$

Assumptions on claim amounts process.

The adjustment coefficient ρ, defined by (18), exists.

6.4.2. Auxiliary processes

We consider the **modified intensity functions**

$$\lambda_{\beta n}(\tau/t_1,...,t_{n-1}) := \beta\lambda_n(\tau/t_1,...,t_{n-1}) \ (0\leq t_1\leq...\leq t_n\leq\tau), \tag{24}$$

where

$$\beta := 1+\alpha\mu(1+\eta)$$

is a parameter depending on the strictly positive parameter α. By (21), (22) and by Ch.4.Th.21, applied to the point process with modified intensity functions, the latter process is non-explosive.

As usual, the risk reserve process is $R_\tau=u+P_\tau-S_\tau$ $(\tau\in\mathbf{R}_+)$, where $u\geq0$ is the initial risk reserve.

The **transformed risk reserve process** is the process, defined for all $\alpha>0$, by

$$Y_{\alpha\tau} := \exp(-\alpha R_\tau) = \exp[\alpha(S_\tau-P_\tau-u)] \ \ (\tau\in\mathbf{R}_+). \tag{25}$$

6.4.3. Basic Theorem

We denote by $p_{\beta\tau n}$ (n=0,1,2,...; $\tau \geq 0$), the probability of n claims exactly in $[0,\tau]$ for the point process defined by the modified intensity functions (24)

Lemma

$$\mathbf{E\ exp[\alpha(S_\tau - P_\tau)] = \sum_{n\geq 0} E^n e^{\alpha X}.\beta^{-n}\ p_{\beta\tau n}\ (\tau\geq 0;\ \alpha>0).} \qquad (26)$$

Proof

By Ch.4.(47), the densities $\pi_{\tau n}(t_1,\ldots,t_n)$ of the claim instants process equal

$$\exp(-\int_{[0,t_1]}\lambda_1)\lambda_1 \exp(-\int_{[t_1,t_2]}\lambda_2)\lambda_2 \ldots \exp(-\int_{[t_{n-1},t_n]}\lambda_n)\lambda_n \exp(-\int_{[t_n,\tau]}\lambda_{n+1}). \quad (27)$$

In (27), and in the rest of the proof, the following abbreviations are used:

$$\lambda_i \equiv \lambda_i(t_i/t_1,\ldots,t_{i-1})\ ,\ \int\lambda_i \equiv \int\lambda_i(\tau/t_1,\ldots,t_{i-1})d\tau.$$

The same notations and abbreviations, completed by the subscript β, are used for the modified intensities (24).

By the first formula of 6.1.2 , since the variables $x_1,\ldots,x_n$ can be integrated out at once,

$$\begin{aligned}
&E\ \exp[\alpha(S_\tau - P_\tau)]\\
&= \sum_{n\geq 0} [E^n e^{\alpha X}] \int_{[0,\tau]} dt_1 \ldots \int_{[t_{n-1},\tau]} dt_n\\
&\quad \times \exp[-\alpha\mu(1+\eta)(\int_{[0,t_1]}\lambda_1 + \ldots + \int_{[t_{n-1},t_n]}\lambda_n + \int_{[t_n,\tau]}\lambda_{n+1})]\\
&\quad\quad \times \exp(-\int_{[0,t_1]}\lambda_1)\lambda_1 \ldots \exp(-\int_{[t_{n-1},t_n]}\lambda_n)\lambda_n \exp(-\int_{[t_n,\tau]}\lambda_{n+1})\\
&= \sum_{n\geq 0} [E^n e^{\alpha X}]\beta^{-n} \int_{[0,\tau]} dt_1 \ldots \int_{[t_{n-1},\tau]} dt_n\\
&\quad \times \exp(-\int_{[0,t_1]}\lambda_{\beta 1})\lambda_{\beta 1} \ldots \exp(-\int_{[t_{n-1},t_n]}\lambda_{\beta n})\lambda_{\beta n} \exp(-\int_{[t_n,\tau]}\lambda_{\beta,n+1})\\
&= \sum_{n\geq 0} E^n e^{\alpha X}.\beta^{-n} \int_{[0,\tau]} dt_1 \ldots \int_{[t_{n-1},\tau]} dt_n\ \pi_{\beta\tau n}(t_1,\ldots,t_n)\\
&= \sum_{n\geq 0} E^n e^{\alpha X}.\beta^{-n}\ p_{\beta\tau n}\ \bullet
\end{aligned}$$

The transformations in the foregoing proof are valid by Fubini because everything is positive. But (26) can be the equality $\infty=\infty$.

We say that α **is admissible** if

$$\alpha > 0 \ , \ \beta \leq Ee^{\alpha X} < \infty, \tag{28}$$

and if the last member of (26) is finite. From the fact that $P_\tau \geq 0$ results that the latter condition is satisfied if

$$E \exp(\alpha S_\tau) < \infty \ (\tau \geq 0) \tag{29}$$

where

$$E \exp(\alpha S_\tau) = \sum_{n\geq 0} P(N_\tau = n)\, E^n e^{\alpha X} \ (\tau \geq 0). \tag{30}$$

The relation (30) results from a simplified version of the proof of the foregoing Lemma. More directly, it results from the iterative relation for conditional expectations

$$E \exp(\alpha S_\tau) = EE[\exp(\alpha S_\tau)/N_\tau].$$

If $\beta = Ee^{\alpha X}$ in (28), then α is the adjustment coefficient ρ defined by the relation (18) of the preceding section.

The filtration $\boldsymbol{F}_\tau$ ($\tau \in \mathbf{R}_+$) is defined in Ch.3.5.1. The instant of ruin T is the first claim instant T_k at which the risk reserve is strictly negative, or $+\infty$ if such instant does not exist. It is a stopping time.

Theorem 5

Let α be admissible in the general risk model satisfying the *Assumptions* of 6.4.1. Then the transformed risk reserve process $Y_{\alpha\tau}$ ($\tau \in \mathbf{R}_+$) is a submartingale. It is a martingale if α equals the adjustment coefficient ρ.

Proof
We have to prove that

$$E(Y_{\alpha s}/\boldsymbol{F}_r) \geq Y_{\alpha r} \text{ a.s. } (0 \leq r \leq s), \tag{31}$$

with equality if $\alpha = \rho$. The first member of that relation equals

$$E[\exp(\alpha(S_s - P_s - u))/\boldsymbol{F}_r] = \exp[\alpha(S_r - P_r - u)]\, E[\exp(\alpha(S_s - S_r) - \alpha(P_s - P_r))/\boldsymbol{F}_r]$$

$$= Y_{\alpha r}\, E[\exp(\alpha(S_s - S_r) - \alpha(P_s - P_r))/\boldsymbol{F}_r].$$

Hence, it is sufficient to prove that

$$E[\exp(\alpha(S_s-S_r)-\alpha(P_s-P_r))/\boldsymbol{F}_r] \geq 1, \tag{32}$$

with equality if $\alpha=\rho$.

Let us first assume that $r=0$. Then, there is no conditioning and (32) results from the Lemma, with $\tau=s$. Indeed, in the last member of (26), the coefficient of $p_{\beta\tau n}$ equals $(Ee^{\alpha X}/\beta)^n$. It is larger than 1, because α is admissible. Hence, by the norm relation in the modified claim instants process (the latter is non-explosive), the last member of (26) is larger than 1. It equals 1 if $\alpha=\rho$.

Let us now assume that $r>0$ and that

$$N_r=m\ ,\ T_1=t_1,\ T_2=t_2,\ \ldots,\ T_m = t_m\ . \tag{33}$$

Then the first member of (32) becomes

$$E[\exp(\alpha(S_s-S_r)-\alpha(P_s-P_r))/\ N_r=m,T_1=t_1,T_2=t_2,\ \ldots,T_m=t_m]$$

It can be calculated in the same way as the first member of (26) from the conditional claim instants process starting at the instant r, with N_r, T_1, ..., T_{N_r} fixed by (33). This is the process with the new origin r and with the new intensity functions λ°_n (n=1,2,...) defined by

$$\lambda^\circ_n(\tau/s_1,\ldots s_n) := \lambda_{m+n}(\tau/t_1,\ldots,t_m,s_1,\ldots,s_n)\quad (r\leq s_1\leq\ldots\leq s_n\leq\tau).$$

By (21), (22) and by Ch.4.Th.21, this conditional claim instants process is non-explosive Then a similar relation as (26) is obtained and (32) follows in the same way as in the case $r=0$ •

6.4.4. Bounds for the Ruin Probability

Theorem 6

Let α be admissible in the general risk model defined in 6.4.1. Then, for all $t\in R_+$,

$$\Psi(t,u) \leq e^{-\alpha u} \textstyle\sum_{n\geq 0} E^n e^{\alpha X}.\beta^{-n}\ p_{\beta t n}. \tag{34}$$

If α is the adjustment coefficient ρ,

$$\Psi(u) \leq e^{-\alpha u}. \tag{35}$$

Proof
We consider the submartingale $Y_{\alpha\tau}$ ($\tau\in\mathbf{R}_+$) of the preceding Theorem. From the implication

$$T \le t \Rightarrow R_{T\wedge t} < 0\,,$$

results that

$$1_{T\le t} \le \exp(-\alpha R_{T\wedge t}) = Y_{\alpha,T\wedge t}.$$

By Doob for the stopping times $T\wedge t$ and t, satisfying $T\wedge t \le t$,

$$\Psi(t,u) = P(T\le t) = E1_{T\le t} \le EY_{\alpha,T\wedge t} \le EY_{\alpha t}$$

$$= e^{-\alpha u}\, E[\alpha(S_t-P_t)] = e^{-\alpha u} \sum_{n\ge 0} E^n e^{\alpha X}.\beta^{-n}\, p_{\beta tn},$$

by the Lemma of 6.4.3. This proves (34).

If $\alpha=\rho$, then the coefficient of $p_{\beta\tau n}$ in the sum of the last member of (34) equals 1, and then this sum equals 1 by the norm relation for the modified claim instants process. This proves the relation

$$\Psi(t,u) \le e^{-\alpha u}.$$

AS $t\uparrow\infty$, the relation (35) is obtained.

6.4.5. Illustrations

Example 1: Classical risk model

We here consider the classical model. It is a particular case of the general model considered in this section. Then the bound (35) is the classical exponential bound. The bound (34) may be much better.

Here the intensities in the first member of (21) all equal the constant $\lambda>0$, and the modified intensities (24) all equal the constant $\beta\lambda$. Hence, the modified claim instants process is a Poisson process with parameter $\lambda\beta$, and then

$$p_{\beta tn} = e^{-\lambda\beta t}\,(\lambda\beta t)^n/n! \ \ (n\ge 0). \tag{36}$$

By (34)

$$\Psi(t,u) \le \exp(-\alpha u-\lambda\beta t + Ee^{\alpha X}) \ \ (\alpha \text{ admissible}). \tag{37}$$

Let us consider the exponential claimsize distribution

$$F(x) = 1-e^{-x}\ (x\geq 0). \tag{38}$$

Then α is admissible iff $\alpha\geq\eta/(1+\eta)$ and then

$$Ee^{\alpha X} = 1/(1-\alpha). \tag{39}$$

For $t=100$, $u=50$, $\eta=0.05$, the classical bound is

$$\Psi(100\ ,\ 50) \leq 0.092.$$

By (37), considering the best admissible α, i.e. that one furnishing the least upper bound:

$$\Psi(100\ ,\ 50) \leq 0.0025.$$

Example 2: Polya case

We consider the intensities

$$\lambda_{n+1}(\tau) := (a+bn)/(1+c\tau)\ \ (n\geq 0)\ ,\ \text{where } a\geq 0,\ b>0,\ c>0).$$

These are the intensities of *Process 3* of Ch.4.6.3, with b replaced by b–a. The intensities of the modified claim instants process are multiplied by β. From this results that

$$p_{\beta t0} = (1+ct)^{-a'}\ ,\ \ p_{\beta tn} = (1+ct)^{-a'}(a''+n-1)^{[n]}/n!\ [1-(1+ct)^{-\beta b'}]^n\ (n\geq 1),$$

where $a':=a/c$, $b':=b/c$, $a'':=a/b$. By (34),

$$\Psi(t,u) \leq e^{-\alpha u}\,(1+ct)^{-\beta a'}\,[1-\beta^{-1}[1-(1+ct)^{-\beta b'}]Ee^{\alpha X}]^{-a''}\ \ (\alpha \text{ admissible})$$

if the expression in the outer square brackets is positive.

For $a=b=c=1$, F defined by (38), $t=100$, $u=50$ and $\eta=0.05$, the best admissible α furnishes the bound

$$\Psi(100\ ,\ 50) \leq 0.029.$$

Chapter 7

Infinite-Time Ruin Probabilities in Classical Risk Model

7.1. Renewal Equations

7.1.1. Risk Model

We consider the classical risk model defined in Ch.3.1.4. The premium income process is $c\tau$ ($\tau \in \mathbf{R}_+$) where c is strictly positive. The premium income rate c is displayed as

$$c = (1+\eta)\lambda\mu,$$

where η is the security loading. It is assumed, when nothing else is specified, that η is strictly positive. We shall make some scarce remarks about the model with $\eta \leq 0$. We define

$$p := \eta/(1+\eta) \quad , \quad q := 1-p = 1/(1+\eta).$$

The concave transform G of the claimsize distribution function F, is defined in Ch.3.2.2. The adjustment coefficient ρ of the couple (G,q) is defined in Ch.3.2.4. It is supposed to exist when it is used.

All results in this and in the next Chapter, are based on the renewal equation of Theorem 3. The densities π_{tn} ($t \geq 0$; n=0,1,2,...) of the claim instants process (i.e. the Poisson process with intensity λ) are considered in the proof of Theorem 3. They result from the relations valid for n=0,1,2,... and $0 \leq t_1 \leq \ldots \leq t_n \leq t$:

$$\pi_{tn}(t_1,\ldots,t_n)dt_1\ldots dt_n := P(N_t=n,\ T_1 \in dt_1,\ldots,T_n \in dt_n) =$$

$$e^{-\lambda t_1}.\lambda dt_1.e^{-\lambda(t_2-t_1)}.\lambda dt_2\ldots.e^{-\lambda(t_n-t_{n-1})}.\lambda dt_n.e^{-\lambda(t-t_n)} = e^{-\lambda t}\lambda^n dt_1\ldots dt_n.$$

We recall that $e^{-\lambda(s-r)}$ is the probability of no claim in the time-interval [r,s].

Hence,

$$\pi_{tn} = e^{-\lambda t}\lambda^n \ (t\geq 0;\ n=0,1,2,...).$$

(see Ch.4.Th.5.Cor. for a complete definition of the Poisson process).

7.1.2. Probabilities U(0) and U(∞)

One of the probabilities U(0) or U(∞) is needed in the proof of Theorem 3. It can be obtained in three different ways. 1: By the following Theorem 2, based on the strong law of large numbers, in full generality. 2: By the following Theorem 1, based on central tendency, under the assumption that $\mu_2<\infty$. 3: By Lundberg's exponential bound (Ch.6.Th.4), based on martingale theory, under the assumption that the adjustment coefficient ρ exists.

Theorem 1

In the classical risk model, let $\mu_2 < \infty$. Then

$$\mathbf{lim}_{t\uparrow\infty}\ \mathbf{F}_t(\mathbf{ct}) = \mathbf{1}, \tag{1}$$

$$\mathbf{U(0)} = \mathbf{lim}_{t\uparrow\infty}\mathbf{U(t,0)} = \mathbf{p}. \tag{2}$$

Proof

The standardized random variable S_t^{01} is asymptotically standardized normal as $t\uparrow\infty$ by Ch.5.Th.1. By Ch.3.Th.5, it equals

$$S_t^{01} = (S_t-\mu\lambda t)(\mu_2\lambda t)^{-1/2}.$$

Let $s\geq 0$.

$$F_t(st) = P(S_t\leq st) = P[S_t^{01} \leq (st-\mu\lambda t)(\mu_2\lambda t)^{-1/2}] = P[S_t^{01} \leq (s-\mu\lambda)t(\mu_2\lambda t)^{-1/2}].$$

Hence, as $t\uparrow\infty$

$$F_t(st) \to P(Z\leq -\infty) = 0 \ \ (0\leq s<\mu\lambda), \tag{3}$$

$$F_t(st) \to P(Z\leq 0) = 1/2 \ \ (s=\mu\lambda), \tag{4}$$

$$F_t(st) \to P(Z\leq +\infty) = 1 \ \ (\mu\lambda<s), \tag{5}$$

where Z is a standardized normal random variable. Then (1) is (5) for s=c. For the proof of (2), we use the relation $U(t,0)=(ct)^{-1}\int_{[0,ct]} F_t(\tau)d\tau$ of Ch.6.Th.2. Let s be a new integration variable related to τ by τ=st. Then

$$U(t,0) = c^{-1}\int_{[0,c]} F_t(st)ds = c^{-1}\int_{[0,(1+\eta)\mu\lambda]} F_t(st)ds$$

$$= c^{-1}\int_{[0,\mu\lambda[} F_t(st)ds + c^{-1}\int_{]\mu\lambda,(1+\eta)\mu\lambda]} F_t(st)ds. \qquad (6)$$

The limit as $t\uparrow\infty$ of the last member equals

$$c^{-1}\int_{[0,\mu\lambda[} 0\ ds + c^{-1}\int_{]\mu\lambda,(1+\eta)\mu\lambda]} 1\ ds = c^{-1}\eta\mu\lambda = \eta/(1+\eta) = p$$

by (3), (5) and by dominated convergence •

If $\eta\le 0$, then

$$U(0) := \lim_{t\uparrow\infty} U(t,0) = 0. \qquad (7)$$

Indeed, then the foregoing proof remains valid, but the last integral of (6) must be replaced by

$$-c^{-1}\int_{](1+\eta)\mu\lambda,\mu\lambda]} F_t(st)ds.$$

By (3), it tends to 0 as $t\uparrow\infty$. The proof of Ch.6.Th.2., used in the foregoing demonstration, does not depend on the condition $\eta>0$. Hence, that Theorem is valid also for negative security loadings.

Theorem 2

In the classical risk model, let $R_\tau:=c\tau-S_\tau$ ($\tau\in R_+$) be the risk reserve corresponding to the initial risk reserve equal to 0. The trajectories of R_τ tend to $+\infty$ a.s. as $\tau\uparrow\infty$ and

$$\Psi(\infty) = \lim_{x\uparrow\infty} \Psi(x) = 0. \qquad (8)$$

Proof

The random variables $D_1:=R_1$, $D_2:=R_2-R_1$, $D_3:=R_3-R_2$,... are i.i.d., with expectation

$$ER_1 = c-ES_1 = (1+\eta)\mu\lambda-\mu\lambda = \eta\mu\lambda.$$

By the strong law of large numbers,

$$R_n/n = (D_1+...+D_n)/n \rightarrow \eta\mu\lambda \text{ a.s. as } n\uparrow\infty.$$

Hence, $R_n\rightarrow\infty$ a.s. as $n\uparrow\infty$. Due to the particular shape of the trajectories of the process R_τ ($\tau\in\mathbf{R}_+$), this implies that $R_\tau\rightarrow\infty$ a.s. as $\tau\uparrow\infty$. Indeed, let us consider a fixed trajectory $R_\tau(\omega)$, where ω is a point of the basic probability space. If $R_{k+1}(\omega)\geq a$, then $R_\tau(\omega)\geq a-c$ ($k\leq\tau\leq k+1$), because the increment of $R_\tau(\omega)$ on the time-interval $[k,k+1]$ is c at most. This proves that $R_\tau\rightarrow+\infty$ a.s.

We now prove (8). Any trajectory $R_\tau(\omega)$ ($\tau\in\mathbf{R}_+$) such that $R_\tau(\omega)\rightarrow+\infty$ as $\tau\uparrow\infty$, is bounded below (explosions of claims can be excluded because their probability equals 0). This implies that $\bigcap_{n\geq0}\{\inf_{\tau\geq0}R_\tau<-n\}$ is a null set. Then

$$\lim_{x\uparrow\infty} \Psi(x) = \lim_{n\uparrow\infty} \Psi(n) = \lim_{n\uparrow\infty} P(\inf_{\tau\geq0}R_\tau<-n)$$

$$= P[\bigcap_{n\geq0}\{\inf_{\tau\geq0}R_\tau<-n\}] = 0 \quad \bullet$$

From an adaptation of the preceding argument results that $\Psi(\infty)=1$ if $\eta<0$. The argument does not allow to tell what happens for $\eta=0$.

7.1.3. Basic Renewal Equation for U

The next Theorem furnishes the **basic renewal equation** $U=p+qU*G$ for the **non-ruin distribution function U**. It is so fundamental that we provide a very detailed proof. In the *Remark* following the demonstration, we indicate how the proof can be abridged and where the ***Quick proofs*** fail to be complete.

Theorem 3 (Basic Renewal Equation)

In the classical risk model, the function U is a probability distribution function on $\mathbf{R}_+$. It is the unique solution of the renewal equation

$$\mathbf{U = p + q\, U*G \quad on\ R_+.} \tag{9}$$

Proof

Let t be fixed for the moment. Let $n\geq1$. We apply Fubini in the last member of relation Ch.6.(3), with $\tau\equiv t_1$, $x\equiv x_1$. The probability of exactly n claims before t, and no ruin, corresponding to the initial risk reserve u, equals

$$U(t,u,n) = \int_{[0,t]} \lambda e^{-\lambda\tau}\, d\tau \int_{[0,u+c\tau]} f(\tau,x)\, dF(x), \tag{10}$$

where

$$f(\tau,x) := \int...\int_{D1} \lambda^{n-1} e^{-\lambda(t-\tau)}\, dt_2...dt_n dF(x_2)...dF(x_n).$$

For fixed $\tau\in[0,t]$ and $x\in[0,u+c\tau]$, the domain D1 is defined by the relations

$$\tau \le t_2 \le \ldots \le t_n \le t \;;\; x_2,\ldots,x_n \ge 0 \;;\; x+x_2 \le u+ct_2 ,\ldots, \; x+x_2+\ldots+x_n \le u+ct_n.$$

We introduce the new integration variables

$$s_1=t_2-\tau,\ldots,\; s_{n-1}=t_n-\tau \;;\; y_1=x_2,\ldots,y_{n-1}=x_n$$

in the multiple integral defining $f(\tau,x)$. Then

$$f(\tau,x) = \int\ldots\int_{D2} \lambda^{n-1} e^{-\lambda(t-\tau)}\, ds_1\ldots ds_{n-1}\, dF(y_1)\ldots dF(y_{n-1}),$$

where the domain D2 is defined by the relations

$$0 \le s_1 \le \ldots \le s_{n-1} \le t-\tau \;;\; y_1,\ldots,y_{n-1} \ge 0;$$

$$y_1 \le (u+c\tau-x)+cs_1 ,\; y_1+y_2 \le (u+c\tau-x)+cs_2 ,\; \ldots ,\; y_1+\ldots+y_{n-1} \le (u+c\tau-x)+cs_{n-1}.$$

This means that

$$f(\tau,x) = U(t-\tau,u+c\tau-x,n-1).$$

Then

$$U(t,u,n) = \int_{[0,t]} \lambda e^{-\lambda\tau} d\tau \int_{[0,u+c\tau]} U(t-\tau,u+c\tau-x,n-1)\, dF(x), \qquad (11)$$

by (10). We now sum (11) over n=1,2,... and we add π_{t0} . By monotone convergence,

$$U(t,u) = \pi_{t0} + \int_{[0,t]} \lambda e^{-\lambda\tau} d\tau \int_{[0,u+c\tau]} U(t-\tau,u+c\tau-x)\, dF(x). \qquad (12)$$

In that relation, we let $t\uparrow\infty$. By dominated convergence,

$$U(u) = \int_{[0,\infty[} \lambda e^{-\lambda\tau} d\tau \int_{[0,u+c\tau]} U(u+c\tau-x)\, dF(x). \qquad (13)$$

The interior integral equals the convolution product U*F at the point $u+c\tau$. Hence

$$U(u) = \int_{[0,\infty[} \lambda e^{-\lambda\tau} (U*F)(u+c\tau)\, d\tau.$$

In the latter integral, we introduce the new integration variable $s=u+c\tau$:

$$U(u) = (\lambda/c)e^{\lambda u/c} \int_{[u,\infty[} e^{-\lambda s/c} (U*F)(s)ds. \qquad (14)$$

From this relation results that the function U has a density (i.e. that it is absolutely continuous on bounded intervals). The derivative equals (Lebesgue a.e.)

$$U'(u) = (\lambda/c)U(u) - (\lambda/c)\,(U*F)(u). \tag{15}$$

This is true for all $u \in \mathbf{R}_+$. Hence

$$U' = (\lambda/c)(1-F)*U.$$

We now take the convolution product by the identity function I on $\mathbf{R}_+$, and we recall that the concave transform G of F is $G = 1/_{\mu}(1-F)*I$. Then

$$U - U(0) = U'*I = (\mu\lambda/c)\,[1/_{\mu}\,(1-F)*I]*U,$$

$$U - U(0) = q\,G*U. \tag{16}$$

We take that relation at the point x, and we let $x \uparrow \infty$. By the factorization Theorem of the convolution product at ∞ (Ch.1.Th.11), we obtain

$$U(\infty) - U(0) = q.1.U(\infty). \tag{17}$$

But $U(\infty)=1$ by Theorem 2. Hence $U(0)=1-q=p$, and then (9) follows from the relation (16).

The unicity of the solution results from Ch.1.Th.14.

The function U is increasing on $\mathbf{R}_+$. It is continuous because it has a density U'. It satisfies $U(\infty)=1$. U is a probability distribution function on $\mathbf{R}_+$ •

Instead of Theorem 2, we can apply Theorem 1, under the assumption that $\mu_2<\infty$. We then have $U(0)=p$ and then $U(\infty)=1$ by (17). If ρ exists, then the relation $U(\infty)=1$, results from Ch.6.Th.4.

If $\eta<0$, then $U(\infty)=0$ by the observation following the proof of Theorem 2, and then $U(0)=0$. This implies that $U \equiv 0$, because U is monotonic. The same conclusion follows from the discussion following the proof of Theorem 1, if $\mu_2<\infty$, for $\eta \leq 0$. Indeed, then $U(0)=0$, and then $U(\infty)=0$ by (17).

Remark (Quick "proofs")

a. The relation (12) can be displayed at once, as follows. Let R_s ($s\in\mathbf{R}_+$) be the risk reserve corresponding to the initial reserve u. Let T be the instant τ of occurrence of the first claim in [0,t]. If no claim occurs in [0,t], then we take T=0. Then (12) results from the relations

$$U(t,u) := P[R_s\geq 0\ (0\leq s\leq t)] = E\ P[R_s\geq 0\ (0\leq s\leq t)/T]. \tag{18}$$

The proof of the equality of the last member of (12) and the last member of (18) is based on easy, but not demonstrated properties of the involved processes.

b. A shorter "proof" goes as follows. In the small time-interval $[0,\varepsilon]$, no claim occurs, one claim occurs (say at the instant $\xi\in[0,\varepsilon]$), or strictly more than one claim occurs. Hence,

$$U(u) = P(N_\varepsilon=0)U(u+c\varepsilon) + P(N_\varepsilon=1)\int_{[0,u+c\xi]} U(u+c\xi-x)dF(x) + \varepsilon\ o(\varepsilon),$$

$$= (1-\lambda\varepsilon)U(u+c\varepsilon) + \lambda\varepsilon \int_{[0,u]} U(u-x)dF(x) + \varepsilon\ o(\varepsilon)$$

$$= (1-\lambda\varepsilon)U(u+c\varepsilon) + \lambda\varepsilon\ (U*F)(u) + \varepsilon\ o(\varepsilon),$$

$$\lambda\ U(u+c\varepsilon) = [U(u+c\varepsilon)-U(u)]/\varepsilon + \lambda\ (U*F)(u) + o(\varepsilon).$$

As $\varepsilon\downarrow 0$:

$$\lambda\ U(u) = c\ U'(u) + \lambda\ (U*F)(u),$$

i.e. (15).

Here the major problem is U'. Indeed, we know, by the modern theory of differentiation of real functions, that U' exists Lebesgue-a.e. But nothing allows us to conclude that U is recuperated by the integration of U'. This is the case iff U is absolutely continuous on bounded intervals. In the proof of the Theorem, this absolute continuity results from (14) and it is only this property that allows to conclude that $U-U(0)=U'*I$. In the abridged proof indicated here, it is not clear at all how the argument could be completed.

7.1.4 Convolutions and Renewal Equations on $\mathbf{R}_+$

The basic theory of convolutions on $\mathbf{R}_+$ and renewal equations on $\mathbf{R}_+$ is developed in Ch.1.4, Ch.1.5 and Ch.1.6. **All convolutions and renewal equations considered in the following Chapters are convolutions and renewal equations on $\mathbf{R}_+$.** The indication "on $\mathbf{R}_+$" shall henceforth mostly be omitted. (In the Appendices A and B, convolutions on $\mathbf{R}$ are introduced.)

We recall that all functions vanish on $\mathbf{R}_{-}$ when convolutions or renewal equations on $\mathbf{R}_{+}$ are considered. Any function f on $\mathbf{R}_{+}$ must be considered as being the function $f(x)1_{x\geq 0}$ on $\mathbf{R}$. See Ch.1.3.1 for implications of this agreement.

By Ch.1.Th.14, the unique solution f of the renewal equation $f=g+qf*H$ ($0<q\leq 1$, H probability distribution function on $\mathbf{R}_{+}$) is

$$f = g*[\textstyle\sum_{k\geq 0} q^k H^{*k}]. \tag{19}$$

This solution is easily remembered as follows. Let us temporarily treat the convolution product f*H as a usual product fH. Then, in a symbolic way,

$$f = g+qfH \;,\; f(1-qH) = g \;,\; f = g(1-qH)^{-1} \;,\; f = g[\textstyle\sum_{k\geq 0} q^k H^k],$$

and (20) results from the latter relation, after restoration of the convolution products.

7.1.5. Renewal Equation for Ψ

If we replace U by $1-\Psi$ in (9), we obtain the following **renewal equation for Ψ**:

$$\Psi = q(1-G) + q\,\Psi*G. \tag{20}$$

7.1.6. Renewal Equation for Ψ_e

We here apply the exponential transformation defined in Ch.1.5.3, to the particular renewal equation (20) for Ψ. **The exponential transform of G** is the probability distribution function G_e defined by

$$G_e(x) := q\int_{[0,x]} e^{\rho y}\, dG(y) \quad (x\in\mathbf{R}_+). \tag{21}$$

The exponential transform of the ruin probability function Ψ is the function Ψ_e defined by

$$\Psi_e(x) := \Psi(x)e^{\rho x} \; (x\in\mathbf{R}_+). \tag{22}$$

Then **the renewal equation for Ψ_e** is

$$\Psi_e = g_e + \Psi_e{*}G_e\,, \tag{23}$$

where

$$g_e(x) := q(1-G(x))e^{\rho x} \quad (x \in \mathbf{R}_+). \tag{24}$$

The renewal equation for Ψ_e is the **exponential transform of the renewal equation for Ψ**.

7.1.7. Exponential Case

Several general results shall be illustrated in the **exponential case**, defined by the claimsize distribution function

$$F(x) := 1-e^{-x/\mu} \quad (x \in \mathbf{R}_+). \tag{25}$$

The parameter μ has the right interpretation: it is the first moment of F. The concave transform of F is

$$G(x) = {}^{1}/_{\mu} \int_{[0,x]} (1-F(y))dy = {}^{1}/_{\mu} \int_{[0,x]} e^{-y/\mu}\, dy = 1-e^{-x/\mu}\ .$$

Hence, G=F in this particular case. Then it is not difficult to verify that the solution of the renewal equation (20) for Ψ is

$$\Psi(x) = q\, e^{-px/\mu} \quad (x \in \mathbf{R}_+). \tag{26}$$

The next Chapter 8 is entirely devoted to claimsize distribution functions furnishing explicit analytic expression for $\Psi(x)$. The simplest of these cases is the exponential one.

7.2. Convolution Power Series Expansions for U

7.2.1. Simple Convolution Power Series Expansion

Theorem 4 (Beekman's Expansion)

The solution of the renewal equation U=p+qU*G is

$$\mathbf{U = p \sum_{k \geq 0} q^k G^{*k}}. \tag{27}$$

Proof

By (19) •

In the following Corollary, two claimsize distribution functions are considered. They are distinguished by the superscripts ^{1} and ^{2}. The security loading η, and then also p and q, are the same in both cases.

Corollary

In the classical risk models with claimsize distributions F^1 and F^2, for any fixed $x \in \mathbf{R}_+$:

a. $U^1(x) = U^2(x)$ **if** $G^1 = G^2$ **on** $[0,x[$.

b. $U^1(x) = U^2(x)$ **if** $F^1 = F^2$ **on** $[0,x[$ **and** $\mu^1 = \mu^2$.

c. $U^1(x) \leq U^2(x)$ **if** $G^1 \leq G^2$ **on** $[0,x[$.

d. $U^1(x) \leq U^2(x)$ **if** $F^2 \leq F^1$ **on** $[0,x[$ **and** $\mu^1 = \mu^2$.

Proof

c. Let $G^1 \leq G^2$ on $[0,x[$. Then $G^1 \leq G^2$ on $[0,x]$ because concave transforms are continuous functions on $\mathbf{R}_+$. Then

$$U^1(x) = \sum_{k\geq 0} (G^1)^{*k}(x) \leq \sum_{k\geq 0} (G^2)^{*k}(x) = U^2(x).$$

a. The assumption of a. implies $G^1 \leq G^2$ and $G^2 \leq G^1$ on $[0,x[$, and then $U_1(x) \leq U_2(x)$ and $U_2(x) \leq U_1(x)$ follows from c.

d. If $F^2 \leq F^1$ on $[0,x[$ and $\mu^1 = \mu^2$, then $G^1 \leq G^2$ on $[0,x]$ by the definition of the concave transform. Hence d. follows from c.

b. By d. •

7.2.2. Alternating Convolution Power Series Expansion

Theorem 5

In the classical risk model, let H_j (j=0,1,2,...) be the distribution function

$$H_j(x) := p(qx/\mu)^j/_{j!}\, e^{qx/\mu} \quad (x \in \mathbf{R}_+). \tag{28}$$

Then

$$U = \sum_{j\geq 0} (-1)^j H_j * F^{*j}. \tag{29}$$

The alternating series in the last member of (29) converges absolutely at each point $x \in \mathbf{R}_+$.

Proof

We recall that the concave transform G of F equals $1/_\mu(1-F)*I$, where I is the identity function on $\mathbf{R}_+$. Then

$$I^{*k}(x) = x^k/_{k!}.$$

Let $r:=q/\mu$ and let the function U_a be defined on $\mathbf{R}_+$, first for a= +1, by

$$U_a := p\sum_{k\geq 0} r^k(1+aF)^{*k}*I^{*k}.$$

We now use the fact that convolution products do have the same associativity, commutativity and distributivity properties as usual products. Then, by monotone convergence, Helly-Bray (Ch.1.Th.8) and by the binomial Theorem,

$$U_a = p\sum_{k\geq 0} r^k(\sum_{0\leq j\leq k} k^{[j]}/_{j!}\, a^jF^{*j})*I^{*k} = p\sum_{j\geq 0}\sum_{k\geq j} r^k k^{[j]}/_{j!}\, a^jF^{*j}*I^{*k}$$

$$= p\sum_{j\geq 0}\sum_{k\geq 0} r^{k+j}(k+j)^{[j]}/_{j!}\, a^jF^{*j}*I^{*(k+j)} = \sum_{j\geq 0} a^jH_j*F^{*j}, \quad (30)$$

with

$$H_j(x) := p\sum_{k\geq 0} r^{k+j}(k+j)^{[j]}/_{j!}\, x^{k+j}/_{(k+j)!}$$

$$= p(rx)^j/_{j!} \sum_{k\geq 0} (rx)^k/_{k!} = p(rx)^j/_{j!}\, e^{rx}.$$

But

$$\sum_{j\geq 0} a^j(Hj*F^{*j})(x) \leq \sum_{j\geq 0} a^jH_j(x) = pe^{arx}e^{rx} < \infty.$$

This implies that the relations (30), hitherto considered for a=+1, are also valid for a=–1, by dominated convergence (or because the involved series do converge absolutely at each point x). Hence,

$$U = p\sum_{k\geq 0} q^kG^{*k} = p\sum_{k\geq 0} r^k(1-F)^{*k}*I^{*k} = \sum_{j\geq 0} (-1)^jH_j*F^{*j} \quad \bullet$$

Corollary (Shiu's Expansion)

In the classical risk model, let the claimsize distribution F be concentrated on the set {1,2,...}. Then

$$\mathbf{U(x) = \sum_{0\leq k\leq [x]} \sum_{0\leq j\leq k} (-1)^j H_j(x-k)[F^{*j}(k)-F^{*j}(k-)] \quad (x\in R_+),} \quad (31)$$

where [x] is the integer part of x.

Proof

The distributions F^{*j} (j=0,1,2,...) are concentrated on {0,1,2,...}. Hence, by the Theorem,

$$U(x) = \sum_{j\geq 0} (-1)^j \int_{[0,x]} H_j(x-y)dF^{*j}(y)$$

$$= \sum_{j\geq 0} (-1)^j \sum_{0\leq k\leq [x]} H_j(x-k)[F^{*j}(k)-F^{*j}(k-)]$$

$$= \sum_{0\leq k\leq [x]} \sum_{j\geq 0} (-1)^j H_j(x-k)[F^{*j}(k)-F^{*j}(k-)],$$

where the square brackets vanish for j>k •

7.2.3. Removing the F-Mass at the Origin

We observe that F(0)=0 in Shiu's formula. This is no real restriction by the following simple Theorem.

Theorem 6

In the classical risk models with claimsize distribution functions F^1 and F^2, $U^1=U^2$ if

$$(1-F^1) = \theta(1-F^2) \quad (0<\theta\leq 1). \tag{32}$$

Proof

F^1 and F^2 do have the same concave transform. Hence U^1 and U^2 are unique solutions of the same renewal equation •

In particular, we can define F^2 from F^1 by (32) with $\theta := 1-F^1(0)$ if $F^1(0)>0$. Then $F^2(0)=0$.

7.3. Elementary Integral Inequalities

7.3.1. +– and –+ Functions

Let g be a function on the interval J. We say that **g is a –+ function on J**, if J can be partitioned in two successive intervals L and R such that $g\leq 0$ on the left interval L, and $g\geq 0$ on the right interval R. We say that **g is a +– function on J**, if J can be partitioned in two successive intervals L and R, such that $g\geq 0$ on the left interval L, and $g\leq 0$ on the right interval R.

Theorem 7 (Elementary Integral Inequalities)

Let g be a Lebesgue-integrable function on the interval J=[a,b[or J=[a,∞[, such that

$$\int_J g(y)dy = 0$$

and let h be a monotonic function on J such that gh is Lebesgue-integrable on J.

a. If g is a –+ function on J, and if h is increasing on J, then

$$\int_J g(y)h(y)dy \geq 0.$$

b. If g is a +– function on J, and if h is increasing on J, then

$$\int_J g(y)h(y)dy \leq 0.$$

c. If g is a –+ function on J and h a positive decreasing function on J, then

$$\int_{[a,x]} g(y)h(y)dy \leq 0 \ (x\in J).$$

d. If g is a +– function on J and h a positive decreasing function on J, then

$$\int_{[a,x]} g(y)h(y)dy \geq 0 \ (x\in J).$$

Proof

In each of the cases a,b,c,d, we denote by c a point in J such that g has a fixed sign on the left of c and the opposite sign on the right of c.

a. $$\int_J g(y)h(y)dy = \int_J g(y)[h(y)-h(c)]dy \geq 0,$$

because g[h–h(c)] is positive on J under the indicated assumptions.

b. $$\int_J g(y)h(y)dy = \int_J g(y)[h(y)-h(c)]dy \leq 0,$$

because g[h–h(c)] is negative on J under the indicated assumptions.

c. If x≤c, the conclusion is direct. Let x≥c. Then

$$\int_{[a,x]} g(y)h(y)dy = \int_{[a,x]} g(y)[h(y)-h(c)]dy + h(c)\int_{[a,x]} g(y)dy. \tag{33}$$

The first integral in the last member is negative, because $g[h-h(c)]$ is negative on $[a,x]$, under the indicated assumptions. The last integral equals $-\int_M g(y)dy$, where M is $[x,b[$ or $[x,\infty[$, and it is also negative.

d. If $x \leq c$, the conclusion is direct. Let $x \geq c$. Then the first integral in the last member of (33) is positive, because $g[h-h(c)]$ is positive on $[a,x]$, under the indicated assumptions. The last integral (33) equals $-\int_M g(y)dy$, where M is $[x,b[$ or $[x,\infty[$, and it is positive •

7.3.2. Comparable Concave Transforms

Theorem 8

In the classical risk models with claimsize distribution functions F^1 and F^2 we assume that $\mu^1=\mu^2$ and that F^1-F^2 is a −+ function on R_+. Then $G^2 \leq G^1$.

Proof

$$\mu[G^2(x)-G^1(x)] = \int_{[0,x]} [(1-F^2(y))-(1-F^1(y))]dy = \int_{[0,x]} [F^1(y)-F^2(y)]dy \leq 0,$$

by Th.7.c with $g:=F^1-F^2$ and $h\equiv 1$ on $\mathbf{R}_+$ •

7.3.3. Comparable Adjustment Coefficients

Theorem 9

In the classical risk models with claimsize distribution functions F^1 and F^2, we assume that $\mu^1=\mu^2$, $\mu^1_2=\mu^2_2$ and that G^1-G^2 is a −+ function on R_+. Then $\rho^2 \leq \rho^1$. The inequality is strict if F^1 and F^2 are not identical.

Proof

We consider the increasing functions of $r \in \mathbf{R}_+$

$$g^1(r) = r\int_{[0,\infty[} (1-G^1(y))e^{ry}dy\ ,\ g^2(r) = r\int_{[0,\infty[} (1-G^2(y))e^{ry}dy.$$

with values in $\mathbf{R}_+ \cup \{\infty\}$. By Ch.3.(8), $g^1(\rho^1)=\eta=g^2(\rho^2)$. Hence g^1 is a finite function on $[0,\rho^1]$. If $g^2(\rho^1)=\infty$, then

$$g^2(\rho^2) = \eta = g^1(\rho^1) < \infty = g^2(\rho^1)$$

and then $\rho^2<\rho^1$ because g^2 is increasing. Hence, we may assume that $g^2(\rho^1)$ is finite and then g^2 is also a finite function on $[0,\rho^1]$. We may also assume that the functions G^1 and G^2 are not identical. By the surface interpretation of the first moment, and by Ch.3.Th.1.c,

$$\int_{[0,\infty[} [(1-G^2(y))-(1-G^1(y))]dy = \mu_1(G^2) - \mu_1(G^1) = 0.$$

Then

$$g^2(r)-g^1(r) = r\int_{[0,\infty[} [(1-G^2(y))-(1-G^1(y)]e^{ry}dy > 0 \quad (0\leq r\leq \rho^1) \tag{34}$$

by Th.7.a, because $(1-G^2)-(1-G^1)=G^1-G^2$ is a $-+$ function and e^{ry} an increasing function of $y\in[0,\infty[$. The strict inequality in (34) results from the proof of Th.7.a, taking into account that the continuous functions G^1 and G^2 are not identical. In particular, for $r=\rho^1$, $g^1(\rho^1)<g^2(\rho^1)$ by (34), and then

$$g^2(\rho^2) = \eta = g^1(\rho^1) < g^2(\rho^1)\ ,\quad g^2(\rho^2) < g^2(\rho^1).$$

The latter strict inequality implies that $\rho^2<\rho^1$ because g^2 is increasing •

7.4. Bounds

7.4.1. Construction of Bounds for Ruin Probabilities

In the classical risk model, let $U^\sim$ and $\Psi^\sim$ be functions on $\mathbf{R}_+$, regarded as approximations of the exact functions U and Ψ. We suppose that $U^\sim+\Psi^\sim=1$. The **error function in the approximation of U by $U^\sim$, or of Ψ by $\Psi^\sim$**, is the function Err defined on $\mathbf{R}_+$ by the relation

$$\mathrm{Err} := p + q\, U^\sim{*}G - U^\sim. \tag{35}$$

An equivalent definition is

$$\mathrm{Err} := \Psi^\sim - q\,\Psi^\sim{*}G - q(1-G). \tag{36}$$

The function Err deserves its name. Indeed,

$$\mathrm{Err} \equiv 0 \iff U^\sim \equiv U \iff \Psi^\sim \equiv \Psi,$$

because U is the unique solution of the renewal equation $U=p+qU*G$.

Theorem 10

In the classical risk model,

$$\mathbf{Err*U = p(U-U^{\sim})}. \tag{37}$$

Proof

$$Err*U = pU+U^{\sim}*(qG*U)-U^{\sim}*U = pU+U^{\sim}*(U-p)-U^{\sim}*U = p(U-U^{\sim}) \bullet$$

Corollary 1

$$\mathbf{Err \geq 0 \Rightarrow U \geq U^{\sim} \quad , \quad Err \leq 0 \Rightarrow U \leq U^{\sim},}$$

$$\mathbf{Err \geq 0 \text{ on } [0,x] \Rightarrow U(x) \geq U^{\sim}(x) \quad , \quad Err \leq 0 \text{ on } [0,x] \Rightarrow U(x) \leq U^{\sim}(x).}$$

Proof
The Corollary results from the Theorem because U is a distribution function, and because (Err*U)(x) only depends on the restriction of Err and U to the interval [0,x] •

Hence, for fixed G, we can try Err with any function $U^{\sim}$. If Err has a fixed sign on [0,x], then $U^{\sim}(x) \leq U(x)$, or $U^{\sim}(x) \geq U(x)$, depending on that sign.

Corollary 2

We assume that $\Psi^{\sim}$ is an approximation of Ψ such that

$$\mathbf{Err \geq -b \text{ on } [0,a[\quad , \quad Err \geq 0 \text{ on } [a,x],}$$

where b>0, 0≤a≤x. Let

$$\mathbf{r := p/(p+b) \quad , \quad s := b/(p+b).}$$

Then

$$\mathbf{\Psi(x) \leq r\, \Psi^{\sim}(x) + s\, \Psi(x-a)} \tag{38}$$

and

$$\mathbf{\Psi(x) \leq r \sum_{0\leq k\leq n-1} s^k\, \Psi^{\sim}(x-ka) + s^n \Psi(x-na) \ (1\leq n < x/a).} \tag{39}$$

Proof
By (37),

$$\Psi^{\sim}(x)-\Psi(x) = p^{-1} \int_{[0,x-a]} Err(x-y)dU(y) + p^{-1} \int_{]x-a,x]} Err(x-y)dU(y)$$

$$\geq p^{-1} \int_{[0,x-a]} 0\, dU(y) + p^{-1} \int_{]x-a,x]} (-b)dU(y)$$

$$= -bp^{-1}[U(x)-U(x-a)] = -bp^{-1}[\Psi(x-a)-\Psi(x)].$$

From this results (38). Then, applying (38) at point x–a instead of x if x–a>a :

$$\Psi(x) \le r\Psi^{\sim}(x) + s\Psi(x-a) \le r\Psi^{\sim}(x) + s[r\Psi^{\sim}(x-a)+s\Psi(x-2a)]$$

$$= r\Psi^{\sim}(x) + rs\,\Psi^{\sim}(x-a)+s^2\,\Psi(x-2a),$$

and so on •

7.4.2. Lundberg's Exponential Upper Bound for Ψ

Theorem 11 (Lundberg's exponential bound)

In the classical risk model,

$$\boldsymbol{\Psi(x) \le e^{-\rho x}\ (x\in \mathbf{R}_+).} \tag{40}$$

Proof

We take $\Psi^{\sim} = e_\rho$, where $e_\rho(x) := e^{-\rho x}$ $(x\in\mathbf{R}_+)$. Then

$$\text{Err} = e_\rho - qe_\rho{*}G - q(1-G),$$

$$q(e_\rho{*}G)(x) = q\int_{[0,x]} e^{-\rho(x-y)}dG(y) \tag{41}$$

$$= e^{-\rho x}[q\int_{[0,\infty[} e^{\rho y}dG(y) - q\int_{]x,\infty[} e^{\rho y}dG(y)] = e^{-\rho x}[1- q\int_{]x,\infty[} e^{\rho y}dG(y)].$$

by Ch.3.(7).

$$e^{\rho x}\,\text{Err}(x) = q\int_{]x,\infty[} e^{\rho y}dG(y) - qe^{\rho x}(1-G(x))$$

$$= q\int_{]x,\infty[} e^{\rho y}dG(y) - qe^{\rho x}\int_{]x,\infty[} dG(y) = q\int_{]x,\infty[} (e^{\rho y}-e^{\rho x})\,dG(y) \ge 0$$

Hence, by Theorem 10.Cor.1, Err≥0, $U\ge U^{\sim}$, $\Psi\le\Psi^{\sim}=e_\rho$ •

Example: The exponential case

From Ch.7.1.7. results that F=G in the exponential case. Then $\rho/q=\eta/\mu$ by the division of the relation Ch.3.(8) by the relation Ch.3.(9). Hence,

$$\rho = q\eta/\mu = p/\mu, \tag{42}$$

and Lundberg's exponential bound for $\Psi(x)$ is $e^{-px/\mu}$, whereas the exact value of $\Psi(x)$ is $qe^{-px/\mu}$.

7.4.3. An Exponential Lower Bound for Ψ

Theorem 12 (Exponential Lower Bound for Ψ)

In the classical risk model, let α be a positive number such that

$$\alpha\rho \int_{[x,\infty[} [1-G(y)]e^{\rho y}dy \leq [1-G(x)]e^{\rho x} \quad (x\in \mathbf{R}_+). \tag{43}$$

Then

$$\alpha/(1+\alpha)\ e^{-\rho x} \leq \Psi(x) \quad (x\in \mathbf{R}_+). \tag{44}$$

Proof

We take $\Psi^{\sim} := \alpha/(1+\alpha)\ e_\rho$, where $e_\rho(x) := e^{-\rho x}$ ($x\in\mathbf{R}_+$). Then

$$(1+\alpha)\ \mathrm{Err} = \alpha\ e_\rho - \alpha q\ e_\rho * G - q(1-G),$$

where $e_\rho * G$ results from (41). Then, by an integration by parts,

$$1/q\ (1+\alpha)e^{\rho x}\ \mathrm{Err}(x) = \alpha\int_{]x,\infty[} e^{\rho y}dG(y) - (1+\alpha)(1-G(x))e^{\rho x}$$

$$= -\alpha\int_{]x,\infty[} e^{\rho y}d(1-G(y)) - (1+\alpha)(1-G(x))e^{\rho x}$$

$$= \alpha e^{\rho x}(1-G(x)) + \alpha\rho\int_{]x,\infty[} (1-G(y))e^{\rho y}dy - (1+\alpha)(1-G(x))e^{\rho x}$$

$$= \alpha\rho\int_{]x,\infty[} (1-G(y))e^{\rho y}dy - (1-G(x))e^{\rho x} \leq 0.$$

Hence, by Th.10.Cor.1, $\mathrm{Err}\leq 0$, $U\leq U^{\sim}$, $\Psi\geq\Psi^{\sim}$ •

Example: Exponential case

In the exponential case, the condition (43) on α becomes

$$\alpha p/\mu \int_{[x,\infty[} e^{-y/\mu}e^{py/\mu}\ dy \leq e^{-x/\mu}e^{px/\mu},$$

$$\alpha p/\mu \int_{[x,\infty[} e^{-qy/\mu}\ dy \leq e^{-qx/\mu}, \quad \alpha p/q\ e^{-qx/\mu} \leq e^{-qx/\mu}.$$

by (42). Hence, we can take $\alpha=q/p=1/\eta$. Then $\alpha/(1+\alpha)=1/(1+\eta)=q$ and (44) becomes $qe^{-\rho x}\leq\Psi(x)$. The lower bound equals the exact value in this case.

7.4.4. A General Lower Bound for Ψ

Theorem 13

In the classical risk model,

$$\mathbf{(1-G)_{/(\eta+1-G)}} \leq \Psi. \tag{45}$$

Proof

For x fixed in $\mathbf{R}_+$, we take $U^\sim \equiv c$ on [0,x]. Then

$$Err(y) = p + qcG(y) - c = p - c[1-qG(y)] \quad (0 \leq y \leq x).$$

Let

$$c := p[1-qG(x)]^{-1}.$$

Then Err(x)=0 and Err≤0 on [0,x] because Err is increasing on that interval. Hence,

$$U(x) \leq p[1-qG(x)]^{-1} \tag{46}$$

by Th.10.Cor 1 This is true for all x. Then

$$U \leq p_{/(1-qG)}\,,\ \Psi \geq 1 - p_{/(1-qG)} = (1-p-qG)_{/(1-qG)} = q(1-G)_{/(1-qG)} \quad \bullet$$

Example: A Pareto case

We here consider the Pareto claimsize distribution defined by

$$F = 0 \text{ on } [0,1[\ ,\ F(x) = 1-x^{-1-\alpha} \quad (x \geq 1), \tag{47}$$

where $\alpha>0$. Then $\mu=(1+\alpha)/\alpha$ and

$$G(x) = \alpha_{/(1+\alpha)}\, x \quad (0 \leq x < 1),$$

$$G(x) = 1 - 1_{/(1+\alpha)}\, x^{-\alpha} \quad (x \geq 1). \tag{48}$$

For r>0, we take

$$\Psi^\sim(x) := q\, g(rx) \quad (x \in \mathbf{R}_+)\,, \tag{49}$$

where $g:=1-G$. For the particular values $\alpha:=0.5$, $\eta:= 0.3$, $r:=0.044$ it is verified numerically that Err≥0 on $\mathbf{R}_+$. Then $\Psi(x) \leq qg(rx)$ by Th.10.Cor.1.

Explicitly,

$$[1+0.45\,x^{1/2}]^{-1} \leq \Psi(x) \leq 1.1\,[0.45\,x^{1/2}]^{-1} \quad (x \geq 23), \tag{50}$$

where the lower bound results from (45). The condition $x \geq 23$ is not necessary for this lower bound. It is the condition $rx \geq 1$, coming from the fact that g has different analytic expressions on $[0,1[$ and on $[1,\infty[$.

7.4.5. Bounds for the Adjustment Coefficient

Theorem 14

In the classical risk model,

$$\boldsymbol{\rho \leq 2\eta\mu/\mu_2}. \tag{51}$$

If the claimsize distribution F is concentrated on the bounded interval [0,b], then

$$\boldsymbol{1/_b \log(1+\eta) \leq \rho}. \tag{52}$$

Proof

We integrate the inequality

$$q(1+\rho x) \leq qe^{\rho x} \; (x \in \mathbf{R}_+)$$

with respect to G(x) on $[0,\infty[$:

$$q(1+\rho\,\mu_1(G)) = \int_{[0,\infty[} q(1+\rho x)dG(x) \leq q\int_{[0,\infty[} e^{\rho x}\,dG(x) = 1,$$

The last equality results from the definition of ρ. In the first member, $\mu_1(G) = \mu_{2/2\mu}$ by Ch.3.Th.1.c. This implies (51).

For (52), we integrate the inequality

$$qe^{\rho x} \leq qe^{\rho b} \quad (0 \leq x \leq b)$$

with respect to G(x) on [0,b]:

$$1 = q\int_{[0,b]} e^{\rho x}\,dG(x) \leq qe^{\rho b}, \quad 1+\eta = 1/q \leq e^{\rho b}, \quad \log(1+\eta) \leq \rho b \;\bullet$$

7.5. Properties of U

7.5.1. Density of U

Theorem 15

In the classical risk model:

a. G(0)=0 and G has the density

$$G' = {}^{1}\!/_{\mu}\,(1-F) \quad \text{on } \mathbf{R}_+. \tag{53}$$

b. U(0)=p and U has the density

$$U' = {}^{q}\!/_{\mu}\,(1-F)*U \quad \text{on } \mathbf{R}_+. \tag{54}$$

c. If F has the density F′ on the interval J=[a,b[or J=[a,∞[in $\mathbf{R}_+$, then U′ has the density

$$U'' = {}^{q^2}\!/_{\mu^2}\,(1-F)^{*2}*U - {}^{pq}\!/_{\mu}\,F' \quad \text{on } \mathbf{J}. \tag{55}$$

Proof
We employ the notation $r := q/\mu$ in this proof.

a. Results from the definition of the concave transform.

b. From the renewal equation $U=p+qU*G$, taken at 0, results that

$$U(0) = p + q\,U(0).G(0) = p,$$

because convolution products are usual products at 0.

From a, the renewal equation $U=p+qU*G$ and the density Theorem for renewal equations (Ch.1.Th.15) results that U has a density U′ on $\mathbf{R}_+$ satisfying the renewal equation

$$U' = qU(0)G' + qU'*G \;\;,\;\; U' = rp(1-F) + qU'*G.$$

By (19), the solution of the latter equation is.

$$U' = rp(1-F)*\sum_{k\geq 0} q^k G^{*k} = r(1-F)*U.$$

c. Let F have the density F′ on J. By the density Theorem for convolutions (Ch.1.Th.12) and by (54) displayed as U′=rU–rU*F, U′ has the density

$$U'' = rU' - rU(0)F' - rU'*F \text{ on } J.$$

Hence, by b,

$$U'' = rU'*(1-F) - rpF' = r^2(1-F)^{*2}*U - rpF' \quad \text{on } J \quad \bullet$$

7.5.2. First Moment of U

Theorem 16

In the classical risk model, the first moment of the probability distribution function U equals

$$\mu_1(U) = 1/\eta\ \mu_1(G) = \mu_2/(2\eta\mu). \tag{56}$$

Proof

From the renewal equation U=p+qU*G follows p(1–U)=q(1–G)*U. We take the convolution product by the identity function I on $\mathbf{R}_+$:

$$p[(1-U)*I] = qU*[(1-G)*I]$$

We take this relation at point x, and we let x↑∞. The functions in square brackets are distribution functions on $\mathbf{R}_+$. By the factorization Theorem of the convolution product at ∞ (Ch.1.Th.11) we obtain

$$p[(1-U)*I](\infty) = qU(\infty).[(1-G)*I](\infty),$$

i.e.

$$p\ \mu_1(U) = q\ \mu_1(G)$$

by the surface interpretation of the first moment. This proves the first equality (56). The second equality results from Ch.3.Th.1.c •

Remark

It is not assumed in the statement or proof of the relation (56), that μ_2 is finite.

7.5.3. Comparison of U-Curves

We here consider the claimsize distributions F^1 and F^2. We assume that $\mu^1=\mu^2$, $\mu^1_2=\mu^2_2<\infty$. Then $\mu_1(U^1)=\mu_1(U^2)$ by the foregoing Theorem. By the surface interpretation of the first moment,

$$\int_{[0,\infty[} [U^1(x)-U^2(x)]dx = 0. \tag{57}$$

The latter relation implies that the total surface between the graphs of U^1 and U^2 on the set where $U^1\leq U^2$ equals the total surface between the graphs on the set where $U^2\leq U^1$. The increasing curves U^1 and U^2 coincide at 0 and at $+\infty$:

$$U^1(0) = p = U^2(0) \ , \ U^1(\infty) = 1 = U^2(\infty).$$

This suggests that the curves U^1 and U^2 must be close to each other.

7.6. Asymptotic Values in Regular Case

7.6.1. Definition of the Regular Case

The classical risk model is regular if the couple (G,q) has an adjustment coefficient ρ such that

$$\int_{[0,\infty[} e^{(\rho+\varepsilon)x}\, dG(x) < \infty, \tag{58}$$

for some $\varepsilon>0$.

If the couple (G,q) has an adjustment coefficient, then the couple corresponding to a small modification of η, still has an adjustment coefficient in all practical cases. Hence, in practice, (58) is satisfied if ρ exists.

We recall the definition

$$[f(x) \sim g(x) \text{ as } x\uparrow\infty] \ :\Leftrightarrow [\lim_{x\uparrow\infty} f(x)/g(x) = 1]. \tag{59}$$

7.6.2. Cramér's Asymptotic Formula

Theorem 17 **(Cramér's Asymptotic Formula)**

In the regular classical risk model,

$$\Psi(x) \sim \alpha\, e^{-\rho x} \text{ as } x\uparrow\infty, \tag{60}$$

where

$$\alpha := \eta\mu/\beta, \tag{61}$$

$$\beta := \rho\mu\int_{[0,\infty[} x e^{\rho x} dG(x) = \rho\int_{[0,\infty[} x(1-F(x))e^{\rho x}\, dx. \tag{62}$$

Proof (main part)

We here admit that Ch.1.Th.17 can be applied to the renewal equation (23) for Ψ_e. Then

$$\Psi_e(\infty) = [\mu_1(G_e)]^{-1} \int_{[0,\infty[} g_e(x)dx. \tag{63}$$

By (24), and by the definition of ρ,

$$\int_{[0,\infty[} g_e(x)dx = q\int_{[0,\infty[} (1-G(x))e^{\rho x}\, dx = q\eta/\rho. \tag{64}$$

By (21),

$$\mu_1(G_e) = \int_{[0,\infty[} x dG_e(x) = q \int_{[0,\infty[} x e^{\rho x}\, dG(x). \tag{65}$$

The latter integral is finite by the regularity assumption because $xe^{\rho x}<e^{(\rho+\varepsilon)x}$, for all x larger than some constant. By (65) and by the definition of the concave transform G,

$$\mu.\mu_1(G_e) = q \int_{[0,\infty[} x(1-F(x))e^{\rho x}\, dx. \tag{66}$$

By (63), (64), (65), (66), $\Psi_e(\infty)=\alpha$, where α is defined by (61) and β by (62). By (22), this relation $\Psi_e(\infty)=\alpha$ is equivalent to (60) •

The complete proof

For the complete proof, we apply the Key Renewal App.A.Th.A4.a to the renewal equation (23) for Ψ_e . It says that (63) holds under the following conditions C1–C5. See the *Usual Assumptions* of App.A.A4.

C1. $G_e(0)=0$.

C2. G_e has a density G_e'.

C3. $\mu_1(G_e) < \infty$.

C4. G_e' is dominated by a continuous decreasing Lebesgue-integrable function g_0.

C5. g_e is directly Riemann-integrable.

Property C1 results from the definition (21) of G_e.

By Th.15.a, by the definition of G and G_e and by the density Theorem for integrals, $G_e(0)=0$ and G_e has the density

$$G_e' = r(1-F(x))e^{\rho x} \text{ on } \mathbf{R}_+, \text{ where } r=q/\mu.$$

Hence, the conditions C1 and C_2 are satisfied.

C3 results from the main part of the proof.

We now prove (C4). Let $\varepsilon>0$ be such that (58) holds. Then, if $x\geq 0$,

$$e^{(\rho+\varepsilon)x}(1-F(x)) = e^{(\rho+\varepsilon)x}\int_{]x,\infty[} dF(y)$$

$$\leq \int_{]x,\infty[} e^{(\rho+\varepsilon)y}\, dF(y) \leq \int_{]0,\infty[} e^{(\rho+\varepsilon)y}\, dF(y) = -\int_{]0,\infty[} e^{(\rho+\varepsilon)y}\, d(1-F(y))$$

$$= 1-F(0) + (\rho+\varepsilon)\int_{]0,\infty[} e^{(\rho+\varepsilon)y}\,(1-F(y))dy$$

$$= 1-F(0) + (\rho+\varepsilon)\mu \int_{]0,\infty[} e^{(\rho+\varepsilon)y}\, dG(y) =: a < \infty,$$

where we integrated by parts. Hence,

$$G_e'(x) = r(1-F(x))e^{\rho x} \leq rae^{-\varepsilon x} \ (x\geq 0).$$

This proves C4 for $g_0(x) := rae^{-\varepsilon x}$ $(x\geq 0)$.

Finally, we prove C5. The function g_e is continuous. It is Lebesgue-integrable by (64). By App.A.Th.A2.c, it is enough to verify the sup-condition of the direct integrability. Let $\delta>0$. We notice that

$$[1-G(n\delta+\delta)]e^{\rho n\delta} \leq [1-G(x)]e^{\rho x} \leq [1-G(n\delta)]e^{\rho(n\delta+\delta)} =: s_n \ (n\delta\leq x<n\delta+\delta).$$

It is enough to verify that $\sum s_n<\infty$.

$$\delta\sum_{k\geq 1} s_n = \delta\sum_{n\geq 0}[1-G(n\delta+\delta)]e^{\rho(n\delta+2\delta)} = \delta e^{2\rho\delta}\sum_{n\geq 0}[1-G(n\delta+\delta)]e^{\rho n\delta}$$

$$\leq e^{2\rho\delta}\sum_{n\geq 0}\int_{[n\delta,n\delta+\delta[}[1-G(x)]e^{\rho x}dx = e^{2\rho\delta}\int_{[0,\infty[}[1-G(x)]e^{\rho x}dx < \infty,$$

by (64) •

Example: Exponential case

In the exponential case, **Cramér's asymptotic value** $\alpha\, e^{-\rho x}$, furnished by (60) coincides with the exact value $qe^{-\rho x}$, by a direct calculation.

7.6.3. Asymptotic Value for U′(x) (x↑∞)

Theorem 18 (Asymptotic Value for U′(x))

In the regular classical model,

$$U'(x) \sim \alpha\rho\, e^{-\rho x} \text{ as } x\uparrow\infty, \tag{67}$$

where the constant α is the same as in the preceding Theorem 17.

Proof (main part)
We consider the renewal equation

$$U' = r\rho(1-F) + qU'{*}G, \text{ where } r:=q/\mu, \tag{68}$$

obtained during the proof of Th.15.b. We apply the exponential transformation defined in Ch.1.5.3 to that equation. The distribution function G_e is still defined by (21).

$$V(x) := U'(x)e^{\rho x}\ ,\ h(x) := r\rho(1-F(x))e^{\rho x}\ (x\in\mathbf{R}_+).$$

Then

$$V = h + V{*}G_e\ . \tag{69}$$

We admit that Ch.1.Th.17 can be applied to that equation. Then

$$V(\infty) = [\mu_1(G_e)]^{-1} \int_{[0,\infty[} h(x)dx \tag{70}$$

The integral in the last member equals

$$\int_{[0,\infty[} h(x)dx = r\rho \int_{[0,\infty[} (1-F(x))e^{\rho x}\, dx = p, \tag{71}$$

by the definition of ρ. The value of $\mu_1(G_\varepsilon)$ is furnished by (65). Then (67) results from (70) •

The complete proof

The complete proof is similar to the complete proof of Theorem 17. Now C5 must be replaced by the direct Riemann-integrability of the function h. It is enough to replace G par F in the last part of the foregoing complete proof •

Extensions

The formal differentiation of (60) with respect to x, i.e. the differentiation according to the usual elementary rules, without paying attention to their validity, furnishes the exact sentence

$$\Psi'(x) \sim -\alpha\rho\, e^{-\rho x} \text{ as } x\uparrow\infty. \tag{72}$$

The proposition is right by the foregoing Theorem, and because $\Psi=1-U$.

Let us assume that F has the density F' on $\mathbf{R}_+$. A F-mass at 0 must not be excluded. Then it results from the density Theorem for renewal equations that U' has a density U'' on $\mathbf{R}_+$, solution of the renewal equation obtained by formal differentiation of renewal equation (68). Then the exponential transformation can be applied to the renewal equation for U'' and then the Key Renewal Theorem applies to the renewal equation obtained in this way. It appears that

$$U''(x) \sim -\alpha\rho^2 e^{-\rho x} \text{ as } x\uparrow\infty. \tag{73}$$

This means that the formal differentiation of (67) again furnishes the correct proposition, and so on for higher order derivatives of U.

7.6.4. Cramér's Asymptotic Value in Practice

Let $\Psi_{CR}(x):=\alpha e^{-\rho x}$ be Cramér's asymptotic value for $\Psi(x)$ furnished by (60), and let ε be a small strictly positive quantity (such that events of probability less than ε are neglected in practice).

The asymptotic value $\Psi_{CR}(x)$ is close to $\Psi(x)$ if x is large enough. But when is x large enough ? The following **pragmatic rule** is adopted in practice:

If $\Psi_{CR}(x) \le \varepsilon$, then x is large enough, and then $\Psi_{CR}(x)$ is close to $\Psi(x)$. (74)

Numerical tests based on the exact values, show that **this is a safe rule**.

7.7. Asymptotic Values in Sub-Exponential Case

7.7.1. Sub-Exponential Distribution Functions

In this section 7.7,

$$g := 1-G. \tag{75}$$

A **sub-exponential distribution function** is a probability distribution function G on $\mathbf{R}_+$ such that G<1 on $\mathbf{R}_+$ and such that the following equivalent conditions are satisfied.

$$\lim_{x\uparrow\infty} [1-G^{*2}(x)]/g(x) = 2, \tag{76}$$

$$\lim_{x\uparrow\infty} [G(x)-G^{*2}(x)]/g(x) = 1, \tag{77}$$

$$\lim_{x\uparrow\infty} [G^2(x)-G^{*2}(x)]/g(x) = 0, \tag{78}$$

$$\lim_{x\uparrow\infty} g^{*2}(x)/g(x) = 0. \tag{79}$$

By the condition G<1, distributions concentrated on a bounded interval cannot be sub-exponential. By the properties of sub-exponential distributions mentioned in 7.7.3, such distributions are heavy-tailed. The foregoing definition applies to any probability distribution function G on $\mathbf{R}_+$, not only to the concave transform G of F in the classical risk model.

7.7.2. Asymptotic Value of Ruin Probability

Theorem 19 (Chistyakov)

Let G be sub-exponential. Then

$$\lim_{x\uparrow\infty} g(x\text{-}a)/g(x) = 1 \quad (a\in\mathbf{R}). \tag{80}$$

Proof

$$G^2(x)-G^{*2}(x) = \int_{[0,x]} [G(x)-G(x-y)]dG(y)$$

$$\geq \int_{]a,x]} [G(x)-G(x-y)]dG(y)$$

$$\geq \int_{]a,x]} [G(x)-G(x-a)]dG(y)$$

$$= [G(x)-G(x-a)][G(x)-G(a)]$$

$$= [g(x-a)-g(x)][G(x)-G(a)] \quad (0<x<a).$$

Then

$$0 \le [g(x-a)-g(x)]/g(x) \le [[G^2(x)-G^{*2}(x)]/g(x)].[G(x)-G(a)]^{-1}.$$

As $x\uparrow\infty$ in the latter relations, we obtain (80), by (78) •

Theorem 20 (Athreya & Ney)

Let G be sub-exponential in the classical risk model. Then

$$\Psi(x) \sim 1/_{\eta}\, g(x) \quad \text{as } x\uparrow\infty. \tag{81}$$

Proof

Let $\varepsilon>0$. We apply the results of 7.4.1. We consider the approximation

$$\Psi^{\sim} := (1+\varepsilon)/_{\eta}\, g$$

of Ψ.

$$Err = p\Psi^{\sim} - qg + q\Psi^{\sim}*g = [\eta(1+\eta)]^{-1}g.[\varepsilon\eta+(1+\varepsilon)(g^{*2}/g)].$$

We take the last factor, in square brackets, at the point x and we let $x\uparrow\infty$. By (79), we obtain the strictly positive value $\varepsilon\eta$. This implies that $a>0$ exists, such that $Err>0$ on $[a,\infty[$. Then (38) is applicable, because Err is bounded on $[0,a]$. Hence, a number r, not depending on x, does exist in $]0,1[$, such that

$$\Psi(x) \le r\Psi^{\sim}(x) + s\Psi(x-a) \quad (x\ge a), \tag{82}$$

where $s:=1-r\in]0,1[$. By (80), we can fix $a'>a$, such that

$$s(1+\varepsilon)\Psi^{\sim}(x-a) \le (s+\varepsilon)\Psi^{\sim}(x) \quad (x>a').$$

Let $\varphi:=\Psi/\Psi^{\sim}$. Then, dividing (82) by $\Psi^{\sim}(x)$, and using the relation

$$\Psi(x-a)/\Psi^{\sim}(x) = \varphi(x-a).\Psi^{\sim}(x-a)/\Psi^{\sim}(x),$$

we obtain

$$\varphi(x) \le r + t\varphi(x-a) \quad (x>a'), \tag{83}$$

where $t:=(s+\varepsilon)/(1+\varepsilon)\in]0,1[$. By successive applications of (83), we have

$$\varphi(x) \le r[1+t+t^2+...+t^{n(x)-1}] + t^{n(x)}\,\varphi[x-an(x)],$$

where n(x) is the first integer such that $x-an(x)\in[0,a']$. Let b be the sup of φ on $[0,a']$ and let $a''>a'$ be such that $bt^{n(a'')}\le\varepsilon$. This is possible because $t\in]0,1[$ and because $n(x)\uparrow\infty$ as $x\uparrow\infty$. Then, for all $x>a''$,

$$\varphi(x) \le r_{/(1-t)} + t^{n(x)}\,\varphi[x-an(x)] \le r_{/(1-t)} + t^{n(a'')}\,b \le (1+\varepsilon)+\varepsilon = 1+2\varepsilon.$$

Then

$$[\eta+g(x)]^{-1} \le \Psi(x)/g(x) \le \eta^{-1}(1+\varepsilon)(1+2\varepsilon) \quad (x>a''),$$

where the first inequality is (45). Letting $x\uparrow\infty$, then $\varepsilon\downarrow 0$, we obtain

$$\lim\sup_{x\uparrow\infty}\,[\Psi(x)/g(x)] = \eta^{-1}.$$

and similarly with lim inf. •

7.7.3. Properties of Sub-Exponential Distributions

Theorem 21

Let G be sub-exponential. No constants α and $r>0$ can exist, such that

$$\mathbf{g(x) \le \alpha e^{-rx} \quad (x\in R_+)} \tag{84}$$

or such that

$$\mathbf{\Psi(x) \le \alpha e^{-rx} \quad (x\in R_+).} \tag{85}$$

No couple (G,q) can have an adjustment coefficient.

Proof

We assume (84) and we prove that this leads to a contradiction. Let $\varepsilon>0$ be such that $(1+\varepsilon)e^{-r}<1$. By (80), $a>0$ exists, such that

$$g(x) \le (1+\varepsilon)g(1+x) \quad (x\ge a).$$

Then, for all $n\ge 0$,

$$\alpha e^{-r(n+a)} \ge g(n+a) \ge (1+\varepsilon)^{-1}g(n-1+a) \ge ... \ge (1+\varepsilon)^{-n}g(a).$$

Then

$$g(a) \le \alpha[(1+\varepsilon)e^{-r}]^n\, e^{-ra} \to 0 \quad \text{as } n\uparrow\infty$$

and $g(a)=0$. This is a contradiction because $G<1$ on $\mathbf{R}_+$.

The relation (85) is impossible, because it implies some inequality (84) by Theorem 20.

The existence of the adjustment coefficient is impossible, because it implies some inequality (85), namely Lundberg's exponential inequality •

The following Theorem shows that **sub-exponentiality is a tail-property**.

Theorem 22

Let G and G_1 be probability distribution functions on R_+ such that $G<1$, $G_1<1$ on R_+ and $G=G_1$ on some interval $[a,\infty[$ where $a\geq 0$. Then G and G_1 are both sub-exponential or both not sub-exponential.

Proof

We suppose that G_1 is sub-exponential. By symmetry, it is sufficient to prove that G is sub-exponential. G_1 has the property expressed by Theorem 19, and then G also has this property because G and G_1 do have the same tail. For $x>a$:

$$0 \leq G^2(x)-G^{*2}(x) = [\int_{[0,a]}+\int_{]a,x[}][G(x)-G(x-y)]dG(y)$$

$$\leq [G(x)-G(x-a)]G(a) + \int_{]a,x]}[G(x)-G(x-y)]dG(y)$$

$$= [G(x)-G(x-a)]G(a) + \int_{]a,x]}[G_1(x)-G_1(x-y)]dG_1(y)$$

$$\leq [G(x)-G(x-a)]G(a) + \int_{[0,x]}[G_1(x)-G_1(x-y)]dG_1(y)$$

$$= [G(x)-G(x-a)]G(a) + [G_1^2(x)-G_1^{*2}(x)].$$

We divide by $g(x)=g_1(x)$ $(x>a)$ and we let $x\uparrow\infty$. Then the sub-exponentiality of G follows from that of G_1 by (78) •

Theorem 23

The probability distribution function $G<1$ on R_+ is sub-exponential if the limit

$$\varphi(r) := \lim_{x\uparrow\infty} g(rx)/g(x) \quad (0<r\leq 1) \tag{86}$$

exists and if the function φ is left-continuous at the point $r=1$.

Proof

Let us assume that G has the indicated properties. Then, for all $\alpha,\beta\in]0,1]$,

$$\lim_{x\uparrow\infty} [G(\alpha x)-G(\beta x)]/g(x) = \lim_{x\uparrow\infty}[g(\beta x)-g(\alpha x)]/g(x) = \varphi(\beta)-\varphi(\alpha).$$

Then, for all $r\in]0,1/2[$, $s:=1-r$, $x>0$,

$$0 \le G^2(x)-G^{*2}(x) = [\int_{[0,rx]}+\int_{]rx,sx]}+\int_{]sx,x]}][G(x)-G(x-y)]dG(y)$$

$$\le [G(x)-G(sx)]G(rx) + [G(x)-G(rx)][G(sx)-G(rx)] + G(x)[G(x)-G(sx)].$$

We divide by g(x), and we let $x\uparrow\infty$:

$$0 \le \limsup_{x\uparrow\infty} [G^2(x)-G^{*2}(x)]/g(x)$$

$$\le [\varphi(s)-\varphi(1)]+0+[\varphi(s)-\varphi(1)] =2[\varphi(s)-1].$$

Now we let $r\downarrow 0$, i.e. $s\uparrow 1$. Then the Theorem follows from the assumptions and from (78) •

Example: Pareto case

We consider the Pareto claimsize distribution F defined by (47), and the corresponding concave transform G expressed by (48). By Theorem 23, G is sub-exponential. By Theorem 20,

$$\Psi(x) \sim {}^{1}/_{\eta(1+\alpha)}\, x^{-\alpha} \text{ as } x\uparrow\infty. \tag{87}$$

7.7.4. Dangerous Asymptotic Values

In the classical risk model, let G be sub-exponential. Let $\Psi_{AN}(x):={}^{1}/_{\eta}g(x)$ be the asymptotic value of $\Psi(x)$ furnished by (81). Let ε be a strictly positive small quantity. The pragmatic rule corresponding to (74) is

$$\text{If } \Psi_{AN}(x) \le \varepsilon, \text{ then } \Psi_{AN}(x) \text{ is close to } \Psi(x). \tag{88}$$

The following example shows that **this can be a dangerous rule**.

Let the claimsize distribution F be the Pareto defined by (47) for $\alpha=3$. Let $x=12$, $\eta=0.1$. Then $\Psi_{AN}(12)=0.0014$ and the business seems to be safe according to the rule (88).

This conclusion is misleading. Indeed, Let

$$F^{\sim}(x) := 1-e^{-2x} \ (x\in\mathbf{R}_+).$$

Then $G\leq G^{\sim}$ and then $\Psi^{\sim}\leq\Psi$ by Th.4.Cor.c. Then $0.10=\Psi^{\sim}(12)\leq\Psi(12)$ by (26). The probability of ruin is 0.10 at least, and not about 0.0014.

Hence, (88) must be applied with care. Preliminary numerical investigations must learn for what classes of sub-exponential distributions G, the pragmatic rule (88) is safe.

7.8. Exponential Approximations

7.8.1. Case of a Small Security Loading η

The compound geometric distribution U_p in Ch.5.Th.4, is the non-ruin distribution function of the classical risk model. Hence, we can use the approximation Ch.5.(60). In the latter formula, μ_1, μ_2 are the moments of G, not of F.

The general relation between the moments of F, and those of its concave transform G is

$$(n+1)\mu_1(F).\mu_n(G) = \mu_{n+1}(F) \ \ (n\geq 1), \tag{89}$$

where the involved moments, except $\mu_1(F)$, may be infinite. Indeed,

$$\mu_n(F) = \int_{]0,\infty[} x^n \, dF(x)$$
$$= -\int_{]0,\infty[} x^n d(1-F(x)) = n\int_{[0,\infty[} (1-F(x))x^{n-1} \, dx$$

by an integration by parts. Then, by the definition of G,

$$(n+1)\mu_1(F).\mu_n(G) = (n+1)\mu_1(F) \int_{[0,\infty[} x^n \, dG(x)$$
$$= (n+1)\int_{[0,\infty[} x^n(1-F(x))dx = \mu_{n+1}(F).$$

Expressed with the moments $\mu \equiv \mu_1$, μ_2, μ_3 of F, Ch.5.(60) becomes

$$\Psi(x) \approx \exp[-1 - (2\eta\mu x - \mu_2)(\mu_2^2 + 4/3\,\eta\mu\mu_3)^{-1/2}] \quad (x \in \mathbf{R}_+, \eta \text{ small}). \qquad (90)$$

7.8.2. A General Approximation

Definition of the approximation

We here consider two classical risk models. The first is the **current model** for which the usual notations are used. In particular, F is the distribution function of any partial claim amount X, and $\mu_k := \mu_k(F)$ (k=1,2,..).

The second model, which we call the **exponential model**, is the classical model with the new security loading η', and the exponential claimsize distribution function

$$F_{\mu'}(x) = q' e^{-p'x/\mu'} \quad (x \in \mathbf{R}_+), \quad \text{where } p' := \eta'/(1+\eta'),\; q' := 1/(1+\eta').$$

In the exponential model, we adopt the usual notations, completed by an accent (never representing a derivative). In particular

$$\mu_k' := \mu_k(F_{\mu'}) \quad (k=1,2,...) \quad , \quad \mu' \equiv \mu_1'.$$

We assume that the claim number process of the exponential model is the Poisson process with the new intensity λ'. The initial risk reserve x is the same in the current model and in the exponential one.

The distributions involved in the exponential model depend on the 3 parameters λ', μ', η'. We will show that they can be specified in such a way that, for all $t \geq 0$, the risk reserve R_t' of the exponential model, has the same moments of order 1,2,3 as the risk reserve R_t of the current model:

$$ER_t^k = ER_t'^k \quad (t \geq 0;\ k=1,2,3). \qquad (91)$$

Then the ruin probability $\Psi'(x)$, calculated in the exponential model, is considered an approximation of the corresponding ruin probability $\Psi(x)$ calculated in the current model:

$$\Psi(x) \approx \Psi'(x) = q' e^{-p'x/\mu'} \quad (x \in \mathbf{R}_+). \qquad (92)$$

As in the case of asymptotic estimates, confidence in approximations can only be acquired via numerical tests. The approximations furnished by (92) are excellent in practice.

Moment Identification

We assume that the moments μ , μ_2 , μ_3 are finite. The characteristic function of the partial claim amount X has the asymptotic expansion,

$$Ee^{i\tau X} \equiv \varphi(\tau) = 1 + i\tau\mu - \tau^2\mu_2/2 - i\tau^3\mu_3/6 + \dots$$

(see Ch.3.2.3). Here the dots represent a term $\tau^3 o(\tau)$ as $\tau\to 0$.

By Ch.3.Th.5.e, the characteristic function of the total claim amount S_t equals

$$Ee^{itS_t} \equiv \varphi_t(\tau) = e^{-\lambda t+\lambda t\varphi(\tau)},$$

where $\varphi\equiv\varphi_F$ is the characteristic function of F. Then the characteristic function of the risk reserve

$$R_t := x+\mu\lambda t(1+\eta)-S_t$$

equals

$$E\exp(i\tau R_t) = \exp[i\tau x+i\tau\mu\lambda t(1+\eta)]\, E\, e^{-i\tau S_t} = \exp[i\tau x+i\tau\mu\lambda t(1+\eta)]\, \varphi_t(-\tau)$$

$$= \exp[i\tau x+i\tau\mu\lambda t(1+\eta)].\ \exp(-\lambda t).\ \exp[\lambda t(1-i\tau\mu-\tau^2\mu_2/2 +i\tau^3\mu_3/6 + \dots)]$$

$$= \exp[i\tau x + i\tau\mu\lambda t\eta - \tau^2\lambda t\mu_2/2 + i\tau^3\lambda t\mu_3/6 + \dots]. \qquad (93)$$

In the exponential model, this becomes

$$E\exp(i\tau R_t') = \exp[i\tau x + i\tau\mu'\lambda' t\eta' - \tau^2\lambda' t\mu_2'/2 + i\tau^3\lambda' t\mu_3'/6 + \dots]$$

$$= \exp[i\tau x + i\tau\mu'\lambda' t\eta' - \tau^2\lambda' t(2\mu'^2)/2 + i\tau^3\lambda' t(6\mu'^3)/6 + \dots], \qquad (94)$$

because

$$\mu_2' = 2\mu'^2 \quad , \quad \mu_3' = 6\mu'^3.$$

We can develop the exponential in (93) and then compare with the development

$$E\exp(i\tau R_t) = 1+i\tau\mu_1(R_t)-\tau^2\mu_2(R_t)/2-i\tau^3\mu_3(R_t)/6+\dots$$

This furnishes the moments $\mu_k(R_t)$ (k=1,2,3) as functions of λ, η, μ, μ_2, μ_3. We can proceed in the same way with (94) and then explicit (91). But clearly, it amounts to the same, to identify directly the coefficients of τ, τ^2, τ^3, resp. in the last member of (93) and (94), without first developing the exponentials.

Approximation

$$\mu\lambda\eta = \mu'\lambda'\eta' \ , \ \lambda\mu_2 = 2\lambda'\mu'^2 \ , \ \lambda\mu_3 = 6\lambda'\mu'^3,$$

by (91). Then

$$\Psi(x) \approx q' e^{-p'x/\mu'} \quad (x \in \mathbf{R}_+) \tag{95}$$

with

$$\mu' = \mu_3/(3\mu_2) \ , \ \eta' = 2\mu\mu_3\eta/(3\mu_2^2).$$

The parameter $\lambda' = 9\mu_2^3\lambda/(2\mu_3^2)$ does not occur in (95). The advantage of the approximations (90) and (95) is that only the 3 first moments of F are needed.

7.9. Numerical Ruin Probabilities

7.9.1. Numerical Algorithm for the Calculation of U(x)

Let Y, Z be independent random variables with distribution function G, U resp. Then the renewal equation $U=p+qU*G$ is identical to the relation

$$P(Z \le x) = p + q\,P(Y+Z \le x) \quad (x \in \mathbf{R}_+). \tag{96}$$

In order to calculate U numerically, we first perform a discretization on G. That means that we take a small span $\delta>0$, and that we replace G by a probability distribution G_δ concentrated on the set $\{0,\delta,2\delta,3\delta,...\}$. Then we consider the solution U_δ of the renewal equation

$$U_\delta = p + qU_\delta * G_\delta.$$

Its convolution power series expansion is

$$U_\delta = p \sum_{k\ge 0} q^k G_\delta^{*k}.$$

Comparing with the corresponding expansion of U, we see that

$$G_\delta \le G \Rightarrow U_\delta \le U,$$

$$G_\delta \ge G \Rightarrow U_\delta \ge U.$$

Hence, we can obtain lower bounds for U, or upper bounds for U, according to the choice of G_δ . If we want U_δ to be close to U, we take G_δ close to G, for instance in such a way that G_δ and G do place the same probability mass on each interval [kh,(k+1)h[, and that moreover $\mu_1(G_\delta) = \mu_1(G)$.

Next, we adopt a new money unit, such that the amounts 0,δ,2δ,... expressed in the old money, become the amounts 0,1,2,..., in the new money. This implies the replacement of G_δ by the corresponding distribution function concentrated on the set {0,1,2,...}.

In the next Theorem, in order to avoid the introduction of more notations, we assume that G is already concentrated on the set {0,1,2...}. Then the random variable Y introduced in the beginning of the discussion can only take the values 0,1,2,... and it will appear that the solution U of the renewal equation U=p+qU*G is also a distribution concentrated on the set {0,1,2,...}. Hence also Z can only take the values 0,1,2,..., and then (96) can be replaced by the relation

$$P(Z \leq k) = p + q\, P(Y+Z \leq k) \quad (k=0,1,2,...). \tag{97}$$

Theorem 24

Let G be concentrated on the set {0,1,2,...}, with probability mass

$$g_k := G(k)-G(k-) \quad (k=0,1,2,...)$$

at the point k. Then the solution U of the renewal equation U=p+qU*G is a distribution concentrated on the set {0,1,2,...}, with probability mass u_k at the point k, resulting from the recurrent relations

$$\begin{aligned} u_0 &= (1-qg_0)^{-1}\, p, \\ u_{k+1} &= (1-qg_0)^{-1}\, q \sum_{1\leq j\leq k+1} g_j u_{k+1-j} \quad (k=0,1,2,...). \end{aligned} \tag{98}$$

Then

$$U(k) = u_0+u_1+...+u_k \quad (k=0,1,2,...). \tag{99}$$

Proof

$$u_0 = P(Z=0) = p+qP(Y+Z=0) = p+qP(Y=0)P(Z=0) = p+qg_0u_0\,,$$

by (97) for k=0. From this results the first relation (98).

From the difference of (97) with the values k+1 and k results that

$$P(Z=k+1) = qP(Y+Z=k+1),$$

$$u_{k+1} = P(Z=k+1) = q\sum_{0\le j\le k+1} P(Y=j,Z=k+1-j) = q\sum_{0\le j\le k+1} P(Y=j)P(Z=k+1-j)$$

$$= q\sum_{0\le j\le k+1} g_j u_{k+1-j} = qg_0 u_{k+1} + q\sum_{1\le j\le k+1} g_j u_{k+1-j}.$$

This implies the last relations (98) •

7.9.2. Connexion with the Panjer Recursions

The basic Theorem 2 of Ch.5 furnishes an algorithm for the numerical calculation of the compound distribution

$$H = \sum_{k\ge 0} p_k F^{*k} \ , \ \text{instead of} \ U = \sum_{k\ge 0} pq^k G^{*k}.$$

The relations (98) result from the relations Ch.5.(23),(24) after the replacement of

$$p_k \ , \ f_k \ , \ h_k \ , \ a \ , \ b$$

by

$$pq^k \ , \ g_k \ , \ u_k \ , \ q \ , \ q$$

resp. See Ch.5.(13).

Chapter 8

Explicit Infinite-Time Ruin Probabilities in Classical Risk Model

8.0. Introduction

We show how explicit analytic infinite-time ruin probabilities can be obtained when the claimsize distribution function $F(x)$ ($x \in \mathbf{R}_+$) is a sum of products of the following functions:

polynomials $P(x)$,

exponential functions e^{ax}, e^{bx}, ...,

trigonometric functions $\sin(ax)$, $\sin(bx)$, ..., $\cos(ax)$, $\cos(bx)$,...

The exponential distribution function

$$F(x) = 1 - e^{-x} \quad (x \in \mathbf{R}_+)$$

considered in the foregoing Chapter, is a very particular case.

Explicit analytic infinite-time ruin probabilities can also be obtained for claimsize distributions concentrated on a bounded interval, with polynomial-exponential-trigonometric expression on that interval.

Power series $\sum_{k\geq 0} a_k x^k$ constitute an essential instrument of the theory of this Chapter. But only some familiarity with the main results of the theory is required. The properties used in the proofs are recalled in section 8.1.1.

The results of this Chapter are not used later in the book.

8.1. Very Regular Renewal Equations on $\mathbf{R}_+$

8.1.1. Power Series

In this Chapter, power series

$$\sum_{k\geq 0} a_k x^k, \tag{1}$$

with real coefficients a_0, a_1, a_2, ... are used.

The power series (1) can be considered with an unspecified variable x. Then, no convergence problems are involved, and the power series can be identified with the sequence $(a_0,a_1,a_2,...)$ of its coefficients. Power series with unspecified variable x are called **formal power series** by some authors.

The power series (1) can also be considered for real (or complex) values of x. **In this Chapter, only positive values of x are employed**. Then the value of the power series (1) is defined by

$$\sum_{k\geq 0} a_k x^k := \lim_{k\uparrow\infty} \sum_{0\leq j\leq k} a_j x^j, \tag{2}$$

if the limit in the last member exists. Hence, the power series (1) has a double meaning. The intended meaning must be obvious from the context.

The power series (1) converges at the point x if the limit (2) exists and if it is finite. **It diverges at the point x**, if the limit (2) does not exists, or if it exists but is infinite. **The power series (1) converges absolutely at the point x** if

$$\sum_{k\geq 0} |a_k| x^k < \infty. \tag{3}$$

The sum in the first member of (3), is meaningful in any case, but it may have the value $+\infty$. **If the power series (1) converges absolutely at the point x, then it converges at that point.**

The radius of convergence r of the power series (1) is the sup of the positive numbers $x\in\mathbf{R}_+$ such that (3) holds.

When $r=\infty$, then **the power series (1) converges absolutely for all $x\in\mathbf{R}_+$**. When $r=0$, then **the power series (1) converges at the point $x=0$ only**. When $0<r<\infty$, then **the power series (1) converges absolutely for $x<r$ and it diverges for $x>r$**. At the point $x=r$, the power series (1) may equally well converge as diverge.

We say that a **property** depending on $x \in \mathbf{R}_+$ **is true everywhere**, if it is true for all $x \in \mathbf{R}_+$. **The property is true near 0** if it is true for all x in some interval $[0,\varepsilon[$ $(\varepsilon>0)$.

The interesting power series are those converging near 0. A power series converges near zero, iff it converges absolutely near 0 and that is the case iff its radius of convergence is strictly positive.

To **calculate sums and products of power series "in the usual way"** means the following: At the first stage, x is treated as an unspecified variable and all terms ax^k with the same k, resulting from the sums and products, are grouped together. The result is a power series (1). Then the value, at the point $x \in \mathbf{R}_+$, is calculated by (2) if the limit exists.

We now recall some basic properties of power series.

a. The power series (1) converges on the interval $[0,c[$, iff it converges absolutely on $[0,c[$.

b. If the power series $\sum_{k\geq 0} a_k x^k$ and $\sum_{k\geq 0} b_k x^k$ converge near 0 and if the have the sam value near 0, then $a_k=b_k$ $(k=0,1,2,\ldots)$. (**Unicity of power series expansion**).

c. The differentiation of a power series converging on the interval $[0,c[$, may be performed termwise at each point $x \in [0,c[$, and then the derivative is a power series converging on $[0,c[$.

d. Sums and products of power series converging on the interval $[0,c[$, can be calculated in the usual way. The result is a power series converging on $[0,c[$.

e. If $f(x):=\sum_{k\geq 0} a_k x^k$ and $g(x):=\sum_{j\geq 0} b_j x^j$ are power series converging near 0, and if $|b_0|$ is strictly less than the radius of convergence of f(x), then the expression

$$f[g(x)] := \sum_{k\geq 0} a_k[\sum_{j\geq 0} b_j x^j]^k.$$

can be calculated in the usual way. The result is a power series converging near 0. (**Substitution of a power series in another power series**).

f. The radius of convergence r of the power series (1) satisfies the relation

$$1/r = \limsup_{k\uparrow\infty} |a_k|^{1/k}. \tag{4}$$

8.1.2. Very Regular Functions and Factorial Transforms

The factorial transform of the power series $\sum_{k\geq 0} a_k x^k$ is the power series

$$T \sum_{k\geq 0} a_k x^k := \sum_{k\geq 0} k! a_k x^k. \tag{5}$$

The inverse factorial transform of the power series $\sum_{k\geq 0} a_k x^k$ is the power series

$$T^{-1} \sum_{k\geq 0} a_k x^k := \sum_{k\geq 0} 1/k!\, a_k x^k. \tag{6}$$

The operations T and T^{-1} are **inverse operations** of each other:

$$TT^{-1} \sum_{k\geq 0} a_k x^k = T^{-1}T \sum_{k\geq 0} a_k x^k = \sum_{k\geq 0} a_k x^k.$$

The functions considered in this Chapter are functions on $\mathbf{R}_+$ or on a bounded interval [0,b[or [0,b]. When convolution products are considered, they are extended to $\mathbf{R}_-$ by annulation on that interval. Functions f with a power series expansion converging near 0, are identified with that power series (on the domain of convergence of the latter). The definitions for power series are adopted in the case of such functions f.

An **entire function** is a function f defined everywhere, with power series expansion $f(x)=\sum_{k\geq 0} a_k x^k$ converging everywhere. A **very regular function** (this is no current terminology) is an entire function f such that the **factorial transform Tf of f** converges near 0. The functions mentioned in **Introduction 8.0** are very regular functions. The function $\exp(-x^2)$ is an entire function, but it is not a very regular function.

Theorem 1

If f is a power series converging near 0, then $T^{-1}f$ is a very regular function.

Proof

Let r and R be the radius of convergence of the power series $\sum_{k\geq 0} a_k x^k$ and $\sum_{k\geq 0} 1/k!\, a_k x^k$ resp. Then r satisfies (4) and R satisfies the relation

$$1/R = \limsup_{k\uparrow\infty} |1/k!\, a_k|^{1/k}.$$

By Stirling, $\lim(1/k!)^{1/k}=0$. Hence, if r>0, then $1/r<\infty$, $1/R=0$, $R=\infty$ •

8.1.3. Convolutions

Entire functions are functions of bounded variation (by classical arguments, because they have derivatives bounded on bounded intervals). Hence, the convolution product u*g is defined on $\mathbf{R}_+$ if u and g are entire functions (Ch.1.3.2). In particular, u*g is defined if u and g are very regular functions.

Theorem 2

Let f and g be very regular functions. Then f*g is a very regular function and

$$\mathbf{T(f*g) = Tf.Tg \quad near\ 0.} \tag{7}$$

Proof

Let $$f(x) = \sum_{i\geq 0} a_i x^i \ , \ \ g(x) = \sum_{j\geq 0} b_j x^j$$

be very regular functions. We first assume that $a_i \geq 0$, $b_j \geq 0$. Then, for all $x \in \mathbf{R}_+$,

$$(f*g)(x) = \int_{[0,x]} f(x-y)dg(y) = \int_{]0,x]} f(x-y)g'(y)dy + f(x)g(0)$$

$$= \int_{]0,x]} \sum_{i\geq 0} a_i(x-y)^i \sum_{j\geq 1} jb_{j-1}y^{j-1}dy + \sum_{i\geq 0} a_i b_0 x^i$$

$$= \sum_{i\geq 0} \sum_{j\geq 1} a_i\, jb_j \int_{]0,x]} (x-y)^i y^{j-1}dy + \sum_{i\geq 0} a_i b_0 x^i$$

$$= \sum_{i\geq 0} \sum_{j\geq 1} a_i b_j\, i!j!_{/(i+j)!}\, x^{i+j} + \sum_{i\geq 0} a_i b_0 x^i = \sum_{i\geq 0} \sum_{j\geq 0} a_i b_j\, i!j!_{/(i+j)!}\, x^{i+j}$$

$$= \sum_{k\geq 0} [\sum_{0\leq i\leq k} a_i b_{k-i}\, i!(k-i)!]\, 1_{/k!}\, x^k. \tag{8}$$

These calculations are allowed by Fubini, because sums are particular integrals and because everything is positive. All sums occurring in the relations leading to (8) are finite, because (f*g)(x) is finite. Then

$$T(f*g)(x) = \sum_{k\geq 0} [\sum_{0\leq i\leq k} a_i b_{k-i}\, i!(k-i)!]\, x^k$$

$$= \sum_{i\geq 0} a_i i! x^i \sum_{j\geq 0} b_j j! x^j = Tf(x).Tg(x), \tag{9}$$

for all $x \in \mathbf{R}_+$, but now the value ∞ is not excluded. From the assumptions results that Tf and Tg are finite near 0. Hence T(f*g) is finite near 0.

We now drop the assumptions $a_i \geq 0$, $b_j \geq 0$. Then the relations leading to (8) remain true when a_i and b_j are replaced everywhere by $|a_i|$ and $|b_j|$ resp. Again, everything is finite because the power series f(x) and g(x) converge absolutely everywhere. Then, by Fubini, the calculations are permitted with the original values a_i and b_i. Hence, f*g is an entire function, and the relations (8) are correct for all values of x.

The relations (9) remain valid when a_i and b_j are replaced everywhere by $|a_i|$ and $|b_j|$. The involved values are finite near 0, because Tf(x) and Tg(x) converge absolutely near 0. Then, by Fubini, the relations (9) are exact near 0, for the original values a_i and b_j. Hence, the power series T(f*g)(x) converges near 0, and it equals Tf(x).Tg(x) near 0 •

In this proof, the justifications by Fubini can be replaced by justifications based on the properties of single and double absolutely convergent series.

Theorem 3

If f and g are entire functions, then f*g is an entire function.

Proof
The conclusion that f*g is an entire function in the foregoing demonstration, is only based on the assumption that f and g are entire functions •

8.1.4. Renewal Equations

A very regular renewal equation on $\mathbf{R}_+$ is a renewal equation $\varphi = f + \varphi * g$ in which the functions f and g are very regular functions. It is not necessarily a renewal equation as defined in Ch.1.4.2, because g must not be a distribution function.

Theorem 4

The very regular renewal equation $\varphi = f + \varphi * g$ has a unique very regular solution φ if $|g(0)| < 1$.

Proof
Let $|g(0)| < 1$. For the proof of the unicity, let φ be a very regular solution. Then by Theorem 2,

$$T\varphi(x) = Tf(x) + T\varphi(x).Tg(x) \text{ near } 0. \qquad (10)$$

The series $T\varphi(x)$, $Tf(x)$ and $Tg(x)$ converge near 0. By the unicity of the power series expansion (8.1.1.a), the coefficient of x^k in the first member of (10) equals the coefficient of x^k in the last member, for all k=0,1,2,... This furnishes a set of relations determining, successively, the coefficients of the power series $\varphi(x)$ as functions of the coefficients of the power series $f(x)$ and $g(x)$. This proves the unicity of the solution, if it exists.

For the proof of the existence, we consider the expansion

$$Tf(x)/[1-Tg(x)] = Tf(x) \sum_{i\geq 0} [Tg(x)]^i = \sum_{k\geq 0} c_k x^k,$$

converging near 0 by 8.1.1.d and e. We define

$$\varphi(x) := T^{-1}[Tf(x)/[1-Tg(x)]] = \sum_{k\geq 0} 1/k!\, c_k x^k.$$

By Theorem 1, φ is an entire function. Then the relation (10) results from the definition of φ. By Theorem 2, it can be displayed as

$$T\varphi(x) = Tf(x) + T(\varphi * g)(x)$$

near 0. By the unicity of the power series expansion, the latter relation is an identity between (formal) power series. We now apply the operator T^{-1} to that relation, and we obtain the identity

$$\varphi(x) = f(x) + (\varphi * g)(x).$$

The involved power series are entire functions. Hence, $\varphi = f + \varphi * g$ •

8.1.5. Complex Extensions

We also consider power series $\sum a_k x^k$ with complex coefficients a_k, and complex functions of $x \in \mathbf{R}_+$ defined by such power series. The definitions and results of 8.1.1 and 8.1.2, remain valid in the complex case. Renewal equations or convolutions with complex functions are not employed.

Power series with complex coefficients only serve as convenient intermediates in some proofs. The imaginary numbers always disappear in the final results.

We agree that the power series and the functions are real, unless the adjective "complex" is mentioned explicitly.

8.2. Simple Functions

8.2.1. Definition

In this Chapter, a **simple function** is a linear combination of functions

$$x^k\, e^{-sx} \sin(tx) \;,\; x^k\, e^{-sx} \cos(tx) \quad (k=0,1,2,\ldots;\ s,t\in\mathbf{R}).$$

Different values of k, s and t may occur in the same simple function.

By the following section 8.2.2, **simple functions are very regular functions.**

8.2.2. Factorial Transform of Simple Functions

We here show how to calculate the factorial transform of a simple function It is enough to indicate the factoriel transform of the particular functions from which the simple functions are built up. It is convenient to calculate the transforms via complex functions.

Let α be a complex parameter. Then, for all k=0,1,2,...,

$$x^k\, e^{-\alpha x} = x^k \textstyle\sum_{j\geq 0} 1/_{j!}\, (-\alpha)^j x^j \ (x\in\mathbf{R}_+)$$

and near 0,

$$T[x^k\, e^{-\alpha x}] = T[\textstyle\sum_{j\geq 0} 1/_{j!}\, (-\alpha)^j x^{j+k}]$$

$$= \textstyle\sum_{j\geq 0} (j+k)!/_{j!}\, (-\alpha)^j x^{j+k} = k!x^k \sum_{j\geq 0} (j+k)!/_{j!k!}\, (-\alpha)^j x^j = k!x^k/(1+\alpha x)^{k+1}. \tag{11}$$

From de Moivre's formulas

$$e^{ix} = \cos(x) + i\sin(x) \;,\; e^{-ix} = \cos(x) - i\sin(x)$$

results that

$$\sin(x) = 1/_{(2i)}\, (e^{ix} - e^{-ix}) \;,\; \cos(x) = 1/_2\, (e^{ix} + e^{-ix}).$$

Then by (11),

$$T[x^k\, e^{-sx} \sin(tx)]$$

$$= 1/_{(2i)}\, T(x^k\, e^{-(s-it)x}) - 1/_{(2i)}\, T(x^k\, e^{-(s+it)x})$$

$$= k!x^k/_{(2i)}\, [[1+(s-it)x]^{-(k+1)} - [1+(s+it)]^{-(k+1)}]. \tag{12}$$

$$T[x^k e^{-sx} \cos(tx)]$$

$$= 1/2\, T(x^k e^{-(s-it)x}) + 1/2\, T(x^k e^{-(s+it)x})$$

$$= k!x^k/2\, [[1+(s-it)x]^{-(k+1)} + [1+(s+it)]^{-(k+1)}]. \tag{13}$$

By (12),

$$T[x^k e^{-sx} \sin(tx)] = k!x^k P_k(x)/[(1+sx)^2+t^2x^2]^{k+1}\ (k=0,1,2,..), \tag{14}$$

where

$$P_k(x) := 1/(2i)\, [[(1+sx)+itx]^{k+1} - [(1+sx)-itx]^{k+1}]. \tag{15}$$

In particular,

$$P_0(x) = tx, \tag{16}$$

$$P_1(x) = 2(1+sx)tx, \tag{17}$$

$$P_2(x) = 3(1+sx)^2tx - t^3x^3. \tag{18}$$

By (13)

$$T[x^k e^{-sx} \cos(tx)] = k!x^k Q_k(x)/[(1+sx)^2+t^2x^2]^{k+1}\ (k=0,1,2,..), \tag{19}$$

where

$$Q_k(x) := 1/2\, [[(1+sx)+itx]^{k+1} + [(1+sx)-itx]^{k+1}]. \tag{20}$$

In particular,

$$Q_0(x) = (1+sx), \tag{21}$$

$$Q_1(x) = (1+sx)^2-t^2x^2, \tag{22}$$

$$Q_2(x) = (1+sx)^3-3(1+sx)t^2x^2. \tag{23}$$

The polynomials $P_k(x)$ and $Q_k(x)$ are real. The denominator in the last member of (14) and (19) is different from 0 for x=0. Hence,

The factorial transform of a simple function is a rational function with no pole at the origin.

We recall that a **rational function** is a function expressible as P(x)/Q(x), where P(x) and Q(x) are polynomials. It can be assumed that P(x) and Q(x) have no common roots (i.e. no common factors). Then the **poles** of the rational function P(x)/Q(x) are the positive roots of the denominator Q(x). (The functions in this Chapter are restricted to $\mathbf{R}_+$. Hence, only positive poles are considered).

The factorial transform of a very regular function is defined near 0. The factorial transform of a simple function, being a rational function, is defined at any point x different from a pole. The indication "near 0", may be omitted when factorial transforms of simple functions are considered.

8.2.3. Inverse Factorial Transform of Rational Functions

Lemma

Let $\alpha_1,\ldots,\alpha_n$ be different complex numbers. Let Q(x) be the complex polynomial

$$Q(x) := (1+\alpha_1 x)^{k_1}(1+\alpha_2 x)^{k_2}\ldots(1+\alpha_n x)^{k_n}, \tag{24}$$

and let P(x) be a complex polynomial with a strictly less degree than the degree of Q(x). Then the complex rational function f(x):=P(x)/Q(x) can be displayed as a linear combination of the terms

$$x^{k-1}/(1+\alpha_j x)^k \ (j=1,\ldots,n;\ k=1,\ldots,k_j). \tag{25}$$

Proof

It is classical that f(x) can be displayed as a linear combination of the terms

$$1/(1+\alpha_j x)^m \ (j=1,\ldots,n;\ m=1,\ldots,k_j). \tag{26}$$

(The explicit calculation of integrals of rational functions is based on this property). For fixed j, the terms (26) for $m=1,\ldots,k_j$, are the terms corresponding to the factor $(1+\alpha_j x)^{k_j}$ in the last member of (24).

Each term (26) is a linear combination of terms (25). Indeed,

$$1/(1+\alpha x)^m = {}^1/_{(1+\alpha x)}\,[1 - {}^{\alpha x}/_{(1+\alpha x)}]^{m-1} = \textstyle\sum_{0\le k\le m-1} c_k\, x^k/(1+\alpha x)^{k+1} \tag{27}$$

by the binomial Theorem. The coefficients c_k are irrelevant •

By (11),

$$T^{-1}[x^k/(1+\alpha x)^{k+1}] = {}^1/_{k!}\, x^k e^{-\alpha x} \ (k=0,1,2,\ldots;\ \alpha \text{ complex}). \tag{28}$$

We now assume that the polynomials P(x), Q(x) in the Lemma are real.

We first consider a factor $(1+rx)^j$ with real r in the last member of the expression (24) of the polynomial Q(x). In the decomposition of f(x), the part corresponding to the factor $(1+rx)^j$ is

$$a_0\, {}^1\!/\!_{(1+rx)} + a_1 {}^x\!/\!_{(1+rx)^2} + \ldots + a_{j-1}\, x^{j-1}/(1+rx)^j.$$

(see proof of Lemma). Its factorial inverse equals, by (28),

$$[a_0+a_1x+ \ldots + a_{j-1}\, {}^1\!/\!_{(j-1)!}\, x^{j-1}]e^{-rx}. \tag{29}$$

We now consider a factor $(1+\alpha x)^k$ of Q(x) with $\alpha=s+it$; $s,t\in\mathbf{R}$; $t\neq 0$. Then the conjugate factor $(1+\beta x)^k$, where $\beta=s-it$, must be present because Q(x) is a real polynomial. The part corresponding to these factors, in the decomposition of f(x) is

$$\begin{aligned} &b_0\, {}^1\!/\!_{(1+\alpha x)} + b_1 {}^x\!/\!_{(1+\alpha x)^2} + \ldots + b_{k-1}\, x^{k-1}/(1+\alpha x)^k \\ &+ c_0\, {}^1\!/\!_{(1+\beta x)} + c_1 {}^x\!/\!_{(1+\beta x)^2} + \ldots + c_{k-1}\, x^{k-1}/(1+\beta x)^k. \end{aligned} \tag{30}$$

The factorial inverse of (30) equals, by (28),

$$[b_0+b_1x+\ldots+b_{j-1}{}^1\!/\!_{(j-1)!}x^{j-1}]e^{-\alpha x}+[c_0+c_1x+\ldots+c_{j-1}{}^1\!/\!_{(j-1)!}x^{j-1}]e^{-\beta x}. \tag{31}$$

But

$$e^{-\alpha x} = e^{-(s+it)x} = e^{-sx}e^{-itx} = e^{-sx}[\cos(tx)-i\sin(tx)],$$

$$e^{-\beta x} = e^{-(s-it)x} = e^{-sx}e^{itx} = e^{-sx}[\cos(tx)+i\sin(tx)].$$

Then (31) can be displayed as

$$(A+iB)e^{-sx}[\cos(tx)-i\sin(tx)] + (C+iD)e^{-sx}[\cos(tx)+i\sin(tx)] =$$

$$[A\cos(tx) + B\sin(tx) + C\cos(tx) - D\sin(tx)]e^{-sx}$$

$$+ i[-A\sin(tx) + B\cos(tx) + C\sin(tx) + D\cos(tx)]e^{-sx}.$$

In these relations, A, B, C and D are real polynomials in x, with a degree strictly less than k. No imaginary quantities may subsist. Hence $A\equiv C$ and $B\equiv -D$. This discussion proves the following Theorem.

Theorem 5

Let $f(x)=P(x)/Q(x)$ where P(x) and Q(x) are polynomials with no common roots satisfying the following assumptions:

a. **The degree of P(x) is strictly less than the degree of Q(x).**

b. **The polynomial Q(x) is a product of different factors of the type**

$$(1+rx)^j \ (r \in R) \tag{32}$$

and of the type

$$(1+\alpha x)^k(1+\beta x)^k \tag{33}$$

where $\alpha=s+it$, $\beta=s-it$, $s \in R$, $0 \neq t \in R$.

Then $T^{-1}f(x)$ is a sum of terms corresponding to the factors (32) and (33). To factor (32) corresponds the term

$$R(x)e^{-rx}, \tag{34}$$

where R(x) is a polynomial with a degree strictly less than j. To factor (33) corresponds the term

$$[S(x)\cos(tx) + T(x)\sin(tx)]e^{-sx}, \tag{35}$$

where S(x) and T(x) are polynomials with a degree strictly less than k •

The Theorem can be applied to any rational function f(x) without pole at the origin. Indeed, f(x) can be displayed as

$$f(x) = R(x) + [P(x)/Q(x)],$$

where R(x), P(x) and Q(x) are polynomials and where the degree of P(x) is strictly less than that of Q(x) and $Q(0) \neq 0$. Then Q(x) can be factorized, and any factor $a+bx$ can be replaced by $a[1+(b/a)x]$. The complex factors can be grouped in products such as (33), because Q(x) is a real polynomial. Then the Theorem can be applied to the rational function P(x)/Q(x). The factorial inverse of the polynomial R(x) results from applications of the formula

$$T^{-1}x^k = {}^1\!/_{k!}\, x^k.$$

The following formulas are factorial inverses of particular rational functions. They can be obtained by the Lemma, or by Theorem 5, used with undeterminate coefficients. Then the latter coefficients result from obvious identifications. We assume that the factors in the denominators are different. For instance, if the product (1+sx)(1+tx) appears in a denominator, then $s \neq t$. It is assumed that

$$\alpha = s+it \ , \ \beta = s-it \ , \ t \neq 0 \text{ and } a,b,c,r,s,t \in \mathbf{R}$$

in the following formulas (36)–(43).

$$T^{-1}[a/(1+sx)] = ae^{-sx}. \tag{36}$$

$$T^{-1}[(a+bx)/[(1+sx)(1+tx)]] = (as-b)_{/(s-t)}\, e^{-sx} - (at-b)_{/(s-t)}\, e^{-tx}. \tag{37}$$

$$T^{-1}[(a+bx)/(1+sx)^2] = ae^{-sx} - (as-b)\, x\, e^{-sx}. \tag{38}$$

$$T^{-1}[(a+bx)/[(1+\alpha x)(1+\beta x)]] = [a\cos(tx) - (as-b)\sin(tx)_{/t}]e^{-sx}. \tag{39}$$

$$\begin{gathered} T^{-1}[(a+bx+cx^2)/[(1+rx)(1+sx)(1+tx)]] \\ =(ar^2-br+c)_{/(r-s)(r-t)}\, e^{-rx}+(as^2-bs+c)_{/(s-r)(s-t)}\, e^{-sx}+(at^2-bt+c)_{/(t-r)(t-c)}\, e^{-tx} \end{gathered} \tag{40}$$

$$\begin{gathered} T^{-1}[(a+bx+cx^2)/[(1+sx)^2(1+tx)]] = 1_{/(s-t)^2}\, (as^2-2ast+bt-c)e^{-sx} \\ - 1_{/(s-t)}\, (as^2-bs+c)x\, e^{-sx} + 1_{/(s-t)^2}\, (at^2-bt+c)e^{-tx}. \end{gathered} \tag{41}$$

$$\begin{gathered} T^{-1}[(a+bx+cx^2)/(1+sx)^3] \\ = a\, e^{-sx} - (2as-b)x\, e^{-sx} + 1_{/2}\, (as^2-bs+c)x^2e^{-sx}. \end{gathered} \tag{42}$$

$$\begin{gathered} T^{-1}[(a+bx+cx^2)/[(1+rx)(1+\alpha x)(1+\beta x)]] \\ = A\, e^{-rx} + [B\cos(tx) - C\sin(tx)_{/t}]\, e^{-sx}, \end{gathered} \tag{43}$$

where

$$A := (ar^2-br+c)/[(r-s)^2+t^2]\ , \ B := a-A\ , \ C := a(s+r)+A(s-r)-b.$$

Particular useful formulas

We now indicate particular useful formulas for the calculation of inverse factorial transforms.

a. If P(x) is a polynomial and $s\neq 0$, then

$$P(x)e^{-x/s}\,dx = d[-s\,e^{-x/s}[P(x)+sP'(x)+s^2P''(x)+\dots]], \tag{44}$$

by direct verification. The number of non-vanishing polynomials P(x), P′(x), P″(x),... is finite.

b. We recall that

$$(f*I)(x) = \int_{[0,x]} f(y)dy, \tag{45}$$

where I is the identity function on $\mathbf{R}_+$ (see end of section 1.3.2). Then, by Theorem 2, if f(x) is very regular,

$$T[\int_{[0,x]} f(y)dy] = x.Tf(x) \text{ near } 0. \tag{46}$$

c. Let g(x) be very regular. Then

$$T^{-1}[xg(x)] = \int_{[0,x]} [T^{-1}g(y)]dy. \tag{47}$$

Indeed, (47) is correct iff it is correct after the application of T. The latter correctness results from (46).

d. Let $t\neq 0$. Then, by (47), (28) and (44),

$$T^{-1}[x/(1+tx)]^{k+1} = T^{-1}[x[x^k/(1+tx)^{k+1}]]$$

$$= \int_{[0,x]} T^{-1}[y^k/(1+ty)^{k+1}]dy = \int_{[0,x]} 1/k!\; y^k e^{-ty}\,dy$$

$$= (1/t^{k+1})[1 - e^{-tx} \textstyle\sum_{0\leq j\leq k} 1/j!\; t^j x^j] \quad (k=0,1,2,\dots). \tag{48}$$

8.3. Very Regular Claimsize Distributions on R_+

8.3.1. Regularity of Concave Transform G

Theorem 6

In the classical risk model, the claimsize distribution function F is very regular iff its concave transform

$$G := 1/_\mu (1-F)*I \tag{49}$$

is very regular. Then the factorial transform of G equals

$$TG(x) = 1/_\mu\, x[1-TF(x)] \ \text{ near } 0. \tag{50}$$

Proof

The identity function I is very regular and $TI(x)=Tx=x$.

If F is very regular, then 1–F is very regular, and the last member of (49) is very regular by Theorem 2. Then (50) results from the application of T to (49), by Theorem 2. Conversely, let

$$G(x) = \sum_{k\geq 1} a_k x^k$$

be very regular. Then

$$G'(x) = \sum_{k\geq 1} k a_k x^{k-1} \ \text{ everywhere,}$$

and

$$TG'(x) = \sum_{k\geq 1} k(k-1)!\, a_k x^{k-1} = \sum_{k\geq 1} k!\, a_k x^{k-1}.$$

The latter power series has the same strictly positive radius of convergence as

$$TG(x) = \sum_{k\geq 1} k!\, a_k x^k.$$

Hence, $G'(x)$ is very regular. Then $F(x)$ is very regular because

$$G'(x) = 1/_\mu [1-F(x)] \ , \ F(x) = 1 - \mu G'(x) \ \bullet$$

If f is very regular, then f′ exists and is very regular. Indeed, the argument used for G and G′ in the foregoing proof is general.

Hence, **if the claimsize distribution function F is very regular, then all derivatives F′, F″,..., exist and are very regular**.

8.3.2. Regularity of Ruin Function Ψ

Theorem 7

In the classical risk model, let G be very regular. Then the ruin function Ψ, satisfying the renewal equation

$$\Psi = q(1-G) + q\Psi*G, \tag{51}$$

is very regular and

$$T\Psi(x) = q[1-TG(x)]/[1-qTG(x)] \text{ near } 0. \tag{52}$$

Proof.
(51) is a very regular renewal equation, with a very regular solution, by Theorem 4. The renewal equation (51) is a renewal equation as defined in Ch.1.4.2. Hence the solution can only be the ruin function Ψ. Then (52) results from the application of T to (51) by Theorem 2 •

8.4. Simple Claimsize Distributions on R_+

8.4.1. Simplicity of Concave Transform G

Theorem 8

In the classical risk model, the claimsize distribution function F is simple iff its concave transform G is simple.

Proof.
Let F(x) be simple. Then TF(x) is a rational function with no pole at 0 by 8.2.2. Then TG(x) is a rational function with no pole at 0 by (50). Then

$$G(x) = T^{-1}TG(x)$$

is simple by Theorem 5.

Conversely, if G(x) is simple, then G′(x) is simple, and then $F(x)=1-\mu G'(x)$ is simple •

Of course, **if the claimsize distribution F is simple, then all derivatives F′, F″,... are simple.**

8.4.2. Structure of Ruin Function Ψ

In the following Theorem, we assume that G(x) is a simple function. Then G′(x) must be bounded by some function ae^{-bx} (a,b>0) and then the couple (G,q) has an adjustment coefficient.

Theorem 9

In the classical risk model, let G be a simple function. Then the ruin function equals

$$\Psi(x) = T^{-1}[q[1-TG(x)]/[1-qTG(x)]]. \tag{53}$$

It is a simple function. It is a sum of terms corresponding to the roots of the rational *characteristic equation*

$$q\,TG(x) = 1, \tag{54}$$

in the following way.

To the real root c with multiplicity j corresponds the term

$$R(x)e^{-rx}, \tag{55}$$

where

$$r := -1/c \in \mathbf{R}_{++} \tag{56}$$

and where R(x) is a polynomial with a degree strictly less than j.

To the couple of conjugate roots γ and δ with multiplicity k corresponds the term

$$[S(x)\cos(tx) + T(x)\sin(tx)]e^{-sx}, \tag{57}$$

where

$$-1/\gamma = s+it\ ,\ -1/\delta = s-it\ ,\ s \in \mathbf{R}_{++}\ ,\ t \in \mathbf{R} \tag{58}$$

and where S(x) and T(x) are polynomials with a degree strictly less than k.

The term (55) with the smallest value of r is Cramér's asymptotic value of Ψ(x) as x↑∞. Then

R(x) is a constant polynomial,

c is the smallest real root of the equation (54),

c is a simple root of that equation,

r is the adjustment coefficient of the couple (G,q).

Proof

The relation (53) results from (52). By 8.2.2, TF(x) is a rational function. Then TG(x) is a rational function by (50). Then (53) can be displayed as

$$\Psi(x) = T^{-1}[P(x)/Q(x)],$$

where P(x) and Q(x) are polynomials without common factors. From $\Psi(0)=q$ results that $P(0)/Q(0)=q$. Hence 0 is not a pole of the rational function P(x)/Q(x). The degree of P(x) is strictly less than the degree of Q(x). Indeed, let us suppose the contrary. Then the division of P(x) by Q(x) furnishes terms ax^k ($a\neq0$, $k\geq0$), with corresponding terms $T^{-1}(ax^k)= ax^k/_{k!}$ in the expression of $\Psi(x)$. But this contradicts the limit relation $\lim_{k\uparrow\infty} \Psi(x)=0$.

Hence, Theorem 5 can be applied to the factorial inversion of the rational function P(x)/Q(x) without a pole at 0. Then the Theorem results from the following observations.

To the real root c with multiplicity j of (54) corresponds the factor $(x-c)^j= (-c)^j(1+rx)^j$ of Q(x). In the corresponding term (55), r must be strictly positive because that term must tend to 0 as $x\uparrow\infty$.

To the couple of conjugate roots γ and δ with multiplicity k of equation (54) corresponds the product of factors

$$(x-\gamma)^k(x-\delta)^k = (\gamma\delta)^k(1+\alpha x)^k(1+\beta x)^k$$

of Q(x). In the corresponding term (57), s must be strictly positive because that term must tend to 0 as $x\uparrow\infty$.

It is clear that Cramér's asymptotic expression must be a particular term ae^{-rx} of the expression of the simple function $\Psi(x)$. It has the property

$$\lim_{x\uparrow\infty}\Psi(x)/[ae^{-rx}] =1.$$

This implies that r must be as small as possible, and that terms such as

$$cx^ne^{-rx}\ (n\geq1)\ ,\ cx^n \sin(tx)e^{-rx}\ (n\geq0)\ ,\ cx^n \cos(tx)\ e^{-rx}\ (n\geq0)$$

cannot figure in the expression of $\Psi(x)$. Hence, r cannot come from a multiple real root, or from a couple of conjugate complex roots of the equation (54) •

8.4.3. Illustrations

Example 1: The usual exponential case

We take $F(x) := 1-e^{-x/\mu}$ $(x \in \mathbf{R}_+)$, $\mu > 0$.

By (11), $1-TF(x) = Te^{-x/\mu} = \mu/_{(x+\mu)}$.

By (50), $TG(x) = x/_{(x+\mu)}$.

By (53),

$$\Psi(x) = q\,T^{-1}\,\mu/_{(x+\mu-qx)} = q\,T^{-1}\,\mu/_{(px+\mu)} = q\,T^{-1}\,1/_{[1+(px/\mu)]}.$$

By (36),

$$\Psi(x) = q\,e^{-px/\mu}\ (x \in \mathbf{R}_+). \tag{59}$$

Example 2: A bi-exponential claimsize distribution

Let

$$F(x) := 1-a'e^{-ax}-b'e^{-bx}\ (x \in \mathbf{R}_+)\ ;\ a',a,b',b > 0\ ;\ a'+b' \leq 1.$$

By the surface interpretation of the first moment,

$$\mu = \int_{[0,\infty[}[1-F(x)]dx = \int_{[0,\infty[}[a'e^{-ax}+b'e^{-bx}]dx = a'/_a + b'/_b.$$

By (11),

$$1-TF(x) = a'\,Te^{-ax} + b'\,Te^{-bx} = a'/_{(1+ax)} + b'/_{(1+bx)}.$$

By (50) and (53),

$$\Psi(x) = q\,T^{-1}[P(x)/Q(x)],$$

where

$$P(x) = \mu(1+ax)(1+bx)-a'x(1+bx)-b'x(1+ax) = \mu + (\mu a+\mu b-a'-b')x,$$

and

$$Q(x) = \mu(1+ax)(1+bx) - qa'x(1+bx) - qb'x(1+ax).$$

We observe that degree 1 of P(x) is strictly less than degree 2 of Q(x). By the expression of μ, the coefficient of x^2 in P(x) is strictly positive, and the coefficient of x^2 in Q(x) vanishes. The quadratic equation Q(x)=0 is equivalent to equation (54). By the last part of Theorem 9, the roots c and d of the equation Q(x)=0 must be real, different, and strictly negative (because otherwise, Cramér's asymptotic expression for $\Psi(x)$ cannot figure in the expression of $\Psi(x)$). This can easily be shown by a direct verification. Then Q(x) can be displayed as

$$Q(x) = (\mu ab - qa'b - qb'a)(1+sx)(1+tx), \text{ where } s = -1/c\ ,\ t = -1/d.$$

Then

$$\Psi(x) = Ae^{-sx} + Be^{-tx}\ , \tag{60}$$

where A and B result from (37). A direct verification shows that A and B are strictly positive.

Example 3: A sinus-exponential claimsize distribution

Let

$$F(x) := 1 - e^{-x}(1+2a \sin x)\ (x \in \mathbf{R}_+),\ \ |a| \le 1/4\ .$$

Then F is a claimsize distribution. An easy calculation shows that $\mu=1+a$. We will hereafter obtain μ indirectly. By (11), (14) and (16),

$$Te^{-x} = 1/(1+x)\ \ ,\ \ T(e^{-x}\sin x) = x/(1+2x+2x^2).$$

By (50),

$$TG(x) = 1/\mu\ x[1+2(1+a)x+2(1+a)x^2]/[(1+x)(1+2x+2x^2)].$$

By (53),

$$\Psi(x) = q\ T^{-1}[P(x)/Q(x)],$$

where

$$P(x) = \mu(1+x)(1+2x+2x^2) - x[1+2(1+a)x+2(1+a)x^2],$$

$$Q(x) = \mu(1+x)(1+2x+2x^2) - qx[1+2(1+a)x+2(1+a)x^2].$$

The degree of P(x) must be strictly less than the degree of Q(x) (see proof of Theorem 9). Hence, $\mu = 1+a$, and then

$$P(x) = \mu+(3\mu-1)x+2\mu x^2.$$

$$Q(x) = \mu+(3\mu-q)x+2(1+p)\mu x^2+2p\mu x^3.$$

The equation (54) is equivalent to the equation Q(x)=0.

We assume that the equation Q(x)=0 has one real root and two imaginary roots. That is the case if $|a|\neq 0$ is small. Indeed, if a=0, then $\mu=1$ and

$$Q(x) = (1+px)(1+2x+2x^2).$$

The roots of the quadratic equation $1+2x+2x^2=0$ are imaginary. Hence, the equation $Q(x)=0$ has one real root and two imaginary roots if $a=0$. For continuity reasons, it has one real root and two imaginary reasons if $|a|\neq 0$ is small enough. We discard the case $a=0$, already discussed in *Example 1*, because then $P(x)=(1+2x+2x^2)$ and then the polynomials $P(x)$ and $Q(x)$ have the factor $(1+2x+2x^2)$ in common. Hence,

$$Q(x) = 2p\mu(1+rx)(1+\alpha x)(1+\beta x)\ ,\ r\in\mathbf{R}_{++}\ ,\ \alpha=s+it\ ,\ \beta=s-it\ ,\ s\in\mathbf{R}_{++}\ ,\ t\in\mathbf{R}.$$

The value of r, s and t can easily be found numerically. Then, by (43),

$$\Psi(x) = A\ e^{-rx} + [B\cos(tx) - C\ {}^{1}/_{t}\sin(tx)]e^{-sx}, \tag{61}$$

where A, B and C result from the relations following (43).

Example 4: F is a convolution of exponentials

Let

$$F := F_1 * F_2 * F_3\ ,$$

$$F_n := 1-e^{-x/\mu_n}\ (x\in\mathbf{R}_+)\ \ ,\ \ \mu_n > 0\ \ (n=1,2,3)\ \ ,\ \mu_1\neq\mu_2\neq\mu_3\neq\mu_1,$$

$$\sigma_1 := \mu_1+\mu_2+\mu_3\ \ ,\ \ \sigma_2 := \mu_1\mu_2+\mu_2\mu_3+\mu_3\mu_1\ \ ,\ \ \sigma_3 := \mu_1\mu_2\mu_3.$$

Then

$$\mu = \mu_1+\mu_2+\mu_3 = \sigma_1.$$

By (11),

$$TF_n(x) = x/(x+\mu_n).$$

By (50) and Theorem 2,

$$TG(x) = {}^{1}/_{\mu}\ x[1-TF_1(x).TF_2(x).TF_3(x)].$$

By (53),

$$\Psi(x) = q\ T^{-1}[P(x)/Q(x)],$$

where

$$P(x) = \mu\sigma_3 + (\mu\sigma_2-\sigma_3)x + (\mu\sigma_1-\sigma_2)x^2,$$

$$Q(x) = \mu\sigma_3 + (\mu\sigma_2-q\sigma_3)x + (\mu\sigma_1-q\sigma_2)x^2 + p\mu x^3.$$

The equation $Q(x)=0$ can have 3 different real roots. Then, by (40),

$$\Psi(x) = Ae^{-rx} + Be^{-sx} + Ce^{-tx},\ \text{ where } r,s,t\in\mathbf{R}_{++}.$$

The numerical values A, B, C, r, s and t are easily found.

The equation Q(x)=0 can have one real root and two imaginary roots. Then, by (43), Ψ(x) has the structure (61), although no trigonometric functions occur in the expression of F.

In order to show analytically that 2 roots can be imaginary, we consider the particular case

$$\mu_1 := 1-\varepsilon \ , \ \mu_2 := 1 \ , \ \mu_3 := 1+\varepsilon \ , p := \varepsilon .$$

Then

$$\mu = \sigma_1 = 3 \ , \ \sigma_2 = 3-\varepsilon^2 \ , \ \sigma_3 = 1-\varepsilon^2 \ , \ q = 1-\varepsilon,$$

$$Q(x) = 3(1-\varepsilon^2) + (8+\varepsilon-2\varepsilon^2-e^3)x + (6+3\varepsilon+\varepsilon^2-\varepsilon^3)x^2 + 3\varepsilon x^3.$$

In the equation Q(x)=0, we replace x by 1/y. Then the equation in y is

$$3(1-\varepsilon^2)y^3 + (8+\varepsilon-2\varepsilon^2-e^3)y^2 + (6+3\varepsilon+\varepsilon^2-\varepsilon^3)y + 3\varepsilon = 0. \qquad (62)$$

For ε=0, it becomes

$$3y^3 + 8y^2 + 6y = 0,$$

i.e.

$$y(3y^2+8y+6) = 0.$$

The latter equation has the 3 roots 0, α≠0, β≠0. The roots α and β can be expressed by elementary algebra. They are imaginary because $8^2-4\times3\times6$ is strictly negative.

We now take ε∈]0,1[. Then (62) has 3 roots $r_\varepsilon \neq 0$, α_ε, β_ε. For continuity reasons, α_ε and β_ε are imaginary if ε is small enough. Then the equation Q(x) =0 has the roots $1/r_\varepsilon$, $1/\alpha_\varepsilon$, $1/\beta_\varepsilon$ and the two latter roots are imaginary.

This example shows that

Sinus or cosinus functions can occur in the expression of Ψ(x) if the claimsize distribution function F(x) is a linear combination of functions $x^k e^{-sx}$ (k=0,1,...; s∈R₊).

8.5. Very Regular Truncated Claimsize Distributions

8.5.1. Definitions

All functions are defined on $\mathbf{R}_+$, unless the contrary is mentioned explicitly. In this section 8.5 and in the following section 8.6, all integrals $\int fdg$ are integrals with respect to some continuous function g of bounded variation, vanishing at 0. Hence, they have no discrete parts, and it is irrelevant to write the integration domains as open, closed, or half-open intervals.

The function H is very regular on the interval $J \subseteq \mathbf{R}_+$ if a very regular function h exists, such that H=h on J.

A very regular truncated claimsize distribution function is a claimsize distribution function F expressible as

$$F = f1_{[0,b[} + 1_{[b,\infty[},$$

where $b \in \mathbf{R}_{++}$ and where f is a very regular function. Then F is very regular on [0,b[and on [b,∞[, but not on $\mathbf{R}_+$. We recall that F≡1 (on $\mathbf{R}_+$) is not a claimsize distribution function (Ch.3.1.1. *General assumption* c). Hence:

Very regular truncated claimsize distribution functions are never very regular functions.

If $F=f1_{[0,b[}+1_{[b,\infty[}$ is a very regular claimsize distribution function, then f may be a distribution function, but that is not necessarily the case. Hence:

A very regular truncated claimsize distribution function is not necessarily the truncation at b of some very regular claimsize distribution.

For instance, the distribution function F defined by F(x):= sin(x) on [0,π/2[and F:=1 on [π/2,∞[, is a very regular truncated claimsize distribution function, but the function sin(x) of $x \in \mathbf{R}_+$ is not a distribution function.

If $F=f1_{[b,\infty[}$ is a very regular truncated claimsize distribution function, then F is very regular on the interval [0,b[, but not on the interval [0,b] if F is discontinuous at b. Indeed, entire functions are continuous functions.

8.5.2. Concave Transform G

Theorem 10

If the claimsize distribution function F, in the classical risk model, is very regular on the interval [0,b[, then its concave transform G is very regular on the interval [0,b].

Proof

Let f be a very regular function such that f=F on [0,b[. Let g be defined by

$$g(x) = {}^1/_\mu \int_{[0,x]} [1-f(y)]dy. \tag{63}$$

Then $g = {}^1/_\mu(1-f)*I$, where I is the identity function on $\mathbf{R}_+$. By Theorem 2, g is very regular. From f=F on [0,b[, results that g=G on [0,b[. Then g=G on [0,b] because both g and G are continuous functions. Hence, G is very regular on [0,b] •

8.5.3. Non-Ruin Distribution U in General Case

The following Theorem 11 will be applied under regularity assumptions only. But it is interesting to notice that no such conditions are involved in its statement or proof.

Theorem 11

We assume the following, in the classical risk model:

a. **G(b) = 1.**

b. **g is a continuous function of bounded variation. g=G on [0,b].**

c. **The function g_b is defined as $g_b(x) := g(b+x)-g(b)$ $(x \in \mathbf{R}_+)$.**

d. **The functions $V_k(k=0,1,2,...)$ satisfy the equations**

$$\mathbf{V_0 = p + q\, V_0{*}g}, \tag{64}$$

$$\mathbf{V_k = qV_k{*}g - qV_{k-1}{*}g_b \ \ (k=1,2,...)}. \tag{65}$$

Then

$$\mathbf{U(nb+x) = \textstyle\sum_{0\le k\le n} V_k[(n-k)b+x] \ \ (n=0,1,2,...;\ 0\le x\le b)}. \tag{66}$$

Proof
We define the functions U_k (k= −1,0,1,2,...) by

$$U_{-1} \equiv 0\ ,\ U_k(x) := U(kb+x) \quad (k=0,1,2,...;\ x\in\mathbf{R}_+).$$

Then

$$(U*G)(kb+x) = \int_{[0,kb+x]} U(kb+x-y)dG(y)$$

$$= \int_{[0,x]} U_k(x-y)dG(y) + \int_{[x,kb+x]} U_{k-1}(b+x-y)dG(y)$$

$$= \int_{[0,x]} U_k(x-y)dG(y) + \int_{[x,b]} U_{k-1}(b+x-y)dG(y)$$

$$= (U_k*G)(x) + \int_{[x,b]} U_{k-1}(b+x-y)dG(y) \quad (k=0,1,2,...;\ 0\le x\le b),$$

because $G([b,\infty[)=0$ by assumption a. We now take the renewal equation $U=p+qU*G$ at point kb+x:

$$U_k(x) = p+q(U_k*G)(x)+q \int_{[x,b]} U_{k-1}(b+x-y)dG(y) \quad (k=0,1,2,...;\ 0\le x\le b). \tag{67}$$

We define the functions u_k (k= −1,0,1,2,...) by

$$u_{-1} \equiv 0\ ,\ u_k(x) := \sum_{0\le j\le k} V_j[(k-j)b+x] \ (k=0,1,2,...;\ x\in\mathbf{R}_+). \tag{68}$$

Then

$$V_k(x) = u_k(x) - u_{k-1}(b+x) \quad (k=0,1,...;\ x\in\mathbf{R}_+). \tag{69}$$

We will prove the relation

$$u_k(x) = p+q(u_k*g)(x)+q \int_{[x,b]} u_{k-1}(b+x-y)dg(y) \quad (k=0,1,2,...;\ x\in\mathbf{R}_+) \tag{70}$$

and then the proof can be finished as follows. Let k=0 in (67) and (70). Then the last term drops, and then relations (67) and (70) are renewal equations on [0,b] determining U_0 and u_0 on that interval. But G=g on [0,b] by assumption b and this implies that $U_0=u_0$ on [0,b]. We now consider (67) and (70) for k=1. These are renewal equations on [0,b], determining U_1 and u_1 on that interval. Then $U_1=u_1$ on [0,b], because G=g and $U_0=u_0$ on that interval. Repeating the argument, we obtain that $U_k=u_k$ on [0,b] (k=0,1,2,...). Then the relation (66) follows from (69) and from the definition of the functions U_k (k=0,1,2,...).

We now demonstrate (70). For k=0, this relation is (64). Hence, we assume that k≥1. For fixed k=1,2,... and $x\in\mathbf{R}_+$, we use the abbreviation

$$[\alpha,\beta](n) \equiv \int_{[\alpha,\beta]} u_{k-n}(nb+x-y)dg(y) \quad (0\le\alpha\le\beta;\ n=0,1,\dots,k).$$

By (65) and (69), for j=0,1,...,k−1,

$$1/_q\, V_{k-j}(jb+x) = (V_{k-j}*g)(jb+x) - (V_{k-j-1}*g_b)(jb+x),$$

$$1/_q\, V_{k-j}(jb+x) = 1/_q[u_{k-j}(jb+x)-u_{k-j-1}(b+jb+x)],$$

$$(V_{k-j}*g)(jb+x) = \int_{[0,jb+x]} u_{k-j}(jb+x-y)dg(y) - \int_{[0,jb+x]} u_{k-j-1}(b+jb+x-y)dg(y)$$

$$= [0,jb+x](j) - [0,jb+x](j+1),$$

$$(V_{k-j-1}*g_b)(x) = \int_{[0,jb+x]} u_{k-j-1}(jb+x-y)dg_b(y) - \int_{[0,jb+x]} u_{k-j-2}(b+jb+x-y)dg_b(y)$$

$$= \int_{[b,b+jb+x]} u_{k-j-1}(b+jb+x-y)dg(y) - \int_{[b,b+jb+x]} u_{k-j-2}(2b+jb+x-y)dg(y)$$

$$= [b,(j+1)b+x](j+1) - [b,(j+1)b+x](j+2),$$

by definition c of g_b. Hence, for j=0,1,2,...,k−1

$$\begin{aligned} &1/_q[u_{k-j}(jb+x)-u_{k-j-1}(b+jb+x)] \\ &= [0,jb+x](j) - [0,jb+x](j+1) - [b,(j+1)b+x](j+1) + [b,(j+1)b+x](j+2). \end{aligned} \tag{71}$$

The relation corresponding to j=k results from (64). It is

$$1/_q\, u_0(kb+x) = p/_q + [0,kb+x](k). \tag{72}$$

The first members of the relations (71) for k=0,1,...,k−1, and of (72) are

$$1/_q[u_k(x)-u_{k-1}(b+x)],$$

$$1/_q[u_{k-1}(b+x)-u_{k-2}(2b+x)],$$

$$\cdots\ \cdots\ \cdots\ \cdots\ \cdots\ \cdots\ \cdots$$

$$1/_q[u_1((k-1)b+x)-u_0(kb+x)],$$

$$1/_q\, u_0(kb+x).$$

Their sum is

$$1/_q\, u_k(x). \tag{73}$$

The last members of the relations (71) for j=0,1,2,...,k−1, and of (72) are

$$[0,x](0) - [0,x](1) - [b,b+x](1) + [b,b+x](2),$$

$$[0,b+x](1) - [0,b+x](2) - [b,2b+x](2) + [b,2b+x](3),$$

$$[0,2b+x](2) - [0,2b+x](3) - [b,3b+x](3) + [b,3b+x](4),$$

$$[0,3b+x](3) - [0,3b+x](4) - [b,4b+x](4) + [b,4b+x](5),$$

... ...

$$[0,(k-2)b+x](k-2)-[0,(k-2)b+x](k-1)-[b,(k-1)b+x](k-1)+[b,(k-1)b+x](k),$$

$$[0,(k-1)b+x](k-1) - [0,(k-1)b+x](k) - [b,kb+x](k),$$

$$p/q + [0,kb+x](k).$$

Their sum is

$$p/q + [0,x](0) + [x,b](1)$$

$$= p/q + \int_{[0,x]} u_k(x-y)dg(y) + \int_{[x,b]} u_{k-1}(b+x-y)dg(y). \qquad (74)$$

Then (73) equals (74), and this proves (70) •

8.5.4. Non-Ruin Distribution U in Very Regular Case

Theorem 12

Let g be a very regular function and let b∈R₊. Then g(b+x) is a very regular function of x∈R₊.

Proof

Let

$$g(x) = \sum_{k\geq 0} a_k x^k.$$

Then

$$g(b+x) = \sum_{k\geq 0} a_k(b+x)^k = \sum_{k\geq 0} a_k \sum_{0\leq j\leq k} k!/j!(k-j)!\ x^j b^{k-j}$$

$$= \sum_{j\geq 0} \sum_{k\geq j} a_k\ k!/j!(k-j)!\ x^j b^{k-j} = \sum_{j\geq 0}[\sum_{k\geq 0} a_{k+j}\ (k+j)!/j!k!\ b^k]x^j. \qquad (75)$$

These calculations are allowed. Indeed, entire functions converge absolutely everywhere. Then the calculations furnish finite results when the coefficients a_k are replaced by $|a_k|$, and in that case they are permitted by Fubini. Then they are also permitted with the initial coefficients a_k. Hence, g(b+x) is an entire function. By (75)

$$Tg(b+x) = \sum_{j\geq 0}[\sum_{k\geq 0} a_{k+j}\, {}^{(k+j)!}/_{k!}\, b^k]x^j.$$

The radius of convergence r of the power series expansion of Tg(x) is strictly positive:

$$\lim\sup_{k\uparrow\infty} (k!|a_k|)^{1/k} = 1/_r < \infty.$$

Let $c>1/_r$. For some k_0, and then all $k\geq k_0$,

$$(k!|a_k|)^{1/k} \leq c \;,\; k!|a_k| \leq c^k.$$

Then, for some B,

$$k!|a_k| \leq B\, c^k \; (k=0,1,2,...).$$

Then, for $x<1/_c$,

$$\sum_{j\geq 0}|\sum_{k\geq 0} a_{k+j}\, {}^{(k+j)!}/_{k!}\, b^k|x^j \leq \sum_{j\geq 0}\sum_{k\geq 0} |a_{k+j}|\, {}^{(k+j)!}/_{k!}\, b^k x^j$$

$$\leq \sum_{j\geq 0}\sum_{k\geq 0} {}^{Bc^{k+j}}/_{k!}\, b^k x^j = B\sum_{j\geq 0}(cx)^j.\sum_{k\geq 0} {}^{(bc)^k}/_{k!} = B.1/_{(1-cx)}.e^{bc} < \infty.$$

This means that the radius of convergence of the power series Tg(b+x) is at least $1/_c$. Hence g(b+x) is a very regular function •

Theorem 13

In Theorem 11, let g be a very regular function. Then g_b and the functions $V_0,V_1,V_2,...$ are very regular, and

$$\mathbf{TV_k = p(-q)^k(Tg_b)^k/(1-qTg)^{k+1} \;\; near\ 0\ \ (k=0,1,2,...).} \qquad (76)$$

Proof

The function g_b is very regular by Theorem 12. Then (64) and (65) for k=1,2,... are successively very regular renewal equations with very regular solutions $V_0,V_1,V_2,...$, by Theorem 2 and Theorem 4. Taking the factorial transforms of (64) and (65), relations connecting $TV_0,TV_1,...,TV_k$ are obtained. Then (76) results from the elimination of $TV_0,TV_1,...,TV_{k-1}$ •

8.6. Simple Truncated Claimsize Distributions

8.6.1. Definitions

The function H is simple on the interval $J \subseteq \mathbf{R}_+$ if a simple function h exists such that H=h on J.

A simple truncated claimsize distribution function is a claimsize distribution function F expressible as $F = f1_{[0,b[} + 1_{[b,\infty[}$, where $b \in \mathbf{R}_{++}$ and where f is a simple function.

The observations about very regular truncated claimsize distributions, made in section 8.5.1, apply to simple truncated claimsize distributions.

8.6.2. Concave Transform G

Theorem 14

If the claimsize distribution function F, in the classical risk model, is simple on the interval [0,b[, then its concave transform G is simple on the interval [0,b].

Proof
The proof is the same as the proof of Theorem 10. Here g(x) is simple if f(x) is simple, because then g(x) is the inverse factorial transform of a rational polynomial without a pole at 0 (Theorem 5):

$$g(x) = {}^{1}/_{\mu}\, T^{-1}[x[1-Tf(x)]] \quad \bullet$$

8.6.3. Non-Ruin Distribution U

Theorem 15

Let g be a simple function and let $b \in \mathbf{R}_+$. Then g(b+x) is a simple function of $x \in \mathbf{R}_+$.

Proof
This is direct by elementary expressions of the functions $(b+x)^k$, $e^{(b+x)}$, sin(b+x) and cos(b+x) •

Theorem 16

In Theorem 11, let g be a simple function. Then g_b and $V_0,V_1,V_2,\ldots$ are simple functions, resulting from the relations

$$V_k = p(-q)^k\, T^{-1}[(Tg_b)^k/(1-qTg)^{k+1}] \quad (k=0,1,2,\ldots) \tag{77}$$

by Theorem 5.

Proof
By Theorem 5, Theorem 11 and Theorem 13 •

8.6.4. Illustrations

In the following illustrations, the notations of Theorem 11 are used. The functions V_k are obtained via relation (76) or (77). The factorial transforms result from the formulas of section 8.2.2, and the inverse factorial transforms from the formulas of section 8.2.3

Example 1: Atomic claimsize distribution

Let

$$F := 0 \text{ on } [0,b[\quad , \quad F := 1 \text{ on } [b,\infty[.$$

Then

$$G(x) = x/b \ (0\le x\le b) \ , \ G = 1 \text{ on } [b,\infty[\ , \ g(x) = g_b(x) = x/b \ (x\in \mathbf{R}_+),$$

$$TV_k(x) = pq^k\,(-1)^k\,(x/b)^k/(1-qx/b)^{k+1},$$

$$V_k(x) = pq^k/k!\,(-1)^k\,(x/b)^k\,e^{qx/b},$$

$$U(nb+x) = \sum_{0\le k\le n} pq^k(-1)^k/k!\,[n-k+(x/b)]^k\,e^{q[n-k+(x/b)]} \quad (n=0,1,2,\ldots;\ 0\le x\le b).$$

Example 2: Uniform claimsize distribution

Let

$$F(x) := x/b \ (0\le x\le b) \ , \ F := 1 \text{ on } [b,\infty[.$$

Then

$$\mu = b/2 \ , \ G(x) = 2(x/b) - (x/b)^2 \ (0\le x\le b),$$

$$g(x) = 2(x/b) - (x/b)^2 \ (x \in \mathbf{R}_+) \ , \quad g_b(x) = -(x/b)^2 \ (x \in \mathbf{R}_+).$$

$$TV_k(x) = p(2q/b^2)^k x^{2k}[1-2q(x/b)+2q(x/b)^2]^{-k-1}.$$

The binomial in square brackets has two complex conjugate roots. It can be displayed as

$$1-2q(x/b)+2q(x/b)^2 = (1+\alpha x)(1+\beta x) = (1+sx)^2+t^2x^2,$$

where

$$\alpha = s+it \ , \ \beta = s-it \ , \ s \in \mathbf{R}_{++} \ , \ t \in \mathbf{R}.$$

Let

$$W_k(s,t,x) := T^{-1}[x^{2k}[(1+sx)^2+t^2x^2]^{-k-1}]. \tag{78}$$

Then

$$U(nb+x) = p\textstyle\sum_{0\le k\le n} (2q/b^2)^k \, W_k(s,t,(n-k)b+x) \ \ (n=0,1,2,\ldots; \ 0\le x\le b).$$

We now explain how the functions $W_k(s,t,x)$ can be obtained. For k=0, by (39),

$$W_0(s,t,x) = [\cos(tx) - s\ {}^{1}\!/_{t} \sin(tx)]e^{-sx}, \tag{79}$$

By (78),

$$W_{k+1}(s,t,x) = -[2(k+1)t]^{-1}\ \partial/\partial t\ W_k(s,t,x) \ \ (k=0,1,2,\ldots). \tag{80}$$

The permutation of the operators T^{-1} and $\partial/\partial t$ can be justified by analytic arguments. Then, starting with $W_0(s,t,x)$ as furnished by (79), the functions $W_1(s,t,x)$, $W_2(s,t,x)$,... result successively from the application of (80).

But the "closed expressions" are soon cumbersome. An easy general expression for $W_k(s,t,x)$ results from the formulas

$$ {}^{1}\!/_{t} \sin(tx) = \textstyle\sum_{k\ge 0} {}^{(-1)^k}\!/_{(2k+1)!}\ t^{2k}\, x^{2k+1}, \tag{81}$$

$$\cos(tx) = \textstyle\sum_{k\ge 0} {}^{(-1)^k}\!/_{(2k)!}\ (tx)^{2k}, \tag{82}$$

to be used in the last member of (79).

Example 3: Truncated exponential claimsize distribution

Let

$$F(x) := 1-ae^{-cx} \ (0\le x<b) \ , \ F := 1 \text{ on } [b,\infty[\ , \ 0<a\le 1 \ , \ c>0.$$

Then

$$G(x) = {}^{a}\!/_{(\mu c)}\,(1-e^{-cx}) \ (0\le x\le b),$$

where μ results from the relation G(b)=1.

$$g(x) = a/(\mu c)\,(1-e^{-cx})\ ,\ g_b(x) = e^{-cb}g(x)\ ,\ Tg(x) = a/\mu\ x/(1+cx),$$

$$TV_k(x) = p(-q)^k e^{-kbc}\,[a/\mu\ x/(1+cx)]^k/[1-q\ a/\mu\ x/(1+cx)]^{k+1}$$

$$= p(-q)^k e^{-kbc} a^k\ \mu\ x^k(1+cx)/[\mu+(\mu c-qa)x]^{k+1}.$$

Case $\mu c = qa$.

$$TV_k(x) = p(-q)^k e^{-kbc} a^k\ \mu^{-k}\ x^k(1+cx),$$

$$V_k(x) = p(-q)^k e^{-kbc} a^k\ \mu^{-k}\ [x^k/k! + cx^{k+1}/(k+1)!].$$

Case $\mu c \neq qa$.

Let $t := c-(qa/\mu)$. Then,

$$TV_k(x) = p(-q)^k e^{-kbc} a^k\ \mu^{-k}[[x^k/(1+tx)^{k+1}] + c[x/(1+tx)]^{k+1}],$$

and by (28) and (48),

$$V_k(x) = p(-q)^k e^{-kbc} a^k\ \mu^{-k}[[x^k/k!\ e^{-tx} + ct^{-k-1}[1 - e^{-tx}\textstyle\sum_{0\le j\le k}(tx)^j/j!]].$$

In each case, the substitution of V_k in (66) furnishes the explicit non-ruin probabilities.

Example 4: Truncated trigonometric claimsize distribution

Let

$$F(x) := 1-\cos(x)\ \ (0\le x\le b=\pi/2)\ ,\ \ F := 1 \text{ on } [b,\infty[.$$

Then

$$G(x) = \sin(x)\ \ (x\le 0\le b)\ ,\ g(x) = \sin(x)\ ,\ g_b(x) = \cos(x)-1\ (x\in\mathbf{R}_+),$$

$$Tg(x) = x/(1+x^2)\ ,\ Tg_b(x) = -x^2/(1+x^2),$$

$$TV_k(x) == p(-q)^k\,[-x^2/(1+x^2)]^k/[1-q(x/1+x^2)]^{k+1}$$

$$= pq^k x^{2k}(1+x^2)/[1-qx+x^2]^{k+1}.$$

The binomial in square brackets has two complex conjugate roots. As in *Example 2*, it can be displayed as

$$1-qx+x^2 = (1+sx)^2+t^2x^2\ ,\ s\in\mathbf{R}_{++}\ ,\ t\in\mathbf{R}.$$

Then, using (47) twice,

$$V_k(x) = pq^k[W_k(s,t,x) + W_k^{II}(s,t,x)], \qquad (83)$$

where the function $W_k(s,t,x)$ is defined by (78), and where

$$W_k^{II}(s,t,x) = \int_{[0,x]} W_k^{I}(s,t,y)dy \ , \ \ W_k^{I}(s,t,x) = \int_{[0,x]} W(s,t,y)dy. \qquad (84)$$

The functions $W_k(s,t,x)$ (k=0,1,2,...) can be found as in *Example 2*. Then the functions $W_k^{II}(s,t,x)$ (k=0,1,2,...) result from (84). The relations soon become lengthy and complicated. Simple general expression are obtained when the expansions (81) and (82) are used.

The non-ruin probabilities result from the introduction of $V_k(x)$, furnished by (83), in (66).

Chapter 9

Infinite-Time Ruin Probabilities in Risk Models with Stochastic Premium Income

9.0. Introduction

In this Chapter, the risk reserve process R_τ ($\tau \geq 0$) is such that

$$R_{\tau+d\tau} = R_\tau + \gamma(R_\tau)d\tau \quad \text{(No claim in the time-interval } d\tau)$$

$$R_\tau = R_{\tau-} - X \quad \text{(One claim with amount X at the instant } \tau).$$

The **premium income intensity** $\gamma(\cdot)$ is a rather arbitrary positive function. The premium income in the infinitesimal time-interval $d\tau$ equals $\gamma(R_\tau)d\tau$.

Hereafter, we consider, as illustrations, some risk models with stochastic premium income. We observe that the same intensity function γ may sometimes be interpreted in different ways and lead to models with different names. We assume, in the examples, that the claim instants process is the Poisson process with constant intensity $\lambda>0$.

a. *Classical risk model*

This model results from the intensity function $\gamma \equiv \mu\lambda(1+\eta)$. The premium income in the interval $d\tau$ does not depend on the risk reserve at τ.

b. *A model with interests*

Let $\gamma(u) := \mu\lambda(1+\eta+cu)$, where c is a positive constant. Then the premium income in the interval $d\tau$ is $\mu\lambda(1+\eta)d\tau + R_\tau c\mu\lambda d\tau$. The part $R_\tau c\mu\lambda d\tau$ of this income can be interpreted as interests produced by the capital R_τ in the interval $d\tau$.

c. ***A model with dividends***

Let $\gamma(u):=\mu\lambda(1+\eta-c1_{u\geq u^\circ})$, where $0<c<\eta$, and where $u^\circ>0$ is a fixed risk reserve. Then the premium income in $d\tau$ is $\mu\lambda(1+\eta)d\tau-c\mu\lambda 1_{R_\tau\geq u^\circ}d\tau$. The negative part can be interpreted as dividends returned by the insurance company as soon as the risk reserve is larger than u°.

d. ***A model with variable security loading***

Let $\gamma(u):=\mu\lambda[1+\eta(u)]$. Then the premium income in $d\tau$ is $\mu\lambda[1+\eta(R_\tau)]d\tau$ and $\eta(R_\tau)$ can be interpreted as being a stochastic security loading. For instance, the function $\eta(u)$ could be $\eta(u)=\eta_1 1_{u\leq u^\circ}+\eta_2 1_{u>u^\circ}$, meaning that the insurer works with the security loading η_1 if the risk reserve is less than u°, and with the security loading η_2 otherwise.

Assumptions on the claim process

In sections 9.1 and 9.2, no special assumptions are made on the claim process $(T_1,X_1,T_2,X_2,...)$. In sections 9.3 to 9.7, the claim process is the same as in the classical risk model. Then the claim instants process is homogeneous Poisson with parameter λ. The partial claim amounts are i.i.d. with distribution F, corresponding concave transform G and expectation $\mu\in]0,\infty[$. The partial claim amounts are independent from the claim instants.

9.1. Deterministic Premium Income Function

9.1.1. Premium Income Function

A **premium income function** is a function $r(t/u)$ defined for $t\in\mathbf{R}_+$ and $u\in\mathbf{R}$, with the following properties, for all $u,v\in\mathbf{R}$ and all $\tau,t\in\mathbf{R}_+$:

$$r(0/u)=u, \tag{1}$$

$$r(t/u)\geq u, \tag{2}$$

$$r(t/u)\leq r(t/v)\quad(u\leq v), \tag{3}$$

$$r(\tau+t/u)=r[t/r(\tau/u)]. \tag{4}$$

Interpretation

Let $s \in \mathbf{R}_+$ be a fixed instant at which the risk reserve equals u. Then r(t/u) is the risk reserve at the instant s+t if no claim occurs in the interval [s,s+t] :

$$R_{s+t} = r(s/R_t) \quad \text{(no claims in [s,s+t])}. \tag{5}$$

The properties (1) to (4) must be satisfied in any consistent premium income model in which the premium earned in any claim-free interval [s,s+t], only depends on the length t of the interval, and on the value u of the risk reserve at the origin s of the interval.

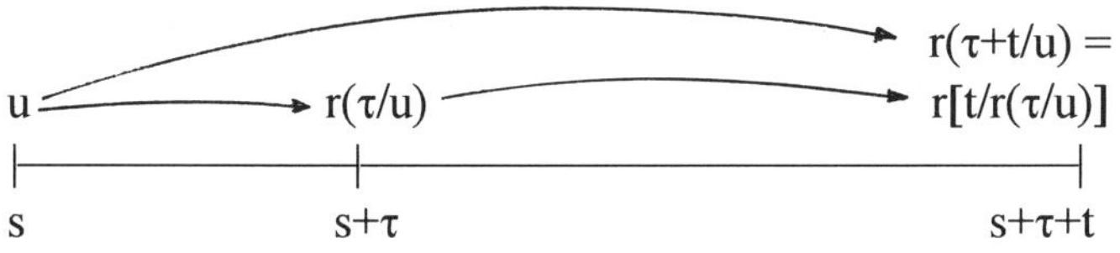

In particular, the **iterativity property** (4) states that, starting from any point s at which the risk reserve equals u, it amounts to the same to evaluate the risk reserve in one step, at s+τ+t, or to evaluate it in two steps: first at s+τ, and then at (s+τ)+t from the value r(τ/u) at s+τ.

The function r(t/u) is an increasing function of t. Indeed, by (4) and (3)

$$r(\tau+t/u) = r[t/r(\tau/u)] \geq r(t/u), \tag{6}$$

because $r(\tau/u) \geq u$ by (2).

In the next section 9.1.2, we show how the premium income function r(t/u) can be constructed from the **premium income intensity function**.

9.1.2. Premium Income Intensity Function

A **premium income intensity function on $\mathbf{R}_+$** is a positive function $\gamma(\cdot)$ on $\mathbf{R}_+$, with the following properties a_+ , b_+ and c_+ :

a_+ γ is bounded on bounded intervals.

b_+ $1/\gamma$ is Lebesgue-integrable on bounded intervals.

c_+ $1/\gamma$ is not Lebesgue integrable on $\mathbf{R}_+$.

A **premium income intensity function on R**, is a positive function $\gamma(\cdot)$ on **R**, with the following properties a, b and c:

a. γ is bounded on bounded intervals.

b. $1/\gamma$ is Lebesgue-integrable on bounded intervals.

c. $1/\gamma$ is not Lebesgue-integrable on $\mathbf{R}_-$ and $1/\gamma$ is not Lebesgue-integrable on $\mathbf{R}_+$.

Interpretations

The premium income in the interval (t,t+dt) is $\gamma(u)dt$ if the risk reserve equals u at the instant t (see following relation (9)).

If we are only interested in finite or infinite-time ruin probabilities, then the evolution of the risk reserve process is irrelevant as soon as it becomes strictly negative. We can agree that it remains constant as soon as it becomes strictly negative, if that happens. Or we can also agree to the fact that the process stops at the first instant T_k such that $R_{T_k}<0$, if such an instant exists. **Then $\gamma(\cdot)$ must only be defined on $\mathbf{R}_+$.**

If fixed-time ruin probabilities are considered, or when general properties of the process are considered (say martingale properties), then it must be specified what happens to the risk reserve process when it becomes strictly negative. **Then $\gamma(\cdot)$ must be defined on R.**

Only infinite-time ruin probabilities are considered later. Hence, we only need $\gamma(\cdot)$ on $\mathbf{R}_+$. But it is convenient to extend $\gamma(\cdot)$ to **R** by the condition $\gamma:\equiv 1$ on $\mathbf{R}_-$ (or in any other way, so that a,b,c hold).

Theorem 1

Let γ be a premium income intensity function on R, and let $\alpha(\cdot)$ be the function on R with values

$$\alpha(x) := \int_{[0,x]} 1/\gamma(y)\, dy \quad (x \in \mathbf{R}). \tag{7}$$

Then $\alpha(\cdot)$ is a continuous strictly increasing function on R and

$$\alpha(-\infty) = -\infty \quad , \quad \alpha(0) = 0 \quad , \quad \alpha(+\infty) = +\infty.$$

Let $\beta(\cdot)$ be the inverse function of $\alpha(\cdot)$. Then $\beta(\cdot)$ is a continuous strictly increasing function on R and

$$\alpha(-\infty) = -\infty \quad , \quad \alpha(0) = 0 \quad , \quad \alpha(+\infty) = +\infty.$$

Let $r(\cdot/\cdot)$ be the function defined by

$$r(t/u) := \beta[t+\alpha(u)] \quad (t\in\mathbf{R}_+, u\in\mathbf{R}). \tag{8}$$

Then $r(\cdot/\cdot)$ is a premium income function. For fixed $u\in\mathbf{R}$, the function $r(t) \equiv r(t/u)$ of $t\in\mathbf{R}_+$ is the solution of the differential equation

$$r'(t) = \gamma[r(t)] \tag{9}$$

with initial value $r(0)=u$.

Proof

The properties of $\alpha(\cdot)$ and $\beta(\cdot)$ are obvious from the assumptions on γ. Then the properties (1) to (4) of $r(\cdot/\cdot)$ are direct. For instance, (4) results from:

$$r[t/r(\tau/u)] = \beta[t+\alpha[r(\tau/u)]] = \beta[t+\alpha[\beta(\tau+\alpha(u))]]$$
$$= \beta[t+(\tau+\alpha(u))] = \beta[(t+\tau)+\alpha(u)] = r(\tau+t/u).$$

By (7), $\alpha'(x)=1/\gamma(x)$. From $\beta(\alpha(x)) = x$, results

$$\beta'(\alpha(x)).\alpha'(x) = 1.$$

Hence

$$\beta'(\alpha(x)) = \gamma(x).$$

Then the derivative of $r(t) \equiv r(t/u) = \beta(t+\alpha(u))$ with respect to t equals

$$r'(t) = \beta'(t+\alpha(u)) = \beta'[\alpha[\beta(t+\alpha(u))]] = \gamma[\beta(t+\alpha(u))] = \gamma[r(t)] \quad \bullet$$

In this Theorem, **oriented integration domains** are implicitly considered: $\int_{[0,x]}$ must be understood as $-\int_{[x,0]}$ when $x<0$.

9.1.3. Too Small and too Large Premium Income Intensities

We here consider two functions γ on $\mathbf{R}_+$ which are no premium income intensity functions. The starting point of the discussion is the differential equation (9).

A too small premium income intensity

Let us consider the function

$$\gamma(x) := x \quad (x \in \mathbf{R}_+).$$

Then the differential equation (9) is

$$r'(t) = r(t)\ , \text{ with solution } \ r(t) = c\,e^t,$$

where c is a constant fixed by the initial condition $r(0)=u$. Hence $c=u$, and

$$r(t/u) := ue^t \ (t,u \in \mathbf{R}_+)$$

is a premium income function with properties (1) to (4) for $u,v,t,\tau \in \mathbf{R}_+$. But the function $1/x$ is not Lebesgue-integrable on the bounded intervals $[0,b]$. It is not a premium income intensity function on $\mathbf{R}_+$ because the condition 9.1.2.b_+ is not satisfied. γ is too small in the neighboorhoud of 0.

The condition 9.1.2.b_+ could be dropped, but this complicates the presentation of the theory. Moreover, risk models in which that condition is not satisfied are most unrealistic, because in such models the premium income becomes very small when the risk reserve is very small already. We observe that the condition 9.1.2.b_+ is satisfied in the classical risk model with a negative security loading $\eta > -1$.

A too large premium income intensity

Let

$$\gamma(x) := (1+x)^2 \quad (x \in \mathbf{R}_+).$$

Then the differential equation (9) is $r'(t) = [1+r(t)]^2$. Its solution is

$$r(t) = (c-t)^{-1} - 1,$$

where $c=(1+u)^{-1}$ is the constant fixed by the initial condition $r(0)=u$.

When t increases, starting at 0, r(t) jumps to the value ∞ at the point $t=c$. Now **the premium income is explosive**. Here γ is not a premium income intensity function because the condition 9.1.2.c_+ is not satisfied. γ is too large.

Non-explosiveness is an essential condition (unless risk models with infinite risk reserves are considered).

9.1.4. Comparable Premium Income Intensity Functions

Theorem 2

Let $\gamma_1 \leq \gamma_2$ be premium income intensity functions on R and let $r_1(\cdot/\cdot)$ and $r_2(\cdot/\cdot)$ be the corresponding premium income functions defined by Theorem 1. Then

$$\mathbf{r_1(t_1/u_1) \leq r_2(t_2/u_2) \quad (0 \leq t_1 \leq t_2 \, , \, u_1 \leq u_2).} \tag{10}$$

Proof

It is sufficient to prove that $r_1(t/u) \leq r_2(t/u)$, because then

$$r_1(t_1/u_1) \leq r_1(t_2/u_1) \leq r_1(t_2/u_2) \leq r_2(t_2/u_2).$$

Let $\delta := \alpha_1 - \alpha_2$ (notations of Theorem 1 completed by subscribts $_1$ or $_2$). Then

$$\delta' = \alpha_1' - \alpha_2' = (1/\gamma_1) - (1/\gamma_2) \geq 0.$$

Hence, δ is an increasing function. The relation $u \leq \beta_1(t+\alpha_1(u))$ holds because it is an equality for t=0, and because the last member increases with t. Then

$$[t+\alpha_1(u)] - [t+\alpha_2(u)] = \delta(u) \leq \delta[\beta_1(t+\alpha_1(u))]$$

$$= \alpha_1[\beta_1(t+\alpha_1(u))] - \alpha_2[\beta_1(t+\alpha_1(u))] = [t+\alpha_1(u)] - \alpha_2[\beta_1(t+\alpha_1(u))],$$

$$\alpha_2[\beta_1(t+\alpha_1(u))] \leq [t+\alpha_2(u)],$$

$$\beta_2[\alpha_2[\beta_1(t+\alpha_1(u))]] \leq \beta_2[t+\alpha_2(u)],$$

$$\beta_1(t+\alpha_1(u)) \leq \beta_2[t+\alpha_2(u)],$$

$$r_1(t/u) \leq r_2(t/u) \quad \bullet$$

9.2. Risk Reserve Process

9.2.1. Definition of Risk Reserve Process

We now define the risk reserve process R_τ ($\tau \in \mathbf{R}_+$) corresponding to the premium income intensity function $\gamma(\cdot)$, the initial risk reserve u and the arbitrary claim process $(T_1, X_1, T_2, X_2, \ldots)$. Of course, the function $r(\cdot/\cdot)$ is the premium income function corresponding to γ, defined by Theorem 1.

Then

$$R_\tau := r(\tau/u) \ \ (0 \le \tau < T_1)\ , \ R_{T_1} := r(T_1/u) - X_1,$$

$$R_\tau := r(\tau - T_1 / R_{T_1}) \ \ (T_1 \le \tau < T_2)\ , \ R_{T_2} := r(T_2 - T_1 / R_{T_1}) - X_2,$$

$$\ldots \ \ldots \ \ldots \ \ldots \ \ldots \ \ldots \ \ldots \ \ldots \ \ldots \ \ldots \ \ldots \ \ldots \ , \ldots$$

If necessary more explicit notations such as $R(\tau/u)$ or $R(\tau/u,\gamma)$ are used. The usual notations for the ruin and non-ruin probabilities, defined in Ch.3.1.2. are employed. If necessary they are completed by the explicit mention of the premium income intensity function γ.

We observe that the risk reserve process is not defined via the total claim amounts process S_τ $(\tau \in \mathbf{R}_+)$.

9.2.2. Comparable Risk Reserves

In the following Theorem, the basic claim process $(T_1, X_1, T_2, X_2, \ldots)$ is the same in all cases. As usual, U denotes non-ruin probabilities.

Theorem 3

Let γ , γ_1 , γ_2 be premium income intensity functions on R. Then, for any $t, \tau \in \mathbf{R}_+$ and any $u, u_1, u_2 \in \mathbf{R}$,

$$\mathbf{R(\tau/u_1,\gamma) \le R(\tau/u_2,\gamma) \ \ (u_1 \le u_2),} \tag{11}$$

$$\mathbf{U(t,u_1/\gamma) \le U(t,u_2/\gamma) \ \ (0 \le u_1 \le u_2),} \tag{12}$$

$$\mathbf{U(u_1/\gamma) \le U(u_2/\gamma) \ \ (0 \le u_1 \le u_2),} \tag{13}$$

$$\mathbf{R(\tau/u,\gamma_1) \le R(\tau/u,\gamma_2) \ \ (\gamma_1 \le \gamma_2),} \tag{14}$$

$$\mathbf{U(t,u/\gamma_1) \le U(t,u/\gamma_2) \ \ (0 \le u \ ; \ \gamma_1 \le \gamma_2 \text{ on } R_+),} \tag{15}$$

$$\mathbf{U(u/\gamma_1) \le U(u/\gamma_2) \ \ (0 \le u \ ; \ \gamma_1 \le \gamma_2 \text{ on } R_+).} \tag{16}$$

Proof
(11) results from the definition of the risk reserve and from the properties of the premium income function. Then (12) and (13) result from (11).

The relation (14) results from the definition of the risk reserve and from Theorem 2. Then (15) and (16) result from (14) and the fact that γ_1 and γ_2 can be modified arbitrarily on $\mathbf{R}_{-}$, in order to have $\gamma_1 \leq \gamma_2$ on $\mathbf{R}$ •

9.3. Semi-Classical Risk Model

9.3.1. Definition of Semi-Classical Risk Model

The **semi-classical risk model** is a model with stochastic premium income defined from some premium income intensity function and with the same claim process $(T_1,X_1,T_2,X_2,...)$ as in the classical risk model. Of course, we do adopt the notations and terminology introduced in earlier Chapters concerning that claim process. Here the premium income intensity function is denoted by $\lambda\mu\gamma(\cdot)$, instead of $\gamma(\cdot)$. Hence, now

$$R_{\tau+d\tau} = R_\tau + \lambda\mu\gamma(R_\tau)d\tau \tag{17}$$

and the relation (7) must be replaced by

$$\alpha(x) = \int_{[0,x]} [\lambda\mu\gamma(y)]^{-1}dy \quad (x\in\mathbf{R}). \tag{18}$$

But the scaling factor $\lambda\mu$ is omitted in notations such as $R(\tau/u,\gamma)$, $U(u/\gamma)$. The function γ must, initially, be defined on $\mathbf{R}_+$ only. It is extended to $\mathbf{R}$ by the condition: $\gamma \equiv 1$ on $\mathbf{R}_{-}$, say.

9.3.2. Integral Equations for U

Theorem 4

In the semi-classical risk model with premium income intensity function $\lambda\mu\gamma(\cdot)$ on R, the infinite-time non-ruin probability function U has a density U' and

$$\mathbf{U(u) = \int_{[0,\infty[} \lambda e^{-\lambda\tau}d\tau \int_{[0,r(\tau/u)]} U(r(\tau/u)-x)dF(x) \quad (u\in R_+),} \tag{19}$$

$$\mathbf{(1-F)*U = \mu\gamma U' \quad on\ R_+,} \tag{20}$$

$$\mathbf{(G*U)(u) = \int_{]0,u]} \gamma(x)dU(x) \quad (u\in R_+).} \tag{21}$$

Proof

For the proof of (19), let U(t,u,n) be the probability of n claims and no ruin in [0,t] corresponding to the initial risk reserve u. We will prove thet

$$U(t,u,n) = \int_{[0,t]} \lambda e^{-\lambda\tau} d\tau \int_{[0,r(\tau/u)]} U(t-\tau, r(\tau/u)-x, n-1)dF(x). \tag{22}$$

From this relation results (19) in the same way that Ch.7.(13) results from Ch.7.(11). We will verify (22) for n=3. The ideas of a general demonstration are clear from this particular proof.

Hereafter, we call the application of the general formula

$$\int_{a<\tau<b} \varphi(\tau)d\tau = \int_{a-c<\tau<b-c} \varphi(\tau+c)d\tau,$$

a c-translation of the integration variable τ.

We now consider U(t,u,3). We denote by $\tau<\tau'<\tau''$ the claim instants in [0,t] and by x, x′, x″ the corresponding claim amounts. Then ruin does not occur iff

$$x \le r(\tau/u),$$

$$x' \le r[\tau'-\tau \,/\, r(\tau/u)-x],$$

$$x'' \le r\{\tau''-\tau' \,/\, r[\tau'-\tau \,/\, r(\tau/u)-x]-x'\}.$$

Hence,

$$U(t,u,3) = \int_{0<\tau<t} d\tau \int_{x\le r(\tau/u)} dF(x) \Big[\int_{\tau<\tau'<t} d\tau' \int_{x'\le r[\tau'-\tau \,/\, r(\tau/u)-x]} dF(x')$$
$$\int_{\tau'<\tau''<t} d\tau'' \int_{x''\le r\{\tau''-\tau' \,/\, r[\tau'-\tau \,/\, r(\tau/u)-x]-x'\}} \lambda^3 e^{-\lambda t} dF(x'')\Big].$$

The integral in square brackets equals

$$Int := \int_{0<\tau'<t-\tau} d\tau' \int_{x'\le r[\tau' \,/\, r(\tau/u)-x]} dF(x')$$
$$\Big[\int_{\tau'+\tau<\tau''<t} d\tau'' \int_{x''\le r\{\tau''-\tau'-\tau \,/\, r[\tau' \,/\, r(\tau/u)-x]-x'\}} \lambda^3 e^{-\lambda t} dF(x'')\Big]$$

by a τ-translation of the integration variable τ'. The integral in the latter square brackets equals

$$\int_{\tau'<\tau''<t-\tau} d\tau'' \int_{x''\le r\{\tau''-\tau' \,/\, r[\tau' \,/\, r(\tau/u)-x]-x'\}} \lambda^3 e^{-\lambda t} dF(x'').$$

by a τ-translation of the integration variable τ''.

Hence,

$$\text{Int} := \lambda e^{-\lambda\tau}\int_{0<\tau'<t-\tau} d\tau' \int_{x'\le r[\tau'/r(\tau/u)-x]} dF(x')$$

$$\int_{\tau'<\tau''<t-\tau} d\tau'' \int_{x''\le r\{\tau''-\tau'/r[\tau'/r(\tau/u)-x]-x'\}} \lambda^2 e^{-\lambda(t-\tau)}\, dF(x'')$$

$$= \lambda e^{-\lambda\tau}\, U(t-\tau, r(\tau/u)-x, 2),$$

$$U(t,u,3) = \int_{0<\tau<t} \lambda e^{-\lambda\tau}\, d\tau \int_{x\le r(\tau/u))} U(t-\tau, r(\tau/u)-x, 2)\, dF(x).$$

This proves (22) for n=3.

For the proof of (20), we observe that the inner integral in the last member of (19) equals $(U*F)(r(\tau/u))$. Hence, by (8),

$$U(u) = \int_{[0,\infty[} \lambda e^{-\lambda\tau}(U*F)[\beta(\tau+\alpha(u))]d\tau.$$

We replace the integration variable τ by $s:=\beta(\tau+\alpha(u))$. Then $\tau=\alpha(s)-\alpha(u)$,

$$U(u) = \int_{[u,\infty[} \lambda e^{-\lambda[\alpha(s)-\alpha(u)]}\, (U*F)(s)\alpha'(s)ds$$

$$= e^{\lambda\alpha(u)} \int_{[u,\infty[} \lambda e^{-\lambda\alpha(s)}\, (U*F)(s)\alpha'(s)ds.$$

From the latter expression and (18) results the absolute continuity of U on bounded intervals, i.e. the existence of the density U'. Then

$$U'(u) = \lambda\alpha'(u)e^{\lambda\alpha(u)}\int_{[u,\infty[}\lambda e^{-\lambda\alpha(s)}(U*F)(s)\alpha'(s)ds - e^{\lambda\alpha(u)}\lambda e^{-\lambda\alpha(u)}\, (U*F)(u)\alpha'(u)$$

$$= \lambda\alpha'(u)U(u) - \lambda\alpha'(u)(U*F)(u).$$

From this results (20), because $\alpha'(u) = [\mu\lambda\gamma(u)]^{-1}$ by (18). For the proof of (21), we display (20) as $U*[\mu^{-1}(1-F)] = \gamma U'$ and we take the convolution product by the identity function I on $\mathbf{R}_+$:

$$U*[\mu^{-1}(1-F)*I] = (\gamma U')*I.$$

The convolution product by I is a Lebesgue-integration. The function in square brackets is the concave transform G of F. This proves (21) •

Remark (Quick "proofs")

a. Relation (19) is direct from a partition of the considered non-ruin event according to the values taken by T_1 and X_1 . But then one must be sure that the risk reserve process has the required properties implying (19).

b. A more direct "proof" of (20) goes as follows. In the small time-interval $[0,\varepsilon]$, no claim occurs, one claim occurs (say at the instant $\xi\in[0,\varepsilon]$) or strictly more than one claim occurs. Hence, by interpretation (17) of the intensity function γ :

$$U(u) = P(N_\varepsilon=0)U(u+\mu\lambda\gamma(u)\varepsilon)+P(N_\varepsilon=1)\int_{[0,u+\mu\lambda\gamma(u)\xi]} U(u+\mu\lambda\gamma(u)\xi-x)dF(x)+\varepsilon o(\varepsilon)$$

$$= (1-\lambda\varepsilon)[U(u) + \mu\lambda\gamma(u)\varepsilon U'(u)] + \lambda\varepsilon\int_{[0,u]} U(u-x)dF(x)+\varepsilon o(\varepsilon)$$

$$= (1-\lambda\varepsilon)[U(u) + \mu\lambda\gamma(u)\varepsilon U'(u)] + \lambda\varepsilon(U*F)(u) + \varepsilon o(\varepsilon),$$

$$U(u) = U(u) -\lambda\varepsilon U(u) + \mu\lambda\gamma(u)\varepsilon U'(u) + \lambda\varepsilon(U*F)(u) + \varepsilon o(\varepsilon).$$

In the latter relation, we simplify by $U(u)$ in each member, then we divide by $\lambda\varepsilon$, and then we let $\varepsilon\downarrow 0$. The result is (20).

9.4. Regular and Practical Semi-Classical Risk Models

9.4.1. Definitions

From (13) results that the infinite-time non-ruin probability function U is increasing.

We say that **the semi-classical risk model is regular** if $U(0)$ is strictly positive and if $U(\infty)=1$. The classical risk model (with strictly positive security loading) is a particular regular semi-classical model.

We say that **the premium income intensity function $\lambda\mu\gamma(\cdot)$ is practical** if $\gamma\geq 1+\varepsilon$ on $\mathbf{R}_+$ for some $\varepsilon>0$. A semi-classical risk model with practical premium income intensity function is a **practical semi-classical risk model.** The classical risk model (with strictly positive security loading) is a practical semi-classical risk model.

9.4.2. Properties

Theorem 5

Any practical semi-classical risk model is regular.

Proof

We consider the practical semi-classical risk model with premium income intensity function $\lambda\mu\gamma(\cdot)$ where $\gamma\geq 1+\varepsilon$ on $\mathbf{R}_+$ and $\varepsilon>0$. Let $\gamma_1\equiv(1+\varepsilon)$, and let us also consider the semi-classical model with premium income intensity function $\lambda\mu\gamma_1$. The latter is a classical model, in which

$$U(0/\gamma_1) > 0 \,,\; U(\infty/\gamma_1) = 1 .$$

From $\gamma_1\leq\gamma$ on $\mathbf{R}_+$ results

$$U(u/\gamma_1) \leq U(u/\gamma) \quad (u\in\mathbf{R}_+)$$

by (16). Hence, for u=0, and as $u\uparrow\infty$,

$$0 < U(0/\gamma_1) \leq U(0/\gamma) \;\;,\;\; 1 = U(\infty/\gamma_1) \leq U(\infty/\gamma).$$

This proves that the model with premium income intensity function $\lambda\mu\gamma(\cdot)$ is regular •

From the fact that equation (21) determines U numerically when the model is regular (by following Theorem 9), it seems clear that this solution must be unique. The next Theorem 6 furnishes a proof of the unicity of the solution in the particular case that the semi-classical model is practical.

Theorem 6

In any practical semi-classical risk model, the infinite-time non-ruin probability function U is the unique solution of the equation (21), or of the equivalent equation (20), with the following properties: U is a probability distribution function with a density and U(0)> 0.

Proof

We consider the practical semi-classical risk model with premium income intensity function $\lambda\mu\gamma(\cdot)$ where $\gamma\geq 1+\varepsilon$ on $\mathbf{R}_+$ and $\varepsilon>0$. The equations (20) and (21) are equivalent because (21) has resulted from (20) in the proof of Theorem 4, and because the differentiation of (21) furnishes (20). By Theorems 4, 5 and 6, the function U has the indicated properties.

Let

$$V(x) := U(x)/U(0) \quad (x \in \mathbf{R}_+).$$

Then by (21),

$$(V^*G)(u) = \int_{]0,u]} \gamma(x)V'(x)dx. \tag{23}$$

By Ch.1.Th.15, V^*G has the density $V(0)G'+V'^*G$ on $\mathbf{R}_+$. Hence, taking the derivative of (23),

$$G'(u) + (V'^*G)(u) = \gamma(u)V'(u) \ \text{ Lebesgue-a.e.} \tag{24}$$

Let U_1 be another solution of (21), with the properties of U. Then the relation (24) holds for $V_1 := U_1/U_1(0)$ and by difference,

$$(f^*G)(u) = \gamma(u)f(u) \ \text{ Lebesgue-a.e., where } f := V' - V_1'.$$

Let N be a Lebesgue-nul set in $\mathbf{R}_+$, such that

$$(f^*G)(u) = \gamma(u)f(u) \quad (u \in \mathbf{C}N), \tag{25}$$

where $\mathbf{C}N$ is the complement of N with respect to $\mathbf{R}_+$. We assume that f is not zero Lebesgue-a.e. and we prove that this leads to a contradiction. Let sup ess(f) be the Lebesgue-essential supremum of f on $\mathbf{R}_+$. We may assume that sup ess(f) >0 because we can replace f by –f. Then a point u_0 exists in $\mathbf{C}N$ such that

$$f(u_0) > (1+\varepsilon)^{-1} \text{ sup ess}(f)$$

At the point u_0, the first member of (25) is less than

$$G(u_0).\text{sup ess}(f) \leq \text{sup ess}(f).$$

By the definition of u_0 and by the assumption on $\gamma(\cdot)$, the last member of (25) is strictly larger than sup ess(f) at the point u_0. From this contradiction results that f=0 and that $V'=V_1'$ Lebesgue-a.e. Then, by integration on]0,x], $V(x)=V_1(x)$ $(x \in \mathbf{R}_+)$ because $V(0)=1=V_1(0)$. Hence

$$U(x)/U(0) = U_1(x)/U_1(0) \quad (x \in \mathbf{R}_+).$$

As $x \uparrow \infty$, we obtain $U(0)=U_1(0)$ because $U(\infty)=1=U_1(\infty)$. Finally, $U=U_1$ on $\mathbf{R}_+$ •

9.5. Explicit Infinite-Time Non-Ruin Probabilities

9.5.1. Semi-Classical Risk Models with Given Non-Ruin Distribution Function U

Let F be any claimsize distribution with a finite strictly positive first moment μ. Let U be any probability distribution function with strictly positive density U' on $\mathbf{R}_+$ and with $U(0)>0$. Let the function $\gamma(\cdot)$ be defined on $\mathbf{R}_+$ by the relation

$$\gamma := [(1-F)*U]/(\mu U'). \tag{26}$$

Then γ is finite and strictly positive on $\mathbf{R}_+$, and very often, $\lambda\mu\gamma(\cdot)$ is a premium income intensity function on $\mathbf{R}_+$. In the latter case, let us consider the semi-classical risk model with the premium income intensity function $\lambda\mu\gamma(\cdot)$. Then relation (20) is satisfied, because it is equivalent to the relation (26) defining γ.

Hence, in this way, we can construct as many semi-classical risk models with explicit infinite-time non-ruin probability distribution function U, as wanted.

9.5.2. Exponential Cases

As an illustration, we here consider exponential cases. Let

$$F(x) := 1-e^{-ax} \ (x\in\mathbf{R}_+), \tag{27}$$

$$U(x) := 1-q'e^{-apx} \ (x\in\mathbf{R}_+), \tag{28}$$

where $a>0$, $p>0$, $0<q'<1$, and let $q:=1-p$, $p':=1-q'$.

Let us first assume that $p\neq1$. Then

$$[(1-F)*U](x) = \int_{[0,x]} e^{-a(x-y)}\, d(1-q'e^{-apy})$$

$$= (1-q')e^{-ax} + apq'e^{-ax}\int_{]0,x]} e^{-aqy}dy = p'e^{-ax} + q'p/q\; e^{-ax}[e^{-aqx}-1]$$

$$= p'e^{-ax} + q'p/q\;[e^{-apx}-e^{-ax}] = 1/q[(p'-p)e^{-ax} + pq'e^{-apx}].$$

Here $\mu=1/a$. Then

$$\mu U'(x) = \mu q' p e^{-px} = pq'\, e^{-apx}.$$

Then, by (26),

$$\gamma(x) = 1/(pqq')\, [pq' + (p'-p)e^{-aqx}].$$

Case p<1.

In the semi-classical risk model with claimsize distribution (27) and premium income intensity function $\lambda\mu\gamma(\cdot)$, the probability of non-ruin corresponding to the initial risk reserve x equals U(x) defined by (28).

Subcase p<p′ Then γ is a strictly increasing function.

Subcase p>p′ Then γ is a strictly decreasing function.

Subcase p=p′ Then $\gamma(x) \equiv 1/q = 1+\eta$ if we define η by this relation. Hence, we obtain the exponential case of the classical risk model considered in Ch.7.1.7

Case p>1. Then $q<0$ .This case is impossible because $\gamma(x)$ increases too fastly with x : it is not a premium income intensity function. The premium income is explosive.

Case p=1. Then $q=0$ and

$$[(1-F)*U](x) = \int_{[0,x]} e^{-a(x-y)}\, d(1-q'e^{-ay})$$

$$= (1-q')e^{-ax} + aq'e^{-ax} \int_{]0,x]} dy = p'e^{-ax} + aq'x\, e^{-ax}.$$

Now the conclusion is: **In the semi-classical risk model with claimsize distribution (27) and premium income intensity function $\lambda\mu\gamma(\cdot)$, where**

$$\gamma(x) := (p'/q') + ax,$$

the probability of non-ruin corresponding to the initial risk reserve x equals U(x) defined by (28).

9.6. Bounds for U

9.6.1. General Result

Theorem 7

In the semi-classical risk model with claimsize distribution F, premium income intensity function $\lambda\mu\gamma(\cdot)$ and infinite-time non-ruin probability function U, let $U^{\sim}$ be a fixed probability distribution function with strictly positive density $U^{\sim\prime}$ such that

$$(1-F)*U^{\sim} \leq \mu\gamma U^{\sim\prime} \quad \text{on } \mathbf{R}_+. \tag{29}$$

Let $$\gamma^{\sim} := [(1-F)*U^{\sim}]/(\mu U^{\sim\prime}). \tag{30}$$

If $\gamma^{\sim}(\cdot)$ is a premium income intensity function on $\mathbf{R}_+$, then $U^{\sim}\leq U$.

Proof
Let us consider the semi-classical risk model with claimsize distribution F and premium income intensity function $\lambda\mu\gamma^{\sim}(\cdot)$. Then $\gamma^{\sim}\leq\gamma$ by (29) and (30). Then $U^{\sim}\leq U$ by (16) •

Of course, if (29) is satisfied with ≤ replaced by ≥, the conclusion is $U^{\sim}\geq U$.

Remark

In the preceding Theorem, the Lebesgue-integrability of $1/\gamma^{\sim}$ on bounded intervals (9.1.2.b_+) is not essential. Indeed, γ and $\gamma^{\sim}$ can be replaced resp. by $\gamma\vee\varepsilon$ and $\gamma^{\sim}\vee\varepsilon$, and then a continuity argument can be used with $\varepsilon\downarrow 0$.

9.6.2. Generalized Exponential Bound

The next Theorem 8 is a beautiful extension, in the semi-classical risk model, of Lundberg's exponential bound in the classical model

We consider a semi-classical risk model with claimsize distribution function F and premium income intensity function $\lambda\mu\gamma(\cdot)$ such that $\gamma>1$. Then, for any fixed $x\in\mathbf{R}_+$, we consider the classical risk model with claimsize distribution F and with constant premium income intensity function $\gamma(x)$. The adjustment coefficient $\rho(x)$ in this model, if it exists, is **the local adjustment coefficient coresponding to $\gamma(x)$**.

Theorem 8 **(Asmussen-Nielsen)**

In the semi-classical risk model with claimsize distribution F, let the premium income intensity function $\lambda\mu\gamma(\cdot)$ have the following properties: $\gamma > 1$, γ is an increasing function, and the local adjustment coefficient $\rho(x)$ corresponding to $\gamma(x)$ exists for all $x \in \mathbf{R}_+$. Then the infinite-time ruin probability $\Psi(x)$ corresponding to the initial risk reserve $x \in \mathbf{R}_+$ satisfies the inequality

$$\Psi(x) \leq \exp[-\int_{[0,x]} \rho(y)dy]. \tag{31}$$

Proof

By 3.2.4.(7),(10):

$$\int_{[0\infty[} e^{\rho(x)y} dG(y) = \gamma(x) \quad (x \in \mathbf{R}_+) \tag{32}$$

and

$$\int_{[0,\infty[} e^{\rho(x)y} dF(y) = 1 + \mu\rho(x)\gamma(x) \quad (x \in \mathbf{R}_+). \tag{33}$$

From (32) results that $\rho(x)$ increases with x. We define the function $\sigma(\cdot)$ by

$$\sigma(x) := \int_{[0,x]} \rho(y)dy \quad (x \in \mathbf{R}_+).$$

Then $\sigma(x) \leq x\rho(x)$, and for $0 \leq y \leq x$,

$$\sigma(x-y) = \int_{[0,x-y]} \rho(z)dz = \int_{[0,x]} \rho(z)dz - \int_{[x-y,x]} \rho(z)dz \geq \sigma(x) - y\rho(x),$$

$$e^{-\sigma(x-y)} \leq e^{-\sigma(x)} e^{y\rho(x)}. \tag{34}$$

We now apply Theorem 7 with

$$U^{\sim} := 1 - \Psi^{\sim}, \text{ where } \Psi^{\sim}(x) := e^{-\sigma(x)}.$$

Then, at point x, the last member of (29) equals

$$\mu\gamma(x)U^{\sim\prime}(x) = \mu\gamma(x)\rho(x)e^{-\sigma(x)}. \tag{35}$$

The first member of (29) equals

$$(1-F)*U^{\sim} = 1 - F - \Psi^{\sim} + \Psi^{\sim}*F,$$

and by (34) and (33)

$$(\Psi^{\sim}*F)(x) = \int_{[0,x]} e^{-\sigma(x-y)} dF(y) \leq \int_{[0,x]} e^{-\sigma(x)} e^{y\rho(x)} dF(y)$$

$$= e^{-\sigma(x)} [\int_{[0,\infty[} - \int_{]x,\infty[}] e^{y\rho(x)} dF(y) = e^{-\sigma(x)} [1 + \mu\rho(x)\gamma(x) - \int_{]x,\infty[} e^{y\rho(x)} dF(y)].$$

We notice that

$$1-F(x) = e^{-x\rho(x)}\int_{]x,\infty[} e^{x\rho(x)}\, dF(y) \le e^{-\sigma(x)}\int_{]x,\infty[} e^{x\rho(x)}\, dF(y).$$

Then the first member of (29) equals, at point x,

$$1-F(x) - e^{-\sigma(x)} + (\Psi^{\sim} * F)(x)$$

$$\le e^{-\sigma(x)}\int_{]x,\infty[} e^{x\rho(x)}\, dF(y) - e^{-\sigma(x)} + e^{-\sigma(x)}\,[1+\mu\rho(x)\gamma(x) - \int_{]x,\infty[} e^{y\rho(x)} dF(y)]$$

$$= e^{-\sigma(x)}\,\mu\rho(x)\gamma(x) - e^{-\sigma(x)}\int_{]x,\infty[} [e^{y\rho(x)} - e^{x\rho(x)}]dF(y)]$$

$$\le \mu\gamma(x)\rho(x)e^{-\sigma(x)}\,.$$

The last member is the same as the last member of (35). This proves (29).Then $\gamma^{\sim}$, defined by (30), is positive and such that $\gamma^{\sim} \le \gamma$. The function $(1-F)*U^{\sim}$ is continuous and strictly positive on $\mathbf{R}_{++}$. Properties 9.1.2.a_+ and c_+ are direct. Then the present Theorem follows from Theorem 7 and its *Remark* •

9.7. Numerical Ruin Probabilities

9.7.1. Method

We consider the probability distribution function U in the regular semi-classical risk model with premium income intensity function $\lambda\mu\gamma(\cdot)$. Then U(0), yet unknown, is strictly positive. We define the distribution function V on $\mathbf{R}_+$ by

$$V(x) = U(x)/U(0) \quad (x \in \mathbf{R}_+). \tag{36}$$

and it is in fact V that we calculate, after the usual discretizations.

Of course, function V is solution of the same integral equation (21) as U. From the value of $V(\infty)$ (i.e. in practice, the value of V(x) for x large enough), we can deduce the value of U(0) by (36), because $U(\infty)=1$. Then the function U results from the relation $U = V.U(0)$.

In the next Theorem, we assume that G has already been discretized and that this distribution is concentrated on the set {1,2,...} (say after a change of the money unit).

9.7.2. Numerical Algorithm

Theorem 9

Let G be concentrated on the set {1,2,...}, with probability mass

$$g_k := G(k)-G(k-) \quad (k=1,2,...)$$

at point k. Then the solution V, with initial value V(0)=1, of the integral equation

$$(G*V)(u) = \int_{]0,u]} \gamma(x)dV(x) \quad (u\in \mathbf{R}_+) \tag{37}$$

is a distribution concentrated on the set {0,1,2,...}, with a mass v_0=1 at the point 0 and a mass v_k at the point k=1,2,..., resulting from the recurrent relations

$$v_{k+1} = [\gamma(k+1)]^{-1} \sum\nolimits_{1\le j\le k+1} g_j v_{k+1-j} \quad (k=0,1,2,...). \tag{38}$$

Proof
At the point u=0 the relation (37) is 0=0, because G(0)=0 and because 0 is not included in the integration domain of the last member. From the difference of (37) for u=k+1 and for u=k results the relation

$$\sum\nolimits_{1\le j\le k+1} g_j v_{k+1-j} = \gamma(k+1)\, v_{k+1}.$$

See the proof of Ch.7.Th. 24 •

Chapter 10

Discrete Risk Models

10.0. Introduction

In this Chapter, we develop discrete risk models. They are approximations resulting from a time and money discretization in the continuous models hitherto studied. The goal is the numerical calculation of ruin probabilities in the continuous models, via the discrete models. Some basic ideas are explained in this Introduction. Complete definitions follow later.

Elementary risk model

We here explain how the **classical risk model** is discretized.

The **time discretization** is defined as follows. Let $\varepsilon>0$. The claim instants in the classical model are approximated and replaced by instants ε, 2ε, ... We then consider a **new unit of time**, such that the instants 0, ε, 2ε, ... in the **old time** become the instants 0, 1, 2, ... in the **new time**. Hence, after the discretization and the change of time-unit, claims can occur only at integer strictly positive instants.

Simultaneously we consider a **money discretization**. Let $\delta>0$. The claim amounts in the classical model are approximated and replaced by amounts 0, δ, 2δ, ...We then consider a **new unit of money**, such that the amounts 0, δ, 2δ, ... in the **old money** become the amounts 0, 1, 2, ... in the **new money**. Hence, in the new money, the claim amounts can only be positive integers.

Further, ε and δ are connected by the following condition: **In the new units, the premium income in any interval]k,k+1] equals 1**. Then, in the discrete model, the risk reserve is an integer at any integer instant k if the initial risk reserve is an integer. This is a very favourable situation for numerical computations.

The discrete model approximating the **classical risk model** is the **elementary risk model** considered in section 10.2.

Semi-elementary risk model

The **semi-elementary risk model**, studied in section 10.4, is a generalization of the elementary risk model. It approximates the **semi-classical risk model**. In this model too, the risk reserve is an integer at any integer instant k if the initial risk reserve is an integer, but now the time-discretization is stochastic in fact.

Ruin probabilities in discrete models

Algorithms for the numerical calculation of **infinite-time ruin probabilities** in the classical and in the semi-classical risk model are furnished by Ch.7.Th.24 and by Ch.9.Th.9. In this Chapter 10, simpler algorithms are developed and moreover algorithms are furnished for the numerical calculation of **finite-time ruin probabilities** in the discrete models and in the classical model.

Ruin probabilities taking the severity of ruin into account

Ruin probabilities taking the severity of ruin into account can be considered as well in continuous as in discrete risk models. We only develop this topic in the discrete case, and we show how these ruin probabilities can be obtained numerically.

Bounds, asymptotic values, martingales,... in discrete models

A rather elementary **theory of discrete risk models**, parallel to the theory of continuous models can be developed. It can precede the continuous theory and it can be presented, from the didactic viewpoint, as an interesting introduction to Ruin Theory. It can even solve most practical problems, making the continuous theory superfluous in practice.

Hereafter, we only develop the components of the discrete theory which are needed in the numerical algorithms.

Notations in old and new units

For quantities expressed in the old units, the usual notations are adopted. For quantities expressed in the new units, we use the superscript °. This precaution is convenient because old and new units are considered simultaneously in the applications. (The superscript ° has other meanings in other Chapters: It denotes a centering when applied to a random variable, or a quantity fixed in the discussion when applied to a real number. No confusions are possible.)

10.1. Sequences and Discrete Renewal Equations

10.1.1. Sequences

In this Chapter we consider finite real functions on $\mathbf{N}_+$, i.e. **infinite sequences**

$$\underline{f} = (f_0, f_1, ...) \ , \ \underline{g} = (g_0, g_1, ...) \ , \ ... \ , \ \underline{F} = (F_0, F_1, ...) \ , \ \underline{G} = (G_0, G_1, ...) \ , \ ...$$

with finite real elements, indexed by $\mathbf{N}_+$. **The family of such sequences is a vector space**, when the linear combinations of sequences (in particular the product of sequences by scalars and the sums and differences of sequences) are defined in the obvious element-wise way. Further operations on sequences are defined in 10.2.

The **restriction** (to $\mathbf{N}_+$) **of the function f** on $\mathbf{R}_+$ is the sequence $\underline{f}$ defined by $f_k := f(k)$ ($k \in \mathbf{N}_+$). The **usual extension** (to $\mathbf{R}_+$) **of the sequence $\underline{f}$ is the jump function** $f(x) := f_{[x]}$. Several Theorems of Chapter 1, in which no densities are involved, have obvious particularizations to sequences, which we do not necessarily mention hereafter.

The sequence $\underline{F}$ is a **distribution (sequence)**, if $\underline{F}$ is positive and increasing. Distribution sequences are denoted by roman capital letters $\underline{F}$, $\underline{G}$, ..., $\underline{U}$, $\underline{V}$, ... More general sequences are denoted by $\underline{f}$, g, ... Of course, $f_\infty := \lim_{k\uparrow\infty} f_k$ if this limit, finite or not, exists. A **probability distribution (sequence)** is a distribution $\underline{F}$ with $F_\infty = 1$.

Let N be a positive integer random variable. The **distribution function** of N is the jump function

$$F(x) := P(N \le x) = P(N \le [x]) \quad (x \in \mathbf{R}_+).$$

The **distribution sequence** of N is the sequence $\underline{F}$ with elements $F_k=P(N\leq k)$ ($k\in\mathbf{N}_+$). Hence, $\underline{F}$ is the restriction of F , and F is the usual extension of $\underline{F}$.

The following sequences receive a special notation:

$$\underline{\delta} := (1,0,0,...)\ ,\ \underline{1} := (1,1,1,...)\ ,\ \underline{S} := (1,2,3,...).$$

10.1.2. Operations on sequences

The **sum sequence** $\Sigma\underline{f}$ of the sequence $\underline{f}$ is the sequence

$$\Sigma\underline{f} := (f_0,f_0+f_1,f_0+f_1+f_2,...).$$

It is defined for all sequences $\underline{f}$. Only sums of a finite number of terms occur in this definition. No convergence problems are involved.

The **difference sequence** $\nabla\underline{f}$ of the sequence $\underline{f}$ is the sequence

$$\nabla\underline{f} := (f_0,f_1-f_0,f_2-f_1,...).$$

It is convenient to define $f_{-1}:=0$ for any sequence $\underline{f}$. Then the difference sequence is the sequence with elements $\nabla f_k=f_k-f_{k-1}$ ($k\in\mathbf{N}_+$).

The three great Theorems for integrals $\int f(x)dG(x)$ (Monotone Convergence, Dominated Convergence, Fubini) apply to sums $\Sigma f_k\nabla G_k$.

The **convolution product** of the sequences $\underline{f}$ and $\underline{h}$ is the sequence $\underline{f}*\underline{h}$ with elements

$$(\underline{f}*\underline{h})_k = \Sigma_{0\leq i\leq k}\, f_{k-i}\nabla h_i.$$

Let f, h be the usual extension of $\underline{f}$, $\underline{h}$. **Then f*h is constant on the intervals [k,k+1[. If $\underline{f*h}$ is the restriction of f*h, then $\underline{f}*\underline{h}=\underline{f*h}$** . Indeed, if $\theta\in[0,1[$,

$$(f*h)(k+\theta) = \int_{[0,k+\theta]} f(k+\theta-x)dh(x)$$

$$= \Sigma_{0\leq i\leq k}\, f(k+\theta-i)\nabla h_i = \Sigma_{0\leq i\leq k}\, f(k-i)\nabla h_i = (\underline{f}*\underline{h})_k.$$

By this property the results proved for **continuous convolutions** (i.e. convolution products of functions) are valid for **discrete convolutions** (i.e. convolution products of sequences).

For instance, the commutativity of the convolution product of sequences follows from

$$\underline{f}*\underline{h} = \underline{f*h} = \underline{h*f} = \underline{h}*\underline{f}.$$

However, we shall give some direct proofs of discrete relations (because these relations might be studied independently of their continuous versions).

Theorem 1

The convolution product of sequences is linear in each factor. It is commutative and associative.

Proof
The linearity is direct. For the commutativity, we have

$$(\underline{f}*g)_k = \sum_{j\le k} f_{k-j}\nabla g_j = \sum_{j\le k}(\sum_{i\le k-j}\nabla f_i)\nabla g_j = \sum\sum_{i+j\le k}\nabla f_i\nabla g_j,$$

$$(g*\underline{f})_k = \sum_{i\le k} g_{k-i}\nabla f_j = \sum_{i\le k}(\sum_{j\le k-i}\nabla g_i)\nabla f_j = \sum\sum_{i+j\le k}\nabla f_i\nabla g_j = (\underline{f}*g)_k.$$

Associativity:

$$((\underline{f}*g)*\underline{h})_n = \sum_{k\le n}(\underline{f}*g)_{n-k}\nabla h_k = \sum_{k\le n}\sum_{j\le n-k} f_{n-k-j}\nabla g_j\nabla h_k$$

$$= \sum_{k\le n}\sum_{j\le n-k}\sum_{i\le n-k-j}\nabla f_i\nabla g_j\nabla h_k = \sum\sum\sum_{i+j+k\le n}\nabla f_i\nabla g_j\nabla h_k$$

$$(\underline{f}*(g*\underline{h}))_n = ((g*\underline{h})*\underline{f})_n = \sum\sum\sum_{j+k+i\le n}\nabla g_j\nabla h_k\nabla f_i = ((\underline{f}*g)*\underline{h})_n \quad \bullet$$

The convolution product of sequences becomes a usual product at the origin: $(\underline{f}*\underline{h})_0=f_0h_0$. A similar factorization takes place at ∞ under assumptions often satisfied. For sequences, Ch.1.Th.11 becomes:

Theorem 2 (Factorization of Convolution Product of Sequences)

$$\mathbf{(\underline{F}*\underline{G})_\infty = F_\infty G_\infty.}$$

If f_∞ exists and is finite and $G_\infty<\infty$, then $(\underline{f}*\underline{G})_\infty=f_\infty G_\infty$ •

We notice the following **particular relations** :

$$\nabla\underline{S} = \underline{1}\ ,\ \nabla\underline{1} = \underline{\delta}\ ,\ \nabla\underline{\delta} = (1,-1,0,0,\ldots)\ ,\ \Sigma\underline{\delta} = \underline{1}\ ,\ \Sigma\underline{1} = \underline{S},$$

$$\underline{f}*\underline{1} = \underline{1}*\underline{f} = \underline{f}\ ,\ \Sigma\nabla\underline{f} = \nabla\Sigma\underline{f} = \underline{f}\ ,\ \nabla\underline{f} = \underline{\delta}*\underline{f}\ ,\ \Sigma\underline{f} = \underline{S}*\underline{f}\,.$$

For instance, the last relation implies that

$$\Sigma(\underline{f}*\underline{g}*\underline{h}) = (\Sigma\underline{f})*\underline{g}*\underline{h} = \underline{f}*(\Sigma\underline{g})*\underline{h} = \underline{f}*\underline{g}*(\Sigma\underline{h}),$$

because the convolution product is commutative and associative. In a similar way, when the operator ∇ is applied to a product, it may be applied to any factor.

10.1.3. Summation by parts

Theorem 3 (Summation by Parts in Finite Sums).

$$\boldsymbol{\sum_{m\le i\le n} f_i\nabla g_i = [f_i g_i]_{m-1}^{n} - \sum_{m\le i\le n} g_{i-1}\nabla f_i.}$$

Proof

The formula results from the application of $\sum_{m\le i\le n}$ to the relation

$$\nabla(f_i g_i) = f_i\nabla g_i + g_{i-1}\nabla f_i \quad \bullet$$

Theorem 4 (Summation by Parts in Infinite Sums).

If $G_\infty<\infty$,

$$\boldsymbol{\sum_{m\le i<\infty} F_i\nabla G_i = F_{m-1}(G_\infty - G_{m-1}) + \sum_{m\le i<\infty} (G_\infty - G_{i-1})\,\nabla F_i} \quad \bullet$$

This is the discrete version of Ch.1.Th.6. It is best remembered as follows. In the summation by parts

$$\sum_{m\le i\le n} F_i\nabla G_i = -\sum_{m\le i\le n} F_i\nabla(G_\infty - G_i)$$

$$= -F_n(G_\infty - G_n) + F_{m-1}(G_\infty - G_{m-1}) + \sum_{m\le i\le n} (G_\infty - G_{i-1})\nabla F_i,$$

we may let $n\uparrow\infty$ and proceed **as if** $F_n(G_\infty - G_n)\to 0$.

As a simple illustration, let N be a positive integer random variable with distribution sequence $\underline{F}$. Then the expectation of N, finite or not, equals

$$E(N) = \sum_{i\ge 0} i\nabla F_i = \sum_{i\ge 1} i\nabla F_i = \sum_{i\ge 1} (1 - F_{i-1}) = \sum_{i\ge 0} (1 - F_i).$$

10.1.4. Renewal Equations

Theorem 5 (Solution of general Renewal Equation)

The renewal equation $\underline{f}=\underline{g}+\underline{f}*\Sigma\underline{h}$ ($h_0\neq 1$) has the unique solution, in recurrent form,

$$\mathbf{f_0 = g_0(1-h_0)^{-1},}$$

$$\mathbf{f_{n+1} = (1-h_0)^{-1}(g_{n+1} + \textstyle\sum_{0<i\leq n} f_i h_{n+1-i})\quad (n\geq 0).}$$

Proof
At the point 0 the renewal equation becomes $f_0=g_0+f_0h_0$ and at n+1 it gives

$$f_{n+1} = g_{n+1} + \textstyle\sum_{0\leq i\leq n+1} f_{n+1-i}\nabla\Sigma h_i$$

$$= g_{n+1} + \textstyle\sum_{0\leq i\leq n+1} f_i h_{n+1-1} = g_{n+1} + \sum_{0\leq i\leq n} f_i h_{n+1-i} + f_{n+1}h_0 \quad \bullet$$

Of course, the Theorem can be applied to the renewal equation $\underline{f}=\underline{g}+\underline{f}*\underline{h}$ if the latter is displayed as

$$\underline{f} = g + \underline{f}*\Sigma(\nabla\underline{h}).$$

The discrete version of Ch.1.Th.14 is the following Theorem.

Theorem 6.

The solution of the renewal equation

$$\mathbf{\underline{f} = \underline{h} + q\underline{f}*\underline{G}\quad (G_0<1=G_\infty,\ 0<q\leq 1)}$$

is $\underline{f}=\underline{h}*\underline{V}_q$, where $\underline{V}_q=\sum_{k\geq 0} q^k\underline{G}^{*k}$. The sequence $\underline{V}_q$ is the solution of the renewal equation

$$\mathbf{\underline{V}_q = \underline{1} + q\,\underline{V}_q*\underline{G}}\quad \bullet$$

10.1.5. Renewal Theorems

We here consider the equations

$$\underline{f} = \underline{h} + \underline{f}*\underline{G}\ ,\ \underline{V} = \underline{1} + \underline{V}*\underline{G}\quad (G_0 <1= G_\infty).$$

We denote by $\underline{v}:=\nabla\underline{V}$ the difference sequence of $\underline{V}$. We consider the renewal Theorems about the limits v_∞ and f_∞. In this Chapter, we prove the weak version of the Theorems, based on the assumption that v_∞ exists. In Appendix B, that assumption is dropped.

The discrete renewal Theorems do not result from the corresponding continuous Theorems, simply via the consideration of the usual extensions of the involved distribution sequences. Indeed, the proof of the continuous Theorems is based on the existence of a density of the distribution G. But the usual extension G of the sequence $\underline{G}$ does not have a density.

Theorem 7 (Weak Version of Renewal Theorem for $\underline{v}:=\nabla\underline{V}$)

If $v_\infty<\infty$ exists and if the first moment μ of $\underline{G}$ is finite, then $v_\infty=1/\mu$.

Proof

Let $g=\nabla\underline{G}$. From the application of the operator ∇ to the equation $\underline{V}=\underline{1}+\underline{V}*\underline{G}$ results that $\underline{v}=\underline{\delta}+\underline{v}*\underline{G}$. Hence

$$\underline{v}*(\underline{1}-\underline{G}) = \underline{\delta}.$$

We take the convolution product by $\underline{S}$ and we divide by μ:

$$\underline{v}*\underline{H} = \mu^{-1}\underline{1}, \text{ where } \underline{H} := \mu^{-1}(\underline{1}-\underline{G})*\underline{S}.$$

Here $H_\infty=1$ because $\mu=\Sigma(1-G_k)$ and because the convolution product by $\underline{S}$ amounts to a summation. At the point k we have $(\underline{v}*\underline{H})_k=1/\mu$. As $k\uparrow\infty$, we obtain $v_\infty H_\infty=1/\mu$ by the factorization Theorem 2 for convolutions•

Theorem 8 (Weak Version of Key Renewal Theorem)

Let $\underline{f}$ be the solution of the renewal equation $\underline{f}=\underline{h}+\underline{f}*\underline{G}$, where

$$\Sigma_{k\geq 0} |h_k| < \infty .$$

Then f_∞ exists and

$$f_\infty = 1/\mu \, \Sigma_{k\geq 0}\, h_k$$

under the assumptions of the foregoing Theorem 7.

Proof

The sequence $\underline{v}$ is bounded because v_∞ exists. By Theorem 6, $\underline{f}=\underline{h}*\underline{V}$. Hence,

$$f_k = \Sigma_{0\leq i\leq k}\, h_{k-i}v_i = \Sigma_{0\leq i\leq k}\, h_i v_{k-i} = \Sigma_{i\geq 0}\, h_i v_{k-i} 1_{i\leq k} \rightarrow \Sigma_{i\geq 0}\, h_i v_\infty = \mu^{-1}\, \Sigma_{i\geq 0}\, h_i$$

as $k\uparrow\infty$ by dominated convergence •

10.1.6. Exponential Transformation

We consider the renewal equation

$$\underline{f} = \underline{h} + q\underline{f}*\underline{G} \quad (G_0<1=G_\infty\,,\ 0<q<1)$$

to which the renewal Theorems cannot be applies.

An **adjustment coefficient** of the couple ($\underline{G}$,q) is a strictly positive number ρ such that

$$q\textstyle\sum_{k\geq 0} e^{\rho k}\nabla G_k = 1.$$

The adjustment coefficient is unique, when it exists.

Let us assume that ρ exists. New sequences $\underline{f}^e$, $\underline{h}^e$, $\underline{G}^e$ are defined by the relations

$$f^e_k = f_k e^{\rho k}\,,\ h^e_k = h_k e^{\rho k}\,,\ G^e_k = q\textstyle\sum_{0\leq j\leq k} e^{\rho k}\nabla G_k.$$

Then $\underline{G}^e$ is a probability distribution sequence and $\underline{\mathbf{f}}^e\mathbf{=}\underline{\mathbf{h}}^e\mathbf{+}\underline{\mathbf{f}}^e\mathbf{*}\underline{\mathbf{G}}^e$. The renewal Theorems can be applied to the latter **exponential transformation** of the initial renewal equation.

10.1.7. Arithmetic Distributions

The **distribution** H is **arithmetic** if a positive number s exists such that H is concentrated on the set {0,s,2s,3s,...}. Then the largest number s with this property is the **span of the arithmetic distribution H**.

The distribution resulting from a sequence $\underline{H}$ is concentrated on set {0,1,2,...}. Hence it is arithmetic. The span is 0 if the distribution is concentrated at 0. It is an integer, at least equal to 1, in all other cases.

Of course, we adopt the same terminology for distribution sequences as for distributions: Let $\underline{h}:=\nabla\underline{H}$. The **atoms** of $\underline{H}$ are the points k such that $h_k>0$. The distribution $\underline{H}$ is concentrated on the set $A\subseteq\mathbf{R}_+$ iff all atoms of $\underline{H}$ belong to A.

The next Theorem shows that the expression of f(∞) furnished by the key renewal Ch.1.Th.17 is not correct when the distribution G of the renewal equation f=g+f*G is arithmetic.

Theorem 9.

Let $\underline{G}$ be a sequence satisfying the assumptions of Theorem 7, and let G be the usual extension of $\underline{G}$. Let f be the solution of the renewal equation f=g+f*G, where g is such that

$$\sum_{k\geq 0} |g(k+\theta)| < \infty \quad (\theta \in [0,1[).$$

Then

$$\lim_{k\uparrow\infty} f(k+\theta) = 1/\mu \sum_{k\geq 0} g(k+\theta).$$

Proof

The function $V=\sum G^{*k}$ is the usual extension of the sequence $\underline{V}=\sum \underline{G}^{*k}$. Hence,

$$V(j)-V(j-) = V_j - V_{j-1} =: v_j.$$

Then

$$f(k+\theta) = \int_{0\leq x\leq k+\theta} g(k+\theta-x)dV(x) = \sum_{j\leq k} g(k+\theta-j)v_j = \sum_{j\leq k} g(\theta+j)v_{k-j}$$

$$= \sum_{j\geq 0} g(\theta+j)v_{k-j}1_{j\leq k} \rightarrow \sum_{j\geq 0} g(\theta+j)v_\infty \quad \text{for } k\uparrow\infty,$$

because f=g*V and by dominated convergence •

Under the assumptions of the foregoing Theorem, the limit $\lim_{k\uparrow\infty} f(k+\theta)$ exists for each θ, but that does not imply that the limit $f(\infty)$ exists. For instance, if we take

$$g(x) := (1-x)1_{x\leq 1}$$

then

$$f(k) \rightarrow 1/\mu \quad \text{and} \quad f(k+0.5) \rightarrow 0.5/\mu \; .$$

Hence, the behaviour of f(x) for large x is different in the arithmetic case (foregoing Theorem 9) and in the non-arithmetic case (Ch.1.Th.17).

We now return to the renewal equations for sequences

$$\underline{V} = \underline{1} + \underline{V}*\underline{G} \;, \quad \underline{v}=\underline{\delta}+\underline{v}*\underline{G}.$$

The assumptions of Theorem 7 can only be satisfied if the span of the distribution $\underline{G}$ is 1. Indeed, suppose that the span is 2. Then $\underline{G}$ is concentrated on the set {0,2,4,...} and then $\underline{V}$ is also concentrated on that set. Hence $0=v_1=v_3=\ldots$ If Theorem 7 applies, we have the contradiction $v_\infty=0$, $\mu=\infty$. Any other span strictly larger than 1 leads to the same contradiction, by the same argument.

The renewal Theorems for span 1 allow to cope with any span. Indeed, let us assume that the span of $\underline{G}$ in the renewal distribution $\underline{V}=\Sigma\underline{G}^{*k}$ is 3 and that the first moment of $\underline{G}$ is μ. Let us take a new unit of length (in fact of **time** in Renewal Theory) 3 times longer than the old one. Then the points 0, 3, 6, ... in the old unit, become the points 0, 1, 2, ... in the new unit. The new distribution $\underline{G}$, say $\underline{G}^{new}$, is concentrated on the set $\{0,1,2,...\}$. Its span equals 1 and its first moment equals $\mu^{new}=\mu/3$. Hence, assuming that the limit v^{new}_{∞} exists, it must be equal to $3/\mu$. This conclusion is translated in the original distributions as follows: $\lim_{k\uparrow\infty} v_{3k}=3/\mu$ and it can be completed by the relations

$$0 = v_1 = v_2 = v_4 = v_5 = v_7 = v_8 = \ldots$$

because $\underline{G}$ is concentrated on the set $\{0,3,6,...\}$ and because then $\underline{V}$ must also be concentrated on that set.

The same method works for arithmetic distributions G with any span s, not necessarily an integer. It is enough to consider a new unit of length (in fact of **time** in Renewal Theory) such that the old points 0, s, 2s, ... become the new points 0, 1, 2, ...

10.2. Elementary Risk Model

10.2.1. Definition of Elementary Model

General assumptions

The **claim process** is the sequence $(T_1°,X_1°,T_2°,X_2°,...)$ where $T_k°$ is the instant of claim number k and $X_k°$ the corresponding claim amount. The **claim instants process** $(T_1°,T_2°,...)$ is independent of the **claim amounts process** $(X_1°,X_2°,...)$. The claim amounts $X_1°,X_2°$,... are i.i.d. The random variable $X° \equiv X_1°$ has a finite strictly positive expectation $\mu°$.

Particular assumptions on claim instants process

The claim instants $T_k°$ are strictly positive integers. No claim can occur at the instant 0. At most one claim can occur in each one of the intervals]0,1],]1,2],.. and when it does, it occurs at the end of the interval. The probability of a claim in any one of the intervals]0,1],]1,2],...equals $\lambda°>0$.

Particular assumptions on claim amounts

The possible values of X° are n=0,1,2,... The distribution of X° is defined by its **claimsize distribution sequence** $\underline{F}^\circ$ or by the corresponding **claimsize masses sequence** $\underline{f}^\circ$. Then

$$\underline{F}^\circ := \Sigma\underline{f}^\circ \, , \, \underline{f}^\circ = \nabla\underline{F}^\circ,$$

$$f^\circ_n := P(X^\circ{=}n) \quad (n{=}0,1,2,...),$$

$$F^\circ_n := P(X^\circ{\le}n) \quad (n{=}0,1,2,...).$$

Assumptions on initial risk reserve and on premium income process

The possible values of the initial risk reserve are m=0,1,2,... The premium income is 1 in each of the intervals [0,1],]1,2],... It is assumed that the premium income is 1 at each instant k=1,2,..., and that this premium is collected before the claim is settled if there is a claim at k.

Assumption on security loading

The expected claim amount in each of the intervals [0,1],]1,2],... is $\lambda^\circ\mu^\circ$ and the premium received in each of these intervals is 1. Then η°, defined by the relation

$$1 = \lambda^\circ\mu^\circ(1{+}\eta^\circ),$$

or

$$\eta^\circ = (\lambda^\circ\mu^\circ)^{-1} - 1.$$

is the **security loading** of the considered discrete model. It must be strictly positive. Hence, we assume that $\lambda^\circ\mu^\circ < 1$. Similarly as in the continuous classical model, we here define

$$q^\circ := (1{+}\eta^\circ)^{-1} \, , \, p^\circ = 1 - q^\circ.$$

Hence,

$$q^\circ = \lambda^\circ\mu^\circ \, , \; p^\circ = 1 - \lambda^\circ\mu^\circ.$$

10.2.2. Finite-Time Non-Ruin Probabilities

Hereafter i,j,k,m,n are positive integers. We denote by $U^\circ_{km} \equiv U^\circ(k,m)$, the probability of non-ruin in the time-interval [0,k] corresponding to the initial risk reserve m. "Ruin" means a strictly negative risk reserve. Risk reserves are defined in discrete models in the same way as in continuous models.

Theorem 10

In the elementary risk model,

$$\mathbf{U^\circ_{k+1,m} = (1-\lambda^\circ)U^\circ_{k,m+1} + \lambda^\circ\textstyle\sum_{0\le i\le m+1} f_i{}^\circ U^\circ_{k,m+1-i}\ (m,k=0,1,2,...).} \qquad (1)$$

Proof
The formula results from the partition of the considered non-ruin event according to the number of claims, 0 or 1, at the instant 1, and in case of a claim, according to the claim amount 0,1,2,... •

Starting with the values

$$U^\circ_{00}=1\ ,\ U^\circ_{01}=1\ ,\dots,\ U^\circ_{0,m+k}=1,$$

the relation (1) allows the successive calculation of the non-ruin probabilities

$$U^\circ_{10}\ ,\ U^\circ_{11}\ ,\ \dots\ ,\ \dots\ ,\ \dots\ ,\ U^\circ_{1,m+k-1}$$

$$U^\circ_{20}\ ,\ U^\circ_{21}\ ,\ \dots\ ,\ \dots\ ,\ U^\circ_{2,m+k-2}$$

$$\dots\ ,\ \dots\ ,\ \dots\ ,\ \dots\ ,$$

$$U^\circ_{k-1,0}\ ,\ \dots\ ,\ U^\circ_{k-1,m+1}.$$

$$U^\circ_{k0}\ ,\ \dots\ ,\ U^\circ_{km}$$

Hence, in order to calculate U°_{km} , we only need the claimsize probability masses

$$f^\circ_0\ ,\ f^\circ_1\ ,\ \dots\ ,\ f^\circ_{k+m}\ .$$

10.2.3. Moments and Concave Transform of Distribution Sequences

Moments

Let M be a random variable with positive integer values, $\underline{F}$ its probability distribution sequence, and let $\underline{f} := \nabla\underline{F}$. Then the moment μ_k of M, or $\underline{F}$, is

$$\mu_k(\underline{F}) := EM^k = \textstyle\sum_{i\ge 0} i^k f_i. \qquad (2)$$

It is defined in any case, but it may be infinite.

From a summation by parts (Theorem 4) results that, for $k \geq 1$,

$$\mu_k(\underline{F}) = \sum_{i\geq 1} i^k \nabla F_i = -\sum_{i\geq 1} i^k \nabla(1-F_i) = \sum_{i\geq 1} (1-F_{i-1}) \nabla i^k .$$

Hence,

$$\mu_k(\underline{F}) = EM^k = \sum_{i\geq 0} (1-F_i) \nabla (1+i)^k. \qquad (3)$$

In particular, for $k=1$,

$$\mu(\underline{F}) \equiv \mu_1(\underline{F}) = EM = \sum_{i\geq 0} (1-F_i). \qquad (4)$$

Concave transform

We now assume that $\mu(\underline{F})$ is finite strictly positive. The **concave transform** of sequence $\underline{F}$ is the sequence

$$\underline{G} := [\mu(\underline{F})]^{-1} \Sigma(\underline{1}-\underline{F}). \qquad (5)$$

The concave transform $\underline{G}$ of the probability distribution sequence $\underline{F}$ is a probability distribution sequence. Indeed $\underline{G}$ is positive and increasing, and by (4),

$$G_\infty = [\mu(\underline{F})]^{-1} \sum_{i\geq 0} (1-F_i) = 1.$$

The original sequence $\underline{F}$ is recuperated from its concave transform $\underline{G}$ if $\mu(F)$ is known. Indeed, by (5),

$$\mu(\underline{F})\, \underline{G} = \Sigma(\underline{1}-\underline{F}), \; \mu(\underline{F})\, \nabla\underline{G} = \nabla\Sigma(\underline{1}-\underline{F}) = \underline{1}-\underline{F}.$$

Hence,

$$\underline{F} = \underline{1} - \mu(\underline{F}) \nabla \underline{G}. \qquad (6)$$

From (5) results that

$$g := \nabla\underline{G} = [\mu(\underline{F})]^{-1} (\underline{1}-\underline{F}). \qquad (7)$$

Then by (3) for $k=1$ and $k=2$,

$$\mu_1(\underline{G}) = \sum_{i\geq 0} i g_i = [\mu(\underline{F})]^{-1} \sum_{i\geq 0} i(1-F_i)$$

$$= [\mu(\underline{F})]^{-1} \sum_{i\geq 0} (1-F_i) \nabla 1/2\, [(1+i)^2-(1+i)] = [2\mu(\underline{F})]^{-1} [\mu_2(\underline{F}) - \mu_1(\underline{F})].$$

Hence,

$$\mu_2(\underline{F}) = \mu_1(\underline{F})\, [1+2\, \mu_1(\underline{G})]. \qquad (8)$$

Concave transform of $\underline{F}°$ in elementary risk model

The concave transform of $\underline{F}°$ is denoted by $\underline{G}°$. Hence,

$$\underline{G}° := 1/_{\mu°}\, \Sigma(\underline{1}-\underline{F}°). \tag{9}$$

$$\underline{F}° = \underline{1}-\mu°\nabla\underline{G}°. \tag{10}$$

$$\mu_2(\underline{F}°) = \mu°\,[1+2\,\mu_1(\underline{G}°)]. \tag{11}$$

The difference sequence of $\underline{G}°$ is denoted by $g°$. Then, by (5),

$$g° := \nabla\underline{G}° := 1/_{\mu°}\,(\underline{1}-\underline{F}°), \tag{12}$$

10.2.4. Infinite-Time Non-Ruin Probabilities

We denote by $U°_i$ (i=0,1,2,...) the probability of non-ruin in the time interval [0,∞[, corresponding to the initial risk reserve i. Then $\underline{U}°$ is the sequence with elements $U°_i$.

Theorem 11

In the elementary risk model,

$$\underline{\mathbf{U}}° = \mathbf{p}°\underline{\mathbf{1}} + \mathbf{q}°\,\underline{\mathbf{U}}°*\underline{\mathbf{G}}°. \tag{13}$$

Proof

We consider the event of non-ruin in [0,∞[corresponding to the initial risk reserve i≥0. From a partition of that event according to the number of claims 0 or 1 at the instant 1, and in case of a claim at 1, according to the claim amounts 0,1,2,..., results the formula

$$U°_i = (1-\lambda°)U°_{i+1} + \lambda°\textstyle\sum_{0\le k\le i+1} U°_{i+1-k}f°_k.$$

Then

$$\nabla U°_{i+1} = \lambda°[U°_{i+1}-(\underline{U}°*\underline{F}°)_{i+1}],$$

$$\nabla U°_{i+1} = \lambda°[\underline{U}°*(\underline{1}-\underline{F}°)]_{i+1}. \tag{14}$$

Then

$$\nabla\underline{U}° - U°_0\,\underline{\delta} = \lambda°\,\underline{U}°*(\underline{1}-\underline{F}°) - \lambda°U°_0(1-F°_0)\,\underline{\delta}. \tag{15}$$

Indeed, by (14), this relation is correct at the point i+1 and at point 0 it becomes 0=0. We apply Σ to (15):

$$\underline{U}° - U°_0\,\underline{1} = \lambda°\mu°\,\underline{U}°*\underline{G}° - \lambda°U°_0(1-F°_0)\,\underline{1}, \tag{16}$$

by (9). We take (16) at the point i, and we let $i\uparrow\infty$:

$$U°_\infty - U°_0 = \lambda°\mu°\,U°_\infty G°_\infty - \lambda°U°_0(1-F°_0),$$

by Theorem 2. But $U°_\infty = 1$ (see following *Remark*). Hence,

$$U°_0 - \lambda°U°_0(1-F°_0) = 1-\lambda°\mu° = 1-q° = p°. \tag{17}$$

Then (13) results from (16) and (17) •

***Remark: The relation* $U°_\infty$=1.**

The relation $U°_\infty=1$, or $\Psi°_\infty=0$ results from the assumption $\lambda°\mu°<1$. It can be proved by obvious adaptations of the arguments leading to Ch.7.Th.1 or to Ch.7.Th.2. We here indicate how the demonstration of the latter Theorem must be modified. Let $Y°_{k+1}$ be the claim amount in the interval]k,k+1]. This random variable takes the value 0 if no claim occurs in that interval. Then $EY°_{k+1}=\lambda°EX°=\lambda°\mu°$. Let $D°_{k+1}:=1-Y°_{k+1}$. Then $D°_{k+1}$ is the increment of the risk reserve in the interval]k,k+1]. The value of the risk reserve at the instant n equals $R°_n=D°_1+...+D°_n$ if the initial risk reserve equals 0. The random variables $D°_1,D°_2,...$ are i.i.d. By the strong law of large numbers

$$1/_n(D°_1 + ... + D°_n) \to ED°_1 = 1-\lambda°\mu° > 0 \ \text{ a.s. as } n\uparrow\infty.$$

Then

$$R°_n \to \infty \ \text{ a.s. as } n\uparrow\infty,$$

and this implies $\Psi°_\infty=0$.

Recurrent numerical solution of renewal equation

By Theorem 5 and (13) displayed as $\underline{U}°=p°\underline{1}+\underline{U}°*(\Sigma q°g)$,

$$U°_0 = p°(1-q°g°_0)^{-1},$$

$$U°_{k+1} = (1-q°g°_0)^{-1}[p° + q° \textstyle\sum_{0\le i\le k} g°_{k+1-i}U°_i] \ \ (k=0,1,2,...). \tag{18}$$

From these relations results that we only need the claimsize probability masses $f^\circ_0, f^\circ_1, \ldots, f^\circ_n$ in order to calculate U°_n.

Continuous integral form of discrete renewal equation

Let the functions $F^\circ, G^\circ, U^\circ$ be the usual extensions of the sequences $\underline{F}^\circ, \underline{G}^\circ, \underline{U}^\circ$ resp. Then

$$G^\circ(x) = 1/\mu^\circ \int_{[0,[x+1]]} [1-F^\circ(y)]dy, \tag{19}$$

because $F^\circ \equiv F^\circ_k$ on $[k,k+1[$. The renewal equation for functions

$$U^\circ = p^\circ + q^\circ\, U^\circ * G^\circ, \tag{20}$$

results from the renewal equation (13) for sequences.

10.2.5. Asymptotic Value of $\Psi^\circ(m)$ as $m\uparrow\infty$

Adjustment coefficient of elementary risk model

Theorem 12 (Equivalent Definitions of Adjustment Coefficient)

In the elementary risk model, the four following relations are equivalent. Each of them defines the adjustment coefficient $\rho^\circ>0$ of the elementary risk model.

$$q^\circ \sum_{k\geq 0} e^{\rho^\circ k} \nabla G^\circ_k = 1, \tag{21}$$

$$(e^{\rho^\circ}-1) \sum_{k\geq 0} (1-G^\circ_k) e^{\rho^\circ k} = \eta^\circ, \tag{22}$$

$$q^\circ \sum_{k\geq 0} (1-F^\circ_k) e^{\rho^\circ k} = \mu^\circ, \tag{23}$$

$$\sum_{k\geq 0} e^{\rho^\circ k} f^\circ_k = 1 + \mu^\circ (e^{\rho^\circ}-1)(1+\eta^\circ). \tag{24}$$

Proof

The equivalence of (21) and (23) results from (12). The equivalence of (21) and (22) results from a summation by parts. Indeed, the sum in the first member of (21) equals

$$\sum_{k\geq 0} e^{\rho^\circ k}\nabla G^\circ_k = G^\circ_0 + \sum_{k\geq 1} e^{\rho^\circ k}\nabla G^\circ_k = G^\circ_0 - \sum_{k\geq 1} e^{\rho^\circ k}\nabla(1-G^\circ_k)$$

$$= G^\circ_0 + (1-G^\circ_0) + \sum_{k\geq 1} (1-G^\circ_{k-1})\nabla e^{\rho^\circ k} = 1 + \sum_{k\geq 0} (1-G^\circ_k)\nabla e^{\rho^\circ(k+1)}$$

$$= 1 + \sum_{k\geq 0} (1-G^\circ_k)[e^{\rho^\circ(k+1)} - e^{\rho^\circ k}] = 1 + (e^{\rho^\circ}-1) \sum_{k\geq 0} (1-G^\circ_k)e^{\rho^\circ k}.$$

For the proof of the equivalence of (23) and (24), we observe that we can replace G° by F° in the foregoing relations. Hence

$$\sum_{k\geq 0} e^{\rho^\circ k}\nabla F^\circ_k = 1 + (e^{\rho^\circ}-1) \sum_{k\geq 0} (1-F^\circ_k)e^{\rho^\circ k}.$$

This implies the equivalence of (23) and the relation

$$\sum_{k\geq 0} e^{\rho^\circ k}\nabla F^\circ_k = 1 + \mu^\circ(e^{\rho^\circ}-1)(1+\eta^\circ).$$

The latter relation is the same as (24) because $\nabla F^\circ_k = f^\circ_k$ •

Exponential transformation

The renewal equation for $\underline{\Psi}^\circ := \underline{1} - \underline{U}^\circ$,

$$\underline{\Psi}^\circ = q^\circ(\underline{1}-\underline{G}^\circ) + q^\circ\, \underline{\Psi}^\circ * \underline{G}^\circ \tag{25}$$

results from renewal equation (13). We suppose that the adjustment coefficient ρ° exists, and we apply the exponential transformation defined in 10.1.6 to (25). The sequences $\underline{\Psi}^e$, $\underline{g}^e$, $\underline{G}^e$ are those with elements

$$\Psi^e_k := e^{\rho^\circ k}\, \Psi^\circ_k,\; g^e_k := q^\circ(1-G^\circ_k)e^{\rho^\circ k},\; G^e_k := q^\circ \sum_{0\leq j\leq k} e^{\rho^\circ k}\nabla G^\circ_k. \tag{26}$$

Then $\underline{G}^e$ is a probability distribution sequence and

$$\underline{\Psi}^e = \underline{g}^e + \underline{\Psi}^e * \underline{G}^e. \tag{27}$$

Elementary version of Cramér's asymptotic formula

We say that **the elementary risk model is regular** if the adjustment coefficient ρ° exists and if $\varepsilon>0$ exists such that the replacement of ρ° by $\rho^\circ+\varepsilon$ keeps the first members of the relations (21) to (24) finite.

By the proof of Theorem 12, it is sufficient to make that assumption for anyone of these relations. When the adjustment coefficient exists, the elementary model is regular in all practical cases.

Theorem 13

In the regular elementary risk model,

$$\Psi^\circ(m) \approx \alpha^\circ e^{-\rho^\circ m} \text{ asymptotically for } m\uparrow\infty, \tag{28}$$

where

$$\alpha^\circ := \eta^\circ q^\circ[(e^{\rho^\circ}-1)\mu^e]^{-1}, \tag{29}$$

$$\mu^e := q^\circ \textstyle\sum_{k\geq 0} k e^{\rho^\circ k} \nabla G^\circ_k = q^\circ/\mu^\circ \sum_{k\geq 0} [1-F^\circ_k] k e^{\rho^\circ k}. \tag{30}$$

Proof (main part)
We assume that Theorem 8 applies to the renewal equation (27). From (12) results that the sequence g° is decreasing. Then the span of $\underline{G}^\circ$, and then also the span of $\underline{G}^e$, equals 1. The condition $\sum g^e_k < \infty$ is satisfied by (22). The first moment of the probability distribution sequence $\underline{G}^e$ equals

$$\mu^e := \mu(\underline{G}^e) = \textstyle\sum_{k\geq 0} k\nabla G^e_k = q^\circ \sum_{k\geq 0} k e^{\rho^\circ k} \nabla G^\circ_k = q^\circ/\mu^\circ \sum_{k\geq 0} [1-F^\circ_k] k e^{\rho^\circ k}.$$

From the regularity assumption and (23) results that μ^e is finite because $k \leq e^{\varepsilon k}$ if k is large enough. Then by (22),

$$\Psi^e_\infty = [\mu^e]^{-1} \textstyle\sum_{k\geq 0} g^e_k = [\mu^e]^{-1} q^\circ \sum_{k\geq 0} (1-G^\circ_k) e^{\rho^\circ k} = [\mu^e]^{-1} q^\circ \eta^\circ [e^{\rho^\circ}-1]^{-1} \quad \bullet$$

For a complete proof, the Key Renewal Theorem B2 of Appendix B is applied.

10.2.6. Ruin Probabilities with Severity of Ruin Taken into Account

The **instant of ruin** is the first instant N such that the risk reserve $R_N<0$, if such an instant exists. Then the random variable $S:= -R_N$ is the **severity of the ruin**. (If ruin does not occur, then the instant of ruin can be defined to be $+\infty$, and the corresponding severity 0).

For k=0,1,2,..., m=0,1,2,... and n=1,2,..., we consider the following ruin probabilities in the elementary risk model:

$\Psi^{o}_{km(n)}$: probability of ruin in [0,k] with severity S=n, corresponding to the initial risk reserve m.

Ψ^{o}_{kmn} : probability of ruin in [0,k] with severity S≤n, corresponding to the initial risk reserve m.

Ψ^{o}_{km} : probability of ruin in [0,k] corresponding to the initial risk reserve m.

Then

$$\Psi^{o}_{kmn} = \sum_{1\leq j\leq n} \Psi^{o}_{km(j)}, \tag{31}$$

$$\Psi^{o}_{km} = \lim_{n\uparrow\infty} \Psi^{o}_{kmn}. \tag{32}$$

Theorem 14

In the elementary risk model, for all values

k = 0,1,2,... ; m = 0,1,2,... ; n = 1,2,... :

$$\begin{gathered}\Psi^{o}_{om(n)} = 0\\ \Psi^{o}_{k+1,m,(n)} = (1-\lambda^{o})\Psi^{o}_{k,m+1,(n)} + \lambda^{o} f^{o}_{m+1+n} + \lambda^{o} \sum_{0\leq i\leq m+1} f^{o}_{i}\Psi^{o}_{k,m+1-i,(n)}\end{gathered} \tag{33}$$

$$\begin{gathered}\Psi^{o}_{omn} = 0\\ \Psi^{o}_{k+1,m,n} = (1-\lambda^{o})\Psi^{o}_{k,m+1,n} + \lambda^{o} \sum_{1\leq j\leq n} f^{o}_{m+1+j} + \lambda^{o} \sum_{0\leq i\leq m+1} f^{o}_{i}\Psi^{o}_{k,m+1-i,n}\end{gathered} \tag{34}$$

$$\begin{gathered}\Psi^{o}_{om} = 0\\ \Psi^{o}_{k+1,m} = (1-\lambda^{o})\Psi^{o}_{k,m+1} + \lambda^{o} \sum_{1\leq j} f^{o}_{m+1+j} + \lambda^{o} \sum_{0\leq i\leq m+1} f^{o}_{i}\Psi^{o}_{k,m+1-i}\end{gathered} \tag{35}$$

Proof

For the proof of the last relation (33), we consider the event of ruin in [0,k], with severity equal to n, corresponding to the initial risk reserve m. Then the last relation (33) results from the partition of that event according to the following possibilities:

1. No claim occurs at the instant 1.
2. A claim occurs at 1 and it produces ruin at 1
    2.1. with severity n
    2.2. with a severity different from n.
3. A claim occurs at 1 and it produces no ruin at 1.

For the proof of the last relation (34), we replace n by j in the last relation (33) and then we sum for j=1,...,n.

The last relation (35) results from the last relation (34) as $n\uparrow\infty$ •

The relations (33) allow the iterative calculation of the probabilities $\Psi^{\circ}_{km(n)}$, the relations (34) the iterative calculation of the probabilities Ψ°_{kmn}, and the relations (35) the iterative calculation of the probabilites Ψ°_{km}.

The sum of the relation (1) and the last relation (35) is the correct relation 1=1.

10.3. Numerical Ruin Probabilities in Classical Risk Model

10.3.1. Introduction of New Time and Money Units

In the classical risk model, we consider old and new time and money units simultaneously. Any duration expressed by t in the old time is expressed by t° in the new time. Any capital expressed by c in the old money is expressed by c° in the new money. More generally, any quantity, stochastic or not, defined in the classical risk model is completed by the superscript $^{\circ}$ when it is expressed in the new units. (Later, this rule is not followed strictly).

We assume that

$$t^{\circ} = t/\varepsilon \quad , \quad c^{\circ} = c/\delta,$$

where ε and δ are strictly positive. Then (see the **Introduction** 10.1) the instants $0,\varepsilon,2\varepsilon,\ldots$ in the old time become the instants 0,1,2,... in the new time and the amounts $0,\delta,2\delta,\ldots$ in the old money become the amounts 0,1,2,... in the new money.

An **invariant** is a quantity, stochastic or not, which value does not depend on the units. For instance N_t and EN_t are invariants:

$$N_t = N^\circ_{t^\circ}\ ,\quad EN_t = EN^\circ_{t^\circ}\ .$$

Indeed, $[0,t]$ and $[0,t^\circ]$ are the same real time interval expressed in different units. Hence, the number N_t of claims in $[0,t]$ equals the number $N^\circ_{t^\circ}$ of claims in $[0,t^\circ]$.

On the contrary S_t is not an invariant, because the value of the total claim amount in $[0,t]$ depends on the money unit.

We define $$\gamma := p_t/ES_t,$$

where p_t is the total premium income in the interval $[0,t]$. Then γ is an invariant, not even depending on t. Of course, $\gamma=1+\eta$, and the value of the security loading does not depend on the units.

The partial claim amounts X and X° are related by $X^\circ = X/\delta$. Hence

$$\mu^\circ = EX^\circ = EX/\delta = \mu/\delta.$$

From the invariance of EN_t results

$$\lambda t = EN_t = EN^\circ_{t^\circ} = \lambda^\circ t^\circ = \lambda^\circ t/\varepsilon.$$

Hence $\lambda^\circ = \varepsilon\lambda$. We now impose the condition $p^\circ_{t^\circ} = t^\circ$ on the new units.

By the invariance of γ,

$$p^\circ_{t^\circ}\, ES_t = p_t\, ES^\circ_{t^\circ},$$

i.e

$$t^\circ.\lambda\mu t = \lambda\mu t(1+\eta).\lambda^\circ\mu^\circ t^\circ,$$

$$1 = (1+\eta)\lambda^\circ\mu^\circ = (1+\eta)\varepsilon\lambda\mu/\delta.$$

Hence, this discussion can be summarized by the formulas

$$c^\circ=c/\delta\ ,\ t^\circ=t/\varepsilon\ ,\ \varepsilon=[\lambda(1+\eta)\mu]^{-1}\delta\ ,\ \mu^\circ=\mu/\delta\ ,\ \lambda^\circ=\varepsilon\lambda\ ,\ \eta^\circ=\eta, \qquad (36)$$

where

c is any amount expressed in the old money and c° is the same amount expressed in the new money,

t is any duration expressed in the old time and t° is the same duration expressed in the new time.

Then the premium income in the interval $[0,t^\circ]$ equals t°.

We consider the ruin probabilities

$$\Psi(u)\,,\ \Psi(t,u)\,,\ \Psi(t,u,x) \tag{37}$$

where $\Psi(t,u,x)$ is the probability of ruin before t, with severity less than x, corresponding to the initial risk reserve u. All probabilities are invariants. Hence

$$\Psi(u) = \Psi^{co}(u^\circ) = \Psi^{co}(u/\delta),$$

$$\Psi(t,u) = \Psi^{co}(t^\circ,u^\circ) = \Psi^{co}(t/\varepsilon,u/\delta),$$

$$\Psi(t,u,x) = \Psi^{co}(t^\circ,u^\circ,x^\circ) = \Psi^{co}(t/\varepsilon,u/\delta,x/\delta),$$

where the notation Ψ^{co} is used for ruin probabilities calculated in the classical continuous model (this is recalled by the superscript ^{c}) with the new units (this is recalled by the superscript $^\circ$).

10.3.2. Approximations Calculated in Elementary Model

The approximations

$$\Psi^{co}(u/\delta) \approx \Psi^\circ[\mathrm{int}(u/\delta)],$$

$$\Psi^{co}(t/\varepsilon,u/\delta) \approx \Psi^\circ[\mathrm{int}(t/\varepsilon),\mathrm{int}(u/\delta)],$$

$$\Psi^{co}(t/\varepsilon,u/\delta,x/\delta) \approx \Psi^\circ[\mathrm{int}(t/\varepsilon),\mathrm{int}(u/\delta),\mathrm{int}(x/\delta)],$$

result from the foregoing discussion. Now the last members are calculated in the elementary risk model. By the discussion of the **Introduction** 10.1 and by the properties of the homogeneous Poisson Process, it is intuitively clear that these approximations are asymptotically exact as $\delta\downarrow 0$ (then $\varepsilon\downarrow 0$ by the third formula (36)). A formal proof is not difficult, at least in case of infinite-time ruin probabilities, because then the continuous and the discrete renewal equations for the non-ruin probabilities can be compared.

We hereafter indicate how this convergence can be accelerated by an adaptation of the claimsize distribution function F and an adaptation of the security loading η.

Hence, the probabilities (37), in the original classical model, are approximated by the probabilities in the elementary model:

$$\Psi(u) \approx \Psi^\circ[\mathrm{int}(u/\delta)], \tag{38}$$

$$\Psi(t,u) \approx \Psi^\circ[\mathrm{int}(t/\varepsilon),\mathrm{int}(u/\delta)], \tag{39}$$

$$\Psi(t,u,x) \approx \Psi^\circ[\mathrm{int}(t/\varepsilon),\mathrm{int}(u/\delta),\mathrm{int}(x/\delta)]. \tag{40}$$

Hereafter δ is fixed in the theoretical discussions. Then ε is fixed by the third relation (36). (In the applications δ receives different decreasing values).

We now summarize and complete the **notation rules** as follows:

No superscripts are used in the **original** classical **model**. The **original** functions F, G, U, Ψ,... do have the usual meanings defined in Chapter 7.

The superscript $^\circ$ is used in the elementary model, and also in the classical model with the new time and money units.

In some cases, differences in the elementary model and in the classical model with the new units, must be emphasized. Then the double superscript ^{co} is used in the classical model with new units and the single superscript $^\circ$ in the elementary model.

We now consider the distribution functions F, F^{co} and F°. The distribution function F^{co} results from the original claimsize distribution function F and the relation $c^\circ = c/\delta$ connecting the old and the new money units:

$$F^{co}(x) = P(X^\circ \leq x) = P(X/\delta \leq x) = P(X \leq \delta x) = F(\delta x). \tag{41}$$

The distribution F° of the elementary model must be concentrated on the set $\mathbf{N}_+$. It results from a **discretization** of F^{co}. The latter can be performed in various ways. **We assume that this discretization does not modify the first moment μ^{co} of F^{co}.**

The claimsize distribution sequence $\underline{F}^\circ$ used in the theory of the elementary model is the restriction of F° to $\mathbf{N}_+$.

It happens that the original claimsize distribution F is already concentrated on the set $\{0,\delta,2\delta,...\}$. Then F^{co} is concentrated on $\{0,1,2,...\}$ and then, of course, we take $F^\circ \equiv F^{co}$.

10.3.3. Claimsize Distribution Adaptation

Lower bound for the original infinite-time ruin probabilities

Numerical investigations show that the last member of (38) is a lower bound of $\Psi(u)$ in most cases. The explanation is given by the following Theorem.

Theorem 15

Let the claimsize distribution F of the classical risk model be concentrated on the set $\{0,\delta,2\delta,...\}$. Then

$$\Psi(k\delta) \geq \Psi^{\circ}(k) \ (k=0,1,2,...). \tag{42}$$

Proof

The classical continuous renewal equation for U^{co} is

$$U^{co} = p + q\, U^{co} * G^{co}, \tag{43}$$

where

$$G^{co}(x) = 1/\mu^{\circ} \int_{[0,x]} [1-F^{co}(y)]dy = 1/\mu^{\circ} \int_{[0,x]} [1-F^{\circ}(y)]dy. \tag{44}$$

Indeed, $F^{co} \equiv F^{\circ}$ (last paragraph of 10.3.2) and p and q are invariants because η is an invariant. The renewal equation (20) for U° is

$$U^{\circ} = p + q\, U^{\circ} * G^{\circ}, \tag{45}$$

where, by (19) and (44)

$$G^{\circ}(x) = 1/\mu^{\circ} \int_{[0,[x+1]]} [1-F^{\circ}(y)]dy$$

$$\geq 1/\mu^{\circ} \int_{[0,x]} [1-F^{\circ}(y)]dy = G^{co}(x). \tag{46}$$

Then, by (43) and (45),

$$U^{co} = p\sum_k q^k (G^{co})^{*k} \leq p\sum_k q^k (G^{\circ})^{*k} = U^{\circ}.$$

Then $\Psi^{co} \geq \Psi^{\circ}$, and

$$\Psi(k\delta) = \Psi^{co}(k) \geq \Psi^{\circ}(k) \ \bullet$$

Upper bound for infinite-time ruin probabilities

Let

$$G^1(x) = 1/\mu^\circ \int_{[0,[x]]} [1-F^\circ(y)]dy \quad (x \in \mathbf{R}_+). \tag{47}$$

Then G^1 is constant on the intervals $[k,k+1[$, and it is the usual extension of its restriction to $\mathbf{N}_+$. This restriction is the probability distribution sequence $\underline{G}^1$ with elements

$$G^1_k = 1/\mu^\circ \int_{[0,[k]]} [1-F^\circ(y)]dy = 1/\mu^\circ \sum_{0\le j\le k-1} (1-F^\circ_j), \tag{48}$$

where the last equality is exact because $F^\circ \equiv F^\circ_j$ on $[j,j+1[$. The last member of (48) equals 0 for k=0.

Let $\underline{U}^1$ be the solution of the discrete renewal equation

$$\underline{U}^1 = p + q\, \underline{U}^1 * \underline{G}^1. \tag{49}$$

The usual extension U^1 of $\underline{U}^1$ is the solution of the renewal equation

$$U^1 = p + q\, U^1 * G^1. \tag{50}$$

Let

$$\Psi^1 := 1-U^1 \;.\quad \underline{\Psi}^1 := 1-\underline{U}^1.$$

Theorem 16

Let the claimsize distribution F of the classical risk model be concentrated on the set {0,δ,2δ,...}. Then

$$\boldsymbol{\Psi(k\delta) \le \Psi^1(k) \quad (k=0,1,2,...).} \tag{51}$$

Proof

The proof is the same as that of Theorem 15. Now, instead of (46):

$$G^1(x) = 1/\mu^\circ \int_{[0,[x]]} [1-F^\circ(y)]dy \le 1/\mu^\circ \int_{[0,x]} [1-F^\circ(y)]dy = G^{co}(x),$$

and then by (43) and (50),

$$U^{co} = p\sum_k q^k (G^{co})^{*k} \ge p\sum_k q^k (G^1)^{*k} = U^1.$$

Then $\Psi^{co} \le \Psi^1$, and

$$\Psi(k\delta) = \Psi^{co}(k) \le \Psi^\circ(k) \;\bullet$$

Improved approximations for original infinite-time ruin probabilities

For $\theta \in [0,1]$, let

$$\underline{G}^{\theta} := (1-\theta)\underline{G}^{\circ} + \theta \underline{G}^{1}, \tag{52}$$

let $\underline{U}^{\theta}$ be the solution of the renewal equation

$$\underline{U}^{\theta} = p + q\, \underline{U}^{\theta} * \underline{G}^{\theta} \tag{53}$$

and let

$$\underline{\Psi}^{\theta} := 1 - \underline{U}^{\theta}.$$

Then, elementwise,

$$\underline{G}^{\circ} \leq \underline{G}^{\theta} \leq \underline{G}^{1}\,,\ \underline{U}^{\circ} \leq \underline{U}^{\theta} \leq \underline{U}^{1}\,,\ \underline{\Psi}^{\circ} \geq \underline{\Psi}^{\theta} \geq \underline{\Psi}^{1}. \tag{54}$$

Instead of (38), we can consider the approximation

$$\Psi(u) \approx \Psi^{\theta}[\mathrm{int}(u/\delta)]. \tag{55}$$

In most cases it furnishes a lower bound for $\Psi(u)$ for $\theta=0$ (Th.15), an upper bound for $\theta=1$ (Th.16) and a rather good approximation for $\theta=1/2$. We do not assume here that the original claimsize distribution F is already concentrated on the set $\{0,\delta,2\delta\ldots\}$.

Let $g^{\theta} := \nabla \underline{G}^{\theta}$. Then the recurrent numerical solution of the renewal equation (53) is furnished by (18) after the obvious substitutions:

U°_{k} , g°_{k} , p° , q° must be replaced by U^{θ}_{k} , g^{θ}_{k} , p , q resp.

Pseudo-probability distribution sequences

The next question is the following: Can we replace the claimsize distribution sequence $\underline{F}^{\circ}$ by a claimsize distribution sequence $\underline{F}^{\theta}$ such that the concave transform of $\underline{F}^{\theta}$ is the function $\underline{G}^{\theta}$ defined by (52)? If the answer is "yes", then we can also calculate the last member of (39) and of (40) with this "improved" claimsize distribution sequence $\underline{F}^{\theta}$ (say with $\theta=1/2$) instead of $\underline{F}^{\circ}$. Then, at least in (39), the approximations must be better for large values of t because they are better for $t=\infty$ by the preceding discussion.

The strict answer to the question is "no", but the indicated improvements can nevertheless be performed numerically. We now justify this answer. Let us assume for the moment, that $\underline{F}^{\theta}$ exists.

Then

$$\underline{G}^{\theta} = {}^{1}\!/_{\mu^{\circ}}\, \Sigma(1-\underline{F}^{\theta}), \tag{56}$$

(because it is understood that the first moment μ° must be preserved), and then (57) can be solved in $\underline{F}^{\theta}$, i.e. $\underline{F}^{\theta}$ can only be

$$\underline{F}^{\theta} = \underline{1} - \mu^{\circ}\nabla\underline{G}^{\theta}. \tag{57}$$

In order to explicit the last member of (59), we display it as

$$\underline{1} - \mu^{\circ}\nabla\underline{G}^{\theta} = \underline{1} - \mu^{\circ}\nabla[(1-\theta)\underline{G}^{\circ} + \theta\underline{G}^{1}]$$

$$= (1-\theta)[\underline{1} - \mu^{\circ}\nabla\underline{G}^{\circ}] + \theta[\underline{1} - \mu^{\circ}\nabla\underline{G}^{1}] = (1-\theta)\underline{F}^{\circ} + \theta[\underline{1} - \mu^{\circ}\nabla\underline{G}^{1}],$$

by (10). By (48), the elements of the difference sequence in the last member are

$$(\nabla\underline{G}^{1})_0 = 0 \quad , \quad (\nabla\underline{G}^{1})_k = {}^{1}\!/_{\mu^{\circ}}(1-F^{\circ}_{k-1}) \ (k\geq 1).$$

Hence, the elements of $\underline{F}^{\theta}$ are

$$\begin{aligned} F^{\theta}_0 &= (1-\theta)F^{\circ}_0 + \theta, \\ F^{\theta}_k &= (1-\theta)F^{\circ}_k + \theta F^{\circ}_{k-1} \ (k\geq 1). \end{aligned} \tag{58}$$

Let

$$\underline{f}^{\theta} := \nabla\underline{F}^{\theta}$$

be the "probability masses" sequence corresponding to $\underline{F}^{\theta}$. Then, by (58):

$$\begin{aligned} f^{\theta}_0 = (1-\theta)f^{\circ}_0 + \theta \quad &, \quad f^{\theta}_1 = -\theta(1-f^{\circ}_0) + (1-\theta)f^{\circ}_1, \\ f^{\theta}_k &= (1-\theta)f^{\circ}_k + \theta f^{\circ}_{k-1} \ \ (k\geq 2). \end{aligned} \tag{59}$$

The surprise now is that f^{θ}_1 can be strictly negative. For $\theta=1$,

$$f^{1}_1 = -(1-f^{\circ}_0) < 0.$$

Hence, $\underline{\mathbf{F}}^{\theta}$ **is not necessarily a probability distribution sequence**. We call $\underline{F}^{\theta}$ a **pseudo-probability distribution sequence.** The sum of the pseudo-probability masses f^{θ}_k is still equal to 1, and the "first moment" $\mu(\underline{F}^{\theta})$ equals μ°. Indeed,

$$\sum_{k\geq 0} f^{\theta}_k = f^{\circ}_0 + (1-\theta)f^{\circ}_1 + \sum_{k\geq 2}[(1-\theta)f^{\circ}_k + \theta f^{\circ}_{k-1}]$$

$$= f^{\circ}_0 + (1-\theta)\sum_{k\geq 1} f^{\circ}_k + \theta \sum_{k\geq 1} f^{\circ}_k = f^{\circ}_0 + (1-\theta)(1-f^{\circ}_0) + \theta(1-f^{\circ}_0) = 1,$$

$$\mu(\underline{F}^{\theta}) := \sum_{k\geq 1} kf^{\theta}_k = -\theta(1-f^{\circ}_0) + (1-\theta)f^{\circ}_1 + \sum_{k\geq 2} k[(1-\theta)f^{\circ}_k + \theta f^{\circ}_{k-1}]$$

$$= -\theta(1-f^{\circ}_0) + (1-\theta)\sum_{k\geq 1} kf^{\circ}_k + \theta\sum_{k\geq 2} (k-1)f^{\circ}_{k-1} + \theta\sum_{k\geq 2} f^{\circ}_{k-1}$$

$$= -\theta(1-f^{\circ}_0) + (1-\theta)\mu^{\circ} + \theta\mu^{\circ} + \theta(1-f^{\circ}_0) = \mu^{\circ}.$$

Improved approximations for the original finite-time ruin probabilities, taking the severity of ruin into account or not

The elementary risk model looses its probabilistic meaning when the claimsize distribution sequence $\underline{F}^{\circ}$ is replaced by a pseudo distribution sequence $\underline{F}^{\theta}$. But the numerical algorithms, based on the relations (1), (33), (34) and (35) can be performed with the probability masses f°_k replaced by the pseudo-masses f^{θ}_k.

We use the superscript θ for the ruin or non-ruin probabilities calculated in this way. We then replace (39) and (40) by the approximations

$$\Psi(t,u) \approx \Psi^{\theta}[\text{int}(t/\varepsilon),\text{int}(u/\delta)], \tag{60}$$

$$\Psi(t,u,x) \approx \Psi^{\theta}[\text{int}(t/\varepsilon),\text{int}(u/\delta),\text{int}(x/\delta)]. \tag{61}$$

Numerical investigations show that they are better than (39) and (40) for $\theta=1/2$, even for small, but still **practical** values of t. (**Practical ruin probabilities** $\Psi(u)$, $\Psi(t,u)$ can be defined as ruin probabilities with values less than 1/100. Then, in the context of ruin problems, **practical parameters** t, u are parameters leading to practical ruin probabilities).

We call **claimsize distribution adaptation**, the replacement of the claimsize distribution sequence $\underline{F}^{\circ}$ by the pseudo-probability distribution sequence $\underline{F}^{\theta}$ (with $\theta=1/2$ if nothing is specified) in the elementary risk model (or in the semi-elementary risk model of the following section 10.4).

10.3.4. Security Loading Adaptation

Improved approximations for original infinite-time ruin probabilities

In the following discussion, we assume that the considered adjustment coefficients and asymptotic values do exist. We also assume that the original claimsize distribution F is already concentrated on the set $\{0,\delta,2\delta,\ldots\}$. Let

$$\Psi^{co}{}_{as}(u) := \alpha^{co}\exp(-\rho^{co}u) \tag{62}$$

be Cramér's classical asymptotic value for the infinite-time ruin probability $\Psi^{co}(u)$, i.e. the ruin probability calculated in the continuous classical model with the new money unit (the time unit is irrelevant in infinite-time ruin probabilities). By Ch.7.Th.16,

$$\alpha^{co} = \eta\mu^{\circ}/\beta^{co}, \tag{63}$$

where

$$\beta^{co} = \rho^{co}\int_{[0,\infty[} x[1-F^{co}(x)]\exp(\rho^{co}x)dx$$

$$= \rho_{co}\sum_{k\geq 0}\int_{[k,(k+1)[} x\exp(\rho^{co}x)[1-F^{\circ}(x)]dx$$

$$= \rho^{co}\sum_{k\geq 0}[1-F^{\circ}{}_k]\int_{[k,k+1[} x\exp(\rho^{co}x)dx$$

$$= (\rho^{co})^{-1}\sum_{k\geq 0}[1-F^{\circ}{}_k][[\rho^{co}(k+1)-1]\exp[\rho^{co}(k+1)] - [\rho^{co}k-1]\exp(\rho^{co}k)]. \tag{64}$$

Here the equation Ch.3.(9) for the adjustment coefficient ρ^{co} becomes

$$1 = q/\mu^{\circ}\,[(\exp\rho^{co}-1)/\rho^{co}]\sum_{k\geq 0}[1-F^{\circ}{}_k]\exp(\rho^{co}k). \tag{65}$$

We now consider the renewal equation (13) of the elementary risk model, with the adapted probability distribution sequence $\underline{G}^{\theta}$ considered in the foregoing section 10.3.3 and with a new security loading η^{θ}, not yet specified. This renewal equation for the new probability distribution sequence which we denote by $\underline{U}^{\theta a}$, is

$$\underline{U}^{\theta a} = p^{\theta}\underline{1} + q^{\theta}\underline{U}^{\theta a} * \underline{G}^{\theta}, \tag{66}$$

where $\qquad q^{\theta} := 1/(1+\eta^{\theta})\,,\ p^{\theta} := 1-q^{\theta}.$

Now Theorem 13 applies to the renewal equation (66), because it is based only on the fact that $\underline{G}^{\circ}$ is a usual probability distribution sequence. We notice $\underline{G}^{\theta}$ is a usual probability distribution sequence indeed, even when the corresponding sequence $\underline{F}^{\theta}$ is a pseudo-probability distribution sequence. Let

$$\Psi^{\theta}{}_{as}(k) := \alpha^{\theta}\exp(-\rho^{\theta}k) \tag{67}$$

be the asymptotic value for

$$\Psi^{\theta a}(k) := 1 - U^{\theta a}(k),$$

furnished by Theorem 13 applied to the renewal equation (66). Then

$$\alpha^{\theta} = \eta^{\theta} q^{\theta}[(\exp \rho^{\theta} - 1)\mu^{e}]^{-1}, \tag{68}$$

where

$$\mu^{e} = (q^{\theta}/\mu^{o})\sum_{k\geq 0} (1 - F^{\theta}_{k})k \exp(\rho^{\theta} k). \tag{69}$$

By (23), the adjustment coefficient ρ^{θ} is the strictly positive root of the equation

$$1 = (q^{\theta}/\mu^{o})\sum_{k\geq 0} (1 - F^{\theta}_{k})\exp(\rho^{\theta} k). \tag{70}$$

By (58), this relation can be displayed as

$$1 = (q^{\theta}/\mu^{o})[(1-\theta) + \theta \exp \rho^{\theta}]\sum_{k\geq 0} (1 - F^{o}_{k})\exp(\rho^{\theta} k). \tag{71}$$

We now compare this equation with (65). We define q^{θ} by the relation

$$(q^{\theta}/\mu^{o})[(1-\theta) + \theta \exp \rho^{\theta}] = q/\mu^{o} \, [(\exp \rho^{co} - 1)/\rho^{co}]$$

i.e.

$$q^{\theta} := q[(1-\theta) + \theta \exp \rho^{\theta}]^{-1}[(\exp \rho^{co} - 1)/\rho^{co}] \tag{72}$$

The solution ρ^{θ} of equation (70) is

$$\rho^{\theta} = \rho^{co}. \tag{73}$$

Then the exact relation

$$\Psi^{co}{}_{as}(k) = (\alpha^{co}/\alpha^{\theta})\, \Psi^{\theta}{}_{as}(k) \tag{74}$$

results from (62) and (67). But

$$\Psi(k\delta) = \Psi^{co}(k)$$

and then (74) suggests the replacement of (55) by the approximation

$$\Psi(u) \approx (\alpha^{co}/\alpha^{\theta})\Psi^{\theta a}[\mathrm{int}(u/\delta)]. \tag{75}$$

From (74) results that, for any value of δ (not necessarily small), relation (75) is asymptotically exact for $u = k\delta$, $k \uparrow \infty$. This explains why the approximation is almost always better than the approximation (55) for large values of the initial risk reserve u. Numerical investigations show that, even for small, but still practical values of u, (75) is rather uniformly better than (55), certainly for $\theta = 0$.

Improved approximations for original finite-time ruin probabilities, taking severity of ruin into account or not

The next step is the replacement of the approximations (60) and (61) by

$$\Psi(t,u) \approx (\alpha^{co}/\alpha^{\theta})\Psi^{\theta a}[\mathrm{int}(t/\varepsilon),\mathrm{int}(u/\delta)], \tag{76}$$

$$\Psi(t,u,x) \approx (\alpha^{co}/\alpha^{\theta})\ \Psi^{\theta a}[\mathrm{int}(t/\varepsilon),\mathrm{int}(u/\delta),\mathrm{int}(x/\delta)], \tag{77}$$

and here also the improvement is rather uniform, for the practical values of the involved parameters.

All probabilities $\Psi^{\theta a}$ are calculated in the elementary risk model, with the pseudo-probability distribution sequence $\underline{F}^{\theta}$, and with the **adapted security loading** η^{θ}. The value of $\rho^{co}=\rho^{\theta}$ results from (65). Then α^{co} results from (63), then η^{θ} from (72) and then α^{θ} from (68).

We call **security loading adaptation** the replacement of the original security loading η by the security loading η^{θ} in numerical calculations in the elementary risk model with pseudo-probability distribution sequence $\underline{F}^{\theta}$. Of course $\theta=0$ is a particular case. Then the security loading adaptation takes place in the elementary model with non adapted claimsize distribution sequence $\underline{F}^{\circ}$.

We say that numerical ruin probabilities are **doubly adapted** if they result from a claimsize distribution adaptation (with $\theta=1/2$ when nothing else is specified), followed by the corresponding security loading adaptation.

Numerical ruin probabilities calculated in the elementary risk model are **non adapted** if they result from the non adapted claimsize distribution sequence $\underline{F}^{\circ}$ and the original security loading η.

10.3.5. Truncation and Discretization of Original Claimsize Distribution Function

Theorem 17

In the classical risk model let F and F^b be claimsize distribution functions such that $\mu(F)=\mu(F^b)$. Then

$$\Psi(u,F) = \Psi(u,F^b) \ \text{ if } \ F = F^b \text{ on } [0,u[,$$

and

$$\Psi(t,u,F) = \Psi(t,u,F^b) \ \text{ if } \ F = F^b \text{ on } [0,u+\mu(1+\eta)\lambda t[.$$

Proof
The equality of the infinite-time ruin probabilities calculated with F and F^b resp., results from Ch.7.Th.4.Cor.

The equality of the finite-time ruin probabilities results from 6.1.2. applied to the classical model. Indeed, then

$$p(\tau) = u + \mu(1+\eta)\lambda\tau,$$

and from the relations Ch.6.(1) to (6) results that F is used on the interval $[0,u+\mu(1+\eta)\lambda t]$ only. Now a modification of F at the end point of that interval does not modify the multiple integral in the last member of Ch.6.(3), because the Lebesgue integrals in the variables $t_1,\ldots,t_n$ are present •

Truncation of original claimsize distribution function

From this Theorem results that F can always be replaced by a distribution $F^{b'}$ concentrated on some bounded interval $[0,b']$.

The re-definition of F, hereafter used, is the following. Let $F(b) < 1$ where b is such that the considered ruin probabilities only depend on $\mu(F)$ and on the restriction of F to the interval $[0,b[$, or such that the F-probability mass outside the interval $[0,b[$ is negligible. Let

$$b' := b + [1-F(b)]^{-1}\int_{[b,\infty[} [1-F(y)]dy. \tag{78}$$

Let $F^{b'}$ be defined by the conditions

$$F^{b'} = F \text{ on } [0,b[\quad , \quad F^{b'} = F(b) \text{ on } [b,b'[\quad , \quad F^{b'} = 1 \text{ on } [b',\infty[. \tag{79}$$

Then $F^{b'}$ is a claimsize distribution concentrated on the bounded interval $[0,b']$ and such that $\mu(F)=\mu(F^{b'})$ by the surface interpretation of the first moment.

Discretization of $F^{b'}$

In the examples of the next section 10.3.6, we apply the preceding numerical algorithms with δ equal to $\delta_\nu := b/\nu$, for different increasing values of ν. We replace $F^{b'}$ by the distribution $F^{b'\nu}$ concentrated on a finite subset of the set

$$\{0,\delta_v,2\delta_v,\ldots\},$$

defined by the relations

$$F^{b'v} = (1/\delta_v) \int_{[k\delta_v,(k+1)\delta_v[} F^{b'}(y)dy \text{ on } [k\delta_v,(k+1)\delta_v[\text{ (k=0,...)}. \qquad (80)$$

Then $\mu(F^{b'v}) = \mu(F^{b'})$ by the surface interpretation of the first moment.

Claimsize distribution sequence $\underline{F}°$

Then the elements of the claimsize distribution sequence $\underline{F}°$ used in the elementary risk model, are

$$F°_k := F^{b'v}(k\delta_v) \text{ (k=0,1,...)}. \qquad (81)$$

L ***function***

Hereafter ε' is a very small quantity, without practical impact on the results, introduced in order to simplify the computer programme. Let

$$L(x) := \int_{[0,x]} F(y)dy \; (x\in\mathbf{R}_+). \qquad (82)$$

The integral in the last member of (78) equals

$$\int_{[b,\infty[} [1-F(y)]dy = \int_{[0,\infty[} [1-F(y)]dy - \int_{[0,b[} [1-F(y)]dy = \mu-b+L(b).$$

Then

$$b' := b + [\varepsilon'+1-F(b)]^{-1}[\mu-b+L(b)]. \qquad (83)$$

This is (78) completed with ε'. The relation (83) is accepted when F(b)=1, i.e. when the original claimsize distribution F is already concentrated on [0,b]. Then it furnishes the right value $b'=b$.

The integral occurring in the relations (80) equals

$$\int_{[k\delta_v,(k+1)\delta_v[} F^{b'}(y)dy = L[(k+1)\delta_v]-L(k\delta_v),$$

where the last equality is correct if the integration domain is contained in the interval [0,b[, because $F=F^{b'}$ on that interval.

Let v' be the integer

$$v' = [(b'+\varepsilon')/\delta_v]-1. \qquad (84)$$

By (81)

$$F^\circ_k = (1/\delta_\nu)[L[(k+1)\delta_\nu]-L(k\delta_\nu)] \quad (k=0,\dots,\nu-1), \tag{85}$$

$$F^\circ_k = F(\nu\delta_\nu) \quad (k=\nu,\dots,\nu'-2), \tag{85}$$

$$F^\circ_{\nu'-1} = (1/\delta_\nu)[b'-(\nu'-1)\delta_\nu]F(\nu\delta_\nu)+(1/\delta_\nu)[\nu'\delta_\nu-b']; \tag{85}$$

$$F^\circ_k = 1 \quad (k=\nu',\nu'+1,\dots). \tag{85}$$

Practical choice of b

Let us call **support of any distribution H**, the smallest closed interval on which H is concentrated. It is the intersection of the closed intervals I such that H is concentrated on I.

The practical choice of b is based on Theorem 17. Let c be the right extremity of the support of the claimsize distribution F. If F is not concentrated on a bounded interval, then $c=+\infty$.

When an infinite-time ruin probability $\Psi(u)$ is considered, we take $b=c\wedge u$. When a finite-time ruin probability $\Psi(t,u)$ is considered, we take

$$b := c\wedge[u+1.1\ \mu(1+\eta)\lambda t], \tag{86}$$

where the factor 1.1 is introduced because the adaptation of η may increase the value of this security loading.

In any case, b can be increased a bit. For instance, b can be replaced by the first integer larger than b. But b can also be decreased. Then the new b must be such that the F-mass in $[b,\infty[$ is negligible. When b is decreased, then also $\delta_\nu = b/\nu$ is decreased (for fixed ν), and then the ruin probability approximations are better. Of course, if b is decreased too much, then the original claimsize distribution differs too much from that one used in the numerical computations.

10.3.6. Numerical Illustrations

We now illustrate the numerical calculation of finite-time and infinite-time ruin probabilities in the classical risk model, and the impact of a claimsize distribution adaptation and the security loading adaptation in the case of 5 particular claimsize distributions. The distributions 1, 2 and 3 are concentrated on the interval [0,1]. For these distributions, we take b=1.

The distributions 4 and 5 are not concentrated on a bounded interval. For these distributions, we take b=u when infinite-time ruin probabilities are considered.

For the finite-time ruin probability corresponding to distribution 4, we take b=18 (the same value as that one considered in the case of the infinite-time ruin probability). Then the F-mass in $[18,\infty[$ equals 1.5 10^{-8}. For the finite time ruin probability corresponding to the distribution 5, we take b=84. This is the first integer larger than (86).

In any case $\lambda=1$, $\eta = 0.25$.

When infinite-time ruin probabilities are calculated, we consider practical values of u, i.e. values such that the corresponding ruin probabilities are not too large or not too small. In the case of finite-time ruin probabilities, the value of u is that one used in the infinite-time case, divided by 2, and then t is such that the corresponding ruin probability is not too small or not too large.

The values of θ that we consider are 0 (no claimsize distribution adaptation), 1/2 and 1. In each of these cases, we consider a non-adapted security loading η=0.25 and an adapted security loading loading η', not specified numerically in the tables of results (and depending on ν).

For ν we first consider small values, then larger and larger values. Here we are limited by two constraints. When ν is too large, the computing times become too long. We have indicated the computing times longer than 1 minute. In other cases, memory overflows do occur for large values of ν. **These constraints prove the interest of the adaptations. For rather small values of ν excellent approximations of the exact values are obtained when the adaptations are applied**. In each table, the ruin probability, with four exact digits after the decimal point, is printed boldface. In some cases, it results from calculations with larger values of ν than those indicated in the tables.

We recall that Theorems 15 and 16 are stated and proved only for infinite-time ruin probabilities, and only for discrete claimsize distributions F, already concentrated on the set $\{0,\delta,2\delta,...\}$.

The following numerical results suggest that they are valid also in the case of finite-time ruin probabilities (when no security loading adaptation is performed). The proof of Theorems 15 and 16 was based on the renewal equations of the classical and of the discrete risk model. No such simple equations do exist for the finite-time ruin probabilities. If the Theorems 15 and 16 do have a finite-time ruin probability version (and this seems about sure), the proof can only be very different.

None of the distributions 1 to 5 is discrete. That (42) and (51) are nevertheless exact in the considered cases is not so surprising (at least for large ν), because the discrete approximations are asymptotically equal to the initial distributions as $\delta \downarrow 0$.

A practical conclusion of the numerical study is the following:

When the claimsize distribution function and the security loading are adapted (or even when only the claimsize distribution adaptation is applied), **the discretization corresponding to a partition of the interval [0,b] in 50 sub-intervals of the same length, furnishes in all cases an approximation of the finite-time or the infinite-time ruin probability, which is safe enough in the practical applications.**

Claimsize distribution 1

We here consider the uniform claimsize distribution on the interval [0,1]:

$$F(x) := x \ (0 \leq x \leq 1) \ , \ F(x) := 1 \ (x > 1)$$

Then

$$\mu = 0.5 \ , \ L(x) = 0.5\, x^2 \ (0 \leq x \leq 1) \ , \ L(x) = x - 0.5 \ (x > 1).$$

The approximations for $\Psi(6)$ are

	ν=25	ν=50	ν=100	ν=200	ν=400
θ=0, η=0.25	0.0149	0.0168	0.0178	0.0183	0.0186
θ=0.5, η=0.25	0.0187	0.0188	0.0188	0.0188	0.0188
θ=1, η=0.25	0.0228	0.0208	0.0198	0.0193	0.0191
θ=0, η'	**0.0189**	**0.0189**	**0.0189**	**0.0189**	**0.0189**
θ=0.5, η'	**0.0189**	**0.0189**	**0.0189**	**0.0189**	**0.0189**
θ=1, η'	**0.0189**	**0.0189**	**0.0189**	**0.0189**	**0.0189**

The approximations for $\Psi(2,3)$ are displayed in the following table.

	ν=25	ν=50	ν=100	ν=200
θ=0 , η=0.25	0.0017	0.0021	0.0024	0.0025
θ=0.5 , η=0.25	0.0021	0.0023	0.0025	**0.0026**
θ=1 , η=0.25	**0.0026**	**0.0026**	**0.0026**	**0.0026**
θ=0 , η′	0.0018	0.0022	0.0024	0.0025
θ=0.5 , η′	0.0021	0.0024	0.0025	**0.0026**
θ=1 , η′	0.0027	**0.0026**	**0.0026**	**0.0026**

Claimsize distribution 2

We here consider the following claimsize distribution F with infinite density at the point 0 :

$$F(x) := x^{1/2} \ (0 \le x \le 1) \quad , \quad F(x) := 1 \ (x>1).$$

Then

$$\mu = 1/3 \quad , \quad L(x) = 2/3 \, x^{3/2} \ (0 \le x \le 1) \quad , \quad L(x) = x - 1/3 \ \ (x>1).$$

The approximations for $\Psi(6)$ are

	ν=25	ν=50	ν=100	ν=200	ν=400
θ=0 , η=0.25	0.0096	0.0111	0.0119	0.0123	0.0125
θ=0.5 , η=0.25	0.0126	0.0126	**0.0127**	**0.0127**	**0.0127**
θ=1 , η=0.25	0.0160	0.0143	0.0135	0.0132	0.0129
θ=0 , η′	0.0128	**0.0127**	**0.0127**	**0.0127**	**0.0127**
θ=0.5 , η′	0.0128	**0.0127**	**0.0127**	**0.0127**	**0.0127**
θ=1 , η′	0.0128	**0.0127**	**0.0127**	**0.0127**	**0.0127**

The approximations for $\Psi(5,3)$ are

	ν=25	ν=50	ν=100	ν=200	
θ=0 , η=0.25	0.0042	0.0050	0.0054	0.0057	(3′25″)
θ=0.5 , η=0.25	0.0052	0.0055	0.0057	**0.0059**	(3′25″)
θ=1 , η=0.25	0.0063	0.0061	0.0060	0.0060	(3′25″)
θ=0 , η′	0.0043	0.0051	0.0056	0.0057	(3′25″)
θ=0.5 , η′	0.0053	0.0056	0.0058	**0.0059**	(3′25″)
θ=1 , η′	0.0063	0.0061	0.0060	0.0060	(3′25″)

Claimsize distribution 3

The following claimsize distribution has an infinite density at point 1.

$$F(x) := 1-(1-x)^{1/2} \ (0 \le x \le 1) \ , \ F(x) := 1 \ (x>1).$$

$$\mu = 2/3 \ , \ L(x) = x - 2/3\,[1-(1-x)^{3/2}]\ (0 \le x \le 1)\ , \ L(x) = x - 2/3\ (x>1).$$

The approximations for $\Psi(8)$ are

	ν=25	ν=50	ν=100	ν=200	ν=400
θ=0 , η=0.25	0.0097	0.0108	0.0114	0.0117	0.0119
θ=0.5 , η=0.25	0.0120	0.0120	0.0120	0.0120	0.0120
θ=1 , η=0.25	0.0145	0.0132	0.0126	0.0123	0.0122
θ=0 , η'	**0.0121**	**0.0121**	**0.0121**	**0.0121**	**0.0121**
θ=0.5 , η'	**0.0121**	**0.0121**	**0.0121**	**0.0121**	**0.0121**
θ=1 , η'	**0.0121**	**0.0121**	**0.0121**	**0.0121**	**0.0121**

Approximations for $\Psi(4,4)$:

	ν=25	ν=50	ν=100	ν=200	
θ=0 , η=0.25	0.0059	0.0068	0.0073	0.0075	(4′40″)
θ=0.5 , η=0.25	0.0070	0.0074	0.0076	**0.0077**	(4′40″)
θ=1 , η=0.25	0.0082	0.0080	0.0079	0.0078	(4′40″)
θ=0 , η'	0.0061	0.0070	0.0073	0.0075	(4′40″)
θ=0.5 , η'	0.0071	0.0075	0.0076	**0.0077**	(4′40″)
θ=1 , η'	0.0080	0.0080	0.0078	0.0078	(4′40″)

Claimsize distribution 4

We now consider the simplest exponential distribution on $[0,\infty[$:

$$F(x) := 1-e^{-x} \ (x \ge 0). \text{ Then } \mu = 1 \ , \ L(x) = x + e^{-x} - 1 \ (x \ge 0).$$

By 7.2.2.(24), $\Psi(18)$= 0.02185898. The approximations for $\Psi(18)$ are,

	ν=25	ν=50	ν=100	ν=200	ν=400	ν=800
θ=0, η=0.25	0.0055	0.0115	0.0161	0.0188	0.0203	0.0211
θ=0.5, η=0.25	0.0236	0.0219	0.0217	0.0217	0.0218	0.0218
θ=1, η=0.25	0.0534	0.0354	0.0248	0.0248	0.0233	0.0226
θ=0, η′	0.0248	0.0226	0.0220	**0.0219**	**0.0219**	**0.0219**
θ=0.5, η′	0.0248	0.0226	0.0220	**0.0219**	**0.0219**	**0.0219**
θ=1, η′	0.0248	0.0226	0.0220	**0.0219**	**0.0219**	**0.0219**

The approximations for Ψ(8,9) are (with b=18),

	ν=25	ν=50	ν=100	ν=200	ν=400	ν=800
θ=0, η=0.25	0.0056	0.0134	0.0181	0.0206	0.0220	0.0228 (3′)
θ=0.5, η=0.25	0.0152	0.0203	0.0219	0.0225	0.0230	**0.0233** (3′)
θ=1, η=0.25	0.0288	0.0283	0.0260	0.0246	0.0240	0.0238 (3′)
θ=0, η′	0.0074	0.0155	0.0195	0.0213	0.0224	0.0230 (3′)
θ=0.5, η′	0.0163	0.0211	0.0223	0.0227	0.0231	0.**0233** (3′)
θ=1, η′	0.0262	0.0267	0.0251	0.0242	0.0238	0.0237 (3′)

Claimsize distribution 5

The final example which we consider is the following long-tailed Pareto distribution

$$F(x) := 0 \ (0 \leq x \leq 1) \quad , \quad F(x) := 1 - x^{-2} \ (x > 1).$$

Then

$$\mu = 2 \ , \ L(x) = 0 \ (0 \leq x \leq 1) \ , \ L(x) = x + x^{-1} - 2 \ \ (x > 1).$$

The approximations for Ψ(80) are (with b=80),

	ν=25	ν=50	ν=100	ν=200	ν=400	ν=800
θ=0, η=0.25	0.0273	0.0290	0.0306	0.0316	0.0321	0.0324
θ=0.5, η=0.25	0.0351	0.0329	**0.0327**	**0.0327**	**0.0327**	**0.0327**
θ=1, η=0.25	0.0503	0.0382	0.0350	0.0338	0.0332	0.0330
θ=0, η′	0.0407	0.0355	0.0339	0.0332	0.0329	0.0328
θ=0.5, η′	0.0365	0.0335	0.0330	0.0328	**0.0327**	**0.0327**
θ=1, η′	0.0353	0.0323	0.0323	0.0324	0.0326	0.0326

The approximations for $\Psi(16,40)$ are (with b=84):

	ν=25	ν=50	ν=100	ν=200	ν=400
θ=0 , η=0.25	0.0074	0.0087	0.0097	0.0104	0.0108
θ=0.5 , η=0.25	0.0102	0.0103	0.0106	0.0109	0.0110
θ=1 , η=0.25	0.0161	0.0163	0.0117	0.0115	0.0113
θ=0 , η'	0.0085	0.0093	0.0100	0.0107	0.0109
θ=0.5 , η'	0.0106	0.0105	0.0107	0.0110	**0.0111**
θ=1 , η'	0.0136	0.0141	0.0112	0.0114	0.0113

10.4. Semi-Elementary Risk Model

10.4.1. Definition of Semi-Elementary Model

The **semi-elementary risk model** is a generalization of the elementary risk model. The only difference is the following. Let $\ldots,\lambda^\circ_{-2},\lambda^\circ_{-1},\lambda^\circ_0,\lambda^\circ_1,\lambda^\circ_2,\ldots$ be a doubly infinite sequence of numbers λ°_m strictly between 0 and 1. Then, in the semi-elementary risk model, the probability of a claim in the interval]k,k+1] (in fact at the end of that interval) equals λ°_m if the amount of the risk reserve at the instant k equals m.

For m<0, λ_m is the probability of a claim in the interval]k,k+1], when the risk reserve has the strictly negative value m at the instant k. Hereafter, we always assume that the process starts with a positive initial risk reserve and we only consider ruin problems. If ruin does occur, we are no longer interested in the process afterwards. This means that the values of ..., λ°_{-2}, λ°_{-1} are irrelevant. We can take them all equal to some fixed value λ° in the interval]0,1[.

The premium income, in any interval]k,k+1] is 1. The expected claim amount in that interval equals $\mu^\circ\lambda^\circ_m$ when the risk reserve is m at k. In that case, let the premium income 1 be displayed as

$$1 = \mu^\circ\lambda^\circ_m(1+\eta_m).$$

The number η_m defined in this way is the **security loading corresponding to the risk reserve m**. A **practical semi-elementary** risk model is a risk model with $\eta_m \geq 1+\varepsilon$ (m=0,1,2,...) for some strictly positive ε.

In the practical semi-elementary risk model, $U^\circ_0>0$ and $U^\circ_\infty=1$. Indeed, this results from a comparison with the elementary risk model with security loading $\eta:=\varepsilon$. In the latter model, $U^\circ_0>0$ and $U^\circ_\infty=1$.

10.4.2. Infinite-Time Non-Ruin Probabilities

Theorem 18

In the semi-elementary risk model

$$\mathbf{U^\circ_{m+1} = [1-\lambda^\circ_m(1-f^\circ_0)]^{-1}[U^\circ_m - \lambda^\circ_m \textstyle\sum_{1\le i\le m+1} f^\circ_i U^\circ_{m+1-i}]\ (m\ge 0).} \quad (87)$$

Proof

We consider the event of non-ruin in $[0,\infty[$ corresponding to the initial risk reserve $m\ge 0$. From a partition of that event according to the number of claims 0 or 1 at the instant 1, and in the case of a claim at 1, according to the possible claim amounts 0,1,2,... results the formula

$$U^\circ_m = (1-\lambda^\circ_m)U^\circ_{m+1} + \lambda^\circ_m \textstyle\sum_{0\le i\le m+1} f^\circ_i U^\circ_{m+1-i}.$$

Then

$$U^\circ_m = (1-\lambda^\circ_m)U^\circ_{m+1} + \lambda^\circ_m f^\circ_0 U^\circ_{m+1} + \lambda^\circ_m \textstyle\sum_{1\le i\le m+1} f^\circ_i U^\circ_{m+1-i},$$

$$U^\circ_m = [1-\lambda^\circ_m(1-f^\circ_0)]\, U^\circ_{m+1} + \lambda^\circ_m \textstyle\sum_{1\le i\le m+1} f^\circ_i U^\circ_{m+1-i} \quad \bullet$$

Although U°_0 is not known, the relation (87) allows the calculation of the probabilities U°_m in the practical semi-elementary risk model as follows. Let

$$V^\circ_m := U^\circ_m/U^\circ_0\ (m=0,1,2,...). \quad (88)$$

Then,

$$V^\circ_0 = 1, \quad (89)$$

$$V^\circ_{m+1} = [1-\lambda^\circ_m(1-f^\circ_0)]^{-1}[V^\circ_m - \lambda^\circ_m \textstyle\sum_{1\le i\le m+1} f^\circ_i V^\circ_{m+1-i}]\ (m\ge 0) \quad (89)$$

by (87) divided by U°_0. Now (89) allows the successive calculation of the numbers V°_1, V°_2,... If m is large enough, then V°_m is an approximation of the limit V°_∞.

As $m\uparrow\infty$ in (88):

$$V^\circ_\infty = 1/U^\circ_0.$$

Then, by (88),

$$U^\circ_m = (V^\circ_\infty)^{-1} V^\circ_m . \quad (90)$$

10.4.3. Finite-Time Non-Ruin Probabilities

Theorem 19

In the semi-elementary risk model,

$$\mathbf{U^\circ_{k+1,m} = (1-\lambda^\circ_m)U^\circ_{k,m+1} + \lambda^\circ_m\sum_{0\le i\le m+1} f_i^\circ U^\circ_{k,m+1-i}\ (m,k=0,1,2,...)} \bullet \quad (91)$$

Starting with

$$U^\circ_{00}=1\ ,\ U^\circ_{01}=1\ ,\ldots,\ U^\circ_{0,m+k}=1,$$

(91) allows the successive calculation of the non-ruin probabilities

$$U^\circ_{10}\ ,\ U^\circ_{11}\ ,\ \ldots\ ,\ \ldots\ ,\ \ldots\ ,\ U^\circ_{1,m+k-1}$$

$$U^\circ_{20}\ ,\ U^\circ_{21}\ ,\ \ldots\ ,\ \ldots\ ,\ U^\circ_{2,m+k-2}$$

$$\ldots\ ,\ \ldots\ ,\ \ldots\ ,\ \ldots\ ,$$

$$U^\circ_{k-1,0}\ ,\ \ldots\ ,\ U^\circ_{k-1,m+1}$$

$$U^\circ_{k0}\ ,\ \ldots\ ,\ U^\circ_{km}\ .$$

Hence, in order to calculate U_{km}, we only need the claimsize probability masses $f^\circ_0,f^\circ_1,\ldots,f^\circ_{k+m}$ and the probabilities $\lambda^\circ_0,\lambda^\circ_1,\ldots,\lambda^\circ_{k+m-1}$.

10.4.4. Ruin Probabilities Taking Severity into Account

Theorem 20

In the semi-elementary risk model, for all values k=0,1,2,..., m = 0,1,2,... and n = 1,2,...,

$$\mathbf{\Psi^\circ_{om(n)} = 0,} \quad (92)$$

$$\mathbf{\Psi^\circ_{k+1,m,(n)} = (1-\lambda^\circ_m)\Psi^\circ_{k,m+1,(n)} + \lambda^\circ_m f^\circ_{m+1+n} + \lambda^\circ_m \sum_{0\le i\le m+1} f^\circ_i \Psi^\circ_{k,m+1-i,(n)}.}$$

$$\mathbf{\Psi^\circ_{omn} = 0,} \quad (93)$$

$$\mathbf{\Psi^\circ_{k+1,m,n} = (1-\lambda^\circ_m)\Psi^\circ_{k,m+1,n} + \lambda^\circ_m\sum_{1\le j\le n} f^\circ_{m+1+j} + \lambda^\circ_m \sum_{0\le i\le m+1} f^\circ_i \Psi^\circ_{k,m+1-i,n}.}$$

$$\mathbf{\Psi^\circ_{om} = 0,} \quad (94)$$

$$\mathbf{\Psi^\circ_{k+1,m} = (1-\lambda^\circ_m)\Psi^\circ_{k,m+1} + \lambda^\circ_m \sum_{1\le j} f^\circ_{m+1+j} + \lambda^\circ_m \sum_{0\le i\le m+1} f^\circ_i \Psi^\circ_{k,m+1-i}} \bullet$$

See proof of Theorem 14.

10.5. Numerical Ruin Probabilities in Semi-Classical Risk Model

10.5.1. New Money, New Time and the Discretization

Old and new money amounts are still connected linearly, in such a way that the amounts 0, δ, 2δ ,... in the old money and in the semi-classical risk model, become the amounts 0, 1, 2,... in the new money and in the semi-elementary model.

Now the relation between old and new times is no longer linear. The instants

$$0\ ,\ t_1 = \varepsilon_0\ ,\ t_2 = \varepsilon_0+\varepsilon_1\ ,\ t_3 = \varepsilon_0+\varepsilon_1+\varepsilon_2\ ,\ \ldots \tag{95}$$

in the old time and in the semi-classical model, become the instants 0, 1, 2, 3,... in the new time and in the semi-elementary model with claim probabilities ...,λ°_{-2}, λ°_{-1}, λ°_0, λ°_1, λ°_2,... The definition of ε_k (k=0,1,2,...) and λ°_m (m= ...,−2,−1,0,1,2,...) results from the following considerations. In the semi-classical model, the old money and time are used. In the semi-elementary model, the new money and time are adopted.

Let us consider the time interval

$$]t_k,t_{k+1}] \tag{96}$$

in the semi-classical risk model and the corresponding interval

$$]k,k+1] \tag{96°}$$

in the semi-elementary model. Let us assume that the risk reserve equals $u=m\delta$ at the instant t_k in the semi-classical risk model and that it equals m at the instant k in the semi-elementary model.

The expected number of claims in the interval (96) is

$$\lambda\ \varepsilon_k \tag{97}$$

and the expected number of claims in the interval (96°) is

$$\lambda^\circ_m. \tag{97°}$$

The premium income in the interval (96) is

$$\mu\lambda\gamma(m\delta)\varepsilon_k + \ldots, \tag{98}$$

Here the dots represent asymptotically negligible terms as $\delta\downarrow 0$. The premium income in the interval (96°) is

$$1. \qquad (98°)$$

The expected claim amount in the interval (96) is

$$\mu\lambda\varepsilon_k. \qquad (99)$$

The expected claim amount in the interval (96°) is

$$\mu^\circ\lambda^\circ_m, \qquad (99°)$$

where $\mu^\circ=\mu/\delta$.

From the equality between invariants

$$(98)/(99) = (98°)/(99°),$$

results the relation

$$\lambda^\circ_m = [\mu\gamma(m\delta)]^{-1}\delta \qquad (100)$$

if the dots in (98) are neglected.

From (100) and from the equality between invariants (97)=(97°), results the relation

$$\varepsilon_k = [\mu\lambda\gamma(m\delta)]^{-1}\delta \text{ (risk reserve at k equal to m).} \qquad (101)$$

In this way, the semi-classical risk model is approximated by the semi-elementary model. The models coincide asymptotically as $\delta\downarrow 0$.

But an important fact must be mentioned: **The times t_1, t_2 ,..., defined by (95) are random variables**. Indeed, the expression (101) of the length ε_k of the interval $]t_k,t_{k+1}]$ depends on the value $m\delta$ of the risk reserve at t_k, and this risk reserve is a random variable. Hence, to the instant k in the semi-elementary model does not correspond a deterministic instant in the original semi-classical model. This makes the calculation of finite-time ruin probabilities in the semi-classical model impossible via the semi-elementary model (it is possible to obtain bounds).

On the contrary, ruin in $[0,\infty[$ in the semi-classical model, corresponds to ruin in $[0,\infty[$ in the semi-elementary model: **Approximations for infinite-time ruin probabilities in the semi-classical risk model can be calculated in the semi-elementary model**. They are asymptotically exact as $\delta\downarrow 0$.

10.5.2. Infinite-Time Ruin Probabilities in Semi-Classical Risk Model

We can consider the semi-classical risk model with any claimsize distribution F and with any practical premium income intensity function $\lambda\mu\gamma(.)$. We consider the particular functions F and γ defined below because then the exact infinite-time ruin probabilities result from Ch.9.5.2, and then a comparison of the approximations obtained by the method of 10.4.2, is possible and interesting. In any case, we take

$$\lambda = 1 \quad , \quad F(x) = 1-e^{-x} \ (x\geq 0)$$

in the semi-classical risk-model. The distribution F is *distribution 4* of 10.3.6. In the semi-elementary model, we use the discretization $\underline{F}°$ of F defined by relations (78), (82) and (85), and we apply a claimsize distribution adaptation. The values of the parameters used are

$$b = 20 \quad , \quad \nu = 800 \quad , \quad \theta = 0.5.$$

(The parameter ν can be replaced by a much smaller value, say ν=100, if the claimsize distribution adaptation is applied.)

For the various functions γ considered hereafter, we define

$$\lambda°_m := [\mu\gamma((m+0.5)\delta)]^{-1}\delta \ (m=0,1,2,...). \tag{102}$$

This is a variant (asymptotically equivalent as $\delta\downarrow 0$) of (100).

We consider three exponential cases with $p<1$ and

$$\gamma(x) := {}^{1}\!/_{pqq'} \ [pq'+(p'-p)e^{-qx}] \ (x\geq 0) \tag{103}$$

and one case with $p=1$ and

$$\gamma(x) := {}^{p'}\!/_{q'} + x \ \ (x\geq 0). \tag{104}$$

In each case,

$$\Psi(x) = q' \, e^{-px} \ \ (x\geq 0), \tag{105}$$

by Ch.9.(28).

From (103) results that

$$\gamma(0) = {}^{p'}\!/_{pq'} \quad , \quad \gamma(\infty) = 1/q.$$

We will take the parameters p and p′ such that

$$\tfrac{1}{2}\,[\gamma(0)+\gamma(\infty)] = 1.25\,. \qquad (106)$$

Then the results of the 3 cases based on (103) can be compared. From this relation results that

$$\eta' := p'/q' = 2.5\,p - p/q. \qquad (107)$$

Premium income intensity function 1

We here take $p=p'=0.2$. Then we obtain the classical case with security loading $\eta=0.25$. The numerical results are

x	V(x)	Ψ(x) approxim.	Ψ(x) exact
0	1.0000	0.79801	0.80000
1	1.7161	0.65336	0.65498
2	2.3024	0.53493	0.53626
4	3.1754	0.35858	0.35946
8	4.1529	0.16113	0.16152
16	4.7896	0.03253	0.03261
32	4.9441	0.00000	0.00000
64	4.9506	0.00000	0.00000
128	4.9506	0.00000	0.00000

Premium income intensity function 2

We now consider (103) with $p=0.1$. Then $\eta'= 0.13888...$ by (107) and then

$$p' = \eta'/(1+\eta') = 0.12195\ 12195...$$

and the numerical results of the following table are easily calculated. Here

$$p < p'$$

and the function γ is strictly decreasing. The numerical values are

x	V(x)	Ψ(x) approxim.	Ψ(x) exact
0	1.0000	0.87671	0.87808
1	1.6767	0.79329	0.79449
2	2.2890	0.71780	0.71889
4	3.3443	0.58760	0.58847
8	4.9158	0.39395	0.39453
16	6.6754	0.17702	0.17727
32	7.8213	0.03574	0.03579
64	8.0994	0.00145	0.00146
128	8.1120	0.00000	0.00000
129	8.1120	0.00000	0.00000

Premium income intensity function 3

We now take p=0.55 in (103). Then p′= 0.1325301204... Now p′<p and γ is a strictly increasing function.

The numerical results are

x	V(x)	Ψ(x) approxim.	Ψ(x) exact
0	1.0000	0.86600	0.86747
1	3.7338	0.49964	0.50049
2	5.3112	0.28828	0.28876
4	6.7464	0.09597	0.09612
8	7.3832	0.01063	0.01065
16	7.4616	0.00013	0.00013
32	7.4626	0.00000	0.00000
64	7.4626	0.00000	0.00000

Premium income intensity function 4

In this last example with Ψ(x) known exactly, we take p′=0.01 in (104). Here the premium income intensity function is not very realistic because it increases too rapidly when no claims do occur. The next premium income function 5 is another linear, more practical function, but it does not allow comparisons with the exact ruin probabilities, because the latter are not known in that case.

The numerical values are

x	V(x)	Ψ(x) approxim.	Ψ(x) exact
0	1.0000	0.99984	0.99000
1	4031.3	0.36787	0.36420
2	5514.2	0.13534	0.13398
4	6260.4	0.01832	0.01813
8	6375.1	0.00034	0.00033
16	6377.2	0.00000	0.00000
32	6377.2	0.00000	0.00000

Premium income intensity function 5

We here take

$$\gamma(x) = 1.05 + 0.01\ x \quad (x \geq 0).$$

The numerical values are displayed in the following table.

x	V(x)	Ψ(x) approxim.
0	1.0000	0.89342
1	1.9129	0.79612
2	2.7675	0.70503
4	4.2903	0.54272
8	6.5810	0.29857
16	8.7483	0.06757
32	9.3711	0.00118
64	9.3822	0.00000
128	9.3822	0.00000

Part II

Optimization Theory

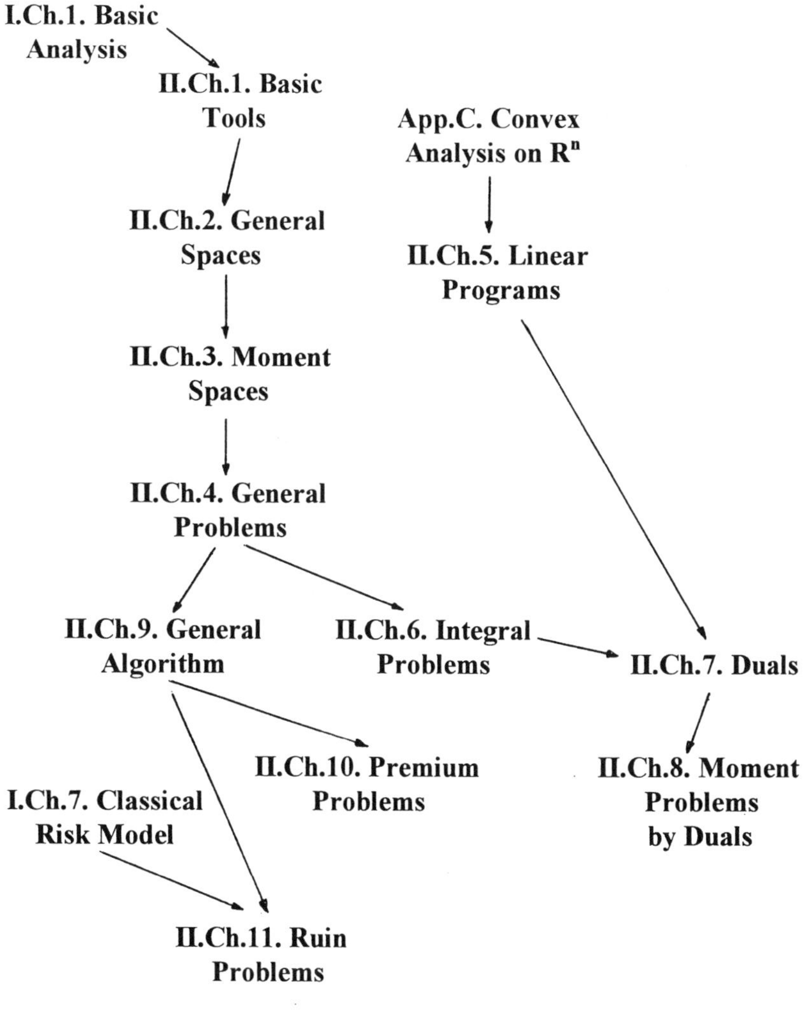
I.Ch.1. Basic Analysis
II.Ch.1. Basic Tools
App.C. Convex Analysis on R^n
II.Ch.2. General Spaces
II.Ch.5. Linear Programs
II.Ch.3. Moment Spaces
II.Ch.4. General Problems
II.Ch.9. General Algorithm
II.Ch.6. Integral Problems
II.Ch.7. Duals
II.Ch.10. Premium Problems
II.Ch.8. Moment Problems by Duals
I.Ch.7. Classical Risk Model
II.Ch.11. Ruin Problems

Chapter 1

Basic Tools

1.0. Introduction: Optimization Problems

Optimization problems on subsets of $\mathbf{R}^2$

Let C be a **bounded, closed, convex** set in $\mathbf{R}^2$. For instance, C can be a closed triangle, or a closed circle.

C is **bounded**. This means that a finite number b exists such that

$$d(0,x) \leq b \quad (x \in C), \tag{Int.1}$$

where d(0,x) is the distance from the origin 0 of $\mathbf{R}^2$ to the point x.

C is **closed**. This means that limits of points in C are points of C. Triangles and circles are closed iff they contain their frontier.

C is **convex**. In order to explain what this means, let us consider two points $x,y \in \mathbf{R}_2$. **The closed line segment with extremities** $\mathbf{x,y \in R^2}$ is the set

$$[x,y] := \{px+qy \,/\, p \geq 0,\ q \geq 0,\ p+q=1\}. \tag{Int.2}$$

An expression such as $px+qy$ $(p \geq 0, q \geq 0, p+q=1)$ is called a **convex combination of the points x and y**. Then C is convex, if all closed line segments with extremities x and y in C, lie entirely in C. Circles are convex sets. Triangles and squares are also convex sets. Other polygons may be convex or not.

Now let us consider a **linear function T on** $\mathbf{R}^2$, i.e. a real function with the property:

$$T(ax+by) = aT(x) + bT(y) \quad (x,y \in \mathbf{R}^2;\ a,b \in \mathbf{R}). \tag{Int.3}$$

This function can be visualized as a plane in $\mathbf{R}^3$, i.e. as a set $\{(x,T(x))/x\in\mathbf{R}^2\}$. We notice that any point $x\in\mathbf{R}^2$, is a couple $x\equiv(x_1,x_2)$ of real numbers x_1,x_2. The **couple** $(x,T(x))$ must be identified with the **triplet** $(x_1,x_2,T(x))\in\mathbf{R}^3$.

Let

$$s := \sup_{x\in C} T(x). \tag{Int.4}$$

We consider the following **optimization problem**: **find a point $x_0\in C$ such that $T(x_0)=s$.** Such a point x_0 is called a **solution of the problem**.

It is obvious, from the geometry of the problem, that the frontier of C contains a solution of the problem. If C is a convex polygon, we can say more: then some vertex must be a solution of the problem.

If we drop parts of the frontier of C, then the sup defined by (Int.4) still exists and s is still a finite number. But then it is not sure that the problem has a solution. If C is not bounded, then s may be infinite, and then no solution exists.

This simple geometry extends to optimization problems on subsets of $\mathbf{R}^n$ and on convex distribution spaces. Then it is convenient to replace the boundedness and closedness conditions by a unique **compactness condition**. The set $C\subseteq\mathbf{R}^2$ is **compact** if any sequence of points $x_n\in C$ (n=1,2,...) has a subsequence $x_{n(k)}$ (k=1,2,...) converging to some point $x\in C$. Any compact set C is closed. Indeed, if C is not closed, a sequence $x_n\in C$ (n=1,2,...) with a limit x not in C exists. Then any subsequence has x as limit and no subsequence can converge to a point of C. Any compact set C is bounded. Indeed, if C is not bounded, a sequence $x_n\in C$ (n=1,2,...) exists, such that $d(0,x_n)\uparrow\infty$ as $n\uparrow\infty$ and then no subsequence can converge to a point of C. In fact **a set in $\mathbf{R}^2$ is compact iff it is closed and bounded** by classical Real Analysis.

The **open line segment with extremities $x,y\in\mathbf{R}^2$** is the set

$$]x,y[:= \{px+qy \,/\, p>0,\ q>0,\ p+q=1\}. \tag{Int.5}$$

An **extremal point of the convex set $C\subseteq\mathbf{R}^2$**, is a point $x\in C$, not belonging to any open line segment in C.

If C is a closed circle, then the extremal points of C are its frontier points. If C is a closed convex polygon, then the extremal points of C are its vertices. The other frontier points of the polygon are not extremal points. Open circles and open convex polygons do not have extremal points.

Compact convex sets are identifiable by their extremal points. Some extremal point x_0 is the solution of the optimization problem defined by the relation (Int.4).

Optimization problems on subsets of $\mathbf{R}^n$

In this discussion, $\mathbf{R}^2$ can be replaced everywhere by $\mathbf{R}^n$ (n=1,2,...). The definitions (Int.2) and (Int.5) of line segments with extremities $x,y \in \mathbf{R}^n$, the definition of convex sets, of linear functions T, of extremal points x, of closed, bounded or compact sets, are the same as in the case n=2. In $\mathbf{R}^n$, sets are compact iff they are bounded and closed.

Examples of compact convex sets are closed n-dimensional balls and closed convex polyhedrons. The extremal points of a closed ball are its frontier points and the extremal points of a closed convex polyhedron are its vertices.

If C is a convex compact subset of $\mathbf{R}^n$ and T a linear function on $\mathbf{R}^n$, then $T(x_0)$ equals s, defined by (Int.4), for some extremal point x_0 of C.

Optimization problems on subsets of ***Prob*****[R]**

We denote by ***Prob*****[R]** the space of probability distributions F on **R**. This space must be "visualized" as a space of **points** F. In ***Prob*****[R]**, the line segments [F,G], and]F,G[are defined by relations (Int.2) and (Int.5), with x, y replaced by F, $G \in$ ***Prob*****[R]** resp. Then the definition of convex sets in ***Prob*****[R]** and of extremal points of such sets, is the same as in $\mathbf{R}^2$. A linear function on the convex set $\boldsymbol{C} \subseteq$ ***Prob*****[R]** is a real function T, called a **functional**, such that

$$T(pF+qG) = pTF+qTG \quad (F,G \in \boldsymbol{C};\ p,q \geq 0;\ p+q=1). \qquad \text{(Int.6)}$$

If $\boldsymbol{C}$ is a convex subset of ***Prob*****[R]** and T a linear functional on $\boldsymbol{C}$, then an extremal point F_0 of $\boldsymbol{C}$ exists, such that $T(F_0)=\sup_{F \in \boldsymbol{C}} T(F)$, under compactness and continuity conditions later indicated.

This discussion suggests that

Compactness, **Convexity** and **Extremal Points**

will be the corner-stones of the theory of optimization problems on subspaces of ***Prob*****[R]**.

A large class of optimization problems on subspaces of ***Prob*[R]** can be treated via the consideration of

Mixtures

Such problems are **optimizations of integrals**

$$\inf_{F\in C}\int\varphi dF\ ,\ \sup_{F\in C}\int\varphi dF,$$

where C is some convex subset of ***Prob*[R]**, defined by **integral constraints** of the type $\int f dF=\alpha$. Here $\alpha\in\mathbf{R}$ and φ and f are fixed functions, integrable with respect to all distributions $F\in C$. Then the explicit definition of the **extremal points** of the space C can be avoided. But these extremal points are automatically involved.

The consideration of **mixtures**, when possible, has another advantage: it may avoid the introduction of weak limits of convex combinations of distributions, because **mixtures** already are such weak limits.

A basic tool in the treatment of some optimization problems is a dualization techique. It is based on a more extensive study of

Convex Analysis on $\mathbf{R}^n$

This topic is developed in Appendix C. We also need some

Convex Analysis on Distribution Spaces

The latter topic is treated in Appendix E.

1.1. General Optimization Problems

1.1.1. Basic Terminology

We will illustrate the terminology on the following **optimization problems**:

$$P := \inf_{s\in Space}[\varphi(s)/Cond(s)], \quad (1)$$

$$Q := \sup_{s\in Space}[\varphi(s)/Cond(s)]. \quad (2)$$

Problem (1) is a **minimization problem**. Problem (2) is **maximization problem**.

The **basic space** Space may be any set. In this book it is mostly a space of distributions on **R**, and sometimes a subset of $\mathbf{R}^n$.

s is the **variable point** of problems (1) and (2). It has a dummy character: it may be replaced by any other symbol. If Space is a space of distributions, then we write F, G, U, ... instead of s. If Space is a subset of $\mathbf{R}^n$, then we write x, y, z, ... instead of s.

φ(s) is a **real finite function** of s∈Space. It is called the **objective function** of the problems.

Cond(s) are conditions on s. They are called the **constraints after the slash** of the problems. The number of constraints after the slash may be finite or infinite. The constraints may be equalities, inequalities, or any other constraints. The set of constraints Cond(s) may be void. The relation

$$s \in \text{Space}$$

is the **basic constraint** of the problems. The **constraints** of the problems are the basic constraint and the constraints after the slash.

The **feasible points** of problem (1) or (2) are the points s satisfying the constraints of the problem. We say that **the problem (1) or (2) has feasible points** if it has at least one feasible point.

We continue the discussion with the problem Q. The terminology is the same for the problem P.

The number defined by the last member of (2) is **the value Q** of **the problem Q**:

$$Q = \sup\{\varphi(s) \,/\, s \text{ feasible point}\}.$$

This value may be a number in **R**, but it can also be +∞ or −∞. The value −∞ occurs if the problem has no feasible points, because $\sup \varnothing = -\infty$. It occurs in that case only.

We notice the **double meaning of Q**: it can denote the **problem Q** as well as the **value Q**. Explicitly, the **problem Q** is the following:

Find the value Q and find the feasible points s such that φ(s)=Q.

Any feasible point s satisfying the relation $\varphi(s)=Q$, is called a **solution of problem Q**. We say that **problem Q has solutions** if it has at least one solution. Very often, the solution is unique when it exists.

The problem Q has a value, finite or not, in any case. It has not necessary a solution. It certainly has no solution if $Q=\pm\infty$, i.e. in the following cases.

The problem has no feasible vectors.

The problem has feasible vectors, but $Q=+\infty$.

The problem Q has not necessarily a solution if its value Q is finite. An example is furnished by the following simple problem

$$\sup_{x\in[0,1[} x. \tag{3}$$

The value of this problem is 1, but the point x=1 is not a solution of the problem because it does not satisfy the basic constraint $x\in[0,1[$.

A **limit solution** of problem Q is a sequence s_ν ($\nu=1,2,...$) of feasible points such that

$$\varphi(s_\nu) \to Q \text{ as } \nu\uparrow\infty.$$

By the very definition of the **sup**, any problem Q with feasible points has limit solutions. For instance, the sequence

$$x_\nu = (\nu-1)/\nu \; (\nu=1,2,...)$$

is a limit solution of problem (3).

1.1.2. Identical and Equivalent Optimization Problems

The problem Q does not change if some constraints after the slash are abandoned, but incorporated in the definition of Space. The problems

$$\sup_{s\in \mathrm{Space}}[\varphi(s)/\mathrm{Cond}(s)]$$

and

$$\sup_{s\in \mathrm{space}}[\varphi(s)/\mathrm{cond}(s)]$$

are **identical problems** if

$$\{s \,/\, s\in\mathrm{Space}, \mathrm{Cond}(s)\} = \{s \,/\, s\in\mathrm{space}, \mathrm{cond}(s)\}.$$

In other words, two optimization problems are **identical** if they are both minimization problems or both maximization problems and if they have the same objective function and the same feasible points.

We notice that the basic constraint can be displayed after the slash. Hence, the problem P defined by (1) is identical to the problem

$$\inf[\varphi(s) \,/\, s\in \text{Space}, \text{Cond}(s)].$$

We say that two optimization problems are **equivalent**, if the characteristics

value, feasible points, solutions, limit solutions

of anyone of the problems result easily from the characteristics of the other problem. This definition depends on the meaning of "easily". In the particular cases we consider in this book, the equivalence is explicited, if it is not too obvious.

Example 1

Problem P defined by (1) is equivalent to problem

$$Q_1 := \sup_{s\in \text{Space}}[-\varphi(s)/\text{Cond}(s)]. \tag{4}$$

Indeed, $Q_1 = -P$ and the problems P and Q_1 have the same feasible points, the same solutions and the same limit solutions.

Example 2

Let
$$Q_1 := \sup_{x\geq 0}[\varphi(x) \,/\, f(x)\leq 1,\ g(x)\leq 2],$$

$$Q_2 := \sup_{x,y,z\geq 0}[\varphi(x) \,/\, f(x)+y=1,\ g(x)+z=2].$$

Here φ, f and g are real finite functions on $\mathbf{R}_+$. In problem Q_1, the variable point x ranges over $\mathbf{R}_+$. In the problem Q_2, the variable triplet (x,y,z) ranges over $\mathbf{R}_+^3$.

Let x be a feasible point of problem Q_1. Then (x,y,z) is a feasible triplet of the problem Q_2 if $y:=1-f(x)$, $z:=2-g(x)$.

Let x be a solution of the problem Q_1. Then (x,y,z) is a solution of the problem Q_2. Obviously, the problems Q_1 and Q_2 have the same value.

Let x_ν (ν=1,2,...) be a limit solution of problem Q_1. Then (x_ν,y_ν,z_ν) (ν=1,2,...) is a limit solution of problem Q_2 if $y_\nu:=1-f(x_\nu)$, $z_\nu:=2-g(x_\nu)$.

Conversely, if (x,y,z) is a feasible triplet or a solution of problem Q_2, then x is a feasible point or a solution resp. of problem Q_1. If (x_ν,y_ν,z_ν)(ν=1,2,...) is a limit solution of problem Q_2, then x_ν(ν=1,2,...) is a limit solution of problem Q_1.

Hence, the problems Q_1 and Q_2 are equivalent.

1.1.3. Optimization Problems With Variable Parameters

Let

$$P(\alpha) := \inf_{s\in \mathrm{Space}(\alpha)}[\varphi(s,\alpha) \,/\, \mathrm{Cond}(s,\alpha)] \tag{5}$$

and

$$Q(\alpha) := \sup_{s\in \mathrm{Space}(\alpha)}[\varphi(s,\alpha) \,/\, \mathrm{Cond}(s,\alpha)] \tag{6}$$

be optimization problems depending on the **n-dimensional parameter** $\alpha:=(\alpha_1,\ldots,\alpha_n)\in\mathbf{R}^n$. The components α_i of α are the **parameters** of the problems.

The function Q with values $Q(\alpha)$ ($\alpha\in\mathbf{R}^n$) is the **value function** of problem $Q(\alpha)$ ($\alpha\in\mathbf{R}^n$). Hence, the **domain** of the function Q is $\mathbf{R}^n$. The **effective domain** of Q is the set

$$\mathrm{dom}\, Q := \{\alpha\in\mathbf{R}^n \,/\, Q(\alpha) \text{ has feasible points}\}.$$

Then

$$\mathrm{dom}\, Q = \{\alpha\in\mathbf{R}^n / -\infty < Q(\alpha)\}$$

because $Q(\alpha)=-\infty$ iff the problem $Q(\alpha)$ has no feasible points.

The function P with values $P(\alpha)$ ($\alpha\in\mathbf{R}^n$) is the **value function** of problem $P(\alpha)$ ($\alpha\in\mathbf{R}^n$). The **domain** of P is $\mathbf{R}^n$ and its **effective domain** is

$$\mathrm{dom}\, P := \{\alpha\in\mathbf{R}^n \,/\, P(\alpha) \text{ has feasible points}\}.$$

Now

$$\mathrm{dom}\, P = \{\alpha\in\mathbf{R}^n / \; P(\alpha) < \infty\}.$$

The problem $P(\alpha)$ or $Q(\alpha)$ is uninteresting if $\alpha \notin \text{dom } P$ or $\alpha \notin \text{dom } Q$. Many problems $P(\alpha)$, $Q(\alpha)$ have a **dual problem** $P^{**}(\alpha)$, $Q^{**}(\alpha)$ (later defined). The definition of **dual problems** is based on the notion of **polar functions** (App. C9) and the latter functions are necessarily defined on the whole space $\mathbf{R}^n$. This explains the consideration of the problems $P(\alpha)$ and $Q(\alpha)$ for values of α outside their effective domain. If no dual problems are involved, it is assumed in almost all cases that $\alpha \in \text{dom } P$ or $\alpha \in \text{dom } Q$.

When the dual problem $P^{**}(\alpha)$ or $Q^{**}(\alpha)$ is considered, the original problem $P(\alpha)$ or $Q(\alpha)$ is called the **primal problem**.

1.2. Compactness, Convexity and Extremal Points

1.2.1. Spaces *Distr*[S] and *Prob*[S]

The space ***Distr***[S] is the family of distributions F concentrated on the set $S \subseteq \mathbf{R}$, **with a finite total mass F(S)**. The space ***Prob***[S] is the family of probability distributions concentrated on S.

The **distribution** F may as well be the **distribution function** (a point function), as the corresponding **measure** (a set function). If F is a probability distribution on **R**, then

$$F(x) = F(]-\infty,x]) \quad (x \in \mathbf{R})$$

and $F(\infty)=1$.

In integrals $\int \varphi dF$, the integration domain is R, whenever it is not mentioned. Of course, if F is concentrated on S, the definition of φ outside S is irrelevant.

1.2.2. Convex Sets and Extremal Points

Let $F,G \in$ ***Distr*[R]**. The **closed line segment [F,G]** and the **open line segment]F,G[** with **extremities F and G**, are the sets

$$[F,G] := \{pF+qG \;/\; p \geq 0,\ q \geq 0,\ p+q=1\}, \tag{7}$$

$$]F,G[:= \{pF+qG \;/\; p>0,\ q>0,\ p+q=1\}. \tag{8}$$

The subset $\boldsymbol{C}$ of ***Distr*****[R]** is **convex** if it contains all closed line segments with extremities in $\boldsymbol{C}$. If $\boldsymbol{C}$ is convex, then $\boldsymbol{C}$ contains all **convex combinations**

$$p_1F_1 + \ldots + p_nF_n \quad (p_1\geq 0,\ldots,p_n\geq 0,\ p_1+\ldots+p_n=1)$$

of points $F_1,\ldots,F_n$ in $\boldsymbol{C}$.

The spaces ***Distr***[S] and ***Prob***[S] are convex, for any $S\subseteq \mathbf{R}$.

The point F is an **extremal point of the convex subset** $\boldsymbol{C}\subseteq$***Distr*****[R]**, if $F\in\boldsymbol{C}$ and if no open line segment]G,H[exists such that $F\in]G,H[\subseteq\boldsymbol{C}$. An equivalent definition is:

F is an **extremal point of the convex subset** $\boldsymbol{C}$ **of** ***Distr*****[R]**, if $F\in\boldsymbol{C}$ and if the following condition is satisfied:

$$[F=pG+qH\ ;\ p,q>0\ ;\ p+q=1\ ;\ G,H\in\boldsymbol{C}] \Rightarrow [F=G=H]. \tag{9}$$

1.2.3. Compact Sets

Weak convergence of functions means convergence at each continuity point of the limit. We write

$$F_n \rightarrow_w F \tag{10}$$

as an abbreviation of the conjunction of the following propositions:

$$F_n\in\textbf{\textit{Distr}}[\mathbf{R}]\ ,\ F\in\textbf{\textit{Distr}}[\mathbf{R}]\ ,\ \lim_{n\uparrow\infty} F_n(x) = F(x)\ \ (x \text{ continuity point of } F).$$

We say that $\mathbf{F_n}$ **converges weakly to F as** $\mathbf{n}\uparrow\infty$ if (10) holds.

The subset $\boldsymbol{Q}$ of ***Distr*****[R]** is **compact** if each sequence $F_n\in\boldsymbol{Q}$ (n=1,2,...) contains a subsequence converging weakly to some point $F\in\boldsymbol{Q}$.

The **closure** $\mathbf{Q^-}$ **of the subset Q of** ***Distr*****[R]** is the set of points of ***Distr*****[R]** which are expressible as a weak limit of a sequence of points in $\boldsymbol{Q}$. In any case $Q\subseteq Q$ (because $F_n\equiv F\rightarrow_w F$). The set Q is **closed** if $Q=Q^-$.

The following is a classical Theorem. For a proof of a more general Theorem, see App.E.Th.E3.

Theorem 1 (General Compactness Theorem)

Any sequence $F_n \in \boldsymbol{Prob}[R]$ (n=1,2,...) has a subsequence converging weakly to some point $F \in \boldsymbol{Distr}[R]$ •

It is not true that any sequence $F_n \in \boldsymbol{Prob}[\mathbf{R}]$ has a subsequence converging weakly to some point $F \in \boldsymbol{Prob}[\mathbf{R}]$. For instance, the sequence $F_n := 1_{[n,\infty[}$ converges weakly to $F \equiv 0 \in \boldsymbol{Distr}[\mathbf{R}]$ and then any subsequence converges weakly to 0, but 0 is not a probability distribution. Here the probability mass **escapes to** $+\infty$ as $n \uparrow \infty$.

In some cases the relations $F_n \to_w F$, $F_n \in \boldsymbol{Prob}[\mathbf{R}]$ imply that $F \in \boldsymbol{Prob}[\mathbf{R}]$. For instance, if the probability distributions F_n are concentrated on the compact interval [a,b] and $F_n \to_w F$, then F is a probability distribution concentrated on [a,b].

1.2.4. Functionals

A **functional T** is any real function defined on some subset $\boldsymbol{A}$ of $\boldsymbol{Distr}[\mathbf{R}]$. The value of T at the point $F \in \boldsymbol{A}$ is denoted by $TF \equiv T(F)$. The **image by T of the subset $\boldsymbol{S}$ of A** is the subset of **R**,

$$T\boldsymbol{S} \equiv T(\boldsymbol{S}) := \{TF \,/\, F \in \boldsymbol{S}\}. \tag{11}$$

The functional T is continuous on $\boldsymbol{A}$ if it has the following property:

$$[F_n \in \boldsymbol{A}\ (n=1,2,...)\,,\ F_n \to_w F \in \boldsymbol{A}] \Rightarrow [TF_n \to TF]. \tag{12}$$

The functional T is linear on the convex subset $\boldsymbol{C}$ of $\boldsymbol{Distr}[\mathbf{R}]$, if

$$T(pF+qG) = p\,TF + q\,TG, \tag{13}$$

for any convex combination pF+qG of points $F,G \in \boldsymbol{C}$. Then

$$T(p_1F_1+...+p_nF_n) = p_1TF_1 + ... + p_nTF_n, \tag{14}$$

for any convex combination $p_1F_1+...+p_nF_n$ of points $F_1,...,F_n \in \boldsymbol{C}$.

Theorem 2

Let T be a continuous functional on the compact subset *Q* of *Distr*[R]. Then a point $F_0 \in Q$ exists such that

$$\mathbf{TF_0 = sup_{F \in Q}\, TF}. \tag{15}$$

Proof
We consider a sequence $F_n \in Q$ such that

$$TF_n \rightarrow sup_{F \in Q}\, TF. \tag{16}$$

By the compactness of Q, a subsequence $F_{n(k)}$ (k=1,2,...) and a point $F_0 \in Q$ exist such that $F_{n(k)} \rightarrow_w F_0$. Then

$$TF_{n(k)} \rightarrow TF_0 \in TQ \tag{17}$$

by the continuity of T. By (16),

$$TF_{n(k)} \rightarrow sup_{F \in Q}\, TF. \tag{18}$$

Then (15) results from (17) and (18) because any sequence in **R** can converge to one point at most •

1.2.5. Convex Hulls

Let *A* be a subset of ***Distr*[R]**. **The convex hull Co*A*≡Co(*A*) of *A*** is the family of all convex combinations $p_1F_1+...+p_nF_n$ of points $F_j \in A$. This convex hull is a convex set, because convex combinations of convex combinations of points of *A* are convex combinations of these points. Obviously Co(*A*) is the smallest convex set in ***Distr*[R]** containing the set *A*.

The **closed convex hull Co^-A of *A*** is the closure of the convex hull of *A*:

$$Co^-A := (CoA)^-.$$

The convex hull and the closed convex hull of a subset of $\mathbf{R^n}$ are defined in the same way. Then $^-$ denotes the usual topological closure in $\mathbf{R^n}$.

1.2.6. Multidimensional Functionals

A n-dimensional functional T is a function defined on a subset of ***Distr***[**R**] with values in $\mathbf{R}^n$. The **linearity** and the **continuity** of a multidimensional functional are defined in the same way as in case n=1, considered in 1.2.4.

Theorem 3

a. **Let T be a continuous n-dimensional functional defined on the compact subset *Q* of *Distr*[R]. Then T*Q* is a compact subset of $\mathbf{R}^n$.**

b. **Let T be a linear n-dimensional functional defined on the convex subset *C* of *Distr*[R]. Then T*C* is a convex subset of $\mathbf{R}^n$.**

Proof

a. Let x_k (k=1,2,...) be a sequence in T***Q***. Then $x_k=TF_k$ for some distribution $F_k \in \boldsymbol{Q}$. By the compactness of ***Q***, a subsequence $F_{k(j)}$ and a point $F_0 \in \boldsymbol{Q}$ exist such that $F_{k(j)} \to_w F_0$. Then $x_{k(j)}=TF_{k(j)} \to TF_0 \in T\boldsymbol{Q}$ by the continuity of T. Hence, any sequence in T***Q*** has a subsequence converging to some point of T***Q***.

b. Let $\sum p_k x_k$ be a convex combination of the points $x_k \in T\boldsymbol{C}$. Then $x_k=TF_k$ for some distribution $F_k \in \boldsymbol{Q}$. By the linearity of T, $\sum p_k x_k = \sum p_k TF_k = T(\sum p_k F_k) \in T\boldsymbol{C}$ because $\sum p_k F_k \in \boldsymbol{C}$ by the convexity of ***C***. Hence, convex combinations of points of ***C*** are points of ***C***.

1.3. Spaces of Mixtures

1.3.1. Mixtures

Let U be a probability distribution concentrated on the subset S of **R** and let $F_\theta(\theta \in S)$ be probability distributions on **R**. Then the function F defined by

$$F(x) = \int_{\theta \in S} F_\theta(x) dU(\theta) \tag{19}$$

is a probability distribution function on $\mathbf{R}_+$ (by dominated convergence). It is called **the mixture of the distributions $F_\theta(\theta \in S)$ with mixing distribution U.**

Convex combinations are particular mixtures. Indeed, let F be the convex combination $F := p_1F_1 + \dots + p_nF_k$ of the probability distributions $F_1,\dots,F_k$. Then relation (19) is true if S:={1,2,...,k} and if U is the k-atomic distribution with mass p_i at the point i (i=1,...,k).

Theorem 4

Let U be a probability distribution on the set $S \subseteq \mathbf{R}$, let $F_\theta(\theta \in S)$ be probability distributions on R, and let f be a function on R. Then

$$\int f(x)d\left[\int_S F_\theta(x)dU(\theta)\right] = \int_S \left[\int f(x)dF_\theta(x)\right]dU(\theta). \tag{20}$$

if $f \geq 0$, or if f is integrable with respect to the distributions $F_\theta(\theta \in S)$ and with respect to their mixture with mixing function U.

Proof
Let

$$F(x) := \int_S F_\theta(x)dU(\theta) \quad (x \in \mathbf{R}).$$

Then (20) becomes

$$\int f(x)dF(x) = \int_S \left[\int f(x)dF_\theta(x)\right]dU(\theta). \tag{21}$$

If f is the indicator function $1_{]-\infty,a]}$ $(a \in \mathbf{R})$, then (21) is the correct relation

$$F(a) = \int_S F_\theta(a)dU(\theta).$$

Then, by linearity, (21) is also correct if f is an indicator function $1_{]a,b]}$ and if f is a linear combination with positive coefficients of such indicator functions.

Then, (21) is correct if $f \geq 0$, by some monotone class argument. Then, (21) is valid for differences of positive functions if the involved integrals are finite.

We observe that the indicated integrability conditions imply the integrability of the function $\int f(x)dF_\theta(x)$ with respect to the distribution $U(\theta)$, because

$$\int_S \left|\int f(x)dF_\theta(x)\right|dU(\theta) \leq \int_S \left[\int |f(x)|dF_\theta(x)\right]dU(\theta) = \int |f(x)|d\left[\int_S F_\theta(x)dU(\theta)\right] \quad \bullet$$

A general rule is that strict inequalities may become equalities when limits are taken: $1/n>0$ $(n=1,2,...)$, but $\lim_{n\uparrow\infty} 1/n=0$. Integrals, i.e. limits of sums, are an exception to the rule. For instance, if $f>0$ on $[0,1]$, then $\int_{[0,1]} f(x)dx>0$. Applying this result to the functions $f-a$ and $b-f$, we see that the relation $a<f<b$ on $[0,1]$ implies $a<\int_{[0,1]} f(x)dx<b$. The following Theorem is an extension of this simple case.

The meaning of $(f_1,\ldots,f_n)\in C$ U-a.e. in the following Theorem is that

$$(f_1(x),\ldots,f_n(x)) \in C \quad (x\in \mathbf{R},\ x\notin N)$$

for some U-null set $N\subseteq \mathbf{R}$, i.e. a set such that $U(N)=0$.

Theorem 5

Let U be a probability distribution on R, C a convex set in $\mathbf{R}^n$, $f_1,\ldots,f_n$ U-integrable functions on R such that $(f_1,\ldots,f_n)\in C$ U-a.e. Then

$$\left(\int f_1 dU,\ldots,\int f_n dU\right) \in C. \tag{22}$$

Proof

We consider the case n=3. Its proof contains the arguments of a general demonstration. Let

$$u_1 = \int f_1 dU\ ,\ u_2 = \int f_2 dU\ ,\ u_3 = \int f_3 dU.$$

We assume that $u:=(u_1,u_2,u_3)\notin C$ and we derive a contradiction. Let P be a plane containing u, such that the convex set C is situated in one of the two closed half-spaces defined by P. Let the equation of P be $a_0+a_1x_1+a_2x_2+a_3x_3=0$. Then $a_0+a_1u_1+a_2u_2+a_3u_3=0$ because $u\in P$. We may assume that

$$a_0 + a_1x_1 + a_2x_2 + a_3x_3 \geq 0 \ ((x_1,x_2,x_3)\in C).$$

because we can replace a_0,a_1,a_2,a_3 by $-a_0,-a_1,-a_2,-a_3$ if necessary. Then

$$a_0 + a_1f_1 + a_2f_2 + a_3f_3 \geq 0 \ \text{ U-a.e.}$$

by the assumption $(f_1,f_2,f_3)\in C$ U-a.e. Then

$$\int(a_0 + a_1f_1 + a_2f_2 + a_3f_3)dU = a_0 + a_1u_1 + a_2u_2 + a_3u_3 = 0.$$

The latter integrand is positive U-a.e. Hence, it must be equal to 0 U-a.e:

$$a_0 + a_1f_1 + a_2f_2 + a_3f_3 = 0 \ \text{ U-a.e,}$$

i.e. $(f_1,f_2,f_3)\in P$ U-a.e. Then $(f_1,f_2,f_3)\in P\cap C$ U-a.e.

This 3-dimensional argument can be repeated and adapted in the plane P: the relation $u \notin P \cap C$ implies that $(f_1,f_2,f_3) \in L \cap C$ U-a.e., where L is some straight line in P (L is determined by the linear equation defining P, completed by another independent linear equation). Then the argument can be repeated and adapted in L: the relation $u \notin L \cap C$ implies that $(f_1,f_2,f_3) \in \{p\} \cap C = \{p\}$ U-a.e., where p is some point of L (p is determined by the linear equations defining L, completed by a third independent linear equation). We then have the contradiction

$$(\int f_1 dU, \int f_2 U, \int f_3 dU) = u = p \in C \quad \bullet$$

1.3.2. Spaces of Mixtures

Let S be a set in **R** and let $F_\theta(\theta \in S)$ be a probability distributions on **R.** Then

$$\boldsymbol{Mixt}[F_\theta(\theta \in S)] := \{F_U \,/\, U \in \boldsymbol{Prob}[S]\} \tag{23}$$

is **the space of mixtures**

$$F_U(x) := \int_S F_\theta(x) dU(\theta) \quad (x \in \mathbf{R}) \tag{24}$$

with **mixing probability distribution** U concentrated on S. Obviously, the space $\boldsymbol{Mixt}[F_\theta(\theta \in S)]$ is a convex space of probability distributions. The set

$$\boldsymbol{B} := \{F_\theta / \theta \in S\} \tag{25}$$

is called **the basis** of the space $\boldsymbol{Mixt}[F_\theta(\theta \in S)]$.

The space (23) is **a regular space of mixtures** if

$$[U,V \in \boldsymbol{Prob}[S];\ F_U = F_V] \Rightarrow U = V. \tag{26}$$

Hence, each distributions of a regular space of mixtures is expressible as mixture of the distributions of the basis, in only one way.

Let f be an integrable function with respect to all distributions in space $\boldsymbol{Mixt}[F_\theta(\theta \in S)]$. Then the **associated function $f^\bullet$** is the function with values

$$f^\bullet(\theta) := \int f(x) dF_\theta(x) \quad (\theta \in S). \tag{27}$$

The **mixture elimination equality** is the following most important relation, resulting from Theorem 4:

$$\int f(x)dF_U(x) = \int f^{\bullet}(\theta)dU(\theta) \quad (U \in \boldsymbol{Prob}[S]). \tag{28}$$

Its application is called a **mixture elimination**. The adjective "associated" is systematically used for functionals, spaces or problems resulting from other functionals, spaces or problems by mixture eliminations.

Theorem 6 (Basic Mixture Theorem)

Let B be the basis of the space of mixtures *Mixt*[$F_\theta(\theta \in S)$]. Let f_1, ..., f_n be functions on R, integrable with respect to each distribution in the space *Mixt*[$F_\theta(\theta \in S)$]. Let T be the n-dimensional functional defined by

$$TF := (\int f_1 dF, \ldots, \int f_n dF) \quad (F \in \boldsymbol{Mixt}[F_\theta(\theta \in S)]). \tag{29}$$

Then

$$T\,\boldsymbol{Mixt}[F_\theta(\theta \in S)] = Co(T\boldsymbol{B}), \tag{30}$$

i.e.

$$\{(\int f_1 dF, \ldots, \int f_n dF) \,/\, F \in \boldsymbol{Mixt}[F_\theta(\theta \in S)]\}$$

$$= Co\{(\int f_1 dF_\theta, \ldots, \int f_n dF_\theta) \,/\, \theta \in S\}. \tag{31}$$

Proof

We prove that

$$T\,\boldsymbol{Mixt}[F_\theta(\theta \in S)] \subseteq Co(T\boldsymbol{B}). \tag{32}$$

Let c be a point in the first member of (32). Then $c=TF_U$ for some $U \in \boldsymbol{Prob}[S]$. Then, by the mixture elimination equality

$$c = (\int f_1 dF_U, \ldots, \int f_n dF_U) = (\int f_1^{\bullet} dU, \ldots, \int f_n^{\bullet} dU)$$

But

$$(f_1^{\bullet}(\theta), \ldots, f_n^{\bullet}(\theta)) = (\int f_1 dF_\theta, \ldots, \int f_1 dF_\theta) = TF_\theta \in T\boldsymbol{B} \subseteq Co(T\boldsymbol{B}) \quad (\theta \in S)$$

and then $c \in Co(T\boldsymbol{B})$ by Theorem 5. We now prove that

$$Co(T\boldsymbol{B}) \subseteq T\,\boldsymbol{Mixt}[F_\theta(\theta \in S)].$$

Let $c \in Co(T\boldsymbol{B})$. Then c can be expressed as a convex combination of points $c_i \in T\boldsymbol{B}$ (i=1,...,k): $c=p_1c_1+...+p_kc_k$. Let $c_i=TF_{\theta_i}$, $\theta_i \in S$. Let U be the probability distribution with masses $p_1,...,p_k$ at the points $\theta_1,...,\theta_k$ resp. Then

$$\textstyle\sum_{0\leq i\leq k} p_iF_{\theta_i} = F_U \in \boldsymbol{Mixt}[F_\theta(\theta \in S)],$$

$$c = \textstyle\sum_{0\leq i\leq k} p_ic_i = \sum_{0\leq i\leq k} p_i \, TF_{\theta_i}$$

$$= T[\textstyle\sum_{0\leq i\leq k} p_iF_{\theta_i}] = TF_U \in T\,\boldsymbol{Mixt}[F_\theta(\theta \in S)] \bullet$$

1.3.3. *Prob*[S] as a Space of Mixtures

We denote by $A_\theta := 1_{[\theta,\infty[}$ the **1-atomic probabilibity distribution** concentrated at the point $\theta \in \mathbf{R}$.

Theorem 7

For any set $S \subseteq \mathbf{R}$,

$$\boldsymbol{Prob}[S] = \boldsymbol{Mixt}[A_\theta(\theta \in S)]. \qquad (33).$$

The space *Mixt*[$A_\theta(\theta \in S)$] is a regular space of mixtures.

Proof

Let $F \in \boldsymbol{Prob}[S]$. Then

$$\int A_\theta(x)dF(\theta) = \int 1_{\theta\leq x}dF(\theta) = F(]-\infty,x]) = F(x) \quad (x \in \mathbf{R}).$$

This shows that F is the mixture of the distributions A_θ ($\theta \in S$) with mixing distribution U=F. It proves the $\subseteq$ part of (33). Conversely, any mixture of distributions concentrated on S, is a distribution concentrated on S. This proves the $\supseteq$ part of (33). For the proof of the regularity, let U,V be probability distributions on S such that

$$\int A_\theta(x)dU(\theta) = \int A_\theta(x)dV(\theta) \quad (x \in \mathbf{R}),$$

Then

$$0 = \int A_\theta(x)dw(\theta) = \int 1_{\theta\leq x}dw(\theta) = w(x) \quad (x \in \mathbf{R}),$$

where $w := U-V$ •

1.3.4. Unimodal Distributions

Continuous case

Let m be a point in **R**, not necessarily an integer. The probability distribution F is **m-unimodal** if it has a density φ on $]-\infty,m[\cup]m,\infty[$, increasing on the interval $]-\infty,m[$ and decreasing on the interval $]m,\infty[$. The **mode** m may be an atom of F.

Densities may be modified arbitrarily on Lebesgue-null sets. Hence, we may assume that φ is right-continuous, or that φ is right continuous at the left of m and left-continuous at the right of m.

An equivalent definition is: F is **m-unimodal** if F can be expressed as a convex combination $pG+qA_m+rH$, where G is a probability distribution concentrated on $]-\infty,m[$, with increasing density on that interval, and H a probability distribution concentrated on $]m,\infty[$, with decreasing density on that interval.

The rectangular m-unimodal distribution $R_{m\theta}$ ($\theta\in$R) is the uniform distribution on the interval with extremities m and θ. Hence, if $m<\theta$, then $R_{m\theta}$ is the distribution with density $1/_{(m-\theta)}$ on the interval $]\theta,m[$. If $m=\theta$, then $R_{mm} = A_m$. If $\theta<m$, then $R_{m\theta}$ is the distribution with density $1/_{(\theta-m)}$ on the interval $]m,\theta[$.

$$R_{m\theta}(x) = 1_{\theta\le x}\,(x-\theta)/_{(m-\theta)} = 1_{\theta\le x}\,1/_{(m-\theta)}\int_{[\theta,x]} dy \quad (\theta<m,\ x<m), \tag{34}$$

$$1-R_{m\theta}(x) = 1_{x\le\theta}\,(\theta-x)/_{(\theta-m)} = 1_{x\le\theta}\,1/_{(\theta-m)}\int_{[x,\theta]} dy \quad (m<\theta,\ m<x). \tag{35}$$

The space

Prob[I;m-unim]

is the space of m-unimodal probability distributions concentrated on the interval $I\subseteq$**R**.

Theorem 8

$$\textit{\textbf{Prob}}[\mathbf{I;m\text{-}unim}] = \textit{\textbf{Mixt}}[\mathbf{R_{m\theta}(\theta\in I)}]. \tag{36}$$

The space *Mixt*[$R_{m\theta}(\theta\in I)$] is a regular space of mixtures.

Proof

a. We start with the proof of the $\subseteq$ part of (36). Let F be a m-unimodal probability distribution concentrated on the interval I, with right-continuous density φ on the set $]-\infty,m[\cup]m,\infty[$. Of course, φ vanishes outside I.

We will prove that F can be displayed as the mixture

$$F(x) = \int_I R_{m\theta}(x)dU(\theta), \tag{37}$$

where U is the distribution function with values

$$\begin{aligned} U(\theta) &:= \int_{]-\infty,\theta]} (m-\tau)d\varphi(\tau) \ (\theta<m), \\ U(\theta) &:= 1-\int_{[\theta,\infty[} (\tau-m)d[-\varphi(\tau)] \ (m<\theta). \end{aligned} \tag{38}$$

This definition is completed by: U(m):=U(m+). Then U is a probability distribution concentrated on I. Indeed, by Fubini,

$$U(\theta) = \int_{]-\infty,\theta]} [\int_{[\tau,m[} dx]d\varphi(\tau) = \int_{]-\infty,m[} [\int_{]-\infty,x\wedge\theta]} d\varphi(\tau)]dx$$

$$= \int_{]-\infty,m[} \varphi(\theta\wedge x)dx \uparrow \int_{]-\infty,m[} \varphi(x)dx = F(]-\infty,m[) \ \text{ as } \theta\uparrow m \ (\theta<m),$$

$$1-U(\theta) = \int_{[\theta,\infty[}[\int_{]m,\tau]}dx]d[-\varphi(\tau)] = \int_{]m,\infty[}[\int_{[x\vee\theta,\infty[} d[-\varphi(\tau)]]dx$$

$$= \int_{]m,\infty[} \varphi(x\vee\theta)dx \uparrow \int_{]m,\infty[} \varphi(x)dx = F(]m,\infty[) \text{ as } \theta\downarrow m \ \ (m<\theta).$$

Now we verify the relation (37). By (34), (35) and Fubini,

$$\int_I R_{m\theta}(x)dU(\theta) = \int_{]-\infty,x]} R_{m\theta}(x)(m-\theta)d\varphi(\theta)$$

$$= \int_{]-\infty,x]} [\int_{[\theta,x]} dy]d\varphi(\theta) = \int_{]-\infty,x]} [\int_{]-\infty,y]} d\varphi(\theta)]dy$$

$$= \int_{]-\infty,x]} \varphi(y)dy = F(x) \ \ (x<m),$$

$$\int_I R_{m\theta}(x)dU(\theta) = 1-\int_I [1-R_{m\theta}(x)]dU(\theta)$$

$$= 1-\int_{[x,\infty[}[1-R_{m\theta}(x)](\theta-m)d[-\varphi(\theta)] = 1-\int_{[x,\infty[}[\int_{[x,\theta]}dy]d[-\varphi(\theta)]$$

$$= 1-\int_{[x,\infty[}[\int_{[y,\infty[} d[-\varphi(\theta)]]dy = 1-\int_{[x,\infty[} \varphi(y)dy = 1-F([x,\infty[)$$

$$= 1-[1-F(x)] = F(x) \ \ (m<x).$$

This proves (37) for x<m and for x>m. Then, letting x↓m, (37) is also correct for x=m by right-continuity and dominated convergence.

b. Now we prove the $\supseteq$ part of (36). Let U be a probability distribution concentrated on I, and let

$$F(x) := \int_I R_{m\theta}(x)dU(\theta).$$

Then F is a probability distribution concentrated on I.

Let function φ be defined on $]-\infty,m[\cup]m,\infty[$ by the relations.

$$\varphi(x) := \int_{]-\infty,x]} 1/(m-\theta)\, dU(\theta) \quad (x<m),$$
$$\varphi(x) := \int_{[x,\infty[} 1/(\theta-m)\, dU(\theta) \quad (m<x). \tag{39}$$

Let F_0 be the distribution with density φ on the set $]-\infty,m[\cup]m,\infty[$ and with mass $F(\{m\})$ at the point m. We will verify that $F=F_0$.

We first suppose $x<m$. Then, by Fubini,

$$F_0(x) = F_0(]-\infty,x]) = \int_{]-\infty,x]} \varphi(y)dy = \int_{]-\infty,x]} [\int_{]-\infty,y]} 1/(m-\theta)\, dU(\theta)]dy$$
$$= \int_{]-\infty,x]} [\int_{[\theta,x]} dy]\, 1/(m-\theta)\, dU(\theta) = \int_{]-\infty,x]} (x-\theta)/(m-\theta)\, dU(\theta).$$

By (34), the latter integral equals

$$\int_I 1_{\theta\le x}\, (x-\theta)/(m-\theta)\, dU(\theta) = \int_I R_{m\theta}(x)\, dU(\theta) = F(x).$$

Hence, $F_0(x)=F(x)$ if $x<m$, and then for $x\uparrow m$, $F_0(m-)=F(m-)$.

In the same way, for $m<x$, by (35),

$$F_0(]x,\infty[) = F_0([x,\infty]) = \int_{[x,\infty[} \varphi(y)dy = \int_{[x,\infty[} [1/(\theta-m) \int_{[y,\infty[} dU(\theta)]dy$$
$$= \int_{[x,\infty[} [\int_{[x,\theta]} dy]\, 1/(\theta-m)\, dU(\theta) = \int_{[x,\infty[} (\theta-x)/(\theta-m)\, dU(\theta)$$
$$= \int_I 1_{x\le\theta}\, (\theta-x)/(\theta-m)\, dU(\theta) = \int_I [1-R_{m\theta}(x)]dU(\theta)$$
$$= 1-\int_I R_{m\theta}(x)dU(\theta) = 1-F(x).$$

Hence,

$$F_0(]x,\infty[) = 1-F(x),$$

and then for $x\downarrow m$,

$$F_0(]m,\infty[) = 1-F(m).$$

Then

$$F_0(\mathbf{R}) = F_0(]-\infty,m[) + F_0(\{m\}) + F_0(]m,\infty[)$$

$$= F_0(m-) + F(\{m\}) + F_0(]m,\infty[)$$

$$= F(m-) + [F(m)-F(m-)] + [1-F(m)] = 1.$$

Hence, F_0 is a probability distribution function. Then $F_0(]x,\infty[)=1-F_0(x)$ $(m<x)$ and then $F_0=F$ on $]m,\infty[$. Then $F_0(m)=F(m)$ by the right-continuity of F_0 and F.

c. For the proof of the regularity, let U,V be probability distributions on I such that

$$\int R_{m\theta}(x)dU(\theta) = \int R_{m\theta}(x)dU(\theta) \quad (x\in\mathbf{R}),$$

and let $w:=U-V$. We first assume that x is strictly less than m. Then, by (34) and Fubini,

$$0 = \int R_{m\theta}(x)dw(\theta) = \int\big[1_{\theta\le x}\ 1/(m-\theta)\int_{[\theta,x]} dy\big]dw(\theta)$$

$$= \int_{]-\infty,x]}\big[1/(m-\theta)\int_{[\theta,x]} dy\big]dw(\theta) = \int_{]-\infty,x]}\big[\int_{]-\infty,y]} 1/(m-\theta)\ dw(\theta)\big]dy \ (x<m).$$

This implies

$$\int_{]-\infty,y]} 1/(m-\theta)\ dw(\theta) = 0 \ \ (y<m)\,,\ w(\theta) = 0 \ \ (\theta<m).$$

Hence, U=V on $]-\infty,m[$. Then, by symmetry, U=V on $]m,\infty[$, and then U(m) =V(m) also, by right-continuity •

Discrete case

We here consider distribution spaces resulting from a **discretization of the density** of the distributions in the space ***Prob***[[a,b];m-unim].

Let S be a finite subset of the compact interval [a,b], containing the extremities a,b, and let $m\in S$. Then

$$\textbf{\textit{Prob}}[[a,b];S,m\text{-unim}] \tag{40}$$

is the space of m-unimodal probability distributions F concentrated on [a,b], with constant density φ on any interval $]\alpha,\beta[$ delimited by two successive points α,β of S. A mass at the mode m is not excluded.

Theorem 9

$$\mathbf{\mathit{Prob}[[a,b];S,m\text{-}unim] = \mathit{Mixt}[R_{m\theta}(\theta \in S)]}. \qquad (41)$$

The space *Mixt*[$R_{m\theta}(\theta \in S)$] is a regular space of mixtures.

Proof
The space in the last member of (41) is the space of mixtures of m-rectangular distributions $R_{m\theta}$, with mixing distribution U concentrated on the set S. The demonstration of Theorem 8 remains valid here. The distribution U of part a. of that proof must be concentrated on S because $d\varphi(\tau)=0$ on intervals $]\alpha,\beta[$ delimited by successive points α,β of S. The function φ of part b. of the proof must be constant on intervals $]\alpha,\beta[$ delimited by successive points of S, because U is concentrated on the set S •

For any interval I in **R**, any subset S of I and any point $m \in I$, we now **define** the space

$$\mathit{Prob}[I;S,m\text{-unim}] := \mathit{Mixt}[R_{m\theta}(\theta \in S)].$$

1.4. Convex Hulls in R^n

1.4.1. Representation of Convex Hulls

Theorem 10 (Carathéodory)

Let Q be a set in R^n.

a. **Each point $x \in \mathrm{Co}\, Q$ is a convex combination of n+1 points of Q.**

b. **Let $x \in \mathrm{Co}\, Q$ and let x be a frontier point of Co Q. Then x is a convex combination of n points of Q.**

c. **Let $x \in (\mathrm{Co}\, Q)^\circ$. Then x is a convex combination with strictly positive coefficients of at least n+1 different points of Q.**

Proof
a. Any point $x \in \mathrm{Co}\, Q$ can be expressed as a convex combination of points $x_i \in Q$ $(i=0,1,\ldots,k)$:

$$x = p_0x_0+\ldots+p_kx_k. \qquad (42)$$

We may drop the terms with a coefficient equal to zero. Hence, we suppose that $p_i>0$ (i=0,1,2,...,k). We assume that k>n and we prove that k can be reduced by one unit at least. Then this argument can be repeated until k becomes equal to n.

The dimension of the vector space $\mathbf{R}^n$ is n. Hence, some linear combination with at least one coefficient different from zero, of the vectors (x_i-x_0) (i=1,...,k), must be the zero vector :

$$0 = b_1(x_1-x_0) + \ldots + b_k(x_k-x_0). \tag{43}$$

We multiply (43) by the scalar s and then we add up (42) and (43):

$$x = [p_0-s(b_1+\ldots+b_n)]x_0 + (p_1+sb_1)x_1 + \ldots + (p_k+sb_k)x_k. \tag{44}$$

In the last member of (44), the sum of the coefficients of $x_0,x_1,\ldots,x_k$, is 1, whatever the value of s may be. For s=0, the last member of (44) is the last member of (42) and then each coefficient is strictly positive. Starting from 0, we can increase or decrease s in a continuous way until some coefficient becomes equal to zero, while the others remain positive. Then we obtain x as a convex combination of strictly less than k+1 vectors.

b. By part a, we can express x as a convex combination of n+1 points of Q:

$$x = p_0x_0 + \ldots + p_nx_n.$$

If some p_i equals zero, then we have finished. Hence, we assume that $p_i>0$ (i=0,...,n). Then

$$x = x_0 + p_1(x_1-x_0) + \ldots + p_n(x_n-x_0).$$

The vectors $(x_1-x_0),\ldots,(x_n-x_0)$ cannot be independent, because then small variations of the coefficients $p_1,\ldots,p_n$ show that x is an interior point of the set Co B. Then the argument of the part a. can be applied.

c. We prove c in case n=2. The demonstration of that particular case includes all the ideas of a general proof. Let $Q\subseteq\mathbf{R}^2$, and let z=(x,y) be a point in the interior of Co Q. Then $\varepsilon>0$ exists, such that the points

$$z_{--} := (x-\varepsilon,y-\varepsilon)\ ,\ z_{-+} := (x-\varepsilon,y+\varepsilon),$$

$$z_{++} := (x+\varepsilon,y+\varepsilon)\ ,\ z_{+-} := (x+\varepsilon,y-\varepsilon)$$

belong to Co Q.

By a, each point z_{++} can be expressed as a convex combination with strictly positive coefficients of 3 not necessarily distinct points of Q:

$$z_{++} = p_{1++}z_{1++} + p_{2++}z_{2++} + p_{3++}z_{3++},$$

$$p_{1++}>0\ ,\ p_{2++}>0\ ,\ p_{3++}>0\ ,\ z_{i++}\in Q\ (i=1,2,3).$$

(The relations $z_{i++}=z_{i++}/2+z_{i++}/2=z_{i++}/3+z_{i++}/3+z_{i++}/3$ can be used). Let $z_1,\ldots,z_k$ be the different points among $z_{i++}(i=1,2,3)$. Then $k\geq 3$. Indeed, if k=2, then the four points z_{++} are convex combinations of z_1 and z_2, i.e. they are situated on the straight line segment connecting z_1 and z_2: this is absurd. If k=1, then we have the contradiction $z_{++}=z_1$.

The point z can be expressed as

$$z = 1/4(z_{--}+z_{-+}+z_{++}+z_{+-})$$

$$= 1/4(p_{1--}z_{1--} + p_{2--}z_{2--} + p_{3--}z_{3--}) + 1/4(p_{1-+}z_{1-+} + p_{2-+}z_{2-+} + p_{3-+}z_{3-+})$$

$$+1/4(p_{1++}z_{1++} + p_{2++}z_{2++} + p_{3++}z_{3++}) + 1/4(p_{1+-}z_{1+-} + p_{2+-}z_{2+-} + p_{3+-}z_{3+-}).$$

We can group the linear combinations of the same point z_i $(i=1,\ldots,k)$:

$$z = p_1z_1 + \ldots + p_kz_k.$$

In the latter expression, $p_1,\ldots,p_k$ are strictly positive, $z_1,\ldots z_k$ are different points in Q and $k\geq 3$ •

1.4.2. Compactness of Convex Hulls

Theorem 11

Let Q be a compact set in R^n. Then Co Q is compact.

Proof

Let $u_k\in$Co Q (k=1,2,...). By Carathéodory, each point u_k can be expressed as a convex combination

$$u_k = p_kx_k + q_ky_k + \ldots + r_kz_k\ (k=1,2,\ldots)$$

of n+1 points $x_k, y_k, \ldots, z_k \in Q$. A subsequence $k_j \equiv k(j)$ of the sequence $k=1,2,\ldots$ exists, such that

$$p_{k(j)},\ q_{k(j)},\ \ldots, r_{k(j)},\ x_{k(j)},\ y_{k(j)},\ldots,\ z_{k(j)}$$

are convergent as $j\uparrow\infty$. Indeed, some subsequence $p_{k(r)}$ $(r=1,2,\ldots)$ of p_k $(k=1,2,\ldots)$ is convergent. Some subsequence $q_{k(r(s))}(s=1,2,\ldots)$ of $q_{k(r)}(r=1,\ldots)$ is convergent... Taking successive subsequences, we obtain the subsequence $k_j(j=1,2,\ldots)$. (The process of taking successive subsequences, must be applied to each one of the n components of x_k, $y_k,\ldots,z_k$). All limits are finite, because the coefficients $p_{k(j)}, q_{k(j)},\ldots,r_{k(j)}$ belong to [0,1], and because the compact set Q is bounded. Let the limits be p, q, ...,r, x, y, ...,z resp. Then,

$$u_{k(j)} \to px + qy + \ldots + rz =: u \ \text{ as } j\uparrow\infty.$$

The compact set Q is closed. The points x,y,...,z belong to Q, because they are limits of points in Q. From the relations

$$p_{k(j)} \geq 0\ ,\ q_{k(j)} \geq 0\ ,\ \ldots,\ r_{k(j)} \geq 0,$$

$$p_{k(j)}+q_{k(j)}+\ldots+r_{k(j)} = 1,$$

results

$$p \geq 0\ ,\ q \geq 0\ ,\ \ldots\ ,\ r \geq 0\ ,\ p+q+\ldots+r = 1$$

as $j\uparrow\infty$. Hence, u is a convex combination of points of Q, and then $u \in \text{Co } Q$. This proves that any sequence in Co Q has a subsequence converging to some point of Co Q. Hence Co Q is compact •

Chapter 2

General Probability Distribution Spaces

2.1. General Notations and Definitions

2.1.1. Probability Distribution Spaces

Pure spaces

An **atom** of the distribution F is a point $\theta \in \mathbf{R}$, such that $F(\{\theta\})>0$, i.e. a point bearing a strictly positive F-mass. We recall that $A_\theta:=1_{[\theta,\infty[}$ is **the 1-atomic probability distribution concentrated at the point $\theta \in \mathbf{R}$**. A **k-atomic probability distribution** is a convex combination

$$F = p_1 A_{\theta_1} + \ldots + p_k A_{\theta_k}$$

of k 1-atomic probability distribution. Then F is concentrated on the set $\{\theta_1, \ldots, \theta_k\}$ and the F-mass at the point θ_j is $p_j \geq 0$ $(j=1,\ldots,k)$. Some coefficients p_j may be equal to zero. Hence, any k-atomic probability distribution has k atoms at most, not necessarily exactly k atoms. All k-atomic probability distributions are called **finite-atomic probability distributions**.

We denote by

$$\boldsymbol{Prob}[S;\text{cond}_1;\ldots;\text{cond}_n]$$

the **pure space** of probability distributions F concentrated on the set $S \subseteq \mathbf{R}$, satisfying the **conditions** (or **constraints**) $\text{cond}_1, \ldots, \text{cond}_n$. These conditions are of the following type:

F is k-atomic (**k-at**),

F is finite-atomic (**finite-at**),

$$\int f dF=\alpha \ (\boldsymbol{\int f=\alpha}) \ , \ \int f dF \leq \alpha \ (\boldsymbol{\int f \leq \alpha}). \tag{1}$$

The abridged forms of the conditions are indicated in brackets. When the **integral constraints** (1) are used, it is assumed that f is integrable with respect to all distributions F concentrated on S.

Unimodal spaces

A **m-unimodal probability distribution** is a probability distribution with an increasing density on the interval $]-\infty,m[$, a decreasing density on the interval $]m,\infty[$, and possible some mass at the **mode** m (Ch.1.3.4). In particular, the **1-rectangular m-unimodal distribution** $R_{m\theta}$ is the uniform probability distribution concentrated on the interval with extremities $m,\theta\in\mathbf{R}$. A **k-rectangular m-unimodal probability distribution** is a convex combination of k distributions $R_{m\theta}$. The k-rectangular m-unimodal probability distributions are **finite-rectangular m-unimodal probability distributions**. We denote by

$$\boldsymbol{Prob}[I;\text{m-unim};\text{cond}_1;\ldots;\text{cond}_n]$$

the **m-unimodal space** of m-unimodal probability distributions F concentrated on the interval I (containing m) and satisfying the constraints $\text{cond}_1,\ldots,\text{cond}_n$. These conditions are the integral conditions (1) or the conditions

F is k-rectangular (**k-rect**),

F is finite-rectangular (**finite-rect**).

Let S be a subset of the interval I, and let $m\in I$. We denote by

$$\boldsymbol{Prob}[I;S,\text{m-unim};\text{cond}_1;\ldots;\text{cond}_n]$$

the subspace of ***Prob***[I;S,m-unim] of distribution functions satisfying the constraints $\text{cond}_1,\ldots,\text{cond}_n$ (see the last paragraph of Ch.1.3).

Spaces of probability mixtures

Let $S\subseteq\mathbf{R}$ and let $F_\theta(\theta\in S)$ be probability distributions. We recall that **the mixture with mixing function** $U\in\boldsymbol{Prob}[S]$ is the probability distribution function F_U with values

$$F_U(x) = \int F_\theta(x)dU(\theta) \quad (x\in\mathbf{R}) \tag{2}$$

and that

$$\boldsymbol{Mixt}[F_\theta(\theta\in S)] := \{F_U \,/\, U\in\boldsymbol{Prob}[S]\} \tag{3}$$

is **the space of mixtures** with **basis** $\{F_\theta/\theta\in S\}$ (See Ch.1.3.2).

Any convex combination G of k distributions $F_\theta(\theta \in S)$ is called a **k-basic distribution of the space *Mixt*[$F_\theta/\theta \in S$]**. G is k-basic iff $G=F_U$ for some k-atomic distribution U concentrated on S. The k-basic distributions are **finite-basic distributions**.

We denote by

$$\boldsymbol{Mixt}[F_\theta(\theta \in S);cond_1;...;cond_n] \tag{4}$$

the space of distributions $F \in \boldsymbol{Mixt}[F_\theta(\theta \in S)]$ satisfying the constraints $cond_1$, ..., $cond_n$. These conditions are the integral conditions (1) or conditions of the type

F is k-basic (**k-basic**) , F is finite-basic (**finite-basic**).

When the integral constraints (1) are used, it is assumed that f is F-integrable for all $F \in \boldsymbol{Mixt}[F_\theta(\theta \in S)]$.

The most important particular case is $F_\theta=A_\theta$ $(\theta \in S)$. Then

$$\boldsymbol{Mixt}[A_\theta(\theta \in S)] = \boldsymbol{Prob}[S] \tag{5}$$

by Ch.1.Th.7. By the same Theorem, (5) is a regular space of mixtures.

Another important particular case is $F_\theta=R_{m\theta}(\theta \in S)$, for fixed mode $m \in S$. Then

$$\boldsymbol{Mixt}[R_{m\theta}(\theta \in I)] = \boldsymbol{Prob}[I;m\text{-unim}] \quad (m \in I,\ I \text{ interval}), \tag{6}$$

$$\boldsymbol{Mixt}[R_{m\theta}(\theta \in S)] = \boldsymbol{Prob}[I;S,m\text{-unim}]\ (S \subseteq I,\ I \text{ interval},\ m \in I) \tag{7}$$

by Ch.1.Th.8 and by the last definition of Ch.1.3.4 .By Ch.1.Th.8, the spaces (6) and (7) are regular spaces of mixtures.

Moment spaces

Moment spaces are spaces of probability distributions F, concentrated on a bounded set S, satisfying the **moment constraints**

$$\int x dF(x)=\mu_1 , \dots , \int x^n dF(x) = \mu_n.$$

Existence of spaces depending on parameters

We say that the **space *Space* exists** if it is not void. The existence question is especiallly relevant in the case of spaces ***Space***$(\alpha_1,...,\alpha_n)$ depending on parameters $\alpha_1,...,\alpha_n \in \mathbf{R}$. Then the set of points $(\alpha_1,...,\alpha_n) \in \mathbf{R}^n$ for which the space exists is called **the effective domain of the space**.

Basic properties of the spaces

The following are imperative questions when optimization problems on some space ***Space*** of probability distributions are considered:

Does *Space* exist? Is *Space* convex? Is *Space* compact?

What are the extremal points of *Space*?

These questions are answered in this Chapter for general spaces of probability mixtures with integral equality constraints. In Chapter 3, more detailed answers are furnished in the case of moment spaces.

2.1.2. General Distribution Spaces

We denote by

$$\textbf{\textit{Distr}}[S], \tag{8}$$

$$\textbf{\textit{Distr}}[S;\text{cond}_1;...;\text{cond}_n], \tag{9}$$

the space of distributions cF with $c \in \mathbf{R}_+$ and, respectively,

$$F \in \textbf{\textit{Prob}}[S], \tag{10}$$

$$F \in \textbf{\textit{Prob}}[S;\text{cond}_1;...;\text{cond}_n]. \tag{11}$$

The consideration of these spaces is convenient in some proofs. They are essential in the duality theory developed in Chapter 7.

2.2. Pure Space Associated to a Space of Mixtures

2.2.1. Definition of the Associated Space

We consider the space

$$\textbf{\textit{Mixt}}[F_\theta(\theta\in S)]. \qquad (12)$$

Let f be an integrable function with respect to all distributions F in that space. We recall that **the associated function** $f^\bullet$ is the function with values

$$f^\bullet(\theta) := \int f(x)dF_\theta(x) \quad (\theta\in S). \qquad (13)$$

We also recall the important **mixture elimination equality** (see Ch.1.(28))

$$\int f(x)dF_U(x) = \int f^\bullet(\theta)dU(\theta) \quad (U\in \textbf{\textit{Prob}}[S]). \qquad (14)$$

Let $\alpha_1,\ldots,\alpha_n\in\mathbf{R}$ and let $f_1,\ldots,f_n$ be integrable functions with respect to all distributions $F\in\textbf{\textit{Mixt}}[F_\theta/\theta\in S]$. **The pure space associated to the space**

$$\textbf{\textit{Mixt}}[F_\theta(\theta\in S);\int f_1=\alpha_1,\ldots\int f_n=\alpha_n] \qquad (15)$$

is the space

$$\textbf{\textit{Prob}}[S;\int f_1^\bullet=\alpha_1,\ldots,\int f_n^\bullet=\alpha_1]. \qquad (16)$$

The associated space (16) results from the space (15), by **the mixture elimination**.

2.2.2. The Linear 1–1 Mapping L

Let L be the function on the space (16) with values

$$L(U) = F_U \quad (U\in \textbf{\textit{Prob}}[S;\int f_1^\bullet=\alpha_1,\ldots,\int f_n^\bullet=\alpha_1]). \qquad (17)$$

Theorem 1

The space of mixtures (15) exists iff its associated pure space (16) exists. The function L defined by (17) is a linear mapping of the convex space (16) onto the convex space (15). It is a 1–1 mapping if the space (12) is a regular space of mixtures.

Proof
For the moment we assume that both spaces (15) and (16) exist. From the following proof it is clear that one of them exists iff the other does.

Let U be concentrated on S. Then

$$F_U \in \boldsymbol{Mixt}[F_\theta(\theta \in S)].$$

If U satisfies the constraints

$$\int f_j^\bullet dU = \alpha_j \ (j=1,\dots,n), \tag{18}$$

then

$$\int f_j dF_U = \alpha_j \ (j=1,\dots,n) \tag{19}$$

by (14). Hence, if U belongs to the space (16), then L(U) belongs to the space (15). This proves that L is a mapping of the space (16) into the space (15). It is a mapping onto the space (15). Indeed, let F be a point in the space (15). Then $F \in \boldsymbol{Mixt}[F_\theta(\theta \in S)]$, and by the definition of the latter space of mixtures, F is expressible as $F=F_U$, where U is concentrated on S. Then F_U satisfies the constraints (19), and then U satisfies the constraints (18) by (14). Hence, U belongs to the space (16) and L(U)=F.

Convex combinations of distributions in the space (15) or (16), are distributions in that space. Hence (15) and (16) are convex spaces. The linearity of L is expressed by the relation

$$L(pU+qV) = pL(U) + qL(V),$$

where pU+qV is any convex combination of distributions U,V in (16).

Finally, if $\boldsymbol{Mixt}[F_\theta(\theta \in S)]$ is a regular space of mixtures, the relation $F_U=F_V$, where U and V are concentrated on S, implies that U=V. Hence, it implies that U=V when U and V belong to the space (16). This proves that the mapping L is 1–1 •

Pure space associated to a pure space

Let $F_\theta=A_\theta(\theta \in S)$. Then

$$\boldsymbol{Mixt}[A_\theta(\theta \in S); \int f_1=\alpha_1,\dots \int f_n=\alpha_n] = \boldsymbol{Prob}[S; \int f_1=\alpha_1,\dots \int f_n=\alpha_n] \tag{20}$$

by (5) and

$$f^\bullet(\theta) = \int f(x) dA_\theta(x) = f(\theta) \ \ (\theta \in S) \tag{21}$$

by (14). Hence,

The pure associated space of a pure space is that space itself.

Pure space associated to a m-unimodal space

Let $F_\theta = R_{m\theta}$ ($\theta \in S$), $m \in S$. Then the functions $f_j^\bullet$($j=1,\ldots,n$) occurring in the definition of the associated space (16) result from the relations

$$f^\bullet(m) = \int f(x)dR_{mm}(x) = \int f(x)dA_m(x) = f(m)$$
$$f^\bullet(\theta) = {}^1/_{(m-\theta)} \int_{]\theta,m[} f(x)dx \quad (\theta \neq m,\ \theta \in S). \tag{22}$$

The latter expression is also valid for $m<\theta$. Then the integral must be considered as an integral with oriented domain, i.e. $\int_{]\theta,m[} := -\int_{]m,\theta[}$.

2.3. General Theorems

2.3.1. Existence Theorems

Theorem 2 (General Existence Theorem)

$$\{(\int f_1 dF,\ldots,\int f_n dF) \,/ F \in \mathit{Mixt}[F_\theta(\theta \in S)]\}$$
$$= \mathrm{Co}\{(f_1^\bullet(\theta),\ldots,f_n^\bullet(\theta))/\theta \in S\}. \tag{23}$$

The space

$$\mathit{Mixt}[F_\theta(\theta \in S);\int f_1=\alpha_1,\ldots\int f_n=\alpha_n] \tag{24}$$

exists iff

$$(\alpha_1,\ldots,\alpha_n) \in \mathrm{Co}\ \{(f_1^\bullet(\theta),\ldots,f_n^\bullet(\theta))\ /\ \theta \in S\}. \tag{25}$$

Proof
The relation (23) is the relation Ch.1.(31), taking the definition of the associated functions into account. The space (24) exists iff

$$(\alpha_1,\ldots,\alpha_n) \in \{(\int f_1 dF,\ldots,\int f_n dF)\ /\ F \in \mathit{Mixt}[F_\theta(\theta \in S)]\}.$$

By (23), this condition is the same as (25) •

Corollary 1 (Existence Theorem of Pure Spaces)

$$\{(\int f_1 dF,...,\int f_n dF) \,/\, F \in \mathit{Prob}[S]\} = \mathrm{Co}\,\{(f_1(\theta),...,f_n(\theta)) \,/\, \theta \in S\}. \quad (26)$$

The space

$$\mathit{Prob}[S;\int f_1=\alpha_1,...\int f_n=\alpha_n] \quad (27)$$

exists iff

$$(\alpha_1,...,\alpha_n) \in \mathrm{Co}\,\{(f_1(\theta),...,f_n(\theta)) \,/\, \theta \in S\} \;\bullet \quad (28)$$

Corollary 2 (Existence Theorem of m-Unimodal Spaces)

The associated functions $f_j^{\bullet}(j=1,...,n)$ are defined by (22).

a. Let $I \subseteq R$ be an interval, $m \in I$. Then

$$\{(\int f_1 dF,...,\int f_n dF) \,/\, F \in \mathit{Prob}[I;\text{m-unim}]\} = \mathrm{Co}\{(f_1^{\bullet}(\theta),...,f_n^{\bullet}(\theta))/\theta \in I\}. \quad (29)$$

The space

$$\mathit{Prob}[I;\text{m-unim};\int f_1=\alpha_1,...\int f_n=\alpha_n] \quad (30)$$

exists iff

$$(\alpha_1,...,\alpha_n) \in \mathrm{Co}\{(f_1^{\bullet}(\theta),...,f_n^{\bullet}(\theta)) \,/\theta \in I\}. \quad (31)$$

b. Let S be a subset of the interval $I \subseteq R$, and let $m \in I$. Then

$$\{(\int f_1 dF,...,\int f_n dF) \,/\, F \in \mathit{Prob}[I;S,\text{m-unim}]\} = \mathrm{Co}\{(f_1^{\bullet}(\theta),...,f_n^{\bullet}(\theta))/\theta \in S\}. \quad (32)$$

The space

$$\mathit{Prob}[I;S,\text{m-unim};\int f_1=\alpha_1,...\int f_n=\alpha_n] \quad (33)$$

exists iff

$$(\alpha_1,...,\alpha_n) \in \mathrm{Co}\{(f_1^{\bullet}(\theta),...,f_n^{\bullet}(\theta)) \,/\theta \in S\}. \quad (34)$$

2.3.2. Convexity of Spaces

The spaces

$$\mathit{Prob}[S;\mathrm{cond}_1,...,\mathrm{cond}_l], \quad (35)$$

$$\mathit{Prob}[I;\text{m-unim};\mathrm{cond}_1,...,\mathrm{cond}_l], \quad (36)$$

$$\textbf{\textit{Prob}}[I;S,\text{m-unim};\text{cond}_1,...,\text{cond}_l], \tag{37}$$

and

$$\textbf{\textit{Mixt}}[F_\theta(\theta\in S);\text{cond}_1,...,\text{cond}_n], \tag{38}$$

are convex if the constraints **k-at**, **k-rect**, **k-basic** do not occur among the conditions $\text{cond}_1,...,\text{cond}_n$. All other conditions of 2.1.1 are allowed.

2.3.3. Compactness Theorems

Theorem 3

Let F_n (n=1,2,...) be probability distributions concentrated on the compact set $S\subseteq R$, such that $F_n\to_w F\in$*Distr*[R]. Then

a. F is a probability distribution concentrated on S.

b. If the distributions F_n(n=1,2,...) are k-atomic, then F is k-atomic.

c. If f is a continuous function on S, then

$$\int_S f dF_n \to \int_S f dF \text{ as } n\uparrow\infty.$$

Proof

a. Obviously F is a probability distribution function. We assume that F is not concentrated on S and we derive a contradiction. Some bounded interval I exists in the complement CS of S such that F(I)>0. We may assume that the extremities of I are continuity points of F. We then have the contradiction

$$0 = F_n(I) \to F(I) > 0 \text{ as } n\uparrow\infty.$$

b. Let F_n be the distribution with mass $p_{1n},...,p_{kn}$ at the points $a_{1n},...,a_{kn}$ in S resp. Then

$$p_{1n}+...+p_{kn} = 1 \text{ , } a_{1n}\in S \text{ ,..., } a_{kn}\in S \text{ (n=1,2,...).}$$

Taking enough subsequences, we may assume that n(ν) (n=1,2,...) is a subsequence of the sequence n=1,2,..., such that all sequences

$$p_{1n(\nu)} \text{ , ... , } p_{kn(\nu)} \text{ , } a_{1n(\nu)} \text{ , ... , } a_{kn(\nu)} \text{ (}\nu\text{=1,2,...)}$$

are convergent as $\nu\uparrow\infty$. Let the limits be p_1, ..., p_k, a_1, ..., a_k resp. Then $p_1+...+p_n=1$, $a_1\in S$, ..., $a_k\in S$. Let G be the k-atomic distribution with mass p_1, ..., p_n at the points a_1, ..., a_k resp. Then $F_{n(\nu)} \to_w G$. But $F_{n(\nu)} \to_w F$. Hence, F=G and F is k-atomic.

c. Let [a,b] be the smallest closed interval containing S. Then $a,b\in S$ because S is closed. The function f has a continuous extension to [a,b]. Indeed, let $x\in]a,b[$, $x\notin S$. Let x_0 be the last point of S before x and x_1 the first point of S after x. These points exist, because S is closed. Then f can be continuously extended to the interval $[x_0,x_1]$ by linearity. Then by Helly-Bray (case of a bounded integration domain),

$$\int_S fdF_n = \int_{[a,b]} fdF_n \to \int_{[a,b]} fdF = \int_S fdF_n \ \text{ as } n\uparrow\infty.$$

We notice that Helly-Bray can be applied because

$$F_n(a-) = 0 \to 0 = F(a-) \text{ as } n\uparrow\infty$$

and

$$F_n(b) = 1 \to 1 = F(b) \text{ as } n\uparrow\infty \quad \bullet$$

Theorem 4 (General Compactness Theorem)

We consider the space of mixtures *Mixt*[$F_\theta(\theta\in S)$] and we assume that F_U is a continuous function of $U\in$*Prob*[S], i.e.

$$[U,U_n\in \textit{Prob}[S]\ (n=1,2,...) \text{ and } U_n\to_w U \text{ as } n\uparrow\infty] \tag{39}$$
$$\Rightarrow\ [F_{U_n}\to_w F_U \text{ as } n\uparrow\infty].$$

Let S be a compact set in R, and let the functions $f_1^\bullet,...,f_n^\bullet$ be continuous on S. Then the spaces

$$\textit{Mixt}[F_\theta(\theta\in S);\textstyle\int f_1=\alpha_1,...,\int f_n=\alpha_n] \tag{40}$$

and

$$\textit{Mixt}[F_\theta(\theta\in S);\text{k-basic};\textstyle\int f_1=\alpha_1,...,\int f_n=\alpha_n] \tag{41}$$

are compact.

Proof
We verify that the pure space

$$\textit{Prob}[S;\textstyle\int f_1^\bullet=\alpha_1,...,\int f_n^\bullet=\alpha_n] \tag{42}$$

associated to the space (40) is compact. Let U_n (n=1,2,...) be a sequence in space (42). By the general compactness Theorem, some subsequence $U_{n(\nu)}$ (ν=1,2,...) exists, such that

$$U_{n(\nu)} \to_w U \in \boldsymbol{Distr}[\mathbf{R}] \text{ as } \nu\uparrow\infty.$$

The constraints of the space (42) are satisfied by the distributions $U_{n(\nu)}$:

$$\int f_j^{\bullet} dU_{n(\nu)} = \alpha_j \ \ (j=1,\ldots,n). \tag{43}$$

By Theorem 3.a, U is a probability distribution concentrated on S. As $\nu\uparrow\infty$ in (43), we obtain $\int f_j^{\bullet} dU=\alpha_j$ (j=1,...,n) by Theorem 3.c. Hence, the constraints of the space (42) are satisfied and U belongs to that space. This proves that the space (42) is compact.

We now prove the compactness of the space (40). Let F_n(n=1,2,...) be a sequence of points in that space. Then $F_n=F_{U_n}$ for some distribution U_n in the space (42) by Theorem 1. By the compactness of the space (42), some subsequence $U_{n(\nu)}$ (ν=1,2,...) exists, such that $U_{n(\nu)} \to_w U\in(42)$ as $\nu\to\infty$. Then

$$F_{U_{n(\nu)}} \to_w F_U \text{ as } \nu\uparrow\infty$$

by the continuity assumption (39). The constraints of the space (40) are satisfied by $F_{n(\nu)}$:

$$\int f_j dF_{n(\nu)} = \alpha_j \ \ (j=1,\ldots,n).$$

Then

$$\int f_j^{\bullet} dU_{n(\nu)} = \alpha_j \ (j=1,\ldots,n)$$

by the mixture elimination equality. As $\nu\uparrow\infty$, we obtain

$$\int f_j^{\bullet} dU_n = \alpha_j \ (j=1,\ldots,n)$$

by Theorem 3.c. Then

$$\int f_j dF_U = \alpha_j \ (j=1,\ldots,n).$$

This proves that $F_U\in(40)$. Hence the space (40) is compact.

The compactness of the space (41) results from the same argument. Indeed, if the distributions F_n (n=1,2,...) are k-basic, then the distributions U_n are k-atomic and then the weak limit U of the sequence $U_{n(\nu)}$ is k-atomic by Theorem 3.b. Then F_U is k-basic •

Corollary 1 (Compactness Theorem for Pure Spaces)

The spaces

$$\boldsymbol{Prob}[S;\int f_1=\alpha_1,\ldots,\int f_n=\alpha_n] \quad (44)$$

and

$$\boldsymbol{Prob}[S;\text{k-at};\int f_1=\alpha_1,\ldots,\int f_n=\alpha_n] \quad (45)$$

are compact if S is a compact set in R and if the functions $f_1,\ldots,f_n$ are continuous on S •

Remark (***non-compact spaces***)

The space ***Prob***[]0,1]] is not compact. Indeed, let F_n (n=1,2,...) be the probability distribution concentrated at the point 1/n and let F be the probability distribution concentrated at the point 0. Then $F_n \to_w F$ and then any subsequence of F_n (n=1,2,...) converges weakly to F. But F does not belong to the space ***Prob***[]0,1]].

The space ***Prob***[[0,1];finite-at] is not compact. Indeed, let F_n (n=1,2,...) be the probability distribution with mass $1/_n$ at each of the points $j/_n$ (j=1,2,...,n), and let F be the uniform probability distribution on [0,1]. Then $F_n \to_w F$ and then any subsequence of F_n (n=1,2,...) converges weakly to F. But F does not belong to the space ***Prob***[[0,1];finite-at].

Corollary 2 (Compactness Theorem for m-Unimodal Spaces)

Let $m\in[a,b]$ and let $f_1,\ldots,f_n$ be bounded functions on [a,b], continuous on some interval $[m-\varepsilon,m+\varepsilon]\cap[a,b]$, where $\varepsilon>0$. Then the following spaces (46) and (47) are compact:

$$\boldsymbol{Prob}[[a,b];\text{m-unim};\int f_1=\alpha_1,\ldots,\int f_n=\alpha_n], \quad (46)$$

$$\boldsymbol{Prob}[[a,b];\text{m-unim,k-rect};\int f_1=\alpha_1,\ldots,\int f_n=\alpha_n]. \quad (47)$$

If S is a compact subset of [a,b], the following spaces (48) and (49) are compact:

$$\boldsymbol{Prob}[[a,b];S,\text{m-unim};\int f_1=\alpha_1,\ldots,\int f_n=\alpha_n]. \quad (48)$$

$$\boldsymbol{Prob}[[a,b];S,\text{m-unim,k-rect};\int f_1=\alpha_1,\ldots,\int f_n=\alpha_n] \quad (49)$$

Proof
The continuity assumption (39) is satisfied by next Theorem 5.a. (no circularity is involved). Let f be bounded on the interval [a,b] and continuous on the interval $[m-\varepsilon,m+\varepsilon]\cap[a,b]$. By the last relation (22), $f^{\bullet}$ is continuous at any point $x\neq m$ in [a,b]. We prove that f is left-continuous at the point m if $a<m$. Let $a<m-\varepsilon<\theta<m$. By the mean value Theorem and the last relation (22), some point $\xi_\theta\in]\theta,m[$ exists such that $f^{\bullet}(\theta)=f(\xi_\theta)$. Then, by the continuity of f at the point m, $\lim_{\theta\uparrow m} f^{\bullet}(\theta)=\lim_{\theta\uparrow m} f(\xi_\theta)=f(m)=f^{\bullet}(m)$. In the same way, $f^{\bullet}$ is right-continuous at the point m if $m<b$. Hence, $f^{\bullet}$ is continuous at m. This conclusion is valid for any function $f_j^{\bullet}(j=1,\ldots,n)$ •

We consider the space

$$\textbf{\textit{Mixt}}[R_{m\theta}(\theta\in\mathbf{R})] = \textbf{\textit{Prob}}[\mathbf{R};\text{m-unim}]. \tag{50}$$

Let U be a probability distribution on **R** and let φ be the density of the m-unimodal probability distribution $F_U\equiv R_{mU}$ on the set $]-\infty,m[\cup]m,\infty[$, Then, by Ch.1.(39),

$$\varphi(x):=\int_{]-\infty,x]}1/(m-\theta)\,dU(\theta)\quad(x<m),$$
$$\varphi(x):=\int_{[x,\infty[}1/(\theta-m)\,dU(\theta)\quad(m<x). \tag{51}$$

Theorem 5

a. **Let $U,U_n\in$ *Prob*[[a,b]] (n=1,2,...) be such that $U_n\to_w U$ as $n\uparrow\infty$. Then**

$$F_n := R_{mU_n} \to_w R_{mU}\ \text{ as } n\uparrow\infty. \tag{52}$$

b. **Let the sequence $F_n\in$ *Prob*[[a,b];m-unim] (n=1,2,...) be such that**

$$F_n\to_w F\in \textbf{\textit{Distr}}[\mathbf{R}]\ \text{ as } n\uparrow\infty. \tag{53}$$

Then

$$F\in\textbf{\textit{Prob}}[[a,b];\text{m-unim}]. \tag{54}$$

Proof
Let φ_n be the density of F_n on the set $]a,m[\cup[m,b[$. By the first relation (51),

$$\varphi_n(x) = \int_{[a,x]} 1/(m-\theta)\, dU_n(\theta)\quad(a\leq x<m).$$

Let x be a continuity point of U. By Helly-Bray (case of a bounded integration domain)

$$\varphi(x) := \lim_{n\uparrow\infty} \varphi_n(x) = \int_{[a,x]} 1/(m-\theta)\, dU(\theta) \quad (a\leq x<m)$$

Then φ (defined arbitrarily at the discontinuity points of U) is the density of R_{mU} on]a,m[. By dominated convergence,

$$F_n([a,x]) = \int_{[a,x]} \varphi_n(y)dy \rightarrow \int_{[a,x]} \varphi(y)dy = R_{mU}([a,x]) \; (x<m).$$

Then $$F_n([x,b]) = \int_{[x,b]} \varphi_n(y)dy \rightarrow \int_{[x,b]} \varphi(y)dy = R_{mU}([x,b]) \; (m<x)$$

by the same argument. These relations imply (52).

b. F_n can be expressed as $F_n := R_{mU_n}$ for some distribution U_n in the space ***Prob***[[a,b]]. By Th.4.Cor.1, (with no integral constraint), ***Prob***[[a,b]] is compact. Some subsequence $U_{n(\nu)}$ (ν=1,2,...) converges weakly to a distribution U in the space. Then $F_{n(\nu)} \rightarrow R_{mU} \in$ ***Prob***[[a,b];m-unim] by a. By (53), $F_{n(\nu)} \rightarrow_w F$. Hence $F=R_{mU}$. This proves (54) •

2.3.4. Extremal Point Theorems

Extremal points of pure spaces

Let S be a subset of **R** with strictly more than n points. We say that the functions $f_0,f_1,...,f_n$ are **independent on S**, if the determinant with elements $f_j(a_i)$ (i,j=0,1,...n) is strictly positive for all points $a_0<a_1<...<a_n$ in S or strictly negative for all points $a_0<a_1<...<a_n$ in S.

For instance, by the properties of Vandermonde determinants, the functions $1,x,x^2,...,x^n$ are independent on any set S with strictly more than n points.

Theorem 6 (Extremal Point Theorem for Pure Spaces)

The set of extremal points of the space

$$\textbf{\textit{Prob}}[S;\textstyle\int f_1=\alpha_1,...,\int f_n=\alpha_n] \tag{55}$$

is a subset of the set

$$\textbf{\textit{Prob}}[S;n+1\text{-at};\textstyle\int f_1=\alpha_1,...,\int f_n=\alpha_n]. \tag{56}$$

If S has strictly more than n points and if the functions $f_0 \equiv 1, f_1, \ldots, f_n$ are independent on S, then the set of extremal points of the space (55) is the set (56).

This is also true, with n=0, if the space (55) has no integral constraints.

Proof
Let F be a point in (55), but not in (56). We prove that F is not an extremal point of the space (55).

R can be partitioned in n+2 successive intervals I,J,...,K bearing a strictly positive F-mass, because F is not n+1-atomic:

$$F(I) > 0\,,\ F(J) > 0\,, \ldots, F(K) > 0. \tag{57}$$

The integral conditions on F, completed by the relation $F(\mathbf{R})=1$, are

$$\int_I f_j\, dF + \int_J f_j dF + \ldots + \int_K f_j dF = \alpha_j \ (j=0,1,\ldots,n), \tag{58}$$

where $\alpha_0 := 1$. The linear homogeneous system

$$x\int_I f_j\, dF + y\int_J f_j dF + \ldots + z\int_K f_j dF = 0 \ (j=0,1,\ldots,n) \tag{59}$$

has n+2 unknown quantities x, y, ..., z and only n+1 equations. It has a solution (x,y,...,z) with at least one number x, y, ... , z different from 0. Multiplying this solution by a small strictly positive scalar, we may assume that $|x|<1$, $|y|<1$,..., $|z|<1$.

Let G be the distribution obtained from F by the multiplication of all F-masses in I by $(1-x)$, all F-masses in J by $(1-y)$,..., all F-masses in K by $(1-z)$. From (58) and (59) results that G is a probability distribution on **R**, satisfying the integral constraints. Then the distribution G belongs to the space (55), because it is concentrated on S. By (57), $G \neq F$.

Let H be the distribution obtained from F by multiplication of all F-masses in I by $(1+x)$, all F-masses in J by $(1+y)$,..., all F-masses in K by $(1+z)$. From (58) and (59) results that H is a probability distribution on **R**, satisfying the integral constraints. Then the distribution H belongs to the space (55), because it is concentrated on S. By (57), $H \neq F$.

But $F=1/_2G+1/_2H$, and this proves that F is not an extremal point of (55).

We now assume that S has strictly more than n points and that the functions $f_0,f_1,\ldots,f_n$ are independent on S. We prove that each point F in the set (56) is an extremal point of the space (55). Let F be the distribution with masses $p_0,p_1,\ldots,p_n$ at the different points $a_0,a_1,\ldots,a_n$ resp. Then the integral conditions, completed by the relation $p_0+p_1+\ldots+p_n=1$ are

$$p_0f_j(a_0) + p_1f_j(a_1) + \ldots + p_nf_j(a_n) = \alpha_j \quad (j=0,1,\ldots,n), \tag{60}$$

where $\alpha_0:=1$. In order to prove that F is an extremal point of the space (55), let

$$F = pG+qH \; ; \; G,H\in(55) \; ; \; p,q>0 \; ; \; p+q=1. \tag{61}$$

From the relations (61) results that G and H must be concentrated on the set $\{a_0,a_1,\ldots,a_n\}$. Let $q_0,q_1,\ldots,q_n$ be the G-masses at the points $a_0,a_1,\ldots,a_n$ resp. and let $r_0,r_1,\ldots,r_n$ be the H-masses at the points $a_0,a_1,\ldots,a_n$ resp. The integral conditions for G and H are

$$q_0f_j(a_0) + q_1f_j(a_1) + \ldots + q_nf_j(a_n) = \alpha_j \quad (j=0,1,\ldots,n), \tag{62}$$

$$r_0f_j(a_0) + r_1f_j(a_1) + \ldots + r_nf_j(a_n) = \alpha_j \quad (j=0,1,\ldots,n). \tag{63}$$

(60) can be regarded as a linear system of n+1 equations with n+1 unknown quantities $p_0,p_1,\ldots,p_n$. By the independence of the functions $f_0,f_1,\ldots,f_n$, it has a unique solution $(p_0,p_1,\ldots,p_n)$. This remark applies to the systems (62) and (63). Hence $p_i=q_i=r_i$ $(i=0,1,\ldots,n)$. Then F=G=H •

Extremal points of spaces of mixtures

Theorem 7 (General Extremal Point Theorem)

We consider the regular space of mixtures *Mixt*[$F_\theta(\theta\in S)$]. The point F_U is an extremal point of the space

$$\textit{Mixt}[F_\theta(\theta\in S);\textstyle\int f_1=\alpha_1,\ldots,\int f_n=\alpha_n] \tag{64}$$

iff U is an extremal point of the associated space

$$\textit{Prob}[S;\textstyle\int f_1^\bullet=\alpha_1,\ldots,\int f_n^\bullet=\alpha_n]. \tag{65}$$

Proof

a. We assume that U is an extremal point of the space (65), and we prove that F_U is an extremal point of the space (64). Let

$$F_U = pG+qH \; ; \; G,H\in(64) \; ; \; p,q>0 \; ; \; p+q=1.$$

By Theorem 1, V,W∈(65) exist, such that $G=F_V$, $H=F_W$. Then

$$F_U = pF_V+qF_W = F_{pV+qW},$$

and then U=pV+qW by the regularity assumption. Then V=W because U is an extremal point of the space (65). Then $G=F_V=F_W=H$. This proves that F_U is an extremal point of the space (64).

b. We assume that U∈(65) and that U is not an extremal point of the space (65). We prove that F_U is not an extremal point of the space (64). The distribution U is expressible as U=pV+qW with

$$V,W\in(65) \; ; \; V\neq W \; ; \; p,q>0 \; ; \; p+q=1.$$

Then $F_U=pF_V+qF_W$ and $F_V\neq F_W$ by the regularity assumption. Hence, F_U is not an extremal point of the space (64) •

Extremal points of m-unimodal spaces

Lemma

Let S be a set in R with strictly more than n points, and let the functions $f_0,f_1,\dots,f_n$ be independent on S. Then the determinant with elements $\int f_j dR_{mc_i}$ (i,j=0,1,...,n) is different from zero for all m∈S and all n+1 different points $c_0,c_1,\dots,c_n\in S$.

Proof

Let the determinant with elements $f_j(c_i)$ (i,j=0,1,...,n) be strictly positive if $c_0<c_1<\dots<c_n$ are points in S. Let a<b<m<c be points in the interval S and let n=3. We verify that the determinant

$$\det\left[\int f_j dR_{ma} \, , \int f_j dR_{mb} \, , \int f_j dR_{mm} \, , \int f_j dR_{mc}\right]_{j=0,1,2,3} \quad (66)$$

is strictly positive. The general argument is clear from that particular example. Determinant (66) is the product of a strictly positive factor by the determinant

$$\det[\int_{a<x<m} f_j(x)dx \, , \int_{b<x<m} f_j(x)dx \, , f_j(m) \, , \int_{m<x<c} f_j(x)dx]_{j=0,1,2,3}$$

$$= \det[\int_{a<x<b} f_j(x)dx + \int_{b<x<m} f(x)dx \, , \int_{b<x<m} f_j(x)dx \, , f_j(m) \, , \int_{m<x<c} f_j(x)dx]_{j=0,1,2,3}.$$

The latter determinant equals

$$\det[\int_{a<x<b} f_j(x)dx \, , \int_{b<y<m} f_j(y)dy \, , f_j(m) \, , \int_{m<z<c} f_j(z)dz]_{j=0,1,2,3}$$

$$= \int_{a<x<b}\int_{b<y<m}\int_{m<z<c} \det[f_j(x) \, , f_j(y) \, , f_j(m) \, , f_j(z)]_{j=0,1,2,3} \, dxdydz > 0 \quad \bullet$$

We observe that Theorem 6 is valid with the following larger definition of independent functions on a set S with strictly more than n points: The functions $f_0,\ldots f_n$ are independent on S if the determinant with elements $f_j(a_i)$ $(i,j=0,1,\ldots,n)$ is different from 0 for any different points $a_0,\ldots,a_n \in S$. Then next Theorem 8 results from the Lemma and from the Theorems 6 and 7.

Theorem 8 (Extremal Point Theorem for m-Unimodal Spaces)

Let $I \subseteq R$ be an interval, m a point of I, S a subset of I. We consider the spaces

$$\textbf{\textit{Prob}}[\mathbf{I;m\text{-}unim;}\int \mathbf{f_1=\alpha_1,\ldots,}\int \mathbf{f_n=\alpha_n}], \tag{67}$$

$$\textbf{\textit{Prob}}[\mathbf{I;S,m\text{-}unim;}\int \mathbf{f_1=\alpha_1,\ldots,}\int \mathbf{f_n=\alpha_n}] \tag{68}$$

and the sets

$$\textbf{\textit{Prob}}[\mathbf{I;m\text{-}unim,n+1\text{-}rect;}\int \mathbf{f_1=\alpha_1,\ldots,}\int \mathbf{f_n=\alpha_n}], \tag{69}$$

$$\textbf{\textit{Prob}}[\mathbf{I;S,m\text{-}unim,n+1\text{-}rect;}\int \mathbf{f_1=\alpha_1,\ldots,}\int \mathbf{f_n=\alpha_n}]. \tag{70}$$

The set of extremal points of the space (67) is a subset of (69). The set of extremal points of the space (68) is a subset of (70). If the functions $f_0 \equiv 1, f_1, \ldots, f_n$ are independent on I, then the set of extremal points of the space (67) equals the set (69). If moreover S has strictly more than n points, then the set of extremal points of the space (68) equals the set (70).

This is also true, for n=0, if no integral constraints do occur in the spaces.

2.4. Krein-Milman Spaces

2.4.1. Definition

Let ***Space*** be a subset of ***Prob*****[R]**. We say that ***Space*** is a **Krein-Milman space** if ***Space*** is convex and compact, and if it is the closed convex hull of the set ***Ext*** of its extremal points:

$$\textit{Space} = \mathbf{Co}^{-}\textit{Ext}. \quad (71)$$

2.4.2. Basic Theorems

The following less elementary Krein-Milman Theorem, is proved in App.E (see Th.E16 and the *Remark* following the proof of that Theorem).

In $\mathbf{R}^n$ it is intuitively obvious that any point of a compact convex set (closed circle, closed convex polygon, ... in $\mathbf{R}^2$; closed ball, closed convex polyhedron, ... in $\mathbf{R}^3$) can be expressed as a convex combination of the extremal points of that set. The following Krein-Milman Theorem is the version of this property valid in the case of convex compact sets of probability distributions.

Theorem 9 (Krein-Milman on *Prob*[[a,b]])

Any compact convex subspace of *Prob*[[a,b]] is a Krein-Milman space •

Theorem 10

Let *Space* be a Krein-Milman space with a finite set *Ext* of extremal points. Then any point of *Space* is a convex combination of points of *Ext*:

$$\textit{Space} = \mathbf{Co}\ \textit{Ext}. \quad (72)$$

Proof

Let H_1, ..., H_k be the points of ***Ext***. In order to prove the $\subseteq$ part of (72), let $G \in \textit{Space}$. By (71) a sequence G_ν (ν=1,2,...) of convex combinations

$$G_\nu = \textstyle\sum_{1 \le i \le k} p_{\nu i} H_i$$

exists such that

$$G_\nu \to_w G \text{ as } \nu \uparrow \infty. \quad (73)$$

A subsequence $\nu(n)$ (n=1,2,...) of the sequence ν=1,2,..., exists such that

$$p_{\nu(n),i} \to p_i \in [0,1] \text{ as } n\uparrow\infty \quad (i=1,\ldots,n).$$

Then $\sum p_i=1$ and

$$G_0 := \sum_{0\leq i\leq k} p_i H_i$$

is a convex combination of the extremal points such that $G_{\nu(n)} \to_w G_0$ as $n\uparrow\infty$. Then $G=G_0$ by (73). Hence $G=G_0 \in \text{Co}$ ***Ext***.

The $\supseteq$ part of (72) holds because ***Ext***$\subseteq$***Space*** and because ***Space*** is convex •

2.4.3. Examples of Krein-Milman Spaces

The following spaces (74), (75) and (76) are Krein-Milman spaces by Theorem 9 and by the Theorems of the section 2.3.

a.

$$\textbf{\textit{Mixt}}[F_\theta(\theta\in S);\textstyle\int f_1=\alpha_1,\ldots,\int f_n=\alpha_n] \tag{74}$$

if S is compact, $f_j^\bullet$ (j=1,...,n) continuous on S and if F_U is a continuous functional of $U\in$***Prob***[S].

b.

$$\textbf{\textit{Prob}}[S;\textstyle\int f_1=\alpha_1,\ldots,\int f_n=\alpha_n] \tag{75}$$

if S is compact and f_j (j=1,...,n) continuous on S. .

c.

$$\textbf{\textit{Prob}}[[a,b];S,\text{m-unim};\textstyle\int f_1=\alpha_1,\ldots,\int f_n=\alpha_n] \tag{76}$$

if S is a closed subset of [a,b] and if f_j (j=1,...,n) is bounded on [a,b] and continuous on some interval $[m-\varepsilon,m+\varepsilon]\cap[a,b]$.

Chapter 3

Moment Spaces

3.1. General Pure Moment Spaces

3.1.1. Definition and Notation of the Spaces

In the notations of the foregoing Chapter 2, the conditions

$$\int f_1 = \mu_1 \, , \; \dots \, , \; \int f_n = \mu_n, \tag{1}$$

where $f_j(x) := x^j$ ($j=1,\dots,n$; $x \in \mathbf{R}$) are called **moment constraints**. Then

$$\boldsymbol{Prob}[S;\mu_1,\dots,\mu_n] \equiv \boldsymbol{Prob}[S;\int f_1=\mu_1,\dots,\int f_n=\mu_n] \tag{2}$$

and the same simplified notation is used when more constraints are involved.

In the following chapters, the **pure moment space** $\boldsymbol{Prob}[S;\mu_1,\dots,\mu_n]$ is considered for bounded subsets S of **R** only.

The **number** μ_j is any number in **R**. The **moment functional** $\mu_j(\cdot)$ is the functional defined on $\boldsymbol{Prob}[S]$ (S bounded set in **R**) with values

$$\mu_j(F) := \int_S x^j dF(x) \;\; (F \in \boldsymbol{Prob}[S]). \tag{3}$$

In any case, the meaning of μ_j, number or functional, is evident from the context.

The space $\boldsymbol{Prob}[S;\mu_1,\dots,\mu_n]$ can be considered for any fixed **parameters** $\mu_1, \dots, \mu_n \in \mathbf{R}$. It can also be considered as a function of $(\mu_1,\dots,\mu_n) \in \mathbf{R}^n$. In the latter case, **the effective domain of the parameters** is the set of points $(\mu_1,\dots,\mu_n)$ for which $\boldsymbol{Prob}[S;\mu_1,\dots,\mu_n] \neq \emptyset$, i.e. the set of points $(\mu_1,\dots,\mu_n)$ for which the space exists. In several statements it is implicitly assumed that $(\mu_1,\dots,\mu_1)$ belongs to the effective domain of the parameters.

We consider ***Prob***[S] as a pure moment space with no moment constraints, i.e. as the particular space ***Prob***[S;μ_1,...,μ_n] with n=0. This is convenient, because some statements remain valid for n=0. An example is furnished by next Theorem 1.a,b.

3.1.2. Properties of Pure Moment Spaces

Theorem 1

Let S be a compact interval or a finite set.

a. The space *Prob*[S;μ_1,...,μ_n] is convex and compact.

b. The extremal points of the space *Prob*[S;μ_1,...,μ_n] are its n+1-atomic distributions. This set of extremal points is compact.

c. The space *Prob*[S;μ_1,...,μ_n] exists iff

$$(\mu_1,...,\mu_n) \in \mathrm{Co}\{(\theta,\theta^2,...,\theta^n) \,/\, \theta \in S\}.$$

Proof

By the results of Ch.2.3 applied to the functions $f_j(x):=x^j$ (j=1,...,n) •

3.1.3. Continuous and Discrete Cases

In the practical optimization problems on ***Prob***[S,μ_1,...μ_n], the set S is a compact interval [a,b]$\subseteq$**R**. We call this the ***continuous case***. Some optimization problems can be solved **analytically** in the continuous case.

Many more problems can be solved **numerically** in the ***discrete case***, defined hereafter.

We consider **intervals of integers**, defined for a,b$\in$**R**, a$\leq$b, by

$$[a,b]_{int} := [a,b]\cap\mathbf{N} \ , \ [a,b[_{int} := [a,b[\cap\mathbf{N},$$

$$]a,b]_{int} :=]a,b]\cap\mathbf{N} \ , \ ]a,b[_{int} :=]a,b[\cap\mathbf{N}.$$

In the ***discrete case***, we mostly assume that S is an interval of integers: S= $[i_0,n_0]_{int}$, where i_0 and n_0 are negative or positive integers.

The ***discrete case*** results from a **discretization** of the ***continuous case***, combined with the introduction of a **new unit of money**. (In most actuarial problems, the involved distributions are distributions of money amounts. Of course, if distributions of other quantities are treated, the corresponding new units must be considered).

Let $\delta>0$ be a fixed small number. In the discretization process, any amount x, positive or not, is replaced by an approximation $i\delta$ ($i\in\mathbf{N}$). The extremities a, b of the interval [a,b] are approximated by $i_0\delta$, $n_0\delta$ resp. Then any distribution concentrated on the interval [a,b] is approximated by a distribution concentrated on the set

$$\{i_0\delta,(i_0+1)\delta,\ldots,n_0\delta\}. \tag{4}$$

The new unit of money is such that the amounts ..., -2δ, $-\delta$, 0, δ, 2δ, ... in the current unit, become the amounts ..., −2, −1, 0, 1, 2, ... when expressed in the new unit. In this way, any distribution concentrated on the set (4) becomes a distribution concentrated on the set $[i_0,n_0]_{int}$. The moment μ_j of any distribution concentrated on the set (4), becomes the moment μ_j/δ^j of the corresponding distribution concentrated on the set $[i_0,n_0]_{int}$.

The solution of the ***discrete problem*** on the space

$$\textbf{\textit{Prob}}[[i_0,n_0]_{int};\mu_1/\delta,\mu_2/\delta^2,\ldots,\mu_n/\delta^n] \tag{5}$$

furnishes an approximation of the initial ***continuous problem*** on the space

$$\textbf{\textit{Prob}}[[a,b];\mu_1,\ldots,\mu_n]. \tag{6}$$

The smaller δ, the better the approximation. The solution of the discrete problem furnishes asymptotically the exact solution of the initial continuous problem as $\delta\downarrow 0$.

If the space (6) exists, if $(\mu_1,\ldots,\mu_n)$ is not a frontier point of the effective domain of the parameters and if δ is small enough, then the space

$$\textbf{\textit{Prob}}[\{i_0\delta,(i_0+1)\delta,\ldots,n_0\delta\};\mu_1,\ldots,\mu_n] \tag{7}$$

exists. This is direct by Theorem 1.c, at least in the cases n=1,2,3 later considered. The space (5) exists iff the space (7) exists.

3.1.4. Existence Problem

The solution of the existence problem of pure moment spaces, results from Theorem 1.c, but that solution is not yet explicited. It is easy to calculate the effective domain

$$Co\{(\theta,\theta^2,...,\theta^n)/\theta\in S\}\subseteq\mathbf{R}^n,$$

in the elementary geometrical way, if n=1,2 or 3. This is done in the next section 3.2. Our visualizations are not precise enough in $\mathbf{R}^n$ (n≥4), and then the geometrical method is useless. The existence problem of the space

$$\boldsymbol{Prob}[[a,b];\mu_1,...,\mu_n]$$

is solved in full generality, by an algebraic method not based on Theorem 1.c, in the section 3.3.

Without loss of continuity, this section 3.3 can be omitted. It is rather exceptional that strictly more than 3 moment constraints are involved in the practical actuarial optimization problems of the type studied in this book.

3.1.5. Enumeration of Extremal Points

The numerical solution of some general optimization problems on the space $\boldsymbol{Prob}[[i_0,n_0]_{int};\mu_1,...,\mu_n]$ is based on a simple explicit enumeration, without omissions or repetitions, of the extremal points of that space. We assume that the set $[i_0,n_0]_{int}$ has n+1 points at least when this **enumeration problem** is considered. By Th.1.b, any extremal distribution of $\boldsymbol{Prob}[[i_0,n_0]_{int};\mu_1,...,\mu_n]$ is expressible as a convex combination

$$p_1A_{i_1} + ... + p_{n+1}A_{i_{n+1}}, \tag{8}$$

with

$$i_0 \leq i_1 < i_2 < ... < i_n < i_{n+1} \leq n_0. \tag{9}$$

Some coefficient p_i may be equal to 0. It is understood that i_1, ..., i_{n+1} are integers. Let $(i_1,...,i_{n+1})$ be a fixed n+1-tuple satisfying the relations (9). Then the coefficients p_1, ..., p_{n+1} in (8) result from the moment constraints

$$p_1i_1^j + p_2i_2^j + ... + p_{n+1}i_{n+1}^j = \mu_j \quad (j=0,1,...,n), \tag{10}$$

completed by the **probability constraint** $p_1+...+p_{n+1}=1$. The latter is the constraint corresponding to the value i=0 in (10), with $\mu_0:=1$. Indeed, the system (10) is a linear system of n+1 equations with n+1 unknown quantities $p_1,...,p_{n+1}$ and a Vandermonde determinant different from zero. It has a unique solution $p_1, ..., p_{n+1}$ (see App.D.D12). Then the distribution (8) is an extremal point of the space ***Prob***$[[i_0,n_0]_{int};\mu_1,...,\mu_n]$ iff $p_1,...,p_{n+1}\geq 0$.

This discussion shows that the number of extremal points is finite, because the number of n+1-tuples $(i_1,...,i_{n+1})$ satisfying the inequalities (9) is finite. It also suggests the following **enumeration method**:

For all integers $i_1, ..., i_{n+1}$ satisfying the constraints

$$i_1\in[i_0,n_0]_{int}\ ,\ i_2\in[i_1+1,n_0]_{int}\ ,\ i_3\in[i_2+1,n_0]_{int}\ ,\ ...\ ,\ i_{n+1}\in[i_n+1,n_0]_{int} \qquad (11)$$

the system (10) is solved and the conditions $p_1\geq 0$, $p_2\geq 0$,..., $p_{n+1}\geq 0$ are tested. Then the n+1-tuple $(i_1,...,i_{n+1})$ is retained iff these conditions are satisfied.

This method works in many cases, but it is not good enough when some non-linear optimization problems are considered. Better enumerations are furnished in the following section 3.2. They are based on assumptions such as "the first moment μ_1 is not an integer". The latter are convenient, because they simplify some computer programs. If they are not initially satisfied, the involved quantities may be modified by ε ($=10^{-10}$ say), without any impact on the results. Hence, such assumptions are not real restrictions.

3.1.6. Feasible n+1-tuples

We say that the n+1-tuple $(i_1,...,i_{n+1})$ of integers is **a feasible n+1-tuple of the space *Prob***$[[i_0,n_0]_{int};\mu_1,...,\mu_n]$ if it satisfies the inequalities (9) and if the corresponding solution of the system (10) satisfies the relations $p_1\geq 0,...,p_n\geq 0$. Hence, the feasible n+1-tuples are exactly those furnishing the extremal points (8). The enumeration problem of the extremal points is equivalent to the enumeration problem of the feasible n+1-tuples.

More generally, the n+1-tuple $(\theta_1,...,\theta_{n+1})$ of real numbers is a **feasible n+1-tuple of the space *Prob***$[S;\mu_1,...,\mu_n]$ if

$$\theta_1,...,\theta_{n+1}\in S\ ;\ \theta_1<\theta_2<...<\theta_{n+1}\ ;\ p_1,...,p_{n+1}\geq 0, \qquad (12)$$

where $p_1, ..., p_{n+1}$ is the unique solution of the system

$$p_1\theta_1^{\,j} + p_2\theta_2^{\,j} + \ldots + p_{n+1}\theta_{n+1}^{\,j} = \mu_j \quad (j=0,1,\ldots,n). \tag{13}$$

Then, and only then, the distribution

$$p_1 A_{\theta_1} + \ldots + p_{n+1} A_{\theta_{n+1}} \tag{14}$$

is an extremal point of the space ***Prob***$[S;\mu_1,\ldots,\mu_n]$.

3.1.7. Central Moments Notation

a. Let X be a bounded random variable with moments $\mu_1 \equiv \mu$, μ_2, μ_3,... We denote by $\mu^\circ_1=0$, μ°_2, μ°_3... the moments of the centered random variable $X^\circ := X-\mu$. We define $\mu_0:=1$, $\mu^\circ_0:=1$.

By the binomial Theorem

$$(X^\circ)^j = (X-\mu)^j = \sum\nolimits_{0\le i\le j} j^{[i]}/i!(-\mu)^i X^{j-i} \quad (j=0,1,2,\ldots), \tag{15}$$

where we use factorial exponents. Taking expectations in (15), we obtain

$$\mu^\circ_j = \sum\nolimits_{0\le i\le j} j^{[i]}/i!(-\mu)^i \mu_{j-i} \quad (j=0,1,2,\ldots). \tag{16}$$

In the same way,

$$X^j = (X^\circ+\mu)^j = \sum\nolimits_{0\le i\le j} j^{[i]}/i!\,\mu^i (X^\circ)^{j-i} \quad (j=0,1,2,\ldots), \tag{17}$$

$$\mu_j = \sum\nolimits_{0\le i\le j} j^{[i]}/i!\,\mu^i \mu^\circ_{j-i} \quad (j=0,1,2,\ldots). \tag{18}$$

b. Now let us drop the assumption that $\mu_1,\mu_2,\ldots$ are the moments of some random variable. For any sequence $\mu_0:=1,\mu_1,\mu_2,\ldots$, we define the sequence $\mu^\circ_0,\mu^\circ_1,\mu^\circ_2,\ldots$ by the relations (16). Then $\mu^\circ_0=1$ and it is not difficult to verify that the relations (18) still hold.

We use the following special symbols:

$$\sigma^2 := \mu^\circ_2\ ,\ \rho^3 := \mu^\circ_3\ ,\ \alpha^4 := \mu^\circ_4\ ,\ \beta^5 := \mu^\circ_5\ ,\ \gamma^6 := \mu^\circ_6. \tag{19}$$

Some relations are simpler when the parameters $\mu,\sigma^2,\rho^3,\ldots$ are used, instead of the original parameters $\mu_1,\mu_2,\mu_3,\ldots$

By (16) and (18) for j=1,2,3,4

$$\mu=\mu_1\ ,\ \sigma^2=\mu_2-\mu_1^2\ ,\ \rho^3=\mu_3-3\mu_1\mu_2+2\mu_1^3\ ,\ \alpha^4=\mu_4-4\mu_1\mu_3+6\mu_1^2\mu_2-3\mu_1^3, \quad (20)$$

$$\mu_1=\mu\ ,\ \mu_2=\sigma^2+\mu^2\ ,\ \mu_3=\rho^3+3\mu\sigma^2+\mu^3\ ,\ \mu_4=\alpha^4+4\mu\rho^3+6\mu^2\sigma^2+\mu^4. \quad (21)$$

When the existence problem of some space is considered, then the parameters μ_j can have any value, and then the parameters $\sigma^2,\alpha^4,...$ can be strictly negative. In most cases, the considered spaces are supposed to exist, and then $\sigma^2,\alpha^4... \geq 0$.

3.2. Particular Pure Moment Spaces

3.2.1. One Moment Constraint

Continuous case

By Theorem 1.c, the space ***Prob***$[[a,b];\mu_1]$ exists iff $\mu_1\in[a,b]$. Indeed,

$$\mathrm{Co}\{\theta/\theta\in[a,b]\} = [a,b].$$

Discrete case

Let $a_1<a_2<...<a_k$. By Theorem 1.c, ***Prob***$[\{a_1,...,a_k\};\mu_1]$ exists iff $\mu_1\in[a_1,a_k]$. Indeed

$$\mathrm{Co}\{\theta/\theta\in\{a_1,...,a_k\}\} = \mathrm{Co}\{a_1,...,a_k\} = [a_1,a_k].$$

The feasible couples of the space ***Prob***$[[i_0,n_0]_{int};\mu_1]$ are the couples (i,j) such that

$$i_0 \leq i < j \leq n_0\ ,\ p \geq 0\ ,\ q \geq 0,$$

where (p,q) is the solution of the system

$$p+q=1\ ,\ pi+qj=\mu. \quad (22)$$

This solution is

$$p = (j-\mu)/(j-i)\ ,\ q = (\mu-i)/(j-i). \quad (23)$$

Hence, (i,j) is a feasible couple of the space $\textit{\textbf{Prob}}[[i_0,n_0]_{int};\mu_1]$ iff

$$i_0 \leq i < j \leq n_0 \ , \ i \leq \mu \leq j.$$

3.2.2. Two Moment Constraints

Continuous case

In $\mathbf{R}^2=\{(x,y)\}$, we denote by Par[a,b] the piece of parabola with equation

$$y = x^2 \ (a \leq x \leq b).$$

Theorem 2

The space $\textit{\textbf{Prob}}[[a,b];\mu_1,\mu_2]$ exists iff one of the following equivalent conditions a, b, c is satisfied.

a. **The point (μ_1,μ_2) belongs to the convex set delimited by Par[a,b] and by the line segment connecting the end points of Par[a,b].**

b.

$$\mathbf{a \leq \mu_1 \leq b \ , \ \mu_1^2 \leq \mu_2 \leq \mu_1(a+b)-ab,} \tag{24}$$

c.

$$\mathbf{a \leq \mu_1 \leq b \ , \ 0 \leq \sigma^2 \leq (b-\mu_1)(\mu_1-a).} \tag{25}$$

Proof

a. By Theorem 1.c, the space exists iff

$$(\mu_1,\mu_2) \in \mathrm{Co}\{(\theta,\theta^2)/\theta\in[a,b]\} = \mathrm{Co}\ \mathrm{Par}[a,b].$$

The convex hull of Par[a,b] is the set delimited by Par[a,b] and by the straight line through the extremities (a,a^2) and (b,b^2) of Par[a,b]. (**Fig.1**).

b. The equation of the straight line through the points (a,a^2), (b,b^2) is

$$y = (a+b)x - ab. \tag{26}$$

The equation of the half plane below the line is

$$y \leq (a+b)x - ab. \tag{27}$$

c. The equivalence of the relations (24) and (25) results from the relations (20) or (21) •

In the geometrical representations in $\mathbf{R}^2$, we do not necessarily use units of the same length on the horizontal x-axis and on the vertical y-axis.

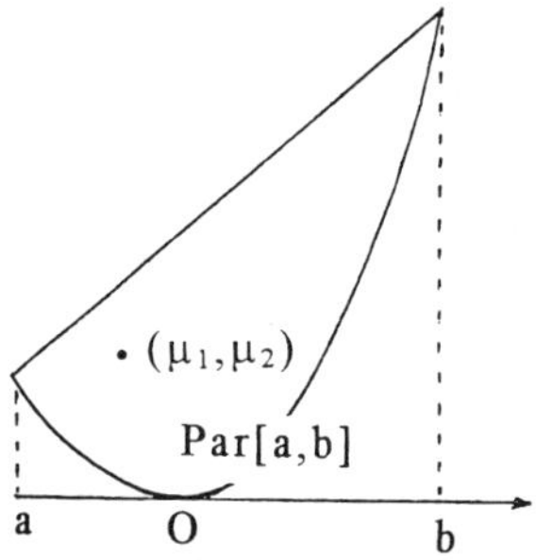

Fig.3. Effective domain of *Prob*[[a,b];μ₁,μ₂]

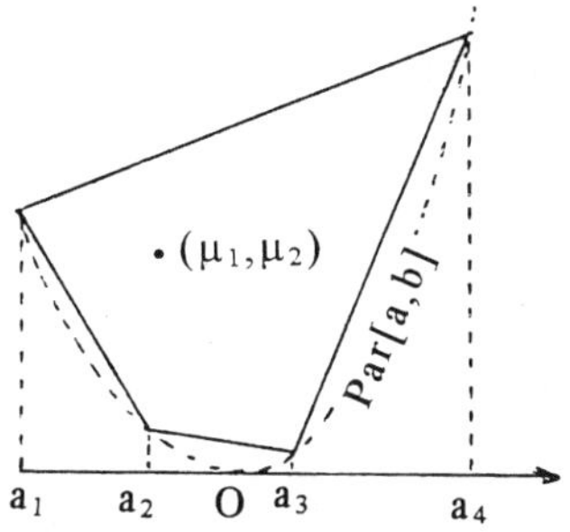

Fig.4. Effective domain of *Prob*[{a₁,a₂,a₃,a₄};μ₁,μ₂]

Discrete case

Theorem 3

The space *Prob*[$\{a_1,...,a_k\};\mu_1,\mu_2$], where $a_1<a_2<...<a_n$, exists iff one of the following equivalent conditions a, b, c is satisfied.

a. **The point (μ_1,μ_2) belongs to the convex polygon with vertices $(a_1,a_1^2),...,(a_k,a_k^2)$ on Par$[a_1,a_k]$.**

b.

$$\begin{aligned} &\mu_2 \le (a_1+a_n)\mu_1 - a_1a_n, \\ &(a_i+a_{i+1})\mu_1 - a_ia_{i+1} \le \mu_2 \quad (i=1,...,k-1). \end{aligned} \tag{28}$$

c.

$$\begin{aligned} &\sigma^2 \le (a_k-\mu)(\mu-a_1) \\ &(a_{i+1}-\mu)(\mu-a_i) \le \sigma^2 \quad (i=1,...,k-1). \end{aligned} \tag{29}$$

Proof

a. By Theorem 3.c, the space exists iff (μ_1,μ_2) belongs to the convex hull of the set

$$\{(\theta,\theta^2)/\theta\in\{a_1,...,a_k\}\} = \{(a_1,a_1^2),...,(a_k,a_k^2)\}.$$

b. The convex polygon of a, is the intersection of the following half-planes delimited by a straight line:

– The half-plane below the line through the points (a_1,a_1^2), (a_k,a_k^2),
– The half-plane above the line through the points (a_1,a_1^2),(a_2,a_2^2),
– The half-plane above the line through the points (a_2,a_2^2),(a_3,a_3^2),

... ...

– The half-plane above the line through the points (a_{k-1},a_{k-1}^2),(a_k,a_k^2).

These lines have an equation such as (26).

b. The equivalence of (28) and (29) results from (20) or (21) •

Let (μ_1,μ_2) be an interior point of the effective domain of $\boldsymbol{Prob}[[a,b];\mu_1,\mu_2]$, defined by Theorem 2.a. Let us consider a partition of the interval [a,b] by k equidistant points

$$a_1:= a < a_2 < \ldots < a_{k-1} < a_k:= b.$$

Then (μ_1,μ_2) belongs to the effective domain of $\boldsymbol{Prob}[\{a_1,\ldots,a_k\};\mu_1,\mu_2]$ if k is large enough. In other words, if the continuous space $\boldsymbol{Prob}[[a,b];\mu_1,\mu_2]$ exists, if (μ_1,μ_2) is an interior point of its effective domain and if k is large enough, then the discrete space $\boldsymbol{Prob}[\{a_1,\ldots,a_k\};\mu_1,\mu_2]$ exists. This justifies the last remark of section 3.1.3 in case n=2.

On the contrary, it happens that the dicrete space $\boldsymbol{Prob}[\{a_1,\ldots,a_k\};\mu_1,\mu_2]$ never exists if (μ_1,μ_2) is a frontier point of the effective domain of the continuous space.

The frontier points of the effective domain of a space, may cause trouble in the numerical and in the analytical solution of the optimization problems on that space. Of course, the frontier cases can be discarded in practice.

We now indicate an enumeration method of the feasible triples of the space $\boldsymbol{Prob}[[i_0,n_0]_{int};\mu_1,\mu_2]$.

Assumption: μ is not an integer and

$$\varphi_{\mu\sigma}(i) := \mu + \sigma^2/(\mu-i) \quad (i=i_0,i_0+1,\ldots,i_n) \tag{30}$$

is not an integer.

The feasible triples of space $\boldsymbol{Prob}[[i_0,n_0]_{int};\mu_1,\mu_2]$ are the triples (i,j,k) satisfying the relations

$$i_0 \le i < j < k \le n_0 \ , \ p \ge 0 \ , \ q \ge 0 \ , \ r \ge 0, \tag{31}$$

where (p,q,r) is the unique solution of the linear system

$$p+q+r = 1 \ , \ pi+qj+rk = \mu_1 \ , \ pi^2+qj^2+rk^2 = \mu_2. \tag{32}$$

This solution is

$$p = [\mu_2-(j+k)\mu_1+jk]/(i-j)(i-k), \tag{33}$$

$$q = [\mu_2-(k+i)\mu_1+ki]/(j-k)(j-i), \tag{33}$$

$$r = [\mu_2-(i+j)\mu_1+ij]/(k-i)(k-j). \tag{33}$$

Hence, the feasible triples are those satisfying the relations

$$i_0 \le i < j < k \le n_0 \tag{34}$$

and the relations

$$\mu_2 \le (i+k)\mu_1 - ik \ , \ \mu_2 \ge (i+j)\mu_1 - ij \ , \ \mu_2 \ge (j+k)\mu_1 - jk. \tag{35}$$

The relations (35) express that the point (μ_1,μ_2) belongs to the triangle with vertices (i,i^2), (j,j^2), (k,k^2).

By projection on the horizontal axis of $\mathbf{R}^2$, they imply the relations

$$i < \mu_1 < k, \tag{36}$$

where the strict inequalities result from the *Assumption*.

It is convenient to replace the couple (μ_1,μ_2) by the couple (μ,σ^2). Then the relations (35) become

$$\sigma^2 \le (k-\mu)(\mu-i) \ , \ \sigma^2 \ge (j-\mu)(\mu-i) \ , \ \sigma^2 \ge (k-\mu)(\mu-j). \tag{37}$$

The first relation (37) remains valid if we replace k by n_0. Then it implies the relation

$$i \le \varphi_{\mu\sigma}(n_0). \tag{38$_1$}$$

By the relations (37),

$$\varphi_{\mu\sigma}(i) \le k, \tag{38$_2$}$$

$$j \leq \varphi_{\mu\sigma}(i), \tag{38$_3$}$$

$$\varphi_{\mu\sigma}(k) \leq j. \tag{38$_4$}$$

Theorem 4

Under the indicated *Assumption*, the feasible triples (i,j,k) of the space *Prob*$[[i_0,n_0]_{int};\mu_1,\mu_2]$, are those satisfying the relations

$$i \in [i_0\,,\, n_0 \wedge [\varphi_{\mu\sigma}(n_0)]]_{int}, \tag{39$_1$}$$

$$k \in [(i+1) \vee [\varphi_{\mu\sigma}(i)+1]\,,\, n_0]_{int}, \tag{39$_2$}$$

$$j \in [(i+1) \vee [\varphi_{\mu\sigma}(k)+1]\,,\, (k-1) \wedge [\varphi_{\mu\sigma}(i)]]_{int}. \tag{39$_3$}$$

Proof
The relations (34) and (35) are **equivalent** to the relations

$$[i_0 \leq i \leq n_0,\ (38_1)]\ ,\ [i+1 \leq k \leq n_0,\ (38_2)]\ ,\ [i+1 \leq j \leq k-1,\ (38_3),\ (38_4)].$$

Each set of relations in square brackets corresponds to one relation (39) •

We recall that [x] is the **integer part** of x, i.e. the integer number smaller than x, closest to x. The 4 inner square brackets, in the relations (39) are integer parts.

3.2.3. Three Moment Constraints

In $\mathbf{R}^3 = \{(x,y,z)\}$, we use the following notations,

Cub[a,b] (a<b) is the piece of cubical curve with parametric equations

$$x = \theta\ ,\ y = \theta^2\ ,\ z = \theta^3\ \ (a \leq \theta \leq b).$$

Line[a,b] ($a \leq b$) is the straight line segment with extremities (a,a^2,a^3), (b,b^2,b^3).

Tri[a,b,c] ($a \leq b \leq c$) is the triangle with vertices (a,a^2,a^3), (b,b^2,b^3), (c,c^3,c^3).

Plane[a,b,c] ($a<b<c$) is the plane containing the triangle Tri[a,b,c].

Tetra[a,b,c,d] ($a\leq b\leq c\leq d$) is the tetrahedron with vertices (a,a^2,a^3), (b,b^2,b^3), (c,c^2,c^3), (d,d^2,d^3).

We consider projections on the horizontal plane $\mathbf{R}^2 = \{(x,y)\}$.

The projection of Cub[a,b] is the piece of parabola Par[a,b] considered in the foregoing section 2.2.2.

The projection of Tri[a,b,c] is the triangle, denoted by $\text{Tri}_2[a,b,c]$, with vertices (a,a^2), (b,b^2), (c,c^2).

The projection of Tetra[a,b,c,d] is the convex quadrilateral Quad[a,b,c,d] with vertices (a,a^2), (b,b^2), (c,c^2), (d,d^2).

Any closed set in $\mathbf{R}^3$ is specified by its projection on the horizontal plane $\mathbf{R}^2$ and by its upper and lower frontier.

The equation of Plane[a,b,c] is

$$z = abc - (ab+bc+ca)x + (a+b+c)y. \tag{40}$$

The equation of the half-space above Plane [a,b,c] is

$$z \geq abc - (ab+bc+ca)x + (a+b+c)y \tag{41}$$

and the equation of the half-space below Plane[a,b,c] is

$$z \leq abc - (ab+bc+ca)x + (a+b+c)y. \tag{42}$$

Continuous case

Theorem 5

The space *Prob*[[a,b];μ_1,μ_2,μ_3] exists iff one of the following equivalent conditions a, b, c is satisfied.

a. **The point (μ_1,μ_2,μ_3) belongs to the set in $\mathbf{R}^3$ of wich the upper frontier is composed of the segments Line[θ,b] ($\theta\in[a,b]$) and of which the lower frontier is composed of the segments Line[a,θ] ($\theta\in[a,b]$).**

b.

$$\mathbf{a \le \mu_1 \le b,} \tag{43_1}$$

$$\mathbf{\mu_1^2 \le \mu_2 \le (a+b)\mu_1 - ab,} \tag{43_2}$$

$$\mathbf{a\mu_2 + (\mu_2 - a\mu_1)^2/(\mu_1 - a) \le \mu_3 \le b\mu_2 - [(b\mu_1 - \mu_2)^2/(b - \mu_1)].} \tag{43_3}$$

c.

$$\mathbf{a \le \mu \le b,} \tag{44_1}$$

$$\mathbf{0 \le \sigma^2 \le (\mu - a)(b - \mu),} \tag{44_2}$$

$$\mathbf{\sigma^4/_{(\mu-a)} - (\mu - a)\sigma^2 \le \rho^3 \le (b - \mu)\sigma^2 - \sigma^4/_{(b-\mu)},} \tag{44_3}$$

The fractions must be replaced by 0, in (43_3) and in (44_3), if the denominator equals 0.

Proof

a. We verify that the upper frontier of CoCub[a,b] is the surface composed of the segments Line[θ,b] (θ∈[a,b]) and that the lower frontier of CoCub[a,b] is the surface composed of the segments Line[a,θ] (θ∈[a,b]). The parametric equations of the first surface are

$$x=p\theta+(1-p)b\ ,\ y=p\theta^2+(1-p)b^2,$$
$$z=p\theta^3+(1-p)b^3\ \ (a\le\theta\le b,\ 0\le p\le 1). \tag{45}$$

They express that (x,y,z) is a convex combination of the points $(\theta,\theta^2,\theta^3)$ and (b,b^2,b^3). The projection of this surface on the horizontal plane is Dom:= CoPar[a,b]. Dom is the set of points (x,y) defined by the following relations (48_1) and (48_2).

The relations (45) can be expressed as

$$b-x=p(b-\theta)\ ,\ b^2-y=p(b^2-\theta^2),$$
$$b^3-z=p(b^3-\theta^3)\ \ (a\le\theta\le b,\ 0\le p\le 1). \tag{46}$$

Then

$$(b^2-y)/_{(b-x)} = b+\theta\ \ ,\ \theta = (bx-y)/_{(b-x)}.$$

by the division of the second relation (46) by the first relation (46).

The division of the last relation (46) by the first relation (46) furnishes the relation

$$(b^3-z)/(b-x) = b^2+b\theta+\theta^2.$$

Using the expression of θ already calculated, we obtain the non parametric equation

$$z = by - (bx-y)^2/(b-x) \quad ((x,y)\in \mathrm{Dom}). \tag{47}$$

of the surface (45). This surface is concave, by elementary geometry. (It is sufficient to verify the concavity of the function $-(b^2-y)^2/(b-x)$ because the difference of this function and the last member of (47) is a linear function. See Ch.6.2.1).

The equation of the surface composed of the segments Line[a,θ] ($\theta\in$[a,b]) results from the replacement of b by a. It is

$$z = ay + (y-ax)^2/(x-a) \quad ((x,y)\in \mathrm{Dom}) \tag{48}$$

This surface is convex.

From the definition of the surfaces (47) and (48) and from their concavity and convexity resp., results that (47) is the upper frontier of the convex hull of Cu[a,b], and (48) the lower frontier.

By Theorem 1.c, the space

$$\boldsymbol{Prob}[[a,b];\mu_1,\mu_2,\mu_3]$$

exists iff

$$(\mu_1,\mu_2,\mu_3) \in \mathrm{Co}\{(\theta,\theta^2,\theta^3)/a\leq\theta\leq b\} = \mathrm{CoCub}[a,b].$$

b. The equations of CoCub[a,b] are

$$a \leq x \leq b, \tag{48$_1$}$$

$$x^2 \leq y \leq (a+b)x - ab, \tag{48$_2$}$$

$$ay + (y-ax)^2/(x-a) \leq z \leq by - (bx-y)^2/(b-x). \tag{48$_3$}$$

The relations (43) result from the replacement of (x,y,z) by (μ_1,μ_2,μ_3) in these equations.

c. The relations (43) and (44) are equivalent by (20) or (21) •

Discrete case

Theorem 6

The space *Prob*$[\{a_1,...,a_k\};\mu_1,\mu_2,\mu_3]$, where $a_1<a_2<...<a_k$, exists iff one of the following equivalent conditions a,b is satisfied.

a. The point (μ_1,μ_2,μ_3) belongs to the polyhedron with upper faces

$$\mathrm{Tri}[a_i,a_{i+1},a_k] \quad (i=1,2,...,k-2) \tag{49}$$

and lower faces

$$\mathrm{Tri}[a_1,a_j,a_{j+1}] \quad (j=1,2,...,k-1). \tag{50}$$

b.

$$\mu_3 \le a_i a_{i+1} a_k - [a_i a_{i+1} + a_{i+1} a_k + a_k a_i]\mu_1 + (a_i + a_{i+1} + a_k)\mu_2 \quad (i=1,2,...,k-2), \tag{51}$$

$$\mu_3 \ge a_1 a_j a_{j+1} - [a_1 a_j + a_j a_{j+1} + a_j a_1]\mu_1 + (a_1 + a_j + a_{j+1})\mu_2 \quad (j=1,2,...,k-1). \tag{51}$$

Proof

a. By Theorem 1.c, the space exists iff (μ_1,μ_2,μ_3) belongs to the set

$$\mathrm{Co}\{(a_1,a_1^2,a_1^3),...,(a_k,a_k^2,a_k^3)\}.$$

This set is the polyhedron with faces (49) and (50). Indeed, it is easy to verify that this polyhedron is convex and that each point (a_i,a_i^2,a_i^3) $(i=1,...,k)$ lies below the planes containing the triangles (49), and above the planes containing the triangles (50).

b. The polyhedron is the intersection of the half-spaces containing the polyhedron, delimited by the planes containing the triangles (49) and (50). The equation of the half-spaces result from relations such as (41) and (42) •

We now consider the enumeration problem of the feasible quadruples of the space ***Prob***$[[i_0,n_0]_{int};\mu_1,\mu_2,\mu_3]$. The quadruple (i,j,k,n) is feasible iff it satisfies the relations

$$i_0 \le i < j < k < n \le n_0 \tag{52}$$

and

$$p \ge 0\,,\ q \ge 0\,,\ r \ge 0\,,\ s \ge 0, \tag{53}$$

where (p,q,r,s) is the unique solution of the system

$$p+q+r+s = 1, \tag{54}$$

$$pi+qj+rk+sn = \mu_1, \tag{54}$$

$$pi^2+qj^2+rk^2+sn^2 = \mu_2, \tag{54}$$

$$pi^3+qj^3+rk^3+sn^3 = \mu_3. \tag{54}$$

This solution is

$$p = [\mu_3-(j+k+n)\mu_2+(jk+kn+nj)\mu_1-jkn]_{/[(i-j)(i-k)(i-n)]}, \tag{55}$$

$$q = [\mu_3-(k+n+i)\mu_2+(kn+ni+ik)\mu_1-kni]_{/[(j-k)(j-n)(j-i)]}, \tag{55}$$

$$r = [\mu_3-(n+i+j)\mu_2+(ni+ij+jn)\mu_1-nij]_{/[(k-n)(k-i)(k-j)]}, \tag{55}$$

$$s = [\mu_3-(i+j+k)\mu_2+(ij+jk+ki)\mu_1-ijk]_{/[(n-i)(n-j)(n-k)]}. \tag{55}$$

Assumptions:

μ is not an integer, and none of the following numbers (56), (57) or (58) is an integer:

$$\sigma^2-(j-\mu)(\mu-i) \quad (i,j=i_0,i_0+1,\ldots,n_0), \tag{56}$$

$$\varphi_{\mu\sigma}(i) := \mu+\sigma^2_{/(\mu-i)} \quad (i=i_0,i_0+1,\ldots,n_0), \tag{57}$$

$$\varphi_{\mu\sigma\rho}(i,j) := \mu-[\rho^3+(\mu-i)\sigma^2+(\mu-j)\sigma^2]_{/[(j-\mu)(\mu-i)-\sigma^2]} \quad (i,j=i_0,\ldots,n_0). \tag{58}$$

The quadruple (i,j,k,n) is extremal iff it satisfies the relations

$$i_0 \le i < j < k < n \le n_0 \tag{59}$$

and

$$\mu_3 \le (j+k+n)\mu_2-(jk+kn+nj)\mu_1+jkn, \tag{60_1}$$

$$\mu_3 \ge (k+n+i)\mu_2-(kn+ni+ik)\mu_1+kni, \tag{60_2}$$

$$\mu_3 \le (n+i+j)\mu_2-(ni+ij+jn)\mu_1+nij, \tag{60_3}$$

$$\mu_3 \ge (i+j+k)\mu_2-(ij+jk+ki)\mu_1+ijk. \tag{60_4}$$

The relations (60) express that the point (μ_1,μ_2,μ_3) belongs to the tetrahedron Tetra[i,j,k,n]. Then, by projection on the horizontal plane, the point (μ_1,μ_2) lies in the quadrilateral Q[i,j,k,n]. Hence, the relations (60) imply the following relations (61):

$$\mu_2 \le (i+n)\mu_1 - in, \tag{61_1}$$

$$\mu_2 \ge (i+j)\mu_1 - ij, \tag{61_2}$$

$$\mu_2 \ge (j+k)\mu_1 - jk, \tag{61_3}$$

$$\mu_2 \ge (k+n)\mu_1 - kn. \tag{61_4}$$

From a projection of the tetrahedron on the x-axis of $\mathbf{R}^2$, results that

$$i \le \mu_1 \le n. \tag{62}$$

At this point, it is convenient to replace the triple (μ_1,μ_2,μ_3) by the triple (μ,σ,ρ). Then the relations (60), (61) and (62) become:

$$\rho^3 \le (j-\mu)(k-\mu)(n-\mu) + [(j-\mu)+(k-\mu)+(n-\mu)]\sigma^2, \tag{63_1}$$

$$\rho^3 \ge (k-\mu)(n-\mu)(i-\mu) + [(k-\mu)+(n-\mu)+(i-\mu)]\sigma^2, \tag{63_2}$$

$$\rho^2 \le (n-\mu)(i-\mu)(j-\mu) + [(n-\mu)+(i-\mu)+(j-\mu)]\sigma^2, \tag{63_3}$$

$$\rho^3 \ge (i-\mu)(j-\mu)(k-\mu) + [(i-\mu)+(j-\mu)+(k-\mu)]\sigma^2. \tag{63_4}$$

$$\sigma^2 < (n-\mu)(\mu-i), \tag{64_1}$$

$$\sigma^2 > (j-\mu)(\mu-i), \tag{64_2}$$

$$\sigma^2 > (k-\mu)(\mu-j), \tag{64_3}$$

$$\sigma^2 > (n-\mu)(\mu-k). \tag{64_4}$$

The strict inequalities result from the *Assumptions*.

The relation (64_1) remains valid if we replace n by n_0. This implies the relation

$$i \le \varphi_{\mu\sigma}(n_0). \tag{65}$$

By (64_1),

$$\varphi_{\mu\sigma}(i) \leq n. \qquad (66)$$

By (64_2),

$$j \leq \varphi_{\mu\sigma}(i). \qquad (67)$$

By (63_3),

$$\rho^3 \leq (\mu-j)[(n-\mu)(\mu-i)-\sigma^2] + [(n-\mu)+(i-\mu)]\sigma^2.$$

Then, by (64_1) and by the definition of the functions $\varphi_{\mu\sigma\rho}$,

$$j \leq \varphi_{\mu\sigma\rho}(i,n). \qquad (68)$$

In the same way, by (63_2) and (64_1),

$$\varphi_{\mu\sigma\rho}(i,n) \leq k. \qquad (69)$$

By (63_4) and (64_2),

$$k \leq \varphi_{\mu\sigma\rho}(i,j). \qquad (70)$$

We partition Q[i,j,k,n] in 2 triangles by the straight segments joining the points (j,j^2) and (n,n^2) in the horizontal plane. Then the point (μ_1,μ_2) can be situated in each of the 2 triangles resulting from that partition. This furnishes the following 2 cases.

Case 1

$$\sigma^2 > (n-\mu)(\mu-j). \qquad (71)$$

Then,

$$\varphi_{\mu\sigma}(n) \leq j. \qquad (72)$$

By (63_1),

$$\varphi_{\mu\sigma\rho}(j,n) \leq k. \qquad (73)$$

Case 2

$$\sigma^2 < (n-\mu)(\mu-j). \qquad (74)$$

Then,

$$j \leq \varphi_{\mu\sigma}(n). \qquad (75)$$

By (63_1),

$$k \leq \varphi_{\mu\sigma\rho}(j,n). \qquad (76)$$

Theorem 7

Under the indicated *Assumption*, the feasible quadruples (i,j,k,n) of the space *Prob*$[[i_0,n_0]_{int};\mu_1,\mu_2,\mu_3]$, are those satisfying the relations

$$\mathbf{i \in [i_0\,,\, n_0\wedge[\varphi_{\mu\sigma}(n_0)]]_{int},} \qquad (77_1)$$

$$\mathbf{n \in [(i+1)\vee[\varphi_{\mu\sigma}(i)+1]\,,\, n_0]_{int},} \qquad (77_2)$$

$$\mathbf{j \in [(i+1)\vee[\varphi_{\mu\sigma}(n)+1]\,,\,(n-1)\wedge[\varphi_{\mu\sigma}(i)]\wedge[\varphi_{\mu\sigma\rho}(i,n)]]_{int},} \qquad (77_3)$$

$$\mathbf{k \in [(j+1)\vee[\varphi_{\mu\sigma\rho}(i,n)+1]\vee[\varphi_{\mu\sigma\rho}(j,n)+1]\,,\,(n-1)\wedge[\varphi_{\mu\sigma\rho}(i,j)]]_{int}.} \qquad (77_4)$$

and those satisfying the relations

$$\mathbf{i \in [i_0\,,\, n_0\wedge[\varphi_{\mu\sigma}(n_0)]]_{int},} \qquad (78_1)$$

$$\mathbf{n \in [(i+1)\vee[\varphi_{\mu\sigma}(i)+1]\,,\, n_0]_{int},} \qquad (78_2)$$

$$\mathbf{j \in [(i+1)\,,\,(n-1)\wedge[\varphi_{\mu\sigma\rho}(i,n)+1]\wedge[\varphi_{\mu\sigma}(n)]]_{int},} \qquad (78_3)$$

$$\mathbf{k\in [(j+1)\vee[\varphi_{\mu\sigma\rho}(i,n)+1]\,,\,(n-1)\wedge[\varphi_{\mu\sigma\rho}(i,j)]\wedge[\varphi_{\mu\sigma\rho}(j,n)]]_{int}.} \qquad (78_4)$$

Proof

In *Case 1* of the foregoing discussion, the relations (59) and (60) are **equivalent** to the following relations:

$$[i_0 \le i \le n_0\,,\,(65)]\ ,\ [i+1 \le n \le n_0\,,\,(65)],$$

$$[i+1 \le j \le k-1\,,\,(67)\,,\,(68)\,,\,(72)]\ ,\ [j+1 \le k \le n-1\,,\,(69)\,,\,(70)\,,\,(73)].$$

The latter relations are equivalent to the relations (77). Each set of relations in square brackets corresponds to one relation (77).

The relations (78) result from the *Case 2* of the foregoing discussion. Then the relations (59) and (60) are **equivalent** to the following relations:

$$[i_0 \le i \le n_0\,,\,(66)]\ ,\ [i+1 \le n \le n_0\,,\,(67)],$$

$$[i+1 \le j \le n-1\,,\,(68)\,,\,(75)]\ ,\ [j+1 \le k \le n-1\,,\,(69)\,,\,(70)\,,\,(76)]\ \bullet$$

3.2.4. n Moment Constraints

The existence problem of space ***Prob***$[[a,b];\mu_1,\dots,\mu_n]$ is solved in full generality in next section 3.3.

The feasible n+1-tuples $(i_1,\dots,i_{n+1})$ of space ***Prob***$[[i_0,n_0]_{int};\mu_1,\dots,\mu_n]$ are those satisfying the relations

$$i_0 \le i_1 < i_2 < \dots < i_n < i_{n+1} \le n_0 \ , \ p_1 \ge 0 \ , \ p_2 \ge 0 \ , \ \dots \ , \ p_{n+1} \ge 0,$$

where $(p_1,\dots,p_{n+1})$ is the unique solution of the linear system

$$p_1 i_1^j + p_2 i_2^j + \dots + p_{n+1} i_{n+1}^j = \mu_j \ (j=0,1,\dots,n). \tag{79}$$

This solution is (see App.D.D12 and particular cases of foregoing sections)

$$p_j = [\mu_n - s_{j1}\mu_{n-1} + s_{j2}\mu_{n-2} - \dots + (-1)^n s_{jn}] / [\Pi_{\alpha=1,\dots,n+1;\alpha\neq j}(i_j - i_\alpha)] (j=1,\dots,n+1), \tag{80}$$

where

$$s_{jk} := \sum\nolimits_{\alpha_1,\dots,\alpha_k} i_{\alpha_1} \dots i_{\alpha_k} \ (k=1,\dots,n).$$

In the latter sum, the summation variables $\alpha_1 < \alpha_2 < \dots < \alpha_k$ take all possible values in the set $\{1,2,\dots,j-1,j+1,\dots,n+1\}$.

3.3. Existence of General Continuous Pure Moment Spaces

3.3.0. Introduction

The visual geometric method for the construction of convex hulls does not work in $\mathbf{R^n}$ ($n \ge 4$), because one does not "see" very much in these spaces. Fortunately a remarquable algebraic method, based on the consideration of quadratic forms, solves the existence problem of space ***Prob***$[[a,b];\mu_1,\dots,\mu_n]$ completely. The proofs are based on Appendix D. The main argument has been found in the Appendix D of Bellman (1960). This section 3.3 can be omitted, without loss of continuity.

3.3.1. Moment Spaces of Distributions

We denote by

$$\boldsymbol{Distr}[[a,b];\mu_0,\mu_1,\ldots,\mu_n] \quad (81)$$

the space of distributions F concentrated on the compact interval [a,b] ($a<b$) with fixed moments $\mu_0,\mu_1,\ldots,\mu_n$. The moment μ_j is defined in the same way as in the case of probability distributions:

$$\mu_j := \int_{[a,b]} x^j dF(x) \quad (j=0,1,2,\ldots),$$

but now μ_0 is the total mass F([a,b]), and it can be any positive number.

We consider the existence problem of the space (81). The general solution of that problem furnishes the existence conditions of the space

$$\boldsymbol{Prob}[[a,b];\mu_1,\ldots,\mu_n] = \boldsymbol{Distr}[[a,b];1,\mu_1,\ldots,\mu_n]$$

3.3.2. Pseudo-Distributions

A pseudo-distribution function is a difference $f=G-F$ of distribution functions (i.e. a function of bounded variation). It can be considered as a **measure** (a set function) with negative or positive masses:

$$f(B) = G(B)-F(B) \quad (B\subseteq \mathbf{R}).$$

A n+1-atomic pseudo-distribution concentrated on [a,b] is a linear combination

$$f = p_0A_{x_0} + p_1A_{x_1} + \ldots + p_nA_{x_n} \quad (82)$$

of atomic distributions A_{x_0}, A_{x_1}, ... , A_{x_n} with $x_0,x_1,\ldots x_n\in[a,b]$. The coefficients $p_0,p_1,\ldots,p_n$ are not necessarily positive.

The moments of pseudo-distributions f are defined in the same way as for usual distributions. For instance, the moment $\mu_j(f)$ of the n+1-atomic pseudo-distribution f is

$$\mu_j(f) := \int_{[a,b]} x^j df(x) = p_0x_0^j + p_1x_1^j + \ldots + p_nx_n^j \quad (j=0,1,\ldots). \quad (83)$$

Theorem 8

Whatever the real numbers μ_0, μ_1, ..., μ_n are, a n+1-atomic pseudo-distribution f with moments μ_0, μ_1, ..., μ_n, concentrated on [a,b], exists.

Proof
Let

$$x_0, x_1, \ldots, x_n \in [a,b], \quad x_0 < x_1 < \ldots < x_n.$$

The linear system in $p_0, p_1, \ldots, p_n$

$$p_0 x_0^j + p_1 x_1^j + \ldots + p_n x_n^j = \mu_j \ (j=0,1,\ldots,n) \tag{84}$$

has a non-vanishing Vandermonde determinant. It has a solution $(p_0, p_1, \ldots, p_n)$. Then

$$f := p_0 A_{x_0} + p_1 A_{x_1} + \ldots + p_n A_{x_n}$$

is a pseudo-distribution concentrated on [a,b], with moments $\mu_0, \mu_1, \ldots, \mu_n$ •

3.3.3. Quadratic Forms

Let $\mu_0, \mu_1, \ldots \in \mathbf{R}$. We define the following quadratic forms in the variables $t_0, t_1, \ldots, t_n$,

$$P_n(t_0, \ldots, t_n) := \sum_{i,j=0,\ldots,n} \mu_{i+j} t_i t_j, \tag{85}$$

$$Q_n(t_0, \ldots, t_n) := \sum_{i,j=0,\ldots,n} \mu_{i+j+1} t_i t_j, \tag{86}$$

$$R_n(t_0, \ldots, t_n) := \sum_{i,j=0,\ldots,n} \mu_{i+j+2} t_i t_j. \tag{87}$$

Of course, when P_n, Q_n or R_n is considered, we assume that the involved numbers μ_k are given. If $\mu_0, \mu_1, \ldots$are the moments of a distribution F, or a pseudo-distribution f, then P_n, Q_n, R_n are called **quadratic forms associated to F or f**.

Theorem 9

Let μ_0, μ_1, μ_2, ... be the moments of some probability distribution F concentrated on [a,b]. Then the quadratic forms

$$\mathbf{P_n \ , \ bP_n - Q_n \ , \ Q_n - aP_n \ , \ -abP_n + (a+b)Q_n - R_n} \tag{88}$$

are semidefinite positive.

Proof

$$0 \le \int_{[a,b]} (\sum_{0\le i\le n} t_i x^i)^2 dF(x)$$
$$= \int_{[a,b]} (\sum_{0\le i\le n} t_i x^i) (\sum_{0\le j\le n} t_j x^j) dF(x)$$
$$= \sum_{i,j=0,\dots,n} \int_{[a,b]} x^{i+j} t_i t_j dF(x) = P_n(t_0,\dots,t_n). \quad (89)$$

$$0 \le \int_{[a,b]} (b-x)(\sum_{0\le i\le n} t_i x^i)^2 dF(x)$$
$$= \int_{[a,b]} (b-x)(\sum_{0\le i\le n} t_i x^i) (\sum_{0\le j\le n} t_j x^j) dF(x)$$
$$= b \sum_{i,j=0,\dots,n} \int_{[a,b]} x^{i+j} t_i t_j dF(x) - \sum_{i,j=0,\dots,n} \int_{[a,b]} x^{i+j+1} t_i t_j dF(x)$$
$$= bP_n(t_0,\dots,t_n) - Q_n(t_0,\dots,t_n).$$

$$0 \le \int_{[a,b]} (x-a)(\sum_{0\le i\le n} t_i x^i)^2 dF(x)$$
$$= \int_{[a,b]} (x-a)(\sum_{0\le i\le n} t_i x^i) (\sum_{0\le j\le n} t_j x^j) dF(x)$$
$$= \sum_{i,j=0,\dots,n} \int_{[a,b]} x^{i+j+1} t_i t_j dF(x) - a\sum_{i,j=0,\dots,n} \int_{[a,b]} x^{i+j} t_i t_j dF(x)$$
$$= Q_n(t_0,\dots,t_n) - aP_n(t_0,\dots,t_n).$$

$$0 \le \int_{[a,b]} (x-a)(b-x)(\sum_{0\le i\le n} t_i x^i)^2 dF(x)$$
$$= \int_{[a,b]} (x-a)(b-x)(\sum_{0\le i\le n} t_i x^i) (\sum_{0\le j\le n} t_j x^j) dF(x)$$
$$= -ab \sum_{i,j=0,\dots,n} \int_{[a,b]} x^{i+j} t_i t_j dF(x)$$
$$+ (a+b) \sum_{i,j=0,\dots,n} \int_{[a,b]} x^{i+j+1} t_i t_j dF(x)$$
$$- \sum_{i,j=0,\dots,n} \int_{[a,b]} x^{i+j+2} t_i t_j dF(x)$$

$$= -abP_n(t_0,\dots,t_n) + (a+b)Q_n(t_0,\dots,t_n) - R_n(t_0,\dots,t_n) \bullet \quad (90)$$

Remark

If F has enough points of increase, then the quadratic forms (88) are definite positive. For instance, let F have a strictly positive continuous density on [a,b]. Then, by the relations (89),

$$[P_n(t_0,t_1,\dots,t_n) = 0] \Leftrightarrow [(\sum_{0\le i\le n} t_i x^i)^2 = 0 \text{ on } [a,b]] \Leftrightarrow [t_0=t_1=\dots=t_n=0].$$

3.3.4. Translations

Let $\mu_0, \mu_1, \mu_2, \ldots$, be a finite sequence of numbers in **R**. By Theorem 8, they can be considered as moments of some pseudo-distribution f concentrated on [a,b]. We now consider **translations** of the interval [a,b] and of the f-mass that it contains.

The c-translation of the interval [a,b] is the interval $[a^\circ,b^\circ]$, where $a^\circ:=a-c$ and $b^\circ:=b-c$. **The c-translation of the pseudo-distribution function f** is the pseudo-distribution f° defined by $f^\circ(x)=f^\circ(x+c)$ $(x\in\mathbf{R})$. **The c-translation of the sequence $\mu_0, \mu_1, \mu_2, \ldots$** is the sequence of moments $\mu^\circ_0, \mu^\circ_1, \mu^\circ_2, \ldots$ of f°.

By the binomial Theorem,

$$\mu^\circ_j = \int_{[a^\circ,b^\circ]} x^j df^\circ(x) = \int_{[a-c,b-c]} x^j df(x+c) = \int_{[a,b]} (x-c)^j df(x)$$

$$= \int_{[a,b]} \sum_{0\le i\le j} j^{[i]}/i!\; x^i(-c)^{j-i}\, df(x) = \sum_{0\le i\le j} j^{[i]}/i!\; (-c)^{j-i} \int_{[a,b]} x^i\, df(x).$$

Hence,

$$\mu^\circ_j = \sum_{0\le i\le j} j^{[i]}/i!\; (-c)^{j-i}\, \mu_i \quad (j=0,1,2,\ldots). \tag{91}$$

We observe that these relations do not depend on the pseudo-distribution f.

The c-translations of the quadratic forms P_n,Q_n,R_n defined by (85), (86) and (87), are the quadratic forms

$$P^\circ_n(t_0,\ldots,t_n) := \sum_{i,j=0,\ldots,n} \mu^\circ_{i+j} t_i t_j, \tag{92}$$

$$Q^\circ_n(t_0,\ldots,t_n) := \sum_{i,j=0,\ldots,n} \mu^\circ_{i+j+1} t_i t_j, \tag{93}$$

$$R^\circ_n(t_0,\ldots,t_n) := \sum_{i,j=0,\ldots,n} \mu^\circ_{i+j+2} t_i t_j, \tag{94}$$

Theorem 10

One of the quadratic forms

$$\mathbf{P_n\ ,\ bP_n-Q_n\ ,\ Q_n-aP_n\ ,\ -abP_n+(a+b)Q_n-R_n} \tag{95}$$

is semidefinite positive (definite positive), iff the corresponding c-translated quadratic form

$$\mathbf{P^\circ_n\ ,\ b^\circ P^\circ_n-Q^\circ_n\ ,\ Q^\circ_n-a^\circ P^\circ_n\ ,\ -a^\circ b^\circ P_n+(a^\circ+b^\circ)Q^\circ_n-R^\circ_n} \tag{96}$$

is semidefinite positive (definite positive).

Proof

It is sufficient to demonstrate that the semidefinite positiveness (definite positiveness) of any of the quadratic forms (85) implies the semidefinite positiveness (definite positiveness) of the corresponding quadratic form (86), because the quadratic forms (85) result from the quadratic forms (86) by a (−c)-translation.

Let the last quadratic form (95) be semidefinite positive. We prove that the last quadratic form (96) is semidefinite positive. The argument is the same for the other quadratic forms.

By Theorem 8, the numbers $\mu_0,\mu_1,\ldots,\mu_{2n+2}$ are the moments of some pseudo-distribution f concentrated on [a,b].

By the relations (90), with F replaced by f,

$$\int_{[a,b]} (x-a)(b-x)(\textstyle\sum_{0\le i\le n} t^\circ_i x^i)^2 df(x) =$$
$$-abP_n(t^\circ_0,\ldots,t^\circ_n)+ (a+b)Q_n(t^\circ_0,\ldots,t^\circ_n) - R_n(t^\circ_0,\ldots,t^\circ_n) \ge 0, \tag{97}$$

for all numbers $t^\circ_0,\ldots,t^\circ_n$. Let $t_0,\ldots,t_n$ be defined by

$$t_i := \textstyle\sum_{i\le j\le n} t^\circ_j\, j^{[i]}/i!\; c^{j-i} \quad (i=0,1,\ldots,n). \tag{98}$$

Then, by (97)

$$0 \le \int_{[a-c,b-c]} (x+c-a)(b-x-c)[\textstyle\sum_{0\le i\le n} t^\circ_i (x+c)^i]^2 df(x+c)$$
$$= \int_{[a^\circ,b^\circ]} (x-a^\circ)(b^\circ-x)[\textstyle\sum_{0\le j\le n} t^\circ_j (x+c)^j]^2 df^\circ(x)$$
$$= \int_{[a^\circ,b^\circ]} (x-a^\circ)(b^\circ-x)[\textstyle\sum_{0\le j\le n} t^\circ_j \sum_{0\le i\le j} j^{[i]}/i!\, x^i c^{j-i}]^2 df^\circ(x)$$
$$= \int_{[a^\circ,b^\circ]} (x-a^\circ)(b^\circ-x)[\textstyle\sum_{0\le i\le n} [\sum_{i\le j\le n} t^\circ_j\, j^{[i]}/i!\, c^{j-i}] x^i]^2 df^\circ(x)$$
$$= \int_{[a^\circ,b^\circ]} (x-a^\circ)(b^\circ-x)[\textstyle\sum_{0\le i\le n} t_i x^i]^2 df^\circ(x)$$
$$= -a^\circ b^\circ P^\circ_n(t_0,\ldots,t_n)+ (a^\circ+b^\circ)Q^\circ_n(t_0,\ldots,t_n) - R^\circ_n(t_0,\ldots,t_n). \tag{99}$$

Hence

$$0 \le -a^\circ b^\circ P^\circ_n(t_0,\ldots,t_n)+ (a^\circ+b^\circ)Q^\circ_n(t_0,\ldots,t_n) - R^\circ_n(t_0,\ldots,t_n), \tag{100}$$

where the latter relation is valid for all $t_0,...,t_n$, because the system (98) can be solved in $t°_0,...,t°_n$. Hence, the last quadratic form (96) is semidefinite positive.

Let us now assume that the last quadratic form (95) is definite positive. In order to prove that the last quadratic form (96) is definite positive, let

$$-a°b°P°_n(t_0,...,t_n)+(a°+b°)Q°_n(t_0,...,t_n)-R°_n(t_0,...,t_n)=0.$$

Then, by the relations (99) and (97)

$$0=\int_{[a-c,b-c]}(x+c-a)(b-x-c)[\textstyle\sum_{0\le i\le n}t°_i(x+c)^i]^2df(x+c)$$

$$=-abP_n(t°_0,...,t°_n).+(a+b)Q_n(t°_0,...,t°_n)-R_n(t°_0,...,t°_n).$$

Then, $t°_0=...=t°_n=0$, because the last quadratic form (95) is definite positive. Then $t_0=...=t_n=0$ by (98) •

3.3.5. Centering Translations

The most important translations of the sequence $\mu_0, \mu_1\equiv\mu, \mu_2, \mu_3, ...$ are its μ-translations, called **centering translations**. Then some elements of the **centered sequence**

$$\mu°_0\ ,\ \mu°_1=0\ ,\ \mu°_2=:\sigma^2\ ,\ \mu°_3=:\rho^3\ ,\ \mu°_4=:\alpha^4\ ,\ \mu°_5=:\beta^5\ ,\ \mu°_6=:\gamma^6\ ,\ ... \qquad (101)$$

receive the indicated special notation (see 3.2).

In the case of centering translations, the relations (91) become

$$\mu°_j=\textstyle\sum_{0\le i\le j}j^{[i]}/i!\,(-\mu)^i\,\mu_{j-i}\ (j=0,1,2,...). \qquad (102)$$

after the replacement of the summation variable i by j–i. Then the initial sequence is recuperated from the centered sequence by the relations

$$\mu_j=\textstyle\sum_{0\le i\le j}j^{[i]}/i!\,\mu^i\,\mu°_{j-i}\ (j=0,1,2,...). \qquad (103)$$

Indeed, the latter relations are those of a (–μ)-translations, and a μ-translation followed by a (–μ)-translation is a null operation.

It is possible and convenient, to keep the untranslated interval [a,b] and to employ simultaneously the centered sequence $\mu°_0, \mu°_1, ...$

3.3.6. Main Theorems

Theorem 11

The space *Distr*[[a,b];$\mu_0,\mu_1,...,\mu_{2n+1}$] exists iff the quadratic forms

$$\mathbf{Q_n - aP_n \text{ and } bP_n - Q_n} \tag{104}$$

are semidefinite positive.

Proof

a. If the space exists, then the quadratic forms (104) are semidefinite positive by Theorem 12.

b. Conversely, we first assume that the quadratic forms (104) are definite positive, and we prove the **existence of a n+1-atomic distribution, concentrated on the interval]a,b[, with moments μ_0, μ_1, ..., μ_{2n+1}.**

The sum of two definite positive quadratic forms is a definite positive quadratic form. Hence, the sum $(b-a)P_n$ of the quadratic forms (104) is a definite positive quadratic form. Then P_n is a definite positive quadratic form.

Let the column $t_{1\times(n+1)}$ and the matrices $p_{(n+1)\times(n+1)}$ and $q_{(n+1)\times(n+1)}$ be defined by

$$t := (t_0,...,t_n)' \ , \ p_{ij} := \mu_{i+j} \ (i,j=0,...,n) \ , \ q_{ij} := \mu_{i+j+1} \ (i,j=0,...,n).$$

Then

$$P_n = t'pt \ , \ Q_n = t'qt.$$

By the simultaneous diagonalization Th. (App.D.Th.D6), a matrix $s_{(n+1)\times(n+1)}$ and a diagonal matrix $d_{(n+1)\times(n+1)}$ exist, such that $p=ss'$, $q=sds'$. Then

$$\mu_{i+j} = p_{ij} = (ss')_{ij} = \textstyle\sum_{0\le k\le n} s_{ik}s'_{kj} = \sum_{0\le k\le n} s_{ik}s_{jk} \ (i,j=0,...,n), \tag{105}$$

$$\mu_{i+j+1} = q_{ij} = (sds')_{ij} = \textstyle\sum_{0\le k\le n} s_{ik}d_k s'_{kj} = \sum_{0\le k\le n} d_k s_{ik}s_{jk} \ (i,j=0,...,n). \tag{106}$$

In (106), we replace j by j−1. Hence,

$$\mu_{i+j} = \textstyle\sum_{0\le k\le n} d_k s_{ik}s_{j-1,k} \ (i=0,...,n;\ j=1,...,n). \tag{107}$$

By substraction of (105) and (107),

$$0 = \textstyle\sum_{0\le k\le n} s_{ik}(s_{jk} - d_k s_{j-1,k}) \ (i=0,...,n;\ j=1,...,n). \tag{108}$$

Let c_j (j=1,...,n) be the column with elements

$$(c_j)_k := s_{jk} - d_k s_{j-1,k} \ (k=0,\dots,n).$$

Then (108) implies that $sc_j=0$, and then $c_j=0$, because s is invertible. Hence

$$s_{jk} - d_k s_{j-1,k} = 0 \quad (k=0,\dots,n;\ j=1,\dots,n).$$

Then

$$s_{jk} = d_k s_{j-1,k} = d_k^2 s_{j-2,k} = \dots = d_k^j s_{0k} \quad (k=0,\dots,n;\ j=1,\dots,n).$$

Hence,

$$s_{jk} = d_k^j\, s_{0k} \ (j,k=0,\dots,n), \tag{109}$$

because this relation is trivially exact for j=0. Let

$$F := \textstyle\sum_{0\le k\le n} s_{0k}^2\, A_{d_k}. \tag{110}$$

We verify that the moments of F are $\mu_0,\dots,\mu_{2n+1}$.

$$\mu_i(F) := \textstyle\sum_{0\le k\le n} s_{0k}^2\, d_k^i \ (i=0,1,\dots).$$

By the relations (105), (106) and (109),

$$\mu_{i+j} = \textstyle\sum_{0\le k\le n} d_k^i\, s_{0k}\, d_k^j\, s_{0k} = \sum_{0\le k\le n} d_k^{i+j}\, s_{0k}^2 = \mu_{i+j}(F) \quad (i,j=0,\dots,n)$$

$$\mu_{i+j+1} = \textstyle\sum_{0\le k\le n} d_k\, d_k^i\, s_{0k}\, d_k^j\, s_{0k} = \sum_{0\le k\le n} d_k^{i+j+1}\, s_{0k}^2 = \mu_{i+j+1}(F) \quad (i,j=0,\dots,n).$$

Hence

$$\mu_i(F) = \mu_i \ (i=0,1,\dots,2n+1).$$

We now verify that F is concentrated on [a,b]. The matrix

$$q - ap = sds' - ass' = s(d - a1)s'$$

is definite positive, because the quadratic form $Q_n - aP_n$ is definite positive. Then the matrix d−a1 is definite positive. Its diagonal elements are strictly positive. Hence

$$d_k - a > 0 \quad (k=0,\dots,n).$$

Similarly, the definite positiveness of the matrix bp−q implies

$$b - d_k > 0 \quad (k=0,\dots,n).$$

c. Finally, we use a continuity argument proving that it is sufficient to assume the semidefinite positiveness of the quadratic forms $Q_n - aP_n$ and $bP_n - Q$ instead of their definite positiveness. Let F_ε be the uniform distribution concentrated on [a,b] with total mass $\varepsilon>0$. Let $\mu_{i\varepsilon}$ (i=0,1,...) be the moments of F_ε, and let $P_{n\varepsilon}$ and $Q_{n\varepsilon}$ be the associated quadratic forms. By Theorem 9, and the *Remark* following its proof, the quadratic forms

$$Q_{n\varepsilon} - aP_{n\varepsilon}\ ,\ bP_{n\varepsilon} - Q_{n\varepsilon}$$

are definite positive. Then the quadratic forms

$$(Q_n + Q_{n\varepsilon}) - a(P_n + P_{n\varepsilon})\ ,\ b(P_n + P_{n\varepsilon}) - (Q_n + Q_{n\varepsilon})$$

are definite positive. By the part already proved, a n+1 -atomic distribution

$$F_\varepsilon = \sum\nolimits_{0\le k\le n} p_{k\varepsilon}\, A x_{k\varepsilon},$$

concentrated on [a,b], with moments $\mu_i + \mu_{i\varepsilon}$ (i=0,...,2n+1), exists. Let $\varepsilon\downarrow 0$ discreetly. Then a subsequence $\varepsilon(\nu)$ (ν=1,2,...) exists, such that the sequences

$$p_{0,\varepsilon(\nu)}\ ,\ \dots\ ,\ p_{n,\varepsilon(\nu)}\ ,\ x_{0,\varepsilon(\nu)}\ ,\ \dots\ ,\ x_{n,\varepsilon(\nu)}\ \ (\nu=1,2,\dots)$$

are convergent. Let the corresponding limits be

$$p_0\ ,\ \dots\ ,\ p_n\ ,\ x_0\ ,\ \dots\ ,\ x_n .$$

Then

$$F := \sum\nolimits_{0\le k\le n} p_k\, A x_k$$

is a distribution concentrated on [a,b], with moments $\mu_0,\dots,\mu_{2n+1}$. Hence, it belongs to the space ***Distr***$[[a,b];\mu_0,\dots,\mu_{2n+1}]$ •

For fixed $\mu_0,\mu_1,\mu_2,\dots$, we denote by (p_n), (q_n), (r_n) the $(n+1)\times(n+1)$ matrices with elements

$$(p_n)_{ij} := \mu_{i+j}\ ,\ (q_n)_{ij} := \mu_{i+j+1}\ ,\ (r_n)_{ij} := \mu_{i+j+2}\ \ (i,j=0,1,\dots,n). \qquad (111)$$

The corresponding quadratic forms are P_n, Q_n, R_n. When spaces of probability distributions are considered, then $\mu_0 := 1$.

If c-translations are considered, then we denote by (p°_n), (q°_n), (r°_n) the $(n+1)\times(n+1)$ matrices with elements

$$(p^\circ_n)_{ij} := \mu^\circ_{i+j}\,,\ (q^\circ_n)_{ij} := \mu^\circ_{i+j+1}\,,\ (r^\circ_n)_{ij} := \mu^\circ_{i+j+2}\quad (i,j=0,1,\ldots,n). \qquad (112)$$

When centering translations are considered, then $\mu := \mu_1$. **Hereafter, in this Chapter, the translations are centering translations when nothing else is specified.**

The following Corollary of Theorem 11 results from Theorem 10.

Corollary

The space *Prob*$[[a,b];\mu_1,\ldots,\mu_{2n+1}]$ exists iff the matrices

$$(q_n)-a(p_n) \text{ and } b(p_n)-(q_n) \qquad (113)$$

are semidefinite positive. The space exists iff the matrices

$$(\mu-a)(p^\circ_n)+(q^\circ_n) \text{ and } (b-\mu)(p^\circ_n)-(q^\circ_n) \qquad (114)$$

are semidefinite positive •

Lemma 1

Let $(p)_{(n+1)\times(n+1)}$ be a definite positive matrix and let $(s)_{(n+1)\times(n+1)}$ be a matrix with vanishing determinant, differing from (p) only by the element in the upper left corner. Then $s_{00}<p_{00}$.

Proof

If the element p_{00} of matrix (p) is replaced by a larger element, then the determinant of the matrix increases, and it remains strictly positive. Indeed, det(p) can be expanded as

$$\det(p) = p_{00}d_{00} + p_{01}d_{01} + \ldots + p_{0n}\, d_{0n},$$

where d_{00} is the determinant of the matrix resulting from (p) by the dropping of the first row and column. The latter matrix is definite positive. Hence $d_{00}>0$. $d_{01},\ldots,d_{0n}$ are determinants not depending on p_{00}. Hence, (s) can only result from (p) by a decrement of p_{00} •

Lemma 2

The quadratic form P_n associated to the n-atomic distribution

$$F := p_1 A_{x_1} + \ldots + p_n A_{x_n},$$

is semidefinite positive, but not definite positive.

Proof

$$\mu_i(F) = \sum_{1\le k\le n} p_k x_k^i \ (i=1,2,\ldots).$$

Hence,

$$P_n = \sum_{i,j=0,\ldots,n} \mu_{i+j}(F) t_i t_j = \sum_{i,j=0,\ldots,n} \sum_{1\le k\le n} p_k x_k^{i+j} t_i t_j$$

$$= \sum_{1\le k\le n} p_k [\sum_{0\le i\le n} x_k^i t_i][\sum_{0\le j\le n} x_k^j t_j] = \sum_{1\le k\le n} p_k [\sum_{0\le i\le n} x_k^i t_i]^2 \ge 0.$$

The linear system in $t_0, t_1, \ldots, t_n$,

$$\sum_{0\le i\le n} x_k^i t_i = 0 \quad (k=1,\ldots,n)$$

has strictly more unknown quantities than equations. It has a solution $(t_0,t_1,\ldots,t_n)$ different from $(0,\ldots,0)$. Then $P_n(t_0,t_1,\ldots,t_n)=0$ •

Theorem 12

The space *Distr*$[[a,b];\mu_0,\mu_1,\ldots,\mu_{2n}]$ exists iff the quadratic forms

$$P_n \text{ and } -abP_{n-1}+(a+b)Q_{n-1}-R_{n-1} \qquad (115)$$

are semidefinite positive.

Proof

a. If the space exists, then the quadratic forms (113) are semidefinite positive by Theorem 9.

b. Conversely, we assume that the quadratic forms (113) are definite positive, and we prove that the space exists. Then the Theorem follows from a continuity argument, similar to that one used in the foregoing proof (and which we do not repeat here). By Theorem 10, we may assume that a=0, because we can perform a a-translation, then prove the Theorem in the case a=0, and then perform a (–a)-translation). Let

$$\mu'_0 := \mu_1 \ , \ \mu'_1 := \mu_2 \ , \ \ldots , \ \mu'_{2n-1} := \mu_{2n}.$$

and let the corresponding quadratic forms be

$$P'_{n-1} := \sum_{i,j=0,\ldots,n-1} \mu'_{i+j} t_i t_j = \sum_{i,j=0,\ldots,n-1} \mu_{i+j+1} t_i t_j = Q_{n-1},$$

$$Q'_{n-1} := \sum_{i,j=0,\ldots,n-1} \mu'_{i+j+1} t_i t_j = \sum_{i,j=0,\ldots,n-1} \mu_{i+j+2} t_i t_j = R_{n-1}.$$

Hence, the quadratic form

$$bP'_{n-1} - Q'_{n-1} = bQ_{n-1} - R_{n-1}$$

is definite positive.

When we drop the first row and the first column of the matrix (p_n) of the quadratic forms P_n, then we obtain the matrix (q'_{n-1}) of the quadratic form Q'_{n-1}. Hence, the latter is definite positive. Hence, the foregoing Theorem 11 applies to the numbers $\mu'_0,\ldots,\mu'_{2n-1}$ and the quadratic forms

$$Q'_{n-1} - 0.P'_{n-1} = Q'_{n-1} \quad \text{and} \quad bP'_{n-1} - Q'_{n-1}.$$

By the part b. of the proof of that Theorem, positive numbers $p'_0,\ldots,p'_{n-1}$ and numbers $x'_0,\ldots,x'_{n-1} \in]0,b[$ exist, such that

$$\mu'_i = \sum_{0\le k\le n-1} p'_k (x'_k)^i \quad (i=0,1,\ldots,2n-1).$$

Let

$$p_k := p'_{k-1}/x'_{k-1} \ (k=1,\ldots,n) \ , \ x_k := x'_{k-1} \ (k=1,\ldots,n)$$

and let

$$F := p_1 A_{x_1} + \ldots + p_n A_{x_n}.$$

For i=1,...,2n,

$$\mu_i(F) = \sum_{1\le k\le n} p_k x_k^i = \sum_{1\le k\le n} (p'_{k-1}/x'_{k-1})(x'_{k-1})^i$$

$$= \sum_{0\le k\le n-1} (p'_k/x'_k)(x'_k)^i = \sum_{0\le k\le n-1} p'_k \, x'^{\,i-1}_k = \mu'_{i-1} = \mu_i.$$

Hence,

$$\mu_i(F) = \mu_i \ (i=1,\ldots,2n), \tag{116}$$

and it is enough to show that we can complete F by a term $p_0 A_0$ ($p_0 \ge 0$) in such a way that

$$\mu_0 = p_0 + p_1 + \ldots + p_n. \tag{117}$$

Indeed, the introduction of a new mass p_0 at the origin does not modify the moments μ_1, ..., μ_{2n}. In fact (117) defines p_0 and then it is sufficient to show that $p_0 \geq 0$, i.e. $p_1+...+p_n \leq \mu_0$ or $\mu_0(F) \leq \mu_0$.

The determinant of the matrix $(p_{nF})_{(n+1)\times(n+1)}$ with elements

$$(p_{nF})_{ij} = \mu_{i+j}(F) \quad (i,j=0,...,n)$$

equals zero. Indeed, by Lemma 2 the quadratic form corresponding to this matrix is semidefinite positive, but not definite positive. Matrix $(p_n)_{(n+1)\times(n+1)}$ defined by (111) is definite positive, because we assume that the corresponding quadratic form P_n is definite positive. By (116), the matrices (p_{nF}) and (p_n) only differ by the element in the upper left corner. By Lemma 1, $\mu_0(F)=(p_{nF})_{00}<(p_n)_{00}=\mu_0$ •

Corollary

The space *Prob*[[a,b];μ_1,...,μ_{2n}] exists iff the matrices

$$(p_n) \text{ and } -ab(p_{n-1})+(a+b)(q_{n-1})-(r_{n-1}) \tag{118}$$

are semidefinite positive. The space exists iff the matrices

$$(p^\circ_n) \text{ and } (b-\mu)(\mu-a)(p^\circ_{n-1})+(a+b-2\mu)(q^\circ_{n-1})-(r^\circ_{n-1}) \tag{119}$$

are semidefinite positive.

Proof
By the Theorem and by Theorem 10.

3.3.7. Illustrations

We now apply the Corollary of Theorem 11 and the Corollary of Theorem 13 to particular cases. We only express the existence conditions of the spaces in centering translated form. That means that we only consider the quadratic forms (114) and (119). We then use the particular notations (101).

We express that the matrices (114) and (119) are definite positive. In this way, we do not completely specify the effective domain of the parameters μ_1, ..., μ_n of the space ***Prob***[[a,b];μ_1,...,μ_n], but only its interior.

It is much simpler to express that a matrix is definite positive, rather than semidefinite positive: The definite positiveness of the matrix $a_{k\times k}$ is equivalent to the strict positiveness of the determinant of the k initial principal submatrices of $a_{k\times k}$. The semidefinite positiveness of $a_{k\times k}$ is equivalent to the positiveness of the determinant of the 2^k-1 principal submatrices of $a_{k\times k}$.

The matrices (p°_n), (q°_n), (r°_n) (n=0,1,2,3) are the initial principal submatrixes of the following matrices (p°_3), (q°_3), (r°_3) resp.

$$(p^\circ_3) = \begin{bmatrix} 1 & 0 & \sigma^2 & \rho^3 \\ 0 & \sigma^2 & \rho^3 & \alpha^4 \\ \sigma^2 & \rho^3 & \alpha^4 & \beta^5 \\ \rho^3 & \alpha^4 & \beta^5 & \gamma^6 \end{bmatrix}$$

$$(q^\circ_3) = \begin{bmatrix} 0 & \sigma^2 & \rho^3 & \alpha^4 \\ \sigma^2 & \rho^3 & \alpha^4 & \beta^5 \\ \rho^3 & \alpha^4 & \beta^5 & \gamma^6 \\ \alpha^4 & \beta^5 & \gamma^6 & \delta^7 \end{bmatrix}$$

$$(r^\circ_3) = \begin{bmatrix} \sigma^2 & \rho^3 & \alpha^4 & \beta^5 \\ \rho^3 & \alpha^4 & \beta^5 & \gamma^6 \\ \alpha^4 & \beta^5 & \gamma^6 & \delta^7 \\ \beta^5 & \gamma^6 & \delta^7 & \varepsilon^8 \end{bmatrix}$$

***Space Prob*[[a,b];μ_1,μ_2]**

The interior of the effective domain of the space is the set of points (μ_1,μ_2) for which the following matrices are definite positive:

$$(p^\circ_1) = \begin{bmatrix} 1 & 0 \\ 0 & \sigma^2 \end{bmatrix}$$

$$(b-\mu)(\mu-a)(p^\circ_0)+(a+b-2\mu)(q^\circ_0)-(r^\circ_0) = (b-\mu)(\mu-a)1-\sigma^2.$$

The latter is a matrix with dimensions 1×1, i.e. a scalar. Hence, this interior is defined by the relations

$$0 < \sigma^2 < (b-\mu)(\mu-a). \tag{120}$$

We notice that the inequality $0<(b-\mu)(\mu-a)$ implies the inequalities

$$a < \mu < b, \tag{121}$$

because $a<b$.

***Space Prob*[[a,b];μ₁,μ₂,μ₃]**

The interior of the effective domain of the space is the set of points (μ_1,μ_2,μ_3) for which the following matrices are definite positive:

$$\begin{bmatrix} \mu-a & \sigma^2 \\ \sigma^2 & (\mu-a)\sigma^2+\rho^3 \end{bmatrix}$$

$$\begin{bmatrix} b-\mu & -\sigma^2 \\ -\sigma^2 & (b-\mu)\sigma^2-\rho^3 \end{bmatrix}$$

This interior is defined by the relations

$$\mu-a > 0 \ , \ b-\mu > 0, \tag{121$_1$}$$

$$(\mu-a)^2\sigma^2 + (\mu-a)\rho^3 - \sigma^4 > 0, \tag{121$_2$}$$

$$(b-\mu)^2\sigma^2 - (b-\mu)\rho^3 - \sigma^4 > 0. \tag{121$_3$}$$

We here seem to miss some relations corresponding to the relations (40) of Theorem 8. In fact, the sum of (121_2) multiplied by $(b-\mu)$ and (121_3) multiplied by $(\mu-a)$ furnishes the relation

$$(b-a)(b-\mu)(\mu-a)\sigma^2 > (b-a)\sigma^4.$$

It implies

$$0 < \sigma^2 < (b-\mu)(\mu-a).$$

Hence, the interior of the effective domain of the space is defined by the relations

$$a < \mu < b, \tag{122$_1$}$$

$$0 < \sigma^2 < (\mu-a)(b-\mu), \tag{122$_2$}$$

$$\sigma^4 - (\mu-a)^2\sigma^2 < (\mu-a)\rho^3 \ , \ (b-\mu)\rho^3 < (b-\mu)^2\sigma^2 - \sigma^4. \tag{122$_3$}$$

The relations (122_1) define the interior of the effective domain of the space

$$\boldsymbol{Prob}[[a,b];\mu_1].$$

The relations (122_1), (122_2) define the interior of the effective domain of the space

$$\boldsymbol{Prob}[[a,b];\mu_1,\mu_2].$$

The relations (122_1), (122_2), (122_3) define the interior of the effective domain of the space

$$\boldsymbol{Prob}[[a,b];\mu_1,\mu_2,\mu_3].$$

The relations (122_1), (122_2) are the relations (122_1) completed by the relations

$$\det(p^\circ_1) > 0 \ , \ \det((b-\mu)(\mu-a)(p^\circ_0)+(a+b-2\mu)(q^\circ_0)-(r^\circ_0)) > 0.$$

The relations (122_1), (122_2), (122_3) are the relations (122_1), (122_2) completed by the relations

$$\det((\mu-a)(p^\circ_1)+(q^\circ_1)) > 0 \ , \ \det((b-\mu)(p^\circ_1)-(q^\circ_1)) > 0.$$

The general rule is clear:

The interior of the effective domain of the space

$$\boldsymbol{Prob}[[a,b];\mu_1,\ldots,\mu_{k-1},\mu_k]$$

is specified by the relations defining the interior of the effective domain of the space

$$\boldsymbol{Prob}[[a,b];\mu_1,\ldots,\mu_{k-1}]$$

completed by the strict inequalities $\det(mat_1)>0$, $\det(mat_2)>0$, where mat_1 and mat_2 are the matrices (114) if $k=2n+1$, the matrices (119) if $k=2n$.

Space $\boldsymbol{Prob}[[a,b];\mu_1,\mu_2,\mu_3,\mu_4]$

The interior of the effective domain of the space is specified by the relations defining the interior of the effective domain of space $\boldsymbol{Prob}[[a,b];\mu_1,\mu_2,\mu_3]$ completed by the following strict inequalities, furnishing the bounds of α^4:

$$\begin{vmatrix} 1 & 0 & \sigma^2 \\ 0 & \sigma^2 & \rho^3 \\ \sigma^2 & \rho^3 & \alpha^4 \end{vmatrix} > 0,$$

$$\begin{vmatrix} (b-\mu)(\mu-a)-\sigma^2 & (a+b-2\mu)\sigma^2-\rho^3 \\ (a+b-2\mu)\sigma^2-\rho^3 & (b-\mu)(\mu-a)\sigma^2+(a+b-2\mu)\rho^3-\alpha^4 \end{vmatrix} > 0$$

***Space Prob*[[a,b];$\mu_1,\mu_2,\mu_3,\mu_4,\mu_5$]**

The interior of the effective domain of the space is specified by the relations defining the interior of the effective domain of space ***Prob***[[a,b];μ_1,μ_2,μ_3,μ_4] completed by the following strict inequalities, furnishing the bounds of β^5,

$$\begin{vmatrix} (\mu-a) & \sigma^2 & (\mu-a)\sigma^2+\rho^3 \\ \sigma^2 & (\mu-a)\sigma^2+\rho^3 & (\mu-a)\rho^3+\alpha^4 \\ (\mu-a)\sigma^2+\rho^3 & (\mu-a)\rho^3+\alpha^4 & (\mu-a)\alpha^4+\beta^5 \end{vmatrix} > 0,$$

$$\begin{vmatrix} (b-\mu) & -\sigma^2 & (b-\mu)\sigma^2-\rho^3 \\ -\sigma^2 & (b-\mu)\sigma^2-\rho^3 & (b-\mu)\rho^3-\alpha^4 \\ (b-\mu)\sigma^2-\rho^3 & (b-\mu)\rho^3-\alpha^4 & (b-\mu)\alpha^4-\beta^5 \end{vmatrix} > 0.$$

3.4. General m-Unimodal Moment Spaces

3.4.1. Definition and Notation of Spaces

In the following sections of this Chapter, we consider the spaces

Prob[[a,b];m-unim;$\mu_1,\dots,\mu_n$], (123)

Prob[[a,b];S,m-unim;$\mu_1,\dots,\mu_n$], (124)

and the more particular spaces

Prob[[i_0,n_0];[i_0,n_0]$_{int}$,m-unim;$\mu_1,\dots,\mu_n$]. (125)

As usual, the indications μ_1, ..., μ_n are abbreviations for the moment constraints

$$\mu_1(F) = \mu_1 , \ldots , \mu_n(F) = \mu_n$$

on the distributions F of the spaces. Whenever the space (123) or (124) is considered, it is implicitly assumed that $m \in [a,b]$. When (124) is used, it is assumed that S is a compact subset of [a,b], with strictly more than n points. When (125) is considered, it is assumed that $m \in [i_0,n_0]$ and that the interval of integers $[i_0,n_0]_{int}$ has strictly more than n points.

The space (125) occurs in numerical optimization problems. It results from a discretization of the space (123), combined with the introduction of a new unit of money (see discussion of 3.1.3).

The family

$$\textbf{\textit{Prob}}[[a,b];\text{m-unim,k-rect};\mu_1,\ldots,\mu_n] \tag{126}$$

is the set of k-rectangular distributions belonging to (123). The introduction of the constraint **k-rect** in (124) or in (125) has the same meaning.

3.4.2. Properties of Unimodal Moment Spaces

Theorem 13

a. **The spaces**

$$\textbf{\textit{Prob}}[[a,b];\text{m-unim};\mu_1,\ldots,\mu_n] \tag{127}$$

and

$$\textbf{\textit{Prob}}[[a,b];\text{S,m-unim};\mu_1,\ldots,\mu_n] \tag{128}$$

are convex and compact.

b. **The extremal points of each of these spaces are its n+1-rectangular distributions. This set of extremal distributions is compact.**

c. **The space (127) exists iff**

$$(\mu_1,\ldots\mu_n) \in \text{Co}\{(\mu_1(R_{m\theta}),\ldots,\mu_n(R_{m\theta}))/\theta\in[a,b]\}. \tag{129}$$

The space (128) exists iff

$$(\mu_1,\ldots\mu_n) \in \mathrm{Co}\{(\mu_1(R_{m\theta}),\ldots,\mu_n(R_{m\theta}))/\theta\in S\}. \qquad (130)$$

The moment $\mu_j(R_{m\theta})$ ($\theta\in R$; $m\in R$;$j=1,2,\ldots$) equals

$$\mu_j(R_{m\theta}) = 1/(j+1)(m^j+m^{j-1}\theta+m^{j-2}\theta^2+\ldots+m^0\theta^j). \qquad (131)$$

Proof
Let $\theta<m$. Then

$$\mu_j(R_{m\theta}) = 1/(m-\theta) \int_{[\theta,m]} x^j dx = 1/(m-\theta)[1/(j+1)(m^{j+1}-\theta^{j+1})],$$

and this furnishes the expression (131). The result is the same if $m=\theta$ and if $m<\theta$. The other propositions result from the Theorems and Corollaries of Chapter 2.3 •

3.5. Associated Pure Moment Spaces of a m-Unimodal Moment Space

3.5.1. Definition of Associated Spaces

We now consider the m-unimodal spaces as mixtures:

$$\textbf{\textit{Prob}}[[a,b];\text{m-unim};\mu_1,\ldots,\mu_n] = \textbf{\textit{Mixt}}[R_{m\theta}(\theta\in[a,b]);\mu_1,\ldots,\mu_n], \qquad (132)$$

$$\textbf{\textit{Prob}}[[a,b];S,\text{m-unim};\mu_1,\ldots,\mu_n] = \textbf{\textit{Mixt}}[R_{m\theta}(\theta\in S);\mu_1,\ldots,\mu_n]. \qquad (133)$$

By Ch.2.2, the associated space of the space (132) is the space

$$\textbf{\textit{Prob}}[S;\textstyle\int f_1^\bullet=\mu_1,\ldots,\int f_n^\bullet=\mu_n], \qquad (134)$$

with $S:=[a,b]$ and

$$f_j^\bullet(\theta) = \int_S x^j dR_{m\theta}(x) = \mu_j(R_{m\theta}) \ \ (\theta\in S). \qquad (135)$$

The associated space of the space (133) is thr space (134).

3.5.2. Properties of Associated Spaces

Theorem 14

The integral constraints on the distribution U∈*Prob*[S],

$$\int f_j^{\bullet}(\theta)dU(\theta) = \mu_j \; (j=1,...,n), \quad (136)$$

where $f_j^{\bullet}$ is defined by (135), are equivalent to the constraints

$$\int \theta^j dU(\theta) = \mu_j^{\bullet} \; (j=1,...,n), \quad (137)$$

where

$$\mu_j^{\bullet} := (j+1)\mu_j - mj\mu_{j-1} \; (j=1,...,n). \quad (138)$$

Proof

By (135) and (131), the constraints (136) are

$$\int 1_{/(j+1)}(m^j+m^{j-1}\theta+m^{j-2}\theta^2+...+m^0\theta^j)dU(\theta) = \mu_j \; (j=1,...,n),$$

$$m^j + m^{j-1}\mu_1(U) + m^{j-2}\mu_2(U) + ... + m^0\mu_j(U) = (j+1)\mu_j \; (j=1,...,n). \quad (139)$$

We replace j by j–1:

$$m^{j-1} + m^{j-2}\mu_1(U) + m^{j-3}\mu_2(U) + ... + m^0\mu_{j-1}(U) = j\mu_{j-1} \; (j=1,...,n). \quad (140)$$

This relation is trivially correct for j=1, with the usual defintion μ_0:=1. We multiply (140) by m, and then we substract that relation form (139):

$$\mu_j(U) = (j+1)\mu_j - mj\mu_{j-1} \; (j=1,...,n). \quad (141)$$

Hence, the relations (139) imply the relations (141). Conversely, it is direct, that the relations (141) imply the relations (139) •

The moments $\mu_1^{\bullet},...,\mu_n^{\bullet}$ defined by (138) are called **the associated moments** of the **original moments** $\mu_1,...,\mu_n$. The original moments are recuperated from the associated moments by the relations

$$\mu_j = 1_{/(j+1)} (m^j + m^{j-1}\mu_1^{\bullet} + m^{j-2}\mu_2^{\bullet} + ... + m^0\mu_j^{\bullet}) \; (j=1,...,n). \quad (142)$$

We recall that R_{mU} (U∈***Prob***[S]) is the distribution function with values

$$R_{mU}(x) := \int_S R_{m\theta}(x)dU(\theta) \; (x\in\mathbf{R}). \quad (143)$$

Theorem 15

a. **The associated space of the space *Prob*[[a,b];m-unim;$\mu_1,\dots,\mu_n$] is the pure moment space *Prob*[[a,b];$\mu_1^\bullet,\dots,\mu_n^\bullet$].**

b. **The associated space of the space *Prob*[[a,b];S,m-unim;$\mu_1,\dots,\mu_n$] is the pure moment space *Prob*[S;$\mu_1^\bullet,\dots,\mu_n^\bullet$].**

c. **The mapping defined by U→R_{mU} is a 1–1 linear continuous mapping of the associated space *Prob*[[a,b];$\mu_1^\bullet,\dots,\mu_n^\bullet$] onto the original space *Prob*[[a,b];m-unim;$\mu_1,\dots,\mu_n$].**

d. **The mapping defined by U→R_{mU} is a 1–1 linear continuous mapping of the associated space *Prob*[S;$\mu_1^\bullet,\dots,\mu_n^\bullet$] onto the original space *Prob*[[a,b];S,m-unim;$\mu_1,\dots,\mu_n$].**

Proof
By Theorem 14, Ch.2.Th.1. and Ch.2.Th.5.a •

3.6. Existence and Extremal Points of m-Unimodal Moment Spaces

3.6.1. Existence Conditions

By Ch.2.Th.1 and by the preceding Theorem 15, the spaces

Prob[[a,b];m-unim;$\mu_1,\dots,\mu_n$] , ***Prob***[[a,b];S,m-unim;$\mu_1,\dots,\mu_n$]

exist iff the corresponding associated spaces

Prob[[a,b];$\mu_1^\bullet,\dots,\mu_n^\bullet$] , ***Prob***[S;$\mu_1^\bullet,\dots,\mu_n^\bullet$]

exist. Hence, the existence problem of m-unimodal moment spaces is reduced to the existence problem of pure moment spaces, and the latter is solved in section 3.2. For small values of n, it is also possible, and instructive, to explicit the conditions (129) and (130).

3.6.2. Associated Central Moments Notation

When m-unimodal moment spaces are considered, then **the associated central moments** are defined by the relations

$$\mu_j^{\bullet\circ} = \sum_{0\le i\le j} j^{[i]}/i!(-\mu^\bullet)^i \mu_{j-i}^\bullet \quad (j=0,1,2,\ldots). \qquad (144)$$

corresponding to the relations (16). Then the inverse relations, corresponding to the relations (18), are

$$\mu_j^\bullet = \sum_{0\le i\le j} j^{[i]}/i!\mu^{\bullet i}\mu_{j-i}^{\bullet\circ} \quad (j=0,1,2,\ldots). \qquad (145)$$

In the relations (144) and (145),

$$\mu^\bullet := \mu_1^\bullet \ , \ \mu_0^\bullet := 1 \ , \ \mu_0^{\bullet\circ} := 1. \qquad (146)$$

We use the following special symbols:

$$\sigma^{\bullet 2} := \mu_2^{\bullet\circ} \ , \ \rho^{\bullet 3} := \mu_3^{\bullet\circ} \ , \ \alpha^{\bullet 4} := \mu_4^{\bullet\circ} \ , \beta^{\bullet 5} := \mu_5^{\bullet\circ} \ , \ \gamma^{\bullet 6} := \mu_6^{\bullet\circ}, \qquad (147)$$

corresponding to the symbols defined by the relations (19).

3.6.3. Extremal Distributions

By Theorem 13, Theorem 15 and by Ch.2.3, the n+1-rectangular distribution

$$p_1 R_{m\theta_1} + \ldots + p_{n+1} R_{m\theta_{n+1}}, \qquad (148)$$

is an extremal point of the space ***Prob***$[[a,b];\text{m-unim};\mu_1,\ldots,\mu_n]$ iff the n+1-atomic distribution

$$p_1 A\theta_1 + \ldots + p_{n+1} A\theta_{n+1} \qquad (149)$$

is an extremal point of the space ***Prob***$[[a,b];\mu_1^\bullet,\ldots,\mu_n^\bullet]$. By the same Theorems, the convex combination (148) is an extremal point of the space ***Prob***$[[a,b];S,\text{m-unim};\mu_1,\ldots,\mu_n]$ iff the corresponding convex combination (149) is an extremal point of the space ***Prob***$[S;\mu_1^\bullet,\ldots,\mu_n^\bullet]$.

Hence, the problem of the determination of the extremal points of the unimodal moment spaces is reduced to the corresponding problem for pure moment spaces. The latter problem has been considered in 3.2.

3.7. Particular m-Unimodal Moment Spaces

3.7.1. Various Moment Notations

In the case of 3 moment constraints, the following moments can be used:

a. The **original moments** μ_1,μ_2,μ_3.

b. The **central moments** μ,σ^2,ρ^3 defined in 3.1.7. (Of course, this terminology is improper in the case of μ).

c. The **associated moments** $\mu_1^\bullet,\mu_2^\bullet,\mu_3^\bullet$ defined in 3.5.2..

d. The **associated central moments** $\mu^\bullet,\sigma^{\bullet 2},\rho^{\bullet 3}$ defined in 3.6.2. (Improper terminology in the case of $\mu^\bullet$).

We here summarize the relations between the triples (μ_1,μ_2,μ_3), (μ,σ^2,ρ^3), $(\mu_1^\bullet,\mu_2^\bullet,\mu_3^\bullet)$ and $(\mu^\bullet,\sigma^{\bullet 2},\rho^{\bullet 3})$.

Relations connecting (μ_1,μ_2,μ_3) *and* (μ,σ^2,ρ^3):

$$\mu := \mu_1, \qquad (150)$$

$$\sigma^2 := \mu_2-\mu_1^2, \qquad (150)$$

$$\rho^3 := \mu_3-3\mu_1\mu_2+2\mu_1^3, \qquad (150)$$

$$\mu_1 = \mu, \qquad (150)$$

$$\mu_2 = \sigma^2+\mu^2, \qquad (151)$$

$$\mu_3 = \rho^3+3\mu\sigma^2+\mu^3. \qquad (151)$$

Relations connecting $(\mu_1^\bullet,\mu_2^\bullet,\mu_3^\bullet)$ *and* $(\mu^\bullet,\sigma^{\bullet 2},\rho^{\bullet 3})$:

$$\mu^\bullet := \mu_1^\bullet, \qquad (152)$$

$$\sigma^{\bullet 2} := \mu_2^\bullet-\mu_1^{\bullet 2}, \qquad (152)$$

$$\rho^{\bullet 3} := \mu_3^\bullet-3\mu_1^\bullet\mu_2^\bullet+2\mu_1^{\bullet 3}, \qquad (152)$$

$$\mu_1^{\bullet} = \mu^{\bullet}, \tag{153}$$

$$\mu_2^{\bullet} = \sigma^{\bullet 2}+\mu^{\bullet 2}, \tag{153}$$

$$\mu_3^{\bullet} = \rho^{\bullet 3}+3\mu^{\bullet}\sigma^{\bullet 2}+\mu^{\bullet 3}. \tag{153}$$

Relations connecting (μ_1,μ_2,μ_3) *and* $(\mu_1^{\bullet},\mu_2^{\bullet},\mu_3^{\bullet})$:

$$\mu_1^{\bullet} := 2\mu_1-m, \tag{154}$$

$$\mu_2^{\bullet} := 3\mu_2-2m\mu_1, \tag{154}$$

$$\mu_3^{\bullet} := 4\mu_3-3m\mu_2, \tag{154}$$

$$\mu_1 = 1/2(\mu_1^{\bullet}+m), \tag{155}$$

$$\mu_2 = 1/3(\mu_2^{\bullet}+m\mu_1^{\bullet}+m^2), \tag{155}$$

$$\mu_3 = 1/4(\mu_3^{\bullet}+m\mu_2^{\bullet}+m^2\mu_1^{\bullet}+m^3). \tag{155}$$

Relations connecting (μ_1,μ_2,μ_3) *and* $(\mu^{\bullet},\sigma^{\bullet 2},\rho^{\bullet 3})$:

$$\mu_1 = 1/2(\mu^{\bullet}+m), \tag{156}$$

$$\mu_2 = 1/3(\sigma^{\bullet 2}+\mu^{\bullet 2}+m\mu^{\bullet}+m^2) \tag{156}$$

$$\mu_3 = 1/4[\rho^{\bullet 3}+3\mu^{\bullet}\sigma^{\bullet 2}+\mu^{\bullet 3}+m(\sigma^{\bullet 2}+\mu^{\bullet 2})+m^2\mu^{\bullet}+m^3], \tag{156}$$

$$\mu^{\bullet} = 2\mu_1-m, \tag{157}$$

$$\sigma^{\bullet 2} = 3\mu_2-4\mu_1^2+2m\mu_1-m^2, \tag{157}$$

$$\rho^{\bullet 3} = 2(2\mu_3-9\mu_1\mu_2+8\mu_1^3)+6m(\mu_2-2\mu_1^2)+6m^2\mu_1-2m^3. \tag{157}$$

Relations connecting (μ,σ^2,ρ^3) *and* $(\mu_1^{\bullet};\mu_2^{\bullet},\mu_3^{\bullet})$:

$$\mu = 1/2(\mu_1^{\bullet}+m), \tag{158}$$

$$\sigma^2 = 1/12(4\mu_2^{\bullet}-3\mu_1^{\bullet 2}-2m\mu_1^{\bullet}+m^2), \tag{158}$$

$$\rho^3 = 1/4[\mu_3^{\bullet}-2\mu_1^{\bullet}\mu_2^{\bullet}+\mu_1^{\bullet 3}-m(\mu_2^{\bullet}-\mu_1^{\bullet 2})], \tag{158}$$

$$\mu_1^{\bullet} = 2\mu - m, \tag{159}$$

$$\mu_2^{\bullet} = 3(\sigma^2+\mu^2) - 2m\mu, \tag{159}$$

$$\mu_3^{\bullet} = 4(\rho^3+3\mu\sigma^2+\mu^3) - 3m(\sigma^2+\mu^2). \tag{159}$$

Relations connecting (μ,σ^2,ρ^3) *and* $(\mu^{\bullet},\sigma^{\bullet 2},\rho^{\bullet 3})$:

$$\mu^{\bullet} = 2\mu - m, \tag{160}$$

$$\sigma^{\bullet 2} = 3\sigma^2 - (\mu-m)^2, \tag{160}$$

$$\rho^{\bullet 3} = 4\rho^3 - 6(\mu-m)\sigma^2 + 2(\mu-m)^3, \tag{160}$$

$$\mu = (\mu^{\bullet}+m)/2, \tag{161}$$

$$\sigma^2 = [4\sigma^{\bullet 2} + (\mu^{\bullet}-m)^2]/12, \tag{161}$$

$$\rho^3 = [\rho^{\bullet 3} + (\mu^{\bullet}-m)\sigma^{\bullet 2}]/4. \tag{161}$$

In this section we explicit the existence conditions of the m-unimodal moment spaces in case of n=1,2,3 moment constraints. These conditions are direct by the method described in 3.6.1, based on the consideration of the associated spaces and on the results of 3.2 and 3.3. However, we shall use the more instructive method based on Theorem 13.c in the cases n=1,2.

3.7.2. One Moment Constraint

The space ***Prob***$[[a,b];m\text{-unim};\mu_1]$ exists iff

$$\mu_1 \in \mathrm{Co}\{1/2(m+\theta) \,/\, \theta \in [a,b]\} = [1/2(a+m), 1/2(m+b)]. \tag{162}$$

Let $a_1=a<a_2<\ldots<a_k=b$. The space

$$\textbf{\textit{Prob}}[[a,b];\{a_1,\ldots,a_k\},m\text{-unim};\mu_1]$$

exists iff

$$\mu_1 \in \mathrm{Co}\{1/2(m+\theta) \,/\, \theta \in \{a_1,\ldots,a_k\}\}$$

$$= \mathrm{Co}\{1/2(m+a_1),\ldots,1/2(m+a_k)\} = [1/2(a+m), 1/2(m+b)]. \tag{163}$$

3.7.3. Two Moment Constraints

In $\mathbf{R}^2 = \{(x,y)\}$, we denote by Par[a,b] the piece of parabola with parametric equations

$$x = 1/2(m+\theta) =: f(\theta)\ ,\ y = 1/3(m^2+m\theta+\theta^2) =: g(\theta)\ \ (a \leq \theta \leq b). \qquad (164)$$

The elimination of θ furnishes the equation

$$y = 1/3(m^2-2mx+4x^3) =: \varphi(x)\ \ (1/2(a+m) \leq x \leq 1/2(m+b)) \qquad (165)$$

of Par[a,b].

For $\alpha,\beta \in [a,b]$, we denote by $P[\alpha]$ the point $(f(\alpha),g(\alpha))$, by $Seg[\alpha,\beta]$ the straight line segment connecting the points $P[\alpha]$ and $P[\beta]$ and by $Line[\alpha,\beta]$ $(\alpha \neq \beta)$ the straight line through the points $P[\alpha]$ and $P[\beta]$.

The equation of $Line[\alpha,\beta]$ is

$$y = 1/3[2x(m+\alpha+\beta)-(m\alpha+m\beta+\alpha\beta)]. \qquad (166)$$

Continuous case

Theorem 16

The space *Prob*[[a,b];m-unim;μ_1,μ_2] exists iff one of the followong equivalent conditions a, b, c is satisfied.

a. **The point (μ_1,μ_2) belongs to the closed convex set with frontier Par[a,b] and Seg[a,b].**

b.

$$\mathbf{1/2(a+m) \leq \mu_1 \leq 1/2(m+b),}$$
$$\mathbf{1/3(m^2-2\mu_1 m+4\mu_1^2) \leq \mu_2 \leq 1/3[2\mu_1(a+m+b)-(am+mb+ab)].} \qquad (167)$$

c.

$$\mathbf{a \leq \mu^{\bullet} \leq b,}$$
$$\mathbf{0 \leq \sigma^{\bullet 2} \leq (b-\mu^{\bullet})(\mu^{\bullet}-a).} \qquad (168)$$

Proof

a. By Theorem 13.c, the space exists iff

$$(\mu_1,\mu_2) \in Co\{(f(\theta),g(\theta)) \,/\, \theta\in[a,b]\}. \qquad (169)$$

The latter convex hull is the set delimited by Par[a,b] and Seg[a,b] (Fig.5).

b. The relations (169) and (167) are equivalent by the equations (165) of Par[a,b] and (166) of Line[α,β] with α:=a, β:=b.

c. The relations (167) and (168) are equivalent by the first two relations (156) and the first two relations (157) •

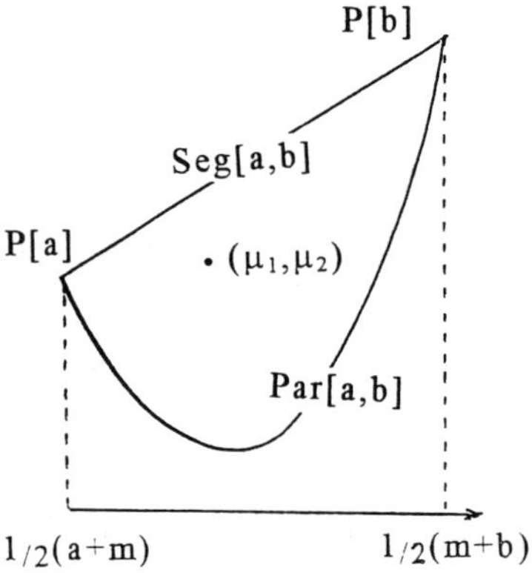

Fig.5. Effective domain of *Prob*[[a,b];m-unim;μ_1,μ_2]

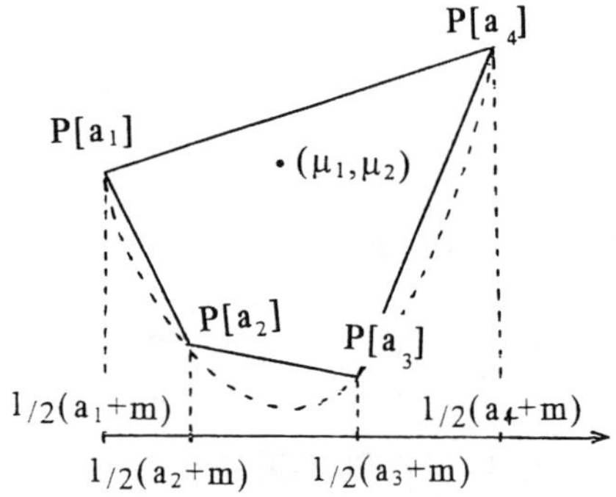

Fig.6. Effective domain of *Prob*[[a,b];{a_1,a_2,a_3,a_4},m-unim;μ_1,μ_2]

Discrete case

Theorem 17

Let a_1:=a <a_2<...<a_k:=b. The space *Prob*[[a,b];{$a_1,...,a_k$},m-unim;μ_1,μ_2] exists if one of the following equivalent conditions a, b is satisfied.

a. The point (μ_1,μ_2) belongs to the convex polygon with vertices P[a_1],...,P[a_k].

b. The point (μ_1,μ_2) is situated under the line Line[a,b] and above the lines Line[a_1,a_2], Line[a_2,a_3],...,Line[a_{k-1},a_k].

Proof

a. By Theorem 1.c, the space exists iff

$$(\mu_1,\mu_2) \in \mathrm{Co}\{(f(\theta),g(\theta)) \,/\, \theta\in\{a_1,...,a_k\}\}$$

$$= \mathrm{Co}\{P[a_1],...,P[a_k]\}.$$

The latter convex hull is the polygon with vertices P[a_1],...,P[a_k]. See Fig.6.

b. The conditions a. and b. are equivalent. See Fig.6 •

The equations of the lines mentioned in b result from (166). Hence, it is easy to translate the condition b in algebraic form.

3.7.4. Three Moment Constraints

Continuous case

Theorem 10

The space *Prob*[[a,b];m-unim;μ_1,μ_2,μ_3] exists iff

$$a \le \mu^{\bullet} \le b, \tag{170}$$

$$0 \le \sigma^{\bullet 2} \le (\mu^{\bullet}-a)(b-\mu^{\bullet}), \tag{170}$$

$$\sigma^{\bullet 4}/(\mu^{\bullet}-a) - (\mu^{\bullet}-a)\sigma^{\bullet 2} \le \rho^{\bullet 3} \le (b-\mu^{\bullet})\sigma^{\bullet 2} - \sigma^{\bullet 4}/(b-\mu^{\bullet}), \tag{170}$$

where the fractions must be replaced by 0 if the denominator is 0.

Proof

The Theorem results from 3.6.1 and Th.5.c •

3.8. Approximation of a finite-rectangular by a finite-atomic distribution

3.8.1. Problem

When numerical calculations are involved, the unimodal distributions are approximated by convex combinations of 1-rectangular distributions R_{mn} ($m,n\in\mathbf{N}$), after a preliminary change of the money unit. Sometimes, the latter convex combinations are not yet suitable for the calculations and they must be replaced by finite-atomic distributions concentrated on $\mathbf{N}$. This happens, for instance, when numerical ruin probabilities must be obtained.

We hereafter indicate how the 1-rectangular distribution R_{0n} can be approximated by a finite-atomic distribution concentrated on the set $[0,n]_{int}$, in such a way that the four first moments μ_1, μ_2, μ_3 and μ_4 are preserved if $n\geq 4$. By a translation, the results can be applied to the 1-rectangular distribution R_{mn}, and then they can be used in any convex combinations of distributions R_{mn} ($m,n\in\mathbf{N}$).

We need the sums

$$\Sigma_{2\leq k\leq n-2}\, k^j \quad (j=1,2,3,4;\ n\geq 4). \tag{171}$$

They can be calculated via the sums

$$\Sigma_{2\leq k\leq n-2}\, k^{[j]} \quad (j=1,2,3,4;\ n\geq 4),$$

by the relations

$$\Delta k^{[j+1]} = (j+1)k^{[j]}\ ,\ \Sigma_{m\leq k\leq n}\, \Delta a_k = a_{n+1}-a_m,$$

where Δ is the ascending difference operator: $\Delta a_k := a_{k+1}-a_k$.

More directly, by App.K. (K34),

$$\Sigma_{1\leq k\leq n}\, k = 1/2\, n + 1/2\, n^2, \tag{172}$$

$$\Sigma_{1\leq k\leq n}\, k^2 = 1/6\, n + 1/2\, n^2 + 1/3\, n^3, \tag{172}$$

$$\Sigma_{1\leq k\leq n}\, k^3 = 1/4\, n^2 + 1/2\, n^3 + 1/4\, n^4, \tag{172}$$

$$\Sigma_{1\leq k\leq n}\, k^4 = -1/30\, n + 1/3\, n^3 + 1/2\, n^4 + 1/5\, n^5 \tag{172}$$

and then

$$\sum_{2\le k\le n-2} k = 1/2\ n(n-3), \qquad (173)$$

$$\sum_{2\le k\le n-2} k^2 = 1/6\ (n-3)(2n^2-3n+4), \qquad (173)$$

$$\sum_{2\le k\le n-2} k^3 = 1/4\ n(n-3)(n^2-3n+4), \qquad (173)$$

$$\sum_{2\le k\le n-2} k^4 = 1/30\ (n-3)[(n-1)(n-2)(6n^2-9n+10)+15n]. \qquad (173)$$

3.8.2. Solution

By (131), $$\mu_j(R_{0n}) = n^j/(j+1).$$

The goal is to approximate R_{0n} by a finite-atomic probability distribution

$$F_n = p_0A_0+p_1A_1+...+p_{n-1}A_{n-1}+p_nA_n$$

in such a way that

$$\mu_j(F_n)=\mu_j(R_{0n})\ (1\le j\le n\wedge 4),$$

i.e.

$$p_0 0^j+p_1 1^j+...+p_{n-1}(n-1)^j+p_n n^j = n^j/(j+1)\ \ (0\le j\le n\wedge 4), \qquad (174)$$

The relation corresponding to j=0 is the probability constraint $\sum p_k=1$.

Case n=0

$$F_0 = R_{00} = A_0. \qquad (175_0)$$

Case n=1

Here $F_1=p_0A_0+p_1A_1$ and (174) is the system

$$p_0+p_1=1,$$

$$0p_0+1p_1= 1/2.$$

Hence

$$F_1 = 1/2\ A_0 + 1/2\ A_1. \qquad (175_1)$$

Case n=2

Here $F_2=p_0A_0+p_1A_1+p_2A_2$ and (174) is the system

$$p_0 + p_1 + p_2 = 1,$$

$$0p_0+1p_1+2p_2 = 1,$$

$$0^2p_0+1^2p_1+2^2p_2 = 4/3.$$

Hence,

$$F_2 = 1/6\ A_0 + 2/3\ A_1 + 1/6\ A_2. \qquad (175_2)$$

Case n=3

Here $F_3 = p_0A_0+p_1A_1+p_2A_2+p_3A_3$ and (174) is the system

$$p_0 + p_1 + p_2 + p_3 = 1,$$

$$0p_0+1p_1+2p_2+3p_3 = 3/2,$$

$$0^2p_0+1^2p_1+2^2p_2+3^2p_3 = 3,$$

$$0^3p_0+1^3p_1+2^3p_2+3^3p_3 = 27/4.$$

Hence,

$$F_3 = 1/8(A_0+3A_1+3A_2+A_3). \qquad (175_3)$$

Case n=4

Here $F_4=p_0A_0+p_1A_1+p_2A_2+p_3A_3+p_4A_4$ and (174) is the system

$$p_0 + p_1 + p_2 + p_3 + p_4 = 1,$$

$$0p_0+1p_1+2p_2+3p_3+4p_4 = 2,$$

$$0^2p_0+1^2p_1+2^2p_2+3^2p_3+4^2p_4 = 16/3,$$

$$0^3p_0+1^3p_1+2^3p_2+3^3p_3+4^3p_4 = 16,$$

$$0^4p_0+1^4p_1+2^4p_2+3^4p_3+4^4p_4=256/5.$$

Hence,

$$F_3 = 1/90(7A_0+32A_1+12A_2+32A_3+7A_4). \qquad (175_4)$$

Case n>4

In this case we display F_n as

$$F_n = p_0A_0 + p_1A_1 + p\textstyle\sum_{2\le k\le n-2} A_k + p_{n-1}A_{n-1} + p_nA_n. \qquad (175_n)$$

Then the 5 unknown quantities p_0, p_1, p, p_{n-1}, p_n must satisfy the system of 5 linear equations

$$0^j p_0 + 1^j p_1 + p\sum_{2\le k\le n-2} k^j + p_{n-1}(n-1)^j + p_n n^j = n^j/(j+1) \quad (j=0,1,2,3,4).$$

(where $0^0:=1$). The sums result from the relations (173). The solution of the system is, after long but direct calcultaions,

$$p_0 = p_n = [5n-6]/[12(n^2-1)], \tag{176}$$

$$p_1 = p_{n-1} = [n(13n-20)]/[12(n-2)(n^2-1)], \tag{176}$$

$$p = [n(n^2-5n+5)]/[(n-2)(n-3)(n^2-1)]. \tag{176}$$

In fact, (175_n) with the coefficients furnished by (176) is valid in the case n=4 also.

Chapter 4

General Optimization Problems

4.1. Components of General Problem

4.1.1. Actuarial Optimization Problems

The insurer wants to calculate the functional $T(F_{true})$ of the distribution F_{true}. But he ignores the true distribution F_{true}. His information on that function is summarized by the relation $F_{true} \in \boldsymbol{Space}$, where ***Space*** is some family of probability distributions. Then

$$\inf_{F \in \boldsymbol{Space}} T(F) \leq T(F_{true}) \leq \sup_{F \in \boldsymbol{Space}} T(F)$$

and the problem is the determination of the values

$$\inf_{F \in \boldsymbol{Space}} T(F)\ ,\ \sup_{F \in \boldsymbol{Space}} T(F). \tag{1}$$

More precisely, the **minimization problem** is the problem

$$P = \inf_{F \in \boldsymbol{Space}} T(F) \tag{2}$$

and the **maximization problem** is the problem

$$Q = \sup_{F \in \boldsymbol{Space}} T(F). \tag{3}$$

The functional $T(\cdot)$ is the **objective functional** of the **optimization** (minimization or maximization) **problems**. ***Space*** is the **hypothetic space**.

If the insurer gathers more information on F_{true}, then he can replace his hypothetic space ***Space*** by some smaller space ***space*** and then he obtains closer bounds for $T(F_{true})$:

$$\inf_{F \in \boldsymbol{Space}} T(F) \leq \inf_{F \in \boldsymbol{space}} T(F) \leq T(F_{true}) \leq \sup_{F \in \boldsymbol{space}} T(F) \leq \sup_{F \in \boldsymbol{Space}} T(F).$$

4.1.2. Examples of Objective Functionals

Premiums

Let X be a risk with distribution F. Then T(F) can be any premium, loaded or not, related to X or to some reinsured part of X.

For instance, X can be a total claim amount in some portfolio and T(F) can be the pure premium of the reinsurer in case of a stop-loss reinsurance with retention limit t. Then

$$T(F) = E_F(X-t)_+ = \int(x-t)_+ dF(x), \tag{4}$$

The pure stop-loss premium optimization problem is extensively treated in Ch.8.4.

The optimization of loaded premiums of reinsured risks, calculated according to various premium principles (expected value premium, variance premium, standard deviation premium, Esscher premium) is treated in Chapter 10.

Compound distributions

Let $p_0, p_1, p_2, \ldots$ be a sequence of positive numbers such that

$$p_0+p_1+p_2+\ldots = 1.$$

For fixed x, we can consider

$$T(F) = 1 - \textstyle\sum_{n\geq 0} p_n F^{*n}(x). \tag{5}$$

In particular, in the **compound Poisson** case,

$$p_n = e^{-\lambda}\lambda^n/n! \ (n=0,1,2,\ldots), \tag{6}$$

where $\lambda>0$.

The last member of (5) can be interpreted as a fixed-time ruin probability in a general risk model. The probabilities (6) correspond to the classical risk model (see I.Ch.5.2.1).

The optimization of the functional (5) is treated in Chapter 11.

Ruin probabilities

T(F) can be any ruin probability in any risk model with i.i.d. partial claim amounts $X_1, X_2, \ldots$, with distribution function F. For instance, in the classical risk model, we can consider the infinite-time ruin probability

$$T(F) = \Psi(F, u, \eta) \qquad (7)$$

corresponding to the fixed initial risk reserve $u \geq 0$ and the fixed security loading $\eta > 0$. Then the optimization of T(F) is called a **Schmitter's problem**. This problem is also treated in Chapter 11.

T(F) can also be the adjustment coefficient ρ corresponding to the security loading η, i.e. the strictly positive root of the equation

$$\int_{[0,\infty[} e^{\rho x} dF(x) = 1 + \rho\mu_1(1+\eta), \qquad (8)$$

where μ_1 is the first moment of F. The optimization of the adjustment coefficients is considered in Ch.11.5.

Distances

Numerous other examples of functionals $T(\cdot)$ can be furnished. We here consider the **mean quadratic distance** between F and some fixed distribution F_{fix} on [a,b], defined as follows:

$$T(F) = [\int_{[0,b]} (F(x) - F_{fix}(x))^2 dx]^{1/2}. \qquad (9)$$

Other definitions of the distance between F and F_{fix} are possible. A distance minimization is performed in Chapter 10.

4.1.3. Examples of Hypothetic Spaces

The following are examples of hypothetic spaces.

$$\boldsymbol{Prob}[[a,b];\mu_1,\ldots,\mu_n], \qquad (10)$$

$$\boldsymbol{Prob}[[a,b];\text{m-unim};\mu_1,\ldots,\mu_n], \qquad (11)$$

$$\textit{\textbf{Prob}}[[a,b];\text{unim};\mu_1,\ldots,\mu_n], \tag{12}$$

$$\textit{\textbf{Mixt}}[F_\theta(\theta\in I);\mu_1,\ldots,\mu_n], \tag{13}$$

$$\textit{\textbf{Prob}}[[a,b];\mu_1,[0,\mu_2]]. \tag{14}$$

The space (12) is the space of unimodal distributions concentrated on [a,b], with moments μ_1, ..., μ_n and with unspecified mode m in [a,b].

The space (14) is the space of probability distributions concentrated on [a,b], with first moment μ_1 and a second moment in the interval $[0,\mu_2]$.

Of course, other constraints than moment constraints can be introduced, for instance more general integral constraints.

4.1.4. Usual Assumptions on Hypothetic Space

In all cases treated in this book, ***Space*** is a Krein-Milman space (Ch.2.4). More specifically, ***Space*** will have the following properties. The assumptions on ***Space*** are always recalled explicitly in the Theorems.

Space is convex

The spaces (10), (11), (13) and (14) are convex. The space (12) is not because a strict convex combination (i.e. a convex combination with strictly positive coefficients) of unimodal distributions with different modes is not a unimodal distribution.

Nevertheless, optimization problems on the space (12) can be solved in two steps. Indeed, let ***Space*** be the space (12) and ***Space***(m) the space (11). Then

$$\sup_{F\in \textit{\textbf{Space}}} T(F) = \sup_{m\in[a,b]} [\sup_{F\in \textit{\textbf{Space}}(m)} T(F)] \tag{15}$$

and a similar relation holds for the minimization problem.

Space is compact

The spaces (10) to (14) are compact.

The extremal points of Space are easily detectable and calculable

This condition is essential in the numerical treatment of the optimization problems. It is not used in the analytical arguments. By the foregoing Theorems of Ch.2 and Ch.3, it is satisfied for the spaces (10), (11) and (13).

Optimization problems on the space (14) can be solved via the problems on the space with 2 moment constraints

$$\boldsymbol{Space}(\mu) = \boldsymbol{Prob}[[a,b];\mu_1,\mu],$$

where the first moment μ_1 is fixed, and the second moment μ is variable. Indeed, if ***Space*** is space (14), then

$$\sup_{F\in \boldsymbol{Space}} T(F) = \sup_{\mu\in[0,\mu_2]}[\sup_{F\in \boldsymbol{Space}(\mu)} T(F)].$$

Space can be approximated by a sequence of subspaces $S_1,S_2,\ldots$ with a finite number of extremal points

This means that any point of ***Space*** is a weak limit of points of $\boldsymbol{S}_1\cup\boldsymbol{S}_2\cup\ldots$ This assumption is satisfied for the spaces (10), (11) and (13). For instance, in the case of the space (10) with a=0, let $\delta:=b/n_0$. Then $\boldsymbol{S}_{n_0}$ can be the subspace of ***Space*** of finite-atomic distributions concentrated on the set $\{0,\delta,2\delta,\ldots,n_0\delta\}$. It becomes the space

$$\boldsymbol{Prob}[[0,n_0]_{int};\mu_1/\delta,\mu_2/\delta^2,\ldots,\mu_n/\delta^n]$$

if a new money unit is introduced in such a way that the amount δ in the current money becomes the amount 1 in the new money.

Again, this condition is not used in analytical arguments.

4.1.5. Usual Assumptions on Objective Functional

An essential assumption on T(F), when numerical optimization problems are considered, is the following:

T(F) is very fastly calculable numerically

Indeed, thousands of values T(F) must be compared to each other in the execution of the numerical algorithms.

The functionals defined by (4), (5) (with p_n defined by (6)), (7), (8) and (9) are calculable quickly enough. Finite-time ruin probabilities in the classical model, or ruin probabilities in more sophisticated models cannot yet be optimized with enough precision, because the computing time of the corresponding functional T(F) is too long.

T(·) is continuous on Space

This is an essential condition in most analytical results. It is not strictly necessary in the numerical algorithms.

The functionals defined by (4), (7), (8) and (9) are continuous.

4.2. General Terminology

4.2.1. Terminology Based on Objective Functional

The structure of the objective functional T(·) leads to the following terminology.

An integral optimization problem is a problem with an objective functional

$$T(F) = \int g\,dF.$$

Here g is a fixed function, integrable with respect to all distributions F of the hypothetic space.

A multiple integral optimization problem is a problem with objective functional

$$T(F) = \Psi\left(\int g_1 dF, \ldots, \int g_k dF\right).$$

Here $g_1, \ldots, g_k$ are fixed functions, integrable with respect to all F in the hypothetic space.

If T(F) is a stop-loss premium, an Esscher premium, a ruin probability,..., then the corresponding optimization problem is a **stop-loss premium problem, an Esscher premium problem, a ruin probability problem,...**

A general optimization problem is an optimization problem with no special structure assumptions on the objective functional T(·).

4.2.2. Terminology Based on Basic Space

In most cases, the hypothetic space is a subspace of some **basic space**

$$\textit{\textbf{Mixt}}[F_\theta(\theta \in S)] \ , \ \textit{\textbf{Prob}}[S] \ , \ \textit{\textbf{Prob}}[[a,b];\text{m-unim}],$$

resulting from the introduction of constraints (moment constraints, or more general integral constraints) on the distributions of the basic space.

The optimization problem is **a mixture problem**, or **a problem on a space of mixtures**, when the basic space is ***Mixt***[$F_\theta(\theta \in S)$]. It is **a pure problem** when the basic space is ***Prob***[S]. It is **a m-unimodal problem** when the basic space is ***Prob***[[a,b];m-unim].

4.2.3. Terminology Based on Constraints

A moment problem is an optimization problem with moment equality constraints

$$\mu_1(F) = \mu_1 \ , \ \dots \ , \ \mu_n(F) = \mu_n.$$

It is **a problem with moment inequality constraints** if the equalities are replaced by weak inequalities. It is **a problem with mixed moment constraints** if only some equalities are replaced by weak inequalities.

A problem with integral constraints is an optimization problem with constraints

$$\int f_1 dF = \alpha_1 \ , \ \dots \ , \ \int f_n dF = \alpha_n.$$

It is **a problem with integral inequality constraints** if the equalities are replaced by weak inequalities. It is **a problem with mixed integral constraints** if only some equalities are replaced by weak inequalities.

4.2.4. Combined Terminology

Of course, the terminology introduced in 4.2.1, 4.2.2 and 4.2.3 is juxtaposed. For instance, the following problem P is **an integral pure moment problem**:

$$P := \inf_{F \in \textit{\textbf{Sp}}}[\int g dF \ / \ \mu_1,\dots,\mu_n], \text{ where } \textit{\textbf{Sp}} = \textit{\textbf{Prob}}[S].$$

It can be displayed as

$$P = \inf_{F\in \boldsymbol{Space}}[\int g dF], \text{ where } \boldsymbol{Space} = \boldsymbol{Prob}[S;\mu_1,\ldots,\mu_n].$$

The hypothetic space of this problem is ***Space*** and its basic space is ***Sp***.

The terminology can be completed by the adjectives

continuous, corresponding to $S=[a,b]$, or
discrete, corresponding to $S=[i_0,n_0]_{int}$,

minimization, corresponding to **inf**, or
maximization, corresponding to **sup**.

Hence, the foregoing problem P is **a continuous integral pure moment minimization problem**.

Of course, a simplified terminology can be used if it is not misleading. Some adjectives can be omitted when they are obvious from the context.

4.3. General Problems with Extremal Solutions

4.3.1. Properties of a Functional on Segments

Let T be a functional on the convex space ***Space*** and let $F,G\in$***Space***. **The restriction of T to the segment [F,G]** is the function T_{FG} on the interval [0,1], with values

$$T_{FG}(\tau) := T[(1-\tau)F+\tau G] \quad (0\leq\tau\leq1). \tag{16}$$

Let ***Pr*** be any property of real functions of one real variable. Instances of ***Pr*** are: to be continuous, to have a derivative, to be monotonic, to be concave,...

We say that **the functional T has the property *Pr* on segments**, if the restriction T_{FG} to any segment [F,G] ($F,G\in$***Space***) has the property ***Pr***.

Examples

T is continuous on segments if $T_{FG}(\tau)$ is a continuous function of $\tau\in[0,1]$, for all distributions $F,G\in$***Space***.

T is differentiable on segments if the derivative T_{FG}' exists on [0,1] for all distributions F,G∈***Space***. Of course $T_{FG}'(0)$ is the right-sided derivative at the point 0 and $T_{FG}'(1)$ is the left-sided derivative at the point 1.

T is convex on segments if $T_{FG}(\tau)$ is a convex function of $\tau\in[0,1]$, for all distributions F,G∈***Space***.

T is concave on segments if $T_{FG}(\tau)$ is a concave function of $\tau\in[0,1]$, for all distributions F,G∈***Space***.

T is monotonic on segments if $T_{FG}(\tau)$ is a monotonic function of $\tau\in[0,1]$, for all distributions F,G∈***Space***.

T is linear on segments if $T_{FG}(\tau)$ is a linear (in the elementary sense; we should say **affine** instead of **linear**) function of $\tau\in[0,1]$ for all F,G∈***Space***.

Remarks

a. We can say that **T is increasing on the particular segment [F,G]**, if $T_{FG}(\tau)$ is an increasing function of $\tau\in[0,1]$. But we do not consider a **functional increasing on segments**. Indeed, in the spirit of the foregoing definitions, this functional must be such that $T_{FG}(\tau)$ is an increasing function of $\tau\in[0,1]$, for all F,G∈***Space***. But then both T_{FG} and T_{GF} must be increasing, and that is only possible if T is constant on the segments [F,G]. In other words, functionals increasing on segments are constant on segments, and then they are constant on ***Space***. For the same reasons, **functionals decreasing on segments** are not considered. We observe that functionals monotonic on segments are increasing on some segments, and decreasing on some other segments.

b. The **convexity**, the **concavity** and the **linearity** of the functional T is defined at once on the whole space ***Space*** by the following relations.

Convexity:

$$T(\sum p_i F_i) \leq \sum p_i T(F_i). \tag{17}$$

Concavity:

$$T(\sum p_i F_i) \geq \sum p_i T(F_i). \tag{18}$$

Linearity:

$$T(\sum p_i F_i) = \sum p_i T(F_i). \tag{19}$$

They must be true for all convex combinations $\sum p_i F_i$ of distributions $F_i \in \boldsymbol{Space}$. This **global convexity, concavity** or **linearity** is equivalent to the **convexity, concavity** or **linearity on segments** resp.

The equivalence results from an argument by induction on the number k of terms of the convex combinations, based on the relation

$$p_1F_1+...+p_kF_k+p_{k+1}F_{k+1}$$
$$= (p_1+...+p_k)[(p_1+...+p_k)^{-1}(p_1F_1+...+p_kF_k)] + p_{k+1}F_{k+1}, \tag{20}$$

where the first member is a convex combination of $F_1, ..., F_k, F_{k+1}$. We observe that the expression in square brackets is a convex combination of the k distributions $F_1, ..., F_k$ and that the last member of (20) is a convex combination of this expression and of F_{k+1}.

c. We recall that **T is continuous on *Space*** (global definition), if

$$[F_n \in \boldsymbol{Space}(n=1,2,...),\ F_n \rightarrow_w F \in \boldsymbol{Space} \text{ as } n\uparrow\infty]$$
$$\Rightarrow\ [T(F_n)\rightarrow T(F) \text{ as } n\uparrow\infty]. \tag{21}$$

This (global) continuity is much stronger than the continuity on segments. For instance, let us consider the very simple functional T defined as

$$T(F) = F(x_0)\ \ (F \in \boldsymbol{Space}), \tag{22}$$

where x_0 is a fixed point in **R**. It is continuous on segments, because

$$T_{FG}(\tau) = (1-\tau)F(x_0)+\tau G(x_0)$$

is a continuous function of $\tau \in [0,1]$. But it is not continuous because the implication (21) is not necessarily satisfied. Indeed, by the very definition of weak convergence of distributions, the relation $F_n \rightarrow_w F$ implies that $F_n(x)\rightarrow F(x)$ when x is a continuity point of F, but not necessarily for all x. For instance, let x_0 be a discontinuity point of F and let F_n (n=1,2,...) be defined as

$$F_n(x) := F(x-n^{-1})\ (x \in \mathbf{R}).$$

Then, if x is any continuity point of F,

$$F_n(x) \to F(x-) = F(x) \text{ for } n\uparrow\infty,$$

Hence, $F_n \to_w F$. But

$$T(F_n) = F_n(x_0) \to F(x_0-) \neq F(x_0) = T(F)$$

and this means that T is not a continuous functional.

4.3.2. Functionals Minimum or Maximum at Segment Extremities

T is maximum at segment extremities if, for all F,G∈***Space***,

$$T_{FG}(\tau) \leq T_{FG}(0) = T(F) \quad (0\leq\tau\leq1) \tag{23}$$

or

$$T_{FG}(\tau) \leq T_{FG}(1) = T(G) \quad (0\leq\tau\leq1). \tag{24}$$

T is minimum at segment extremities if, for all F,G∈***Space***,

$$T_{FG}(\tau) \geq T_{FG}(0) = T(F) \quad (0\leq\tau\leq1) \tag{25}$$

or

$$T_{FG}(\tau) \geq T_{FG}(1) = T(G) \quad (0\leq\tau\leq1). \tag{26}$$

The following implications are direct

$$\text{T convex on segments} \Rightarrow \text{T maximum at segment extremities,} \tag{27}$$

$$\text{T concave on segments} \Rightarrow \text{T minimum at segment extremities,} \tag{28}$$

$$\text{T monotonic on segments} \Rightarrow \text{T maximum at segment extremities,} \tag{29}$$

$$\text{T monotonic on segments} \Rightarrow \text{T minimum at segments extremities.} \tag{30}$$

4.3.3. Existence of Extremal Solutions

By the relation

$$\inf_{F\in \boldsymbol{Space}} T(F) = -\sup_{F\in \boldsymbol{Space}}[-T(F)], \tag{31}$$

the minimization and maximization problems correspond symmetrically to each other. Mostly hereafter, only the maximization problem is treated.

Lemma

Let T be a functional, maximum at segment extremities, defined on the convex space *Space*, and let $G:=p_1H_1+...+p_kH_k$ be a convex combination of the points $H_j \in$ *Space* (j=1,...,k). Then

$$\mathbf{T(G) \leq T(H_j)} \tag{32}$$

for some j=1,...,k.

Proof
We may assume that $p_1,...,p_k>0$ and $k>1$. Then $p_1,...,p_k<1$. We can display G as

$$G = \tau H + (1-\tau)H_k, \tag{33}$$

with

$$H := q_1H_1 + ... + q_{k-1}H_{k-1}, \tag{34}$$

$$q_j := p_j/(p_1+...+p_{k-1}) \ (j=1,...,k-1) \ , \ \tau := p_1+...+p_{k-1}.$$

Then $T(G) \leq T(H)$ or $T(G) \leq T(H_k)$ because T is maximum at segment extremities. If $T(G) \leq T(H_k)$, we have finished. If $T(G) \leq T(H)$, then we repeat the argument with the convex combination (34), and we conclude that $T(H) \leq T(H_{k-1})$ or that T(H) is smaller than the value of T at some convex combination of the points H_1, ..., H_{k-2}. If necessary, the argument is repeated until only the point H_1 is left •

Theorem 1

Let T be a continuous functional, maximum at segment extremities, defined on the Krein-Milman space *Space*. Then a sequence of extremal points H_ν (ν=1,2,...) of *Space* exists, such that

$$\mathbf{T(H_\nu) \rightarrow \sup_{F \in \mathit{Space}} T(F)} \text{ as } \nu \uparrow \infty. \tag{35}$$

If the set *Ext* of extremal points of *Space* is compact, then an extremal point H_0 of *Space* exists, such that

$$\mathbf{T(H_0) = \sup_{F \in \mathit{Space}} T(F)}. \tag{36}$$

Proof
By Ch.1.Th.2, a point $G_0 \in$ ***Space*** exists, such that

$$TG_0 = \sup_{F \in \textit{Space}} TF =: s.$$

A sequence $G_\nu \in$Co ***Ext*** (ν=1,2,...) exists, such that

$$G_\nu \to_w G_0 \text{ as } \nu \uparrow \infty.$$

By the continuity of T,

$$T(G_\nu) \to T(G_0) = s \text{ as } \nu \uparrow \infty. \tag{37}$$

The point G_ν is a convex combination of extremal points $H_{\nu j}$ of ***Space***:

$$G_\nu = p_{\nu 1} H_{\nu 1} + \ldots + p_{\nu,k(\nu)} H_{\nu,k(\nu)}. \tag{38}$$

By the Lemma, some point $H_{\nu j}$=:H_ν exists, such that $T(G_\nu) \leq T(H_\nu)$. Then

$$T(H_\nu) \to s \text{ as } \nu \uparrow \infty \tag{39}$$

by (37). This proves (35).

We now assume that ***Ext*** is compact. Then a subsequence H_{ν_k} (k=1,2,...) and an extremal point H_0 of ***Ext*** exist, such that $H_{\nu_k} \to_w H_0$. Then $T(H_{\nu_k}) \to T(H_0)$ by the continuity of T. By (39), $T(H_{\nu_k}) \to s$. Hence, $T(H_0)=s$ •

We notice that Theorem 1 can be applied to the maximization of functionals convex on segments, by (27). The inf version of Theorem 1 can be applied to the minimization of functionals concave on segments, by (28). But no version can be applied to the maximization of functionals concave on segments, or to the minimization of functionals convex on segments.

Both Theorem 1 and its inf version can be applied to functionals linear on segments. In particular, they can be applied to the optimization of integral functionals $\int f dF$ (f fixed).

An extremal solution of the problems $\inf_{F \in \textit{Space}} T(F)$ or $\sup_{F \in \textit{Space}} T(F)$ is a solution belonging to the set ***Ext*** of extremal points of the hypothetic space ***Space***. Hence, the following is a tautological Corollary of Theorem 1:

Corollary

Let T be a continuous functional, maximum at segment extremities, on the Krein-Milman space *Space* and let the set *Ext* of extremal points of *Space* be compact. Then the problem $\sup_{F \in \textit{Space}} T(F)$ has an extremal solution •

A different, more instructive proof of this result, not based on the theory of Krein-Milman spaces, is furnished by Ch.6.Th.1. in the case of integral maximization problems on a space of mixtures with integral constraints. The latter proof uses the basic mixture Theorem (Ch.1.Th.6).

4.4. Multiple Integral Problems with Integral Constraints

4.4.1. Problem

We consider the problem

$$Q := \sup_{F \in \boldsymbol{Space}} T(F), \tag{40}$$

with hypothetic space

$$\boldsymbol{Space} := \boldsymbol{Mixt}[F_\theta(\theta \in S); \int f_1 = \alpha_1, \ldots, \int f_n = \alpha_n] \tag{41}$$

and objective functional

$$T(F) := \Psi(\int g_1 dF, \ldots, \int g_k dF) \tag{42}$$

on ***Space***. The functions $f_1, \ldots, f_n, g_1, \ldots, g_k, \Psi$ are fixed. The functions $f_1, \ldots, f_n, g_1, \ldots, g_k$ are supposed to be integrable with respect to all distributions F in the basic space $\boldsymbol{Mixt}[F_\theta(\theta \in S)]$.

We recall (Ch.2.1.1) that **a j-basic distribution of** $\boldsymbol{Mixt}[F_\theta(\theta \in S)]$ is a convex combination of j distributions $F_\theta(\theta \in S)$.

4.4.2. Existence of Finite-Basic Solutions

Theorem 2

In the maximization problem Q of 4.4.1, let *Space* be compact, and let T(F) be a continuous functional of F∈*Space*. Then the problem has an (n+k+1)-basic solution.

Proof
By Ch.1.Th.6,

$$\{(\int g_1 dF, \ldots, \int g_k dF, \int f_1 dF, \ldots, \int f_n dF) / F \in \boldsymbol{Mixt}[F_\theta(\theta \in S)]\}$$

$$= \mathrm{Co}\{(\int g_1 dF_\theta, \ldots, \int g_k dF_\theta, \int f_1 dF_\theta, \ldots, \int f_n dF_\theta) / \theta \in S\} \subseteq \mathbf{R}^{k+n}. \tag{43}$$

By Ch.1.Th.2, the problem (40) has a solution F∈***Space***. Then

$$F \in \textbf{\textit{Mixt}}[F_\theta(\theta \in S)]\ ,\ \int f_i dF = \alpha_i\ (i=1,\dots,n).$$

By (43),

$$(\int g_1 dF,\dots,\int g_k dF,\int f_1 dF,\dots,\int f_n dF)$$

$$\in \mathrm{Co}\{(\int g_1 dF_\theta,\dots,\int g_k dF_\theta,\int f_1 dF_\theta,\dots,\int f_n dF_\theta)\ /\ \theta \in S\}.$$

By Carathéodory (Ch.1.Th.10.a), the point

$$(\int g_1 dF,\dots,\int g_k dF,\int f_1 dF,\dots,\int f_n dF)$$

is a convex combination of k+n+1 points

$$(\int g_1 dF_\theta,\dots,\int g_k dF_\theta,\int f_1 dF_\theta,\dots,\int f_n dF_\theta)\ \ (\theta \in S).$$

Let this convex combination be

$$(\int g_1 dF,\dots,\int g_k dF,\int f_1 dF,\dots,\int f_n dF)$$

$$= \sum_{1\le j\le k+n+1} p_j(\int g_1 dF_{\theta_j},\dots,\int g_k dF_{\theta_j},\int f_1 dF_{\theta_j},\dots,\int f_n dF_{\theta_j}). \tag{44}$$

Let

$$G := \sum_{1\le j\le k+n+1} p_j F_{\theta_j}. \tag{45}$$

Then (44) becomes

$$(\int g_1 dF,\dots,\int g_k dF,\int f_1 dF,\dots,\int f_n dF) = (\int g_1 dG,\dots,\int g_k dG,\int f_1 dG,\dots,\int f_n dG),$$

i.e.

$$\int g_i dG = \int g_i dF\ \ (i=1,\dots,k), \tag{46}$$

$$\int f_i dG = \int f_i dF = \alpha_i\ \ (i=1,\dots,n). \tag{47}$$

By (46),

$$T(G) = \Psi(\int g_1 dG,\dots,\int g_k dG) = \Psi(\int g_1 dF,\dots,\int g_k dF) = T(F) = Q. \tag{48}$$

Let

$$U := \sum_{1\le j\le k+n+1} p_j A_{\theta_j}.$$

Then

$$G = F_U \in \textbf{\textit{Mixt}}[F_\theta(\theta \in S)]. \tag{49}$$

By the relations (47) and (49), G is a feasible distribution of the problem (40). By (48) the maximum Q is reached at the point G. Hence G is a solution of the problem •

The numerical computation of the solution, via the general optimization algorithm of Ch.10, shows that many problems covered by the Theorem, have a j-basic solution, with $j<k+n+1$.

4.5. Associated Pure Problem of an Optimization Problem With Integral Constraints

4.5.1. Definition of Associated Problem

We consider the problem

$$\mathrm{Sup}_{F\in \boldsymbol{Mixt}[F_\theta(\theta\in S)]}[T(F)/\textstyle\int f_1dF=\alpha_1,\ldots,\int f_ndF=\alpha_n]. \tag{50}$$

We replace the variable point F by F_U where U ranges over ***Prob***[S]. Then, by the definition of the space of mixtures, F_U ranges over ***Mixt***[$F_\theta(\theta\in S)$]. Hence, with the new variable point U, problem (50) becomes

$$\mathrm{Sup}_{U\in \boldsymbol{Prob}[S]}[T(F_U)/\textstyle\int f_1dF_U=\alpha_1,\ldots,\int f_ndF_U=\alpha_n]. \tag{51}$$

By the mixture elimination equality,

$$\int f_idF_U = \int f_i^\bullet dU \quad (i=1,\ldots,n), \tag{52}$$

where $f_i^\bullet$ is the associated function of f_i (Ch.1.3.2). Then (51) becomes the problem

$$\mathrm{Sup}_{U\in \boldsymbol{Prob}[S]}[T(F_U)/\textstyle\int f_1^\bullet dU=\alpha_1,\ldots,\int f_n^\bullet dU=\alpha_n]. \tag{53}$$

The latter is a pure problem because its basic space is the pure space ***Prob***[S]. The problem (53) is **the pure problem associated to the problem (50)**. As the foregoing discussion shows, the pure problem results from **the original problem** (50) by the introduction of the new variable point U instead of F.

The hypothetic space of the original problem (50) is

$$\boldsymbol{Space} := \boldsymbol{Mixt}[F_\theta(\theta\in S);\textstyle\int f_1=\alpha_1,\ldots,\int f_n=\alpha_n]. \tag{54}$$

The hypothetic space of the associated problem (51) is

$$\boldsymbol{Space}^{\bullet} := \boldsymbol{Prob}[S;\int f_1^{\bullet}=\alpha_1,\ldots,\int f_n^{\bullet}=\alpha_n]. \quad (55)$$

Hence, the hypothetic space of the associated problem is the associated space of the hypothetic space of the original problem.

The replacement of a problem (50) by its associated problem (53) is called **a mixture elimination**.

4.5.2. Particular Cases

a. Multiple integral problems

Let

$$T(F) = \Psi[\int g_1 dF,\ldots,\int g_k dF]. \quad (56)$$

Then

$$T(F_U) = \Psi[\int g_1 dF_U,\ldots,\int g_k dF_U]$$
$$= \Psi[\int g_1^{\bullet} dU,\ldots,\int g_k^{\bullet} dU] =: T^{\bullet}(U) \quad (57)$$

and the associated problem of the problem (50) is the problem

$$\mathrm{Sup}_{U\in \boldsymbol{Prob}[S]}[T^{\bullet}(U)/\int f_1^{\bullet} dU=\alpha_1,\ldots,\int f_n^{\bullet} dU=\alpha_n]. \quad (58)$$

The latter is a multiple integral problem.

Hence, **the associated problem of a multiple integral optimization problem is a multiple integral optimization problem.**

b. Pure problems

If F_θ is the 1-atomic distribution A_θ, then

$$\boldsymbol{Mixt}[F_\theta(\theta\in S)] = \boldsymbol{Prob}[S],$$

and then the original problem (50) is already a pure problem.

The associated problem of a pure optimization problem is that problem itself.

c. *m-unimodal problems*

Let the original problem be

$$\text{Sup}_{F\in \textbf{\textit{Prob}}[[a,b];S,m\text{-unim}]}[T(F)/\textstyle\int f_1 dF=\alpha_1,\ldots,\int f_n dF=\alpha_n]. \qquad (59)$$

Its basic space is

$$\textbf{\textit{Prob}}[[a,b];S,m\text{-unim}] = \textbf{\textit{Mixt}}[R_{m\theta}(\theta\in S)]. \qquad (60)$$

The problem (59) is a particular problem (50). Its associated problem is the problem (53) where the associated functions are defined by Ch.2.(22).

In the case of m-unimodal problems, a mixture elimination is called **a mode elimination**.

d. *m-unimodal moment problems*

We consider the problem

$$\text{Sup}_{F\in \textbf{\textit{Prob}}[[a,b];S,m\text{-unim}]}[T(F)/\mu_1,\ldots,\mu_n], \qquad (61)$$

i.e. the problem (59) with $f_j(x)=x^j$ ($x\in\mathbf{R}, j=1,\ldots,n$). The associated problem is a problem (53) with integral constraints

$$\int f_j^{\bullet}(\theta)dU(\theta) = \mu_j \; (j=1,\ldots,n), \qquad (62)$$

where the associated functions $f_j^{\bullet}$ result from Ch.3.(135). By Ch.3.Th.14, the constraints (62) are equivalent to the constraints

$$\int \theta^j dU(\theta) = \mu_j^{\bullet} \; (j=1,\ldots,n), \qquad (63)$$

where

$$\mu_j^{\bullet} := (j+1)\mu_j - mj\mu_{j-1} \; (j=1,\ldots,n)\,,\; \mu_0:=1. \qquad (64)$$

Hence, the associated problem of the problem (61) is the problem

$$\text{Sup}_{U\in \textbf{\textit{Prob}}[S]}[T(F_U)/\mu_1^{\bullet},\ldots,\mu_n^{\bullet}], \qquad (65)$$

where $\mu_1^{\bullet},\ldots,\mu_n^{\bullet}$ are the fixed moments of the distribution U.

The associated problem of a m-unimodal moment problem is a pure moment problem.

e. Multiple integral m-unimodal moment problems

We can combine the conclusions of *a.* and *d.* Let us consider the problem (61) with T(F) defined by (56). Then the associated problem is

$$\mathrm{Sup}_{U \in \boldsymbol{Prob}[S]}[T^{\bullet}(U)/\mu_1^{\bullet},\ldots,\mu_n^{\bullet}], \tag{66}$$

where the associated objective functional $T^{\bullet}$ is defined by (57) and the associated moments $\mu_1^{\bullet},\ldots, \mu_n^{\bullet}$ by (64).

The associated problem of a multiple integral m-unimodal moment problem is a multiple integral pure moment problem.

f. Integral problems

All conclusions about multiple integral problems remain valid in the case of integral problems.

4.6. Discretizations in Original and Extremal Point Optimization Problems

4.6.1. Extremal Point Problems

Let

$$\sup_{F \in \boldsymbol{Space}} T(F) \tag{67}$$

be an optimization problem on the convex hypothetic space ***Space***. Then the corresponding **extremal point problem** is the optimization problem

$$\sup_{F \in \boldsymbol{Ext}} T(F), \tag{68}$$

where ***Ext*** is the set of extremal points of ***Space***.

Very often, the solution of the extremal point problem is also the solution of the original problem. This happens whenever the Corollary of Theorem 1 can be applied. In particular, it occurs in the case of integral optimization problems on a space of mixtures with integral constraints (under compactness and continuity assumptions), because then the objective functional is linear. More particularly, all stop-loss premium problems on pure or m-unimodel moment spaces, have extremal solutions.

In this section 4.6, we show how extremal point problems with integral constraints (in particular, with moment constraints) can be solved numerically.

4.6.2. Discretization

Original optimization problem

We consider the original problem

$$\sup_{F\in \textbf{\textit{Space}}} T(F), \tag{69}$$

with

$$\textbf{\textit{Space}} := \textbf{\textit{Mixt}}[F_\theta(\theta\in[a,b]);\textstyle\int f_1=\alpha_1,\ldots,\int f_n=\alpha_n]. \tag{70}$$

Pure optimization problem

The associated pure problem of problem (69) is problem

$$\sup_{U\in \textbf{\textit{Space}}\bullet} T(F_U) \tag{71}$$

with

$$\textbf{\textit{Space}}\bullet := \textbf{\textit{Prob}}[[a,b]:\textstyle\int f_1^\bullet=\alpha_1,\ldots,\int f_n^\bullet=\alpha_n]. \tag{72}$$

We assume that the basic space of mixtures of the problem (69) is regular. Then, by Ch.2.3.4, the point U of the space (72) is an extremal point of that space iff the point F_U is an extremal point of the space (70).

Hence, the extremal points problem corresponding to (69) can be solved via the extremal points problem corresponding to its pure associated problem (71). Then it is enough to consider original pure problems.

We hereafter treat the problem

$$\sup_{F\in \textbf{\textit{Space}}} T(F), \tag{73}$$

where

$$\textbf{\textit{Space}} = \textbf{\textit{Prob}}[[0,b];\textstyle\int f_1=\alpha_1,\ldots,\int f_n=\alpha_n]. \tag{74}$$

Discretized problem

Let n_0 be an integer, $n_0\geq n$, and let $\delta:=b/n_0$. We replace the interval [0,b] of the problem (73) by the discrete set $\{0,\delta,2\delta,\ldots,n_0\delta\}$. Then the problem (73) becomes

$$\sup_{F\in \textbf{\textit{Space}}'} T(F) \tag{75}$$

where

$$\textbf{\textit{Space}}' := \textbf{\textit{Prob}}[\{0,\delta,2\delta,\ldots,n_0\delta\};\textstyle\int f_1=\alpha_1,\ldots,\int f_n=\alpha_n]. \tag{76}$$

Discretized problem in new money

For any function φ on **R** and c>0, let $\varphi_c \equiv (\varphi)_c$ be the function with values

$$\varphi_c(x) \equiv (\varphi)_c(x) := \varphi(x/c). \tag{77}$$

Then,

$$\int_{[0,b]} f(x)dG_\delta(x) = \int_{[0,b/\delta]} f(\delta x)dG_\delta(\delta x) = \int_{[0,n_0]} f_{1/\delta}(x)dG(x) \tag{78}$$

if the integrals do exist. In the problem (75), we replace F by G_δ and we take G as new variable point. When G ranges over

$$\textbf{\textit{Prob}}[\{0,1,\ldots,n_0\}] \equiv \textbf{\textit{Prob}}[[0,n_0]], \tag{79}$$

then $F=G_\delta$ ranges over

$$\textbf{\textit{Prob}}[\{0,\delta,2\delta,\ldots,n_0\delta\}]. \tag{80}$$

Indeed, let G be a point in the space (79). Then the jumps of G are at the points $k\in\{0,1,\ldots,n_0\}$, and then the jumps of the function

$$F(x) = G_\delta(x) = G(x/\delta)$$

are at the points x such that $x/\delta=k\in\{0,1,\ldots,n_0\}$, i.e. $x\in\{0,\delta,,2\delta,\ldots,n_0\delta\}$.

The integral constraints on $F=G_\delta$, in the last member of (76), are

$$\int f_j(x)dG_\delta(x) = \alpha_j \quad (j=1,\ldots,n),$$

i.e.

$$\int (f_j)_{1/\delta}dG = \alpha_j \quad (j=1,\ldots,n)$$

by (78). Hence, when G ranges over

$$\textbf{\textit{Space}}'' := \textbf{\textit{Prob}}[[0,n_0]_{int};\int(f_1)_{1/\delta}=\alpha_1,\ldots,\int(f_n)_{1/\delta}=\alpha_n], \tag{81}$$

then $F=G_\delta$ ranges over ***Space′***.

The conclusion of this discussion is that the problem (73) is equivalent to the problem

$$\sup_{G\in \textbf{\textit{Space}}''} T(G_\delta). \tag{82}$$

The replacement of problem (75) by problem (82) amounts to the adoption of a new money unit, such that the amounts $0,\delta,2\delta,...$ in the old money become the amounts $0,1,2,...$ in the new money.

Approximative solution of problem (73)

If G is a solution of the problem (82), then $F=G_\delta$ is a solution of the problem (75). This solution is an approximation of the solution of the problem (73). The approximation is asymptotically exact as $n_0\uparrow\infty$.

Approximative solution of extremal point problem

We now consider the extremal points problem

$$\sup_{F\in \boldsymbol{Ext}} T(F) \tag{83}$$

corresponding to the problem (73), i.e. ***Ext*** is the set of extremal points of the space (74).

The set ***Ext'*** of extremal points of the space (76) is an approximation of the set ***Ext*** if n_0 is large enough. In fact

$$\boldsymbol{Ext'} \subseteq \boldsymbol{Ext},. \tag{84}$$

by Ch.2.3.4 (we suppose that the regularity assumptions are satisfied).

The discretized extremal point problem is the problem

$$\sup_{F\in \boldsymbol{Ext'}} T(F). \tag{85}$$

Its solution is an approximation, asymptotically exact as $n_0\uparrow\infty$, of the extremal point problem (83). An equivalent problem is the problem

$$\sup_{F\in \boldsymbol{Ext''}} T(G_\delta), \tag{86}$$

where ***Ext''*** is the set of extremal points of the space (81).

4.6.3. Particular Cases

a. Multiple integral problems

Let T(F), in (73), be the multiple integral functional

$$T(F) = \Psi[\int g_1 dF,\dots,\int g_k dF]. \quad (87)$$

Then, by (78),

$$T(G_\delta) = \Psi[\int g_1 dG_\delta,\dots,\int g_k dG_\delta] = \Psi[\int (g_1)_{1/\delta} dG,\dots,\int (g_k)_{1/\delta} G] =: T''(G).$$

Then the problem (82) is the multiple integral optimization problem

$$\sup_{G\in \boldsymbol{Space}''} T''(G). \quad (88)$$

b. Moment spaces

Let the hypothetic space (74) of the problem (73) be the moment space

$$\boldsymbol{Space} = \boldsymbol{Prob}[[0,b];\mu_1,\dots,\mu_n]. \quad (89)$$

This is the space (74) with the particular functions

$$f_j(x) := x^j \ (x\in \mathbf{R},\ j=1,\dots,n) \quad (90)$$

and the moment values $\mu_1,\dots,\mu_n$ instead of $\alpha_1,\dots,\alpha_n$. Then the integral constraints on G in (81) are

$$\int (f_j)_{1/\delta}(x) dG(x) = \mu_j \ \ (j=1,\dots,n). \quad (91)$$

By (77), $(f_j)_{1/\delta}(x) = f_j(\delta x) = (\delta x)^j = \delta^j x^j$. Hence, the constraints (91) are

$$\int x^j dG(x) = \mu_j/\delta^j =: \mu''_j \ \ (j=1,\dots,n).$$

Then (81) is the moment space

$$\boldsymbol{Space}'' := \boldsymbol{Prob}[[0,n_0]_{int};\mu''_1,\dots,\mu''_n]. \quad (92)$$

4.6.4. Rough and Fine Discretizations

The discretization used in 4.6.2 is called a **n_0-discretization** with **span** $\delta := b/n_0$. It replaces the distributions concentrated on the interval [0,b] by distributions concentrated on the finite set $\{0, \delta, 2\delta, \ldots, n_0\delta\}$.

In the case of the interval [a,b] ($a,b \in \mathbf{R}$), the **n_0-discretization** is the replacement of distributions concentrated on that interval by distributions concentrated on the set $\{a, a+\delta, a+2\delta, \ldots, a+n_0\delta\}$, where $\delta := (b-a)/n_0$ is the **span**. We use the following adjectives for the discretizations.

$n \le n_0 < 20$:	**very rough discretizations,**
$20 \le n_0 < 200$:	**rough discretizations,**
$200 \le n_0 < 3200$:	**fine discretizations,**
$3200 \le n_0 < 10^5$:	**very fine discretizations,**
$10^5 \le n_0 \le 10^{12}$:	**hyper-fine discretizations**.

All numerical algorithms are based on some discretization. The following difficulties can occur when the discretization is too fine:

a. The computing time is excessive.
b. Not enough computer memory is available.
c. Numerical computing errors occur.

The latter case may happen with very large values of n_0 ($n_0 > 10^{12}$ for instance).

Some multiple integral optimization moment problems can be solved with hyper-fine discretizations. We notice that the involved integrals $\int \varphi dG$ become finite sums when G is concentrated on a finite set.

Other optimization problems, like infinite-time ruin probability problems, can be solved with fine discretizations. They cannot be considered with very fine discretizations because then they do not enter in the computer (see b.).

Other problems can still be treated with rough or only very rough discretizations, because of a. Optimization problems for which the numerical calculation of one single value T(F) takes several minutes, cannot be treated at all.

This is the situation today, in 1996.

4.7. Numerical Algorithms for Extremal Point Optimization Problems

4.7.1. Problem

We consider the problem (73), here called **the original problem**, and the corresponding extremal point problem

$$\sup_{F\in \boldsymbol{Ext}} T(F), \tag{93}$$

where ***Ext*** is the set of extremal points of ***Space*** (74). We now display ***Space″*** (81) as

$$\boldsymbol{Space}''(n_0) = \boldsymbol{Prob}\left[[0,n_0]_{int}; \int h_1=\alpha_1,\ldots,\int h_n=\alpha_n\right]. \tag{94}$$

Hence, for fixed n_0 and $\delta:=b/n_0$, the function h_j is $(f_j)_{1/\delta}$ $(j=1,\ldots,n)$. We here use the more explicit notation ***Space′***(n_0) for the space (76).

The goal of this section 4.7 is the numerical solution of the extremal point problem (93) via its corresponding discrete problem

$$\sup_{F\in \boldsymbol{Ext}''} T(G_\delta), \tag{95}$$

where ***Ext″***≡***Ext″***(n_0) is the set of extremal points of ***Space″***(n_0).

4.7.2. Feasible n+1-tuples

We assume that the set $[0,n_0]_{int}$ has strictly more than n points and that the functions $1, f_1, \ldots, f_n$ are independent on [0,b]. See Ch.2.3.4.

The n+1-tuple $(i_1,\ldots,i_{n+1})$ of integers, is called a **n_0-feasible n+1-tuple** if

$$0 \le i_1 < i_2 < \ldots < i_n < i_{n+1} \le n_0 \tag{96}$$

and

$$p_1,\ldots,p_{n+1} \ge 0, \tag{97}$$

where $(p_1,\ldots,p_{n+1})$ is the unique solution of the linear system

$$p_1 + \ldots + p_{n+1} = 1 \tag{98}$$

$$p_1h_j(i_1)+ \ldots + p_{n+1}h_j(i_{n+1}) = \alpha_j \ (j=1,\ldots,n). \tag{98}$$

The relations (96), (97) and (98) express that the n+1-atomic distribution

$$G := p_1 A_{i_1} + \ldots + p_{n+1} A_{i_{n+1}} \tag{99}$$

belongs to ***Space***″(n_0). By Ch.2.Th.6, it is an extremal point of that space. By the same Theorem, all extremal points can be expressed in this way. The extremal point of the original ***Space*** (74), corresponding to the extremal point (99), is

$$F = G_\delta = p_1 A_{\delta i_1} + \ldots + p_{n+1} A_{\delta i_{n+1}}. \tag{100}$$

We notice that

$$\begin{aligned} &\mathbf{(i_1,\ldots,i_n) \text{ is a } n_0\text{-feasible } n+1\text{-tuple}} \\ &\Rightarrow \mathbf{(2i_1,\ldots,2i_2) \text{ is a } 2n_0\text{- feasible } n+1\text{-tuple}}. \end{aligned} \tag{101}$$

Indeed, let $(i_1,\ldots,i_n)$ be a n_0-feasible n+1-tuple. Then F (100) belongs to the original space ***Space***. The distribution F is concentrated on the set

$$\{0,(\delta/2),2(\delta/2),3(\delta/2),\ldots,2n_0(\delta/2)\}.$$

Hence F∈***Space***′($2n_0$). Then

$$p_1 A_{2i_1} + \ldots + p_{n+1} A_{2i_{n+1}} \in \textit{\textbf{Space}}''(2n_0) \tag{102}$$

and then $(2i_1,\ldots,2i_n)$ is a $2n_0$-feasible n+1-tuple.

4.7.3. Reduction to a Lattice Problem

The n_0-feasible n+1-tuples are called the **n_0-lattice points**, or simply **the lattice points** when n_0 is fixed in the discussion.

We denote by Latt≡Latt(n_0) the set of all n_0-lattice points. **The value function** V is defined on Latt by

$$V(\underline{i}) \equiv V(i_1,\ldots,i_{n+1}) := T(F) = T(G_\delta) \quad (\underline{i}:=(i_1,\ldots,i_{n+1})\in \text{Latt}), \tag{103}$$

where F and G are defined by (100) and (99) resp. Then the discrete extremal points optimization problem (95) is equivalent to **lattice problem**

$$\sup_{\underline{i}\in \text{Latt}} V(\underline{i}). \tag{104}$$

We say that **the lattice point $\underline{k}$ is better than the lattice point $\underline{i}$** if $V(\underline{k})\geq V(\underline{i})$. Hence, the problem (104) is the determination of the best lattice point.

4.7.4. Algorithm Based on a Complete Enumeration of Lattice Points

Let

$$\text{Latt} = \{\underline{i}_1, \underline{i}_2, \ldots, \underline{i}_\omega\}.$$

Then the lattice problem (104) is solved as follows. We compare $V(\underline{i}_1)$ and $V(\underline{i}_2)$ and we denote the best of the points $\underline{i}_1$, $\underline{i}_2$ by $\underline{k}_2$.

Then we compare $V(\underline{k}_2)$ and $V(\underline{i}_3)$ and we denote the best of the points $\underline{k}_2$, $\underline{i}_3$ by $\underline{k}_3$ ... Then the point $\underline{k}_\omega$ is the solution of the problem (104).

It is not necessary, when this algorithm is executed, to stock the whole sequence $\underline{I}_1$, $\underline{I}_2$, ..., $\underline{i}_\omega$ of lattice points. It is sufficient to have some **enumeration rule** allowing to calculate successively the points $\underline{I}_1$, $\underline{I}_2$, ... At each stage, only the best point $\underline{k}$ must be remembered.

In case of problems with n moment constraints, the enumeration rule results from the last relations of Ch.3.2.1 when n=1, from Ch.3.Th.4 when n=2, and from Ch.3.Th.7 when n=3.

A more general enumeration rule is the following. The lattice points $(i_1,\ldots,i_{n+1})$ must satisfy the relations (96). We consider the integers

$$i_1 \in [0, n_0 - n]_{\text{int}},$$

then for fixed i_1 the integers

$$i_2 \in \,]i_1, n_0 - n + 1]_{\text{int}},$$

then for fixed i_2 the integers

$$i_3 \in \,]i_2, n_0 - n + 2]_{\text{int}},$$

... ...

$$\ldots \quad \ldots \quad \ldots \quad \ldots$$

then for fixed i_n the integers

$$i_{n+1} \in \,]i_n, n_0]_{\text{int}}.$$

For each n+1-tuple $(i_1,\ldots,i_{n+1})$, we solve the system (98) and we only retain the n+1-tuple if the inequalities (97) are satisfied. In this way, all lattice points are finally obtained. Of course, the enumeration based on this rule takes much more computing time than those based on the results of Ch.3 in the case of moment problems.

4.7.5. Algorithm Based on Local Comparisons

k_0-algorithm with fixed n_0-discretization

Let n_0 be fixed, and let k_0 be a small strictly positive integer. We say that the lattice points

$$(i_1,\dots,i_{n+1}) \text{ and } (j_1,\dots,j_{n+1}) \tag{105}$$

are k_0-neighbours if

$$|i_1-j_1| \le k_0,\ |i_2-j_2| \le k_0,\ \dots ,\ |i_{n+1}-j_{n+1}| \le k_0. \tag{106}$$

The k_0-neighbours of the lattice point $(i_1,\dots,i_{n+1})$ are among the n+1-tuples

$$(i_1+k_1,\dots,i_{n+1}+k_{n+1})\ (k_1,\dots,k_{n+1}\in\{-k,-k+1,\dots, -1,0,1,\dots,k-1,k\}). \tag{107}$$

Hence, any lattice point has $(n+1)^{2k_0+1}$ k_0-neighbours at most.

An enumeration of the k_0-neighbours of $\underline{i}=(i_1,\dots,i_{n+1})$ is easy. It can be obtained from the consideration of all the points (107), and the verification of the relation (96) and (97) corresponding to each of them.

We notice that any lattice point is a k_0-neighbour of itself.

We then proceed as follows.

Round 1: We start with a fixed **first initial lattice point** $\underline{i}_1$. We search for its best k_0-neighbour, and we denote it by $\underline{i}_2$. The research of $\underline{i}_2$ is based on an enumeration of the k_0-neighbours $\underline{k}$ of $\underline{i}_1$ and on a comparison of the values $V(\underline{k})$. If $\underline{i}_2=\underline{i}_1$, then $\underline{i}_2$ is called **a local k_0-maximum** of the lattice problem, and then the execution is stopped.

Round 2: If $\underline{i}_2\neq\underline{i}_1$, then $\underline{i}_2$ is adopted as a **second initial lattice point**, and then the foregoing procedure is repeated with the latter. It furnishes a best k_0-neighbour $\underline{i}_3$ of $\underline{i}_2$. If $\underline{i}_3=\underline{i}_2$, then $\underline{i}_3$ is a local k_0-maximum, and then the execution is stopped.

Round 3: If $\underline{i}_3\neq\underline{i}_2$, then $\underline{i}_2$ is adopted as **third initial lattice point**, and then the foregoing procedure is repeated with the latter. It furnishes a best k_0-neighbour $\underline{i}_4$ of $\underline{i}_3$. If $\underline{i}_4=\underline{i}_3$, then $\underline{i}_4$ is a local k_0-maximum, and then the execution is stopped

… … …

The execution necessarily stops and furnishes a local k_0-maximum, after a finite number of rounds, because the number of lattice points is finite.

Then it is hoped that this local k_0-maximum is the **global maximum**, i.e. the solution of lattice problem (104). This happens (even with k_0=1) if the first initial lattice point is good enough. It always happens if k_0 is large enough, whatever the first initial lattice point is.

k_0-algorithm with variable discretization

We consider a small value of n_0, say n_0=50 or n_0=100. By the algorithm of 4.7.4, we find a **n_0-solution**, i.e. a solution of the lattice problem (104) with Latt=Latt(n_0). By (101), we transform this n_0-lattice point in a $2n_0$-lattice point. The latter is adopted as first initial point of the k_0-algorithm with $2n_0$-discretisation. The corresponding $2n_0$-solution is transformed in a 2^2n_0-lattice point by (101). The latter is adopted as first initial point of the k_0-algorithm with 2^2n_0-discretization, ...

The algorithm is stopped in the following cases:

a. As soon as a solution with enough precision of the original extremal point problem (93), is obtained.

b. When memory overflows do occur.

c. When the computing time becomes excessive.

d. When numerical errors occur because the discretization becomes too fine.

4.7.6. Variants

a. In the algorithm with fixed discretization, each round can be interrupted as soon as a better lattice point $\underline{k}$ than the initial lattice point $\underline{i}$ is obtained. Then $\underline{k}$ is adopted as initial point of the following round. The execution stops when no improved point is obtained in a complete round.

b. In the algorithm with variable discretization, the value k_0 defining the k_0-neighbours, may vary with the discretization. Smaller values of k_0 can be used when the discretization becomes finer.

4.7.7. Quality, Safety and Execution Time

The **complete algorithm**, i.e. the algorithm of 4.7.4, is based on the comparison of the values V(k̲) when k̲ ranges over all n_0-lattice points. It is completely safe: it furnishes the solution of the lattice problem (104), i.e. the global maximum, in any case. Unfortunately it can be applied with rough, or very rough discretizations only, because otherwise the execution time becomes excessive. This solution may furnish a poor approximation of the solution of the original problem (93), but it is nevertheless good enough in many practical actuarial applications.

The k_0-algorithm of 4.7.5, based on the comparison of the values V(k̲) when k̲ ranges over the set of k_0-neighbours of the lattice points previously obtained, is not completely safe in general: it may furnish some k_0-local maximum instead of the global maximum. Everything depends on the choice of the first initial lattice point i̲ and on the value of k_0. Mostly, a good choice of i̲ results from a preliminary execution of the complete algorithm, with a rough discretization. Then the solution can be transformed into an approximative solution (a first initial lattice point) of the lattice problem with a much finer discretization, by (101).

The goal is to keep k_0 as small as possible. An increment of k_0 by 1 multiplies the execution time by about

$$(n+1)^{2(k_0+1)+1}/(n+1)^{2k_0+1} = (n+1)^2.$$

In most cases, the value $k_0=1$ is safe. In other cases it may be necessary to take $k_0=2$ or $k_0=3$. Everything depends on the original objective functional T and on the corresponding value function V on Latt.

The discretization finally used in the k_0-algorithm with variable discretization may be hyper-fine in some cases. This happens in many multiple-integral extremal points optimization problems.

In other problems, like ruin probability optimization problems, the use of a n_0-discretization implies the manipultion of several vectors with n_0 components (or more). Then some fine discretizations can be used, but very fine discretizations become impossible because then memory overflows do occur.

4.8. Special Extremal Distributions

4.8.1. Special Finite-Atomic Distributions

Every moment space

$$\boldsymbol{Space_n} := \boldsymbol{Prob}[[a,b];\mu_1,\dots,\mu_n] \tag{108}$$

has two special extremal distributions. We assume that the point $(\mu_1,\dots,\mu_n)$ is a fixed interior point of the effective domain dom_n of $\boldsymbol{Space_n}$. By definition, dom_n is the set of points $(\mu_1,\dots,\mu_n)$ for which $\boldsymbol{Space_n}$ is not void.

These special distributions occur so often in the optimization problems that they deserve special names.

The initial k+1-atomic distribution of $\boldsymbol{Space_{2k}}$ is its unique distribution

$$p_1 A_a + p_2 A_{x_2} + \dots + p_{k+1} A_{x_{k+1}} \tag{109}$$

with $a<x_2<\dots<x_{k+1}\leq b$. The k atoms $x_2,\dots,x_{k+1}$ and the k+1 masses $p_1,\dots,p_{k+1}$ are determined by the 2k moment constraints completed by the probability constraint $\sum p_i=1$.

The final k+1-atomic distribution of $\boldsymbol{Space_{2k}}$ is its unique distribution

$$p_1 A_{x_1} + \dots + p_k A_{x_k} + p_{k+1} A_b \tag{110}$$

with $a\leq x_1<x_2<\dots<x_k<b$. The k atoms $x_1,\dots,x_k$ and the k+1 masses $p_1,\dots,p_{k+1}$ are determined by the 2k moment constraints completed by the probability constraint.

The narrow k+1-atomic distribution of $\boldsymbol{Space_{2k+1}}$ is its unique distribution

$$p_1 A_{x_1} + \dots + p_{k+1} A_{x_{k+1}} \tag{111}$$

with $a<x_1<\dots<x_{k+1}<b$. The k+1 atoms $x_1,\dots,x_{k+1}$ and the k+1 masses $p_1,\dots,p_{k+1}$ are determined by the 2k+1 moment constraints completed by the probability constraint.

The broad k+2-atomic distribution of $\boldsymbol{Space_{2k+1}}$ is its unique distribution

$$p_1 A_a + p_2 A_{x_2} + \dots + p_{k+1} A_{x_{k+1}} + p_{k+2} A_b \tag{112}$$

with $a<x_2<...<x_{k+1}<b$. The k atoms $x_2,...,x_{k+1}$ and the k+2 masses $p_1,...,p_{k+2}$ are determined by the 2k+1 moment constraints completed by the probability constraint.

.

The existence of these **special atomic distribitions** results from next Ch.8. Th.5.

4.8.2. Special Finite-Basic Distributions

We now consider the space of mixtures

$$\boldsymbol{Space_n} := \boldsymbol{Mixt}[F_\theta(\theta\in[a,b]);\mu_1,...,\mu_n]. \tag{113}$$

We assume that the point $(\mu_1,...,\mu_n)$ is a fixed interior point of the effective domain dom_n of $\boldsymbol{Space_n}$.

The initial k+1-basic distribution of $\boldsymbol{Space_{2k}}$ is its unique distribution

$$p_1F_a + p_2F_{x_2} + ... + p_{k+1}F_{x_{k+1}} \tag{114}$$

with $a<x_2<...<x_{k+1}\leq b$. The k points $x_2,...,x_{k+1}$ and the k+1 masses $p_1,...,p_{k+1}$ are determined by the 2k moment constraints completed by the probability constraint $\sum p_i=1$.

The final k+1-basic distribution of $\boldsymbol{Space_{2k}}$ is its unique distribution

$$p_1F_{x_1} + ... + p_kF_{x_k} + p_{k+1}F_b \tag{115}$$

with $a\leq x_1<x_2<...<x_k<b$. The k points $x_1,...,x_k$ and the k+1 masses $p_1,...,p_{k+1}$ are determined by the 2k moment constraints completed by the probability constraint.

The narrow k+1-basic distribution of $\boldsymbol{Space_{2k+1}}$ is its unique distribution

$$p_1F_{x_1} + ... + p_{k+1}F_{x_{k+1}} \tag{116}$$

with $a<x_1<...<x_{k+1}<b$. The k+1 points $x_1,...,x_{k+1}$ and the k+1 masses $p_1,...,p_{k+1}$ are determined by the 2k+1 moment constraints completed by the probability constraint.

.

The broad k+2-basic distribution of ***Space***$_{2k+1}$ is its unique distribution

$$p_1F_a + p_2F_{x_2} + \ldots + p_{k+1}F_{x_{k+1}} + p_{k+2}F_b \quad (117)$$

with $a<x_2<\ldots<x_{k+1}<b$. The k points $x_2,\ldots,x_{k+1}$ and the k+2 masses $p_1,\ldots,p_{k+2}$ are determined by the 2k+1 moment constraints completed by the probability constraint. •

The existence of these **special basic distribitions** results from the Theorems mentioned at the end of section 4.8.1, applied to the pure space associated to the space of mixtures.

Of course, if the space of mixtures is a space of m-unimodal distributions, then "basic" is replaced by "m-rectangular" in the foregoing terminology.

Chapter 5

Linear Programs and Games

5.0. Introduction

A linear program is an optimization problem of a linear function of a finite number of real variables, subject to a finite number of linear constraints. Linear programs are very popular and very useful. They can be solved numerically by the celebrated **Dantzig simplex method**.

An extended linear program is an optimization problem of a linear function of a finite number of real variables, subject to any number of linear constraints. The duals of the optimization problems of integrals $\int \varphi dF$, considered in Chapter 7, are extended linear programs. Extended linear programs can be solved numerically, at least approximatively, by the methods of usual linear programs: if the set of constraints is infinite, it is replaced by a properly chosen large finite subset.

A huge literature exists about linear programming. Only very general basic results of this theory are developed in section 5.1. In 5.2, we demonstrate a general Theorem used in Chapter 7.

In section 5.3, we develop the duality theory of linear programs. It is based on the consideration of the polar functions defined in App.C.C9 and on the Fenchel-Moreau Theorem. This theory is not used later in the book, but it is a good introduction to the duality theory of Chapter 7: the methodology is identical in the discrete case of 5.3 and in the continuous case of Chapter 7. In both cases the value function of the dual problem arises in the most natural way, as a bipolar function of the value function of the primal problem.

One of the most beautiful applications of the duality theory of linear programs, is the proof of the existence of a solution of any matrix game (von Neumann's Theorem in Matrix Game Theory). Some very general simple results about zero-sum two-person games are proved in 5.4, and the main Theorem of Matrix Games is demonstrated in 5.5.

The basic Theorem of two-person games with complete information is proved in section 5.6

Sections 5.3, 5.4, 5.5 and 5.6 can be omitted without loss of continuity.

5.1. Linear Programs

5.1.1. Linear Programs on R_+^m

A linear program on R_+^m, or a **linear optimization problem on R_+^m**, is an optimization problem

$$P := \inf_{x_1,\ldots,x_m\geq 0}[\varphi(x_1,\ldots,x_m) / \text{cond}(x_1,\ldots,x_m)] \qquad (1)$$

or

$$Q := \sup_{x_1,\ldots,x_m\geq 0}[\varphi(x_1,\ldots,x_m) / \text{cond}(x_1,\ldots,x_m)], \qquad (2)$$

with a linear objective function

$$\varphi(x_1,\ldots,x_m) = c_1x_1+\ldots+c_nx_m \qquad (3)$$

and a finite number of linear constraints $\text{cond}(x_1,\ldots,x_m)$. The latter may be of the type

$$a_1x_1+\ldots+a_mx_m \leq \alpha \;,\; a_1x_1+\ldots+a_mx_m \geq \alpha \;,\; a_1x_1+\ldots+a_mx_m = \alpha. \qquad (4)$$

The constraints (4) are called a **≤-constraint**, a **≥-constraint** and an **equality constraint** respectively.

The relation

$$\inf_{x_1,\ldots,x_m\geq 0}[\varphi(x_1,\ldots,x_m) / \text{cond}(x_1,\ldots,x_m)]$$
$$= -\sup_{x_1,\ldots,x_m\geq 0}[-\varphi(x_1,\ldots,x_m) / \text{cond}(x_1,\ldots,x_m)] \qquad (5)$$

implies the following.

a. Any linear minimization problem on R_+^m is equivalent to a linear maximization problem on R_+^m. See the *example 1* of Ch.1.1.2.

Any general statement about a linear maximization problem on $\mathbf{R}_+^m$ has an obvious corresponding version, resulting from (5), about the linear minimization problem. We often omit the statement concerning the minimization problem.

b. Any linear maximization problem on $\mathbf{R}_+^m$ can be displayed as a problem with ≤-constraints only.

Indeed, this is obvious by the equivalences

$$a_1x_1+...+a_mx_m \geq 0 \Leftrightarrow (-a_1)x_1+...+(-a_m)x_m \leq 0, \quad (6)$$

$$a_1x_1+...+a_mx_m = 0 \Leftrightarrow [a_1x_1+...+a_mx_m \leq 0, (-a_1)x_1+...+(-a_m)x_m \leq 0]. \quad (7)$$

Theorem 1

Any linear maximization problem Q on $\mathbf{R}_+^m$ is equivalent to a linear maximization problem $Q_=$ on some space $\mathbf{R}_+^n$, with equality constraints only, and with the same value $Q_=$=Q.

Proof

By the equivalence (6), we may assume that the problem Q only has equality constraints and ≤-constraints. Let $a_1x_1+...+a_mx_m \leq \alpha$ be a fixed constraint of the problem Q. We introduce a new variable $x_{m+1} \geq 0$ and we replace the constraint $a_1x_1+...+a_mx_m \leq \alpha$ by the equality constraint

$$a_1x_1+...+a_mx_m+x_{m+1} = \alpha.$$

The problem obtained in this way is a maximization problem on $\mathbf{R}_+^{m+1}$, equivalent to the problem Q, and with the same value. See *example 2* of Ch.1. 1.2. By a repetition of this operation, all ≤-constraints can be eliminated •

5.1.2. Linear Programs on $\mathbf{R}^m$

A linear program on $\mathbf{R}^m$, or a **linear optimization problem on $\mathbf{R}^m$**, is an optimization problem

$$P_\pm := \inf_{x_1,...,x_m}[\varphi(x_1,...,x_m) \,/\, \mathrm{cond}(x_1,...,x_m)] \quad (8)$$

or

$$Q_\pm := \sup_{x_1,...,x_m}[\varphi(x_1,...,x_m) \,/\, \mathrm{cond}(x_1,...,x_m)], \quad (9)$$

with a linear objective function (3) and linear constraints (4). The variables $x_1,\dots,x_m$ may take negative as well as positive values in the problems $P_\pm$ and $Q_\pm$. This is suggested by the subscript $_\pm$.

a. Any linear optimization problem on $\mathbf{R}_+^m$ can be displayed as a linear optimization problem on $\mathbf{R}^m$, because the constraints $x_1,\dots,x_m \geq 0$ can be placed after the slash.

b. Any linear minimization problem on $\mathbf{R}^m$ is equivalent to a linear maximization problem on $\mathbf{R}^m$, by the relation corresponding to (5).

c. Any linear maximization problem on $\mathbf{R}^m$ can be displayed as a problem with $\leq$-constraints only, by the equivalences (6) and (7).

The argument of the proof of Theorem 1 does not work in the case of maximization problems on $\mathbf{R}^m$. In general, a maximization problem on $\mathbf{R}^m$ cannot be reduced to a single equivalent maximization problem on some space $\mathbf{R}^n$ with equality constraints only.

Theorem 2

Any maximization problem on $\mathbf{R}^m$ can be reduced to 2^m maximization problems on $\mathbf{R}_+^m$.

Proof

We prove the Theorem and clarify its meaning, in the case of the linear problem

$$\sup_{x,y}[\varphi(x,y) \,/\, \mathrm{cond}(x,y)]. \tag{10}$$

on $\mathbf{R}^2$. This particular case contains all the ideas of a general proof.

The value (10) is the maximum of the four values

$$\sup_{x\geq 0,y\geq 0}[\varphi(x,y) \,/\, \mathrm{cond}(x,y)], \tag{11}$$

$$\sup_{x\leq 0,y\geq 0}[\varphi(x,y) \,/\, \mathrm{cond}(x,y)] = \sup_{x\geq 0,y\geq 0}[\varphi(-x,y) \,/\, \mathrm{cond}(-x,y)], \tag{12}$$

$$\sup_{x\leq 0,y\leq 0}[\varphi(x,y) \,/\, \mathrm{cond}(x,y)] = \sup_{x\geq 0,y\geq 0}[\varphi(-x,-y) \,/\, \mathrm{cond}(-x,-y)], \tag{13}$$

$$\sup_{x\geq 0,y\leq 0}[\varphi(x,y) \,/\, \mathrm{cond}(x,y)] = \sup_{x\geq 0,y\geq 0}[\varphi(x,-y) \,/\, \mathrm{cond}(x,-y)]. \tag{14}$$

The relation (11) and the last member of the relations (12), (13) and (14) define four optimization problems on $\mathbf{R}_+^2$. The value, the feasible points, the solutions and the limit solutions of each of these four problems furnish the value, the feasible points, the solutions and the limit solutions of problem (10) •

5.1.3. Matrix Notations

In this Chapter, $\mathbf{R}^k$ and $\mathbf{R}_+^k$ (k=1,2,...) are spaces of columns $x=(x_1,...,x_k)'$.

A notation such as $u \leq v$ between matrices (in particular between rows or columns) indicates that the elements of u are smaller than the corresponding elements of v. The notation $u \geq 0$ indicates that all components of u are positive. The relation $u \neq 0$ means that at least one component of u is different from zero.

We consider the maximization problems

$$Q := \sup_{x \geq 0}[c'x \,/\, ax \leq \alpha] \;,\; Q_= := \sup_{x \geq 0}[c'x \,/\, ax = \alpha], \tag{15}$$

$$Q_\pm := \sup_x[c'x \,/\, ax \leq \alpha] \;,\; Q_{\pm=} := \sup_x[c'x \,/\, ax = \alpha]. \tag{16}$$

and similar minimization problems. In all these programs, $a_{n \times m}$ is a matrix, and $c_{m \times 1}$ and $\alpha_{n \times 1}$ are columns. The variable point $x_{m \times 1}$ ranges over $\mathbf{R}_+^m$ in the case of problems Q and $Q_=$. It ranges over $\mathbf{R}^m$ in the case of the problem $Q_\pm$ and $Q_{\pm=}$. The problems Q, $Q_=$, $Q_\pm$ and $Q_{\pm=}$ are resp., the most general maximization problem on $\mathbf{R}_+^m$ with $\leq$-constraints, the most general maximization problem on $\mathbf{R}_+^m$ with equality constraints, the most general maximization problem on $\mathbf{R}^m$ with $\leq$-constraints, and the most general maximization problem on $\mathbf{R}^m$ with equality constraints.

5.1.4. Direction of a Sequence in $\mathbf{R}^m$

We recall that $\|y\| := (y_1^2+...+y_m^2)^{1/2}$ is the norm of the point $y:=(y_1,...,y_m)'$ in $\mathbf{R}^m$. Let

$$x_\nu := (x_{\nu 1},...x_{\nu m})' \in \mathbf{R}^m \; (\nu=1,2,...) \tag{17}$$

be a sequence of points with the following properties

a. $\qquad x_\nu \neq 0 \; (\nu=1,2,...).$

b. $\qquad \lim_{\nu \uparrow \infty} \|x_\nu\| = \infty.$

c. $\qquad \lim_{\nu \uparrow \infty} x_\nu / \|x_\nu\| = z = (z_1,...,z_m)'.$

The point z is called **the direction of the sequence x_ν (ν=1,2,...)**. Obviously, $||z||=1$.

Let $x_\nu \in \mathbf{R}_+^m$(ν=1,2,...) We assume a,b,c and moreover, for all j=1,...,m:

d. $$z_j>0 \Rightarrow [x_{\nu j}>0 \ (\nu=1,2,...)].$$

Let $$\rho_\nu := \min_i[x_{\nu i}/z_i] \ \ (\nu=1,2,...), \tag{18}$$

where i ranges over the subscripts 1,...,m such that $z_i>0$. The sequence

$$y_\nu := x_\nu - \rho_\nu z \ \ (\nu=1,2,...) \tag{19}$$

is called **the direction-transformed sequence of the sequence x_ν (ν=1,2,...)**.

Theorem 3

Let $x_\nu \in \mathbf{R}_+^m$ (ν=1,2,...) be a sequence of points with the properties a,b,c and d, and let y_ν (ν=1,2,...) be the direction-transformed sequence of the sequence x_ν (ν=1,2,...). Then $y_\nu \in \mathbf{R}_+^m$ and each point y_ν has strictly more components equal to 0 than the corresponding point x_ν(ν=1,2,...).

Each unbounded sequence in $\mathbf{R}_+^m$ has a subsequence with the properties a,b,c and d.

Proof

We first prove that y_ν(ν fixed) has strictly more 0 components than x_ν. If $x_{\nu j}=0$, then $z_j=0$ by d, and then $y_{\nu j}=0$ by (19).

Let the minimum (18) be attained for the subscript i(ν):

$$\rho_\nu = x_{\nu,i(\nu)}/z_{i(\nu)}.$$

Then $z_{i(\nu)}>0$ and then $x_{\nu,i(\nu)}>0$ by d. But

$$y_{\nu,i(\nu)} = x_{\nu,i(\nu)} - \rho_\nu z_{i(\nu)} = 0.$$

We now verify that $y_{\nu j} \geq 0$ for all j=1,...,m. If $z_j=0$, then $y_{\nu j}=x_{\nu j} \geq 0$. If $z_j>0$, then

$$y_{\nu j} = x_{\nu j} - \rho_\nu z_j = z_j[(x_{\nu j}/z_j) - \rho_\nu] \geq 0,$$

by definition of ρ_ν.

We now demonstrate the last part of the Theorem. Let $x_\nu \in \mathbf{R}_+^m$ ($\nu=1,2,\ldots$) be any unbounded sequence. Then the sequence $\|x_\nu\|$ ($\nu=1,2,\ldots$) is unbounded. Taking a subsequence (but keeping the same notation), we may assume that $\|x_\nu\| \to \infty$ for $\nu \uparrow \infty$ and that $x_\nu \neq 0$ ($\nu=1,2,\ldots$).

The sequence $x_\nu/\|x_\nu\|$ ($\nu=1,2,\ldots$) is bounded, because the norm of each term equals 1. Hence, taking a subsequence, we may assume that $x_\nu/\|x_\nu\|$ converges to some point $z \in \mathbf{R}_+^m$ for $x\uparrow\infty$. Hence a,b and c are satisfied already (for a subsequence).

Let i be fixed, such that $z_i>0$. Then $x_{\nu i}/\|x_\nu\| >0$ if ν is large enough, and then $x_{\nu i}>0$ if ν is large enough, because $\|x_\nu\| \to \infty$. Hence, dropping a finite number of initial points $x_1,\ldots,x_k$, we may assume that $x_{\nu i}>0$ ($\nu=1,2,\ldots$). This operation can be repeated with any subscript i such that $z_i>0$. Hence d is satisfied (for a subsequence) •

5.1.5. Existence of Solutions

Theorem 4

Each of the following problems has a solution if it has a finite value:

$$\mathbf{Q := \sup_{x\geq 0}[c'x \,/\, ax\leq\alpha] \ , \ Q_= := \sup_{x\geq 0}[c'x \,/\, ax=\alpha],}$$

$$\mathbf{Q_\pm := \sup_x[c'x \,/\, ax\leq\alpha] \ , \ Q_{\pm=} := \sup_x[c'x \,/\, ax=\alpha],}$$

$$\mathbf{P := \inf_{x\geq 0}[c'x \,/\, ax\geq\alpha] \ , \ P_= := \inf_{x\geq 0}[c'x \,/\, ax=\alpha],}$$

$$\mathbf{P_\pm := \inf_x[c'x \,/\, ax\geq\alpha] \ , \ P_{\pm=} := \sup_x[c'x \,/\, ax=\alpha].}$$

Proof

By 5.1.1.a and 5.1.2.b, it is sufficient to consider the maximization problems. By Theorem 1 and by 5.1.2.c, it is enough to consider the problems $Q_=$ and $Q_\pm$.

a. We start with the problem $Q_=$. Let $Q_= \in \mathbf{R}$. Let the sequence $x_\nu \in \mathbf{R}_+^m$ ($\nu=1,2,\ldots$) be a limit solution of problem $Q_=$.

Case 1: The sequence x_ν (ν=1,2,...) is bounded.

Taking a subsequence, we may assume that $x_\nu \rightarrow x \in \mathbf{R}_+^m$ for $\nu\uparrow\infty$. By the feasibility of x_ν: $ax_\nu=\alpha$. Then $ax=\alpha$ as $\nu\uparrow\infty$. Hence, x is a feasible point of problem $Q_=$.

$$c'x_\nu \rightarrow Q \text{ as } \nu\uparrow\infty,$$

because the sequence x_ν (ν=1,2,...) is a limit solution. But also $c'x_\nu \rightarrow c'x$, because $x_\nu \rightarrow x$. Hence $Q_= = c'x$. This proves that x is a solution.

Case 2: The sequence x_ν (ν=1,2,...) is unbounded.

Taking a subsequence, we may assume, by Theorem 3, that the assumptions a,b,c and d of 5.1.4 are satisfied. We consider the direction z of the sequence x_ν (ν=1,2,...). By the feasibility of x_ν: $ax_\nu=\alpha$. We divide this relation by $||x_\nu||$ and then we let $\nu\uparrow\infty$. By b and c, we obtain $az=0$. By b and c, the limit relation $c'x_\nu \rightarrow Q_= \in \mathbf{R}$ implies

$$c'z = \lim_{\nu\uparrow\infty} c'[x_\nu/||x_\nu||] = \lim_{\nu\uparrow\infty} Q_=/||x_\nu|| = 0.$$

We consider the direction-transformed sequence $y_\nu := x_\nu - \rho_\nu z$ (ν=1,2,...) of the sequence x_ν (ν=1,2,...). By Theorem 3, $y_\nu \in \mathbf{R}_+^m$, and from the relation $az=0$ results that y_ν is a feasible point of problem $Q_=$. Moreover

$$c'y_\nu = c'x_\nu - \rho_\nu(c'z) = c'x_\nu \rightarrow Q \text{ as } \nu\uparrow\infty.$$

This implies that the sequence y_ν (ν=1,2,...) is a limit solution of problem $Q_=$, and then we can start the discussion again with this new sequence y_ν (ν=1,2,...), and we can start again and again, until *Case 1* happens. This necessarily occurs after m steps at most, because the number of zeros in the components of the terms of the successively direction-transformed sequences augments strictly in each step, by Theorem 3. We finally obtain the bounded sequence 0, 0,..., unless *Case 1* happens before. This proves that problem $Q_=$ has a solution if it has a finite value.

b. We now consider the problem $Q_\pm$. Let its value be finite. By Theorem 2, problem $Q_\pm$ can be reduced to a finite number of problems $Q_1, Q_2,...,Q_k$ of the type Q (see proof of Theorem 2). None of them can have the value $+\infty$, because then $Q_\pm=+\infty$. Some of them may have no feasible points, and then they have the value $-\infty$.

We omit the problems Q_j with $Q_j=-\infty$. We consider the problems Q_j with a finite value. Obviously such problems exist, because the problem $Q_\pm$ has feasible points, and each feasible point of $Q_\pm$ is a feasible point of some problem Q_j, and then $Q_j \in \mathbf{R}$. By b, each of the problems Q_j with a finite value has a solution x_j. The solution x_j such that $c'x_j$ is largest, is a solution of problem $Q_\pm$ •

By equivalences such as (6) and (7), the problem $Q_\pm$ ($P_\pm$) of the foregoing Theorem is the most general linear maximization (minimization) program with equality and weak inequality constraints. Hence, Theorem 4 can be summarized as follows:

Any linear optimization program, with equality and weak inequality constraints, and with a finite value, has a solution.

5.2. Programs with Linear Objective Function

5.2.1. Extended Linear Programs

An extended linear program is an optimization problem of a linear objective function of a finite number of variables $x_1,...,x_m$, subject to any number of linear equality constraints or weak inequality constraints.

Let S be any set. Let $\alpha(\theta)$, $a_1(\theta),..., a_m(\theta)$ be finite real numbers defined for all $\theta \in S$ and let $c \in \mathbf{R}^m$. Then the most general extended linear minimization program on $\mathbf{R}^m$ is

$$P_{ext} := \inf_x[c'x \,/\, a(\theta)x \geq \alpha(\theta)\ (\theta \in S)], \tag{20}$$

where $x := (x_1,...,x_m)'$ ranges over $\mathbf{R}^m$. In the last member of (20), $c \in \mathbf{R}^m$ and $a(\theta)$ is the row

$$a(\theta) := (a_1(\theta),...,a_m(\theta)).$$

Then

$$a(\theta)x = a_1(\theta)x_1 + ... + a_m(\theta)x_m$$

is the usual matrix product of row $a(\theta)$ by column x.

The generality of the problem (20) results from the fact that $\geq$-constraints and equality constraints can be replaced by $\leq$-constraints, by the general equivalences (6) and (7).

The most general extended linear maximization program on $\mathbf{R}^m$ is the problem

$$Q_{ext} := \sup_x[c'x \,/\, a(\theta)x \geq \alpha(\theta)\ (\theta \in S)], \tag{21}$$

where x ranges over $\mathbf{R}^m$.

Theorem 5

Let the value of the problem P_{ext} (20) or Q_{ext} (21) be finite, and let

$$[z \neq 0\,,\ a(\theta)z \geq 0\ (\theta \in S)] \Rightarrow c'z \neq 0, \tag{22}$$

for all $z \in \mathbf{R}^m$. Then the problem has a solution.

Proof
We consider the problem P_{ext}. The adaptations to be made in the case of the problem Q_{ext} are obvious. Let sequence $x_\nu \in \mathbf{R}^m$ (ν=1,2,...) be a limit solution of problem P_{ext}. Then

$$a(\theta)x_\nu \geq \alpha(\theta)\ \ (\theta \in S,\ \nu=1,2,\ldots) \tag{23}$$

and

$$c'x_\nu \rightarrow P_{ext} \in \mathbf{R}\ \text{ as } \nu\uparrow\infty. \tag{24}$$

Case 1: The sequence x_ν (ν=1,2,...) is bounded.

Then we may assume that $x_\nu \rightarrow x \in \mathbf{R}$ as $\nu\uparrow\infty$, because we can replace the sequence by a convergent subsequence. Then by (23), for $\nu\uparrow\infty$:

$$a(\theta)x \geq \alpha(\theta)\ \ (\theta \in S). \tag{25}$$

The relation $x_\nu \rightarrow x$ implies $c'x_\nu \rightarrow c'x$. Then $c'x = P_{ext}$ by (24). This means that x is a solution of the problem P_{ext}. The feasibility of x results from (25).

Case 2: The sequence x_ν (ν=1,2,...) is unbounded.

Taking a subsequence, we may assume that the conditions 5.1.4.a,b,c are satisfied. We divide (23) by $||x_\nu||$ and then we let $\nu\uparrow\infty$:

$$a(\theta)z \geq 0\ \ (\theta \in S). \tag{26}$$

by 5.1.4.b,c. Then by (24),

$$c'z = \lim_{\nu\uparrow\infty} c'[x_\nu/\|x_\nu\|] = \lim_{\nu\uparrow\infty} P_{ext}/\|x_\nu\| = 0. \tag{27}$$

The relation $\|z\|=1$, hence $z\neq 0$, and (26) and (27) contradict the assumption (22). Hence, this *Case 2* is impossible •

5.2.2. Programs with Arbitrary Constraints

Let B be any set in $\mathbf{R}^m$ and $c_{m\times 1}$ a fixed point in $\mathbf{R}^m$. The problems

$$P_{gen} := \inf_x[c'x \,/\, x\in B] \tag{28}$$

and

$$Q_{gen} := \sup_x[c'x \,/\, x\in B], \tag{29}$$

where x ranges over $\mathbf{R}^m$, generalize all the problems considered hitherto. In the foregoing problems, the constraints define a closed convex subset B.

A direction of B is any point z that can be obtained as the direction of a sequence $x_\nu\in B$ ($\nu=1,2,\ldots$) with properties 5.1.4.a,b,c. Bounded sets do not have directions. Any unbounded set has directions (by the consideration of subsequences). The following is an easy generalization of Theorem 5.

Theorem 6

We consider the problem P_{gen} (28) or Q_{gen} (29), and we suppose that B is a closed (not necessarily convex) subset of $\mathbf{R}^m$. If the value of the problem is finite, and if $c'z\neq 0$ for any direction z of the set B, then the problem has a solution

Proof
We consider the problem P_{gen}. The proof is the same in the case of the problem Q_{gen}. Let $P_{gen}\in\mathbf{R}$, and let $c'z\neq 0$ for any direction z of B. We consider a limit solution, and the same cases *Case 1* and *Case 2* as in the proof of Theorem 5. Only the following adaptations must be introduced:

Case 1. Now (23) must be replaced by the relation $x_\nu\in B$ ($\nu=1,2,\ldots$). For $\nu\uparrow\infty$, it implies $x\in B$, because B is closed. Then x is a solution of the problem.

Case 2. Now z is a direction of set B, and it still satisfies the relations (27), i.e. $c'z=0$. But this contradicts the assumptions: *Case 2* is impossible •

5.2.3. Illustration

We here discuss the connexion between the problems P_{ext} and P_{gen} and the meaning of condition $c'z\neq 0$ in case of a particular problem on $\mathbf{R}^2$. It is convenient to interpret $p:=(p_1,p_2)'$ as a point p of $\mathbf{R}^2$ as well as a vector with origin $O:=(0,0)'$ and extremity point p.

We consider the problem

$$P_{gen}(c_1,c_2) := \inf_x[c_1x_1+c_2x_2/\ x_2\geq x_1^{-1}\ ,\ x_1>0], \tag{30}$$

where $x:=(x_1,x_2)'$ ranges over $\mathbf{R}^2$. We assume that

$$||c||=c_1^2+c_2^2=1. \tag{31}$$

The set of feasible points is

$$B := \{(x_1,x_2)\ /\ x_2\geq x_1^{-1},\ x_1>0\}. \tag{32}$$

Let

$$a_1(\theta)x_1+a_2(\theta)x_2 = \alpha(\theta)\quad (\theta>0) \tag{33}$$

be the equation of the tangent line to the curve $x_2=1/x_1$ ($x_1>0$) at the point with abscissa θ. The functions $a_1(\cdot)$, $a_2(\cdot)$ and $\alpha(\cdot)$ are easily found. They are irrelevant in the following discussion. The feasible points are those situated above all the tangents. Hence problem (30) is identical to problem

$$P_{ext}(c_1,c_2) = \inf_x[c_1x_1+c_2x_2/\ a_1(\theta)x_1+a_2(\theta)x_2 \geq \alpha(\theta)\quad (\theta>0)]. \tag{34}$$

This shows **that some problems P_{gen} with non-linear constraints are identical to extended linear programs P_{ext}.**

The objective function is the scalar product $c'x=c_1x_1+c_2x_2$. It has the well known geometrical interpretation: it is the algebraic (positive or negative) length of the segment [O,proj(x/c)], where proj(x/c) is the orthogonal projection of the point x on the line containing the vector c. See Fig.7.

The directions of the set B are the vectors $z\in\mathbf{R}_+^2$ with norm $||z||=1$.

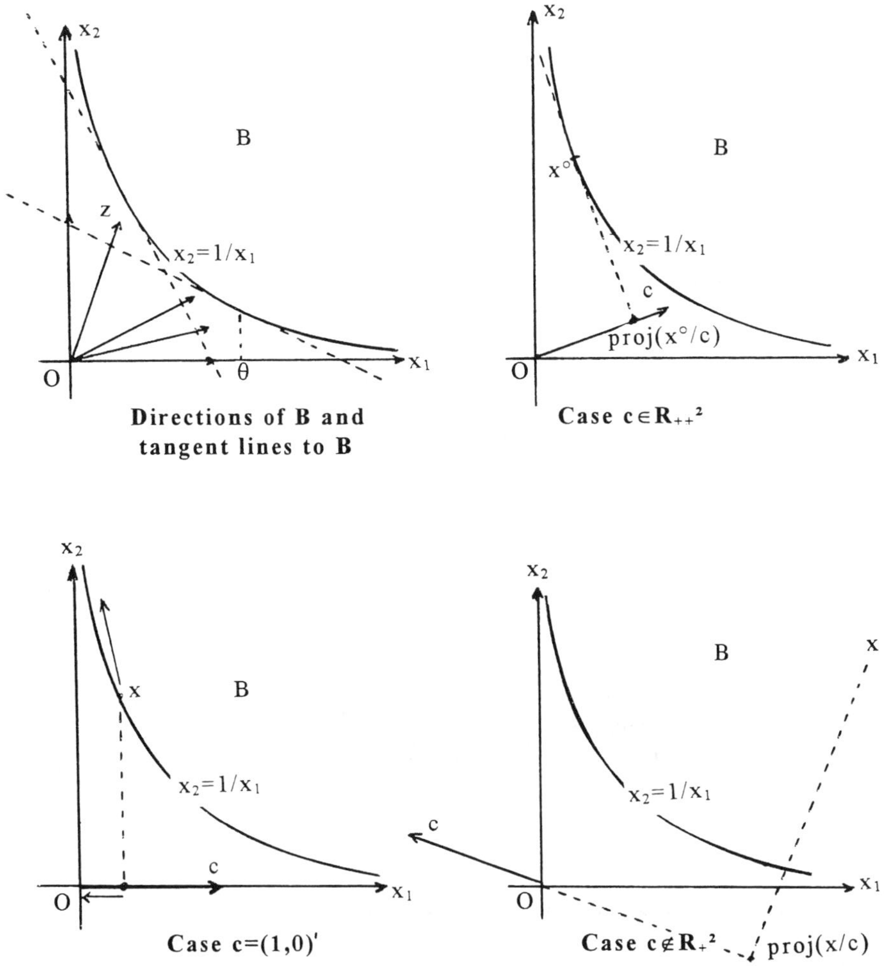

Fig.7. Different cases in illustration of 5.2.3

Case $c \in \mathbf{R}_{++}^2$. The problem $P_{gen}(c_1,c_2)$ has a finite value and a solution x°. The latter is the contact point of the tangent line to the set B, orthogonal to the line containing the vector c. The condition $c'z \neq 0$ is satisfied for all directions $z \in B$.

Case $c=(1,0)'$. The problem $P_{gen}(0,1)$ has the finite value 0, but it has no solution. The tangent line to B orthogonal to the horizontal axis becomes an asymptote. The condition $z'c\neq 0$ is not satisfied for the vertical direction $z=(0,1)'$.

Case $c=(0,1)'$. It is similar to the foregoing case: finite value, no solution.

Case $c\notin\mathbf{R}_+^2$. The value is $-\infty$. The problem cannot have a solution.

5.3. Duality Theory of Linear Programs

5.3.1. Primal Maximization Problem

The **primal linear problem** of this section is the problem

$$Q(\alpha) := \sup_{x\geq 0}[c'x \,/\, ax\leq\alpha]. \tag{35}$$

on $\mathbf{R}_+^m$. This is the first problem (15), but now the point $\alpha\in\mathbf{R}^n$ is considered as parameter, and therefore explicitly mentioned in the notation $Q(\alpha)$. We also consider the auxiliary problem

$$Q_=(\alpha) = \sup_{x\geq 0}[c'x \,/\, ax=\alpha], \tag{36}$$

in demonstrations of results concerning problem $Q(\alpha)$. The **effective domains** dom Q and dom $Q_=$ are defined in Ch.1.1.3.

Lemma

Let $Q_=(\alpha_0)=+\infty$ for some $\alpha_0\in\mathbf{R}^n$. Then $Q_=(\alpha)=+\infty$ for all $\alpha\in$dom $Q_=$.

Proof
The point α_0 belongs to dom $Q_=$. Let $x_\nu\in\mathbf{R}_+^m$ (ν=1,2,...) be a limit solution of problem $Q_=(\alpha_0)$. Then

$$ax_\nu = \alpha_0 \; (\nu=1,2,...), \tag{37}$$

$$c'x_\nu\rightarrow Q_=(\alpha_0) = +\infty \text{ as } \nu\uparrow\infty. \tag{38}$$

This implies that the sequence x_ν (ν=1,2,...) is unbounded. By Theorem 3, we may assume that the conditions 5.1.4.a,b,c,d are satisfied, because we can replace the sequence by a subsequence. Let z be the direction of the sequence x_ν (ν=1,2,...).

We divide relation (37) by $\|x_\nu\|$, and we let $\nu\uparrow\infty$. By 5.1.4.b,c,

$$az = 0. \tag{39}$$

Let $\alpha\in$ dom $Q_=$, and let x^α be a feasible point of the problem $Q_=(\alpha)$.

Case 1: $c'z>0$.

Let $u_\nu:=x^\alpha+\nu z$ ($\nu=1,2,\ldots$). Then $u_\nu\geq 0$, $au_\nu=ax^\alpha+\nu.az=ax^\alpha=\alpha$ by (39). Hence, u_ν is a feasible point of problem $Q_=(\alpha)$. Then

$$Q_=(\alpha) \geq c'u_\nu = c'x^\alpha + \nu.c'z \to +\infty \text{ as } \nu\uparrow\infty.$$

Hence, $Q_=(\alpha)= +\infty$.

Case 2: $c'z\leq 0$.

Let $y_\nu:=x_\nu-\rho_\nu.z$ ($\nu=1,2,\ldots$) be the direction-transformed sequence of the sequence x_ν ($\nu=1,2,\ldots$). By Theorem 3, $y_\nu\in\mathbf{R}_+^{\mathbf{m}}$. By (37) and (39),

$$ay_\nu = ax_\nu-\rho_\nu.az = ax_\nu = \alpha_0 \ (\nu=1,2,\ldots).$$

Hence, y_ν is a feasible point of problem $Q_=(\alpha_0)$. By (38),

$$c'y_\nu = c'x_\nu-\rho_\nu.c'z \geq c'x_\nu \to +\infty=Q_=(\alpha_0) \text{ as } \nu\uparrow\infty.$$

This implies that sequence y_ν ($\nu=1,2,\ldots$) is a limit solution of problem $Q_=(\alpha_0)$, and then we can start the discussion again with this new sequence, and we can start again and again, until *Case 1* happens. This necessarily occurs after m steps at most, because the number of zeros in the components of the terms of the successively direction-transformed sequences increases strictly in each step, by Theorem 3. Indeed, if *Case 1* does not occur, we finally obtain the sequence 0,0,..., and this is contradictory because we always leave *Case 2* with some sequence y_ν ($\nu=1,2,\ldots$) such that $c'y_\nu\to+\infty$ as $\nu\uparrow\infty$ •

We recall that **the value function Q**, is the function with values $Q(\alpha)$ ($\alpha\in\mathbf{R}^{\mathbf{n}}$).

Theorem 7

If the value function Q has one finite value, then Q is finite on dom Q and the problem Q(α) has a solution for all α∈dom Q.

Proof

By Theorem 1, it is sufficient to prove the Theorem for problem $Q_=(\alpha)$ ($\alpha\in\mathbf{R}^{\mathbf{n}}$). Then the first part results from the Lemma, and the rest from Theorem 4 •

Theorem 8

The value function Q is a concave function on $\mathbf{R}^n$. If Q has one finite value, then Q is a proper concave upper semi-continuous function on $\mathbf{R}^n$.

Proof

a. We prove that Q is concave. We have to verify that

$$Q(p\alpha+(1-p)\beta) \geq pQ(\alpha) + (1-p)Q(\beta) \quad (\alpha,\beta \in \mathbf{R}^n;\ 0 \leq p \leq 1). \tag{40}$$

That relation is correct if $p=0$ or $p=1$. Hence, we may assume that $0<p<1$. Then (40) is correct if $Q(\alpha)= -\infty$ or $Q(\beta)= -\infty$ (see App.C.C5). Hence, we may assume that

$$-\infty < Q(\alpha) \ , \ -\infty < Q(\beta).$$

Let

$$-\infty < a < Q(\alpha) \ , \ -\infty < b < Q(\beta).$$

Then the problem $Q(\alpha)$ has a feasible point x and the problem $Q(\beta)$ a feasible point y, such that

$$a < c'x \ , \ b < c'y.$$

The feasibility conditions are

$$x \geq 0 \ , \ ax \leq \alpha \ , \ y \geq 0 \ , \ ay \leq \alpha.$$

Let

$$z := px + (1-p)y.$$

Then

$$z \geq 0 \ , \ az = p\ ax + (1-p)\ ay \leq p\alpha + q\beta.$$

Hence, z is a feasible point of problem $Q(p\alpha+(1-p)\beta)$. This implies that

$$Q(p\alpha+(1-p)\beta) \geq c'z = p\ c'x + (1-p)c'y \geq pa + (1-p)b.$$

Hence,

$$Q(p\alpha+(1-p)\beta) \geq pa + (1-p)b.$$

For $a\uparrow Q(\alpha)$ and $b\uparrow Q(\beta)$, we obtain (40).

b. If Q has a finite value, then dom $Q\neq\emptyset$, $Q\equiv-\infty$ outside dom Q, and by Theorem 7, Q is finite on dom Q. Hence, Q is a proper concave function if it has a finite value (see App.C.C5).

c. We now assume that the problem $Q_=(\alpha)$ has a finite value, and we prove that the value function $Q_=$ is upper semi-continuous. By Theorem 1, this implies the upper semi-continuity of the value function Q, if it has a finite value.

We assume that

$$\alpha_\nu \to \alpha \in \mathbf{R}^n \text{ and } Q_=(\alpha_\nu) \to b \in \mathbf{R}\cup\{-\infty,+\infty\} \text{ as } \nu\uparrow\infty. \tag{41}$$

We must prove that $b \le Q_=(\alpha)$. This relation is correct if $b=-\infty$. Hence, we may assume that $-\infty<b$. Then $-\infty<Q_=(\alpha_\nu)$ if ν is large enough. Hence, we may assume that $\alpha_\nu \in \text{dom } Q_=$ (ν=1,2,...). Then the problem $Q_=(\alpha_\nu)$ has a solution x_ν by the $Q_=$-version of the Theorem 7. Hence,

$$x_\nu \ge 0 \;,\; ax_\nu = \alpha_\nu \;,\; c'x_\nu = Q_=(\alpha_\nu) \;\; (\nu=1,2,...). \tag{42}$$

Case 1: The sequence x_ν (ν=1,2,...) is bounded.

We may assume that

$$x_\nu \to x \in \mathbf{R}^m \text{ as } \nu\uparrow\infty,$$

because we can take a subsequence. As $\nu\uparrow\infty$, by (41) and (42):

$$x \ge 0 \;,\; ax = \alpha \;,\; c'x = b.$$

This implies that x is a feasible point of the problem $Q_=(\alpha)$ and that $b \le Q_=(\alpha)$. Hence, in this *Case 1*, we have finished.

Case 2: The sequence x_ν (ν=1,2,...) is unbounded.

By Theorem 3, we may assume that the conditions 5.1.4.a,b,c,d are satisfied, because we can take a subsequence. Let z be the direction of the sequence x_ν (ν=1,2,...). The sequence α_ν (ν=1,2,...) is bounded, because it converges to point $\alpha \in \mathbf{R}^n$ by (41). We divide the second relation (42) by $\|x_\nu\|$, and we let $\nu\uparrow\infty$. Then, by 5.1.4.b,c:

$$az = 0. \tag{43}$$

Subcase 2_1: $c'z > 0$.

Let α_0 be a fixed point in dom $Q_=$ and let x_0 be a feasible point of the problem $Q_=(\alpha_0)$. Let

$$u_\nu := x_0 + \nu.z \; (\nu=1,2,...).$$

Then

$$u_\nu \geq 0 \ , \ au_\nu = ax_0 + \nu.az = ax_0 = \alpha_0 \ (\nu=1,2,...),$$

by (43). Hence, u_ν is a feasible point of the problem $Q_=(\alpha_0)$. Then

$$Q_=(\alpha_0) \geq c'u_\nu = c'x_0 + \nu.c'z \to \infty \ \text{as} \ \nu\uparrow\infty.$$

Hence $Q_=(\alpha_0)=+\infty$. But this contradicts the $Q_=$-version of Theorem 7. Hence, *Subcase 2_1* cannot occur.

Subcase 2_2: $c'z \leq 0$.

Let

$$y_\nu := x_\nu - \rho_\nu.z \ (\nu=1,2,...)$$

be the direction-transformed sequence of the sequence x_ν (ν=1,2,...). By Theorem 3, $y_\nu \geq 0$. By the second relation (42) and by (43),

$$ay_\nu = ax_\nu - \rho_\nu.az = ax_\nu = \alpha_\nu \ (\nu=1,2,...).$$

Hence, y_ν is a feasible point of the problem $Q_=(\alpha_\nu)$. Then, by the last relation (42),

$$Q_=(\alpha_\nu) \geq c'y_\nu = c'x_\nu - \rho_\nu.c'z \geq c'x_\nu = Q_=(\alpha_\nu) \ (\nu=1,2,...).$$

Hence, $c'y_\nu = Q_=(\alpha_\nu)$ and y_ν is a solution of problem $Q_=(\alpha_\nu)$. Then we can start the discussion again with sequence y_ν (ν=1,2,...) instead of x_ν (ν=1,2,...), and we can start again and again as long as *Case 1* does not occur. Sooner or later, this case must occur. Indeed, by Theorem 3, we finish with the bounded sequence 0, 0,..., if *Case 1* does not happen before •

Remark

Now two definitions of the **effective domain dom Q** are available. By **the problem definition** of Ch.1.1.3, adopted hitherto,

$$\text{dom } Q := \{\alpha \in \mathbf{R}^n \ / \ \text{The problem } Q(\alpha) \text{ has feasible points}\}.$$

By **the function definition** of App.C.C5,

$$\text{dom } Q := \{\alpha \in \mathbf{R}^n \ / \ -\infty < Q(\alpha)\}.$$

Of course, these definitions do agree because $Q(\alpha) = -\infty$ iff the problem $Q(\alpha)$ has no feasible vectors.

The **problem definition** of the effective domain is general. It is valid for any optimization problem depending on parameters. The **function definition** of the effective domain is available for concave and convex functions only.

If P is a convex function on $\mathbf{R}^n$, then dom P is the set of points $\alpha \in \mathbf{R}^n$ such that $P(\alpha) < \infty$. In any case hereafter considered, the two definitions coincide when they are both available.

5.3.2. Dual Problem

We continue with the problem $Q(\alpha)$ ($\alpha \in \mathbf{R}^n$) defined by (35).

Theorem 9

The bipolar function of the value function Q is the function Q with values**

$$\mathbf{Q^{**}(\alpha) = \inf_{y\geq 0}[\alpha' y \,/\, a' y \geq c] \quad (\alpha \in R^n)} \tag{44}$$

where y ranges over $\mathbf{R_+^n}$.

Proof

Let $\beta = (\beta_1,\ldots,\beta_n) \in \mathbf{R}^n$. Then, by App.C.C9,

$$Q^*(\beta) = \inf_\alpha[\beta'\alpha - Q(\alpha)] = \inf_\alpha[\beta'\alpha - \sup_{x\geq 0}[c'x \,/\, ax \leq \alpha]]$$

$$= \inf_\alpha[\beta'\alpha + \inf_{x\geq 0}[-c'x \,/\, ax \leq \alpha]] = \inf_\alpha \inf_{x\geq 0}[\beta'\alpha - c'x \,/\, ax \leq \alpha]$$

$$= \inf_{x\geq 0} \inf_\alpha[\beta'\alpha - c'x \,/\, ax \leq \alpha] = \inf_{x\geq 0}[\inf_\alpha[\beta'\alpha \,/\, ax \leq \alpha] - c'x], \tag{45}$$

where α ranges over $\mathbf{R}^n$. The $\inf_\alpha$, in the last member of (45), is attained for $\alpha = ax$ if $\beta \geq 0$. It equals $-\infty$ if not$(\beta \geq 0)$, i.e. if some component β_j is strictly negative, because then we can let $\alpha_j \uparrow \infty$. Hence,

$$Q^*(\beta) = \inf_{x\geq 0}[\beta' ax\, 1_{\beta\geq 0} - \infty\, 1_{\text{not}(\beta\geq 0)} - c'x]$$

$$= \inf_{x\geq 0}[(\beta' a - c')x] - \infty\, 1_{\text{not}(\beta\geq 0} = 0\, 1_{\beta' a - c' \geq 0} - \infty\, 1_{\text{not}(\beta' a - c' \geq 0)} - \infty\, 1_{\text{not}(\beta\geq 0)},$$

$$\text{dom } Q^* = \{\beta \,/\, \beta\geq 0,\ \beta' a - c'\geq 0\}.$$

Then

$$Q^{**}(\alpha) = \inf_{\beta\in \text{dom } Q^*}[\alpha'\beta - Q^*(\beta)]$$

$$= \inf_{\beta\geq 0, \beta' a - c'\geq 0}[\alpha'\beta - 0] = \inf_{\beta\geq 0}[\alpha'\beta \,/\, a'\beta\geq c] \ \bullet$$

The problem $Q^{**}(\alpha)$ ($\alpha\in\mathbf{R}^n$) defined by (44) is the **dual problem** of the problem $Q(\alpha)$ ($\alpha\in\mathbf{R}^n$).

We notice that the parameter α occurs in the constraints of the problem $Q(\alpha)$, not in its objective function. In the problem $Q^{**}(\alpha)$, the parameter α occurs in the objective function, not in the constraints.

Theorem 10

If the value function Q has a finite value, then $Q(\alpha)=Q^{**}(\alpha)$ ($\alpha\in\mathbf{R}^n$). In any case $Q(\alpha)\leq Q^{**}(\alpha)$ ($\alpha\in\mathbf{R}^n$).

Proof
If Q has a finite value, then it is a proper concave upper semi-continuous function by Theorem 2. Then $Q=Q^{**}$ by Fenchel-Moreau (App.C.Th.C17.c). In any case, $Q\leq Q^{**}$ by App.C.Th.C16.Cor. •

5.3.3. Primal Minimization Problem and Its Dual

We consider the problem

$$P(c) := \inf_{y\geq 0}[\alpha' y \,/\, a' y\geq c] \quad (c\in\mathbf{R}^m) \tag{46}$$

where y ranges over $\mathbf{R}_+^n$. The matrix $a_{n\times m}$ and the column $\alpha_{n\times 1}$ are the same as in problem $P(\alpha)$. The problem $P(c)$ is problem (44), but now c is regarded as parameter and α is fixed. The problem $P(c)$ is equivalent to a problem of type $Q(\alpha)$, because

$$\inf_{y\geq 0}[\alpha' y \,/\, a' y\geq c] = -\sup_{y\geq 0}[-\alpha' y \,/\, (-a')y\leq -c] \quad (c\in\mathbf{R}^m). \tag{47}$$

Any result valid for problem $Q(\alpha)$ ($\alpha\in\mathbf{R}^m$) has an obvious P-version. The following Theorem 11 is a combination of the P-version of Theorem 7 and the P-version of Theorem 8.

Theorem 11

If the value function P has one finite value, then P is finite on dom P and then the problem P(c) has a solution for all $c\in$dom P.

The function P is a convex function on R^m. If P has one finite value, then P is a proper convex lower semi-continuous function on R^m •

The following Theorem 12 is the P-version of Theorem 9. The polar functions used in the calculation of the bipolar function P** are sup-polars (see App.C. C9 and C10).

Theorem 12

The bipolar function of the value function P is the function P with values**

$$P^{**}(c) = \sup_{x\geq 0}[c'x \,/\, ax\leq\alpha] \quad (c\in \mathbf{R}^m), \tag{48}$$

where x ranges over R_+^m •

The problem defined by (48) is **the dual problem of problem P(c) ($c\in\mathbf{R}^m$)**.

The following Theorem 13 is the P-version of Theorem 10.

Theorem 13

If the value function P has one finite value, then P(c)=P(c) ($c\in\mathbf{R}^n$). In any case P**(c)≤P(c) ($c\in\mathbf{R}^n$) •**

It is possible to **define** the dual problem of the problem P(c) ($c\in\mathbf{R}^n$) by the last member of relation (48). Then Theorem 13 results from the results proved for the problems Q(α) and Q**(α) by the exploitation of relations such as (47). In this way, the theory of convex functions becomes superfluous.

5.3.4. Duality Theorem

In the following Theorem, we consider the problems

$$P = \inf_{y\geq 0}[\alpha' y \,/\, a' y \geq c]\,,\; Q = \sup_{x\geq 0}[c' x \,/\, ax \leq \alpha], \tag{49}$$

where $a_{n\times m}$ is a fixed matrix, and $c_{m\times 1}$, $\alpha_{n\times 1}$ fixed columns. In the first problem, y ranges over $\mathbf{R}_+^n$. In the last problem x ranges over $\mathbf{R}_+^m$. These problems are those of the preceding sections, but now c and α are fixed.

Theorem 14 (Duality Theorem)

We consider the problems P and Q.

a. **If one of the problems has a finite value, then both problems have a solution.**

b. **If both problems have feasible points, then both problems have a solution.**

c. **If one of the problems has feasible points, then the problems have the same value P=Q.**

d. **Let x be a feasible point of the problem Q, and y a feasible point of the problem P. Then $c'x \leq \alpha'y$. The equality $c'x=\alpha'y$ holds iff x is a solution of the problem Q and y a solution of the problem P.**

Proof
We notice that

$$Q = Q(\alpha) = P^{**}(c)\;\;,\;\; P = P(c) = Q^{**}(\alpha), \tag{50}$$

where the problems $Q(\alpha)$, $P^{**}(c)$, $P(c)$, $Q^{**}(\alpha)$ are those considered in the foregoing sections.

a. Let the value $Q=Q(\alpha)$ be finite. Then problem $Q(\alpha)$ has a solution by Theorem 4, and $Q(\alpha)=Q^{**}(\alpha)$ by Theorem 10. Then the value $P=Q^{**}(\alpha)$ is finite, and problem P has a solution by Theorem 4. Hence, both problems P and Q have a solution if value Q is finite. By symmetry, both problems have a solution if value P is finite.

b. Let P and Q have feasible points. Then, by (50) and by Theorem 10,

$$-\infty < Q = Q(\alpha) \leq Q^{**}(\alpha) = P < +\infty,$$

where the strict inequalities result from the existence of feasible points. Hence, the values P and Q are finite, and then both problems P and Q have a solution by a.

c. Let the problem Q have feasible points. Then $-\infty<Q$. If Q is finite, then $Q=Q(\alpha)=Q^{**}(\alpha)=P$ by (50) and by Theorem 10. If $Q=+\infty$, then $+\infty=Q=Q(\alpha) \leq Q^{**}(\alpha)=P$ by (50) and by Theorem 10, and then $P=Q=+\infty$. In any case $P=Q$. By symmetry, $P=Q$ if the problem P has feasible points.

d.

$$c'x \leq Q = P \leq \alpha'y, \tag{51}$$

where the inequalities result from the feasibility of x and y, and the equality from c. If x is a solution of the problem P and y a solution of the problem Q, then

$$c'x = P = Q = \alpha'y. \tag{52}$$

If $c'x=\alpha'y$, then (52) results from (51) and then x is a solution of the problem Q and y is a solution of the problem P •

5.4. Zero-Sum Two-Person Games

5.4.1. Definition of Game

Let S and T be any sets. We call S **the set of strategies of the first player Sophie**, and T **the set of strategies of the second player Thomas**. Let $\varphi(s,t)$ be any real finite function defined for $s \in S$ and $t \in T$. The function φ is **the pay-off function** of the game.

We consider the game with the following simple rules.

Sophie chooses a point $s \in S$ and Thomas chooses, independently, a point $t \in T$. Then Thomas pays Sophie the amount $\varphi(s,t)$.

We have here two players. Hence we speak of **a two-person game**. One player wins what the other loses or, in other words, the sum of their gains is zero. Hence the name: **zero-sum game**.

5.4.2. Solutions

A solution of the game (S,T,φ) is a couple (σ,τ) $(\sigma\in S,\ \tau\in T)$ of strategies satisfying the inequalities

$$\varphi(s,\tau) \le \varphi(\sigma,\tau) \le \varphi(\sigma,t) \quad (s\in S,\ t\in T). \tag{53}$$

Not every game has solutions (see 5.5.1).

Let us assume that the game (S,T,φ) has a solution (σ,τ). If Thomas adopts strategy τ, then the best thing that Sophie can do is to play strategy σ. Indeed, by the first inequality (53), her gain diminishes (not necessarily strictly) if she plays another strategy. If Sophie adopts strategy σ, then the best thing that Thomas can do is to play strategy τ. His loss augments if he adopts any other strategy, by the last inequality (53).

Of course, each player ignores the strategy of its opponent. Nevertheless, we shall justify, at least in a particular case (See 5.4.5) that σ and τ are the unique clever strategies of Sophie and Thomas respectively.

A solution of a game is also called **an optimal couple of strategies**. The inequalities (53) state that solution (σ,τ) is **a saddle point of the function φ**.

Theorem 15

Let (σ,τ) and (σ_0,τ_0) be solutions of the game (S,T,φ). Then (σ,τ_0) and (σ_0,τ) are solutions and

$$\varphi(\sigma,\tau) = \varphi(\sigma_0,\tau_0). \tag{54}$$

Proof

For all $s\in S$ and $t\in T$, we assume (53) and

$$\varphi(s,\tau_0) \le \varphi(\sigma_0,\tau_0) \le \varphi(\sigma_0,t). \tag{55}$$

We have to prove that

$$\varphi(s,\tau_0) \le \varphi(\sigma,\tau_0) \le \varphi(\sigma,t), \tag{56}$$

$$\varphi(s,\tau) \le \varphi(\sigma_0,\tau) \le \varphi(\sigma_0,t). \tag{57}$$

We can use (53) and (55) with $s=\sigma$, $s=\sigma_0$, $t=\tau$, $t=\tau_0$. Hence,

$$\begin{aligned}\boldsymbol{\varphi(s,\tau_0)} &\le \varphi(\sigma_0,\tau_0) \le \varphi(\sigma_0,\tau) \le \varphi(\sigma,\tau) \le \boldsymbol{\varphi(\sigma,\tau_0)} \\ &\le \varphi(\sigma_0,\tau_0) \le \varphi(\sigma_0,\tau) \le \varphi(\sigma,\tau) \le \boldsymbol{\varphi(\sigma,t)}.\end{aligned} \tag{58}$$

This proves (56). In (58) we may permute (σ,τ) and (σ_0,τ_0). Then (57) is obtained. In (56) we can take $s=\sigma_0$, $t=\tau$. Hence,

$$\varphi(\sigma_0,\tau_0) \le \varphi(\sigma,\tau).$$

By symmetry,

$$\varphi(\sigma,\tau) \le \varphi(\sigma_0,\tau_0).$$

This proves (54) •

5.4.3. Value of Game

We consider a game (S,T,φ) with solutions (i.e. with at least one solution). The **value of the game** is

$$\mathrm{Val}(S,T,\varphi) := \varphi(\sigma,\tau), \tag{59}$$

where (σ,τ) is any solution of the game. By Theorem 15, this value does not depend on the particular solution (σ,τ).

5.4.4. Minimax Criterion

Let us consider $\sup_{x\in D} f(x)$, where f is a real function on the set D.

This **sup is attained at the point $\xi\in D$** if $f(\xi)=\sup_{x\in D}f(x)$. Then $\sup_{x\in D}f(x)$ can also be represented as $\max_{x\in D} f(x)$.

Hence, a **max** is an attained **sup**. By the very use of the notation **max**, it is assumed that the **sup** is attained.

Of course, a similar notation and terminology applies to the couple **inf**, **min**.

Theorem 16

a. **In any game (S,T,φ),**

$$\sup_{s\in S} \inf_{t\in T} \varphi(s,t) \le \inf_{t\in T} \sup_{s\in S} \varphi(s,t). \tag{60}$$

b. **If the game (S,T,φ) has solutions, then**

$$Val(S,T,\varphi) = \sup_{s\in S} \inf_{t\in T} \varphi(s,t) = \inf_{t\in T} \sup_{s\in S} \varphi(s,t). \tag{61}$$

c. **Let**

$$\max_{s\in S} \inf_{t\in T} \varphi(s,t) = \min_{t\in T} \sup_{s\in S} \varphi(s,t), \tag{62}$$

where the max is attained at the point $\sigma\in S$ and the min at the point $\tau\in T$. Then (σ,τ) is a solution of the game, and its value equals $\varphi(\sigma,\tau)$.

Proof

a. Successively,

$$\varphi(s,t) \le \sup_{t\in T} \varphi(s,t) \quad (s\in S,\ t\in T),$$

$$\inf_{s\in S} \varphi(s,t) \le \inf_{s\in S} \sup_{t\in T} \varphi(s,t) \quad (t\in T),$$

$$\sup_{t\in T} \inf_{s\in S} \varphi(s,t) \le \inf_{s\in S} \sup_{t\in T} \varphi(s,t).$$

b. Let (σ,τ) be a solution of the game. Then, successively, by (53) and (59),

$$\varphi(s,\tau) \le Val(S,T,\varphi) \le \varphi(\sigma,t) \quad (s\in S,\ t\in T),$$

$$\sup_{s\in S} \varphi(s,\tau) \le Val(S,T,\varphi) \le \inf_{t\in T} \varphi(\sigma,t).$$

But

$$\inf_{t\in T} \sup_{s\in S} \varphi(s,t) \le \sup_{s\in S} \varphi(s,\tau)\ ,\ \inf_{t\in T} \varphi(\sigma,\tau) \le \sup_{s\in S} \inf_{t\in T} \varphi(\sigma,t).$$

Hence,

$$\inf_{t\in T} \sup_{s\in S} \varphi(s,t) \le Val(S,T,\varphi) \le \sup_{s\in S} \inf_{t\in T} \varphi(\sigma,t)$$

and then b. results from a.

c. Let

$$f(s) := \inf_{t\in T} \varphi(s,t)\ (s\in S)\ ,\ g(t) := \sup_{s\in S} \varphi(s,t)\ (t\in T).$$

Then

$$f(\sigma) = \max_{s\in S} f(s) \ , \ g(\tau) = \min_{t\in T} g(t).$$

$$\varphi(s,t) \le g(t) \ \ (s\in S,\ t\in T), \tag{63}$$

$$f(s) \le \varphi(s,t) \ \ (s\in S,\ t\in T), \tag{64}$$

Assumption (62) is

$$f(\sigma) = g(\tau). \tag{65}$$

For s=σ, t=τ in (63) and (64), we obtain

$$\varphi(\sigma,\tau) \le g(\tau)\ ,\ f(\sigma) \le \varphi(\sigma,\tau).$$

Then

$$\varphi(\sigma,\tau) \le g(\tau) = f(\sigma) \le \varphi(\sigma,\tau)$$

by (65). Hence,

$$\varphi(\sigma,\tau) = g(\tau) = f(\sigma). \tag{66}$$

By (63) with t=τ,

$$\varphi(s,\tau) \le g(\tau).$$

By (64) with s=σ,

$$f(\sigma) \le \varphi(\sigma,t).$$

Then by (66),

$$\varphi(s,\tau) \le \varphi(\sigma,\tau) \le \varphi(\sigma,t) \ \ (s\in S,\ t\in T).$$

This proves that (σ,τ) is a solution of the game. By definition, the value of the game is φ(σ,τ) •

Theorem 17

Let S be a compact subset of $\mathbf{R}^m$, T a compact subset of $\mathbf{R}^n$, and let the function φ(·,·) be continuous on the cartesion product $S\times T\subseteq \mathbf{R}^{m+n}$. Then the min's and the max's involved in the expressions

$$\max_{s\in S} \min_{t\in T} \varphi(s,t)\ ,\ \min_{t\in T} \max_{s\in S} \varphi(s,t) \tag{67}$$

are attained.

Proof

It is classical that a continuous function attains its minimum value and its maximum value on any compact set. For fixed s∈S, the function φ(s,t) of t∈T is continuous. Hence, τ_s exists such that

$$\varphi(s,\tau_s) = \min_{t\in T} \varphi(s,t) \ \ (s\in S).$$

Let f be the function with values

$$f(s) := \min_{t\in T} \varphi(s,t) \quad (s\in S).$$

We will prove that f is continuous on S. Then the maximum of f is attained at some point of S, and then the min and the max involved in the first expression (67) exist. Then the last expression (67) can be treated in the same way.

In order to prove the continuity of f, let $s,s'\in S$. Then

$$\varphi(s,t) \le \varphi(s',t) + |\varphi(s,t)-\varphi(s',t)|\ ,\ \varphi(s',t) \le \varphi(s,t) + |\varphi(s',t)-\varphi(s,t)|,$$

$$\max_{t\in T} \varphi(s,t) \le \max_{t\in T} \varphi(s',t) + \max_{t\in T} |\varphi(s,t)-\varphi(s',t)|,$$

$$\max_{t\in T} \varphi(s',t) \le \max_{t\in T} \varphi(s,t) + \max_{t\in T} |\varphi(s',t)-\varphi(s,t)|.$$

Hence,

$$f(s) \le f(s') + \max_{t\in T} |\varphi(s,t)-\varphi(s',t)|,$$

$$f(s') \le f(s) + \max_{t\in T} |\varphi(s',t)-\varphi(s,t)|.$$

Then

$$|f(s')-f(s)| \le \max_{t\in T} |\varphi(s',t)-\varphi(s,t)|.$$

This relation implies the continuity of f because continuous functions are uniformly continuous on compact sets. In particular φ is uniformly continuous on $S\times T$ •

If φ satisfies the conditions of the foregoing Theorem, then the game (S,T,φ) has a solution iff

$$\max_{s\in S} \min_{t\in T} \varphi(s,t) = \min_{t\in T} \max_{s\in S} \varphi(s,t). \qquad (68)$$

This is **the minimax criterion**.

5.4.5. Symmetrical Games

The game (S,T,φ) is **symmetrical** if S=T and if φ is an **anti-symmetrical function** on $S\times T$, i.e. a function such that

$$\varphi(s,t) = -\ \varphi(t,s) \quad (s,t\in S). \qquad (69).$$

Let the game be symmetrical. If Sophie plays the strategy s and Thomas the strategie t, then Sophie wins the amount $\varphi(s,t)$. If Thomas plays the strategy s and Sophie the strategy t, then Thomas wins the same amount $-\varphi(t,s) = \varphi(s,t)$. Hence, Sophie and Thomas are in a completely symmetrical situation.

Theorem 18

Let (S,T,φ) be a symmetrical game. Then

$$\mathbf{sup}_{s\in S}\mathbf{inf}_{t\in T}\, \varphi(s,t) = -\, \mathbf{inf}_{t\in T}\mathbf{sup}_{s\in S}\, \varphi(s,t). \tag{70}$$

If φ satisfies the assumptions of Theorem 17, then the game has a solution iff the first or the last member of (70) equals zero. Then the value of the game equals zero.

Proof
By the anti-symmetry of φ,

$$\sup_s \inf_t \varphi(s,t) = \sup_s \inf_t[-\varphi(t,s)] = \sup_s[-\sup_t \varphi(t,s)]$$

$$= -\inf_s \sup_t \varphi(t,s) = -\inf_t \sup_s \varphi(s,t).$$

This proves (70), and then the other conclusions are obvious by the minimax criterion and by Theorem 16.b •

Let (S,T,φ) be a symmetrical game with a solution (σ,τ) satisfying the relations

$$\varphi(s,\tau) < \varphi(\sigma,\tau) = 0 < \varphi(\sigma,t) \quad (s,t\in S;\ (s,t)\neq(\sigma,\tau)). \tag{71}$$

If Sophie plays strategy the σ, and Thomas a strategy $t\neq\tau$, then he loses the amount $\varphi(\sigma,t)>0$. If Thomas plays the strategy τ and Sophie a strategy $s\neq\sigma$, then she loses the amount $-\varphi(s,\tau)>0$.

In a symmetrical game, any strategy leading to a stricly positive loss, is a bad strategy. Sophie and Thomas's unique clever strategies are σ and τ respectively.

An example of a symmetrical game satisfying (71) is the following. Let S=T=[0,1] and let φ be any anti-symmetrical function defined on the square $[0,1]\times[0,1]$ such that

$$\varphi(s,t)>0\ (s>t)\ ,\ \varphi(s,t)<0\ (s<t)\ ,\ \varphi(s,s)=0.$$

Then

$$\sup_s\varphi(s,t) > 0\ (t\neq 1)\ ,\ \sup_s\varphi(s,1) = 0\ ,\ \inf_t\sup_s\varphi(s,t) = 0 \text{ attained at } t=1,$$

$$\inf_t\varphi(s,t) < 0\ (s\neq 1)\ ,\ \inf_t\varphi(1,t) = 0\ ,\ \sup_s\inf_t\varphi(s,t) = 0 \text{ attained at } s=1,$$

By Theorem 16.c, $(\sigma,\tau):=(1,1)$ is a solution of the game. For this game, the relations (71) are satisfied.

5.5. Matrix Games

5.5.1. Matrix Game with One Move

Let $a_{m\times n}$ be a matrix with elements a_{ij} (i=1,...,m; j=1,...,n). Now Sophie chooses a row $i\in\{1,...,m\}$ and Thomas a column $j\in\{1,..,n\}$. Then Sophie wins the amount a_{ij}.

The **matrix game with one move** defined in this way is the zero-sum two-person game

$$(\{1,...,m\},\{1,...,n\},\varphi),$$

where φ is the function with values

$$\varphi(i,j) := a_{ij}\ (i=1,...,m;\ j=1,...,n).$$

By Theorem 16.a,

$$\max_{i=1,...,m}\min_{j=1,...n} a_{ij} \leq \min_{j=1,...,n}\max_{i=1,...,m} a_{ij}. \tag{72}$$

By Theorem 16.c, the game has a solution iff (72) is an equality. Most matrix games with one move do not have solutions.

Example: **Matching Pennies**, played once.

Sophie and Thomas put down a penny, head or tail up. The pennies are uncovered and Sophie takes both if they show the same side. Otherwise Thomas gets both.

Here Sophie and Thomas's set of strategies is

$$S = T = \{\text{head, tail}\}$$

and the pay-off function has the values

$$\varphi(\text{head,head}) = \varphi(\text{tail,tail}) = 1 \ , \ \varphi(\text{head,tail}) = \varphi(\text{tail,head}) = -1.$$

Let head ≡ 1 , tail ≡ 2. Then the matrix of the game is

$$a = \begin{bmatrix} 1 & -1 \\ -1 & 1 \end{bmatrix}$$

Now (72) is the strict inequality $-1 < +1$. No solutions exist.

5.5.2. Matrix Game with Several Moves

Now Sophie and Thomas play repeatedly, a large number of times, the matrix game of the foregoing section. A strategy of Sophie is any column

$$s = (s_1,\ldots,s_m)' \in \mathbf{R}^m,$$

with elements s_i satisfying the relations

$$s_1 \geq 0 \ , \ \ldots \ , \ s_m \geq 0 \ , \ s_1+\ldots+s_m = 1.$$

The interpretation is that Sophie plays row i with frequency s_i. Sophie's set of strategies is denoted by S. Similarly, a strategy of Thomas is any column

$$t = (t_1,\ldots,t_n)' \in \mathbf{R}^n$$

with

$$t_1 \geq 0 \ , \ \ldots \ , \ t_n \geq 0 \ , \ t_1+\ldots+t_n = 1.$$

Thomas plays column j with frequency t_j. Thomas's set of strategies is denoted by T.

The **average gain** of Sophie is

$$\sum_{i=1,\ldots,m} \sum_{j=1,\ldots,n} s_i t_j a_{ij} = s'at, \tag{73}$$

in matrix notations.

We regard this **game with repeated moves**, as the zero-sum two-person game (S,T,φ), where the values of φ are

$$\varphi(s,t) = s'at \ (s \in S,\ t \in T).$$

This game is denoted as $(S,T,a_{m\times n})$. It is completely specified by the matrix $a_{m\times n}$.

By Theorem 17, inf and sup can systematically be replaced by min and max, when the game $(S,T,a_{m\times n})$ is considered. Indeed, $S\times T$ is a compact subset of $\mathbf{R}^{m+n}$, and φ is continuous on that set.

By (53), the couple (σ,τ) is a solution of the game $(S,T,a_{m\times n})$ iff

$$s'a\tau \le \sigma'a\tau \le \sigma'at \ \ (s \in S,\ t \in T). \tag{74}$$

The following Theorem is one of the first and most beautiful results of Game Theory.

Theorem 19 (von Neumann)

Any matrix game $(S,T,a_{m\times n})$ played repeatedly has a solution.

Proof

Let $b_{m\times n}$ be the matrix with all elements equal to k. Then $s'bt=k$ $(s \in S,\ t \in T)$ and

$$s'(a+b)t = s'at + k \ \ (s \in S,\ t \in T).$$

By (74), (σ,τ) is a solution of the game (S,T,a) iff it is a solution of the game $(S,T,a+b)$. If k is large enough then $a+b>0$, i.e. all elements of the matrix $a+b$ are strictly positive. Hence, we may assume that $a>0$.

Let $\alpha_{m\times 1}$ and $c_{n\times 1}$ be columns with all elements equal to 1. We consider the optimization problems

$$P = \inf_{x\ge 0}[\alpha'x \,/\, a'x \ge c] \ \ , \ Q = \sup_{y\ge 0}[c'y \,/\, ay \le \alpha]$$

where y ranges over $\mathbf{R}_+^{\,n}$ and x over $\mathbf{R}_+^{\,m}$. The set of feasible vectors of the problem Q is non-void and bounded. Indeed, it contains the vector 0, and the set of vectors y satisfying the relations $y\ge 0$, $ay\le\alpha$ is bounded because $a>0$ and $\alpha>0$. Hence, the value Q is finite. By the duality Theorem 14.a, both problems P and Q have solutions. Let η be a solution of the problem Q and ξ a solution of the problem P. By the duality Theorem 6.d, $c'\eta=\alpha'\xi$:

$$v := \eta_1+\ldots+\eta_n = \xi_1+\ldots+\xi_m.$$

Then v>0 because

$$\xi \geq 0 \ , \ a'\xi \geq c > 0.$$

Let

$$\sigma := \xi/v \ , \ \tau := \eta/v.$$

Then $\sigma \in S$, $\tau \in T$. We now verify that (σ,τ) is a solution of the game (S,T,a). The solution η satisfies the constraints after the slash of problem Q: $a\eta \leq \alpha$. We pre-multiply this relation by ξ' and by s':

$$\xi' a\eta \leq \xi'\alpha = \xi_1+\ldots+\xi_m = v,$$

$$s'a\eta \leq s'\alpha = s_1+\ldots+s_m = 1 \ \ (s\in S).$$

The solution ξ satisfies the constraints after the slash of problem P: $\xi' a \geq c'$. We post-multiply this relation by η and by t:

$$\xi' a\eta \geq c'\eta = \eta_1+\ldots+\eta_n = v,$$

$$\xi' at \geq c't = t_1+\ldots+t_n = 1 \ \ (t\in T).$$

Hence,

$$\xi' a\eta = v \ , \ v.s'a\eta \leq \xi' a\eta \leq v.\xi' at \ \ (s\in S,\ t\in T). \tag{75}$$

Then the relations (74) result from the division of the inequalities (75) by v^2 •

This Theorem proves the existence of the solution (σ,τ) of the game $(S,T,a_{m\times n})$ and, at the same time, its demonstration shows how to find it numerically via linear programming.

In the next *example*, the solution is found in a direct, independent way.

Example: **Matching Pennies**, played repeatedly.

We augment each element of matrix $a_{2\times 2}$ of the game by 1. We get the matrix $2.1_{1\times 1}$. The games $(S,T,a_{2\times 2})$ and $(S,T,1_{2\times 2})$ have the same solutions (see first lines of proof of Theorem 19). By (74), the couple $(\sigma,\tau) = ((\sigma_1,\sigma_2)',(\tau_1,\tau_2)')$ is a solution of the game $(S,T,1_{2\times 2})$ iff

$$s'\tau \leq \tau'\sigma \leq \sigma' t \ \ (s=(s_1,s_2)'\in S,\ t=(t_1,t_2)'\in T),$$

or

$$s_1\tau_1+s_2\tau_2 \le \tau_1\sigma_1+\tau_2\sigma_2 \le \sigma_1 t_1+\sigma_2 t_2,$$

or

$$s_1\tau_1+(1-s_1)(1-\tau_1) \le \tau_1\sigma_1+(1-\tau_1)(1-\sigma_1) \le \sigma_1 t_1+(1-\sigma_1)(1-t_1),$$

or

$$(2\tau_1-1)(s_1-\sigma_1) \le 0 \le (2\sigma_1-1)(t_1-\tau_1) \quad (0\le s_1\le 1,\ 0\le t_1\le 1). \tag{76}$$

If $(2\tau_1-1)\neq 0$, $\sigma_1\neq 0$ and $\sigma_1\neq 1$, then we can contradict the first inequality (76) by taking $s_1>\sigma_1$ or $s_1<\sigma_1$. Hence,

$$\tau_1 = 1/2 \text{ or } \sigma_1 = 0 \text{ or } \sigma_1 = 1.$$

In the same way

$$\sigma_1 = 1/2 \text{ or } \tau_1 = 0 \text{ or } \tau_1 = 1,$$

by the last inequality (76). The potential solutions (σ,τ) with $\sigma_1=0$ or 1, or $\tau_1=0$ or 1, contradict (76) by the obvious right choice of s_1 and t_1. Hence,

$$\sigma_1 = 1/2 = \sigma_2 \ , \ \tau_1 = 1/2 = \tau_2.$$

The conclusion of this discussion is the following: the unique possible solution of Matching Pennies played repeatedly is

$$(\sigma,\tau) := ((1/2,1/2)',(1/2,1/2)').$$

By Theorem 19, it is a solution indeed. The value of the game is $\sigma' a\tau=0$.

5.6. Two-Person Games with Complete Information

5.6.1. Mathematical Logic Notation

Some of the following statements are most convenient in the mathematical logic notation.

Let M, M(x), M(x,y) be sets, P, P(x), P(x,y), P(x,y,z) propositions. Then

$$\neg P :\Leftrightarrow P \text{ is false},$$

$$\forall x\in M{:}P(x) \ :\Leftrightarrow \ \text{For all x in M, P(x) is true},$$

$$\exists x \in M : P(x) \;:\Leftrightarrow\; \text{For some x in M, P(x) is true,}$$

$$\exists x \in M : \forall y \in M(x) : P(x,y) \;:\Leftrightarrow\; \exists x \in M : [\forall y \in M(x) : P(x,y)]$$

$$\forall x \in M : \exists y \in M(x) : V z \in M(x,y) : P(x,y,z) \;:\Leftrightarrow$$

$$\forall x \in M : [\exists y \in M(x) : V z \in M(x,y) : P(x,y,z)],$$

and similarly when more symbols $\forall, \exists$ are involved.

Obviously

$$\neg[\forall x \in M : P(x)] \;\Leftrightarrow\; \exists x \in M : \neg P(x),$$

$$\neg[\exists x \in M : P(x)] \;\Leftrightarrow\; \forall x \in M : \neg P(x).$$

These equivalences can be applied successively. For instance:

$$\neg[\forall x \in M : \exists y \in M(x) : V z \in M(x,y) : P(x,y,z)]$$

$$\Leftrightarrow\; \exists x \in M : \forall y \in M(x) : \exists z \in M(x,y) : \neg P(x,y,z).$$

5.6.2. Definition of Game

We now consider the game with the following rules.

Sophie chooses her first move s_1 in the set M:

$$s_1 \in M. \tag{77}$$

Then Thomas chooses his first move t_1 in the set $M(s_1)$:

$$t_1 \in M(s_1). \tag{77}$$

Then Sophie chooses her second move s_2 in the set $M(s_1,t_1)$:

$$s_2 \in M(s_1,t_1). \tag{77}$$

Then Thomas chooses his second move t_2 in the set $M(s_1,t_1,s_2)$:

$$t_2 \in M(s_1,t_1,s_2). \tag{77}$$

... ...

Then Sophie chooses her last move s_n in the set $M(s_1,t_1,...,s_{n-1},t_{n-1})$:

$$s_n \in M(s_1,t_1,...,s_{n-1},t_{n-1}). \qquad (77)$$

Then Thomas chooses his last move t_n in the set $M(s_1,t_1,...,s_{n-1},t_{n-1},s_n)$:

$$t_n \in M(s_1,t_1,...,s_{n-1},t_{n-1},s_n). \qquad (77)$$

Here n is a fixed integer and M, $M(s_1)$, $M(s_1,t_1)$,...,$M(s_1,t_1,...,s_{n-1},t_{n-1},s_n)$ are any sets successively defined for the moves $s_1,t_1,...,s_n,t_n$ satisfying the relations (77).

A **realization of the game** is any 2n-tuple $(s_1,t_1,...,s_n,t_n)$ satisfying the relations (77). Let $\boldsymbol{R}$ be the set of realizations. It is partitioned in 3 subsets

$$\boldsymbol{R} = \boldsymbol{R}_S+\boldsymbol{R}_T+\boldsymbol{R}_{ST}.$$

For any realization in $\boldsymbol{R}_S$, **Sophie wins the game**. For any realization in $\boldsymbol{R}_T$, **Thomas wins the game**. For any realization in $\boldsymbol{R}_{ST}$, **there is no winner**.

We say that **Sophie has a winning strategy** if

$$\exists s_1 \in M: \forall t_1 \in M(s_1): \exists s_2 \in M(s_1,t_1): \forall t_2 \in M(s_1,t_1,s_2): \ldots \ldots \ldots$$
$$\exists s_n \in M(s_1,t_t,...,s_{n-1},t_{n-1}): \forall t_n \in M(s_1,t_1,...,s_{n-1},t_{n-1},s_n):$$
$$(s_1,t_1,...,s_n,t_n) \in \boldsymbol{R}_S. \qquad (78)$$

We say that **Sophie has a non-losing strategy** if

$$\exists s_1 \in M: \forall t_1 \in M(s_1): \exists s_2 \in M(s_1,t_1): \forall t_2 \in M(s_1,t_1,s_2): \ldots \ldots \ldots$$
$$\exists s_n \in M(s_1,t_t,...,s_{n-1},t_{n-1}): \forall t_n \in M(s_1,t_1,...,s_{n-1},t_{n-1},s_n):$$
$$(s_1,t_1,...,s_n,t_n) \in \boldsymbol{R}_S+\boldsymbol{R}_{ST}. \qquad (79)$$

We say that **Thomas has a winning strategy** if

$$\forall s_1 \in M: \exists t_1 \in M(s_1): \forall s_2 \in M(s_1,t_1): \exists t_2 \in M(s_1,t_1,s_2): \ldots \ldots \ldots$$
$$\forall s_n \in M(s_1,t_t,...,s_{n-1},t_{n-1}): \exists t_n \in M(s_1,t_1,...,s_{n-1},t_{n-1},s_n):$$
$$(s_1,t_1,...,s_n,t_n) \in \boldsymbol{R}_T. \qquad (80)$$

We say that **Thomas has a non-losing strategy** if

$$\forall s_1\in M:\exists t_1\in M(s_1):\forall s_2\in M(s_1,t_1):\exists t_2\in M(s_1,t_1,s_2):\ \dots\ \dots\ \dots$$
$$\forall s_n\in M(s_1,t_t,\dots,s_{n-1},t_{n-1}):\exists t_n\in M(s_1,t_1,\dots,s_{n-1},t_{n-1},s_n):$$
$$(s_1,t_1,\dots,s_n,t_n)\in \boldsymbol{R}_T+\boldsymbol{R}_{ST}. \qquad (81)$$

5.6.3. Examples

The foregoing model is so general that it covers almost all real two-person games with no chance moves: chess, draugths, several games with matches,...

The constraint that the total number of moves equals a fixed number 2n is no restriction, because any game can be completed with dummy moves when it is finished. For instance, in chess we can take $2n=100^{100}$. If a real play is finished in 63 moves, we can complete it with $100^{100}-63$ moves consisting in doing nothing.

The set $\boldsymbol{R}_{ST}$ can be void. Then Sophie or Thomas wins the game.

5.6.4. Basic Theorem

Theorem 20 (von Neumann)

For the game defined in 5.6.2, each of the following propositions a,b,c is true.

a. **Sophie has a winning strategy or Thomas has a non-losing strategy.**

b. **Thomas has a winning strategy or Sophie has a non-losing strategy.**

c. **If $\boldsymbol{R}_{ST}=\emptyset$, then Sophie has a winning strategy or Thomas has a winning strategy.**

Proof

a. One of the propositions (78) or ¬(78) is true. By the remarks of 5.6.1, ¬(78) is equivalent to the proposition

$$\forall s_1 \in M : \exists t_1 \in M(s_1) : \forall s_2 \in M(s_1,t_1) : \exists t_2 \in M(s_1,t_1,s_2) : \ldots \ldots \quad \ldots$$

$$\forall s_n \in M(s_1,t_t,\ldots,s_{n-1},t_{n-1}) : \exists t_n \in M(s_1,t_1,\ldots,s_{n-1},t_{n-1},s_n) :$$

$$\neg[(s_1,t_1,\ldots,s_n,t_n) \in \boldsymbol{R}_S].$$

But

$$\neg[(s_1,t_1,\ldots,s_n,t_n) \in \boldsymbol{R}_S] \Leftrightarrow (s_1,t_1,\ldots,s_n,t_n) \in \boldsymbol{R}_T + \boldsymbol{R}_{ST}. \tag{82}$$

Hence,

$$\neg(78) \Leftrightarrow (81).$$

b. One of the propositions (80) or $\neg$(80) is true, and

$$\neg(80) \Leftrightarrow (79).$$

c. One of the propositions (78) or $\neg$(78) is true, and

$$\neg(78) \Leftrightarrow (80)$$

if $\boldsymbol{R}_{ST} = \varnothing$ •

This Theorem proves the existence of winning or non-losing strategies, but it gives no way to find them out. It implies that at least one of the players has a non-losing strategy, but it does not allow to discover which one it is. For super-clever people (not yet born), chess is uninteresting, because they could reveal the non-losing, or perhaps winning strategy of one of the players.

The sets M, $M(s_1)$, $M(s_1,t_1)$,... may be infinite in the foregoing Theorem. This occurs in the following game. In turn, Sophie and Thomas put a small object on a table. No object may touch the objects already on the table. The winner is the player putting down the last object. It is assumed that enough objects are available. Here $\boldsymbol{R}_{ST} = \varnothing$, and either Sophie or Thomas has a winning strategy, whatever the shape of the table or the shapes of the objects are.

For instance, if the table is round and the objects are identical pieces of money, then the first player Sophie has the following winning strategy: she places her first coin in the center of the table and for any coin placed by Thomas, she places a coin in a symmetrical position with respect to the center of the table.

Of course, this strategy cannot be applied if the table has a hole in the middle (for the parasol). Then the second player Thomas has the obvious winning strategy.

Chapter 6

Integral Optimization Problems

6.1. Analytical Finite-Basic Solution: Theory

6.1.1. Integral Optimization Problems

The main problem of this section is the integral problem on a space of mixtures with integral equality constraints

$$Q(\alpha_1,\dots,\alpha_n) := \sup_{F\in \boldsymbol{Sp}}[\int f_{n+1}dF \;/\; \int f_1 dF=\alpha_1,\dots,\int f_n dF=\alpha_n] \qquad (1)$$

where the **basic space** is

$$\boldsymbol{Sp} = \boldsymbol{Mixt}[F_\theta(\theta\in S)]. \qquad (2)$$

The functions $f_1,\dots,f_n,f_{n+1}$ are supposed to be integrable with respect to all distributions $F\in\boldsymbol{Sp}$. The **parameters** $\alpha_1,\dots,\alpha_n$ are any real finite numbers, but the interesting n-tuples $(\alpha_1,\dots,\alpha_n)$ are those in the **effective domain** dom Q of the problem (see the general terminology in Ch.1.1.3). Problem (1) is identical to problem

$$Q(\alpha_1,\dots,\alpha_n) = \sup_{F\in \boldsymbol{Space}}[\int f_{n+1}dF], \qquad (3)$$

where the **hypothetic space** (depending on $\alpha_1,\dots,\alpha_n$) is

$$\boldsymbol{Space} = \boldsymbol{Mixt}[F_\theta(\theta\in S);\int f_1=\alpha_1,\dots,\int f_n=\alpha_n]. \qquad (4)$$

Then dom Q is the set of points $(\alpha_1,\dots,\alpha_n)$ for which ***Space*** exists (i.e. is non void). ***Space*** is the family of **feasible distributions** of problem (1).

The important particular basic spaces ***Sp*** are

$$\boldsymbol{Mixt}[A_\theta/\theta\in S] = \boldsymbol{Prob}[S], \qquad (5)$$

$$\boldsymbol{Mixt}[R_{m\theta}/\theta\in[a,b]] = \boldsymbol{Prob}[[a,b];\text{m-unim}] \;(m\in[a,b]), \qquad (6)$$

$$\boldsymbol{Mixt}[R_{m\theta}/\theta\in S] = \boldsymbol{Prob}[[a,b];S,\text{m-unim}] \;(S\subseteq[a,b]). \qquad (7)$$

The most important integral constraints are moment constraints.

The problem

$$Q(\mu_1,\ldots,\mu_n) := \sup_{F\in Sp}\left[\int f_{n+1}dF \;/\; \int x dF(x)=\mu_1,\ldots,\int x^n dF(x)=\mu_n\right] \tag{8}$$

is a problem with **moment constraints** or a **moment problem**. The notation of moment problem (8) is abbreviated as

$$Q(\mu_1,\ldots,\mu_n) := \sup_{F\in Sp}\left[\int f_{n+1}dF \;/\; \mu_1,\ldots,\mu_n\right] \tag{9}$$

Of course, minimization problems

$$P(\alpha_1,\ldots,\alpha_n) := \inf_{F\in Sp}\left[\int f_{n+1}dF \;/\; \int f_1 dF=\alpha_1,\ldots,\int f_n dF=\alpha_n\right] \tag{10}$$

are considered as well.

Every terminology, notation, particularization, statement,... concerning the maximization problem (1) has an obvious corresponding version concerning the minimization problem (10). In this book, primal maximization problems are systematically denoted by Q, with subscripts or not. Then the corresponding minimization problem, resulting from the replacement of sup by inf, is denoted by P with the same subscripts, if any.

A rather general rule is **that we do not repeat the definitions, results,..., for the minimization problems**, but we do use them in the applications.

By relations such as

$$\inf_{F\in Sp}\left[\int \varphi dF \;/\; \int f dF=\alpha\right] = -\sup_{F\in Sp}\left[\int(-\varphi)dF \;/\; \int f dF=\alpha\right], \tag{11}$$

any integral minimization problem is equivalent to an integral maximization problem.

Exceptionally, we consider problems with inequality constraints, or with mixed equality and inequality constraints, such as

$$\sup_{F\in Sp}\left[\int f_{n+1}dF \;/\; \int f_1 dF\le\beta,\int f_2 dF=\alpha_2,\ldots,\int f_n dF=\alpha_n\right]. \tag{12}$$

By the relation

$$\sup_{F\in Sp}\left[\int f_{n+1}dF \;/\; \int f_1 dF\le\beta,\int f_2 dF=\alpha_2,\ldots,\int f_n dF=\alpha_n\right] = \sup_{\alpha_1\le\beta} Q(\alpha_1,\ldots,\alpha_n), \tag{13}$$

the value of problem (12) results from the value of the problems $Q(\alpha_1,\dots,\alpha_n)$ $(\alpha_1 \le \beta)$ defined by (1). Very often, the solution of the problems $Q(\alpha_1,\dots,\alpha_n)$ $(\alpha_1 \le \beta)$ furnishes the solution of problem (12).

Hereafter, the continuous problems are always considered with S=[a,b]. Problems with distributions concentrated on non compact intervals can be reduced to problems on [a,b]. For instance, the value of problem

$$\sup_{F \in \textbf{\textit{Prob}}[[a,\infty[]} \left[\int \varphi dF \,/\, \int f dF = \alpha\right] \tag{14}$$

equals

$$\sup_{b \ge a} \sup_{F \in \textbf{\textit{Prob}}[[a,b]]} \left[\int \varphi dF \,/\, \int f dF = \alpha\right]. \tag{15}$$

It results from the value of the problems

$$\sup_{F \in \textbf{\textit{Prob}}[[a,b]]} \left[\int \varphi dF \,/\, \int f dF = \alpha\right] \ (b \ge a). \tag{16}$$

If the value (15) is infinite, then problem (14) has no solution. If it is finite, then it may be that problem (14) has a solution, and that this solution can be deduced from the solution of the problems (16).

In many cases, the value of a problem is much more important than its eventual solutions. In any case, the values (12) and (14) result from (13) and (15) respectively.

6.1.2. Finite-Basic Solution

We recall that the **associated function $f^{\bullet}$ of the function f**, with respect to the basic space of mixtures ***Sp***=***Mixt***$[F_\theta(\theta \in S)]$, is the function with values

$$f^{\bullet}(\theta) := \int f(x) dF_\theta(x) \ \ (\theta \in S). \tag{17}$$

By Ch.4.Th.1.Cor, we already know that problem (1) has an extremal solution on the hypothetic space (under compactness and continuity conditions). This extremal distribution of ***Space*** is an n+1-basic distribution of ***Sp***, i.e. a convex combination of n+1 distributions of the basis $\{F_\theta / \theta \in S\}$ of ***Sp***.

The following Theorem provides a new instructive proof of this result. This other demonstration not only shows the existence of the n+1-basic solution, but it indicates how to find it.

The proof of the next Theorem is an adaptation of the proof of Ch.4.Th.2. By the latter Theorem, the problem has an n+2-basic solution (under continuity and compactness assumptions). Hence, the next Theorem is more precise in the case of integral optimization problems.

Theorem 1

Let S be a compact set in R and let the functions $f_1^\bullet,...,f_n^\bullet,f_{n+1}^\bullet$ be continuous on S. Then the integral maximization problem

$$\mathbf{Q(\alpha_1,...,\alpha_n)\ \ ((\alpha_1,...,\alpha_n)\in dom\ Q)} \tag{18}$$

defined by (1) or (3) has an n+1-basic solution.

Proof

a. Let

$$\mathrm{Cur}_{n+1}Q := \{(f_1^\bullet(\theta),...,f_n^\bullet(\theta),f_{n+1}^\bullet(\theta))\ /\ \theta\in S\} \subseteq \mathbf{R}^{n+1}. \tag{19}$$

The set $\mathrm{Cur}_{n+1}Q$ is compact. Indeed, let $x_\nu\in\mathrm{Cur}_{n+1}Q$ (ν=1,2,...). Then $\theta_\nu\in S$ exists, such that

$$x_\nu = (f_1^\bullet(\theta_\nu),...,f_n^\bullet(\theta_\nu),f_{n+1}^\bullet(\theta_\nu))\ \ (\nu=1,2,...).$$

By the compactness of S, some subsequence $\theta_{\nu(k)}$ (k=1,2,...) of the sequence θ_ν (ν=1,2,...), converges to a point $\theta\in S$. Then

$$f_j^\bullet(\theta_{\nu(k)}) \to f_j^\bullet(\theta)\ \text{ as } k\uparrow\infty\ \ (j=1,...,n,n+1),$$

by the continuity of $f_j^\bullet$ on S. Let

$$x := (f_1^\bullet(\theta),...,f_n^\bullet(\theta),f_{n+1}^\bullet(\theta)). \tag{20}$$

Then $x_{\nu(k)} \to x$ as $k\uparrow\infty$. This proves the compactness of $\mathrm{Cur}_{n+1}Q$.

b.. By Ch.1.Th.6

$$\{(\textstyle\int f_1dF,...,\int f_ndF,\ \int f_{n+1}dF)\ /\ F\in \boldsymbol{Sp}\} = \mathrm{Co\ Cur}_{n+1}Q. \tag{21}$$

Then

$$(\alpha_1, ...,\alpha_n, \textstyle\int f_{n+1}dF) = (\int f_1dF,...,\int f_ndF,\ \int f_{n+1}dF) \in \mathrm{Co\ Cur}_{n+1}Q, \tag{22}$$

for any feasible distribution F of problem $Q(\alpha_1,...,\alpha_n)$. Let the sequence F_ν (ν=1,2,...) be a limit solution of problem $Q(\alpha_1,...,\alpha_n)$. Then

$$\int f_{n+1}dF_\nu \to Q(\alpha_1,\ldots,\alpha_n) \text{ as } \nu\uparrow\infty. \tag{23}$$

By (21),

$$(\alpha_1, \ldots,\alpha_n, \int f_{n+1}dF_\nu) \in \mathrm{CoCur}_{n+1}Q \quad (\nu=1,2,\ldots),$$

and then as $\nu\uparrow\infty$,

$$(\alpha_1, \ldots,\alpha_n, Q(\alpha_1,\ldots,\alpha_n)) \in \mathrm{CoCur}_{n+1}Q, \tag{24}$$

because the set $\mathrm{CoCur}_{n+1}Q$ is compact, hence closed, by Ch.1.Th.11.

c. We now prove that the point $(\alpha_1, \ldots,\alpha_n, Q(\alpha_1,\ldots,\alpha_n))$ is a frontier point of the set $\mathrm{CoCur}_{n+1}Q$. Indeed, let us assume that it is an interior point. Then $\varepsilon>0$ exists, such that

$$(\alpha_1, \ldots,\alpha_n, Q(\alpha_1,\ldots,\alpha_n)+\varepsilon) \in \mathrm{CoCur}_{n+1}Q. \tag{25}$$

By (21), a distribution $F\in \boldsymbol{Sp}$ exists, such that

$$\int f_1dF = \alpha_1 ,\ldots, \int f_ndF = \alpha_n , \int f_{n+1}dF = Q(\alpha_1,\ldots,\alpha_n)+\varepsilon. \tag{26}$$

By the first n relations (26), F is a feasible distribution of problem $Q(\alpha_1,\ldots,\alpha_n)$. Then the last relation (26) contradicts the fact that the value of the problem is $Q(\alpha_1,\ldots,\alpha_n)$.

d. By Carathéodory (Ch.1.Th.10.b), the point $(\alpha_1,\ldots,\alpha_n,Q(\alpha_1,\ldots,\alpha_n))$ is a convex combination of n+1 points of $\mathrm{Cur}_{n+1}Q$. Let

$$(\alpha_1,\ldots,\alpha_n,Q(\alpha_1,\ldots,\alpha_n)) = \sum_{1\le i\le n+1} p_i(f_1^\bullet(\theta_i),\ldots,f_n^\bullet(\theta_i),f_{n+1}^\bullet(\theta_i)), \tag{27}$$

where

$$\theta_1,\ldots,\theta_n,\theta_{n+1} \in S.$$

Let

$$F := \sum_{1\le i\le n+1} p_iF_{\theta_i}. \tag{28}$$

Then

$$F\in \boldsymbol{Sp} \tag{29}$$

and

$$(\alpha_1,\ldots,\alpha_n,Q(\alpha_1,\ldots,\alpha_n)) = \sum_{1\le i\le n+1} p_i(\int f_1dF_{\theta_i},\ldots,\int f_ndF_{\theta_i}, \int f_{n+1}dF_{\theta_i})$$

$$= (\int f_1dF,\ldots,\int f_ndF,\int f_{n+1}dF). \tag{30}$$

Then

$$\alpha_1 = \int f_1dF , \ldots , \alpha_n = \int f_ndF, \tag{31}$$

$$Q(\alpha_1,\ldots,\alpha_n) = \int f_{n+1} dF. \tag{32}$$

By (28), F is an n+1-basic distribution. By (29) and (31), F is a feasible distribution of problem $Q(\alpha_1,\ldots,\alpha_n)$. Then by (32), F is a solution of the problem •

In most practical problems S is a compact interval, or a finite set (when discretizations are involved). Any finite subset of **R** is compact, and any function is continuous on any finite set.

The next Corollaries result from the application of the Theorem to the basic spaces (5) and (6) with S:=[a,b]. The next Corollary 2 results from Ch.2.Th.4. Cor.2 and from the proof of the latter Corollary.

Corollary 1 (Taylor)

Let the functions f_1, ..., f_{n+1} be continuous on [a,b]. Then the problem

$$\sup_{F\in Prob[a,b]]}[\int f_{n+1}dF \ / \ \int f_1 dF=\alpha_1,\ldots,\int f_n dF=\alpha_n]$$

has an n+1-atomic solution •

Corollary 2 (Taylor)

Let the functions f_1 ,..., f_{n+1} be bounded on the interval [a,b] and continuous on $[m-\varepsilon,m+\varepsilon]\cap[a,b]$, where $\varepsilon>0$. Then the problem

$$\sup_{F\in Prob[a,b];m\text{-}unim]}[\int f_{n+1}dF \ / \ \int f_1 dF=\alpha_1,\ldots,\int f_n dF=\alpha_n]$$

has an n+1-rectangular solution •

6.1.3. Geometrical Research of Analytic Solution

The research of the explicit analytical solution of the problem $Q(\alpha_1,\ldots,\alpha_n)$ can be based on Theorem 2, and on its proof, if n is small. In the space $\mathbf{R}^{n+1} = \{(\alpha_1,\ldots,\alpha_n,y)\}$, we imagine that the y-axis is vertical, and the $(\alpha_1,\ldots,\alpha_n)$-space horizontal. Then the surface with equation

$$y = Q(\alpha_1,\ldots,\alpha_n) \ ((\alpha_1,\ldots,\alpha_n)\in \mathrm{dom}\ Q) \tag{33}$$

is the **upper frontier** of the set $CoCur_{n+1}Q$.

The geometrical steps to be executed in the research of the analytical solution of problem $Q(\alpha_1,...,\alpha_n)$ are the following (see Fig.8 in case n=2).

a. Construct the convex hull

$$\mathrm{CoCur}_n Q = \mathrm{dom}\ Q \subseteq \mathbf{R}^n$$

of the curve

$$\mathrm{Cur}_n Q := \{(f_1^\bullet(\theta),...,f_n^\bullet(\theta)) \ / \ \theta \in S\} \subseteq \mathbf{R}^n.$$

Only points $(\alpha_1,...,\alpha_n)$ belonging to $\mathrm{CoCur}_n Q$ are considered.

b. Construct the upper frontier $\mathrm{UpFro}_{n+1}Q \subseteq \mathbf{R}^{n+1}$ of the convex hull

$$\mathrm{CoCur}_{n+1}Q \subseteq \mathbf{R}^{n+1}$$

of the curve

$$\mathrm{Cur}_{n+1}Q := \{(f_1^\bullet(\theta),...,f_n^\bullet(\theta),f_{n+1}^\bullet(\theta)) \ / \ \theta \in S\} \subseteq \mathbf{R}^{n+1}.$$

c. Then the intersection B of the vertical line through the point $(\alpha_1,...,\alpha_n,0)$ with $\mathrm{UpFro}_{n+1}Q$ furnishes the value $Q(\alpha_1,...,\alpha_n)$ of the problem.

d. By Carathéodory, point B can be expressed as a convex combination

$$B = p_1 B_1 + ... + p_{n+1} B_{n+1}$$

of n+1 points $B_j \in \mathrm{Cur}_{n+1}Q$ $(j=1,...,n+1)$. Let $\theta_j \in S$ be such that

$$B_j = (f_1^\bullet(\theta_j),...,f_n^\bullet(\theta_j),f_{n+1}^\bullet(\theta_j)) \quad (j=1,...,n+1).$$

Then

$$F = p_1 F_{\theta_1} + ... + p_{n+1} F_{\theta_{n+1}}$$

is a solution of problem $Q(\alpha_1,...,\alpha_n)$.

This construction is illustrated in the following figure corresponding to case n=2. Curve $\mathrm{Cur}_{n+1}Q$ is the fat 3-dimensional polygonal curve $B_1B_2B_3B_4$. Its projection $\mathrm{Cur}_n Q$ on the horizontal plane is the fat 2-dimensional polygonal curve $A_1A_2A_3A_4$. The convex hull $\mathrm{CoCur}_{n+1}Q$ of $\mathrm{Cur}_{n+1}Q$ is the tetrahedron with vertices B_1,B_2,B_3,B_4. The convex hull $\mathrm{CoCur}_n Q$ of $\mathrm{Cur}_n Q$ is the quadrilateral with vertices A_1,A_3,A_4,A_2. The upper frontier $\mathrm{UpFro}_{n+1}Q$ of the convex hull $\mathrm{CoCur}_{n+1}Q$ is the triangle with vertices B_2,B_3,B_4.

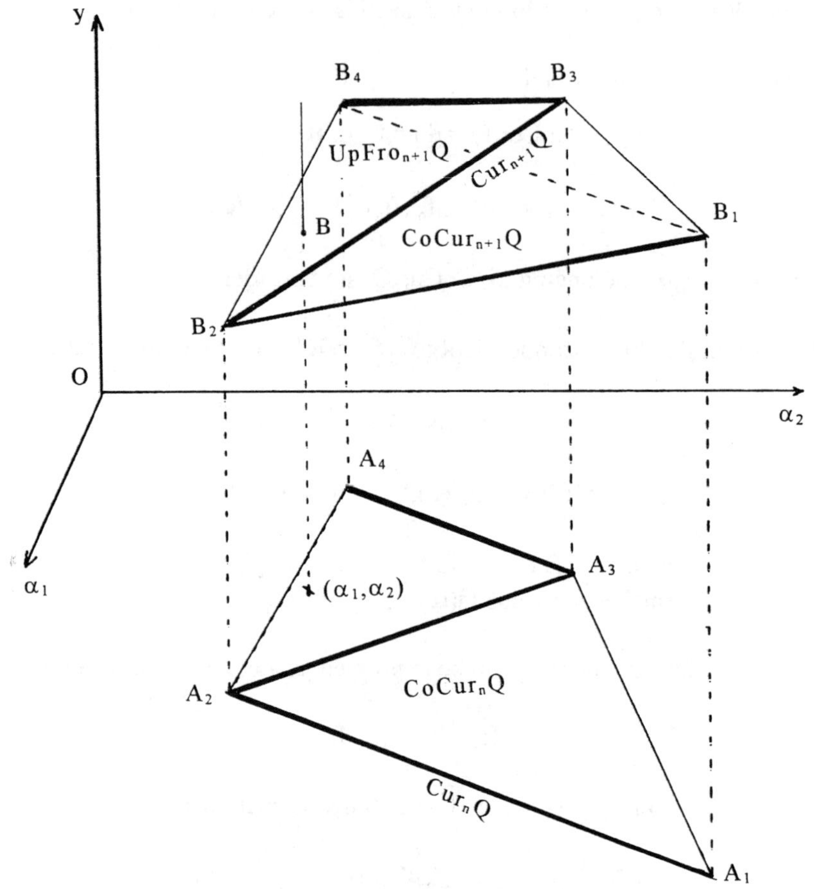

Fig.8. Geometrical construction of analytic solution in case n=2

Remarks

a. The foregoing construction works, at least partially, if the compactness and the continuity assumptions leading to the compactness of the set $Cur_{n+1}Q$ are not satisfied. Then the surface (33) is still the upper frontier of the set $CoCur_{n+1}Q$, but it does not necessarily belong to that set and it can have infinite points $(\alpha_1,\ldots,\alpha_n,\infty)$. The following can happen:

b1. $(\alpha_1,\ldots,\alpha_n,Q(\alpha_1,\ldots,\alpha_n)) \in CoCur_{n+1}Q$.
Then the value $Q(\alpha_1,\ldots,\alpha_n)$ of the problem still results from step c and its solution from step d.

b2. $Q(\alpha_1,...,\alpha_n) < \infty$, but $(\alpha_1,...,\alpha_n,Q(\alpha_1,...,\alpha_n)) \notin \mathrm{CoCur}_{n+1}Q$. Then $Q(\alpha_1,...,\alpha_n)$ still results from step c, but step d cannot be executed, and the problem has no solution.

b3. $Q(\alpha_1,..,\alpha_n)=\infty$.
Then this infinite value still results from step c, but step d cannot be executed and the problem has no solution.

b. The minimization problem $P(\alpha_1,...,\alpha_n)$ can be solved in the same way. Then the lower frontier $\mathrm{LoFro}_{n+1}Q$ of the $\mathrm{CoCur}_{n+1}Q$ must be considered.

6.1.4. Problems with Mixed Constraints

Under compactness and continuity assumptions, **integral problems with n mixed integral constraints have an n+1-basic solutions**. The general argument is translucent enough from the following particular case.

We consider the problem

$$Q_{\leq}(\alpha,\beta) := \sup_{F\in \boldsymbol{Sp}}[\textstyle\int\varphi dF \;/\; \int f dF\leq\alpha,\ \int g dF=\beta], \tag{34}$$

where ***Sp*** is the general space of mixtures $\boldsymbol{Mixt}[F_\theta(\theta\in S)]$. It can be displayed as

$$Q_{\leq}(\alpha,\beta) = \sup_{F\in \boldsymbol{Space}}[\textstyle\int\varphi dF], \tag{35}$$

where the hypothetic space is

$$\boldsymbol{Space} := \boldsymbol{Mixt}[F_\theta(\theta\in S);\textstyle\int f dF\leq\alpha;\int g dF=\beta].$$

Let ***Space*** be compact, and let $\int\varphi dF$ be a continuous function of $F\in\boldsymbol{Space}$. By Ch.1.Th.2, the problem (35) has a solution F_0. Let $\int f dF_0=\alpha_0$ and let us consider the problem

$$Q_{=}(\alpha_0,\beta) := \sup_{F\in \boldsymbol{Sp}}[\textstyle\int\varphi dF \;/\; \int f dF=\alpha_0,\ \int g dF=\beta].$$

This is a problem with integral equality constraints and with feasible distributions, because F_0 is such a distribution. By Theorem 1, the problem $Q_{=}(\alpha_0,\beta)$ has a 3-basic solution. Obviously, the latter solution is a solution of the initial problem $Q_{\leq}(\alpha,\beta)$.

6.2. Analytical Finite-Basic Solutions: Illustrations

6.2.1. Reminders of Elementary Geometry

The main problem in the research of explicit analytic solutions, by the method of 6.1.3, is the construction of convex hulls. The following simple results in $\mathbf{R}^2=\{(x,y)$ and in $\mathbf{R}^3=\{(x,y,z)\}$ may be useful. We hereafter assume that the functions have the regularity properties implicitly used, i.e. we assume the existence of the involved derivatives and partial derivatives. We recall the elementary definitions of convexity and concavity in $\mathbf{R}^2$ and $\mathbf{R}^3$ and the practical conditions allowing to verify this convexity or concavity. Of course, the elementary definitions (based on the existence hypothesis of derivatives and tangent lines and planes), coincide with the more general definitions of App.C.

Linear interpolation

The equation of the straight line through the points (r,s) and (u,v) $(r\neq u)$ is

$$y = [(x-r)v+(u-x)s]/(u-r). \tag{36}$$

Indeed, the last member is linear in x. It equals s for x=r and v for x=u.

***Tangent lines in* R²**

The infinitesimal form of the equation of the tangent to the curve y=f(x), with point of contact (u,f(u)), is dy=f′(u)du. The usual equation results from the replacement of du, dy by (x−u), (y−f(u)), resp. It is

$$y = f(u) + f'(u).(x-u). \tag{37}$$

Convex and concave curves in* R² *(usual equation)

An elementary definition of convexity is the following. **The curve y=f(x) $(a\leq x\leq b)$ is convex on [a,b]** if it is situated above its tangent lines on that interval. This condition is translated as

$$f(x)+f'(x)\Delta x \leq f(x+\Delta x) \quad (x,x+\Delta x\in[a,b]), \tag{38}$$

where $\Delta x \in \mathbf{R}$. By Taylor,

$$f(x+\Delta x) = f(x) + f'(x)\Delta x + 1/2\, f''(x+\theta\Delta x)\Delta x^2, \tag{39}$$

for some number θ between 0 and 1. Then, by (68), a sufficient condition for the convexity on [a,b] is $f''(x) \geq 0$ ($a \leq x \leq b$), and it is not difficult to see that this condition is also necessary.

Of course, **the curve $y=f(x)$ ($a \leq x \leq b$) is concave on [a,b]** if the symmetric curve $y= -f(x)$ ($a \leq x \leq b$) is convex on that interval.

Convex and concave curves in $\mathbf{R}^2$ *(parametric equations)*

We consider the curve with parametric equations

$$x = x(\theta)\ ,\ y = y(\theta)\ \ (a \leq \theta \leq b). \tag{40}$$

We assume that the function $x(\cdot)$ is strictly monotonic on [a,b]. Let I be the interval $x([a,b])$ (i.e. the image of interval [a,b] under the mapping $x(.)$), and let $\theta=\theta(x)$ ($x \in I$) be the solution of equation $x=x(\theta)$. At any time, as well $\theta \in [a,b]$ as $x \in I$ can be considered as independent variable.

The differentiation of the identity $x(\theta(x))=x$ furnishes the relation $x'_\theta \theta'_x = 1$ between the partial derivatives x'_θ and θ'_x. Hence, $\theta'_x=[x'_\theta]^{-1}$. By the differentiation of the identity $x'_\theta(\theta(x))\theta'_x(x)=1$,

$$x''_{\theta\theta}[\theta'_x]^2 + x'_\theta\theta''_{xx} = 0\ \ ,\ \ \theta''_{xx} = -x''_{\theta\theta}[x'_\theta]^{-3}.$$

We now consider y as a function $y(\theta(x))$ of $x \in I$. Then

$$y'_x = y'_\theta(\theta(x))\theta'_x(x)\ \ ,\ \ y''_{xx} = y''_{\theta\theta}[\theta'_x]^2 + y'_\theta\theta''_{xx}.$$

Hence,

$$\mathbf{y'_x = y'_\theta[x'_\theta]^{-1}}, \tag{41}$$

$$\mathbf{y''_{xx} = [y''_{\theta\theta}x'_\theta - x''_{\theta\theta}y'_\theta][x'_\theta]^{-3}}. \tag{41}$$

We now write $f(\cdot)$, $g(\cdot)$ instead of $x(\cdot)$, $y(\cdot)$. Then the following proposition results from the last relation (41).

In R^2, let Cur be the curve with parametric equations

$$x = f(\theta)\ ,\ y = g(\theta)\ \ (a \le \theta \le b). \tag{42}$$

If f is strictly increasing on [a,b], the convexity condition of Cur is

$$f'(\theta)g''(\theta) - g'(\theta)f''(\theta) \ge 0\ \ (a \le \theta \le b). \tag{43}$$

If f is strictly decreasing on [a,b], the convexity condition of Cur is

$$f'(\theta)g''(\theta) - g'(\theta)f''(\theta) \le 0\ \ (a \le \theta \le b). \tag{44}$$

If f is strictly increasing, the concavity condition of Cur is (34).

If f is strictly decreasing, the concavity condition of Cur is (33).

Tangent planes in R^3

The infinitesimal form of the equation of the tangent plane to the surface $z=f(x,y)$, with point of contact $(u,v,f(u,v))$, is $dz=f'_u du+f'_v dv$. The usual equation results from the replacement of du,dv,dz by $(x-u),(y-v),(z-f(u,v))$ resp. It is

$$z = f(u,v) + f'_u(u,v).(x-u) + f'_v(u,v).(y-v). \tag{45}$$

Convex and concave surfaces in R^3 *(usual equations)*

The surface $z=f(x,y)$ is convex on the convex set $C \subseteq R^2$ if it is situated above its tangent planes, on C:

$$f(x,y)+f'_x(x,y)\Delta x+f'_y(x,y)\Delta y \le f(x+\Delta x,y+\Delta y)\ \ ((x,y),(x+\Delta x,y+\Delta y)\in C). \tag{46}$$

By Taylor,

$$f(x+\Delta x,y+\Delta y) = f(x,y)+f'_x(x,y)\Delta x+f'_y(x,y)\Delta y+1/2R(x,y,\Delta x,\Delta y),$$

where

$$R(x,y,\Delta x,\Delta y) =$$

$$f''_{xx}(x+\theta\Delta x,y+\theta\Delta y)\Delta x^2+2f''_{xy}(x+\theta\Delta x,y+\theta\Delta y)\Delta x\Delta y+f''_{yy}(x+\theta\Delta x,y+\theta\Delta y)\Delta y^2$$

for some $\theta \in]0,1[$. Hence, by (46), the surface $y=f(x,y)$ is convex on C if

$$f''_{xx}(x,y)\Delta x^2+2f''_{xy}(x,y)\Delta x\Delta y+f''_{yy}(x,y)\Delta y^2\geq 0 \ ((x,y),(x+\Delta x,y+\Delta y)\in C).$$

This relation expresses that the quadratic form in Δx and Δy of the first member is semidefinite positive. This proves the following proposition.

The convexity conditions of the surface y=f(x,y) ((x,y)∈C) are

$$\mathbf{f''_{xx}(x,y).f''_{yy}(x,y) - [f''_{xy}(x,y)]^2 \geq 0,} \qquad (47)$$

$$\mathbf{f''_{xx}(x,y) \geq 0 \ , f''_{yy}(x,y) \geq 0. \ ((x,y)\in C).}$$

The concavity conditions of the surface y=f(x,y) ((x,y)∈C) are

$$\mathbf{f''_{xx}(x,y).f''_{yy}(x,y) - [f''_{xy}(x,y)]^2 \leq 0,} \qquad (48)$$

$$\mathbf{f''_{xx}(x,y) \leq 0 \ , f''_{yy}(x,y) \leq 0. \ ((x,y)\in C).}$$

Of course, **the surface z=f(x,y) ((x,y)∈C) is concave on the convex set C** if the symmetrical surface z= –f(x,y) ((x,y)∈C) is convex on that set.

Convex and concave surfaces in $\mathbf{R}^3$ *(parametric equations)*

a. We consider the surface with parametric equations

$$x = f(\alpha,\beta) \ , \ y = g(\alpha,\beta) \ , \ z = h(\alpha,\beta) \ \ ((\alpha,\beta)\in B). \qquad (49)$$

We assume that the the mapping $(f,g):B\rightarrow\mathbf{R}^2$ is invertible on B. Let the first two equations (49) be equivalent to the equations

$$\alpha = \rho(x,y) \ , \ \beta = \sigma(x,y) \ \ ((x,y)\in C). \qquad (50)$$

We assume that C is convex. The usual non parametric equation of the surface (49) is

$$z = h(\rho(x,y),\sigma(x,y)) =:\varphi(x,y) \ \ ((x,y)\in C). \qquad (51)$$

The first two relations (49) imply

$$dx = f'_\alpha d\alpha + f'_\beta d\beta \ , \ \ dy = g'_\alpha d\alpha + g'_\beta d\beta. \qquad (52)$$

Let

$$d(\alpha,\beta) := f'_\alpha(\alpha,\beta)g'_\beta(\alpha,\beta) - f'_\beta(\alpha,\beta)g'_\alpha(\alpha,\beta) \; ((\alpha,\beta)\in B). \tag{53}$$

We assume that d>0 on B, or d<0 on B. (By the general theory of implicit functions, this assumption is superfluous because the mapping (f,g) is supposed to be invertible on B).

b. For the moment, we take x and y as independent variables. By (51),

$$\varphi'_x = h'_\rho\rho'_x + h'_\sigma\sigma'_x \, , \; \varphi'_y = h'_\rho\rho'_y + h'_\sigma\sigma'_y, \tag{54}$$

$$\varphi''_{xx} = h''_{\rho\rho}\rho'_x\rho'_x + h''_{\rho\sigma}\rho'_x\sigma'_x + h''_{\rho\sigma}\rho'_x\sigma'_x + h''_{\sigma\sigma}.\sigma'_x\sigma'_x + h'_\rho\rho''_{xx} + h'_\sigma\sigma''_{xx}, \tag{55}$$

$$\varphi''_{xy} = h''_{\rho\rho}\rho'_x\rho'_y + h''_{\rho\sigma}\rho'_x\sigma'_y + h''_{\rho\sigma}\rho'_y\sigma'_x + h''_{\sigma\sigma}.\sigma'_x\sigma'_y + h'_\rho\rho''_{xy} + h'_\sigma\sigma''_{xy}, \tag{55}$$

$$\varphi''_{yy} = h''_{\rho\rho}\rho'_y\rho'_y + h''_{\rho\sigma}\rho'_y\sigma'_y + h''_{\rho\sigma}\rho'_y\sigma'_y + h''_{\sigma\sigma}.\sigma'_y\sigma'_y + h'_\rho\rho''_{yy} + h'_\sigma\sigma''_{yy}. \tag{55}$$

c. The solution of the linear system in X and Y,

$$0 = A + f'_\rho X + f'_\sigma Y, \tag{56}$$

$$0 = B + g'_\rho X + g'_\sigma Y, \tag{56}$$

is

$$X = -[Ag'_\sigma - Bf'_\sigma]/d \; , \; Y = [Ag'_\rho - Bf'_\rho]/d. \tag{57}$$

d. In order to find the partial derivatives of ρ and σ with respect to x and y, we start from the identities

$$0 = -x + f(\rho(x,y),\sigma(x,y)) \, , \; 0 = -y + g(\rho(x,y),\sigma(x,y)). \tag{58}$$

By differentiation,

$$0 = -1 + f'_\rho\rho'_x + f'_\sigma\sigma'_x \, , \; 0 = 0 + g'_\rho\rho'_x + g'_\sigma\sigma'_x. \tag{59}$$

By c,

$$\rho'_x = g'_\sigma/d \; , \; \sigma'_x = -g'_\rho/d. \tag{60}$$

By differentiation of the relations (58) with respect to y,

$$0 = 0 + f'_\rho\rho'_y + f'_\sigma\sigma'_y \, , \; 0 = -1 + g'_\rho\rho'_y + g'_\sigma\sigma'_y. \tag{61}$$

By c,

$$\rho'_y = -f'_\sigma/d \; , \; \sigma'_y = f'_\rho/d. \tag{62}$$

By differentiation of the relations (59) with respect to x,

$$0 = [f''_{\rho\rho}\rho'_x\rho'_x+f''_{\rho\sigma}\rho'_x\sigma'_x+f''_{\rho\sigma}\rho'_x\sigma'_x+f''_{\sigma\sigma}\sigma'_x\sigma'_x]+f'_\rho\rho''_{xx}+f'_\sigma\sigma''_{xx}, \quad (63)$$

$$0 = [g''_{\rho\rho}\rho'_x\rho'_x+g''_{\rho\sigma}\rho'_x\sigma'_x+g''_{\rho\sigma}\rho'_x\sigma'_x+g''_{\sigma\sigma}\sigma'_x\sigma'_x]+g'_\rho\rho''_{xx}+g'_\sigma\sigma''_{xx}. \quad (63)$$

By c, and by the relations (60),

$$\rho''_{xx} = -[f''_{\rho\rho}g'_\sigma g'_\sigma -2f''_{\rho\sigma}g'_\rho g'_\sigma+f''_{\sigma\sigma}g'_\rho g'_\rho]g'_\sigma/d^3$$

$$+[g''_{\rho\rho}g'_\sigma g'_\sigma-2g''_{\rho\sigma}g'_\rho g'_\sigma+g''_{\sigma\sigma}g'_\rho g'_\rho]f'_\sigma/d^3. \quad (64)$$

$$\sigma''_{xx} = [f''_{\rho\rho}g'_\sigma g'_\sigma -2f''_{\rho\sigma}g'_\rho g'_\sigma+f''_{\sigma\sigma}g'_\rho g'_\rho]g'_\rho/d^3$$

$$-[g''_{\rho\rho}g'_\sigma g'_\sigma-2g''_{\rho\sigma}g'_\rho g'_\sigma+g''_{\sigma\sigma}g'_\rho g'_\rho]f'_\rho/d^3. \quad (64)$$

By differentiation of the relations (59) with respect to y,

$$0 = [f''_{\rho\rho}\rho'_x\rho'_y+f''_{\rho\sigma}\rho'_x\sigma'_y+f''_{\rho\sigma}\rho'_y\sigma'_x+f''_{\sigma\sigma}f\sigma'_x\sigma'_y]+f'_\rho f\rho''_{xy}+f'_\sigma\sigma''_{xy}, \quad (65)$$

$$0 = [g''_{\rho\rho}\rho'_x\rho'_y+g''_{\rho\sigma}\rho'_x\sigma'_y+g''_{\rho\sigma}\rho'_y\sigma'_x+g''_{\sigma\sigma}\sigma'_x\sigma'_y]+g'_\rho\rho''_{xy}+g'_\sigma\sigma''_{xy}\sigma. \quad (65)$$

By c and by the relations (60) and (62),

$$\rho''_{xy} = -[-f''_{\rho\rho}f'_\sigma g'_\sigma+f''_{\rho\sigma}f'_\rho g'_\sigma+f''_{\rho\sigma}f'_\sigma g'_\rho-f''_{\sigma\sigma}f'_\rho g'_\rho]g'_\sigma/d^3$$

$$+[-g''_{\rho\rho}f'_\sigma g'_\sigma+g''_{\rho\sigma}f'_\rho g'_\sigma+g''_{\rho\sigma}f'_\sigma g'_\rho-g''_{\sigma\sigma}f'_\rho g'_\rho]f'_\sigma/d^3. \quad (66)$$

$$\sigma''_{xy} = [-f''_{\rho\rho}f'_\sigma g'_\sigma+f''_{\rho\sigma}f'_\rho g'_\sigma+f''_{\rho\sigma}f'_\sigma g'_\rho-f''_{\sigma\sigma}f'_\rho g'_\rho]g'_\rho/d^3$$

$$-[-g''_{\rho\rho}f'_\sigma g'_\sigma+g''_{\rho\sigma}f'_\rho g'_\sigma+g''_{\rho\sigma}f'_\sigma g'_\rho-g''_{\sigma\sigma}f'_\rho g'_\rho]f'_\rho/d^3. \quad (66)$$

By differentiation of the relations (61) with respect to y,

$$0 = [f''_{\rho\rho}\rho'_y\rho'_y+f''_{\rho\sigma}\rho'_y\sigma'_y+f''_{\rho\sigma}\rho'_y\sigma'_y+f''_{\sigma\sigma}\sigma'_y\sigma'_y]+f'_\rho f\rho''_{yy}+f'_\sigma\sigma''_{yy}, \quad (67)$$

$$0 = [g''_{\rho\rho}\rho'_y\rho'_y+g''_{\rho\sigma}\rho'_y\sigma'_y+g''_{\rho\sigma}\rho'_y\sigma'_y+g''_{\sigma\sigma}\sigma'_y\sigma'_y]+g'_\rho\rho''_{yy}+g'_\sigma\sigma''_{yy}. \quad (67)$$

By c and (62),

$$\rho''_{yy} = -[f''_{\rho\rho}f'_\sigma f'_\sigma-2f''_{\rho\sigma}f'_\rho f'_\sigma+f''_{\sigma\sigma}f'_\rho f'_\rho]g'_\sigma/d^3$$

$$+[g''_{\rho\rho}f'_\sigma f'_\sigma-2g''_{\rho\sigma}f'_\rho f'_\sigma+g''_{\sigma\sigma}f'_\rho f'_\rho]f'_\sigma/d^3. \quad (68)$$

$$\sigma''_{yy} = [f''_{\rho\rho}f'_{\sigma}f'_{\sigma} - 2f''_{\rho\sigma}f'_{\rho}f'_{\sigma} + f''_{\sigma\sigma}f'_{\rho}f'_{\rho}]g'_{\rho}/d^3$$

$$-[g''_{\rho\rho}f'_{\sigma}f'_{\sigma} - 2g''_{\rho\sigma}f'_{\rho}f'_{\sigma} + g''_{\sigma\sigma}f'_{\rho}f'_{\rho}]f'_{\rho}/d^3. \quad (68)$$

e. We now take α,β as independent variables. For any $F,G,H \in \{f,g,h\}$, we define the following functions of $(\alpha,\beta) \in B$:

$$D_{FG} := F'_{\alpha}G'_{\beta} - F'_{\beta}G'_{\alpha}, \quad (69)$$

$$A_{F,GH} := F''_{\alpha\alpha}G'_{\beta}H'_{\beta} - F''_{\alpha\beta}G'_{\alpha}H'_{\beta} - F''_{\alpha\beta}G'_{\beta}H'_{\alpha} + F''_{\beta\beta}G'_{\alpha}H'_{\alpha}. \quad (70)$$

Let

$$B_{ff} := D_{fg}A_{h,ff} + D_{gh}A_{f,ff} + D_{hf}A_{g,ff}, \quad (71)$$

$$B_{fg} := D_{fg}A_{h,fg} + D_{gh}A_{f,fg} + D_{hf}A_{g,fg}, \quad (71)$$

$$B_{gg} := D_{fg}A_{h,gg} + D_{gh}A_{f,gg} + D_{hf}A_{g,gg}. \quad (71)$$

Then $d \equiv D_{fg}$ and by the relations (55), (60), (62), (64), (66) and (68),

$$\varphi''_{xx} = B_{gg}/[D_{fg}]^3, \quad (72)$$

$$\varphi''_{xy} = -B_{fg}/[D_{fg}]^3, \quad (72)$$

$$\varphi''_{yy} = B_{ff}/[D_{fg}]^3. \quad (72)$$

This proves the following result.

If $D_{fg}>0$ on B, the convexity conditions of the surface (49) are

$$\mathbf{B_{ff} \geq 0 \;,\; B_{gg} \geq 0 \;,\; B_{ff}B_{gg}-(B_{fg})^2 \geq 0 \;\; on\; B}. \quad (73)$$

If $D_{fg}<0$ on B, the convexity conditions of the surface (49) are

$$\mathbf{B_{ff} \leq 0 \;,\; B_{gg} \leq 0 \;,\; B_{ff}B_{gg}-(B_{fg})^2 \leq 0 \;\; on\; B}. \quad (74)$$

If $D_{fg}>0$ on B, the concavity conditions of the surface (49) are the relations (74).

If $D_{fg}<0$ on B, the concavity conditions of the surface (49) are the relations (73).

6.2.2. A Pure 1-Constraint Problem

We consider the maximization problem

$$Q(\alpha) = \sup_{F\in \mathit{Prob}[[0,b]]}[\int u^{1/2}(1+u)^{-1}dF(u) \,/\, \int u^{1/2}dF(u)=\alpha] \qquad (75)$$

and the corresponding minimization problem $P(\alpha)$. Let

$$f(u) := u^{1/2} \ , \ g(u) := u^{1/2}(1+u)^{-1} \ \ (0\leq u\leq b). \qquad (76)$$

We apply the method of 6.1.3. Here $f^{\bullet}=f$, $g^{\bullet}=g$. The curves and domains are represented in Fig.9. (The same figure is used for different illustrations. Only the shape of the curves is relevant.)

a. $\mathrm{Cur}_1Q = \{f(\theta) \,/\, \theta\in[0,b]\} = [0,b^{1/2}]$, dom $Q = \mathrm{CoCur}_1Q = [0,b^{1/2}]$.

b. Cur_2Q is the curve with parametric equations, in $\mathbf{R}^2=\{(x,y)\}$,

$$x = \theta^{1/2} =: f(\theta) \ , \ y = \theta^{1/2}(1+\theta)^{-1} =: g(\theta) \quad (0\leq\theta\leq b).$$

The usual equation of Cur_2Q results from the elimination of θ. It is

$$y = x(1+x^2)^{-1} =: \varphi(x) \ (0\leq x\leq b^{1/2}=:a).$$

The upper frontier of CoCur_2Q is composed of the curve $y=\varphi(x)$ $(0\leq x\leq x_0)$ and the segment

$$[(x_0,\varphi(x_0)),(a,\varphi(a))], \qquad (77)$$

tangent to Cur_2Q, with point of contact $(x_0,\varphi(x_0))$. The point x_0 results from the equation

$$\varphi'(x_0) = [\varphi(a)-\varphi(x_0)]/(a-x_0), \qquad (78)$$

expressing that the slope of the segment (77) equals the derivative $\varphi'(x_0)$.

c. Hence, the value of problem $Q(\alpha)$ is

$$Q(\alpha) = \varphi(\alpha) \ \ (0\leq\alpha\leq x_0), \qquad (79)$$

$$Q(\alpha) = [(a-\alpha)\varphi(x_0)+(\alpha-x_0)\varphi(a)]/(a-x_0) \ \ (x_0\leq\alpha\leq a). \qquad (79)$$

d. The values α, x_0, a of x correspond to the values α^2, x_0^2, b of θ. Hence, the solution F of the problem Q(α) is the distribution

$$F = A_{\alpha^2}\ (0\leq\alpha\leq x_0), \tag{80}$$

$$F = [(a-\alpha)A_{x_0^2} + (\alpha-x_0)A_b]/(a-x_0)\ \ (x_0\leq\alpha\leq a). \tag{80}$$

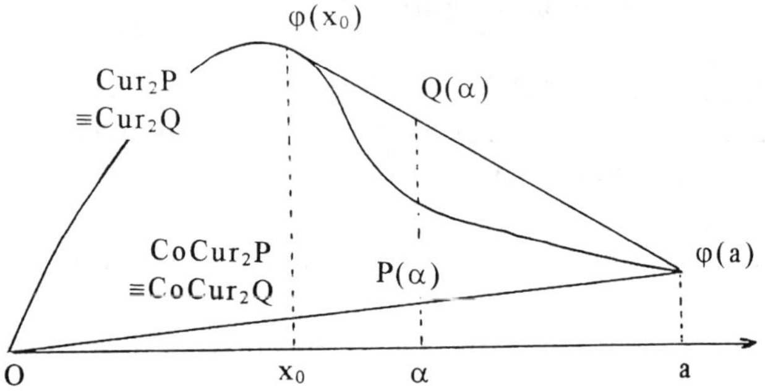

Fig.9. Convex hull of problem 6.2.2.

Minimization problem

The value and solution of the minimization problem P(α) result from the same Fig.9. The lower frontier of the convex hull $CoCur_2P$ ($=CoCur_2Q$) is the line segment [(0,0),(a,φ(a))]. The value of problem P(α) is

$$P(\alpha) = [(a-\alpha).0 + (\alpha-0)\varphi(a)]/(a-0) = \alpha/_a\ \varphi(a)\ \ (0\leq\alpha\leq a). \tag{81}$$

The solution of problem P(α) is distribution

$$F = 1/_a[(a-\alpha)A_0+\alpha A_b]\ \ (0\leq\alpha\leq a). \tag{82}$$

Numerical results

By (78), x_0 is the root of the equation

$$(1-x^2)(a-x) = a/_{(1+a^2)}\,(1+x^2)^2 - x(1+x^2).$$

Then, for b=36, i.e. a=6, we obtain x_0=1.180. Then for α=3,

$$P(3) = \inf_{F\in \boldsymbol{Prob}[[0,36]]}[\int u^{1/2}(1+u)^{-1}dF(u)\ /\ \int u^{1/2}dF(u)=3] = 0.081 \qquad (83)$$

$$Q(3) = \sup_{F\in \boldsymbol{Prob}[[0,36]]}[\int u^{1/2}(1+u)^{-1}dF(u)\ /\ \int u^{1/2}dF(u)=3] = 0.368 \qquad (83)$$

6.2.3. A 0-Unimodal 1-Constraint Problem

We here consider the problem

$$Q_0(\alpha) = \sup_{F\in \boldsymbol{Prob}[[0,b];0\text{-unim}]}[\int u^{1/2}(1+u)^{-1}dF(u)\ /\ \int u^{1/2}dF(u)=\alpha] \qquad (84)$$

and the corresponding minimization problem $P_0(\alpha)$.

The problem can be displayed as

$$Q_0(\alpha) = \sup_{F\in \boldsymbol{Sp}}[\int g dF\ /\ \int f dF(u)=\alpha]$$

where

$$\boldsymbol{Sp} := \boldsymbol{Mixt}[R_{0\theta}/\theta\in[0,b]],$$

and where the functions f and g are defined by (76).

The value and the solution of problem $Q_0(\alpha)$ result from the value and the solution of the associated problem

$$Q_0^{\bullet}(\alpha) = \sup_{F\in \boldsymbol{Prob}[[0,b]]}[\int g^{\bullet}dF\ /\ \int f^{\bullet}dF=\alpha].$$

Here

$$f^{\bullet}(\theta) = \int_{[0,b]}f(x)dR_{0\theta}(x) = {}^{1}/_{\theta}\int_{[0,\theta]} x^{1/2}dx = {}^{2}/_{3}\ \theta^{1/2} \quad (0\leq\theta\leq b),$$

$$g^{\bullet}(\theta) = \int_{[0,b]}g(x)dR_{0\theta}(x) = {}^{1}/_{\theta}\int_{[0,\theta]} {}^{x^{1/2}}/_{(1+x)}\ dx = {}^{2}/_{\theta}[\theta^{1/2}-\mathrm{arc\ tan}(\theta^{1/2})].$$

We now apply the method of 6.1.3 to problem $Q_0^{\bullet}(\alpha)$.

a. $$\mathrm{Cur}_1Q_0^{\bullet} = \{f^{\bullet}(\theta)\ /\ \theta\in[0,b]\} = [0,{}^{2}/_{3}b^{1/2}] = [0,a],$$

where $$a := {}^{2}/_{3}\ b^{1/2}.$$

Then $$\mathrm{dom}\ Q_0^{\bullet} = \mathrm{CoCur}_1Q_0^{\bullet} = [0,a].$$

b. $Cur_2Q_0^\bullet$ is the curve in $\mathbf{R}^2=\{(x,y)\}$ with parametric equations

$$x = f^\bullet(\theta)\ ,\ y = g^\bullet(\theta)\ \ (0\leq\theta\leq b).$$

The usual equation of $Cur_2Q_0^\bullet$ results from the elimination of θ. It is

$$y = 4/3\ x^{-1} - 8/9\ x^{-2} \text{ arc tan}(3x/2) =: \varphi(x)\ \ (0\leq x\leq a:=2/3 b^{1/2}).$$

$Cur_2Q_0^\bullet$ has a similar shape as curve Cur_2Q of the illustration of 6.2.2. Fig.9 can still be used here: P and Q must be replaced everywhere by $P_0^\bullet$, $Q_0^\bullet$.

The upper frontier of $CoCur_2Q_0^\bullet$ is composed of the curve $y=\varphi(x)$ $(0\leq x\leq x_0)$ and of the segment

$$[(x_0,\varphi(x_0)),(a,\varphi(a))]$$

tangent to $Cur_2Q_0^\bullet$ with point of contact $(x_0,\varphi(x_0))$. The point x_0 results from the equation

$$\varphi'(x_0) = [\varphi(a)-\varphi(x_0)]/(a-x_0).$$

c. Hence, the value of the problem $Q_0^\bullet(\alpha)$ is

$$Q_0^\bullet(\alpha) = \varphi(\alpha)\ \ (0\leq\alpha\leq x_0), \tag{85}$$

$$Q_0^\bullet(\alpha) = [(a-\alpha)\varphi(x_0)+(\alpha-x_0)\varphi(a)]/(a-x_0)\ \ (x_0\leq\alpha\leq a). \tag{86}$$

The problems $Q_0(\alpha)$ and $Q_0^\bullet(\alpha)$ have the same value.

d. The values α,x_0,a of x correspond to the values $9/4\alpha^2$, $9/4x_0^2$, b of θ. Hence, the solution U of the problem $Q_0^\bullet(\alpha)$ is the distribution

$$U = A_{9\alpha^2/4}\ (0\leq\alpha\leq x_0), \tag{87}$$

$$U = [(a-\alpha)A_{9x_0^2/4} + (\alpha-x_0)A_b]/(a-x_0)\ \ (x_0\leq\alpha\leq a). \tag{87}$$

The solution F of problem $Q(\alpha)$ is

$$F = R_{0,9\alpha^2/4}\ (0\leq\alpha\leq x_0), \tag{88}$$

$$F = [(a-\alpha)R_{0,9x_0^2/4} + (\alpha-x_0)R_{0b}]/(a-x_0)\ \ (x_0\leq\alpha\leq a). \tag{88}$$

Minimization problem

The value of the problems $P_0^{\bullet}(\alpha)$ and $P_0(\alpha)$ is

$$P_0^{\bullet}(\alpha) = P_0(\alpha) = [(a-\alpha).0 + (\alpha-0)\varphi(a)]/(a-0) = \alpha/_{a}\, \varphi(a) \quad (0\leq\alpha\leq a). \quad (89)$$

The solution U of the problem $P_0^{\bullet}(\alpha)$ and the solution F of the problem $P_0(\alpha)$ are

$$U = 1/_{a}[(a-\alpha)A_0+\alpha A_b] \quad (0\leq\alpha\leq a). \quad (90)$$

$$F = 1/_{a}[(a-\alpha)R_{00}+\alpha R_{0b}] \quad (0\leq\alpha\leq a). \quad (91)$$

Numerical results

For b=36, i.e. a=4 we obtain x_0=1.352. Then, for α=3,

$$P_0(3) = \inf_{F\in \boldsymbol{Prob}[[0,36];0\text{-unim}]}\Big[\int u^{1/2}(1+u)^{-1}dF(u) \,/\, \int u^{1/2}dF(u)=3\Big]= 0.191 \quad (92)$$

$$Q_0(3) = \sup_{F\in \boldsymbol{Prob}[[0,36];0\text{-unim}]}\Big[\int u^{1/2}(1+u)^{-1}dF(u) \,/\, \int u^{1/2}dF(u)=3\Big]= 0.327 \quad (92)$$

6.2.4. A General Pure 2-Moment Problem

We consider the problem

$$Q(\mu_1,\mu_2) = \sup_{F\in \boldsymbol{Prob}[[a,b]]}\Big[\int\varphi dF \,/\, \mu_1,\mu_2\Big]. \quad (93)$$

We here extend the construction of the proof of Ch.3.Th.5, corresponding to the particular case $\varphi(x)=x^3 (a\leq x\leq b)$.

a. Cur_2Q is the curve with parametric equations

$$x = \theta \ , \ y = \theta^2 \quad (a\leq\theta\leq b).$$

dom Q is the set of points (x,y) satisfying the relations Ch.3.(48_1),(48_2).

b. Cur_3Q is the curve with parametric equations

$$x = \theta \ , \ y = \theta^2 \ , \ z = \varphi(\theta) \quad (a\leq\theta\leq b).$$

Let Surf be the surface composed of the line segments

$$[(\theta,\theta^2,\varphi(\theta)),(b,b^2,\varphi(b))] \quad (a\leq\theta\leq b)$$

connecting the variable point $(\theta,\theta^2,\varphi(\theta))$ and the fixed point $(b,b^2,\varphi(b))$ of Cur_3Q. The parametric equations of Surf are

$$x = f(p,\theta)\ ,\ y = g(p,\theta)\ ,\ z = h(p,\theta) \quad (0\leq p\leq 1,\ a\leq\theta\leq b),$$

where

$$f(p,\theta) := p\theta+(1-p)b = b-p(b-\theta),$$

$$g(p,\theta) := p\theta^2+(1-p)b^2 = b^2-p(b^2-\theta^2),$$

$$h(p,\theta) := p\varphi(\theta)+(1-p)\varphi(b) = \varphi(b)-p[\varphi(b)-\varphi(\theta)].$$

They express that the point (x,y,z) is a convex combination of the points $(\theta,\theta^2,\varphi(\theta))$ and $(b,b^2,\varphi(b))$.

We look for conditions under which Surf is concave. Then Surf is the upper frontier of $CoCur_3Q$ and the value Q result from the usual non-parametric equation of Surf.

Hence, we calculate the functions B_{ff}, B_{fg} and B_{gg} defined by (71). Here $(\alpha,\beta)=(p,\theta)$.

The intermediate results are the following:

$$f'_p = -(b-\theta)\ ,\ f'_\theta = p\ ,\ f''_{pp} = 0\ ,\ f''_{p\theta} = 1\ ,\ f''_{\theta\theta} = 0,$$

$$g'_p = -(b^2-\theta^2)\ ,\ g'_\theta = 2p\theta\ ,\ g''_{pp} = 0\ ,\ g''_{p\theta} = 2\theta\ ,\ g''_{\theta\theta} = 2p,$$

$$h'_p = -[\varphi(b)-\varphi(\theta)]\ ,\ h'_\theta = p\varphi'(\theta)\ ,\ h''_{pp} = 0\ ,\ h''_{p\theta} = \varphi'(\theta)\ ,\ h''_{\theta\theta} = p\varphi''(\theta).$$

$$D_{fg} = p(b-\theta)^2 \geq 0,$$

$$D_{gh} = 2p\theta[\varphi(b)-\varphi(\theta)] - p(b^2-\theta^2)\varphi'(\theta),$$

$$D_{hf} = p(b-\theta)\varphi'(\theta) - p[\varphi(b)-\varphi(\theta)].$$

$$A_{h,ff} = 2p(b-\theta)\varphi'(\theta) + p\varphi''(\theta)(b-\theta)^2,$$

$$A_{f,ff} = 2p(b-\theta)\ ,\ A_{g,ff} = 2p(b^2-\theta^2),$$

$$A_{h,fg} = p(b-\theta)(b+3\theta)\varphi'(\theta) + p(b-\theta)(b^2-\theta^2)\varphi''(\theta),$$

$$A_{f,}fg = p(b-\theta)(b+3\theta)\ ,\ A_{g,}fg = 2p(b-\theta)(b^2+b\theta+2\theta^2),$$

$$A_{h,gg} = 4p\theta(b^2-\theta^2)\varphi'(\theta) + p(b^2-\theta^2)^2\varphi''(\theta),$$

$$A_{f,gg} = 4p\theta(b^2-\theta^2)\ ,\ A_{g,gg} = 2p(b^2-\theta^2)(b^2+3\theta^2).$$

$$B_{ff} = -2p^2(b-\theta)^2[\varphi(b)-[\varphi(\theta)+(b-\theta)\varphi'(\theta)+ 1/2(b-\theta)^2\varphi''(\theta)]],$$

$$B_{fg} = -2p^2(b-\theta)(b^2-\theta^2)[\varphi(b)-[\varphi(\theta)+(b-\theta)\varphi'(\theta)+ 1/2(b-\theta)^2\varphi''(\theta)]],$$

$$B_{gg} = -2p^2(b^2-\theta^2)^2[\varphi(b)-[\varphi(\theta)+(b-\theta)\varphi'(\theta)+ 1/2(b-\theta)^2\varphi''(\theta)]].$$

We observe that

$$(B_{fg})^2 = B_{ff}B_{gg}.$$

Hence, the last condition (73) or (74) is satisfied in any case.

Surf is a continuous surface on the closed convex set dom Q. Then the concavity of Surf on dom Q results from its concavity on the interior (dom Q)° of dom Q. Hence, we may assume, in the discussion of the concavity of Surf, that $0<p<1$, $a<\theta<b$. Then $D_{fg}>0$, and the concavity is equivalent to the relations $B_{ff}\leq 0$, $B_{gg}\leq 0$. Hence, **Surf is concave if**

$$\varphi(\theta)+(b-\theta)\varphi'(\theta)+ 1/2(b-\theta)^2\varphi''(\theta) \leq \varphi(b)\quad (a<\theta<b). \tag{94}$$

We now assume that $\varphi'''\geq 0$ on [a,b]. Then the relation (94) is verified. Indeed, by Taylor $\varphi(b)$ equals the first member of (94) augmented by the term

$$1/6\ (b-\theta)^3\varphi'''(\xi) \geq 0, \text{ where } \xi\in[\theta,b].$$

c. We need the usual non parametric equation of Surf on dom Q. We consider points $(x,y)\in(\text{dom Q})°$, i.e. points (p,θ) such that $0<p<1$, $a<\theta<b$. Then the solution of the system

$$x = p\theta+(1-p)b\ ,\ y = p\theta^2+(1-p)b^2$$

is $$p(x,y) = (b-x)^2/(b^2-2bx+y) \ , \ \theta(x,y) = (bx-y)/(b-x).$$

The usual equation of Surf is

$$z = p(x,y)\varphi[\theta(x,y)] + [1-p(x,y)]\ \varphi(b) \ \ ((x,y)\in(\text{dom } Q)^{\circ}).$$

d. Let $x=\mu_1$, $y=\mu_2$. Then the solution of the problem Q is $pA_\theta+(1-p)A_b$, where p and θ must be replaced by $p(\mu_1,\mu_2)$ and $\theta(\mu_1,\mu_2)$.

The minimization problem $P(\mu_1,\mu_2)$ can be treated in the same way. This proves the following Theorem.

Theorem 2

Let φ be a function with a positive third order derivative on [a,b], and let

$$a<\mu_1<b \ , \ \mu_1^2<\mu_2<(a+b)\mu_1-ab.$$

a. The value of the problem

$$Q(\mu_1,\mu_2) = \sup_{F\in Prob[[a,b]]}[\textstyle\int\varphi dF \ / \ \mu_1,\mu_2]$$

equals $$Q(\mu_1,\mu_2) = p\varphi(\theta)+(1-p)\varphi(b),$$

where $$p := (b-\mu_1)^2/(b^2-2b\mu_1+\mu_2),$$

and $$\theta := (b\mu_1-\mu_2)/(b-\mu_1).$$

The solution of the problem is the bi-atomic distribution

$$pA_\theta+(1-p)A_b.$$

b. The value of the problem

$$P(\mu_1,\mu_2) = \inf_{F\in Prob[[a,b]]}[\textstyle\int\varphi dF \ / \ \mu_1,\mu_2]$$

equals $$P(\mu_1,\mu_2) = (1-p)\varphi(a) + p\varphi(\theta),$$

where $$p := (\mu_1-a)^2/(a^2-2a\mu_1+\mu_2),$$

and $$\theta := (\mu_2-a\mu_1)/(\mu_1-a).$$

The solution of the problem is the bi-atomic distribution

$$(1-p)A_a+pA_\theta \ \bullet$$

6.3. Numerical Finite-Basic Solutions

6.3.1. Problems

We here consider the problems

$$Q(\mu_1,\dots,\mu_n) := \sup_{F\in \boldsymbol{Prob}[[0,20]]}\left[\int e^x dF(x)/\mu_1(F)=\mu_1,\dots,\mu_n(F)=\mu_n\right], \qquad (95)$$

$$Q_0(\mu_1,\dots,\mu_n) := \sup_{F\in \boldsymbol{Prob}[[0,20];0\text{-unim}]}\left[\int e^x dF(x)/\mu_1(F)=\mu_1,\dots,\mu_n(F)=\mu_n\right], \qquad (96)$$

$$P(\mu_1,\dots,\mu_n) := \min_{F\in \boldsymbol{Prob}[[0,20]]}\left[\int e^x dF(x)/\mu_1(F)=\mu_1,\dots,\mu_n(F)=\mu_n\right], \qquad (97)$$

$$P_0(\mu_1,\dots,\mu_n) := \min_{F\in \boldsymbol{Prob}[[0,20];0\text{-unim}]}\left[\int e^x dF(x)/\mu_1(F)=\mu_1,\dots,\mu_n(F)=\mu_n\right], \qquad (98)$$

for n=1,2,3,4. The moments μ_1,μ_2,μ_3,μ_4 are those of the 6-rectangular distribution

$$1/6(R_{0,0} + R_{0,4} + R_{0,8} + R_{0,12} + R_{0,16} + R_{0,20}).$$

Then

$$\mu_1 = 5\ ,\ \mu_2 = 48.888\dots\ ,\ \mu_3 = 600\ ,\ \mu_4 = 8354.1333\dots\ .$$

The solution of these problems is denoted by

$$F_{k,max,pure}\ ,\ F_{k,max,m}\ ,\ F_{k,min,pure}\ ,\ F_{k,min,m}$$

resp., and the corresponding values by

$$Val_{k,max,pure}\ ,\ Val_{k,max,m}\ ,\ Val_{k,min,pure}\ ,\ Val_{k,min,m}.$$

6.3.2. Numerical Solutions

Problem (96) is solved via its associated problem. This is the pure moment problem

$$Q_0^{\bullet}(2\mu_1,3\mu_2,\dots,(n+1)\mu_n)$$

$$= \sup_{\boldsymbol{Prob}[[0,20]]}\left[\int 1/x(e^x-1)dF(x)/2\mu_1,3\mu_2,\dots,(n+1)\mu_n\right].$$

and problem (98) is treated in the same way.

By Theorem 1, the solutions are n+1-basic distributions, i.e. extremal points of the hypothetic space ***Space***. Then the problems on ***Space*** can be replaced by the corresponding problem on the set ***Ext*** of extremal points of ***Space***. The latter are solved by the *k_0-algorithm with variable discretization* of Ch.4.7.5. The following numerical results correspond to hyper-fine discretizations. The exact values are indicated in the following table.

	k=1	k=2	k=3	k=4
$Val_{k,min,pure}$	148.41316	9019.6213	111318.74	575741.91
$Val_{k,min,m}$	2202.5466	108890.66	606171.93	1854801.4
$Val_{k,max,m}$	12129130	7718563.5	5661435.5	4928052.5
$Val_{k,max,pure}$	121299300	46567222	22957940	13973311

The solutions are the following special finite-atomic or finite-rectangular (see Ch.4.8) distributions, with m=0:

$$F_{1,min,pure} = A_5 \text{ (Narrow 1-atomic)}$$

$$F_{1,min,m} = R_{m,10} \text{ (Narrow 1-rectangular)}$$

$$F_{1,max,m} = 0.05R_{m,0}+0.05R_{m,20} \text{ (Broad 2-rectangular)}$$

$$F_{1,max,pure} = 0.075A_0+0.25A_{20} \text{ (Broad 2-atomic)}$$

$$F_{2,min,pure} = 0.488636A_0+0.511364A_{9.777778} \text{ (Initial 2-atomic)}$$

$$F_{2,min,m} = 0.318182R_{m,0}+0.681818R_{m,14.666667} \text{ (Initial 2-rectangular)}$$

$$F_{2,max,m} = 0.681818R_{m,5.333333}+0.318182R_{m,20} \text{ (Final 2-rectangular)}$$

$$F_{2,max,pure} = 0.904018A_{3.407407}+0.095982A_{20} \text{ (Final 2-atomic)}$$

$$F_{3,min,pure} = 0.723464A_{1.978201}+0.276536A_{12.905520} \text{ (Narrow 2-atomic)}$$

$$F_{3,min,m} = 0.865963R_{m,3.168699}+0.134037R_{m,16.831301} \text{ (Narrow 2-rectangular)}$$

$$F_{3,max,m} = 0.233333R_{m,0}+0.533333R_{m,10}+0.233333R_{0,20} \text{ (Broad 3-rect.)}$$

$F_{3,max,pure} = 0.404248A_0+0.548434A_{7.391304}+0.047318A_{20}$ (Broad 3-atomic)

$F_{4,min,pure} = 0.331524A_0+0.517437A_{5.239738}+0.151039A_{15.153460}$ (Initial 3-at.)

$F_{4,min,m} = 0.202899R_{m,0}+0.448718R_{m,8}+0.348384R_{m,18.4}$ (Initial 3-rect.)

$F_{4,max,m} = 0.348384R_{m,1.6}+0.448718R_{m,12}+0.202899R_{0,20}$ (Final 3-rect.)

$F_{4,max,pure} = 0.622400A_{1.403118}+0.348818A_{10.180261}+0.028782A_{20}$ (Final 3-at.)

Chapter 7

Duals of Integral Optimization Problems

7.0. Introduction

Integral optimization problems can be solved numerically when the number of constraints is fairly large, by the algorithms of Ch.4.7. They can be solved analytically by the method of Ch.6.1.3 when the number n of constraints equals 0, 1 or 2. The latter method is based on the construction of convex hulls in $\mathbf{R}^{n+1}$. It becomes impracticable when $n \geq 3$, because our geometrical visualizations are not precise enough in $\mathbf{R}^4$ and in spaces of higher dimensions.

In this Chapter 7, we consider a pure integral optimization problem, called **the primal problem**, and we define a corresponding **dual problem**. This dual problem appears in the most natural way: it results from the calculation of the bipolar function (App.C.C9) of the value function of the primal problem.

Under very general conditions, the primal problem and the dual problem have the same value. From the study of the properties of the couple (primal problem, dual problem) results a method permitting the analytic research of the solution of the primal problem whatever the number n of its integral constraints is.

The dual problem is a linear program (Ch.5.1) if the set S, on which the distributions are concentrated, is finite. When numerical solutions are considered, the practical problems are discretized (at least if no simple analytic solution is available), and then S becomes finite. Hence, the value of any primal integral problem can be calculated via its dual and the latter can be found by the algorithms available in the case of usual linear programs (Dantzig simplex method, or any other algorithm).

In any case, the dual problem is an extended linear program (Ch.5.2.1), i.e. an optimization problem of a linear function of a finite number of variables, under a set, not necessarily finite, of linear constraints.

The existence proof of a solution of the dual problem is based on Ch.5.Th.5.

7.1. Discovery of Dual Problem

7.1.1. Definition of Primal Problem

We consider the **primal maximization problem**

$$Q(\alpha_0,\ldots,\alpha_n) := \sup_{F\in \boldsymbol{Distr}[S]}\left[\int f_{n+1}dF \,/\, \int f_0 dF=\alpha_0,\ldots,\int f_n dF=\alpha_n\right] \quad (1)$$

and the corresponding **primal minimization problem**

$$P(\alpha_0,\ldots,\alpha_n) := \inf_{F\in \boldsymbol{Distr}[S]}\left[\int f_{n+1}dF \,/\, \int f_0 dF=\alpha_0,\ldots,\int f_n dF=\alpha_n\right].$$

The space ***Distr***[S] and subspaces of the latter, are defined in Ch.2.1.2.

We mostly consider the maximization problem only, when general theoretical results are developed. These results have obvious versions concerning the minimization problem.

The functions $f_0,\ldots,f_{n+1}$ are supposed to be F-integrable for all distributions $F\in$***Distr***[S].

The **parameters** $\alpha_0,\ldots,\alpha_n$ are any real finite numbers, but the interesting n+1-tuples $(\alpha_0,\ldots,\alpha_n)$ are those in the **effective domain** dom Q of the problem. The latter is the set of points $(\alpha_0,\ldots,\alpha_n)$ such that the problem has **feasible distributions**. The set of feasible distributions of problem $Q(\alpha_0,\ldots,\alpha_n)$ is the space

$$\boldsymbol{Distr}\left[S;\int f_0=\alpha_0,\ldots,\int f_n=\alpha_n\right]. \quad (2)$$

The **probability constraint** on $F\in$***Distr***[S] is the integral constraint $\int dF=1$. The problem

$$Q_1(\alpha_1,\ldots,\alpha_n) := \sup_{F\in \boldsymbol{Distr}[S]}\left[\int f_{n+1}dF \,/\, \int dF=1,\int f_1 dF=\alpha_1,\ldots,\int f_n dF=\alpha_n\right]$$

$$= \sup_{F\in \boldsymbol{Prob}[S]}\left[\int f_{n+1}dF \,/\, \int f_1 dF=\alpha_1,\ldots,\int f_n dF=\alpha_n\right] \quad (3)$$

is **the probability problem** corresponding to problem (1). The problem

$$\sup_{F\in \boldsymbol{Distr}[S]}\left[\int f_{n+1}dF \,/\, \int dF=\alpha_0,\int f_1 dF=\alpha_1,\ldots,\int f_n dF=\alpha_n\right] \quad (4)$$

is **the distribution problem** corresponding to problem (3).

Only probability problems are interesting in practice, but only the dual theory of distribution problems is convenient. This explains the consideration of both types of problems. By the consideration of corresponding problems, the dual theory can be applied to practical probability problems.

7.1.2. Definition of Dual Problem

Theorem 1

The bipolar function of the function Q defined on $\mathbf{R}^{n+1}$ by (1), is the function with values

$$\mathbf{Q^{**}(\alpha_0,\ldots,\alpha_n)}$$

$$= \inf_y[\textstyle\sum_{0\le j\le n} y_j\alpha_j \;/\; \sum_{0\le j\le n} y_jf_j \ge f_{n+1} \text{ on } S]\;((\alpha_0,\ldots,\alpha_n)\in\mathbf{R}^{n+1}), \qquad (5)$$

where $y:=(y_0,\ldots,y_n)$ ranges over $\mathbf{R}^{n+1}$.

Proof

Let $$x := (x_0,\ldots,x_n)\in\mathbf{R}^{n+1}.$$

Then $$Q^*(y) = \inf_x[\langle x,y\rangle - Q(x)]$$

$$= \inf_x\big[\textstyle\sum_{0\le j\le n} x_jy_j - \sup_{F\in \mathit{Distr}[S]}[\int f_{n+1}dF \;/\; \int f_jdF=x_j\ (j=0,\ldots,n)]\big]$$

$$= \inf_x\big[\inf_{F\in \mathit{Distr}[S]}[\textstyle\sum_{0\le j\le n} x_jy_j - \int f_{n+1}dF \;/\; \int f_jdF=x_j\ (j=0,\ldots,n)]\big]$$

$$= \inf_{F\in \mathit{Distr}[S]}\big[\inf_x[\textstyle\sum_{0\le j\le n} x_jy_j - \int f_{n+1}dF \;/\; \int f_jdF=x_j\ (j=0,\ldots,n)]\big]$$

$$= \inf_{F\in \mathit{Distr}[S]}\big[\inf_x[\textstyle\sum_{0\le j\le n} x_jy_j \;/\; \int f_jdF=x_j\ (j=0,\ldots,n)] - \int f_{n+1}dF\big]$$

$$= \inf_{F\in \mathit{Distr}[S]}[\textstyle\sum_{0\le j\le n} y_j\int f_jdF - \int f_{n+1}dF]$$

$$= \inf_{F\in \mathit{Distr}[S]}[\textstyle\int(\sum_{0\le j\le n} y_jf_j - f_{n+1})dF]. \qquad (6)$$

Hence,

$$Q^*(y) = 0 \text{ if } \textstyle\sum_{0\le j\le n} y_jf_j - f_{n+1} \ge 0 \text{ on } S$$

and

$$Q^*(y) = -\infty \text{ if } \textstyle\sum_{0\le j\le n} y_jf_j - f_{n+1} < 0 \text{ at some point of } S.$$

Indeed, if $\sum_{0\le j\le n} y_j f_j - f_{n+1} \ge 0$ on S, then the integral in square brackets in (6) is positive. Its minimum value is obtained for $F\equiv 0$. If $\sum_{0\le j\le n} y_j f_j(\theta_0) - f_{n+1}(\theta_0) < 0$, $\theta_0 \in S$, then we can take for F the distribution with mass c at the point θ_0, and we may let $c\uparrow\infty$. This furnishes the $\inf = -\infty$.

The effective domain of the function Q* is

$$\text{dom } Q^* = \{y\in \mathbf{R}^{n+1} / \textstyle\sum_{0\le j\le n} y_j f_j - f_{n+1} \ge 0 \text{ on } S\}.$$

Let

$$\alpha := (\alpha_0,\ldots,\alpha_n) \in \mathbf{R}^{n+1}.$$

Then

$$Q^{**}(\alpha) = \inf_{y\in \text{dom } Q^*}[<\alpha,y> - Q^*(y)]$$

$$= \inf_y[\textstyle\sum_{0\le j\le n} y_j\alpha_j - 0 / \sum_{1\le j\le n} y_j f_j \ge f_{n+1} \text{ on } S] \quad \bullet$$

The problem $Q^{**}(\alpha_1,\ldots,\alpha_n)$ defined by the relation (5) is **the dual problem of the problem $Q(\alpha_1,\ldots,\alpha_n)$** defined by (1).

Dual of problem with mixed constraints

We prove some scarce results about the **problem $Q_\le(\alpha_0,\ldots,\alpha_n)$ with mixed integral contstraints**, i.e. the problem defined by the last member of (1) with some equality constraints $\int f_j dF=\alpha_j$ replaced by the corresponding weak inequality constraints $\int f_j dF \le \alpha_j$ (j=0,...,n). Let J be the set of subscripts j for which this replacement is made.

Theorem 2

The bipolar function of the function $Q_\le$ is the function with values

$$Q_\le^{**}(\alpha_0,\ldots,\alpha_n)$$

$$= \inf_y[\textstyle\sum_{0\le j\le n} y_j\alpha_j / \sum_{0\le j\le n} y_j f_j \ge f_{n+1} \text{ on } S] \; ((\alpha_0,\ldots,\alpha_n)\in \mathbf{R}^{n+1}), \qquad (7)$$

where y_j ($j\notin J$) ranges over R and y_j ($j\in J$) over R_+.

Proof

Let $x := (x_0,\dots,x_n) \in \mathbf{R}^{n+1}$.

Then

$$Q_\leq^*(y) = \inf_x[<x,y> - Q_\leq(x)]$$

$$= \inf_x\Big[\sum_{0\leq j\leq n} x_j y_j - \sup_{F\in \mathit{Distr}[S]}\Big[\int f_{n+1}dF \,/\, \int f_j dF = x_j\ (j\notin J), \int f_j dF \leq x_j\ (j\in J)\Big]\Big].$$

By the same transformations as in the foregoing proof,

$$Q_\leq(y) = \inf_{F\in \mathit{Distr}[S]}\Big[\inf_x\Big[\sum_{0\leq j\leq n} x_j y_j \,/\, \int f_j dF = x_j\ (j\notin J), \int f_j dF \leq x_j\ (j\in J)\Big] - \int f_{n+1}dF\Big]$$

$$= \inf_{F\in \mathit{Distr}[S]}\Big[\varphi(y,F) - \int f_{n+1}dF\Big],$$

where

$$\varphi(y,F) := \inf_x\Big[\sum_{0\leq j\leq n} x_j y_j \,/\, \int f_j dF = x_j\ (j\notin J), \int f_j dF \leq x_j\ (j\in J)\Big].$$

If $y_j \geq 0$ $(j\in J)$, then

$$\varphi(y,F) = \sum_{0\leq j\leq n} y_j \int f_j dF = \int\Big(\sum_{0\leq j\leq n} y_j f_j\Big)dF,$$

because then the inf is attained for $x_j = \int f_j dF$ $(j=0,\dots,n)$.

If $j_0 \in J$ exists such that $y_{j_0} < 0$, then $\varphi(y,F) = -\infty$, because then we can let $x_{j_0} \uparrow +\infty$. Hence,

$$Q_\leq^*(y) = \inf_{F\in \mathit{Distr}[S]}\Big[\int\Big(\sum_{0\leq j\leq n} y_j f_j - f_{n+1}\Big)dF\Big]\mathbf{1}_{y_j\geq 0\ (j\in J)} - \infty\mathbf{1}_{y_j<0 \text{ for some } j\in J}.$$

The $\inf_F$ equals zero if

$$\sum_{0\leq j\leq n} y_j f_j - f_{n+1} \geq 0 \text{ on } S,$$

because then we can take $F\equiv 0$. It equals $-\infty$ if

$$\sum_{0\leq j\leq n} y_j f_j - f_{n+1} < 0 \text{ at some point } \theta_0 \text{ of } S,$$

because then we can put the mass c at θ_0 and let $c\uparrow +\infty$. Hence

$$Q_\leq^*(y) = 0 \text{ if } y_j \geq 0\ (j\in J) \text{ and } \sum_{0\leq j\leq n} y_j f_j - f_{n+1} \geq 0 \text{ on } S,$$

$$Q_\leq(y) = -\infty \text{ in all other cases.}$$

Then

$$\mathrm{dom}\ Q_{\leq}^* = \{y\in\mathbf{R}^{n+1} \ / \ y_j\geq 0\ (j\in J) \text{ and } \textstyle\sum_{0\leq j\leq n} y_j f_j - f_{n+1}\geq 0 \text{ on } S\},$$

and

$$Q_{\leq}^{**}(\alpha) = \inf_{y\in \mathrm{dom}\, Q_{\leq}^*}[<\alpha,y> - Q_{\leq}^*(y)]$$

$$= \inf_y[\textstyle\sum_{0\leq j\leq n} y_j\alpha_j - 0 \ / \ y_j\geq 0\ (j\in J) \text{ and } \sum_{0\leq j\leq n} y_j f_j - f_{n+1}\geq 0 \text{ on } S] \ \bullet$$

The problem $Q_{\leq}^{**}(\alpha_0,\ldots,\alpha_n)$ defined by the relation (7) is **the dual problem of the problem $Q_{\leq}(\alpha_0,\ldots,\alpha_n)$**.

Dual of primal minimization problem

The bipolar function $P^{**}(\alpha_0,\ldots,\alpha_n)$ $(\alpha_0,\ldots,\alpha_n\in\mathbf{R})$ of the value function $P(\alpha_0,\ldots,\alpha_n)$ of the minimization problem corresponding to problem $Q(\alpha_0,\ldots,\alpha_n)$ can be calculated in the same way as in the proof of Theorem 1. But then sup-polars must be used, i.e. $\inf_x$ and $\inf_y$ must be replaced by $\sup_x$ and $\sup_y$ (see App.C.C9 and C10). The result is

$$P^{**}(\alpha_0,\ldots,\alpha_n)$$

$$= \sup_y[\textstyle\sum_{0\leq j\leq n} y_j\alpha_j \ / \ \sum_{0\leq j\leq n} y_j f_j \leq f_{n+1} \text{ on } S] \ ((\alpha_0,\ldots,\alpha_n)\in R^{n+1}), \qquad (8)$$

where $y:=(y_0,\ldots,y_n)$ ranges over R^{n+1}.

The problem defined by (8) is **the dual problem of the minimization problem $P(\alpha_0,..,\alpha_n)$**. We observe that

$$P(\alpha_0,\ldots,\alpha_n) := \inf_{F\in \mathit{Distr}[S]}[\textstyle\int f_{n+1}dF \ / \ \int f_0 dF=\alpha_0,\ldots,\int f_n dF=\alpha_n]$$

$$= -\sup_{F\in \mathit{Distr}[S]}[\textstyle\int(-f_{n+1})dF \ / \ \int(-f_0)dF=-\alpha_0,\ldots,\int(-f_n)dF=-\alpha_n]$$

$$=: -(Q_-)(-\alpha_0,\ldots,-\alpha_n). \qquad (9)$$

Then, by Theorem 1,

$$(Q_-)^{**}(-\alpha_0,\ldots,-\alpha_n)$$

$$= \inf_y[\textstyle\sum_{0\leq j\leq n} -y_j\alpha_j \ / \ \sum_{0\leq j\leq n} -y_j f_j \geq -f_{n+1} \text{ on } S]$$

$$= -\sup_y[\textstyle\sum_{0\leq j\leq n} y_j\alpha_j \ / \ \sum_{0\leq j\leq n} y_j f_j \leq f_{n+1} \text{ on } S] \ \ ((\alpha_0,\ldots,\alpha_n)\in R^{n+1}).$$

Hence, by (8),

$$P^{**}(\alpha_0,\dots,\alpha_n) = -(Q_-)^{**}(-\alpha_0,\dots,-\alpha_n) \quad (\alpha_0,\dots,\alpha_n \in \mathbf{R}). \qquad (10)$$

The dual problem $P^{**}(\alpha_0,\dots,\alpha_n)$ can be **defined** by (10), where Q_- is defined by (9). Then the properties of the problem $P^{**}(\alpha_0,\dots,\alpha_n)$ and of its value function P^{**} can be deduced from the corresponding properties of the dual of the maximization problem. In this way, the theory of convex functions and the consideration of sup-polar functions can be avoided.

7.2. Properties of Primal and Dual Problems

7.2.1. Properties of Primal Problem

We continue with the primal maximization problem $Q(\alpha_0,\dots,\alpha_n)$ defined by (1), and **we henceforth assume that $f_0 \equiv 1$ on** S. We also consider the following assumptions.

***Boundedness assumption*: The function f_{n+1} is bounded on** S.

***Compactness-continuity assumption*: The set S is a compact subset of R and the functions $f_1,\dots,f_{n+1}$ are continuous on** S.

Any continuous function on a compact set is bounded on that set. Hence, the *compactness-continuity assumption* implies the *boundedness assumption*. The *compactness-continuity assumption* is satisfied if S is a finite set, because any function f is continuous on any finite set S.

A **k-atomic distribution** is a distribution expressible as cF where $c \geq 0$ and where F is a k-atomic probability distribution.

Theorem 3

a. **The value function Q defined by (1) on $\mathbf{R}^{n+1}$ has an affine upper bound if the *boundedness assumption* is satisfied.**

b. **Q is a concave function on $\mathbf{R}^{n+1}$. It is a proper concave function on $\mathbf{R}^{n+1}$ if the *boundedness assumption* is satisfied.**

c. **Q is a proper concave upper semi-continuous function on $\mathbf{R}^{n+1}$ if the *compactness-continuity assumption* is satisfied.**

d. If the *compactness-continuity assumption* is satisfied, then the problem

$$\mathbf{Q(\alpha_0,...,\alpha_n)\ \ ((\alpha_0,...,\alpha_n)\in dom\ Q)} \tag{11}$$

has an n+1-atomic solution.

Proof

Let $\alpha := (\alpha_0,\ldots,\alpha_n)$, $\beta := (\beta_0,\ldots,\beta_n)$.

a. Let $f_{n+1} \le b < \infty$ on S. For any feasible distribution F of problem $Q(\alpha)$,

$$\alpha_0 = \int dF = F(S)\ ,\ \int f_{n+1}dF \le b\ F(S) \le b\alpha_0.$$

Hence, $Q(\alpha) \le b\alpha_0$ ($\alpha\in$dom Q). Then $Q(\alpha)\le\alpha_0 b$ ($\alpha\in\mathbf{R}^{n+1}$), because $Q(\alpha)=-\infty$ ($\alpha\notin$dom Q).

b. We prove that

$$Q((1-p)\alpha+p\beta) \ge (1-p)Q(\alpha) + pQ(\beta)\ (\alpha,\beta\in\mathbf{R}^{n+1};\ 0\le p\le 1). \tag{12}$$

If p=0 or p=1, then (12) is an equality. Hence, we may assume that $0<p<1$. If $Q(\alpha)= -\infty$ or $Q(\beta)= -\infty$, then the last member of (12) must be understood as being equal to $-\infty$. Hence, we may assume that $-\infty < Q(\alpha)$, $-\infty < Q(\beta)$. Let a,b be such that

$$-\infty < a < Q(\alpha)\ ,\ -\infty < b < Q(\beta).$$

Then a feasible distribution F of problem $Q(\alpha)$ exists and a feasible distribution G of problem $Q(\beta)$ exists, such that

$$a < \int f_{n+1}dF\ ,\ b < \int f_{n+1}dG.$$

The feasibility conditions are

$$F\in \boldsymbol{Distr}[S]\ ,\ G\in \boldsymbol{Distr}[S]\ ,\ \int f_j dF = \alpha_j\ (j=0,\ldots,n)\ ,\ \int f_j dG = \beta_j\ (0=1,\ldots,n).$$

Let $H:=(1-p)F+pG$. Then

$$H\in \boldsymbol{Distr}[S]\ ,\ \int f_j dH = (1-p)\alpha_j+p\beta_j\ \ (j=0,\ldots,n).$$

Hence, H is a feasible distribution of problem $Q((1-p)\alpha+p\beta)$. Then

$$Q((1-p)\alpha+p\beta) \geq \int f_{n+1}dH = (1-p)\int f_{n+1}dF + p\int f_{n+1}dG > (1-p)a + pb,$$

$$Q((1-p)\alpha+p\beta) \geq (1-p)a + pb,$$

and then (12) results from $a\uparrow Q(\alpha)$ and $b\uparrow Q(\beta)$ in the latter relation. This proves that Q is concave.

Let the *boundedness assumption* be satisfied. Then $Q<\infty$ by a. The effective domain dom Q is not void. Indeed, $F\equiv 0\in$ ***Distr***[S], and this implies that the n+1-tuple (0,...,0) belongs to dom Q. Hence, Q is a proper concave function.

c. We now suppose that the *compactness-continuity assumption* is satisfied, and we prove that Q is upper semi-continuous. Let

$$\beta_\nu := (\beta_{\nu 0},\ldots,\beta_{\nu n}) \to (\alpha_0,\ldots,\alpha_n) =: \alpha \in \mathbf{R}^{n+1} \text{ as } \nu\uparrow\infty$$

and

$$Q(\beta_\nu) \to c \in \mathbf{R}\cup\{-\infty,+\infty\} \text{ as } \nu\uparrow\infty.$$

We have to prove that $c\leq Q(\alpha)$. We may assume that $-\infty < c$. Let b be such that $-\infty<b<c$. Then ν_0 exists, such that $b<Q(\beta_\nu)$ $(\nu\geq\nu_0)$. Only values $\nu\geq\nu_0$ are considered hereafter. A feasible distribution G_ν of the problem $Q(\beta_\nu)$ exists, such that

$$b < \int f_{n+1}dG_\nu \tag{13}$$

The integral constraints of the problem $Q(\beta_\nu)$ are satisfied for the feasible distribution G_ν:

$$\beta_{\nu j} = \int f_j dG_\nu \quad (j=0,\ldots,n). \tag{14}$$

$$G_\nu(S) = \int dG_\nu = \int f_0 dG_\nu = \beta_{\nu 0} \to \alpha_0 \text{ as } \nu\uparrow\infty. \tag{15}$$

This implies that the sequence $G_\nu(S)$ $(\nu=\nu_0,\nu_0+1,\ldots)$ is bounded. By the general compactness Theorem for distributions (App.E.Th.E3), some subsequence $G_{\nu(k)}$ (k=1,2,...) converges weakly to some distribution $G\in$ ***Distr***[S]. Then by Ch.2.Th.3.c (applied to the probability distributions $G_{\nu(k)}/G_{\nu(k)}(S)$),

$$\int f_j dG_{\nu(k)} \to \int f_j dG \text{ as } k\uparrow\infty \quad (j=0,\ldots,n+1). \tag{16}$$

In (13) and (14), we replace ν by $\nu(k)$, and then we let $k\uparrow\infty$:

$$b \leq \int f_{n+1} dG, \tag{17}$$

$$\alpha_j = \int f_j dG \quad (j=0,...,n). \tag{18}$$

By (18), G is a feasible distribution of the problem $Q(\alpha)$. Then, by (17), $b \leq Q(\alpha)$. For $b \uparrow c$, we obtain $c \leq Q(\alpha)$. This proves that Q is upper semi-continuous. By b, Q is a proper concave function.

d. Let the *compactness-continuity assumption* be satisfied, let $\alpha \in$ dom Q and let F be a feasible distribution of problem $Q(\alpha)$. Then

$$F(S) = \int dF = \int f_0 dF = \alpha_0.$$

Hence $\alpha_0 \geq 0$. If $\alpha_0=0$, then $F(\mathbf{R})=0$ and then $\alpha_1=...=\alpha_n=0$. Then the n+1-atomic distribution F=0 is a solution of the problem $Q(\alpha)$. Hence, we may assume that $\alpha_0>0$. Let us consider the probability problem

$$Q_0(\alpha_1/\alpha_0,...,\alpha_n/\alpha_0) := \sup_{G \in \mathbf{\mathit{Prob}}[S]} \left[\int f_{n+1} dG \;/\; \int f_1 dG = \alpha_1/\alpha_0, ..., \int f_n dG = \alpha_n/\alpha_0 \right].$$

Let F be a feasible distribution of the problem $Q(\alpha)$. Then $G:=F/\alpha_0$ is a feasible distribution of the problem $Q_0(\alpha_1/\alpha_0,...,\alpha_n/\alpha_0)$. Hence

$$(\alpha_1/\alpha_0,...,\alpha_n/\alpha_0) \in \text{dom } Q_0.$$

By Ch.6.Th.1, problem $Q_0(\alpha_1/\alpha_0,...,\alpha_n/\alpha_0)$ has a n+1-atomic solution G. Then $F:=\alpha_0 G$ is an n+1-atomic solution of the problem $Q(\alpha)$ •

Theorem 4

We consider the problem $Q(\alpha_0,\alpha_1,...,\alpha_n)$ $(\alpha_0,...,\alpha_n \in \mathbf{R})$ and the correspon-ding probability problem

$$\mathbf{Q_1(\alpha_1,...,\alpha_n) = Q(1,\alpha_1,...,\alpha_n) \quad (\alpha_1,...,\alpha_n \in R).}$$

Then

$$\mathbf{(\alpha_1,...,\alpha_n) \in \text{dom } Q_1 \Leftrightarrow (1,\alpha_1,...,\alpha_n) \in \text{dom } Q,}$$

$$\mathbf{(\alpha_1,...,\alpha_n) \in (\text{dom } Q_1)^\circ \Leftrightarrow (1,\alpha_1,...,\alpha_n) \in (\text{dom } Q)^\circ.}$$

Proof
The Theorem results from the following equivalences.

$$(\alpha_1,\dots,\alpha_n) \in \text{dom } Q_1 \Leftrightarrow (c, c\alpha_1,\dots,c\alpha_n) \in \text{dom } Q,$$

for all c>0.

$$(\alpha_1,\dots,\alpha_n)\in(\text{dom } Q_1)^\circ \quad :\Leftrightarrow$$

$$[\alpha_1-\varepsilon,\alpha_1+\varepsilon]\times\dots\times[\alpha_n-\varepsilon,\alpha_n+\varepsilon]\subseteq\text{dom } Q_1 \text{ for some } \varepsilon>0,$$

$$(\alpha_0,\dots,\alpha_n)\in(\text{dom } Q)^\circ \quad :\Leftrightarrow$$

$$[\alpha_0-\delta,\alpha_0+\delta]\times\dots\times[\alpha_n-\delta,\alpha_n+\delta]\subseteq\text{dom } Q \text{ for some } \delta>0 \quad \bullet$$

7.2.2. Connexions between Primal and Dual Problem

We continue with problem $Q(\alpha_0,\dots\alpha_n)$ ($\alpha_0,\dots,\alpha_n\in\mathbf{R}$) with $f_0\equiv1$ on S, and its dual problem $Q^{**}(\alpha_0,\dots,\alpha_n)$.

Theorem 5

a. **$Q\le Q^{**}$.**

b. **If the *boundedness assumption* is satisfied, then $Q=Q^{**}$ on the interior $(\text{dom } Q)^\circ$ of dom Q.**

c. **If the *compactness-continuity assumption* is satisfied, then $Q=Q^{**}$ on dom Q.**

Proof

a. By App.C.Th.C16.Cor.

b. Let the *boundedness assumption* be satisfied. By App.C.Th.C17.b, $Q^{**}=Q^{-}$. By Theorem 3.a,b, and App.C.Th.C7, Q is continuous on $(\text{dom } Q)^\circ$. Then by App.C.Th.C10.b, $Q=Q^{-}$ on $(\text{dom } Q)^\circ$.

c. If the *compactness-continuity assumption* is satisfied, then $Q=Q^{**}$ by Theorem 3.c and by App.C.Th.C17.c •

Theorem 6

We consider the problems $Q(\alpha)$ and $Q^{**}(\alpha)$ for fixed $\alpha:=(\alpha_0,\ldots,\alpha_n)$ in R^{n+1}. We suppose that $Q(\alpha)=Q^{**}(\alpha)$.

a. **Let F be a feasible distribution of problem $Q(\alpha)$, $y:=(y_0,\ldots,y_n)$ a feasible point of problem $Q^{**}(\alpha)$. Then**

$$\sum_{0\le j\le n} y_j f_j(\theta) \ge f_{n+1}(\theta) \quad (\theta\in S) \tag{19}$$

and

$$\int f_{n+1} dF \le \sum_{0\le j\le n} y_j\alpha_j. \tag{20}$$

The relation

$$\int f_{n+1} dF = \sum_{0\le j\le n} y_j\alpha_j. \tag{21}$$

holds iff F is a solution of $Q(\alpha)$ and y a solution of $Q^{**}(\alpha)$.

b. **Let**

$$F = p_1 A_{\theta_1} + \ldots + p_k A_{\theta_k}, \tag{22}$$

where $\theta_1,\ldots,\theta_k\in S$ and $p_1,\ldots,p_k>0$, be a k-atomic solution of problem $Q(\alpha)$, and let y be a solution of problem $Q^{**}(\alpha)$. Then $\theta_1,\ldots,\theta_k$ are roots of the equation

$$\sum_{0\le j\le n} y_j f_j(\theta) = f_{n+1}(\theta) \quad (\theta\in S). \tag{23}$$

Proof

a. The relation (19) is correct because y is a feasible point of $Q^{**}(\alpha)$. By the feasibility of F,

$$\alpha_j = \int f_j(\theta) dF(\theta) \quad (j=0,\ldots,n). \tag{24}$$

Then

$$\sum_{0\le j\le n} y_j\alpha_j = \sum_{0\le j\le n} y_j \int f_j(\theta) dF(\theta) \ge \int f_{n+1}(\theta) dF(\theta).$$

This proves (20).

Let F be a solution of problem $Q(\alpha)$ and y a solution of problem $Q^{**}(\alpha)$. Then

$$\int f_{n+1} dF = Q(\alpha) = Q^{**}(\alpha) = \sum_{0\le j\le n} y_j\alpha_j.$$

Conversely, let us assume (21). If F is not a solution of problem $Q(\alpha)$, then a feasible distribution F_0 exists, such that

$$\int f_{n+1}\, dF < \int f_{n+1} dF_0,$$

and then (20) is contradicted by the couple (F_0,y). In the same way, (20) is contradicted if y is not a solution of problem $Q^{**}(\alpha)$.

b. By (21), (22) and (24),

$$0 = \sum_{0\leq j\leq n} y_j\alpha_j - \int f_{n+1}dF = \sum_{0\leq j\leq n} y_j\int f_j dF - \int f_{n+1}dF$$

$$= \sum_{1\leq i\leq k} p_i[\sum_{0\leq j\leq n} y_j f_j(\theta_i) - f_{n+1}(\theta_i)]$$

By (19), the term in square brackets is positive for all $i=1,\dots,k$. It must vanish because $p_i>0$ •

7.2.3. Properties of Dual Problem

We consider the problem $Q(1,\alpha_1,\dots,\alpha_n)=Q_1(\alpha_1,\dots,\alpha_n)$, with $f_0\equiv 1$ on S, and the dual problem

$$Q^{**}(1,\alpha_1,\dots,\alpha_n) = \inf_y[y_0+\alpha_1 y_1+\dots+\alpha_n y_n \,/\, y_0+f_1 y_1+\dots+f_n y_n \geq f_{n+1} \text{ on S}], \quad (25)$$

for fixed $\alpha=(\alpha_1,\dots,\alpha_n)\in\mathbf{R}^n$. The **independence of functions** is defined in Ch.2.3.4.

Theorem 7

We assume that the *compactness-continuity assumption* is satisfied, that the functions $1,f_1,\dots,f_n$ are independent on S, and that $\alpha\in(\text{dom } Q_1)^\circ$. Then the dual problem $Q^{**}(1,\alpha)$ has a solution.

Proof
By Theorem 3.d, the problem $Q(1,\alpha)$ has a solution. Hence, the value $Q(1,\alpha)$ is finite. From the general relation $Q\leq Q^{**}$ (Theorem 5.a) results that $-\infty<Q(1,\alpha)\leq Q^{**}(1,\alpha)$. The problem $Q^{**}(1,\alpha)$ has feasible points. Indeed, f_{n+1} is bounded on S, by the *compactness-continuity assumption*. Let y_0 be so large that $y_0\geq f_{n+1}$ on S. Then the n+1-tuple $(y_0,0,\dots,0)$ satisfies the constraints of problem $Q^{**}(1,\alpha)$. The existence of feasible points implies that $Q^{**}(1,\alpha)<\infty$. Hence $Q^{**}(1,\alpha)\in\mathbf{R}$.

Then it is enough to prove that the condition Ch.5.(22) of Ch.5.Th.5 is verified. Here the relations in the first member of Ch.5.(22) become

$$(z_0,z) \neq (0,0) \;,\; z_0+f(\theta)z' \geq 0 \;(\theta\in S), \tag{26}$$

where

$$z_0\in \mathbf{R} \;,\; z:=(z_1,...,z_n)\in \mathbf{R}^n \;,\; f(\theta) := (f_1(\theta),...,f_n(\theta)).$$

Here, the function c′z in the last member of Ch.5.(22) becomes $z_0+\alpha z'$. We will prove that

$$(26) \Rightarrow z_0+\alpha z' > 0.$$

By Ch.2.Th.2.Cor.1, dom Q_1=Co$\{f(\theta)/\theta\in S\}$. It is assumed that α is an interior point of dom Q_1. Then, by Ch.1.Th.10.c, α is expressible as a convex combination with strictly positive coefficients, of at least n+1 different points of $\{f(\theta)/\theta\in S\}$. Let $\theta_1,...,\theta_k$ ($k\geq n+1$) be different points in S, such that

$$\alpha = \textstyle\sum_{1\leq j\leq k} p_j f(\theta_j) \;;\; k \geq n+1 \;;\; p_1,...,p_k > 0 \;;\; p_1+...+p_k = 1. \tag{27}$$

By (27),

$$z_0+\alpha z' = \textstyle\sum_{1\leq j\leq k} p_j[z_0+f(\theta_j)z']. \tag{28}$$

By (26),

$$z_0+f(\theta_j)z' \geq 0 \;\; (j=1,...,k). \tag{29}$$

At least one of the relations (29) is a strict inequality. Indeed if none is, then $z_0=0$ and $z=0$ by the independence assumption, but this contradicts the first relation (26). Hence, $z_0+\alpha z'>0$, because the coefficients $p_1,...,p_k$ are strictly positive •

7.3. Analytical Solutions by Dual Method

7.3.1. Basic Theorem

In this section 7.3, we consider the probability problems

$$Q(\alpha_1,...,\alpha_n) := \sup_{F\in \mathbf{\mathit{Prob}}[[a,b]]}\left[\textstyle\int f_{n+1}dF \;/\; \int f_1 dF=\alpha_1,...,\int f_n dF=\alpha_n\right] \tag{30}$$

and

$$P(\alpha_1,...,\alpha_n) := \inf_{F\in \mathbf{\mathit{Prob}}[[a,b]]}\left[\textstyle\int f_{n+1}dF \;/\; \int f_1 dF=\alpha_1,...,\int f_n dF=\alpha_n\right]. \tag{31}$$

We indicate a method, called **dual method**, allowing to find the analytic solution of the problems (30) and (31), even if the number of constraints is strictly larger than 2. It is based on the following Theorem 8, which proof does not depend on any previous results. But Theorem 3.d, Theorem 6, and Theorem 7, justify the existence of the curves involved in the statement of Theorem 8. They explain why the method must work when the assumptions on which the previous Theorems are based, are verified.

The dual method has the following advantage on the multi-dimensional method of Ch.6.1.3: All its geometry takes place in the usual plane $\mathbf{R}^2=\{(x,y)\}$. One of its inconvenients, when compared to the multi-dimensional method, is that is does not allow a global geometrical visualization of the problems and their solutions, simultaneously for all values of the parameters.

The dual method applies to pure integral optimization problems only. When the basic space of the problem is not a pure space, then the optimization problem must be replaced by its associated pure problem, before the dual method can be used.

Theorem 8

We consider the problem $Q(\alpha_1,\ldots,\alpha_n)$ defined by (30) and we assume that $(\alpha_1,\ldots,\alpha_n)\in$dom Q. Let Cur be the curve with equation

$$y = f_{n+1}(x) \quad (a\leq x\leq b). \tag{32}$$

Let Cur$(\alpha,\beta,\ldots,\gamma)$ be a curve with equation

$$y = c_0 + c_1f_1(x) + \ldots + c_nf_n(x) \quad (a\leq x\leq b), \tag{33}$$

situated above the fixed curve Cur, touching it at the points with absciss $\alpha,\beta,\ldots,\gamma\in[a,b]$.

Let the finite-atomic distribution

$$F := pA_\alpha+qA_\beta+\ldots+rA_\gamma \tag{34}$$

be a feasible distribution of the problem. Then F is a solution of the problem and its value is

$$Q(\alpha_1,\ldots,\alpha_n) = c_0 + c_1\alpha_1 + \ldots + c_n\alpha_n. \tag{35}$$

Proof
By the feasibility conditions on F,

$$pf_j(\alpha)+qf_j(\beta)+...+rf_j(\gamma) = \alpha_j \ (j=1,...,n). \qquad (36)$$

Let G be a feasible distribution of the problem. Then

$$c_0 + c_1\alpha_1 + ... + c_n\alpha_n = c_0 + c_1\int f_1 dG + ... + c_n\int f_n dG$$

$$= \int[c_0+c_1f_1(x)+...+c_nf_n(x)]dG(x) \geq \int f_{n+1}(x)dG(x),$$

because Cur(α,β,...,γ) is situated above Cur. Hence, $c_0+c_1\alpha_1+...+c_n\alpha_n$ is an upper bound of the integrals $\int f_{n+1}dG$ (G feasible distribution). The upper bound $c_0+c_1\alpha_1+...+c_n\alpha_n$ is attained at the point F. Indeed,

$$c_0 + c_1\alpha_1 + ... + c_n\alpha_n = c_0 + c_1\int f_1 dF + ... + c_n\int f_n dF$$

$$= \int[c_0+c_1f_1(x)+...+c_nf_n(x)]dF(x)$$

$$= p[c_0+c_1f_1(\alpha)+...+c_nf_n(\alpha)] + q[c_0+c_1f_1(\beta)+...+c_nf_n(\beta)] + ...$$

$$+ r[c_0+c_1f_1(\gamma)+...+c_nf_n(\gamma)]$$

$$= pf_{n+1}(\alpha) + qf_{n+1}(\beta) + ... + rf_{n+1}(\gamma) = \int f_{n+1}dF$$

because Cur(α,β,...,γ) touches Cur at the points α,β,...,γ •

This Theorem is valid in case of the minimization problem (31). Then the curve Cur(α,β,...,γ) must be situated under the fixed curve Cur.

7.3.2. Dual Method in Practice

Maximization problem

We consider the maximization problem $Q(\alpha_1,...,\alpha_n)$. We suppose that the *assumptions of the dual method*, explicited in the following section 7.3.3, are satisfied.

a. Research of the feasible subsets of [a,b]

A variable curve of the problem $Q(\alpha_1,...,\alpha_n)$ is any curve with an equation such as (33), where $c_0,c_1,...,c_n \in \mathbf{R}$. Let $\alpha,\beta,...,\gamma$ be $k \leq n+1$ points in [a,b]. We say that a variable curve is **a feasible curve of the set** $\{\alpha,\beta,...,\gamma\}$, if it is situated above **the fixed curve** $y=f_{n+1}(x)$ $(a \leq x \leq b)$ on [a,b], and if it touches the fixed curve at the points with absciss $\alpha,\beta,...,\gamma$. **A feasible subset of [a,b]**, is a subset $\{\alpha,\beta,...,\gamma\}$ with $k \leq n+1$ points, such that a corresponding feasible curve exists.

The first step of the dual method is the research of all feasible subsets $\{\alpha,\beta,...,\gamma\}$ of [a,b]. They are composed of **fixed points** (such as a,b), **variable points** (defined by inequalities) and **partially variable points** (defined by equalities). See the illustrations of Ch.8.3 for examples of feasible sets.

We notice that the feasible sets only depend on the functions $f_1,...,f_n,f_{n+1}$ and not on $\alpha_1,...,\alpha_n$.

b. Fixation of the probabilities, the variable and the partially variable points

By the next Theorem 9, a feasible set $\{\alpha,\beta,...,\gamma\}$ exists, such that some finite-atomic distribution

$$F := pA_\alpha + qA_\beta + ... + rA_\gamma \tag{37}$$

is a solution of the optimization problem. Then F is a feasible distribution. The feasibility constraints must allow to fix the unknown probabilities p,q,...,r and the variable and partially variable points of the feasible set $\{\alpha,\beta,...,\gamma\}$.

In most cases, the solution F is unique when the parameters $\alpha_1,...,\alpha_n$ are fixed. If the parameters $\alpha_1,...,\alpha_n$ are unspecified, then several potential analytic solutions F_k (k=1,...,m} corresponding to several classes $\{\alpha_k,\beta_k,...,\gamma_k\}$ of feasible sets, occur. Then (dom Q)° can be partitioned in m subsets D_k (k=1,...m) such that F_k is the solution of the maximization problem with parameters $(\alpha_1,...,\alpha_n) \in D_k$.

This partition is necessary when explicit analytic solutions must be furnished. If the goal is the numerical solution of the problem for fixed values of the parameters $\alpha_1,...,\alpha_n$, then this partition is superfluous, because the feasibility conditions can be tested for each potential solution F_k (k=1,...,m).

Minimization problem

The technique is identical in the case of the minimization problem $P(\alpha_1,...,\alpha_n)$, with feasible curves situated under the fixed curve.

7.3.3. Applicability of Dual Method

The ***assumptions of the dual method*** are the following.

a. The *compactness-continuity assumption* (7.2.1).

b. The functions $1,f_1,...,f_n$ are independent on [a,b] (Ch.2.3.4).

c. $(\alpha_1,...,\alpha_n)\in(\text{dom } Q)^\circ$

Theorem 9

Let the *assumptions of the dual method* be satisfied. Then the problem $Q(\alpha_1,...,\alpha_n)$ has a k-atomic solution F, with $k\leq n+1$, and such that the set of atoms of F is a feasible subset of [a,b].

Proof

We consider the problem $Q(\alpha_0,\alpha_1,...,\alpha_n)$ of section 7.2, and its dual problem $Q^{**}(\alpha_0,\alpha_n,...,\alpha_n)$ for $S:=[a,b]$, $\alpha_0:=1$, $f_0\equiv1$ on [a,b]. The problem $Q(\alpha_1,...,\alpha_n)$ of Theorem 8 is the same as problem $Q(\alpha_0,\alpha_1,...,\alpha_n)$ of 7.2 and it is also the same as problem $Q_1(\alpha_1,...,\alpha_n)$ of Th.7.

By Th.3.d, the problem $Q(\alpha_0,\alpha_1,...,\alpha_n)$ has an n+1-atomic solution F. It can be displayed as a convex combination

$$F = p_1A_{\theta_1} + ... + p_kA_{\theta_k},$$

where $\theta_1,...,\theta_k\in S$ and $p_1,...,p_k>0$, because the terms with a coefficient $p_i=0$ can be dropped. By Th.7, the dual problem $Q^{**}(\alpha_0,\alpha_1,...,\alpha_n)$ has a solution $(y_0,y_1,...,y_n)$. By Th.5.c, $Q=Q^{**}$ on dom Q. Hence,

$$Q(\alpha_0,\alpha_1,...,\alpha_n) =Q^{**}(\alpha_0,\alpha_1,...,\alpha_n). \quad (38)$$

We notice that $(1,\alpha_1,\dots,\alpha_n)\in(\text{dom } Q)^\circ\subseteq\text{dom } Q$, by Th.4. By (38) and by (19) and (23) of Th.6, the curve $\text{Cur}(\theta_1,\dots,\theta_k)$,

$$y = y_0 + y_1f_1(x) + \dots + y_nf_n(x) \quad (a\leq x\leq b)$$

is a feasible curve of the set $\{\theta_1,\dots,\theta_k\}$ •

It happens that the dual method works when *the assumptions of the dual method* are not satisfied. For instance, the assumption $(\alpha_1,\dots,\alpha_n)\in(\text{dom } Q)^\circ$ can be replaced by$(\alpha_1,\dots,\alpha_n)\in\text{dom } Q$ if the dual problem $Q^{**}(1,\alpha_1,\dots,\alpha_n)$ has a solution. Mostly we do not discuss the exceptional cases in which $(\alpha_1,\dots,\alpha_n)$ belongs to the frontier of dom Q. The practical importance of these cases is negligible.

In the case of moment problems, the effective domain dom Q results from the Theorems of Chapter 3. In case of more general problems, the effective domain of the problems

$$Q_k(\alpha_1,\dots,\alpha_k) := \sup_{F\in \boldsymbol{prob}[[a,b]]}[\textstyle\int f_{n+1}dF \;/\; \int f_1dF=\alpha_1,\dots,\int f_kdF=\alpha_k]$$

can be found, successively for k=1,2,... by the dual method itself. Indeed,

$$\text{dom } Q_k = \boldsymbol{Prob}[[a,b];\textstyle\int f_1dF=\alpha_1,\dots,\int f_kdF=\alpha_k].$$

If dom Q_{k-1} is known, then dom Q_k is the set of points $(\alpha_1,\dots,\alpha_{k-1},\alpha_k)$ with $(\alpha_1,\dots,\alpha_{k-1})\in\text{dom } Q_{k-1}$ and such that

$$P_{k-1}(\alpha_1,\dots,\alpha_{k-1}) \leq \alpha_k \leq Q_{k-1}(\alpha_1,\dots,\alpha_{k-1}),$$

where $P_{k-1}(\alpha_1,\dots,\alpha_k)$ is the value of the minimization problem corresponding to problem $Q_{k-1}(\alpha_1,\dots,\alpha_{k-1})$.

Chapter 8

Moment Problems by Dual Method

8.1. Feasible Sets and Polynomials

8.1.1. Moment Problems

In this Chapter we consider the integral maximization moment problem

$$Q(\mu_1,\ldots,\mu_n) := \sup_{F\in \boldsymbol{Prob}[a,b]}\left[\int\varphi dF \,/\, \mu_1,\ldots,\mu_n\right] \tag{1}$$

and the corresponding minimization problem

$$P(\mu_1,\ldots,\mu_n) := \inf_{F\in \boldsymbol{Prob}[a,b]}\left[\int\varphi dF \,/\, \mu_1,\ldots,\mu_n\right]. \tag{2}$$

We call $\int\varphi dF$ the **objective functional** of the problem and φ its **objective function**. The hypothetic space of the problems is the pure moment space

$$\boldsymbol{Prob}[[a,b];\mu_1,\ldots,\mu_n]. \tag{3}$$

It is the space of feasible distributions of problems (1) or (2). We here denote by

$$\mathrm{dom}_n[a,b] := \{(\mu_1,\ldots,\mu_n) \,/\, \boldsymbol{Prob}[[a,b];\mu_1,\ldots,\mu_n]\neq\varnothing\} \tag{4}$$

the effective domain of space (3). Then $\mathrm{dom}_n[a,b]$ is also the effective domain of problems (1) and (2). The topological interior of $\mathrm{dom}_n[a,b]$ is denoted by $\mathrm{dom}_n^\circ[a,b]$.

We recall that an atom of a distribution is a point bearing a strictly positive mass and that a k-atomic distribution may have strictly less than k atoms.

Let $A:=\{\theta_1,\ldots,\theta_k\}$ be a subset of [a,b], $\theta_1<\ldots<\theta_k$. We say that **A is an initial subset of [a,b]** if $\theta_1=a$, **a final subset** if $\theta_k=b$, **a narrow subset** if $a<\theta_1$ and $\theta_k<b$, **a broad subset** if $\theta_1=a$ and $\theta_k=b$.

An internal point of A (with respect to [a,b]) is a point $\theta_j \in A$ such that $a<\theta_j<b$. The points a and b are **external points of A**, if they belong to A.

Hence, the number of external points of a broad, initial, final, narrow subset of [a,b] is 2, 1, 1, 0 resp.

8.1.2. Feasible Finite-Atomic Distributions

Theorem 1

Let $(\mu_1,\ldots,\mu_n) \in \mathrm{dom}_n{}^\circ[a,b]$.

a. **The space**

$$\textit{Space} := \textit{Prob}[[a,b];\mu_1,\ldots,\mu_n]$$

has finite-atomic distributions with strictly more than n atoms.

b. **Let $G \in \textit{Space}$ be a finite-atomic distribution, A the set of atoms of G, i the number of internal points of A and e the number of external points of A. Then $2i+e \geq n+1$.**

Proof

Let $A=\{\theta_1,\ldots,\theta_k\}$, $\theta_1<\ldots<\theta_k$. Then b is equivalent to the following implications

$$a<\theta_1<\ldots<\theta_k<b \Rightarrow 2k\geq n+1, \tag{5}$$

$$a=\theta_1<\ldots<\theta_k<b \Rightarrow 2k\geq n+2, \tag{6}$$

$$a<\theta_1<\ldots<\theta_k=b \Rightarrow 2k\geq n+2, \tag{7}$$

$$a=\theta_1<\ldots<\theta_k=b \Rightarrow 2k\geq n+3, \tag{8}$$

because $k=i+e$ and resp. $e=0$, $e=1$, $e=1$, $e=2$ in (5), (6), (7), (8).

a. By Ch.2.Th.2.Cor.1, with $f_j(x):=x^j$ $(j=1,\ldots,n)$,

$$\mathrm{Dom}_n[a,b] = \mathrm{Co}\{(\theta,\theta^2,\ldots,\theta^n)/a\leq\theta\leq b\}. \tag{9}$$

By Ch.1.Th.10.c, the point $(\mu_1,\ldots,\mu_n)$ can be displayed as a convex combination

$$(\mu_1,\ldots,\mu_n) = \sum_{1\le i\le m} p_i(\theta_i,\theta_i^2,\ldots,\theta_i^n)$$

with

$$m\ge n+1 \ ;\ p_1,\ldots,p_m>0 \ ;\ \theta_1,\ldots,\theta_m \text{ different points in } [a,b]. \tag{10}$$

Then

$$\mu_j = p_1\theta_1^j + \ldots + p_m\theta_m^j \ (j=1,\ldots,n).$$

and then

$$F := p_1A_{\theta_1} + \ldots + p_mA_{\theta_m}. \tag{11}$$

belongs to ***Space***. This proofs the first part of the Theorem.

b. The implications (5), (6), (7) and (8) are proved for particular values of k. Then the general argument is transparent.

For the proof of (5), we take k=3, we assume that $2k=6\le n$ and we derive a contradiction. We consider the distribution (11) with $m\ge n+1\ge 7$. Let X,Y,Z,U be 4 independent random variables with distribution F. Then

$$E[(X-Y)^2(X-Z)^2(X-U)^2\,(Y-Z)^2(Y-U)^2\,(Z-U)^2] \tag{12}$$

$$= \iiint(x-y)^2(x-z)^2(x-u)^2(y-z)^2(y-u)^2(z-u)^2dF(x)dF(y)dF(z)dF(z)$$

$$= \sum\sum\sum\sum_{\alpha\beta\gamma\delta}p_\alpha p_\beta p_\gamma p_\delta\iiint(x-y)^2(x-z)^2(x-u)^2(y-z)^2(y-u)^2(z-u)^2$$
$$dA_{\theta_\alpha}(x)dA_{\theta_\beta}(y)dA_{\theta_\gamma}(z)dA_{\theta_\delta}(z)$$

$$= \sum\sum\sum\sum_{\alpha\beta\gamma\delta}p_\alpha p_\beta p_\gamma p_\delta(\theta_\alpha-\theta_\beta)^2(\theta_\alpha-\theta_\gamma)^2(\theta_\alpha-\theta_\delta)^2(\theta_\beta-\theta_\gamma)^2(\theta_\beta-\theta_\delta)^2(\theta_\gamma-\theta_\delta)^2, \tag{13}$$

where $\alpha,\beta,\gamma,\delta$ range over the set $\{1,\ldots,m\}$. The sum (13) is strictly positive because 4 different values $\alpha,\beta,\gamma,\delta$ can be selected in the set $\{1,\ldots,m\}$.

The expectation (12) equals a sum

$$\sum_{pqrs} a_{pqrs}E(X^pY^qZ^rU^s) = \sum_{pqrs} a_{pqrs}\mu_p\mu_q\mu_r\mu_s \tag{14}$$

with $p,q,r,s\le 6$. Hence, it depends on the moments $\mu_1,\ldots,\mu_6$ only. Then the expectation (12) is strictly positive if X, Y, Z, U are independent random variables with any distribution of ***Space***. The latter property is contradicted by

$$G := p_1 A_{\theta_1} + p_2 A_{\theta_2} + p_3 A_{\theta_3}, \quad \text{where } a<\theta_1 \text{ and } \theta_k<b.$$

Indeed, Let X,Y,Z,U be four independent random variables with distribution G. Then the expectation (12) still equals (13), but now $\alpha,\beta,\gamma,\delta$ range over the set $\{1,2,3\}$. Hence, at least two values $\alpha,\beta,\gamma,\delta$ are equal and then (13) vanishes.

For the proof of (6), we take k=3, we assume that $2k=6\le n+1$ and we derive a contradiction. We consider the distribution (11) with $m\ge n+1\ge 6$. Let X,Y,Z be 3 independent random variables with distribution F. Then

$$E[(X-Y)^2(Y-Z)^2(Z-X)^2(X-a)(Y-a)(Z-a)] \tag{15}$$

is a sum of terms

$$(\theta_\alpha-\theta_\beta)^2(\theta_\beta-\theta_\gamma)^2(\theta_\gamma-\theta_\alpha)^2(\theta_\alpha-a)(\theta_\beta-a)(\theta_\gamma-a) \tag{16}$$

with strictly positive coefficients. The expectation (15) depends only on the moments $\mu_1,\ldots,\mu_5$ and $n\ge 5$. Hence, (15) remains strictly positive if F is replaced by any distribution of ***Space***. This is contradicted by

$$G:= p_1 A_{\theta_1} + p_2 A_{\theta_2} + p_3 A_{\theta_3}, \text{ with } \theta_1:=a.$$

Indeed, the α,β,γ range over the set $\{1,2,3\}$. If α, β or γ equals 1, then term (16) vanishes with the factor $\theta_\alpha-a$, $\theta_\beta-a$ or $\theta_\gamma-a$. Hence α,β,γ range over the set $\{2,3\}$ and then the subscripts cannot be different. Then (16) vanishes again.

The proof of (7) is similar.

For the proof of (8), we take k=4, we assume that $2k=8\le n+2$ and we derive a contradiction. We consider the distribution (11) with $m\ge n+1\ge 7$. Let X,Y,Z be 3 independent random variables with distribution F. Then

$$E[(X-Y)^2(Y-Z)^2(Z-X)^2(X-a)(b-X)(Y-a)(b-Y)(Z-a)(b-Z)] \tag{17}$$

is a sum of terms

$$(\theta_\alpha-\theta_\beta)^2(\theta_\beta-\theta_\gamma)^2(\theta_\gamma-\theta_\alpha)^2(\theta_\alpha-a)(b-\theta_\alpha)(\theta_\beta-a)(b-\theta_\beta)(\theta_\gamma-a)(b-\theta_\gamma) \tag{18}$$

with strictly positive coefficients. Hence, (17) is strictly positive and remains so when F is replaced by any distribution of ***Space***. This is contradicted by

$$G:= p_1 A_{\theta_1} + p_2 A_{\theta_2} + p_3 A_{\theta_3} + p_4 A_{\theta_4}, \text{ with } \theta_1:=a \text{ and } \theta_4:=b.$$

Indeed, $\alpha,\beta,\gamma\in\{1,2,3,4\}$ in (18) and then (18) vanishes if $\alpha,\beta,\gamma=1$ or 4. Hence $\alpha,\beta,\gamma\in\{2,3\}$ and then (18) vanishes again •

8.1.3. Good Feasible Sets

We here recall some definitions connected to the dual method (Ch.7.3.2), and we adapt them to the case of the moment problems of this Chapter 8. **The fixed function** of the problems (1) and (2) is the function φ, and the corresponding **fixed curve** is the curve with equation

$$y = \varphi(x) \quad (a\leq x\leq b) \tag{19}$$

in $\mathbf{R}^2=\{(x,y)\}$. The **variable functions** are any polynomials

$$f(x) := c_0+c_1x+c_2x^2+\ldots+c_nx^n \; (c_0,\ldots c_n\in\mathbf{R}) \tag{20}$$

of degree n (We say that (12) is a polynomial of degree n, even if $c_n=0$). The corresponding **variable curves** are the curves with equation

$$y = f(x) \quad (a\leq x\leq b). \tag{21}$$

Let $\{\alpha_1,\ldots,\alpha_k\}$ be a set of k different points in [a,b] and let $k\leq n+1$. In the case of the maximizationn problem (1), the polynomial (20) is a **feasible polynomial** of the set $\{\alpha_1,\ldots,\alpha_k\}$, if it satisfies the conditions

$$\varphi(x) \leq f(x) \; (a\leq x\leq b) \;,\; \varphi(\alpha_j) = f(\alpha_j) \; (j=1,\ldots,k). \tag{22}$$

In case of the minimization problem (2), the polynomial (20) is a **feasible polynomial** of the set $\{\alpha_1,\ldots,\alpha_k\}$, if it satisfies the conditions

$$f(x) \leq \varphi(x) \; (a\leq x\leq b) \;,\; \varphi(\alpha_j) = f(\alpha_j) \; (j=1,\ldots,k). \tag{23}$$

The set $\{\alpha_1,\ldots,\alpha_k\}$ is **a feasible set** of problem (1) or (2), if it has some feasible polynomial. The set $\{\alpha_1,\ldots,\alpha_k\}$ is **a good feasible set** if it is a feasible set and if moreover $2i+e\geq n+1$, where i is the number of internal points of the set, and e its number of external points.

Hereafter, the problems (1) and (2) are considered for $(\mu_1,\ldots,\mu_n)\in\mathrm{dom}_n{}^\circ[a,b]$ only.

Then the set of atoms of any finite-atomic feasible distribution is a good feasible set by Theorem 1.b. Now Ch.7.Th.9 becomes the following Th.2.

Theorem 2

Let $(\mu_1,\ldots,\mu_n)\in \mathrm{dom}_n{}^\circ[a,b]$ and let the objective function φ of the problem

$$\sup_{F\in Prob[a,b]}\left[\int\varphi dF/\mu_1,\ldots,\mu_n\right] \text{ or } \inf_{F\in Prob[a,b]}\left[\int\varphi dF/\mu_1,\ldots,\mu_n\right]$$

be continuous on [a,b]. Then the problem has a k-atomic solution F, with $k\leq n+1$ atoms and such that the set of atoms of F is a good feasible set.

8.1.4. Polynomial Interpolation

In the research of feasible polynomials and feasible sets, we have to construct polynomials f with fixed values $f(\alpha)$, $f(\beta)$, ..., $f(\gamma)$, and some fixed values $f'(\alpha)$, $f''(\alpha)$, ..., $f'(\beta)$,$f''(\beta)$,..., ..., ..., $f'(\gamma)$, $f''(\gamma)$, ... They can most easily be found by **Newton's interpolation method**. The general method is clear from the following particular examples. All points $\alpha,\beta,\ldots$ are supposed to be different.

Example: **$f(\alpha)$, $f(\beta)$, $f(\gamma)$, $f(\delta)$ are fixed**

Then the polynomial f is displayed as

$$f(x) = a + b(x-\alpha) + c(x-\alpha)(x-\beta) + d(x-\alpha)(x-\beta)(x-\gamma). \qquad (24)$$

The coefficients a,b,c,d result from the replacement of x by $\alpha,\beta,\gamma,\delta$.

Let $\beta=\alpha+\varepsilon$. As $\varepsilon\to 0$, the polynomial (24) becomes

$$f(x) = a + b(x-\alpha) + c(x-\alpha)^2 + d(x-\alpha)^2(x-\gamma).$$

The fixation of $f(\alpha)$ and $f'\alpha)$ can be considered as the fixation of $f(\alpha)$ and $f(\alpha+\varepsilon)$ for small $\varepsilon\neq 0$. Even simpler: we imagine that $f(\alpha)$ is fixed twice, or that $f(\alpha),f(\alpha)$ is fixed. This explains the choice of the polynomial f(x) of the following example.

Example: **f(α), f′(α), f(β), f(γ) are fixed**

The polynomial f is displayed as

$$f(x) = a + b(x-\alpha) + c(x-\alpha)^2 + d(x-\alpha)^2(x-b). \tag{25}$$

Then

$$f'(x) = b + 2c(x-\alpha) + +2d(x-\alpha)(x-\beta) + d(x-\alpha)^2. \tag{26}$$

The coefficients a,b,c,d result from the replacement of x by α,β,γ in (25) or (26).

Now it is obvious how f must be displayed in the general case:

General case without derivatives: **f(α), f(β), ..., f(γ) fixed**

The polynomial f is displayed as

$$f(x) = a + b(x-\alpha) + c(x-\alpha)(x-\beta) + \ldots + d(x-\alpha)(x-\beta)\ldots(x-\gamma). \tag{27}$$

General case: **f(α), f(β), ..., f(γ) and some derivatives fixed**

Let θ be one of the numbers α,β,...,γ. If f(θ) and f′(θ) are fixed, then we apply the *general case without derivatives* with f(θ),f(θ) fixed. If f(θ),f′(θ),f″(θ) are fixed, then we apply the *general case without derivatives* with f(θ),f(θ),f(θ) fixed,... Any other number α,β,...,γ is treated similarly.

Example: **f(α), f′(α), f(β), f′(β), f″(β) fixed**

We apply the *general case without derivatives* with f(α),f(α),f(β),f(β),f(β) fixed. Hence, we display f as

$$f(x) = a + b(x-\alpha) + c(x-\alpha)^2 + d(x-\alpha)^2(x-\beta) + e(x-\alpha)^2(x-\beta)^2. \tag{28}$$

Five quantities are fixed. Hence, we stop with a formula with five unknown coefficients a,b,c,d,e. In order to find them, we calculate f′(x) and f″(x), from (28). Then the replacement of x by α or β in the expression of f(x), f′(x) or f″(x), furnishes the coefficients a,b,c,d,e.

We notice that the expression of f(x) depends on the order in which the fixed quantities are considered. If we take the fixed quantities of the foregoing example in the order, $f(\beta), f'(\beta), f''(\beta), f(\alpha), f'(\alpha)$, then we display f as

$$f(x) = a + b(x-\beta) + c(x-\beta)^2 + d(x-\beta)^3 + (x-\beta)^3(x-\alpha). \tag{29}$$

The polynomials (28) and (29) are represented in different ways, but they are identical by the following classical Theorem applied to their difference.

Theorem 3

Let f be a polynomial of degree n satisfying n+1 conditions

$$\mathbf{f(\alpha)=0\ ,\ f'(\alpha)=0\ ,\ \dots\ ,\ f(\beta)=0\ ,\ f'(\beta)=0\ ,\ \dots\ ,\ f(\gamma)=0\ ,\ f'(\gamma)=0, \dots}$$

where α, β, γ,... are different real numbers. Then $f \equiv 0$.

Proof
We demonstrate a particular case by a general argument. Let n=5, and let

$$f(\alpha)=0\ ,\ f'(\alpha)=0\ ,\ f''(\alpha)=0\ ,\ f(\beta)=0\ ,\ f(\gamma)=0\ ,\ f'(\gamma)=0. \tag{30}$$

The 6 particular polynomials

$$1\ ,\ (x-\alpha)\ ,\ (x-\alpha)^2\ ,\ (x-\alpha)^3\ ,\ (x-\alpha)^3(x-\beta)\ ,\ (x-\alpha)^3(x-\beta)(x-\gamma) \tag{31}$$

are independent. They form a basis of the vector space of polynomials of degree 5. Hence f(x) is a linear combination of polynomials (31):

$$f(x) = c_0 + c_1(x-\alpha) + c_2(x-\alpha)^2$$
$$+c_3(x-\alpha)^3 + c_4(x-\alpha)^3(x-\beta) + c_5(x-\alpha)^3(x-\beta)(x-\gamma).$$

Then

$$f(x) = c_0+c_1(x-\alpha)+c_2(x-\alpha)^2+(x-\alpha)^3 g(x)$$

where

$$g(x) := c_3+c_4(x-\beta)+c_5(x-\beta)(x-\gamma).$$

Then

$$f'(x) = c_1+2c_2(x-\alpha)+3(x-\alpha)^2 g(x)+(x-\alpha)^3 g'(x),$$

$$f''(x) = 2c_2+6(x-\alpha)g(x)+6(x-\alpha)^2 g'(x)+(x-\alpha)^3 g''(x),$$

$$g'(x) = c_4+c_5(x-\beta)+c_5(x-\gamma).$$

Then

$$0 = f(\alpha) = c_0 , 0 = f'(\alpha) = c_1 , 0 = f''(\alpha) = 2c_2,$$

$$0 = f(\beta) = (\beta-\alpha)^3 g(\beta) = (\beta-\alpha)^3 c_3 , c_3=0$$

$$0 = f(\gamma) = (\beta-\alpha)^3 g(\gamma) = (\beta-\alpha)^3(\gamma-\beta)c_4 , c_4=0,$$

$$0 = f'(\gamma) = 3(\gamma-\alpha)^3 g(\gamma)+(\gamma-\alpha)^3 g'(\gamma) = (\gamma-\alpha)^3(\gamma-\beta)c_5 , c_5=0 \bullet$$

8.2. Special Finite-Atomic Distributions

8.2.1. Notations

We denote by $s_{k,xy\ldots z}$ the sum of all products of k different elements x,y,...,z. In particular

$$s_{0,x} := 1 , s_{0,xy} := 1 , s_{0,xyz} := 1 , \ldots,$$

$$s_{1,x} := x , s_{1,xy} := x+y , s_{1,xyz} := x+y+z , \ldots,$$

$$s_{2,xy} := xy,$$

$$s_{2,xyz} := xy+xz+yz,$$

$$s_{2,xyzu} := xy+xz+xu+yz+yu+zu, \ldots,$$

$$s_{3,xyz} := xyz ,$$

$$s_{3,xyzu} := xyz+xyu+xzu+yzu,\ldots$$

We also use the notations

$$\mu_0:=1 , \mu_{j,x} := \mu_j-x\mu_{j-1} = s_{0,x}\mu_1-s_{1,x}\mu_{j-1} \text{ (j=1,2,...)}$$

$$\mu_{j,xy} := \mu_{j,x}-y\mu_{j-1,x}$$

$$= s_{0,xy}\mu_j-s_{1,xy}\mu_{j-1}+s_{2,xy}\mu_{j-2} \text{ (j=2,3,...)},$$

$$\mu_{j,xyz} := \mu_{j,xy}-z\mu_{j-1,xy}$$

$$= s_{0,xyz}\mu_j-s_{1,xyz}\mu_{j-1}+s_{2,xyz}\mu_{j-2}-s_{3,xyz}\mu_{j-3} \text{ (j=3,4,...)},$$

... ...

8.2.2. Finite-Atomic Distributions with Variable Atoms

We here consider finite-atomic distributions such as

$$p_1A_{\alpha_1} + \ldots + p_iA_{\alpha_i} + q_1A_{\theta_1} + \ldots + q_jA_{\theta_j}, \tag{32}$$

where $\alpha_1,\ldots,\alpha_i$ are fixed points, $\theta_1,\ldots,\theta_j$ are unknown points, called **variable points** (varying with $\mu_1,\ldots,\mu_n$) and $p_1,\ldots,p_i,q_1,\ldots,q_j$ are unknown coefficients.

Theorem 4

Let

$$p_1A_{\alpha_1}+\ldots+p_iA_{\alpha_i}+q_1A_{\theta_1}+\ldots+q_jA_{\theta_j} \in \textit{Prob}[[a,b];\mu_1,\ldots,\mu_{i+2j-1}]. \tag{33}$$

Then $\theta_1,\ldots,\theta_j$ are the roots of the equation

$$\begin{vmatrix} 1 & x & x^2 & \ldots & x^j \\ \mu_{i,\alpha_1,\ldots,\alpha_j} & \mu_{i+1,\alpha_1,\ldots,\alpha_j} & \mu_{i+2,\alpha_1,\ldots,\alpha_j} & \ldots & \mu_{i+j,\alpha_1,\ldots,\alpha_j} \\ \mu_{i+1,\alpha_1,\ldots,\alpha_j} & \mu_{i+2,\alpha_1,\ldots,\alpha_j} & \mu_{i+3,\alpha_1,\ldots,\alpha_j} & \ldots & \mu_{i+j+1,\alpha_1,\ldots,\alpha_j} \\ \ldots & \ldots & \ldots & \ldots & \ldots \\ \mu_{i+j-1,\alpha_1,\ldots,\alpha_j} & \mu_{i+j,\alpha_1,\ldots,\alpha_j} & \mu_{i+j+1,\alpha_1,\ldots,\alpha_j} & \ldots & \mu_{i+2j-1,\alpha_1,\ldots,\alpha_j} \end{vmatrix} = 0 \tag{34}$$

and $p_1, \ldots, p_i, q_1, \ldots, q_j$ satisfy the relations

$$p_1\alpha_1^k + \ldots + p_i\alpha_i^k + q_1\theta_1^k + \ldots + q_j\theta_j^k = \mu_k \ (k=0,1,\ldots,i+j-1). \tag{35}$$

Proof

We consider the case of i=2 fixed atoms $\alpha,\beta\in[a,b]$ and j=3 variable atoms θ,η,ξ. Then the general argument is translucent. Hence, the unknown distribution is

$$pA_\alpha+qA_\beta+rA_\theta+sA_\eta+tA_\xi.$$

The feasibility conditions are

$$p\alpha^k + q\beta^k + r\theta^k + s\eta^k + t\xi^k = \mu_k \ (k=0,1,\ldots,7). \tag{36}$$

Then

$$p\alpha^{k-1} + q\beta^{k-1} + r\theta^{k-1} + s\eta^{k-1} + t\xi^{k-1} = \mu_{k-1} \ (k=1,\ldots,7). \tag{37}$$

We substract (37), multiplied by α, from (36):

$$q\beta^{k-1}\beta_\alpha + r\theta^{k-1}\theta_\alpha + s\eta^{k-1}\eta_\alpha + t\xi^{k-1}\xi_\alpha = \mu_{k,\alpha} \ (k=1,\ldots,7), \tag{38}$$

where $x_y:=x-y$ ($x,y\in\mathbf{R}$). Then

$$q\beta^{k-2}\beta_\alpha + r\theta^{k-2}\theta_\alpha + s\eta^{k-2}\eta_\alpha + t\xi^{k-2}\xi_\alpha = \mu_{k-1,\alpha} \ (k=2,\ldots,7). \tag{39}$$

We substract (39), multiplied by β, from (38):

$$r\theta^{k-2}\theta_\alpha\theta_\beta + s\eta^{k-2}\eta_\alpha\eta_\beta + t\xi^{k-2}\xi_\alpha\xi_\beta = \mu_{k,\alpha\beta} \ (k=2,\ldots,7). \tag{40}$$

Then

$$r\theta^{k-3}\theta_\alpha\theta_\beta + s\eta^{k-3}\eta_\alpha\eta_\beta + t\xi^{k-3}\xi_\alpha\xi_\beta = \mu_{k-1,\alpha\beta} \ (k=3,\ldots,7). \tag{41}$$

We substract (41), multiplied by θ, from (40):

$$s\eta^{k-3}\eta_\alpha\eta_\beta\eta_\theta + t\xi^{k-3}\xi_\alpha\xi_\beta\xi_\theta = \mu_{k,\alpha\beta\theta} \ (k=3,\ldots,7). \tag{42}$$

Then

$$s\eta^{k-4}\eta_\alpha\eta_\beta\eta_\theta + t\xi^{k-4}\xi_\alpha\xi_\beta\xi_\theta = \mu_{k-1,\alpha\beta\theta} \ (k=4,5,6,7). \tag{43}$$

We substract (43), multiplied by η, from (42):

$$t\xi^{k-4}\xi_\alpha\xi_\beta\xi_\theta\xi_\eta = \mu_{k,\alpha\beta\theta\eta} \ (k=4,5,6,7). \tag{44}$$

Then

$$t\xi^{k-5}\xi_\alpha\xi_\beta\xi_\theta\xi_\eta = \mu_{k-1,\alpha\beta\theta\eta} \ (k=5,6,7). \tag{45}$$

We substract (45), multiplied by ξ, from (44):

$$\mu_{k,\alpha\beta\theta\eta\xi} = 0 \ \ (k=5,6,7). \tag{46}$$

The relation

$$\mu_{k,\alpha\beta\theta\eta\xi} = \mu_{k,\alpha\beta} - (\theta+\eta+\xi)\mu_{k-1,\alpha\beta} + (\theta\eta+\eta\xi+\xi\theta)\mu_{k-2,\alpha\beta} - \theta\eta\xi\mu_{k-3,\alpha\beta}$$

is direct. Hence, the system (46) for the unknown atoms θ,η,ξ is

$$\mu_{5,\alpha\beta} - (\theta+\eta+\xi)\mu_{4,\alpha\beta} + (\theta\eta+\eta\xi+\xi\theta)\mu_{3,\alpha\beta} - \theta\eta\xi\mu_{2,\alpha\beta} = 0, \tag{47}$$

$$\mu_{6,\alpha\beta} - (\theta+\eta+\xi)\mu_{5,\alpha\beta} + (\theta\eta+\eta\xi+\xi\theta)\mu_{4,\alpha\beta} - \theta\eta\xi\mu_{3,\alpha\beta} = 0, \tag{47}$$

$$\mu_{7,\alpha\beta} - (\theta+\eta+\xi)\mu_{6,\alpha\beta} + (\theta\eta+\eta\xi+\xi\theta)\mu_{5,\alpha\beta} - \theta\eta\xi\mu_{4,\alpha\beta} = 0. \tag{47}$$

The numbers θ,η,ξ satisfy the equation of the third degree

$$(x-\theta)(x-\eta)(x-\xi) = 0,$$

i.e.

$$x^3 - (\theta+\eta+\xi)x^3 + (\theta\eta+\eta\xi+\xi\theta)x - \theta\eta\xi = 0. \tag{48}$$

The coefficients $(\theta+\eta+\xi)$, $(\theta\eta+\eta\xi+\xi\theta)$, $\theta\eta\xi$ result from the system (47) by Cramer's rule. Then the equation (48) can be displayed as

$$\begin{vmatrix} 1 & x & x^2 & x^3 \\ \mu_{2,\alpha\beta} & \mu_{3,\alpha\beta} & \mu_{4,\alpha\beta} & \mu_{5,\alpha\beta} \\ \mu_{3,\alpha\beta} & \mu_{4,\alpha\beta} & \mu_{5,\alpha\beta} & \mu_{6,\alpha\beta} \\ \mu_{4,\alpha\beta} & \mu_{5,\alpha\beta} & \mu_{6,\alpha\beta} & \mu_{7,\alpha\beta} \end{vmatrix} = 0. \qquad \bullet$$

8.2.3. Moment Problems

We consider **the moment optimization problems** with moment constraints

$$Q_{mom}(\mu_1,\dots,\mu_n) := \sup_{F\in \mathbf{\mathit{Prob}}[a,b]}[\int x^{n+1}dF(x) \,/\, \mu_1,\dots,\mu_n] \tag{49}$$

and

$$P_{mom}(\mu_1,\dots,\mu_n) := \inf_{F\in \mathbf{\mathit{Prob}}[a,b]}[\int x^{n+1}dF(x) \,/\, \mu_1,\dots,\mu_n]. \tag{50}$$

Lemma 1

Let Feas be a feasible set of problem (49) or (50). Then $2i+e\leq n+1$, where i is the number of internal points of Feas and e its number of external points.

Proof

Let f be a feasible polynomial (of degree n) of the set Feas and let $g:=\varphi-f$, where $\varphi(x):=x^{n+1}$. Let c be an internal point of Feas. Then $f(c)=\varphi(c)$ by definition of feasible polynomial of a set, and $f'(c)=\varphi'(c)$ because otherwise it is impossible that $f\leq\varphi$ or $\varphi\leq f$ on [a,b]. Hence

$$g(c)=0\ ,\ g'(c)=0\ \text{(c internal point of Feas)}. \tag{51}$$

If d is an external point of Feas, then $f(d)=\varphi(d)$:

$$g(d)=0 \quad \text{(d external point of Feas).} \tag{52}$$

The relations (51) and (52) define 2i+e conditions on the polynomial g of degree n+1. If 2i+e>n+1, then $g\equiv 0$ by Theorem 3. Then $\varphi=f$ and this is impossible because the degree of f is n and $\varphi(x)=x^{n+1}$. Hence $2i+e\leq n+1$ •

Lemma 2

Let $(\mu_1,\ldots,\mu_n)\in \mathrm{dom}_n°[a,b]$ (n=2j or n=2j−1).

a. The good feasible sets of the problem $P_{mom}(\mu_1,\ldots,\mu_{2j-1})$ are sets

$$\{\theta_1,\ldots,\theta_j\} \text{ with } a<\theta_1<\ldots<\theta_j<b. \tag{53}$$

b. The good feasible sets of the problem $P_{mom}(\mu_1,\ldots,\mu_{2j})$ are sets

$$\{a,\theta_1,\ldots,\theta_j\} \text{ with } a<\theta_1<\ldots<\theta_j<b. \tag{54}$$

c. The good feasible sets of the problem $Q_{mom}(\mu_1,\ldots,\mu_{2j}\}$ are sets

$$\{\theta_1,\ldots,\theta_j,b\} \text{ with } a<\theta_1<\ldots<\theta_j<b. \tag{55}$$

d. The good feasible sets of the problem $Q_{mom}(\mu_1,\ldots,\mu_{2j-1})$ are sets

$$\{a,\theta_1,\ldots,\theta_{j-1},b\} \text{ with } a<\theta_1<\ldots<\theta_{j-1}<b. \tag{56}$$

Proof

Let Feas be a good feasible set of $Q_{mom}(\mu_1,\ldots,\mu_n)$ or $P_{mom}(\mu_1,\ldots,\mu_n)$ with i internal points and e external points. Then $2i+e\geq n+1$ by the definition of a good feasible set (8.1.3) and $2i+e\leq n+1$ by Lemma 1. Hence 2i+e=n+1. If n=2j, then 2i+e=2j+1 and then e−1 is an even integer. Hence, then e=1 and i=j:

The good feasible sets of the problem $P_{mom}(\mu_1,\ldots,\mu_{2j})$ or $Q_{mom}(\mu_1,\ldots,\mu_{2j})$ are sets (54) or (55). (57)

If n=2j−1, then 2i+e=2j and e is an even integer. If e=0 then i=j. If e=2, then i=j−1. Hence,

The good feasible sets of the problem $P_{mom}(\mu_1,\ldots,\mu_{2j-1})$ or $Q_{mom}(\mu_1,\ldots,\mu_{2j-1})$ are sets (53) or (56). (58)

But

$$\text{(53) cannot be a good feasible set of } Q_{mom}(\mu_1,\ldots,\mu_{2j-1}), \tag{59}$$

$$\text{(56) cannot be a good feasible set of } P_{mom}(\mu_1,\ldots,\mu_{2j-1}), \tag{60}$$

$$\text{(54) cannot be a good feasible set of } Q_{mom}(\mu_1,\ldots,\mu_{2j}), \tag{61}$$

$$\text{(55) cannot be a good feasible set of } P_{mom}(\mu_1,\ldots,\mu_{2j}). \tag{62}$$

Indeed, the propositions (59), (60), (61) and (62) are direct by Theorem 3 and by the consideration of the involved polynomials on **R** (instead of on [a,b]).

As an example, we treat (59) with j=3. We assume that that narrow set $\{\theta_1,\theta_2,\theta_3\}$ is a good feasible set of problem $Q_{mom}(\mu_1,\ldots\mu_5)$ and that f is the corresponding feasible polynomial. This cannot be, by Theorem 3 and by the argument of the Lemma, because the curve y=f(x) has an intersection with the fixed curve $y=x^6$ on $]b,\infty[$. Indeed, x^6 goes faster to $+\infty$ as $x\uparrow\infty$ than any power $x^1,\ldots,x^5$. (See Fig.10) •

Some good feasible sets and corresponding feasible polynomials are represented in figures 11, 12, 13 and 14.

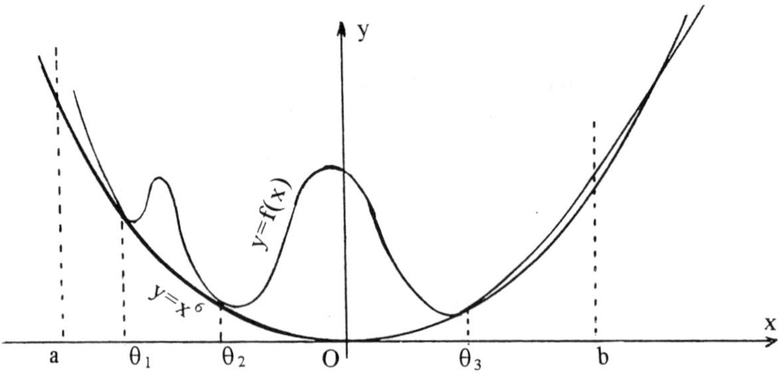

Fig.10. $\{\theta_1,\theta_2,\theta_3\}$ cannot be a good feasible set of $Q_{mom}(\mu_1,\ldots,\mu_5)$

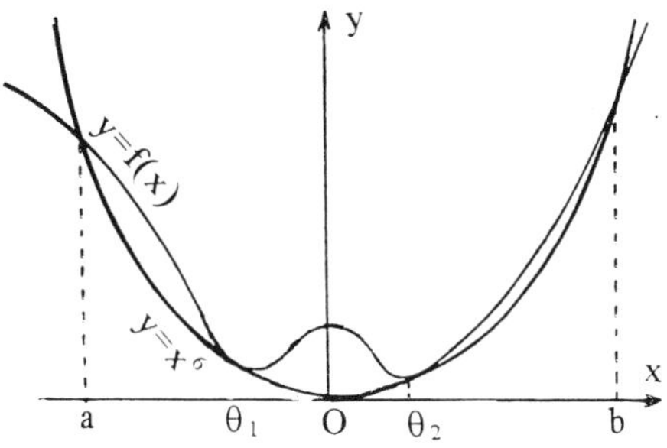

Fig.11. $\{a,\theta_1,\theta_2,b\}$ is a good feasible set of $Q_{mom}(\mu_1,\ldots,\mu_5\}$

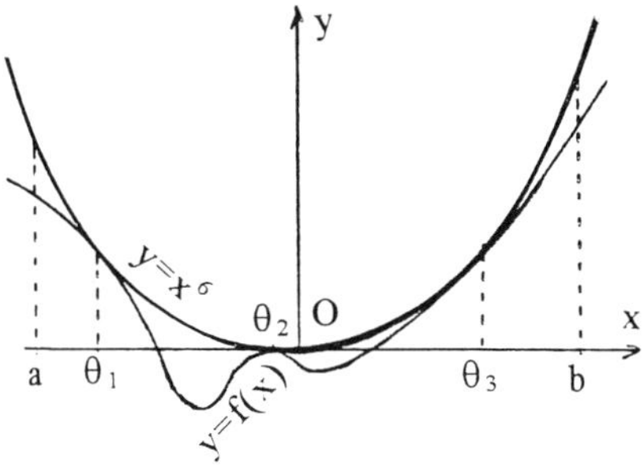

Fig.12. $\{\theta_1,\theta_2,\theta_3\}$ is a good feasible set of $P_{mom}(\mu_1,\ldots,\mu_5\}$

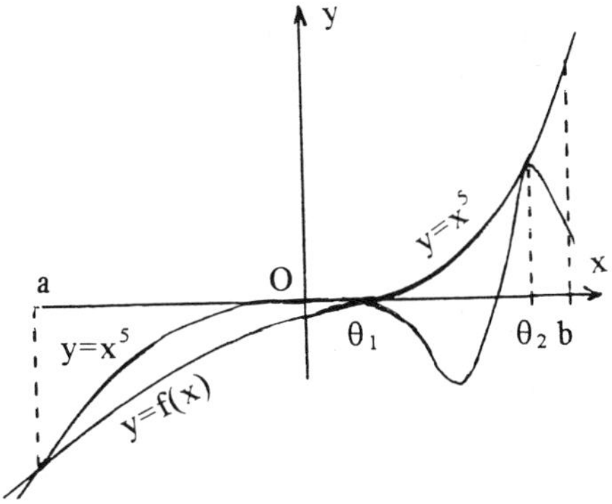

Fig.13. $\{a,\theta_1,\theta_2\}$ is a good feasible set of $Q_{mom}(\mu_1,\ldots,\mu_4\}$

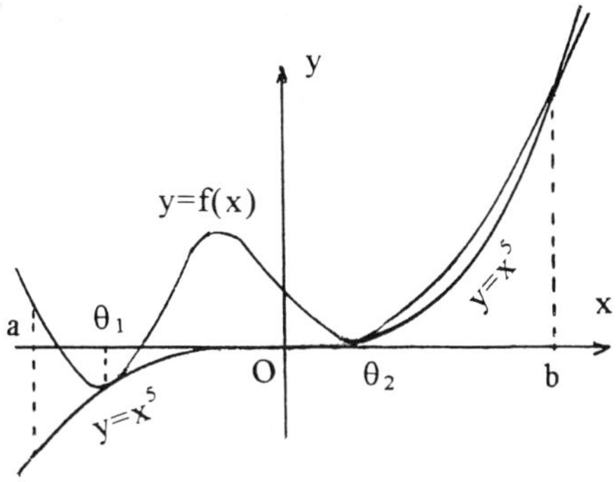

Fig.14. $\{\theta_1,\theta_2,b\}$ is a good feasible set of $P_{mom}(\mu_1,\ldots,\mu_4\}$

8.2.4. Existence of Special Extremal Distributions

Theorem 5

a. (Existence of narrow special distribution)

Let $(\mu_1,...,\mu_{2j-1}) \in \mathrm{Dom}_{2j-1}°[a,b]$. Let $\theta_1,...,\theta_j$ be the roots of the equation

$$\begin{vmatrix} 1 & x & x^2 & \cdots & x^j \\ \mu_0 & \mu_1 & \mu_2 & \cdots & \mu_j \\ \mu_1 & \mu_2 & \mu_3 & \cdots & \mu_{j+1} \\ \cdots & \cdots & \cdots & \cdots & \cdots \\ \mu_{j-1} & \mu_j & \mu_{j+1} & \cdots & \mu_{2j-1} \end{vmatrix} = 0. \tag{63}$$

Then $\theta_1,...,\theta_j$ are different numbers in $]a,b[$. Let $q_1,...,q_j$ be the numbers defined by the Vandermonde system

$$q_1\theta_1^k + ... + q_j\theta_j^k = \mu_k \ (k=0,1,...,j-1). \tag{64}$$

Then $q_1,...q_j$ are strictly positive and

$$q_1 A_{\theta_1} + ... + q_j A_{\theta_j} \in \mathbf{\mathit{Prob}}[[a,b];\mu_1,...,\mu_{2j-1}]. \tag{65}$$

b. (Existence of initial special distribution)

Let $(\mu_1,...,\mu_{2j}) \in \mathrm{Dom}_{2j}°[a,b]$. Let $\theta_1,...,\theta_j$ be the roots of the equation

$$\begin{vmatrix} 1 & x & x^2 & \cdots & x^j \\ \mu_{1,a} & \mu_{2,a} & \mu_{3,a} & \cdots & \mu_{j+1,a} \\ \mu_{2,a} & \mu_{3,a} & \mu_{4,a} & \cdots & \mu_{j+2,a} \\ \cdots & \cdots & \cdots & \cdots & \cdots \\ \mu_{j,a} & \mu_{j+1,a} & \mu_{j+2,a} & \cdots & \mu_{2j,a} \end{vmatrix} = 0. \tag{66}$$

Then $\theta_1,...,\theta_j$ are different numbers in $]a,b[$. Let $p,q_1,...,q_j$ be the solution of the Vandermonde system

$$pa^k + q_1\theta_1^k + ... + q_j\theta_j^k = \mu_k \ (k=0,1,...,j). \tag{67}$$

Then $p,q_1,...q_j$ are strictly positive and

$$pA_a + q_1A_{\theta_1} + \ldots + q_jA_{\theta_j} \in \mathit{Prob}[[a,b];\mu_1,\ldots,\mu_{2j}]. \quad (68)$$

c. (Existence of final special distribution)

Let $(\mu_1,\ldots,\mu_{2j})\in \mathrm{Dom}_{2j}°[a,b]$. Let $\theta_1,\ldots,\theta_j$ be the roots of the equation

$$\begin{vmatrix} 1 & x & x^2 & \ldots & x^j \\ \mu_{1,b} & \mu_{2,b} & \mu_{3,b} & \ldots & \mu_{j+1,b} \\ \mu_{2,b} & \mu_{3,b} & \mu_{4,b} & \ldots & \mu_{j+2,b} \\ \ldots & \ldots & \ldots & \ldots & \ldots \\ \mu_{j,b} & \mu_{j+1,b} & \mu_{j+2,b} & \ldots & \mu_{2j,b} \end{vmatrix} = 0. \quad (69)$$

Then $\theta_1,\ldots,\theta_j$ are different numbers in $]a,b[$. Let $q_1,\ldots,q_j,p$ be the numbers defined by the Vandermonde system

$$q_1\theta_1^k + \ldots + q_j\theta_j^k + pb^k = \mu_k \ (k=0,1,\ldots,j). \quad (70)$$

Then $q_1,\ldots q_j,p$ are strictly positive and

$$q_1A_{\theta_1} + \ldots + q_jA_{\theta_j} + pA_b \in \mathit{Prob}[[a,b];\mu_1,\ldots,\mu_{2j}]. \quad (71)$$

d. (Existence of broad special distribution)

Let $(\mu_1,\ldots,\mu_{2j+1})\in \mathrm{Dom}_{2j+1}°[a,b]$. Let $\theta_1,\ldots,\theta_j$ be the roots of the equation

$$\begin{vmatrix} 1 & x & x^2 & \ldots & x^j \\ \mu_{2,ab} & \mu_{3,ab} & \mu_{4,ab} & \ldots & \mu_{j+2,ab} \\ \mu_{3,ab} & \mu_{4,ab} & \mu_{5,ab} & \ldots & \mu_{j+3,ab} \\ \ldots & \ldots & \ldots & \ldots & \ldots \\ \mu_{j+1,ab} & \mu_{j+2,ab} & \mu_{j+3,ab} & \ldots & \mu_{2j+1,ab} \end{vmatrix} = 0. \quad (72)$$

Then $\theta_1,\ldots,\theta_j$ are different numbers in $]a,b[$. Let $p_1,q_1,\ldots q_j,p_2$ be the numbers defined by the Vandermonde system

$$p_1a^k + q_1\theta_1^k + \ldots + q_j\theta_j^k + p_2b^k = \mu_k \ (k=0,1,\ldots,j+1). \quad (73)$$

Then $p_1,q_1,\ldots q_j,p_2$ are strictly positive and

$$p_1A_a + q_1A_{\theta_1} + \ldots + q_jA_{\theta_j} + p_2A_b \in \mathit{Prob}[[a,b];\mu_1,\ldots,\mu_{2j+1}]. \quad (74)$$

Proof

a. By Theorem 2, problem $P_{mom}(\mu_1,\dots,\mu_{2j-1})$ has a finite-atomic solution F with a good feasible set of atoms. By Lemma 2, this set is some set (53). Then F can be displayed as the distribution in the first member of (65). The moment constraints and the probability constraint are satisfied by F. By Theorem 4, relations (63) and (64) are satisfied.

b. Same proof, but now based on Lemma 2.b.

c. By Lemma 2.c.

d. By Lemma 2.d •

8.2.5. Particular Special Distributions

We assume that $(\mu_1,\dots,\mu_n)$ is an interior point of the effective domain in the following examples. We explicit the atoms of the special distributions in case of n=1,2,3 or 4 moment constraints. If the number of atoms is k (k=2 or 3 if n= 1,2,3 or 4), then the corresponding masses (p,q if k=2; p,q,r if k=3) result from the Vandermonde system expressing that the probability constraint and the first k–1 moment constraints are satisfied.

One moment constraint

The **narrow finite-atomic distribution** of the space ***Prob***$[[a,b];\mu_1]$ is the 1-atomic distribution A_{μ_1}. Its **broad finite-atomic distribution** is the 2-atomic distribution

$$pA_a + qA_b, \tag{75}$$

Two moment constraints

The **initial finite-atomic distribution** of the space ***Prob***$[[a,b];\mu_1,\mu_2]$ is the 2-atomic distribution (Th.5.b, j=1)

$$pA_a + qA_\theta, \tag{76}$$

where

$$\theta = \mu_{2,a}/\mu_{1,a} = (\mu_2 - a\mu_1)/(\mu_1 - a). \tag{77}$$

The **final finite-atomic distribution** of the space ***Prob***$[[a,b];\mu_1,\mu_2]$ is the 2-atomic distribution (Th.5.c, j=1)

$$pA_\theta + qA_b, \tag{78}$$

where

$$\theta = \mu_{2,b}/\mu_{1,b} = (b\mu_1-\mu_2)/(b-\mu_1). \tag{79}$$

Three moment constraints

The **narrow finite-atomic distribution** of ***Prob***$[[a,b];\mu_1,\mu_2,\mu_3]$ is the 2-atomic distribution (Th.5.a, j=2)

$$pA_\theta + qA_\eta, \tag{80}$$

where

$$\theta = [-(\mu_1\mu_2-\mu_3)-[(\mu_1\mu_2-\mu_3)^2-4(\mu_2-\mu_1^2)(\mu_1\mu_3-\mu_2^2)]^{1/2}]/[2(\mu_2-\mu_1^2)], \quad (81)$$

$$\eta = [-(\mu_1\mu_2-\mu_3)+[(\mu_1\mu_2-\mu_3)^2-4(\mu_2-\mu_1^2)(\mu_1\mu_3-\mu_2^2)]^{1/2}]/[2(\mu_2-\mu_1^2)]. \quad (81)$$

The **broad finite-atomic distribution** of ***Prob***$[[a,b];\mu_1,\mu_2,\mu_3]$ is the 3-atomic distribution (Th.5.d, j=1)

$$pA_a + qA_\theta + rA_b, \tag{82}$$

where

$$\theta = \mu_{3,ab}/\mu_{2,ab} = [\mu_3-(a+b)\mu_2+ab\mu_1]/[\mu_2-(a+b)\mu_1+ab]. \tag{83}$$

Four moment constraints

The **initial finite-atomic distribution** of ***Prob***$[[a,b];\mu_1,\mu_2,\mu_3,\mu_4]$ is the 3-atomic distribution (Th.5.b, j=2)

$$pA_a + qA_\theta + rA_\eta, \tag{84}$$

where

$$\theta = [-\mu_{2314,a}-[(\mu_{2314,a})^2-4\mu_{1322,a}\mu_{2433,a}]^{1/2}]/(2\mu_{1322,a}), \quad (85)$$

$$\eta = [-\mu_{2314,a}+[(\mu_{2314,a})^2-4\mu_{1322,a}\mu_{2433,a}]^{1/2}]/(2\mu_{1322,a}), \quad (85)$$

$$\begin{aligned}\mu_{ijk\nu,x} &:= \mu_{i,x}\mu_{j,x} - \mu_{k,x}\mu_{\nu,x} \\ &= (\mu_i-x\mu_{i-1})(\mu_j-x\mu_{j-1})-(\mu_k-x\mu_{k-1})(\mu_\nu-x\mu_{\nu-1}) \ , \ \ \mu_0:=1.\end{aligned} \tag{86}$$

The **final finite-atomic distribution** of ***Prob***$[[a,b];\mu_1,\mu_2,\mu_3,\mu_4]$ is the 3-atomic distribution (Th.5.c, j=2)

$$pA_\theta + qA_\eta + rA_b, \tag{87}$$

where

$$\theta = [-\mu_{2314,b} - [(\mu_{2314,b})^2 - 4\mu_{1322,b}\mu_{2433,b}]^{1/2}]/(2\mu_{1322,b}), \tag{88}$$

$$\eta = [-\mu_{2314,b} + [(\mu_{2314,b})^2 - 4\mu_{1322,b}\mu_{2433,b}]^{1/2}]/(2\mu_{1322,b}). \quad (88)$$

8.3. Illustrations: Unloaded Stop-Loss Premium Maximization

8.3.1. Problems and Method of Solution

We consider the **stop-loss problems**

$$Q_{SL}(\mu_1,\ldots,\mu_n) := \sup_{F\in \boldsymbol{Prob}[[a,b]]}[\int\varphi(x)dF(x) \,/\, \mu_1,\ldots,\mu_n], \tag{89}$$

$$Q_{SL,m}(\mu_1,\ldots,\mu_n) := \sup_{F\in \boldsymbol{Prob}[[a,b];m\text{-unim}]}[\int\varphi(x)dF(x) \,/\, \mu_1,\ldots,\mu_n], \tag{90}$$

with $[a,b]\subseteq \mathbf{R}_+$, t fixed in]a,b[, m fixed in [a,b] and

$$\varphi(x) := (x-t)_+ \ (a\le x\le b). \tag{91}$$

Interpretation

Let $X\ge 0$ be a random variable, interpreted as a risk covered by an insurance company. The risk is reinsured by an excess of loss treaty with **retention limit** t. This means that the reinsurance company covers the part

$$(X-t)_+ := \max(0,X-t) \tag{92}$$

of the risk X. The hypothetic space of the reinsurer is

$$\boldsymbol{Space_{SL}} := \boldsymbol{Prob}[[a,b];\mu_1,\ldots,\mu_n] \tag{93}$$

in case of problem $Q_{SL}(\mu_1,\ldots,\mu_n)$ and

$$\boldsymbol{Space_{SL,m}} := \boldsymbol{Prob}[[a,b];m\text{-unim};\mu_1,\ldots,\mu_n] \tag{94}$$

in case of problem $Q_{SL,m}(\mu_1,\ldots,\mu_n)$.

We always assume that

$$(\mu_1,\ldots,\mu_n)\in \mathrm{Dom}_n{}^{\circ}[a,b]. \tag{95}$$

It is clear that the points $(\mu_1,\ldots,\mu_n)$ on the frontier of $\mathrm{Dom}_n[a,b]$ can be neglected in all practical considerations, and that the discussion of these frontier points is a loss of time. (It may be interesting from the theoretical viewpoint).

Fixed, variable and partially variable points

The pure problem $Q_{SL}(\mu_1,\ldots,\mu_n)$ is solved by the dual method. The m-unimodal problem $Q_{SL,m}(\mu_1,\ldots,\mu_n)$ is replaced by its pure associated problem and the latter is solved by the dual method.

Three types of points can occur in the feasible sets:

a. **The fixed points** a,b and t.
b. **Variable points** $\theta,\eta,\xi,\ldots$
c. **Partially variable points** u,v,w,...

The variable points satisfy inequality conditions only. The partially variable points satisfy equality relations.

The fixed function of problem $Q_{SL}(\mu_1,\ldots,\mu_n)$ is φ. The variable functions are the polynomials of degree n. We recall that, by Newton's method of 8.1.4, a polynomial f of degree n with n+1 pre-assigned values $f(\alpha),f'(\alpha),\ldots, f(\beta), f'(\beta), \ldots$ can be constructed. Some feasible polynomials f of degree n are specified by strictly more than n+1 equality relations

$$f(a)=\varphi(a)\ ,\ f(u)=\varphi(u)\ ,\ f'(u)=\varphi'(u)\ ,\ f(v)=\varphi(v)\ ,\ f'(v)=\varphi'(v)\ ,\ldots$$

Then the points u,v,... must be connected by equality relations $g(u,v,\ldots)=0$. In this way partially variable points u,v,... occur.

The value of the problems

The value of any optimization problem is direct from its solution. If the finite-atomic distribution

$$F = pA_\alpha + qA_\beta + \ldots + rA_\gamma \tag{96}$$

is a solution of problem $Q_{SL}(\mu_1,\ldots,\mu_n)$, then the value of that problem is

$$\int\varphi dF = p\varphi(\alpha)+q\varphi(\beta)+\ldots+r\varphi(\gamma) = p(\alpha-t)_+ + q(\beta-t)_+ + \ldots + r(\gamma-t)_+. \qquad (97)$$

This value can be explicited and transformed in various ways.

If the feasible polynomial has been calculated, then the general relation Ch.7. Th.8.(35) can be used. In many cases, the value can be explicited as a function of the parameters of the problem (a, b, t, the moments $\mu_1,\ldots,\mu_n$ and the mode m when it is fixed). We do not mention such analytic expressions. They result from elementary algebra.

General method of solution

Step 1. We make an inventory of the good feasible sets and corresponding feasible polynomials. Then different cases occur.

Step 2. We indicate the potential solution of the problem corresponding to each case.

Step 3. For any fixed point $(\mu_1,\ldots,\mu_n) \in Dom_n°[a,b]$, we indicate what case does occur. In the following sections, the latter step appears under the heading *Classification of the solutions*.

By Theorem 2, all possibilities must be exhausted, i.e. no points $(\mu_1,\ldots,\mu_n)$ of $Dom_n°[a,b]$ can be forgotten if all good feasible sets are considered in step 1.

In principle, the method works for any number n of moment constraints, but we only treat the cases n=1,2,3. The consideration of more constraints is much less interesting because then the problems are less practical, the possible cases become too numerous and the discussions too lengthy. Moreover, the numerical algorithms of Ch.4.7 are much easier to program than the analytical solutions corresponding to all possible cases, and they furnish the exact solution of the problem, and its value, in less than one minute.

Needless to say that the general method can be applied to the minimization problems $P_{SL}(\mu_1,\ldots,\mu_n)$ and $P_{SL,m}(\mu_1,\ldots,\mu_n)$ (after the mode elimination) corresponding to the problems $Q_{SL}(\mu_1,\ldots,\mu_n)$ and $Q_{SL,m}(\mu_1,\ldots,\mu_n)$.

8.3.2. Pure Maximization Problem

One moment constraint

The variable curves of the problem $Q_{SL}(\mu_1)$ are straight lines. The set $\{a,b\}$ is the unique feasible set. The corresponding feasible curve is the straight line through the points $(a,\varphi(a))$, $(b,\varphi(b))$. See Fig.15. The solution of the problem is the distribution

$$pA_a+qA_b \tag{98}$$

where p and q result from the probability and the moment constraint.

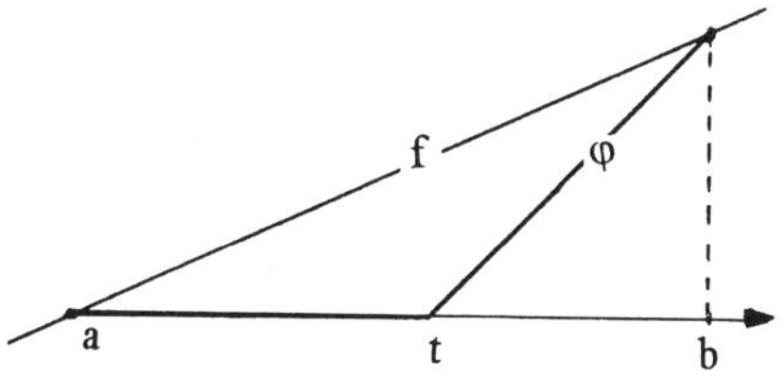

Fig.15. Feasible line and set of problem $Q_{SL}(\mu_1)$

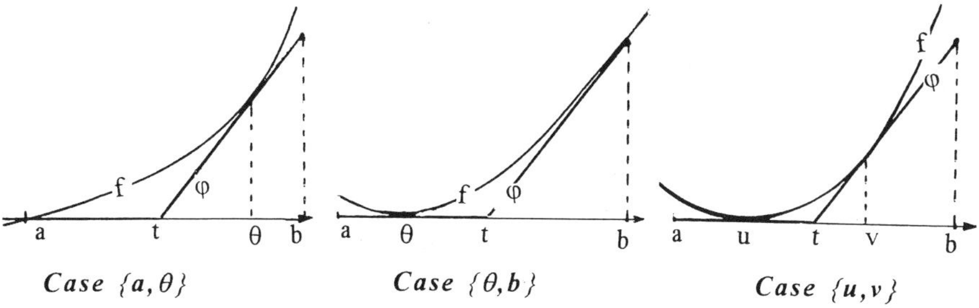

Fig.16. Feasible parabolas and sets of problem $Q_{SL}(\mu_1,\mu_2)$

Two moment constraints

The variable functions of the problem $Q(\mu_1,\mu_2)$ are polynomials f of the second degree. The feasible parabolas, and the corresponding good feasible sets, are represented in Fig.16. By the condition $2i+e\geq n+1=3$ of Theorem 1, the set $\{a,b\}$ is not a good feasible set.

Case $\{a,\theta\}$

The feasible polynomial f satisfies the conditions

$$t<\theta\leq b \text{ , } f'(a)\geq 0 \text{ , } f(a)=\varphi(a) \text{ , } f(\theta)=\varphi(\theta) \text{ , } f'(\theta)=\varphi'(\theta).$$

By Newton's interpolation, we diplay f(x) as

$$f(x) = c_0+c_1(x-a)+c_2(x-a)(x-\theta).$$

Then

$$f'(x) = c_1+c_2(x-\theta)+c_2(x-a),$$

$$0 = \varphi(a) = f(a) = c_0 \text{ , } \theta\text{-}t = \varphi(\theta) = f(\theta) = c_1(\theta\text{-}a),$$

$$1 = \varphi'(\theta) = f'(\theta) = c_1+c_2(\theta-a) \text{ , } \theta-a = c_1(\theta-a)+c_2(\theta-a)^2 = \theta-t + c_2(\theta-a)^2,$$

$$f'(a)(\theta-a) = c_1(\theta-a) + c_2(a-\theta)(\theta-a) = (\theta-t) - (t-a) = a+\theta-2t.$$

Hence, θ satisfies the relations

$$t < \theta \leq b \text{ , } 2t \leq a + \theta. \tag{99}$$

Case $\{\theta,b\}$

The feasible polynomial f is specified by the conditions

$$a\leq\theta<t \text{ , } f'(b)\leq 1 \text{ , } f(\theta)=\varphi(\theta) \text{ , } f'(\theta)=\varphi'(\theta) \text{ , } f(b)=\varphi(b).$$

By Newton's interpolation method, we display f(x) as

$$f(x) = c_0+c_1(x-\theta)+c_2(x-\theta)^2.$$

Then

$$f'(x) = c_1+2c_2(x-\theta),$$

$$0 = \varphi(\theta) = f(\theta) = c_0 \ , \ 0 = \varphi'(\theta) = f'(\theta) = c_1,$$

$$b-t = \varphi(b) = f(b) = c_2(b-\theta)^2,$$

$$f'(b)(b-\theta) = 2c_2(b-\theta)^2 = 2(b-t).$$

Hence, θ satisfies the relations

$$a \leq \theta < t \ , \ b+\theta \leq 2t. \tag{100}$$

Case {u,v}

In this case the feasible polynomial f satisfies the relations

$$a<u<t<v<b \ , \ f(u)=\varphi(u) \ , \ f'(u)=\varphi'(u) \ , \ f(v)=\varphi(v) \ , \ f'(v)=\varphi'(v). \tag{101}$$

The feasible polynomial f of the second degree must satisfy 4 equality constraints. This is only possible if the points u,v are connected. Newton's interpolation method can still be applied. We consider a polynomial f of the third degree satisfying the equalities (101) and then we relate the points u,v in such a way that the coefficient of the term x^3 vanishes. (In the later applications of this method, the supplementary term is dropped at the start). We can display f as

$$f(x) = c_0 + c_1(x-u) + c_2(x-u)^2 + c_3(x-u)^2(x-v).$$

Then

$$f'(x) = c_1 + 2c_2(x-u) + 2c_3(x-u)(x-v) + c_3(x-u)^2.$$

By the conditions (101),

$$0 = \varphi(u) = f(u) = c_0 \ , \ 0 = \varphi'(u) = f'(u) = c_1,$$

$$v-t = \varphi(v) = f(v) = c_2(v-u)^2 \ , \ 1 = \varphi'(v) = f'(v) = 2c_2(v-u)+c_3(v-u)^2.$$

Hence, the condition $c_3=0$ is $u+v=2t$. The feasibility conditions on the 2-atomic distribution

$$pA_u + qA_v, \tag{102}$$

completed by the condition $c_3=0$ and by the probability condition $p+q=1$, are

$$p+q=1 \ , \ pu+qv=\mu_1 \ , \ pu^2+qv^2=\mu_2 \ , \ u+v=2t. \tag{103}$$

The system (103) is a system of 4 equations for the 4 unknown quantities p, q, u, v. We eliminate p in the two first equations and in the two equations in the middle:

$$q(v-u) = \mu_1-u \ , \ qv(v-u) = \mu_2-u\mu_1.$$

Hence $v(\mu_1-u)=\mu_2-u\mu_1$, and then, by the last equation (103),

$$(2t-u)(\mu_1-u) = \mu_2-u\mu_1.$$

Hence, u is a root of the equation of the second degree

$$x^2 - 2tx + 2t\mu_1-\mu_2 = 0. \tag{104}$$

For reasons of symmetry (or by a direct verification), v satisfies the same equation. The roots are calculated by elementary algebra. Then p and q result from the first equations (103). The result is

$$u = t-[(t-\mu_1)^2+(\mu_2-\mu_1^2)]^{1/2}, \tag{105}$$

$$v = t+[(t-\mu_1)^2+(\mu_2-\mu_1^2)]^{1/2}, \tag{105}$$

$$p = (v-\mu_1)/(v-u), \tag{105}$$

$$q = (\mu_1-u)/(v-u). \tag{105}$$

Classification of the solutions of problem $Q_{SL}(\mu_1,\mu_2)$

a. The initial distribution pA_a+qA_θ is the solution of the problem if the conditions (99) are satisfied.

b. The final distribution $pA_\theta+qA_b$ is the solution of the problem if the conditions (100) are satisfied.

c. Otherwise, the solution is the 2-atomic distribution pA_u+qA_v, with u,v,p,q defined by (105).

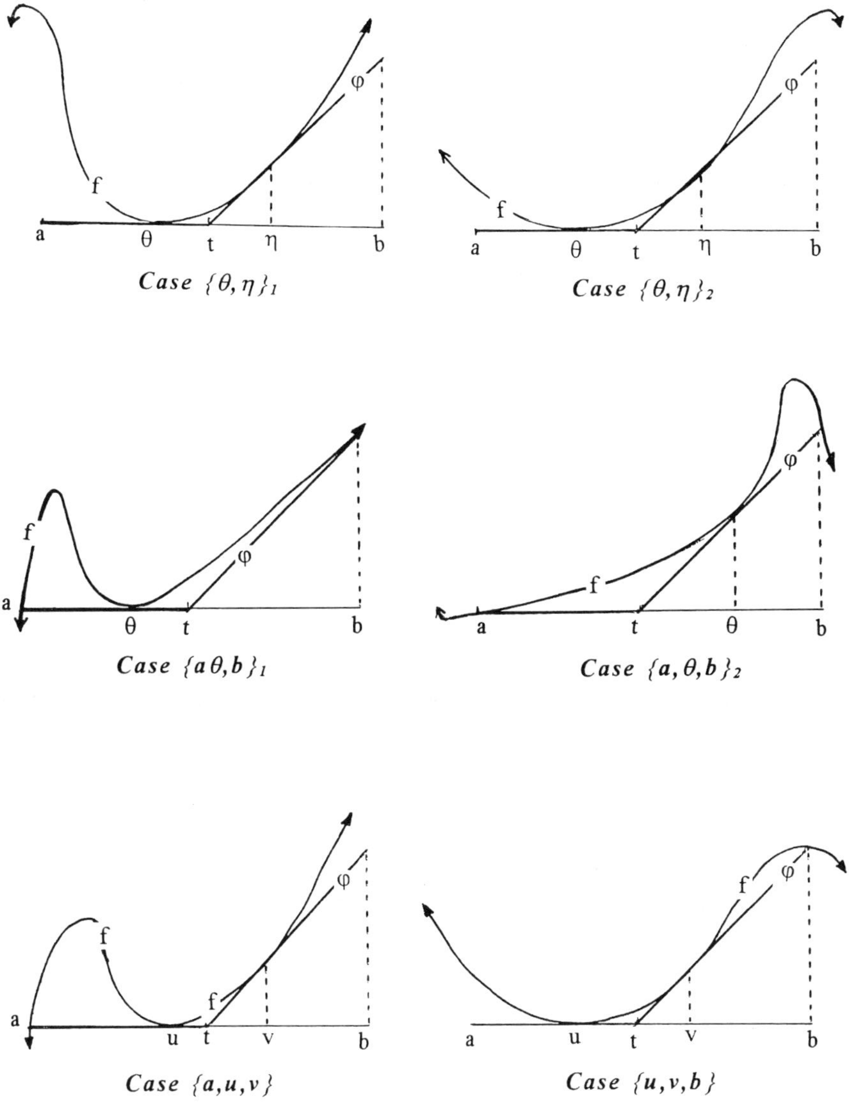

Fig.17. Feasible polynomials and sets of problem $Q_{SL}(\mu_1,\mu_2,\mu_3)$

Three moment constraints

The variable functions of the problem $Q(\mu_1,\mu_2,\mu_3)$ are polynomials of the third degree. The graphs of all feasible polynomials and the corresponding feasible sets, are represented in Fig.17. The case $\{\theta,\eta\}$ has two versions, denoted by $\{\theta,\eta\}_1$ and $\{\theta,\eta\}_2$. The case $\{a,\theta,b\}$ has two versions denoted by $\{a,\theta,b\}_1$ and $\{a,\theta,b\}_2$.

In the versions with subscript 1, feasible polynomial f is such that

$$\lim_{x\downarrow-\infty} f(x) = -\infty \ , \ \lim_{x\uparrow+\infty} f(x) = +\infty. \tag{106}$$

In the versions with subscript 2, it is such that

$$\lim_{x\downarrow-\infty} f(x) = +\infty \ , \ \lim_{x\uparrow+\infty} f(x) = -\infty. \tag{107}$$

Case $\{\theta,\eta\}$

The feasible polynomial f satisfies the relations

$$a\leq\theta<t<\eta\leq b \ , \ \varphi(\theta)=f(\theta) \ , \ \varphi'(\theta)=f'(\theta) \ , \ \varphi(\eta)=f(\eta) \ , \ \varphi'(\eta) = f'(\eta).$$

These conditions do specify the polynomial f, but they do not imply its feasibility. Hence, we must have a closer look at f. By Newton's method, we obtain

$$(\eta-\theta)^3 f(x) = (\eta-t)(\eta-\theta)(x-\theta)^2 + (2t-\theta-\eta)(x-\theta)^2(x-\eta). \tag{108}$$

Subcase $\{\theta,\eta\}_1$ is characterized by the conditions (106) and $f(a)\geq0$, i.e. by the relations

$$2t-\theta-\eta \geq 0 \tag{109}$$

and

$$(\eta-t)(\eta-\theta) + (2t-\theta-\eta)(a-\eta) \geq 0. \tag{109}$$

Subcase $\{\theta,\eta\}_2$ is characterized by the conditions (107) and $f(b)\geq\varphi(b)$. The latter condition is

$$(\eta-t)(\eta-\theta)(b-\theta)^2 + (2t-\theta-\eta)(b-\theta)^2(b-\eta) \geq (b-t)(\eta-\theta)^3.$$

The difference of the term in the last member and the first term of the first member is divisible by $(b-\eta)$. Hence, the conditions of the *subcase* $\{\theta,\eta\}_2$ are

$$2t-\theta-\eta \leq 0 \tag{110}$$

and

$$(2t-\theta-\eta)(b-\theta)^2 \geq (\eta-\theta)[(t-\theta)^2-(\eta-t)(b-t)]. \tag{110}$$

Case {a,θ,b}

The feasible polynomial f satisfies the conditions

$$a<\theta<b\ ,\ \varphi(a)=f(a)\ ,\ \varphi(\theta)=f(\theta)\ ,\ \varphi'(\theta)=f'(\theta)\ ,\ \varphi(b)=f(b).$$

We first consider the *subcase* $\{a,\theta,b\}_1$, characterized by the conditions $a<\theta<t$ and $f'(b)\leq\varphi'(b)$. Then, by Newton's interpolation method, taking the points in the order a,θ,b,

$$(b-a)(b-\theta)^2f(x) = (b-t)(x-a)(x-\theta)^2,$$

$$(b-a)(b-\theta)^2f'(x) = (b-t)(x-\theta)^2 + 2(b-t)(x-a)(x-\theta).$$

Hence, this subcase is characterized by the conditions

$$a<\theta<t\ ,\ (b-t)(b-\theta)^2 + 2(b-t)(b-a)(b-\theta) \leq (b-a)(b-\theta)^2,$$

i.e.

$$a<\theta<t\ ,\ 2(b-t)(b-a) \leq (t-a)(b-\theta). \tag{111}$$

We now consider *subcase* $\{a,\theta,b\}_2$, characterized by the conditions $t<\theta<b$ and $\varphi'(a)\leq f'(a)$. Then, by Newton's method, taking the points in the order θ,b,a,

$$(b-a)(\theta-a)^2f(x)$$

$$= (b-a)(\theta-a)^2(\theta-t) + (b-a)(\theta-a)^2(x-\theta) - (t-a)(x-\theta)^2(x-b), \tag{112}$$

$$(b-a)(\theta-a)^2f'(x)$$

$$= (b-a)(\theta-a)^2 - 2(t-a)(x-\theta)(x-b) - (t-a)(x-\theta)^2. \tag{113}$$

Hence, the conditions of *subcase* $\{a,\theta,b\}_2$ are

$$t<\theta<b\ ,\ (b-t)(\theta-a) \geq 2(t-a)(b-a). \tag{114}$$

The solution of the problem, in both *subcases* is the 3-atomic distribution

$$pA_a + qA_\theta + rA_b, \tag{115}$$

where p,q,r result from the probability constraint and two moment constraints.

Case {a,u,v}

The feasible polynomial f satisfies the conditions

$$a<u<t<v<b,\ \varphi(a)=f(a),\ \varphi(u)=f(u),\ \varphi'(u)=f'(u),\ \varphi(v)=f(v),\ \varphi'(v)=f'(v). \quad (116)$$

The partially variable points u,v are connected by some equality relation. By Newton's interpolation method, we find that

$$(v-a)(2t-u-v) = (v-t)(v-u). \quad (117)$$

Let

$$pA_a + qA_u + rA_v \quad (118)$$

be the feasible distribution corresponding to the feasible set {a,u,v}. Then, with the notations of 8.2.1,

$$u = t-[(2v-a-t)(v-t)/(t-a)], \quad (119)$$

$$\mu_{3a} - (u+v)\mu_{2a} + uv\mu_{1a} = 0, \quad (119)$$

$$p = [\mu_2-(u+v)\mu_1+uv]/[a-u)(a-v)], \quad (120)$$

$$q = [\mu_2-(a+v)\mu_1+av]/[(u-a)(u-v)], \quad (120)$$

$$r = [\mu_2-(a+u)\mu_1+au]/[(v-a)(v-u)]. \quad (120)$$

Indeed, the first relation (119) results from (117). The feasibility conditions on the distribution (118) are

$$p+q+r = 1, \quad (121)$$

$$pa+qu+rv = \mu_1, \quad (121)$$

$$pa^2+qu^2+rv^2 = \mu_2, \quad (121)$$

$$pa^3+qu^3+rv^3 = \mu_3. \quad (121)$$

The second relation (119) results from the elimination of p,q,r, and (120) is the solution of the system defined by the first three relations (121).

The substitution of the expression of u furnished by the first relation (119), in the second relation (119), leads to a cubic equation for v.

Case {u,v,b}

The feasible polynomial f satisfies the conditions

$$a<u<t<v<b,\ \varphi(u)=f(u),\ \varphi'(u)=f'(u),\ \varphi(v)=f(v),\ \varphi'(v)=f'(v),\ \varphi(b)=f(b). \quad (122)$$

In order to find the equality relation connecting the partially variable points u and v, we apply Newton's interpolation method, and we display f as

$$f(x) = c_0+c_1(x-u)+c_2(x-u)(x-v)+c_3(x-u)(x-v)(x-b).$$

Then

$$f'(x) = c_1+c_2(x-v)+c_2(x-u)+c_3(x-v)(x-b)+c_3(x-u)(x-b)+c_3(x-u)(x-v).$$

Then the conditions $f(u)=0$, $f(v)=v-t$, $f(b)=b-t$ furnish the coefficients c_0, c_1 and c_2:

$$c_0 = 0\ ,\ c_1(v-u) = v-t\ ,\ c_2(b-u)(v-u) = t-u.$$

Then c_3 must satisfy the two relations $f'(u)=0$, $f'(v)=0$. Then

$$(v-t)(b-u)-(v-u)(t-u) = (b-u)(t-u) \quad (123)$$

by the elimination of c_3. Let the feasible distribution corresponding to the feasible set {u,v,b} be

$$pA_u + qA_v + rA_b. \quad (124)$$

Then, similarly as in the foregoing case, we obtain the relations

$$v = t+[(b+t-2u)(t-u)/(b-t)], \quad (125)$$

$$\mu_{3b} - (u+v)\mu_{2b} + uv\mu_{1b} = 0, \quad (125)$$

$$p = [\mu_2-(v+b)\mu_1+vb]/[(u-v)(u-b)], \quad (126)$$

$$q = [\mu_2-(u+b)\mu_1+ub]/[(v-u)(v-b)], \quad (126)$$

$$r = [\mu_2-(u+v)\mu_1+uv]/[(b-u)(b-v)]. \quad (126)$$

The substitution of the expression of v furnished by the first relation (125), in the second relation (125), leads to a cubic equation for u.

Classification of the solutions of problem $Q_{SL}(\mu_1,\mu_2,\mu_3)$

a. The narrow distribution $pA_\theta+qA_\eta$ is the solution of the problem if the relations (109) or (110) are satisfied.

b. The broad distribution $pA_a+qA_\theta+rA_b$ is the solution of the problem if the relations (111) or (114) are satisfied.

c. The 3-atomic distribution $pA_a+qA_u+rA_v$ is the solution if the system (119) has a solution (u,v) such that $a<u<t<v<b$ and $p,q,r\geq 0$.

d. The 3-atomic distribution $pA_u+qA_v+rA_b$ is the solution if the system (125) has a solution (u,v) such that $a<u<t<v<b$ and $p,q,r\geq 0$.

8.3.3. m-Unimodal Maximization Problem

Associated problem

The associated problem of the problem $Q_{SL,m}(\mu_1,\dots,\mu_n)$ is the problem

$$Q_{SL,m}^\bullet(\mu_1^\bullet,\dots,\mu_n^\bullet) := \sup_{F\in \mathbf{Prob}[[a,b]]}\left[\int\varphi^\bullet dF/\mu_1^\bullet,\dots,\mu_n^\bullet\right], \tag{127}$$

where

$$\varphi^\bullet(x) := \int\varphi(y)dR_{mx}(y) \tag{128}$$

and where the **associated moments** $\mu_j^\bullet$ are defined by Ch.3.(138). If the k-atomic distribution

$$pA_\alpha+qA_\beta+\dots+rA_\gamma \tag{129}$$

is a solution of the associated problem (127), then the k-rectangular distribution

$$pR_{m\alpha}+qR_{m\beta}+\dots+rR_{m\gamma} \tag{130}$$

is a solution of the original problem $Q_m(\mu_1,\dots,\mu_n)$. Then the value of both problems is

$$Q_{SL,m}(\mu_1,\dots,\mu_n) = Q_{SL,m}^\bullet(\mu_1^\bullet,\dots,\mu_n^\bullet) = p\varphi^\bullet(\alpha)+q\varphi^\bullet(\beta)+\dots+r\varphi^\bullet(\gamma). \tag{131}$$

For n=1,2,3, we will solve the more general problem

$$Q_m^\circ(\mu_1,\dots,\mu_n) := \sup_{F\in \mathbf{Prob}[[a,b]]}[\int\gamma(x)dF(x) \,/\, \mu_1,\dots,\mu_n], \qquad (132)$$

where

$$\gamma=2\varphi^\bullet\ ,\ (\mu_1,\dots,\mu_n)\in \mathrm{Dom}_n^\circ[a,b]. \qquad (133)$$

Hence, in (132), $\mu_1,\dots,\mu_n$ are any moments satisfying (133), not necessarily associated moments. The solution of the problem (127) is the solution of problem (132) with $\mu_1,\dots,\mu_n$ replaced by $\mu_1^\bullet,\dots,\mu_n^\bullet$. Then the value of the problem (132) equals twice the value of problem (127). Of course the factor 2 is completely irrelevant. It simplifies the typography a little bit.

We assume that a<m<t<b. This is the practical situation: the retention limit t is strictly larger than the mode m when the claimsize distribution X has a unimodal distribution. Of course, the case t≤m could be treated as well.

$$\gamma(x) = 2\varphi^\bullet(x)= 2\int(y-t)_+dR_{mx}(y) = {}^2/_{(x-m)}\int_{[t,x]}(y-t)dy = {}^{(x-t)^2}/_{(x-m)}\ \ (t\le x\le b).$$

Hence,

$$\gamma(x) = (x-t)_+{}^2/(x-m)\ \ (a\le x\le b). \qquad (134)$$

By

$$(x-t)^2 = [(x-m)-(t-m)]^2 = (x-m)^2 - 2(x-m)(t-m) + (t-m)^2,$$

we have

$$\gamma(x) = {}^{(t-m)^2}/_{(x-m)} + (x-m) - 2(t-m)\ \ (t\le x\le b), \qquad (135)$$

$$\gamma'(x) = -{}^{(t-m)^2}/_{(x-m)^2} + 1 \ge 0\ \ (t\le x\le b), \qquad (136)$$

$$\gamma''(x) = {}^{2(t-m)^2}/_{(x-m)^3} \ge 0\ \ (t\le x\le b). \qquad (137)$$

$\gamma\equiv 0$ on [a,t]. Hence, γ is continuous, concave and increasing on [a,b].

The fixed curve of problem $Q_m^\circ(\mu_1,\dots,\mu_n)$ is $y=\gamma(x)$ ($a<x<b$). The variable functions are the polynomials of degree n.

There is an obvious parallelism between the treatment of the problems $Q(\mu_1,\dots,\mu_n)$ and $Q_m^\circ(\mu_1,\dots,\mu_n)$. The discussions will be much shorter in case of the latter problem.

One moment constraint

The solution of the problem $Q_m°(\mu_1)$ is the 2-atomic distribution

$$pA_a+qA_b, \tag{138}$$

where (see Fig.18)

$$p = (b-\mu_1)/(b-a)\ ,\ q = (\mu_1-a)/(b-a). \tag{139}$$

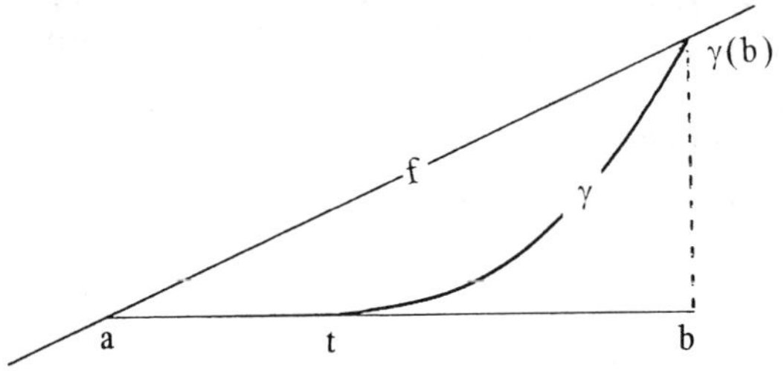

Fig.18. Feasible line and set of problem $Q_m°(\mu_1)$

Two moment constraints

The feasible sets and parabolas of the problem $Q_m°(\mu_1,\mu_2)$ are represented in Fig.19.

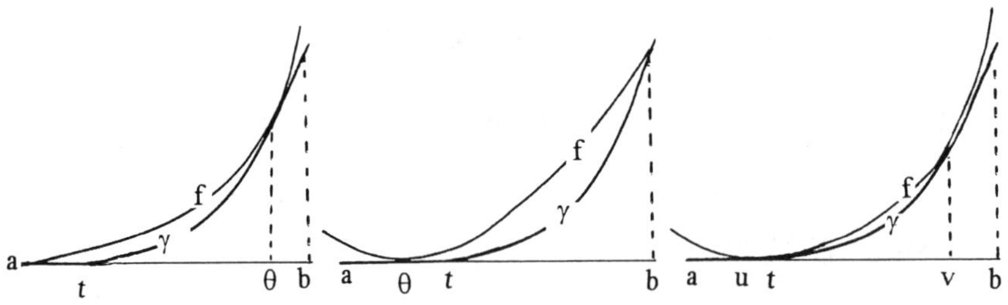

Fig.19. Feasible parabolas and sets of problem $Q_m°(\mu_1,\mu_2)$

***Case* $\{a,\theta\}$**

The solution of the problem is the initial 2-atomic distribution

$$pA_a + qA_\theta, \tag{140}$$

with

$$t \le \theta \le b \ , \ \gamma'(\theta)(\theta-a) \le 2\gamma(\theta), \tag{141}$$

The latter inequality translates that $\gamma'(a)\ge 0$.

***Case* $\{\theta,b\}$**

The solution of the problem is the final 2-atomic distribution

$$pA_b + qA_\theta, \tag{142}$$

with

$$a \le \theta \le t \ , \ 2\gamma(b) \le \gamma'(b)(b-\theta). \tag{143}$$

The latter relation expresses condition $f'(b)\le\gamma'(b)$.

***Case* $\{u,v\}$**

The feasible polynomial f, of the second degree, satisfies the relations

$$a<u<t<v<b \ , \ \gamma(u)=f(u) \ , \ \gamma'(u)=f'(u) \ , \ \gamma(v)=f(v) \ , \ \gamma'(v)=f'(v). \tag{144}$$

We display f(x) as

$$f(x) = c_0 + c_1(x-u) + c_2(x-u)^2.$$

Then

$$f'(x) = c_1 + 2c_2(x-u),$$

and $c_0=c_1=0$ by the first equalities (144). Then

$$\gamma(v) = c_2(v-u)^2 \ , \ \gamma'(v) = 2c_2(v-u) \ , \ v-u = 2\gamma(v)/\gamma'(v). \tag{145}$$

Then

$$pA_u + qA_v \tag{146}$$

is a feasible distribution if

$$p+q=1 \ , \ pu+qv=\mu_1 \ , \ pu^2+qv^2=\mu_2. \tag{147}$$

Then

$$\mu_2 - (u+v)\mu_1 + uv = 0, \tag{148}$$

by the elimination of p and q. Then

$$v-u = (\mu_2-2v\mu_1+v^2)/(v-\mu_1). \tag{149}$$

Hence

$$(\mu_2-2v\mu_1+v^2)/(v-\mu_1) = 2\gamma(v)/\gamma'(v), \qquad (150)$$

$$u = (v\mu_1-\mu_2)/v-\mu_1), \qquad (150)$$

$$p = (v-\mu_1)/(v-u), \qquad (150)$$

$$q = (\mu_1-u)/(v-u). \qquad (150)$$

Classification of the solutions of problem $Q_m{}^\circ(\mu_1,\mu_2)$

a. **The initial distribution pA_a+qA_θ is the solution if (141) is true.**

b. **The final distribution $pA_\theta+qA_b$ is the solution if (143) is true.**

c. **Otherwise the solution is the 2-atomic distribution pA_u+qA_v with u, v,p,q defined by (150).**

9.4.4. Three moment constraints

The feasible sets and polynomials of problem $Q_m{}^\circ(\mu_1,\mu_2,\mu_3)$ are represented in Fig.20.

Case $\{\theta,\eta\}$

In both *subcases* $\{\theta,\eta\}_1$, $\{\theta,\eta\}_2$ the feasible polynomial is

$$f(x) = \frac{1}{(\eta-\theta)^3}[\gamma(\eta)(\eta-\theta)(x-\theta)^2 + [\gamma'(\eta)(\eta-\theta)-2\gamma(\eta)](x-\theta)^2(x-\eta)]. \tag{151}$$

In both *subcases*

$$a \le \theta < \eta \le b \ , \ f(a) \ge 0 \ , \ \gamma(b) \le f(b). \tag{152}$$

and the solution is the narrow 2-atomic distribution

$$pA_\theta + qA_\eta. \tag{153}$$

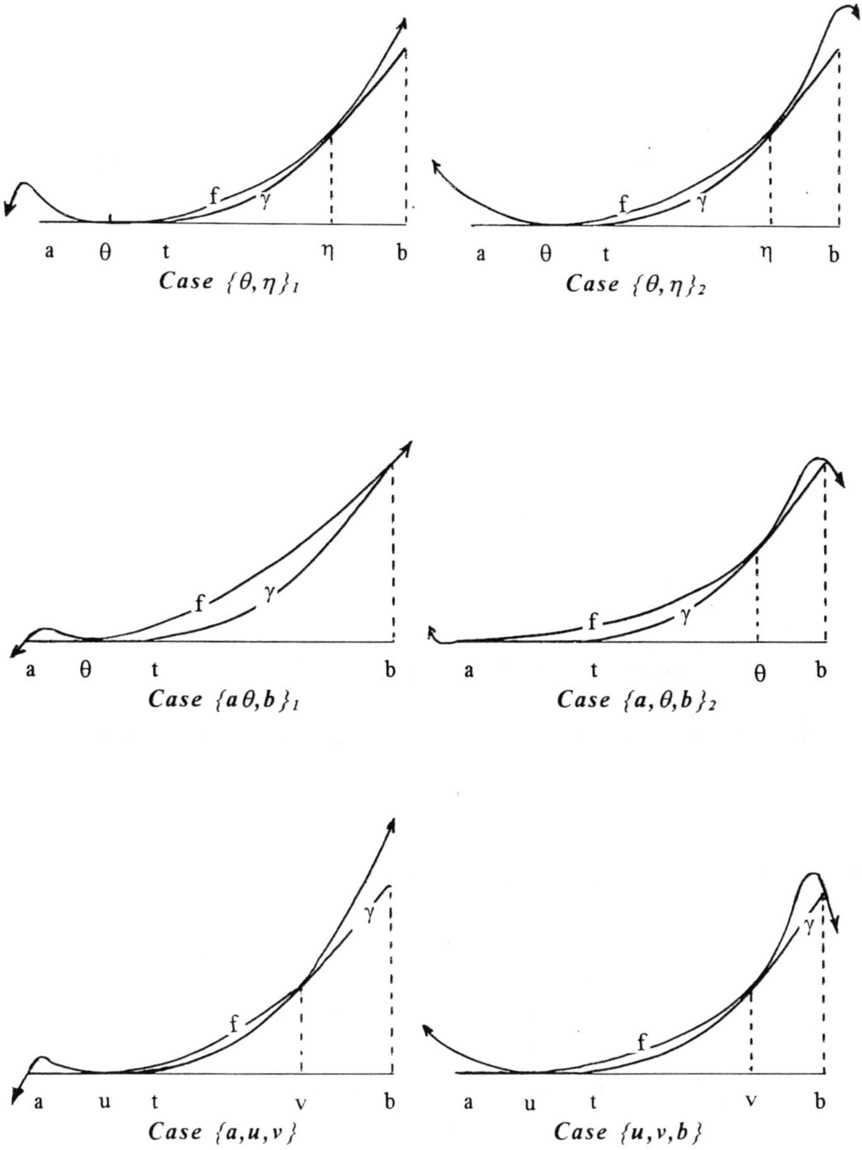

Fig.20. Feasible polynomials and sets of problem $Q_m°(\mu_1,\mu_2,\mu_3)$

Case {a,θ,b}

In both *subcases* $\{a,\theta,b\}_1$ and $\{a,\theta,b\}_2$, the feasible polynomial is

$$f(x) = c_0+c_1(x-\theta)+c_2(x-\theta)^2+c_3(x-\theta)^2(x-\eta), \tag{154}$$

with

$$c_0 := \gamma(\theta)\ ,\ c_1 := \gamma'(\theta)\ ,\ c_2 := {}^1\!/\!_{(\eta-\theta)^2}[\gamma(\eta)-c_0-c_1(\eta-\theta)], \tag{155}$$

$$c_3 := {}^1\!/\!_{(\eta-\theta)^2}[\gamma'(\eta)-c_1-2c_2(\eta-\theta)]. \tag{156}$$

In both subcases

$$a<\theta<b\ ,\ 0\le f'(a)\ ,\ f'(b)\le\gamma'(b). \tag{157}$$

and the solution is the broad 3-atomic distribution

$$pA_\alpha + qA_b + rA_\theta. \tag{158}$$

Case {a,u,v}

The feasible polynomial is

$$f(x) = {}^1\!/\!_{(v-u)^3}[\gamma(v)(v-u)(x-u)^2 + [\gamma'(v)(v-u)-2\gamma(v)](x-u)^2(x-v)], \tag{159}$$

where the partially variable points u and v are connected by the second relation (161). Let

$$pA_a + qA_u + rA_v \tag{160}$$

be the feasible distribution corresponding to the feasible set {a,u,v}. Then

$$f(a) = 0, \tag{161}$$

$$\mu_{3a} - (u+v)\mu_{2a} + uv\mu_{1a} = 0, \tag{161}$$

$$p = [\mu_2-(u+v)\mu_1+uv]/[a-u)(a-v)], \tag{162}$$

$$q = [\mu_2-(a+v)\mu_1+av]/[(u-a)(u-v)], \tag{162}$$

$$r = [\mu_2-(a+u)\mu_1+au]/[(v-a)(v-u)], \tag{162}$$

with

$$a<u<v\le b\ ,\ f'(a)\ge 0\ ,\ f(b)\ge\gamma(b). \tag{163}$$

Case {u,v,b}

The feasible polynomial is the polynomial (159), but now u and v are connected by the second relation (164). Let the feasible distribution corresponding to the feasible set {u,v,b} be

$$pA_u + qA_v + rA_b. \tag{164}$$

Then,

$$f(b) = \gamma(b), \tag{165}$$

$$\mu_{3b} - (u+v)\mu_{2b} + uv\mu_{1b} = 0, \tag{165}$$

$$p = [\mu_2-(v+b)\mu_1+vb]/[(u-v)(u-b)], \tag{166}$$

$$q = [\mu_2-(u+b)\mu_1+ub]/[(v-u)(v-b)], \tag{166}$$

$$r = [\mu_2-(u+v)\mu_1+uv]/[(b-u)(b-v)], \tag{166}$$

and

$$a \le u < v < b \ , \ f(a) \ge 0 \ , \ f'(b) \le \gamma'(b). \tag{167}$$

Classification of the solutions of problem $\mathbf{Q_m{}^\circ(\mu_1,\mu_2,\mu_3)}$

a. The narrow distribution $pA_\theta+qA_\eta$ is the solution if (152) is true.

b. The broad distribution $pA_a+qA_\theta+rA_b$ is the solution if (157) is true.

c. The 3-atomic distribution $pA_a+qA_u+rA_v$ is the solution if the system (161) has a solution (u,v) satisfying (163) and $p,q,r\ge 0$.

d. The 3-atomic distribution $pA_u+qA_v+rA_b$ is the solution if the system (165) has a solution satisfying (167) and $p,q,r\ge 0$.

Chapter 9

General Optimization Algorithm

9.1. Local Maxima

9.1.1. General Maximization Problem

In this Chapter we consider the general maximization problem

$$\sup_{F \in \textbf{\textit{Space}}} T(F). \tag{1}$$

All definitions and propositions have symmetrical versions, not mentioned (but used in the applications), concerning the corresponding minimization problem $\inf_{F \in \textbf{\textit{Space}}} T(F)$.

F,G,H,... with subscripts or not, are points of ***Space***. We always assume that ***Space*** is convex and we denote by ***Ext*** the set of its extremal points.

We use the restrictions to segments T_{FG} of the functional T (Ch.4.3.1) and we assume that ***Space*** is a Krein-Milman space (Ch.2.4) in the basic results of this Chapter.

9.1.2. Directional Derivatives

We say that **T has a derivative at the point F, in the direction of the point G**, if $T_{FG}(\tau)$ has a finite right-sided derivative $T'_{FG}(0)$ at the origin $\tau=0$. Then the latter derivative is denoted by T′(F,G). The derivative T′(F,G) is a **directional derivative**, or a **Gâteaux-derivative**. **T has a directional derivative on *Space*** if T has a derivative T′(F,G) at any point F, in any direction G.

T′ is direction-linear if T′(F,G) is linear in G, for any fixed point F:

$$T'(F,\sum p_i G_i) = \sum p_i T'(F,G_i), \tag{2}$$

for any convex combination $\sum p_i G_i$ of points G_i in ***Space***.

T′ is direction-continuous if $T'(F,G)$ is a continuous function of $G \in$ ***Space*** for any fixed point $F \in$ ***Space***

The **directional continuity of T′** is explicited as

$$[G, G_\nu \in \textbf{\textit{Space}}\ (\nu=1,2,\ldots) \text{ and } G_\nu \to_w G \text{ as } \nu \uparrow \infty] \Rightarrow [T'(F,G_\nu) \to T'(F,G) \text{ as } \nu \uparrow \infty]\ \ (F \in \textbf{\textit{Space}}). \quad (3)$$

9.1.3. Global and Local Maxima

The directional derivative T′ is supposed to exist whenever it is used.

The point $F \in$ *Space* is a local maximum of T if

$$T'(F,G) \le 0 \ \ (G \in \textbf{\textit{Space}}). \quad (4)$$

The point $F \in$ *Space* is a global maximum of T if

$$T(F) \ge T(G) \ \ (G \in \textbf{\textit{Space}}) \quad (5)$$

i.e. if it is a solution of the problem $\sup_{F \in \textbf{\textit{Space}}} T(F)$.

Theorem 1

Let T be a functional with direction-linear derivative T′ on the Krein-Milman space *Space*, with the set of extremal points *Ext*. Let T′ be direction-continuous or let *Ext* be a finite set. Then the point F of *Space* is a local maximum of T iff

$$\mathbf{T'(F,G) \le 0\ (G \in \textbf{\textit{Ext}})}. \quad (6)$$

Proof

Let (6) be satisfied. Let us first assume that ***Ext*** is finite. Then any point $H \in$ ***Space*** is a convex combination

$$H = \Sigma p_i G_i$$

of points $G_i \in$ ***Ext*** by Ch.2.Th.10. Then

$$T'(F,H) = T'(F, \Sigma p_i G_i) = \Sigma p_i T'(F,G_i) \le 0, \quad (7)$$

by the directional linearity of T′ and by (6).

Let us now assume that T′ is direction-continuous, but ***Ext*** not necessarily finite. Then, for any point $H \in$***Space***, a sequence H_ν ($\nu=1,2,...$) of convex combinations of extremal points exists, such that

$$H_\nu \rightarrow_w H \text{ as } \nu\uparrow\infty.$$

Then

$$T'(F,H_\nu) \leq 0 \ (\nu=1,2,...)$$

by the argument of the first part of the proof, and then

$$T'(F,H) = \lim_{\nu\uparrow\infty} T'(F,H_\nu) \leq 0$$

by the directional continuity •

Theorem 2

Let T be a functional with directional derivative T′ on the convex space *Space*. Then any global maximum of T is a local maximum.

Proof

We assume that the point $F \in$***Space*** is not a local maximum, and we verify that it is not a global maximum. A point $G \in$***Space*** exists, such that

$$T'(F,G) > 0.$$

By the definition of the right-sided derivative of $T_{FG}(\tau)$ at $\tau=0$, some $\varepsilon>0$ exists such that

$$T_{FG}(\varepsilon) - T_{FG}(0) > 0,$$

i.e.

$$T(F) < T[(1-\varepsilon)F + \varepsilon G] \ \bullet$$

9.1.4. Directional Linearity of Directional Derivatives

By the following Theorem 3, the directional linearity of T′ is a rather general property. The function φ defined by (8) is **the restriction of T to the triangle FGH**. In some problems (say multiple integral problems) it is easily explicited and the conditions of the Theorem are obviously satisfied.

Theorem 3

We assume that for any F,G,H$\in$*Space*, the function with values

$$\varphi(s,t) := T((1-s-t)F+sG+tH) \quad (s\geq 0,\ t\geq 0,\ s+t\leq 1) \tag{8}$$

has continuous partial derivatives

$$\varphi_1(s,t) := \partial/\partial s\ \varphi(s,t)\ ,\ \varphi_2(s,t) := \partial/\partial t\ \varphi(s,t). \tag{9}$$

Then T′(F,G) (F,G$\in$*Space*) exists and is linear in G.

Proof

$$\varphi(s,0) = T((1-s)F+sG) = T_{FG}(s)\ ,\ \varphi_1(0,0) = T'(F,G), \tag{10}$$

$$\varphi(0,t) = T((1-t)F+tH) = T_{FH}(t)\ ,\ \varphi_2(0,0) = T'(F,H). \tag{11}$$

The derivative T′(F,G) exists by (10).

We now prove the linearity. Let pG+qH be a convex combination of G and H. Then

$$T((1-\tau)F+\tau(pG+qH)) = T((1-\tau p-\tau q)F+\tau pG+\tau qH)$$
$$= \varphi(\tau p,\tau q) \quad (0\leq\tau\leq 1)$$

and

$$\partial/\partial\tau\ T((1-\tau)F+\tau(pG+qH)) = \partial/\partial\tau\ \varphi(\tau p,\tau q)$$
$$= p\varphi_1(\tau p,\tau q) + q\varphi_2(\tau p,\tau q)$$

by the chain rule. For $\tau=0$, by (10) and (11):

$$T'(F,pG+qH) = pT'(F,G) + qT'(F,H) \quad \bullet$$

9.2. General Numerical Algorithm

9.2.1. ε-Local Maxima

The point F$\in$*Space* is an ε-local maximum of T, where $\varepsilon\geq 0$, if

$$T'(F,G) \leq \varepsilon \quad (G\in \textbf{\textit{Space}}). \tag{12}$$

The following Theorem 4 is the ε-version of Theorem 1.

Theorem 4

Let T be a functional with direction-linear derivative T′ on the Krein-Milman space *Space*, with the set of extremal points *Ext*. Let T′ be direction-continuous or let *Ext* be a finite set. Then the point $F \in$ *Space* is an ε-local maximum iff

$$T'(F,G) \leq \varepsilon \ (G \in Ext) \ \bullet \tag{13}$$

Proof
By the same arguments as in the proof of Theorem 1. For instance, now the relations (7) become

$$T'(F,H) = T'(F,\sum p_i G_i) = \sum p_i T'(F,G_i) \leq \sum p_i \varepsilon = \varepsilon \ \bullet$$

9.2.2. Description of Algorithm

Problem

The problem is the numerical determination of the solution of the maximization problem $\sup_{F \in Space} T(F)$.

Assumptions

Space is a Krein-Milman space with a finite number of extremal points G_1, $G_2, \ldots, G_\omega$. The functional T has a directional derivative T′ and T′ is direction-linear.

Execution (see Fig.21)

Preliminary step. Some **first initial approximation** F_{init} of the solution is fixed.

Round 1. The **optimal direction** G_{opt}, viewed from the point F_{init}, is determined. It is the solution of the optimization problem

$$\sup_{G \in Ext} T'(F_{init},G). \tag{14}$$

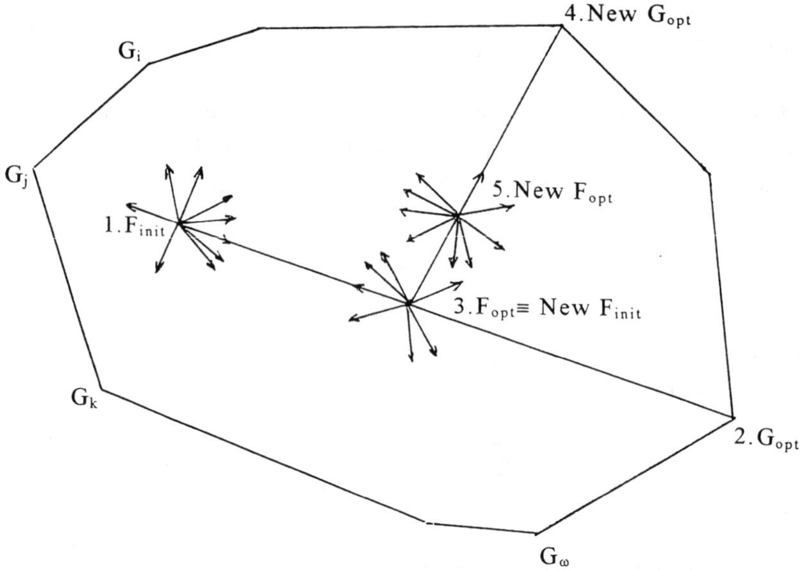

Fig.21. General optimization algorithm

The optimal point F_{opt} is determined on the segment $[F_{init}, G_{opt}]$. It is the point

$$F_{opt} = (1-\tau)F_{init} + \tau G_{opt}, \tag{15}$$

where τ is the solution of the optimization problem

$$\sup_{\tau\in[0,1]} T((1-\tau)F_{init} + \tau G_{opt}). \tag{16}$$

Round 2. The optimal point (15) is used as a **second initial approximation** of the solution. The round 1 is repeated with this new F_{init}. Hence, a new G_{opt} and a new F_{opt} are found.

Round 3. The latter new F_{opt} used as a **third initial opproximation** and the round 1 is repeated with it

... ...

End of execution

Let $F_1, F_2, \ldots$ be the successive initial approximations. The execution is stopped as soon as an approximation F_k is obtained such that

$$T'(F_k, G) \leq \varepsilon \quad (G \in \boldsymbol{Ext}). \tag{17}$$

Then F_k is an ε-local maximum by Theorem 4. If ε is small enough, F_k can be considered as a local maximum and then F_k is the global maximum in many cases. Some justifications are furnished in the following paragraph.

Global and local character of algorithm

The value of the derivative of a function at a point informs on its increment in the neighbourhood of that point: it is a local information. The research of the optimal direction G_{opt} is local. On the contrary, the research of the optimal point on the segment $[F_{init}, G_{opt}]$ has a global character. It explains why the practical global maximum is furnished by the algorithm in most cases.

9.2.3. Algorithm in Practice

Problem

We consider the continuous maximization problem $\sup_{F \in \boldsymbol{Space}} T(F)$ where the hypothetic space is the space of mixtures with integral constraints

$$\boldsymbol{Space} := \boldsymbol{Mixt}[F_\theta(\theta \in [0,b]; \int f_1 = \alpha_1, \ldots, \int f_n = \alpha_n]. \tag{18}$$

Discretization

This space is discretized and a new money unit is introduced, as explained in Ch.4.6.2. Then the original optimization problem becomes the n_0-discretized problem and then the numerical algorithm is applied to the latter.

In order to avoid the introduction of new symbols, we now use the notations ***Space***, ***Ext*** and T in case of the n_0-discretized problem.

First initial approximation

As first initial approximation F_{init} we take the solution of the maximization problem $\sup_{F \in \boldsymbol{Ext}} T(F)$. This is an extremal point problem. It can be solved by the *k_0-algorithm with fixed n_0-discretization* of Ch.4.7.5.

Numerical calculation of directional derivatives

The directional derivative $T'(F,G)$ is approximated by the value

$$[T_{FG}(\varepsilon')-T_{FG}(0)]/\varepsilon', \tag{19}$$

where ε' is a strictly positive small number (not necessarily the same as the number ε occurring in the paragraph *end of execution* of 9.2.2).

Determination of the optimal direction

The problem (14) is an optimal point problem again. It can be solved by the *k_0-algorithm with fixed n_0-discretization* of Ch.4.7.5.

Determination of the optimal point in the optimal direction

Let $\varphi(\tau)$ $(0\leq\tau\leq1)$ be the restriction of T to the segment $[F_{init},G_{opt}]$. Then the solution τ of problem (16) is such that $\varphi'(\tau)=0$ if it lies in the interval $]0,1[$. It can be found by any classical method. No sophisticated methods are needed. We apply the elementary **dichotomy algorithm**: if $\varphi'(c)\varphi'(d)<0$, then $]c,d[$ contains a root of φ' and then we consider $e:=\varphi'[1/2(c+d)]$ and we replace c or d by $1/2(c+d)$ according to the sign of e. It is enough to repeat this procedure in order to obtain a root of φ' with any required precision.

The derivative $\varphi'(\tau)$ is approximated by

$$[\varphi(\tau\pm\varepsilon')-\varphi(\tau)]/(\pm\varepsilon'),$$

say with $+\varepsilon'$ if $\tau\in[0,1/2]$ and with $-\varepsilon'$ if $\tau\in]1/2,1]$.

Convergence

The practical convergence of the sequence $F_1,F_2,\ldots$ of successive initial approximations is observed in almost all cases and an approximation F_k satisfying (17) is obtained if ε is not too small. The convergence may be very slow when the solution is not an extremal point. Some fine discretizations $(n_0\leq400)$ can be used, but the computing time is already excessive with $n_0=400$ in some cases.

9.2.4. Research of Structure of Solution

In most cases, the observation of the successive approximations $F_1, F_2, \ldots$ reveals the structure of the solution of the optimization problem very quickly. In many actuarial problems the practical convergence to some extremal distribution is obvious. Very often, the convergence to some special extremal distribution (See Ch.4.8) is evident.

Of course, when it becomes sure that the solution is an extremal distribution, the initial problem can be replaced by the extremal point problem $\sup_{F\in \mathbf{\mathit{Ext}}} T(F)$ and the latter can be solved by the algorithms of Ch.4.7.

In the illustration of the following section 9.3, the solution (not an extremal point) is revealed by the numerical algorithm and then it is completed by an analytic method.

9.2.5. Discontinuous Objective Functional

Elementary example

Let f be the function on [0,2] defined by the relations

$$f(x):=x\ (0\le x<1)\ ,\ f(x):=0\ (1\le x\le 2). \tag{20}$$

We consider the problem $\sup_{x\in[0,2]} f(x)$. When we replace the interval [0,2] by the discrete set $\{0,\delta,2\delta,\ldots,2n\delta\}$, where $\delta:=1/(2n)$, then the solution of the corresponding 2n-discretized problem is the point $x_n=(n-1)/n$.

The original continuous problem has no solution, but the sequence x_n (n=1,2,...) is a limit solution. The limit value $\lim_{n\uparrow\infty} f(x_n)=f(1-)=1$ is the value of the original problem. It is convenient to summarize this conclusion by the statement: the point $1-$ is the solution of the problem $\sup_{x\in[0,2]} f(x)$.

Optimizations on Space

Very similar things may occur with the problem $\sup_{F\in \mathbf{\mathit{Space}}} T(F)$ if T is not continuous on ***Space***. Then the following can happen.

a. The original problem has no solution.

b. The corresponding n_0-discretized problem has a solution for any n_0.

c. The numerical algorithms reveal limit solutions with atoms $\theta\pm$.

The discontinuity of T may be compatible with the existence of the directional derivative. See Ch.4.3.1.Rem.c.

9.3. Illustration: a Distance Minimization

9.3.1. Problem

We consider the hypothetic space

$$\boldsymbol{Space} := \boldsymbol{Prob}[[0,b];\mu_1,\mu_2] \tag{21}$$

and the fixed already discretized distribution

$$F_{fix} = \sum_{0\leq n\leq m} c_n A_{\delta n}, \tag{22}$$

where $m=b/\delta$. We assume that F_{fix} does not belong to ***Space*** and we want to approximate it by some

$$F = \sum_{0\leq n\leq m} p_n A_{\delta n} \tag{23}$$

of ***Space***. The distance from F_{fix} to F is defined as

$$d(F,F_{fix}) = [\sum_{0\leq n\leq m} ((p_n-c_n)^2]^{1/2}$$

and we want to minimize it by the right choice of coefficients p_n (n=1,...,m), such that $F\in$***Space***. Equivalently, the problem is the minimization problem of the functional

$$T(F) = \sum_{0\leq n\leq m} (p_n-c_n)^2. \tag{24}$$

9.3.2. Numerical Solution

In case of the values

$$b=100\ ,\ \mu_1=1.5\ ,\ \mu_2=43, \tag{25}$$

$$c_n=1/(m+1)\ (n=0,1,2,...,m) \tag{26}$$

and m=100, the general optimization algorithm furnishes the solution

$$F_{100} = 0.3806A_0+0.2881A_1+0.1974A_2+0.1085A_3+0.0213A_4+0.0041A_{100}.$$

It is calculated with the rough (see Ch.4.6.4) 100-discretization of ***Space***. In case of fine discretizations, the computing time is excessively long (on a 1994 P.C.).

9.3.3. Analytic Solution

Several tests with different values of m show that j(m) exists such that the solution F_m corresponding to the m-discretization has the structure

$$F_m = \sum_{0\leq n\leq j(m)} p_n A_{n\delta} + p_m A_{m\delta} ,$$

where the coefficients $p_0, p_1, \ldots , p_{j(m)} , p_m$ are strictly positive.

In the general case, let us assume that $F_m=\sum_{n\geq 0} p_n A_n=\sum_{n\in S} p_n A_n$, where

$$S = \{n / n\in\{0,1,2,\ldots,m\}, p_n>0\}.$$

S depends on m and on the fixed coefficients $c_0, c_1,\ldots,c_n$. For the moment we assume that S is known. Then the minimization problem can be solved by classical methods. Indeed, then it is equivalent to the minimization of the function

$$\sum_{n\in S} (p_n-c_n)^2 \qquad (27)$$

of the variables p_n ($n\in S$), under the constraints

$$\sum_{n\in S} p_n = 1 \;,\; \sum_{n\in S} np_n = \mu_1 \;,\; \sum_{n\in S} n^2p_n = \mu_2 \qquad (28)$$

because then the constraints $p_n>0$ ($n\in S$) are automatically satisfied. Hence, using Lagrange multipliers λ_1, λ_2, λ_3, the minimization of (27) under the constraints (28) amounts to the unconstrained minimization of

$$Q = 1/2 \sum_{n\in S} (p_n-c_n)^2 - \lambda_1 \sum_{n\in S} p_n - \lambda_2 \sum_{n\in S} np_n - \lambda_3 \sum_{n\in S} n^2p_n.$$

Taking the derivative with respect to p_n, we obtain that p_n ($n\in S$) must satisfy the relations

$$p_n = c_n + \lambda_1 + n\lambda_2 + n^2\lambda_3 \; (n\in S), \qquad (29)$$

We multiply by n and by n^2 and we sum over $n\in S$. Taking the constraints (28) into account, we obtain that λ_1, λ_2, λ_2 satisfy the linear system

$$1-\sum_{n\in S} c_n = \lambda_1 S_0 + \lambda_2 S_1 + \lambda_3 S_2,$$

$$\mu_1 - \sum_{n\in S} nc_n = \lambda_1 S_1 + \lambda_2 S_2 + \lambda_3 S_3,$$

$$\mu_2 - \sum_{n\in S} n^2 c_n = \lambda_1 S_2 + \lambda_2 S_3 + \lambda_3 S_4,$$

where

$$S_i := \sum_{n\in S} n^i \; (i=0,1,2,3,4).$$

In the general case, the set S is the largest subset of $\{0,1,...,m\}$ such that the coefficients p_n furnished by (29) are strictly positive.

We now consider the values defined by (25) and (26). Then

$$S = \{0,1,2,...,j(m),m\}, \tag{30}$$

where $j(m)$ is the largest integer such that the coefficients p_n furnished by the relations (29) are strictly positive.

For $m=1600$, we obtain $j(m)=53$ and then the solution of the minimization problem is

$$F_{1600} = \sum_{0\le n\le 53} p_n A_{0.0625n} + p_{1600} A_{100}.$$

Here p_n is defined by (29) with

$$\lambda_1 = 0.036155 \;,\; \lambda_2 = -0.000707284 \;,\; \lambda_3 = 0.000000429294.$$

It is not difficult to solve the minimization problem with hyper-fine discretizations. The discretizations with

$$m = 3200 \;,\; 2\times 32.000 \;,\; 2^2\times 32000 \;,\; ...$$

can be treated successively. Then the value of $j(2^{2n+1}m)$ must be sought near the value of $2j(2^n m)$.

Chapter 10

Loaded Premium Problems

10.1. Premium Calculation Principles

10.1.1. Pure Premium

In insurance, a **risk X** is any positive random variable with a finite expectation. The **pure premium of the risk X** is the expectation

$$E_F X = \mu_1(F) = \int x dF(x). \tag{1}$$

The subscript F emphasizes that the expectation of X is calculated with respect to the distribution function F. This precaution is necessary because several hypothetical distributions $F \in \boldsymbol{Space}$, for the same risk X, are considered in this Chapter.

10.1.2. Loaded Premium

A premium calculation principle on *Space* is a functional T on ***Space*** such that

$$T(F) \geq E_F X \quad (F \in \boldsymbol{Space}). \tag{2}$$

Then T(F) is the corresponding **loaded premium** of the risk X. Practical premium calculation principles should satisfy more properties than (2). For a discussion of these properties, and for the origin of some principles, the reader can consult Gerber (1979) or Goovaerts et al. (1983). The following are examples of premium calculation principles. The parameter γ is a strictly positive number.

Expected value principle:

$$T(F) := (1+\gamma) E_F X. \tag{3}$$

Variance principle:

$$T(F) := E_F X + \gamma \mathrm{Var}_F X. \tag{4}$$

Standard deviation principle:

$$T(F) := E_F X + \gamma [\mathrm{Var}_F X]^{1/2}. \tag{5}$$

Esscher principle:

$$T(F) := E_F(Xe^{\gamma X})/E_F(e^{\gamma X}). \tag{6}$$

In any case, ***Space*** is supposed to be such that T(F) is finite for all distributions $F \in$ ***Space***.

The premiums (3), (4), (5) and (6) are called, resp., **the expected value premium, the variance premium, the standard deviation premium, the Esscher premium, with parameter γ of the risk X**.

Let X and Y be independent random variables with the same distribution F. Then

$$(Y-X)(e^{\gamma Y}-e^{\gamma X}) \geq 0$$

because $e^{\gamma x}$ is an increasing function of $x \in \mathbf{R}$, and then

$$\begin{aligned} 0 \leq E[(Y-X)(e^{\gamma Y}-e^{\gamma X})] &= E(Ye^{\gamma Y}) + E(Xe^{\gamma X}) - E(X)E(e^{\gamma Y}) - E(Y)E(e^{\gamma X}) \\ &= 2E(Xe^{\gamma X}) - 2E(X)E(e^{\gamma X}). \end{aligned}$$

This proves (2) in the case of the Esscher premium.

10.1.3. Reinsured Risk

Let $\rho(\cdot)$ be a function on $\mathbf{R}_+$ such that

$$0 \leq \rho(x) \leq x \quad (x \in \mathbf{R}_+).$$

The new risk

$$X_\rho := \rho(X)$$

can be considered as the part of the initial risk X covered by a reinsurer. It can also represent the part of the risk kept by the first insurer. In particular, if $\rho(x)=x$ $(x \in \mathbf{R}_+)$, then no reinsurance is involved, and then $X_\rho = X$.

In the particular case of a stop-loss reinsurance contract with retention limit t, the first insurer covers the part

$$X \wedge t := \min(X,t)$$

of the initial risk X, and the reinsurer the part

$$(X-t)_+ = (X-t)1_{X>t}$$

The first insurer and the reinsurer can apply, independently, any premium calculation principle.

10.1.4. Optimization Problems

Let us assume that the reinsurer uses the variance principle. He cannot calculate the premium

$$T(F) = E_F X_\rho + \gamma Var_F X_\rho,$$

because he ignores the distribution function F of the initial risk X. The safest strategy that he can adopt, is to charge the premium

$$\sup_{F \in \boldsymbol{Space}} T(F), \tag{7}$$

where ***Space*** is the hypothetic space. This kind of strategy probably originated in the beginning of the 1970's in the mind of famous Swiss actuaries (Straub, Bichsel, Bühlmann,...).

Of course, the problem is the same for the first insurer, even when no reinsurance is involved, if he applies a premium calculation principle based on more characteristics of F than the moments $\mu_1(F)$ and $\mu_2(F)$. For instance, the distribution F must be completely specified if he uses the Esscher premium.

The maximization problem (7) can be considered for any premium calculation principle, for any function $\rho(\cdot)$ and for any hypothetic space ***Space***.

The following sections illustrate the general method allowing to solve numerically about any practical maximization problem (7). All solutions can be found by the general optimization algorithm of foregoing Chapter 9. In any case the objective functional is a multiple integral functional.

Needless to say that the minimization problems as well as the corresponding maximization problems can be considered and solved.

10.2. Relevant Functionals of Loaded Premiums

For the moment, the hypothetic space ***Space*** is any Krein-Milman space, ρ is any function on $\mathbf{R}_+$ such that $0 \le \rho(x) \le x$ and we consider the risk $X_\rho := \rho(X)$. Only distribution functions F,G belonging to ***Space*** are considered and τ is a variable with values in [0,1].

10.2.1. Expected Value Premium

Objective functional

The objective functional of the optimization problems (maximization or minimization) is

$$T(F) = (1+\gamma)\int \rho dF. \tag{8}$$

Restriction to segments

$$\begin{aligned} T_{FG}(\tau) &= T[(1-\tau)F+\tau G] = T[F+\tau(G-F)] \\ &= (1+\gamma)[\int \rho dF + \tau \int \rho d(G-F)] \end{aligned} \tag{9}$$

Hence, **the objective functional T is linear on segments**. The solutions are extremal points of ***Space***. The numerical algorithms of Ch.4.7 can be applied if ***Space*** is a space of mixtures with integral constraints, in particular if ***Space*** is a pure moment space, or an m-unimodal moment ***Space***.

10.2.2. Variance Premium

Objective functional

The objective functional of the optimization problems is

$$T(F) = E_F\rho(X) + \gamma Var_F\rho(X) = \int \rho dF + \gamma[\int \rho^2 dF - [\int \rho dF]^2]. \tag{10}$$

Restriction to segments

$$\begin{aligned} T_{FG}(\tau) &= T[(1-\tau)F+\tau G] = T[F+\tau(G-F)] \\ &= \int \rho dF + \tau \int \rho d(G-F) + \gamma[\int \rho^2 dF + \tau \int \rho^2 d(G-F) - [\int \rho dF + \tau \int \rho d(G-F)]^2]. \end{aligned}$$

Hence

$$T_{FG}(\tau) = T_0 + \tau T_1 + \tau^2 T_2, \tag{11}$$

where

$$T_0 := \int \rho dF + \gamma[\int \rho^2 dF - [\int \rho dF]^2],$$

$$T_1 := \int \rho d(G-F) + \gamma[\int \rho^2 d(G-F) - 2\int \rho dF . \int \rho d(G-F)]$$

$$T_2 := \gamma[\int \rho d(G-F)]^2$$

We observe that $T_2 \geq 0$. Hence, **the objective functional T is convex on segments**. Functionals convex on segments are maximum at segment extremities. By Ch.4.Th.1.Cor., the solution of the maximization problem is an extremal point of ***Space***. The numerical algorithms of Ch.4.7 can be applied if ***Space*** is a space of mixtures with integral constraints, in particular if ***Space*** is a pure moment space, or a m-unimodal moment ***Space***.

Directional derivative

$$T'(F,G) = T_1.$$

T_1 is linear in G. Hence, **the directional derivative T′ is direction-linear**.

10.2.3. Standard Deviation Premium

Objective functional

The objective functional of the optimization problems is

$$T(F) = E_F\rho(X) + \gamma[Var_F\rho(X)]^{1/2} = \int \rho dF + \gamma[\int \rho^2 dF - [\int \rho dF]^2]^{1/2}. \tag{12}$$

Restriction to segments

$$T_{FG}(\tau) = T[(1-\tau)F+\tau G] = T[F+\tau(G-F)]$$

$$= \int \rho dF + \tau\int \rho d(G-F) + \gamma[\int \rho^2 dF + \tau\int \rho^2 d(G-F) - [\int \rho dF + \tau\int \rho d(G-F)]^2]^{1/2}.$$

Hence

$$T_{FG}(\tau) = S_0 + \tau S_1 + \gamma[T_0 + \tau T_1 + \tau^2 T_2]^{1/2}, \tag{13}$$

where

$$S_0 := \int \rho dF \ , \ S_1 := \int \rho d(G-F),$$

$$T_0 := \int \rho^2 dF - [\int \rho dF]^2 \ , \ T_1 := \int \rho^2 d(G-F) - 2\int \rho dF . \int \rho d(G-F),$$

$$T_2 := [\int \rho d(G-F)]^2.$$

Directional derivative

By (13),

$$T'_{FG}(\tau) = S_1 + \gamma/2\ [T_0+\tau T_1+\tau^2 T_2]^{-1/2}[T_1+2\tau T_2]. \qquad (14)$$

Then

$$T'(F,G) = S_1 + \gamma/2\ [T_0]^{-1/2} T_1. \qquad (15)$$

We notice that T_0 does not depend on G, and that S_1 and T_1 are linear in G. Hence, **the directional derivative T′ is direction-linear**.

10.2.4. Esscher Premium

Objective functional

$$T(F) = [\int \rho e^{\gamma\rho} dF]/[\int e^{\gamma\rho} dF]. \qquad (16)$$

Restriction to segments

$$T_{FG}(\tau) = [\int \rho e^{\gamma\rho} dF + \tau \int \rho e^{\gamma\rho} d(G-F)]/[\int e^{\gamma\rho} dF + \tau \int e^{\gamma\rho} d(G-F)].$$

Hence

$$T_{FG}(\tau) = [S_0+\tau S_1]/[T_0+\tau T_1], \qquad (17)$$

where

$$S_0 := \int \rho e^{\gamma\rho} dF \ , \ S_1 := \int \rho e^{\gamma\rho} d(G-F) \ , \ T_0 := \int e^{\gamma\rho} dF \ , \ T_1 := \int e^{\gamma\rho} d(G-F).$$

Directional derivative

$$T'_{FG}(\tau) = [S_1(T_0+\tau T_1) - T_1(S_0+\tau S_1)]/[T_0+\tau T_1]^2. \qquad (18)$$

Then

$$T'(F,G) = (S_1 T_0 - T_1 S_0)/T_0^2. \qquad (19)$$

The directional derivative is direction-linear.

10.3. Particular Optimization Problems

10.3.1. Definition of Particular Problems

In the following sections, we consider the maximization and the minimization of loaded premiums. We develop numerical examples in the case of a stop-loss reinsurance. For all premium calculation principles we consider a pure hypothetic space with one, two or three fixed moments. We also consider a subspace specified by an m-unimodality constraint. In all cases, the distributions are concentrated on some interval [0,b] and we call b the **maximal claim**. The maximal claim b is such that the probability of a claim strictly larger than b is zero or negligible. The maximal claim b can have other interpretations. A modification of stop-loss reinsurance often introduced is for the amount of the reinsurance liabilility to be restricted to the amount b–t, so that the payment is limited to this if the claim exceeds b. In another variant of stop-loss reinsurance, the reinsurer's liability is limited to a certain percentage p(b–t) ($0<p<t$) of b–t, the balance being met by the cedent. Needless to say that the methodology of this Chapter applies to these cases.

10.3.2. Relevant Functions of Stop-Loss Reinsurance

In the numerical illustrations we consider the following particular function with $0<t<b$, and with $0<m<t<b$ in case of an m-unimodal uncertainty space.

$$\rho(x) = (x-t)_+ \quad (0 \le x \le b). \tag{20}$$

Case of a pure hypothetic space

In case of a pure hypothetic space, the following integrals and the corresponding integrals with G instead of F, occur in the expression of the objective functional and of its restriction to segments:

$$\int \rho dF = \int_{[0,b]} (x-t)_+ dF(x) \ , \ \int \rho^2 dF = \int_{[0,b]} (x-t)_+^2 dF(x). \tag{21}$$

$$\int \rho e^{\gamma\rho} dF = \int (x-t)_+ e^{\gamma(x-t)_+} \, dF(x), \tag{22}$$

$$\int e^{\gamma\rho} dF = \int e^{\gamma(x-t)_+} \, dF(x). \tag{23}$$

Case of an m-unimodal hypothetic space

The expressions of the associated moments are

$$\mu_1^\bullet=2\mu_1-m\ ,\ \mu_2^\bullet=3\mu_2-2m\mu_1\ ,\ \mu_3^\bullet=4\mu_3-3m\mu_2\ ,\ \mu_4^\bullet=5\mu_4-4m\mu_3 \tag{24}$$

by Ch.3.(138).

We need the associated functions $\rho^\bullet$, $(\rho^2)^\bullet$, $(\rho e^{\gamma\rho})^\bullet$, $(e^{\gamma\rho})^\bullet$ of the functions ρ , ρ^2 , $\rho e^{\gamma\rho}$, $e^{\gamma\rho}$ occurring in the integrals (21), (22) and (23).

$$\rho^\bullet(x) := \int_{[0,b]} \rho(y)dR_{mx}(y) = \int_{[0,b]}(y-t)_+dR_{mx}(y)$$
$$= 1/2\ [(x-t)^2/(x-m)]\ 1_{t\le x\le b}\ \ (0\le x\le b), \tag{25}$$

$$(\rho^2)^\bullet(x) := \int_{[0,b]} \rho^2(y)dR_{mx}(y) = \int_{[0,b]}(y-t)_+^2\, dR_{mx}(y).$$
$$= 1/3\ [(x-t)^3/(x-m)]\ 1_{t\le x\le b}\ \ (0\le x\le b). \tag{26}$$

For $t\le x\le b$:

$$(\rho e^{\gamma\rho})^\bullet(x) = \int_{[0,b]}\rho(y)e^{\rho(y)}dR_{mx}(y) = 1/(x-m)\int_{[t,x]}(y-t)e^{\gamma(y-t)}dy$$
$$= 1/[\gamma^2(x-m)]\int_{[t,x]}\gamma(y-t)e^{\gamma(y-t)}d[\gamma(y-t)] = 1/\gamma^2(x-m)\int_{[0,\gamma(x-t)]} ze^z dz$$
$$=1/[\gamma^2(x-m)]\int_{[0,\gamma(x-t)]} d[e^z(z-1)].$$

Hence,

$$(\rho e^{\gamma\rho})^\bullet(x) = 1/[\gamma^2(x-m)]\ [e^{\gamma(x-t)}(\gamma(x-t)-1)+1]1_{t\le x\le b}\ \ (0\le x\le b). \tag{27}$$

For $0\le x<t$:

$$(e^{\gamma\rho})(x) = 1.$$

For $t\le x\le b$:

$$(e^{\gamma\rho})^\bullet(x) = \int_{[0,b]}e^{\rho(y)}dR_{mx}(y)$$
$$= \int_{[m,t]}e^{\rho(y)}dR_{mx}(y) + \int_{[t,x]}e^{\rho(y)}dR_{mx}(y),$$

where

$$\int_{[m,t]}e^{\rho(y)}dR_{mx}(y) = (t-m)/(x-m),$$

and

$$\int_{[t,x]}e^{\rho(y)}dR_{mx}(y) = 1/(x-m)\int_{[t,x]}e^{\gamma(y-t)}dy$$
$$= 1/[\gamma(x-m)]\int_{[t,x]}e^{\gamma(y-t)}d[\gamma(y-t)]$$

$$= 1/[\gamma(x-m)] \int_{[0,\gamma(x-t)]} e^z dz = 1/[\gamma(x-m)]\ [e^{\gamma(x-t)}-1].$$

Hence,

$$(e^{\gamma\rho})^{\bullet}(x) = 1_{0\leq x<t} + 1/[\gamma(x-m)]\ [e^{\gamma(x-t)}+\gamma(t-m)-1]\,1_{t\leq x\leq b}. \tag{28}$$

10.3.3. Numerical Values of Parameters

The optimizations are performed on the hypothetic spaces

$$\textbf{\textit{Prob}}[[0,b];\mu_1]\ ,\ \textbf{\textit{Prob}}[[0,b];\mu_1,\mu_2]\ ,\ \textbf{\textit{Prob}}[[0,b];\mu_1,\mu_2,\mu_3], \tag{29}$$

$$\textbf{\textit{Prob}}[[0,b];\text{m-unim};\mu_1]\ ,\ \textbf{\textit{Prob}}[[0,b];\text{m-unim};\mu_1,\mu_2], \tag{29}$$

$$\textbf{\textit{Prob}}[[0,b]\text{m-unim};\mu_1,\mu_2,\mu_3], \tag{29}$$

in case of numerical values μ_1,μ_2,μ_3,b,m hereafter specified.

T(F) is the expected value premium, the variance premium, the standard deviation premium or the Esscher premium in case of a stop-loss reinsured risk with retention limit t. Hence, the function $\rho(\cdot)$ defined by (20) is used.

We use the following notations already introduced in Ch.6.3.1:

$Val_{k,max,pure}$ is the value of a maximization problem on a hypothetic space with k moment constraints and no unimodality constraint. If $_{pure}$ is replaced by $_{m}$, then the m-unimodality constraint is used. If $_{max}$ is replaced by $_{min}$, then the minimization problem is considered.

Moments, mode m, maximal claim b and retention limit t

We adopt the moments μ_1,μ_2 and μ_3 of the m-unimodal distribution

$$0.75R_{m,3} + 0.25R_{m,50} \text{ with m:=5.} \tag{30}$$

Then

$$\mu_1{:=}9.875\ ,\ \mu_2{=}243.5\ ,\ \mu_3{=}8730.6875 \tag{31}$$

by Ch.3.(131).

We consider the maximal claim b:=100. When an m-unimodality constraint is introduced we take m:=5. The distribution (30) is irrelevant. The moments (31) are also used when no unimodality constraint is involved. We take the retention limit t:=12.

Loading parameter γ

The meaning of γ is different in the various premium calculation principles of 10.1.2. Even more, γ has different dimensions. Indeed, let M be the dimension of money (in the same way, L is the dimension of length in physics).

Then γ is dimensionless in the expected value principle.

The dimension of $E_F X$ and $Var_F X$ is M and M^2 resp. Hence, the dimension of γ is M^{-1} in the variance principle.

The dimension of $[Var_F X]^{1/2}$ is M. Hence, γ is dimensionless in the standard deviation principle.

In the Esscher principle, the dimension of γ is M^{-1} because γX must be dimensionless.

These dimensions learn how γ must be transformed when real changes of money units are considered.

In the numerical examples, we fix γ as follows.

Expected value premium

$$\gamma = 0.4. \tag{32}$$

Then the expected value premium is $1.04 \times 9.875 = 13.825$ if no reinsurance is involved.

Variance premium

We take γ in such a way that the variance premium equals 13.825 if no reinsurance is involved and if μ_1 and μ_2 are fixed by (31).Hence

$$1.4\mu_1 = \mu_1 + \gamma[\mu_2 - \mu_1^2]$$

and then

$$\gamma = 0.027058. \tag{33}$$

Standard deviation premium

We take γ in such a way that the variance premium equals 13.825 if no reinsurance is involved and if μ_1 and μ_2 are fixed by (31). Hence

$$1.4\mu_1 = \mu_1 + \gamma[\mu_2 - \mu_1^2]^{1/2}$$

and then

$$\gamma = 0.326922. \tag{34}$$

Esscher premium

Here the rule of the two foregoing cases does not work. We fix γ by the condition

$$Val_{2,max,pure}(\text{Expected value premium}) = Val_{2,max,pure}(\text{Esscher premium}), \tag{35}$$

where the first member is calculated with γ=0.4 and the last member with the γ of the Esscher premium. Then the Esscher γ equals

$$\gamma := 0.018734. \tag{36}$$

10.3.4. Numerical Results

		k=1	k=2	k=3
Expected value premium	$Val_{k,max,pure}$	12.1660	7.0970	6.4114
	$Val_{k,max,m}$	8.4165	6.0570	5.7778
	$Val_{k,min,m}$	0.5429	2.9353	5.1494
	$Val_{k,min,pure}$	0	1.7500	3.7659
Variance premium	$Val_{k,max,pure}$	27.3385	6.5136	6.4720
	$Val_{k,max,m}$	14.5770	6.3253	6.3253
	$Val_{k,min,m}$	0.4030	5.2477	5.9617
	$Val_{k,min,pure}$	0	4.1851	5.0030
Standard deviation premium	$Val_{k,max,pure}$	17.2726	7.3659	7.2460
	$Val_{k,max,m}$	11.8283	7.0789	7.0345
	$Val_{k,min,m}$	0.6326	5.6368	6.6846
	$Val_{k,min,pure}$	0	4.6543	5.7126
Esscher premium	$Val_{k,max,pure}$	88.0000	7.5762	6.4114
	$Val_{k,max,m}$	58.6667	6.6453	6.0371
	$Val_{k,min,m}$	1.8333	5.6128	5.6621
	$Val_{k,min,pure}$	0	4.7661	4.7915

The functional T(F) is a function of 1 or 2 integrals. By Ch.4.Th.2, the solution of the problems is a 4- or a 5-atomic distribution in the pure case. It is a 4- or a 5-rectangular distribution in the m-unimodal case. In fact, the numerical computations show that the solution is a 3-atomic, or a 3-rectangular distribution for the numerical values of the parameters indicated in 10.3.2. The numerical values of the optimization problems are obtained in two stages. First the general algorithm of Chapter 9 is applied in order to verify that the solutions are extremal points. Then the algorithms of Ch.4.7 can be applied with hyper-fine discretizations. The values indicated in the foregoing table are exact values.

Chapter 11

Ruin Problems

11.1. Ruin Problems and Numerical Solutions

11.1.1. Numerically Solvable Problems

In this Chapter we consider a portfolio with i.i.d. claim amounts $X_1, X_2, \ldots$ Now F represents the distribution of any partial risk X_k and the hypothetic space ***Space*** is a family of such distributions.

We treat the optimization problems

$$\inf_{F \in \textbf{\textit{Space}}} T(F)\ ,\ \sup_{F \in \textbf{\textit{Space}}} T(F), \tag{1}$$

where T(F) is some ruin probability depending on fixed parameters such as the security loading, the initial risk reserve and the expected number of claims in one year.

A related problem considered in 11.5 is the optimization of the adjustment coefficient ρ_F of F.

The optimization of

fixed-time ruin probabilities in the classical risk model

and

infinite-time ruin probabilities in the classical risk model

can be performed numerically on a rather general hypothetic space.

Fixed-time ruin probabilities T(F) can be calculated very quickly by Panjer's recursions (Part I.Ch.5.Th.2) after the usual discretization. Infinite-time ruin probabilities T(F) can be obtained very fastly via the elementary risk model (Part I.Ch.10.2 and 10.3).

In case of fixed-time ruin probabilities, the total number N_t of claims in the time-interval [0,t] can be **a binomial negative random variable**, **a geometric random variable** or **a binomial random variable**, instead of **a Poisson random variable** as in the classical model. Panjer's algorithm can be used in each case.

11.1.2. Not Yet Numerically Solvable Problems

The optimization of infinite-time ruin probabilities in models with stochastic premium income (Vol.I.Ch.9), the optimization of finite-time ruin probabilities in the classical or in more general ruin models, cannot yet be executed in a satisfactory way. Indeed, then the computing times are excessive, even when very rough discretizations are considered.

11.1.3. Extremal Solutions

The optimization problems of the numerical illustrations of this Chapter are solved by the general algorithm of Chapter 9. In any case, this algorithm reveals that the solution is an extremal point of ***Space***. Then the numerical algorithms of Ch.4.7 can be applied and fine discretizations can be used when ruin problems are considered. Very fine discretizations are mostly excluded because then too long vectors must be manipulated. The latter remark does not apply to adjustment coefficient problems: they can be solved with hyper-fine discretizations on pure or m-unimodal moment spaces.

11.1.4. Discretization of Objective Functional

Any problem on a space of mixtures with integral constraints is replaced by the corresponding associated problem on a pure space (Ch.4.5). The mixture elimination can be performed in the integral constraints by the relations Ch.4.(52). In case of ruin problems, the mixture cannot be eliminated in the objective functional $T(F_U)$.

Let us assume that the original problem is a problem on an m-unimodal hypothetic space. Then, after the usual discretization and introduction of a new money unit, $T(F_U)$ becomes a ruin probability (fixed-time or infinite-time) corresponding to some finite-rectangular distribution

$$p_0R_{m,0} + p_1R_{m,1} + \ldots + p_{n_0}R_{m,n_0}. \tag{2}$$

Panjer's algorithm or the calculation of infinite-time ruin probabilities via the elementary risk model can be applied to finite-atomic distributions

$$F = q_0A_0 + q_1A_1 + \dots + q_{n_0}A_{n_0} \tag{3}$$

but not to finite-rectangular distributions (2). Hence, then some new discretization is necessary. In that case, we apply the approximation described in Ch.3.8 to each term $R_{m,j}$ ($j=1,\dots,n_0$) of (2). The result is some finite-atomic distribution (3).

In case of infinite-time ruin probabilities, a claimsize distribution adaptation (Part I.Ch.10.3.3) is applied to (3) before it is used.

11.2. Numerical Fixed-Time Ruin Probabilities

11.2.1. Objective Functional

In the classical actuarial risk model, the total claim amount in the time interval [0,t] is

$$S_t := X_1+X_2+\dots+X_{N_t} \ (=0 \text{ if } N_t=0), \tag{4}$$

where N_t is the number of claims in [0,t]. The random variable N_t is Poisson, with parameter $\lambda>0$. The expected number of claims in [0,t] is λt and the expected claim amount in [0,t] is $\lambda t\mu_1$ where $\mu_1=EX_k=\mu_1(F)<\infty$ is the first moment of the unknown distribution F of X_k. The distribution function F_t of S_t is the compound Poisson distribution (Part I.Ch.3.Th.5.c)

$$F_t = \textstyle\sum_{k\geq 0} p_{kt}F^{*k}, \text{ with } p_{kt} = e^{-\lambda t}(\lambda t)^k/k!. \tag{5}$$

The insurer starts with the initial risk reserve $u\geq 0$ and he earns the total premium $\lambda t\mu_1(1+\eta)$ ($\eta>0$ is the security loading) in the interval [0,t]. At the instant t he owns the amount $u+\lambda t\mu_1(1+\eta)$. He is **ruined at the fixed instant t** if

$$S_t > u+\lambda t\mu_1(1+\eta).$$

Hence, **the fixed-time ruin probability** at the instant t is

$$\begin{aligned} T(F) &:= P[S_t>u+\lambda t\mu_1(1+\eta)] = 1-P[S_t\leq u+\lambda t\mu_1(1+\eta)] \\ &= 1-F_t(u+\lambda t\mu_1(1+\eta)) = 1-F_t(x), \end{aligned} \tag{6}$$

where

$$x := u+\lambda t\mu_1(1+\eta). \tag{7}$$

Only x and λt are relevant: the ruin probability is the same if the parameters are modified in such a way that x and λt remain the same.

11.2.2. Numerical Algorithm

We assume that the claimsize distribution F is (3) (after discretizations, change of money unit and mode elimination if necessary). Then T(F) equals $1-F_t(k_0)$, where the integer k_0 corresponds to the value x defined by the relation (7). Now $F_t(k_0)$ results from Panjer's recursions. They say that

$$F_t(k_0) = h_0 + h_1 + \ldots + h_{k_0}, \tag{8}$$

where

$$h_0 = \textstyle\sum_{k\geq 0} p_k f_0^{\,k} = e^{\lambda t(f_0-1)} \tag{9}$$

and

$$h_k = \lambda t/k \textstyle\sum_{1\leq j\leq k} j f_j h_{k-j} \; (k=1,2,\ldots,k_0). \tag{10}$$

11.2.3. Numerical Results

Parameters of hypothetic spaces

We consider the hypothetic spaces Ch.10.(29) with the following values of the parameters:

$$b=100\,,\; m=1\,,\; \mu_1=1.5\,,\; \mu_2=43\,,\; \mu_3=2550. \tag{11}$$

Parameters of objective functional

$$\lambda t=10\,,\; x=100. \tag{12}$$

Value of problems

The values of the problems are displayed in the following table. The notations are the same as in Ch.10.3.3.

	k=1	k=2	k=3
$Val_{k,max,pure}$	0.1340	0.0442	0.0218
$Val_{k,max,m}$	0.0182	0.0140	0.0108
$Val_{k,min,m}$	0.0000	0.0058	0.0061
$Val_{k,min,pure}$	0.0000	0.0009	0.0033

Solution of problems

The functional T(F) defined by (6) and (5) is not continuous. For instance, T(F) contains the discontinuous term $-p_{1t}F^{*1}(x)=-p_{1t}F(x)$ (see Ch.4.(22)).

In some cases, the optimization problem has limit solutions only (see Ch.9.2.5).

In other cases, the solution is a special extremal distribution. For instance, the values $Val_{1,max,m}$, $Val_{2,max,m}$ and $Val_{3,max,m}$ are attained at the broad 2-rectangular, the final 2-rectangular and the broad 3-rectangular distribution resp.

11.3. Numerical Infinite-Time Ruin Probabilities

11.3.1. Objective Functional

Here T(F) is the infinite-time ruin probability

$$T(F) := \Psi_F(u) = 1-U_F(u) \qquad (13)$$

of the classical risk model with claimsize distribution F corresponding to the fixed initial risk reserve $u \geq 0$ (Vol.I.Ch.7.1).

11.3.2. Numerical Algorithm

We assume that the claimsize distribution F is (3) (after discretizations, change of money unit, mode elimination if necessary and claimsize distribution adaptation). Then T(F) equals 1−U(k) where k corresponds to the initial risk reserve u. By Part 1.Ch.10.(18),

$$U(0) = p/[1-qg_0],$$

$$U(k) = [p+q\sum_{1\le j\le k} g_j U(k-j)]/[1-qg_0] \quad (k=1,2,...), \tag{14}$$

with

$$g_j := [1-F(j)]/\mu_1(F) \quad (j=0,1,2,...)\ ,\ p:=\eta/(1+\eta)\ ,\ q:=1/(1+\eta). \tag{15}$$

11.3.3. Numerical Results

Hypothetic spaces

The same hypothetical spaces are considered as in 11.2, with the same numerical values (11).

Parameters of objective functional

$$u=200\ ,\ \eta=0.3. \tag{16}$$

Value of problems

	k=1	k=2	k=3
$Val_{k,max,pure}$	0.3083	0.0477	0.0371
$Val_{k,max,m}$	0.1019	0.0409	0.0364
$Val_{k,min,m}$	0.0000	0.0317	0.0360
$Val_{k,min,pure}$	0.0000	0.0252	0.0359

Solution of problems

	k=1	k=1	k=1
$F_{k,max,pure}$	Broad 2-at	Final 2-at	Broad 3-at
$F_{k,max,m}$	Br. 2-rect	Fin 2-rect	Br. 3-rect
$F_{k,min,m}$	Narr 1-rect	Init 2-rect	Narr 2-rect
$F_{k,min,pure}$	Narr 1-at	Init 2-at	Narr 2-at

Of course

$$F_{k,max,pure},\ F_{k,min,m},\ F_{k,min,m},\ F_{k,min,pure}$$

denotes the distribution furnishing the value

$$Val_{k,max,pure},\ Val_{k,min,m},\ Val_{k,min,m},\ Val_{k,min,pure}$$

resp.

11.4. Numerical Adjustment Coefficients

11.4.1. Objective Functional

T(F) is the strictly positive root ρ of the equation

$$\int_{[0,b]} e^{\rho x} dF(x) = 1+\rho\mu_1(1+\eta), \tag{17}$$

where μ_1 is the first moment of F and $\eta>0$ the security laoding (Part I.Ch.3. Th.3).

11.4.2. Numerical Algorithm

We use the elementary dichotomy algorithm for the calculation of the root ρ of the equation (17). See Ch.9.2.3.

11.4.3. Numerical Results

Hypothetic spaces and parameter of objective functional

The hypothetic spaces are the same as in 11.2 and 11.3. Again $\eta=0.3$.

Value of problems

	k=1	k=2	k=3
$Val_{k,max,pure}$	0.335757	0.017569	0.015143
$Val_{k,max,m}$	0.321922	0.015978	0.015084
$Val_{k,min,m}$	0.010129	0.014180	0.014945
$Val_{k,min,pure}$	0.005036	0.013034	0.014720

Solution of problems

	k=1	k=2	k=3
$F_{k,max,pure}$	Narr 1-at	Init 2-at	Narr 2-at
$F_{k,max,m}$	Narr 1-rect	Init 2-rect	Narr 2-rect
$F_{k,min,m}$	Br. 2-rect	Fin 2-rect	Br. 3-rect
$F_{k,min,pure}$	Broad 2-at	Final 2-at	Broad 3-at

The connection between this table and the corresponding table of solutions of 11.3.3 is intuitively obvious. Indeed, by Cramér's asymptotic formula (Part I.Ch.7.Th.17), the largest adjustment coefficient corresponds to the smallest ruin probability if the initial risk reserve u is large enough. The tables show that this condition on u must here be satisfied.

As a general rule, the final finite-atomic or the broad finite-atomic distribution is the solution of the maximization problem if u is large enough. See the following Theorem 5 for a particular case.

11.5. Theoretical Infinite-Time Ruin Probabilities

11.5.1. Problem

In the rest of this Chapter, the hypothetic space is

$$\boldsymbol{Space} = \boldsymbol{Prob}[[a,b];\mu_1,\mu_2]. \quad (18)$$

The problem is the optimization (minimization or maximazation) of the functional

$$T(F) := U(F,u) \ \ (F \in \boldsymbol{Space}), \quad (19)$$

where u is fixed, and U(F,u) is the infinite-time non-ruin probability in the classical risk model with distribution function F and initial risk reserve $u \geq a$. This problem has been treated numerically in the foregoing section 11.3 in case $a=0$. Here it is more convenient to work with non-ruin probabilities U instead of ruin probabilities Ψ. We use a rather flexible notation. Instead of U(F,u), we also write $U_F(u)$.

By Vol.I.Ch.7.Th.3, the renewal equation for the function $U_F(u)$ of $u \in \mathbf{R}_+$ is

$$U_F = p + qU_F * G_F, \quad (20)$$

where $p := \eta/(1+\eta)$, $q := 1-p$, and where G_F is the concave transform of F. The functions F, G_F, U_F are considered on $\mathbf{R}_+$ only.

11.5.2. Directional Derivative

We recall that

$$T_{F_0F_1}(t) := T[(1-t)F_0+tF_1] \ (F_0,F_1 \in \boldsymbol{Space};\ 0 \leq t \leq 1), \quad (21)$$

$$T'(F_0,F_1) := T'_{F_0F_1}(0) \ \ (F_0,F_1 \in \boldsymbol{Space}). \quad (22)$$

Theorem 1

Let $F_0, F_1 \in$ *Space*. $U_t \equiv U_{F_t}$ $(0 \leq t \leq 1)$ and

$$F_t := (1-t)F_0 + tF_1 \quad (0 \leq t \leq 1),$$

$$G_t \equiv G_{F_t} = (1-t)G_{F_0} + tG_{F_1} \quad (0 \leq t \leq 1),$$

a. The derivative $T'_{F_0F_1}(t)$ $(0 \leq t \leq 1)$ exists. It equals

$$T'_{F_0F_1}(t) = {}^{q}/_{p}\, ((G_1 - G_0)*U_t*U_t)(u) \quad (0 \leq t \leq 1). \tag{23}$$

b.

$$T'(F_0, F_1) = {}^{q}/_{p}\, ((G_{F_1} - G_{F_0})*U_{F_0}*U_{F_0})(u). \tag{24}$$

Proof

a. Hereafter $s, t \in [0,1]$, $s \neq t$. The relation

$$U_t - U_s = {}^{q}/_{p}\, (G_t - G_s)*U_t*U_s \tag{25}$$

results from the convolution product of the relations

$$U_t = p + qU_t*G_t \ , \ \ p + qU_s*G_s = U_s.$$

We notice that

$$G_t = (1-t)G_0 + tG_1 = G_0 + t(G_1 - G_0),$$

$$G_s = (1-t)G_0 + sG_1 = G_0 + s(G_1 - G_0),$$

$$G_t - G_s = (t-s)(G_1 - G_0),$$

and then by (25),

$$U_t - U_s = (t-s)\ {}^{q}/_{p}\, (G_1 - G_0)*U_s*U_t. \tag{26}$$

The functions G_0, G_1, U_s, U_t are probability distribution functions on $\mathbf{R}_+$. Hence the functions $G_1*U_s*U_t$ and $G_0*U_s*U_t$ are probability distribution functions on $\mathbf{R}_+$ and the function

$$|(G_1 - G_0)*U_s*U_t| = |G_1*U_s*U_t - G_0*U_s*U_t|$$

is bounded on $\mathbf{R}_+$. Then, by (26),

$$\lim_{s \to t} U_s = U_t\ \text{, uniformly on } \mathbf{R}_+ \tag{27}$$

and

$$(U_t-U_s)_{/(t-s)} = {}^{q}/_{p}\,(G_1-G_0)*U_s*U_t \rightarrow {}^{q}/_{p}\,(G_1-G_0)*U_t*U_t \text{ as } s\rightarrow t. \quad (28)$$

Hence,

$$U'_t = {}^{q}/_{p}\,(G_1-G_0)*U_t*U_t \ (0\leq t\leq 1), \quad (29)$$

where the accent represents a derivative with respect to t. This relation, at the fixed point $u\in\mathbf{R}_+$, proves a.

b. The relation (24) is the relation (23) at the particular point t=0 •

Remarks

a. Higher-order derivatives of the function $T_{F_0F_1}$ can be successively obtained by the argument of the preceeding proof. For instance, by the difference of (29) with the same relation for s, we obtain

$$(U'_t-U'_s)_{/(t-s)}$$

$$= {}^{q}/_{p}\,(G_1-G_0)*(U_t-U_s)_{/(t-s)}*U_s + {}^{q}/_{p}\,(G_1-G_0)*(U_t-U_s)_{/(t-s)}*U_t.$$

As s→t, we obtain

$$U''_t = 2{}^{q}/_{p}\,(G_1-G_0)*U'_t*U_t. \quad (30)$$

b. The same argument can be applied to the discrete renewal equation I.Ch.10.(13) of the elementary risk model

$$\underline{U} = p\underline{1} + q\underline{U}*\underline{G}. \quad (31)$$

Then, with the obvious notations, (29) becomes

$$\underline{U}'_t = {}^{q}/_{p}\,(\underline{G}_1-\underline{G}_0)*\underline{U}_t*\underline{U}_t \ (0\leq t\leq 1). \quad (32)$$

11.5.3. Existence of a Solution

Theorem 2

The problems

$$\mathbf{inf}_{F\in Space}\,\mathbf{T(F)}\ ,\ \mathbf{sup}_{F\in Space}\,\mathbf{T(F)} \quad (33)$$

defined by (18) and (19), have a solution.

Proof

Space is compact by Ch.3.Th.1.a. By Ch.1.Th.2, it is enough to verify that the functional T is continuous on ***Space***.

We first observe that, for any functions $F, F_1, F_2, \ldots \in$ ***Space***,

$$[F_n \to_w F] \Rightarrow [G_{F_n} \to G_F \text{ uniformly on } \mathbf{R}_+ \text{ as } n\uparrow\infty]. \tag{34}$$

Indeed,

$$\mu_1|G_{F_n}(x)-G_F(x)| \le \int_{[0,x]} |F_n(y)-F(y)|dy \le \int_{[0,b]} |F_n(y)-F(y)|dy \quad (0\le x\le b)$$

and

$$G_{F_n} = G_F = 1 \text{ on } [b,\infty[.$$

Then

$$F_n \to_w F \Rightarrow T(F_n) \to T(F)$$

Indeed, by (25),

$$|T(F_n)-T(F)| = |U_{F_n}(u)-U_F(u)| =$$

$$q/p\ |((G_{F_n}-G_F)*U_{F_n}*U_F)(u)| \le q/p\ \sup_{x\ge 0}|G_{F_n}(x)-G_F(x)| \quad \bullet$$

The solution of the problems (33) is probably unique if $b\le u$. No proof has been furnished hitherto.

The solution is not necessarily unique if $u<b$. Indeed, let $u<b$ and let F be a solution of one of the problems (33). Then $T(F)=U_F(u)$ depends only on the restriction of F to the interval $[0,u]$, by Part.I.Ch.7.Th.4.Cor.b. Hence F remains a solution if we modify that distribution on $]u,b]$ in such a way that it still belongs to ***Space***.

11.5.4. Atomicity of Solution

For any $F\in$ ***Space***, we denote by V_F the function with values

$$V_F(x) := (U_F*U_F)'(u-x) \quad (0\le x\le u). \tag{35}$$

We notice that the derivative $(U_F)'$ exists on $\mathbf{R}_+$ by Part I.Ch.7.Th.15.b. Then the derivative $(U_F*U_F)'$ exists on $\mathbf{R}_+$ by Part I.Ch.1.Th.12, and it equals

$$(U_F*U_F)' = U_F(0)(U_F)'+(U_F)'*U_F. \tag{36}$$

Theorem 3

Let F be a function in *Space* and I a closed interval in $[a,b\wedge u]$, such that V_F is strictly increasing or strictly decreasing on the interior $I°$ of I. If F is a solution of one of the problems (33), then the F-mass in $I°$ is zero or it is concentrated at a single atom of $I°$.

Proof

We assume that the F-mass in $I°$ is not zero, that it is not concentrated at a single atom and that F is a solution of one of the problems (33). We then derive a contradiction. We consider the last problem (33), i.e. the maximization problem, and we assume that V_F is strictly increasing on $I°$. The following argument can easily be adapted to the other cases. We assume that $I:=[c,d]$. By Ch.9.Th.2,

$$T'(F,F_0) \leq 0 \quad (F_0 \in \boldsymbol{Space}). \tag{37}$$

We will prove that this relation is contradicted. The concave transform G_F of F is a continuous function on $\mathbf{R}_+$. We consider its graph on the interval $[c,d]$, the right-sided tangent at the point $C:=(c,G_F(c))$, and the left-sided tangent at the point $D:=(d,G_F(d))$. See Fig.22. These tangents are not identical because the F-mass in $I°$ is not zero. They meet at some point P situated strictly above the graph of G_F because G_F is concave and because the F-mass in $I°$ is not concentrated at a single atom.

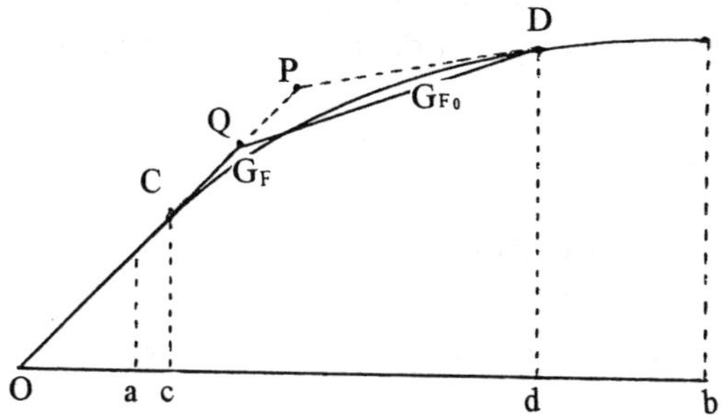

Fig.22. Function G of proof of Theorem 3

Let Q be a point on the segment $]C,P[$, and let G be the continuous function on $\mathbf{R}_+$ with the same graph as G_F outside $[c,d]$, and which graph is the polygonal line CQD on $[c,d]$. We take Q in such a way that

$$\int_I G_F(x)dx = \int_I G(x)dx. \tag{38}$$

The function G is a probability distribution function, and $\mu_1(G_F)=\mu_1(G)$ by (38) and by the surface interpretation of the first moment (Part I.Ch.1.1.5). The function G is the concave transform G_{F_0} of some distribution $F_0\in$***Space***, by Part I.Ch.3.Th.1.b. Then, by (24),

$$p/q\ T'(F,F_0) = ((G_{F_0}-G_F)*U_F*U_F)(u) = \int_{[0,u]} (G_{F_0}-G_F)(u\text{-}x)d(U_F*U_F)(x)$$

$$= \int_{]0,u[} (G_{F_0}-G_F)(u-x)(U_F*U_F)'(x)dx = \int_{]0,u[} (G_{F_0}-G_F)(x)(U_F*U_F)'(u-x)dx$$

$$= \int_{]c,d[} (G_{F_0}-G_F)(x)V_F(x)dx > 0. \tag{39}$$

The latter inequality results from an elementary integral inequality (Part I.Ch.7. Th.7.a.). Here the inequality is strict (see proof of elementary inequality). Then (37) is contradicted by (39) •

Let us call the distribution $F\in$***Space*** a **regular distribution** (with respect to the optimization problems (44)) if a finite number of points $c_0,c_1,\dots,c_k$ exist such that

$$a = c_0 < c_1 < c_2 < \dots < c_k = b\wedge u \tag{40}$$

and such that V_F is strictly positive or strictly negative on each of the intervals $]c_j,c_{j+1}[$ $(j=0,1,\dots,k-1)$. The function $F\in$***Space*** is an **irregular distribution** if it is not a regular one. The irregularity occurs if $V_F\equiv0$ on some open sub-interval of $[a,b\wedge u]$, or if V_F has an infinity of sign alternations on $[a,b\wedge u]$.

We say that **the distribution F is finite-atomic on the interval I** if the F-mass in I is concentrated at a finite number of atoms in I.

Corollary

Let F be a solution of one of the problems (33). Then F is finite-atomic on the interval [a,b∧u] or F is irregular.

Proof
Let us assume that F is regular. Let V_F be strictly positive or strictly negative on each interval $]c_j,c_{j+1}[$ $(j=0,\dots,k-1)$ considered in the foregoing definition. Then, by the Theorem, only the points c_j $(j=0,\dots,k)$ and at most one point $d_j\in]c_j,c_{j+1}[$ $(j=0,\dots,k-1)$ can be atoms of F and there is no F-mass elsewhere in $[a,b\wedge u]$ •

Irregular solutions do probably not exist, but no proof has been furnished hitherto.

11.5.5. Case of Large Initial Risk Reserves

Problem

We here denote by

$$P(u) = \inf_{F\in \textbf{\textit{Space}}} U(F,u) \qquad (41)$$

the problem already treated in the foregoing sections, but now different values of the risk reserve u≥a are considered. We are mainly interested in large values of u. We denote by

$$F_{fin} := pA_\theta + qA_b \qquad (42)$$

the final bi-atomic distribution of the hypothetic space (18).

Concave transform of F_{fin}

In Fig.23 are represented the graph of the concave transform G_{fin} of F_{fin} and the graph of the concave transform G_F of another distribution $F\in$***Space***. The relations

$$\mu_1(F_{fin}) = \mu_1(F) \ , \ \mu_2(F_{fin}) = \mu_2(F)$$

imply that

$$\mu_1(G_{fin}) = \mu_1(G_F) \text{ , i.e. } \int_{[0,b]} G_{fin}(x)dx = \int_{[0,b]} G_F(x)dx \qquad (43)$$

by the surface interpretation of the first moment.

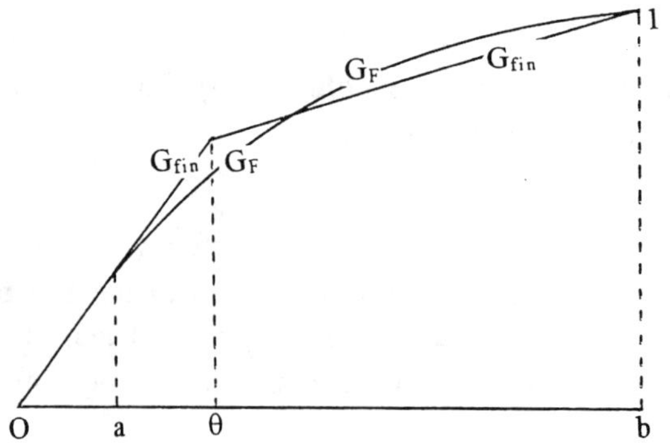

Fig.23. Concave transform G_{fin} of F_{fin}

Uniform solution of problems P(u)

The function $G_F - G_{fin}$ is a −+ function. By Part I.Ch.7.Th.9, the adjustments coefficients ρ_F and ρ_{fin} satisfy the relation

$$\rho_{fin} < \rho_F \ (F \in \textbf{\textit{Space}},\ F \neq F_{fin}). \tag{44}$$

Then u_F exists such that

$$U_{fin} < U_F \ \text{ on } [u_F, \infty[\tag{45}$$

by Cramér's asymptotic formula (Part I.Ch.7.Th.17). In (45), F is any feasible distribution different from the final bi-atomic distribution F_{fin}. Hence

$$\text{For all } F \in \textbf{\textit{Space}},\ u_F \text{ exists such that } U_{fin} \leq U_F \text{ on } [u_F, \infty[. \tag{46}$$

We notice that u_F in (46) may depend on F. The proposition (46) does not logically imply the proposition

$$\text{Some } u_0 \text{ exists such that } U_{fin} \leq U_F \text{ on } [u_0, \infty[\text{ for all } F \in \textbf{\textit{Space}}. \tag{47}$$

The proposition (47) is nevertheless correct. Its proof is based on the following Theorem 4. A proof can be found in the Reference 101.

Theorem 4

Some interval $[c_0, \infty[\subseteq R_+$ exists on which all distribution functions

$$U_{F_1} * U_{F_2} \ (F_1, F_2 \in \textbf{\textit{Space}}) \tag{48}$$

are concave (i.e. have a decreasing derivative) •

Theorem 5

Some $u_0 \geq b$ exist such that for all $u \geq u_0$, the final bi-atomic distribution F_{fin} is a solution of the problem P(u) defined by (41).

Proof
The assertion is equivalent to (47). Let $u_0 := c_0 + b$, where c_0 is the number existing by Theorem 4. Let $u \geq u_0$ and let F be any distribution in ***Space***. The function $G_F - G_{fin}$ is a −+ function. The function $(U_{fin} * U_F)'(u-x)$ is an increasing function of $x \in [0,b]$. Hence, by (25) and by an elementary integral inequality (Part I.Ch.7.Th.7.a),

$$p/q\,(U_F(u)-U_{fin}(u)) = ((G_F-G_{fin})*U_{fin}*U_F))(u)$$

$$= \int_{[0,u]}(G_F-G_{fin})(u-x)(U_{fin}*U_F)'(x)dx$$

$$= \int_{[0,u]}(G_F-G_{fin})(x)(U_{fin}*U_F)'(u-x)dx$$

$$= \int_{[0,b]}(G_F-G_{fin})(x)(U_{fin}*U_F)'(u-x)dx \geq 0 \quad \bullet$$

Part III

Credibility Theory

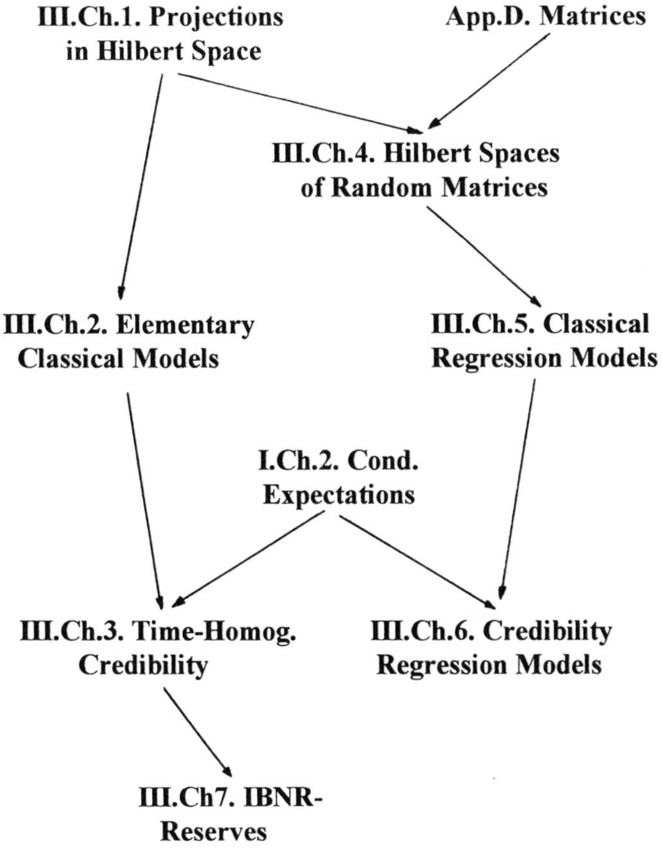
III.Ch.1. Projections in Hilbert Space
App.D. Matrices
III.Ch.4. Hilbert Spaces of Random Matrices
III.Ch.2. Elementary Classical Models
III.Ch.5. Classical Regression Models
I.Ch.2. Cond. Expectations
III.Ch.3. Time-Homog. Credibility
III.Ch.6. Credibility Regression Models
III.Ch7. IBNR-Reserves

Chapter 1

Projections in Hilbert Space

1.1. Projections in R^n

1.1.1. R^n as a Linear Space

For fixed $n \geq 1$, we consider the n-dimensional eucledean space $\mathbf{R}^n$, and we call it the **basic space** in this section 1.1. We here represent **points** of $\mathbf{R}^n$ by capital letters X,Y,... , with subscripts or not. (In all other places, X,Y,...are random variables or random vectors). **Scalars**, i.e. real numbers, are represented by small letters a,b,...,x,y,...

A **vector** is a couple (X,Y) of points X and Y in the basic space. The point X is the **origin** of the vector (X,Y), and the point Y is its **end**. Very often, points are regarded as vectors: the point X is identified with the vector (O,X), where O is the origin of the basic space. The point Y−X, with the explicit representation as a difference of Y and X, can be interpreted as being the vector (X,Y). The vector notations (O,X) or (X,Y) are not used hereafter. The context is always clear enough about the meaning, vector or point, of X or Y−X.

A **linear combination** of points $X_1,\ldots,X_k$ is a sum $Y := \sum_{1\leq j\leq k} a_j X_j$, with scalar **coefficients** $a_1,\ldots,a_k$. Linear combinations are, always, sums of a **finite** number of terms. Precisely, this linear combination is defined as follows. Let

$$X_j := (x_{j1}, x_{j2}, \ldots, x_{jn}) \quad (j=1,2,\ldots,k).$$

Then

$$Y := (\textstyle\sum_{1\leq j\leq k} a_j x_{j1}\,,\ \sum_{1\leq j\leq k} a_j x_{j2}\,,\ \ldots\,,\ \sum_{1\leq j\leq k} a_j x_{jn}).$$

We observe that Y is a point of the basic space. Hence,

Linear combinations of points in the basic space are points in the basic space.

This property is stated in the following equivalent way:

The basic space is a linear space.

Vector space is synonymous of **linear space.**

1.1.2. Planes

An **affine combination** of points in the basic space is a linear combination with coefficients adding up to 1. A **plane** is a subset of the basic space, containing all affine combinations of its points. We will clarify the intuitive content of this definition after the following Theorem.

Theorem 1

Let *P* be a subset of the basic space. Then *P* is a plane iff *P* contains all affine combinations of couples of points in *P*.

Proof

If ***P*** contains all affine combinations of points in ***P***, then ***P*** contains all affine combinations of couples of points in ***P***.

Conversely let us assume that ***P*** contains all affine combinations of couples of points in ***P***. By recurrence, we assume that ***P*** contains the affine combinations of k points of ***P*** and we prove that ***P*** contains the affine combination

$$Y := a_1X_1+...+a_kX_k+a_{k+1}X_{k+1}$$

of the k+1 points $X_j \in \boldsymbol{P}$. At least one of the coefficients a_j is not equal to 1. We may assume that $a_{k+1} \neq 1$. Then $a_1+...+a_k \neq 0$. Let

$$a:=(a_1+...+a_k)^{-1}.$$

Then

$$Z := aa_1X_1 + aa_2X_2 + ... + aa_kX_k$$

is an affine combination of the k points $X_1,...,X_k$ in ***P***. By the recurrence assumption, $Z \in \boldsymbol{P}$. Then

$$Y = (a_1+...+a_k)Z + a_{k+1}X_{k+1}$$

is an affine combination of the 2 points Z and X_{k+1} of ***P***. Hence $Y \in \boldsymbol{P}$ •

Let us consider two points X and Y in the basic space. If $X \neq Y$, then the set of affine combinations

$$Z := (1-a)X + aY \quad (a \in \mathbf{R})$$

of X and Y, is the **straight line** through the points X and Y. If a=0, then Z=X. If a=1 then Z=Y. If X=Y, then $Z \equiv X$.

Hence, by Theorem 1, a plane is a subset ***P*** of the basic space such that the straight line through any two of its points lies entirely in ***P***.

According to this definition, the planes of $\mathbf{R}^3$ are the following sets:

$\mathbf{R}^3$, usual planes, straigth lines, points.

Void subsets of the basic space are not regarded as planes.

Similarly, the basic space $\mathbf{R}^n$ contains planes of dimension 1,2,...,n. From the dimensional viewpoint, the terminology might be a bit misleading. But there is no real danger, because the dimensions are completely irrelevant later. Planes are also called **affine subsets**.

Let ***S*** be a subset of the basic space. The **plane generated by *S*** is the smallest plane containing ***S***. Obviously,

The plane generated by *S* is the set of affine combinations of points of S,

because any affine combination of affine combinations of points $X_1,\ldots,X_k$, is an affine combination of these points.

But the following statement, inspired by Theorem 1, is false:

The plane generated by ***S*** is the set of affine combinations of couples of points of ***S***.

Indeed if ***S*** is a set with three different points, for instance, then the set of affine combinations of couples of points of ***S*** is a set formed by three different straight lines, and such a set is not a plane.

1.1.3. Planes through the Origin

A **linear subspace** of the basic space is a subset containig all linear combinations of its points.

Theorem 2

Let *L* be a subset of the basic space. Then *L* is a linear subspace iff *L* contains all linear combinations of couples of points in *L*.

Proof
The proof is similar to that of Theorem 1 •

Let ***S*** be a subset of the basic space. The **linear subspace generated by *S*** is the smallest plane containing ***S***. Obviously,

The linear subspace generated by *S* is the set of linear combinations of points of S,

because any linear combination of linear combinations of points $X_1,...,X_k$, is a linear combination of these points.

But the following statement, inspired by Theorem 2, is false: the linear subspace generated by ***S*** is the set of linear combinations of couples of points of ***S***.

Any linear subspace ***L*** contains O. Indeed, if X is any point of ***L***, then 0.X=O is a linear combination of points in ***L***. Any linear space is a plane, because affine combinations are particular linear combinations.

Theorem 3

A plane in the basic space is a linear space iff it contains O.

Proof
Let ***P*** be a plane containing O. Any linear combination $a_1X_1+...+a_kX_k$ of points in ***P*** can be completed, without modification, as affine combination

$$a_1X_1+...+a_kX_k+(1-a_1-...-a_k)O.$$

of points in ***P***.

Hence, it belongs to ***P***. This proves that ***P*** is linear.

Conversely, if ***P*** is a linear subspace then ***P*** contains O •

Hence, **plane through the origin** is synonymous of **linear subspace**.

1.1.4. Scalar Product, Norm and Orthogonality

The **scalar product** of the points

$$X := (x_1,...,x_n) \ , \ Y := (y_1,...,y_n)$$

(considered as vectors with origin O), is the scalar

$$<X,Y> \ := x_1y_1+...+x_ny_n \ .$$

The scalar product is commutative:

$$<X,Y> = <Y,X>. \tag{1}$$

The scalar product is bi-linear, i.e. linear in each argument:

$$<a_1X_1+...+a_kX_k \ , Y> \ = \ a_1<X_1,Y> + \ ... \ + a_k <X_k,Y>, \tag{2}$$

$$<X \ , a_1Y_1+...+a_kY_k> = a_1 <X,Y_1> + \ ... \ + a_k <X,Y_k>. \tag{3}$$

Other properties of the scalar product are

$$<X,X> \ \geq \ 0, \tag{4}$$

$$<X,X> = 0 \ \Leftrightarrow \ X=O. \tag{5}$$

The vectors X and Y are **orthogonal** if their scalar product <X,Y> is 0. The symbol $\perp$ indicates orthogonality:

$$X\perp Y \ \Leftrightarrow \ <X,Y> = 0.$$

The **length**, or **norm** ||X|| of the vector X is the positive square root of <X,X> :

$$||X|| = <X,X>^{1/2} \ .$$

The **distance** d(X,Y) of the points X and Y is defined by

$$d(X,Y) = ||Y-X||.$$

Theorem 4

For any points X, Y in the basic space,

$$||aX|| = |a|.||X||, \quad (6)$$

$$||X+Y||^2 = ||X||^2 + ||Y||^2 + 2 <X,Y> \quad \textbf{(Triangle Equality).} \quad (7)$$

Proof

$$||aX||^2 = <aX,aX> = a<X,aX> = a^2<X,X>,$$

by the bi-linearity of the scalar product. This proves (6).

$$||X+Y||^2 = <X+Y,X+Y> = <X,X+Y> + <Y,X+Y>$$

$$= <X,X> + <X,Y> + <Y,X> + <Y,Y> = ||X||^2 + ||Y||^2 + 2 <X,Y>,$$

by the bi-linearity and the commutativity of the scalar product. This proves (7)
•

1.1.5. Projections on Planes

Let ***P*** be a plane and X any point in the basic space. The (orthogonal) **projection of X on *P*** is the point Y of ***P*** such that X–Y is orthogonal to any vector with an origin and end in ***P*** :

$$X-Y \perp V-W \quad (V,W \in \boldsymbol{P}). \quad (8)$$

Let ***P*** be a plane through the origin O of the basic space. Then (8) is equivalent to the condition

$$X-Y \perp V \ (V \in \boldsymbol{P}). \quad (9)$$

Indeed, if (8) is true, then we can take W=O in that relation and then we obtain the relation (9). Conversely, if (9) is true, then we can write it for V and for W in ***P*** and then we obtain (8) by difference.

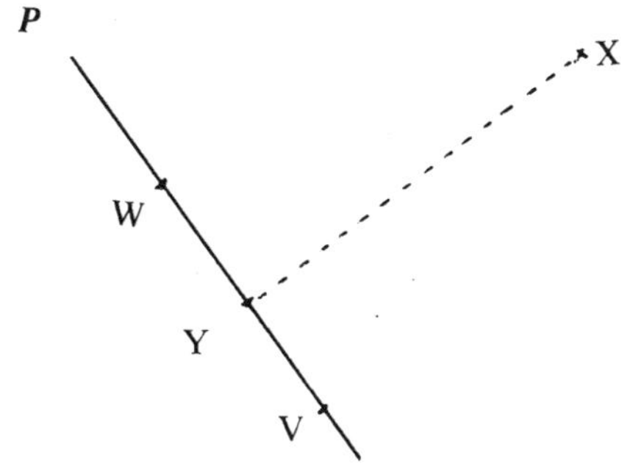

Fig.24. Projection on a plane: X–Y⊥V–W

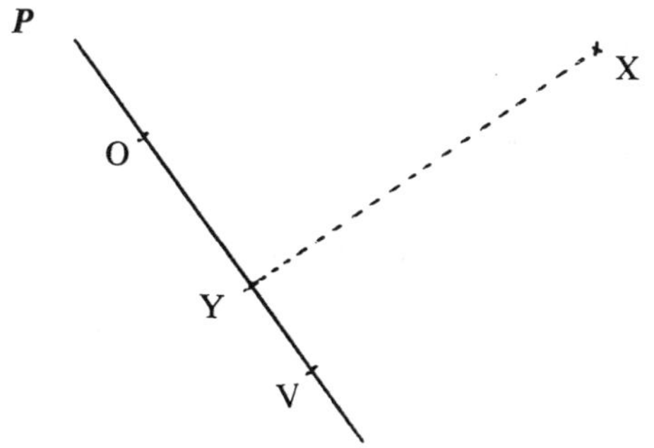

Fig.25. Projection on a plane through O: X–Y⊥V

We denote by Proj(X/***P***) the projection of X on the plane ***P***.

The existence and unicity of projections on planes is obvious in $\mathbf{R}^2$ (in which the planes are the complete space, straight lines or points) and in $\mathbf{R}^3$ (in which the planes are the complete space, usual planes, straight lines or points).

In most applications, the projections are found explicitly, proving their existence in the particular cases considered. The existence and unicity of general projections is proved in Appendix F.

1.1.6. Distance Minimization

Theorem 5

Let *P* be a plane and X a point in the basic space. Then Proj(X/*P*) is the point of *P* closest to X:

$$\mathbf{d(X,Proj(X/\mathit{P})) \leq d(X,Z) \quad (Z \in \mathit{P}).} \tag{10}$$

Proof
Let

$$Y := \mathrm{Proj}(X/\boldsymbol{P}).$$

Let Z be any point in ***P***. By the triangle equality

$$\|X-Z\|^2 = \|(X-Y)+(Y-Z)\|^2 = \|X-Y\|^2 + \|Y-Z\|^2 + 2\langle X-Y, Y-Z\rangle,$$

where the latter scalar product is zero because $X-Y \perp Y-Z$ by the definition of the projection Y. Hence

$$d^2(X,Y) = \|X-Y\|^2 \leq \|X-Y\|^2 + \|Y-Z\|^2 = \|X-Z\|^2 = d^2(X,Z)$$

i.e.

$$d(X,Y) \leq d(X,Z) \quad (Z \in \boldsymbol{P})$$

because distances are positive •

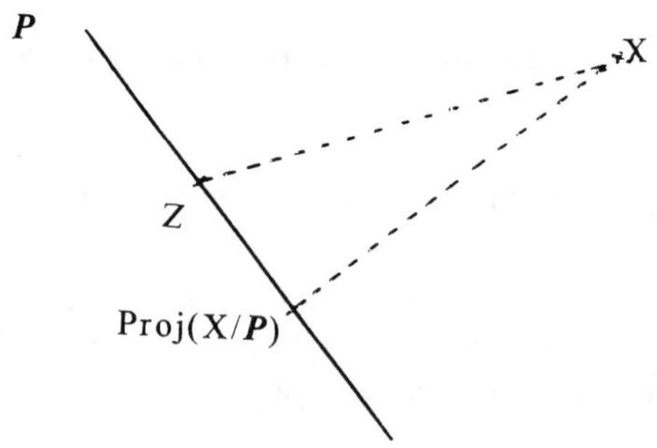

Fig.26. Distance minimization resulting from a projection

1.2. Projections in Hilbert Spaces

1.2.1. General Hilbert Spaces

A **Hilbert space** is a linear space of elements, called **points** or **vectors**, equipped with a **scalar product** $<\cdot,\cdot>$ having the properties (1) to (5) and having topological properties (not needed here), defined in App.F.

Hilbert space is closely related, especially in its elementary geometrical aspects, to $\mathbf{R}^n$. The definition and notation of

linear combination, affine combination, plane, plane generated by a set, linear subspace, linear subspace generated by a set, orthogonality, length or **norm, distance, projection on a plane,**

given in $\mathbf{R}^n$ are adopted in any Hilbert space $\boldsymbol{H}$. It is enough to replace **basic space** by $\boldsymbol{H}$ everywhere in the definitions of 1.1.

In the preceding section 1.1, the explicit definition of the scalar product $<X,Y>$ in $\mathbf{R}^n$ has never been used in the proof of the Theorems, but only the properties (1) to (5). Hence,

The results of the preceding section 1.1 are valid in any Hilbert space *H*.

1.2.2. Hilbert Space L_2 of Square-Integrable Random Variables

All the random variables considered hereafter are supposed to be defined on some fixed probability space. We denote by $\boldsymbol{L_2}$ the space of **square-integrable random variables**, i.e. the space of random variables X such that $EX^2<\infty$. Almost surely equal random variables are regarded as identical.

We recall the classical **Schwarz's inequality** (I.Ch.2.Th.7):

$$E^2|XY| \leq EX^2.EY^2 \text{ (X,Y any random variables).} \tag{11}$$

It shows that

The product XY is integrable if $X,Y\in L_2$.

L_2 is a space of integrable random variables

The latter property results from (11) with $Y \equiv 1$.

In next chapters we mainly project points X on finite-dimensional planes $\boldsymbol{P}$ in $\boldsymbol{L_2}$. (An exception occurs in the model developed in Ch.3.6.6). Then we can consider the linear subspace $\boldsymbol{R}$ of $\boldsymbol{L_2}$ generated by X and $\boldsymbol{P}$ and we can forget the points of $\boldsymbol{L_2}$ outside $\boldsymbol{R}$. The finite-dimensional space $\boldsymbol{R}$ can be identified with some euclidean space $\mathbf{R}^n$.

These considerations do reduce the projections to projections in $\mathbf{R}^n$. Hence, the topology is reduced to the topology of $\mathbf{R}^n$ and, strictly speaking, we do not need the more complicated topological structure of $\boldsymbol{L_2}$ when projections on finite-dimensional planes are considered.

Hence, for the applications of next Chapters, it is enough to prove the algebraic part only of the following classical Theorem of Probability Theory.

Theorem 6

$\boldsymbol{L_2}$ is a Hilbert space for the scalar product defined by

$$\langle X,Y \rangle := E(XY) \quad (X,Y \in \boldsymbol{L_2}).$$

Proof (algebraic part)

$\boldsymbol{L_2}$ is a linear space. Indeed, if $X,Y \in \boldsymbol{L_2}$,

$$E|aX+bY|^2 \leq E(a^2X^2 + 2|abXY| + b^2Y^2) \leq a^2EX^2 + 2|ab|\, E|XY| + b^2EY^2 < \infty.$$

The scalar product is obviously commutative and bi-linear. The property (4) amounts to $EX^2 \geq 0$. The part $\Leftarrow$ of (5) is direct. For the part $\Rightarrow$, let us assume that $\langle X,X \rangle = 0$. Then $EX^2=0$ and this implies that $X=0$ a.s. Then X is zero because almost surely equal random variables are identified •

1.2.3. Projection Theorems in L_2

Let $\boldsymbol{S}$ be a finite subset of $\boldsymbol{L_2}$. We denote by $\boldsymbol{P}(\boldsymbol{S})$ the plane through the origin generated by $\boldsymbol{S}$. For any real number μ, we denote by $\boldsymbol{P}_\mu(\boldsymbol{S})$ the set of random variables X in $\boldsymbol{P}(\boldsymbol{S})$ with an expectation equal to μ.

A sufficient condition in order to have $\boldsymbol{P}_{\mu}(\boldsymbol{S})\neq\emptyset$ is that $\boldsymbol{S}$ contains at least one random variable X with $EX\neq 0$. Indeed, then the random variable $\mu(EX)^{-1}X$ belongs to $\boldsymbol{P}_{\mu}(\boldsymbol{S})$. We implicitly assume that $\boldsymbol{S}$ contains some random variable with expectation different from 0 whenever the notation $\boldsymbol{P}_{\mu}(\boldsymbol{S})$ is used.

$\boldsymbol{P}_{\mu}(\boldsymbol{S})$ is a plane.

Indeed, let

$$Y := a_1X_1+...+a_nX_n$$

be an affine combination of points $X_1,...,X_n\in\boldsymbol{P}_{\mu}(\boldsymbol{S})$. Then $Y\in\boldsymbol{P}(\boldsymbol{S})$ and

$$EY = a_1EX_1+...+a_nEX_n = (a_1+...+a_n)\mu = \mu,$$

and then $Y\in \boldsymbol{P}_m(\boldsymbol{S})$

The notations $\boldsymbol{P}(\boldsymbol{S})$ and $\boldsymbol{P}_{\mu}(\boldsymbol{S})$ are also used with the explicit expression of the variables in $\boldsymbol{S}$. For instance

$$\boldsymbol{P}(X_1,...,X_k) \equiv \boldsymbol{P}(\boldsymbol{S}) \text{ with } \boldsymbol{S} := \{X_1,...,X_n\},$$

$$\boldsymbol{P}_{\mu}[X_{ij}(i\in I;j\in J)] \equiv \boldsymbol{P}_{\mu}(X_{ij};i\in I;j\in J) \equiv \boldsymbol{P}_{\mu}(\boldsymbol{S}) \text{ with } \boldsymbol{S} := \{X_{ij}/i\in I,j\in J\}.$$

Of course, in the next Theorem 7, $\boldsymbol{P}(1,\boldsymbol{S})$ is the plane through the origin generated by 1 and by the random variables of $\boldsymbol{S}$.

In the following Theorems, $\boldsymbol{S}$ is a finite subset of $\boldsymbol{L_2}$, X and Y are points in $\boldsymbol{L_2}$

Theorem 7 (Projection Theorem on Planes through O)

$$\mathbf{Y = Proj[X/}\boldsymbol{P}(\boldsymbol{S})\mathbf{]}$$

iff the following conditions a,b are satisfied:

a. $\qquad Y \in \boldsymbol{P}(\boldsymbol{S}).$

b. $\qquad E(YZ) = E(XZ) \quad (Z\in\boldsymbol{S}).$

Proof

For any $Y\in\boldsymbol{P}(\boldsymbol{S})$:

$$Y=\text{Proj}[X/\boldsymbol{P}(\boldsymbol{S})] \Leftrightarrow X-Y\perp Z\ (Z\in\boldsymbol{P}(\boldsymbol{S}))$$

$$\Leftrightarrow X-Y\perp Z\ (Z\in\boldsymbol{S}) \Leftrightarrow E(YZ)=E(XZ)\ (Z\in\boldsymbol{S}).$$

The $\Leftarrow$ part of the second equivalence results from the fact that each random variable in ***P***(***S***) can be displayed as a linear combination

$$a_1Z_1+\ldots+a_nZ_n$$

of random variables in ***S*** and

$$X-Y\perp Z_i\ (i=1,\ldots,n) \Rightarrow X-Y\perp a_1Z_1+\ldots+a_nZ_n \quad \bullet$$

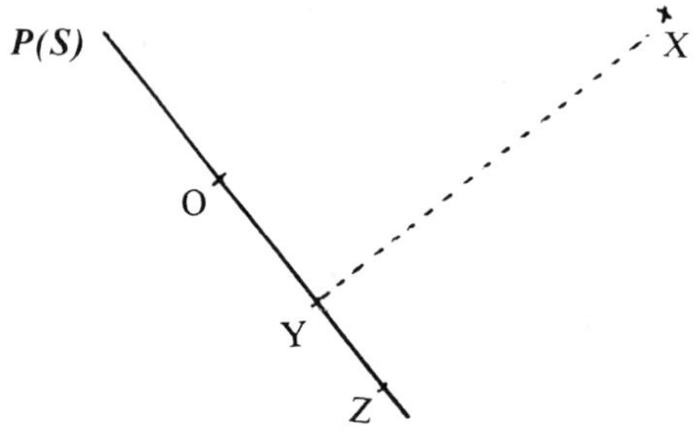

Fig.27. Projection on *P*(*S*).

Theorem 8 (Optimal Projection Theorem of Random Variables)

$$\mathbf{Y = Proj[X/}\boldsymbol{P}\mathbf{(1,}\boldsymbol{S}\mathbf{)]}$$

iff the following conditions a,b,c are satisfied:

a. (Linearity Condition)

$$\mathbf{Y\in}\ \boldsymbol{P}\mathbf{(1,}\boldsymbol{S}\mathbf{).}$$

b. (Unbiasedness Condition)

$$\mathbf{EY = EX.}$$

c. (Covariance Conditions)

$$\mathbf{Cov(Y,Z) = Cov(X,Z)\quad (Z\in}\boldsymbol{S}\mathbf{).}$$

Proof
Let Y be the projection of X on ***P***(1,***S***). In Theorem 7.b, we can take Z=1 and then we obtain EY=EX. From the relation of Theorem 7.b, we substract the relation EY.EZ=EX.EZ. Then we obtain the condition c above.

Conversely, if b and c are verified, then we add relation EY.EZ=EX.EZ to the relation of c and we obtain the relation of Theorem 7.b $\bullet$

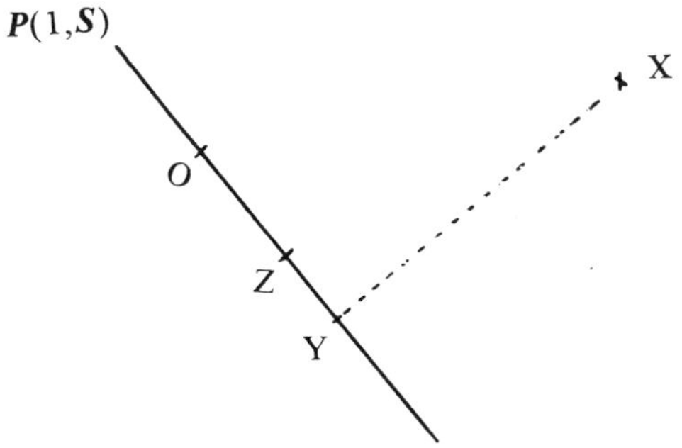

Fig.28. Projection on P(1,S)

Theorem 9 (Optimal Projection Theorem on Planes not through O)

Let EX≠0. Then

$$\mathbf{Y = Proj[X/}\boldsymbol{P}_{\mathbf{EX}}(\boldsymbol{S})\mathbf{]} \qquad (12)$$

iff the following conditions a,b,c are satisfied:

a. (Linearity Condition)

$$\mathbf{Y} \in \boldsymbol{P}(\boldsymbol{S}).$$

b. (Unbiasedness Condition)

$$\mathbf{EY = EX.}$$

c. (Covariance Condition)

Some constant c exists, so that Cov(X−Y,Z) = c EZ (Z∈*S*).

Proof

We assume (12). Then a,b are direct. In order to prove c, let V be a fixed random variable in ***S*** with expectation different from 0. Then

$$V_1 := (EV)^{-1}.EX.V \in \boldsymbol{P}_{EX}(\boldsymbol{S}).$$

Let Z∈***S***. We assume first that EZ≠0. Then

$$Z_1 := (EZ)^{-1}.EX.Z \in \boldsymbol{P}_{EX}(\boldsymbol{S}).$$

By (12),

$$X-Y \perp Z_1-V_1.$$

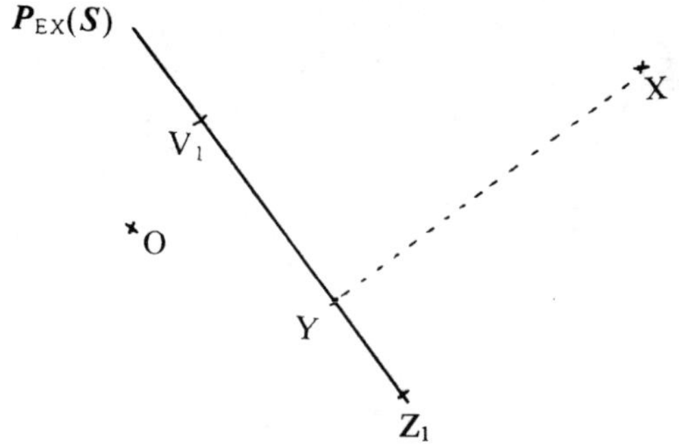

Fig.29. Projection on $\boldsymbol{P}_{EX}(\boldsymbol{S})$

Then

$$0 = E[(X-Y)(Z_1-V_1)] = E[(X-Y)(Z_1-V_1)] - E(X-Y).E(Z_1-V_1)$$

$$= Cov(X-Y,Z_1-V_1) = Cov(X-Y,Z_1) - Cov(X-Y,V_1).$$

Then

$$Cov(X-Y,Z_1) = Cov(X-Y,V_1),$$

$$Cov(X-Y,Z) = [(EX)^{-1}Cov(X-Y,V_1)]\ EZ.$$

The factor in square brackets, in the last member, does not depend on Z. This proves c for $EZ\neq 0$.

Let us now assume that EZ=0. Then V_1 and V_1+Z belong to $\boldsymbol{P}_{EX}(\boldsymbol{S})$. Then by (12),

$$X-Y \perp (V_1+Z)-V_1 = Z,$$

$$0 = E[(X-Y)Z] = E[(X-Y)Z] - E(X-Y).EZ = Cov(X-Y,Z)$$

and

$$Cov(X-Y,Z) = 0 = c\ EZ,$$

and we do have c again.

Now we assume a,b,c and we prove (12). Let the random variables of $\boldsymbol{S}$ be $Z_1,\ldots,Z_k$. Let

$$V := \Sigma a_i Z_i \in \boldsymbol{P}_{EX}(\boldsymbol{S})\ ,\ W := \Sigma b_i Z_i \in \boldsymbol{P}_{EX}(\boldsymbol{S})$$

Then

$$E[(X-Y)(V-W)] = E[(X-Y)(V-W)] - E(X-Y).E(V-W)$$

$$= \mathrm{Cov}(X-Y,V-W) = \mathrm{Cov}(X-Y,V) - \mathrm{Cov}(X-Y,W)$$

$$= \sum a_i \,\mathrm{Cov}(X-Y,Z_i) - \sum b_i \,\mathrm{Cov}(X-Y,Z_i) = \sum a_i \, c\, EZ_i - \sum b_i \, c\, EZ_i$$

$$= c\, EV - c\, EW = c\, EX - c\, EX = 0.$$

Hence

$$X-Y \perp V-W \quad (V,W \in \boldsymbol{P}_{EX}(\boldsymbol{S}))$$

and this is (12) •

Theorem 10 (Optimal Projection Theorem of Constants)

Let μ be a constant different from 0 and M a point in L_2. Then

$$\mathbf{M = Proj[\mu/\boldsymbol{P}_\mu(\boldsymbol{S})]} \tag{13}$$

iff the following conditions a,b,c are satisfied:

a. (Linearity Condition)

$$\mathbf{M \in \boldsymbol{P}(\boldsymbol{S}).}$$

b. (Unbiasedness Condition)

$$\mathbf{EM = \mu.}$$

c. (Covariance Condition)

Some constant c exists, so that Cov(M,Z) = c EZ ($Z \in \boldsymbol{S}$).

The projection M defined by (13) is the unbiased minimum-variance estimator of m in $\boldsymbol{P}(\boldsymbol{S})$.

Proof

The first part of the Theorem results from Theorem 9 with $X \equiv \mu$, $Y \equiv M$. For the last part, let M be defined by (13). Then, by Theorem 5,

$$\mathrm{Var}\, M = E(M-\mu)^2 = d^2(\mu,M) \le d^2(\mu,Z) = E(Z-\mu)^2 = \mathrm{Var}\, Z \quad (Z \in \boldsymbol{P}_\mu(\boldsymbol{S})) \; \bullet$$

In the foregoing Theorems 7,8,9 and 10, the set $\boldsymbol{S}$ is supposed to be a set of **observable random variables**, in the applications.

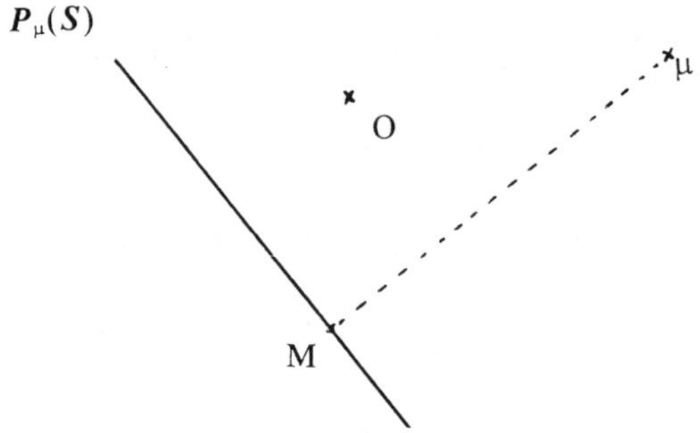

Fig.30. Projection of a constant μ

The projections furnished by the Theorems are **approximations** of the **not observable random variable** X or **estimators** of the **not observable constant parameter** μ. The random variable X is approximated by a linear function of the observable random variables in Theorem 7 and in Theorem 9. It is approximated by a linear function of 1 and of the observable random variables in Theorem 8.

We say that an approximation of a random X by a random variable Y in a given family is **optimal**, if it minimizes the distance d(Y,X) and if moreover, it is unbiased: EY=EX. All projections furnish a distance minimization by Theorem 5. The projections of the Theorems 8, 9 and 10 are unbiased, hence optimal.

If X is a constant μ in Th. 8, then the projection Y is also μ. Hence, Theorem 8 cannot be used for the estimation of constants. But Theorem 10 can be. There **optimal** is synonymous of **unbiased and of minimum-variance.**

Chapter 2

Elementary Classical Statistical Models

2.1. Random Variables with Fourth Order Moment

2.1.1. Definition and Properties of L_4

As usual, all random variables are supposed to be defined on the same probability space and almost surely equal random variables are identified.

We denote by L_4 the space of random variables having a fourth order moment, i.e. the space of random variables X such that $EX^4 < \infty$.

$$\textbf{The product XYZU is integrable if } X,Y,Z,U \in L_4. \tag{1}$$

Indeed, by Schwarz, for any random variables X,Y,Z,U :

$$E^4|XYZU| = [E^2(|XY|.|ZU|)]^2 \leq [E|XY|^2.E|XY|^2]^2$$

$$= E^2(X^2Y^2).E^2(Z^2U^2) \leq EX^4.EY^4.EZ^4.EU^4,$$

where the last member is finite if $X,Y,Z,U \in L_4$.

By (1), $L_4 \subseteq L_2$. Indeed, let $X \in L_4$. We apply (1) to the random variables X,X,1,1. The conclusion is that X^2 is integrable: $X \in L_2$.

L_4 is a linear space. Indeed, let $X,Y \in L_4$. Then

$$(aX+bY)^4 = a^4X^4 + 4a^3bX^3Y + 6a^2b^2X^2Y^2 + 4ab^3XY^3 + b^4Y^4,$$

where each term in the last member is integrable by (1).

2.1.2. Excess of a Random Variable

For any random variable X with first moment, we denote by X° the **centered random variable** $X° := X-EX$. Of course $X^{\circ 2} \equiv (X^\circ)^2$, $X^{\circ 4} \equiv (X^\circ)^4$.

Let $X \in \boldsymbol{L_4}$ The **excess** of X is the number defined by

$$e(X) := (EX^{\circ 4}/E^2X^{\circ 2})-3$$

if $EX^{\circ 2} > 0$. If $EX^{\circ 2}=0$, then we take $e(X):=0$.

This terminology is used in Cramér (1958). Other names for **excess** are **kurtosis** and **Fisher's coefficient** γ_2 .

Examples

a. If X is normal, then $e(X)=0$.

b. If X is Poisson with parameter $\lambda>0$, then $e(X)= 1/\lambda$.

c. If N is binomial with parameters $n,p,q:=1-p$ $(0<p<1)$, then

$$e(N) = (1-6pq)/(npq).$$

d. If N is uniform on $\{0,1,\dots,n\}$, then

$$e(N) = -6/5[2/n(n+1) + 1].$$

e. If X is uniform on $[0,a]$, then $e(X) = -6/5$.

f. If X is gamma with density

$$1/\Gamma(a)\, x^{a-1}e^{-x} \quad (x\geq 0),$$

where $a>0$, then $e(X)= 6/a$.

g. If X is Pareto with density $ax^{-(1+a)}$ on $[1,\infty[$, where $a>4$, then

$$e(X) = [[3(a-2)(3a^2+a+2]/[(a-4)(a-3)a]] - 6.$$

h. If X is lognormal with density

$$[x\sigma(2\pi)^{1/2}]^{-1} \exp[-(\log x - m)^2/(2\sigma^2)] \quad (x>0),$$

where $\sigma \in \mathbf{R}_{++}$ and $m \in \mathbf{R}$, then

$$e(X) = \exp(4\sigma^2) + 2\exp(3\sigma^2) + 3\exp(2\sigma^2) - 6.$$

Theorem 1 (Properties of Excess)

Let $X \in L_4$. Then

a. $$e(a+bX) = e(X) \quad (b \neq 0).$$

b. $$e(X) \geq -2.$$

c. $e(X) = -2$ iff X takes two different values, each with a probability equal to 1/2.

Proof
The relation $e(a+bX)=e(X)$ is direct. For b we have:

$$\begin{aligned} e(X).E^2X^{\circ 2} &= EX^{\circ 4} - 3E^2X^{\circ 2} = (EX^{\circ 4} - E^2X^{\circ 2}) - 2E^2X^{\circ 2} \\ &= \operatorname{Var} X^{\circ 2} - 2E^2X^{\circ 2} \geq -2E^2X^{\circ 2}. \end{aligned} \tag{2}$$

For c, it is direct that $e(X) = -2$ if $P(X=-1)=P(X=+1)=1/2$. Then, by a, $e(X) = -2$ if X takes any two different values with a probability equal to 1/2, each.

Conversely, let us assume that $e(X) = -2$. Then $EX^{\circ 2}>0$, and by the relations (2), $\operatorname{Var} X^{\circ 2}=0$, $X^{\circ 2}=c$ for some constant $c>0$. Then positive probabilities p,q exist such that

$$P(X^\circ = -c^{1/2}) = p \ , \quad P(X^\circ = +c^{1/2}) = q.$$

But $EX^\circ=0$. Hence $p=q=1/2$ •

2.1.3. Expectations of Homogeneous Forms of Degree 4

In the next Theorem 2, δ_{ij} is **Kronecker's symbol**, taking the value 1 if i=j and the value 0 if i≠j. We also use the symbol δ_{ijpq} taking the value 1 if i=j=p=q and the value 0 in all other cases. The subscripts i,j,p,q range over the values 1,2,...,n.

Theorem 2

Let $Y_1,...,Y_n$ be centered independent random variables in L_4. Let

$$u_i := EY_i^2 \quad , \quad e_i := e(Y_i).$$

Then

$$E(Y_iY_j) = \delta_{ij}u_i, \tag{3}$$

$$E(Y_iY_jY_pY_q) = \delta_{ij}\delta_{pq}u_iu_p + \delta_{ip}\delta_{jq}u_iu_j + \delta_{iq}\delta_{jp}u_iu_j + \delta_{ijpq}u_i^2e_i, \tag{4}$$

$$E(\sum_{ijpq} a_{ijpq}Y_iY_jY_pY_q) = \sum_{ij}(a_{iijj}+a_{ijij}+a_{ijji})u_iu_j + \sum_i a_{iiii}\, u_i^2\, e_i. \tag{5}$$

Proof
The relation (3) is direct for i=j and for i≠j. In the latter case, we observe that

$$E(Y_iY_j)=EY_i.EY_j=0.0,$$

by the independence of Y_i and Y_j and because Y_i and Y_j are centered.

The relation (4) is true in all possible cases. For instance, if i=j=p=q, then (4) becomes

$$EY_i^4 = 3u_i^2 + u_i^2(u_i^{-2}EY_i^4 - 3)$$

If i=j=p≠q , then (4) results from the relations

$$E(Y_i^3Y_q) = EY_i^3.EY_q = 0$$

and if i=j≠p=q, then it results from the relations

$$E(Y_i^2Y_p^2) = EY_i^2.EY_p^2 = u_iu_p$$

(5) results from (4) by summation •

Of course, for (3) it is enough to assume that $Y_1,...,Y_n$ are independent centered random variables in $\boldsymbol{L}_2$.

2.2. Classical Model with Unweighted Observations

2.2.1. Definition of the model. Problems

The **classical model with unweighted observations** is defined by n independent observable random variables $X_1,...,X_n$ with the same expectation μ, the same variance σ^2 and the same excess e.

The problems are

a. The estimation of μ.

b. The estimation of σ^2 when μ is known.

c. The estimation of σ^2 when μ is unknown.

We use the abbreviations

$$X_\Sigma := X_1+...+X_n \ , \ X_A := 1/_n X_\Sigma .$$

Of course, $_\Sigma$ and $_A$ are fixed subscripts. The random variable X_Σ results from X_i by the elimination of i by summation over all possible values of that index. The random variable X_A results from X_i by the elimination of the subscript i by the formation of a usual Arithmetic mean.

2.2.2. Estimation of μ

As possible estimators of μ, we consider the random variables of the family

$$\boldsymbol{P}(X_1,...,X_n).$$

The optimal estimator of μ in that family is

$$\mu_{proj} := \mathrm{Proj}[\mu/\ \boldsymbol{P}_\mu(X_1,...,X_n)].$$

By the symmetry of the model, we must have

$$\mu_{proj} = X_A.$$

This is easily verified by the optimal projection Theorem of constants (see the model with weighted observations of next section 2.3).

2.2.3. Estimation of σ^2 when μ Is Known

As possible estimators of σ^2, we consider the random varialbles in the family

$$\boldsymbol{P}(X_1^{o2},\dots,X_n^{o2}).$$

The optimal estimator in that family is

$$S_\mu^2 := \mathrm{Proj}[\sigma^2/\boldsymbol{P}_{\sigma^2}(X_1^{o2},\dots,X_n^{o2})].$$

For reasons of symmetry, the optimal estimator can only be

$$S_\mu^2 = 1/n\ [(X_1-\mu)^2 + \dots + (X_n-\mu)^2].$$

A confirmation of this is furnished by the optimal projection Theorem of constants (see the model with weighted observations of 2.3).

2.2.4. Estimation of σ^2 when μ Is Unknown

We observe that

$$n(X_i-X_A) = nX_i - X_\Sigma = \Sigma_j(X_i-X_j) = \Sigma_i(X_i^o-X_j^o),$$

$$n^2(X_i-X_A)^2 = \Sigma_{jk}(X_i^o-X_j^o)(X_i^o-X_k^o) = \Sigma_{jk}(X_i^oX_i^o-X_i^oX_k^o-X_i^oX_j^o+X_j^oX_k^o).$$

We apply E and we use the relation (3), i.e. $E(X_i^oX_j^o) = \delta_{ij}\sigma^2$:

$$n^2\ E(X_i-X_A)^2 = \Sigma_{jk}(\delta_{ii}-\delta_{ik}-\delta_{ij}+\delta_{jk})\sigma^2 = (n^2-n-n+n)s^2 = n(n-1)\sigma^2. \quad (6)$$

Hence, we can consider the family of estimators

$$\boldsymbol{P}((X_i-X_A)^2;i=1,\dots,n).$$

The optimal estimator of σ^2 in that family is

$$S^2 := \text{Proj}(\sigma^2/\boldsymbol{P}_{\sigma^2}((X_i-X_A)^2;i=1,...,n).$$

For reasons of symmetry, and by (6) (see the model of 2.3),

$$S^2 = 1/(n-1)\,[(X_1-X_A)^2 +...+ (X_n-X_A)^2].$$

2.2.5. Grouping of Observations

We here assume that

$$X_{11}, X_{12}, \dots, X_{1w_1},$$

$$X_{21}, X_{22}, \dots, X_{2w_2},$$

$$\dots \quad \dots \quad \dots \quad \dots \quad \dots$$

$$X_{n1}, X_{n2}, \dots, X_{nw_n},$$

are independent random variables with expectation μ, variance σ^2, excess e. Let

$$X_{i\Sigma} := X_{i1}+X_{i2}+...+X_{iw_i}, \quad X_{iA} := X_{i\Sigma}/w_i \quad (i=1,...,n).$$

Theorem 3

Under the indicated assumptions, X_{1A}, X_{2A}, ..., X_{nA} are independent random variables with

$$\mathbf{EX_{iA} = \mu \;,\; Var\, X_{iA} = \sigma^2/w_i \;,\; e(X_{iA}) = e/w_i \;\; (i=1,2,...,n).} \qquad (7)$$

Proof

The relations for EX_{iA} and Var X_{iA} are direct. In order to prove the relation for $e(X_{iA})$, we use the notations, for fixed i:

$$k := w_i \;,\; Y_j := X_{ij}^{\circ} = X_{ij}-m \;\; (j=1,...,k) \;,\; Y_\Sigma := Y_1+...+Y_k \,.$$

Then

$$E(Y_\Sigma)^2 = E(\textstyle\sum_{ij} Y_iY_j) = \sum_{ij} \delta_{ij}\, \sigma^2 = k\sigma^2 ,$$

$$E(Y_\Sigma)^4 = \textstyle\sum_{ijpq} E(Y_iY_jY_pY_q) = \sum_{ij} (1+1+1)\sigma^2\sigma^2 + \sum_i \sigma^4 e = 3k^2\sigma^4 + k\sigma^4 e,$$

by (5). Then

$$e(Y_\Sigma) = [E(Y_\Sigma)^4/E^2(Y_\Sigma)^2] - 3 = e/k,$$

and then

$$e(X_{iA}) = e(Y_\Sigma/k) = e(Y_\Sigma) = e/k = e/w_i,$$

by Th.1.a. •

Since excesses are discussed, it is implicitly assumed that the random variables X_{ij} above, belong to $\boldsymbol{L_4}$. If only the first two relations of (7) are considered, then it is sufficient to suppose that the involved random variables belong to $\boldsymbol{L_2}$ (we shall mostly not repeat this kind of observations hereafter).

2.3. Classical Model with Weighted Observations

2.3.1. Definition of Model. Classical Estimators

The model is defined by n independent observable random variables $X_1,\ldots,X_n$ satisfying the assumptions

$$EX_i = \mu \quad , \quad \text{Var}\, X_i = \sigma^2/w_i \quad , \quad e(X_i) = e/w_i \quad (i=1,\ldots,n). \tag{8}$$

By 2.2.5, this model results from a model with independent observations with the same expectation, the same variance and the same excess, by a grouping and averaging of some random variables. Here the weights w_i are supposed to be strictly positive, not necessarily integer.

In order to avoid some dull discussions, we assume $\mu\neq0$, $\sigma^2\neq0$.

The model is mostly used with e=0. Then it is still a generalization of the corresponding classical model with normal observations (see 2.1.2.Ex.1).

The classical estimator for μ is,

$$X_W := \textstyle\sum_i (w_i/w_\Sigma)\, X_i \ , \ \text{ where } \ w_\Sigma := w_1+\ldots+w_n \ . \tag{9}$$

The classical estimators for σ^2 are, under normal assumptions,

$$S_\mu^2 = 1/n \textstyle\sum_i w_i(X_i-\mu)^2 \ , \text{ if } \mu \text{ is known,} \tag{10}$$

$$S^2 = 1/(n-1) \textstyle\sum_i w_i(X_i-X_W)^2 \ , \text{ if } \mu \text{ is unknown.} \tag{11}$$

We will prove that the classical estimators X_W , S_μ^2, S^2 are optimal when it is only supposed that e=0, a much weaker assumption than the hypothesis that the observable random variables are normally distributed. In fact, the optimality of X_W is general, whatever the value of e is, and even if e does not exist (i.e. when the random variables do not have a finite fourth-order moment).

Hereafter i,j,k,p,q,r,s are subscripts taking the values 1,...,n, independently.

For any numbers a_i we denote by a_Σ the sum $a_\Sigma = a_1+...+a_n$.

2.3.2. Optimal Estimation of μ

Theorem 4

The optimal estimator of μ in the family *P*(X_1,...,X_n) is the classical estimator X_W.

Proof
The optimal estimator in the indicated family is

$$\mu_{\mathbf{proj}} := \mathrm{Proj}[\mu/\boldsymbol{P}_\mu(X_1,...,X_n)] =: a_1X_1+...+a_nX_n \ .$$

In order to find the coefficients a_i , we apply the optimal projection Theorem of constants. By the unbiasedness condition,

$$\mu = E\mu_{\mathbf{proj}} = E(a_1X_1+...+a_nX_n) = \mu a_\Sigma \ , \quad a_\Sigma = 1.$$

By the covariance condition,

$$\mathrm{const.} = \mathrm{Cov}(\mu_{\mathbf{proj}},X_i)$$

$$= \mathrm{Cov}(a_1X_1+...+a_nX_n,X_i) = a_i \ \mathrm{Var}\ X_i = a_i\ \sigma^2/w_i \ .$$

Hence, (different occurences of const. do not necessarily represent the same constant).

$$a_i = \mathrm{const}.w_i,$$

$$1 = a_\Sigma = \mathrm{const}.w_\Sigma \ ,$$

and the latter const. must be equal to $(w_\Sigma)^{-1}$ •

2.3.3. Unbiased Estimation of σ^2 when μ Is Known

Theorem 5

The random variable

$$\mathbf{V := a_1(X_1-\mu)^2 + ... + a_n(X_n-\mu)^2}$$

is an unbiased estimator of s^2 iff

$$\textstyle\sum_i a_i/w_i = 1. \tag{12}$$

Proof

$$EV = \textstyle\sum_i E(X_i-\mu)^2 = \sum_i a_i \text{ Var } X_i = (\sum_i a_i/w_i)\sigma^2 \quad \bullet$$

2.3.4. Optimal Estimation of σ^2 when μ and e Are Known

Theorem 6

The optimal estimator $S_\mu{}^2$ of σ^2 in the family $P((X_i-\mu)^2;i=1,...,n)$ is

$$S_\mu{}^2 = c \textstyle\sum_i [w_i/(2+eu_i)](X_i-\mu)^2,$$

where $u_i = 1/w_i$ and where c is defined by the relation

$$c \textstyle\sum_i[1/(2+eu_i)] = 1.$$

Proof
The optimal estimator of σ^2 in the indicated family is

$$S_\mu{}^2 = \text{Proj}[s^2/\boldsymbol{P}_{\sigma^2}((X_i-\mu)^2;i=1,...,n)]$$

$$=: \textstyle\sum_i a_i(X_i-\mu)^2 = \sum_i a_i X_i^{o2}.$$

In order to find the coefficients a_i , we apply the optimal projection Theorem of constants. The unbiasedness condition is (12):

$$\textstyle\sum_i a_i u_i = 1. \tag{13}$$

Covariance condition :

$$\text{const.}EX_j^{o2} = \text{Cov}(S_\mu{}^2,X_j^{o2}),$$

$$\text{const. } u_j = a_j \operatorname{Cov}(X_j^{\circ 2}, X_j^{\circ 2})$$

$$= a_j(EX_j^{\circ 4} - E^2X_j^{\circ 2})$$

$$= a_j(3u_j^2\sigma^4 + u_j^2\sigma^4 e u_j - u_j^2\sigma^4)$$

by Theorem 2, taking into account that $EX_j^{\circ 2} = u_j\sigma^2$ here. Hence

$$a_j = \text{const. } (2u_j + eu_j^2)^{-1} .$$

where the latter const. results from the unbiasedness condition (13):

$$1 = \text{const. } \textstyle\sum_j (2+eu_j)^{-1} \quad \bullet$$

Corollary

If e=0, the optimal estimator of σ^2 in the family $P((X_i-\mu)^2; i=1,\ldots,n)$, is the classical estimator S_μ^2 explicited in (10) •

2.3.5. Unbiased Estimation of σ^2 when μ Is Unknown

As in Theorem 6, we use the notation $u_i := 1/w_i$.

Lemma

$$\mathbf{w_\Sigma(X_r - X_W) = \textstyle\sum_i a_{ri}X_i^\circ}, \tag{14}$$

$$\mathbf{w_\Sigma^2(X_r - X_W)^2 = \textstyle\sum_{ij} a_{ri}a_{rj}X_i^\circ X_j^\circ}, \tag{15}$$

$$\mathbf{w_\Sigma E(X_r - X_W)^2 = (w_\Sigma u_r - 1)\sigma^2}, \tag{16}$$

where

$$\mathbf{a_{ri} := w_\Sigma\, \delta_{ri} - w_i}. \tag{17}$$

Proof

$$w_\Sigma(X_r - X_W) = w_\Sigma X_r - \textstyle\sum_i w_iX_i = w_\Sigma(X_r^\circ + \mu) - \sum_i w_i(X_i^\circ + \mu)$$

$$= w_\Sigma X_r^\circ - \textstyle\sum_i w_iX_i^\circ = \sum_i (w_\Sigma\delta_{ri} - w_i)X_i^\circ .$$

This proves (14). Then (15) results from (14) squared. For (16), we apply E to (15):

$$w_\Sigma^2 E(X_r - X_W)^2 = \sum_{ij} a_{ri}a_{rj} E(X_i^\circ X_j^\circ) = \sum_{ij} a_{ri}a_{rj}\delta_{ij}u_i\sigma^2$$

$$= \sigma^2\sum_i a_{ri}a_{ri}u_i = \sigma^2\sum_i (w_\Sigma^2\delta_{ri} - 2w_\Sigma w_i\delta_{ri} + w_i^2)u_i$$

$$= \sigma^2(w_\Sigma^2 u_r - 2w_\Sigma + w_\Sigma) = \sigma^2 w_\Sigma(w_\Sigma u_r - 1) \quad \bullet$$

Theorem 7

$$\mathbf{V := a_1(X_1 - X_W)^2 + \ldots + a_n(X_n - X_W)^2}$$

is an unbiased estimator of σ^2 iff

$$\mathbf{w_\Sigma = \sum_i a_i(w_\Sigma u_i - 1).} \tag{18}$$

Proof
The Theorem is direct by (16) •

2.3.6. Optimal Estimation of σ^2 when μ Is Unknown and e=0

Theorem 8

Let e=0. The optimal estimator of σ^2 in the family $\boldsymbol{P}((X_i - X_W)^2; i=1,\ldots,n)$ is the classical estimator S^2 defined by (11).

Proof
The optimal estimator of σ^2 in the indicated family is the random variable

$$V := \mathrm{Proj}[\sigma^2/\boldsymbol{P}_{\sigma^2}((X_r - X_W)^2; r=1,\ldots,n)] =: \sum_r a_r(X_r - X_W)^2.$$

In order to find the coefficients a_r, we apply the optimal projection Theorem of constants. The unbiasedness condition is (18). The covariance condition is

$$\mathrm{Cov}(V,(X_s - X_W)^2) = \mathrm{const.}E(X_s - X_W)^2,$$

$$w_\Sigma^4\, E[V(X_s - X_W)^2] - w_\Sigma^2\, EV.w_\Sigma^2\, E(X_s - X_W)^2 = \mathrm{const.}w_\Sigma^2\, E(X_s - X_W)^2. \tag{19}$$

By (14),

$$w_\Sigma^2(X_r - X_W)^2.w_\Sigma^2(X_s - X_W)^2 = \sum_{ijpq} a_{ri}a_{rj}a_{sp}a_{sq}X_i^\circ X_j^\circ X_p^\circ X_q^\circ$$

and then by (5),

$$E[w_\Sigma^2(X_r-X_W)^2.w_\Sigma^2(X_s-X_W)^2] = E[\sum_{ijpq} a_{ri}a_{rj}a_{sp}a_{sq}\, X_i^\circ X_j^\circ X_p^\circ X_q^\circ]$$

$$= \sigma^4 \sum_{ij} (a_{ri}a_{ri}a_{sj}a_{sj}+a_{ri}a_{rj}a_{si}a_{sj}+a_{ri}a_{rj}a_{sj}a_{si})u_iu_j$$

$$= \sigma^4 \sum_i a_{ri}a_{ri}u_i \sum_j a_{sj}a_{sj}u_j + 2\sigma^2 \sum_i a_{ri}a_{si}u_i \sum_j a_{rj}a_{sj}u_j$$

$$= \sigma^4(b_{rr}b_{ss}+2b_{rs}b_{rs}) ,$$

where

$$b_{rs} := \sum_i a_{ri}a_{si}u_i = \sum_i (w_\Sigma\delta_{ri}-w_i)(w_\Sigma\delta_{si}-w_i)u_i$$

$$= \sum_i (w_\Sigma^2\delta_{ri}\delta_{si}u_i-w_\Sigma\delta_{si}-w_\Sigma\delta_{ri}+w_i) = w_\Sigma^2\delta_{rs}u_r-w_\Sigma-w_\Sigma+w_\Sigma = w_\Sigma(w_\Sigma\delta_{rs}u_r-1).$$

Then

$$w_\Sigma^4\, E[V(X_s-X_W)^2] =\sigma^4 \sum_r a_r\, E[w_\Sigma^2(X_r-X_W)^2.w_\Sigma^2(X_s-X_W)^2]$$

$$= \sigma^4 \sum_r a_r(b_{rr}b_{ss}+2b_{rs}b_{rs}).$$

By (14),

$$w_\Sigma^2\, EV =w_\Sigma^2 \sum_r a_r(X_r-X_W)^2 = \sum_r a_r \sum_{ij} a_{ri}a_{rj}E(X_i^\circ X_j^\circ)$$

$$= \sigma^2 \sum_r a_r \sum_{ij} a_{ri}a_{rj}\, \delta_{ij}u_i = \sigma^2 \sum_r a_r \sum_i a_{ri}a_{ri}\, u_i = \sigma^2 \sum_r a_rb_{rr} ,$$

$$w_\Sigma^2(X_s-X_W)^2 = \sum_{ij} a_{si}a_{sj}E(X_i^\circ X_j^\circ) = \sigma^2 b_{ss} .$$

Then the covariance condition (19) becomes

$$\sum_r a_r(b_{rr}b_{ss}+2b_{rs}b_{rs})- (\sum_r a_rb_{rr})b_{ss} = \text{const}.b_{ss}$$

$$\sum_r a_rb_{rs}b_{rs} = \text{const}.b_{ss} \tag{20}$$

This relation, and the unbiasedness relation (18), are satisfied for

$$a_r=w_r/(n-1).$$

Indeed, then the verification of (18) is direct, and the first member of (20), multiplied by $(n-1)w_\Sigma^{-2}$, equals

$$\sum_r w_r(w_\Sigma\delta_{rs}u_r - 1)^2 = \sum_r w_r(w_\Sigma{}^2\delta_{rs}u_r{}^2 - 2w_\Sigma\delta_{rs}u_r + 1)$$

$$= w_\Sigma{}^2u_s - 2w_\Sigma + w_\Sigma = w_\Sigma{}^2u_s - w_\Sigma = b_{ss} \quad \bullet$$

If $e\neq 0$, then the fourth-order expressions of the foregoing proof must be completed as follows

$$E[w_\Sigma{}^2(X_r-X_W)^2.w_\Sigma{}^2(X_s-X_W)^2]$$

$$= \sigma^4(b_{rr}b_{ss}+2b_{rs}b_{rs}) + e\sigma^4\sum_i a_{ri}a_{ri}a_{si}a_{si}u_i{}^3,$$

$$w_\Sigma{}^4\, E[V(X_s-X_W)^2] = \sigma^4 \sum_r a_r(b_{rr}b_{ss}+2b_{rs}b_{rs}) + e\sigma^4 \sum_r a_r \sum_i a_{ri}a_{ri}a_{si}a_{si}u_i{}^3$$

and then the covariance condition becomes

$$\sum_r a_rb_{rs}b_{rs} + e\sum_r a_r \sum_i a_{ri}a_{ri}a_{si}a_{si}u_i{}^3 = \text{const.}b_{ss}.$$

This condition, and the unbiasedness condition (18), form a system of n+1 linear equations for the n+1 unknown quantities $a_1,\dots,a_n$, const. It could be solved numerically. From (17) results that

$$\sum_i a_{ri}a_{ri}a_{si}a_{si}u_i{}^3$$

$$= w_\Sigma{}^4\delta_{rs}u_r{}^3 - 4w_\Sigma{}^3\delta_{rs}u_r{}^2 + 4w_\Sigma{}^2\delta_{rs}u_r + w_\Sigma{}^2(u_r+u_s) - 3w_\Sigma\,.$$

2.3.7. Approximatively Optimal Estimation of σ^2 when μ Is Unknown and e Known

If μ is unknown and e known, we suggest the following estimator for σ^2:

$$S_e{}^2 = c\sum_i [w_i/(2+eu_i)](X_i-X_W)^2,$$

where the constant c is defined by the unbiasedness relation (18), becoming here

$$w_\Sigma = c\sum_i [w_i/(2+eu_i)](w_\Sigma u_i-1).$$

The estimator $S_e{}^2$ is the optimal estimator $S_\mu{}^2$ introduced in Theorem 6, with μ replaced by its optimal estimator X_W and then c adapted in order to preserve the unbiasedness.

2.3.8. Expectation and Variance of Classical Estimator S^2

Theorem 9

The classical estimator S^2 explicited in (11) is an unbiased estimator of σ^2 with variance

$$\mathbf{Var}\ S^2 = [2/(n-1)]\sigma^4 + [(w_\Sigma u_\Sigma - 2n+1)/((n-1)^2 w_\Sigma)]e\sigma^4,$$

where

$$u_i := 1/w_i \quad , \quad u_\Sigma := u_1+\ldots+u_n\ .$$

Proof

The unbiasedness results from Theorem 7 with $a_i := w_i/(n-1)$. By (15),

$$w_\Sigma^2(n-1)S^2 = w_\Sigma^2(n-1)\sum_r w_r(X_r - X_W)^2 = \sum_{ijr} w_r a_{ri} a_{rj} X_i^\circ X_j^\circ = \sum_{ij} c_{ij} X_i^\circ X_j^\circ,$$

where

$$c_{ij} := \sum_r w_r a_{ri} a_{rj} = w_\Sigma(w_\Sigma w_i \delta_{ij} - w_i w_j).$$

Hence, by (5),

$$w_\Sigma^4(n-1)^2 ES^4 = \sum_{ijpq} c_{ij} c_{pq}\, E(X_i^\circ X_j^\circ X_p^\circ X_q^\circ)$$

$$= \sigma^4 \sum_{ij}(c_{ii}c_{jj} + c_{ij}c_{ij} + c_{ij}c_{ji})u_i u_j + \sigma^4 \sum_i d_{ii} d_{ii} u_i^2\, e u_i$$

$$= \sigma^4 w_\Sigma^4(n^2-1) + e\sigma^4 w_\Sigma^3(w_\Sigma u_\Sigma - 2n+1)$$

The substraction of $w_\Sigma^4(n-1)^2E^2S^2 = w_\Sigma^4(n-1)^2\sigma^4$ and then the division by $w_\Sigma^4(n-1)^2$ furnishes the announced value of $\text{Var}\ S^2$ •

Chapter 3

Time-Homogeneous Credibility Theory

3.0. Introduction

We will illustrate some basic ideas of Credibility Theory on a portfolio in automobile insurance. We assume that the claim number process of each contract of the portfolio is a usual Poisson process, with parameter λ depending on the contract. We consider the estimation of the parameter λ of a fixed contract. We recall that λ is the expected number of claims in one year.

a. *Individual estimator*

Let N be the number of claims of the considered contract, observed during t years. As estimator of λ, we can adopt

$$\Lambda_{ind} := N/t .$$

This is a rather poor estimator in practice, because t is never large enough.

b. *Portfolio, or collective estimator*

Let N_{port} be the total number of claims in the portfolio, observed during t years, and let k be the fixed number of contracts in the portfolio. Then the parameter λ of the considered contract could be estimated by

$$\Lambda_{port} := N_{port}/(kt).$$

One inconvenience of this estimator is that it does not distinguish between the contracts. In the construction of a bonus-malus system, the consideration of this portfolio estimator only, is useless.

c. *Credibility estimator*

The **credibility estimator** Λ_{cred} of the parameter λ of a fixed contract, is a convex combination of Λ_{ind} and Λ_{port} :

$$\Lambda_{cred} := z\Lambda_{ind}+(1-z)\Lambda_{port}$$

Then $z\in[0,1]$ is the **credibility (weight) of the individual observations**. The science and art of credibility theory, is the determination of z.

In the section 3.1, we develop the North American approach, called **limited fluctuation theory**. Everywhere else, only the **modern theory**, initiated by H. Bühlmann (1967) in his historical paper, is considered.

Now we indicate the general characteristics of **credibility situations**, i.e. situations in which the application of credibility theory can be considered.

The **general problem of credibility theory** is the estimation of parameters (expected number of claims, expected amount of claims,...) akin to **individuals** (persons, contracts, portfolios,...), for which the available observations are too restricted in order to furnish thrustful estimations, but for which more extensive **surrounding information** can be used. Mostly, when credibility theory can be applied, the individual is embedded in some heterogeneous collectivity, furnishing the surrounding information. Of course, this vague description shall take precise forms in the various models hereafter considered.

In the example above, the surrounding information results from the contracts of the portfolio, other than the considered one. Characteristic of Credibility Theory is that the portfolio may be heterogeneous. It may contain good and bad drivers. In a homogeneous portfolio the common value of the parameter λ is of course estimated by λ_{port}, and then no Credibility Theory is necessary.

The limited fluctuation Credibility Theory is based on central tendency assumptions. In its practical application, two paramaters ε and p must be prefixed. They are such that fluctuations (defined precisely later) in the credibility estimator larger than p, have a probability less than ε.

In modern Credibility Theory, no parameters such as ε or p are involved and no central tendency assumptions are necessary. The theory is **distribution-free**. This means that no hypothesis is made on the distribution of the number of claims or of the amount of claims. Poisson distribution assumptions, such as in the introductory example, do not occur in the general theory.

Credibility situations do occur about everywhere. For instance, the estimation of the mortality of aids patients (in a country, in a continent or in the world) could be approached by Credibility Theory. The surrounding information might be furnished by statistics in other countires or in other continents, or by general mortality tables.

3.1. Limited Fluctuation Credibility Theory

3.1.1. Assumptions and Problem

We consider a portfolio with k independent contracts 1,2,...,j,...,k, during a fixed period (not mentioned explicitly in the formulas). The **number of claims of the contract** j is a Poisson random variable N_j with parameter λ_j. The **total claim amount** X_j of the contract j is the sum of its **partial claim amounts**: $X_j=X_{j1}+...+X_{jN_j}$. These partial claim amounts are i.i.d., for fixed j, with first moment $\mu_{j1}:=EX_{jn}$ and second finite moment $\mu_{j2}:=EX_{jn}^2$ (n=1,2,...,N_j). The **total number of claims in the portfolio** is $N:=N_1+ ... +N_k$ and the **total claim amount in the portfolio** is $S=X_1+ ... +X_k$.

The standardized random variable S^{01} (Part I.Ch.3.4.3) is treated as standardized normal hereafter. This is legitimated by Part I.Ch.5.Th.1, at least when all partial claims X_{jn} are i.i.d. and if the expected number of claims in the portfolio is large enough, Of course, S^{01} is approximatively standardized normal in much more general situations.

The problem is the estimation of the expected total claim amount ES. Here, the **individual**, in the spirit of Credibility Theory, is the considered portfolio. The **credibility estimator** of ES will be a random variable denoted by $(ES)_{cred}$. It is assumed that the insurer does already possess the general estimate $(ES)_{gen}$ of ES, provided by **surrounding information**. This surrounding information must be understood in a very large sense. For instance $(ES)_{gen}$ might result from

- earlier statistics in the portfolio
- statistics in similar portfolios
- statistics in a larger portfolio containing the considered one
- subjective estimations
- mathematical speculations

.. ..

3.1.2. Limited Fluctuation Credibility Estimator of ES

We now consider the following **credibility estimator** of ES:

$$(ES)_{cred} = zS + (1-z)(ES)_{gen} ,$$

where $0 \le z \le 1$. We display it as

$$(ES)_{cred} = z(S-ES) + z\,ES + (1-z)(ES)_{gen} .$$

We call z(S–ES) **the fluctuating part of $(ES)_{cred}$** .

The **credibility weight** z is the largest number in]0,1] such that

$$P[z|S-ES| \ge p\,ES] \le \varepsilon, \qquad (1)$$

where ε and p are small strictly positive constants, fixed in advance. Hence, by this constraint on z, the probability of a large fluctuating part must be small.

Let Z be a standardized normal random variable, and let y_ε be defined by the relation

$$P(|Z| \ge y_\varepsilon) = \varepsilon. \qquad (2)$$

For instance, by means of tables of the normal distribution, the following values are obtained:

$$y_{0.1} = 1.6449$$
$$y_{0.05} = 1.9600$$
$$z_{0.01} = 2.5758$$
$$z_{0.001} = 3.2905$$

By Part I.Ch.3.Th.5.b,

$$EX_j = \lambda_j\mu_{j1} ,\ Var\ X_j = \lambda_j\mu_{j2}\ \ (j=1,\dots,k).$$

Let

$$\lambda := \lambda_1+\dots+\lambda_k ,\ \mu_1 := (\lambda_1\mu_{11}+\dots+\lambda_k\mu_{k1})/\lambda ,\ \ \mu_2 := (\lambda_1\mu_{12}+\dots+\lambda_k\mu_{k2})/\lambda.$$

Then,

$$ES = EX_1+\dots+EX_k = \lambda_1\mu_{11}+\dots+\lambda_k\mu_{k1} = \lambda\mu_1,$$

$$Var\ S = Var\ X_1 + \dots + Var\ X_k = \lambda_1\mu_{12}+\dots+\lambda_k\mu_{k2} = \lambda\mu_2,$$

$$S^{01} = (S-ES)/(\text{Var } S)^{1/2} = (S-\lambda\mu_1)/(\lambda\mu_2)^{1/2}. \tag{3}$$

We divide by $z(\lambda\mu_2)^{1/2}$ in the square brackets in the first member of (1). Then, by (3),

$$P[|S^{01}| \geq p\lambda^{1/2}/(zr)] \leq \varepsilon, \text{ where } r := \mu_2/\mu_1^2.$$

A comparison with (2) shows that z is the largest number in]0,1] such that

$$p\lambda^{1/2}/(zr) \geq y_\varepsilon, \; z \leq p\lambda^{1/2}/(ry_\varepsilon). \tag{4}$$

If the last member of the last inequality of (4) is larger than 1, then $z=1$, and then it is said that there is **full credibility**. Hence, there is full credibility iff

$$\lambda \geq \lambda_S := (ry_\varepsilon)^2/p^2 \tag{5}$$

If $z<1$, then it is said that there is **partial credibility**.

3.1.3. Limited Fluctuation Credibility Estimator of EN

The foregoing discussion applies to the estimation of the expected number of claims EN. The random variable N can be considered as a total claim amount in a portfolio in which each partial cost X equals 1. Hence, the preceding formulas are valid, with μ_1, μ_2, r replaced by 1. In particular, from (5) results that there is full credibility in the estimation of EN iff

$$\lambda \geq \lambda_N := y_\varepsilon^2/p^2. \tag{6}$$

Some numerical values of λ_N are given in the next Table.

	p=0.3	p=0.2	p=0.1	p=0.05	p=0.01
ε=0.1	30	68	271	1082	27057
ε=0.05	43	96	384	1537	38416
ε=0.01	74	166	663	2654	66347
ε=0.001	120	271	1083	4331	108274

Value of λ_N for which there is full credibility in the estimation of EN

3.1.4. Limited Fluctuation Credibility in Practice

By (5) and (6), $\lambda_S = r^2\,\lambda_N.$ (7)

The last member of (4) equals, by (5) and (7),

$$[p^2\lambda/(ry_\varepsilon)^2]^{1/2} = [\lambda/\lambda_S]^{1/2} = [\lambda/(r^2\lambda_N)]^{1/2}.$$

Hence, **the limited fluctuation credibility estimator of ES equals**

$$\mathbf{(ES)_{cred} = zS + (1-z)(ES)_{gen},} \quad (8)$$

where

$$\mathbf{z= 1\wedge[\lambda/(r^2\lambda_N)]^{1/2}}.$$

The expected number of claims λ is replaced by an estimate in the expression of z and $r{:=}\mu_2/\mu_1^2$ results from partial claim statistics in the considered portfolio, but maybe also in other similar portfolios. According to Beard et al. (1969) page 69, "The variation of r depends significantly on the degree of heterogeneity of the risk sums ... The value of r may often be of the order of 3 to 5, but in cases where very large risk sums can occur, the value can be much larger."

The limited fluctuation credibility estimator of λ=EN equals

$$\mathbf{(EN)_{cred} = zN + (1-z)(EN)_{gen},}$$

where

$$\mathbf{z= 1\wedge[\lambda/(\lambda_N)]^{1/2}}. \quad (9)$$

$(EN)_{gen}$ is an estimate of EN resulting from the surrounding information. Here, circularity is involved because z depends on the parameter λ to be estimated. In practice, λ is replaced by a rough estimate in (9) (the realization of N or the value $(EN)_{gen}$). But $(EN)_{cred}$ can also be treated as a pseudo-estimator of EN, to be used iteratively (see the following section 3.3.7).

If $(ES)_{gen}$ is an unbiased estimator of ES, then $(ES)_{cred}$ is an unbiased estimater of ES, whatever the value of z is. Indeed, if $E(ES)_{gen} = ES$, then

$$E(ES)_{cred} = zES + (1-z)E(ES)_{gen} = zES + (1-z)ES = ES.$$

Similarly, if $(EN)_{gen}$ is an unbiased estimator of EN, then $(EN)_{cred}$ is an unbiased estimater of EN, whatever the value of z is.

3.2. General Notations in Modern Credibility Theory

Only modern credibility models are considered from now on. In the sequel, we adopt the notation system described hereafter.

3.2.1. Subscripts

The **variable subscripts** are denoted by i,j,k,...,r,s,t,..., and the **fixed subscripts** by k°,...,t°,... All these subscripts are strictly positive integers.

Propositions and relations depending on variable subscripts are supposed to be valid for all values of these subscripts. For instance, if a_i and b_i are numbers defined for i=1,2,...,i°, then $a_i=b_i$ is in fact an abbreviation of $a_i=b_i$ (i=1,2,...,i°). Similarly, in sums over variable subscripts, the latter must take all possible values, if this is not mentioned explicitly. For instance,

$$\sum_i a_i \equiv \sum_{1\leq i\leq i^\circ} a_i \,.$$

When we consider portfolios with several contracts, the latter will be denoted by 1,2,...,k°, and the subscripts i,j,k will always be **contract subscripts** with possible values 1,2,...,k°. The subscripts r,s,t will always be **time subscripts**.

Beyond the subscripts i,j,...,t°,... we will also use subscripts $_\Sigma$, $_A$, $_W$, $_Z$,... The latter subscripts cannot take numerical values. Their meaning is defined hereafter.

3.2.2. Elimination of Variable Subscripts

When a variable subscript is replaced by Σ, this means that it must be eliminated by summation over its possible value. For instance, let X_t (a random variable or not) be defined for t=1,2,...,t°. Then

$$X_\Sigma := \sum_{1\leq t\leq t^\circ} X_t.$$

When a variable subscript is replaced by A, this means that it must be eliminated by the formation of the usual Arithmetic mean. For instance,

$$X_A := X_\Sigma/t^\circ.$$

Let us assume now that a symbol, say Y_k (a random variable or not) is defined for k=1,2,...,k° and that corresponding strictly positive numbers w_k (k=1,2, ...k°), or z_k (k=1,2,...,k°), called **weights**, are given. Then Y_W results from Y_k by the formation of the weighted mean value with weights w_k:

$$Y_W := \sum_k (w_k/w_\Sigma)\, Y_k.$$

Similarly, Y_Z results from Y_k by the formation of the weighted mean value with weights z_k:

$$Y_Z := \sum_k (z_k/z_\Sigma)\, Y_k.$$

These rules are applied to symbols with more than one subscript. .

3.2.3. Random Variables

All random variables involved in a fixed model, are supposed to be defined on the same basic probability space. In modern Credibility Theory two kinds of random variables occur.

a. *Observable random variables*

The observable random variables are denoted by X, with subscripts. These random variables are always supposed to be square-integrable. As indicated by their name, they can be observed and replaced by the observed realizations in applications. Mostly, in Risk Theory, the observable random variables are claim amounts or claim numbers. In the latter case they are often replaced by N, with subscripts.

b. *Conditioning random variables*

The conditioning random variables are denoted by Θ, with subscripts or not. No square-integrability constraints are imposed on them. They have a hidden character and cannot be observed.

The formalism of the models is the same if each random variable Θ is replaced by a random vector $(\Theta_1,...,\Theta_n)$ (or by a random family, or even by a sub-σ-algebra of the basic σ-algebra on the probability space on which all random variables are defined).

3.2.4. Centered Random Variables

If Y is any random variable having a first moment, then $Y^\circ := Y - EY$ is the corresponding **centered random variable**. It is direct that

$$(\sum_k a_k Y_k)^\circ = \sum_k a_k (Y_k{}^\circ).$$

Hence, $Y_W{}^\circ$ can be viewed as $(Y_W)^\circ$, but also as a random variable defined from the random variables $Y_k{}^\circ$ ($k=1,2,\ldots,k^\circ$) by the elimination of k. We notice the double meaning of the superscript °. When applied to a constant it means "fixed". When applied to a random variable it means "centered".

3.2.5. Projections and Other Estimators

The optimal projection Theorem of random variables (Ch.1.Th.8) and the optimal projection Theorem of constants (Ch.1.Th.10), will be used over and over again.

Hereafter, the subscript $_{\text{proj}}$ is used for projections on a plane of observable random variables. Credibility estimators are such projections, but for them, the subscript $_{\text{cred}}$ is adopted.

Estimators of parameters $a, \sigma^2, \ldots$, are denoted by the corresponding Roman capitals $A, S^2, \ldots$

3.2.6. Conditional Expectations, Variances and Covariances

In the following sections, extensive use is made of the properties of modern conditional expectations, variances and covariances (Part I.Ch.2). It is indispensable to learn these properties by rote. No further references to Part I.Ch. 2 will be made hereafter.

3.3. Credibility Theory Model with Unweighted Observation (Bühlmann 1967)

3.3.1. Model with 1 Contract

We here develop the first modern credibility model of this book. Only for this model, the interpretations are explained in full detail. They are similar in the other models hereafter considered. They are essential for the intuitive understanding of the concepts, but not necessary for the comprehension of the mathematics.

In the spirit of modern distribution-free Credibility Theory, the model with 1 contract is not practical, because it contains parameters that cannot be estimated from the observable random variables of the model itself. Nevertheless we develop it for the following reasons.

a. It contains the essential ingredients of modern Credibility Theory.

b. It already allows the construction of the credibility estimator of the practical model with several contracts, expounded later.

Assumptions

The model with 1 contract is defined by the random variables

$$\begin{array}{l} \Theta, \\ X_1, \\ X_2, \\ \dots \\ X_{t^\circ}, \end{array} \qquad (10)$$

such that for fixed Θ, the observable random variables $X_1, X_2, \ldots X_{t^\circ}$ are conditionally i.i.d.

Interpretations

Let us consider a fixed insurance contract. The random variable X_t ($1 \le t \le t^\circ$) might be the total claim amount, or the total number of claims of that contract during the observation year t.

We assume that the distribution of the vector $(X_1,...,X_{t^\circ})$ depends on some parameter θ, a fixed but unknown real number. For instance, θ might be the Poisson parameter λ if claim numbers are considered and if the claim number process is Poisson. We consider θ as a particular realization of some random variable Θ.

Then we obtain a random vector $(\Theta,X_1,...,X_{t^\circ})$, and the initial vector $(X_1,...,X_{t^\circ})$ is in fact the conditional vector $(X_1,...,X_{t^\circ})/_{\Theta=\theta}$ of the vector $(\Theta,X_1,...,X_{t^\circ})$. But now we can also consider other realizations $\theta',\theta'',...$ of Θ, than the unique **true realization** θ, and corresponding conditional vectors

$$(X_1,...,X_{t^\circ})/_{\Theta=\theta'}\ ,\ (X_1,...,X_{t^\circ})/_{\Theta=\theta''}\ ,...$$

This means that our initial contract is embedded in a **theoretical portfolio** of **hypothetical contracts**. The distributions involved in the theoretical portfolio are irrelevant, except for 3 parameters μ, a, σ^2 later defined.

In the models with several contracts, it can be assumed that the theoretical portfolio coincides, more or less, with the real portfolio from which the considered contract is extracted, and that values θ', θ'',... other than θ, do correspond to contracts other than the original one. For the moment, only one contract is supposed to be real.

We must be very careful with interpretations of expectations such as EX_t, because the complete theoretical portfolio is involved in such an expectation. In fact, EX_t has no practical meaning. Only $E(X_t/\Theta=\theta)$ has a real sense. The conditional expectations $E(X_t/\Theta=\theta')$, $E(X_t/\Theta=\theta'')$,... are akin to hypothetical contracts, and the formula $EX_t = EE(X_t/\Theta)$ shows that EX_t is an expectation of such theoretical, not real, expectations. EX_t is an expectation, corresponding to a contract chosen at random in the theoretical portfolio.

Another important point is the following. The independence of the random variables $X_1,...,X_{t^\circ}$ of the initial contract, with fixed θ, does not imply the independence of the random variables appearing in (10). Indeed, it results from the assumptions about the random varables (10) that

$$E[f_1(X_1)f_2(X_2)...f_{t^\circ}(X_{t^\circ})/\Theta] = E[f_1(X_1)/\Theta].E[f_2(X_2)/\Theta]...E[f_{t^\circ}(X_{t^\circ})/\Theta].$$

But this does not imply any factorization of

$$E[f_1(X_1)f_2(X_2)...f_{t°}(X_{t°})] = EE[f_1(X_1)f_2(X_2)...f_{t°}(X_{t°})/\Theta]$$

$$= E\{E[f_1(X_1)/\Theta].E[f_2(X_2)/\Theta]...E[f_{t°}(X_{t°})/\Theta]\}$$

But then the following question arises: Are the observable random variables X_t of the original contract, the same as those appearing in (10)? The answer is "No" in theory, but "Yes" in practice. "No" because, the original random variables are such that

$$E[f_1(X_1)f_2(X_2)...f_{t°}(X_{t°})] = E[f_1(X_1)].E[f_2(X_2)]...E[f_{t°}(X_{t°})]$$

by their independence and because this relation does not hold in the model defined by the random variables (10), as we just observed. "Yes" because the general random variables X_t cannot be observed if only one contract is considered. Only the random variables X_t of the given contract are accessible to observation, and in this contract, the random variable Θ takes the fixed value θ: In fact, only the random variables X_t of the conditional random vector $(X_1,...,X_{t°})_{/\Theta=\theta}$ can be observed, and the latter are independent. The random variable X_t of (10) is an observation corresponding to a contract chosen at random it the theoretical portfolio. The independence of observations akin to fixed contracts, does not imply the independence of observations akin to contracts selected at random.

Notations

$$\mu(\Theta) := E(X_t/\Theta) \ , \ \mu := E\mu(\Theta) \ , \ a := Var\ \mu(\Theta),$$

$$\sigma^2(\Theta) := Var(X_t/\Theta) \ , \ \sigma^2 := E\sigma^2(\Theta),$$

$$z := at°/(\sigma^2+at°),$$

$$\mu(\Theta)_{cred} := Proj[\mu(\Theta)/\boldsymbol{P}(1,X_1,X_2,...,X_{t°})].$$

Notice that we use the same symbol for the constant μ and for the function $\mu(\cdot)$, and also for the constant σ^2 and for the function $\sigma^2(\cdot)$.

The numbers μ, a, σ^2 are the **parameters** of the considered model. They will also occur in the model with several contracts, in which they can be estimated.

The constant z is the **credibility weight** of the considered contract. The random variable $\mu(\Theta)_{cred}$ is the **credibility approximation** of the random variable $\mu(\Theta)$. The sense of that terminology will become clear by the following Theorem 2.

More interpretations

By its very definition, $\mu(\Theta)_{cred}$ can be explicited as

$$\mu(\Theta)_{cred} = c + a_1X_1 + a_2X_2 \ldots + a_{t^\circ}X_{t^\circ}. \tag{11}$$

We are interested in the value $\mu(\theta) := E(X_t/\Theta=\theta)$. Here θ is the true unknown parameter of the considered contract. Let $(\theta, x_1, x_2, \ldots, x_{t^\circ})$ be a realization of the vector $(\Theta, X_1, X_2, \ldots, X_{t^\circ})$. The random variable $\mu(\Theta)_{cred}$, i.e.

$$c + a_1X_1 + \ldots + a_{t^\circ}X_{t^\circ},$$

is an approximation of the random variable $\mu(\Theta)$, and then the number

$$c + a_1x_1 + \ldots + a_{t^\circ}x_{t^\circ}$$

is regarded as an approximation of $\mu(\theta)$. In other words, the last member of (11) is an estimator of the constant $\mu(\theta)$.

$\mu(\Theta)_{cred}$ is the **credibility approximation** of $\mu(\Theta)$ as well as the **credibility estimator** of $\mu(\theta)$.

Covariance relations

Theorem 1

$$\mathbf{EX_t = \mu,} \tag{12}$$

$$\mathbf{Cov(X_s,X_t) = a + \delta_{st}\,\sigma^2,} \tag{13}$$

$$\mathbf{Cov(X_t,X_A) = Cov(X_A,X_A) = a + (\sigma^2/t^\circ) = a/z,} \tag{14}$$

$$\mathbf{Cov(X_t,\mu(\Theta)) = a.} \tag{15}$$

Proof

(12)

$$EX_t = EE(X_t/\Theta)) = E\mu(\Theta) = \mu.$$

(13)

$$\text{Cov}(X_s,X_t) = E\,\text{Cov}(X_s,X_t/\Theta) + \text{Cov}[E(X_s/\Theta),E(X_t/\Theta)]$$

$$= \delta_{st}\,E\,\text{Var}(X_t/\Theta) + \text{Var}\,\mu(\Theta) = \delta_{st}\sigma^2 + a.$$

(14)

$$\mathrm{Cov}(X_t,X_\Sigma) = \sum_s \mathrm{Cov}(X_t,X_s) = \sum_s (\delta_{st}\sigma^2 + a) = \sigma^2 + t°a.$$

Then, dividing by t°,

$$\mathrm{Cov}(X_t,X_A) = a + (\sigma^2/t°).$$

$$\mathrm{Cov}(X_\Sigma,X_A) = \sum_t \mathrm{Cov}(X_t,X_A) = \sum_t(a + (\sigma^2/t°) = at° + \sigma^2.$$

Dividing by t°, we obtain the second relation(14). The last relation (14) results from the definition of z.

(15)

$$\mathrm{Cov}(X_t,\mu(\Theta)) = E\,\mathrm{Cov}[X_t,\mu(\Theta)/\Theta] + \mathrm{Cov}[E(X_t/\Theta),E(\mu(\Theta)/\Theta)]$$

$$= E\,0 + \mathrm{Cov}[\mu(\Theta),\mu(\Theta)] = \mathrm{Var}\,\mu(\Theta) = a \;\bullet$$

Credibility estimator

Theorem 2 (Bühlmann)

In the model with 1 contract and unweighted observations defined by the random variables (10),

$$\mu(\Theta)_{cred} = zX_A + (1-z)\mu. \tag{16}$$

Proof

It is sufficient to verify the unbiasedness and covariance conditions of the optimal projection Theorem of random variables. This is direct by the covariance relations of Theorem 1.

Rather than to verify that the announced expression for $\mu(\Theta)_{cred}$ is the exact one, it is more instructive to discover this expression. The projection $\mu(\Theta)_{cred}$ can be expressed by (11). The unbiasedness condition says that $\mu(\Theta)$ and its projection $\mu(\Theta)_{cred}$ must have the same expectation:

$$E\mu(\Theta) = c + \sum_s a_s\, EX_s \quad , \quad \mu = c + \mu a_\Sigma \quad , \quad c = (1-a_\Sigma)\mu, \tag{17}$$

by (12). The covariance condition states that $\mu(\Theta)$ and its projection must have the same covariance with any observable random variable X_t:

$$\mathrm{Cov}[\mu(\Theta),X_t] = \textstyle\sum_s a_s\,\mathrm{Cov}(X_s,X_t) \;\;,\;\; a = \sum_s a_s(a+\delta_{st}\sigma^2),$$

$$a = aa_\Sigma + a_t\sigma^2 \;\;,\;\; a_t = a(1-a_\Sigma)/\sigma^2. \tag{18}$$

In the first relation of (18), we sum over t :

$$t°a = t°aa_\Sigma + \sigma^2 a_\Sigma \;\;,\;\; a_\Sigma = t°a/(t°a+\sigma^2) = z.$$

Then $a_t = z/t°$ by the last relation (18), and $c=(1-z)\mu$ by the last relation (17). Then by (11)

$$\mu(\Theta)_{cred} = (1-z)\mu + zX_\Sigma/t° = (1-z)\mu + zX_A \;\bullet$$

Estimation of σ^2

Theorem 3

In the model with 1 contract and unweighted observations defined by the random variables (10),

$$\mathbf{S_0^2 := {}^1/_{(t°-1)} \textstyle\sum_{1\le t\le t°} (X_t-X_A)^2} \tag{19}$$

is an unbiased estimator of σ^2**.**

Proof

$$(t°-1)S_0^2 = \textstyle\sum_t (X_t°-X_A°)^2 = \sum_t [(X_t°)^2 - 2X_t°X_A° + (X_A°)^2]\,,$$

and then, by the covariance relations,

$$(t°-1)ES_0^2 = \textstyle\sum_t [E(X_t°)^2 - 2E(X_t°X_A°) + E(X_A°)^2]$$

$$= \textstyle\sum_t[\mathrm{Var}\,X_t - 2\mathrm{Cov}(X_t,X_A) + \mathrm{Var}\,X_A]$$

$$= \textstyle\sum_t[a+\sigma^2 - 2(a+\sigma^2/_{t°}) + (a+\sigma^2/_{t°})]$$

$$= \textstyle\sum_t [\sigma^2 - \sigma^2/_{t°}] = (t°-1)\sigma^2 \;\bullet$$

3.3.2. Model with 1 Contract Completed by 1 Observation

Let us consider the random variables

$$\begin{array}{c}\Theta,\\ X_1,\\ X_2,\\ \ldots\\ X_{t^\circ},\\ X_{t^\circ+1}\end{array} \qquad (20)$$

and let us assume that for fixed Θ, the random variables $X_1, \ldots, X_{t^\circ}, X_{t^\circ+1}$ are still conditionally i.i.d.

The random variables $X_1,\ldots,X_{t^\circ}$ are still supposed to be observable, but $X_{t^\circ+1}$ is not. This is the case if thc present instant is the end of the year t°. Now the problem is to find the credibility approximation for $X_{t^\circ+1}$. This approximation is

$$(X_{t^\circ+1})_{cred} := \mathrm{Proj}[X_{t^\circ+1}/\boldsymbol{P}(1,X_1,\ldots X_{t^\circ})].$$

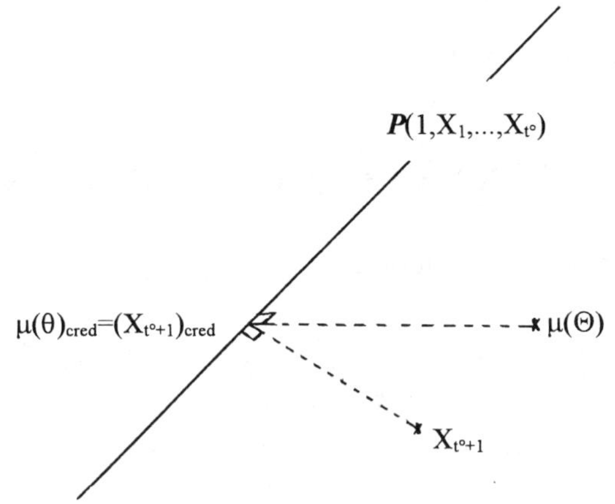

Fig.31. Identity of credibility projection of $\mu(\Theta)$ and of $X_{t^\circ+1}$

Theorem 4

$$(X_{t°+1})_{cred} = \mu(\Theta)_{cred} \tag{21}$$

Proof

$$EX_{t°+1} = \mu = E\mu(\Theta) \ , \ Cov(X_{t°+1}, X_t) = a = Cov(\mu(\Theta), X_t) \ \ (t \le t°)$$

and then $\mu(\Theta)$ can be replaced by $X_{t°+1}$ everywhere in the proof of Theorem 2 •

In the initial contract with parameter θ, the number $\mu(\theta)$ is the expected value of any random variable X_t, also of $X_{t°+1}$. If the variables X_t are claim amounts, then $\mu(\theta)$ is the **yearly pure premium** of the contract. It is estimated, for the year t°+1, by $\mu(\Theta)_{cred}$, from the observation $X_1,...,X_{t°}$.

It may perhaps look more natural to estimate the pure premium of the year t°+1 by $(X_{t°+1})_{cred}$ instead of $\mu(\Theta)_{cred}$. Fortunately, by the foregoing Theorem there is no difference.

3.3.3. Conditional Expectations Considered Estimators

Let Y be a square-integrable random variable and X a random vector. Then

$$E(Y/X) = Proj[Y/\boldsymbol{F}(X)], \tag{22}$$

where $\boldsymbol{F}(X)$ is the plane, through the origin, of square-integrable functions f(X) of X. Indeed, E(Y/X) belongs to $\boldsymbol{F}(X)$ and it is enough to verify the orthogonality

$$Y - E(Y/X) \perp f(X)$$

for any point f(X) of $\boldsymbol{F}(X)$. This orthogonality is equivalent to the relation

$$E[[Y - E(Y/X)]f(X)] = 0,$$

or

$$E[Y\ f(X)] = E[f(X)E[Y/X]],$$

where the last member of the last relation equals

$$E[E[f(X)Y/X]] = E[f(X)Y].$$

The random variable

$$\mu(\Theta)_{cond} := E[\mu(\Theta)/X_1,X_2,\ldots,X_{t^\circ}] \tag{23}$$

is a better approximation of $\mu(\Theta)$ than $\mu(\Theta)_{cred}$. Indeed, by (22),

$$E[\mu(\Theta)/X_1,X_2,\ldots,X_{t^\circ}] = \mathrm{Proj}[\mu(\Theta)/\boldsymbol{F}(X_1,X_2,\ldots,X_{t^\circ})]. \tag{24}$$

Moreover

$$\boldsymbol{P}(1,X_1,\ldots,X_{t^\circ}) \subseteq \boldsymbol{F}(X_1,X_2,\ldots,X_{t^\circ}),$$

and it is geometrically obvious that the projection $\mu(\Theta)_{cond}$ of $\mu(\Theta)$ on the plane $\boldsymbol{F}(X_1,X_2,\ldots,X_{t^\circ})$ is closer to $\mu(\Theta)$ than the projection $\mu(\Theta)_{cred}$ of $\mu(\Theta)$ on the sub-plane $\boldsymbol{P}(1,X_1,\ldots,X_{t^\circ})$ (see Fig.32).

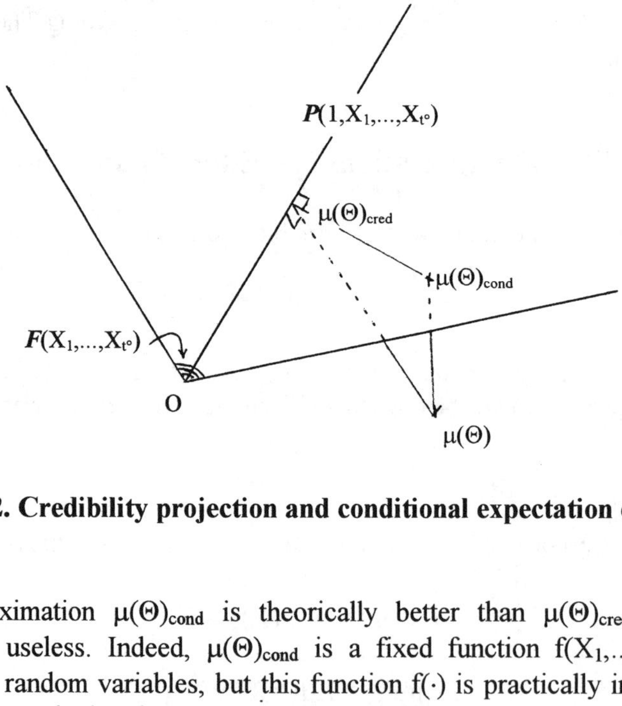

Fig.32. Credibility projection and conditional expectation of $\mu(\Theta)$

The approximation $\mu(\Theta)_{cond}$ is theorically better than $\mu(\Theta)_{cred}$, but it is practically useless. Indeed, $\mu(\Theta)_{cond}$ is a fixed function $f(X_1,\ldots X_{t^\circ})$ of the observable random variables, but this function $f(\cdot)$ is practically impossible to estimate in real situations (unless, in opposition to the spirit of modern Credibility Theory, assumptions are made on the involved distributions). On the contrary, $\mu(\Theta)_{cred}$ depends only on the 3, rather easily estimated parameters μ, a, σ^2 , in the model with several contracts.

From the geometry of the problem results the relation

$$\mu(\Theta)_{cred} = [\mu(\Theta)_{cond}]_{cred}, \tag{25}$$

where the subscript $_{cred}$ is used for projections on the plane $\boldsymbol{P}(1,X_1,...,X_t$ in the last member also. This relation (25) can be summarized in the following way:

The credibility estimator is the optimally linearized conditional expectation.

Now, let us assume that the model with t° observations is completed by an observation $X_{t°+1}$, as in section 3.3.2. Then the relation corresponding to (21) is

$$\mathbf{(X_{t°+1})_{cond} = \mu(\Theta)_{cond}}, \tag{26}$$

where

$$(X_{t°+1})_{cond} := E(X_{t°+1}/X_1,...,X_{t°}). \tag{27}$$

Indeed, by the conditional independence of $X_1,...,X_{t°+1}$ for fixed Θ,

$$\mu(\Theta) = E(X_{t°+1}/\Theta) = E(X_{t°+1}/\Theta,X_1,...,X_{t°})$$

and then

$$\mu(\Theta)_{cond} = E[\mu(\Theta)/X_1,...,X_{t°}]$$

$$= E[E(X_{t°+1}/\Theta,X_1,...,X_{t°})/X_1,...,X_{t°}]$$

$$= E(X_{t°+1}/X_1,...,X_{t°}) = (X_{t°+1})_{cond},$$

by general iterativity.

3.3.4. Practical Model with Several Contracts

Assumptions

The practical **model with several contracts and unweighted observations** is defined by the array of random variables

$$\begin{array}{ccccc}
\Theta_1 & \cdots & \Theta_k & \cdots & \Theta_{k°} \\
X_{11} & \cdots & X_{k1} & \cdots & X_{k°1} \\
X_{12} & \cdots & X_{k2} & \cdots & X_{k°2} \\
\cdots & \cdots & \cdots & \cdots & \cdots \\
X_{1t°} & \cdots & X_{kt°} & \cdots & x_{k°t°}
\end{array}$$

with i.i.d. columns, and such that, in each column

$$(\Theta_k, X_{k1}, X_{k2},\ldots,X_{kt^\circ})', \tag{28}$$

the observable random variables $X_{k1}, X_{k2},\ldots,X_{kt^\circ}$ are conditionally i.i.d. for fixed Θ_k .

Interpretations

Each column (28) of the array is called a **contract**. It corresponds to a real contract in which Θ_k has a fixed, unknown value θ_k.

Hence, the contracts are independent and identically distributed. Credibility Theory copes with **heterogeneous portfolios** and here we have the paradoxal situation that such portfolios are modelled by identically distributed contracts! The explanation is simple: the true values of the parameters $\theta_1, \theta_2,\ldots, \theta_{k^\circ}$ are generally different.

It can be assumed that the contracts are extracted from the same theoretical portfolio and that the real portfolio is a good image of the theoretical one if k° is large enough. But the mathematics of the model are not based on this interpretation.

Notations

$$\mu := EX_{kt} \quad , \quad \mu(\Theta_k) := E(X_{kt}/\Theta_k) \quad , \quad a := Var\ \mu(\Theta_k),$$

$$\sigma^2(\Theta_k) := Var(X_{kt}/\Theta_k) \ , \ \sigma^2 := E\sigma^2(\Theta_k),$$

$$z := at^\circ/(\sigma^2+at^\circ),$$

$$\mu(\Theta_k)_{cred} := Proj[\mu(\Theta_k)/\boldsymbol{P}(1,X_{kt}(k=1,\ldots k^\circ;t=1,\ldots,t^\circ))]$$

From the equidistribution assumptions results that the numbers μ, a, σ^2, and the functions $\mu(\cdot)$, $\sigma^2(\cdot)$, do not depend on k or t. The random variable $\mu(\Theta_k)_{cred}$ is the **credibility approximation** of the random variable $\mu(\Theta_k)$, or the **credibility estimator** of the unknown constant

$$\mu(\theta_k) := E(X_{kt}/\Theta_k=\theta_k).$$

3.3.5. Covariance Relations (Several Contracts)

Theorem 5

In the model with several contracts and unweighted observations,

$$\mathbf{EX_{kt} = EX_{kA} = EX_{AA} = E\mu(\Theta_k) = \mu,} \tag{29}$$

$$\mathbf{Cov(X_{ks},X_{kt}) = a + \delta_{st}\,\sigma^2,} \tag{30}$$

$$\mathbf{Cov(X_{kt},X_{kA}) = Cov(X_{kA},X_{kA}) = a+(\sigma^2/t^\circ) = a/z,} \tag{31}$$

$$\mathbf{Cov(X_{kt},X_{AA}) = Cov(X_{kA},X_{AA}) = Cov(X_{AA},X_{AA})}$$
$$\mathbf{= [a + \sigma^2/t^\circ]/k^\circ = a/(k^\circ z),} \tag{32}$$

$$\mathbf{Cov(X_{kt},\mu(\Theta_k)) = Cov(X_{kA},\mu(\Theta_k)) = a,} \tag{33}$$

$$\mathbf{Cov(X_{AA},\mu(\Theta_k)) = a/k^\circ.} \tag{34}$$

Proof

The relations (29) are direct. The relations (30), (31) result from Theorem 1 because each contract k of the model with several contracts is a model with one contract. For (31), we observe that $Cov(X_{kt},X_{jA})=0$ if $k\neq j$ because then the contracts j and k are independent. Hence

$$Cov(X_{kt},X_{\Sigma A}) = \textstyle\sum_j Cov(X_{kt},X_{jA})$$
$$= Cov(X_{kt},X_{kA}) = a+(\sigma^2/t^\circ) = a/z,$$

by (31). Dividing by k°, we obtain the expressions (33) for $Cov(X_{kt},X_{AA})$. They do not depend on k or t. This implies the two first relations (32). The equality between the first and the last member of (33) results from Theorem 1. Then the first relation (33) results from the fact that the covariance $Cov(X_{kt},\mu(\Theta_k))$ does not depend on t. Relation (34) results from (33) and relation

$$Cov(X_{jA},\mu(\Theta_k))=0\ (k\neq j)\ \bullet$$

3.3.6. Credibility Estimator (Several Contracts)

Theorem 6

In the model with several contracts and unweighted observations,

$$\mu(\Theta_k)_{cred} = zX_{kA} + (1-z)\mu. \tag{35}$$

Proof

From (16) applied to the contract k results that

$$\text{Proj}[\mu(\Theta_k)/\boldsymbol{P}(1,X_{k1},...,X_{kt^\circ})] = zX_{kA} + (1-z)\mu.$$

Hence, by the definition of $\mu(\Theta_k)_{cred}$, it is enough to verify that

$$\text{Proj}[\mu(\Theta_k)/\boldsymbol{P}(1,X_{jt}(j=1,...k^\circ;t=1,...,t^\circ))]$$

$$= \text{Proj}[\mu(\Theta_k)/\boldsymbol{P}(1,X_{k1},...,X_{kt^\circ})]. \tag{36}$$

This is intuitively evident, because $\mu(\Theta_k)$ is a random variable defined in the contract k, and this contract is independent of the contracts $j \neq k$. For an analytical verification of (36), let Y be the last member of (36). Then, in order to prove that Y equals the first member of (36), we have to verify the unbiasedness relation $E\mu(\Theta_k)=EY$ and the covariance relations

$$\text{Cov}(\mu(\Theta_k),X_{jt}) = \text{Cov}(Y,X_{jt}) \tag{37}$$

of the optimal projection Theorem of random variables. These conditions are satisfied for j=k, because then they are the same as those for the projection on the plane $\boldsymbol{P}(1,X_{k1},...,X_{kt^\circ})]$. For $j \neq k$, (37) is also exact, because then it becomes 0=0, because Y and $\mu(\Theta_k)$ are random variables defined in the contract k and X_{jt} is a random variable of the contract j, independent of k •

In the last member of (35), μ is estimated by X_{AA} , and it is in fact the following estimator

$$\mu(\Theta_k)_{CRED} := zX_{kA} + (1-z)X_{AA}, \tag{38}$$

of $\mu(\theta_k)$, with z replaced by an estimate, which is adopted in practice. By the following Theorem, $\mu(\Theta_k)_{CRED}$ is also a projection on a plane of observable random variables.

Theorem 7

$$\mu(\Theta_k)_{CRED} = \mathbf{Proj}[\mu\Theta)/P_\mu(X_{kt}(k=1,...,k°;t=1,...,t°))]. \tag{39}$$

Proof
In order to prove the relation

$$\mathrm{Proj}[\mu\Theta)/P_\mu(X_{kt}(k=1,...,k°;t=1,...,t°))] = zX_{kA} + (1-z)X_{AA}, \tag{40}$$

it is sufficient to verify the unbiasedness and covariance conditions of the optimal projection Theorem of random variables on planes not through the origin (Ch.1.Th.9). Here, they are

$$E[zX_{kA} + (1-z)X_{AA}] = E\mu(\Theta_k) \tag{41}$$

and

$$\mathrm{Cov}[zX_{kA} + (1-z)X_{AA} - \mu(\Theta_k)\,,\, X_{jt}] = \text{const.}, \tag{42}$$

where const. must be understood as a number not depending on j or k.

By (29), each member of (41) equals μ. By the independence of the contracts and the covariance relations of Theorem 5, the first member of (42) equals

$$z\ \mathrm{Cov}(X_{kA},X_{jt}) + (1-z)\,\mathrm{Cov}(X_{AA},X_{jt}) - \mathrm{Cov}(\mu(\Theta_k),X_{jt})$$

$$= \delta_{kj}\, z\mathrm{Cov}(X_{kA},X_{kt}) + (1-z)\,\mathrm{Cov}(X_{AA},X_{jt}) - \delta_{kj}\,\mathrm{Cov}(\mu(\Theta_k),X_{jt})$$

$$= \delta_{kj}\, z(a/z) + (1-z)a_{/(k°z)} - \delta_{kj}\, a = (1-z)a_{/(k°z)} \quad \bullet$$

Interpretations

The simple formula (16), discovered by Hans Bühlmann, and its practical version (38), is one of the most fascinating and useful achievements of Risk Theory. Here we discuss (38).

The formula (38) has the form of the rather empirical old American credibility theory formula

[Credibility estimate] = z [Individual estimate] + (1−z)[General estimate]

The American formula is based on a prefixed number ε, a prefixed number p, and central tendency assumptions. Nothing of this is needed in Bühlmann's fantastic approach.

Moreover, the **credibility weight z of the random variable** X_{kA} has a great intuitive content. Hereafter we explain why this is so.

From the definition of the parameter **a** and from the expression of the following estimators of **a** results that this parameter can be interpreted as a **measure of the heterogeneity of the portfolio**. From the definition of σ^2, and from the estimator (19) of that parameter, results that σ^2 must be interpreted as a measure of the **variability of the observations in the contracts**.

Now let us consider

$$z := at°/(\sigma^2+at°).$$

a. z increases with the number t° of observation years.

The larger t°, the larger the credibility z of X_{kA}. This is exactly what we do expect. In the limit, as $t°\uparrow\infty$, X_{kA} receives full credibility, in complete agreement with the law of large numbers. Of course, the latter remark is purely academic, because t° is never large enough in practice.

b. z increases with a.

The larger the heterogeneity of the portfolio, the larger the credibility z of X_{kA}. This is exactly what we do expect. In very heterogeneous portfolios, the surrounding information furnished by the other contracts is not thrustworthy: its credibility weight (1−z) must be close to 0, and then the credibility weight z of X_{kA} can only be close to 1. On the contrary, in nearly homogeneous portfolios, the information furnished by the other contracts must receive a large weight and then the credibility weight z of the contract k can only be small.

c. z increases when σ^2 decreases.

The smaller the variability of the observations in the individual contracts, the larger the credibility z of the observations of these contracts. This is also what we do expect intuitively. Indeed, by (21), the credibility estimator in any contract k, is also an approximation of the coming observation $X_{k,t°+1}$.

If the past observations $X_{k1},...,X_{kt^\circ}$ do not differ very much, then we do expect an outcome $X_{k,t^\circ+1}$ not very different from the preceding ones, i.e. then X_{kA} must receive a large credibility z. On the contrary, if great oscillations do occur in the observations $X_{k1},...,X_{kt^\circ}$, then they cannot be very useful in the prediction of $X_{k,t^\circ+1}$, i.e. then X_{kA} must receive small credibility.

3.3.7. Parameter Estimators (Several Contracts)

The following Theorem provides estimators for the parameters σ^2, a occurring in the credibility weight z. A **pseudo-estimator** is an estimator depending on the estimated parameters. After the next Theorem, we explain how such pseudo-estimators can be used in practice.

Theorem 8

In the model with several contracts and unweighted observations, an unbiased estimator of σ^2 is

$$S^2 := 1/_{k^\circ(t^\circ-1)} \sum_{1\leq k\leq k^\circ} \sum_{1\leq t\leq t^\circ} (X_{kt}-X_{kA})^2. \tag{43}$$

An unbiased estimator of a is

$$A := 1/_{(k^\circ-1)} \sum_{1\leq k\leq k^\circ} (X_{kA}-X_{AA})^2 - 1/_{t^\circ} S^2. \tag{44}$$

An unbiased pseudo-estimator of a is

$$A_{pseu} := z/_{(k^\circ-1)} \sum_{1\leq k\leq k^\circ} (X_{kA}-X_{AA})^2. \tag{45}$$

Proof

From (19) results an unbiased estimator of σ^2 in each contract k. The usual arithmetic mean of these estimators is (43). It is still unbiased.

For the proof of the unbiasedness of A_{pseu}, we consider the random variables

$$X_{1A}, X_{2A}, \ldots, X_{k^\circ A}.$$

They have the same expectation μ and the same variance a/z, by the last relation (31). Hence, they constitute an elementary classical model, in which

$$V := 1/(k°-1) \sum_{1 \le k \le k°} (X_{kA}-X_{AA})^2$$

is an unbiased estimator of the variance a/z by Ch.2.2.4. Hence A_{pseu}=zV is an unbiased pseudo-estimator of a.

The unbiasedness of A results from the relations

$$EV = a/z = a + (\sigma^2/t°) = a + ES^2/t° \; , \; EA = E(V - S^2/t°) = a \; \bullet$$

In order to explain how pseudo-estimators can be used, let us assume that the observations in the last member of (45) have been replaced by realizations, and that σ^2 , occurring in z, has been replaced by the realization of S^2. Then a function f(a) of **a** is left. Some initial value a_0 is fixed and then a_i is defined by recurrence on i :

$$a_{i+1} = f(a_i) \quad (i=0,1,2,...).$$

Then **a** is estimated by $\lim_{i\uparrow\infty} a_i$. The following double condition must be fulfilled when pseudo-estimators are used in this way:

The limit $\lim_{i\uparrow\infty} a_i$ must exist, whatever the initial value a_0 is and it may not depend on that initial value.

In some cases this condition can be proved to be verified. We shall do it later for the pseudo-estimater A_{pseu}, under more general circumstances than those considered here (see next 3.4.7). In practice, it is sufficient to verify numerically that the condition is verified by the consideration of different initial values a_0,

Experience shows that the pseudo-estimators used in Credibility Theory converge very fastly.

The foregoing is an example of 1 pseudo-estimator for 1 parameter. More generally, n pseudo-estimators for n parameters, can be treated iteratively in the same way.

The pseudo-estimators that we will encounter, are **theorically unbiased**. For instance, EA_{pseu}=a. But in that formula, it is assumed that **a** has already the exact value in the first member, and that is generally not the case, because **a** is replaced by some approximation a_i in the iterative procedure. This means, that pseudo-estimators are **practically biased**.

This is no reason to prefer the classical estimator A. Indeed, the latter may furnish strictly negative values. But **a** is a variance. Hence $a \geq 0$ and negative estimates are replaced by 0. This means that A is in fact replaced by $A \vee 0$, introducing a bias again.

The preceding discussion can be applied to all pseudo-estimators or systems of pseudo-estimators. We will not repeat it in the sequel, for other pseudo-estimators than A_{pseu} .

3.3.8. Groupings in a Contract with Several Observations the Same Year

We here consider a model with 1 contract and t° observation years, but now the contract is the family of random variables

$$\Theta \,,\; X_{tn}\; (t=1,\ldots,t_0;\; n=1,\ldots,w_t). \tag{46}$$

This contract corresponds to a real contract in which Θ has a fixed value θ.

The random variables

$$X_{t1}\,,\; X_{t2}\,,\; \ldots\,,\; X_{tw_t} \tag{47}$$

are w_t different observations of the year t. For instance, the contract might cover w_t different cars in automobile insurance, during the year t, and X_{tn} might be the claim amount corresponding to car number n.

We assume that, for fixed Θ, the random variables X_{tn} are conditionally i.i.d., with conditional mean $\mu(\Theta)$ and conditional variance $\sigma^2(\Theta)$.

Let X_{tA} be the usual arithmetic mean of the random variables (47). Then

$$\Theta,\; X_{1A}\,,\; X_{2A}\,,\; \ldots\,,\; X_{t°A} \tag{48}$$

is a sequence of random variables with the following properties:

a. For fixed Θ, the random variables X_{1A}, X_{2A}, ... ,$X_{t°A}$ are conditionally independent.

b. $$E(X_{tA}/\Theta) = \mu(\Theta).$$

c. $$Var(X_{tA}/\Theta) = \sigma^2(\Theta)/w_t.$$

The number w_t is called the **natural weight** of the observation X_{tA}. The natural weight w_t is also the **precision** of the observation X_{tA}. To a great precision corresponds a small variance of the conditional random variable $X_{tA/\Theta}$.

3.4. Credibility Theory Model with Weighted Observations (Bühlmann & Straub 1970)

3.4.1. Model with 1 Contract

Here the contract is defined by the following conditioning random variable, observable random variables and corresponding weights

$$\Theta$$
$$(X_1,w_1)$$
$$\ldots$$
$$(X_t,w_t)$$
$$\ldots$$
$$(X_{t^\circ},w_{t^\circ})$$

satisfying the assumptions

a. For fixed Θ, the random variables $X_1,\ldots,X_{t^\circ}$ are conditionally independent.

b. A function $\mu(\cdot)$ exists, such that

$$E(X_t/\Theta) = \mu(\Theta). \tag{49}$$

c. A function $\sigma^2(\cdot)$ exists, such that

$$Var(X_t/\Theta) = \sigma^2(\Theta)/w_t. \tag{50}$$

This contract corresponds to a real contract in which Θ has a fixed unknown value θ.

By the preceding section 3.3.8, the contract might result from a grouping and averaging of observations in a contract with several i.i.d. observations X_{tn} during the year t. But the contract may have a different provenance. Here, we assume that the weights w_t are strictly positive, but we do not suppose that w_t is an integer.

Notations

$$\mu := E\mu(\Theta) \quad , \quad \sigma^2 := E\sigma^2(\Theta) \quad , \quad a := \mathrm{Var}\ \mu(\Theta),$$

$$z := aw_{\Sigma}/(\sigma^2+aw_{\Sigma}),$$

$$\mu(\Theta)_{cred} := \mathrm{Proj}(\mu(\Theta)/\boldsymbol{P}(1,X_1,\dots,X_{t^\circ})).$$

The same terminology is used as in the case of a contract with unweighted observations: μ, a , σ^2 are the **parameters** of the model (estimated completely in the model with several contracts) and z is the **credibility weight** of the contract.

Covariance relations

Theorem 9

$$\mathbf{EX_t = E\mu(\Theta) = \mu,} \tag{51}$$

$$\mathbf{Cov(X_s,X_t) = a + \delta_{st}(\sigma^2/w_s),} \tag{52}$$

$$\mathbf{Cov(X_t,X_W) = Cov(X_W,X_W) = a + (\sigma^2/w_{\Sigma}) = a/z,} \tag{53}$$

$$\mathbf{Cov(X_t,\mu(\Theta)) = a.} \tag{54}$$

Proof

(51)

$$EX_t = EE(X_t/\Theta) = E\mu(\Theta) = \mu.$$

(52)

$$\mathrm{Cov}(X_s,X_t) = E\ \mathrm{Cov}(X_s,X_t/\Theta) + \mathrm{Cov}[E(X_s/\Theta),E(X_t/\Theta)]$$

$$= \delta_{st}\ E\ \mathrm{Var}(X_s/\Theta) + \mathrm{Var}\ \mu(\Theta) = \delta_{st}\ (\sigma^2/w_s) + a.$$

(53)

The last equality of (53) results from the definition of z.

$$w_{\Sigma}\ \mathrm{Cov}(X_t,X_W) = \textstyle\sum_s w_s\ \mathrm{Cov}(X_t,X_s) = \sum_s w_s[a + \delta_{st}(\sigma^2/w_s)] = aw_{\Sigma} + \sigma^2.$$

Then the two first equalities of (53) follow from these relations, taking into account that the last member does not depend on t.

(54)

$$\mathrm{Cov}(X_t,\mu(\Theta)) = E\ \mathrm{Cov}[X_t,\mu(\Theta)/\Theta] + \mathrm{Cov}[E(X_t/\Theta),E[\mu(\Theta)/\Theta]]$$

$$= 0 + \mathrm{Var}\ \mu(\Theta) = a \quad \bullet$$

Credibility estimator

Theorem 10

In the model with 1 contract and weighted observations,

$$\mu(\Theta)_{cred} = zX_W + (1-z)\mu. \tag{55}$$

Proof

It is sufficient to verify the unbiasedness and covariance relations of the optimal projection Theorem of random variables. This is direct by the covariance relations of Theorem 9.

We here prefer to discover the relation (55). The first member can be displayed as

$$\mu(\Theta)_{cred} = c + \textstyle\sum_s a_s X_s.$$

Then

$$\mu = c + \textstyle\sum_s a_s\mu = c + \mu a_\Sigma\,, \tag{56}$$

by the unbiasedness condition, and

$$a = \mathrm{Cov}(\mu(\Theta),X_t) = \mathrm{Cov}[\mu(\Theta)_{cred}\,,X_t]$$

$$= \mathrm{Cov}[X_t\,,c + \textstyle\sum_s a_s X_s] = \sum_s a_s\,\mathrm{Cov}(X_t,X_s)$$

$$= \textstyle\sum_s a_s[a+\delta_{st}(\sigma^2/w_s)] = aa_\Sigma + a_t(\sigma^2/w_t),$$

by the covariance conditions of the projection Theorem, and by the covariance relations of Theorem 9. Hence

$$aw_t = aa_\Sigma w_t + a_t\sigma^2, \tag{57}$$

and by summation,

$$aw_\Sigma = aa_\Sigma w_\Sigma + a_\Sigma\sigma^2. \tag{58}$$

Then $a_t = (w_t/w_\Sigma)z$ by (57) and $c = (1\text{-}z)\mu$ by (58) •

Estimation of σ^2

Theorem 11

$$S_0^2 := 1/(t^\circ-1) \sum_{1\le t\le t^\circ} w_t(X_t-X_W)^2$$

is an unbiased estimator of σ^2.

Proof.

$$(t^\circ-1)S_0^2 = \sum_t w_t(X_t^\circ - X_W^\circ)^2$$

$$= \sum_t w_t\,(X_t^\circ X_t^\circ - 2X_t^\circ X_W^\circ + X_W^\circ X_W^\circ).$$

We apply E. By the covariance relations, we obtain $(t^\circ-1)S_0^2 = (t^\circ-1)\sigma^2$ •

Variance of S_0^2 *under zero excess assumptions*

For any random variable Y with first moment, we define **the conditionally centered random variable**

$$Y^\Theta = Y - E(Y/\Theta).$$

If $EY^4<\infty$, then **the conditional excess of Y, for fixed Θ** is defined by

$$e(Y/\Theta) := (EY^{\Theta 4}/E^2Y^{\Theta 2})-3. \tag{59}$$

This excess is the excess of the conditional random variable $Y_{/\Theta}$. We say that **the model with 1 contract is a model with no conditional excesses** if $e(X_t/\Theta)=0$ for all observable random variables X_t. Then it is of course understood that these variables do have a fourth-order moment.

This assumption, with the same meaning in the model with several contracts considered hereafter, will only be used in the discussion of the optimality of some parameter estimators. It is satisfied approximatively, in contracts in which the obervations result from a grouping and averaging of a large number of partial obervations, as explained in 3.3.8. Indeed, then the excess of the partial observations is divided by the number of grouped observations, by the last formula Ch.2.(7). This is compatible with the fact that the excess of normal random variables is zero, because some central tendency is involved in grouping and averaging of i.i.d. random variables.

Lemma

In the model with 1 contract and weighted observations,

$$\mathbf{E(S_0^2/\Theta) = \sigma^2(\Theta).} \tag{60}$$

In the model with 1 contract, weighted observations and no conditional excesses,

$$\mathbf{Var(S_0^2/\Theta) = \sigma^4(\Theta)_{/(t^\circ-1)}.} \tag{61}$$

Proof

The conditional random variables $X_{1/\Theta},\ldots,X_{t^\circ/\Theta}$ are such that

$$E(X_t/\Theta) = \mu(\Theta) \quad , \quad Var(X_t/\Theta) = \sigma^2(\Theta)/w_t \quad , \quad e(X_t/\Theta) = 0.$$

Hence, for fixed Θ, they do satisfy the assumptions Ch.2.(8), with e=0, of the classical model considered in Ch.2.3. Then (60) and (61) result from Ch.2.Th.8. (The proof of this Theorem can be repeated with conditional expectations $E(\cdot/\Theta)$ and conditionally centered random variables X_t^{Θ}) •

Theorem 12

In the model with 1 contract, weighted observations and no conditional excesses,

$$\mathbf{Var\ S_0^2 = \sigma^4{}_{/(t^\circ-1)} + v^2,} \tag{62}$$

where

$$\mathbf{v^2 := Var\ \sigma^2(\Theta).}$$

Proof

By the Lemma,

$$Var(S_0^2) = E\ Var(S_0^2/\Theta) + Var\ E(S_0^2/\Theta) = \sigma^4{}_{/(t^\circ-1)} + v^2 \quad \bullet$$

3.4.2. Practical Model with Several Contracts

The credibility model with several contracts and weighted observations is defined by the k° **independent contracts**,

$$\begin{array}{ccccc}
\Theta_1 & & \Theta_k & & \Theta_{k^\circ} \\
(X_{11},w_{11}) & \dots & (X_{k1},w_{k1}) & \dots & (X_{k^\circ 1},w_{k^\circ 1}) \\
(X_{12},w_{12}) & \dots & (X_{k2},w_{k2}) & \dots & (X_{k^\circ 2},w_{k^\circ 2}) \\
\dots & \dots & \dots & \dots & \dots \\
(X_{1t},w_{1t}) & \dots & (X_{kt},w_{kt}) & \dots & (X_{k^\circ t},w_{k^\circ t}) \\
\dots & \dots & \dots & \dots & \dots \\
(X_{1t_1},w_{1t_1}) & \dots & \dots & \dots & (X_{k^\circ,t_{k^\circ}},w_{k^\circ,t_{k^\circ}}) \\
 & & (X_{kt_k},w_{kt_k}) & &
\end{array}$$

satisfying the assumptions of 3.4.1. **for the same functions $\mu(\cdot)$ and $\sigma^2(\cdot)$**. The possible values of the variable contract subscript k are 1,2,..., k°. The number t_k of observable random variables of the contract k, may depend on k. In an expression in which k is fixed, the possible values of the variable time index t are $1,2,\dots,t_k$. We call t_k **the length of the contract k**. Explicitly, the ***assumptions*** are the following.

a. For fixed Θ_k, the random variables $X_{k1},\dots,X_{kt_k}$ are conditionally independent.

b. A function $\mu(\cdot)$ exists, such that

$$E(X_{kt}/\Theta_k) = \mu(\Theta_k). \tag{63}$$

c. A function $\sigma^2(\cdot)$ exists such that

$$Var(X_{kt}/\Theta_k) = \sigma^2(\Theta_k)/w_{kt}. \tag{64}$$

d. The k° contracts 1,2,...,k° are independent.

e. The random variables $\Theta_1,\Theta_2,\dots,\Theta_{k^\circ}$ are identically distributed.

Notations

$$\mu := E\mu(\Theta_k)\ ,\ \sigma^2 := E\sigma^2(\Theta_k)\ ,\ a := Var\ \mu(\Theta_k),$$

$$z_k := aw_{k\Sigma}/(\sigma^2+aw_{k\Sigma}),$$

$$\mu(\Theta_k)_{cred} := Proj[\mu(\Theta_k)/\boldsymbol{P}(1,X_{kt}(k=1,\dots,k^\circ;t=1,\dots,t_k))].$$

Now each contract k has its own **credibility weight z_k**. We call w_{kt} the **natural weight of the observation X_{kt}**, and $w_{k\Sigma}$ the **natural weight of the contract k.**

From the observations $X_{k1},\ldots,X_{kt_k}$ of the contract k, we can form the **weighted observation**

$$X_{kW} := \sum_t (w_{kt}/w_{k\Sigma}) X_{kt}$$

of that contract. From the weighted observations $X_{1W},\ldots,X_{k^\circ W}$, we can form the **naturally weighted portfolio observation**

$$X_{WW} := \sum_k (w_{k\Sigma}/w_{\Sigma\Sigma}) X_{kW}$$

and also the **credibility weighted observation**

$$X_{ZW} := \sum_k (z_k/z_\Sigma) X_{kW}.$$

3.4.3. Covariance Relations (Several Contracts)

Theorem 13

$$\mathbf{E}X_{kt} = \mathbf{E}X_{kW} = \mathbf{E}X_{WW} = \mathbf{E}X_{ZW} = \mathbf{E}\mu(\Theta) = \mu, \tag{65}$$

$$\mathrm{Cov}(X_{ks}, X_{kt}) = a + \delta_{st}(\sigma^2/w_{ks}), \tag{66}$$

$$\mathrm{Cov}(X_{kt}, X_{kW}) = \mathrm{Cov}(X_{kW}, X_{kW}) = a + (\sigma^2/w_{k\Sigma}) = a/z_k, \tag{67}$$

$$\mathrm{Cov}(X_{kt}, X_{ZW}) = \mathrm{Cov}(X_{kW}, X_{ZW}) = \mathrm{Cov}(X_{ZW}, X_{ZW}) = a/z_\Sigma, \tag{68}$$

$$\mathrm{Cov}(X_{kt}, X_{WW}) = \mathrm{Cov}(X_{kW}, X_{WW}) = (\sigma^2/w_{\Sigma\Sigma}) + a(w_{k\Sigma}/w_{\Sigma\Sigma}), \tag{69}$$

$$\mathrm{Cov}(X_{WW}, X_{WW}) = (\sigma^2/w_{\Sigma\Sigma}) + a \sum_k (w_{k\Sigma}^2/w_{\Sigma\Sigma}^2), \tag{70}$$

$$\mathrm{Cov}(X_{kt}, \mu(\Theta_k)) = a. \tag{71}$$

Proof

The relations (65) are direct. The relations (66), (67), (71) result from the covariance relations for one contract of Theorem 9. The relations (68), (69), (70) result from (67) by the linearity properties of the covariance and by the independence of the contracts •

3.4.4. Credibility Estimator (Several Contracts)

Theorem 14 (Bühlmann & Straub)

In the model with several contracts and weighted observations,

$$\mu(\Theta_k)_{cred} = z_k X_{kW} + (1-z_k)\mu. \tag{72}$$

Proof
(72) results from (55) in the same way that (35) results from (16) •

Optimal estimation of μ

Theorem 15

In the model with several contracts and weighted observations, the optimal estimator of μ in the plane $P(X_{kt};k=1,\ldots,k°;t=1,\ldots,t_k)$ is

$$\mu_{proj} := \text{Proj}[\mu / P_\mu(X_{kt};k=1,\ldots,k°;t=1,\ldots,t_k)] = X_{ZW}. \tag{73}$$

Proof
The unbiasedness and covariance conditions of the optimal projection Theorem of constants, are direct for X_{ZW}, by (65) and (68) •

Practically, μ is replaced by X_{ZW} in the last member of (72). By the following Theorem, the estimator $\mu(\Theta_k)_{CRED}$ obtained in this way, results directly from the projection on a plane of observable random variables.

Theorem 16

In the model with several contracts and weighted observations,

$$\begin{aligned}\mu(\Theta_k)_{CRED} &:= \text{Proj}[\mu(\Theta_k) / P_\mu(X_{jt};j=1,\ldots,k°;t=1,\ldots,t_j)] \\ &= z_k X_{kW} + (1-z_k)X_{ZW}.\end{aligned} \tag{74}$$

Proof
It is enough to verify the unbiasedness and covariance conditions of the optimal projection Theorem of random variables on planes not through the origin (Ch.1.Th.9),

$$E[z_k X_{kW}+(1-z_k)X_{ZW}] = E\mu(\Theta_k), \tag{75}$$

$$Cov[z_k X_{kW}+(1-z_k)X_{ZW} - \mu(\Theta_k), X_{jt}] = \text{const.} \tag{76}$$

The relation (75) results from (65). By the independence of the contracts and by the covariance relations of Theorem 13, the first member of (76) equals

$$z_k\delta_{kj}Cov(X_{kW},X_{jt}) + (1-z_k)Cov(X_{ZW},X_{jt}) - \delta_{kj}Cov(\mu(\Theta_k),X_{jt})$$

$$= \delta_{kj}\, z_k(a/z_k) + (1-z_k)(a/z_\Sigma) - \delta_{ij}\, a = (1-z_k)(a/z_\Sigma) \quad \bullet$$

In fact, it is the credibility estimator (74) that Bühlmann and Straub (1970) have published. That estimator solves, automatically, the problem of the right estimation of μ: the correct estimator is X_{ZW}, not X_{WW} .

3.4.5. General Remarks on Optimal Parameter Estimation

a. Let c be a parameter, and let $C_1,\ldots,C_n$ be unbiased estimators of c, called **the basic estimators of c**. Then, whatever the positive weights $p_1,\ldots,p_n$ are, not all zero,

$$C_P = \sum\nolimits_{1\le i\le n} (p_i/p_\Sigma)C_i$$

is an unbiased estimator of c. We observe that C_P does not change when the weights p_i are multiplied by the same strictly positive constant.

b. The problem of optimal parameter estimation is the determination of **the optimal weights p_i** (up to a constant factor), i.e. the weights for which C_P is the optimal estimator of c in the family of linear combinations of the estimators C_i. We recall that "optimal" is synonymous of "unbiased and of minimum variance". This optimal estimator is

$$c_{proj} := Proj[c/\boldsymbol{P}_c(C_1,\ldots,C_n)].$$

It is furnished by the the optimal projection Theorem of constants. In Credibility Theory, some optimal estimators are in fact pseudo-estimators.

c. As an example, let us consider the problem of the optimal estimation of μ in the model with several contracts and unweighted observations. As basic estimators, we take all the observable random variables X_{kt}. By Theorem 15, the optimal estimator of μ is X_{ZW}. It is not the intuitively expected unbiased estimator X_{WW} .

d. **In symmetrical situations, there is no optimal estimation problem**.

Indeed, then the optimal estimator results from symmetry considerations.

We will illustrate this remark by the estimation of μ in the model with k° contracts of the same length t° and unweighted observations. Now the optimal estimator

$$\sum_{kt} p_{kt}X_{kt} \text{ , with } p_{\Sigma\Sigma} = 1,$$

can only be that one with equal weights p_{kt}. Indeed, for symmetry reasons, two observations X_{kt} and X_{ks} in the same contract k, must necessarily receive the same weight $p_{kt}=p_{ks}$. For the same reasons, two observations X_{jt} and X_{kt} in the same year, must also receive the same weight $p_{jt}=p_{kt}$. Without any doubt, the optimal estimator of μ can only be X_{WW} .

e. Let us now assume that the basic estimators $C_1,\dots,C_n$ of c are independent random variables satisfying the relations

$$EC_i = c \quad , \quad \text{Var } C_i = v^2/v_i \quad .$$

Then we are in an elementary classical situation and the optimal estimator of c is C_P , constructed from the weigths $p_i := v_i$, by Ch.2.Th.4. At this stage, the constant v^2 is completely irrelevant and it is equivalent to say that

The optimal estimator of c is C_P, with $p_i = 1/\text{Var } C_i$.

Now we make the supplementary assumptions that the random variables C_i have no excess, $e(C_i)=0$, and we consider the problem of the estimations of v^2. As basic estimators, we can take the random variables

$$\text{const.}(C_i-C_P)^2,$$

where the const. is irrelevant (it is mentioned because basic estimators are unbiased by definition), and where C_P is the optimal estimator of c. Then, by Ch.2.Th.8, the optimal estimator of v^2 is

$$V^2 := 1/(n-1) \sum_{1 \leq i \leq n} v_i(C_i - C_P)^2. \quad (77)$$

f. In Credibility Theory, some optimal estimators or pseudo-estimators can only be obtained explicitly under particular assumptions, certainly not strictly satisfied in practical portfolio's. In the model with several contracts and weighted observations, such assumptions are

No conditional excesses: $e(X_{kt}/\Theta) = 0$.

and

No contract excesses: $e(X_{kw}) = 0$.

We summarize the conclusion of the discussion preceding the Lemma of Theorem 12: In contracts with observations resulting from groupings and averagings of numerous partial i.i.d. observations, the excesses of these observations are small. Hence, in a lot of practical situations, the no-excess assumptions are satisfied at least approximatively.

g. The optimal estimators or pseudo-estimators in Credibility Theory, are theoretically unbiased, in any case. (The practical unbiasedness of pseudo-estimators **and of classical estimators**, is another problem mentioned at the end of 3.3.7). Estimators and pseudo-estimators, proved to be optimal under particular assumptions, are nevertheless used when these assumptions are not necessarily satisfied. Then, some optimality may be lost. The estimator is not necessarily of minimum-variance in the considered family of estimators, but the theoretical unbiasedness remains preserved.

h. The credibility estimators of modern Credibility Theory are distribution-free. This is one of its great properties, making the applicability to real situations very large. The optimality conditions on the parameter estimators are formulated in the same distribution-free spirit, hereafter. For instance, a no-excess condition is much less restrictive than the supposition that the corresponding distribution is normal.

3.4.6. Estimation of σ^2 (Several Contracts)

From Theorem 11, applied to the contract k, results that

$$S_k^2 := (t_k-1)^{-1} \sum_{1\le t\le t_k} w_{kt}(X_{kt}-X_{kW}) \tag{78}$$

is an unbiased estimator of σ^2. In the estimation problem of σ^2, we consider the random variables $S_1^2,\ldots,S_{k^\circ}^2$ as basic estimators. We denote by

$$S_P^2 := \sum_k (p_k/p_\Sigma)S_k^2$$

the unbiased estimator of σ^2 defined from the weights p_k. The **usual estimator** for σ^2,

$$S^2 := [\sum_j(t_j-1)]^{-1} \sum_k(t_k-1)S_k^2 \tag{79}$$

corresponds to the weights $p_k = t_k-1$.

Theorem 17

In the model with several contracts, weighted observations and no conditional excesses, the optimal pseudo-estimator of σ^2 is the estimator S_P^2 defined from the weights

$$p_k := [\sigma^4(t_k-1)^{-1} + v^2]^{-1} \tag{80}$$

where

$$v^2 := \mathrm{Var}\ \sigma^2(\Theta).$$

Proof
The sequence $S_1^2,\ldots,S_{k^\circ}^2$ is a sequence of independent random variables, and

$$ES_k^2 = \sigma^2 \ , \ \mathrm{Var}\ S_k^2 = \sigma^4(t_k-1)^{-1} + v =: u_k\ ,$$

by Theorem 12. By 3.4.5.e, the optimal estimator S_P^2 is that one defined from the weights $p_k:=1/u_k$ •

The optimal pseudo-estimator furnished by the preceding Theorem is not practical, because v is not known in the distribution-free model. In parametric models it may happen that v is known.

Mostly, the contracts do have the same length $t_1=t_2=...=t_{k°}$ and then the following Corollary applies.

Corollary

In the model with several contracts, weighted observations and no conditional excesses, the usual estimator S^2 for σ^2 is optimal if all the contracts have the same length, or if $v^2=0$.

Proof

When the contracts have the same length, then

$$\text{Var } S_k^2 = \text{const.},$$

and as well in the usual estimator as in the optimal one, the weigths p_k are equal. If $v^2=0$, then

$$p_k = \sigma^{-4}(t_k-1)$$

in the optimal estimator, by (80). These weights differ from the corresponding weights (t_k-1) of the usual estimator, by the irrelevant constant factor σ^4 •

The optimal pseudo-estimator S_P^2 is the estimator with weights (80), or what amounts to the same, with weights

$$[(t_k-1)^{-1} + (v^2/\sigma^4)\,]^{-1}$$

If $r:=v^2/\sigma^4$ is small, compared to $(t_k-1)^{-1}$, then v^2/σ^4 can be neglected and then the usual estimator is approximatively optimal. On the contrary, if r is large, compared to $(t_k-1)^{-1}$, then the latter term can be neglected, and then the estimator with equal weights

$$1/k° \sum_k S_k^2$$

is approximatively optimal. Hence, in such a case, short contracts and long contracts should receive the same weight when the estimation of σ^2 is considered. Unfortunately, r is not known, and it seems difficult to estimate v from the observations X_{kt}. Only assumptions on the involved distributions could furnish some information on r.

3.4.7. Estimation of a (Several Contracts)

***Optimal pseudo-estimation of* a**

From (65), (67) and from the independence of the contracts, results that $X_{1W},\dots,X_{k^\circ W}$ are independent random variables, such that

$$EX_{kW} = \mu \ , \ Var(X_{kW}) = a/z_k \ .$$

This is a classical elementary situation, allowing the optimal estimation of μ and **a** by 3.4.5.e. Then the optimal estimator of μ is the estimator X_{ZW} already obtained in Theorem 15. Under no excess assumptions, the optimal estimator **a** is the **Bichsel-Straub pseudo-estimator A_{pseu}** (indicated in an unpublished paper, Reference 22) defined in the following Theorem.

Theorem 18

In the model with several contracts, weighted observations, and no contract excesses, the optimal pseudo-estimator of a is the *Bichsel-Straub estimator*

$$A_{pseu} := 1/(k^\circ-1) \sum_{1\le k\le k^\circ} z_k(X_{kW}-X_{ZW})^2 \ \bullet \qquad (81)$$

As explained in 15.3.7, pseudo-estimators are used iteratively. The convergence of A_{pseu} and the non dependence of the limit on the initial value $a_0>0$ result from the following Theorem.

Theorem 19

Let f(x) be a continuous positive increasing function of $x\ge 0$. For $x>0$, let $g(x):=f(x)/x$. We assume that g is a strictly decreasing function and that $g(\infty):=\lim_{x\uparrow\infty} g(x)=0$. Let $g(0):=\lim_{x\downarrow 0} g(x)$.

Then the sequence x_0, $x_1:=f(x_0)$, $x_2:=f(x_1)$, ... converges to a finite limit r not depending on the initial value $x_0>0$. If $g(0)\le 1$, then $r=0$. If $g(0)>1$, then r is the unique strictly positive root of the equation $x=f(x)$.

Proof

Let us first assume that $g(0)>1$. A unique strictly positive number r exists, such that $g(r)=1$, i.e. $f(r)=r$, because $g(\infty)=0$ and g is strictly decreasing,

If $0<x\leq r$, then $f(x)/x=g(x)\geq g(r)=1$ and then $x\leq f(x)\leq f(r)=r$. Hence, $0<x\leq r \Rightarrow x\leq f(x)\leq r$. This means that, when we start with a value x_0 in the interval $]0,r]$, then $x_n\leq f(x_n)=x_{n+1}\leq r$. Then x_n is a bounded increasing sequence, and as $n\uparrow\infty$, $\lim x_n\leq f(\lim x_n)=\lim x_n\leq r$, where the inequalities can only be equalities because $\lim x_n$ satisfies the equation defining r. Hence, $\lim x_n=r$.

If $r<x$, then $f(x)/x=g(x)<g(r)=1$ and then $x>f(x)\geq f(r)=r$. Hence, $r<x \Rightarrow r\leq f(x)<x$. This means that, when we start with a value x_0 in the interval $]r,\infty[$, then $r\leq f(x_n) =x_{n+1}<x_n$. Then x_n is a decreasing sequence, and as $n\uparrow\infty$, $r\leq f(\lim x_n)=\lim x_n\leq \lim x_n$. Again, the inequalities must be equalities.

Finally, let us assume that $g(0)\leq 1$. Then 0 is the unique root of the equation $x=f(x)$. Let $x>0$. Then $f(x)/x=g(x)\leq g(0)\leq 1$, and $f(x)\leq x$. This means that, when we start with a value x_0, then $0\leq f(x_n)=x_{n+1}\leq x_n$, and as $n\uparrow\infty$, $f(\lim x_n)=\lim x_n$. Then $\lim x_n=0$ •

Now we verify that the conditions of this Theorem are satisfied for A_{pseu}, considered as function of **a** only. Let accents represent derivatives with respect to **a**. Then by (81),

$$(k^\circ-1)(A_{pseu})'$$

$$= \sum_k (z_k)'(X_{kw}-X_{zw})^2 - 2(X_{zw})' \sum_k z_k(X_{kw}-X_{zw})$$

$$= \sum_k (z_k)'(X_{kw}-X_{zw})^2 - 0 \geq 0,$$

because $(z_k)'\geq 0$.

For $a>0$, let $y_k := z_k/a$. Then,

$$(k^\circ-1)(A_{pseu}/a) = \sum_k y_k(X_{kw}-X_{zw})^2,$$

and

$$(k^\circ-1)(A_{pseu}/a)'$$

$$= \sum_k (y_k)'(X_{kw}-X_{zw})^2 - 2(X_{zw})' \sum_k y_k(X_{kw}-X_{zw})$$

$$= \sum_k (y_k)'(X_{kW}-X_{ZW})^2 - 2(X_{ZW})' \, a^{-1} \sum_k z_k(X_{kW}-X_{ZW})$$

$$= \sum_k (y_k)'(X_{kW}-X_{ZW})^2 - 0 < 0,$$

because $(y_k)' < 0$.

Classical estimation of **a**

Classical (i.e. non-pseudo-) estimators of **a** can be constructed in the following way. Let $p_1,...p_{k^\circ}$ be any weights, and let us consider the statistic

$$Q := \sum_k p_k(X_{kW}-X_{WW})^2. \tag{82}$$

Then

$$Q = \sum_k p_k(X_{kW}{}^\circ - X_{WW}{}^\circ)^2$$

$$= \sum_k p_k(X_{kW}{}^\circ X_{kW}{}^\circ - 2X_{kW}{}^\circ X_{WW}{}^\circ + X_{WW}{}^\circ X_{WW}{}^\circ).$$

and

$$EQ = \sum_k p_k \, [\mathrm{Cov}(X_{kW},X_{kW}) - 2\mathrm{Cov}(X_{kW},X_{WW}) + \mathrm{Cov}(X_{WW},X_{WW})]$$

The covariances can be explicited by the second relation (67), the second relation (69), and relation (70). The result is an expression

$$EQ = \alpha \, a + \beta \, \sigma^2 ,$$

where α and β only depend on the weights p_k and on the natural weights $w_{k\Sigma}$. This implies that

$$1/\alpha \; Q - \beta/\alpha \; S^2$$

is an unbiased estimator of **a**. In fact, the unbiasedness is a practical illusion, because strictly negative estimates are replaced by 0. This "unbiasedness" cannot be used as argument in favor of classical estimators, againts pseudo-estimators (also biased in practice).

The estimator A defined in the following Theorem is the **Bühlmann-Straub (1970) classical estimator** of **a**.

Theorem 20

In the model with several contracts and weighted observations, the following estimator A is an unbiased estimator of a:

$$\mathbf{A := [w_{\Sigma\Sigma}/(w_{\Sigma\Sigma}^2 - \Sigma_j w_{j\Sigma}^2)][\Sigma_k\, w_{k\Sigma}(X_{kw} - X_{ww})^2 - (k^\circ - 1)S^2].}$$

Proof

The estimator A results from the statistic (82) with $p_k := w_{k\Sigma}$. Indeed, then

$$EQ = \Sigma_k\, w_{k\Sigma}\,[Cov(X_{kw}, X_{kw}) - 2Cov(X_{kw}, X_{ww}) + Cov(X_{ww}, X_{ww})] = \alpha a + \beta\sigma^2,$$

where

$$\alpha := \Sigma_k\, w_{k\Sigma}[1 - 2(w_{k\Sigma}/w_{\Sigma\Sigma}) + \Sigma_j\, (w_{j\Sigma}^2/w_{\Sigma\Sigma}^2)]$$

$$= w_{\Sigma\Sigma} - 2\Sigma_k(w_{k\Sigma}^2/w_{\Sigma\Sigma}) + w_{\Sigma\Sigma}\Sigma_j\, (w_{j\Sigma}^2/w_{\Sigma\Sigma}^2) = [w_{\Sigma\Sigma}^2 - \Sigma_j\, w_{j\Sigma}^2]/w_{\Sigma\Sigma}\,,$$

and

$$\beta := \Sigma_k\, w_{k\Sigma}[(1/w_{k\Sigma}) - (2/w_{\Sigma\Sigma}) + (1/w_{\Sigma\Sigma})] = k^\circ - 1 \quad \bullet$$

3.5. Hierarchical Credibility (Jewell 1975)

3.5.1. Hierarchical Model with Weighted Observations

We consider **the hierarchical credibility model with 3 levels and weighted observations** defined by the conditioning random variables, observable random variables and corresponding weights

$$\Theta_m\,,\ \Theta_{mn}\,,\ \Theta_{mnp}\,,\ X_{mnpq}\,,\ w_{mnpq} \tag{83}$$

for

$$m = 1,2,\ldots,m^\circ\ ;\ n = 1,2,\ldots,\ n_m\ ;\ p = 1,2,\ldots,\ p_{mn}\ ;\ q = 1,2,\ldots,\ q_{mnp}.$$

The insurance company m is the set of random variables

$$\Theta_m\,,\ \Theta_{mn}\,,\ \Theta_{mnp}\,,\ X_{mnpq}\,,\ w_{mnpq}\ \text{(n,p,q: variable subscripts).}$$

The portfolio mn (or **the portfolio m of the company n**) is the set of random variables

$$\Theta_{mn}\,,\ \Theta_{mnp}\,,\ X_{mnpq}\,,\ w_{mnpq}\ \text{(p,q: variable subscripts).}$$

The contract mnp (or **the contract p of the portfolio n of the company m**) is the set of random variables

$$\Theta_{mnp}\ ,\ X_{mnpq}\ ,\ w_{mnpq}\ \text{(q: variable subscript).}$$

The observation mnpq (or **the observation q of the contract p of the portfolio n of the company m**) is the random variable X_{mnpq}. It has the strictly positive **natural weight** w_{mnpq} .

We use the abbreviations

$$\Theta_{m+} \equiv \Theta_m,$$

$$\Theta_{mn+} \equiv (\Theta_m,\Theta_{mn}),$$

$$\Theta_{mnp+} \equiv (\Theta_m,\Theta_{mn},\Theta_{mnp}).$$

With these definitions, the ***Assumptions*** on the model are the following:

a. The companies are independent.

b. In each company m, the portfolios are conditionally independent for fixed Θ_m.

c. In each portfolio mn, the contracts are conditionally independent for fixed Θ_{mn+} .

d. In each contract mnp, the observations are conditionally independent for fixed Θ_{mnp+} .

e. A function $\mu(\cdot,\cdot,\cdot)$ exists, such that

$$E(X_{mnpq}/\Theta_{mnp+}) = \mu(\Theta_{mnp+}). \tag{84}$$

f. A function $\sigma^2(\cdot,\cdot,\cdot)$ exists, such that

$$Var(X_{mnpq}/\Theta_{mnp+}) = \sigma^2(\Theta_{mnp+})/w_{mnpq}. \tag{85}$$

h. The random triplets Θ_{mnp+} are identically distributed.

In practical situations, the random variables Θ_m, Θ_{mn}, Θ_{mnp} have fixed unknown values θ_m, θ_{mn}, θ_{mnp}.

Other interpretations than

company - portfolio - contract - observation

are possible. For instance

continent - state - region - observation

We develop the theory of the model with 3 levels. It contains all the ideas of the model with any number n of levels. The Bühlmann-Straub model is a model with 1 level.

Notations

$$\mu(\Theta_{mn+}) := E(\mu(\Theta_{mnp+})/\Theta_{mn+}) \ , \ \mu(\Theta_m) := E(\mu(\Theta_{mn+})/\Theta_m) \ , \ \mu := E\mu(\Theta_m),$$

$$\sigma^2 := E\sigma^2(\Theta_{mnp+}).$$

We notice the four different meanings of μ in μ, $\mu(\cdot)$, $\mu(\cdot,\cdot)$, $\mu(\cdot,\cdot,\cdot)$ and the two different meanings of σ^2 in σ^2, $\sigma^2(\cdot)$.

Let ***Obs*** be the family of all observable random variables X_{mnpq}. Then **the problem** is the calculation of the following **credibility estimators**

$$\mu(\Theta_{mnp+})_{cred} := \text{Proj}[\mu(\Theta_{mnp+})/\boldsymbol{P}(1,\boldsymbol{Obs})]$$

$$\mu(\Theta_{mn+})_{cred} := \text{Proj}[\mu(\Theta_{mn+})/\boldsymbol{P}(1,\boldsymbol{Obs})]$$

$$\mu(\Theta_{m+})_{cred} := \text{Proj}[\mu(\Theta_{m+})/\boldsymbol{P}(1,\boldsymbol{Obs})]$$

By (84), $\mu(\Theta_{mnp+})_{cred}$ is an estimator of the expectation of the observations of the real contract mnp, because Θ_{mnp+} has a fixed value in the real contract p of the real portfolio n of the real company m. Similarly, by the relations of the following Theorem, $\mu(\Theta_{mn+})_{cred}$ is an estimator of the expectation of the observations of the real portfolio mn, and $\mu(\Theta_{m+})_{cred}$ is an estimator of the expectation of the observations of the real company m.

3.5.2. Expectations and Covariance Relations

Theorem 21 **(Expectations)**

1.

$$\mathbf{E(X_{mnpq}/\Theta_{mnp+}) = \mu(\Theta_{mnp+}).}$$

2.

$$\mathbf{E(X_{mnpq}/\Theta_{mn+}) = \mu(\Theta_{mn+}).}$$

3.

$$\mathbf{E(X_{mnpq}/\Theta_{m+}) = \mu(\Theta_{m+}).}$$

4.

$$\mathbf{EX_{mnpq} = \mu.}$$

5.

$$\mathbf{E(\mu(\Theta_{mnp+})/\Theta_{mn+}) = \mu(\Theta_{mn+}).}$$

6.

$$\mathbf{E(\mu(\Theta_{mnp+})/\Theta_{m+}) = \mu(\Theta_{m+}).}$$

7.

$$\mathbf{E\mu(\Theta_{mnp+}) = \mu.}$$

8.

$$\mathbf{E(\mu(\Theta_{mn+})/\Theta_{m+}) = \mu(\Theta_{m+}).}$$

9.

$$\mathbf{E\mu(\Theta_{mn+}) = \mu.}$$

10.

$$\mathbf{E\mu(\Theta_{m}) = \mu.}$$

Proof
Relation 1 is an assumption, and 5,8,10 are notations. For 2,

$$E(X_{mnpq}/\Theta_{mn+}) = E[E(X_{mnpq}/\Theta_{mnp+})/\Theta_{mn+}] = E[\mu(\Theta_{mnp+})/\Theta_{mn+}] = \mu(\Theta_{mn+})$$

by 1 and 5. For 6,

$$E(\mu(\Theta_{mnp+})/\Theta_{m+}) = E[E(\mu(\Theta_{mnp+})/\Theta_{mn+})/\Theta_{m+}] = E[\mu(\Theta_{mn+})/\Theta_{m+}] = \mu(\Theta_{m+})$$

by 5 and 8. The proof of the other relations is similar •

The general structure of these relations is

$$E(X_{subscr}\ /\Theta_{sub+}) = \mu(\Theta_{sub+}) \quad , \quad E(\mu(\Theta_{subscr+})/\Theta_{sub+}) = \mu(\Theta_{sub+})$$

where $_{subscr}$ are subscripts $_{mn\ldots}$ and where $_{sub}$ is an initial segment $_{m\ldots}$ of $_{subscr}$.

Theorem 22 (Covariance Relations)

Unique constants a, b, c exist, such that

$$\mathbf{Cov(X_{mnpq},X_{mijk}) = \delta_{ni}\delta_{pj}\delta_{qk}(\sigma^2/w_{mnpq}) + \delta_{ni}\delta_{pj}\, a + \delta_{ni}\, b + c,} \tag{86}$$

$$\mathbf{Cov(X_{mnpq},\mu(\Theta_{mij+})) = \delta_{ni}\delta_{pj}\, a + \delta_{ni}\, b + c,} \tag{87}$$

$$\mathbf{Cov(X_{mnpq},\mu(\Theta_{mi+})) = \delta_{ni}\, b + c,} \tag{88}$$

$$\mathbf{Cov(X_{mnpq},\mu(\Theta_{m+})) = c.} \tag{89}$$

Proof

The relations (86) to (89) are equivalent to (89) and to the relations

$$Cov(X_{mnpq},X_{mijk}-\mu(\Theta_{mij+})) =\delta_{ni}\delta_{pj}\delta_{qk}(\sigma^2/w_{mnpq}), \tag{90}$$

$$Cov(X_{mnpq},\mu(\Theta_{mij+})-\mu(\Theta_{mi+})) = \delta_{ni}\delta_{pj}\, a, \tag{91}$$

$$Cov(X_{mnpq},\mu(\Theta_{mi+})-\mu(\Theta_{m+})) = \delta_{ni}\, b, \tag{92}$$

resulting from the differences (86)–(87) , (87)–(88) , (88)–(89).

Let Cov be the first member of (90). Then

$$Cov = E\, Cov(X_{mnpq},X_{mijk}-\mu(\Theta_{mij+})/\Theta_m) + 0, \tag{93}$$

where the 0 results from the relation

$$E(X_{mijk}-\mu(\Theta_{mij+})/\Theta_m) = 0$$

implied by Theorem 21. The last member of (93) equals 0 if $n\neq i$ by the conditional independence of the portfolios of the company m for fixed Θ_m. Hence,

$$Cov = \delta_{ni}\, Cov = \delta_{ni}\, E\, Cov(X_{mnpq},X_{mnjk}-\mu(\Theta_{mnj+})/\Theta_{mn+}).$$

The last member equals 0 if $p\neq j$ by the conditional independence of the contracts of the portfolio mn for fixed Θ_{mn+} . Hence

$$Cov = \delta_{ni}\delta_{pj}\, Cov = \delta_{ni}\delta_{pj}\, E\, Cov(X_{mnpq},X_{mnpk}-\mu(\Theta_{mnp+})/\Theta_{mnp+})$$

$$= \delta_{ni}\delta_{pj}\, E\, Cov(X_{mnpq},X_{mnpk}/\Theta_{mnp+}),$$

where the last member equals 0 if $q \neq k$ by the conditional independence of the observations of the contract mnp for fixed Θ_{mnp+} . Hence,

$$Cov = \delta_{ni}\delta_{pj}\delta_{qk}\, Cov = \delta_{ni}\delta_{pj}\delta_{qk}\, E\, Var(X_{mnpq}/\Theta_{mnp+})$$

$$= \delta_{ni}\delta_{pj}\delta_{qk}\, E\, \sigma^2(\Theta_{mnp+})/w_{mnpq} = \delta_{ni}\delta_{pj}\delta_{qk}\, \sigma^2/w_{mnpq}.$$

This proves (90). For the proof of (91) and the definition of a, let Cov now be the first member of (91). Then, by the same argument as that already used,

$$Cov = E\, Cov(X_{mnpq}, \mu(\Theta_{mij+}) - \mu(\Theta_{mi+})/\Theta_m) = \delta_{ni}\, Cov$$

$$= E\, Cov(X_{mnpq}, \mu(\Theta_{mnj+}) - \mu(\Theta_{mn+})/\Theta_{mn+}) = \delta_{ni}\delta_{pj}\, Cov$$

$$= \delta_{ni}\delta_{pj}\, E\, Cov(X_{mnpq}, \mu(\Theta_{mnp+}) - \mu(\Theta_{mn+})/\Theta_{mnp+})$$

$$+ \delta_{ni}\delta_{pj}\, Cov[E(X_{mnpq}/\Theta_{mnp+}), E(\mu(\Theta_{mnp+}) - \mu(\Theta_{mn+})/\Theta_{mnp+})]$$

$$= 0 + \delta_{ni}\delta_{pj}\, Cov[\mu(\Theta_{mnp+}), \mu(\Theta_{mnp+}) - \mu(\Theta_{mn+})] = \delta_{ni}\delta_{pj}\, a,$$

where

$$a := Cov[\mu(\Theta_{mnp+}), \mu(\Theta_{mnp+}) - \mu(\Theta_{mn+})].$$

This proves (91). For the proof of (92) and the definition of b, let Cov now be the first member of (92). Then

$$Cov = E\, Cov(X_{mnpq}, \mu(\Theta_{mi+}) - \mu(\Theta_{m+})/\Theta_m) = \delta_{ni}\, Cov$$

$$= \delta_{ni}\, E\, Cov(X_{mnpq}, \mu(\Theta_{mn+}) - \mu(\Theta_{m+})/\Theta_{mn+})$$

$$+ \delta_{ni}\, Cov[E(X_{mnpq}/\Theta_{mn+}), E(\mu(\Theta_{mn+}) - \mu(\Theta_{m+})/\Theta_{mn+})]$$

$$= 0 + \delta_{ni}\, Cov[\mu(\Theta_{mn+}), \mu(\Theta_{mn+}) - \mu(\Theta_{m+})] = \delta_{ni}\, b\, ,$$

where

$$b := Cov[\mu(\Theta_{mn+}), \mu(\Theta_{mn+}) - \mu(\Theta_{m+})].$$

This proves (92). From the involved equidistributions results that a,b do not depend on the subscripts m,n,p,q. The constant c defined by (89) does not depend on m,n,p,q because

$$c = Cov(X_{mnpq}, \mu(\Theta_m)) = 0 + Cov[E(X_{mnpq}/\Theta_m), E(\mu(\Theta_m)/\Theta_m)]$$

$$= Cov[\mu(\Theta_m), \mu(\Theta_m)] = Var\, \mu(\Theta_m) \quad \bullet$$

Notations

The **credibility weight z_{mnp} of the contract mnp**, **the credibility weight z_{mn} of the portfolio mn**, and **the credibility weight z_m of the company m** are defined successively by the relations

$$z_{mnp} := aw_{mnp\Sigma}/(\sigma^2+aw_{mnp\Sigma}),$$

$$z_{mn} := bz_{mn\Sigma}/(a+bz_{mn\Sigma}),$$

$$z_m := cz_{m\Sigma}/(b+cz_{m\Sigma}),$$

where a,b,c are the constants of the preceding Theorem.

The averages X_{mnpW} , X_{mnZW} , X_{mZZW} , X_{ZZZW} used in the following Theorem are formed according to the general rules. Explicitly, here

$$X_{mnpW} := \sum_{1\leq q\leq q_{mnp}} (w_{mnpq}/w_{mnp\Sigma})X_{mnpq},$$

$$X_{mnZW} := \sum_{1\leq p\leq p_{mn}} (z_{mnp}/z_{mn\Sigma})\, X_{mnpW},$$

$$X_{mZZW} := \sum_{1\leq n\leq n_m} (z_{mn}/z_{m\Sigma})\, X_{mnZW},$$

$$X_{ZZZW} := \sum_{1\leq m\leq m^\circ} (z_m/z_\Sigma)\, X_{mZZW}.$$

Theorem 23

$$\mathbf{Cov(X_{sub},X_{mijW}) = \delta_{ni}\delta_{pj}(a/z_{mnp}) + \delta_{ni}b + c,}$$

for sub ≡ mnpq, mnpW.

$$\mathbf{Cov(X_{sub},X_{miZW}) = \delta_{ni}(b/z_{mn}) + c,}$$

for sub ≡ mnpq, mnpW, mnZW.

$$\mathbf{Cov(X_{sub},X_{mZZW}) = c/z_m,}$$

for sub ≡ mnpq, mnpW, mnZW, mZZW

$$\mathbf{Cov(X_{sub},X_{ZZZW}) = c/z_\Sigma,}$$

for sub ≡ mnpq, mnpW, mnZW, mZZW, ZZZW.

Proof

$$\mathrm{Cov}(X_{mnpq},X_{mijW}) = \sum_k (w_{mijk}/w_{mij\Sigma})\,\mathrm{Cov}(X_{mnpq},X_{mijk})$$

$$=\sum_k (w_{mijk}/w_{mij\Sigma})[\delta_{ni}\delta_{pj}\delta_{qk}(\sigma^2/w_{mnpq})+\delta_{ni}\delta_{pj}a+\delta_{ni}b+c]$$

$$=\sum_k (w_{mijk}/w_{mij\Sigma})\delta_{ni}\delta_{pj}\delta_{qk}(\sigma^2/w_{mnpq}) + \sum_k (w_{mijk}/w_{mij\Sigma})[\delta_{ni}\delta_{pj}a+\delta_{ni}b+c]$$

$$= (1/w_{mnp\Sigma})\delta_{ni}\delta_{pj}\sigma^2 + \delta_{ni}\delta_{pj}a+\delta_{ni}b+c = \delta_{ni}\delta_{pj}(a/z_{mnp}) + \delta_{ni}b + c$$

by (86) and by the definition of z_{mnp} . This proves the first relation of the Theorem for sub≡mnpq. The result does not depend on q. Hence it is also valid for sub≡mnpW.

Then, by the relation already proved and by the definition of z_{mn}

$$\mathrm{Cov}(X_{mnpq},X_{mizW}) = \sum_j (z_{mij}/z_{mi\Sigma})\,\mathrm{Cov}(X_{mnpq},X_{mijW})$$

$$= \sum_j (z_{mij}/z_{mi\Sigma})[\delta_{ni}\delta_{pj}(a/z_{mnp}) + \delta_{ni}b + c] = \delta_{ni}(a/z_{mn\Sigma})+\delta_{ni}b + c$$

$$= \delta_{ni}(b/z_{mn}) + c.$$

This proves the second relation of the Theorem for sub≡mnpq. The result does not depend on p,q. Hence, it is valid for sub=mnpW and then for sub≡mnZW also. The other relations are proved in the same way •

The following relations result from Theorem 21.4:

$$\mathbf{EX_{mnpq} = EX_{mnpW} = EX_{mnZW} = EX_{mZZW} = EX_{ZZZW}}\ .$$

3.5.3. Credibility Estimators

Theorem 24

$$\mu(\Theta_m)_{cred} = z_m X_{mZZW} + (1-z_m)\mu,$$

$$\mu(\Theta_{mn+})_{cred} = z_{mn} X_{mnZW} + (1-z_{mn})\,\mu(\Theta_m)_{cred},$$

$$\mu(\Theta_{mnp+})_{cred} = z_{mnp} X_{mnpW} + (1-z_{mnp})\,\mu(\Theta_{mn+})_{cred}.$$

Proof
For the first relation, the unbiasedness condition of the optimal projection Theorem of random variables is the direct relation

$$E\mu(\Theta_m) = E[z_m X_{mZZW} + (1-z_m)\mu].$$

The covariance condition is

$$Cov(\mu(\Theta_m), X_{ijpq}) = Cov(z_m X_{mZZW} + (1-z_m)\mu, X_{ijpq}).$$

For $m \neq i$ it is 0=0 because the companies are independent. Hence, it is enough to verify that

$$Cov(\mu(\Theta_m), X_{mjpq}) = z_m\, Cov(X_{mZZW}, X_{ijpq}).$$

By (89), the first member equals c. By the third relation of Theorem 23, the last member equals $z_m.c/z_m$.

We now consider the second relation of the Theorem. The unbiasedness condition of the optimal projection Theorem of random variables is

$$E\mu(\Theta_{mn+}) = E[z_{mn} X_{mnZW} + (1-z_{mn})\mu(\Theta_m)_{cred}].$$

It results from Th.21.9 and from the formula already proved for $\mu(\Theta_m)_{cred}$. The covariance condition is

$$Cov(\mu(\Theta_{mn+}), X_{ijpq}) = Cov[z_{mn} X_{mnZW} + (1-z_{mn})\mu(\Theta_m)_{cred}\ ,\ X_{ijpq}\ ].$$

If $i \neq m$, then this relation is 0=0, because the companies are independent. Hence, it is enough to verify that

$$Cov(\mu(\Theta_{mn+}), X_{mjpq}) = z_{mn} Cov(X_{mnZW}, X_{mjpq}) + (1-z_{mn}) Cov[\mu(\Theta_m)_{cred}\ ,\ X_{mjpq}],$$

or by the relation for $\mu(\Theta_m)_{cred}$ already proved, that

$$Cov(\mu(\Theta_{mn+}), X_{mjpq}) = z_{mn} Cov(X_{mnZW}, X_{mjpq}) + (1-z_{mn}) z_m Cov[X_{mZZW}, X_{mjpq}].$$

By (88), the first member equals $\delta_{nj}b+c$. By Theorem 23, the last member equals

$$z_{mn}\ [\delta_{nj}(b/z_{mn})+c] + (1-z_{mn})z_m(c/z_m) = \delta_{nj}b + cz_{mn} + (1-z_{mn})c = \delta_{nj}b+c.$$

The verification of the last relation of the Theorem is similar •

3.5.4. Parameter Estimation

Theorem 25

An optimal estimator of μ is

$$\mu_{proj} := \mathrm{Proj}[\mu/P_\mu(Obs)] = X_{ZZZW}\,.$$

Proof
The unbiasedness condition of the optimal projection Theorem of constants is the direct relation $EX_{ZZZW}=\mu$. The covariance condition is

$$\mathrm{Cov}(X_{ZZZW},X_{mnpq}) = \mathrm{const.}$$

It results from the last relation of Theorem 23 •

Theorem 26

The following random variable S^2 is an unbiased estimator of the parameter σ^2. The random variables A, B, C, are unbiased pseudo-estimators of the parameters a, b, c, resp.

$$S^2 := [\Sigma_{mnp}(q_{mnp}-1)]^{-1}\,\Sigma_{mnpq}\, w_{mnpq}(X_{mnpq}-X_{mnpW})^2,$$

$$A := [\Sigma_{mn}(p_{mn}-1)]^{-1}\,\Sigma_{mnp}\, z_{mnp}(X_{mnpW}-X_{mnZW})^2,$$

$$B := [\Sigma_{m}(n_{m}-1)]^{-1}\,\Sigma_{mn}\, z_{mn}(X_{mnZW}-X_{mZZW})^2,$$

$$C := [m^\circ-1]^{-1}\,\Sigma_{m}\, z_{m}(X_{mZZW}-X_{ZZZW})^2.$$

Proof
We verify that B is unbiased. The other verifications are similar. Let

$$Q := \Sigma_{mn}\, z_{mn}(X_{mnZW}-X_{mZZW})^2 = \Sigma_{mn}\, z_{mn}(X_{mnZW}^\circ - X_{mZZW}^\circ)^2$$

$$= \Sigma_{mn}\, z_{mn}\,(X_{mnZW}^\circ X_{mnZW}^\circ - 2X_{mnZW}^\circ X_{mZZW}^\circ + X_{mZZW}^\circ X_{mZZW}^\circ).$$

Then by Theorem 23,

$$EQ := \sum_{mn} z_{mn}[(b/z_{mn})+c-2(c/z_m)+(c/z_m)] = \sum_m\sum_n [b+cz_{mn}[1-(1/z_m)]] =$$

$$\sum_m [bn_m+\sum_n cz_{mn}[1-(1/z_m)]] = \sum_m [bn_m + cz_{m\Sigma}[1-(1/z_m)]] = \sum_m[bn_m-b] \bullet$$

3.6. Semilinear Credibility Theory

3.6.0. Introduction

Let us again consider the first contract with random variables $\Theta, X_1, \ldots, X_{t^\circ}$ of modern Credibility Theory introduced in this Chapter. In 3.3.1, the unknown random variable $\mu(\Theta) := E(X_t/\Theta)$ is approximated by a linear combination

$$\mu(\Theta)_{cred} = c + a_1X_1 + a_2X_2 + \ldots + a_{t^\circ}X_{t^\circ}$$

of 1 and of the observable random variables X_t. In **practical semilinear credibility**, $\mu(\Theta)$ is approximated by a linear combination

$$c + a_1f(X_1) + a_2f(X_2) + \ldots + a_{t^\circ}f(X_{t^\circ}) \tag{94}$$

of 1 and of the random variables $f(X_t)$, where $f(\cdot)$ is a known fixed function.

In **optimal semilinear credibility**, the unknown function f is that one for which (94) is closest to $\mu(\Theta)$.

A possible choice of $f(X_t)$ is $f(X_t) := X_t \wedge b$. In this case, the claim amounts, say, are truncated at the fixed value b. The known bonus-malus systems in automobile insurance are based on the number, not on the amount of claims. One of the reasons is that the premium would be much too high for some unlucky drivers in systems taking the complete amounts X_t into account. A system with truncated amounts could be useful.

In the following sections, we develop a model with several contracts and weighted observations. The observation of the contract k and the year t is the arithmetic mean X_{ktA} of w_{kt} **partial observations** $X_{kt1}, X_{kt2}, \ldots, X_{ktw_{kt}}$. For instance, for fixed k and t, the variables X_{ktn} may be claim amounts akin to w_{kt} cars covered by the same contract k during the year t. Then the function f (say some truncation), can be applied to the average X_{ktA}, or to the partial claims X_{ktn}. It is the second choice that is made later.

It is also possible to display all the observations X_{ktn} of the same year k in a single column

$$(X_{k1}, X_{k2},..., X_{kt_k})'.$$

Then we have a model with unweighted observations, but contracts of different length and observations X_{kt} in which t can no longer be interpreted as a time index. For the formulas of the latter model, it is enough to take all weights w_{kt} equal to 1 in the model studied hereafter.

3.6.1. Groupings in Contracts with Several Observations the Same Year

We consider the portfolio defined by the random variables

$$\Theta_k \, , \, X_{ktn}$$

for

$$k = 1,2,...,k° \quad ; \quad t = 1,2,...,t_k \quad ; \quad n = 1,2,...,w_{tk}.$$

The contract k is the set of random variables Θ_k, X_{ktn} $(t{=}1,...t_k;n{=}1,...,w_{tk})$.

Assumptions

a. The contracts are independent.

b. In each contract k, **the observations**

$$X_{ktn} \ (t{=}1,...t_k;n{=}1,...,w_{tk})$$

are square-integrable random variables, conditionally independent for fixed Θ_k.

c. All couples (Θ_k, X_{ktn}) are identically distributed.

d. $f(\cdot)$ is a function such that $f(X_{ktn})$ are square integrable random variables.

In the real portfolio, $\Theta_1,...,\Theta_{k°}$ have fixed unknown values $\theta_1,...,\theta_{k°}$.

Notations

$$\mu_1(\Theta_k) := E(X_{ktn}/\Theta_k) \quad , \quad \mu_2(\Theta_k) := E(f(X_{ktn})/\Theta_k),$$

$$\sigma_{11}(\Theta_k) := Var(X_{ktn}/\Theta_k),$$

$$\sigma_{12}(\Theta_k) := Cov[X_{ktn}, f(X_{ktn})/\Theta_k],$$

$$\sigma_{22}(\Theta_k) := Var[f(X_{ktn})/\Theta_k],$$

$$a_{ij} := Cov[\mu_i(\Theta_k), \mu_j(\Theta_k)] \quad (i,j=1,2),$$

$$X_{kt} := (X_{kt1} + X_{kt2} + ... + X_{ktw_{kt}})/w_{kt},$$

$$Y_{kt} := [f(X_{kt1}) + f(X_{kt2}) + ... + f(X_{ktw_{kt}})]/w_{kt}.$$

3.6.2. Practical Semilinear Credibility Theory Model

The model is defined by **the conditioning random variables Θ_k, the observable random couples (X_{kt}, Y_{kt}) and corresponding weights w_{kt}** of the following array:

Θ_1	...	Θ_k	...	Θ_{k°
(X_{11}, Y_{11}, w_{11})	...	(X_{k1}, Y_{k1}, w_{k1})	...	$(X_{k^\circ 1}, Y_{k^\circ 1}, w_{k^\circ 1})$
(X_{12}, Y_{12}, w_{12})	...	(X_{k2}, Y_{k2}, w_{k2})	...	$(X_{k^\circ 2}, Y_{k^\circ 2}, w_{k^\circ 2})$
...	...	...	...	...
(X_{1t}, Y_{1t}, w_{tt})	...	(X_{kt}, Y_{kt}, w_{kt})	...	$(X_{k^\circ t}, Y_{k^\circ t}, w_{k^\circ t})$
	...	...	...	... ...
$(X_{1t_1}, Y_{1t_1}, w_{1t_1})$		...		$(X_{k^\circ t_{k^\circ}}, Y_{k^\circ t_{k^\circ}}, w_{k^\circ t_{k^\circ}})$
		$(X_{kt_k}, Y_{kt_k}, w_{kt_k})$		

Each columns of that array is called a **contract**.

Assumptions

a. In each contract k, the random couples (X_{kt}, Y_{kt}) are conditionally independent for fixed Θ_k .

b. Functions $\mu_1(\cdot)$, $\mu_2(\cdot)$ exist, such that

$$E(X_{kt}/\Theta_k) = \mu_1(\Theta_k) \quad , \quad E(Y_{kt}/\Theta_k) = \mu_2(\Theta_k).$$

c. Functions $\sigma_{11}(\cdot)$, $\sigma_{22}(\cdot)$, $\sigma_{12}(\cdot)$ exist, such that

$$Var(X_{kt}/\Theta_k) = \sigma_{11}(\Theta_k)/w_{kt},$$

$$Var(Y_{kt}/\Theta_k) = \sigma_{22}(\Theta_k)/w_{kt}.$$

$$Cov(X_{kt}, Y_{kt}/\Theta_k) = \sigma_{12}(\Theta_k)/w_{kt}.$$

d. The contracts $1,2,\ldots,k°$ are independent.

e. The random variables $\Theta_1,\ldots,\Theta_{k°}$ are identically distributed.

As usual, the observations X_{kt}, Y_{kt} are square-integrable, and the weights w_{kt} are strictly positive real numbers.

The preceding assumptions are verified for the random variables and weights

$$\Theta_k, X_{kt}, Y_{kt}, w_{kt}$$

considered in the preceding section 3.6.1.

Notations

$$\mu_1 := E\mu_1(\Theta_k) \quad , \quad \mu_2 := E\mu_2(\Theta_k),$$

$$\sigma_{11} := E\sigma_{11}(\Theta_k) \quad , \quad \sigma_{22} := E\sigma_{22}(\Theta_k) \quad , \quad \sigma_{12} := E\sigma_{12}(\Theta_k),$$

$$a_{11} := Var\ \mu_1(\Theta_k) \quad , \quad a_{22} := Var\ \mu_2(\Theta_k),$$

$$a_{12} := Cov[\mu_1(\Theta_k), \mu_2(\Theta_k)],$$

$$\boldsymbol{Obs}_1 := \{X_{kt} / k=1,\ldots,k°;\ t=1,\ldots,t_k\},$$

$$\boldsymbol{Obs}_2 := \{Y_{kt} / k=1,\ldots,k°;\ t=1,\ldots,t_k\},$$

$$\mu_1(\Theta_k)_{cred} := Proj[\mu_1(\Theta_k)/\boldsymbol{P}(1,\boldsymbol{Obs}_1)],$$

$$\mu_2(\Theta_k)_{cred} := Proj[\mu_2(\Theta_k)/\boldsymbol{P}(1,\boldsymbol{Obs}_2)],$$

$$\mu_{1/2}(\Theta_k)_{cred} := Proj[\mu_1(\Theta_k)/\boldsymbol{P}(1,\boldsymbol{Obs}_2)],$$

$$z_{1,k} := a_{11}w_{k\Sigma}/(\sigma_{11}+a_{11}w_{k\Sigma}),$$

$$z_{2,k} := a_{22}w_{k\Sigma}/(\sigma_{22}+a_{22}w_{k\Sigma}),$$

$$z_{12,k} := a_{12}w_{k\Sigma}/(\sigma_{12}+a_{12}w_{k\Sigma}),$$

$$z_{1/2,k} := a_{12}w_{k\Sigma}/(\sigma_{22}+a_{22}w_{k\Sigma}).$$

The estimators $\mu_1(\Theta_k)_{cred}$ and $\mu_2(\Theta_k)_{cred}$ are of the same type as those considered in the Bühlmann-Straub model defined in 3.4.2. Indeed such a model results from the suppression of the random variables Y_{kt} or X_{kt}. The covariance relations of Theorem 13 are valid for the random variables X_{kt} if μ, a, σ^2, z_k are replaced by μ_1, a_{11}, σ_{11}, $z_{1,k}$ resp. They are valid for the random variables Y_{kt} if μ, a, σ^2, z_k are replaced by μ_2, a_{22}, σ_{22}, $z_{2,k}$ resp.

New here is the estimator $\mu_{1/2}(\Theta_k)_{cred}$, typical of semilinear credibility if X_{kt} and Y_{kt} are the random variables considered in 3.6.2. Hence, now our **problem** is the determination of **the semilinear credibility estimator** $\mu_{1/2}(\Theta_k)_{cred}$ and the estimation of the involved structure parameters.

3.6.3. Semilinear Credibility Estimator

The formulas of the following Theorem are proved in the usual way.

Theorem 27

$$\mathbf{EX_{kt} = \mu_1 \;,\; EY_{kt} = \mu_2,}$$

$$\mathbf{Cov(X_{ks},X_{kt}) = a_{11} + \delta_{st}(\sigma_{11}/w_{kt}),}$$

$$\mathbf{Cov(Y_{kt},Y_{ks}) = a_{22} + \delta_{st}(\sigma_{22}/w_{kt}),}$$

$$\mathbf{Cov(X_{ks},Y_{kt}) = a_{12} + \delta_{st}(\sigma_{12}/w_{kt}),}$$

$$\mathbf{Cov(X_{kt},X_{kw}) = Cov(X_{kw},X_{kw}) = a_{11} + (\sigma_{11}/w_{k\Sigma}) = a_{11}/z_{11,k},}$$

$$\mathbf{Cov(Y_{kt},Y_{kw}) = Cov(Y_{kw},Y_{kw}) = a_{22} + (\sigma_{22}/w_{k\Sigma}) = a_{22}/z_{22,k},}$$

$$\mathbf{Cov(X_{kt},Y_{kw}) = Cov(X_{kw},Y_{kt}) = Cov(X_{kw},Y_{kw}) = a_{12} + (\sigma_{12}/w_{k\Sigma}) = a_{12}/z_{12,k},}$$

$$\mathbf{Cov}[\mu_1(\Theta_k), X_{kt}] = a_{11},$$

$$\mathbf{Cov}[\mu_2(\Theta_k), Y_{kt}] = a_{22},$$

$$\mathbf{Cov}[\mu_1(\Theta_k), Y_{kt}] = \mathbf{Cov}[\mu_2(\Theta_k), X_{kt}] = a_{12} \bullet$$

Theorem 28

$$\mu_{1/2}(\Theta_k)_{cred} = \mu_1 - z_{1/2,k}\, \mu_2 + z_{1/2,k}\, Y_{kw}. \tag{95}$$

Proof

The unbiasedness condition of the optimal projection Theorem of random variables is

$$E\mu_1(\Theta_k) = E(\mu_2 - z_{1/2,k}\, \mu_1 + z_{1/2,k}\, Y_{kw}).$$

The first member of this relation equals μ_1 and the second also, because $EY_{kw} = EY_{ks} = \mu_2$. The covariance condition is

$$\mathrm{Cov}[\mu_1(\Theta_k), Y_{js}] = \mathrm{Cov}[\mu_1 - z_{1/2,k}\, \mu_2 + z_{1/2,k}\, Y_{kw}, Y_{js}].$$

For $j \neq k$, the relation is 0=0 because the contracts are independent. Hence, we assume that j=k. Then, by foregoing Theorem, the first member equals a_{12} , and the last

$$z_{1/2,k}\, \mathrm{Cov}(Y_{kw}, Y_{ks}) = z_{1/2,k}\, a_{22}/z_{22,k} = a_{12} \quad \bullet$$

3.6.4. Mean Quadratic Error

Theorem 29

The mean quadratic error in the approximation of $\mu_1(\Theta_k)$ by its semilinear credibility estimator $\mu_{1/2}(\Theta_k)_{cred}$ equals

$$\mathbf{E}[\mu_{1/2}(\Theta_k)_{cred} - \mu_1(\Theta_k)]^2 = a_{11} - a_{12}\, z_{1/2,k}. \tag{96}$$

Proof

$$E[\mu_{1/2}(\Theta_k)_{cred} - \mu_1(\Theta_k)]^2$$

$$= E[\mu_1 + z_{1/2,k}\, Y_{kw}^{\circ} - \mu_1(\Theta_k)]^2$$

$$= E[z_{1/2,k}\, Y_{kw}{}^{\circ} - \mu_1{}^{\circ}(\Theta_k)]^2$$

$$= (z_{1/2,k})^2 \mathrm{Var}\, Y_{kw} - 2z_{1/2;k}\, \mathrm{Cov}(Y_{kw}, \mu_1(\Theta_k)) + \mathrm{Var}\, \mu_1(\Theta_k)$$

$$= a_{22}[(z_{1/2,k})^2/z_{22,k}] - 2\, z_{1/2,k}\, a_{12} + a_{11}$$

$$= z_{1/2,k}\, a_{12} - 2\, z_{1/2,k}\, a_{12} + a_{11} \quad \bullet$$

Let us assume that Y_{kt} is defined by the last relation of 3.6.1 and that different functions f are considered, for instance truncations at different heights b. Let p_k be weights not depending on f, for instance $p_k := w_{k\Sigma}$. Then, one can look for the function f minimizing the averaged mean quadratic error

$$\textstyle\sum_k (p_k/p_\Sigma)\, E[\mu_{1/2}(\Theta_k)_{cred} - \mu_1(\Theta_k)]^2 = a_{11} - a_{12} \sum_k p_k\, z_{1/2,k}. \qquad (97)$$

But a_{11} does not depend on f. Hence,

The function f minimizing the first member of (97) is that one maximizing $a_{12}\sum_k p_k z_{1/2,k}$.

As a particular case, let us consider a bonus-malus system in automobile insurance, based on the claim amounts. Then all observations have the same weight 1, and all contracts have the same length t°. Then the credibility weights $z_{1/2}$ do not depend on k, the weights p_k are irrelevant and the optimization problem is the maximization of

$$a_{12}\, z_{1/2} = a_{12}t^{\circ}/(\sigma_{12}+a_{12}t^{\circ}) = \alpha/(1+\alpha),$$

where

$$\alpha := a_{12}t^{\circ}/\sigma_{12}\, .$$

Hence, finally the optimization problem is the maximization of a_{12}/σ_{12} .

3.6.5. Parameter Estimation

The parameters μ_1, μ_2, σ_{11}, σ_{22}, a_{11}, a_{22} can be estimated as in the Bühlmann-Straub model. Hence only the estimation of σ_{12} and a_{12} is left.

Theorem 30

An unbiased estimator of σ_{12} is

$$S_{12} := [\Sigma_k(t_k-1)]^{-1} \Sigma_{kt} w_{kt}(X_{kt}-X_{kW})(Y_{kt}-Y_{kW}). \quad (98)$$

An unbiased pseudo-estimator of a_{12} is

$$A_{12,pseu} := [k^\circ-1]^{-1} \Sigma_k z_{12,k} (X_{kW}-X_{z_{12}W})(Y_{kW}-Y_{z_{12}W}), \quad (99)$$

where

$$X_{z_{12}W} := \Sigma_t (z_{12,t}/z_{12,\Sigma})X_{tW},$$

$$Y_{z_{12}W} := \Sigma_t (z_{12,t}/z_{12,\Sigma})Y_{tW}$$

Proof
The proof is as usual. For the estimator S_{12}, some covariance relations of Theorem 27 are used. The proof of the unbiasedness of $A_{12,pseu}$ is based on the following covariance relations

$$\text{Cov}(X_{z_{12}W}, Y_{kW}) = \text{Cov}(X_{kW}, Y_{z_{12}W})$$

$$= \text{Cov}(X_{z_{12}W}, Y_{z_{12}W}) = a_{12}/z_{12,\Sigma} \quad \bullet$$

The construction of a classical unbiased estimator A_{12} ("unbiased" before the adaptations; see following *Remark*) of a_{12} is easy. It is enough to calculate the expectation of the statistic

$$Q := \Sigma_k w_{kt}(X_{kW}-X_{WW})(Y_{kW}-Y_{WW})$$

and to proceed as in the discussion preceding Theorem 20. Preliminarily, the covariances $\text{Cov}(X_{kW}, Y_{WW})$, $\text{Cov}(X_{WW}, Y_{kW})$, $\text{Cov}(X_{WW}, Y_{WW})$ must be calculated.

Remark

The covariance matrix of the vector $(\mu_1(\Theta_k), \mu_2(\Theta_k))'$ is the matrix with elements a_{ij}. Covariance matrices are semidefinite positive. This implies that

$$a_{11} \geq 0 \quad , \quad a_{22} \geq 0 \quad , \quad a_{12}^2 \leq a_{11}\, a_{22}$$

Estimates which do not satisfy these conditions must be adapted (see Ch.4. 5.3). Then the unbiasedness is lost in most cases.

3.6.6. Optimal Semilinear Credibility

We here consider again the credibility theory contract with random variables $\Theta, X_1, \ldots, X_{t^\circ}$ such that for fixed Θ, the observable random variables $X_1, \ldots, X_{t^\circ}$ are conditionally i.i.d. We complete it by a supplementary observation $X_{t^\circ+1}$ as in 3.3.3, but only $X_1, \ldots, X_{t^\circ}$ are considered as observable, and the variable indices s and t take only the values $1, 2, \ldots, t^\circ$.

The problem is the determination of the function f and of the constants c, $a_1, \ldots, a_{t^\circ}$ such that $c+\Sigma_t a_t f(X_t)$ is closest to $\mu(\Theta)$. For reasons of symmetry, the coefficients a_t must be equal in **the optimal approximation** $c+\Sigma_t a_t f(X_t)$ of $\mu(\Theta)$. We can take $a_1 = \ldots = a_t = 1$. Then c can be incorporated in the terms $f(X_t)$, i.e., we can re-define f by $f+(c/t^\circ)$. Hence the optimal approximation must be of the form $\Sigma_t f(X_t)$.

After this preliminary discussion, we can define the optimal approximation as

$$\mu(\Theta)_{\mathbf{opt}} := \text{Proj}[\mu(\Theta)/\boldsymbol{LF})$$

where $\boldsymbol{LF}$ is the plane through the origin of square-integrable random variables which can be displayed as $\Sigma_t f(X_t)$. Then

$$\mu(\Theta)_{\mathbf{opt}} = \Sigma_t f^*(X_t) ,$$

for some **optimal function f*** and our problem is the determination of f^*.

We start with a result similar to (21) and (26).

Theorem 31

$$\mathbf{Proj}[\mu(\Theta)/\boldsymbol{LF}] = \mathbf{Proj}(X_{t^\circ+1}/\boldsymbol{LF})$$

Proof
Geometrically, it is obvious that it is sufficient to prove that the vector

$$\mu(\Theta) - X_{t^\circ+1}$$

is orthogonal to $\boldsymbol{LF}$, i.e.

$$\mu(\Theta) - X_{t^\circ+1} \perp \Sigma_t f(X_t),$$

where the latter sum is any point of $\boldsymbol{LF}$.

This orthogonality condition is successively equivalent to

$$E[[\mu(\Theta)-X_{t°+1}]\sum_t f(X_t)] = 0,$$

$$E[[\mu°(\Theta)-X_{t°+1}°]\sum_t f(X_t)] = 0\ ,$$

$$E[[\mu°(\Theta)-X_{t°+1}°]\sum_t f°(X_t)] =0,$$

$$Cov[\mu(\Theta),\sum_t f(X_t)] = Cov[X_{t°+1},\sum_t f(X_t)],$$

$$Cov[\mu(\Theta),f(X_1)] = Cov(X_{t°+1},f(X_1)]. \tag{100}$$

The first member of the latter relation equals

$$E\ Cov[\mu(\Theta),f(X_1)/\Theta] + Cov[E(\mu(\Theta)/\Theta),E(f(X_1)/\Theta)]$$

$$= 0 + Cov[\mu(\Theta),E(f(X_1)/\Theta)]$$

The last member of (100) equals

$$E\ Cov(X_{t°+1},f(X_1)/\Theta] + Cov[E(X_{t°+1}/\Theta),E(f(X_1)/\Theta)] =$$

$$= 0 + Cov[\mu(\Theta),E(f(X_1)/\Theta)]\ \bullet$$

Theorem 32

The optimal function f* is the solution of the integral equation

$$\mathbf{E(X_2/X_1) = f^*(X_1) + (t°-1)E[f^*(X_2)/X_1].} \tag{101}$$

Proof

We apply the foregoing Theorem and we translate that

$$Proj(X_{t°+1}/\boldsymbol{LF}) = \sum_s f^*(X_s).$$

Hence,

$$X_{t°+1} - \sum_s f^*(X_s) \perp \sum_t f(X_t),$$

where the latter sum is any point in ***LF***.

This orthogonality condition is successively equivalent to the following conditions

$$E[X_{t^\circ+1}\sum_t f(X_t)] = E[\sum_s f^*(X_s) \sum_t f(X_t)],$$

$$t^\circ\ E[X_{t^\circ+1}\ f(X_1)] = t^\circ\ E[f^*(X_1)f(X_1)] + t^\circ(t^\circ-1)E[f^*(X_2)f(X_1)],$$

$$E[X_2f(X_1)] = E[f^*(X_1)f(X_1)] + (t^\circ-1)E[f^*(X_2)f(X_1)],$$

$$E[f(X_1)[X_2-f^*(X_1)-(t^\circ-1)f^*(X_2)]] = 0,$$

$$E[f(X_1)[E(X_2/X_1) - f^*(X_1)-(t^\circ-1)E[f^*(X_2)/X_1]]] = 0.$$

We now take f so that

$$f(X_1) = E(X_2/X_1) - f^*(X_1)-(t^\circ-1)E[f^*(X_2)/X_1].$$

Then $Ef^2(X_1)=0$, i.e. $f(X_1)=0$ a.s. •

If the couple (X_1,X_2) has a density $\varphi(\cdot,\cdot)$ then (101) is equivalent to the integral equation

$$\int y\varphi(x,y)dy = f^*(x)\int\varphi(x,y)dy + (t^\circ-1)\int f^*(y)\varphi(x,y)dy$$

for f^*. If the random variables X_t are discrete, with values $x_1 , ... x_n$, and if

$$p_{ij} = P(X_1=x_i,X_2=x_j)\ \ (i,j=1,2,...,n),$$

then (101) is equivalent to the following linear system of n equations for the n unknown quantities $f(x_1), \ldots , f(x_n)$:

$$\sum_{1\le j\le n} x_i p_{ij} = f^*(x_i)\sum_{1\le j\le n} p_{ij} + (t^\circ-1)\sum_{1\le j\le n} f^*(x_j)p_{ij}\ \ (i=1,...,n).$$

Remark

The approximation

$$\mu(\Theta)_{cred}\ ,\ \ \mu(\Theta)_{opt}\ ,\ \ \mu(\Theta)_{cond}$$

is the projection of $\mu(\Theta)$ on the plane through the origin

$$\boldsymbol{P}(1,X_1,\ldots,X_{t^\circ})\ ,\ \ \boldsymbol{LF}\ ,\ \ \boldsymbol{F}(X_1,\ldots,X_{t^\circ})\ \text{(see 3.3.3)}$$

respectively. These planes are such that

$$\boldsymbol{P}(1,X_1,...,X_{t^\circ}) \subseteq \boldsymbol{LF} \subseteq \boldsymbol{F}(X_1,...,X_{t^\circ})$$

Then

$$d(\mu(\Theta),\mu(\Theta)_{cond}) \leq d(\mu(\Theta)\,,\,\mu(\Theta)_{opt}) \leq d(\mu(\Theta),\mu(\Theta)_{cred}),$$

where $d(\cdot,\cdot)$ is the distance function. The optimal semilinear approximation $\mu(\Theta)_{opt}$ is a kind of compromise between the approximations $\mu(\Theta)_{cred}$ and $\mu(\Theta)_{cond}$. It is closer to $\mu(\Theta)$ than $\mu(\Theta)_{cred}$, but it is much more difficult to calculate in practice. The still closer approximation $\mu(\Theta)_{cond}$ is not practical at all.

3.7. Parametric Credibility Theory. Exact Credibility

3.7.1. Parametric Credibility Theory

As in the preceding section 3.6.6, we consider the credibility model with random vector

$$(\Theta,X_1,...,X_{t^\circ}\,,X_{t^\circ+1}), \tag{102}$$

where, for fixed Θ, the random variables $X_1,...,X_{t^\circ+1}$ are i.i.d. Only $X_1,...,X_{t^\circ}$ are considered as observable, but not $X_{t^\circ+1}$.

Let X be any fixed random variable X_t. The distribution of the vector (102) is completely specified by the couple

$$(\text{Distribution of } X_{/\Theta}\,,\ \text{Distribution of } \Theta). \tag{103}$$

In **parametric Credibility Theory**, the analytic form of the distributions of the couple (103) is specified. The distributions may be normal, Poisson, gamma, binomial negative,... They depend on parameters, and only the latter keep some freedom in the **parametric models**. In this way, "parametric" is the opposite of "distribution-free". Parametric Credibility Theory is much older than distribution-free Credibility, innovated by Hans Bühlmann only in 1967.

A theoretical portfolio with distributions specified by (103) is associated to the random vector (102). This portfolio can be a model of the real portfolio. Then it is assumed that the real contracts $1,2,...,k^\circ$ correspond to values θ_1, ..., θ_{k°, chosen at random, of Θ.

Then extensive distributive information is mostly available on X, because all realizations of the observable random variables X_{kt} can be considered as realizations of X. The empirical distribution of X resulting from these observations must be compatible with the theoretical distribution of X, resulting from the elimination of Θ in the couple (103).

3.7.2. Exact Credibility

We consider the usual credibility approximations $\mu(\Theta)_{cred}$ and $(X_{t^\circ+1})_{cred}$, equal to each other by (21). They are projections on the plane $\boldsymbol{P}(1,X_1,...,X_{t^\circ})$. We also consider the better approximations

$$\mu(\Theta)_{cond} := E(\mu(\Theta)/X_1,...,X_{t^\circ}) \ , \ (X_{t^\circ+1})_{cond} := E(X_{t^\circ+1}/X_1,...,X_{t^\circ}), \quad (104)$$

also equal to each other by (25). They are projections on the much larger plane $\boldsymbol{F}(X_1,...,X_{t^\circ})$. It happens that all these projections fall together. Then it is said that **exact credibility** does occur. Exact credibility, or not, only depends on the distribution of the couple (103).

We will adopt the following definition: The couple (103) is **an exact credibility couple** if the conditional expectations (104) are linear in $X_1,...,X_{t^\circ}$. With this definition, the random variables X_t must only be assumed to be integrable, not necessarily square-integrable. If they are square integrable, then projections can be considered, and then all the projections fall together if (103) is an exact credibility couple. In the sequel, we always assume the integrability of X_t. When usual credibility estimators are considered, then the square-integrability is supposed.

3.7.3. Explicit Expressions

Notations

We denote by $H(\cdot)$ the distribution function of Θ, and by $h(\cdot)$ the corresponding density (supposed to exist when it is used).

In the **continuous case,** we assume that the conditional random variable $X_{/\Theta=\theta}$ has the density $f(\cdot/\theta)$.

In the **discrete case**, we assume that X_t are positive integer random variables Then we adopt the notations N, N_t instead of X, X_t and we assume that the distribution of the conditional random variable $N_{/\Theta=\theta}$ is defined by the probabilities

$$p(n/\theta) := P(N=n/\Theta=\theta) \ (n=0,1,\ldots).$$

***Distribution of* N *or* X**

In the discrete case, let $p(n) := P(N=n)$ (n=0,1,2,...). Then

$$p(n) = \int p(n/\theta)\, dH(\theta) \quad \text{(Discrete case)}.$$

In the continuous case, we denote by $f(\cdot)$ the density of X. Then

$$f(x) = \int f(x/\theta)\, dH(\theta) \quad \text{(Continuous case)}.$$

The same symbol f is used for the obvious densities and conditional densities.

Conditional expectations

We mainly consider exact credibility couples in the rest of this Chapter.

In the **discrete case**, exact credibility does occur iff

$$E(N_{t^\circ+1}/n_1,\ldots,n_{t^\circ}) \equiv E(N_{t^\circ+1}/N_1=n_1,\ldots,N_{t^\circ}=n_{t^\circ}) \tag{105}$$

is linear in the integer positive variables $n_1,\ldots,n_{t^\circ}$. We have

$$E(N_{t^\circ+1}/n_1,\ldots,n_{t^\circ}) = \sum_n n\, P(N_{t^\circ+1}=n \,/\, N_1=n_1,\ldots,N_{t^\circ}=n_{t^\circ})$$

$$= \sum_n n\, P(N_1=n_1,\ldots,N_{t^\circ}=n_{t^\circ}, N_{t^\circ+1}=n) \,\big/\, P(N_1=n_1,\ldots,N_{t^\circ}=n_{t^\circ}), \tag{106}$$

where

$$P(N_1=n_1,\ldots,N_{t^\circ}=n_{t^\circ}) = \int P(N_1=n_1,\ldots,N_{t^\circ}=n_{t^\circ}/\Theta=\theta)\, dH(\theta)$$

$$= \int P(N_1=n_1/\theta)\ldots P(N_{t^\circ}=n_{t^\circ}/\theta)\, dH(\theta) = \int p(n_1/\theta)\ldots p(n_{t^\circ}/\theta) dH(\theta).$$

In the same way, the numerator of (106) equals

$$\sum_n n\, P(N_1=n_1,\ldots,N_{t^\circ}=n_{t^\circ}, N_{t^\circ+1}=n)$$

$$= \sum_n n \int p(n_1/\theta)\ldots p(n_{t^\circ}/\theta)p(n/\theta)dH(\theta).$$

$$= \int p(n_1/\theta)\ldots p(n_{t^\circ}/\theta) \left[\sum_n n\, p(n/\theta)\right] dH(\theta).$$

$$= \int p(n_1/\theta)\ldots p(n_{t^\circ}/\theta)\, E(N/\theta)\, dH(\theta).$$

Hence,

$$E(N_{t^\circ+1}/n_1,\ldots,n_{t^\circ}) \tag{107}$$

$$= \int p(n_1/\theta)\ldots p(n_{t^\circ}/\theta)\, E(N/\theta)\, dH(\theta) \Big/ \int p(n_1/\theta)\ldots p(n_{t^\circ}/\theta)dH(\theta)$$

In the **continuous case**, exact credibility occurs iff

$$E(X_{t^\circ+1}/x_1,\ldots,x_{t^\circ}) \equiv E(X_{t^\circ+1}/X_1=x_1,\ldots,X_{t^\circ}=x_{t^\circ})$$

is linear in the variables $x_1,\ldots,x_{t^\circ}$. We have

$$E(X_{t^\circ+1}/x_1,\ldots,x_{t^\circ}) = \int x\, f(x/x_1,\ldots,x_{t^\circ})\, dx$$

$$= \int x\, f(x_1,\ldots,x_{t^\circ},x)dx \Big/ f(x_1,\ldots,x_{t^\circ}). \tag{108}$$

In the last member of (108)

$$f(x_1,\ldots,x_{t^\circ}) = \int f(x_1,\ldots,x_{t^\circ}/\theta)dH(\theta) = \int f(x_1/\theta)\ldots f(x_{t^\circ}/\theta)dH(\theta),$$

and

$$\int_x x\, f(x_1,\ldots,x_{t^\circ},x)dx = \int_x x \int_\theta f(x_1,\ldots,x_{t^\circ},x/\theta)dH(\theta)\, dx$$

$$= \int_x x \int_\theta f(x_1/\theta)\ldots f(x_{t^\circ}/\theta)f(x/\theta)\, dH(\theta)\, dx$$

$$= \int_\theta f(x_1/\theta)\ldots f(x_{t^\circ}/\theta)\left[\int_x x\, f(x/\theta)\, dx\right]dH(\theta)$$

$$= \int f(x_1/\theta)\ldots f(x_{t^\circ}/\theta)\, E(X/\theta)dH(\theta).$$

Hence,

$$E(X_{t^\circ+1}/x_1,\ldots,x_{t^\circ})$$
$$= \int f(x_1/\theta)\ldots f(x_{t^\circ}/\theta)\, E(X/\theta)dH(\theta) \,/ \int f(x_1/\theta)\ldots f(x_{t^\circ}/\theta)dH(\theta) \qquad (109)$$

Credibility estimators

In the credibility estimators

$$(N_{t^\circ+1})_{cred} = z(N_1+\ldots+N_{t^\circ})/t^\circ + (1-z)\mu,$$

$$(X_{t^\circ+1})_{cred} = z(X_1+\ldots+X_{t^\circ})/t^\circ + (1-z)\mu,$$

we need μ and $z = at^\circ/(\sigma^2+at^\circ)$ and in z we need σ^2 and a.

$$\mu(\Theta) = E(N/\Theta) \quad , \quad \mu = EN \quad \text{(Discrete case)} \; ,$$

$$\mu(\Theta) = E(X/\Theta) \;,\; \mu = EX \text{ (Continuous case)},$$

$$\mu = E\mu(\Theta) = \int \mu(\theta)\, dH(\theta),$$

$$a = \text{Var } \mu(\Theta) = E\mu^2(\Theta) - E^2\mu(\Theta) = \int\mu^2(\theta)dH(\theta) - [\int\mu(\theta)dH(\theta)]^2,$$

$$\mu(\theta) = \textstyle\sum_n n\, p(n/\theta) \;\; \text{(Discrete case)},$$

$$\mu(\theta) = \int x\, f(x/\theta)\, dx \;\; \text{(Continuous case)},$$

$$\sigma^2(\Theta) = \text{Var}(N/\Theta) \;\; \text{(Discrete case)} \;,\; \sigma^2(\Theta) = \text{Var}(X/\Theta) \;\; \text{(Continuous case)},$$

$$\sigma^2 = E\sigma^2(\Theta) = \int \sigma^2(\theta)\, dH(\theta),$$

$$\sigma^2(\theta) = E(N^2/\theta) - E^2(N/\theta)$$

$$= \textstyle\sum_n n^2\, p(n/\theta) - [\mu(\theta)]^2 \text{ (Discrete case)},$$

$$\sigma^2(\theta) = E(X^2/\theta) - E^2(X/\theta)$$

$$= \int x^2 f(x/\theta)dx - [\mu(\theta)]^2 \text{ (Continuous case)}.$$

Exact credibility is a rather old topic in actuarial science. The exact credibility couples

(Poisson , Gamma) (3.7.4)

(Negative binomial , Bêta) (3.7.5)

(Normal, Normal) (3.7.6)

have been known for a very long time. The discovery, by Bill Jewell (1974) of the general exponential couple of the next section 3.7.7, is more recent. By the right parametrization, it contains in fact the other couples as particular cases.

3.7.4. The (Poisson, Gamma) Couple

Definition of the (Poisson, Gamma) couple

In this discrete case, α, β are strictly positive parameters and the density of Θ is the gamma density

$$h(\theta) := \alpha^{\beta}/(\beta-1)!\ \theta^{\beta-1}\ e^{-\alpha\theta}\ (\theta > 0). \tag{110}$$

If $\beta-1$ is not a positive integer, then $(\beta-1)!$ must be understood as the value $\Gamma(\beta)$ of the Γ-function at the point β.

The conditional random variable $N_{/\Theta=\theta}$ is Poisson:

$$p(n/\theta) = e^{-\theta}\,\theta^{n}/n!\ (n=0,1,2,\ldots). \tag{111}$$

We use the formula

$$\int_{]0,\infty[} \theta^{\beta-1} e^{-\alpha\theta} d\theta = (\beta-1)!/\alpha^{\beta}$$

resulting from the formula with $\alpha=1$. (The latter formula is direct, by recurrence, when β is a strictly positive integer. It is the definition of $\Gamma(\beta)$ whatever the value of $\beta>0$ is).

***Distribution of* N**

$$P(N=n) = \int_{]0,\infty[} e^{-\theta}\,\theta^{n}/n!\ \alpha^{\beta}/(\beta-1)!\ \theta^{\beta-1}\ e^{-\alpha\theta}\ d\theta$$

$$= \alpha^{\beta}\ [n!(\beta-1)!]^{-1} \int_{]0,\infty[} \theta^{n+\beta-1}\ e^{-(1+\alpha)\theta}\ d\theta$$

$$= \alpha^{\beta}\ [n!(\beta-1)!]^{-1}\ [(1+\alpha)^{n+\beta}]^{-1}\ (n+\beta-1)!\ .$$

Hence,

$$P(N=n) = (n+\beta-1)^{[n]}/n!\ [\alpha/1+\alpha]^{\beta}[1/1+\alpha]^{n}\ (n=0,1,2,\ldots),$$

where

$$x^{[n]} = x(x-1)\ldots(x-n+1).$$

Hence, N is a binomial negative random variable.

Conditional expectation

The denominator of the fraction in the last member of (107) equals

$$\alpha^{\beta}[n_1!\ldots n_t!(\beta-1)!]^{-1}\int_{]0,\infty[} e^{-\theta}\,\theta^{n_1}\ldots e^{-\theta}\theta^{n_{t^\circ}}\,\theta^{\beta-1}\,e^{-\alpha\theta}\,d\theta$$

$$= \alpha^{\beta}[n_1!\ldots n_t!(\beta-1)!]^{-1}\int_{]0,\infty[} \theta^{n_1+\ldots+n_{t^\circ}+\beta-1}\,e^{-(t^\circ+\alpha)\theta}\,d\theta \qquad (112)$$

$$= \alpha^{\beta}\,(n_1+\ldots+n_{t^\circ}+\beta-1)!\,[n_1!\ldots n_t!(\beta-1)!(t^\circ+\alpha)^{n_1+\ldots+n_{t^\circ}+\beta}]^{-1}.$$

The random variable $N_{/\Theta=\theta}$ is Poisson with parameter θ. Then the expectation is also θ, i.e. $E(N/\theta)=\theta$. Then the numerator of the the fraction in the last member of (107) differs only by the factor θ in the interior of integral (112). Hence, this numerator equals

$$\alpha^{\beta}\,(n_1+\ldots+n_{t^\circ}+\beta)!\,[n_1!\ldots n_t!(\beta-1)!(t^\circ+\alpha)^{n_1+\ldots+n_{t^\circ}+\beta+1}]^{-1}.$$

Hence

$$E(N_{t^\circ+1}/n_1,\ldots,n_{t^\circ}) = (n_1+\ldots+n_{t^\circ}+\beta)/(t^\circ+\alpha). \qquad (113)$$

The last member is linear in $n_1,\ldots,n_{t^\circ}$:

The (Poisson, Gamma) couple defined by distributions (110) and (111) is an exact credibility couple.

Credibility estimator

From (113) results the credibility estimator

$$(N_{t^\circ+1})_{cred} = z(N_1+\ldots+N_{t^\circ})/t^\circ + (1-z)\mu \qquad (114)$$

where

$$z = t^\circ/(t^\circ+\alpha)\ ,\quad \mu = \beta/\alpha. \qquad (115)$$

Here we calculate μ and z by the usual credibility formulas.

The expectation and variance of a Poisson random variable with parameter λ are equal to λ. Hence, by (111),

$$\mu(\Theta) = E(N/\Theta) = \Theta \quad , \quad \sigma^2(\Theta) = Var(N/\Theta) = \Theta.$$

Then

$$\mu = \sigma^2 = E\Theta = \int_{]0,\infty[} \theta\, h(\theta)d\theta$$

$$= {\alpha^\beta}/{(\beta-1)!} \int_{]0,\infty[} \theta^\beta\, e^{-\alpha\theta}\, d\theta$$

$$= {\alpha^\beta}/{(\beta-1)!} \cdot \beta!/\alpha^{\beta+1} = \beta/\alpha\ .$$

$$E\Theta^2 = \int_{]0,\infty[} \theta^2\, h(\theta)d\theta = {\alpha^\beta}/{(\beta-1)!} \int_{]0,\infty[} \theta^{\beta+1}\, e^{-\alpha\theta}\, d\theta$$

$$= {\alpha^\beta}/{(\beta-1)!} \cdot (\beta+1)\,!/\alpha^{\beta+2} = \beta(\beta+1)/\alpha^2\ .$$

$$a = Var\ \Theta = E\Theta^2 - E^2\Theta = \beta/\alpha^2\ .$$

The relations (115) result from these values..

3.7.5. The (Binomial Negative, Bêta) Couple

Definition of the (Binomial negative, Bêta) couple

In this discrete case, $\alpha > 1$, $\beta > 0$ and $\gamma > 0$ are fixed parameters. The density of Θ is the bêta density

$$h(\theta) := (\alpha+\beta-1)!/{[(\alpha-1)!(\beta-1)!]}\ \theta^{\alpha-1}(1-\theta)^{\beta-1} \quad (0 \le \theta \le 1). \qquad (116)$$

The conditional random variable $N_{/\Theta=\theta}$ is the binomial negative with distribution defined by

$$p(n/\theta) := (\gamma+n-1)^{[n]}/{n!}\ \theta^\gamma(1-\theta)^n \quad (n=0,1,2,\dots). \qquad (117)$$

As usual x! must be understood as being $\Gamma(1+x)$ if x is not a positive integer.

We will use the classical power series expansion

$$\sum_{n\geq 0} (\gamma+n)^{[n]}/_{n!}\, x^n = 1/(1-x)^{1+\gamma} \ (|x| < 1). \qquad (118)$$

From a differentiation, then a multiplication by x, results that

$$\sum_{n\geq 0} n(\gamma+n)^{[n]}/_{n!}\, x^n = (1+\gamma)x/(1-x)^{2+\gamma} \ (|x| < 1). \qquad (119)$$

In the same way,

$$\sum_{n\geq 0} n^2(\gamma+n)^{[n]}/_{n!}\, x^n = [(1+\gamma)x(1+x+\gamma x)]/(1-x)^{3+\gamma} \ (|x| < 1). \qquad (120)$$

Another formula useful here is

$$\int_{[0,1]} \theta^{\alpha-1}(1-\theta)^{\beta-1}\, d\theta = (\alpha-1)!(\beta-1)!/_{(\alpha+\beta-1)!} \ (\alpha,\beta>0). \qquad (121)$$

Conditional expectation

The denominator of the fraction in the last member of (107) equals

$$c \int_{[0,1]} \theta^{t\gamma+\alpha-1}(1-\theta)^{n_1+\ldots+n_{t^\circ}+\beta-1}\, d\theta$$

$$= c\, [(t^\circ\gamma+\alpha-1)!(n_1+\ldots+n_{t^\circ}+\beta-1)!]/[(t\gamma+\alpha+n_1+\ldots+n_{t^\circ}+\beta-1)!]\,,$$

where c is the obvious constant. From (117) and (119):

$$E(N/\theta) = \gamma(1-\theta)/_\theta. \qquad (122)$$

Then the numerator of the fraction in the last member of (107) equals

$$c\gamma \int_{[0,1]} \theta^{t\gamma+\alpha-2}(1-\theta)^{n_1+\ldots+n_{t^\circ}+\beta}\, d\theta$$

$$= c\gamma\, [(t^\circ\gamma+\alpha-2)!(n_1+\ldots+n_{t^\circ}+\beta)!]/[(t\gamma+\alpha+n_1+\ldots+n_{t^\circ}+\beta-1)!],$$

Hence,

$$E(N_{t^\circ+1}/n_1,\ldots,n_{t^\circ}) = \gamma(n_1+\ldots+n_{t^\circ}+\beta)/_{(t^\circ\gamma+\alpha-1)}. \qquad (123)$$

The (Binomial negative, Bêta) couple defined by distributions (117) and (116) is an exact credibility couple.

Credibility estimator

From (123) results the usual credibility estimator $(N_{t°+1})_{cred}$, explicited in (114), with

$$\mu = \beta\gamma/(\alpha-1) \quad , \quad z = t°\gamma/(t°\gamma+\alpha-1). \tag{124}$$

Now we calculate these values by the usual credibility formulas.

By (122),

$$\mu(\Theta) = E(N/\Theta) = \gamma(1-\Theta)/\Theta \; .$$

By (117) and (120),

$$E(N^2/\Theta) = \gamma(1-\Theta)(1+\gamma-\gamma\Theta)/\Theta^2 \; .$$

Then

$$\sigma^2(\Theta) = E(N^2/\Theta)-\mu^2(\Theta) = \gamma(1-\Theta)/\Theta^2 \; .$$

By (116) and (121),

$$\mu = E\mu(\Theta)$$

$$= \gamma(\alpha+\beta-1)!/[(\alpha-1)!(\beta-1)!] \int_{[0,1]} \theta^{\alpha-2}(1-\theta)^{\beta}\, d\theta = \beta\gamma/(\alpha-1) \; .$$

This is the value furished by the first relation (124).

$$\sigma^2 = E\sigma^2(\Theta) = \gamma(\alpha+\beta-1)!/[(\alpha-1)!(\beta-1)!] \int_{[0,1]} \theta^{\alpha-3}(1-\theta)^{\beta}\, d\theta$$

$$= (\alpha+\beta-1)\beta\gamma/[(\alpha-1)(\alpha-2)]$$

$$E\mu^2(\Theta) = \gamma^2(\alpha+\beta-1)!/[(\alpha-1)!(\beta-1)!] \int_{[0,1]} \theta^{\alpha-3}(1-\theta)^{\beta+1}\, d\theta$$

$$= \beta(\beta+1)\, \gamma^2/[(\alpha-1)(\alpha-2)]$$

$$a = E\mu^2(\Theta)-\mu^2 = (\alpha+\beta-1)\beta\gamma^2/[(\alpha-1)^2(\alpha-2)]$$

This calculation shows that we must assume $\alpha>2$ here.

From the values of σ^2 and a , the last relation (124) is obtained again.

3.7.6. The (Normal, Normal) Couple

Definition of the (Normal, Normal) couple

In this continuous couple, the parameters are $\alpha\in\mathbf{R}$, $\beta>0$, $\sigma>0$. The density of Θ is the normal density

$$h(\theta) := \beta^{-1}(2\pi)^{-1/2}\exp[-{}^1/_{2\beta^2}(\theta-\alpha)^2] \quad (\theta\in\mathbf{R}). \tag{125}$$

The conditional random variable $X/_\Theta$ has the normal density

$$f(x/\theta) := \sigma^{-1}(2\pi)^{-1/2}\exp[-{}^1/_{2\sigma^2}(x-\theta)^2] \quad (x\in\mathbf{R}). \tag{126}$$

Conditional expectation

The denominator of the fraction in the last member of (109) can be displayed as

$$\gamma\int_R e^{-p(\theta)}\,d\theta$$

where γ is a constant and where $p(\theta)$ is the polynomial

$$p(\theta) := {}^1/_{2\sigma^2}[(x_1-\theta)^2+\ldots+(x_t-\theta)^2] + {}^1/_{2\beta^2}(\theta-\alpha)^2$$

$$= a^2\theta^2 + 2b\theta + c = (a\theta+b')^2 + c-b'^2\,,$$

where a, b, c are constants defined in the obvious way, and where $b':=b/a$. Then, with the new integration variable $x:= a\theta+b'$,

$$\int_R e^{-p(\theta)}\,d\theta = \exp(b'^2-c)\int_R \exp[-(a\theta+b')^2]d\theta = {}^1/_a\exp(b'^2-c)\int_R e^{-x^2}\,dx.$$

The numerator of the fraction in the last member of (109) equals

$$\gamma\int_R \theta\, e^{-p(\theta)}\,d\theta$$

because $E(X/\theta)=\theta$.

$$\int_R \theta e^{-p(\theta)}\,d\theta = \exp(b'^2-c)\int_R \theta\exp[-(a\theta+b')^2]d\theta =$$

$$1/_{a^2}\exp(b'^2-c)\int_R (x-b')\, e^{-x^2}\, dx. = -b'/_{a^2}\exp(b'^2-c)\int_R e^{-x^2}\, dx\,,$$

because

$$\int_R x\, e^{-x^2}\, dx = 0.$$

Hence, the last member of (109) equals $-b'/a = -b/a^2$:

$$E(X_{t^\circ+1}/x_1,\ldots,x_{t^\circ}) = \left[1/_{2\sigma^2}(x_1+\ldots+x_{t^\circ}) + \alpha/_{2\beta^2}\right]/\left[t/_{2\sigma^2} + 1/_{2\beta^2}\right]. \qquad (127)$$

The (Normal, Normal) couple defined by densities (126) and (125) is an exact credibility couple.

Credibility estimator

From (127) results that

$$(X_{t^\circ+1})_{cred} = z(X_1+\ldots+X_{t^\circ})/_{t^\circ} + (1-z)\mu,$$

where

$$\mu = \alpha \ , \ z = t^\circ\beta^2/_{(t^\circ\beta^2+\sigma^2)}. \cdot$$

These values result from the credibility formulas, via the parameters σ^2 , a of the general theory. Indeed, here

$$\mu(\Theta) = E(X/\Theta) = \Theta,$$

$$\mu = E\Theta = \alpha,$$

$$\sigma^2(\Theta) = Var(X/\Theta) = \sigma^2\,,$$

$$E\sigma^2(\Theta) = \sigma^2,$$

where the σ^2 in the first member is the parameter of the general Credibility Theory, and where the σ^2 in the last member is the parameter occurring in the density (126).

$$a = Var\ \Theta = \beta^2.$$

From these values of σ^2, a , results the expression for z already mentioned.

3.7.7. The General (Exponential, Exponential) Exact Credibility Couple (Jewell 1974)

We consider the **continuous case** only. (The discrete case results from obvious adaptations). The density of Θ is

$$h(\theta) := {}^1/_c\, [\beta(\theta)]^{-t'}\, e^{-x'\theta} \quad (\theta \in B) \tag{128}$$

and that of $X/_{\Theta=\theta}$ is

$$f(x/\theta) := {}^1/_{\beta(\theta)}\, \alpha(x)\, e^{-\theta x} \quad (x \in A), \tag{129}$$

where A is an open interval $A =]a_1, a_2[$, bounded or not, and where B is an open interval $B =]b_1, b_2[$, bounded or not. The following assumptions are made on the fixed parameters $t' > 0$, x', c and on the functions $\alpha(\cdot)$, $\beta(\cdot)$.

Assumptions

$f(\cdot/\theta)$ is supposed to be a density on A, for any fixed $\theta \in B$. Hence, the function $\beta(\cdot)$ results from the positive function $\alpha(\cdot)$ by the relation

$$\beta(\theta) = \int_A \alpha(x) e^{-\theta x}\, dx \quad (\theta \in B). \tag{130}$$

We assume that $\beta(\cdot)$ is a finite, strictly positive function on B. We assume that $\beta(\cdot)$ has finite derivatives $\beta'(\cdot)$, $\beta''(\cdot)$, and that they can be taken under the integral sign in the last member of (130):

$$\beta'(\theta) = -\int_A x\, \alpha(x) e^{-\theta x}\, dx \quad (\theta \in B),$$

$$\beta''(\theta) = \int_A x^2 \alpha(x) e^{-\theta x}\, dx \quad (\theta \in B).$$

Here, accents on functions denote derivatives with respect to θ.

The function $h(\cdot)$ is a density on B. Hence c is the norming constant.

Further assumptions on the triplet $(\alpha(\cdot), t', x')$ are

$$\lim h(\theta) = 0\ , \quad \lim\ h'(\theta) = 0, \quad \text{as } \theta \downarrow b_1 \text{ and as } \theta \uparrow b_2\, .$$

For any values $x_1,...,x_{t°}$ fixed in A, the limit of the function of θ,

$$e^{-\theta(x_1+...+x_{t°})}\,[\beta(\theta)]^{-t'-t°}$$

is also supposed to be zero as $\theta\downarrow b_1$ and as $\theta\uparrow b_2$. As usual, t° is the fixed number of observable random variables $X_1,...,X_{t°}$.

Theorem 33 (Jewell)

Under the indicated assumptions, the (Exponential, Exponential) couple defined by the distributions (129) and (128) is an exact credibility couple, and

$$\mu = x'/t' \ , \ s^2/a = t' \ , \ z = t°/(t'+t°) .$$

Proof

$$\mu(\theta) = E(X/\theta) = 1/\beta(\theta) \int_A x\,\alpha(x)\,e^{-\theta x}\,d(x) = -\beta'(\theta)/\beta(\theta), \tag{131}$$

$$-\mu'(\theta) = [\beta(\theta)\beta''(\theta)-\beta'(\theta)\beta'(\theta)]/\beta^2(\theta) = 1/\beta(\theta) \int_A x^2\alpha(x)e^{-\theta x}\,dx - \mu^2(\theta)$$

$$= E(X^2/\theta) - E^2(X/\theta) = Var(X/\theta) = \sigma^2(\theta). \tag{132}$$

$$c\,h'(\theta) = -t'[\beta(\theta)]^{-t'-1}\beta'(\theta)e^{-x'\theta} - x'[\beta(\theta)]^{-t'}e^{-x'\theta}$$

$$= t'[-\beta'(\theta)/\beta(\theta)].[\beta(\theta)]^{-1}e^{-x'\theta} - cx'h(\theta) = ct'\mu(\theta)h(\theta) - cx'h(\theta).$$

Hence,

$$\mu(\theta)h(\theta) = 1/t'\ h'(\theta) + x'/t'\ h(\theta), \tag{133}$$

and then,

$$\mu = E\mu(\Theta) = \int_B \mu(\theta)h(\theta)d\theta = 1/t' \int_B h'(\theta)d\theta + x'/t' \int_B h(\theta)d\theta = 0 + x'/t' .$$

Then (133) becomes

$$t'[\mu(\theta)-\mu]h(\theta) = h'(\theta)$$

and then

$$t'\mu'(\theta)h(\theta) + t'[\mu(\theta)-\mu]h'(\theta) = h''(\theta),$$

$$t'\mu'(\theta)h(\theta) + t'^2[\mu(\theta)-\mu]^2h(\theta) = h''(\theta),$$

and then, by (132)

$$-t'\sigma^2(\theta)h(\theta) + t'^2[\mu(\theta)-\mu]^2h(\theta) = h''(\theta).$$

Then, by an integration over $\theta \in B$,

$$-t'\ E\sigma^2(\Theta) + t'^2E[\mu(\Theta)-\mu]^2 = 0\ ,\ \ \sigma^2 = t'\ \mathrm{Var}\mu(\Theta) = t'a\ .$$

Hence, $\sigma^2/a = t'$, and then z has the announced value.

Now we prove that the couple is an exact credibility couple. By (109), (128), (129) and (131),

$$E(X_{t°+1}/x_1,\ldots,x_{t°}) =$$

$$[-\int_B e^{-\theta(x_1+\ldots+x_{t°})}\ [\beta(\theta)]^{-t'-t°-1}\ \beta'(\theta)d\theta]/[\int_B e^{-\theta(x_1+\ldots+x_{t°})}\ [\beta(\theta)]^{-t'-t°}d\theta]$$

The numerator in the last member equals

$$-\int_B e^{-\theta(x_1+\ldots+x_{t°})}\ [\beta(\theta)]^{-t'-t°-1}\ \beta'(\theta)d\theta = -\int_B e^{-\theta(x_1+\ldots+x_{t°})}\ d[\beta(\theta)]^{-t'-t°}$$

$$= (x_1+\ldots+x_{t°})/(t'+t°) \int_B e^{-\theta(x_1+\ldots+x_{t°})}\ [\beta(\theta)]^{-t'-t°}d\theta$$

by an integration by parts. Hence,

$$E(X_{t°+1}/x_1,\ldots,x_{t°}) = (x_1+\ldots+x_{t°})/(t'+t°)\ \ \bullet$$

Chapter 4

Hilbert Spaces of Random Vectors and Random Matrices

4.1. Matrices

4.1.1. Scalar Matrices

The notations, definitions and main properties of scalar matrices are developed in App.D.

4.1.2. Random Matrices

Random matrices, or **stochastic matrices**, are matrices of which the elements are random variables. Such matrices are always represented by capital letters A,B,...,X,Y,... hereafter. Random vectors, rows or columns, are particular random matrices.

The **expectation** $EA \equiv E(A)$ of the random matrix $A_{m\times n}$ with elements A_{ij} , is the matrix $(EA)_{m\times n}$ with elements $(EA)_{ij} = E(A_{ij})$. Of course, EA is defined only when the expectations $E(A_{ij})$ exist.

The relations

$$E(aA) = a(EA) \ , \ E(Ab) = (EA)b \ , \ E(aAb) = a(EA)b$$

are obvious. Here A is a random matrix and a, b are scalar matrices such that the products aA, Ab, aAb are meaningful.

The operators E and tr commute:

$$tr(EA) = E(tr\ A).$$

4.2. $L_{2,m\times n}$, $L_{2,n}$ and L_2 Spaces

4.2.1. $L_{2,m\times n}$ Spaces

We recall some properties of L_2. The space L_2 is the Hilbert space of square-integrable random variables defined on some fixed probability space. The scalar product in L_2 is $<X,Y>=E(XY)$. The corresponding distance is $d(X,Y) = E^{1/2}(X-Y)^2$. Almost surely equal random variables are identified in L_2. The sentence

$$X_k \to X \text{ in } L_2$$

is an abridgment of the following propositions:

$$X_k \in L_2 \; (k=1,2,...) \;,\; X \in L_2 \;,\; E(X_k - X)^2 \to 0 \text{ as } k\uparrow\infty.$$

Definition of the space $L_{2,m\times n}(p,q)$

The space $L_{2,m\times n}$ is the space of random matrices $A_{m\times n}$ with elements $A_{ij} \in L_2$. Linear combinations of random matrices $A_{m\times n}$ with elements in L_2 are matrices with elements in L_2. Hence, $L_{2,m\times n}$ **is a linear space**.

Let $p_{m\times m}$ and $q_{n\times n}$ be definite positive matrices. Then

$$<A,B> := \operatorname{tr} E(A'pBq) \quad (A,B \in L_{2,m\times n}). \tag{1}$$

The expectations involved in the last member of (1) exist because the product of two square-integrable random variables is an integrable random variable.

We hereafter prove that the function defined by (1) is a scalar product on $L_{2,m\times n}$, i.e. a function with the properties Ch.1.(1) to (5), and that the space $L_{2,m\times n}$ is topologically complete for the corresponding distance. This means that $L_{2,m\times n}$, endowed with the scalar product (1) is an Hilbert space (see App.F. F1). This Hilbert space is denoted by $L_{2,m\times n}(p,q)$. The definite positive matrices p and q are always fixed. Very often, they are omitted in the notations. They are essential for the complete definition of the space $L_{2,m\times n}(p,q)$, but several interesting results proved in particular spaces $L_{2,m\times n}(p,q)$ do not depend on the matrices defining the scalar product.

Theorem 1

The function $<\cdot,\cdot>$ defined by (1) is a scalar product on $\boldsymbol{L}_{2,m\times n}$.

Proof

The linearity of $<A,B>$ in A and in B is direct. For the symmetry, we observe that the trace of a matrix and that of the transposed matrix is the same. Hence,

$$<A,B> \; = \text{tr}\; E(A'pBq) = E\; \text{tr}(A'pBq)$$

$$= E\; \text{tr}[(A'pBq)'] = E\; \text{tr}(qB'pA)$$

$$= E\; \text{tr}(B'pAq) = \text{tr}\; E(B'pAq) = \; <B,A> ,$$

by the cyclical property of the trace.

Now we prove that $<A,A>$ is positive. Matrices $s_{m\times m}$ and t_{nxn} exist, such that $p=s's$, $q=t't$. Then, with $R_{m\times n}:= sAt'$,

$$<A,A> = E\; \text{tr}(A'pAq) = E\; \text{tr}(A's'sAt't)$$

$$= E\; \text{tr}(tA's'sAt') = E\; \text{tr}[(sAt')'(sAt')]$$

$$= E\; \text{tr}(R'R) = E \sum_{ij} R'_{ji}R_{ij} = E \sum_{ij} (R_{ij})^2 \geq 0.$$

Finally, we assume that $<A,A> = 0$, and we prove that this implies $A=0$. By the assumption and by the expression obtained above for $<A,A>$,

$$0 = \; <A,A> \; = E \sum_{ij} (R_{ji})^2 .$$

Then $\sum_{ij} (R_{ji})^2=0$ (where the a.s. indication can be dropped, because almost surely equal random variables are identified). Hence, $R_{ji}=0$ for all i,j. Then $sAt' =R=0$ and then $A=0$, because the matrices s and t are invertible •

The **norm** in $\boldsymbol{L}_{2,m\times n}$ is

$$||A|| := \; <A,A>^{1/2} \quad (A\in \boldsymbol{L}_{2,m\times n}). \tag{2}$$

Let $A,A_k\in \boldsymbol{L}_{2,m\times n}$ (k=1,2,...). Then, **the convergence of A_k to A in $\boldsymbol{L}_{2,m\times n}$** is defined by the equivalence

$$[A_k \to A \text{ in } \boldsymbol{L}_{2,m\times n} \text{ as } k\uparrow\infty] \;:\Leftrightarrow$$

$$[\|A-A_k\| \to 0 \text{ as } k\uparrow\infty].$$

The elements of any matrix are also called its **components**.

Theorem 2

Convergence in $\boldsymbol{L}_{2,m\times n}$ is equivalent to componentwise convergence in $\boldsymbol{L}_2$. Explicitly:

$$[A_k \to A \text{ in } \boldsymbol{L}_{2,m\times n} \text{ as } k\uparrow\infty] \Leftrightarrow$$

$$[(A_k)_{ij} \to A_{ij} \text{ in } \boldsymbol{L}_2 \text{ as } k\uparrow\infty \ (i=1,\ldots,m;\ j=1,\ldots,n)].$$

Proof
Let $B_k:=A-A_k$. As in the foregoing proof, let $p=s's$, $q=t't$, where s and t are square invertible matrices. Let

$$(R_k)_{m\times n} := sB_kt'.$$

Then

$$\langle B_k,B_k\rangle = E\,tr(B_k'pB_kq) = E\,tr(B_k's'sB_kt't)$$

$$= E\,tr(tB_k's'sB_kt') = E\,tr[(sB_kt')'(sB_kt')]$$

$$= E\,tr(R_k'R_k) = E\sum_{ij}[(R_k)_{ij}]^2 = \sum_{ij} E[(R_k)_{ij}]^2$$

and as $k\uparrow\infty$,

$$\langle B_k,B_k\rangle \to 0 \Leftrightarrow$$

$$E[(R_k)_{ij}]^2 \to 0 \ (i=1,\ldots,m;\ j=1,\ldots,n) \Leftrightarrow$$

$$R_k \to 0 \text{ componentwise in } \boldsymbol{L}_2 \Leftrightarrow$$

$$B_k \to 0 \text{ componentwise in } \boldsymbol{L}_2\,,$$

where the latter equivalence results from the relations

$$R_k = sB_kt' \quad , \quad B_k = s^{-1}R_kt'^{-1}\,.$$

Indeed, these relations imply that the components of R_k are linear combinations of the components and B_k, and that the components of B_k are linear combinations of the components of R_k •

Theorem 3

The space $\boldsymbol{L}_{2,m\times n}$ is complete for the norm defined by (2). Hence, $\boldsymbol{L}_{2,m\times n}$, endowed with the scalar product (1), is a Hilbert space.

Proof
Let A_k (k=1,2,...) be a Cauchy sequence in $\boldsymbol{L}_{2,m\times n}$. This means that the doubly indexed sequence $D_{kk'}:=A_k-A_{k'}$ converges to 0 in $\boldsymbol{L}_{2,m\times n}$ as $k,k'\uparrow\infty$. The preceding Theorem 2 can be applied in case of doubly indexed sequences (with the same proof). Hence, for any fixed i and j, the sequence

$$(D_{kk'})_{ij} = (A_k)_{ij}-(A_{k'})_{ij}$$

converges to 0 in $\boldsymbol{L}_2$ as $k,k'\uparrow\infty$. Then $(A_k)_{ij}$ (k=1,2,...) is a Cauchy sequence in the complete space $\boldsymbol{L}_2$. This implies the existence of a random variable A_{ij} in $\boldsymbol{L}_2$ such that $(A_k)_{ij}$ converges to A_{ij} in $\boldsymbol{L}_2$. Hence $A_k\to A$ componentwise in $\boldsymbol{L}_2$, and then, again by Theorem 2, $A_k\to A$ in $\boldsymbol{L}_{2,m\times n}$.

This proves that any Cauchy sequence in $\boldsymbol{L}_{2,m\times n}$ converges to some point in $\boldsymbol{L}_{2,m\times n}$, i.e. the space $\boldsymbol{L}_{2,m\times n}$ is complete •

4.2.2. $\boldsymbol{L}_{2,n}$ Spaces

$\boldsymbol{L}_{2,n}$ is the space of random columns $X_{n\times 1}$ with elements $X_i\in\boldsymbol{L}_2$ (i=1,...,n). Columns are particular matrices. Hence $\boldsymbol{L}_{2,n}\equiv\boldsymbol{L}_{2,n\times 1}$. The scalar product $<\cdot,\cdot>$ is defined from definite positive matrices $p_{n\times n}$ and $q_{1\times 1}$ in $\boldsymbol{L}_{2,n\times 1}$. The matrix $q_{1\times 1}$ is identified with its unique strictly positive element q_{11}. This element is irrelevant, and it can be replaced by 1. Hence, the scalar product is defined by

$$<X,Y> := E(X'pY) \quad (X,Y\in\boldsymbol{L}_{2,n}) \tag{3}$$

in $\boldsymbol{L}_{2,n}$. A more complete notation for $\boldsymbol{L}_{2,n}$ is $\boldsymbol{L}_{2,n}(p)$.

4.2.3. Space $\boldsymbol{L}_{2,1}\equiv\boldsymbol{L}_2$

In the space $\boldsymbol{L}_{2,1}\equiv\boldsymbol{L}_2$, the matrix $p_{1\times 1}$ is identified with its unique strictly positive element p_{11}, and we can take $p_{11}=1$. Then the scalar product is the same in $\boldsymbol{L}_{2,1}$ and in $\boldsymbol{L}_2$.

4.3. Projection Theorems

4.3.1. Planes

Hereafter, only projections on topologically closed planes are considered in $\boldsymbol{L}_{2,m\times n}(p,q)$. "Plane" must be understood everywhere as "closed plane", when projections are involved. In fact, the considered planes are finite-dimensional in the applications, and such planes are closed by a general Theorem (App.F. Th.F5).

The projection of the point $A\in\boldsymbol{L}_{2,m\times n}$ on the plane $\boldsymbol{P}\subseteq\boldsymbol{L}_{2,m\times n}$ is denoted, as usual, by

$$\mathrm{Proj}(A/\boldsymbol{P}).$$

It happens that this projection does not depend on p or q. This can be made explicit by a statement such as

$$B = \mathrm{Proj}(A/\boldsymbol{P}) \text{ in } \boldsymbol{L}_{2,m\times n}, \text{ independently of p.}$$

In the latter case, B remains the same when p is replaced by any other definite positive matrix of dimensions m×m, but B may depend on the not mentioned matrix q.

Let $\varnothing\neq\boldsymbol{S}\subseteq\boldsymbol{L}_{2,m\times n}$. Then, as in Ch.1.2.3, we denote by $\boldsymbol{P}(\boldsymbol{S})$ the plane through the origin generated by $\boldsymbol{S}$, i.e. the family of all linear combinations of points in $\boldsymbol{S}$. Often, $\boldsymbol{S}$ is a finite set, and then $\boldsymbol{P}(\boldsymbol{S})$ is a finite-dimensional plane.

Let $v_{m\times n}$ be a matrix. Then $\boldsymbol{P}_v(\boldsymbol{S})$ is the set of matrices $A\in\boldsymbol{P}(\boldsymbol{S})$ such that EA=v. Any affine combination of matrices with expectation v, is a matrix with expectation v. Hence **$\boldsymbol{P}_v(\boldsymbol{S})$ is a plane**.

Hereafter, we prove particular projection Theorems. In any case, we can use the general definition of a projection on a plane $\boldsymbol{P}$:

$$[B = \mathrm{Proj}(A/\boldsymbol{P})] \;:\Leftrightarrow\; [B\in\boldsymbol{P},\ A-B\perp V-W\ (V,W\in\boldsymbol{P})], \tag{4}$$

stated in Ch.1.1.5 (for projections in $\mathbf{R}^n$, but valid in any Hilbert space by Ch.1.2.1). If $\boldsymbol{P}$ is a plane through the origin, then (4) can be replaced by

$$[B = \mathrm{Proj}(A/\boldsymbol{P})] \;\Leftrightarrow\; [B\in\boldsymbol{P},\ A-B\perp V\ (V\in\boldsymbol{P})]. \tag{5}$$

4.3.2. Projections in $L_{2,m\times n}$

Theorem 4

Let $S \subseteq L_{2,m\times n}$ and let $a_{m\times n}$ be a scalar matrix. Then

$$[A = \mathrm{Proj}(a/P(S))] \Leftrightarrow [A \in P(S),\ \langle A,V\rangle = \langle a,EV\rangle\ (V \in S)]. \quad (6)$$

Proof

By (5), for any $A \in P(S)$,

$$A = \mathrm{Proj}(a/P(S)) \Leftrightarrow A-a \perp V\ (V \in P(S) \Leftrightarrow A-a \perp V\ (V \in S)$$

$$\Leftrightarrow \langle A-a, V\rangle = 0\ (V \in S) \Leftrightarrow \langle A,V\rangle = \langle a,V\rangle\ (V \in S),$$

where the latter scalar product equals

$$\langle a,V\rangle = \mathrm{tr}\, E(a'pVq) = \mathrm{tr}\,[a'p(EV)q] = \langle a,EV\rangle \quad \bullet$$

4.3.3. Projections in $L_{2,n\times n}$

Let $S \subseteq L_{2,n\times n}$. We say that **$S$ is closed under left matrix multiplication** if $aV \in S$ for any scalar matrix $a_{n\times n}$ and any matrix $V \in S$. **If S is closed under left matrix multiplication, then S contains the origin $0_{n\times n}$**, because we can take $a=0_{n\times n}$ in the definition. Hence, **planes closed under left matrix multiplication, are planes through the origin**.

Theorem 5

Let Q be a plane in $L_{2,n\times n}$, closed under left matrix multiplication and containing a matrix B such that EB is invertible. Then, for any matrix $a_{n\times n}$:

$$A = \mathrm{Proj}(a/P_a(Q)) \Leftrightarrow$$

$$[A \in P_a(Q),\ \langle A,V\rangle = \langle A,W\rangle\ (V,W \in Q;\ EV=EW=1_{n\times n})]. \quad (7)$$

Proof

Let $I := (EB)^{-1}B$. Then $I \in Q$, $EI = 1_{n\times n}$, $aI \in Q$, $E(aI) = a$. Hence $aI \in P_a(Q)$ and then $P_a(Q) \neq \varnothing$.

We now prove the following relation.

$$\{T-U \,/\, T,U\in \boldsymbol{P}_a(\boldsymbol{Q})\} = \{V-W \,/\, V,W\in \boldsymbol{Q}\,;\, EV = EW = 1_{nxn}\}. \qquad (8)$$

For the $\subseteq$ part, let $T,U\in \boldsymbol{P}_a(\boldsymbol{Q})$. Then $T,U\in \boldsymbol{Q}$ and ET=EU=a. Let

$$V := T-aI+I \;\;,\;\; W := U-aI+I.$$

Then $V,W\in \boldsymbol{Q}$ and EV=EW=1. Hence T−U=V−W belongs to the last member of (8). For the $\supseteq$ part of (8), let $V,W\in \boldsymbol{Q}$ and $EV=EW=1_{nxn}$. Let

$$T := V-I+aI \;\;,\;\; U := W-I+aI.$$

Then $T,U\in \boldsymbol{Q}$ and ET=EU=a. Hence, $T,U\in \boldsymbol{P}_a(\boldsymbol{Q})$ and V−W=T−U belongs to the first member of (8). This proves (8). Then

$$A = \mathrm{Proj}(a/\boldsymbol{P}_a(\boldsymbol{Q})) \Leftrightarrow A-a\perp T-U \;(T,U\in \boldsymbol{P}_a(\boldsymbol{Q}))$$

$$\Leftrightarrow A-a\perp V-W \;(V,W\in \boldsymbol{Q}\,;\, EV=EW=1\}$$

$$\Leftrightarrow <A-a, V-W> =0 \;(V,W\in \boldsymbol{Q}\,;\, EV=EW=1\}$$

$$\Leftrightarrow <A, V-W> =0 \;(V,W\in \boldsymbol{Q}\,;\, EV=EW=1\},$$

where the last equivalence results from the relations

$$<a, V-W> = \mathrm{tr}\, E[a'p(V-W)q] = \mathrm{tr}\, [a'p[E(V-W)]q] = \mathrm{tr}\, [a'p0q] = 0 \quad \bullet$$

Theorem 6

Let $\boldsymbol{Q}$ be a plane in $\boldsymbol{L}_{2,n\times n}(p,q)$, closed under left matrix multiplication, and containing a matrix B such that EB is invertible. Let $a_{n\times n}$ be an invertible matrix. Let

$$\mathbf{A := Proj(a/\boldsymbol{Q}) \text{ in } \boldsymbol{L}_{2,n\times n}(p,q), \text{ independently of } p}$$

and let EA be invertible. Then

$$\mathbf{Proj(a/\boldsymbol{P}_a(\boldsymbol{Q})) = a(EA)^{-1}A.}$$

Proof

A belongs to $\boldsymbol{Q}$ and then $B:=a(EA)^{-1}A\in \boldsymbol{Q}$. Then $B\in \boldsymbol{P}_a(\boldsymbol{Q})$ because EB=a.

We now prove that

$$<B,V> = <B,W> \text{ in } \boldsymbol{L}_{2,n\times n}(p,q) \quad (V,W\in\boldsymbol{Q}\,;\, EV=EW=1) \tag{9}$$

Let $V,W\in\boldsymbol{Q}$ and $EV=EW=1$. Let $c_{n\times n}:=a(EA)^{-1}$. The matrix c is invertible and $B=cA$. By the definition of A,

$$A-a \perp c^{-1}(V-W) \text{ in } \boldsymbol{L}_{2,n\times n}(c'pc,q),$$

because $c^{-1}(V-W)\in\boldsymbol{Q}$ and because $\boldsymbol{Q}$ is a plane through the origin $\boldsymbol{Q}$. Hence,

$$<A-a,c^{-1}(V-W)> = 0 \text{ in } \boldsymbol{L}_{2,n\times n}(c'pc,q),$$

$$0 = \text{tr } E[(A-a)'(c'pc)c^{-1}(V-W)q]$$

$$= \text{tr } E[(cA-ca)'p(V-W)q]$$

$$= \text{tr } E[B'p(V-W)q] - \text{tr } E[(ca)'p(V-W)q]$$

$$= <B,V-W> - \text{tr}[(ca)'p(EV-EW)q] = <B,V-W> - 0.$$

This proves (9). Then $B= \text{Proj}(a/\boldsymbol{P}_a(\boldsymbol{Q}))$ by Theorem 5 •

Hence, in order to find $\text{Proj}(a/\boldsymbol{P}_a(\boldsymbol{Q}))$, we may first calculate $A:=\text{Proj}(a/\boldsymbol{Q})$, and then, if Theorem 6 can be applied, just take the bias away by pre-multiplying by $a(EA)^{-1}$.

4.3.4. Projections in $\boldsymbol{L}_2$

The following Theorem is Ch.1.Th.10, stated here in a different way, and slightly generalized, because now the set $\boldsymbol{S}$ may be infinite.

Theorem 7

Let $\boldsymbol{S}$ be a set in $\boldsymbol{L}_2$ containing a random variable B with $EB\neq 0$, and let a be a constant. Then

$$A = \text{Proj}(a/\boldsymbol{P}_a(\boldsymbol{S})) \Leftrightarrow$$

$$[A\in\boldsymbol{P}_a(\boldsymbol{S}),\ E(AV)EW = E(AW)EV\ (V,W\in\boldsymbol{S})] \tag{10}$$

Proof

For $A \in \boldsymbol{P}_a(\boldsymbol{S})$, $A = \text{Proj}(a/\boldsymbol{P}_a(\boldsymbol{S})) \Leftrightarrow$

$$A - a \perp C - D \quad (C, D \in \boldsymbol{P}_a(\boldsymbol{S})) \tag{11}$$

$$\Leftrightarrow$$

$$A - a \perp EV.W - EW.V \quad (V, W \in \boldsymbol{S}) \tag{12}$$

$$\Leftrightarrow A \perp EV.W - EW.V \ (V, W \in \boldsymbol{S})$$

$$\Leftrightarrow E[A(EV.W - EW.V)] = 0 \ (V, W \in \boldsymbol{S}).$$

For the proof of $(11) \Leftrightarrow (12)$, let us first assume (11). Let $V, W \in \boldsymbol{S}$. We define C and D by

$$C := a(EB)^{-1}B + EV.W - EW.V,$$

$$D := a(EB)^{-1}B.$$

Then $C, D \in \boldsymbol{P}_a(\boldsymbol{S})$, and by (11),

$$A - a \perp C - D = EV.W - EW.V.$$

Let us now assume (12). Let $C, D \in \boldsymbol{P}_a(\boldsymbol{S})$. It is enough to prove that

$$A - a \perp C - a(EB)^{-1}B. \tag{13}$$

Indeed, then also

$$A - a \perp D - a(EB)^{-1}B,$$

and then (11) follows by difference. For the proof of (13), we observe that C is a linear combination $\sum c_i V_i$ of points V_i in $\boldsymbol{S}$. Then

$$C - a(EB)^{-1}B =$$

$$\sum c_i (EB)^{-1}(EB.V_i - EV_i.B),$$

because

$$\sum c_i \, EV_i = E(\sum c_i V_i) = EC = a.$$

By (12),

$$A - a \perp EB.V_i - EV_i.B,$$

and then

$$A - a \perp \sum c_i (EB)^{-1}(EB.V_i - EV_i.B)$$

$$= C - a(EB)^{-1}B \quad \bullet$$

Theorem 8

Let S be a set in L_2 containing a random variable B with EB≠0. Let a≠0, A:=Proj(a/P(S)), EA≠0. Then

$$\mathbf{Proj(a/}P_a(S)\mathbf{) = a(EA)^{-1}A.}$$

Proof
In L_2, all planes are closed under left matrix multiplication, because this multiplication is a multiplication by scalars. The projections do not depend on the matrices $p_{1\times 1}$, $q_{1\times 1}$ defining the scalar product. Hence, the Theorem results from Theorem 6 with $Q:=P(S)$. Indeed, then $P_a(Q)=P_a(S)$ •

4.4. Covariance Matrices

4.4.1. Definitions

Let $X\in L_{2,m}$, $Y\in L_{2,n}$. We recall that the superscript ° denotes centerings:

$$X^\circ := X-EX \ , \ Y^\circ := Y-EY.$$

The **covariance matrix of X and Y** is the m×n-dimensional matrix

$$\mathrm{Cov}(X,Y') := E(X^\circ Y^{\circ\prime}),$$

The **covariance matrix of X** is the matrix

$$\mathrm{Cov}\ X \equiv \mathrm{Cov}(X,X') = E(X^\circ X^{\circ\prime}).$$

Let Θ be any vector of random variables. For any matrix $A_{m\times n}$ such that EA exists, **the conditional expectation of A for fixed Θ** is the matrix E(A/Θ) with dimensions m×n and with elements

$$[E(A/\Theta)]_{ij} := E(A_{ij}/\Theta).$$

The **conditional covariance matrix of X and Y for fixed Θ,** is the matrix

$$\mathrm{Cov}(X,Y'/\Theta) := E(X^{\Theta}Y^{\Theta\prime}/\Theta),$$

where X^{Θ} and Y^{Θ} are **the conditionally centered vectors**

$$X^{\Theta} := X - E(X/\Theta)\,,\ Y^{\Theta} := Y - E(Y/\Theta).$$

The **conditional covariance matrix of X, for fixed Θ,** is the matrix

$$\mathrm{Cov}(X/\Theta) \equiv \mathrm{Cov}(X,X'/\Theta) = E(X^{\Theta}X^{\Theta\prime}/\Theta).$$

If Z is any row with square-integrable components, then

$$\mathrm{Cov}(X,Z) := \mathrm{Cov}(X,(Z')'),$$

$$\mathrm{Cov}(X,Z/\Theta) := \mathrm{Cov}(X,(Z')'/\Theta).$$

In particular, for any matrices $a_{r\times m}$ and $b_{n\times s}$,

$$\mathrm{Cov}(aX,Y'b) := \mathrm{Cov}[(aX),(b'Y)'],$$

$$\mathrm{Cov}(aX,Y'b/\Theta) := \mathrm{Cov}[(aX),(b'Y)'/\Theta].$$

4.4.2. Properties

We always assume that the vectors X, Y and Z occurring in

$$\mathrm{Cov}(X,Y')\ ,\ \mathrm{Cov}(X,Y'/\Theta)\ ,\ \mathrm{Cov}(X,Z)\ ,\ \mathrm{Cov}(X,Z/\Theta)$$

are vectors with square-integrable components.

Theorem 9

a.

Cov(X,Y′) and Cov(X,Y′/Θ) are bilinear, i.e. linear in X and in Y.

b.

$$\mathbf{Cov(aX,Y'b) = a\ Cov(X,Y')\ b,}$$

$$\mathbf{Cov[a(\Theta)X,Y'b(\Theta)/\Theta) = a(\Theta)\ Cov(X,Y')\ b(\Theta).}$$

c.

$$\mathbf{Cov(Y,X') = [Cov(X,Y')]',}$$

$$\mathbf{Cov(Y,X'/\Theta) = [Cov(X,Y'/\Theta)]'},$$

$$\mathbf{Cov(X/\Theta) = [Cov(X/\Theta)]'}.$$

d.

$$\textbf{Cov(X) is a semidefinite positive matrix.}$$

e.

$$\mathbf{Cov(X,Y') = E(XY') - (EX)(EY')},$$

$$\mathbf{Cov(X,Y'/\Theta) = E(XY'/\Theta) - E(X/\Theta)E(Y'/\Theta)}.$$

f.

$$\mathbf{Cov(X,Y') = E\ Cov(X,Y'/\Theta) + Cov[E(X/\Theta),E(Y'/\Theta)]},$$

$$\mathbf{Cov\ X = E\ Cov(X/\Theta) + Cov\ E(X/\Theta)}.$$

Proof

The verification of all these relations is direct. For the proof of d, we first notice that Cov X is a symmetric matrix by c. Let $X \in \boldsymbol{L}_{2,n}$ and let $x_{n\times 1}$ be any scalar column. Then

$$x'(\text{Cov X})x = x'E(X^\circ X^{\circ\prime})x = E(x'X^\circ X^{\circ\prime}x)$$

$$= E[(X^{\circ\prime}x)'(X^{\circ\prime}x)] = E(X^{\circ\prime}x)^2 \geq 0,$$

because $(X^{\circ\prime}x)$ is a matrix of dimensions 1×1, i.e. a scalar •

4.5. Spaces of Scalar Matrices

4.5.1. Definition of the Spaces

We denote by $\mathbf{R}_{m\times n}$ the space of scalar matrices with dimensions m×n. The scalar product is defined on $\mathbf{R}_{m\times n}$ by

$$<a,b> := \text{tr}(a'pbq) \quad (a,b \in \mathbf{R}_{m\times n}),$$

where $p_{m\times m}$ and $q_{n\times n}$ are fixed definite positive matrices. That this is a scalar product indeed, results from a simplified version of the proof of Theorem 1. The space $\mathbf{R}_{m\times n}$ is denoted more explicitly by $\mathbf{R}_{m\times n}(p,q)$ when the attention is drawn on the matrices p and q defining the scalar product.

From a simplified version of the proof of Theorem 2, results that **convergence in $\mathbf{R}_{m\times n}$ is equivalent to componentwise convergence of the matrices**.

The space $\mathbf{R}_n \equiv \mathbf{R}_{n\times 1}$ is the space of scalar columns of length n. Now the matrix $q_{1\times 1}$ can be dropped. Then $\mathbf{R}_n(p)$ is the space $\mathbf{R}_n$ endowed with the scalar product

$$<x,y> := tr(x'py) \quad (x,y\in\mathbf{R}_n),$$

where $p_{n\times n}$ is a fixed definite positive matrix. The usual scalar product, and corresponding distance, result from the matrix $p:= 1_{n\times n}$.

The space $\mathbf{R}^n \equiv \mathbf{R}_{1\times n}$ is the space of scalar rows of length n.

4.5.2. Projections on Convex Sets

Let $\boldsymbol{C}$ be a closed convex set in $\mathbf{R}_{m\times n}(p,q)$ and let v be a fixed point in that space. Then $\boldsymbol{C}$ contains a unique point w, such that (see Fig.33)

$$d(v,w) \leq d(v,u) \quad (u\in\boldsymbol{C}).$$

Hence, w is the unique point in $\boldsymbol{C}$, closest to v. The point w is **the projection Proj(v/*C*) of v on *C***. The distance function d(·,·) is that one resulting from the scalar product defined from the matrices p and q :

$$d(u,v) := \left[tr[(u-v)'p(u-v)q]\right]^{1/2}$$

The existence and unicity of Proj(v/*C*) is rather obvious in $\mathbf{R}_2$ and $\mathbf{R}_3$, with the usual distance. See App.F.Th.F1 for a general proof in arbitrary Hilbert spaces.

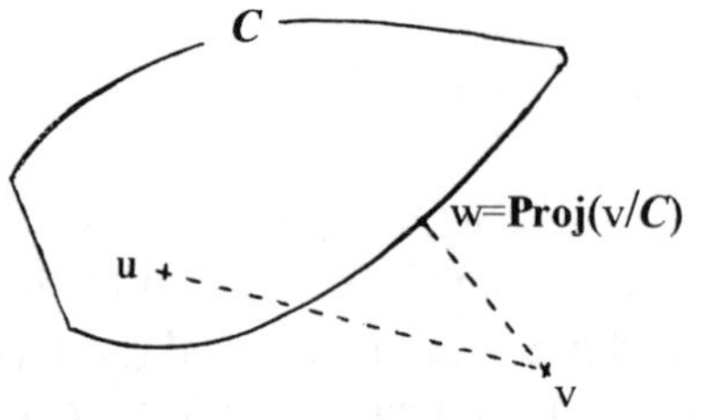

Fig.33. Projection on a convex set

4.5.3. Correction of an Estimated Covariance Matrix

Let $X \in \boldsymbol{L}_{2,n}$. By Th.9.d, Cov X is a semidefinite positive matrix. Let $v_{n\times n}$ be some estimate of Cov X. Hence, v is a scalar matrix considered to be an approximation of Cov X. Mostly v results from an estimator V (a random matrix) of Cov X in which the observable random variables have been replaced by observed realizations.

It is frequent in Credibility Theory that v is not semidefinite positive. Then v must be corrected, i.e. replaced by the semidefinite positive matrix w "closest" to v. Hereafter we explain how w is defined precisely, and how that matrix can be calculated.

Let $\boldsymbol{C}_{n\times n}$ be **the space of covariance matrices Cov X ($X \in \boldsymbol{L}_{2,n}$).** Then $\boldsymbol{C}_{n\times n}$ **is the space of all semidefinite positive matrices $p_{n\times n}$**. Indeed by Theorem 9.d, each matrix in $\boldsymbol{C}_{m\times n}$ is semidefinite positive. Conversely, let $p_{n\times n}$ be a semidefinite positive matrix. We prove that p is the covariance matrix Cov Y of some vector $Y \in \boldsymbol{L}_{2,n}$. Let $X_{n\times 1}$ be a column of i.i.d random variables with variance 1. Then Cov $X = 1_{n\times n}$. Let s_{nxn} be a matrix such that $p = ss'$ and let $Y := sX$. Then

$$\text{Cov } Y = \text{Co}(Y,Y') = \text{Cov}(sX,X's') = s\,\text{Cov}(X,X)\,s' = ss' = p.$$

Let $\boldsymbol{S}_{n\times n}$ be **the space of symmetric matrices of dimensions n×n**.

We consider $\mathbf{R}_{n\times n}$ with scalar product

$$<a,b> := \text{tr}(ab') = \text{tr}(a'b) = \textstyle\sum_j (a'b)_{jj} = \sum_{ij} a'_{ji}b_{ij} = \sum_{ij} a_{ij}b_{ij} \quad (a,b \in \mathbf{R}_{n\times n}).$$

This is the scalar product defined from the definite positive matrices $p := 1_{n\times n}$ and $q := 1_{n\times n}$. The corresponding distance is

$$d(a,b) := <a-b,a-b>^{1/2} = [\textstyle\sum_{ij}(a_{ij}-b_{ij})^2]^{1/2} .$$

Hence, if we identify each point $a \in \mathbf{R}_{n\times n}$ with the row

$$(a_{11},\ldots,a_{1n},a_{21},\ldots,a_{2n},\ldots,\ldots,\ldots,a_{n1},\ldots,a_{nn}),$$

then $\mathbf{R}_{n\times n}$ is the usual space $\mathbf{R}^{n^2}$, with the usual scalar product and hence, with the usual distance and the usual orthogonality.

A **cone**, is a set containing the linear combinations with positive coefficients of its points. **Any cone is a convex set.**

Theorem 10

$C_{n\times n}$ is a closed cone in $R_{n\times n}$. For any point $v\in R_{n\times n}$, the projection

$$w := Proj(v/C_{n\times n})$$

can be obtained in the following way. Let $u:=(v+v')/2$. Let $t_{n\times n}$ be an orthogonal matrix such that $d := t'ut$ is diagonal. Let d_+ be the matrix d in which each strictly negative diagonal element is replaced by 0. Then $w=td_+t'$. The same matrix w is obtained if other orthogonal matrices t are considered.

Proof

Let c_i (i=1,...,k) be matrices in $C_{n\times n}$ and let p_i (i=1,...,k) be positive scalars. For any column $x_{n\times 1}$,

$$x'(\sum_i p_ic_i)x = \sum_i p_i(x'c_ix) \geq 0.$$

Hence,

$$\sum_i p_ic_i \in C_{n\times n},$$

because $\sum p_ic_i$ is symmetric. This proves that $C_{n\times n}$ is a cone.

Let $c_k\in C_{n\times n}$ (k=1,2,...) be such that $c_k\to c\in R_{n\times n}$ as $k\uparrow\infty$. Then $c\in C_{n\times n}$. Indeed, for any column $x_{n\times 1}$,

$$x'c_kx \to x'cx \text{ as } k\uparrow\infty,$$

because the convergence of c_k to c is componentwise convergence. But $x'c_kx$ is positive, and then $x'cx$ is also positive. Obviously, c is symmetric. Hence $c\in C_{n\times n}$. This proves that $C_{n\times n}$ is closed.

Linear combinations of symmetric matrices are symmetric matrices. Hence, $S_{n\times n}$ is a plane through the origin and $C_{n\times n}$ is a closed convex set in that plane. The projection w of v on $C_{n\times n}$ can be calculated in two steps: v is projected on $S_{n\times n}$ and then this projection u is projected on $C_{n\times n}$:

$$u := Proj(v/S_{n\times n}) \quad , \quad w := Proj(u/C_{n\times n}).$$

Then $u = 1/2(v+v')$ iff

$$v - 1/2\,(v+v') \perp s \quad (s \in \boldsymbol{S}_{n\times n}).$$

This orthogonality is equivalent to the relation

$$<2v-(v+v'),s> = 0 \;\;, \;\; \text{or} \;\; <v-v',s> = 0,$$

$$\text{or} \;\; tr[(v-v')s'] = 0 \;\;, \;\; \text{or} \;\; tr(vs') = tr(v's').$$

The latter relation is exact. Indeed,

$$tr(v's') = tr(v's) = tr(v's)' = tr(s'v) = tr(vs')$$

because $s=s'$, because the trace remains unchanged after transposition, and by the cyclical property of the trace. Hence $u = 1/2(v+v')$.

Now we prove that w can be obtained in the indicated way from the symmetric matrix u.

Any diagonal element p_{ii} of a semidefinite positive matrix p is positive. This implies that for any diagonal matrix $d_{n\times n}$, the semidefinite positive matrix closest to d is d_+.

For any matrices $a_{n\times n}$, b_{nxn} and any orthogonal matrix $t_{n\times n}$,

$$d(a,b) = d(t'at,t'bt).$$

Indeed, the square of the last member equals, with $e:=a-b$,

$$d^2(t'at,t'bt) = <t'at-t'bt,t'at-t'bt> = <t'et,t'et> = tr[(t'et)(t'et)']$$

$$= tr(t'ett'e't) = tr(tt'ett'e') = tr(1e1e') = tr(ee') = <e,e> = d^2(a,b).$$

Now let t be orthogonal such that $d:=t'ut$ is diagonal, and let $w:=td_+t'$. Let c be any matrix in $\boldsymbol{C}_{n\times n}$ Then we have to verify that

$$d(u,w) \leq d(u,c) \;\;, \;\; \text{or} \;\; d(t'ut,t'wt) \leq d(t'ut,t'ct),$$

$$\text{or} \;\; d(d,d_+) \leq d(d,t'ct).$$

The latter inequality is correct, because t′ct belongs to $\mathbf{C}_{n\times n}$, and because d_+ is the point of $\mathbf{C}_{n\times n}$ closest to d. This proves that w can be calculted as indicated in the statement of the Theorem.

The projection of a point on a closed convex set is a well defined unique point of that set. Hence, the orthogonal matrix t used in the preceding discussion is irrelevant. It can be replaced by any other orthogonal matrix with the required property •

The foregoing Theorem furnishes the solution of the initial problem of this section: If v is an estimate of the covariance matrix Cov X and if v is not semidefinite positive, then v is replaced by $w:=P(v/\mathbf{C}_{n\times n})$. The Theorem shows how to calculate w.

4.6. Zero-Excess Random Vectors

4.6.1. Definitions and Examples

Definitions

A **zero-excess random variable** is a random variable X such that

$$E(X^\circ)^4 = 3E^2(X^\circ)^2 < \infty. \tag{14}$$

A **basic zero-excess vector $\mathbf{Z}_{n\times 1}$** is a random column

$$Z = (Z_1,...,Z_n)',$$

such that for any subscripts $i,j,k,m \in \{1,...,n\}$, $EZ_i^4 < \infty$ and

$$E(Z_i^\circ Z_j^\circ) = \delta_{ij}u_i, \tag{15}$$

$$E(Z_i^\circ Z_j^\circ Z_k^\circ Z_m^\circ) = \delta_{ij}\delta_{km}u_iu_k + \delta_{ik}\delta_{jm}u_iu_j + \delta_{im}\delta_{jk}u_iu_j, \tag{16}$$

where

$$u_i := \mathrm{Var}\, Z_i = E(Z_i^\circ)^2. \tag{17}$$

A **zero-excess vector $\mathbf{Y}_{n\times 1}$** is a random column which can be displayed as Y=sZ, where $s_{n\times n}$ is a scalar matrix and $Z_{n\times 1}$ a basic zero-excess vector.

Comments and examples

By Ch.1.1.2, a zero-excess random variable X is a random variable of wich the excess e(X) equals zero.

For i=j=k=m in (16), we obtain $E(Z_i°)^4=3E^2(Z_i°)^2$. Hence, **the components of any basic zero-excess random vector are zero-excess random variables**. This result is generalized in the following Theorem 11.

By Ch.2.Th.2, **any random column of wich the components are independent zero-excess random variables, is a basic zero-excess vector.**

Any normal random vector $Y_{n\times1}$ is a zero-excess vector. Indeed, it is classical that Y can be displayed as Y=sZ, where Z is a random column with independent normal random variables. Hence, all results proved hereafter for zero-excess vectors can be applied to normal vectors.

Several classical results, concerning point estimators, proved for normal vectors in multivariate statistical analysis, are in fact valid for any zero-excess vectors. The essential part of Credibility Theory is not based on zero-excess vectors. The latter do only occur when the quality of some estimators is discussed. In distribution-free Credibility Theory, only point estimators are involved, and then the introduction of zero-excess vectors (rather than normal vectors) keeps the theory rather distribution-free.

Theorem 11

a. **Let $Y_{n\times1}$ be a zero-excess vector. Then $X_{m\times1}:=a_{m\times n}Y_{n\times1}$ is a zero-excess vector.**

b. **The zero-excess vector X is a basic zero-excess vector iff Cov X is a diagonal matrix.**

c. **Any sub-vector of a zero-excess vector is a zero-excess vector.**

d. **Any component of a zero-excess vector is a zero-excess random variable.**

Proof

a. Let $Y_{n\times 1}=s_{n\times n}Z_{n\times 1}$ where Z is the basic zero-excess vector satisfying (15), (16) and (17). Let $v_{m\times m}$:=Cov X. Let $t_{m\times m}$ be an orthogonal matrix such that $w_{m\times m}:= tvt'$ is diagonal. Let $U_{m\times 1}:= tX$. Then

$$\text{Cov } U = \text{Cov}(U,U') = t(\text{Cov } X)t' = tvt' = w =: \text{Diagonal}(w_1,\ldots,w_m).$$

We have

$$U = tX = taY = tasZ = cZ, \text{ where } c_{m\times n} := tas.$$

We will verify that U is a basic zero-excess vector. Hereafter

$$i,j,p,q \in \{1,\ldots,n\} \text{ and } \alpha,\beta,\mu,\nu \in \{1,\ldots,m\}.$$

Then

$$\delta_{\alpha\beta}w_\alpha = \text{Cov}(U_\alpha,U_\beta) = E(U_\alpha{}^\circ U_\beta{}^\circ) = \textstyle\sum_{ij} c_{\alpha i}c_{\beta j}E(Z_i{}^\circ Z_j{}^\circ)$$

$$= \textstyle\sum_{ij} c_{\alpha i}c_{\beta j}\delta_{ij}u_i = \sum_i c_{\alpha i}c_{\beta i}u_i .$$

Hence,

$$\textstyle\sum_i c_{\alpha i}c_{\beta i}u_i = \delta_{\alpha\beta}w_\alpha.$$

The property of U corresponding to (15) results from the foregoing formulas:

$$E(U_\alpha{}^\circ U_\beta{}^\circ) = \delta_{\alpha\beta}w_\alpha.$$

We now verify the property corresponding to (16).

$$E(U_\alpha{}^\circ U_\beta{}^\circ U_\mu{}^\circ U_\nu{}^\circ) = \textstyle\sum_{ijpq} c_{\alpha i}c_{\beta j}c_{\mu p}c_{\nu q}\, E(Z_i{}^\circ Z_j{}^\circ Z_p{}^\circ Z_q{}^\circ)$$

$$= \textstyle\sum_{ijpq} c_{\alpha i}c_{\beta j}c_{\mu p}c_{\nu q}\, (\delta_{ij}\delta_{pq}u_iu_p + \delta_{ip}\delta_{jq}u_iu_j + \delta_{iq}\delta_{jp}u_iu_j)$$

$$= \textstyle\sum_{ip} c_{\alpha i}c_{\beta i}c_{\mu p}c_{\nu p}u_iu_p + \sum_{ij} c_{\alpha i}c_{\beta j}c_{\mu i}c_{\nu j}u_iu_j + \sum_{ij} c_{\alpha i}c_{\beta j}c_{\mu j}c_{\nu i}u_iu_j$$

$$= \textstyle\sum_i c_{\alpha i}c_{\beta i}u_i\sum_p c_{\mu p}c_{\nu p}u_p + \sum_i c_{\alpha i}c_{\mu i}u_i\sum_j c_{\beta j}c_{\nu j}u_j + \sum_i c_{\alpha i}c_{\nu i}u_i\sum_j c_{\beta j}c_{\mu j}u_j$$

$$= \delta_{\alpha\beta}w_\alpha\delta_{\mu\nu}w_\mu + \delta_{\alpha\mu}w_\alpha\delta_{\beta\nu}w_\nu + \delta_{\alpha\nu}w_\alpha\delta_{\beta\mu}w_\beta.$$

This proves that U is a basic zero-excess vector. Then from U=tX, results X=t′U, because t is orthogonal (hence invertible with $t^{-1}=t'$). From the relation $X_{m\times m}=(t')_{m\times m}U_{m\times 1}$ then results that X is a zero-excess vector.

b. From (15) results that the covariance matrix of any basic zero-excess vector Z is a diagonal matrix. Conversely, let $X_{n\times 1}$ be a zero-excess vector with diagonal covariance matrix. Then X can be displayed as $X_{n\times 1}=a_{n\times n}Z_{n\times 1}$, where Z is a basic zero-excess vector. Now we can repeat the argument of a, with m=n. As orthogonal matrix t, we can take the unit matrix $1_{n\times n}$. Then the conclusion is that U:=1X is a basic zero-excess vector.

c. Let $X_{n\times 1}=a_{n\times n}Z_{n\times 1}$ be a zero-excess vector, Z a basic zero excess vector. Let $Y_{m\times 1}$ be the sub-vector of $X_{n\times 1}$ composed of the first m<n components of X. Let $b_{m\times n}$ be the sub-matrix of $a_{n\times n}$ composed of the first m rows of that matrix. Then Y=bZ. By a, Y is a zero-excess vector. The argument can be adapted to any sub-vector of X.

d. Each component of a zero-excess vector is a particular sub-vector. By c, it is a zero-excess vector. A zero-excess vector of length 1 is a zero-excess random variable •

4.6.2. Independent Centered Zero-Excess Random Vectors

When the covariance matrix Cov X of a random vector $X_{n\times 1}$ is considered, it is implicitly supposed that X has square-integrable components.

Theorem 12

Let $X_{n\times 1}$ be a centered random vector and let v:=Cov X. Then, for any scalar matrix $a_{n\times n}$,

$$\mathbf{E(X'aX) = tr(av).} \tag{18}$$

Proof

$$E(X'aX) = E\,tr(X'aX) = E\,tr\,(aXX')$$

$$= tr\,E(aXX') = tr\,[aE(XX')] = tr(av) \quad \bullet$$

Non-degenerated random vectors

The **random vector** $X_{n\times 1}$ is said to be **non-degenerated** if its covariance matrix Cov X is invertible.

Let $X_{n\times1}=s_{n\times n}Y_{n\times1}$. Then X is non-degenerated iff s is invertible and Y is non-degenerated. Indeed,

$$\mathrm{Cov}\,X = \mathrm{Cov}(X,X') = \mathrm{Cov}(sY,Y's') = s\,\mathrm{Cov}(Y,Y')\,s' = s\,(\mathrm{Cov}\,Y)\,s'\,,$$

and then, taking determinants,

$$\det(\mathrm{Cov}\,X) = \det(s).\det(\mathrm{Cov}\,Y).\det(s') = [\det(s)]^2\det(\mathrm{Cov}\,Y).$$

Hence,

$$[\det(\mathrm{Cov}\,X) \neq 0] \Leftrightarrow [\det(s) \neq 0\ ,\ \det(\mathrm{Cov}\,Y) \neq 0].$$

Let $X_{m\times1}=s_{m\times m}U_{m\times1}$, $Y_{n\times1}=t_{n\times n}V_{n\times1}$. If the random vectors X and Y are independent and non-degenerated, then the random vectors U and V are independent. Indeed, from the preceding observation results that s and t are invertible when X and Y are non-degenerated, and then

$$U = s^{-1}X\ ,\ V = t^{-1}Y.$$

Of course, this observation is true for any number of random vectors.

Theorem 13

Let $X_{n\times1}$ and $Y_{n\times1}$ be independent centered zero-excess vectors and let

$$\mathbf{v := Cov\,X\ ,\ w := Cov\,Y.}$$

Then, for any scalar matrices $a_{n\times n}$ and $b_{n\times n}$,

$$\mathbf{E(X'aXX'bX) = tr(av)tr(bv) + tr(avbv) + tr(a'vbv).} \qquad (19)$$

If X and Y are non-degenerated, then

$$\mathbf{E(X'aYY'bX) = tr(awbv),} \qquad (20)$$

$$\mathbf{E(X'aYX'bY) = tr(a'vbw).} \qquad (21)$$

Proof

In this proof, the subscripts i,j,k,m take all possible values 1,...,n. Let

$$X_{n\times1} = s_{n\times n}U_{n\times1}\ ,\ Y_{n\times1} = t_{n\times n}V_{n\times1}\ ,\ \ x_i := EU_i^2\ ,\ \ y_i := EV_i^2,$$

where U and V are basic zero-excess vectors.

Let

$$P_{n\times n} := UU' \ , \ Q_{n\times n} := VV' \ , \ p := EP \ , \ q := EQ \ .$$

Then, by (15) and (16)

$$p_{ij} = E(U_iU_j) = \delta_{ij}x_i \quad , \quad q_{ij} = E(V_iV_j) = \delta_{ij}y_i. \tag{22}$$

$$E(U_iU_jU_kU_m) = \delta_{ij}\delta_{km}x_ix_k + \delta_{ik}\delta_{jm}x_ix_j + \delta_{im}\delta_{jk}x_ix_j \ . \tag{23}$$

Now we consider the traces in the last member of (19),(20),(21).

$$v := Cov(X) = Cov(X,X') = Cov(sU,U's')$$

$$= s\ Cov(U,U')\ s' = s\ E(UU')\ s' = sps'.$$

In the same way, we calculate w. Hence,

$$v = sps' \quad , \quad w = tqt'.$$

Then

$$tr(av) = tr(asps') = tr(s'asp)$$

$$tr(av) = \textstyle\sum_i [(s'as)p]_{ii} = \sum_{ij} (s'as)_{ij}p_{ji} = \sum_{ij} (s'as)_{ij}\delta_{ij}x_i = \sum_i (s'as)_{ii}x_i.$$

Then also

$$tr(bv) = = \textstyle\sum_i (s'bs)_{ii}x_i,$$

and

$$tr(av)tr(bv) = \textstyle\sum_{ijkm} (s'as)_{ii}x_i\ (s'bs)_{jj}x_j\ (*)$$

$$tr(avbv) = tr(asps'bsps') = tr[(s'as)p(s'bs)p]\ ,$$

and

$$tr(avbv) = \textstyle\sum_{ijkm} (s'as)_{ij}p_{jk}(s'bs)_{km}p_{mi} = \sum_{ijkm} (s'as)_{ij}\delta_{jk}x_j\ (s'bs)_{km}\delta_{mi}x_m,$$

$$tr(avbv) = \textstyle\sum_{jm} (s'as)_{mj}x_j\ (s'bs)_{jm}x_m\ (*)$$

We replace a by a′:

$$tr(a'vbv) = \textstyle\sum_{jm} (s'a's)_{mj}x_j(s'bs)_{jm}x_m\ (*)$$

$$tr(awbv) = tr(atqt'bsps') = tr[(s'at)q(t'bs)p],$$

$$\mathrm{tr}(awbv) = \sum_{ijkm} (s'at)_{ij}q_{jk}(t'bs)_{km}p_{mi} = \sum_{ijkm} (s'at)_{ij}\delta_{jk}y_j(t'bs)_{km}\delta_{mi}x_m,$$

$$\mathrm{tr}(awbv) = \sum_{jm} (s'at)_{mj}y_j(t'bs)_{jm}x_m \ (*)$$

$$\mathrm{tr}(a'vbw) = \mathrm{tr}(a'sps'btqt') = \mathrm{tr}[(t'a's)p(s'bt)q],$$

and

$$\mathrm{tr}(a'vbw) = \sum_{ijkm} (t'a's)_{ij}p_{jk}(s'bt)_{km}q_{mi} = \sum_{ijkm} (t'a's)_{ij}\delta_{jk}x_j(s'bt)_{km}\delta_{mi}y_m,$$

$$\mathrm{tr}(a'vbw) = \sum_{jm} (t'a's)_{mj}x_j(s'bt)_{jm}y_m \ (*)$$

The first member of (19) equals, by (23),

$$E(X'aXX'bX) = E(U's'asUU's'bsU) = E\ \mathrm{tr}(U's'asUU's'bsU)$$

$$= E\ \mathrm{tr}[(s'as)(UU')(s'bs)(UU')] = = E\sum_{ijkm} (s'as)_{ij}(UU')_{jk}(s'bs)_{km}(UU')_{mi}$$

$$= E\sum_{ijkm} (s'as)_{ij}U_jU_k(s'bs)_{km}U_mU_i = \sum_{ijkm} (s'as)_{ij}(s'bs)_{km}\ E(U_iU_jU_kU_m)$$

$$= \sum_{ijkm} (s'as)_{ij}(s'bs)_{km}\ (\delta_{ij}\delta_{km}x_ix_k + \delta_{ik}\delta_{jm}x_ix_j + \delta_{im}\delta_{jk}x_ix_j)$$

$$= \sum_{ik} (s'as)_{ii}(s'bs)_{kk}x_ix_k + \sum_{ij} (s'as)_{ij}(s'bs)_{ij}x_ix_j + \sum_{ij} (s'as)_{ij}(s'bs)_{ji}x_ix_j$$

$$= \sum_{ik} (s'as)_{ii}(s'bs)_{kk}x_ix_k + \sum_{ij} (s'a's)_{ji}(s'bs)_{ij}x_ix_j + \sum_{ij} (s'as)_{ij}(s'bs)_{ji}x_ix_j.$$

This last member equals the last member of (19) by the first three formulas marked with an asterisk.

By (22) and by the independence of U and V, the first member of (20) equals

$$E(X'aYY'bX) = E(U's'atVV't'bsU) = E\ \mathrm{tr}[(s'at)(VV')(t'bs)(UU')]$$

$$= E\sum_{ijkm} (s'at)_{ij}(VV')_{jk}(t'bs)_{km}(UU')_{mi}$$

$$= E\sum_{ijkm} (s'at)_{ij}V_jV_k\ (t'bs)_{km}U_mU_i$$

$$= \sum_{ijkm} (s'at)_{ij}E(V_jV_k)(t'bs)_{km}E(U_mU_i)$$

$$= \sum_{ijkm} (s'at)_{ij}\delta_{jk}y_k(t'bs)_{km}\delta_{mi}x_i = \sum_{jm} (s'at)_{mj}y_j(t'bs)_{jm}x_m = \mathrm{tr}(awbv),$$

by the fourth formula marked with an asterisk.

Similarly, the first member of (21) equals

$$E(X'aYX'bY) = E(U's'atVU's'btV) = E\ tr[(s'at)(VU')(s'bt)(VU')]$$

$$= E \sum_{ijkm} (s'at)_{ij}(VU')_{jk}(s'bt)_{km}(VU')_{mi}$$

$$= E \sum_{ijkm} (s'at)_{ij} V_j U_k (s'bt)_{km} V_m U_i$$

$$= \sum_{ijkm} (s'at)_{ij}(s'bt)_{km} E(U_i U_k) E(V_j V_m)$$

$$= \sum_{ijkm} (s'at)_{ij}(s'bt)_{km}\delta_{ik}x_i\delta_{jm}y_m = \sum_{ij} (s'at)_{ij}(s'bt)_{ij}x_i y_j$$

$$= \sum_{ij} (t'a's)_{ji}x_i(s'bt)_{ij}y_j = tr(a'vbw),$$

by the last formula marked with an asterisk •

Theorem 14

Let $(X_1)_{n\times 1}$,..., $(X_{k^\circ})_{n\times 1}$ be independent centered zero-excess vectors. Then, for any scalar matrices $a_{n\times n}$ and $b_{n\times n}$, and all values of the subscripts $i,j,k,m \in \{1,...,k^\circ\}$,

$$E(X_i'aX_jX_k'bX_m)$$

$$= \delta_{ij}\delta_{km}tr(av_i)tr(bv_k) + \delta_{ik}\delta_{jm}tr(a'v_ibv_j) + \delta_{im}\delta_{jk}tr(bv_iav_j), \quad (24)$$

where

$$v_i := Cov\ X_i\ .$$

Proof

For fixed subscripts i,j,k,m, the following cases can occur

(i=j=k=m) , (i=j≠k=m) , (i=k≠j=m) , (i=m≠j=k) , other cases.

The other cases, hereafter denoted by "other" are:

– three of the subscripts are equal, the fourth is different
– the four subscripts are different

Then

$$1 = 1_{i=j=k=m} + 1_{i=j\neq k=m} + 1_{i=k\neq j=m} + 1_{i=m\neq j=k} + 1_{other}\,,$$

and

$$E(X_i'aX_jX_k'bX_m) = E_1 + E_2 + E_3 + E_4 + E_5\,,$$

with

$$E_1 := E(X_i'aX_jX_k'bX_m)\, 1_{i=j=k=m}$$

$$= 1_{i=j=k=m}[tr(av_i)tr(bv_i) + tr(av_ibv_i) + tr(a'v_ibv_i)],$$

$$E_2 := E(X_i'aX_jX_k'bX_m)\, 1_{i=j\neq k=m} = 1_{i=j\neq k=m}E(X_i'aX_i)E(X_k'bX_k)$$

$$= 1_{i=j\neq k=m}\, tr(av_i)tr(bv_k),$$

$$E_3 := E(X_i'aX_jX_k'bX_m)\, 1_{i=k\neq j=m} = 1_{i=k\neq j=m}\, tr(a'v_ibv_j),$$

$$E_4 := E(X_i'aX_jX_k'bX_m)\, 1_{i=m\neq j=k} = 1_{i=m\neq j=k}\, tr(av_jbv_i),$$

$$E_5 := E(X_i'aX_jX_k'bX_m)\, 1_{other} = 0,$$

by Theorem 12 and Theorem 13. But

$$1_{i=j\neq k=m} = \delta_{ij}\delta_{km} - 1_{i=j=k=m},$$

$$1_{i=k\neq j=m} = \delta_{ik}\delta_{jm} - 1_{i=j=k=m},$$

$$1_{i=m\neq j=k} = \delta_{im}\delta_{jk} - 1_{i=j=k=m}$$

and then

$$E_2 = \delta_{ij}\delta_{km}\, tr(av_i)tr(bv_k) - 1_{i=j=k=m}\, tr(av_i)tr(bv_k),$$

$$E_3 = \delta_{ik}\delta_{jm}\, tr(a'v_ibv_j) - 1_{i=j=k=m}\, tr(a'v_ibv_j),$$

$$E_4 = \delta_{im}\delta_{jk}\, tr(av_jbv_i) - 1_{i=j=k=m}\, tr(av_jbv_i).$$

Then the sum $E_1+E_2+E_3+E_4+E_5$ furnishes the announced expression •

Chapter 5

Classical Regression Models

5.1. Deterministic Regression

5.1.1. Problem

Introduction: particular problems

We look for the straight line "closest" to the points

$$(1,x_1)\,,\,(2,x_2)\,,\,\ldots\,,\,(n,x_n)$$

in

$$\mathbf{R}^2 = \{(\eta,\xi)/\ \eta,\xi\in\mathbf{R}\}.$$

(In this Chapter, $\mathbf{R}^m$ is a space of rows and $\mathbf{R}_m$ a space of columns). Let the equation of the unknown line be $\xi = b_1 + \eta b_2$. Then the unknown quantities are b_1 and b_2 and we want that

$$\begin{aligned} x_1 &\approx b_1 + 1.b_2 \\ x_2 &\approx b_1 + 2.b_2 \\ \ldots &\quad \ldots \quad \ldots \\ x_n &\approx b_1 + n.b_n \end{aligned}$$

These relations can be displayed as

$$x_{n\times 1} \approx y_{n\times 2}\, b_{2\times n}\,, \tag{1}$$

where

$$x := (x_1,\ldots,x_n)' \quad , \quad b := (b_1,b_2)'$$

and where y is the matrix

$$\begin{bmatrix} 1 & 1 \\ 1 & 2 \\ \ldots & \ldots \\ 1 & n \end{bmatrix}$$

The unknown vector b is a point in $\mathbf{R}_2$, and x and yb are points in $\mathbf{R}_n$. Now we can formulate the problem more precisely:

Find the point $b \in \mathbf{R}_2$ such that yb is closest to x in $\mathbf{R}_n$.

But the formulation is not yet complete, because we still have to explain how distances are measured in $\mathbf{R}_n$. By Ch.4.5.1, we can consider any definite positive matrix $p_{n\times n}$, and then define the distance function $d(\cdot,\cdot)$ to be that one resulting from the scalar product

$$<x,z> = x'pz \quad (x,z \in \mathbf{R}_n), \tag{2}$$

i.e.

$$d(x,z) := <x-z,x-z>^{1/2} = [(x-z)'p(x-z)]^{1/2}. \tag{3}$$

The usual distance corresponds to $p := 1_{n\times n}$. It is the adopted matrix if nothing else is specified.

Our problem is a **deterministic linear regression problem.** It is **deterministic** because no random variables are involved. It is a **linear problem** because yb is linear in the unknown vector b.

Although parabolas are considered in the following problem, instead of straight lines, it is also a linear problem. Now we look for the parabola

$$\xi = b_1 + \eta b_2 + \eta^2 b_3$$

closest to the points (k,x_k) $(k=1,\ldots,n)$. Here we want

$$\begin{aligned} x_1 &\approx b_1 + 1b_2 + 1^2 b_3 \\ x_2 &\approx b_1 + 2b_2 + 2^2 b_3 \\ &\cdots \quad \cdots \quad \cdots \quad \cdots \quad \cdots \\ x_n &\approx b_1 + nb_2 + n^2 b_3 \end{aligned}$$

i.e.

$$x_{n\times 1} \approx y_{n\times 3}\, b_{3\times 1}.$$

Here

$$x := (x_1,\ldots,x_n)' \quad , \quad b := (b_1,b_2,b_3)'$$

and y is the matrix

$$\begin{bmatrix} 1 & 1 & 1^2 \\ 1 & 2 & 2^2 \\ \cdots & \cdots & \cdots \\ 1 & n & n^2 \end{bmatrix}$$

Here, the precise problem is the determination of the point $b \in \mathbf{R}_3$ such that yb is closest to x in the space $\mathbf{R}_n$ in which distances are defined by (3).

General problem

Let $x_{n\times 1}$ be a fixed vector, and $y_{n\times m}$ a fixed matrix. Then the general problem is to find the vector $b_{m\times 1}$ such that yb is closes to x in the space $\mathbf{R}_n(p)$.

Usual assumptions

$m \leq n$ and the the **design matrix** $y_{n\times m}$ is of full rank m.

Rank of a matrix

We recall that the **rank of a matrix** is the dimension of the linear space generated by its rows, or the dimension of the linear space generated by its columns. These dimensions are equal.

An equivalent definition, adopted in App.D, is the following: The **rank of the matrix** c is the largest number k such that c contains an invertible sub-matrix with dimensions $k\times k$.

If the dimensions of the matrix c are $m\times n$, then the rank of c can be $m\wedge n$ at most. A **matrix of full rank** is a matrix of dimensions $m\times n$ and rank $m\wedge n$.

Let $p_{n\times n}$ be definite positive and let $y_{n\times m}$ be a matrix of full rank $m\leq n$. Then $(y'py)_{m\times m}$ is a definite positive matrix. Hence $y'py$ is invertible.

Indeed, let $x_{m\times 1}$ be any column of length m. Then

$$x'(y'py)x = (yx)'p(yx) \geq 0,$$

because p is semidefinite positive. Let us assume now that the latter inequality is an equality. Then yx=0 because p is definite positive. Let $a_{m\times m}$ be an invertible submatrix of y. Then the relation yx=0 implies that ax=0, and then x=0. Hence $(y'py)$ is definite positive. All definite positive matrices are invertible.

5.1.2. Solution of General Problem

The **general problem** stated in the foregoing section is easily solved by a projection technique. The set

$$\boldsymbol{P} := \{y_{n\times m}b_{m\times 1} \,/\, b\in\mathbf{R}_m\}$$

is a plane through the origin of $\mathbf{R}_n$. Let $c{:=}\text{Proj}(x_{n\times 1}/\boldsymbol{P})$. Then $c=yb$ for some point $b\in\mathbf{R}_m$ and then b is the solution. Under the usual assumptions, the point b is unique. It is furnished by the following Theorem.

Theorem 1

Under the usual assumptions, the solution $b_{m\times 1}$ of the deterministic regression problem defined by the vector $x_{n\times 1}$, the design matrix $y_{n\times m}$ and the definite positive matrix $p_{n\times n}$ (defining the scalar product in $\mathbf{R}_n$) is

$$\mathbf{b = (y'py)^{-1}y'px.}$$

Proof
Rather than to prove that the indicated solution is correct, it is more instructive to find it. The vector b is such that for all $z\in\mathbf{R}_m$,

$$x - yb \perp yz \ , \ \langle x{-}yb, yz\rangle = 0 \ , \ (yz)'p(x{-}yb) = 0 \ , \ z'[y'p(x{-}yb)] = 0.$$

Then

$$y'p(x{-}yb) = 0 \ , \ y'px = (y'py)b \ , \ b = (y'py)^{-1}y'px \ \bullet$$

5.2. Regression Model with One Observable Random Vector

5.2.1. Definition of the Model

The model considered here is defined by the non-degenerated **observable random vector** $X\in\boldsymbol{L}_{2,n}$ satisfying the relations

$$EX = yb \ , \ \text{Cov}\, X = \sigma^2 v, \tag{4}$$

where $y_{n\times m}$ is a known **design matrix** of full rank m<n, $v_{n\times n}$ is a known definite positive matrix, $b_{m\times 1}$ is an unknown column, and σ^2 is an unknown strictly positive scalar.

5.2.2. Estimation of b

Classical estimator of b

The **classical estimator of b** is

$$B := (y'v^{-1}y)^{-1}y'v^{-1}X. \tag{5}$$

The existence of the matrix $(y'v^{-1}y)^{-1}$ results from the assumptions. Indeed, the matrix v is invertible because v is definite positive. **The matrix v^{-1} is definite positive**. Indeed, v = s′s for some matrix $s_{n\times n}$. Then

$$0 \neq \det(v) = \det(s')\det(s),$$

$$\det(s) = \det(s') \neq 0.$$

This implies that s and s′ are invertible , and that

$$v^{-1} = s^{-1}s'^{-1} = t't \ , \ \text{where } t := s'^{-1} = s^{-1\prime}.$$

From v^{-1}= t′t results that v^{-1} is semidefinite positive, and then v^{-1} is definite positive because it is invertible. By 5.1.1, **the matrix $(y'v^{-1}y)$ is definite positive**, hence invertible.

Strongly unbiased estimators of b

We say that any estimator of b is **strongly unbiased** (in the considered model) if it can be displayed as aX, where $a_{m\times n}$ is such that $a_{m\times n}y_{n\times m}=1_{m\times m}$. If aX is strongly unbiased, then E(aX)=a.EX=ayb=b. Hence **strongly unbiased estimators are unbiased estimators of b**. The classical estimator B is a strongly unbiased estimator of b.

We represent by $\boldsymbol{B}_{str}$ the set of strongly unbiased estimators of b. Affine combinations of strongly unbiased estimators of b, are strongly unbiased estimators of b. Hence, **$\boldsymbol{B}_{str}$ is a plane in $\boldsymbol{L}_{2,m}$** .

The plane $\boldsymbol{B}_{str}$ is a sub-plane of the plane $\{cX/c\in\mathbf{R}_{m\times n}\}$ through the origin. The latter is a linear space with dimension mn at most: **$\boldsymbol{B}_{str}$ is a finite-dimensional plane**.

Although this is irrelevant for the sequel, we here explain how the strongly unbiased estimators of b can be obtained. In order to simplify the discussion, we assume that the sub-matrix $(y_1)_{m\times m}$ of y, formed by the m first rows of y, is invertible. We denote by $(y_2)_{(n-m)\times m}$ the submatrix of y formed by the n–m last rows of y. We consider a corresponding partition of the matrix $a_{m\times n}$ occurring in the strongly unbiased estimator aX. We denote by $(a_1)_{m\times m}$ the submatrix of $a_{m\times n}$ formed by the m first columns of $a_{m\times n}$ and by $(a_2)_{m\times(n-m)}$ the submatrix formed by the n–m last columns. Then

$$1_{m\times m} = ay = a_1y_1 + a_2y_2,$$

because matrices can be multiplied by blocks. Then

$$a_1y_1 = 1-a_2y_2,$$

$$a_1 = (1-a_2y_2)y_2^{-1}.$$

In the latter relation, the (n–m)m elements of a_2 can be chosen arbitrarily.

The optimality of the classical estimator B results from the following Theorem, in which $p_{m\times m}$ is the definite positive matrix defining the scalar product in $\boldsymbol{L}_{2,m}$. This matrix is necessary for the complete definition of Hilbert space $\boldsymbol{L}_{2,m}(p)$, but the projection B of b on $\boldsymbol{B}_{str}$ does not depend on p.

Theorem 2 (Gauss-Markov)

In the regression model with one observable vector defined by the relations (4),

$$\mathbf{B = Proj(b/\boldsymbol{B}_{str})\ \text{in}\ \boldsymbol{L}_{2,m}(p), \text{independently of p.}}$$

Proof

We have to verify that

$$B-b \perp B_1-B_2 \ (B_1,B_2\in\boldsymbol{B}_{str}).$$

Let

$$B_1 = a_1X\ ,\ B_2 = a_2X\ ,\ a_1y = 1\ ,\ a_2y = 1\ ,\ c := a_1-a_2.$$

Then

$$B_1-B_2 = cX\ ,\ cy=0\ ,$$

and it is enough to verify that

$$B-b \perp cX \quad , \text{ or } <B-b,cX> = 0 \quad , \text{ or } E[(cX)'p(B-b)]=0.$$

The first member of the latter relation equals

$$E(X'c'pB^\circ) = E(X'^\circ c'pB^\circ)$$
$$= E\ tr(X'^\circ c'pB^\circ) = E\ tr(B^\circ X'^\circ c'p)$$
$$= tr\ E(B^\circ X'^\circ c'p) = tr\ E[(y'v^{-1}y)^{-1}y'v^{-1}X^\circ X'^\circ c'p)]$$
$$= tr\ [y'v^{-1}y)^{-1}y'v^{-1}E(X^\circ X'^\circ)c'p]$$
$$= \sigma^2\ tr[y'v^{-1}y)^{-1}y'v^{-1}vc'p] = \sigma^2\ tr[y'v^{-1}y)^{-1}y'c'p]$$
$$=\sigma^2\ tr[y'v^{-1}y)^{-1}(cy)'p] = \sigma^2\ tr[y'v^{-1}y)^{-1}0p] = 0 \quad \bullet$$

Remark

In the proof of Theorem 2, we can regard v as a definition of Cov X and drop the factor σ^2. This means that the result is in fact not based on the last relation (4), Cov X = σ^2v.

The **Gauss-Markov formula**,

$$Proj(b/\boldsymbol{B}_{str}) = [y'(Cov\ X)^{-1}y]^{-1}y'(Cov\ X)^{-1}X \text{ in } \boldsymbol{L}_{2,m}(p). \qquad (6)$$

is valid, under the usual integrability, rank and non-degeneracy conditions, provided only EX = yb.

5.2.3. Estimation of σ^2

Classical estimator of σ^2

The **classical estimator of σ^2** is

$$S^2 := {}^1/_{(n-m)}\ (X-yB)'v^{-1}(X-yB). \qquad (7)$$

Then

$$S^2 := {}^1/_{(n-m)}\ (X^\circ-yB^\circ)'v^{-1}(X^\circ-yB^\circ). \qquad (8)$$

By the expression (5) of B,

$$S^2 = 1/(n-m)\, X^{\circ\prime} c X^{\circ}\,, \tag{9}$$

where

$$c_{n\times n} := v^{-1} - v^{-1}y(y'v^{-1}y)^{-1}y'v^{-1}\,.$$

By Ch.4.6.2.(18),

$$E(X^{\circ\prime}cX^{\circ}) = \sigma^2\, tr(cv) = \sigma^2\,[tr(1_{n\times n}) - tr[v^{-1}y(y'v^{-1}y)^{-1}y']]$$

$$= \sigma^2\,[tr(1_{n\times n}) - tr[y'v^{-1}y(y'v^{-1}y)^{-1}]] = \sigma^2\,[tr(1_{n\times n}) - tr(1_{m\times m})] = \sigma^2(n-m). \tag{10}$$

Hence, **S^2 is an unbiased estimator of σ^2**.

Strongly centered vectors

We say that any random vector $Y_{k\times 1}$ is **strongly centered** (in the considered model) if it can be displayed as Y=aX, where the matrix $a_{k\times n}$ is such that $a_{k\times n}y_{n\times m}=0_{k\times m}$. Then $Y=aX^{\circ}$, because

$$Y = aX = aX - ayb = a(X\text{-}yb) = aX^{\circ}.$$

If $Y_{k\times 1}=a_{k\times n}X_{n\times 1}$ is strongly centered, then $s_{j\times k}Y_{k\times 1}$ is strongly centered because the latter vector equals (sa)X , where (sa)y = s(ay)=0.

The family of strongly centered vectors is a plane through the origin of $\boldsymbol{L}_{2,n}$.

Strongly centered vectors can be obtained as follows. The relation

$$a_{k\times n}y_{n\times m} = 0_{k\times m}$$

is equivalent to the k relations

$$a_i y = 0 \;(i=1,\dots,k),$$

where a_i is the row i of the matrix $a_{k\times n}$. Hence, the rows of $a_{k\times n}$ may be any solutions $s_{1\times n}$ of the matrix equation sy=o. The space of solutions of this equation is a linear space with dimensions n–m, and the k rows of $a_{k\times n}$ can be chosen arbitrarily in this space.

An example of a strongly centered vector is

$$Y := X - yB = [1 - y(y'v^{-1}y)^{-1}y'v^{-1}]X.$$

The matrix v^{-1} in the last member of (7) is definite positive. It can be displayed as $v=s's$. Let

$$Z := [1/(n-m)]^{1/2}\, sY.$$

Then Z is strongly centered, and by (7), $S^2=Z'Z$.

Theorem 3

In the regression model with one observable vector defined by the relations (4), let

$$\mathbf{Y}_{k\times 1} = \mathbf{a}_{k\times n}\mathbf{X}_{n\times 1} \quad , \quad \mathbf{Z}_{k\times 1} = \mathbf{b}_{k\times n}\mathbf{X}_{n\times 1} \, ,$$

be strongly centered vectors. Then

$$\mathbf{E(Y'Z) = tr(a'bv)}\, \boldsymbol{\sigma^2}. \tag{11}$$

Proof
Because of the strong centering, $Y=aX^\circ$ and $Z=bX^\circ$. Then, by 16.6.2.(18),

$$E(Y'Z) = E(X^{\circ\prime}a'bX^\circ) = tr(a'bv)\, \sigma^2 \;\bullet$$

Hence, if $tr(a'bv)\neq 0$, then

$$1/tr(a'bv)\; Y'Z$$

is an unbiased estimator of σ^2.

We represent by $\boldsymbol{S}_{str}$ the family of random variables $Y'Z$, where $Y_{k\times 1}$ and $Z_{k\times 1}$ are strongly centered vectors of any length k. The classical estimator S^2 is a particular point of $\boldsymbol{S}_{str}$, by the discussion preceding Theorem 3.

The random variables of $\boldsymbol{S}_{str}$ are linear combinations of the n^2 products X_iX_j (i,j=1,...,n). Hence, they are integrable.

If the components of X have a finite fourth-order moment, then $\boldsymbol{S}_{str}$ is a subset of $\boldsymbol{L}_2$ and then the plane through the origin $\boldsymbol{P}(\boldsymbol{S}_{str})$ generated by $\boldsymbol{S}_{str}$ in $\boldsymbol{L}_2$ is finite-dimensional. Its dimension is n^2 at most.

By the following Theorem, the classical estimator S^2 is the optimal (unbiased and of minimum variance) estimator of σ^2 in the family $\boldsymbol{P}(\boldsymbol{S}_{str})$ when the observable vector X is a zero-excess vector.

Theorem 4

In the regression model defined by the relations (4), let us assume that the observable vector X is a zero-excess vector. Then

$$\mathbf{S^2 = Proj[\sigma^2/\boldsymbol{P}_{\sigma^2}(\boldsymbol{S}_{str})] \ \ in\ \boldsymbol{L}_2.}$$

Proof

We start with the proof of the relation

$$E(S^2Y'Z) = (n-m+2)/(n-m)\ tr(a'bv)\ \sigma^4, \tag{12}$$

where Y and Z are the strongly centered vectors considered in Theorem 3. Because of the strong centering, Y=aX°, Z=bX°. By (9) and Ch.4.(20), and because c is symmetric,

$$(n-m)\sigma^{-4}\ E(S^2Y'Z) = \sigma^{-4}\ E(X°'cX°X°'a'bX°)$$

$$= tr(cv)tr(a'bv) + 2tr(cva'bv).$$

Here

$$tr(cv) = n-m,$$

by (10), and

$$tr(cva'bv) = tr(a'bv) - tr[v^{-1}y(y'v^{-1}y)^{-1}.y'a'.bv],$$

where the latter trace is zero because Y is strongly centered. Indeed,

$$y'a' = (ay)'=0.$$

This proves (12).

We now apply Ch.4.Th.7. S^2 belongs to $\boldsymbol{P}_{\sigma^2}(\boldsymbol{S}_{str})$ because $S^2 \in \boldsymbol{S}_{str}$ and $ES^2=\sigma^2$. Hence, it is enough to verify that

$$E(S^2S_1)E(S_2) = E(S^2S_2)E(S_1)\ \ (S_1,S_2 \in \boldsymbol{S}_{str}). \tag{13}$$

Let

$$S_1 = Y_1'Z_1\ ,\ Y_1 = a_1X\ ,\ Z_1 = b_1X\ ,\ a_1y = 0\ ,\ b_1y = 0,$$

$$S_2 = Y_2'Z_2\ ,\ Y_1 = a_2X\ ,\ Z_1 = b_2X\ ,\ a_2y = 0\ ,\ b_2y = 0.$$

By (11), (12),

$$(n-m)\ E(S^2S_1)E(S_2)$$

$$= (n-m)E(S^2Y_1'Z_1)E(Y_2'Z_2)$$

$$= (n-m+2)tr(a_1'b_1v)\sigma^4.tr(a_2'b_2v)\sigma^2.$$

This implies (13) by symmetry •

In the regression model defined by the relations (4), let us assume that the observable vector X is a zero-excess vector. Then

$$\textbf{Var } S^2 = 2/_{(n-m)}\, \sigma^4 .$$

Indeed,

$$\text{Var } S^2 = ES^4 - E^2S^2 = ES^4 - \sigma^4 ,$$

By (9) and Ch.4.(20),

$$(n-m)^2ES^4 = E(X^{\circ\prime}cX^\circ X^{\circ\prime}cX^\circ) = \sigma^4\, tr(cv)tr(cv) + 2\sigma^4 tr(cvcv),$$

where tr(cv)=n–m by (10), and

$$tr(cvcv) = tr(1-v^{-1}yuy')^2 \text{ , where } u_{m\times m} := (y'v^{-1}y)^{-1} .$$

Hence

$$tr(cvcv) = tr(1_{n\times n} - 2\, v^{-1}yuy' + v^{-1}yu.y'v^{-1}yu.y')$$

$$= tr(1_{n\times n} - 2\, v^{-1}yuy' + v^{-1}yuy') = n - tr(v^{-1}yuy')$$

$$= n - tr(y'v^{-1}yu) = n - tr\, 1_{m\times m} = n-m.$$

Then

$$(n-m)^2ES^4 = \sigma^4[(n-m)^2+2(n-m)],$$

$$ES^4 = [1 + 2/_{(n-m)}]\sigma^4.$$

5.3. General Model with Several Observable Random Vectors

5.3.1. Assumptions

Here we consider a general (yet incomplete) model defined by k° independent non-degenerated observable random vectors

$$(X_1)_{n\times 1} , (X_2)_{n\times 1} , \dots , (X_{k^\circ})_{n\times 1} \tag{14}$$

with square-integrable components, such that

$$EX_k = \mu_{n\times 1} \quad (k=1,\dots,k^\circ). \tag{15}$$

Hereafter, the subscripts i,j,k,m range over the set $\{1,2,...,k°\}$.

We denote

$$(v_k)_{n\times n} := \text{Cov } X_k \tag{16}$$

The particular Models I, II and III, later considered, are specified by assumptions on the invertible matrices $(v_k)_{n\times n}$.

No regression assumption occurs in the model considered here, or in the Models I, II and III hereafter defined. But, as indicated in the following section 5.3.2, they can be treated as regression models, and their study is based on the regression model of 5.2.

We do not consider rather direct generalizations (models with observable random vectors of different length or models with regression assumption on the observable vectors), because such generalizations are not used in the following chapter on Credibility Theory.

5.3.2. Associated Regression Model

Matrices partitioned in blocks

It is convenient to work with matrices partitioned in submatrices, called **blocks**. In particular

$$\text{Column}(a_1,...a_s)$$

is the matrix with the blocks $a_1,...,a_s$ displayed on a vertical line, in the indicated order. It is assumed, when that notation is used, that all the blocks have the same number of columns.

$$\text{Row}(a_1,...,a_s)$$

is the matrix with the blocks $a_1,...,a_s$ displayed on a horizontal line, in the indicated order. It is assumed, when that notation is used, that all the blocks have the same number of rows.

$$\text{Diagonal}(a_1,...,a_s)$$

is the matrix with the blocks $a_1,...,a_s$ on a descending diagonal line, in the indicated order. It is assumed, when that notation is used, that all the blocks are square matrices.

Matrices can be multiplied by blocks, provided the products of the involved blocks are defined.

Matrices can also be inverted by blocks. The formula

$$[\text{Diagonal}(a_1,\dots,a_s)]^{-1} = \text{Diagonal}(a_1^{-1},\dots,a_s^{-1})$$

is valid, if the inverse matrices in the last member do exist.

Associated regression model

Let

$$X_{nk°\times 1} := \text{Column}(X_1,X_2,\dots,X_{k°}),$$

$$y_{nk°\times n} := \text{Column}(1_{n\times n},\ 1_{n\times n},\dots,1_{n\times n}),$$

$$v_{nk°\times nk°} := \text{Diagonal}(v_1,\ v_2,\dots,v_{k°}).$$

Then

$$EX_{nk°\times 1} = y_{nk°\times n}\,\mu_{n\times 1}\quad,\ \text{Cov } X = v_{nk°\times nk°}\ . \tag{17}$$

5.3.3. Strongly Unbiased Estimators of μ

We now apply the definitions introduced in 5.2 to the model (17). A **strongly unbiased estimator of μ** is an estimator aX, with

$$a_{n\times nk°}\, y_{nk°\times n} = 1_{n\times n}.$$

Let

$$a = \text{row}(a_1,\dots,a_{k°})$$

be the partition of $a_{n\times nk°}$ in k° blocks with n columns. Then

$$aX = a_1X_1 + \dots + a_{k°}X_{k°},$$

$$ay = a_1 1_{n\times n} + \dots + a_{k°}1_{n\times n} = a_1 + \dots + a_{k°} = a_\Sigma.$$

Hence, **the strongly unbiased estimators of μ are**

$$\textstyle\sum_k a_k X_k \tag{18}$$

where $(a_k)_{n\times n}$ are matrices such that $a_\Sigma = 1_{n\times n}$.

We represent by $\boldsymbol{M}_{str}$ the plane in $\boldsymbol{L}_{2,n}$ of strongly unbiased estimators of μ.

From the Gauss-Markov formula (6) results that

$$\mathrm{Proj}(\mu/\boldsymbol{M}_{str}) = [y'(\mathrm{Cov}\ X)^{-1}y]^{-1}y'(\mathrm{Cov}\ X)^{-1}X \ \text{ in } \boldsymbol{L}_{2,n}(p).$$

Here

$$(\mathrm{Cov}\ X)^{-1} = [\mathrm{Diagonal}(v_1,\ldots,v_{k^\circ})]^{-1} = \mathrm{Diagonal}(v_1^{-1},\ldots,v_{k^\circ}^{-1}),$$

$$y'(\mathrm{Cov}\ X)^{-1}y = \textstyle\sum_k 1_{n\times n}\, v_k^{-1}\, 1_{n\times n} = \sum_k v_k^{-1},$$

$$y'(\mathrm{Cov}\ X)^{-1}X = \textstyle\sum_k 1_{n\times n}\, v_k^{-1}X_k = \sum_k v_k^{-1}X_k.$$

Hence,

$$\mathrm{Proj}(\mu/\boldsymbol{M}_{str}) = [\textstyle\sum_k v_k^{-1}]^{-1}\sum_k v_k^{-1}X_k \ \text{ in } \boldsymbol{L}_{2,n}(p). \tag{19}$$

This relation will furnish an optimal estimator for μ in Model I and in Model II. In Model III, (19) furnishes an optimal pseudo-estimator.

5.3.4. The Zero-Excess Assumption

The **zero-excess assumption** is that the vectors $X_1,\ldots,X_{k^\circ}$ are zero-excess vectors. This assumption is mentioned explicitly, whenever it is used. It implies that X is a zero-excess vector. Indeed, let

$$(X_k)_{n\times 1} = (s_k)_{n\times n}\,(Z_k)_{n\times 1}\,,$$

where $Z_1,\ldots,Z_{k^\circ}$ are basic zero-excess vectors. Let

$$s_{nk^\circ\times nk^\circ} := \mathrm{Diagonal}(s_1,\ldots,s_{k^\circ}),$$

$$Z_{nk^\circ\times 1} := \mathrm{Column}(Z_1,\ldots,Z_{k^\circ}). \tag{20}$$

Then

$$X_{nk^\circ\times 1} = s_{nk^\circ\times nk^\circ}\, Z_{nk^\circ\times 1}.$$

The independence of the vectors $Z_1,\ldots,Z_{k^\circ}$ results from the non-degeneracy and independence of the vectors $X_1,\ldots,X_{k^\circ}$. From the fact that $Z_1,\ldots,Z_{k^\circ}$ are independent basic zero-excess vectors results that Z is a basic zero-excess vector, by the following Remark. Then, from X=sZ results that **X is a zero-excess vector**.

Remark

Let $Z_1,...,Z_{k^\circ}$ be independent basic zero-excess vectors. Then the vector Z:= Column($Z_1,...,Z_{k^\circ}$) is a basic zero-excess vector.

Indeed, for the simplicity of the notations we assume that all vectors Z_k have the same length n. This is the case for Z defined by (20). We also assume that the vectors Z_k are centered already. Hereafter

$$i,j,k,m \in \{1,...,k^\circ\} \text{ and } p,q,r,s \in \{1,...,n\}.$$

The components of Z_k are denoted by Z_{ks}. The value of $\delta_{ip,jq}$ is 1 if i=j and p=q. It is 0 in all other cases.

Then the relations Ch.4.(15),(16), defining the basic zero-excess, are

$$E(Z_{ip}Z_{jq}) = \delta_{ip,jq}\, u_{ip}, \tag{21}$$

$$E(Z_{ip}Z_{jq}Z_{kr}Z_{ms})$$

$$= \delta_{ip,jq}\delta_{kr,ms}u_{ip}u_{kr} + \delta_{ip,kr}\delta_{jq,ms}u_{ip}u_{jq} + \delta_{ip,ms}\delta_{jq,kr}u_{ip}u_{jq}, \tag{22}$$

where

$$u_{ip} := \text{Var } Z_{ip} = E(Z_{ip})^2.$$

For i=j (21) is exact because Z_i is a basic zero-excess vector. Let i≠j. Then the last member of (21) equals 0. The first equals 0 because

$$E(Z_{ip}Z_{jq}) = EZ_{ip}.EZ_{jq} = 0.0,$$

by the independence of Z_i and Z_j. Hence (21) is correct.

Let us now verify (22). We consider the following cases.

Case i=j=k=m.

Then (22) is true because Z_i is a basic zero excess vector.

Case i=j≠k=m.

Then (22) becomes

$$E(Z_{ip}Z_{iq}Z_{kr}Z_{ks}) = \delta_{ip,iq}\delta_{kr,ks}u_{ip}u_{kr}$$

This relation is correct, because the first member equals

$$E(Z_{ip}Z_{iq})\ E(Z_{kr}Z_{ks}) = \delta_{ip,iq}u_{ip}\ \delta_{kr,ks}u_{kr}\ ,$$

by the independence of Z_i and Z_k , and by (21).

Cases resulting from a permutation of i,j,k,m in i=j≠k=m.

Then (22) is correct by symmetry.

Cases with 3 or 4 different subscripts i,j,km.

Then (22) becomes 0=0, because of the factorizations in the first member allowed by the independence of $Z_1,\ldots,Z_{k°}$.

5.4. Model I with Several Random Vectors

5.4.1. Definition of Model I

We here consider the model defined by k° independent non-degenerated observable random vectors

$$(X_1)_{n\times 1}\ ,\ (X_2)_{n\times 1}\ ,\ \ldots\ ,\ (X_{k°})_{n\times 1} \tag{23}$$

with square-integrable components, such that

$$EX_k = \mu_{n\times 1}\ ,\ \ v_k := \mathrm{Cov}\ X_k = \sigma^2 w_k^{-1}\ \ (k=1,\ldots,k°). \tag{24}$$

μ is an unknown vector, σ^2 an unknown scalar and $(w_k)_{n\times n}$ are known definite positive matrices, called **matrix weights**. The problem is the estimation of μ and σ^2.

5.4.2. Estimation of μ

The **classical estimator of** μ is

$$(X_W)_{n\times 1} := w_\Sigma^{-1}\ \textstyle\sum_k w_k X_k. \tag{25}$$

It is the estimator resulting from the replacement of $v_k$by $\sigma^2 w_k^{-1}$ in the last member of (19). Hence,

$$X_W = \mathrm{Proj}(\mu/\boldsymbol{M}_{str})\ \text{ in } \boldsymbol{L}_{2,n}(p). \tag{26}$$

This relation indicates the optimal character of X_W.

5.4.3. Estimation of σ^2

Classical estimator of σ^2

The **classical estimator of σ^2** is

$$S^2 := 1/_{n(k^\circ-1)} \Sigma_k (X_k - X_W)' w_k (X_k - X_W). \quad (27)$$

Associated regression model

The regression model (17) associated to Model I, is defined by the relations

$$EX = y\mu \quad , \quad \text{Cov } X = \sigma^2 u, \quad (28)$$

where

$$u := \text{Diagonal}(w_1^{-1}, \ldots, w_{k^\circ}^{-1}).$$

The classical estimator of σ^2 in that regression model equals

$$1/_{(nk^\circ-n)} (X - yX_W)' u^{-1} (X - yX_W)$$

$$= 1/_{(nk^\circ-n)} (X - yX_W) u^{-1} (X - yX_W)$$

$$= 1/_{(nk^\circ-n)} \Sigma_k (X_k - 1_{n\times n} X_W)' w_k (X_k - 1_{n\times n} - X_W)$$

$$= 1/_{(nk^\circ-n)} \Sigma_k (X_k - X_W)' w_k (X_k - X_W) = S^2.$$

by (7) adapted to the model (28). Hence, the classical estimator of σ^2 in the regression model (28) is the estimator S^2 defined by (27).

Optimality of S^2 under the zero-excess assumption

By Theorem 4, adapted to model (28); the estimator S^2 has an optimal character, that we here clarify. By the definition of 5.2.3, here applied to model (28), a **strongly centered vector** of length r is a column $a_{r\times nk^\circ} X_{nk^\circ\times 1}$ such that

$$a_{r\times nk^\circ}\, y_{nk^\circ\times n} = 0_{r\times n}.$$

Let

$$a = \text{row}(a_1,\ldots,a_{k^\circ})$$

be the partition of $a_{r\times nk^\circ}$ in k° blocks with n columns. Then

$$aX = a_1X_1 + \ldots + a_{k^\circ}X_{k^\circ} \, ,$$

$$ay = a_1 1_{n\times n} + \ldots + a_{k^\circ} 1_{n\times n} = a_1 + \ldots + a_{k^\circ} = a_\Sigma \, .$$

Hence, **the strongly centered vectors of length r are the vectors**

$$\boldsymbol{\Sigma_k\, a_kX_k} \tag{29}$$

where $(a_k)_{r\times n}$ are matrices such that $a_\Sigma=0_{r\times n}$.

We denote by $\boldsymbol{S}_{str}$ the family of random variables Y′Z, where $Y_{r\times 1}$ and $Z_{r\times 1}$ are strongly centered vectors of any length r. Then, by Theorem 4, and by 5.3.4,

$$S^2 = \text{Proj}[\sigma^2/\boldsymbol{P}_{\sigma^2}(\boldsymbol{S}_{str})] \quad \text{in } \boldsymbol{L}_2 \tag{30}$$

if the observable vectors X_k are zero-excess vectors.

This relation implies that S^2 is the optimal (i.e. unbiased and of minimum variance) estimator of σ^2 in the family $\boldsymbol{P}(\boldsymbol{S}_{str})$, under the indicated assumptions.

5.5. Model II with Several Random Vectors

5.5.1. Definition of Model II

We here consider the model defined by k° independent non-degenerated observable random vectors

$$(X_1)_{n\times 1}\, ,\ (X_2)_{n\times 1}\, ,\ \ldots\, ,\ (X_{k^\circ})_{n\times 1} \tag{31}$$

with square-integrable components, such that

$$EX_k = \mu_{n\times 1} \;\; , \;\; \text{Cov}\, X_k \; = (1/w_k)v \;\; (k=1,\ldots,k^\circ). \tag{32}$$

Here $\mu_{n\times 1}$ is an unknown vector, $v_{n\times n}$ is an unknown definite positive matrix, and w_k are known strictly positive numbers, called **weights**. The problem is the estimation of μ and v.

5.5.2. Estimation of μ

The **classical estimator of μ** is

$$(X_W)_{n\times 1} := (1/w_\Sigma)\, \Sigma_k\, w_k X_k. \tag{33}$$

It is the estimator resulting from the replacement of v_k by $(1/w_k)v$ in the last member of (19). Hence,

$$X_W = \text{Proj}(\mu/\boldsymbol{M}_{str}) \text{ in } \boldsymbol{L}_{2,n}(p). \tag{34}$$

This relation indicates the optimal character of X_W.

5.5.3. Estimation of v

Classical estimator

The **classical estimator** of v is

$$V := {}^1\!/\!_{(k^\circ-1)}\, \Sigma_k\, w_k(X_k-X_W)(X_k-X_W)'. \tag{35}$$

Another expression for V is the double sum

$$V = [2(k^\circ-1)w_\Sigma]^{-1}\, \Sigma_{jk}\, w_j w_k\, (X_j-X_k)(X_j-X_k)'. \tag{36}$$

Indeed,

$$w_\Sigma(X_k-X_W) = w_\Sigma X_k - \Sigma_i w_i X_i = \Sigma_i w_i(X_k-X_i),$$

$$2(k^\circ-1)w_\Sigma{}^2 V = 2\, w_\Sigma{}^2\, \Sigma_k w_k(X_k-X_W)(X_k-X_w)'$$

$$= \Sigma_{ijk}\, w_i w_j w_k\, 2(X_k-X_i)(X_k-X_j)'.$$

By the symmetry of X_iX_j' as a function of (i,j), and by the dummy character of the summation subscripts, we may replace

$$2(X_k-X_i)(X_k-X_j)' = 2(X_kX_k'-X_iX_k'-X_jX_k'+X_iX_j')$$

by

$$2(X_kX_k'-X_jX_k'),$$

and then by

$$(X_kX_k'+X_jX_j'-X_jX_k'-X_kX_j').$$

Then

$$2(k^\circ-1)w_\Sigma^2 V = \textstyle\sum_{ijk} w_iw_jw_k(X_kX_k'+X_jX_j'-X_jX_k'-X_kX_j')$$

$$= w_\Sigma \textstyle\sum_{jk} w_jw_k (X_j-X_k)(X_j-X_k)'.$$

This proves (36). From this relation, it is easily verified that **V is an unbiased estimator of v**. Indeed,

$$2(k^\circ-1)w_\Sigma\, EV = \textstyle\sum_{jk} w_jw_k\, E[(X_j-X_k)(X_j-X_k)']$$

$$= \textstyle\sum_{jk} w_jw_k\, E[(X_j^\circ-X_k^\circ)(X_j^\circ-X_k^\circ)']$$

$$= \textstyle\sum_{jk} w_jw_k\, E(X_j^\circ X_j^{\circ\prime}-X_j^\circ X_k^{\circ\prime}-X_k^\circ X_j^{\circ\prime}+X_k^\circ X_k^{\circ\prime})$$

$$= 2\textstyle\sum_{jk} w_jw_k\, E(X_j^\circ X_j^{\circ\prime}-X_j^\circ X_k^{\circ\prime}) = 2\sum_{jk} w_jw_k[\mathrm{Var}\, X_j - \mathrm{Cov}(X_j,X_k)]$$

$$= 2\textstyle\sum_{jk} w_jw_k[w_j^{-1}v - \delta_{jk}w_j^{-1}v] = 2[k^\circ w_\Sigma\, v - w_\Sigma\, v] = 2(k^\circ-1)w_\Sigma\, v.$$

Optimality of V

We here define a **strongly centered vector with scalar coefficients**, as any linear combination

$$Y_{n\times 1} = \textstyle\sum_k a_kX_k\,, \text{ with } a_\Sigma = 1. \tag{37}$$

From (37) results that

$$Y = \textstyle\sum_k a_kX_k = \sum_k a_kX_k^\circ.$$

In order to test that some linear combination $\sum a_kX_k$ is strongly centered, it is sufficient to replace the vectors X_k by the scalar 1 and then the result must be 0. An example of a strongly centered vector with scalar coefficients is

$$X_i-X_W = w_\Sigma^{-1}\textstyle\sum_j w_j(X_i-X_j). \tag{38}$$

Let Y and Z be strongly centered vectors with scalar coefficients:

$$Y = \sum_i a_i X_i = \sum_i a_i X_i^\circ \,, \quad Z = \sum_j b_j X_j = \sum_j b_j X_j^\circ \,, \quad a_\Sigma = 0 \,, \quad b_\Sigma = 0.$$

Then

$$E(YZ') = \sum_{ij} a_i b_j \, E(X_i^\circ X_j^{\circ\prime}) = \sum_{ij} a_i b_j \, \mathrm{Cov}(X_i, X_j')$$

$$= \sum_{ij} a_i b_j \, \delta_{ij} \, \mathrm{Var}\, X_i = \sum_i a_i b_i \;\; \mathrm{Var}\, X_i = [\sum_i (a_i b_i / w_i)] \, v.$$

Hence, linear combinations of matrices such as YZ' can be used as unbiased estimators of v. By (32) and (35), the classical estimator V is such a linear combination. The following Theorem shows that, under the zero-excess assumption, V is the linear unbiased combination closest to v in $\boldsymbol{L}_{2,n\times n}(p,q)$, whatever the definite positive matrices $p_{n\times n}$ and $q_{n\times n}$ defining the scalar product in $\boldsymbol{L}_{2,n\times n}$ are.

We denote by $\boldsymbol{V}_{str}$ the family of matrices YZ' in $\boldsymbol{L}_{2,n\times n}$, where Y and Z are strongly unbiased vectors with scalar coefficients. The plane through the origin generated by this family, i.e. $\boldsymbol{P}(\boldsymbol{V}_{str})$ is finite-dimensional. Indeed, each of the n^2 components of any matrix in $\boldsymbol{P}(\boldsymbol{V}_{str})$ is a linear combination of products of two components of the vectors $X_1,\ldots,X_{k^\circ}$. Hence,

$$\dim[\boldsymbol{P}(\boldsymbol{V}_{str})] \le n^2 (k^\circ n)^2 \,.$$

The classical estimator V defined by (35) belongs to $\boldsymbol{P}(\boldsymbol{V}_{str})$ because the vectors (38) are stongly centered vectors with scalar coefficients. Each point in $\boldsymbol{P}(\boldsymbol{V}_{str})$ can be displayed as a linear combination

$$\sum_r c_r Y_r Z_r'$$

of matrices $Y_r Z_r'$, where Y_r and Z_r are strongly centered vectors with scalar coefficients. Then c_r can be incorporated in Y_r, i.e we can define the new Y_r by $c_r Y_r$. This new Y_r is still a strongly centered vector with scalar coefficients. Hence, the points of $\boldsymbol{P}(\boldsymbol{V}_{str})$ can be displayed as sums

$$\sum_r Y_r Z_r' . \tag{39}$$

of matrices $Y_r Z_r'$ in $\boldsymbol{V}_{str}$. Then **any difference $V_1 - V_2$ of points in $\boldsymbol{P}(\boldsymbol{V}_{str})$ can be displayed as a sum (39) of matrices $Y_r Z_r'$ in $\boldsymbol{V}_{str}$,** because the scalar -1, as any other scalar, can be incorporated in any strongly centered vector with scalar coefficients.

Theorem 5

In the Model II, we assume that the observable vectors $X_1,\dots,X_{k^\circ}$ are zero-excess vectors. Then

$$\mathbf{V = Proj[v/}\boldsymbol{P}_{\mathbf{v}}(\boldsymbol{V}_{\mathbf{str}})] \ \textbf{ in } \boldsymbol{L}_{\mathbf{2,nxn}}(\mathbf{p,q}), \qquad (40)$$

where V is the classical estimator of v defined by (25).

Proof
We have to verify that

$$V-v \perp V_1-V_2 \ \ (V_1,V_2\in \boldsymbol{P}_v(\boldsymbol{V}_{str})).$$

But

$$v \perp V_1-V_2\,,$$

because

$$E(V_1-V_2) = v-v = 0.$$

Hence, it is sufficient to verify that

$$V \perp V_1-V_2,$$

or, by the definition Ch.4.(1) of the scalar product and the corresponding orthogonality in $\boldsymbol{L}_{2,n\times n}(p,q)$, that

$$E\ \mathrm{tr}[Vp(V_1-V_2)q] = 0 \ \ (V_1,V_2\in \boldsymbol{P}_v(\boldsymbol{V}_{str})), \qquad (41)$$

because v is symmetric. By (36)

$$2(k^\circ-1)w_\Sigma V = \textstyle\sum_{ij} w_iw_j(X_i^\circ-X_j^\circ)(X_i^\circ-X_j^{\circ\prime})$$

$$= \textstyle\sum_{ij} w_iw_j(X_i^\circ X_i^{\circ\prime}-X_i^\circ X_j^{\circ\prime}-X_j^\circ X_i^{\circ\prime}+X_j^\circ X_j^{\circ\prime})$$

$$= \textstyle\sum_{ijkm} w_iw_j(\delta_{ik}\delta_{im}-\delta_{ik}\delta_{jm}-\delta_{jk}\delta_{im}+\delta_{jk}\delta_{jm})X_k^\circ X_m^{\circ\prime}$$

$$= \textstyle\sum_{km} (w_kw_\Sigma\delta_{km}-w_kw_m-w_mw_k+w_\Sigma\delta_{km})X_k^\circ X_m^{\circ\prime}.$$

Hence,

$$(k^\circ-1)w_\Sigma V = \textstyle\sum_{km} c_{km}X_k^\circ X_m^{\circ\prime}\ , \quad \text{where} \quad c_{km} := w_kw_\Sigma\delta_{km}-w_kw_m. \qquad (42)$$

By the discussion preceding the statement of the Theorem, the difference V_1-V_2 in (41), can be displayed as a sum

$$V_1-V_2 = \textstyle\sum_r Y_rZ_r',$$

where

$$Y_r = \sum_i a_{ri}X_i = \sum_i a_{ri}X_i^\circ$$

and

$$Z_r = \sum_j b_{rj}X_j = \sum_j b_{rj}X_j^\circ$$

are strongly centered vectors with scalar coefficients a_{ri}, b_{rj}. Then

$$V_1-V_2 = \sum_{rij} a_{ri}b_{rj}X_i^\circ X_j^{\circ\prime} = \sum_{ij} d_{ij}X_i^\circ X_j^{\circ\prime}, \text{ where } d_{ij} = \sum_r a_{ri}b_{rj} .$$

Let $u_i{:=}1/w_i$. By the strong centering of the vectors Y_r and Z_r, and because $E(V_1-V_2)=0$:

$$\sum_i d_{ij} = 0 \ , \ \sum_j d_{ij} = 0 \ , \ \sum_i d_{ii}u_i = 0.$$

Then

$$(k^\circ-1)w_\Sigma \, E \, tr[Vp(V_1-V_2)q] = \sum_{ijkm} d_{ij}c_{km} \, E \, tr(X_k^\circ X_m^{\circ\prime}pX_i^\circ X_j^{\circ\prime}q)$$

$$= \sum_{ijkm} d_{ij}c_{km} \, E \, tr(X_m^{\circ\prime}pX_i^\circ X_j^{\circ\prime}qX_k^\circ).$$

By Ch.4.(19), the last member is the sum of the following 3 terms Σ_1 , Σ_2 , Σ_3:

$$\Sigma_1 := \sum_{ijkm} d_{ij}c_{km} \, \delta_{mi}\delta_{jk} \, tr(pu_m v)tr(qu_j v),$$

$$\Sigma_2 := \sum_{ijkm} d_{ij}c_{km} \, \delta_{mj}\delta_{ik} \, tr(pu_m vqu_i v),$$

$$\Sigma_3 := \sum_{ijkm} d_{ij}c_{km} \, \delta_{mk}\delta_{ij} \, tr(qu_m vpu_i v).$$

Then (41) is correct because each of these terms equals 0. Indeed, let

$$\alpha := tr(pv)tr(qv) \ , \ \beta := tr(pvqv).$$

Then

$$\Sigma_1 = \alpha \sum_{ijkm} d_{ij}c_{km} \, \delta_{mi}\delta_{jk}u_m u_j = \alpha \sum_{mj} d_{mj}c_{jm} \, u_m u_j$$

$$= \alpha\sum_{mj} d_{mj}(w_j w_\Sigma \delta_{jm} - w_j w_m)u_m u_j = \alpha \sum_j d_{jj}u_j w_\Sigma - \alpha\sum_{mj} d_{mj} = 0.$$

$$\Sigma_2 = \beta \sum_{ijkm} d_{ij}c_{km} \, \delta_{mj}\delta_{ik} \, u_m u_i = \beta \sum_{mi} d_{im}c_{im} \, u_m u_i$$

$$= \beta \sum_{mi} d_{im}(w_i w_\Sigma \delta_{im} - w_i w_m)u_m u_i = \beta \sum_I d_{ii}u_i w_\Sigma - \beta \sum_{mi} d_{mi} = 0.$$

$$\Sigma_3 = \beta \sum_{ijkm} d_{ij}c_{km} \, \delta_{mk}\delta_{ij} \, u_m u_i = \beta\sum_{mi} d_{ii}c_{mm}u_m u_i$$

$$= \beta \left(\sum_m c_{mm}u_m\right)\left(\sum_i d_{ii}u_i\right) = 0 \ \bullet$$

5.6. Model III with Several Random Vectors

5.6.1. Definition of Model III

We here consider the model defined by k° independent non-degenerated observable random vectors

$$(X_1)_{n\times 1}\ ,\ (X_2)_{n\times 1}\ ,\ \ldots\ ,\ (X_{k^\circ})_{n\times 1} \tag{43}$$

with square-integrable components, such that

$$EX_k = \mu_{n\times 1}\ ,\ \ \text{Cov}\ X_k\ = v+u_k\ \ (k=1,\ldots,k^\circ). \tag{44}$$

Here $\mu_{n\times 1}$ is an unknown vector, $v_{n\times n}$ is an unknown definite positive matrix, and u_k are known definite positive matrices. The problem is the estimation of μ and v.

We use the notations

$$v_k := v+u_k\ ,\ \ z_k := v_k^{-1} = (v+u_k)^{-1}\ .$$

The matrices z_k are **matrix pseudo-weights**. We use the prefix "pseudo" because they depend on the unknown matrix v.

This Model III arises in Hachemeister's regression model in Credibility Theory. In Model III no obvious classical estimators for μ or v exist. The research of optimal estimators leads to pseudo-estimators. Hereafter, we indicate general classes of unbiased estimators and particular optimal pseudo-estimators.

5.6.2. Estimation of μ

Optimal pseudo-estimator

Here Cov $X_k=z_k^{-1}$. Then by (19), the **optimal pseudo-estimator**

$$\text{Proj}(\mu/\boldsymbol{M}_{str})\ \text{ in } \boldsymbol{L}_{2,n}(p)$$

of μ, equals

$$X_Z := z_\Sigma^{-1} \textstyle\sum_k z_k X_k. \tag{45}$$

The estimator X_Z can be used with v replaced by some estimate in z_k. More frequently, it is used simultaneously with a pseudo-estimator of v in Credibility Theory. The technique is explained in section Ch.3.3.7.

Unbiased estimators

For any matrix weights $(c_k)_{n\times n}$,

$$X_C := c_\Sigma^{-1} \textstyle\sum_k c_k X_k \tag{46}$$

is an unbiased estimator of μ.

If $c_{n\times n}$ is any invertible matrix, then the replacement of c_k by the product cc_k does not modify the estimator X_C .

The pseudo-estimator (45) equals

$$X_Z := z_\Sigma^{-1} \textstyle\sum_k (v+u_k)^{-1} X_k \,.$$

Hence, if it is known that the elements of v are small compared to the corresponding elements of the matrices u_k, then v can be neglected and then the right estimator of μ is

$$X_W := w_\Sigma^{-1} \textstyle\sum_k w_k X_k. \tag{47}$$

If it is known that the elements of v are large compared to the corresponding elements of the matrices u_k, then the latter can be neglected, and then the right estimator of μ is

$$X_A := 1/k^\circ \textstyle\sum_k X_k \,. \tag{48}$$

5.6.3. Estimation of v

Spaces of random matrices

V_μ is the space of random matrices

$$\textstyle\sum_k (a_k)_{n\times n} (X_k-\mu)(X_k-\mu)'. \tag{49}$$

V_Z is the space of random matrices

$$\textstyle\sum_k (a_k)_{n\times n} (X_k-X_Z)(X_k-X_Z)'. \tag{50}$$

V is the space of random matrices

$$\sum_{ij} (a_{ij})_{n\times n} (X_i-X_j)(X_i-X_j). \tag{51}$$

In these definitions, a_k and a_{ij} are any matrices in $\mathbf{R}_{n\times n}$. The spaces V_μ, V_Z and V are planes through the origin, closed under left matrix multiplication.

Theorem 6

$$\sum_k (\mathbf{a}_k)_{n\times n} (\mathbf{X}_k-\mu)(\mathbf{X}_k-\mu)' = \sum_k \mathbf{a}_k \mathbf{X}_k{}^\circ\mathbf{X}_k{}^{\circ\prime}, \tag{52}$$

$$\sum_k (\mathbf{a}_k)_{n\times n} (\mathbf{X}_k-\mathbf{X}_Z)(\mathbf{X}_k-\mathbf{X}_Z)'$$

$$=\sum_{ij}(\delta_{ij}\mathbf{a}_i\mathbf{X}_i{}^\circ\mathbf{X}_j{}^{\circ\prime}-\mathbf{a}_i\mathbf{X}_i{}^\circ\mathbf{X}_j{}^{\circ\prime}\mathbf{z}_j\mathbf{z}_\Sigma{}^{-1}-\mathbf{a}_j\mathbf{z}_\Sigma{}^{-1}\mathbf{z}_i\mathbf{X}_i{}^\circ\mathbf{X}_j{}^{\circ\prime}+\mathbf{a}_\Sigma\mathbf{z}_\Sigma{}^{-1}\mathbf{z}_i\mathbf{X}_i{}^\circ\mathbf{X}_j{}^{\circ\prime}\mathbf{z}_j\mathbf{z}_\Sigma{}^{-1}), \tag{53}$$

$$\sum_{ij} (\mathbf{a}_{ij})_{n\times n} (\mathbf{X}_i-\mathbf{X}_j)(\mathbf{X}_i-\mathbf{X}_j)' = \sum_{ij} (\delta_{ij}\mathbf{a}_{i\Sigma} + \delta_{ij}\mathbf{a}_{\Sigma i} -\mathbf{a}_{ij} -\mathbf{a}_{ji})\mathbf{X}_i{}^\circ\mathbf{X}_j{}^{\circ\prime}. \tag{54}$$

Proof
Relation (52) is obvious.

$$X_k-X_Z = X_k - z_\Sigma{}^{-1}\sum_i z_iX_i = z_\Sigma{}^{-1}\sum_i z_i(X_k-X_i) = z_\Sigma{}^{-1}\sum_i z_i(X_k{}^\circ-X_i{}^\circ).$$

Then

$$\sum_k a_k (X_k-X_Z)(X_k-X_Z)' = \sum_{ijk} a_k z_\Sigma{}^{-1}z_i(X_k{}^\circ-X_i{}^\circ)(X_k{}^\circ-X_j{}^\circ)'z_j'z_\Sigma{}^{-1\prime}$$

$$=\sum_{ijk} a_k z_\Sigma{}^{-1}z_i(X_k{}^\circ X_k{}^{\circ\prime}- X_k{}^\circ X_j{}^{\circ\prime}-X_i{}^\circ X_k{}'+X_i{}^\circ X_j{}^{\circ\prime})z_jz_\Sigma{}^{-1}$$

$$=\sum_k a_kX_k{}^\circ X_k{}^{\circ\prime}-\sum_{jk}a_kX_k{}^\circ X_j{}^{\circ\prime}z_jz_\Sigma{}^{-1}-\sum_{ik}a_kz_\Sigma{}^{-1}z_iX_i{}^\circ X_k{}^{\circ\prime}$$
$$+\sum_{ij} a_\Sigma z_\Sigma{}^{-1}z_iX_i{}^\circ X_j{}^{\circ\prime}z_jz_\Sigma{}^{-1}.$$

We used the fact that z_j and z_Σ are symmetrical matrices. For (54),

$$\sum_{ij} a_{ij} (X_i-X_j)(X_i-X_j)' = \sum_{ij} a_{ij} (X_i{}^\circ-X_j{}^\circ)(X_i{}^\circ-X_j{}^\circ)'$$

$$=\sum_{ij} a_{ij} (X_i{}^\circ X_i{}^{\circ\prime}+X_j{}^\circ X_j{}^{\circ\prime}-X_i{}^\circ X_j{}^{\circ\prime}-X_j{}^\circ X_i{}^{\circ\prime})$$

$$=\sum_{ijkm} a_{ij} (\delta_{ik}\delta_{im}+\delta_{jk}\delta_{jm}-\delta_{ik}\delta_{jm}-\delta_{jk}\delta_{im})X_k{}^\circ X_m{}^{\circ\prime}$$

$$=\sum_{km} (a_{m\Sigma}\delta_{km}+a_{\Sigma m}\delta_{km}-a_{km}-a_{mk}) X_k{}^\circ X_m{}^{\circ\prime} \bullet$$

Expectations

Theorem 7

$$\mathbf{E} \textstyle\sum_k (\mathbf{a}_k)_{n\times n} (\mathbf{X}_k-\mu)(\mathbf{X}_k-\mu)' = \sum_k \mathbf{a}_k\mathbf{v}_k, \tag{55}$$

$$\mathbf{E} \textstyle\sum_k (\mathbf{a}_k)_{n\times n} (\mathbf{X}_k-\mathbf{X}_Z)(\mathbf{X}_k-\mathbf{X}_Z)' = [\sum_k \mathbf{a}_k\mathbf{v}_k] - \mathbf{a}_\Sigma \mathbf{z}_\Sigma^{-1}, \tag{56}$$

$$\mathbf{E} \textstyle\sum_{ij} (\mathbf{a}_{ij})_{n\times n} (\mathbf{X}_i-\mathbf{X}_j)(\mathbf{X}_i-\mathbf{X}_j)' = \sum_k (\mathbf{a}_{k\Sigma}+\mathbf{a}_{\Sigma k}-2\mathbf{a}_{kk})\mathbf{v}_k. \tag{57}$$

Proof

$$\mathrm{E} \textstyle\sum_k (a_k)_{n\times n} (X_k-\mu)(X_k-\mu)'$$

$$= \textstyle\sum_k a_k \mathrm{E}(X_k^\circ X_k^{\circ\prime}) = \sum_k a_k v_k.$$

This proves (57). For (58),

$$\mathrm{E} \textstyle\sum_k (a_k)_{n\times n} (X_k-X_Z)(X_k-X_Z)'$$

$$= \textstyle\sum_{ij}[\delta_{ij}a_i\mathrm{E}(X_i^\circ X_j^{\circ\prime})-a_i\mathrm{E}(X_i^\circ X_j^{\circ\prime})z_jz_\Sigma^{-1}$$

$$-a_jz_\Sigma^{-1}z_i\mathrm{E}(X_i^\circ X_j^{\circ\prime})+a_\Sigma z_\Sigma^{-1}z_i\mathrm{E}(X_i^\circ X_j^{\circ\prime})z_jz_\Sigma^{-1}]$$

$$= \textstyle\sum_{ij}[\delta_{ij}a_i\delta_{ij}v_i - a_i\delta_{ij}v_i\, z_jz_\Sigma^{-1} - a_jz_\Sigma^{-1}z_i\delta_{ij}v_i + a_\Sigma z_\Sigma^{-1}z_i\delta_{ij}v_i\, z_jz_\Sigma^{-1}]$$

$$= \textstyle\sum_i[a_iv_i - a_iv_i\, z_iz_\Sigma^{-1} - a_iz_\Sigma^{-1}z_iv_i + a_\Sigma z_\Sigma^{-1}z_iv_i\, z_iz_\Sigma^{-1}]$$

$$= \textstyle\sum_i[a_iv_i - a_iz_\Sigma^{-1} - a_iz_\Sigma^{-1} + a_\Sigma z_\Sigma^{-1}z_iz_\Sigma^{-1}] = \sum_i a_iv_i - a_\Sigma z_\Sigma^{-1}.$$

This proves (58). For (59),

$$\mathrm{E} \textstyle\sum_{ij} a_{ij} (X_i-X_j)(X_i-X_j)' = \sum_{ij} (\delta_{ij}a_{i\Sigma} + \delta_{ij}a_{\Sigma i} - a_{ij} - a_{ji})\mathrm{E}(X_i^\circ X_j^{\circ\prime})$$

$$= \textstyle\sum_{ij} (\delta_{ij}a_{i\Sigma} + \delta_{ij}a_{\Sigma i} - a_{ij} - a_{ji})\delta_{ij}v_i = \sum_i (a_{i\Sigma} + a_{\Sigma i} - a_{ii} - a_{ii})v_i \quad \bullet$$

***Unbiased estimators of* v**

In the last member of (57), v_k equals $v+u_k$. Hence

$$\mathrm{E} \textstyle\sum_{ij} a_{ij}(X_i-X_j)(X_i-X_j)'$$

$$= \textstyle\sum_k (a_{k\Sigma}+a_{\Sigma k}-2a_{kk})(v+u_k)$$

$$= [2a_{\Sigma\Sigma} - 2\textstyle\sum_k a_{kk}]v + \sum_k (a_{k\Sigma}+a_{\Sigma k}-2a_{kk})u_k.$$

This proves the following Theorem.

Theorem 8

In the Model III,

$$\mathbf{V_a := [2a_{\Sigma\Sigma} - 2\textstyle\sum_k a_{kk}]^{-1}[\sum_{ij} a_{ij}(X_i - X_j)(X_i - X_j)' - \sum_k (a_{k\Sigma} + a_{\Sigma k} - 2a_{kk})u_k]} \quad (58)$$

is an unbiased estimator of v, whatever the matrix weights $(a_{ij})_{n\times n}$ are, but such that the inverse matrix appearing in the last member exists •

We observe that **V_a does not change if all the matrices a_{ij} are premultiplied by any invertible matrix $a_{n\times n}$** .

Scalar weights are particular matrix weights. The scalar s "works" like the matrix $s1_{n\times n}$ in matrix operations.

It happens that $u_k = w_k u_{n\times n}$, where w_k is a scalar. Then arguments can be found in favor of scalar weights such as

$$a_{ij} = w_i w_j \quad , \quad a_{ij} = (w_i w_j)^{1/2} \quad , \quad a_{ij} = 1. \qquad (59)$$

(See the discussion following next Theorem 10).

If a_{ij} are scalar weights, then V_a is symmetric. This is not the case (or only exceptionally) if a_{ij} are matrix weights. If the estimate furnished by V_a is not a semidefinite positive matrix, then the latter must be corrected, as explained in Ch.4.5.3.

In the construction of unbiased usual estimators of v, one could try to start with symmetric statistics such as

$$S := \textstyle\sum_{ij} a_{ij}(X_i - X_j)(X_i - X_j)' a_{ij}',$$

where $(a_{ij})_{n\times n}$ are matrices. This does not work because then ES looks like

$$ES = (a)_{n\times n} v(a')_{n\times n} + (b)_{n\times n} v(b')_{n\times n} + \ldots$$

and then it is not possible to extract v from that relation. For the same reasons, statistics such as

$$\sum_k (a_k)_{n\times n}(X_k - X_C)(X_k - X_C)' \tag{60}$$

and

$$\sum_k (a_k)_{n\times n}(X_k - X_C)(X_k - X_C)'(a_k')_{n\times n},$$

where X_C is defined by (46), are unsuccessful in the construction of unbiased estimators of v.

In the particular case in which X_C is the optimal pseudo-estimator X_Z of μ, statistics such as (60) can be used for the construction of pseudo-estimators.

***Pseudo-estimators of* v *in the space* V_Z**

The optimal estimator of v in the space $\boldsymbol{V}_Z$ is the projection

$$\text{Proj}[v/\boldsymbol{P}_v(\boldsymbol{V}_Z)] \text{ in } \boldsymbol{L}_{2,n\times n}(p,q). \tag{61}$$

This projection can be calculated under the zero-excess assumption. But its expression is complicated, and ipso-facto, uninteresting. Rather than to calculate the exact projection, we obain an approximation as follows. We first calculate

$$\text{Proj}[v/\boldsymbol{P}_v(\boldsymbol{V}_\mu)] \text{ in } \boldsymbol{L}_{2,n\times n}(p,q). \tag{62}$$

This projection, furnished by the following Theorem 9, is some expression (49), in which we replace μ by its optimal estimator X_Z. This replacement introduces some bias. The latter is easily corrected by the use of (56).

Theorem 9

In the Model III, under the zero-excess assumption,

$$\mathbf{Proj}[v/\boldsymbol{P}_v(\boldsymbol{V}_\mu)] = v\,[\textstyle\sum_k w_{opt,k}\, v_k]^{-1} \sum_k w_{opt,k}\,(X_k-\mu)(X_k-\mu)' \tag{63}$$

in $\boldsymbol{L}_{2,n\times n}(p,q)$, where the optimal matrix weigths $w_{opt,k}$ are

$$w_{opt,k} := [v_k q + \text{tr}(v_k q).1_{n\times n}]^{-1}. \tag{64}$$

Proof

Rather than to verify that the indicated projection is correct, we discover it. Let

$$V = \sum_j c_j(X_j-\mu)(X_j-\mu)' = \sum_j c_j X_j^\circ X_j^{\circ\prime},$$

be the projection of v on $\boldsymbol{P}_v(\boldsymbol{V}_\mu)$. By Ch.4.Th.5, the unknown matrices c_j are such that EV=v , i.e.

$$\sum_i c_i v_i = v \tag{65}$$

and such that for any matrix

$$A := \sum_i a_i(X_i-\mu)(X_i-\mu)' = \sum_i a_i X_i^\circ X_i^{\circ\prime} \in \boldsymbol{V}_\mu,$$

the scalar product <V,A> does not depend on A if EA=1. By Ch.4.Th.14,

$$<V,A> = E\,\mathrm{tr}(V'pAq) = \sum_{ij} E\,\mathrm{tr}(X_j^\circ X_j^{\circ\prime} c_j' p a_i X_i^\circ X_i^{\circ\prime} q)$$

$$= \sum_{ij} E\,\mathrm{tr}(X_j^{\circ\prime} c_j' p a_i X_i^\circ X_i^{\circ\prime} q X_j^\circ) = \Sigma_1 + \Sigma_2 + \Sigma_3,$$

where

$$\Sigma_1 := \sum_{ij} \delta_{ji}\delta_{ij}\mathrm{tr}(c_j' p a_i v_j)\mathrm{tr}(q v_i) = \sum_i \mathrm{tr}(c_i' p a_i v_i)\mathrm{tr}(q v_i)$$

$$= \sum_i \mathrm{tr}(v_i a_i' p c_i)\mathrm{tr}(v_i q) = \sum_i \mathrm{tr}[v_i a_i' p c_i . \mathrm{tr}(v_i q) 1_{n\times n}],$$

$$\Sigma_2 := \sum_{ij} \delta_{ji}\delta_{ij}\mathrm{tr}(a_i' p c_j v_j q v_i) = \sum_i \mathrm{tr}(a_i' p c_i v_i q v_i) = \sum_i \mathrm{tr}(v_i a_i' p c_i v_i q),$$

$$\Sigma_3 := \sum_{ij} \delta_{jj}\delta_{ii}\mathrm{tr}(q v_j c_j' p a_i v_i) = \mathrm{tr}[q(\textstyle\sum_j v_j c_j')p(\sum_i a_i v_i)]$$

$$= \mathrm{tr}(q.EV'.p.EA) = \mathrm{tr}(qvp.EA).$$

Hence,

$$<V,A> = \sum_i \mathrm{tr}[v_i a_i' p.[c_i(v_i q + \mathrm{tr}(v_i q) 1_{n\times n})]] + \mathrm{tr}(qvp.EA).$$

We take c_i in such a way that the matrix in the inner square brackets of the last member is a constant matrix c:

$$c_i(v_i q + \mathrm{tr}(v_i q)1_{n\times n}) = c \;,\; c_i := c\, w_{opt,i}$$

We fix $c_{n\times n}$ so that (65) is satisfied:

$$c \sum_i w_{opt,i}\, v_i = v \;,\; c = v[\textstyle\sum_i w_{opt,i}\, v_i]^{-1}.$$

Then

$$<V,A> = \sum_i \mathrm{tr}[v_i a_i' pc] + \mathrm{tr}(qvp.EA) = \mathrm{tr}[(\textstyle\sum_i v_i a_i')pc] + \mathrm{tr}(qvp.EA)$$

$$= \mathrm{tr}(EA'.pc) + \mathrm{tr}(qvp.EA).$$

The latter member does not depend on A if EA=1 •

By the discussion preceding the statement of the Theorem, the approximatively optimal pseudo-estimator of v which we propose, is

$$\mathbf{V_{Z,pseu} := c \textstyle\sum_k w_{opt,k} (X_k - X_Z)(X_k - X_Z)'}, \tag{66}$$

where the weights $w_{opt,k}$ are defined by (64), and where $c_{n\times n}$ is such that $V_{Z,pseu}$ is unbiased. By (56),

$$\mathbf{c = v\ [(\textstyle\sum_k w_{opt,k} v_k) - w_{opt,\Sigma}\, z_\Sigma^{-1}]^{-1}}. \tag{67}$$

Another unbiased pseudo-estimator of v in the space $\boldsymbol{V}_Z$ is

$$v/(k^\circ-1) \cdot \textstyle\sum_k z_k (X_k - X_Z)(X_k - X_Z)'. \tag{68}$$

The unbiasedness results from the relation (56) of which the last member equals $k^\circ-1$ when $a_k=z_k$. This pseudo-estimator coincides with the pseudo-estimator (66) if n=1. Indeed, in the latter case, the scalar weights $w_{opt,k}$ and z_k differ only by the constant factor 2q :

$$w_{opt,k} = (2qv_k)^{-1} = (1/2q)\, z_k$$

If n>1, the pseudo-estimator (68) does not seem to have any optimal character.

Pseudo-estimators of v in the space V

The optimal pseudo-estimator of v in $\boldsymbol{V}$ is the projection

$$\mathrm{Proj}[v/\boldsymbol{P}_v(\boldsymbol{V})]. \tag{69}$$

It can be calculated, under the zero-excess assumption, but its general expression is too complicated to be useful.

The comparison of (35) and (36) suggests that (51), with

$$a_{ij} := c\ w_{opt,i}\ w_{opt,j}$$

might be optimal in some sense. Next Theorem shows that this pseudo-estimator equals the projection (69), under the supplementary commutativity assumption (73).

The pseudo-estimator V_{pseu} obtained in this way can be used in any case, also if the commutativity assumption is satisfied only approximatively. It is unbiased by the right choice of the matrix $c_{n\times n}$.

The commutativity assumption is satisfied exactly in the following case (often satisfied, with an excellent approximation, in the regression credibility model of the next Chapter):

$$u_i = w_i\, u_{n\times n}\ ,\quad w_i \text{ scalar.} \tag{70}$$

Indeed, then for $q := v^{-1}$,

$$v_iq+tr(v_iq)1_{n\times n} = (v+u_i)q+tr(v_iq)1_{n\times n} = w_iuv^{-1}+\alpha_i1_{n\times n},$$

where α_i is a scalar. Then

$$[v_iq + tr(v_iq)1_{n\times n}][v_jq + tr(v_jq)1_{n\times n}] = [w_iuv^{-1}+\alpha_i1_{n\times n}][w_juv^{-1}+\alpha_j1_{n\times n}]$$

$$= w_iw_juv^{-1}uv^{-1} + (w_i\alpha_j+w_j\alpha_i)uv^{-1} + \alpha_i\alpha_j1_{n\times n}$$

$$= [w_juv^{-1}+\alpha_j1_{n\times n}][w_iuv^{-1}+\alpha_i1_{n\times n}]= [v_jq + tr(v_jq)1_{n\times n}][v_iq + tr(v_iq)1_{n\times n}].$$

This shows the commutativity of $(w_{opt,i})^{-1}$ and $(w_{opt,j})^{-1}$. The latter implies the commutativity of $w_{opt,i}$ and $w_{opt,j}$.

We define

$$\mathbf{V_{pseu} = c\,\textstyle\sum_{ij}\, w_{opt,i}\, w_{opt,j}\, (X_i{-}X_j)(X_i{-}X_j)'}, \tag{71}$$

where the weights $w_{opt,i}$ are defined by (64) and where $c_{n\times n}$ is such that the pseudo-estimator V_{pseu} of v is unbiased. By (57),

$$\mathbf{c = v\,[\textstyle\sum_k(w_{opt,k}\, w_{opt,\Sigma}+ w_{opt,\Sigma} w_{opt,k} - 2w_{opt,k}\, w_{opt,k})v_k]^{-1}}. \tag{72}$$

Theorem 10

We adopt the zero-excess assumption, and we suppose that

$$\mathbf{w_{opt,i}\, w_{opt,j} = w_{opt,j}\, w_{opt,i}} \tag{73}$$

in the Model III. Then

$$\mathbf{V_{pseu} = Proj[v/\mathit{P}_v(\mathit{V})]\ \ in\ \mathit{L}_{2,nxn}(p,q)}. \tag{74}$$

Proof
In this proof, let

$$V := V_{pseu} \quad , \quad c_i := w_{opt,i} \quad , \quad c_{ij} := cc_ic_j,$$

Then, by (54),

$$V = c \textstyle\sum_{ij} c_ic_j(X_i - X_j)(X_i - X_j)' = 2c \sum_{ij} (\delta_{ij}c_ic_\Sigma - c_ic_j)X_i^\circ X_j^{\circ\prime}.$$

Let

$$A := \textstyle\sum_{km} (a_{ij})_{n\times n} (X_k - X_m)(X_k - X_m)'$$

be any point in $\boldsymbol{L}_{2,n\times n}$. We may assume that $a_{km}=a_{mk}$ because

$$\textstyle\sum_{km} a_{km} (X_k - X_m)(X_k - X_m)' = 1/2 \sum_{km} (a_{km}+a_{mk}) (X_k - X_m)(X_k - X_m)',$$

Then, by (54),

$$A = 2 \textstyle\sum_{km} (\delta_{km}a_{k\Sigma} - a_{km})X_k^\circ X_m^{\circ\prime}.$$

By Ch.4.Th.5, it is enough to verify that $<V,A>$ does not depend on A if $EA=1$, because we already know that $EV_{pseu}=v$, by the choice of c Let

$$d_{ij} := c(\delta_{ij}c_ic_\Sigma - c_ic_j) = d_{ji} \quad , \quad b_{km} := \delta_{km}a_{k\Sigma} - a_{km} = b_{mk}\,.$$

Then

$$V = 2 \textstyle\sum_{ij} d_{ij}X_i^\circ X_j^{\circ\prime} \quad , \quad A = 2 \sum_{km} b_{km} X_k^\circ X_m^{\circ\prime}.$$

By Ch.4.Th.14,

$$1/4 <V,A> = E\, tr(V'pAq)$$

$$= \textstyle\sum_{ijkm} E\, tr(X_j^\circ X_i^{\circ\prime} d_{ij}'pb_{km}X_k^\circ X_m^{\circ\prime} q)$$

$$= \textstyle\sum_{ijkm} E\, (X_i^{\circ\prime} d_{ij}'pb_{km}X_k^\circ X_m^{\circ\prime} qX_j^\circ) = \Sigma_1 + \Sigma_2 + \Sigma_3,$$

where

$$\Sigma_1 := \textstyle\sum_{ijkm} \delta_{ik}\delta_{mj}\, tr(d_{ij}'pb_{km}v_i)tr(qv_m) = \sum_{im} tr(d_{im}'pb_{im}v_i)tr(qv_m)$$

$$= \textstyle\sum_{ij} tr(d_{ij}'pb_{ij}v_i)tr(qv_j) = \sum_{ij} tr(v_ib_{ij}'pd_{ij})tr(v_jq),$$

$$\Sigma_2 := \textstyle\sum_{ijkm} \delta_{im}\delta_{kj}\, tr(b_{km}'pd_{ij}v_iqv_k) = \sum_{ik} tr(b_{ki}'pd_{ik}v_iqv_k)$$

$$= \textstyle\sum_{ij} tr(v_jb_{ij}'pd_{ij}v_iq) = \sum_{ij} tr(v_ib_{ij}'pd_{ij}v_jq),$$

$$\Sigma_3 = \Sigma_{ijkm}\ \delta_{ij}\delta_{km}\mathrm{tr}(qv_id_{ij}'pb_{km}v_k) = \Sigma_{ik}\ \mathrm{tr}(qv_id_{ii}'pb_{kk}v_k)$$

$$= \mathrm{tr}[q(\Sigma_i d_{ii}v_i)'p(\Sigma_k b_{kk}v_k)] = 1/4\ \mathrm{tr}(q.EV'.p.EA)$$

by (57). Hence, Σ_3 does not depend on A if EA=1. Then it is enough to prove that $\Sigma_1+\Sigma_2$ does not depend on A if EA=1.

The sum $\Sigma_1+\Sigma_2$ is the trace of the matrix

$$\Sigma_{ij}\ v_ib_{ij}'pd_{ij}.\mathrm{tr}(v_jq)1_{n\times n} + \Sigma_{ij}\ v_ib_{ij}'pd_{ij}v_jq = \Sigma_{ij}\ v_ib_{ij}'pd_{ij}[v_jq+\mathrm{tr}(v_jq)1_{n\times n}]$$

$$= \Sigma_{ij}\ v_ib_{ij}'pc(\delta_{ij}c_ic_\Sigma-c_ic_j)\ [v_jq+\mathrm{tr}(v_jq)1_{n\times n}]$$

$$=\Sigma_{ij}\ v_ib_{ij}'pc(\delta_{ij}c_\Sigma-c_i).c_j[v_jq+\mathrm{tr}(v_jq)1_{n\times n}] = \Sigma_{ij}\ v_ib_{ij}'pc(\delta_{ij}c_\Sigma-c_i)$$

$$= (\Sigma_i b_{ii}v_i)pcc_\Sigma - \Sigma_{ij}\ v_ib_{ij}'pcc_i = =EA'.pcc_\Sigma - \Sigma_i\ v_i(\Sigma_j b_{ij})'pcc_i = EA'.pcc_\Sigma\ ,$$

because

$$\Sigma_j\ b_{ij} = \Sigma_j(\delta_{ij}a_{i\Sigma}-a_{ij}) = a_{i\Sigma}-a_{i\Sigma} = 0.$$

Hence, $\Sigma_1+\Sigma_2$ does not depend on A if EA=1 •

Let us now assume (70) and let us take $q=v^{-1}$. Then v_kq, in (64), equals

$$v_kq = (v+u_k)q = (v+w_iu)v^{-1} = 1_{n\times n} + w_iuv^{-1}. \tag{75}$$

The optimal matrix weights a_{ij} in the estimator (58) are

$$a_{ij} = w_{opt,i}\ w_{opt,j},$$

but they cannot be used if V_a must be a usual estimator, not a pseudo-estimator. However, from (64) and (75), we learn that the scalar weights

$$a_{ij} = w_iw_j$$

should be used when $1_{n\times n}$ is small compared to uv^{-1}, and that the constant scalar weights $a_{ij}=1$ are right when $1_{n\times n}$ is large compared to uv^{-1}. Mostly, no prior information is available on the magnitude of uv^{-1}, and then the intermediate scalar weights

$$a_{ij} := (w_iw_j)^\alpha\ ,\ \ \alpha = 1/2\ ,$$

could be adopted.

Chapter 6

Credibility Regression Models

6.1. Regression Model with One Contract

6.1.1. Definitions

Definition of the regression model with one contract

Hachemeister's regression model with one contract is defined by the equations

$$E(X/\Theta) = y\ \beta(\Theta) \quad , \quad Cov(X/\Theta) = \sigma^2(\Theta)v \qquad (1)$$

with the following components.

$X_{t\times 1}$ is an **observable random vector** in $\boldsymbol{L}_{2,t\times 1}$. Hence the **number t of observation years** (or periods) is a strictly positive integer. Θ is any random variable. (The formalism is the same if Θ is any random vector). The function β(·) is such that $\beta(\Theta)\in\boldsymbol{L}_{2,n\times 1}$ where n is a strictly positive integer, strictly less than t. The **design matrix** $y_{t\times n}$ is of full rank n. The function $\sigma^2(\cdot)$ is such that $\sigma^2(\Theta)$ is a square-integrable random variable. The matrix $v_{t\times t}$ is definite positive.

In the real contract, Θ has a fixed, unknown value θ.

We want to find an optimal approximation, defined precisely hereafter, of the **unknown random vector β(Θ)**, by a vector of which the components are linear combinations of 1 and of the components of the observable vector X. Unknown parameters do occur in this **credibility approximation**. They can only be estimated in the practical **regression model with several contracts** studied later. But the credibility approximation can already be constructed in the model with one contract considered in this section 6.1.

Linear combinations with matrix coefficients

Let ***S*** be a set of random columns of the same length n. We recall that ***P*(*S*)** is the plane generated by ***S***, i.e. the family of linear combinations $\sum a_i Y_i$ of vectors Y_i in ***S***. The coefficients a_i , in any **linear combination**, are scalars, by the very definition of such a combination.

A **linear combination with matrix coefficients**, of elements of ***S***, is any sum such as $\sum a_i Y_i$, with matrix coefficients $(a_i)_{m\times n}$ and $Y_i \in \boldsymbol{S}$.

We denote by $\boldsymbol{P}_{m\times 1}(\boldsymbol{S})$ the space of linear combinations $\sum a_i Y_i$ with matrix coefficients $(a_i)_{m\times n}$, of vectors Y_i in ***S***.

Of course, if $\boldsymbol{S}=\{Y_1,\ldots,Y_k\}$, then $\boldsymbol{P}_{m\times 1}(\boldsymbol{S})\equiv\boldsymbol{P}_{m\times 1}(Y_1,\ldots,Y_k)$

The vectors of $\boldsymbol{P}_{m\times 1}(\boldsymbol{S})$ are columns of length m. Hence, if the vectors of ***S*** are columns of length n, the matrix coefficients involved in the definition of $\boldsymbol{P}_{m\times 1}(\boldsymbol{S})$ can only be matrices with dimensions m×n.

Definition of the credibility approximation

After these general definitions, we return to the regression model (1) with one contract. The space $\boldsymbol{P}_{n\times 1}(1_{t\times 1},X_{t\times 1})$ is a finite-dimensional plane through the origin of $\boldsymbol{L}_{2,n\times 1}$. The **credibility approximation** $\beta(\Theta)_{cred}$ of the random variable $\beta(\Theta)$ is defined by

$$\beta(\Theta)_{cred} = \mathrm{Proj}[\beta(\Theta)/\boldsymbol{P}_{n\times 1}(1,X)] \text{ in } \boldsymbol{L}_{2,n\times 1}(p). \qquad (2)$$

It is the **credibility estimator** of the unknown constant $\beta(\theta)$.

The definite positive matrix $p_{n\times n}$ is that one defining the scalar product in $\boldsymbol{L}_{2,n\times 1}$, but we will see that the projection (2) does not depend on p.

Notations

$$b_{n\times 1} := E\beta(\Theta) \quad , \quad a_{n\times n} := \mathrm{Cov}\,\beta(\Theta) \quad , \quad \sigma^2 = E\,\sigma^2(\Theta).$$

By Ch.5.2.2, the matrix $y'v^{-1}y$ is definite positive. The vector

$$B_{n\times 1} := (y'v^{-1}y)^{-1}y'v^{-1}X = uy'v^{-1}X,$$

.where

$$u_{n\times n} := (y'v^{-1}y)^{-1}$$

is the **regression estimator of β(Θ)** (later called the **individual estimator of β(Θ)** in the model with several contracts). It is the regression vector calculated in the determinisitic way from the vector X. The definite positive matrix v^{-1} appears automatically in later developments. In Ch.5.1.2.Th.1, an arbitrary definite positive matrix p has been used.

6.1.2. Deterministic Results

Theorem 1

a. **Let $a_{1\times m}$ be a row and $b_{n\times 1}$ be a column. Then axb=0 for all matrices $x_{m\times n}$ iff ba=0.**

b. **For any matrices a,b,c,d such that the following sums, products and inverses are defined,**

$$(1+ab)^{-1} = 1-a(1+ba)^{-1}b, \tag{3}$$

$$d(a+bcd)^{-1} = [c+(da^{-1}b)^{-1}]^{-1}(da^{-1}b)^{-1}da^{-1}. \tag{4}$$

Proof

a. results from the relations

$$axb = tr(axb) = tr(x.ba)$$

$$= \textstyle\sum_i (x.ba)_{ii} = \sum_{ij} x_{ij}(ba)_{ji}\ .$$

Indeed, the latter sum is zero, for all x_{ij} iff $(ba)_{ji}$=0 for all subscripts i,j , i.e. iff ba=0.

The relation (3) is equivalent to the relation

$$1 = [1-a(1+ba)^{-1}b](1+ab),$$

where the last member equals

$$(1+ab) - a(1+ba)^{-1}b(1+ab)$$

$$= (1+ab) - a(1+ba)^{-1}(b+bab)$$

$$=(1+ab) - a(1+ba)^{-1}(1+ba)b = (1+ab) - a1b = 1.$$

The relation (4) is equivalent to the relation

$$d = [c+(da^{-1}b)^{-1}]^{-1}(da^{-1}b)^{-1}da^{-1}(a+bcd),$$

where the last member equals

$$[c+(da^{-1}b)^{-1}]^{-1}(da^{-1}b)^{-1}(d+da^{-1}bcd)$$

$$= [c+(da^{-1}b)^{-1}]^{-1}(da^{-1}b)^{-1}[1+(da^{-1}b)c]d$$

$$=[c+(da^{-1}b)^{-1}]^{-1}[(da^{-1}b)^{-1}+c]d = d \bullet$$

6.1.3. Basic Theorem

Theorem 2

In the regression model with one observable vector defined by (1),

$$\mathbf{EX = yb \quad , \quad E(B/\Theta) = \beta(\Theta) \quad , \quad EB = b,}$$

$$\mathbf{Cov\ X = yay'+\sigma^2 v \quad , \quad Cov[\beta(\Theta),X'] = ay',}$$

$$\mathbf{Cov\ B = a+\sigma^2 u \quad , \quad Cov[\beta(\Theta),B'] = a,}$$

$$\mathbf{Cov(B,X') = (a+\sigma^2 u)y' = (Cov\ B)y'.}$$

Proof

These relations are direct from the definitions, by the general formulas for expectations and conditional expectations, covariances and conditional covariances:

$$EX = EE(X/\Theta) = E[y\beta(\Theta)] = y\, E\beta(\Theta) = yb.$$

$$E(B/\Theta) = uy'v^{-1}E(X/\Theta) = uy'v^{-1}y\beta(\Theta) = \beta(\Theta).$$

$$EB = EE(B/\Theta) = E\beta(\Theta) = b.$$

$$\text{Cov } X = \text{E Cov}(X/\Theta) + \text{Cov E}(X/\Theta) = \sigma^2 v + \text{Cov}[y\beta(\Theta)]$$

$$= \sigma^2 v + \text{Cov}[y\beta(\Theta),\beta'(\Theta)y'] = \sigma^2 v + y\,[\text{Cov } \beta(\Theta)]y' = \sigma^2 v + yay'.$$

$$\text{Cov}[\beta(\Theta),X'] = \text{E Cov}[\beta(\Theta),X'/\Theta] + \text{Cov}[E(\beta(\Theta)/\Theta),E(X'/\Theta)]$$

$$= 0 + \text{Cov}[\beta(\Theta),\beta'(\Theta)y'] = [\text{Cov } \beta(\Theta)]y' = ay'.$$

$$\text{Cov } B = \text{Cov}(B,B') = \text{Cov}(uy'v^{-1}X,X'v^{-1}yu)$$

$$= uy'v^{-1}(\text{Cov } X)v^{-1}yu = uy'v^{-1} +(yay'+\sigma^2 v)v^{-1}yu$$

$$= uy'v^{-1}yay'v^{-1}yu + \sigma^2 uy'v^{-1}vv^{-1}yu$$

$$= u.y'v^{-1}y.a.y'v^{-1}y.u + \sigma^2 u.y'v^{-1}y.u = a+\sigma^2 u.$$

$$\text{Cov}[\beta(\Theta),B'] = 0 + \text{Cov}[\beta(\Theta),E(B'/\Theta)]$$

$$= \text{Cov}[\beta(\Theta),\beta'(\Theta)] = a.$$

$$\text{Cov}(B,X') = uy'v^{-1}\text{ Cov } X = uy'v^{-1}(yay'+\sigma^2 v)$$

$$= u.y'v^{-1}y.ay' + \sigma^2 uy' = ay' + \sigma^2 uy' \quad \bullet$$

Lemma

Let $Y_{1\times m}$ be a random row and $Z_{n\times 1}$ a random column with square-integrable components. Then $E(YxZ)=0$ for all matrices $x_{m\times n}$ iff $E(ZY)=0$.

Proof
The Lemma results from the relations

$$E(YxZ) = E\text{ tr}(YxZ) = E\text{ tr}(xZY) = \text{tr }E(xZY) = \text{tr }[x.E(ZY)]$$

$$= \textstyle\sum_i [x.E(ZY)]_{ii} = \sum_{ij} x_{ij}[E(ZY)]_{ji}\,.$$

Indeed, the latter sum is zero for all x_{ij} iff $[E(ZY)]_{ji}=0$ for all i,j •

Theorem 3 (Hachemeister)

In the regression model with one observable vector defined by (1),

$$\beta(\Theta)_{cred} = zB + (1-z)b, \tag{5}$$

where

$$z_{n\times n} = a(a+\sigma^2 u)^{-1}. \tag{6}$$

Proof

Rather than to verify that the announced projection is correct, we will discover it. Let

$$c_{n\times 1} + d_{n\times t}X_{t\times 1}$$

be the projection of $\beta(\Theta)$ on the plane through the origin $\boldsymbol{P}_{n\times 1}(1,X)$ in $\boldsymbol{L}_{2,n\times 1}(p)$. Then $c+dX-\beta(\Theta)$ is orthogonal to any vector $Y := \gamma_{n\times 1} + \delta_{n\times t}X$ in that plane:

$$c+dX - \beta(\Theta) \perp \gamma+\delta X \quad , \quad E[(\gamma'+X'\delta')p(c+dX-\beta(\Theta))] = 0, \tag{7}$$

for all $\gamma_{n\times 1}$ and all $\delta_{n\times t}$. For $\delta':=0$, we must have,

$$E[\gamma' p(c+dX-\beta(\Theta))] = 0,$$

$$\gamma' p\, E[c+dX-\beta(\Theta)] = 0,$$

for all γ'. This implies

$$p\, E[c+dX-\beta(\Theta)] = 0,$$

and then

$$E[c+dX-\beta(\Theta)] = 0,$$

because p is inversible. Hence,

$$E(c+dX) = E\,\beta(\Theta). \tag{8}$$

For $\gamma':=0$, in the last relation (7), we must have

$$E[X'\delta' p(c+dX-\beta(\Theta))] = 0,$$

for all δ'. By the Lemma, this implies

$$E[p(c+dX-\beta(\Theta))X'] = 0,$$

$$p\, E[(c+dX-\beta(\Theta))X'] = 0.$$

Then p can be dropped in the last relation and we obtain

$$E[(c+dX)X'] = E[\beta(\Theta)X']. \tag{9}$$

From (9) we substract (8) post-multiplied by EX' :

$$Cov(c+dX,X') = Cov[\beta(\Theta),X'],$$

$$d\ Cov\ X = Cov[\beta(\Theta),X'],$$

and then, by Theorem 3,

$$d(\sigma^2v+yay') = ay',$$

and by Theorem 1.b,

$$d = a.y'(\sigma^2v+yay')^{-1}$$

$$= a.[a+\sigma^2(y'v^{-1}y)^{-1}]^{-1}(y'v^{-1}y)^{-1}y'v^{-1}$$

$$= a(a+\sigma^2u)^{-1}uy'v^{-1}.$$

Then

$$dX = a(a+\sigma^2u)^{-1}\ uy'v^{-1}X = a(a+\sigma^2u)^{-1}B = zB\ ,$$

where z is defined by (6). Then by (8)

$$c + E(dX) = b \quad , \quad c + z\ EB = b,$$

$$c + zb = b \quad , \quad c = (1-z)b.$$

Hence,

$$c+dX = zB+(1-z)b \quad \bullet$$

The matrix $z_{n\times n}$ defined by (6) is the **credibility weight** of the observable vector X.

By (5), the credibility estimator $\beta(\Theta)_{cred}$ of $\beta(\Theta)$ is a **convex combination with matrix coefficients z and (1–z)** of the **individual estimator B** and the **portfolio estimator b** (where we anticipate the terminology of the model with several contracts).

6.1.4. The Particular Bühlmann-Straub Model

Let n=1 and let the design matrix y be the particular column

$$y_{t\times 1} = (1,...,1)'.$$

Let us assume that v is the diagonal matrix

$$v := \text{Diagonal}(w_1^{-1},...,w_t^{-1}),$$

where $w_1,...,w_t$ are strictly positive weights. Then the assumptions (1) become, for r,s=1,...,t:

$$EX_s = \beta(\Theta),$$

$$Var(X_s/\Theta) = \sigma^2(\Theta)/w_s,$$

$$Cov(X_r,X_s/\Theta) = 0 \ (r\neq s),$$

The latter equality expresses the conditional uncorrelation of the observable random variables $X_1,...,X_t$, for fixed Θ.

These are, in a sligthly generalized form, the assumptions of the Bühlmann-Straub model considered in Ch.3.4, where $\mu(\Theta)\equiv\beta(\Theta)$. The conditional independence assumption Ch.3.4.1.a, could be replaced everywhere by the weaker conditional uncorrelation assumption.

Now

$$v^{-1} = \text{Diagonal}(w_1,...,w_t)$$

and $y'v^{-1}y$ is the scalar

$$y'v^{-1}y = (1,...,1).\text{Diagonal}(w_1,...,w_t).(1,...,1)' = w_\Sigma.$$

Then u is the scalar $u = 1/w_\Sigma$

and z is the scalar

$$z = a(a+\sigma^2u)^{-1} = aw_\Sigma/(\sigma^2+aw_\Sigma).$$

Then $y'v^{-1}X$ is the scalar

$$y'v^{-1}X = (1,...1).\text{Diagonal}(w_1,...,w_t).(X_1,...,X_t)' = \textstyle\sum_j w_jX_j.$$

Finally B is the scalar

$$B = u.y'v^{-1}X = (1/w_\Sigma)\Sigma_j\, w_jX_j = X_W\,.$$

Of course, these results are in complete agreement with those of Ch.3.4.

6.1.5. Estimation of σ^2

The parameter σ^2 can already be estimated in the regression model with one contract. **The classical estimator of σ^2** is

$$S_0^2 := 1_{/(t-n)}\,(X-yB)'v^{-1}(X-yB). \tag{10}$$

S_0^2 is an unbiased estimator of σ^2. Indeed, by Theorem 2,

$$(t-n)S_0^2 = (X^\circ-yB^\circ)'v^{-1}(X^\circ-yB^\circ),$$

$$(t-n)ES_0^2 = E[(X^\circ-yB^\circ)'v^{-1}(X^\circ-yB^\circ)]$$

$$= E\ \mathrm{tr}[(X^\circ-yB^\circ)'v^{-1}(X^\circ-yB^\circ)]$$

$$= E\ \mathrm{tr}[(X^\circ-yB^\circ)(X^\circ-yB^\circ)'v^{-1}]$$

$$= \mathrm{tr}\ E[(X^\circ-yB^\circ)(X^\circ-yB^\circ)'v^{-1}]$$

$$= \mathrm{tr}\ E[(X^\circ X^{\circ\prime}-yB^\circ X^{\circ\prime}-X^\circ B^{\circ\prime}y'+yB^\circ B^{\circ\prime}y')v^{-1}]$$

$$= \mathrm{tr}\ [[\mathrm{Cov}\,X - y\,\mathrm{Cov}(B,X') - \mathrm{Cov}(X,B').y' + y\,\mathrm{Cov}(B,B').y']v^{-1}]$$

$$= \mathrm{tr}\ [[yay'+\sigma^2v - y(a+\sigma^2u)y' - y(a+\sigma^2u)y' + y(a+\sigma^2u)y]v^{-1}]$$

$$= \mathrm{tr}\ [\sigma^2 1_{t\times t} - \sigma^2yuy'v^{-1}] = \sigma^2t-\sigma^2\ \mathrm{tr}(yuy'v^{-1})$$

$$= \sigma^2t - \mathrm{tr}(u.y'v^{-1}y)$$

$$= \sigma^2t-\ \mathrm{tr}\ 1_{n\times n} = \sigma^2(t-n).$$

This proves the unbiasedness of S_0^2.

A more direct proof goes as follows. Let

$$X^{\Theta} := X - E(X/\Theta) = X - y\beta(\Theta),$$

$$B^{\Theta} := B - E(B/\Theta) = B - \beta(\Theta) = uy'v^{-1}X^{\Theta}$$

Then

$$E(S_0^2/\Theta) = \sigma^2(\Theta), \tag{11}$$

by Ch.5.2.3, because, for fixed Θ, the credibility regression model with one contract is the classical model considered in Ch.5.2. Applying E to (11), we obtain another proof of the unbiasedness of S_0^2.

6.1.6. Conditional Zero-Excess Vectors

We will prove the optimal character of S_0^2 , under a conditional zero-excess assumption. The definition of a conditional zero-excess vector, is a direct adaptation of the definition of a usual zero-excess vector, given in section Ch.4.6.1. Let

$$Z_{n\times 1} = (Z_1,\ldots,Z_n)'$$

be a random vector and let Θ be any random variable (or random vector). We say that **the conditional vector $Z_{/\Theta}$ is a basic zero-excess vector** if, for any subscripts $i,j,k,m \in \{1,\ldots,n\}$, $EZ_i^4 < \infty$ and

$$E(Z_i^{\Theta}Z_j^{\Theta}) = \delta_{ij}u_i(\Theta),$$

$$E(Z_i^{\Theta}Z_j^{\Theta}Z_k^{\Theta}Z_m^{\Theta}) = \delta_{ij}\delta_{km}u_i(\Theta)u_k(\Theta) + \delta_{ik}\delta_{jm}u_i(\Theta)u_j(\Theta) + \delta_{im}\delta_{jk}u_i(\Theta)u_j(\Theta),$$

where

$$Z_i^{\Theta} := Z_i - E(Z_i/\Theta),$$

and

$$u_i(\Theta) := \mathrm{Var}(Z_i/\Theta) = E(Z_i^{\Theta})^2.$$

Let $Y_{n\times 1}$ be a random column and let Θ be any random variable (or random column). We say that **$Y_{/\Theta}$ is a zero-excess vector** if Y can be displayed as $Y_{n\times 1} = s_{nxn}Z_{n\times 1}$ where s is a scalar matrix and Z a random vector such that $Z_{/\Theta}$ is a basic zero-excess vector.

The results of Ch.4.6 have obvious **conditional versions**, obtained by direct adaptations of the arguments used in that section:

– Usual expectations $E(\cdot)$ must be replaced by conditional expectations $E(\cdot/\Theta)$.

– Usual centerings denoted by $^{\circ}$, must be replaced by conditional centerings denoted by $^{\Theta}$.

– Usual covariance matrices $v := \text{Cov } X$, must be replaced by conditional covariance matrices $v(\Theta) := \text{Cov}(X/\Theta)$.

6.1.7. Optimality of S_0^2

We now return to the credibility regression model with one contract. We prove the optimal character of S_0^2 by an adaptation of the arguments in the classical regression model developed in Ch.5.2.3.

Here Ch.5.(8) and (9) become

$$S_0^2 = 1/(t-n)\ (X^{\Theta}-yB^{\Theta})'v^{-1}(X^{\Theta}-yB^{\Theta})$$

$$S_0^2 = 1/(t-n)\ X^{\Theta\prime}cX^{\Theta},$$

where

$$c := v^{-1} - v^{-1}yuy'v^{-1}.$$

A **strongly centered vector**, in the credibility regression model with one contract, is a column $Y_{k\times 1}$ which can be displayed as $Y=eX$, where the matrix $e_{k\times t}$ is such that $e_{k\times t}y_{t\times n}=0_{k\times n}$. Then $Y=eX^{\Theta}$, because

$$Y = eX = eX - ey\beta(\Theta) = e[X-y\beta(\Theta)]$$

$$= e[X-E(X/\Theta)] = eX^{\Theta}.$$

We denote by $\boldsymbol{S}_{str}$ the family of random variables $Y'Z$, where $Y_{k\times 1}$ and $Z_{k\times 1}$ are strongly centered vectors of any length k. The classical estimator S_0^2 belongs to $\boldsymbol{S}_{str}$.

By the following Theorem, S_0^2 is the optimal (unbiased and of minimum variance) estimator of σ^2, under the indicated assumptions.

Theorem 4

In the credibility regression model with one contract defined by the relations (1), let us assume that $X_{/\Theta}$ is a conditional zero-excess vector. Then

$$\mathbf{S_0^2 = Proj[\sigma^2/\mathit{P}_{\sigma^2}(\mathit{S}_{str})].}$$

Proof
The proof of Ch.5.Th.4 remains valid. Indeed, it is based on the relations Ch.5.(11) and (12) only. The conditional versions of these relations are valid here (of course, a,b are general matrices, not those of the regression model).

$$E(Y'Z/\Theta) = tr(a'bv)\sigma^2(\Theta),$$

$$E(S_0^2Y'Z/\Theta) = (t-n+2)_{/(t-n)}\ tr(a'bv)\sigma^4(\Theta).$$

Taking expectations, the usual versions are also valid •

6.1.8. The Zero-Excess Assumption on B

In the credibility regression model with several contracts, the optimality of (pseudo-)estimators of the matrix $a_{n\times n}$ will be based on the assumption that regression vectors such as B are zero-excess vectors. Here we consider theoretical cases in which the latter zero-excess assumption is verified.

In practical situations, the zero-excess assumptions we make, can only be satisfied approximatively, but our estimators or pseudo-estimators, are theoretically unbiased anyway, and they can be used in any case.

If the zero-excess assumptions are met with a good approximation, then we have good estimators. If not, then we might have bad estimators. The fact is that nobody knows what the right estimators look like in the latter case.

Theorem 5

In the credibility regression model with one contract defined by the relations (1), let X be a zero-excess vector. Then B is a zero-excess vector •

This Theorem results from Ch.4.Th.11.a.

In next Theorem 6, the zero-excess of B results from the zero-excess of $X_{/\Theta}$ and the zero-excess of $\beta(\Theta)$, under the indicated assumptions.

We say that **the vector X has vanishing centered third order moments** if

$$E(X_i^\circ X_j^\circ X_k^\circ) = 0 \quad (i,j,k = 1,\ldots,t).$$

Normal vectors have vanishing centered third order moments. We say that **the vector $X_{/\Theta}$ has vanishing centered third order moments** if

$$E(X_i^\Theta X_j^\Theta X_k^\Theta/\Theta) = 0 \quad (i,j,k = 1,\ldots,t).$$

Theorem 6

In the credibility regression model with one contract, defined by the relations (1), we assume that $\beta(\Theta)$ is a zero-excess vector, that $X_{/\Theta}$ is a zero-excess vector with vanishing centered third order moments, and that $\sigma^2(\Theta) \equiv \sigma^2$. Then B is a zero-excess vector.

Proof

Let $s_{n\times n}$ be an orthogonal matrix such that

$$w := s(a+\sigma^2 u)s'$$

is a diagonal matrix. The diagonal elements of w are denoted by $w_1,\ldots,w_n$. Let $Z := sB$. Then $B=s^{-1}Z$ because orthogonal matrices are invertible, and then it is sufficient to prove that Z is a basic zero-excess vector satisfying the relations corresponding to Ch.4.(15) and (16).

From Theorem 2 results that

$$\text{Cov } Z = \text{Cov}(sB,B's') = s(\text{Cov } B)s' = s(a+\sigma^2 u)s' = w.$$

Hence

$$E(Z_i^\circ Z_j^\circ) = (\text{Cov } Z)_{ij} = \delta_{ij}w_i.$$

This is the relation corresponding to Ch.4.6.1.(15). For the proof of the relation corresponding to Ch.4.6.1.(16), we use the notations

$$c := uy'v^{-1} \quad , \quad e := sc.$$

Then, by Theorem 2,

$$B = cX \quad , \quad Z = sB = scX = eX ,$$

$$Z° = eX° = e(X-yb) = e[X-y\beta(\Theta) + y\beta(\Theta)-yb] = e[X^{\Theta}+y\beta°(\Theta)]$$

$$= eX^{\Theta}+ey\beta°(\Theta) = eX^{\Theta}+scy\beta°(\Theta) = eX^{\Theta}+s\beta°(\Theta).$$

Hence

$$Z° = eX^{\Theta}+s\beta°(\Theta).$$

Then

$$Z_i° = e_iX^{\Theta}+s_i\beta°(\Theta) ,$$

where e_i is the row i of the matrix e, and s_i the row i of the matrix s. The matrices e_iX^{Θ} and $s_i\beta°(\Theta)$ are scalars. They equal the transposed matrices $X^{\Theta\prime}e_i'$, $\beta°(\Theta)s_i'$. In a product of matrices they can be permuted with other matrices. Let

$$U_i := e_iX^{\Theta} \quad , \quad V_i := s_i\beta°(\Theta).$$

Then

$$Z_i°Z_j°Z_k°Z_m° = (U_i+V_i)(U_j+V_j)(U_k+V_k)(U_m+V_m) = \tag{12}$$

$$U_iU_jU_kU_m + U_iU_jV_kV_m + U_iV_jU_kV_m + U_iV_jV_kU_m$$

$$+ V_iU_jU_kV_m + V_iU_jV_kU_m + V_iV_jU_kU_m + V_iV_jV_kV_m + 8 \text{ other terms.}$$

In the other terms, the number of occurrences of a factor U_r is 1 or 3. The expectation of any such term equals 0. Indeed, let us consider, for instance, the term $U_iU_jU_kV_m$:

$$E(U_iU_jU_kV_m) = EE(U_iU_jU_kV_m/\Theta),$$

where

$$E(U_iU_jU_kV_m/\Theta) = V_mE(e_iX^{\Theta}e_jX^{\Theta}e_kX^{\Theta}/\Theta) = V_m \textstyle\sum_{\alpha\beta\gamma} (e_{i\alpha}X_\alpha{}^{\Theta}e_{j\beta}X_\beta{}^{\Theta}e_{k\gamma}X_\gamma{}^{\Theta}/\Theta)$$

$$= V_m \textstyle\sum_{\alpha\beta\gamma} e_{i\alpha}e_{j\beta}e_{k\gamma}E(X_\alpha{}^{\Theta}X_\beta{}^{\Theta}X_\gamma{}^{\Theta}/\Theta) = 0,$$

because $X/_{\Theta}$ has vanishing centered third order moments. For a term such as $U_lV_jV_kV_m$ in which U occurs only once, we have

$$E(U_lV_jV_kV_m) = EE(U_lV_jV_kV_m/\Theta) = V_jV_kV_mE(e_mX^{\Theta}/\Theta),$$

where

$$E(e_mX^{\Theta}/\Theta) = \textstyle\sum_\alpha e_{m\alpha} E(X^{\Theta}/\Theta) = 0.$$

We now apply Ch.4.6.2.(16) in order to calculate the expectation of the terms in the last member of (12).

We use the relations

$$Cov(X/\Theta) = \sigma^2 v \quad , \quad Cov\ \beta(\Theta) = a.$$

Then

$$E(U_iU_jU_kU_m) = EE(U_iU_jU_kU_m/\Theta),$$

where

$$E(U_iU_jU_kU_m/\Theta)= E(X^{\Theta\prime}e_i'e_jX^{\Theta}X^{\Theta\prime}e_k'e_mX^{\Theta})$$

$$= \sigma^4[tr(e_i'e_jv)tr(e_k'e_mv) + tr(e_i'e_jve_k'e_mv) + tr(e_j'e_ive_k'e_mv)]$$

$$= \sigma^4[tr(e_jve_i')tr(e_mve_k') + tr(e_jve_k'.e_mve_i') + tr(e_ive_k'.e_mve_j')]$$

$$=\sigma^4[e_jve_i'.e_mve_k' + e_jve_k'.e_mve_i' + e_ive_k'.e_mve_j'],$$

because the matrices $e_\alpha ve_\beta'$ are scalars. The scalar $e_\alpha ve_\beta'$ is the $\alpha\beta$-element of the symmetric matrix eve:

$$e_\alpha ve_\beta' = (eve')_{\alpha\beta}\ .$$

Hence,

$$E(U_iU_jU_kU_m) = \sigma^4[(eve')_{ij}(eve')_{km} + (eve')_{ik}(eve')_{jm} + (eve')_{im}(eve')_{jk}] \quad (*)$$

$$E(U_iU_jV_kV_m) = EE(U_iU_jV_kV_m/\Theta),$$

where

$$E(U_iU_jV_kV_m/\Theta) = V_kV_mE(U_iU_j/\Theta) = V_kV_mE(X^{\Theta\prime}e_i'e_jX^{\Theta})$$

$$= V_kV_m\,\sigma^2\,tr(e_i'e_jv)= V_kV_m\,\sigma^2\,tr(e_jve_i') = V_kV_m\,\sigma^2\,e_jve_i' = V_kV_m\,\sigma^2\,(eve')_{ij},$$

$$E(U_iU_jV_kV_m) = \sigma^2\,(eve')_{ij}\,E(V_kV_m) = \sigma^2\,(eve')_{ij}\,E[\beta^{\circ\prime}(\Theta)s_k's_m\beta^{\circ}(\Theta)]$$

$$\sigma^2\,(eve')_{ij}\,tr(s_k's_ma) = \sigma^2\,(eve')_{ij}\,tr(s_mas_k')$$

$$=\sigma^2\,(eve')_{ij}\,s_mas_k' = \sigma^2(eve')_{ij}(sas')_{km}.$$

Hence,

$$E(U_iU_jV_kV_m) = \sigma^2(eve')_{ij}(sas')_{km} \quad (*)$$

In the same way

$$E(U_iU_kV_jV_m) = \sigma^2(eve')_{ik}(sas')_{jm} \quad (*)$$

$$E(U_iU_mV_jV_k) = \sigma^2(eve')_{im}(sas')_{jk} \quad (*)$$

$$E(U_jU_kV_iV_m) = \sigma^2(eve')_{jk}(sas')_{im} \quad (*)$$

$$E(U_jU_mV_iV_k) = \sigma^2(eve')_{jm}(sas')_{ik} \quad (*)$$

$$E(U_kU_mV_iV_j) = \sigma^2(eve')_{km}(sas')_{ij} \quad (*)$$

$$E(V_iV_jV_kV_m) = E[\beta^{\circ\prime}(\Theta)s_i's_j\beta^\circ(\Theta)\beta^{\circ\prime}(\Theta)s_k's_m\beta^\circ(\Theta)]$$

$$= tr(s_i's_ja)tr(s_k's_ma) + tr(s_i's_jas_k's_ma) + tr(s_j's_ias_k's_ma)$$

$$= tr(s_jas_i')tr(s_mas_k') + tr(s_jas_k's_mas_i') + tr(s_ias_k's_mas_j')$$

$$= s_jas_i'.s_mas_k' + s_jas_k'.s_mas_i' + s_ias_k'.s_mas_j'.$$

Hence,

$$E(V_iV_jV_kV_m) = (sas')_{ij}(sas')_{km} + (sas')_{ik}(sas')_{jm} + (sas')_{im}(sas')_{jk} \quad (*)$$

Then, from the sum of the relations marked with an asterisk results that

$$\begin{aligned} E(Z_i^\circ Z_j^\circ Z_k^\circ Z_m^\circ) = {} & [[sas')_{ij}+\sigma^2(eve')_{ij}][(sas')_{km}+\sigma^2(eve')_{km}] \\ & +[sas')_{ik}+\sigma^2(eve')_{ik}][(sas')_{jm}+\sigma^2(eve')_{jm}] \\ & +[sas')_{im}+\sigma^2(eve')_{im}][(sas')_{jk}+\sigma^2(eve')_{jk}]] \end{aligned}$$

But

$$eve' = scvc's' = s.uy'v^{-1}.v.v^{-1}yu.s' = s.u.y'v^{-1}y.u.s' = sus',$$

and then

$$sas' + \sigma^2 eve' = sas' + \sigma^2 sus' = s(a+\sigma^2 u)s' = w,$$

$$[sas')_{ij}+\sigma^2(eve')_{ij}] = w_{ij} = \delta_{ij}w_i \quad (i,j = 1,...,n).$$

Then

$$E(Z_i^\circ Z_j^\circ Z_k^\circ Z_m^\circ) = \delta_{ij}w_i\,\delta_{km}w_m + \delta_{ik}w_k\,\delta_{jm}w_j + \delta_{im}w_i\,\delta_{jk}w_j.$$

This is the relation corresponding to Ch.4.(16) •

We now indicate another general result concerning zero-excess vectors. Of course, we say that **$Y_{/X}$ has vanishing centered third order moments** if

$$E(Y_i^XY_j^XY_k^X) = 0$$

for all i,j,k, where

$$Y_i^X = Y_i - E(Y_i/X).$$

Theorem 7

Let $X_{n\times 1}$, $Y_{n\times 1}$ be a couple of random vectors such that X is a zero-excess vector, and such that $Y_{/X}$ is a zero-excess vector with vanishing centered third order moments and with constant covariance matrix v:=Cov(Y/X). Then Y is a zero-excess vector.

Proof

Let

$$u := \text{Cov } X.$$

Then

$$\text{Cov } Y = \text{E Cov}(Y/X) + \text{Cov E}(Y/X) = v + \text{Cov } X = u+v.$$

Let $s_{n\times n}$ be an orthogonal matrix such that

$$w := s(u+v)s'$$

is a diagonal matrix. Let $Z_{n\times 1}$=sY. Then

$$\text{Cov } Z = s(u+v)s' = w.$$

Then Y=s′Z and it is sufficient to prove that Z is a basic zero-excess vector. This can be done as in the preceding proof. Here the developments are simpler

•

There is an obvious correspondence between results concerning zero-excess vectors and results concerning normal vectors. As an illustration of this remark we prove the "normal version" of the foregoing zero-excess Theorem 7. The proof is based on the following result indicated in Cramér (1958), section 11.12.

Let $p_{n\times n}$ be a definite positive matrix and $b_{n\times 1}$ any vector. Then

$$\int_{x\in R^n} \exp(b'x-{}_{1/2}\, x'px)dx = (2\pi)^{n/2}\,(\det p)^{-1/2}\,\exp({}_{1/2}\, b'p^{-1}b). \qquad (13)$$

We say that **the random vector $X_{n\times 1}$ is Normal(μ,v)** if X has a normal distribution defined by the conditions EX=$\mu_{n\times 1}$, Cov X=$v_{n\times n}$. Of course, then it is assumed that matrix v is semidefinite positive. If moreover, X is not degenerated, v is definite positive.

Theorem 8

Let $(X_{n\times 1}, Y_{n\times 1})$ be a couple of non degenerated random vectors such that the conditional vector $Y/_{X=x}$ is Normal(x,u) for all $x \in R^n$ and such that the vector X is Normal(μ,v). Then the vector Y is Normal(μ,u+v).

Proof

The density of $Y/_{X=x}$ and Y are

$$f_{Y/x}(y) = (2\pi)^{-n/2} (\det u)^{-1/2} \exp[-1/2(y-x)'u^{-1}(y-x)],$$

$$f_X(x) = (2\pi)^{-n/2} (\det v)^{-1/2} \exp[-1/2(x-\mu)'v^{-1}(x-\mu)].$$

The density of Y equals

$$f_Y(y) = \int_{x\in R^n} f_{Y/x}(y) f_X(x) dx$$

$$= (2\pi)^{-n} (\det u)^{-1/2} (\det v)^{-1/2} \int_{x\in R^n} \exp(Q) dx,$$

where $$Q := -1/2\,[(y-x)'u^{-1}(y-x) + (x-\mu)'v^{-1}(x-\mu)]$$

$$= -1/2[(y'u^{-1}y + \mu'v^{-1}\mu) - (y'u^{-1}x + x'u^{-1}y + x'v^{-1}\mu + \mu'v^{-1}x) + x'(u^{-1}+v^{-1})x]$$

and then

$$\exp(Q) = \exp[-1/2(y'u^{-1}y + \mu'v^{-1}\mu)]\exp[(y'u^{-1} + \mu'v^{-1})x - 1/2\, x'(u^{-1}+v^{-1})x].$$

By (13)

$$f_Y(y) = (2\pi)^{-n/é} (\det u)^{-1/2} (\det v)^{-1/2} [\det(u^{-1}+v^{-1})]^{-1/2} \exp(P),$$

where

$$P := -1/2(y'u^{-1}y + \mu'v^{-1}\mu) + 1/2(y'u^{-1} + \mu'v^{-1})(u^{-1}+v^{-1})^{-1}(u^{-1}y + v^{-1}\mu).$$

By the relations

$$(u+v) = u(u^{-1}+v^{-1})v\,,\ (u+v)^{-1} = v^{-1}(u^{-1}+v^{-1})^{-1}u^{-1},$$

$$u^{-1} - u^{-1}(u^{-1}+v^{-1})^{-1}u^{-1} = u^{-1} - (u^{-1}+v^{-1}-v^{-1})(u^{-1}+v^{-1})^{-1}u^{-1}$$

$$= u^{-1} - 1.u^{-1} + v^{-1}(u^{-1}+v^{-1})^{-1}u^{-1} = (u+v)^{-1},$$

and by the corresponding relations resulting from a permutation of u and v, and also by the relation for the determinant of a product of square matrices,

$$f_Y(y) = (2\pi)^{-n/2} [\det(u+v)]^{-1/2} \exp[-1/2\,(y-\mu)'(u+v)^{-1}(y-\mu)] \quad \bullet$$

The next Theorem is the normal version of the zero-excess Theorem 6. We recall that Θ may be any random vector. Then the assumption, in the following Theorem 9, that **conditionings by Θ and by $\beta(\Theta)$ are equivalent**, is satisfied if the components of Θ are functions of the components of $\beta(\Theta)$. See I.Ch.2.(27).

Theorem 9

In the credibility regression model with one contract, defined by the relations (1), we assume that the conditionings by Θ and by $\beta(\Theta)$ are equivalent, that $\beta(\Theta)$ is a normal vector, and that $X_{/\Theta}$ is normal with constant covariance matrix. Then B is a normal vector.

Proof

Let $Z := \beta(\Theta)$. Theorem 8 can be applied to the couple (B,Z). Indeed, Z is normal, and $B_{/Z}$ is normal with constant covariance matrix, because $X_{/Z}$ is normal with constant covariance matrix. By Theorem 2,

$$E(B/Z) = E[B/\beta(\Theta)] = E(B/\Theta) = \beta(\Theta) = Z,$$

i.e. the first moment of $B_{/Z=z}$ is z •

6.2. Regression Model with Several Contracts

6.2.1. Definition of the Model

Hachemeister's credibility regression model with k° contracts is defined by the random variables, random vectors and scalar matrices of the following array

$$\begin{array}{ccccc} \Theta_1 & \ldots & \Theta_k & \ldots & \Theta_{k^\circ} \\ X_1 & \ldots & X_k & \ldots & X_{k^\circ} \\ y_1 & \ldots & y_k & \ldots & y_{k^\circ} \\ v_1 & \ldots & v_k & \ldots & v_{k^\circ} \end{array}$$

in which each column is a contract satisfying, **for the same vector function $[\beta(\cdot)]_{n\times 1}$ and the same scalar function $\sigma^2(\cdot)$**, the assumptions 6.1.1. of the credibility regression model with one contract. Further assumptions are indicated hereafter.

The possible values of the variable contract subscripts i,j,k are 1,...,k°. As usual Θ_k is any random variable (or any random vector). The dimensions of

$$X_k \;,\; y_k \;,\; v_k$$

are resp.
$$t_k\times 1 \;,\; t_k\times n \;,\; t_k\times t_k \,.$$

t_k is **the length of the observable vector k**. We say that **the contracts have the same length** if $t_1=\ldots=t_{k^\circ}$.

Assumptions

a.
$$E(X_k/\Theta_k) = y_k\beta(\Theta_k) \;,\; Cov(X_k/\Theta_k) = \sigma^2(\Theta_k)v_k. \tag{14}$$

b. The contracts are independent.

c. The random variables $\Theta_1,\ldots,\Theta_{k^\circ}$ are identically distributed.

Of course, these assumptions must be completed by the usual square-integrability assumptions, the full-rank assumption on y_k, the definite positive-ness assumption on v_k.

Credibility estimator

The **credibility estimator of $\beta(\Theta_k)$** is

$$\beta(\Theta_k)_{cred} := \mathrm{Proj}[\beta(\Theta_k)/\boldsymbol{P}_{n\times 1}(1,X_1,\ldots,X_{k^\circ})] \quad \text{in } \boldsymbol{L}_{2,n\times 1}(p). \tag{15}$$

Here $\boldsymbol{P}_{n\times 1}(1,X_1,\ldots,X_{k^\circ})$ is the family of random columns of length n which can be displayed as $c+\sum c_k X_k$, where c is a scalar column, necessarily of length n, and c_k a random matrix, necessarily with dimensions $n\times t_k$.

Notations

$$b_{n\times 1} := E\beta(\Theta_k) \;,\; a_{n\times n} := Cov\ \beta(\Theta_k) \;,\; \sigma^2 = E\sigma^2(\Theta_k),$$

$$u_k := (y_k' v_k^{-1} y_k)^{-1}$$

$$(B_k)_{n\times 1} := (y_k' v_k^{-1} y_k)^{-1} y_k' v_k^{-1} X_k = u_k y'_k v_k^{-1} X_k,$$

$$(z_k)_{n\times n} := a(a+\sigma^2 u_k)^{-1} \;,\; (B_Z)_{n\times 1} := \textstyle\sum_k z_\Sigma^{-1} z_k B_k.$$

6.2.2. Basic Theorem

In the following Theorem, the formulas of Theorem 2, completed with the subscript k in the right places, are displayed.

Theorem 10

In the credibility regression model with several contracts,

$$\mathbf{EX_k = y_k b \quad , \quad E(B_k/\Theta_k) = \beta(\Theta_k) \quad , \quad EB_k = b,}$$

$$\mathbf{Cov\ X_k = y_k a y_k' + \sigma^2 v_k \quad , \quad Cov[\beta(\Theta_k), X_k'] = a y_k',}$$

$$\mathbf{Cov\ B_k = a + \sigma^2 u_k \quad , \quad Cov[\beta(\Theta_k), B_k'] = a,}$$

$$\mathbf{Cov(B_k, X_k') = (a + \sigma^2 u_k) y_k' = (Cov\ B_k) y_k'} \quad \bullet$$

Theorem 11 (Hachemeister)

In the credibility regression model with several contracts,

$$\mathbf{\beta(\Theta_k)_{cred} = z_k B_k + (1 - z_k) b.}$$

Proof
Obviously

$$z_k B_k + (1 - z_k) b \in \boldsymbol{P}_{n\times 1}(1, X_1, \ldots, X_{k^\circ})]$$

We will verify that

$$[z_k B_k + (1 - z_k) b] - \beta(\Theta_k) \perp Z,$$

where

$$Z = c + \sum_j c_j X_j$$

is any point in the plane trough the origin $\boldsymbol{P}_{n\times 1}(1, X_1, \ldots, X_{k^\circ})]$ in $\boldsymbol{L}_{2,n\times 1}(p)$. Let

$$V_k := z_k B_k + (1 - z_k) b - \beta(\Theta_k)$$

Then, by Theorem 2, $EV_k = 0$, i.e. $V_k = V_k^\circ$. By Theorem 3,

$$V_k \perp c + c_k EX_k.$$

and it is sufficient to verify that

$$V_k \perp c_jX_j \ (j\neq k), \quad \text{or} \quad E(V_k'pc_jX_j) = 0.$$

The first member of the last relation equals

$$E(V_k^{\circ\prime}pc_jX_j) = E(V_k^{\circ\prime}pc_jX_j^{\circ}) = E\,\mathrm{tr}(V_k^{\circ\prime}pc_jX_j^{\circ})$$

$$= E\,\mathrm{tr}(pc_jX_j^{\circ}V_k^{\circ\prime}) = \mathrm{tr}\,E(pc_jX_j^{\circ}V_k^{\circ\prime})$$

$$= \mathrm{tr}\,[pc_jE(X_j^{\circ}V_k^{\circ\prime})] = \mathrm{tr}[pc_j\mathrm{Cov}(X_j, V_k)] = 0.$$

Indeed, $\mathrm{Cov}(X_j,V_k)=0$, because X_j and V_k are independent, since $j\neq k$ •

6.2.3. Estimation of b

A **strongly unbiased estimator of b** is a random vector $Y_{n\times 1}$ which can be displayed as

$$Y = \sum_k c_kX_k$$

where $c_1,\ldots,c_{k^\circ}$ are matrices such that

$$\sum_k c_ky_k = 1_{n\times n}.$$

The dimensions of c_k can only be $n\times t_k$. If Y is strongly unbiased, then

$$EY = \sum_k c_kEX_k = \sum_k c_ky_kb = \sum_k c_ky_k.b = b.$$

Hence, **strongly unbiased estimators of b are unbiased estimators of b**. We represent by $\boldsymbol{B}_{str}$ the family of strongly unbiased estimators of b. Obviously, $\boldsymbol{B}_{str}$ is a plane in $\boldsymbol{L}_{n\times 1}$.

The estimator B_Z (in fact a pseudo-estimator) of b belongs to $\boldsymbol{B}_{str}$. Indeed,

$$B_Z = \sum_k z_\Sigma^{-1}z_kB_k = \sum_k z_\Sigma^{-1}z_ku_ky_k'v_k^{-1}X_k\,,$$

and

$$\sum_k z_\Sigma^{-1}z_ku_ky_k'v_k^{-1}y_k = \sum_k z_\Sigma^{-1}z_k.u_k.y_k'v_k^{-1}y_k$$

$$= \sum_k z_\Sigma^{-1}z_k = z_\Sigma^{-1}z_\Sigma = 1.$$

The optimality of B_Z, as an estimator of b, results from the following Theorem.

Theorem 12

In the credibility regression model with several contracts,

$$\mathbf{B_Z = Proj(b/\boldsymbol{B}_{str}) \ \ in\ \boldsymbol{L}_{2,n\times 1}(p).}$$

Proof

We already know that $B_Z \in \boldsymbol{B}_{str}$. We will verify that

$$B_Z - b \perp Y_1 - Y_2 ,$$

where Y_1, Y_2 are any points in $\boldsymbol{B}_{str}$. Let

$$Y_1 := \textstyle\sum_k c_{1k}X_k \ , \ \sum_k c_{1k}y_k = 1 \ , \ Y_2 := \sum_k c_{2k}X_k \ , \ \sum_k c_{1k}y_k = 1,$$

$$V := Y_1 - Y_2 = \textstyle\sum_k (c_{1k} - c_{2k})X_k = \sum_k c_k X_k \, , \ \text{where } \ c := c_1 - c_2. \qquad (16)$$

Then

$$\textstyle\sum_k c_k y_k = 0,$$

and we have to verify that

$$B_Z{}^\circ \perp V, \quad \text{or} \quad E(V'pB_Z{}^\circ) = 0.$$

The first member of the latter relation equals

$$\textstyle\sum_{jk} E(X_k{}'c_k{}'pz_\Sigma{}^{-1}z_jB_j{}^\circ) = \sum_{jk} E(X_k{}^{\circ\prime}c_k{}'pz_\Sigma{}^{-1}z_jB_j{}^\circ).$$

$$= \textstyle\sum_{jk} E(X_k{}^{\circ\prime}c_k{}'pz_\Sigma{}^{-1}z_jB_j{}^\circ) = \sum_{jk} E\ tr(c_k{}'pz_\Sigma{}^{-1}z_jB_j{}^\circ X_k{}^{\circ\prime})$$

$$= \textstyle\sum_{jk} tr\ E(c_k{}'pz_\Sigma{}^{-1}z_jB_j{}^\circ X_k{}^{\circ\prime}) = \sum_{jk} tr\ [c_k{}'pz_\Sigma{}^{-1}z_j\, E(B_j{}^\circ X_k{}^{\circ\prime})]$$

$$= \textstyle\sum_{jk} tr\ E[c_k{}'pz_\Sigma{}^{-1}z_j Cov(B_j, X_k{}')] = \sum_k tr\ E[c_k{}'pz_\Sigma{}^{-1}z_k Cov(B_j, X_k{}')]$$

$$= \textstyle\sum_k tr\ E[c_k{}'pz_\Sigma{}^{-1}z_k(a+\sigma^2u_k)y_k{}'] = \sum_k tr\ E[pz_\Sigma{}^{-1}.z_k(a+\sigma^2u_k).y_k{}'c_k{}']$$

$$= \textstyle\sum_k tr\ E[pz_\Sigma{}^{-1}.a.y_k{}'c_k{}'] = tr\ E[pz_\Sigma{}^{-1}a\sum_k y_k{}'c_k{}'] = tr\ E[pz_\Sigma{}^{-1}a0] = 0.$$

In these relations, we used the fact that B_j and X_k are independent if $j \neq k$, the expression of $Cov(B_k, X_k')$ furnished by Theorem 10 and the definition of z_k•

Let

$$\beta(\Theta_k)_{CRED} := z_kB_k + (1-z_k)B_Z. \tag{17}$$

This is the credibility estimator $\beta(\Theta_k)_{cred}$, furnished by Theorem 11, in which the vector b has been replaced by its optimal estimator B_Z. By the next Theorem, $\beta(\Theta_k)_{CRED}$ can be obtained in one step, as a projection of $\beta(\Theta_k)$ on $\boldsymbol{B}_{str}$ in $\boldsymbol{L}_{2,n\times1}(p)$.

Theorem 13

In the credibility regression model with several contracts,

$$\beta(\Theta_k)_{CRED} = \mathrm{Proj}[\beta(\Theta_k)/\boldsymbol{B}_{str}] \text{ in } \boldsymbol{L}_{2,n\times1}.$$

Proof

It is direct that B_k belongs to $\boldsymbol{B}_{str}$ .Hence, it is enough to verify that $C_k \perp Y_1-Y_2$, where Y_1,Y_2 are any points in $\boldsymbol{B}_{str}$, and where

$$C_k := z_kB_k + (1-z_k)B_Z - \beta(\Theta_k) = z_k(B_k-B_Z) + [B_Z-b] + b-\beta(\Theta_k).$$

By Theorem 12, the term in square-brackets is orthogonal to Y_1-Y_2 .
Let

$$D_k = z_k(B_k-B_Z) + b-\beta(\Theta_k)$$

Then

$$D_k := z_k(B_k{}^\circ-B_Z{}^\circ) - \beta^\circ(\Theta) = \textstyle\sum_j z_kz_\Sigma{}^{-1}z_j(B_k{}^\circ-B_j{}^\circ) - \beta^\circ(\Theta_k).$$

Let Y_1,Y_2,V be defined by (16). Then

$$Y_1-Y_2 = V = \textstyle\sum_i c_iX_i \ , \ \ \sum_i c_iy_i = 0,$$

and it is sufficient to prove that

$$D_k \perp V \ , \quad \text{or } \ E(V'pD_k) = 0.$$

The first member of the latter relation equals, by Theorem 10 and by the independence of the contracts,

$$\textstyle\sum_{ij} E[X_i'c_i'pz_kz_\Sigma{}^{-1}z_j(B_k{}^\circ-B_j{}^\circ)] - \sum_i E[X_i'c_i'p\beta^\circ(\Theta_k)] \tag{18}$$

$$= \sum_{ij} E[X_i^{\circ\prime}c_i'pz_kz_\Sigma^{-1}z_j(B_k^\circ - B_j^\circ)] - \sum_i E[X_i^{\circ\prime}c_i'p\beta^\circ(\Theta_k)]$$

$$= \sum_{ij} E\,tr[X_i^{\circ\prime}c_i'pz_kz_\Sigma^{-1}z_j(B_k^\circ - B_j^\circ)] - \sum_i E\,tr[X_i^{\circ\prime}c_i'p\beta^\circ(\Theta_k)]$$

$$= \sum_{ij} E\,tr[pz_kz_\Sigma^{-1}z_j(B_k^\circ - B_j^\circ)X_i^{\circ\prime}c_i'] - \sum_i E\,tr[p\beta^\circ(\Theta_k)X_i^{\circ\prime}c_i']$$

$$= \sum_{ij} tr\,E[pz_kz_\Sigma^{-1}z_j(B_k^\circ - B_j^\circ)X_i^{\circ\prime}c_i'] - \sum_i tr\,E[p\beta^\circ(\Theta_k)X_i^{\circ\prime}c_i']$$

$$= \sum_{ij} tr\,[[pz_kz_\Sigma^{-1}z_jE[(B_k^\circ - B_j^\circ)X_i^{\circ\prime}]c_i'] - \sum_i tr\,[pE[\beta^\circ(\Theta_k)X_i^{\circ\prime}]c_i']$$

$$= \sum_{ij} tr\,[[pz_kz_\Sigma^{-1}z_jE[(B_k^\circ X_i^{\circ\prime}]c_i'] - \sum_{ij} tr\,[[pz_kz_\Sigma^{-1}z_jE[(B_j^\circ X_i^{\circ\prime}]c_i'] \\ - \sum_i tr\,[pE[\beta^\circ(\Theta_k)X_i^{\circ\prime}]c_i']$$

$$= \sum_{ij} tr\,[[pz_kz_\Sigma^{-1}z_jCov(B_k,X_i)c_i'] - \sum_{ij} tr\,[[pz_kz_\Sigma^{-1}z_jCov(B_j,X_i')c_i'] \\ - \sum_i tr\,[pCov[\beta^\circ(\Theta_k),X_i']c_i']$$

$$= \sum_{j} tr\,[[pz_kz_\Sigma^{-1}z_jCov(B_k,X_k)c_k'] - \sum_{i} tr\,[[pz_kz_\Sigma^{-1}z_iCov(B_i,X_i')c_i'] \\ - tr\,[pCov[\beta^\circ(\Theta_k),X_k']c_k']$$

$$= \sum_{j} tr\,[[pz_kz_\Sigma^{-1}z_j(a+\sigma^2u_k)y_k'c_k'] - \sum_{i} tr\,[[pz_kz_\Sigma^{-1}z_i(a+\sigma^2u_i)y_i'c_i'] \\ - tr\,[pay_k'c_k']$$

$$= tr\,[[pz_kz_\Sigma^{-1}z_\Sigma(a+\sigma^2u_k)y_k'c_k'] - \sum_i tr\,[[pz_kz_\Sigma^{-1}ay_i'c_i'] - tr\,[pay_k'c_k']$$

$$= tr\,[[pz_k(a+\sigma^2u_k)y_k'c_k'] - tr\,[[pz_kz_\Sigma^{-1}a\sum_i y_i'c_i'] - tr\,[pay_k'c_k']$$

$$= tr\,[[pay_k'c_k'] - tr\,[[pz_kz_\Sigma^{-1}a0] - tr\,[pay_k'c_k'] = 0 \quad \bullet$$

6.2.4. The Credibility Regression Model in Practice

We consider a fixed contract k. The vector B_k is the **individual estimator of $\beta(\Theta_k)$**. Mostly this estimator is not safe enough. The vector B_Z is the **portfolio estimator of $\beta(\Theta_k)$**. This estimator is not sufficiently "individual". The **credibility estimator $\beta(\Theta_k)_{CRED}$ of $\beta(\Theta_k)$** is expected to be safe enough and sufficiently individual.

The vector yB_k is the **individual estimator of $E(X_k/\Theta)$**, the vector yB_Z is its **portfolio estimator**, and the vector $y\beta(\Theta_k)_{CRED}$ **its credibility estimator**. Let

$$X_k = (X_{k1},...X_{t_k})'.$$

The actuary needs an estimator of $E(X_{k\tau}/\Theta_k)$, where $X_{k\tau}$ is a future observation, say of the year $\tau=t_k+1$. The foregoing theory does not furnish this estimator. In order to obtain it, we must assume that the observable vector X_k is completed by the non-observable random variable $X_{k\tau}$ and that the design matrix y_k is completed by a row, say $y_{k\tau}$. In practice, the definition of this supplementary row is obvious. For instance, if y_k is a matrix with 3 columns, and if the row t is

$$y_{kt} = (1,t,t^2) \quad (t=1,...,t_k),$$

then it is rather evident that the new row $y_{k\tau}$ must be

$$y_{k\tau} := (1,\tau,\tau^2).$$

The credibility approximation of $E(X_k/\Theta_k)$ is

$$y_k\beta(\Theta_k)_{CRED} = y_k z_k B_k + y_k(1-z_k)B_Z.$$

The component t $(t=1,...,t_k)$ of that column is

$$y_{kt}\beta(\Theta_k)_{CRED} = y_{kt}z_k B_k + y_{kt}(1-z_k)B_Z,$$

and the latter is the credibility approximation of the random variable $E(X_{kt}/\Theta)$. By an obvious extrapolation,

$$y_{k\tau}\beta(\Theta_k)_{CRED} = y_{k\tau}z_k B_k + y_{k\tau}(1-z_k)B_Z, \tag{19}$$

is defined to be the **credibility estimator of $E(X_{k\tau}/\Theta_k)$**.

The **individual,** the **portfolio estimator** of that random variable is $y_{k\tau}B_k$, $y_{k\tau}B_Z$ resp.

6.2.5. Alternate Definition of Credibility Estimators

Taking the relation $E(X_k/\Theta_k)=y_k\beta(\Theta_k)$ into account, the credibility approximation of $E(X_k/\Theta_k)$ has been defined as the credibility approximation of $\beta(\Theta_k)$ pre-multiplied by y_k in the preceding section 6.2.4. In fact, the credibility approximation of $E(X_k/\Theta_k)$ can be defined directly, in a more satisfactory way, as follows:

$$E(X_k/\Theta_k)_{cred} := \text{Proj}[E(X_k/\Theta_k)/\boldsymbol{P}_{t_k\times 1}(1,X_1,\ldots X_{k^\circ})] \text{ in } \boldsymbol{L}_{2,t_k\times 1}(p_k), \qquad (20)$$

where

$$\boldsymbol{P}_{t_k\times 1}(1,X_1,\ldots X_{k^\circ})$$

is the space of random columns of length t_k,

$$c + \sum c_k X_k \text{ (c vector, } c_k \text{ matrices).}$$

The matrix p_k occurring in $\boldsymbol{L}_{2,t_k\times 1}(p_k)$ is the definite positive matrix of dimensions $t_k \times t_k$ defining the scalar product in the space $\boldsymbol{L}_{2,t_k\times 1}$. The matrix p_k is essential in the definition of the Hilbert space, but it will not occur in the projection defined by (20).

The space $\boldsymbol{P}_{t_k\times 1}(1,X_1,\ldots X_{k^\circ})$ is a finite-dimensional plane through the origin of $\boldsymbol{L}_{2,t_k\times 1}$.

$$E(X_k/\Theta_k)_{CRED} := \text{Proj}[E(X_k/\Theta_k)/y_k\boldsymbol{B}_{str}] \text{ in } \boldsymbol{L}_{2,t_k\times 1}(p_k), \qquad (21)$$

where

$$y_k\boldsymbol{B}_{str} := \{y_k Y \,/\, Y \in \boldsymbol{B}_{str}\}.$$

The space $y_k\boldsymbol{B}_{str}$ is a sub-plane of $\boldsymbol{P}_{t_k\times 1}(1,X_1,\ldots X_{k^\circ})$, (mostly) not through the origin of $\boldsymbol{L}_{2,t_k\times 1}$. By the next Theorem, the credibility estimator defined by (21) is that one considered in section 6.2.4.

Theorem 14

In the credibility regression model with several contracts,

$$\mathbf{E(X_k/\Theta_k)_{cred} = y_k\beta(\Theta_k)_{cred}}$$

and

$$\mathbf{E(X_k/\Theta_k)_{CRED} = y_k\beta(\Theta_k)_{CRED}}.$$

Proof

$$y_k\beta(\Theta_k)_{cred} = y_k[z_kB_k+(1-z_k)b] = y_k(z_kB_k^\circ+b),$$

$$y_k\beta(\Theta_k)_{cred} - E(X_k/\Theta_k) = y_k\beta(\Theta_k)_{cred} - y_k\beta(\Theta_k) = y_k[z_kB_k^\circ-\beta^\circ(\Theta_k)].$$

Hence, for the first relation of the Theorem, we have to verify that

$$y_k[z_kB_k^\circ-\beta^\circ(\Theta_k)] \perp c+\sum_j c_jX_j,$$

where c is a column of length t_k and c_j a matrix of dimensions $t_k \times t_j$. This orthogonality relation, in $\boldsymbol{L}_{2,t_k\times 1}(p_k)$, is equivalent to the relation

$$E[(c+\sum_j X_j'c_j')p_k y_k[z_k B_k^\circ - \beta^\circ(\Theta_k)]] = 0.$$

The first member of the latter relation equals

$$\sum_j E[X_j^{\circ\prime} c_j' p_k y_k[z_k B_k^\circ - \beta^\circ(\Theta_k)]] = \sum_j E\,\mathrm{tr}[X_j^{\circ\prime} c_j' p_k y_k[z_k B_k^\circ - \beta^\circ(\Theta_k)]]$$

$$= \sum_j E\,\mathrm{tr}[c_j' p_k y_k[z_k B_k^\circ - \beta^\circ(\Theta_k)]X_j^{\circ\prime}]$$

$$= \sum_j E\,\mathrm{tr}[c_j' p_k y_k z_k B_k^\circ X_j^{\circ\prime}] - \sum_j E\,\mathrm{tr}[c_j' p_k y_k \beta^\circ(\Theta_k) X_j^{\circ\prime}]$$

$$= \sum_j \mathrm{tr}\,E[c_j' p_k y_k z_k B_k^\circ X_j^{\circ\prime}] - \sum_j \mathrm{tr}\,E[c_j' p_k y_k \beta^\circ(\Theta_k) X_j^{\circ\prime}]$$

$$= \sum_j \mathrm{tr}\,[c_j' p_k y_k z_k E(B_k^\circ X_j^{\circ\prime})] - \sum_j \mathrm{tr}\,[c_j' p_k y_k E(\beta^\circ(\Theta_k) X_j^{\circ\prime})]$$

$$= \mathrm{tr}\,[c_k' p_k y_k z_k \mathrm{Cov}(B_k, X_k')] - \mathrm{tr}\,[c_k' p_k y_k \mathrm{Cov}(\beta(\Theta_k), X_k')]$$

$$= \mathrm{tr}\,[c_k' p_k y_k z_k (a+\sigma^2 u_k) y_k'\,] - \mathrm{tr}\,[c_k' p_k y_k a y_k']$$

$$= \mathrm{tr}\,[c_k' p_k y_k a y_k'\,] - \mathrm{tr}\,[c_k' p_k y_k a y_k'] = 0.$$

This proves the first relation of the Theorem. For the last relation, we have

$$y_k \beta(\Theta_k)_{CRED} - E(X_k/\Theta_k) = y_k[z_k B_k + (1-z_k)B_Z] - E(X_k/\Theta_k)$$

$$= y_k[z_k B_k + (1-z_k)(b + B_Z - b)] - E(X_k/\Theta_k)$$

$$= y_k[z_k B_k + (1-z_k)b] - E(X_k/\Theta_k) + y_k(1-z_k)(B_Z - b)$$

$$= [y_k \beta(\Theta_k)_{cred} - E(X_k/\Theta_k)] + y_k(1-z_k)B_Z^\circ.$$

We have to prove that

$$[y_k \beta(\Theta_k)_{cred} - E(X_k/\Theta_k)] + y_k(1-z_k)B_Z^\circ \perp y_k(Y_1 - Y_2),$$

where $Y_1, Y_2 \in \boldsymbol{B}_{str}$.

$$y_k(Y_1-Y_2) \in \boldsymbol{P}_{t_k\times 1}(1,X_1,\ldots X_{k^\circ})$$

and by the first formula already proved,

$$[y_k\beta(\Theta_k)_{cred} - E(X_k/\Theta_k)] \perp y_k(Y_1-Y_2)$$

Hence, it is enough to verify that

$$y_k(1-z_k)B_Z{}^\circ \perp y_k(Y_1-Y_2),$$

or, if Y_1 and Y_2 are defined by (16),

$$\textstyle\sum_j y_k(1-z_k)z_\Sigma{}^{-1}z_jB_j{}^\circ \perp \sum_i c_iX_i\text{ , where } \sum_i c_iy_i=0.$$

Then it is enough to verify that

$$E[\textstyle\sum_i X_i'c_i'p_k\sum_j y_k(1-z_k)z_\Sigma{}^{-1}z_jB_j{}^\circ] = 0.$$

The first member of that relation equals

$$\textstyle\sum_{ij} E[X_i{}^{\circ\prime}c_i'p_ky_k(1-z_k)z_\Sigma{}^{-1}z_jB_j{}^\circ] = \sum_{ij} E\ tr[X_i{}^{\circ\prime}c_i'p_ky_k(1-z_k)z_\Sigma{}^{-1}z_jB_j{}^\circ]$$

$$=\textstyle\sum_{ij} E\ tr[p_ky_k(1-z_k)z_\Sigma{}^{-1}z_jB_j{}^\circ X_i{}^{\circ\prime}c_i']$$

$$=\textstyle\sum_i E\ tr[p_ky_k(1-z_k)z_\Sigma{}^{-1}z_iCov(B_i,X_i)c_i']$$

$$=\textstyle\sum_i E\ tr[p_ky_k(1-z_k)z_\Sigma{}^{-1}z_i(a+\sigma^2u_i)y_i'c_i']$$

$$=\textstyle\sum_i E\ tr[p_ky_k(1-z_k)z_\Sigma{}^{-1}ay_i'c_i'] = E\ tr[p_ky_k(1-z_k)z_\Sigma{}^{-1}a\sum_i y_i'c_i']$$

$$= E\ tr[p_ky_k(1-z_k)z_\Sigma{}^{-1}a0] = 0 \quad \bullet$$

6.2.6. Estimation of σ^2

The **classical estimator of σ^2** is

$$S^2 := [\textstyle\sum_k(t_k-n)]^{-1} \sum_k (t_k-n)S_k{}^2, \tag{22}$$

where

$$S_k{}^2 := (t_k-n)^{-1} (X_k-y_kB_k)'v_k{}^{-1}(X_k-y_kB_k). \tag{23}$$

The estimator $S_k{}^2$ is the estimator (10) defined here in contract k. Hence, it is an unbiased estimator of σ^2. Then (22) is also an unbiased estimator of σ^2.

The estimator S^2 is a point of the plane

$$\boldsymbol{P}(S_1^2,\ldots,S_{k^\circ}^2)$$

through the origin of $\boldsymbol{L}_2$. By the following Theorem, it is the optimal (unbiased and of minimum variance) estimator in that family, under the indicated assumptions.

Theorem 15

In the credibility regression model with several contracts, we assume that the conditional vectors X_k/Θ_k are zero-excess vectors. Then

$$\mathbf{S^2 = Proj[\sigma^2/\boldsymbol{P}_{\sigma^2}(S_1^2,\ldots,S_{k^\circ}^2)]}$$

if $\sigma^2(\Theta_k)\equiv\sigma^2$ or if all contracts have the same length.

Proof
By Ch.5.Th.5,

$$\text{Var}(S_k^2/\Theta_k) = 2(t_k-1)^{-1}\,\sigma^4(\Theta_k)$$

because the assumptions (14) imply that, for fixed Θ, the contract k is the classical regression model of Ch.5.2 (see last paragraph of Ch.6.1.5). Then

$$\text{Var}\,S_k^2 = \text{E Var}(S_k^2/\Theta_k) + \text{Var E}(S_k^2/\Theta) = 2(t_k-1)^{-1}\,\text{E}\sigma^4(\Theta_k) + \text{Var}\,\sigma^2(\Theta).$$

Hence,

$$\text{Var}\,S_k^2 = [1+2(t_k-1)^{-1}]\,\text{E}\sigma^4(\Theta_k) - \sigma^4. \tag{24}$$

By the optimal projection Theorem Ch.1.Th.10 of constants, it is enough to verify that

$$\text{Cov}(S^2,S_k^2)/\text{E}S_k^2$$

does not depend on k. But $\text{E}S_k^2=\sigma^2$. Hence, it is sufficient to verify that $\text{Cov}(S^2,S_k^2)$ does not depend on k. Let

$$c_j := [\Sigma_k(t_k-n)]^{-1}\,(t_j-n).$$

Then $S^2 = \Sigma c_jS_j^2$, and by the independence of the contracts,

$$\mathrm{Cov}(S^2, S_k^2) = c_k \mathrm{Var}\, S_k^2.$$

If $\sigma^2(\Theta_k) \equiv \sigma^2$, then $\sigma^4(\Theta_k) \equiv \sigma^4$, $E\sigma^4(\Theta_k) = \sigma^4$, and then

$$\mathrm{Var}\, S_k^2 = 2(t_k - 1)^{-1}\sigma^4$$

by (24). Then

$$\mathrm{Cov}(S^2, S_k^2) = 2[\Sigma_k(t_k - n)]^{-1}\sigma^4,$$

where the last member does not depend on k.

If all the contracts have the same length $t_k \equiv t°$, then Var S_k^2 does not depend on k, c_k does not depend on k, and then the product c_kVar S_k^2 does not depend on k •

6.2.7. Estimation of a

By Theorem 10, the independent vectors

$$(B_1)_{n\times 1}\,,\ (B_2)_{n\times 1}\,,\ \ldots\,,\ (B_{k°})_{n\times 1} \tag{25}$$

are such that

$$EB_k = b \quad , \quad \mathrm{Cov}\, B_k = a + \sigma^2 u_k\,. \tag{26}$$

Hence they satisfy the assumptions Ch.5.(43),(44) of the Modell III considered in Chapter 5. The matrix corresponding to the matrix z_k of Ch.5.6.1, is

$$z_k^{cl} := (a + \sigma^2 u_k)^{-1}. \tag{27}$$

Then $z_k = a z_k^{cl}$ and this implies that $B_Z = B_{Z^{cl}}$. By Ch.5.6.2, B_Z is also the optimal estimator of b in the model defined by the relations (25) and (26).

Hereafter the superscript ^{cl} is used for the vectors and matrices defined in the classical model III of Chapter 5. The correspondence with the vectors and matrices of the credibility regression model with several contracts is:

$$X_k^{cl} = B_k \quad , \quad \mu^{cl} = b$$

$$v^{cl} = a \quad , \quad u_k^{cl} = \sigma^2 u_k \quad , \quad v_k^{cl} = a + \sigma^2 u_k = (z_k^{cl})^{-1} = z_k^{-1} a \quad , \quad z_k^{cl} = a^{-1} z_k.$$

The result of Ch.5.6.3 can be transposed to the the estimation of the matrix $a_{n\times n}$. The next Theorem results from Ch.5.Th.8.

Theorem 16

In the credibility regression model with several contracts,

$$\mathbf{A_c := [2c_{\Sigma\Sigma}-2\Sigma_k c_{kk}]^{-1}[\Sigma_{ij}c_{ij}(B_i-B_j)(B_i-B_j)'-\Sigma_k(c_{k\Sigma}+c_{\Sigma k}-2c_{kk})v_kS^2]},$$

is an unbiased estimator of $a_{n\times n}$ whatever the matrix weights $(c_{ij})_{n\times n}$ are, but such that the inverse matrix occurring in the last member exists •

We now consider pseudo-estimators of $a_{n\times n}$. The simplest pseudo-estimator of that matrix, corresponding to Ch.5.(8), is

$$1/(k^\circ-1)\ \Sigma_k\ z_k(B_k-B_Z)(B_k-B_Z)'. \tag{28}$$

Arguments in favor of this pseudo-estimator are its theoretical unbiasedness and its simplicity. It does not deserve a special notation. We did not discover any optimal character of (28). The pseudo-estimator (28) is the n-dimensional extension of the optimal pseudo-estimator A_{pseu} of Ch.3.(81).

As usual, optimal pseudo-estimators can be constructed as projections on large planes. The planes that we consider hereafter are now defined.

$\boldsymbol{A}_b$ is the space of random matrices

$$\Sigma_k\ (c_k)_{n\times n}\ (B_k-b)(B_k-b)'.$$

$\boldsymbol{A}_Z$ is the space of random matrices

$$\Sigma_k\ (c_k)_{n\times n}\ (B_k-B_Z)(B_k-B_Z)'.$$

$\boldsymbol{A}$ is the space of random matrices

$$\Sigma_{ij}\ (c_{ij})_{n\times n}\ (B_i-B_j)(B_i-B_j)'.$$

In these definitions, c_k and c_{ij} are any matrices in $\mathbf{R}_{n\times n}$. The spaces $\boldsymbol{A}_b$, $\boldsymbol{A}_Z$ and $\boldsymbol{A}$ are finite dimensional planes through the origin of $\boldsymbol{L}_{2,n\times n}(p,q)$. The definite positive matrices p,q are those defining the scalar product in the space $\boldsymbol{L}_{2,n\times n}$, by Ch.4.(1).

The **modified credibility matrices** are

$$z_k^{\circ} := [z_k^{-1} + (\mathrm{tr}\ z_k^{-1})1_{n\times n}]^{-1}.$$

Theorem 17

If the vectors B_k of the credibility regression model are zero-excess vectors, then

$$\mathbf{A_{b,pseu} := c \textstyle\sum_k z_k^{\circ}(B_k - b)(B_k - b)' = Proj[(a/\mathit{P}_a(\mathit{A}_b)]},$$

in $L_{2,n\times n}(p,a^{-1})$, where c_{nxn} is such that $EA_{b,pseu}$=a , i.e.

$$\mathbf{c := [\textstyle\sum_k z_k^{\circ} z_k^{-1}]^{-1}}.$$

Proof

The Theorem results from Ch.5.Th.9 with $q^{cl} := a^{-1}$. Then

$$v_k^{cl} q^{cl} = z_k^{-1} a a^{-1} = z_k^{-1} \quad , \quad (w_{opt,k})^{cl} = [z_k^{-1} + (\mathrm{tr}\ z_k^{-1})1_{n\times n}]^{-1} = z_k^{\circ},$$

$$v^{cl}[\textstyle\sum_k (w_{opt,k})^{cl} v_k^{cl}]^{-1} = a[\sum_k z_k^{\circ} z_k^{-1} a]^{-1} = [\sum_k z_k^{\circ} z_k^{-1}]^{-1} \quad \bullet$$

$A_{b,pseu}$ could be used as a pseudo-estimator for $a_{n\times n}$, simultaneously with the pseudo-estimator B_Z of b. A better pseudo-estimator, in which b is already replaced by B_Z is the projection of $a_{n\times n}$ on $\mathit{P}_a(\mathit{A}_Z)$. It can be calculated under the assumption that the vectors B_k are zero-excess vectors, but its expression is rather complicated. A simple approximation of the latter projection results from the replacement of b by B_Z in $A_{b,pseu}$, and a simultaneous correction of c, in order to preserve the unbiasedness. The result is the following pseudo-estimator A_{pseu} corresponding to the pseudo-estimator Ch.5.(66).

$$\mathbf{A_{pseu} := [\textstyle\sum_k z_k^{\circ} z_k^{-1} - z_\Sigma^{\circ} z_\Sigma^{-1}]^{-1} \sum_k z_k^{\circ}(B_k - B_Z)(B_k - B_Z)'}. \qquad (29)$$

The pseudo-estimator A_{pseu} is approximatively optimal if the vectors B_k are zero-excess vectors. It is unbiased, and it can be used in any case.

The variability of the length of the contracts and the dependence on k of the design matrix y_k , are not a luxury. They allow to cope with missing data. But, in most cases, t_k and y_k do not depend on the contract k, and v_k is a diagonal matrix. We now consider the latter situation.

The practical credibility regression model with several contracts

In the **practical credibility regression model with several contracts,**

$$t_k \equiv t^\circ \;,\; y_k \equiv y_{t^\circ \times n} \;,\; v_k = \text{Diagonal}(w_{k1}^{-1},...,w_{kt^\circ}^{-1}).$$

Then the strictly positive number w_{kt} is the **volume** (or **the natural weight) of the observation X_{kt}** of the contract k and the year t. We denote by w_{kA} the arithmetic mean of the natural weights of the contract k:

$$w_{kA} = 1/t^\circ\,(w_{k1}+...+w_{kt^\circ}).$$

The volumes of different contracts may be very different, but very often the volume of any fixed contract k does not vary much with t. The case of **contracts of constant volume,** $w_{kt} \equiv w_{kA}$ is not exceptional.

In the practical model with contracts of constant volume,

$$v_k^{-1} = w_{kA} 1_{t^\circ \times t^\circ} \;,\; u_k = (y' v_k^{-1} y)^{-1} = w_{kA}(y'y)^{-1}$$

and then

$$z_k = a[a + w_{kA}\sigma^2 (y'y)^{-1}]^{-1} = [1_{n\times n} + w_{kA}\sigma^2 (ay'y)^{-1}]^{-1}$$

$$z_k^{-1} = 1_{n\times n} + w_{kA}\sigma^2 (ay'y)^{-1}. \tag{30}$$

Then

$$z_j^{-1} z_k^{-1} = z_k^{-1} z_j^{-1}$$

and this implies that

$$z_j^\circ z_k^\circ = z_k^\circ z_j^\circ.$$

During the proof of Theorem 17, we have obtained that z_k° equals $(w_{opt,k})^{cl}$. Hence, the following Theorem results from Ch.5.Th.10.

Theorem 18

In the practical credibility regression model with several contracts of constant volume,

$$\mathbf{A^\circ_{pseu} := [\textstyle\sum_k (z_k^\circ z_\Sigma^\circ + z_\Sigma^\circ z_k^\circ - 2 z_k^\circ) z_k^{-1}]^{-1} \sum_{ij} z_i^\circ z_j^\circ (B_i - B_j)(B_i - B_j)'} \tag{31}$$

$$\mathbf{= Proj[a/\mathit{P}_a(\mathit{A})] \;\; in\; \mathit{L}_{2,nxn}(p,a^{-1}),}$$

if the vectors B_k are zero-excess vectors •

The term in square brackets in the last member of (31) equals

$$2\sum_k (z_k{}^\circ z_\Sigma{}^\circ - z_k{}^\circ) z_k{}^{-1},$$

because $z_k{}^\circ z_\Sigma{}^\circ = z_\Sigma{}^\circ z_k{}^\circ$ in the practical model with contracts of constant volume.

The pseudo-estimator A°_{pseu} defined by (30), is unbiased in any case. It can be used in any practical model. If the volumes of the contracts do not vary too much in time, and if the the vectors B_k do not differ too much from zero-excess vectors, then A°_{pseu} will remain approximatively optimal. If the contracts result from groupings of a large number of i.i.d. contracts, then, by central tendency, the vectors B_k are approximatively normal, and this implies approximative zero-excess. Hence, the assumptions on which the optimality of A°_{pseu} is based are far from unrealistic.

Let us now re-consider the general usual estimator A_c of Theorem 16, in the practical credibility regression model. We cannot use it with the "optimal weights"

$$c_{ij} = z_i{}^\circ z_j{}^\circ,$$

because then it becomes a pseudo-estimator. But the foregoing study furnishes arguments for the scalar weights

$$c_{ij} = w_{iA} w_{jA},$$

in case $1_{n\times n}$ is small compared to $w_{kA}\sigma^2(ay'y)^{-1}$ by (30), and arguments for constant weights in case $1_{n\times n}$ is large compared to $w_{kA}\sigma^2(ay'y)^{-1}$. In intermediate situations, or when no information is available on the order of magnitude of $\sigma^2(ay'y)^{-1}$ (this is mostly the case), the statistician allergic to pseudo-estimators can for instance use the usual estimator A_c with the scalar weights

$$c_{ij} := (w_{iA} w_{jA})^\alpha \ , \ \alpha = 1/2.$$

6.3. Variants of the Credibility Regression Model

6.3.1. Impossible Credibility Estimates

We consider a fixed contract in the credibility regression model, and we omit the fixed subscript k in the notations. By (19), the **credibility estimator** of $E(X_\tau/\Theta)$, where τ is some future year, is

$$y_\tau\beta(\Theta)_{CRED} = y_\tau zB + y_\tau(1-z)B_Z. \tag{31}$$

Here y_τ is a supplementary row by which the initial design matrix y must be completed. The **individual estimator** of $E(X_\tau/\Theta)$ is $y_\tau B$, and the **portfolio estimator** of $E(X_\tau/\Theta)$ is $y_\tau B_Z$. From (31) does not result that the credibility estimator of $E(X_\tau/\Theta)$ lies in the interval delimited by the portfolio estimator and by the individual estimator.

The credibility regression model hitherto developed can furnish a **portfolio premium** equal to 1000 $, an **individual premium** equal to 2000 $ and a **credibility adjusted individual premium** equal to 2500 $. Nobody can accept this, and certainly not the insured to whom this happens.

The reason of this impossible situation is that z is a matrix, not just a scalar. Indeed, let us assume, that z in (31) is a scalar. Then (31) can be displayed as

$$y_\tau\beta(\Theta)_{CRED} = z.y_\tau B + (1-z).y_\tau B_Z. \tag{32}$$

Moreover if $0 \le z \le 1$, then the last member of (32) is a number in the interval with extremities $y_\tau B$ and $y_\tau B_Z$.

In the following section 18.3.2, we develop a credibility regression model in which z necessarily is a diagonal matrix. In this model, the practical impossibility here discussed occurs less often than in the original model, but it is not completely excluded. In the section 6.3.3, we develop a model in which z is a scalar between 0 and 1. In the latter model, as we have just seen, no impossible credibility estimates can occur. In the adapted models, the distance, in $\boldsymbol{L}_{2,n\times 1}(p)$, separating $\beta(\Theta)$ and its credibility approximation, are larger than in the original model. The order of preference of the models should be

1. Original model
2. Model with diagonal credibility matrix (6.3.2)
3. Model with credibility matrix reduced to a scalar (6.3.3).

Only in case of practical impossibilities, the first model should be replaced by the second one, and the second model by the third.

We develop the theory of the adapted models in the case of a portfolio reduced to one contract. The parameters $b_{n\times 1}$, a_{nxn} and σ^2 are the same as in the original model. They should be estimated in the original model with several contracts.

In the practical portfolio with several contracts, the original regression model can be used for some contracts, the adapted models for other contracts in which practical impossibilities do occur.

6.3.2. Regression Model with Diagonal Credibility Matrix

We consider the regression model with one contract defined by the relations (1) and we adopt the notations of 6.1. The credibility estimator of $\beta(\Theta)$ that we consider now is

$$\beta(\Theta)_{diag} := \text{Proj}[\beta(\Theta)/\boldsymbol{P}_{b,n\times 1,diag}(B,b)] \text{ in } \boldsymbol{L}_{2,n\times 1}(p)$$

where

$$\boldsymbol{P}_{b,n\times 1,diag}(B,b),$$

is the space of random vectors of length n,

$$cB + eb \ (c_{n\times n}\ ,\ e_{n\times n} \text{ diagonal matrices})$$

such that

$$E(cB+eb) = b.$$

The space $\boldsymbol{P}_{b,n\times 1,diag}(B,b)$ is a finite-dimensional plane in $\boldsymbol{L}_{2,n\times 1}$.

Deterministic results

Let $a_{m\times n}$ and $b_{m\times n}$ be matrices Then the "product" $(a_\circ b)_{m\times n}$ is the matrix with elements

$$(a_\circ b)_{ij} = a_{ij}b_{ij}.$$

For any square matrix $c_{n\times n}$, the matrix $(c_{DC})_{n\times 1}$ is the Diagonal of c displayed as a Column:

$$c_{DC} = \text{Column}(c_{11},\dots,c_{nn}).$$

Theorem 19

a. Let a, b be matrices of dimensions n×n and let c be a diagonal matrix of dimensions n×n. Then

$$(acb)_{DC} = (a_\circ b')c_{DC}\,.$$

b. Let $p_{n\times n}$ and $q_{n\times n}$ be semidefinite positive matrices. Then $p_\circ q$ is a semidefinite positive matrix. If p and q are definite positive matrices, then $p_\circ q$ is a definite positive matrix.

c. Let p be a semidefinite positive matrix. Then tr(p)≥0. If p is definite positive, then tr(p)>0.

d. Let p_{nxn} and q_{nxn} be semidefinite positive matrices. Then tr(pq)>0. If p and q are definite positive, then tr(pq)>0.

Proof

a. The element i of $(axb)_{DC}$ equals

$$[(acb)_{DC}]_i = (acb)_{ii} = \textstyle\sum_{jk} a_{ij}c_{jk}b_{ki} = \sum_j a_{ij}c_{jj}b_{ji}$$

$$= \textstyle\sum_j a_{ij}(b')_{ij}\, c_{jj} = \sum_j (a_\circ b')_{ij}(c_{DC})_j = [(a_\circ b')c_{DC}]_i.$$

b. Let $x_{n\times 1}$ be any column. We have to verify that $x'(p_\circ q)x \ge 0$. The semidefinite positive matrix q can be displayed as product q=ss′ , where s is square. Let s_k be the column k of the matrix s. Then

$$x'(p_\circ q)x = \textstyle\sum_k (x_\circ s_k)'p(x_\circ s_k).$$

Indeed, the right member of that relation equals

$$\textstyle\sum_k\sum_{ij} (x_\circ s_k)_i p_{ij}(x_\circ s_k)_j = \sum_{ijk} x_i s_{ik} p_{ij} x_j s_{jk} = \sum_{ij} x_i p_{ij} x_j \sum_k s_{ik}s_{jk}$$

$$\textstyle\sum_{ij} x_i p_{ij} x_j \sum_k s_{ik}s_{jk} = \sum_{ij} x_i p_{ij} x_j \sum_k s_{ik}(s')_{kj}$$

$$= \textstyle\sum_{ij} x_i p_{ij} x_j (ss')_{ij} = \sum_{ij} x_i p_{ij} x_j q_{ij} = \sum_{ij} x_i p_{ij} q_{ij} x_j$$

$$= \textstyle\sum_{ij} x_i (p_\circ q)_{ij} x_j = x'(p_\circ q)x.$$

But $(x_\circ s_k)'p(x_\circ s_k)\geq 0$ because p is semidefinite positive. Then $x'(p_\circ q)x \geq 0$ and this proves that $p_\circ q$ is semidefinite positive.

Now let us assume that p and q are definite positive, and let us suppose that $x'(p_\circ q)x = 0$. Then $(x_\circ s_k)'p(x_\circ s_k)=0$ for all k, and then $x_\circ s_k = 0$ for all k, because p is definite positive. Then x=0, because the definite positiveness of q implies the invertibility of s. This proves that $p_\circ q$ is definite positive.

c. Let s be an orthogonal matrix such that d:=sps′ is diagonal. Then d is semidefinite positive and its diagonal elements are positive. Then

$$0 \leq \mathrm{tr}(d) = \mathrm{tr}(sps') = \mathrm{tr}(pss') = \mathrm{tr}(p).$$

The inequality is strict if p is definite positive, because then d is invertible, and then its diagonal elements must be strictly positive.

d. The semidefinite matrix q can be displayed as q=ss′, where s is square. Then

$$\mathrm{tr}(pq)= \mathrm{tr}(pss') = \mathrm{tr}(s'ps) \geq 0,$$

by c. because s′ps is semidefinite positive.

If q is definite positive, then s is invertible, because then

$$0 \neq \det(q) = \det(s).\det(s').$$

Moreover if p is definite positive then s′ps is invertible. Then sps′ is definite positive, and tr(sps′) > 0 by c •

The trace of the product of 3 definite positive matrices can be strictly negative. Here is an example:

$$\begin{bmatrix} 2 & 1 \\ 1 & 1 \end{bmatrix} \begin{bmatrix} 1+\varepsilon & -1 \\ -1 & 1 \end{bmatrix} \begin{bmatrix} 1 & 2 \\ 2 & 4+\varepsilon \end{bmatrix} = \begin{bmatrix} -1+2\varepsilon & -2+3\varepsilon \\ \varepsilon & 2\varepsilon \end{bmatrix}$$

For ε>0, the 3 matrices in the first member have strictly positive diagonal elements and a strictly positive determinant. Hence, they are definite positive. The trace of the matrix in the last member equals −1+4ε. It is strictly negative when ε<0.25.

The credibility estimator with diagonal credibility matrix z

Lemma

Let $A_{1\times n}$ be a random row and $B_{n\times 1}$ a random column with square-integrable components. Then E(AxB)=0 for any scalar diagonal matrix $x_{n\times n}$ iff $E(BA)_{DC} = 0$.

Proof

$$E(AxB) = \sum_{ij} E(A_i x_{ij} B_j) = \sum_i x_{ii} E(A_i B_i) = \sum_i x_{ii}\, E(BA)_{ii}\,.$$

The last sum equals 0, far all x_{ii} iff $E(BA)_{ii}$ =0 for all ii, i.e. iff the column $E(BA)_{DC}$ =0 •

Theorem 20

In the credibility regression model with one contract defined by the relations (1),

$$\beta(\Theta)_{\mathbf{diag}} = \mathbf{zB + (1-z)b},$$

where $z_{n\times n}$ is the diagonal matrix such that

$$\mathbf{z_{DC} = [p_\bullet(a+\sigma^2u)]^{-1}(pa)_{DC}}\,.$$

Proof
Let

$$\beta(\Theta)_{\mathbf{diag}} = cB+eb,$$

where e and c are diagonal matrices. Then

$$E(cB+eb) = b \tag{33}$$

and

$$cB+eb-\beta(\Theta) \perp Y_1-Y_2, \tag{34}$$

where Y_1 and Y_2 are any vectors in $\boldsymbol{P}_{b,n\times 1,\mathbf{diag}}(B,b)$. Let

$$Y_1 = c_1B+e_1b\ ,\ \ Y_2 = c_2B+e_2b.$$

Then

$$b = EY_1 = c_1EB + e_1b = (c_1+e_1)b.$$

$$b = EY_2 = c_2EB + e_2b = (c_2+e_2)b.$$

By (33),

$$b = (e+c)b.$$

Then

$$cB+eb = c(B-b)+(c+e)b = cB^\circ+b,$$

$$cB+eb-\beta(\Theta) = cB^\circ-[\beta(\Theta)-b] = cB^\circ-\beta^\circ(\Theta),$$

$$Y_1 = c_1B^\circ+b, \quad Y_2 = c_2B^\circ+b, \quad Y_1-Y_2 = xB^\circ,$$

where $x_{n\times n}:=c_1-c_2$ is any diagonal matrix. The orthogonality relation (34) now becomes

$$cB^\circ-\beta^\circ(\Theta) \perp xB^\circ,$$

or

$$E[B^{\circ\prime}x'p[cB^\circ-\beta^\circ(\Theta)]] = 0. \tag{35}$$

By the Lemma, the latter relation implies that

$$E[p[cB^\circ-\beta^\circ(\Theta)]B^{\circ\prime}]_{DC} = 0,$$

$$[pcE(B^\circ B^{\circ\prime}) - pE[\beta^\circ(\Theta)B^{\circ\prime}]]_{DC} = 0,$$

$$[pc(\mathrm{Cov}\, B) - p\mathrm{Cov}[\beta(\Theta),B']]_{DC} = 0.$$

Then, by Theorem 2

$$[pc(a+\sigma^2u) - pa]]_{DC} = 0,$$

$$[pc(a+\sigma^2u)]_{DC} = (pa)_{DC}$$

and by Theorem 19.a,

$$[p_\circ(a+\sigma^2u)]c_{DC} = (pa)_{DC},$$

$$c_{DC} = [p_\circ(a+\sigma^2u)]^{-1}(pa)_{DC}.$$

The inverse matrix in the last member exists by Theorem 19.b, because the matrices p,a,u are definite positive •

The diagonal matrix z of the preceding Theorem depends on the definite positive matrix p defining the scalar product in $\boldsymbol{L}_{2,n\times 1}$. As matrix p, the matrix $a_{n\times n}$ can be taken.

6.3.3. Regression Model with z Reduced to a Scalar

We consider the regression model with one contract defined by the relations (1) and we adopt the notations of 6.1. The credibility estimator of $\beta(\Theta)$ which we now consider is

$$\beta(\Theta)_{scal} := \text{Proj}[\beta(\Theta)/\boldsymbol{P}_{b,n\times 1,scal}(B,b)] \ \text{ in } \boldsymbol{L}_{2,n\times 1}(p)$$

where

$$\boldsymbol{P}_{b,n\times 1,scal}(B,b),$$

is the space of random vectors of length n,

$$cB + eb \ (c,e\in\mathbf{R})$$

such that

$$E(cB+eb) = b.$$

The space $\boldsymbol{P}_{b,n\times 1,scal}(B,b)$ is a finite dimensional plane in $\boldsymbol{L}_{2,n\times 1}(p)$. In fact, it is the straight line through the points B and b.

Theorem 21

In the credibility regression model with one contract defined by the relations (1),

$$\boldsymbol{\beta(\Theta)_{scal} = zB + (1-z)b,} \tag{36}$$

where z is the scalar

$$\boldsymbol{z = tr(pa)/tr[p(a+\sigma^2u)]}. \tag{37}$$

Then 0<z<1.

Proof

In order to find $\beta(\Theta)_{scal}$, we proceed as in the proof of Theorem 19. but now c,e,c_1,e_1,c_2,e_2,x are scalars. Now (35) must be true for any scalar x. Hence,

$$0 = E[B^{\circ\prime}p[cB^\circ-\beta^\circ(\Theta)]] = E\ \text{tr}[B^{\circ\prime}p[cB^\circ-\beta^\circ(\Theta)]]$$

$$= E\ \text{tr}[p[cB^\circ-\beta^\circ(\Theta)]B^{\circ\prime}] = \text{tr}\ E[p[cB^\circ-\beta^\circ(\Theta)]B^{\circ\prime}]$$

$$\text{tr}[pcE(B^\circ B^{\circ\prime})-pE[\beta^\circ(\Theta)B^{\circ\prime}]] = \text{tr}[pc(\text{Cov } B)-p\text{Cov}[\beta(\Theta),B']]$$

$$= \text{tr}[pc(a+\sigma^2u)-pa] = c\ \text{tr}[p(a+\sigma^2u)]-\text{tr}(pa).$$

$$= tr[pc(a+\sigma^2u)-pa] = c\ tr[p(a+\sigma^2u)]-tr(pa).$$

This proves the relation (36), with the value (37) of z=c.

The denominator in the last member of (37) equals

$$tr(pa) + \sigma^2 tr(pu).$$

Then $0 < z < 1$ because the trace of a product of two definite positive matrices is strictly positive by Theorem 19.d •

The scalar z of the preceding Theorem depends on the definite positive matrix p defining the scalar product in $\boldsymbol{L}_{2,n\times 1}$. The matrix $a_{n\times n}$ can be taken as matrix p.

Chapter 7

Introduction to IBNR-Reserves

7.0. Introduction

We consider a fixed portfolio of an insurance company. As a rule, losses will not all be paid at the end of a bookyear. A loss reserve must be created for the unpaid losses.

A loss may be unpaid because it has not yet been reported or because its size has not yet been settled. "IBNR" (Incurred But Not Reported) must be understood as "IBNP" (Incurred But Not Paid) in most cases.

IBNR-models are mathematical models allowing to estimate the future losses akin to casualties which have already occurred.

Rough classifications of IBNR-models are the following.

> **Micro-models**: the partial claim amounts are taken into account

and

> **Macro-models**: the claim amounts are aggregated.

> **Deterministic models**: no random variables are involved

and

> **Stochastic models**: the claim amounts are regarded as realizations of random variables.

A sub-classification of stochastic models is:

> **Parametric models**: the involved distributions are supposed to be known (normal, Poisson,...) but some parameters must be estimated

and

> **Distribution-free models**: no particular assumptions are made on the involved distributions.

Clearly, IBNR-reserves is not a typical topic of credibility theory. We treat it here because our last model is a **credibility theory model**. The latter will be a distribution-free stochastic model.

7.1. Chain-Ladder Method

7.1.1. Data

The data of the **chain-ladder method** are furnished in an array such as the following:

Development year t \ Year of origin k	1	2	3	4	5	6
0	x_{10}	x_{20}	x_{30}	x_{40}	x_{50}	x_{60}
1	x_{11}	x_{21}	x_{31}	x_{41}	x_{51}	
2	x_{12}	x_{22}	x_{32}	x_{42}		
3	x_{13}	x_{23}	x_{33}			
4	x_{14}	x_{24}				

In that array, we are at the end of the year 6 and we have to make forecasts for the years 7, 8, ... The number x_{kt} is the amount paid by the insurer for casualties occurred during the year k with a **delay of settlement** equal to t. The delay of settlement of a casualty is 0 if it is paid during the bookyear of its origin. It is 1 if it is paid one bookyear later. It is 2 if it is paid two bookyears later,... Hence, the amount x_{kt} of the array has been paid during the bookyear k+t. The integer t is also called the **development year** of the casualty.

To one casualty may correspond several amounts x_{kt}, $x_{kt'}$, $x_{kt''}$, ... and several development years t, t′, t″,...

The problem is to fill in the array and to obtain the following array, where the numbers below the staircase line are estimates.

	1	2	3	4	5	6
0	x_{10}	x_{20}	x_{30}	x_{40}	x_{50}	x_{60}
1	x_{11}	x_{21}	x_{31}	x_{41}	x_{51}	x_{61}
2	x_{12}	x_{22}	x_{32}	x_{42}	x_{52}	x_{62}
3	x_{13}	x_{23}	x_{33}	x_{43}	x_{53}	x_{63}
4	x_{14}	x_{24}	x_{34}	x_{44}	x_{54}	x_{64}

7.1.2. Cumulative Data

The initial array with amounts x_{kt} is replaced by the following array with cumulative amounts y_{kt}

y_{10}	y_{20}	y_{30}	y_{40}	y_{50}	y_{60}
y_{11}	y_{21}	y_{31}	y_{41}	y_{51}	
y_{12}	y_{22}	y_{32}	y_{42}		
y_{13}	y_{23}	y_{33}			
y_{14}	y_{24}				

The amounts y_{kt} are vertical sums:

$$\begin{array}{r} x_{k0} \\ +x_{k1} \\ +\ldots \\ +x_{kt} \\ \hline =y_{kt} \end{array}$$

The effect of the replacement of the amounts x_{kt} by the amounts y_{kt} is a **smoothing** of the original rough data.

7.1.3. Completion of the Cumulative Data

The array with y_{kt} data is completed as follows

y_{10}	y_{20}	y_{30}	y_{40}	y_{50}	y_{60}
y_{11}	y_{21}	y_{31}	y_{41}	y_{51}	y_{61}
y_{12}	y_{22}	y_{32}	y_{42}	y_{52}	y_{62}
y_{13}	y_{23}	y_{33}	y_{43}	y_{53}	y_{63}
y_{14}	y_{24}	y_{34}	y_{44}	y_{54}	y_{64}

The numbers below the staircase line result, successively, from the formulas

$$\frac{y_{10}+y_{20}+y_{30}+y_{40}+y_{50}}{y_{11}+y_{21}+y_{31}+y_{41}+y_{51}}=\frac{y_{60}}{\mathbf{y_{61}}}$$

$$\frac{y_{11}+y_{21}+y_{31}+y_{41}}{y_{12}+y_{22}+y_{32}+y_{42}}=\frac{y_{51}}{\mathbf{y_{52}}}=\frac{y_{61}}{\mathbf{y_{62}}}$$

$$\frac{y_{12}+y_{22}+y_{32}}{y_{13}+y_{23}+y_{33}} = \frac{y_{42}}{y_{43}} = \frac{y_{52}}{y_{53}} = \frac{y_{62}}{y_{63}}$$

$$\frac{y_{13}+y_{23}}{y_{14}+y_{24}} = \frac{y_{33}}{y_{34}} = \frac{y_{43}}{y_{44}} = \frac{y_{53}}{y_{54}} = \frac{y_{63}}{y_{64}}$$

7.1.4. Solution of the Initial Problem

Then the amounts below the staircase line in the second array of 7.1.1 are obtained as differences:

$$x_{61} = y_{61}-y_{60},$$

$$x_{52} = y_{52}-y_{51}\ ,\ x_{62} = y_{62}-y_{61},$$

$$x_{43} = y_{43}-y_{42}\ ,\ x_{53} = y_{53}-y_{52}\ ,\ x_{63} = y_{63}-y_{62},$$

$$x_{34} = y_{34}-y_{33}\ ,\ x_{44} = y_{44}-y_{43}\ ,\ x_{54} = y_{54}-y_{53}\ ,\ x_{64} = y_{64}-y_{63}.$$

7.2. Deterministic Least-Squares Method

7.2.1. Incomplete Data

We now present a method allowing to deal with incomplete data, such as in the following array

$$\begin{array}{cccccc}
 & & x_{30} & x_{40} & x_{50} & x_{60} \\
 & x_{21} & x_{31} & x_{41} & x_{51} & \\
x_{12} & x_{22} & & x_{42} & & \\
x_{13} & x_{23} & x_{33} & & & \\
x_{14} & x_{24} & & & &
\end{array}$$

This is the same array as the first array of 7.1.1, but here the amounts x_{10}, x_{11}, x_{20} are missing (say because they are too old) and the amount x_{32} is missing (say because it is too irregular).

Now the cumulative array of 7.1.2 cannot be formed and hence, the chain-ladder method cannot be applied.

In the general case, we denote by D the set of couples (k,t) such that x_{kt} figures in the array. Let the columns of the array be 1, 2,..., k° and let its rows be 0, 1,..., t°. Further, let

$$T_k := \{t / (k,t) \in D\} \quad (k=1,\ldots,k°),$$

$$K_t := \{k / (k,t) \in D\} \ (t=0,1,\ldots,t°\}.$$

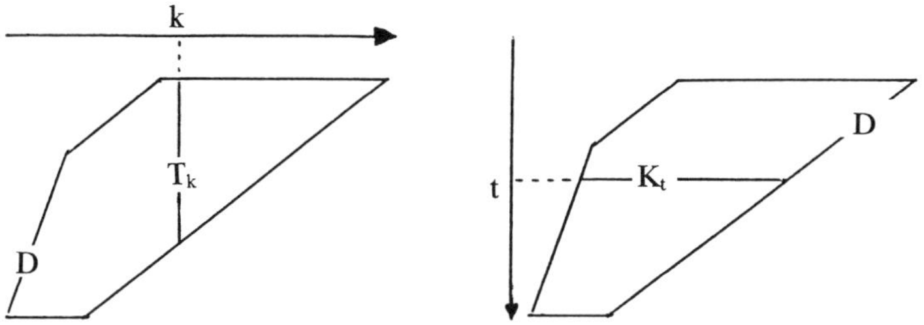

Fig.34. Schematic representation of T_k and K_t

7.2.2. Theoretical Array

We consider the **theoretical array** with numbers $b_k y_t$ ((k,t)∈D).

	b_1	b_2	b_3	b_4	b_5	b_6
y_0			b_3y_0	b_4y_0	b_5y_0	b_6y_0
y_1		b_2y_1	b_3y_1	b_4y_1	b_5y_1	
y_2	b_1y_2	b_2y_2		b_4y_2		
y_3	b_1y_3	b_2y_3	b_3y_3			
y_4	b_1y_4	b_2y_4				

We interpret b_k as the total claim amount paid by the insurer for all claims with year of origin k, and y_t as the proportion of b_k corresponding to the development year t.

The (square of the) distance between the **real array** with numbers x_{kt} ((k,t)∈D) and the theoretical array with numbers $b_k y_t$ ((k,t)∈D) is

$$Q(b_1,\ldots,b_{k°},y_0,\ldots,y_{t°}) = \sum_{(k,t)\in D} w_{kt}(b_k y_t - x_{kt})^2,$$

where w_{kt} ((k,t)∈D) are known weights.

Of course, if no arguments can be found in favour of particular weights, we take $w_{kt}=1$.

7.2.3. Solution of the Initial Problem

Now we take $b_1,\dots,b_{k^\circ},y_0,\dots,y_{t^\circ}$ in such a way that distance $Q(b_1,\dots,b_{k^\circ},y_0,\dots,y_{t^\circ})$ is minimum. We express that the partial derivatives in b_k and y_t vanish. We notice that

$$\sum_{(k,t)\in D} = \sum_{k=1,\dots,k^\circ} \sum_{t\in T_k} = \sum_{t=0,\dots,t^\circ} \sum_{k\in K_t}.$$

Hence,

$$1/2\ (\partial Q/\partial b_k) = \sum_{t\in T_k} w_{kt} y_t (b_k y_t - x_{kt}) = 0 \quad (k=1,\dots,k^\circ),$$

$$1/2\ (\partial Q/\partial y_t) = \sum_{k\in K_t} w_{kt} b_k (b_k y_t - x_{kt}) = 0 \quad (t=0,\dots,t^\circ).$$

Then

$$b_k = [\sum_{t\in T_k} w_{kt} x_{kt} y_t]/[\sum_{t\in T_k} w_{kt} y_t^2] \ (k=1,\dots,k^\circ), \tag{1}$$

$$y_t = [\sum_{k\in K_t} w_{kt} x_{kt} b_k]/[\sum_{k\in K_t} w_{kt} b_k^2] \ (t=0,\dots,t^\circ). \tag{2}$$

The system (1), (2) can be solved recursively as follows. We calculate the last member of (1) with arbitrary strictly positive initial values y_t ($t=0,\dots,t^\circ$). The resulting values b_k ($k=1,\dots,k^\circ$) are introduced in the last member of (2). They furnish new values y_t ($t=0,\dots,t^\circ$). We treat the latter as new initial values and we repeat the procedure again and again. The algorithm furnishes limiting values $y_{t,\infty}$ ($t=0,\dots,t^\circ$) and $b_{k,\infty}$ ($k=1,\dots,k^\circ$). The following is observed:

a. Convergence takes place whatever the initial values y_t are.

b. The products $b_{k,\infty} y_{t,\infty}$ ($k=1,\dots,k^\circ$; $t=0,\dots,t^\circ$) do not depend on the initial values y_t.

Then, for any (k,t) ($k=1,\dots,k^\circ$; $t=0,\dots,t^\circ$) such that $(k,t)\notin D$, we take

$$x_{kt} = b_{k,\infty} y_{t,\infty}.$$

In this way, the initial array of 7.2.1 is completed.

Remark

If we want to keep the interpretation of the numbers y_0, y_1, ..., $y_{t°}$ as proportions, we must replace them by

$$y_0/y_\Sigma\,,\ y_1/y_\Sigma\,,\ \dots\,,\ y_{t°}/y_\Sigma$$

resp., where

$$y_\Sigma := y_0+y_1+\dots+y_{t°}.$$

At the same time, we must replace b_1, ..., $b_{k°}$ by b_1y_Σ, ..., $b_{k°}y_\Sigma$ resp.

In this way, we solve the minimization problem of $Q(b_1,\dots,b_{k°},y_0,\dots,y_{t°})$ under the constraint $y_0+y_1+\dots+y_{t°}=1$.

7.3. Credibility Theory Model

7.3.1. Definition of the Model

As an example, we consider the same array as in 7.2.1, but now the amounts x_{kt} ($(k,t)\in D$) are regarded as realizations of square-integrable random variables X_{kt}. Moreover, the columns of the array are completed by conditioning random variables Θ_k.

Θ_1	Θ_2	Θ_3	Θ_4	Θ_5	Θ_6
		X_{30}	X_{40}	X_{50}	X_{60}
	X_{21}	X_{31}	X_{41}	X_{51}	
X_{12}	X_{22}		X_{42}		
X_{13}	X_{23}	X_{33}			
X_{14}	X_{24}				

The familiar interpretation of credibility theory is adopted here: The distribution of the column k with elements X_{kt} ($t\in T_k$) depends on a (multidimensional) parameter θ_k. The latter is unknown. It is treated as a realization of some random variable Θ_k.

The **column k of the model** ($k=1,\dots,k°$) is the set of random variables X_{kt} ($t\in T_k$) completed by the random variable Θ_k.

The ***assumptions*** on the model are the following.

a. For fixed Θ_k, the random variables X_{kt} ($t \in T_k$) are conditionally independent.

b. A function $\beta(\cdot)$ and random variables Y_{kt} ($(k,t) \in D$) exist such that

$$X_{kt} = \beta(\Theta_k) Y_{kt} \quad ((k,t) \in D). \tag{3}$$

For any fixed k, the random variables Y_{kt} ($t \in T_k$) are independent of Θ_k.

The expectation

$$EY_{kt} =: y_t \neq 0 \tag{4}$$

does not depend on k.

c. A scalar ρ^2 exists such that

$$\text{Var } Y_{kt} = \rho^2 / w_k, \tag{5}$$

where $w_k > 0$ is the **natural weight** (supposed to be known) of the accident year k.

d. The k° columns 1,2,...,k° are independent.

e. The random variables $\Theta_1, \Theta_2, \ldots, \Theta_k$ are identically distributed.

f.

$$E\beta(\Theta_k) = 1. \tag{6}$$

The condition (6) is no restriction, because only the products $\beta(\Theta_k) Y_{kt}$ are relevant and because $\beta(\Theta_k)$ and Y_{kt} can be replaced resp. by

$$\beta(\Theta_k)/E\beta(\Theta_k) \text{ and } Y_{kt}.E\beta(\Theta_k).$$

7.3.2. Origin of the Model

The idea of approximating X_{kt} by a multiplicative expression $b_k y_t$ is already subjacent in the chain-ladder method and in its least-squares variant of 7.2 (see the theoretical array of 7.2.2).

A corresponding stochastic model is

$$X_{kt} = b_k y_t + Err_{kt}, \tag{7}$$

where Err_{kt} is a random variable with vanishing expectation.

The next step is to replace y_t by a random variable Y_t and to consider the model

$$X_{kt} = b_k Y_t + Err_{kt}, \tag{8}$$

where Y_t and Err_{kt} can be supposed to be independent.

The latter model is close to the model

$$X_{kt} = B_k Y_{kt}, \tag{9}$$

where B_k is a random variable independent of Y_{kt} (in the model (8). Y_t and Err_{kt} are supposed to be amalgameted in a unique random variable Y_{kt}).

Finally, taking $B_k=\beta(\Theta_k)$, we have the basic idea of the credibility model of 7.3.1.

7.3.3. Solution of the IBNR-Problem

Estimation of $y_1,\ldots,y_{t^\circ}$

By the *assumptions* of the model

$$EX_{kt} = E\beta(\Theta_k).EY_{kt} = 1.y_t = y_t.$$

Hence, X_{kt} is an unbiased estimator of y_t. We adopt

$$\textstyle\sum_{k\in K_t} (w_k/w_{t,\Sigma})X_{kt} \tag{10}$$

as an estimator of y_t. Here

$$w_{t,\Sigma} := \textstyle\sum_{k\in K_t} w_k.$$

Hereafter we assume that $y_1,\ldots,y_{t^\circ}$ are known.

Credibility approximation of $\boldsymbol{\beta(\Theta_k)}$

Let

$$Z_{kt} := X_{kt}/y_t \quad ((k,t)\in D). \tag{11}$$

We consider the following array, called **transformed array**

Θ_1	Θ_2	Θ_3	Θ_4	Θ_5	Θ_6
		Z_{30}	Z_{40}	Z_{50}	Z_{60}
	Z_{21}	Z_{31}	Z_{41}	Z_{51}	
Z_{12}	Z_{22}		Z_{42}		
Z_{13}	Z_{23}	Z_{33}			
Z_{14}	Z_{24}				

Let

$$\sigma^2(\Theta_k) := \rho^2\beta^2(\Theta_k), \tag{12}$$

$$w_{kt} := w_k y_t^2. \tag{13}$$

Theorem 1

a. **For fixed Θ_k, the random variables Z_{kt} $(t\in T_k)$ are conditionally independent.**

b.

$$\mathbf{E(Z_{kt}/\Theta_k) = \beta(\Theta_k) \quad ((k,t)\in D).}$$

c.

$$\mathbf{Var(Z_{kt}/\Theta_k) = \sigma^2(\Theta_k)/w_{kt} \quad ((k,t)\in D).}$$

d. **The columns of the transformed array are independent.**

e. **The random variables $\Theta_1,\ldots,\Theta_{k^\circ}$ are identically distributed.**

Proof

b.

$$E(Z_{kt}/\Theta_k) = E(X_{kt}/\Theta_k)/y_t = E[\beta(\Theta_k)Y_{kt}/\Theta_k]/y_t$$

$$= \beta(\Theta_k)E(Y_{kt}/\Theta_k)/y_t = \beta(\Theta_k)E(Y_{kt})/y_t = \beta(\Theta_k).$$

c.

$$\begin{aligned}\mathrm{Var}\,(Z_{kt}/\Theta_k) &= \mathrm{Var}(X_{kt}/\Theta_k)/y_t^2 = \mathrm{Var}[\beta(\Theta_k)Y_{kt}/\Theta_k]/y_t^2\\ &= \beta^2(\Theta_k)\mathrm{Var}(Y_{kt}/\Theta_k)/y_t^2 = \beta^2(\Theta_k)\mathrm{Var}(Y_{kt})/y_t^2\\ &= \rho^2\beta^2(\Theta_k)/(w_k y_t^2) = \sigma^2(\Theta_k)/w_{kt}.\end{aligned}$$

The points a, d and e are obvious from the *assumptions* •

Solution of the problem

Comparing the points a–c of Theorem 1 to the points a–c of Ch.3.4.2, we conclude that the transformed array defines a Bühlmann & Straub credibility model. Hence, we can calculate the credibility estimator $\beta(\Theta_k)_{cred}$ of $\beta(\Theta_k)$ from the observable random variables Z_{kt} ($(k,t)\in D$) of the transformed array. (Obviously the vertical positions and the vertical numberings of the observable random variables Z_{kt} are irrelevant.). Then

$$X_{kt,cred} := \beta(\Theta_k)_{cred}\, y_t \ (k=1,\ldots,k^\circ;\ t=0,1,\ldots,t^\circ). \tag{14}$$

The random variables $X_{kt,cred}$ ($(k,t)\notin D$) are the **credibility estimators** of the corresponding unknown amounts x_{kt}.

We notice that

$$E(X_{kt}/\Theta_k) = \beta(\Theta_k)\, y_t \ ((k,t)\in D)$$

by (3) and (4). The definition (14) is based on this relation and on its extension to couples $(k,t)\notin D$. Hence, implicitly we assume that the *assumptions* 7.3.1.a–c are satisfied for all $k=1,\ldots,k^\circ$ and all $t=0,1,\ldots,t^\circ$.

Particularity of the transformed array model

In the general Bühlmann & Straub model, the portfolio mean $\mu:=E\mu(\Theta_k)$ is not known. In the transformed array model, the corresponding mean $E\beta(\Theta_k)$ equals 1 by 7.3.1.f. This simplifies the estimation of the heterogeneity parameter a. Here the pseudo-estimator Ch.3.(81) can be replaced by

$$A_{pseu} = 1/k^\circ \sum_{1\le k\le k^\circ} z_k(Z_{kw}-1)^2. \tag{15}$$

See Ch.2.Th.6.Cor.

7.3.4. Variants

In the foregoing model,

$$\mathrm{Var}(X_{kt}/\Theta_k) = \rho^2\beta^2(\Theta_k)/w_k. \tag{16}$$

This means that the observation X_{kt} has the **natural weight** w_k. Mack (1990) and Goovaerts et al. (1990) propose variants in which the assumption (5) is dropped and replaced by the following assumption:

For some function $\sigma^2(\cdot)$,

$$\mathrm{Var}(X_{kt}/\Theta_k) = y_t^{\alpha}\,\sigma^2(\Theta_k)/w_k, \tag{17}$$

where α is some exponent (say in the interval [0,2]).

Then the observation X_{kt} has the natural weight w_k/y_t^{α} and

$$\mathrm{Var}(Z_{kt}/\Theta_k) = y_t^{\alpha}\sigma^2(\Theta_k)/(w_k y_t^2) = \sigma^2(\Theta_k)/w_{kt,\alpha}, \tag{18}$$

where $w_{kt,\alpha} := y_t^{2-\alpha}w_k$. The foregoing discussion remains valid with the weights w_{kt} replaced by $w_{kt,\alpha}$ everywhere. We denote by $X_{kt,\alpha,cred}$ the corresponding credibility estimators (14).

The choice of the value α can be based on practical or theoretical arguments (for instance on micro-decompositions of the involved claim amounts). We here suggest the following pragmatic way for the determination of α.

The (square) distance of the initial array with amounts X_{kt} $((k,t)\in D)$ and the array with estimated amounts $X_{kt,\alpha,cred}$ is defined as

$$Q(\alpha) = \textstyle\sum_{(k,t)\in D} v_{kt,\alpha}(X_{kt}-X_{kt,\alpha,cred})^2, \tag{19}$$

where $v_{kt,\alpha}$ $((k,t)\in D)$ are fixed (natural or credibility) weights. The random variables in the last member of (19) are replaced by their realizations. We then adopt the value of α minimizing $Q(\alpha)$.

Practically, we consider a finite number of close equidistant values of α and for each of them we calculate the credibility estimators and the corresponding distance $Q(\alpha)$. Then we retain the value furnishing the smallest distance $Q(\alpha)$. With today's computers, these calculations are performed within reasonable times.

This pragmatic procedure can be extended to the consideration of more general functions $\varphi(y_t)$ instead of y_t^{α} in the last member of (17).

Appendices

App.A. Continuous Renewal Theorems
↓
I.Ch.7.6.

App.B. Discrete Renewal Theorems
↓
I.Ch.10.2.5

App.C. Convex Analysis on R^n
↓
I.Ch.5.3
II.Ch.8

App.D. Matrices
↓
II.Ch.3.3
III.Ch.4
III.Ch.5

App.E. Krein-Milman
↓
II.Ch.2.4
II.Ch.9

App.F. Projections in Hilbert Space
↓
I.Ch.2.2
III.Ch.4
III.Ch.5

App.G. Characteristic Functions
→ **I.Ch.5.1**, **I.Ch.5.3**
→ **App.H. Generating Functions**
→ **App.I. Moment Functions**

App.H. Generating Functions
→ **App.J. Laplace Transforms**

App.I. Moment Functions

App.J. Laplace Transforms
↓
I.Ch.4.5.6

App.K. Sums, ...
↓
I.Ch.4.6
I.Ch.8.1.2
I.Ch.8.4.3
I.Ch.8.6.4
II.Ch.3.8

Appendix A

Continuous Renewal Theorems on R_+

A1. Cantor's Diagonal Process

The following is a classical Theorem used in several places in the Appendices.

Theorem A1 (Cantor's Diagonal Process)

Let D be a denumerable set and let $\gamma(r,n)$ ($r \in D$; $n=1,2,\ldots$) be real numbers. For some sequence $1=n_1<n_2<\ldots$, the limit $\lim_{k\uparrow\infty} \gamma(r,n_k)$, finite or not, exists for all $r \in D$.

Proof
The proof is based on the following properties: For any sequence of real numbers, a convergent subsequence exists, possibly with infinite limit. Any subsequence of a convergent sequence is a convergent sequence.

Let $r_1,r_2,\ldots$ be an enumeration without repetitions of the points of D. Let us consider the following array A_0

$$\begin{array}{cccc} \gamma(r_1,1) & \gamma(r_2,1) & \gamma(r_3,1) & \cdots \\ \gamma(r_1,2) & \gamma(r_2,2) & \gamma(r_3,2) & \cdots \\ \gamma(r_1,3) & \gamma(r_2,3) & \gamma(r_3,3) & \cdots \\ \cdots & \cdots & \cdots & \cdots \end{array}$$

Let us cross out lines other than the first one in this array, in such a way that an infinite number of lines is still left, and that the first column of the new array A_1 converges to some number, finite or not. In A_1 let us cross out lines, other than the two first lines, in such a way that an infinite number of lines is still left, and that the second column of the new array A_2 converges to some number, finite or not. In A_2 let us cross out lines, other than the three first lines, in such a way that an infinite numbers of lines is still left, and that the third column of the new array A_3 converges to some number, finite or not... In this way, we define recursively a sequence of arrays A_1, A_2, A_3,...

Then the limit array finally left is the intersection (in the obvious sense) of the arrays A_1, A_2, A_3,... Let the limit array be

$$\begin{array}{cccc} \gamma(r_1,n_1) & \gamma(r_2,n_1) & \gamma(r_3,n_1) & \dots \\ \gamma(r_1,n_2) & \gamma(r_2,n_2) & \gamma(r_3,n_2) & \dots \\ \gamma(r_1,n_3) & \gamma(r_2,n_3) & \gamma(r_3,n_3) & \dots \\ \dots & \dots & \dots & \dots \end{array}$$

Each column of this array converges to some number, finite or not •

The set D, in Theorem A1, may be finite. Then the arrays of the preceding proof have a finite number of columns, and only a finite number of sub-arrays must be considered.

A2. Direct Riemann-Integrability on $\mathbf{R}_+$

Let g be a function on $\mathbf{R}_+$, I an interval in $\mathbf{R}_+$. Then

$$\inf_I g := \inf_{x\in I} g(x) \ , \ \sup_I g := \sup_{x\in I} g(x) \ , \ \text{osc}_I\, g := \sup_I g - \inf_I g.$$

The number $\text{osc}_I\, g$ is the **oscillation of g on I**. Let $\delta>0$. We consider the partition of $\mathbf{R}_+$ by the points $n\delta$ ($n=0,1,2,\ldots$) and we define

$$g_\delta := \textstyle\sum_{n\geq 0} \inf_{[n\delta,n\delta+\delta]} g.1_{[n\delta,n\delta+\delta[} \ , \ g^\delta := \sum_{n\geq 0} \sup_{[n\delta,n\delta+\delta]} g.1_{[n\delta,n\delta+\delta[},$$

$$|g|^\delta := \textstyle\sum_{n\geq 0} \sup_{[n\delta,n\delta+\delta]} |g|.1_{[n\delta,n\delta+\delta[}.$$

The function g is **directly (Riemann-) integrable (on $\mathbf{R}_+$)** if it satisfies the **sup-condition**

$$\textstyle\int_{[0,\infty[} |g|^\delta(x)dx = \delta\sum_{n\geq 0} \sup_{[n\delta,n\delta+\delta]} |g| < \infty \quad (\delta>0)$$

and the **osc-condition**

$$\textstyle\int_{[0,\infty[} g^\delta(x)dx - \int_{[0,\infty[} g_\delta(x)dx = \delta\sum_{n\geq 0} \text{osc}_{[n\delta,n\delta+\delta]}\, g \to 0 \text{ as } \delta\downarrow 0.$$

Theorem A2 (Direct Integrability Theorem)

a. **Let g be directly integrable. Then g is Lebesgue-integrable and**

$$\textstyle\int_{[0,\infty[} g_\delta(x)dx \to \int_{[0,\infty[} g(x)dx \ , \ \int_{[0,\infty[} g^\delta(x)dx \to \int_{[0,\infty[} g(x)dx \quad \text{as } \delta\downarrow 0.$$

b. **The family of directly integrable functions is a vector space.**

c. g is directly integrable iff g_- and g_+ are directly integrable.

d. Let $g\geq 0$ be decreasing. Then g is directly integrable iff g is Lebesgue-integrable.

e. We assume that g has at most a finite number of discontinuity points c and that the limits $g(c\pm)<\infty$ exist at these points. Let the sup-condition be satisfied. Then g is directly integrable.

Proof

In this proof, we write $\int f \equiv \int_{[0,\infty[} f(x)dx$ for any function f.

a. $\int|g|\leq\int|g|^\delta<\infty$ by the sup-condition. Hence g is Lebesgue-integrable. In the relations $\int g_\delta\leq\int g\leq\int g^\delta$, the limit as $\delta\downarrow 0$ of the difference of the extreme members equals 0 by the osc-condition.

b. By the relations $\sup_I|f+g|\leq\sup_I|f|+\sup_I|g|$, $\operatorname{osc}_I(f+g)\leq\operatorname{osc}_I f+\operatorname{osc}_I g$, $\sup_I|af|= |a|\sup_I|f|$, $\operatorname{osc}_I(af)=|a|\operatorname{osc}_I f$.

c. If g_+ and g_- are directly integrable, then $g=g_+-g_-$ is directly integrable by statement b. If g is directly integrable, the direct integrability of g_+, g_- results from the relations $\sup_I f_+\leq\sup_I|f|$, $\sup_I f_-\leq\sup_I|f|$, $\operatorname{osc}_I f_+\leq\operatorname{osc}_I f$, $\operatorname{osc}_I f_-\leq\operatorname{osc}_I f$.

d. If g is directly integrable, then g is Lebesgue-integrable by a. Conversely, let g be Lebesgue-integrable. Then

$$\int g_\delta\leq\int g<\infty\ ,\ \int(g^\delta-g_\delta)=\delta\sum_{n\geq 0}\operatorname{osc}_{[n\delta,n\delta+\delta]}g=\delta\sum_{n\geq 0}[g(n\delta)-g(n\delta+\delta)]=\delta g(0).$$

This implies the osc-condition, but also the sup-condition because

$$\int g^\delta=\delta g(0)+\int g_\delta<\infty.$$

e. By c, we may assume that $g\geq 0$. We prove the osc-condition. Let $0<\delta<1$, $k\geq 1$. Then

$$\int_{[k,k+1]}g^\delta\leq\sup_{[k-1,k]}g+\sup_{[k,k+1]}g+\sup_{[k+1,k+2]}g,$$

$$\int_{[n,\infty[}g^\delta\leq 3\sum_{k\leq n-1}\sup_{[k,k+1]}g.$$

By the sup-condition with $\delta=1$, we can fix n in such a way that the last member of the latter relation is less than $\varepsilon>0$. We assume that g is continuous for the moment. Let $\delta_0\in]0,1[$ be so small that the oscillation of g on any interval with a length less than δ_0 in $[0,n+1]$ is less than ε/n. This is possible because continuous functions are uniformly continuous on compact intervals.

Then, if $0\le\delta\le\delta_0$,

$$\int_{[0,\infty[}(f^\delta - f_\delta) \le \int_{[0,n[}(f^\delta - f_\delta) + \int_{[n,\infty[} f^\delta \le n(\varepsilon/n) + \varepsilon = 2\varepsilon.$$

This proves the osc-condition in case g is continuous on $\mathbf{R}_+$.

Let us now assume that g has 1 discontinuity point c. We consider the function $g_1 := g1_{[0,c]}$ with g(c) re-defined as g(c−) and the function $g_2 := g1_{[c,\infty[}$ with g(c) re-defined as g(c+). Then g_1 is continuous on the compact interval [0,c], hence uniformly continuous on that interval, and this implies the osc-condition for g_1. The osc-condition is satisfied for g_2 by the initial argument because g_2 is continuous on $[c,\infty[$. The sup-condition is satisfied for g_1 and g_2 because it is satisfied for g. Hence g_1 and g_2 are directly integrable, and then g_1+g_2 is directly integrable by b. The argument is easily adapted in case of more discontinuity points •

The following is the graph of a positive continuous function which is Lebesgue-integrable, but not directly integrable. The basis and the height of the k-th triangle measure 1/k. The Lebesgue-integral equals $(1/2)\sum_{k\ge1}k^{-2}<\infty$. The sup-condition is not satisfied with $\delta=1$ because $\sum_{k\ge1}k^{-1}=\infty$.

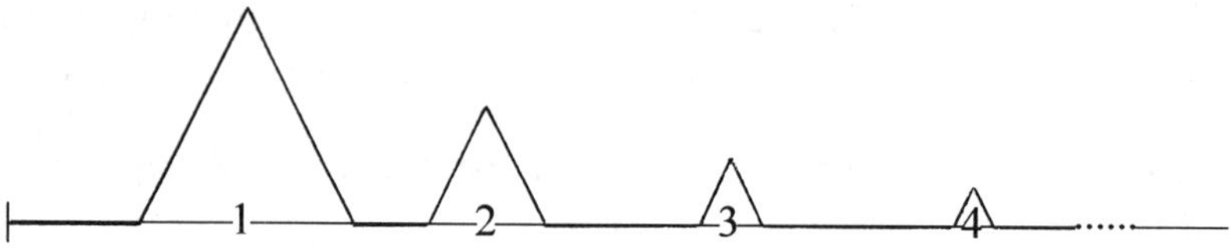

Fig.35. Graph of a function wich is not directly integrable

A3. Convolution Products on R

In this Appendix, we prove renewal Theorems on $\mathbf{R}_+$, but some proofs lead outside $\mathbf{R}_+$ and we have to consider functions and convolutions on $\mathbf{R}$.

Let f be a bounded function on $\mathbf{R}$, g a difference of bounded distribution functions on $\mathbf{R}_+$. In particular, g can be a probability distribution function on $\mathbf{R}_+$. The **convolution product** f*g is the function defined on $\mathbf{R}$ by

$$(f*g)(x) = \int_{[0,\infty[} f(x-y)dg(y) \quad (x\in\mathbf{R}).$$

This convolution product has similar properties, with similar proofs, as the convolution product on $\mathbf{R}_+$ defined in I.Ch.1.3.2. All integration domains will be intervals in $\mathbf{R}_+$. Functions defined on $\mathbf{R}_+$ must be extended to $\mathbf{R}$ by annulation on $\mathbf{R}_-$.

Let f be a bounded function on **R** and h a positive number. The **increment function** f^h is defined on **R** by

$$f^h(x) := f(x)-f(x-h) \quad (x\in\mathbf{R}), \text{ i.e. } f^h = f*1_{[0,h[}\,.$$

We recall that the function f, defined on **R**, is **uniformly continuous on the set S in R**, if for any $\varepsilon>0$, some $\delta>0$ exists such that

$$|f(x)-f(y)| \le \varepsilon \;(x,y\in S\,;\,|x-y|\le\delta).$$

The function f is **uniformly continuous** if it is uniformly continuous on **R.**

Lemma 1

Let f be a function on $\mathbf{R}_+$, bounded and uniformly continuous on some interval $[b,\infty[$ and let $s_k\uparrow\infty$ be a sequence in R. Then a bounded and uniformly continuous function f_0 exists on R, and a subsequence t_k of s_k exists, such that

$$\lim_{k\uparrow\infty} f(x+t_k) = f_0(x)\,,\ \text{uniformly on bounded intervals in } \mathbf{R}.$$

Proof

We consider the numbers $f(r+s_k)$ (r rational, $k\in\mathbf{N}_+$). The set of rational numbers is denumerable. By Cantor, a function f_0 exists on the set of rational numbers, such that

$$f(r+t_k) \to f_0(r) \quad (r \text{ rational}) \tag{A1}$$

for some subsequence t_k of s_k .

The function f_0 is bounded on the set of rationals. Indeed, a positive number c exists such that $|f(x)|\le c$ $(x\ge b)$. If the rational number r is fixed, then $r+t_k\ge b$ for all k larger than some k_0. Then $|f_0(r)|\le c$ by (A1).

The function f_0 is uniformly continuous on the set of rationals. Indeed, let $\varepsilon>0$. A number $\delta>0$ exists such that

$$|f(y)-f(x)| \le \varepsilon \quad (b\le x,\ b\le y,\ |y-x|\le\delta). \tag{A2}$$

Let r, s be rational numbers such that $|s-r|\le\delta$ and let k_0 be such that $r+t_k\ge b$, $s+t_k\le b$ $(k\ge k_0)$. By (A2),

$$|f(s+t_k)-f(r+t_k)| \le \varepsilon \quad (k\ge k_0)$$

and as $k\uparrow\infty$,

$$|f_0(s)-f_0(r)| \le \varepsilon \quad (r,s \text{ rational}; |s-r|\le\delta). \tag{A3}$$

We now extend the definition of f_0 to R. Let $x\in\mathbf{R}$. Then

$$f_0(x) := \lim_{s\to x, s \text{ rational}} f_0(s).$$

We must show that this limit exists. Let r be a rational number such that $|x-r| <\delta$. Then $|s-r|<\delta$ if s is close enough to x and by (A3), as $s\to x$ (s rational):

$$|\liminf f_0(s)- f_0(r)| \le \delta \quad , \quad |\limsup f_0(s)- f_0(r)| \le \delta.$$

Then

$$|\limsup f_0(s) - \liminf f_0(s)| \le 2\delta,$$

and as $\delta\downarrow 0$:

$$\liminf f_0(s) = \limsup f_0(s).$$

The function f_0 is bounded on R. Indeed, it is bounded on the set of rationals.

The function f_0 is uniformly continuous on R. Indeed, let x and y be numbers such that $|y-x|\le\delta/2$. Let $r\to x$, $s\to y$ (r,s rational). For r close enough to x and s close enough to y: $|s-r|\le\delta$. Then, by (A3),

$$|f_0(y)-f_0(x)| \le \varepsilon \quad (x,y\in\mathbf{R}; |y-x|\le\delta). \tag{A4}$$

Finally, we prove the **uniform convergence on bounded intervals**, announced in the statement of the Theorem.Let J be a bounded interval. Let $\varepsilon>0$. Let $\delta>0$ be such that (A2) and (A4) hold. Let $J=J_1+\ldots+J_j$ where $J_1,\ldots,J_j$ are intervals with length less than δ. Let us consider a fixed interval J_i $(0\le i\le j)$. Let a_i be the left extremity of J_i and let r be a fixed rational number in J_i. Let k(i) be a positive integer such that $a_i+t_{k(i)}>b$ and

$$|f_0(r)-f(r+t_k)| \le \varepsilon \ (k\ge k(i)).$$

This is possible by (A1). Then, for any $x\in J_i$ and $k\ge k(i)$:

$$|f_0(x)-f(x+t_k)| \le |f_0(x)-f_0(r)| + |f_0(r)-f(r+t_k)| + |f(r+t_k)-f(x+t_k)| \le 3\varepsilon.$$

Then, if $k_0= k(1)\vee\ldots\vee k(j)$: $|f_0(x)-f(x+t_k)|\le 3\varepsilon$ $(x\in J, k\ge k_0)$ •

Lemma 2

Let f be a bounded, uniformly continuous function on R, such that f=f*G on R, where G is a probability distribution function on R₊, vanishing at 0, with right-continuous density G′ on R₊. Then f is a constant function on R.

Proof
From the right-continuity of G′ results that G′ is strictly positive on some interval [a,b] with 0<a<b.

We assume that f is not a constant function and we derive a contradiction. Let $c-h<c$ be such that $f(c-h)\neq f(c)$. Replacing f by $-f$ if necessary, we may assume $f(c-h)<f(c)$. Post-multiplying the relation $f=f*G$ by $*1_{[0,h[}$ and using the commutativity of the convolution product, we obtain

$$f^h = f^h * G \ , \quad \sup f^h := \sup\{f^h(x)/x\in\mathbf{R}\} > 0 \ .$$

Let us first assume that sup f^h is attained, i.e. that $x_0\in\mathbf{R}$ exists such that $f^h(x_0)=\sup f^h$. Then

$$\sup f^h = f^h(x_0) = \int_{[0,\infty[} f^h(x_0-y)dG(y)\ ,$$

$$0 = \int_{[0,\infty[}(\sup f^h - f^h(x_0-y)dG(y) \geq \int_{[a,b]}(\sup f^h - f^h(x_0-y))G'(y)dy.$$

Then

$$\sup f^h - f^h(x_0-y) = 0 \quad (a\leq y\leq b)\ , \quad f^h \equiv \sup f^h \ \text{ on } \ [x_0-b, x_0-a]\ .$$

By a repetition of the argument:

$$f^h \equiv \sup f^h \ \text{ on } \ [x_0-2b, x_0-2a]\ ,$$

$$f^h \equiv \sup f^h \ \text{ on } \ [x_0-3b, x_0-3a]\ ,$$

$$\dots \quad \dots \quad \dots \quad \dots \quad \dots$$

The union of the intervals [ka,kb] ($k\in\mathbf{N}_{++}$) contains some interval $[c,\infty[$. Hence d exists such that $f^h\equiv\sup f^h$ on $]-\infty,d]$. We now show that $f^h\equiv\sup f^h$ on $]d,\infty]$.

Let us fix $x>d$. The relation $f^h=f^h*G^{*k}$ ($k\in\mathbf{N}_+$) results from a repeated use of relation $f^h=f^h*G$. Then

$$\begin{aligned} f^h(x) &= \int_{[0,x-d]} f^h(x-y)dG^{*k}(y) + \int_{]x-d,\infty[} f^h(x-y)dG^{*k}(y) \\ &= \int_{[0,x-d]} f^h(x-y)dG^{*k}(y) + \sup f^h.(1-G^{*k}(x-d)) \\ &\geq \inf f^h.\ G^{*k}(x-d) + \sup f^h.(1-G^{*k}(x-d)). \end{aligned}$$

$G^{*k}(x-d)\to 0$ as $k\uparrow\infty$ by the Lemma of I.Ch.1.Th.13. Hence $f^h(x)\geq\sup f^h$, and this implies that $f^h(x)=\sup f^h$. This proves that $f^h\equiv\sup f^h$. Hence, for m=1,2,...,n:

$$f(mh)-f((m-1)h) = \sup f^h\ .$$

Adding up these relations, we obtain,

$$f(nh)-f(0) = n \sup f^h \quad (n \in \mathbf{N}_+).$$

This leads to a contradiction as $n\uparrow\infty$ because f is bounded.

Let us now assume that $\sup f^h$ is not attained. Then a sequence $s_k\downarrow-\infty$, or $s_k\uparrow+\infty$ exists such that $f^h(s_k)\to\sup f^h$. By Lemma 2 (or by an obvious variant if $s_k\downarrow-\infty$), a bounded and uniformly continuous function f_0 exists on **R**, such that

$$\lim_{k\uparrow\infty} f^h(x+t_k) = f_0(x), \text{ uniformly on bounded sets,}$$

for some subsequence t_k of s_k. From $k\uparrow\infty$ in the relation

$$f^h(x+t_k) = \int_{[0,\infty[} f^h(x+t_k)dG(y),$$

follows that

$$f_0(x)= \int_{[0,\infty[} f_0(x-y)dG(y) \ (x\in\mathbf{R}), \text{ i.e. } f_0 = f_0*G.$$

But $\sup f_0=\sup f^h$ and $\sup f_0$ is attained at the point 0. Hence, $f_0\equiv\sup f^h>0$ by the case already proved. Then

$$\lim_{k\uparrow\infty} f^h(x+t_k) = \sup f^h, \text{ uniformly on bounded sets.} \tag{A5}$$

Let us fix n such that

$$n > 2(\sup f - \inf f)/\sup f^h .$$

Let k be such that

$$f^h(x+t_k) > \sup f^h /2 \quad (0\le x\le nh).$$

This is possible by (A5). Then

$$f(mh+t_k)-f((m-1)h+t_k) = f^h(mh+t_k) > \sup f^h /2 \quad (m=1,\dots,n).$$

Adding up these relations, we obtain the contradiction

$$f(nh+t_k)-f(t_k) > n \sup f^h /2 > \sup f - \inf f \ \bullet$$

A4. Renewal Theorems on $\mathbf{R}_+$

Usual Assumptions on G

In the following Lemmas and Theorems of this Appendix, V is the unique solution, by I.Ch.1.Th.14.a, of the renewal equation $V=1+V*G$ on $\mathbf{R}_+$.

The ***Usual Assumptions*** **on the probability distribution G** appearing in the renewal equations $V=1+V*G$ and $f=g+f*G$ on $\mathbf{R}_+$, are the following.

a. **$G(0)=0$.**

b. **G has a density G' on $\mathbf{R}_+$.**

c. **The first moment μ of G is finite.**

d. **G' is dominated by a continuous decreasing Lebesgue-integrable function g_0 on $\mathbf{R}_+$: $0 \le G' \le g_0$.**

These assumptions, used in the proof of the renewal Theorems, may seem rather restrictive. In fact, they are not, when the renewal Theorems are applied to the classical actuarial risk model, because there the claimsize distribution undergoes a preliminary transformation making a, b and d true. (It is replaced by its concave transform). The proofs in this Appendix A, are essentially due to Feller (1966), but the *Usual Assumptions* we make, allow interesting simplifications.

Lemma 3

Let $G(0)<0$. Positive constants c_1, c_2 exist, such that

$$V(y)-V(x) \le c_1+c_2(y-x) \quad (0 \le x \le y).$$

Proof
The distribution G is not concentrated at the origin. A strictly positive number h such that $G(h)<1$ exists because $G(0)<1$ and because G is right-continuous. From the renewal equation $V=1+V*G$ results that $1=(1-G)*V$. For any $x>h$,

$$1 = \int_{[0,x]}(1-G(x-y))dV(y) \ge \int_{]x-h,x]}(1-G(x-y))dV(y)$$

$$\ge \int_{]x-h,x]}(1-G(h))dV(y) = (1-G(h))(V(x)-V(x-h)) .$$

Hence

$$V(x)-V(x-h) \le (1-G(h))^{-1} =: c_1 .$$

We replace x by $x+h$, $x+2h$,..., $x+kh$, and we add up the corresponding relations:

$$V(x+kh)-V(x) \le kc_1 \quad (x \in \mathbf{R}_+ ,\ k \in \mathbf{N}_+).$$

Let $y:=x+a>x$. Then $kh \le a<(k+1)h$ for some integer k. With $c_2:=c_1h^{-1}$, we have

$$V(y)-V(x) = V(x+a)-V(x) \le V(x+(k+1)h)-V(x)$$

$$\le (k+1)c_1 \le c_1+c_2a \quad \bullet$$

Lemma 4

Under the *Usual Assumptions* on G, the renewal function V has a bounded density V′ on $\mathbf{R}_+$, satisfying the renewal equation V′=G′+V′*G on $\mathbf{R}_+$. The function V is uniformly continuous on $\mathbf{R}_+$.

Proof
By Ch.Th.16, V′=G′+V′*G, because here V(0)=1 (consider V=1+V*G at 0). Hence, for the boundedness of V′, it is sufficient to verify that V′*G is bounded on $\mathbf{R}_+$.

$$(V'*G)(x) = \int_{[0,x]} V'(x-y)dG(y) = \int_{]0,x[} V'(x-y)G'(y)dy = \int_{]0,x[} V'(y)G'(x-y)dy$$

$$\leq \int_{]0,x[} V'(y)g_0(x-y)dy = -\int_{]0,x[} g_0(x-y)d_y(V(x)-V(y))$$

($\int$ by parts)

$$= g_0(x)(V(x)-V(0)) + \int_{]0,x[}(V(x)-V(y))d_y g_0(x-y)$$

(by Lemma 3)

$$\leq g_0(x)(c_1+c_2x) + \int_{]0,x[}[c_1+c_2(x-y)]d_y g_0(x-y)$$

($\int$ by parts)

$$= g_0(x)(c_1+c_2x) + c_1g_0(0) - (c_1+c_2x)g_0(x) + c_2\int_{]0,x[} g_0(x-y)dy$$

$$= c_1g_0(0) + c_2\int_{]0,x[} g_0(y)dy \leq c_1g_0(0) + c_2\int_{]0,\infty[} g_0(y)dy < \infty.$$

Hence, V′ is bounded on $\mathbf{R}_+$. This implies that V is uniformly continuous on $\mathbf{R}_+$. Indeed, let $0 \leq x \leq y$. Then

$$V(y)-V(x) = \int_{]x,y]} V'(s)ds \leq \sup_{s\in[0,\infty[} V'(s).(y-x) \quad \bullet$$

Theorem A3 (Renewal Theorem for the Increments of V)

Under the *Usual Assumptions* on G, the solution V of the renewal equation V=1+V*G on $\mathbf{R}_+$, is such that

$$\mathbf{\lim_{x\uparrow\infty} [V(x)-V(x-h)] = h/\mu \quad (h\in R_+).}$$

Proof
It is enough to prove that each sequence $s_k\uparrow\infty$ has a subsequence t_k such that

$$V^h(t_k) \to h/\mu \text{ as } k\uparrow\infty. \tag{A6}$$

(Indeed, if the limit of the statement of the Theorem does not exist, or is different from h/μ, then $V^h(x)$ has at least one limit point different from h/μ as $x\uparrow\infty$. From some sequence $s_k\uparrow\infty$, $V^h(s_k)$ tends to this limit point. Then any subsequence also tends to this limit different from h/μ).

By Lemma 4, V is uniformly continuous on $\mathbf{R}_+$. Then V^h is uniformly continuous on $[h,\infty[$. By Lemma 3, V^h is bounded. By Lemma 1, a bounded and uniformly continuous function V_0 exists on $\mathbf{R}$, such that

$$\lim_{k\uparrow\infty} V^h(x+t_k) = V_0(x) \quad (x\in\mathbf{R})$$

for some subsequence t_k of s_k. From the convolution multiplication of relation $V=1+V*G$ by $1_{[o,h[}$ results the relation

$$V^h = 1_{[0,h[} + V^h * G. \qquad \text{(A7)}$$

Hence

$$V^h(x+t_k) = 1_{[0,h[}(x+t_k) + \int_{[0,x+t_k[} V^h(x+t_k-y)dG(y)$$

As $k\uparrow\infty$,

$$V_0(x) = \int_{[0,\infty[} V_0(x-y)dG(y) \quad (x\in\mathbf{R}), \text{ i.e. } V_0=V_0*G \text{ on } \mathbf{R}.$$

By Lemma 2, $V_0\equiv c$ for some $c\in\mathbf{R}$. Hence,

$$\lim_{k\uparrow\infty} V^h(x+t_k) = c \quad (x\in\mathbf{R}). \qquad \text{(A8)}$$

By (A7),

$$V^h *(1-G) = 1_{[0,h[}.$$

We take the convolution product of the latter relation by $1/_\mu I$ (I: identity function on $\mathbf{R}_+$):

$$V^h *[1/_\mu (1-G)*I] = 1/_\mu\, 1_{[0,h[}*I.$$

Let $H:=1/_\mu (1-G)*I$ be the concave transform of G. Then H is a probability distribution function. We take the relation $V^h*H=1/_\mu 1_{[0,h[}*I$ at the point t_k. Then the last member equals h/μ if $t_k>h$, and the first member equals

$$\int_{[0,\infty]} V^h(t_k-x)dH(x) \to \int_{[0,\infty[} c\,dH(x) = c \text{ as } t_k\uparrow\infty,$$

by (A8) and by dominated convergence. Hence $c=h/\mu$. Taking $x=0$ in (A8), we have $V^h(t_k)\to h/\mu$, i.e. (A6) •

Theorem A4 (Key Renewal Theorem)

Under the *Usual Assumptions* on G, let f be the solution of the renewal equation f=g+f*G. Then f(∞) exists and

$$\mathbf{f(\infty) = 1/\mu \int_{[x,\infty[} g(x)dx,} \tag{A9}$$

if the following conditions a. or b. are satisfied:

a. g is directly Riemann-integrable on $\mathbf{R_+}$.

b. G′ is directly Riemann-integrable on $\mathbf{R_+}$, g(∞)=0 and g is Lebesgue-integrable on $\mathbf{R_+}$.

Theorem A5 (Renewal Theorem for the Density V′ of V)

We adopt the *Usual Assumptions* on G and we suppose that G′ is directly Riemann-integrable on $\mathbf{R_+}$. Then the solution V of the renewal equation V=1+V*G has a bounded density V′ on $\mathbf{R_+}$, the limit V′(∞) exists and it equals 1/μ.

Proof of Th.A8 and Th.A9.

By I.Ch.1.Th.14, f=g*V, where V is the solution of the renewal equation V=1+V*G. Hence (A9) is equivalent to the relation

$$\lim_{x\uparrow\infty} (g*V)(x) = 1/\mu \int_{[0,\infty[} g(x)dx. \tag{A10}$$

The relation (A10) is exact for $g:=1_{[a,a+h[}$ $(a\geq 0)$. Indeed, if $x>a+h$,

$$(1_{[a,a+h[}*V)(x) = \int_{[0,x]} 1_{[a,a+h[}(x-y)dV(y) = \int_{]x-a-h,x-a]} dV(y)$$

$$= V(x-a)-V(x-a-h) = V^h(x-a) \rightarrow \mu^{-1}h = \mu^{-1}\int_{[0,\infty[} 1_{[a,a+h[}(x)dx, \tag{A11}$$

by Theorem A3. By the first three relations of (A11) and by Lemma 3,

$$(1_{[a,a+h[}*V)(x) = V(x-a)-V(x-a-h) \leq c_1+c_2h. \tag{A12}$$

We now consider a partition of $\mathbf{R}_+$ by points nδ (n=0,1,2,...) and a function

$$g := \sum_{n\geq 0} c_n\, 1_{[n\delta,n\delta+1[}, \text{ where } \sum_{n\geq 0} |c_n| < \infty. \tag{A13}$$

We prove that (A10) is valid for this g. By (A12),

$$|(g*V)(x)-\sum_{n\le m}c_n(1_{[n\delta,n\delta+1[}*V)(x)|$$

$$= |\sum_{n\ge m+1}c_n(1_{[n\delta,n\delta+1[}*V)(x)| \le (c_1+c_2h)\ \sum_{n\ge m+1}|c_n|.$$

As $x\uparrow\infty$,

$$|\limsup_{x\uparrow\infty}\ (g*V)(x)-\sum_{n\le m}c_n.\delta/\mu| \le (c_1+c_2h)\ \sum_{n\ge m+1}|c_n|,$$

by (A11). As $m\uparrow\infty$,

$$|\limsup_{x\uparrow\infty}\ (g*V)(x)-\sum_{n\ge 0}c_n.\delta/\mu| \le (c_1+c_2h)\ \lim_{m\uparrow\infty}\sum_{n\ge m+1}|c_n| = 0.$$

In this argument, lim sup can be replaced by lim inf everywhere. The conclusion is

$$\lim_{x\uparrow\infty}\ (g*V)(x) = \sum_{n\ge 0}c_n.\delta/\mu = 1/\mu\int_{[0,\infty[}\ g(x)dx,$$

i.e. (A10) is correct for the function g defined by (A13).

Let g be directly integrable. We prove that (A10) is valid in that case. By section A2, $g_\delta\le g\le g^\delta$ where g_δ and g^δ are functions such as g defined by (A13) for which (A10) is valid. Hence, for $x\uparrow\infty$ in the relations

$$(g_\delta*V)(x) \le (g*V)(x) \le (g^\delta*V)(x),$$

we obtain

$$1/\mu\int_{[0,\infty[}g_\delta(x)dx \le \limsup_{x\uparrow\infty}\ (g*V)(x) \le 1/\mu\int_{[0,\infty[}g^\delta(x)dx.$$

As $\delta\downarrow 0$,

$$1/\mu\int_{[0,\infty[}g(x)dx \le \limsup_{x\uparrow\infty}\ (g*V)(x) \le 1/\mu\int_{[0,\infty[}g(x)dx$$

by Th.A2.a. Lim sup can be replaced by lim inf in these relations. The conclusion is that (A10) is correct for any directly integrable function g. This proves Th.A4.a.

We now apply the case already proved to the renewal equation $V'=G'+V'*G$. Hence, if G' is directly integrable, then

$$V'(\infty)=1/\mu\int_{[0,\infty[}G'(x)dx=1/\mu.$$

This proves Theorem A5. Then Th.A4.b results from I.Ch.1.Th.17 •

Theorem A6 (Elementary Renewal Theorem)

Under the *Usual Assumptions* on G, the solution V of the renewal equation V=1+V*G is such that

$$\lim_{x\uparrow\infty} V(x)/x = 1/\mu.$$

Proof

For any positive number b and x>b,

$$\frac{V(x)}{x} = \frac{V(x)-V(b)}{x-b}\cdot\frac{x-b}{x} + \frac{V(b)}{x}\ .$$

Hence, as $x\uparrow\infty$,

$$\limsup[V(x)/x] = \limsup\,[[V(x)-V(b)]/(x-b)].$$

Let $\varepsilon>0$. Let us fix b in such a way that

$$\mu^{-1} - \varepsilon \le V'(y) \le \mu^{-1} + \varepsilon \quad (y\ge b).$$

This is possible by the renewal Theorem A5 for the density V'. We integrate that relation over $]b,x]$, then we divide by x–b, and then we take the lim sup as $x\uparrow\infty$:

$$\mu^{-1} - \varepsilon \le \limsup_{x\uparrow\infty} V(x)/x \le \mu^{-1} + \varepsilon.$$

As $\varepsilon\downarrow 0$:

$$\limsup_{x\uparrow\infty} V(x)/x = \mu^{-1}.$$

Similarly,

$$\liminf_{x\uparrow\infty} V(x)/x = \mu^{-1} \quad \bullet$$

Appendix B

Discrete Renewal Theorems on $\mathbf{N}_+$

B1. Convolution Products on N

In I.Ch.10, sequences on $\mathbf{N}_+$, such as

$$\underline{f} = (f_0, f_1, f_2, \ldots) \equiv (f(0), f(1), f(2), \ldots)$$

are considered. In this Appendix, we prove renewal Theorems for renewal equations built up from such sequences, but sequences and convolutions on **N** occur in the proofs. We use the same notations $\underline{f}$, $\underline{g}$,... for sequences on **N** and on $\mathbf{N}_+$, but we specify in the context what sequences are considered. For instance, the following is a **sequence $\underline{g}$ on N**:

$$\underline{g} = (\ldots, g_{-2}, g_{-1}, g_0, g_1, g_2, \ldots) \equiv (\ldots, g(-2), g(-1), g(0), g(1), g(2), \ldots).$$

Sequences defined on $\mathbf{N}_+$ must be extended to **N** by annulation on $\mathbf{N}_{-}$. For instance, the sequence $\underline{f}$ considered above, must be identified with the sequence

$$\underline{f} = (\ldots, 0, 0, f_0, f_1, f_2, \ldots)$$

on **N**, for which it is not necessary to introduce a new notation. This is compatible with the definition $\nabla f_0 := f_0 - f_{-1} = f_0$ adopted for sequences on $\mathbf{N}_+$.

The **convolution product** of the bounded sequence $\underline{f}$ on **N** and the probability distribution sequence $\underline{G}$ on $\mathbf{N}_+$ is the sequence $\underline{f}*\underline{G}$ on **N** defined by

$$(\underline{f}*\underline{G})_k := \textstyle\sum_{j\geq 0} f_{k-j} \nabla G_j \quad (k \in \mathbf{N}).$$

This convolution product is associative:

$$(\underline{f}*\underline{G})*\underline{H} = \underline{f}*(\underline{G}*\underline{H}),$$

if $\underline{H}$ is also a probability distribution sequence.

B2. Renewal Theorems on $\mathbf{N}_+$

Usual Assumptions on $\underline{\mathbf{G}}$

Hereafter we consider the following renewal equations on $\mathbf{N}_+$

$$\underline{V} = \underline{1} + \underline{V}*\underline{G} \quad , \ \underline{v} = \underline{\delta} + \underline{v}*\underline{G} \ , \ \underline{f} = \underline{h} + \underline{f}*\underline{G}, \qquad \text{(B1)}$$

where $\underline{v}:=\nabla\underline{V}$ (see the notations of I.Ch.10.1). The second of the equations (B1) results from an application of the operator ∇ to the first. We define $\underline{g}:=\nabla\underline{G}$. The following are the ***Usual Assumptions*** on $\underline{G}$, used in the rest of this Appendix B:

a. **$\underline{G}$ is a probability distribution sequence on $\mathbf{N}_+$.**

b. **$\underline{G}$ is not concentrated at 0.**

c. **$\underline{G}$ has a finite first moment μ.**

d. **The span of the arithmetic distribution $\underline{G}$ is 1 (see I.Ch.10.1.7).**

Lemma 1

The atoms of $\underline{V}$ are the linear combinations, with positive integer coefficients, of the atoms of $\underline{G}$.

Proof
The lemma results from the following observations.

a. By Ch.10.Th.6. the solution of the first renewal equation (B1) is $\underline{V}= \sum_{k\geq 0} \underline{G}^{*k}$. From this results that a point j is an atom of $\underline{V}$ iff it is an atom of some distribution $\underline{G}^{*k}$ ($k\in N_+$).

b. If A_1 is the set of atoms of the distribution $\underline{F_1}$ on N_+, and A_2 the set of atoms of the distribution $\underline{F_2}$ on N_+, then $A_1+A_2:=\{i+j/i\in A_1, j\in A_2\}$ is the set of atoms of $\underline{F_1}*\underline{F_2}$.

c. 0 is a linear combination, with coefficients equal to 0, of any atoms of G. The point 0 is the unique atom of $\underline{G}^{*0}$ •

Lemma 2

A point $j_0 \in \mathbf{N}_+$ exists, such that each point $j \geq j_0$ is an atom of $\underline{V}$.

Proof

Let A be the set of atoms of $\underline{G}$. Let L the set of linear combinations with coefficients in **N** of the points of A. Let k_0 be the first strictly positive integer of L. Then

$$A \subseteq \{0, k_0, 2k_0, 3k_0, \ldots\}. \tag{B2}$$

Indeed, let $j \in A$. Then j is in some interval $[ik_0,(i+1)k_0[$, $i \in \mathbf{N}_+$. This implies that $j-ik_0 \in L$. But $j-ik_0<k_0$. By the definition of k_0, this is only possible if $j-ik_0=0$. This proves (B2). From (B2) results that $\underline{G}$ is concentrated on the set $\{0,k_0,2k_0,3k_0,\ldots\}$. This implies that $k_0=1$, because the span of $\underline{G}$ is 1. Hence $1 \in L$, and 1 is a linear combination of atoms of $\underline{G}$, with coefficients in **N**. We can separate the positive and the negative terms in this linear combination. This means that we can display 1 as difference of two positive integers k+1 and k, each of wich is a linear combination of atoms of $\underline{G}$ with positive integer coefficients. Then k and k+1 are atoms of $\underline{V}$ by the Lemma 1. If k=0, then 1 is an atom of V, and then 2,3,... are also atoms of $\underline{V}$. Then we can take $j_0=0$. Let us now assume that k>0. The intervals

$$[(k+j)k\,,\ (k+j)k+(k+j)] \quad (j=0,1,2,\ldots) \tag{B3}$$

recover $[k^2,\infty[$, because the left extremity of the first interval, corresponding to j=0, is k^2 , and because any couple of successive intervals overlap. For fixed j, the integers of the interval (B3) are $(k+j)k+i$ $(i=0,1,\ldots,k+j)$, i.e.

$$(k+j-i)k+i(k+1) \quad (i=0,1,\ldots,k+j).$$

The latter points are atoms of $\underline{V}$, because k and k+1 are atoms of $\underline{V}$. Hence, we can take $j_0=k^2$ •

Lemma 3

Let $\underline{w}$ be a bounded sequence on N, such that $\underline{w}=\underline{w}*\underline{G}$ on N. Then $\underline{w}$ is a constant sequence on N.

Proof

We assume that $\underline{w}$ is not a constant sequence and we derive a contradiction. A point $j \in \mathbf{N}$ exists such that $w_{j-1} \neq w_j$. Replacing $\underline{w}$ by $-\underline{w}$ if necessary, we may assume that $w_{j-1}<w_j$.

Let $\underline{u} := \nabla \underline{w}$ on $\mathbf{N}$. Then sup $\underline{u}>0$ and $\underline{u}=\underline{u}*\underline{G}$ by the application of ∇ to the equation $\underline{w}=\underline{w}*\underline{G}$.

Let us first assume that sup $\underline{u}$ is attained, i.e. that $i_0 \in \mathbf{N}$ exists such that $u(i_0)=\sup \underline{u}$. Then

$$\sup \underline{u} = u(i_0) = \textstyle\sum_{i\geq 0} u(i_0-i)g(i) \ , \ 0 = \sum_{i\geq 0}(\sup \underline{u} - u(i_0-i))g(i).$$

Hence,

$$u(i_0-i) = \sup \underline{u} \quad (i \text{ atom of } \underline{G}).$$

The same argument can be applied to the equation $\underline{u}=\underline{u}*\underline{G}^{*k}$, resulting from repeated convolution products of $\underline{u}=\underline{u}*\underline{G}$ by $\underline{G}$. Hence

$$u(i_0-i) = \sup \underline{u} \quad (i \text{ atom of } \underline{G}^{*k}),$$

for all $k \in \mathbf{N}_+$ and then

$$u(i_0-i) = \sup \underline{u} \quad (i \text{ atom of } \underline{V}).$$

By Lemma 2, this implies the existence of $j_0 \in \mathbf{N}$ such that

$$u(j) = \sup \underline{u} \quad (j \leq j_0).$$

Then

$$u(j_0+1) = \textstyle\sum_{j\geq 0} u(j_0+1-j)g(j) = u(j_0+1)g(0) + \sum_{j\geq 1} u(j_0+1-j)g(j)$$

$$= u(j_0+1)g(0) + \sup \underline{u} \textstyle\sum_{j\geq 1} g(j) = g(0)u(j_0+1) + (1-g(0))\sup \underline{u}.$$

Hence

$$u(j_0+1) = \sup \underline{u}\,,$$

because $g(0)\neq 1$. Repeating this argument, we conclude that

$$u(j) = \sup \underline{u} \quad (j \in \mathbf{N}).$$

Then

$$w(k)-w(0) = \textstyle\sum_{1\leq j\leq k} \nabla w_j = \sum_{1\leq j\leq k} u(j) = k \sup \underline{u}$$

and this provides a contradiction as $k\uparrow\infty$ because the first member is bounded.

Let us assume now that sup $\underline{u}$ is not attained. Then a sequence $i_n \downarrow -\infty$, or $i_n \uparrow +\infty$ exists such that $u(i_n) \to \sup \underline{u}$ as $n\uparrow\infty$. Let us consider the numbers

$$u(k+i_n) \ (k \in \mathbf{N},\ n \in \mathbf{N}_+). \tag{B4}$$

By Cantor's diagonal process (App.A.Th.A1), a sequence $\underline{u}_0$ on $\mathbf{N}$, and a subsequence j_n of i_n exist, such that

$$\lim_{n\uparrow\infty} u(k+j_n) = u_0(k) \quad (k \in \mathbf{N}).$$

The sequence $\underline{u}_0$ is bounded, because $\underline{u}$ is bounded. The sequence $\underline{u}_0$ satisfies the renewal equation $\underline{u}_0=\underline{u}_0*\underline{G}$. Indeed,

$$u(k+j_n) = \sum_{j\geq 0} u(k+j_n-j)g(j).$$

As $n\uparrow\infty$:

$$u_0(k) = \sum_{j\geq 0} u_0(k-j)g(j),$$

by dominated convergence. Here sup $\underline{u}_0$=sup $\underline{u}=u_0(0)$. Hence, sup $\underline{u}_0$ is attained at the point 0. By the case already treated, $u_0(k)$=sup $\underline{u}$ ($k\in\mathbf{N}$) and then

$$\lim_{n\uparrow\infty} u(k+j_n) = \sup \underline{u} \quad (k\in\mathbf{N}). \tag{B5}$$

Let us fix m such that

$$m > 2(\sup \underline{w} - \inf \underline{w})/(\sup \underline{u}),$$

then n such that

$$u(k+j_n) > (\sup \underline{u})/2 \quad (k=1,2,\ldots m).$$

This is possible by (B5). Then we obtain the contradiction

$$w(m+j_n) - w(j_n) = \sum_{1\leq k\leq m} u(k+j_n) > m(\sup \underline{u})/2 > \sup \underline{w} - \inf \underline{w} \bullet$$

Lemma 4

The sequence $\underline{v}$ is bounded on $\mathbf{N}_+$.

Proof

By the relation $\underline{1}=(\underline{1}-\underline{G})*\underline{V}$ at the point $k\in\mathbf{N}_+$:

$$1 = \sum_{0\leq j\leq k} (1-G_{k-j})v_j \geq (1-G_0)v_k.$$

Hence, $v_k\leq(1-G_0)^{-1}$ ($k\in\mathbf{N}_+$) •

Theorem B1 (Renewal Theorem for $\underline{v}:=\nabla\underline{V}$)

Under the *Usual Assumptions* on $\underline{G}$, let $\underline{V}$ be the solution of the renewal equation $\underline{V}=\underline{1}+\underline{V}*\underline{G}$ on $\mathbf{N}_+$, and let $\underline{v}:=\nabla\underline{V}$. Then the limit v_∞ exists, and it equals $1/\mu$.

Proof

It is enough to prove that each sequence $i_n\uparrow\infty$ has a subsequence j_n such that

$$\lim_{n\uparrow\infty} v(j_n) = \mu^{-1}, \tag{B6}$$

because then only μ^{-1} can be a limit point of v(k) as $k\uparrow\infty$.

Let us consider the numbers

$$v(k+i_n)\ (k\in\mathbf{N},\ n\in\mathbf{N}_+).$$

By Cantor's diagonal process (App.A.Th.A1), a sequence $\underline{v}_0$ on **N**, and a subsequence j_n of i_n exist, such that

$$\lim_{n\uparrow\infty} v(k+j_n) = v_0(k)\ \ (k\in\mathbf{N}).$$

The sequence $\underline{v}_0$ is bounded, because $\underline{v}$ is bounded by Lemma 4. The sequence $\underline{v}_0$ satisfies the renewal equation $\underline{v}_0=\underline{v}_0*\underline{G}$. Indeed, from the second relation (B1) follows that

$$v(k+j_n) = \delta(k+j_n) + \sum_{j\geq 0} v(k+j_n-j)g(j),$$

for any $k\in\mathbf{N}$, $k+j_n>0$. Then, as $n\uparrow\infty$,

$$v_0(k) = \sum_{j\geq 0} v_0(k-j)g(j)\ \ (k\in\mathbf{N}),$$

by dominated convergence. From the equation $\underline{v}_0=\underline{v}_0*\underline{G}$ and Lemma 3 results that $\underline{v}_0$ is a constant sequence, say $v_0(k)=c\in\mathbf{R}_+$ ($k\in\mathbf{N}$). Hence,

$$\lim_{n\uparrow\infty} v(k+j_n) = c\ \ (k\in\mathbf{N}). \tag{B7}$$

We have $\underline{v}*\underline{H}=\mu^{-1}\underline{1}$ for some probability distribution sequence $\underline{H}$ on $\mathbf{N}_+$ (see proof of I.Ch.10.Th.7). At the point j_n, this relation gives

$$\mu^{-1} = \mu^{-1}1(j_n) = (\underline{v}*\underline{H})(j_n) = \sum_{j\geq 0} v(j_n-j)\nabla H_j \to \sum_{j\geq 0} c\ \nabla H_j = c,$$

as $n\uparrow\infty$, by (B7) and by dominated convergence. Hence $c=\mu^{-1}$ and then (B6) results from k=0 in (B7) •

Theorem B2 (Key Renewal Theorem)

Under the *Usual Assumptions* on $\underline{G}$, let $\underline{f}$ be the solution of the renewal equation $\underline{f}=\underline{h}+\underline{f}*\underline{G}$. Then f_∞ exists and $f_\infty=1/_\mu \sum_{k\geq 0} h_k$ if $\sum_{k\geq 0}|h_k|<\infty$.

Proof

By the preceding Theorem B1, v_∞ exists and is finite and then I.Ch.10.Th.8 can be applied •

Appendix C

Convex Analysis on $\mathbf{R}^n$

The following Theorems C1 to C13 are rather intuitively obvious in $\mathbf{R}$, $\mathbf{R}^2$ or $\mathbf{R}^3$. Their validity in $\mathbf{R}^n$ can easily be admitted. At least, the proofs can be omitted at first reading.

C1. Convex Sets in $\mathbf{R}^n$

We here consider $\mathbf{R}^n$ as a space of columns $x=(x_1,\ldots,x_n)'$ with elements $x_j \in \mathbf{R}$ $(1,\ldots,n)$. This allows some convenient matrix notations.

We recall that **the scalar product $<x,y>$** of

$$x = (x_1,\ldots,x_n)' \in \mathbf{R}^n \text{ and } y = (y_1,\ldots,y_n)' \in \mathbf{R}^n$$

is defined as

$$<x,y> := x_1y_1 + \ldots + x_ny_n = x'y = y'x. \qquad \text{(C1)}$$

The norm $||x||$ is

$$||x|| := <x,y>^{1/2} = (x'y)^{1/2} \qquad \text{(C2)}$$

and **the distance from x to y** is $||x-y||$.

The intervals with **extremities** $x,y \in \mathbf{R}^n$, are the following sets in $\mathbf{R}^n$:

$$[x,y] := \{(1-p)x+py \ / \ 0 \le p \le 1\} \text{ (closed interval),}$$

$$[x,y[:= \{(1-p)x+py \ / \ 0 \le p < 1\} \text{ (half-open interval excluding y),}$$

$$]x,y] := \{(1-p)x+py \ / \ 0 < p \le 1\} \text{ (half-open interval excluding x),}$$

$$]x,y[:= \{(1-p)x+py \ / \ 0 < p < 1\} \text{ (open interval).}$$

The open ball, closed ball with center $x \in \mathbf{R}^n$ and radius $\rho > 0$ is the set

$$\{y / y \in \mathbf{R}^n, ||x-y|| < \rho\} \ , \ \{y / y \in \mathbf{R}^n, ||x-y|| \le \rho\} \text{ resp.}$$

In $\mathbf{R}^1$, $\mathbf{R}^2$, $\mathbf{R}^3$, the open balls are open intervals, circles, spheres resp.

The point x is an **interior point** of the set $E \subseteq \mathbf{R}^n$ if an open ball V exists such that $x \in V \subseteq E$. **The interior** of the set $E \subseteq \mathbf{R}^n$ is the set of interior points of E. It is denoted by E^0. **The closure** of E is the set of points $x \in E$ expressible as a limit of a sequence of points in E. It is denoted by E^-.

$$E^{0-} := (E^0)^-, E^{-0} := (E^-)^0, E^{00} := (E^0)^0 = E^0, E^{--} := (E^-)^- = E^-.$$

The set E is **open** if $E^0=E$. It is **closed** if $E^-=E$. The set E is open iff it has the following property: for all $x \in E$, an open set V exists such that $x \in V \subseteq E$.

A flat convex set in $\mathbf{R}^n$ is a convex set with no interior points (this terminology is justified by the following Lemma of Theorem C2). **A fat convex set** in $\mathbf{R}^n$, or **a convex body**, is a convex set with interior points.

We notice that

$$]x,y[^0 = [x,y[\text{ in } \mathbf{R}^1, \quad]x,y[^0 = \varnothing \text{ in } \mathbf{R}^n \ (n>1).$$

Hence, the open interval $]x,y[$ $(x \neq y)$ is not an open set in $\mathbf{R}^n$ $(n>1)$.

If $U,V \subseteq \mathbf{R}^n$ and $a,b \in \mathbf{R}$,

$$a + bU := \{a+bx \,/\, x \in U\},$$

$$aU+bV := \{ax+by \,/\, x \in U, y \in V\}.$$

C2. Interior and Closure of a Convex Set

Theorem C1

Let C be a convex set in $\mathbf{R}^n$. Then C^- and C^0 are convex sets.

Proof

a. Let $x,y \in C^-$ and let $p \in [0,1]$. Sequences $x_i,y_i \in C$ $(i=1,2,...)$ exist, such that $x_i \to x$, $y_i \to y$ as $i \to \infty$. Then $(1-p)x_i+py_i \in C$ and

$$(1-p)x_i + p\, y_i \to (1-p)x + py \in C^-.$$

b. Let $x,y \in C^0$ and let $p \in [0,1]$. Open balls U,V exist such that $x \in U \subseteq C$, $y \in V \subseteq C$. Then $(1-p)U+pV$ is an open set in C, containing $(1-p)x+py$. This proves that $(1-p)x+py \in C^0$ •

Lemma

Any flat convex set in $\mathbf{R}^n$ is contained in a (n–1)-dimensional plane.

Proof
Let C be a flat convex set in $\mathbf{R}^n$. By a translation, if necessary, we may assume that that the origin 0 of $\mathbf{R}^n$ belongs to C. Let P be the vector space generated by C, i.e. the set of all linear combinations of points of C. If $P=\mathbf{R}^n$, then C contains n independent vectors $x_1,\dots,x_n$ and then the point $(x_1+\dots+x_n+0)/(n+1)$ is an interior point of C. This contradiction proves that the dimension of P is strictly less than n •

Theorem C2

If C is a convex set in $\mathbf{R}^n$, then $C^{-0}=C^0$. If C is a convex body in $\mathbf{R}^n$, then $C^{0-}=C^-$.

Proof
The proof is based on the following preliminary results a. and b.

a. Let C be a flat convex set in $\mathbf{R}^n$. Then $C^{-0}=\varnothing$.

By the Lemma a plane P exists such that $C\subseteq P$. Then $C^-\subseteq P$ and then $C^{-0}\subseteq P^0=\varnothing$. Hence $C^{-0}=\varnothing$.

b. Let C be a convex set in $\mathbf{R}^n$, $x\in C^0$, $y\in C^-$. Then $[x,y[\in C^0$.

Indeed, any point $z\in[x,y[$ can be displayed as $z=(1-p)x+py$, with $p\in[0,1[$. Let V be an open ball such that $x\in V\subseteq C$. Let $y_i\in C$ $(i=1,2,\dots)$ be a sequence of points such that $y_i\to y$. Then

$$z-py_i \to z-py = (1-p)x \in (1-p)V.$$

The set $(1-p)V$ is open. Hence, for fixed i, large enough, $z-py_i\in(1-p)V$. Then $z\in py_i+(1-p)V$. The set $py_i+(1-p)V$ is an open set in C. Hence, $z\in C^0$.

c. Let C be a convex body in $\mathbf{R}^n$. Then $C^{0-}=C^-$.

Indeed, $C^{0-}\subseteq C^-$, and it is enough to prove that $C^-\subseteq C^{0-}$. Let $y\in C^-$. The set C^0 contains a point x. Let $p_i\uparrow 1$ as $i\uparrow\infty$, $0\le p_i<1$ and let $y_i:=(1-p_i)x+p_iy$. Then $y_i\to y$, and by b, $y_i\in C^0$. Hence $y\in C^{0-}$.

d. Let C be a convex set in $\mathbf{R}^n$. Then $C^{-0}=C^0$.

Indeed, $C^0 \subseteq C^{-0}$, and it is enough to prove that $C^{-0} \subseteq C^0$. If $C^0=\emptyset$, then $C^{-0}=\emptyset$ by a. Hence, we may assume that $C^0 \neq \emptyset$. Let $x \in C^0$. Let $y \in C^{-0}$ and let V be an open ball such that $y \in V \subseteq C^-$. It is enough to prove that $V \subseteq C$ because then $y \in C^0$. Let $z \in V$. A point u exists in V such that $z \in [x,u[$, because V is open. Then $u \in V^- \subseteq C^-$ and then $[x,u[\in C^0 \subseteq C$ by b. Then $z \in C$ •

C3. Separation Theorems

Theorem C3 (Strict Separation Theorem in $\mathbf{R}^n$. Hahn-Banach)

Let $C \neq \emptyset$ be a closed convex set in $\mathbf{R}^n$, $y \notin C$. Then $c \in \mathbf{R}$ and $\alpha \in \mathbf{R}^n$ exist, such that

$$\alpha' x < c < \alpha' y \quad (x \in C). \tag{C3}$$

Proof

Let $d := \inf_{x \in C} ||y-x||$ be the distance from y to C. Let $x_i \in C$ (i=1,2,...) be a sequence such that $||y-x_i|| \to d$. The sequence x_i(i=1,2,...) is bounded. A sub-sequence $x_{i(j)}$, converging to some point $x_0 \in \mathbf{R}^n$ exists. Then $x_0 \in C$, because $x_i \in C$ and because C is closed. Then $||y-x_{i(j)}|| \to ||y-x_0||$. Hence, $||y-x_0||=d>0$.

For $x \in C$ and $\varepsilon \in]0,1[$,

$$x_0 + \varepsilon(x-x_0) = \varepsilon x + (1-\varepsilon)x_0 \in C.$$

Then

$$||y-x_0||^2 \leq ||y-[x_0+\varepsilon(x-x_0)]||^2 = ||(y-x_0)-\varepsilon(x-x_0)||^2$$

$$= ||y-x_0||^2 - 2\varepsilon <y-x_0,x-x_0> + \varepsilon^2||x-x_0||^2.$$

Hence

$$2 <y-x_0,x-x_0> \leq \varepsilon||x-x_0||^2,$$

and as $\varepsilon \downarrow 0$,

$$<y-x_0,x-x_0> \leq 0 \quad (x \in C).$$

Further,

$$<y-x_0,y-x_0> = ||y-x_0||^2 = d^2 > 0.$$

Then

$$<x,y-x_0> \leq <x_0,y-x_0> < <y,y-x_0> \quad (x \in C).$$

Let $\alpha := y-x_0$ and let c be a number strictly between $<x_0,\alpha>$ and $<y,\alpha>$. Then $<x,\alpha> < c < <y,\alpha>$, for all $x \in C$ •

We now explain the geometrical meaning of the strict separation Theorem in $\mathbf{R}^3 = \{(z_1,z_2 z_3)'\}$. In the relations (C3), let $\alpha=(\alpha_1,\alpha_2,\alpha_3)'$, $y=(y_1,y_2,y_3)'$. We consider the plane P with equation

$$\alpha_1 z_1 + \alpha_2 z_2 + \alpha_3 z_3 - c = 0.$$

Then the relations (C3) are explicited as follows

$$\alpha_1 x_1 + \alpha_2 x_2 + \alpha_3 x_3 - c < 0 \quad ((x_1,x_2,x_3)' \in C),$$

$$\alpha_1 y_1 + \alpha_2 y_2 + \alpha_3 y_3 - c > 0.$$

They mean that the convex set C is situated on one side of P and that the point y lies on the other side. The strict inequalities imply that $C \cap P = \varnothing$, $y \notin P$. Hence, Theorem 3 says, in geometrical language, that

Any closed convex set can strictly be separated by a plane from any point y not belonging to the set.

If the set C has points belonging to the plane, but still lies on one side of it, or if y is in the plane, then C and y are **weakly separated** by the plane. The following Theorem 13 states, in geometrical language, that

Any convex set C can weakly be separated by a plane from any point not belonging to the interior of C. Here the point may belong to the frontier of C, and hence to C.

The separation Theorems C3 and C4 are the simplest cases of the numerous versions of the Hahn-Banach Theorem. By these other versions, convex sets can be strictly or weakly separated by planes, not only in $\mathbf{R}^n$, but in very general topological vector spaces. Linear functions defined on subspaces can be extended to the complete space. The general Hahn-Banach Theorem is one of the most powerful tools of Functional Analysis.

Lemma

Let y be a frontier point of the closed convex set C in $\mathbf{R}^n$. Then $\alpha \neq 0$ exists in $\mathbf{R}^n$ such that

$$\boldsymbol{\alpha' x \leq \alpha' y \quad (x \in C).}$$

Proof

Let $y_i \notin C$ (i=1,2,...) be a sequence of points, such that $y_i \to y$ as $i \uparrow \infty$. By Theorem C3, α_i (i=1,2,...) exists in $\mathbf{R}^n$ such that $(\alpha_i)'x_i < (\alpha_i)'y_i$ $(x \in C)$. Then $\alpha_i \neq 0$, and we may divide by $\|\alpha_i\|$. Hence, we may assume that $\|\alpha_i\| = 1$. Taking a subsequence, we may assume that $\alpha_i \to \alpha \in \mathbf{R}^n$ as $i \uparrow \infty$. Then $\|\alpha\| = 1$ and $\alpha' x \leq \alpha' y$ $(x \in C)$ •

Theorem C4 (Weak Separation Theorem in $\mathbf{R}^n$. Hahn-Banach)

Let $C \neq \varnothing$ be a convex set in $\mathbf{R}^n$, $y \notin C^0$. Then $\alpha \neq 0$ exists in $\mathbf{R}^n$, such that

$$\alpha' x \leq \alpha' y \quad (x \in C). \tag{C4}$$

Proof

Let us first assume that $y \notin C^-$. Then $\alpha \in \mathbf{R}^n$ exists, by Theorem C3, such that $\alpha' x < \alpha' y$ $(x \in C^-)$. Then $\alpha \neq 0$, and $\alpha' x \leq \alpha' y$ $(x \in C)$.

Let us now assume that $y \in C^-$. Then, by Theorem C2, $y \notin C^0 = C^{-0}$. Hence, y is a frontier point of the closed convex set C^-. By the Lemma, $\alpha \neq 0$ exists in $\mathbf{R}^n$ such that $\alpha' x \leq \alpha' y$ for all $x \in C^- \supseteq C$ •

C4. Hypographs

We consider functions $P(\cdot)$, $Q(\cdot)$,... on $\mathbf{R}^n$ with values in $\mathbf{R} \cup \{-\infty, +\infty\}$.

For any column $x = (x_1, \ldots, x_n)' \in \mathbf{R}^n$ and any scalar $a \in \mathbf{R}$, we define the column

$$[x,a] := (x_1, \ldots, x_n, a)' \in \mathbf{R}^{n+1}.$$

Such columns cannot be confused with closed intervals.

The hypograph of the function Q is the set

$$\text{hypo } Q := \{[x,a] \in \mathbf{R}^{n+1} \;/\; x \in \mathbf{R}^n,\ a \in \mathbf{R},\ a \leq Q(x)\}. \tag{C5}$$

It is a subset of $\mathbf{R}^{n+1}$, even if Q takes the value $\pm\infty$. For functions with values in $\mathbf{R}$, the hypograph is the set of points situated under the graph of the function.

The function Q can be recuperated from its hypograph as follows. For any set $H \subseteq \mathbf{R}^{n+1} = \mathbf{R}^n \times \mathbf{R}$, and any point $x \in \mathbf{R}^n$, we define **the section of H at x**, as

$$\text{sect}_x(H) := \{a \in \mathbf{R} \;/\; [x,a] \in H\}.$$

Then

$$Q(x) = \sup(\text{sect}_x(\text{hypo } Q)) \quad (x \in \mathbf{R}^n).$$

A section of a hypograph can be any of the sets $\varnothing$, $\mathbf{R}$, or $]-\infty, b]$ $(b \in \mathbf{R})$. Conversely, if H is a set in $\mathbf{R}^{n+1}$ such that $\text{sect}_x(H)$ is $\varnothing$, $\mathbf{R}$ or $]-\infty, b]$, then H is the hypograph of a unique function Q.

The set $H \subseteq \mathbf{R}^{n+1}$ is an hypograph iff, for all $x \in \mathbf{R}^n$ and all $a,b \in \mathbf{R}$, the section $\mathrm{sect}_x(H)$ is a closed subset of R, and

$$[b \in \mathrm{sect}_x(H),\ a<b] \Rightarrow [a \in \mathrm{sect}_x(H)].$$

C5. Concave Functions

The function $Q:\mathbf{R}^n \to \mathbf{R} \cup \{-\infty,+\infty\}$ is **concave** if

$$Q(px+(1-p)y) \geq pQ(x)+(1-p)Q(y) \quad (x,y \in \mathbf{R}^n;\ 0 \leq p \leq 1), \tag{C6}$$

whenever the last member is defined. This relation must hold for all $x,y \in \mathbf{R}^n$ and all $p \in [0,1]$ if the following definitions are adopted:

$$0.(\pm\infty) = (\pm\infty).0 = 0 \ , \ +\infty-\infty = -\infty+\infty = -\infty.$$

A proper concave function is a concave function Q, different from the function $-\infty$, and such that $Q<\infty$.

The effective domain of the concave function Q is the set

$$\mathrm{dom}\ Q := \{x \in \mathbf{R}^n \,/\, -\infty < Q(x)\}. \tag{C7}$$

For any concave function Q, **dom Q is a convex set in $\mathbf{R}^n$**. Indeed, if $Q(x)>-\infty$ and $Q(y)>-\infty$, then the relation (C6) shows that $Q(px+(1-p)y)>-\infty$. Hence, dom Q contains the convex combinations of any couple of its points.

A non-degenerated concave function is a proper concave function Q such that dom Q is a convex body.

Examples

a. Let $I \neq \varnothing$ be an interval in **R**, and let Q be the function defined on **R** by the relations

$$Q(x) := -x^2\ (x \in I) \ , \ Q(x) := -\infty \ (x \notin I).$$

Then Q is a non-degenerated concave function, and $\mathrm{dom}\ Q = I$.

b. Let I be an interval in **R**, and let Q be the function defined on **R** by the relations

$$Q(x) := +\infty \ (x \in I) \ , \ Q(x) := -\infty \ (x \notin I).$$

Then Q is an improper concave function, and dom Q = I.

c. **An affine function on $\mathbf{R}^n$** is a function f with values

$$f(x) = \alpha' x + c \ (x \in \mathbf{R}^n), \tag{C8}$$

where $\alpha \in \mathbf{R}^n$ and $c \in \mathbf{R}$. **A linear function** is an affine function (48) with c=0. (In older and more elementary terminology, affine functions with $c \neq 0$ are also called **linear functions**). Any affine function f is finite, concave and non-degenerated. Its effective domain is $\mathbf{R}^n$.

The upper and lower bounds of the functions hereafter considered, are defined pointwise. For instance, if the functions Q_s are defined on $\mathbf{R}^n$ for $s \in S$ (S is any set), then $\inf_{s \in S} Q_s$ is the function with values

$$(\inf_{s \in S} Q_s)(x) := \inf_{s \in S}[Q_s(x)] \ \ (x \in \mathbf{R}^n). \tag{C9}$$

Theorem C5

Let the functions $Q_s (s \in S)$ be concave functions on $\mathbf{R}^n$. Then $\inf_{s \in S} Q_s$ is a concave function on $\mathbf{R}^n$.

Proof

$$\inf_{s \in S}(Q_s(px+(1-p)y)) \geq \inf_{s \in S}(pQ_s(x)+(1-p)Q_s(y))$$

$$\geq p \inf_{s \in S} Q_s(x) + (1-p) \inf_{s \in S} Q_s(y) \ \ (x,y \in \mathbf{R}^n;\ 0 \leq p \leq 1) \ \bullet$$

Theorem C6

The function Q on $\mathbf{R}^n$ is concave iff its hypograph is convex.

Proof

a. Let Q be concave. Let [x,a] and [y,b] be points of hypo Q and let $p \in [0,1]$. Then

$$Q(x) \geq a \in \mathbf{R}\ ,\ Q(y) \geq b \in \mathbf{R},$$

and

$$Q(px+(1-p)y) \geq pQ(x)+(1-p)Q(y) \geq pa+(1-p)b.$$

Hence,

$$p[x,a]+(1-p)[y,b] = [px+(1-p)y\ ,\ pa+(1-p)Q(b)] \in \text{hypo } Q.$$

b. Let hypo Q be convex. We will verify that

$$Q(px+(1-p)y) \geq pQ(x) + (1-p)Q(y) \quad (x,y\in\mathbf{R}^n;\ 0\leq p\leq 1).$$

The relation is correct if $Q(x)=-\infty$ or $Q(y)=-\infty$. Hence, we may assume that $Q(x)>-\infty$ and $Q(y)>-\infty$. Let $a,b\in\mathbf{R}$ be such that $Q(x)>a$ and $Q(y)>b$. Then $[x,a]$ and $[y,b]$ belong to hypo q, and

$$[px+(1-p)y\ ,\ pa+(1-p)b] = p[x,a] + (1-p)[y,b] \in \text{hypo } Q \quad (0\leq c\leq 1).$$

Hence

$$Q(px+(1-p)y) \geq pa+(1-p)b.$$

Then, as $a\uparrow Q(x)$ and $b\uparrow Q(y)$,

$$Q(px+(1-p)y) \geq pQ(x)+(1-p)Q(y) \quad \bullet$$

Lemma 1

Let Q be a concave function on $\mathbf{R}^n$ with a finite value at the point $x_0\in\mathbf{R}^n$. Let $c\in\mathbf{R}_{++}$ and let V be an open ball, centered at 0, such that

$$\mathbf{Q(x_0) - Q(x_0+x) \leq c \quad (x\in V).} \tag{C10}$$

Then

$$\mathbf{|Q(x_0) - Q(x_0+\varepsilon x)| \leq \varepsilon c \quad (x\in V,\ 0<\varepsilon\leq 1).} \tag{C11}$$

Proof

Let $x\in V$. Then

$$x_0+\varepsilon x = (1-\varepsilon)x_0+\varepsilon(x_0+x)\ ,\quad x_0 = {}^{1}\!/_{(1+\varepsilon)}(x_0+\varepsilon x) + {}^{\varepsilon}\!/_{(1+\varepsilon)}(x_0-x),$$

where $-x\in V$ because V is a ball. Then

$$Q(x_0+\varepsilon x) \geq (1-\varepsilon)Q(x_0) + \varepsilon Q(x_0+x) \geq (1-\varepsilon)Q(x_0) + \varepsilon(Q(x_0)-c) = Q(x_0)-\varepsilon c,$$

$$Q(x_0) - Q(x_0+\varepsilon x_0) \leq \varepsilon c.$$

This proves one part of the statement. Further,

$$Q(x_0) \geq {}^{1}\!/_{(1+\varepsilon)}Q(x_0+\varepsilon x) + {}^{\varepsilon}\!/_{(1+\varepsilon)}Q(x_0-x)$$

$$\geq {}^{1}\!/_{(1+\varepsilon)}Q(x_0+\varepsilon x) + {}^{\varepsilon}\!/_{(1+\varepsilon)}(Q(x_0)-c).$$

Hence,

$$(1+\varepsilon)Q(x_0) \geq Q(x_0+\varepsilon x) + \varepsilon(Q(x_0)-c)\ ,\quad Q(x_0+\varepsilon x) - Q(x_0) \leq \varepsilon c \quad \bullet$$

Lemma 2

Let Q be a concave function on $\mathbf{R}^n$, with a finite value at the point $x_0 \in \mathbf{R}^n$. Let the function Q have a finite lower constant bound on some neighbourhood of x_0. Then Q is continuous at the point x_0.

Proof
The assumptions imply the existence of c and V such that the assumptions of the Lemma 1 are satisfied. Then (C11) implies the continuity of Q at x_0 •

Theorem C7

Any proper concave function Q on $\mathbf{R}^n$ is continuous on $(\text{dom } Q)^0$.

Proof
Let Q be a proper concave function and let $x_0 \in (\text{dom } Q)^0$. Then x_0 is the center of some open n-dimensional cube K contained in dom Q. Let $x_1,\dots,x_m$ $(m=2^n)$ be the vertices of this cube. Then any point $x \in K$ is some convex combination $p_1x_1+\dots+p_mx_m$. Let $c:=\min(Q(x_1),\dots,Q(x_m))$. Then $c \in \mathbf{R}$, and

$$Q(x) = Q(p_1x_1+\dots+p_mx_m) \geq p_1Q(x_1) + \dots + p_mQ(x_m) \geq c \quad (x \in K).$$

Hence c is a lower bound of Q on K. By the Lemma 2, Q is continuous at the point x_0 •

C6. Upper Semi-Continuous Functions

The function Q on $\mathbf{R}^n$ is **upper semi-continuous at the point $x \in \mathbf{R}^n$** if, for any sequence $x_i \in \mathbf{R}^n$ (i=1,2,...) and any point $c \in \mathbf{R} \cup \{-\infty,+\infty\}$,

$$[x_i \to x \text{ and } Q(x_i) \to c \text{ as } i \uparrow \infty] \Rightarrow [c \leq Q(x)]. \qquad \text{(C12)}$$

The function Q is **upper semi-continuous** if it is upper semi-continuous at each point $x \in \mathbf{R}^n$.

Examples

a. Let Q be a function on **R**, not necessarily finite, such that the left and right limits $Q(x-)$ and $Q(x+)$ exist at each point $x \in \mathbf{R}$. Then Q is upper semi-continuous iff $Q(x)=\max[Q(x-),Q(x+)]$ $(x \in \mathbf{R})$.

b. Increasing functions on **R** are upper semi-continuous iff they are right-continuous. Decreasing functions on **R** are upper semi-continuous iff they are left-continuous.

c. The continuous finite functions Q on $\mathbf{R}^n$ are upper semi-continuous, because

$$[x_i \to x \text{ and } Q(x_i) \to c \text{ as } i\uparrow\infty] \Rightarrow [c = Q(x)]$$

if Q is continuous.

d. In particular, affine functions are upper semi-continuous.

Let Q be a function on $\mathbf{R}^n$ and let x be a point in $\mathbf{R}^n$. We recall that the point $c \in \mathbf{R} \cup \{-\infty, +\infty\}$ is **a limit point of Q(y) as y→x**, if a sequence $x_i (i=1,2,\ldots)$ exists, such that $x_i \to x$ and $Q(x_i) \to c$ as $i\uparrow\infty$. It is not assumed here that $x_i \neq x$. (When notations such as $x_i \uparrow x$ are used in **R**, then it is supposed that $x_i < x$). The upper bound of the limit points of Q(y) as y→x is **the lim sup of Q(y) as y→x**. This upper bound is a particular limit point of Q(y) as y→x. It is denoted by $\mathbf{\limsup_{y\to x} q(y)}$. As a particular sequence x_i, we can take $x_i \equiv x$ $(i=1,2,\ldots)$. Then $Q(x_i) \equiv Q(x)$. Hence Q(x) is a particular limit point of Q(y) as y→x and

$$\limsup_{y\to x} Q(y) \geq Q(x). \tag{C13}$$

An equivalent definition of lim sup is

$$\limsup_{y\to x} Q(y) := \inf_V (\sup_{y\in V} Q(y)),$$

where V ranges over the open balls with center x.

We recall that, for any set $S \subseteq \mathbf{R} \cup \{-\infty, +\infty\}$, $Q^{-1}(S) := \{x \in \mathbf{R}^n \,/\, Q(x) \in S\}$.

Theorem C8

a. The function Q on $\mathbf{R}^n$ is upper semi-continuous iff $Q^{-1}([a,\infty])$ is a closed subset of $\mathbf{R}^n$, for any $a \in \mathbf{R}$.

b. The function Q on $\mathbf{R}^n$ is upper semi-continuous iff hypo Q is a closed set in $\mathbf{R}^{n+1}$.

c. The function Q on $\mathbf{R}^n$ is upper semi-continuous iff

$$\limsup_{y\to x} Q(y) = Q(x) \quad (x \in \mathbf{R}^n). \tag{C14}$$

Proof

a. Let $Q^{-1}([a,\infty])$ be closed ($a\in\mathbf{R}$). We prove that Q is upper semi-continuous. Let $x_i\to x$, $Q(x_i)\to c$. If $c=-\infty$, then $c\leq Q(x)$. Hence, we may assume that $-\infty<c$. Let $-\infty<a<c$. Then i_0 exists, such that $a\leq Q(x_i)$ ($i\geq i_0$). Hence, $x_i\in Q^{-1}([a,\infty])$ ($i\geq i_0$). Then $x\in Q^{-1}([a,\infty])$ because $Q^{-1}([a,\infty])$ is closed. Hence, $a\leq Q(x)$. As $a\uparrow c$, we obtain $c\leq Q(x)$. Hence Q is upper semi-continuous.

We now assume that $Q^{-1}([c,\infty])$ is not closed for some $c\in\mathbf{R}$, and we prove that Q is not upper semi-continuous. Points x_i($i=1,2,\ldots$) and x exist, such that $x_i\in Q^{-1}([c,\infty])$ and $x_i\to x\notin Q^{-1}([c,\infty])$. Then $Q(x)<c$. Hence Q is not upper semi-continuous at the point x.

b. Let Q be upper semi-continuous. We prove that hypo Q is closed. Let $[x_i,a_i]$ ($i=1,2,\ldots$) and $[x,a]$ be points in $\mathbf{R}^{n+1}$ such that

$$[x_i,a_i] \in \text{hypo } Q \text{ and } [x_i,a_i]\to[x,a] \text{ as } i\uparrow\infty.$$

Then $Q(x_i)\geq a_i$, $x_i\to x$ and $a_i\to a$. A subsequence $x_{i(j)}$ ($j=1,2,\ldots$) exists, such that $Q(x_{i(j)})\to c\in\mathbf{R}\cup\{-\infty,+\infty\}$ as $j\uparrow\infty$. Then $x_{i(j)}\to x$ and $c\leq Q(x)$ because Q is upper semi-continuous at the point x. On the other side, $Q(x_{i(j)})\geq a_{i(j)}$ and then $c\geq a$ as $j\uparrow\infty$. Hence $a\leq Q(x)$, i.e. $[x,a]\in$ hypo Q. This proves that hypo Q is closed.

We now assume that hypo Q is closed and we prove that Q is upper semi-continuous. Let $x_i\to x$, $Q(x_i)\to c$. If $c=-\infty$, then $c\leq Q(x)$. Hence, we may assume that $-\infty<c$. Let $-\infty<a<c$. Then $(x_i,Q(x_i)\wedge a)\in$hypo Q, and $[x_i,q(x_i)\wedge a]\to[x,a]$ $\in$hypo q, because hypo Q is closed. Then $a\leq Q(x)$, and then $c\leq Q(x)$, as $a\uparrow c$. Hence, Q is upper semi-continuous.

c. Let Q be upper semi-continuous. Then any limit point of Q(y) as $y\to x$ is less than Q(x) by (C12). Hence, $\limsup_{y\to x} Q(y)\leq Q(x)$. By (C13), this inequality must be an equality. This proves (C14).

Let us now assume (C14). Then any limit point of Q(y) as $y\to x$ is less than Q(x), and then (C12) is satisfied. Hence Q is upper semi-continuous •

Theorem C9

Let Q_s($s\in S$) be upper semi-continuous functions on $\mathbf{R}^n$. Then the function $Q:=\inf_{s\in S} Q_s$ is an upper semi-continuous function on $\mathbf{R}^n$.

Proof

For all $x \in \mathbf{R}^n$ and $a \in \mathbf{R}$,

$$x \in Q^{-1}([a,\infty]) \Leftrightarrow a \leq Q(x) \Leftrightarrow [\text{For all } s \in S,\ a \leq Q_s(x)]$$

$$\Leftrightarrow [\text{For all } s \in S,\ x \in Q_s^{-1}([a,\infty])] \Leftrightarrow x \in \bigcap_{s \in S} Q_s^{-1}([a,\infty]).$$

Hence,

$$Q^{-1}([a,\infty]) = \bigcap_{s \in S} Q_s^{-1}([a,\infty]) \quad (a \in \mathbf{R}).$$

By Th.C8.a, the last member is an intersection of closed sets. It is a closed set. Then, again by Th.C8.a, Q is upper semi-continuous •

C7. Upper Semi-Continuous Regularizations

Loosely speaking, a **regularization of a function** is the replacement of that function by some more regular function.

The upper semi-continuous regularization of the function Q on $\mathbf{R}^n$ is the function Q^- defined as

$$Q^- := \inf\{P \mid Q \leq P,\ P \text{ upper semi-continuous}\}.$$

By Theorem C9, Q^- is an upper semi-continuous functions. From the definition results that $Q \leq Q^-$ and that $Q^- \leq P$ for any upper semi-continuous upper bound P of Q. Hence,

The upper semi-continuous regularization Q^- is the smallest upper semi-continuous upper bound of Q.

Theorem C10

For any function Q on $\mathbf{R}^n$,

a. Q^- is the function with hypograph $(\text{hypo } Q)^-$:

$$\text{hypo}(Q^-) = (\text{hypo } Q)^-. \tag{C15}$$

b.

$$Q^-(x) = \limsup_{y \to x} Q(y) \quad (x \in \mathbf{R}^n). \tag{C16}$$

Proof

a.

We first prove that $(\text{hypo } Q)^{-}$ is an hypograph. The set $\text{sect}_x((\text{hypo } Q)^{-})$ is closed because $(\text{hypo } Q)^{-}$ is closed. Let

$$b \in \text{sect}_x((\text{hypo } Q)^{-}) \;,\; -\infty < a < b. \tag{C17}$$

We verify that

$$a \in \text{sect}_x((\text{hypo } Q)^{-}). \tag{C18}$$

By (C17), $[x,b]\in(\text{hypo } Q)^{-}$. Then a sequence $[x_i,b_i]\in\text{hypo } Q$ (I=1,2,...) exists, such that $[x_i,b_i]\rightarrow[x,b]$ as $I\uparrow\infty$. Then

$$x_i \rightarrow x \text{ and } b_i\rightarrow b \text{ as } i\uparrow\infty \;,\; b_i \le Q(x_i) \; (i=1,2,...).$$

Let $a_i:=b_i\wedge a$ (i=1,2,...) Then

$$a_i\rightarrow a \text{ as } i\uparrow\infty \,,\, a_i\le Q_i(x_i) \; (i=1,2,...),$$

$$[x_i,a_i] \in \text{hypo } q \;,\; [x_i,a_i] \rightarrow [x,a].$$

Hence, $[x,a]\in(\text{hypo } Q)^{-}$. This proves (C18).

We now prove the $\subseteq$ part of (C15). Let P be the function on $\mathbf{R}^n$ such that

$$\text{hypo } P = (\text{hypo } Q)^{-}.$$

By Theorem C8..b, P is upper semi-continuous, and

$$\text{hypo } Q \subseteq (\text{hypo } Q)^{-} = \text{hypo } P \;,\; Q \le P.$$

Hence, P is an upper semi-continuous upper bound of Q. This implies

$$Q^{-} \le P \,,\, \text{hypo } Q^{-} \subseteq \text{hypo } P = (\text{hypo } Q)^{-}.$$

We now prove the $\supseteq$ part of (C15). We successively have,

$$Q \le Q^{-} \;,\; \text{hypo } Q \subseteq \text{hypo } Q^{-} \;,\; (\text{hypo } Q)^{-} \subseteq (\text{hypo } Q^{-})^{-} = \text{hypo } Q^{-},$$

where the latter equality holds because $\text{hypo } Q^{-}$ is closed by Theorem C8.b.

b. The function Q^{-} is upper semi-continuous, and $Q\le Q^{-}$. Then, by Theorem C8.c,

$$\limsup_{y\rightarrow x} Q(y) \le \limsup_{y\rightarrow x} Q^{-}(x) = Q^{-}(x).$$

This proves the $\geq$ part of (C16). For the proof of the $\leq$ part, we may assume that $-\infty<Q^-(x)$. Let $-\infty<a<Q^-(x)$. Then, by a,

$$[x,a] \in \text{hypo } Q^- = (\text{hypo } Q)^-.$$

A sequence $[x_i,a_i]$ (i=1,2,...) exists, such that

$$[x_i,a_i] \in \text{hypo } Q \ , \ [x_i,a_i] \to [x,a] \ \text{ as } i\uparrow\infty.$$

Then

$$x_i \to x \ , \ a_i \to a \ , \ Q(x_i) \geq a_i.$$

A subsequence $x_{i(j)}$ (j=1,2,...) exists, such that

$$Q(x_{i(j)}) \to c \in \mathbf{R}\cup\{-\infty,+\infty\} \text{ as } j\uparrow\infty.$$

Then $x_{i(j)}\to x$, and c is a limit point of Q(y) as $y\to x$. Then

$$\limsup_{y\to x} Q(y) \geq c = \lim_{j\uparrow\infty} Q(x_{i(j)}) \geq \lim_{j\uparrow\infty} a_{i(j)} = a.$$

Hence $a\leq\limsup_{y\to x} Q(y)$ and then, as $a\uparrow Q^-(x)$, $Q^-(x)\leq\limsup_{y\to x} Q(y)$ •

C8. Concave Upper Semi-Continuous Regularizations

The concave upper semi-continuous regularization of the function Q on $\mathbf{R}^n$ is the function Q^- defined as

$$Q\hat{} := \inf\{P \ / \ Q\leq P, \ P \text{ concave upper semi-continuous}\}.$$

By Theorem C5, Q^ is a concave function. By Theorem C9, Q^ is an upper semi-continuous functions. From the definition results that $Q\leq Q\hat{}$ and that $Q\hat{} \leq P$ for any concave upper semi-continuous upper bound P of Q. Hence,

The concave upper semi-continuous regularization Q^ is the smallest concave upper semi-continuous upper bound of Q.

Theorem C11

For any function Q on $\mathbf{R}^n$, $(\text{Co hypo } Q)^-$ is an hypograph, and Q^ is the function with that hypograph:

$$\textbf{hypo}(Q\hat{}) = (\textbf{Co hypo } Q)^-. \tag{C19}$$

Proof

a. Let $[x,b]\in$Co hypo Q, $-\infty<a<b$. Then $[x,a]\in$Co hypo Q.

Indeed, $[x,b]$ is a convex combination $[x,b]=\sum_{1\le i\le m} p_i[x_i,b_i]$ of points $[x_i,b_i]\in$ hypo Q. Then

$$x=\sum_{1\le i\le m} p_i x_i \ , \ b=\sum_{1\le i\le m} p_i b_i.$$

Let $a_i \in \mathbf{R}$ (i=1,...,m) be such that $a_i\le b_i$, $\sum_{1\le i\le m} p_i a_i = a$. Then

$$Q(x_i)\ge b_i\ge a_i \ , \ [x_i,a_i]\in \text{hypo } Q \ , \ [x,a]=\sum_{1\le i\le m} p_i[x_i,a_i]\in \text{Co hypo } Q.$$

b. We now prove that $(\text{Co hypo } Q)^-$ is an hypograph.

For all $x\in\mathbf{R}^n$, $\text{sect}_x(\text{Co hypo } Q)^-$ is a closed subset of $\mathbf{R}$, because $(\text{Co hypo } Q)^-$ is a closed subset of $\mathbf{R}^{n+1}$. Let

$$b\in \text{sect}_x(\text{Co hypo } Q)^- \ , \ -\infty<a<b. \tag{C20}$$

It is enough to verify that

$$a\in \text{sect}_x(\text{Co hypo } Q)^-. \tag{C21}$$

By (C20), $[x,b]\in(\text{Co hypo } Q)^-$. By a, $[x,a]\in(\text{Co hypo } Q)^-$. This proves (C21).

c. We now prove the $\subseteq$ part of (C19).

By b, P exists, such that hypo $P=(\text{Co hypo } Q)^-$. The set $(\text{Co hypo } Q)^-$ is closed, and convex by Theorem C1. By Theorem C6 and Theorem C8.b, the function P is concave upper semi-continuous. Then

$$Q^\wedge\le P \ , \ \text{hypo } Q^\wedge\subseteq \text{hypo } P=(\text{Co hypo } Q)^-.$$

d. We finally prove the $\supseteq$ part of (C19).

From $Q\le Q^\wedge$ results $(\text{Co hypo } Q)^-\subseteq(\text{Co hypo } Q^\wedge)^-=\text{hypo } Q^\wedge$, where the latter equality holds because hypo $Q^\wedge$ is convex by Th.C6, and closed by Th.C8.b •

Lemma

Let Q be a proper concave function on $\mathbf{R}^n$, such that $Q(x_0)\in\mathbf{R}$ and such that Q has a finite constant upper bound on some neighbourhood of the fixed point x_0. Then Q has an affine upper bound.

Proof

Let V be a neighbourhood of the point x_0 such that $Q(x)\le b_0\in\mathbf{R}$ $(x\in V)$. Let $\varepsilon>0$ and a_0 be such that $b_0+\varepsilon<a_0\in\mathbf{R}$. Then

$$W := V\times]a_0-\varepsilon,a_0+\varepsilon[:= \{[x,c] \,/\, x\in V,\ c\in]a_0-\varepsilon,a_0+\varepsilon[\}$$

is a neighbourhood of the point $[x_0,a_0]$. Let $[x,a]\in W\cap(\text{hypo } Q)$. Then

$$[x,a] \in W \ ,\ a \in\ ]a_0-\varepsilon,a_0+\varepsilon[\ ,\ a_0-\varepsilon < a,$$

and

$$[x,a] \in \text{hypo } Q \ ,\ a \le Q(x) \le b_0 < a_0-\varepsilon \ ,\ a < a_0-\varepsilon.$$

This contradiction shows that $W\cap(\text{hypo } Q)=\varnothing$. Then $[x_0,a_0]\notin(\text{hypo } Q)^{-}$. By the strict separation Theorem C3, $[\alpha,a]\in\mathbf{R}^{n+1}$ exist, such that

$$[\alpha,a]'[x,b] < [\alpha,a]'[x_0,a_0] \ \ ([x,b]\in(\text{hypo } Q)^{-}),$$

i.e.,

$$\alpha'x + ab \ < \alpha'x_0 + aa_0 \ \ ([x,b]\in\text{hypo } Q^{-}) \qquad \text{(C22)}$$

by Theorem C6.a. The point $[x_0,Q(x_0)]$ belongs to hypo Q^{-} because $Q^{-}(x_0)\ge Q(x_0)$. Hence, we can take $x=x_0$, $b=Q(x_0)$ in (C22). Then

$$aQ(x_0) < aa_0 \ ,\ 0 < a[a_0-Q(x_0)].$$

This implies that $a>0$ because $Q(x_0)\le b_0<a_0-\varepsilon\le a_0$. Then, by (C22),

$$\beta'x + b \ < \beta'x_0 + a_0 \ \ ([x,b]\in\text{hypo } Q^{-}), \qquad \text{(C23)}$$

where $\beta := \alpha/a$. If $Q(x)\in\mathbf{R}$, then we can take $b=Q(x)$ in (C23):

$$Q(x) < [a_0 + \beta'x_0] - \beta'x \ \ (x\in\mathbf{R}^n,\ Q(x)\in\mathbf{R}).$$

If $Q(x)\notin\mathbf{R}$, then $Q(x)=-\infty$, because Q is a proper concave function. Hence

$$Q(x) < [a_0 + \beta'x_0] - \beta'x \ \ (x\in\mathbf{R}^n).\bullet$$

Theorem C12

a. Any proper concave upper semi-continuous function Q on $\mathbf{R}^n$ has an affine upper bound.

b. Any non-degenerated concave function Q on $\mathbf{R}^n$ has an affine upper bound.

Proof

a. Let $Q(x_0)\in\mathbf{R}$. Let a_0 be such that $Q(x_0)<a_0<\infty$. Then $[x_0,a_0]$ does not belong to hypo Q. The set hypo Q is closed by Theorem C8.b. Then the strict separation Theorem C3 can be applied to the couple $[x_0,a_0]$, hypo Q. The affine upper bound is obtained by the argument of the proof of the Lemma.

b. By Theorem C7, Q is continuous on the non void set $(\text{dom } Q)^0$. Let $x_0\in(\text{dom } Q)^0$ and let B be a closed ball such that $x_0\in B^0\subseteq B\subseteq(\text{dom } Q)^0$. Then some finite constant is an upper bound of Q on B, because continuous functions are bounded on compact sets. The interior B^0 of B is a neighbourhood of x_0. Hence, the Lemma can be applied •

Theorem C13

Let Q be a function on $\mathbf{R}^n$ with an affine upper bound. Then

$$Q\hat{} = \inf\{f \,/\, Q\leq f,\ f \text{ affine function}\}. \tag{C24}$$

Proof

Let

$$P := \inf\{f \,/\, Q\leq f,\ f \text{ affine function}\}.$$

Affine functions are concave upper semi-continuous. Hence, P is concave upper semi-continuous by Theorem C5 and Theorem C9. Then $Q\hat{}\leq P$.

We now prove that $P\leq Q\hat{}$. Let f_0 be an affine function such that $Q\leq f_0$. Then f_0 is concave upper semi-continuous. Hence $Q\hat{}\leq f_0$. The funtion f_0 has only finite values. Hence $Q\hat{}$ cannot take the value $+\infty$.

Let $x_0\in\mathbf{R}^n$. Let $a_0\in\mathbf{R}$ be such that $Q\hat{}(x_0)<a_0$. It is enough to prove the existence of an affine upper bound f of $Q\hat{}$ such that $f(x_0)\leq a_0$. Indeed, then $P(x_0)\leq f(x_0)\leq a_0$, because f is an affine upper bound of Q. Then, as $a_0\downarrow Q\hat{}(x_0)$, we obtain $P(x_0)\leq Q\hat{}(x_0)$ $(x_0\in\mathbf{R}^n)$. This implies that $P\leq Q\hat{}$ because x_0 is any point in $\mathbf{R}^n$.

Now, for fixed x_0 and a_0, we prove the existence of f. By Theorem C8.b, the set hypo $Q\hat{}$ is closed. By the condition $Q\hat{}(x_0)<a_0$, the point $[x_0,a_0]$ does not belong to hypo $Q\hat{}$. By the strict separation Theorem C3, $c\in\mathbf{R}$ and $[\alpha,a]\in\mathbf{R}^{n+1}$ exist, such that

$$[\alpha,a]'[x,b] < c < [\alpha,a]'[x_0,a_0] \quad ([x,b]\in\text{hypo } Q\hat{}),$$

i.e.,

$$\alpha' x + ab < c < \alpha' x_0 + aa_0 \quad ([x,b] \in \text{hypo } Q\hat{}\,). \tag{C25}$$

We first assume that $-\infty < Q\hat{}(x_0)$. Then $[x_0, Q\hat{}(x_0)]$ belongs to hypo $Q\hat{}$ and we can take $x = x_0$, $b = Q\hat{}(x_0)$ in (C25). Then

$$aQ\hat{}(x_0) < aa_0 \;,\;\; 0 < a[a_0 - Q\hat{}(x_0)].$$

This implies $a>0$ because $Q\hat{}(x_0) < a_0$. Hence, by (C25),

$$\beta' x + b < \beta' x_0 + a_0 \quad ([x,b] \in \text{hypo } Q\hat{}\,), \tag{C26}$$

where $\beta := \alpha / a$. If $Q\hat{}(x) \in \mathbf{R}$, then we can take $b = Q\hat{}(x)$ in (C26):

$$Q\hat{}(x) < [a_0 + \beta' x_0] - \beta' x \quad (x \in \mathbf{R}^n,\; Q\hat{}(x) \in \mathbf{R}).$$

If $Q\hat{}(x) \notin \mathbf{R}$, then $Q\hat{}(x) = -\infty$, because $q\hat{}$ cannot take the value $+\infty$. Hence

$$Q\hat{}(x) < [a_0 + \beta' x_0] - \beta' x \quad (x \in \mathbf{R}^n)$$

if $-\infty < Q\hat{}(x_0)$.

We now assume that $Q\hat{}(x_0) = -\infty$. If $a>0$, we can proceed as in the foregoing case. Hence, we may assume that $a \le 0$. We first assume that $a=0$. Then (C25) becomes

$$\alpha' x < c < \alpha' x_0 \quad ([x,b] \in \text{hypo } Q\hat{}\,),$$

i.e.,

$$\alpha' x < c < \alpha' x_0 \quad (x \in \text{dom } Q\hat{}\,).$$

Then

$$f(x) := c + f_0(x) - \alpha' x \quad (x \in \mathbf{R}^n)$$

is an affine function. It is an upper bound of $Q\hat{}(x)$. Indeed, if $x \in \text{dom } Q\hat{}$, then

$$f(x) = f_0(x) + (c - \alpha' x) \ge f_0(x) \ge Q\hat{}(x),$$

and if $x \notin \text{dom } Q\hat{}$,

$$f(x) > -\infty = Q\hat{}(x).$$

We finally consider the case $a<0$. This is an impossible case. Indeed, let x be fixed in dom $Q\hat{}$. Then the first inequality of (C25) leads to a contradiction as $b \downarrow -\infty$ •

Theorem C14

Let Q be a concave function on $\mathbf{R}^n$ with an affine upper bound. Then

$$Q^{-} = Q^{\wedge} = \inf\{f \,/\, Q \le f,\ f \text{ affine function}\}.$$

Proof

The last equality results from the preceding Theorem. By Th.C11, Th.C6 and Th.C10.a,

$$\text{hypo } Q^{\wedge} = (\text{Co hypo } Q)^{-} = (\text{hypo } Q)^{-} = \text{hypo } Q^{-}.$$

Functions with the same hypograph are identical. Hence $Q^{\wedge}=Q^{-}$. Then the Theorem follows from Th.C13 •

Remark

The foregoing proof shows that the relation $Q^{-}=Q^{\wedge}$ is valid for any concave function Q. The existence of an affine upper bound of Q is not used in the proof of that equality.

C9. Polar Functions

We continue with functions $Q:\mathbf{R}^n \to \mathbf{R} \cup \{-\infty,+\infty\}$.

The polar function of Q is the function Q* with values

$$Q^*(x) := \inf_y [x'y - Q(y)],$$

where y ranges over $\mathbf{R}^n$, or equivalently, over dom Q. **The bipolar function of Q** is the function $Q^{**}:=(Q^*)^*$. **The tripolar function of Q** is the function $Q^{***}:=(Q^{**})^*=(Q^*)^{**}$. More explicitly, the polar functions considered here are **inf-polar functions**.

Examples

In the following *examples*, functions Q on **R** are considered.

a. Let $Q\equiv 1$. Then

$$Q^*(x) = \inf_y[xy-1] = -\infty\, 1_{x\neq 0} - 1_{x=0}\ , \quad \text{dom } Q^* = \{0\},$$

$$Q^{**}(x) = \inf_y[xy-Q^*(y)] = \inf_{y=0}[xy-(-1)] = 1 = Q(x).$$

b. Let $Q(x) := x$ ($x \in \mathbf{R}$). Then

$$Q^*(x) = \inf_y[xy - y] = \inf_y (x-1)y = -\infty\, 1_{x\neq 1} + 0.1_{x=1},\ \text{dom}\, Q^* = \{1\},$$

$$Q^{**}(x) = \inf_y[xy - Q^*(y)] = \inf_{y=1}[x-0] = x = Q(x).$$

c. Let $Q(x) := -x^2$ ($x \in \mathbf{R}$). Then

$$Q^*(x) = \inf_y[xy + y^2] = -x^2/4\ ,\quad \text{dom}\, Q^* = \mathbf{R},$$

$$Q^{**}(x) = \inf_y[xy + y^2/4] = -x^2 = Q(x).$$

d. Let $Q(x) := x^2$. Then

$$Q^*(x) = \inf_y[xy - y^2] = -\infty\ ,\ Q^{**}(x) = \inf_y[xy + \infty] = \infty,$$

$$Q^{***}(x) = \inf_y[xy - \infty] = -\infty.$$

Theorem C15

For any function Q on $\mathbf{R}^n$, the polar function Q^* is concave upper semi-continuous.

Proof

If Q takes the value $+\infty$, then $Q^* \equiv -\infty$. Hence, we may assume that $Q<\infty$. Then, for fixed y in dom Q,

$$f_y(x) := y'x - Q(y) \tag{C27}$$

is an affine function of $x \in \mathbf{R}^n$, and $Q^* = \inf_{y\in \text{dom}} f_y$. Affine functions are concave upper semi-continuous. Then Q^* is concave upper semi-continuous by Theorem C5 and Theorem C10 •

Theorem C16

For any function Q on $\mathbf{R}^n$,

$$\mathbf{Q^{**} = \inf\{f\, /\, Q \leq f\, ,\ f \text{ affine function}\}.} \tag{C28}$$

Proof

Let $P := \inf\{f\, /\, Q \leq f\, ,\ f \text{ affine function}\}$.

Any affine function f is expressible as $f(x) = y'x - a$, with $y \in \mathbf{R}^n$ and $a \in \mathbf{R}$.

Hence,

$$P(x) = \inf_{y,a} \{y'x-a \,/\, Q(z) \le y'z-a \ (z\in \mathbf{R^n})\}. \qquad (C29)$$

The condition after the slash in the last member of (C29), is successively equivalent to the following conditions:

$$a \le y'z - Q(z)\ (z\in \mathbf{R^n})\ ,\ a \le \inf_z[y'z - Q(z)]\ ,\ a \le Q^*(y).$$

Hence,

$$P(x) = \inf_{y,a} \{x'y-a \,/\, a\le Q^*(y)\} = \inf_y[\inf_a\{x'y-a \,/\, a\le Q^*(y)\}]$$

$$= \inf_y [x'y-Q^*(y)] = Q^{**}(x) \ \bullet$$

Corollary

For any function Q on $\mathbf{R^n}$, $Q \le Q^{**}$.

Proof
By the Theorem, Q^{**} is the inf of functions which are upper bounds of Q. Hence $Q\le Q^{**}$ •

Theorem C17 (Fenchel-Moreau)

a. **For any function Q on $\mathbf{R^n}$ with an affine upper bound, $Q^{**} = Q^\wedge$.**

b. **For any concave function Q on $\mathbf{R^n}$ with an affine upper bound, $Q^{**} = Q^-$.**

c. **For any proper concave upper semi-continuous function Q on $\mathbf{R^n}$, $Q^{**} = Q$.**

Proof
a. and b. follow from the Theorems C13, C14 and C16. We now prove c. By Th.C12.a, Q has an affine upper bound. Then $Q^{**}=Q^-$ by b. By the upper semi-continuity of Q, $Q^-=Q$ •

Theorem C18

a. **For any functions P,Q on $\mathbf{R^n}$: $Q\le P \Rightarrow P^*\le Q^*$.**

b. **For any function Q on $\mathbf{R^n}$, $Q^{***} = Q^*$.**

Proof

a. If Q≤P, then $x'y-P(x) \leq x'y-P(y)$ $(x,y\in\mathbf{R}^n)$.

b. By the Corollary of Th.C16, Q≤Q**. Then (Q**)*≤Q* by a. By the Corollary of Th.C16 applied to Q*, Q*≤(Q*)**. Then

$$Q^{***} = (Q^{**})^* \leq Q^* \leq (Q^*)^{**} = Q^{***} \quad \bullet$$

C10. Convex Functions

The theory developed in the foregoing sections is a theory of **concave functions** The corresponding symmetric theory of **convex functions** is direct. The basic concepts of the theory of concave functions, i.e

Hypographs hypo Q
Concave functions
Upper semi-continuous functions
Upper semi-continuous regularizations
Concave upper semi-continuous regularizations
Inf-polar functions,

must be replaced by the following corresponding concepts, in the theory of **convex functions**:

Epigraphs epi P
Convex functions
Lower semi-continuous functions
Lower semi-continuous regularizations
Convex lower semi-continuous regularizations
Sup-polar functions.

Obvious correspondences exist. For instance,

$$P \text{ is convex } \Leftrightarrow (-P) \text{ is concave,}$$

$$P \text{ is lower semi-continuous } \Leftrightarrow (-P) \text{ is upper semi-continuous.}$$

They could be used as definitions.

Appendix D

Matrices

D1. Notations and Definitions

We use a rather flexible notation for matrices and their elements. The **matrix** with elements c_{ij} (i=1,...,m; j=1,...,n) is denoted by (c), c, $(c)_{m\times n}$, $c_{m\times n}$ or, in extended form, by

$$\begin{bmatrix} c_{11} & c_{12} & \dots & c_{1n} \\ c_{21} & c_{22} & \dots & c_{2n} \\ \dots & \dots & \dots & \dots \\ c_{n1} & c_{n2} & \dots & c_{nn} \end{bmatrix}$$

Then m×n are **the dimensions of matrix c**.

The **determinant of square matrix $c_{n\times n}$** is denoted by det(c), $\det(c)_{n\times n}$ or in extended form, by

$$\begin{vmatrix} c_{11} & c_{12} & \dots & c_{1n} \\ c_{21} & c_{22} & \dots & c_{2n} \\ \dots & \dots & \dots & \dots \\ c_{n1} & c_{n2} & \dots & c_{nn} \end{vmatrix}$$

The **transposed matrix of matrix $a_{m\times n}$** is the matrix $(a')_{n\times m}$ with elements

$$(a')_{ij} \equiv a'_{ij} := a_{ji} \quad (i=1,\dots,n;\ j=1,\dots,m).$$

The matrix (s) is symmetric if s=s′, i.e if $s_{ij}=s_{ji}$ (i,j=1,...,n).

A row is a matrix $x_{1\times n}$. Then n is the **length** of the row. The row $x_{1\times n}$ is explicited as

$$(x_1,\dots,x_n).$$

A column is a matrix $x_{n\times 1}$. Then n is the **length** of the column.

The column $x_{n\times 1}$ is explicited as

$$\begin{bmatrix} x_1 \\ x_2 \\ \dots \\ x_n \end{bmatrix}$$

or as $(x_1,\dots,x_n)'$.

Rows and columns are called **vectors**. Matrices $c_{1\times 1}$ can be identified with scalars.

The diagonal elements of the square matrix $a_{n\times n}$ are the elements a_{ii} $(i=1,\dots,n)$. **A diagonal matrix** is a square matrix $d_{n\times n}$ such that $d_{ij}=0$ $(i,j=1,\dots,n,$ $i\neq j)$. It is represented as

$$\text{diag}(d_{11},\dots,d_{nn})$$

or as

$$\begin{bmatrix} d_{11} & & & \\ & d_{22} & & \\ & & \dots & \\ & & & d_{nn} \end{bmatrix}$$

We assume that the reader is familiar with the usual algebraic operations on matrices (sums, differences, products, multiplication by scalars) and with their basic properties.

The unit matrix $1_{n\times n}$ is the diagonal matrix with all diagonal elements equal to 1. It is such that $a1=1a=a$, for any matrix $a_{n\times n}$.

The zero matrix $0_{m\times n}$ is a matrix with all elements equal to 0. **A non-zero matrix** is a matrix with at least one element different from 0.

The inverse matrix of the square matrix $a_{n\times n}$ is denoted by a^{-1} when it exists. It is such that $aa^{-1}=a^{-1}a=1_{n\times n}$. **A matrix is invertible** if it has an inverse matrix.

An orthogonal matrix is a square invertible matrix $s_{n\times n}$ such that the inverse matrix s^{-1} coincides with the transposed matrix s'. **The matrix s is orthogonal iff the transposed matrix s' is orthogonal**, because $(s')^{-1}=(s^{-1})'$ for any invertible matrix s.

We assume that all displayed sums, products, inverses, determinants,... are meaningful. For instance, when we consider c^{-1}, we implicitly assume that c is invertible. If a product cd of matrices c and d occurs somewhere, it is assumed that the number of columns of c equals the number of rows of d.

D2. Determinants

We assume that the reader can calculate determinants, and that he is familiar with the results of the following Theorem.

Theorem D1

$$\mathbf{det(c)_{n\times n} = det(c')_{n\times n},} \tag{D1}$$

$$\mathbf{det(c)_{n\times n} \neq 0 \;\Leftrightarrow\; c_{n\times n} \text{ is invertible},} \tag{D2}$$

$$\mathbf{det(ab)_{n\times n} = det(a)_{n\times n}\, det(b)_{n\times n}} \;\bullet \tag{D3}$$

D3. Submatrices

Let $c_{m\times n}$ be a matrix and let $i_1,\ldots,i_r$, $j_1,\ldots,j_s$ be integers such that $1\le i_1<\ldots<i_r\le m$, $1\le j_1<\ldots<j_s\le n$. We denote by $(c)_{i_1\ldots i_r;j_1\ldots j_s}$ the submatrix of (c) with rows $i_1,\ldots,i_r$ and columns $j_1,\ldots,j_s$.

The principal submatrices of the matrix $c_{n\times n}$ are the matrices $(c)_{i_1\ldots i_r;i_1\ldots i_r}$ $(1\le i_1<\ldots<i_r\le n)$. The matrix $c_{n\times n}$ has 2^n-1 principal submatrices. We call the n submatrices $c_{1;1}$, $c_{12;12}$, ..., $c_{1\ldots n;1\ldots n}$ **the initial principal submatrices of c**.

D4. Partitions in Blocks

The matrix $c_{m\times n}$ can be partitioned in submatrices, called **blocks**, by horizontal and vertical lines. Let the blocks be $\gamma_{\mu\nu}$ ($\mu=1,\ldots,\rho$; $\nu=1,\ldots,\sigma$). Then c can be represented in **block form**:

$$c = \begin{bmatrix} \gamma_{11} & \gamma_{12} & \cdots & \gamma_{1\nu} \\ \gamma_{21} & \gamma_{22} & \cdots & \gamma_{2\nu} \\ \cdots & \cdots & \cdots & \cdots \\ \gamma_{\mu 1} & \gamma_{\mu 2} & \cdots & \gamma_{\mu\nu} \end{bmatrix}$$

Matrices in block form can be multiplied according to the usual rule of matrix multiplication if all involved block products are meaningful.

D5. Linear Equations

We consider the **linear system** of m equations with n **unknown quantities** $x_1,\ldots,x_n$.

$$a_{11}x_1 + a_{12}x_2 + \ldots + a_{1n}x_n = b_1,$$
$$a_{21}x_1 + a_{22}x_2 + \ldots + a_{2n}x_n = b_2,$$
$$\ldots \quad \ldots \quad \ldots \quad \ldots \quad \ldots \quad \ldots \quad \ldots$$
$$a_{m1}x_1 + a_{m2}x_2 + \ldots + a_{mn}x_n = b_m,$$

It is called a **homogeneous system** if $b_1=b_2=\ldots=b_n=0$. **A non-zero solution** is a solution $x_1,\ldots,x_n$, with at least one value $x_1,\ldots,x_n$ different from 0

The system can be displayed in matrix form as ax=b, where $x:= (x_1,\ldots,x_n)'$, $b:= (b_1,\ldots,b_m)'$ and where $a_{m\times n}$ is the matrix with elements a_{ij}. If $a_{m\times n}$ is invertible (hence, square: m=n), we can **pre-multiply** the relation ax=b by a^{-1}. We then obtain the **unique solution** $x=a^{-1}b$.

Theorem D2

Any linear homogeneous system of equations with strictly more unknown quantities than equations, has a non-zero solution •

D6. Diagonalization Theorem

Theorem D3 (Diagonalization Theorem)

For any symmetric matrix p, an orthogonal matrix s exists such that sps′ is a diagonal matrix •

D7. Semidefinite Positive Matrices and Quadratic Forms

Let $p_{n\times n}$ be a matrix, and let x be the column $(x_1,\ldots,x_n)'$. Then

$$x'px = \sum_{i,j=1,\ldots,n} p_{ij}x_ix_j$$

is **the quadratic form** with variables $x_1,\ldots,x_n$ **associated to p**.

The matrix p is semidefinite positive if it is symmetric, and if $x'px \geq 0$ for all vectors x. **The matrix p is definite positive** if it is symmetric and if $x'px > 0$ for all non-zero vectors x.

Theorem D4

a. **The matrix p is definite positive iff p is semidefinite positive and**

$$\mathbf{x'px = 0 \Rightarrow x = 0.}$$

b. **If p is semidefinite positive (definite positive), then any principal submatrix of p is semidefinite positive (definite positive). In particular, then any diagonal element of p is positive (strictly positive).**

c. **Let p be semidefinite positive (definite positive), and let s be a square (invertible) matrix with the same dimensions as p. Then s′ps is semidefinite positive (definite positive).**

d. **The matrix p is semidefinite positive (definite positive) iff a square (invertible) matrix s exists such that p=s′s.**

e. **If p is semidefinite positive, then det(p)≥0. If p is definite positive, then det(p)>0.**

f. **The matrix p is definite positive iff it is semidefinite positive and invertible.**

Proof

a. Direct from the definitions.

b. We consider $p_{124;124}$. The general case is similar. Let

$$x = (x_1,x_2,0,x_4,0,\ldots,0).$$

Then

$$(x_1,x_2,x_4)\, p_{124;124}(x_1,x_2x_4)' = x'px.$$

If p is semidefinite positive, then the last member is positive for all x_1,x_2,x_4. Then $p_{124;124}$ is semidefinite positive. If p is definite positive, then the last member is strictly positive for all non-zero vectors (x_1,x_2,x_4). Then $p_{124;124}$ is definite positive.

c. Let $p_{n\times n}$ be semidefinite positive. For any column $y_{n\times 1}$, let x:=sy. Then

$$y'(s'ps)y = (sy)'p(sy) = x'px. \geq 0$$

Hence, s′ps is semidefinite positive. Let p be definite positive, and s invertible. Then

$$y'(s'ps)y = 0 \Rightarrow x'px = 0 \Rightarrow x = 0 \Rightarrow sy = 0 \Rightarrow y = 0.$$

Hence, s′ps is definite positive by a.

d. The unit matrix $1_{n\times n}$ is definite positive because $x'1x=x_1^2 + ... + x_n^2$, for any column $x_{n\times 1}$. Hence, s′s=s′1s is semidefinite positive by c. If s is invertible, then s′s = s′1s is definite positive by c.

Conversely, let p be semidefinite positive. By the diagonalization Theorem, an orthogonal matrix r exists, such that d:= rpr′ is diagonal. Then

$$p = r^{-1}d(r')^{-1} = r'd(r^{-1})' = r'd(r')' = r'dr.$$

By c, the matrix d is semidefinite positive. By b, its diagonal elements are positive. Let $d^{1/2}$ be the diagonal matrix with the positive diagonal elements $(d^{1/2})_{ii}:=(d_{ii})^{1/2}$ and let $s:=d^{1/2}r$. Then

$$s' = r'(d^{1/2})' = r'd^{1/2}$$

and

$$p = r'dr = r'd^{1/2}d^{1/2}r = s's.$$

We now assume that p is definite positive. Then d is definite positive, by c. By b, the diagonal elements of d are strictly positive. Then the diagonal elements of $d^{1/2}$ are strictly positive and then the latter matrix is invertible. Then $s:=d^{1/2}r$ is invertible, because the orthogonal matrix r is invertible.

e. Let p be semidefinite positive. By d, p=s′s for some square matrix s. By Theorem D1,

$$\det(p) = \det(s')\det(s) = [\det(s)]^2 \geq 0.$$

If p is definite positive, then s is invertible, and det(s)≠0 by Theorem D1. Then det(p)>0.

f. Results from d. Indeed, if p=s′s, then $\det(p)=[\det(s)]^2$ by Theorem D1 and then p is invertible iff s is invertible •

Lemma

The matrix q with elements $q_{ij}:= a_i a_j$ (i,j=1,...,n) is semidefinite positive.

Proof
Let $a:= (a_1,...,a_n)$. Then $q=a'a$. For any column $x_{n\times 1}$, ax is a scalar, and

$$x'qx = x'a'ax = (ax)'(ax) = (ax)^2 \geq 0 \quad \bullet$$

Theorem D5

a. **The symmetric matrix p is definite positive iff all its initial principal submatrices have a strictly positive determinant.**

b. **The symmetric matrix p is semidefinite positive iff all its principal submatrices have a positive determinant.**

Proof
The indicated conditions are necessary conditions for definite positiveness or semidefinite positiveness by Theorem D4.b,e. We prove that they are sufficient.

a. Let $p_{n\times n}$ be a symmetric matrix, such that the determinant of each of its initial principal submatrices is strictly positive. We prove that p is definite positive by recurrence on n. We may assume that $p_{11}=1$. Let

$$p_{n\times n} = \begin{bmatrix} 1 & p_{12} & p_{13} & \cdots \\ p_{21} & p_{22} & p_{23} & \cdots \\ p_{31} & p_{32} & p_{33} & \cdots \\ \cdots & \cdots & \cdots & \cdots \end{bmatrix}$$

$$q_{n\times n} = \begin{bmatrix} 1 & p_{12} & p_{13} & \cdots \\ p_{21} & p_{21}p_{12} & p_{21}p_{13} & \cdots \\ p_{31} & p_{31}p_{12} & p_{31}p_{13} & \cdots \\ \cdots & \cdots & \cdots & \cdots \end{bmatrix}$$

$$r_{n\times n} = \begin{bmatrix} 0 & 0 & 0 & \cdots \\ 0 & p_{22}-p_{21}p_{12} & p_{23}-p_{21}p_{13} & \cdots \\ 0 & p_{32}-p_{31}p_{12} & p_{33}-p_{31}p_{13} & \cdots \\ \cdots & \cdots & \cdots & \cdots \end{bmatrix}$$

Then, by the familiar properties of determinants,

$$\det(r_{2;2}) = \det(p_{12;12}) > 0,$$

$$\det(r_{23;23}) = \det(p_{123;123}) > 0, \ \ldots$$

Then the matrix $r_{23\ldots n;23\ldots n}$ is definite positive by the recurrence assumption and then r is semidefinite positive. The matrix q is semidefinite positive by the Lemma. The sum of two semidefinite positive matrices is a semidefinite positive matrices. Hence, p=q+r is semidefinite positive. But p is an initial principal submatrix of itself. Hence det(p)>0 and p is invertible by Theorem D1. Then p is definite positive by Theorem D4.f.

b. Let the principal submatrices of the symmetric matrix $p_{n\times n}$ have a positive determinant. For $\varepsilon>0$, let $(p_\varepsilon)_{n\times n}:=p_{n\times n}+\varepsilon 1_{n\times n}$. Then the initial principal submatrices of p_ε have a strictly positive determinant. Indeed, for instance,

$$\det(p_\varepsilon)_{123;123} = \det(p)_{123;123} + \varepsilon[\det(p)_{12;12} + \det(p)_{13;13} + \det(p)_{23;23}]$$

$$+ \varepsilon^2[\det(p)_{1;1} + \det(p)_{2;2} + \det(p)_{3;3}] + \varepsilon^3 > 0.$$

By a, p_ε is definite positive. Then $p=\lim_{\varepsilon\downarrow 0} p_\varepsilon$ is semidefinite positive, because $x'px=\lim_{\varepsilon\downarrow 0} x'p_\varepsilon x\geq 0$ for all columns x •

Remark

Let p be a symmetric matrix, such that all initial principal submatrices of p have a positive determinant. Then p is not necessarily semidefinite positive. An example is furnished by the matrix

$$p = \begin{bmatrix} 1 & 1 & 2 \\ 1 & 1 & 2 \\ 2 & 2 & 1 \end{bmatrix}$$

Then

$$\det(p)_{11} = 1 > 0 \ , \ \det(p)_{12;12} = 0 \ , \ \det(p)_{123;123} = 0.$$

But $\det(p)_{23:23}= -3<0$ and then p is not semidefinite positive by Theorem D4.b.

D8. Simultaneous Diagonalization

Theorem D6 (Simultaneous Diagonalization Theorem)

Let $p_{n\times n}$ be a definite positive matrix and $a_{n\times n}$ a symmetric matrix. Then an invertible matrix $s_{n\times n}$ and a diagonal matrix $d_{n\times n}$ exist, such that $p=ss'$ and $a=sds'$.

Proof

By Theorem D4.d, p can be displayed as $p=tt'$, where $t_{n\times n}$ is invertible. By the usual diagonalization Theorem D3 applied to the symmetric matrix $t^{-1}at'^{-1}$, an orthogonal matrix $r_{n\times n}$ exists, such that

$$d := r(t^{-1}at'^{-1})r' = r(t^{-1}at'^{-1})r^{-1}$$

is diagonal. Let $s:=tr^{-1}=tr'$. Then

$$ss' = tr^{-1}rt' = tt' = p \ , \ \ sds' = tr^{-1}(rt^{-1}at'^{-1}r^{-1})rt' = a \ \bullet$$

D9. Rank of a Matrix

The rank of the non-zero matrix $c_{m\times n}$ is the largest number k such that c contains an invertible submatrix with dimensions $k\times k$. **The rank of any zero matrix** is zero. The matrix $c_{m\times n}$ is **a matrix of full rank** if its rank is $m\wedge n$.

Theorem D7

a. **Let $p_{n\times n}$ be a semidefinite positive matrix, and let $y_{n\times m}$ be any matrix. Then $y'py$ is a semidefinite positive matrix.**

b. **Let $p_{n\times n}$ be a definite positive matrix, and let $y_{n\times m}$ be a matrix of full rank $m\leq n$. Then $y'py$ is a definite positive matrix.**

Proof

a. The dimensions of $y'py$ are $m\times m$. Let $x_{m\times 1}$ be any column. Then $(yx)_{n\times 1}$ is a column and

$$x'(y'py)x = (yx)'p(yx) \geq 0,$$

because p is semidefinite positive. Hence $y'py$ is semidefinite positive.

b. Let $x'(y'py)x=0$. Then $(yx)'p(yx)=0$, and $yx=0$, because p is definite positive. We prove that

$$yx=0 \Rightarrow x=0.$$

The matrix $y_{n\times m}$ contains an invertible sub-matrix $a_{m\times m}$. We may assume that this submatrix is $(y)_{1...m;1...m}$. By an horizontal line, we partition the matrix y in the two blocks

$$(y)_{1...m;1...m},$$

$$(y)_{m+1...n;1...m}.$$

Then, by block multiplication, the equality $yx=0$ is equivalent to the two equalities

$$(y)_{1...m;1...m}\, x = 0,$$

$$(y)_{m+1...n;1...m}\, x = 0.$$

Then $x=0$ by the first equality, because $(y)_{1...m;1...m}$ is invertible •

D10. Trace of a Matrix

The trace tr(c) of the square matrix $c_{n\times n}$ is the sum of its diagonal elements:

$$tr(c) := \sum_{1\le i\le n} c_{ii}.$$

Theorem D8 (Cyclical Property of Trace)

Let $c_1,c_2...,c_v$ be matrices such that the product $c_1c_2...c_v$ is defined and is a square matrix. Then the products

$$c_1c_2...c_v\ ,\ c_2...c_vc_1\ ,\ c_3...c_vc_1c_2c_3\ ,\ ...\ ,\ c_{v-1}c_vc_1...c_{v-2}\ ,\ c_vc_1...c_{v-1}$$

are defined, are square matrices, and they all have the same trace.

Proof

Let $a_{m\times n}$ and $b_{n\times m}$ be matrices. By the associativity of the matrix product, it is enough to verify that $tr(ab) = tr(ba)$.

$$tr(ab) = \sum_{1\le i\le m} (ab)_{ii} = \sum_{1\le i\le m} [\sum_{1\le j\le n} a_{ij}b_{ji}]$$

$$= \sum_{1\le j\le n} [\sum_{1\le i\le m} b_{ji}a_{ij}] = \sum_{1\le j\le n} (ba)_{jj} = tr(ba)\ \bullet$$

D11. Markov Matrices

A Markov matrix $p_{n°\times n°}$ is a square matrix with positive elements p_{ij} such that the sum of the elements in each row equals 1: $\sum_j p_{ij}=1$.

In this section D11, all subscripts i,j,k,n range over the set {1,2,...,n°}.

The product of two Markov matrices $p_{n°\times n°}$ and $q_{n°\times n°}$ is a Markov matrix. Indeed,

$$\sum_j (pq)_{ij} = \sum_j \sum_k p_{ik} q_{kj} = \sum_k p_{ik} \sum_j q_{kj} = \sum_k p_{ik}.1 = 1. \qquad \text{(D4)}$$

In the following Theorem, the powers p^m of the Markov matrix $p_{n°\times n°}$ are considered. The elements of p^m are denoted by $p^m{}_{ij}$. Hence, m is an exponent in the notation p^m, but it is a superscript in the notation $p^m{}_{ij}$.

Limits of matrices are defined element-wise:

$$\lim_{m\uparrow\infty} p^m = q \;:\Leftrightarrow\; \lim_{m\uparrow\infty} p^m{}_{ij} = q_{ij} \; (i,j=1,2,\ldots,n°). \qquad \text{(D5)}$$

Theorem D9

Let $p_{n°\times n°}$ be a Markov matrix such that some power p^r contains a column with strictly positive elements only. Then the limit $q:=\lim_{m\uparrow\infty} p^m$ exists and $q_{n°\times n°}$ is a Markov matrix with n° identical rows.

Proof

Let $\qquad p^r{}_{min,j} := \mathrm{Min}_i \, p^r{}_{ij} \;,\; p^r{}_{min,\Sigma} := \sum_j p^r{}_{min,j} > 0,$

where the strict inequality results from the assumptions. For all m=1,2,..., let

$$p^m{}_{max,n} := \mathrm{Max}_i \, p^m{}_{in} \;,\; p^m{}_{min,n} := \mathrm{Min}_i \, p^m{}_{in} \;,\; d^m{}_n := p^m{}_{max,n} - p^m{}_{min,n}.$$

Hereafter, n is a fixed column. We will prove that

$$p^m{}_{max,n} \text{ increases with m,} \qquad \text{(D6)}$$

$$p^m{}_{min,n} \text{ decreases when m increases,} \qquad \text{(D7)}$$

$$d^m{}_n \to 0 \text{ for } m\uparrow\infty. \qquad \text{(D8)}$$

This will prove the Theorem, because then all the elements of the column n must converge to the same limit. Obviously, a limit of Markov matrices is a Markov matrix.

We start with the proof of (D6).

$$p^{m+1}{}_{max,n} = \mathrm{Max}_i\, p^{1+m}{}_{in} = \mathrm{Max}_i \sum_k p_{ik}p^m{}_{kn} \le \mathrm{Max}_i \sum_k p_{ik}p^m{}_{max,n}$$

$$= p^m{}_{max,n}\, \mathrm{Max}_i \sum_k p_{ik} = p^m{}_{max,n}\, \mathrm{Max}_i\, 1 = p^m{}_{max,n}.$$

The proof of (D7) is similar:

$$p^{m+1}{}_{min,n} = \mathrm{Min}_i\, p^{1+m}{}_{in} = \mathrm{Min}_i \sum_k p_{ik}p^m{}_{kn} \ge \mathrm{Min}_i \sum_k p_{ik}p^m{}_{min,n}$$

$$= p^m{}_{min,n}\, \mathrm{Min}_i \sum_k p_{ik} = p^m{}_{min,n}\, \mathrm{Min}_i\, 1 = p^m{}_{min,n}.$$

We recall the notations $(c)_+ := \mathrm{Max}(c,0)$, $(c)_- := -\mathrm{Min}(c,0)$. Then

$$(c)_+ \ge 0 \;,\; (c)_- \ge 0 \;,\; c = (c)_+ - (c)_- \;,\; a \le b \Rightarrow (a)_+ \le (b)_+.$$

We apply $(\cdot)_+$ to the relation $p^r{}_{ik} - p^r{}_{jk} \le p^r{}_{ik} - p^r{}_{min,k}$, where the last member is positive, and we sum over k:

$$0 \le \sum_k (p^r{}_{ik} - p^r{}_{jk})_+ \le \sum_k (p^r{}_{ik} - p^r{}_{min,k}) = \sum_k p^r{}_{ik} - \sum_k p^r{}_{min,k} = 1 - p^r{}_{min,\Sigma} < 1. \quad \text{(D9)}$$

The relations

$$\sum_k (p^r{}_{ik} - p^r{}_{jk})_+ - \sum_k (p^r{}_{ik} - p^r{}_{jk})_- = \sum_k (p^r{}_{ik} - p^r{}_{jk}) = \sum_k p^r{}_{ik} - \sum_k p^r{}_{jk} = 1 - 1 = 0$$

imply

$$\sum_k (p^r{}_{ik} - p^r{}_{jk})_+ = \sum_k (p^r{}_{ik} - p^r{}_{jk})_- \,. \quad \text{(D10)}$$

We observe that

$$d^r{}_n = \mathrm{Max}_i\, p^r{}_{in} - \mathrm{Min}_j\, p^r{}_{jn} = \mathrm{Max}_i\, p^r{}_{in} + \mathrm{Max}_j\, (-p^r{}_{jn}) = \mathrm{Max}_{ij}(p^r{}_{in} - p^r{}_{jn})$$

$$\le \mathrm{Max}_{ij}(p^r{}_{in} - p^r{}_{jn})_+ \le \mathrm{Max}_{ij} \sum_k (p^r{}_{ik} - p^r{}_{jk})_+ \le 1 - p^r{}_{min,\Sigma}, \quad \text{(D11)}$$

by (D9).

Let s be a strictly positive integer. Then

$$d^{r+s}{}_n = \mathrm{Max}_{ij}(p^{r+s}{}_{in} - p^{r+s}{}_{jn}) = \mathrm{Max}_{ij} \sum_k (p^r{}_{ik} - p^r{}_{jk}) p^s{}_{kn}$$

$$= \mathrm{Max}_{ij} \left[\sum_k (p^r{}_{ik} - p^r{}_{jk})_+\, p^s{}_{kn} - \sum_k (p^r{}_{ik} - p^r{}_{jk})_-\, p^s{}_{kn}\right]$$

$$\le \mathrm{Max}_{ij} \left[\sum_k (p^r{}_{ik} - p^r{}_{jk})_+\, p^s{}_{max,n} - \sum_k (p^r{}_{ik} - p^r{}_{jk})_-\, p^s{}_{min,n}\right]$$

by (D10)

$$= \mathrm{Max}_{ij} \left[\sum_k (p^r{}_{ik} - p^r{}_{jk})_+\, p^s{}_{max,n} - \sum_k (p^r{}_{ik} - p^r{}_{jk})_+\, p^s{}_{min,n}\right]$$

$$= \left[\mathrm{Max}_{ij} \sum_k (p^r{}_{ik} - p^r{}_{jk})_+\right](p^s{}_{max,n} - p^s{}_{min,n})$$

by (D9)

$$\le \mathrm{Max}_{ij}(1 - p^r{}_{min,\Sigma})d^s{}_n = (1 - p^r{}_{min,\Sigma})d^s{}_n. \quad \text{(D12)}$$

Then

$$d^{mr}{}_n \leq (1-p^r{}_{min,\Sigma})^m. \qquad \text{(D13)}$$

Indeed, by successive applications of (D12) and by (D11),

$$d^{mr}{}_n = d^{r+(m-1)r}{}_n \leq (1-p^r{}_{min,\Sigma})d^{(m-1)r}{}_n \leq (1-p^r{}_{min,\Sigma})^2 d^{(m-2)r}{}_n$$
$$\leq \ldots \leq (1-p^r{}_{min,\Sigma})^{m-1}\, d^r{}_n \leq (1-p^r{}_{min,\Sigma})^m .$$

From (D6) and (D7) results that $d^m{}_n$ decreases when m increases. The subsequence $d^{mr}{}_n$ (m=1,2,...) of the sequence $d^m{}_n$ (m=1,2,...) converges to 0 as $m\uparrow\infty$ by (D9) and (D13). This proves (D8) •

Interpretation

We consider a collectivity C, partitioned in classes $C_1,C_2,\ldots,C_{n^\circ}$ and observed at the instants t=0,1,2,...Let $c^t{}_i$ (not necessarily an integer), be the number of members of the class C_i at the instant t. The row $c^t := (c^t{}_1,c^t{}_2,\ldots,c^t{}_{n^\circ})$ is called **the partition of the collectivity at the instant t**. We assume that during one period (delimited by two successive instants t, t+1), the proportion p_{ij} of members of the class C_i leaves that class and enters in the class C_j. Hence, $c^{t+1}{}_j = \sum_i c^t{}_i p_{ij}$. This means that the partition c^{t+1} results from the partition c^t by the matrix relation

$$c^{t+1} = c^t\, p, \qquad \text{(D14)}$$

where p is the Markov matrix with elements p_{ij}. Let $c^t{}_\Sigma$ be the total number of members in the collectivity at the instant t. Then

$$c^{t+1}{}_\Sigma = \sum_j c^{t+1}{}_j = \sum_j \sum_i c^t{}_i p_{ij} = \sum_i c^t{}_i \sum_j p_{ij} = \sum_i c^t{}_i.1 = c^t{}_\Sigma.$$

Hence

$$c^t{}_\Sigma = c^0{}_\Sigma \text{ (t=0,1,2,...)}. \qquad \text{(D15)}$$

By successive applications of (D14), we obtain

$$c^t = c^0 p^t, \qquad \text{(D16)}$$

and then by Th.D9, as $t\uparrow\infty$:

$$c^\infty := \lim_{t\uparrow\infty} c^t = c^0\, q. \qquad \text{(D17)}$$

(we admit that the assumptions of that Theorem are satisfied) Let each row of q be $(q_1,q_2,\ldots,q_{n^\circ}):=q^\circ$. Then

$$c^\infty{}_i = (c^0 q)_i = \sum_j c^0{}_j q_i = c^0{}_\Sigma\, q_i.$$

Hence, by (D17), $c^{\infty} = c^{0}_{\Sigma}.q^{o}$: **the limit partition c^{∞} does not depend on the initial partition c^{0}** (for a fixed total number of members c^{0}_{Σ}).

Remarks

a. The foregoing deterministic model can be "stochastified". Then c^{t}_{i} must be regarded as the expected number of members in the class C_i at the instant t, and the proportions p_{ij} must be interpreted as probabilities.

b. Markov matrices $p_{\infty\times\infty}$ with elements p_{ij} (i,j=1,2,...), with infinite dimensions, are defined in the obvious way. Th.D9 has an obvious version valid in that case: It is sufficient to assume that some power p^{r} has a column with all elements larger than some $\varepsilon>0$, and to replace Max and Min by Sup and Inf resp. in the foregoing proof.

D12. Vandermonde Systems

A Vandermonde system of equations is a linear system such as

$$\begin{aligned}
p_0 + p_1 + \ldots + p_n &= \mu_0\\
p_0a_0 + p_1a_1 + \ldots + p_na_n &= \mu_1\\
p_0a_0^2 + p_1a_1^2 + \ldots + p_na_n^2 &= \mu_2\\
\ldots \quad \ldots \quad \ldots \quad \ldots &\quad \ldots \quad \ldots\\
p_0a_0^n + p_1a_1^n + \ldots + p_na_n^n &= \mu_n
\end{aligned}$$

The unknown quantities are $p_0,p_1,\ldots,p_n$. The parameters $a_0,a_1,\ldots,a_n$ are n+1 different real numbers. The parameters $\mu_0,\mu_1,\ldots,\mu_n$ are any real numbers. The solution of the system is

$$p_i = [\mu_n - s_{1i}\mu_{n-1} + s_{2i}\mu_{n-2} - \ldots + (-1)^n s_{ni}] / [\Pi_{j;\, j\neq i}(a_i - a_j)] \quad (i=0,1,\ldots,n),$$

where

$$s_{1i} := \textstyle\sum_{j;\, j\neq i} a_j$$

$$s_{2i} := \textstyle\sum_{jk;\, j,k\neq i;\, j<k} a_ja_k$$

$$s_{3i} := \textstyle\sum_{jkm;\, j,k,m\neq i;\, j<k<m} a_ja_ka_m$$

$$\ldots \quad \ldots \quad \ldots \quad \ldots \quad \ldots \quad \ldots \quad \ldots$$

$$s_{ni} := a_0a_1\ldots a_{i-1}a_{i+1}\ldots a_n.$$

The subscripts j,k,m,... must range over the set {0,1,...,n} and they must satisfy the indicated coditions.

Appendix E

Krein-Milman Theorem for Spaces of Probability Distributions

E1. Weak Convergence

As usual, a **distribution** can be a **distribution function** (a point function) as well as a **measure** (a set function). The capital letters F, G, ... denote distributions. No different symbols are used for a distribution function and for the corresponding measure.

The distribution functions F and F+c define the same measure. In case of probability distribution functions, c is fixed by the condition $F(-\infty)=0$.

DISTR is the set of all distributions F, not necessarily with a finite total mass F(**R**).

***Prob*[R**$_+$;finite] is the set of probability distributions F on **R**$_+$ with a finite first moment $\mu(F)$.

***Prob*[R**$_+$;$[0,\mu_1]$**]** is the set of probability distributions F on **R**$_+$ with first moment $\mu(F)\in[0,\mu_1]$. We assume that μ_1 is finite when that notation is used.

We recall that **weak convergence** of functions means convergence at the continuity points of the limit. The symbol $\rightarrow_w$ denotes weak convergence. Hence

$$[F_n \rightarrow_w F] \;:\Leftrightarrow\; [F_n(x) \rightarrow F(x) \text{ as } n\uparrow\infty \text{ (x continuity point of F)}].$$

A pointwise bounded sequence of functions is a sequence f_k (k=1,2,...) such that the sequence $f_1(x)$, $f_2(x)$, ... is bounded at each point $x\in\mathbf{R}$. The bound may depend on x.

Theorem E1

The set of discontinuity points of the distribution function F is enumerable.

Proof
It is enough to prove that F has an enumerable (not excluding finite) number of discontinuities on each interval $]n,n+1]$ ($n \in \mathbf{N}$). The jump $F(d)-F(d-)$ of the discontinuity $d \in]n,n+1]$ of F lies in one of the intervals

$$\ldots, [1/4,1/3[, [1/3,1/2[, [1/2,1[, [1,0[$$

The number of jumps in each of these intervals, corresponding to discontinuities $d \in]n,n+1]$, is finite because otherwise $F(n+1)-F(n)=\infty$ •

Remark on integration theory (tacitly used hereafter)

The monotone and dominated convergence Theorems of I.Ch.1 are stated for usual pointwise convergence. When integrations are performed with respect to Lebesgue measure, the pointwise convergence of integrands may be replaced by their weak convergence in these Theorems. Indeed, pointwise and weak convergence differ at most on the denumerable set of discontinuities of the limit function (Th.E1). The integrals do not change when this set is substracted from the integration domain.

Theorem E2

a. **If a sequence of distributions converges weakly to F, then any subsequence converges weakly to F.**

b. **If a sequence of distributions converges weakly to F and to G, then F=G.**

Proof.
a. is obvious. For b, let $F_n \rightarrow_w F$ and $F_n \rightarrow_w G$. Then F=G on the set of common continuity points of F and G, and then F=G by the right-continuity of F and G •

Theorem E3 (General Compactness Theorem for Distributions)

Let F_n (n=1,2,...) be a pointwise bounded sequence in *DISTR*. Then some subsequence F_{n_k} (k=1,2,...) converges weakly to some function $F \in$ *DISTR*.

Proof
We consider the numbers $F_n(r)$ (n=1,2,...; r rational). By Cantor's diagonal principle (App.A.Th.A1), a subsequence F_{n_k}(k=1,2,...) and a function F_0 exist, such that

$$\lim_{k\uparrow\infty} F_{n_k}(r) = F_0(r) \quad (r \text{ rational}).$$

Then F_0 is a finite function, because the sequence F_{n_k} is pointwise bounded. It is an increasing function because each F_{n_k} is increasing. We define F on $\mathbf{R}_+$ as follows: $F(x):=\inf_{r>x,\ r\ \text{rational}} F_0(r)$ ($x\in\mathbf{R}_+$). Then $F\in$ ***DISTR***. Indeed, F is increasing. We prove the right-continuity of F at the point $x\in\mathbf{R}$. Let $\varepsilon>0$. Let $s>x$ be a rational point such that $F_0(s)-F(x)<\varepsilon$. Then $x\le y<s \Rightarrow F(y)-F(x)<2\varepsilon$. Indeed, let $x\le y<s$ and let r be a rational number such that $y<r<s$, $F_0(r)-F(y)<\varepsilon$. Then

$$|F(y)-F(x)| \le |F(y)-F_0(r)| + |F_0(r)-F(x)| \le \varepsilon + F_0(s)-F(x) \le 2\varepsilon.$$

We now prove that $F_{n_k} \to_w F$. Let $c>0$ be a continuity point of F. Let x,y and then r,s be points such that $x<r<c<s<y$, r and s rational, and such that

$$F(c)-F(x)<\varepsilon\ ,\ F(y)-F(c)<\varepsilon\ ,\ F_0(r)-F(x)<\varepsilon\ ,\ F_0(s)-F(c)<\varepsilon\ .$$

The first two relations are possible by the continuity of F at c and the last two by the definition of F(x) and F(c). Let k_0 be such that

$$|F_{n_k}(r)-F_0(r)|<\varepsilon\ \ ,\ \ |F_{n_k}(s)-F_0(s)|<\varepsilon\ \ (k\ge k_0)\ .$$

The relations

$$F_{n_k}(r)-F(c) \le F_{n_k}(c)-F(c) \le F_{n_k}(s)-F(c)$$

imply, for $k\ge k_0$,

$$|F_{n_k}(c)-F(c)| \le |F_{n_k}(r)-F(c)| + |F_{n_k}(s)-F(c)| \le |F_{n_k}(r)-F_0(r)| + |F_0(r)-F(x)|$$

$$+ |F(x)-F(c)| + |F_{n_k}(s)-F_0(s)|+|F_0(s)-F(c)| <5\varepsilon \quad \bullet$$

Theorem E4 (Basic Inequalities)

For all functions $\alpha(\cdot)$, $\beta(\cdot)$, $\alpha_1(\cdot)$, ..., $\alpha_m(\cdot)$ on R and $F\in$ *DISTR*,

$$\left[\int_{\mathbf{R}}(\alpha+\beta)^2 dF\right]^{1/2} \le \left[\int_{\mathbf{R}}\alpha^2 dF\right]^{1/2} + \left[\int_{\mathbf{R}}\beta^2 dF\right]^{1/2} \ \textbf{(Minkowski)},$$

$$\left[\int_{\mathbf{R}}|\alpha\beta| dF\right]^2 \le \int_{\mathbf{R}}\alpha^2 dF \ .\ \int_{\mathbf{R}}\beta^2 dF \ \ \textbf{(Schwarz)},$$

$$\int_{\mathbf{R}}(\alpha_1+...+\alpha_m)^2 dF \le m^2\int_{\mathbf{R}}\alpha_1^2 dF +...+ m^2\int_{\mathbf{R}}\alpha_m^2 dF \ \ \textbf{(Elementary inequality)}.$$

Proof
We may assume that α, β, α_1, ..., α_m are positive functions.

We recall **Schwarz for positive random variables**: $E^2(XY) \le EX^2.EY^2$ (I.Ch.2. Th.7). If X is a random variable with distribution F, it can be applied to the random variables $\alpha(X)$ and $\beta(Y)$. Hence, Schwarz (of the statement) is true if $F(\mathbf{R})=1$. Schwarz is correct if $0<F(\mathbf{R})<\infty$, because then we can replace F by $F/F(\mathbf{R})$. If $F(\mathbf{R})=\infty$, then Schwarz holds for the functions $\alpha 1_{[-n,+n]}$ and $\beta 1_{[-n,+n]}$ because $F([-n,+n])<\infty$. Letting $n\uparrow\infty$, we obtain Schwarz for α and β by monotone convergence.

By a similar argument, Minkowski results from **Minkowski for positive random variables**,

$$E^{1/2}(X+Y)^2 \le E^{1/2}X^2 + E^{1/2}Y^2.$$

The latter relation is equivalent to the relation

$$EX^2 + EY^2 + 2E(XY) \le EX^2 + EY^2 + 2E^{1/2}X^2.E^{1/2}Y^2.$$

It is correct ($\infty=\infty$) if $EX^2=\infty$ or $EY^2=\infty$. If EX^2 and EY^2 are finite, we can simplify by these terms and then the relation is equivalent to Schwarz for positive random variables.

The elementary integral inequality results from the inequalities

$$(a_1+...+a_m)^2 \le (a+...+a)^2 = m^2a^2 \le m^2a_1^2 + ... + m^2a_m^2 \quad (a_1,...,a_m\in\mathbf{R}),$$

where $a:=\max(|a_1|,...,|a_m|)$ •

E2. Convergence in Distance

The **mean quadratic distance**, or briefly **the distance**, of the distributions F,G $\in$***Prob***[$\mathbf{R}_+$;finite] is the number

$$d(F,G) := [\int(F-G)^2dI]^{1/2} \equiv [\int[F(x)-G(x)]^2dx]^{1/2},$$

where I is the identitiy function on $\mathbf{R}_+$. In this Appendix, the integration domain is $\mathbf{R}_+$ whenever it is not specified. The distance is finite because

$$d^2(F,G) = \int(F-G)^2dI \le \int|F-G|dI = \int|g-f|dI \le \int fdI + \int gdI = \mu(F) + \mu(G),$$

by the surface interpretation of the first moment. In this Appendix, we use the notations $f:=1-F$, $g:=1-G$, ... when F, G,... are probability distributions on $\mathbf{R}_+$.

$F_n \to_d F$ means that F_n (n=1,2,...) and F belong to the space ***Prob***[**R**$_+$;finite] and that $d(F_n,F) \to 0$ as $n\uparrow\infty$. This convergence is called **d-convergence**, or **convergence in distance**.

Theorem E5

a. d-convergence $\Rightarrow$ weak convergence, on *Prob*[R$_+$;finite].

b. d-convergence $\Leftrightarrow$ weak convergence, on *Prob*[R$_+$;[0,μ_1]].

Proof
For the proof of a, we assume that F_n converges to F in distance, but not weakly, and we derive a contradiction. A continuity point c of F exists, such that $F_n(c)$ does not converge to F(c). Using a subsequence, we may assume that $F_n(c) \to a \neq F(c)$. Using a further subsequence, we may assume that $F_n \to_w G$ $\in$***DISTR*** by the general compactness Th.E3. We let $n\uparrow\infty$ in the relation

$$\int_{[0,c+1]} (F_n - F)^2 dI \le d^2(F_n,F).$$

Hence, $\int_{[0,c+1]}(G-F)^2dI=0$ by dominated convergence in the first member. Then F=G Lebesgue-a.e. on [c,c+1]. By right-continuity, F=G on [0,c+1[. This implies that c is a continuity point of G, and then we have the contradiction $F_n(c) \to G(c)=F(c)$.

The $\Rightarrow$ part of b. results from a.

We now demonsrate the $\Leftarrow$ part of b. Let $F,F_n \in$***Prob***[**R**$_+$;[0,μ_1]] be such that $F_n \to_w F$. Let $\varepsilon>0$. Let c be a continuity point of F, so large that $f(c)<\varepsilon$. Let n_0 be such that

$$|f_n(c)-f(c)| = |F_n(c)-F(c)| < \varepsilon \ \ (n \ge n_0) .$$

Then

$$f_n(c) \le |f_n(c)-f(c)|+f(c) \le 2\varepsilon \ (n \ge n_0)$$

and

$$d^2(F,F_n) = \int_{[0,c[} (F-F_n)^2 dI + \int_{[c,\infty[} (F-F_n)^2 dI.$$

where

$$\int_{[c,\infty[} (F-F_n)^2 dI = \int_{[c,\infty[} (f-f_n)^2 dI \le 4\int_{[c,\infty[} f^2 dI + 4\int_{[c,\infty[} f_n^2 dI$$

$$\le 4f(c)\int_{[c,\infty[} f dI + 4f_n(c) \int_{[c,\infty[} f_n dI \le 4\varepsilon\mu(F) + 8\varepsilon\mu(F_n) \le 12\varepsilon\mu_1 \ (n \ge n_0).$$

by the elementary integral inequality and because f and f_n are decreasing functions.

Hence, $|d^2(F,F_n)-\int_{[0,c[} (F-F_n)^2 dI| \le 12\varepsilon\mu_1$.

As $n\uparrow\infty$, the integral in the first member tends to 0 by dominated convergence. Hence

$$\limsup_{n\uparrow\infty} d^2(F,F_n) \le 12\varepsilon\mu_1 \quad \bullet$$

The following example shows that weak convergence and d-convergence are not equivalent on ***Prob***[$\mathbf{R}_+$;finite]. Let F_0 be the probability distribution concentrated at 0, i.e. $F_0\equiv 1$ (on $\mathbf{R}_+$). Let F_n(n=1,2,...) be the probability distribution with mass (n−1)/n at 0 and mass 1/n at the point n^2. Then $F_n\to F$ weakly. But $d(F_0,F_n)=1$, and F_n does not converge to F_0 in distance.

In the rest of this Appendix, we remain in the space *Prob*[$\mathbf{R}_+$;finite]. called the *basic space*, and only d-convergence is considered.

Theorem E6

Let F,G,H be distributions in the basic space. Then

$$\mathbf{d(F,G)=0 \Leftrightarrow F=G\,,}$$

$$\mathbf{d(F,G) = d(G,F)\ \ (Symmetry)\,,}$$

$$\mathbf{d(F,H) \le d(F,G)+d(G,H)\ \ (Triangle\ inequality)\,.}$$

Proof
If d(F,G)=0, then F=G Lebesgue-a.e., and then F=G everywhere, by the right-continuity of F and G. This proves the $\Rightarrow$ part of the equivalence. The $\Leftarrow$ part is obvious. The symmetry relation is direct.

For the triangle inequaliy, we have by Minkowski,

$$d(F,H) = \left[\int((F-G)+(G-H))^2 dI\right]^{1/2}$$

$$\le \left[\int(F-G)^2 dI\right]^{1/2} + \left[\int(G-H)^2 dI\right]^{1/2} = d(F,G)+d(G,H) \quad \bullet$$

This Theorem states that d is a **distance** (or a **metric**) on the basic space.

(The following definitions do not coincide with those of II.Ch.1.2.3. No contradictions are involved. See the final *Remark* of this Appendix.)

The set ***A***, in the basic space, is **compact** if each sequence in ***A*** contains a subsequence F_n (n=1,2,...) such that $F_n\to_d F\in\boldsymbol{A}$.

The set $\boldsymbol{A}$, in the basic space, is **closed**, if it has the following property:

$$[F_n \in \boldsymbol{A}\ (n=1,2,...)\ ,\ F_n \to_d F] \Rightarrow F \in \boldsymbol{A}.$$

A **limit point** of the set $\boldsymbol{A}$ in the basic space, is a point F such that $F_n \to_d F$ for some sequence $F_n \in \boldsymbol{A}$ (n=1,2,...). Each point $F \in \boldsymbol{A}$ is a limit point of $\boldsymbol{A}$ because we can consider the sequence $F_n := F$ (n=1,2,...). The **closure** $\boldsymbol{A}^-$ of $\boldsymbol{A}$ is the set of limits points of $\boldsymbol{A}$.

Theorem E7

a. **If $F_n \to_d F$ and $G_n \to_d G$, then $d(F_n,G_n) \to d(F,G)$ as $n \uparrow \infty$.**

b. **If $F_n \to_d F$ and $F_n \to_d G$, then F=G.**

c. **The closure A^- of the set A in the basic space, is a closed set.**

Proof

a. By the triangle inequality,

$$d(F_n,G_n) \le d(F_n,F)+d(F,G_n) \le d(F_n,F)+d(F,G)+d(G,G_n),$$

$$d(F,G) \le d(F,F_n)+d(F_n,G) \le d(F,F_n)+d(F_n,G_n)+d(G_n,G).$$

Hence,

$$d(F_n,G_n) - d(F,G) \le d(F_n,F) + d(G,G_n),$$

$$d(F,G) - d(F_n,G_n) \le d(F,F_n) + d(G_n,G).$$

Then

$$|d(F_n,G_n) - d(F,G)| \le d(F_n,F) + d(G,G_n) \to 0 \text{ as } n \uparrow \infty$$

if $d(F_n,F) \to 0$ and $d(G,G_n) \to 0$ as $n \uparrow \infty$.

b. Let $F_n \to_d F$ and $F_n \to_d G$. Then $0 = d(F_n,F_n) \to d(F,G)$ by a. Hence d(F,G) =0 and then F=G.

c. Let $F_n \in \boldsymbol{A}^-$ (n=1,2,...), $F_n \to_d F$. F_n is a limit point of $\boldsymbol{A}$. Hence a distribution $G_n \in \boldsymbol{A}$ exists, such that $d(F_n,G_n) \le 1/n$. Then, by the triangle inequality

$$d(G_n,F) \le d(G_n,F_n) + d(F_n,F) \to 0 \text{ as } n \uparrow \infty.$$

Hence $G_n \to_d F$ and F is a limit point of $\boldsymbol{A}$. Then $F \in \boldsymbol{A}^-$. Hence $\boldsymbol{A}$ is closed •

Theorem E8

Any closed subset of a compact set in the basic space is compact. Any compact set in the basic space is closed.

Proof
Let $\boldsymbol{A} \subseteq \boldsymbol{B}$, $\boldsymbol{B}$ compact, $\boldsymbol{A}$ closed. In order to prove that $\boldsymbol{A}$ is compact, we consider a sequence $F_n \in \boldsymbol{A}$ (n=1,2,...). Then $F_n \in \boldsymbol{B}$ and some subsequence converges to a point $F \in \boldsymbol{B}$ because $\boldsymbol{B}$ is compact. Then $F \in \boldsymbol{A}$ because $\boldsymbol{A}$ is closed. This proves the first proposition.

For the proof of the second proposition, let $\boldsymbol{B}$ be compact and let $F_n \in B$ (n=1,2,...) be a sequence such that $F_n \to_d F$. A subsequence F_{n_k} and a point G exist, such that $F_{n_k} \to_d G \in \boldsymbol{B}$. But also $F_{n_k} \to_d F$. Hence $F = G \in \boldsymbol{B}$ by Th.E17.b •

E3. Convex Sets and Linear Functionals

The subset $\boldsymbol{A}$ of the basic space is **convex** if it contains the convex combinations of its points. The **convex hull Co*A*** of $\boldsymbol{A}$ is the set of all convex combinations of points of $\boldsymbol{A}$. The **closed convex hull** of $\boldsymbol{A}$ is the closure $Co^{-}\boldsymbol{A} := (Co\boldsymbol{A})^{-}$ of the convex hull of $\boldsymbol{A}$.

The basic space is convex because $\mu(\sum p_i F_i) = \sum p_i \mu(F_i)$.

A **functional** is a real finite function defined on a subset of the basic space. A **linear functional** on the convex subset $\boldsymbol{C}$ of the basic space, is a functional T on $\boldsymbol{C}$ such that $T(\sum p_i F_i) = \sum p_i T(F_i)$ for all convex combinations $\sum p_i F_i$ of points $F_i \in \boldsymbol{C}$. A **continuous functional** on the subset $\boldsymbol{A}$ of the basic space, is a functional T on $\boldsymbol{A}$ with the following property:

$$[F_n \in \boldsymbol{A} \text{ (n=1,2,...)}, F \in \boldsymbol{A}, F_n \to_d F] \Rightarrow [T(F_n) \to T(F) \text{ as } n \uparrow \infty].$$

Theorem E9

a. **Let C be a subset of the basic space containing the convex combinations of couples of its points. Then C is convex.**

b. **Let T be a functional on the convex subset C of the basic space such that T(pF+qG)=pTF+qTG for convex combinations pF+qG of couples of points F,G of C. Then T is a linear functional.**

c. **The convex hull Co*A* of the subset *A* of the basic space is convex.**

Proof

a. Let $F:=p_1F_1 + \dots + p_nF_n$ be a convex combination of points $F_k\in \boldsymbol{C}$. We prove that $F\in\boldsymbol{C}$ by induction on n. The induction assumption is that the property is true for the convex combinations of n−1 points. If $p_n=1$, then $p_1=\dots=p_{n-1}=0$ and $F=F_n\in\boldsymbol{C}$. Hence, we may suppose that $p_n\neq 1$. Then $p:= p_1+\dots+p_{n-1}\in]0,1]$ and

$$F = p[p_{1/p}\, F_1 + \dots + p_{n-1/p}\, F_{n-1}] + (1-p)F_n.$$

The term in square brackects is a convex combination of the distributions F_1, ..., F_{n-1}. It belongs to $\boldsymbol{C}$ by the induction assumption. Then F is a convex combination of 2 points of $\boldsymbol{C}$ and it belongs to $\boldsymbol{C}$.

b. We consider the same convex combination and the same decomposition as in the proof a. Then

$$T(p_1F_1+\dots+p_nF_n) = T[p[p_{1/p}\, F_1 + \dots + p_{n-1/p}\, F_{n-1}] + (1-p)F_n]$$

$$= p\, T[p_{1/p}\, F_1 + \dots + p_{n-1/p}\, F_{n-1}] + (1-p)TF_n$$

and the proof can be completed by induction.

c. Any convex combination of convex combinations of points in $\boldsymbol{A}$ is a convex combination of points in $\boldsymbol{A}$.

Theorem E10

a. Let $F_n:=p_nG_n+q_nH_n$ (n=1,2,...) be a convex combinations of points G_n and H_n of the basic space such that $p_n\to p$, $q_n\to q$, $G_n\to_d G$, $H_n\to_d H$ as $n\uparrow\infty$. Then $F:=pG+qH$ belongs to the basic space and $F_n\to_d F$.

b. Let $\boldsymbol{C}$ be a convex set in the basic space. Then $\boldsymbol{C}^-$ is convex.

Proof

The relation $p_n\geq 0$, $q_n\geq 0$, $p_n+q_n=1$ imply $p\geq 0$, $q\geq 0$, $p+q=1$ as $n\uparrow\infty$. Hence F belongs to the basic space.

$$f := 1-F = (p+q)-(pG+qH) = p(1-G) + q(1-H) = pg + qh.$$

Similarly,

$$f_n = p_ng_n + q_nh_n.$$

Then

$$p_ng_n - pg = p_n(g_n-g) + (p_n-p)g\ ,\ q_nh_n - qh = q_n(h_n-h) + (q_n-q)h$$

and by the elementary inequality

$$d^2(F_n,F) = \int(F_n-F)^2dI = \int(f_n-f)^2dI = \int[\, p_n(g_n-g)+(p_n-p)g+q_n(h_n-h)+(q_n-q)h]^2dI$$

$$\leq 16p_n^2\int(g_n-g)^2dI + 16(p_n-p)^2\int g^2dI + 16q_n^2\int(h_n-h)^2 + 16(q_n-q)^2\int h^2dI$$

$$\leq 16d^2(G,G_n) + 16(p_n-p)^2\int gdI + 16d^2(H,H_n) + 16(q_n-q)^2\int hdI$$

$$= 16d^2(G,G_n) + 16(p_n-p)^2\mu(G) + 16d^2(H,H_n) + 16(q_n-q)^2\mu(H) \to 0 \text{ as } n\uparrow\infty.$$

b. Let $F=pG+qH$ be a convex combination of points $G,H\in\boldsymbol{C}^-$. Sequences G_n and H_n ($n=1,2,\ldots$) exist in $\boldsymbol{C}$ such that $G_n\to_d G$ and $H_n\to_d H$. Then $F_n := pG_n+qH_n\in\boldsymbol{C}$, because $\boldsymbol{C}$ is convex and $F_n\to_d F\in\boldsymbol{C}^-$ by a. This proves that any convex combination of any couple of points in $\boldsymbol{C}^-$, is a point in $\boldsymbol{C}^-$ •

Theorem E11

Let $\varphi:=F_0-G_0$ be a difference of function F_0 and G_0 in the basic space and let T be the functional on the basic space with values $TF:=\int F\varphi dI$. Then T is a continuous linear functional on the basic space.

Proof

The function $F\varphi$ is I-integrable, because $|F\varphi|\leq|\varphi|\leq f_0+g_0$. The linearity of T is direct. For the proof of the continuity, let $F_n\to_d F$. Then

$$|TF_n-TF| \leq \int|F_n-F|\varphi dI,$$

and by Schwarz,

$$|TF_n-TF|^2 \leq \int|F_n-F|^2dI.\int\varphi^2dI = d^2(F_n,F).d^2(F_0,G_0) \to 0 \text{ as } n\uparrow\infty \text{ •}$$

Theorem E12

Let S be a compact set in the basic space and let G_0 be a point in the basic space. Let $s_1:=\inf_{F\in S} d(G_0,F)$ and $s_2:=\sup_{F\in S} d(G_0,F)$. Then F_1 and F_2 exist in S, such that $s_1=d(G_0,F_1)$ and $s_2=d(G_0,F_2)$.

Proof

Let $H_n\in\boldsymbol{S}$ ($n=1,2,\ldots$) be such that $d(G_0,H_n)\to s_1$ as $n\uparrow\infty$. By the compactness of $\boldsymbol{S}$, a subsequence H_{n_k} ($k=1,2,\ldots$) and a function $F_1\in\boldsymbol{S}$ exist, such that $H_{n_k}\to_d F_1$. Then $d(G_0,H_{n_k})\to d(G_0,F_1)$. But also $d(G_0,H_{n_k})\to s_1$. Hence, $d(G_0,F_1)=s_1$. The existence of F_2 is proved in the same way •

Theorem E13 (Hahn-Banach on *Prob*[R_+;finite])

Let *C* be a convex compact set in the basic space and let G_0 be a point in the basic space not belonging to *C*. Then a continuous linear functional T exists on the basic space and a number $a \in R$ exists, such that

$$TG_0 < a \leq TF \quad (F \in C). \tag{E7}$$

Proof
Let $s := \inf_{F\in C} d(F,G_0)$. By Theorem E12, a point $F_0 \in C$ exists, such that $d(F_0,G_0) = s$. Let $F \in C$, $p \in]0,1]$. Then

$$F_0 + p(F-F_0) = (1-p)F_0 + pF \in C$$

because *C* is convex. Then, by the definition of s,

$$d^2(F_0,G_0) = s^2 \leq d^2[F_0+p(F-F_0),G_0],$$

$$\int (F_0-G_0)^2 dI \leq \int [(F_0-G_0)+p(F-F_0)]^2 dI,$$

$$0 \leq 2p\int (F_0-G_0)(F-F_0)dI + p^2\int (F-F_0)^2 dI.$$

We divide by p and then we let $p\downarrow 0$. This gives

$$0 \leq \int (F_0-G_0)(F-F_0)dI = \int (F-F_0)\varphi dI,$$

where $\varphi := F_0 - G_0$.

$$0 < \int (F_0-G_0)^2 dI = \int (F_0-G_0)\varphi dI,$$

where the strict inequality holds because $F_0 \in C$, $G_0 \notin C$, $F_0 \neq G_0$. Hence

$$\int G_0\varphi dI < \int F_0\varphi dI \leq \int F\varphi dI \quad (F \in C),$$

and we can take

$$a := \int F_0\varphi dI \ , \ TF := \int F\varphi dI$$

by Theorem E11 •

E4. Extremal Points

Let *C* be a convex subset of the basic space. The point F is an **extremal point of *C***, if it belongs to *C* and if it cannot be displayed as a convex combination of two points of $C-\{F\}$. An equivalent definition is the following. F is an **extremal point of *C*** if $F \in C$ and if the following condition is satisfied:

$$[F=pG+qH \,;\, p+q=1 \,;\, p,q>0 \,;\, G,H\in \boldsymbol{C}] \Rightarrow [F=G=H].$$

The set $\boldsymbol{A}$ is an **extremal set of $\boldsymbol{C}$** if $\boldsymbol{A}\subseteq\boldsymbol{C}$ and if the following condition is satisfied:

$$[F=pG+qH\in \boldsymbol{A} \,;\, p+q=1 \,;\, p,q>0 \,;\, G,H\in \boldsymbol{C}] \Rightarrow [G,H\in \boldsymbol{A}].$$

Hence, **F is an extremal point of $\boldsymbol{C}$ iff {F} is an extremal set of $\boldsymbol{C}$**.

Theorem E14

Let $\boldsymbol{C}$ be a convex compact subset of the basic space and let $\boldsymbol{A}$ be a closed extremal set of $\boldsymbol{C}$. Then $\boldsymbol{A}$ contains an extremal point of $\boldsymbol{C}$.

Proof
$\boldsymbol{A}$ is compact, because closed subsets of compact sets are compact sets by Th.E8. Let F_0 be fixed in $\boldsymbol{A}$. Let $s:=\sup_{F\in A} d(F_0,F)$. By Theorem E12, a point $F\in\boldsymbol{A}$ exists, such that $d(F_0,F)=s$. In order to show that F is an extremal point of $\boldsymbol{C}$, we assume that

$$F=pG+qH \,;\, p+q=1 \,;\, p,q>0 \,;\, G,H\in \boldsymbol{C}.$$

From these relations, and $F\in\boldsymbol{A}$, results that $G,H\in\boldsymbol{A}$ because $\boldsymbol{A}$ is an extremal set of $\boldsymbol{C}$. Then $d(F_0,G)\leq s$, $d(F_0,H)\leq s$, by the definition of s. Hence,

$$pd^2(F_0,G)+qd^2(F_0,H) \leq s^2 = d^2(F_0,F) = d^2(F_0,pG+qH),$$

$$p\int(F_0-G)^2dI + q\int(F_0-H)^2dI \leq \int[p(F_0-G)+q(F_0-H)]^2dI\,.$$

The development of the square in the last integral furnishes the inequality

$$pq\int(G-H)^2dI \leq 0.$$

Hence, $d^2(G,H)=0$, $G=H=F$ •

Corollary

Any convex compact set $\boldsymbol{C}$ in the basic space has extremal points.

Proof
$\boldsymbol{C}$ is an extremal set of itself •

Theorem E15

Let T be a continuous linear functional on the basic space and *C* a convex compact set in this space. Let s:=inf$_{F\in C}$ TF, *A*:={F/F∈*C*, TF=s}. Then *A*≠∅, *A* is an extremal set of *C* and TF$_0$=s for some extremal point F$_0$ of *C*.

Proof
We prove that *A*≠∅. Let F_n∈*C* (n=1,2,...) be a sequence such that $TF_n \to s$ as n↑∞. By the compactness of *C*, a subsequence F_{n_k} (k=1,2,...) and a function F∈*C* exist, such that $F_{n_k} \to_d F$. Then $TF_{n_k} \to TF$ by the continuity of T. But also $TF_{n_k} \to s$. Hence, TF=s, F∈*A*, *A*≠∅.

In order to prove that *A* is an extremal set of *C*, we assume that

$$F=pG+qH\in \boldsymbol{A}\ ;\ p+q=1\ ;\ p,q>0\ ;\ G,H\in \boldsymbol{C}\ .$$

Then s=TF=pTG+qTH. This is only possible if TG=TH=s, because TG≥s and TH≥s by the definition of s. Hence, G,H∈*A*.

The set *A* is closed. Indeed, let us assume that F_n∈*A*, $F_n \to_d F$. Then F∈*C*, because *C* is closed. By the continuity of T on *C*, $s=TF_n \to TF$. Hence, TF=s, F∈*A*, *A* is closed.

By Theorem E14, *A* contains an extremal point F_0 of *C* and then s=TF_0 •

Theorem E16 (Krein-Milman on *Prob*[R$_+$;finite])

Let *C* be a convex compact subset of the basic space *Prob*[R$_+$;finite] and let *E* be the set of extremal points of *C*. Then *E*≠∅ and C=Co$^-$*E*.

Proof
The set *E* is not void by the Corollary of Theorem E14.

E is a subset of the closed convex set *C*. This implies that co$^-$*E*⊆*C*. We derive a contradiction from the assumption that this inclusion is strict.

Let G_0∈*C*−co$^-$*E*. The set Co$^-$E is compact by Th.E8, because it is a closed subset of the compact set *C*. By the Hahn-Banach Theorem E13, applied to Co$^-$E and G_0, a continuous linear functional T exists on the basic space and a number a∈**R** exists, such that

$$TG_0 < a \leq TF \quad (F \in Co^- \boldsymbol{E}). \tag{E1}$$

By Theorem E15, an extremal point F_0 of $\boldsymbol{C}$ exists, such that

$$TF_0 = \inf_{F \in \boldsymbol{C}} TF =: s.$$

Then $F_0 \in \boldsymbol{E} \subseteq Co^- \boldsymbol{E}$ and by (E1), we have the contradiction

$$s \leq TG_0 < a \leq TF_0 = s,$$

where the first inequality results from the definition of s and because $G_0 \in \boldsymbol{C}$ •

Remark

The foregoing Krein-Milman Theorem is valid in case of subsets $\boldsymbol{C}$ of the space ***Prob***[$\mathbf{R}_+$;[0,μ_1]]. Then d-convergence may be replaced everywhere (also in the definition of compact sets) by weak convergence. Indeed, these convergences are equivalent on ***Prob***[$\mathbf{R}_+$;[0,μ_1]] by Th.E5.b.

In particular, the weak convergence version of the Krein-Milman Theorem is valid in case of subsets $\boldsymbol{C}$ of the space ***Prob***[[a,b]] of probability distributions concentrated on the compact interval $[a,b] \subseteq \mathbf{R}_+$. Obviously, the Theorem remains valid after translations of [a,b]. Hence,

The weak convergence version of the Krein-Milman Theorem is valid in case of subsets *C* of the space *Prob*[[a,b]] of probability distributions concentrated on the compact interval [a,b]⊆R.

II.Ch.2.Th.9 is the latter version of the Krein-Milman Theorem. In Part II, only weak convergence of distributions is considered.

Extension

With a couple of modifications in the proofs, the Krein-Milman Theorem remains valid when the basic space is replaced by the space of probability distributions F on $\mathbf{R}$ with finite first absolute moment

$$\int_{\mathbf{R}} |x| dF(x) = \int_{]-\infty,0]} F dI + \int_{[0,\infty[} (1-F) dI < \infty$$

Then

$$d^2(F,G) := \int_{\mathbf{R}} (F-G)^2 dI \leq \int_{\mathbf{R}} |F-G| dI$$

$$\leq \int_{]-\infty,0]} F dI + \int_{]-\infty,0]} G dI + \int_{[0,\infty[} (1-F) dI + \int_{[0,\infty[} (1-G) dI < \infty,$$

for any distributions F and G in the new larger basic space.

Appendix F

Orthogonal Projections in Hilbert Space

Hilbert spaces are finite or infinite-dimensional spaces with a geometrical structure very close to that of the familiar eucledean spaces $\mathbf{R}^n$.

F1. Definition of Hilbert Space

A Hilbert space *H*

a. **Is a linear space**

b. **Equipped with a scalar product $<\cdot,\cdot>$**

c. **Such that the normed space resulting from the corresponding norm is complete.**

We explain the different components of this definition.

a. ***H* is a linear space.**

This means that all linear combinations of points X,Y,... in ***H*** belong to ***H*** and that they can be transformed according to the usual rules:

$$X+Y=Y+X\ ,\ a(bX+cY)=(ab)X+(ac)Y\ ,\ \ldots$$

The usual practical Hilbert spaces are **functional spaces**, i.e. families of real functions defined on some fixed space and then the usual transformation rules are automatically valid.

b. ***H* is equipped with a scalar product $<\cdot,\cdot>$**

A **scalar product on a linear space *H*** is a real function $<X,Y>$ of $X,Y\in \boldsymbol{H}$, with the following properties, to be valid for all points $X,Y,X_1,\ldots,X_k$ in ***H***:

$$<X,X> \geq 0, \qquad \text{(F1)}$$

$$<X,X> = 0 \Leftrightarrow X=0, \qquad \text{(F1)}$$

$$<X,Y> = <Y,X>, \qquad \text{(F1)}$$

$$<a_1X_1+...+a_kX_k,Y> = a_1<X_1,Y>+...+a_k<X_k,Y>. \qquad (F1)$$

The latter property is the **linearity in the first variable.** Of course, the linearity in the first variable and the **commutativity** (third relation) imply the **linearity in the second variable**.

A **norm on a linear space *H*** is a real function $||X||$ of $X \in \boldsymbol{H}$, with the following properties, valid for all X,Y,Z in ***H*** :

$$||X|| \geq 0, \qquad (F2)$$

$$||X||=0 \Leftrightarrow X=0, \qquad (F2)$$

$$||aX|| = |a|.||X||, \qquad (F2)$$

$$||X+Y|| \leq ||X||+||Y||. \qquad (F2)$$

The norm is defined from the scalar product by the relation

$$||X|| := <X,X>^{1/2} \ (X \in \boldsymbol{H}). \qquad (F3)$$

The following relations (F4) and (F5), and then also the relations (F2), result from (F1) and from the definition (F3).

$$||X+Y||^2 = ||X||^2 + ||Y||^2 +2 <X,Y>, \qquad (F4)$$

$$||X+Y||^2+||X-Y||^2 = 2||X||^2 + 2||Y||^2 \ \text{(Parallelogram identity)}, \qquad (F5)$$

$$|<X,Y>| \leq ||X||.||Y|| \ \text{(Schwarz)}.$$

The relations (F4), (F5) are direct from the definitions. Schwarz is obvious when $||Y||=0$. If $||Y||\neq 0$, then Schwarz results from

$$0 \leq ||X+aY||^2 = ||X||^2 + a^2||Y||^2 + 2a<X,Y> \text{, with } a= ||X||/||Y|| .$$

The last relation (F2), squared, results from Schwarz.

c. ***H*, equipped with the norm $||\cdot||$, is a complete normed space**.

A **normed space** is a linear space ***H*** equipped with a norm $||\cdot||$. This norm induces a topology on ***H*** for which the convergence of single and double sequences is defined as follows:

$$\lim_{n\uparrow\infty} X_n = X :\Leftrightarrow \lim_{n\uparrow\infty} ||X_n-X|| =0,$$

$$\lim_{m\uparrow\infty,n\uparrow\infty} X_{mn} = X :\Leftrightarrow \lim_{m\uparrow\infty,n\uparrow\infty} ||X_{mn}-X|| =0.$$

A **Cauchy sequence** in a normed space ***H*** is a sequence X_n such that

$$\lim_{m\uparrow\infty,n\uparrow\infty} (X_m - X_n) = 0.$$

The normed space ***H*** is **complete** if each Cauchy sequence in ***H*** converges to some point of ***H***. A **Banach space** is a complete normed space. Hence, **Hilbert spaces are particular Banach spaces.**

Orthogonality in Hilbert space H

The **orthogonality** of $X,Y\in\boldsymbol{H}$ is defined and denoted as follows:

$$X\perp Y :\Leftrightarrow \langle X,Y\rangle = 0.$$

Example

$\mathbf{R}^n$ is a Hilbert space, for the usual scalar product defined by

$$\langle x,y\rangle = x_1y_1+\ldots+x_ny_n \quad (x,y\in\mathbf{R}^n),$$

where $x_1,\ldots,x_n$ are the coordinates of x and $y_1,\ldots,y_n$ those of y. $\mathbf{R}^n$ can be regarded as the family of real functions defined on the set $\{1,\ldots,n\}$. Hence, $\mathbf{R}^n$ is a functional space.

F2. Projections

The **distance of the points** X,Y in the Hilbert space ***H*** is the number

$$d(X,Y) := ||X-Y||.$$

The **distance of the point** $X\in\boldsymbol{H}$ **to the set** $\boldsymbol{A}\subseteq\boldsymbol{H}$ is the number

$$d(X,\boldsymbol{A}) = \inf_{Z\in\boldsymbol{A}} d(X,Z).$$

Theorem F1 (Existence of Projections Theorem)

Let *C* be a closed convex set in the Hilbert space *H* and let X be a point of *H*. Then *C* contains a unique point Y such that d(X,Y)=d(X,*C*).

Proof
Let Z_m be a sequence of points in ***C*** such that $d(X,Z_m)\to d(X,\boldsymbol{C})$ as $m\uparrow\infty$. We prove that Z_m is a Cauchy sequence. By the parallelogram identity:

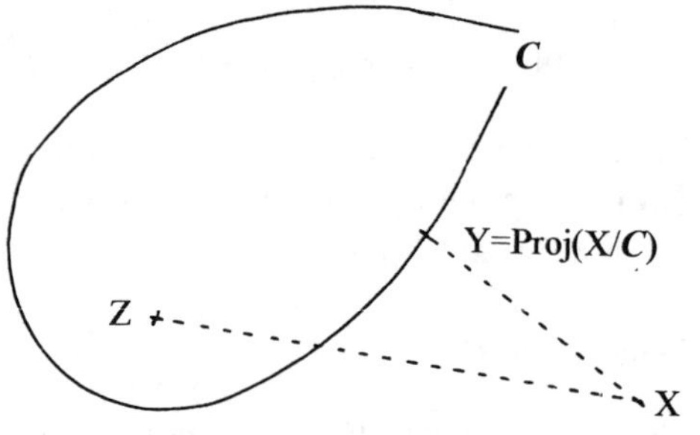

Fig.36. Projection on a convex set

$$||(X-Z_m)+(X-Z_n)||^2 + ||Z_n-Z_m||^2 =$$

$$||(X-Z_m)+(X-Z_n)||^2 + ||(X-Z_m)-(X-Z_n)||^2 = 2||X-Z_m||^2 + 2||X-Z_n||^2.$$

The point $1/2(Z_m+Z_n)$ belongs to $\boldsymbol{C}$ because $\boldsymbol{C}$ is convex. Hence

$$4d^2(X,\boldsymbol{C}) \leq 4||X-1/2(Z_m+Z_n)||^2 = ||(X-Z_m)+(X-Z_n)||^2.$$

Then

$$4d^2(X,\boldsymbol{C}|| + ||Z_n-Z_m||^2 \leq 2||X-Z_m||^2 + 2||X-Z_n||^2.$$

We take the double limit for $m\uparrow\infty, n\uparrow\infty$. The last member tends to $4d^2(X,\boldsymbol{C})$. Hence

$$\lim_{m\uparrow\infty,n\uparrow\infty} ||Z_n-Z_m|| \leq 0.$$

This inequality must be an equality. This proves that Z_m is a Cauchy sequence. Then Z_m converges to some point Y in $\boldsymbol{H}$. This point Y belongs to $\boldsymbol{C}$ because $\boldsymbol{C}$ is closed. Then

$$d(X,Y) = \lim_{m\uparrow\infty} d(X,Z_m) = d(X,\boldsymbol{C}).$$

This proves the existence of Y. For the unicity, let Y and Z be points in $\boldsymbol{C}$ such that

$$d(X,Y) = d(X,\boldsymbol{C}) \ , \ d(X,Z) = d(X,\boldsymbol{C}).$$

Then the point $1/2\,(Y+Z)$ belongs to $\boldsymbol{C}$ and

$$2||X-Y||^2 + 2||X-Z||^2 = 4d^2(X,\boldsymbol{C}) \leq 4||X-1/2(Y+Z)||^2$$

$$= ||(X-Y)+(X-Z)||^2 = ||X-Y||^2 + ||X-Z||^2 + 2<X-Y,X-Z>,$$

$$||X-Y||^2 + ||X-Z||^2 - 2<X-Y,X-Z> \leq 0.$$

The first member of the latter relation equals

$$||(X-Y)-(X-Z)||^2 = ||Z-Y||^2.$$

Hence $||Z-Y||=0$, $Z=Y$ •

The unique point Y occurring in the statement of Theorem F1, is the (orthogonal) **projection of X on *C***. We denote it by Proj(X/*C*). It is the point of *C* closest to X.

A **plane,** in a linear space *H*, is a subspace containing the affine combinations of its points. We recall that an **affine combination** is a linear combination $\Sigma_i a_i X_i$ with $\Sigma_i a_i=1$. A plane is also called an **affine subspace** of *H*.

A **linear subspace** (or a **vector subspace**) of *H*, is a subspace containing the linear combinations of its points. The linear subspaces of *H* contain the point 0. Indeed, if X is any point of the linear subspace *L* of *H*, then the linear combination $0.X=0$ belongs to *L*. Planes do not necessarily contain the origin 0.

A plane is a linear subspace iff it contains 0. Indeed, if the plane *P* contains 0, then the linear combination $a_1X_1+...+a_kX_k$ of points $X_1,...,X_k$ in *P* equals the affine combination $a_1X_1+...+a_kX_k+[1-(a_1+...+a_k)].0$ of the points $X_1,...,X_k,0$ in *P*. Hence, the linear subspaces of *H* are its **planes through the origin.**

Theorem F2 (Projection Theorem)

Let *P* be a closed plane in the Hilbert space *H* and let X,Y∈*H*. Then

$$\mathbf{Y = Proj(X/\mathit{P}) \quad \Leftrightarrow \quad Y \in \mathit{P},\ X-Y \perp Z-Y\ (Z \in \mathit{P}).} \tag{F6}$$

If *P* is a linear closed subspace of *H*, then

$$\mathbf{Y = Proj(X/\mathit{P}) \quad \Leftrightarrow \quad Y \in \mathit{P},\ X-Y \perp Z\ (Z \in \mathit{P}).} \tag{F7}$$

Proof

In order to prove the ⇒ part of (F6), let Y=Proj(X/*P*) and let Z∈*P*. For any Z′ in *P*,

$$||X-Y||^2 \leq ||X-Z'||^2 = ||X-Y||^2 + ||Y-Z'||^2 + 2<X-Y, Y-Z'>,$$

$$0 \leq ||Y-Z'||^2 + 2<X-Y, Y-Z'>.$$

In particular, for

$$Z' := Y+a(Z-Y) = (1-a)Y+aZ \in \mathit{P},$$

we obtain

$$0 \leq a^2||Z-Y||^2 - 2a<X-Y, Z-Y>$$

and if a is replaced by −a:

$$0 \le a^2\|Z-Y\|^2 + 2a\langle X-Y, Z-Y\rangle.$$

Now we consider the latter relations for a>0, we divide by a, and we let $a\downarrow 0$. The conclusion is that $\langle X-Y, Z-Y\rangle$ is both positive and negative. Hence, this scalar product equals 0, i.e. $X-Y\perp Z-Y$.

In order to prove the $\Leftarrow$ part of (F6), we suppose $Y\in \boldsymbol{P}$, $X-Y\perp Z-Y$ $(Z\in \boldsymbol{P})$. Then, for all $Z\in \boldsymbol{P}$,

$$\|X-Z\|^2 = \|X-Y\|^2 + \|Y-Z\|^2 \ , \ \|X-Y\|^2 \le \|X-Z\|^2.$$

In the latter relation, we take the inf for $Z\in \boldsymbol{P}$: $\|X-Y\|^2 \le d^2(X,\boldsymbol{P})$. This inequality can only be an equality, because $Y\in \boldsymbol{P}$.

In order to prove (F7), let $\boldsymbol{P}$ be linear. It is sufficient to prove the equivalence

$$X-Y\perp Z-Y \ (Z\in \boldsymbol{P}) \Leftrightarrow X-Y\perp Z' \ (Z'\in \boldsymbol{P}),$$

for fixed Y in $\boldsymbol{P}$ and X in $\boldsymbol{H}$. The $\Rightarrow$ part holds because we can take $Z=Z'+Y$ in the left member. The $\Leftarrow$ part is true, because we can take $Z'=Z-Y$ in the right member •

Theorem F3 (Iterated Projections on Planes)

Let $\boldsymbol{P},\boldsymbol{Q}$ be closed planes in the Hilbert space $\boldsymbol{H}$, $\boldsymbol{P}\subseteq\boldsymbol{Q}$ and $X\in\boldsymbol{H}$. Then

$$\mathbf{Proj(Proj(X/\boldsymbol{P})/\boldsymbol{Q}) = Proj(X/\boldsymbol{P})} \ , \ \mathbf{Proj(Proj(X/\boldsymbol{Q})/\boldsymbol{P}) = Proj(X/\boldsymbol{P})} .$$

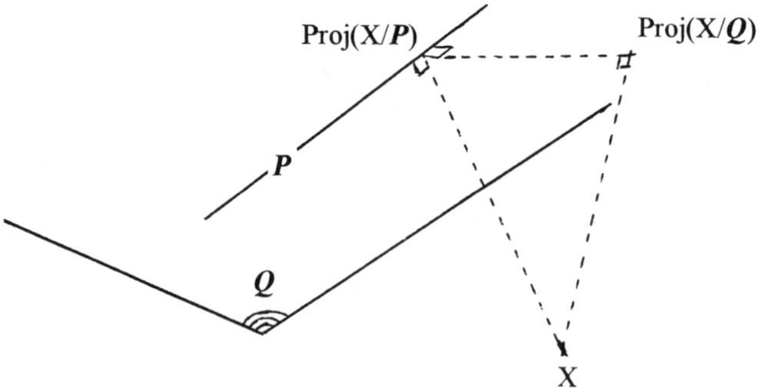

Fig.37. Iterated projection

Proof
The first formula is tautological because the projection of X on $\boldsymbol{P}$ is already a point of $\boldsymbol{Q}$. The second relation is obvious from the geometry of Fig.37 (an analytical proof based on the projection Theorem F2 is easy) •

Theorem F4 (Linearity of Projection on a Linear Space)

Let $\boldsymbol{P}$ be a closed linear subspace of the Hilbert space $\boldsymbol{H}$ and let X,Y be points in $\boldsymbol{H}$. Then

$$\mathrm{Proj}(aX+bY/\boldsymbol{P}) = a\,\mathrm{Proj}(X/\boldsymbol{P}) + b\,\mathrm{Proj}(Y/\boldsymbol{P}).$$

Proof
The Theorem results from three applications of the equivalence (F7) of the projection Theorem F3. Let $U:=\mathrm{Proj}(X/\boldsymbol{P})$, $V:=\mathrm{Proj}(Y/\boldsymbol{P})$. Let Z be any point in $\boldsymbol{P}$. Then

$$X-U \perp Z\ ,\ X-V \perp Z\ ,\ (aX+bY)-(aU+bV) = a(X-U)+b(Y-V) \perp Z.$$

Hence,

$$(aX+bY)-(aU+bV) \perp Z\ (Z\in\boldsymbol{P})\ ,\ aU+bV = \mathrm{Proj}(aX+bY/\boldsymbol{P})\ \bullet$$

Theorem F5

Any finite dimensional plane, in a Hilbert space, is closed.

Proof
For any set $\boldsymbol{S}$ in the Hilbert space $\boldsymbol{H}$ and any point X_0 of $\boldsymbol{H}$, we define the **translated set** $\boldsymbol{S}+X_0:=\{X+X_0/X\in\boldsymbol{S}\}$. Then $\boldsymbol{S}$ is closed iff $\boldsymbol{S}_0$ is closed.

Let $\boldsymbol{P}$ be an n-dimensional plane in $\boldsymbol{H}$. Let X_0 be a fixed point of $\boldsymbol{P}$ and let $\boldsymbol{P}_0$ be the translated set $\boldsymbol{P}_0:=\boldsymbol{P}-X_0\equiv\boldsymbol{P}+(-X_0)$. Then $\boldsymbol{P}_0$ is a plane through the origin, i.e. a linear subspace of $\boldsymbol{H}$. We prove that $\boldsymbol{P}_0$ is closed. The n-dimensional vector space $\boldsymbol{P}_0$, endowed with the scalar product $<\ ,\ >$, has an **orthonormal basis**, i.e. a basis $X_1,\dots,X_n$ such that

$$<X_i,X_i> = 1\ ,\ <X_i,X_j> = 0\ (i\neq j).$$

Let Y_k (k=1,2,...) be a sequence of points in $\boldsymbol{P}_0$ such that $Y_k\to Y\in\boldsymbol{H}$ as $k\uparrow\infty$. We have to prove that $Y\in\boldsymbol{P}_0$. Each vector Y_k can be displayed as a linear combination of the vectors $X_1,\dots,X_n$ of the basis:

$$Y_k = a_{k1}X_1 + \dots + a_{kn}X_n.$$

Then

$$\|Y-Y_k\|^2 = \langle Y-\textstyle\sum_{1\le i\le n} a_{ki}X_i , Y-\sum_{1\le i\le n} a_{ki}X_i\rangle$$
$$= \|Y\|^2 - 2\textstyle\sum_i a_{ki}\langle Y,X_i\rangle + \sum_i (a_{ki})^2.$$

The last member converges to 0 as $k\uparrow\infty$. This implies that the n sequences a_{k0}, ..., a_{kn} (k=1,2,...) are bounded. Indeed, if the sequence a_{ki} (i fixed) is not bounded, we can take a subsequence, and we may assume that $\lim_{k\uparrow\infty} a_{ki} = \pm\infty$. But then

$$(a_{ki})^2 - 2a_{ki}\langle Y,X_i\rangle \to +\infty \text{ as } k\uparrow\infty$$

and then it is clear that $\|Y-Y_k\|^2 \to \infty$. Hence, taking subsequences, we may assume that $\lim_{k\uparrow\infty} a_{ki} =: a_i < \infty$ (i=1,2,...,n). Then

$$\|Y-Y_k\| \to \|Y\|^2 - 2\textstyle\sum_i a_i\langle Y,X_i\rangle + \sum_i (a_i)^2 = \|Y-\sum_i a_iX_i\| .$$

This limit is 0, because $Y_k \to Y$. Hence $Y=\sum_i a_iX_i \in \boldsymbol{P}_0$ •

F3. Spaces of Random Variables

The space $\boldsymbol{L}$ is **the space of finite random variables** defined on some fixed probability space **($\Omega, \mathfrak{I}$, P). Almost surely equal random variables are identified**. Hence, **X=Y** means in fact that **X=Y a.s.** Mostly, we omit the **a.s.** indication. We consider the spaces

$\boldsymbol{L}_1 = \{X\in\boldsymbol{L} \,/\, E|X| < \infty\}$ (Space of **integrable random variables**),

$\boldsymbol{L}_2 = \{X\in\boldsymbol{L} \,/\, E(X^2) < \infty\}$ (Space of **square-integrable random variables**).

$\boldsymbol{L}_+$ is the space of positive random variables, possibly with infinite values. The products $0.\infty$ and $\infty.0$ equal 0 by definition.

The spaces $\boldsymbol{L}$, $\boldsymbol{L}_1$, $\boldsymbol{L}_2$ are linear. The space $\boldsymbol{L}_+$ is conical (i.e. it contains the linear combinations with positive coefficients of its points).

The expectation E(X) of any positive random variable exists, but it may be infinite. The **Schwarz inequality, for random variables $X,Y\in\boldsymbol{L}_+$** is

$$E^2(XY) \le E(X^2)E(Y^2) \quad (X,Y\in\boldsymbol{L}_+) \quad \text{(Schwarz).} \qquad \text{(F8)}$$

For $Y\equiv1$:

$$E(X^2)<\infty \Rightarrow E(X)<\infty \text{ , i.e. } \boldsymbol{L}_2\subseteq\boldsymbol{L}_1.$$

$$[E(X^2)<\infty, E(Y^2)<\infty] \Rightarrow E|XY|<\infty,$$

by Schwarz, i.e.

$$X,Y \in \boldsymbol{L}_2 \Rightarrow XY \in \boldsymbol{L}_1.$$

It is a classical result of MeasureTheory that $\boldsymbol{L}_2$ **is a complete normed space (i.e. a Banach space) when it is equipped with the norm**

$$||X|| = E^{1/2}(X^2) \quad (X \in \boldsymbol{L}_2). \tag{F9}$$

Several types of convergence can be considered on $\boldsymbol{L}_2$. Hereafter it is always norm-convergence.

The function $<\cdot,\cdot>$ with values

$$<X,Y> = E(XY) \quad (X,Y \in \boldsymbol{L}_2) \tag{F10}$$

is a scalar product on $\boldsymbol{L}_2$ and the corresponding norm is (F9). Hence, $\boldsymbol{L}_2$ **equipped with the scalar product (F10), is a Hilbert space**.

An **interval in $\mathbf{R}^n$** is the cartesian product of n intervals in **R**. The **Borel σ-algebra on $\mathbf{R}^n$** is the smallest σ-algebra containing the intervals of $\mathbf{R}^n$. A **Borel set in $\mathbf{R}^n$** is a set belonging to the Borel σ–algebra on $\mathbf{R}^n$. The mapping $\varphi:\mathbf{R}^m \to \mathbf{R}^n$, is a **Borel mapping** if it is measurable with respect to the Borel σ-algebra on $\mathbf{R}^m$ and the Borel σ-algebra on $\mathbf{R}^n$ (i.e. if $\varphi^{-1}(B)$ is a Borel set in $\mathbf{R}^m$ for any Borel set B in $\mathbf{R}^n$). A **Borel function on $\mathbf{R}^n$** is a Borel mapping defined on $\mathbf{R}^n$, with values in **R**. Positive functions f with infinite values are considered on $\mathbf{R}^n$. Then f is a **Borel function on $\mathbf{R}^n$** if $f^{-1}(\infty)$ is a Borel set in $\mathbf{R}^n$ and if $f^{-1}(B)$ is a Borel set in $\mathbf{R}^n$ for any Borel set B in **R**.

Hereafter, f, g, ... denote Borel functions on some $\mathbf{R}^n$. The value of the integer n is clear from the context in any particular case.

A random vector is a vector $Y=(Y_1,\ldots,Y_n)$ with elements $Y_k \in \boldsymbol{L}$. For any random vector Y, we consider the space

$$\boldsymbol{F}_2(Y) := \{f(Y) \,/\, f \text{ finite Borel function such that } f(Y) \in \boldsymbol{L}_2\}.$$

Theorem F6

The space $\boldsymbol{F}_2(Y)$ (Y random vector) is a closed linear subspace of the Hilbert space $\boldsymbol{L}_2$.

Proof

The linearity is evident. In order to prove that $\boldsymbol{F}_2(Y)$ is closed, let $f_k(Y)$ be a sequence in $\boldsymbol{F}_2(Y)$ and let Z be a point in $\boldsymbol{L}_2$ such that $f_k(Y) \to Z$ as $k \uparrow \infty$. Replacing $f_k(Y)$ by a subsequence, we may assume that $f_k(Y) \to Z$ a.s. (Convergence of a sequence in $\boldsymbol{L}_2$ implies convergence a.s. for some subsequence). Let g and f be the functions defined on $\mathbf{R}^n$ by

$$g := \lim \sup_{k \uparrow \infty} f_k \ , \quad f = g 1_{g<\infty}.$$

Then f is a Borel function on $\mathbf{R}^n$, and $Z=f(Y)$ a.s. Indeed, for all ω in the set $\Omega_0 \subseteq \Omega$ on which $f_k(Y)$ converges to Z,

$$g(Y(\omega)) = \lim \sup_{k \uparrow \infty} f_k(Y(\omega))$$

$$= \lim_{k \uparrow \infty} f_k(Y(\omega)) = Z(\omega) < \infty.$$

Hence, $f(Y)=Z \in \boldsymbol{L}_2$, i.e. $Z \in \boldsymbol{F}_2(Y)$ •

In the preceding proof, f_k converges on the set $Y(\Omega_0)$, but not necessarily on its complement. This explains the consideration of the lim sup. Of course, the lim inf could do the job as well.

Planes in Hilbert spaces are not necessarily closed, and projections on non-closed planes do not necessarily exist. This can be reconciled with our 3-dimensional **visualization** as follows. We **imagine** that not closed planes are full of infinitesimal gaps (such as the gaps in the line of rational points). If we try to project a point on such a plane, we can fall in a gap, and then the projection does not exist.

Here is a simple **example of a plane through the origin, not closed in $\boldsymbol{L}_2$**. Let the basic probability space be]0,1] with the Lebesgue measure on the Borel subsets. Let $\boldsymbol{B}$ be the space of bounded Borel functions on]0,1]. Then $\boldsymbol{B}$ is a linear subspace of $\boldsymbol{L}_2$. In order to show that $\boldsymbol{B}$ is not closed in $\boldsymbol{L}_2$, let f be an unbounded positive square-integrable Borel function on]0,1], for instance $f(x):=x^{-1/3}$ $(0<x\leq 1)$. Let $f_k:=f 1_{f\leq k}$. Then $f_k \in \boldsymbol{B}$, and as $k \uparrow \infty$, by dominated convergence,

$$\|f-f_k\|^2 = \|f\, 1_{f>k}\|^2$$

$$= \int_{]0,1]} f^2(x) 1_{f(x)>k}\, dx \downarrow 0 \text{ as } k \uparrow \infty.$$

This means that $f_k \to f \notin B$ in $\boldsymbol{L}_2$.

F4. Conditional Expectations

The conditional expectation of the random variable $X \in L_2$, for fixed random vector Y, is defined by

$$\mathbf{E(X/Y) := Proj(X/}\boldsymbol{F}_2\mathbf{(Y))}. \qquad \text{(F11)}$$

By (F7),

$$[f(Y) = E(X/Y)] \Leftrightarrow [f(Y) \in \boldsymbol{F}_2(Y), X - f(Y) \perp Z \ (Z \in \boldsymbol{F}_2(Y))]$$

$$\Leftrightarrow [f(Y) \in \boldsymbol{F}_2(Y), E[f(Y)Z] = E[XZ] \ (Z \in \boldsymbol{F}_2(Y))].$$

It is direct that $Z \in \boldsymbol{F}_2(Y)$ can be replaced by Z=h(Y), where h is any bounded positive Borel function, in the latter equivalences. Hence, we can re-formulate the definition (F11) and combine it with the existence and unicity of the projection (Theorem F1), as follows.

Theorem F7 (Definition of E(X/Y) for Square-Integrable X)

Let Y be a random vector, X a square-integrable random variable. Then a unique square-integrable random variable f(Y) exists, such that

$$\mathbf{E[f(Y)h(Y)] = E[Xh(Y)]} \quad \textbf{(h bounded positive Borel function).}$$

Then E(X/Y):= f(Y) is ***the conditional expectation of X for fixed Y*** •

If X_1, X_2 are square-integrable, such that $X_1 \leq X_2$, then I.Ch.2.Th.1 implies that $E(X_1/Y) \leq E(X_2/Y)$. In particular, if X is square-integrable positive, then E(X/Y) is square-integrable positive.

Let X be any positive random variable. Then $X1_{X \leq k}$ is a bounded random variable and the preceding Theorem can be applied to it. Letting $k \uparrow \infty$, the following Theorem-Definition is obtained. The unicity results from I.Ch.2. Th.1.

Theorem F8 (Definition of E(X/Y) for Positive X)

Let Y be a random vector, X a positive random variable. Then a unique positive random variable f(Y) exists, such that

$$\mathbf{E[f(Y)h(Y)] = E[Xh(Y)]} \quad \textbf{(h bounded positive Borel function).}$$

Then E(X/Y):= f(Y) is ***the conditional expectation of X for fixed Y*** •

In this Theorem X and E(X/Y) may have infinite values.

For $h \equiv 1$ in Theorem F8, we obtain E[E(X/Y)]=EX. Hence,

If X is positive and integrable, then E(X/Y) is positive and integrable.

Integrable random variables are finite (a.s.). Hence differences of such random variables can be considered. For X integrable, Theorem F8, applied to X_+ and X_- furnishes the following Theorem-Definition. Again the unicity results from I.Ch.2.Th.1.

Theorem F9 (Definition of E(X/Y) for Integrable X)

Let Y be a random vector, X an integrable random variable. Then a unique integrable random variable f(Y) exists, such that

$$E[f(Y)h(Y)] = E[Xh(Y)] \quad \text{(h bounded positive Borel function).}$$

Then E(X/Y):= f(Y) is *the conditional expectation of X for fixed Y* •

$E(X/Y)=E(X/\beta_Y)$, where β_Y is the σ-algebra generated by Y (i.e. the smallest σ-algebra for which the components of Y are measurable). Conditionings by sub-σ-algebras (of the σ-algebra on the basic probability space on which all random variables are defined) are not considered in this book.

In Modern Credibility Theory, the conditionings by a random variable Θ can be replaced everywhere by conditionings by a σ-algebra β. This generalizes the mathematics, but it obscures the interpretations.

Appendix G

Characteristic Functions

G1. The Subsequence Criterion for Weak Convergence

Theorem G1 **(Subsequence Criterion for Weak Convergence)**

Let F_n (n=1,2,...) be a pointwise bounded sequence (App.E.E1) of distribution functions. Then $F_n \to_w F$ iff the following condition is satisfied:

Any subsequence $F_{n'}$ of F_n has a subsequence $F_{n''}$ such that $F_{n''} \to_w F$. (G1)

Proof
If $F_n \to_w F$, then (G1) is satisfied by App.E.Th.E2.a.

Conversely let (G1) be satisfied. We assume that F is not the weak limit of the sequence F_n (n=1,2,...) and we derive a contradiction. A continuity point c of F exists such that $F_n(c)$ does not converge to F(c). Then a subsequence $F_{n'}$ exists such that $F_{n'}(c) \to a \neq F(c)$. By the general compactness Theorem (App.E.Th.E3), a subsequence $F_{n''}$ of $F_{n'}$ and a distribution G exist such that $F_{n''} \to_w G$. By (G1), a subsequence $F_{n'''}$ of $F_{n''}$ exists such that $F_{n'''} \to_w F$. By App.E.Th.E2, $F_{n'''} \to_w G$ because $F_{n''} \to_w G$, and then F=G. Hence, c is a continuity point of G and $F_{n'''}(c) \to G(c)=F(c)$. But $F_{n'''}(c) \to a$ because $F_{n'}(c) \to a$. We then have the contradiction F(c)=a •

G2. Helly-Bray Theorem

A continuous function of bounded variation, defined on the interval $I \subseteq \mathbf{R}$, is a function f expressible as a difference F–G of continuous increasing functions F and G on I. All "elementary" continuous functions on compact intervals are continuous functions of bounded variation. We now prove a particular case of the Helly-Bray Theorem (I.Ch.1.Th.7). Only this particular case is used in the applications.

Theorem G2 (Helly-Bray)

See statement I.Ch.1.Th.7.

Proof (in case f is a continuous function of bounded variation on compact intervals)

a. (Case of bounded integration domain). We may assume that f is a continuous increasing function on $[a-1,b+1]$ because f can be displayed as a difference of two functions of this kind, and the result can be applied to each of them. Then, by an integration by parts, by dominated convergence and by another integration by parts,

$$\int_{(a\pm,b\pm)} f dF_n = f(b\pm)F_n(b\pm)-f(a\pm)F_n(a\pm) - \int_{(a\pm,b\pm)} F_n df$$

$$\to f(b\pm)F(b\pm)-f(a\pm)F(a\pm) - \int_{(a\pm,b\pm)} F df = \int_{(a\pm,b\pm)} f dF.$$

b. (Case of integrand f vanishing at $\pm\infty$). Let c and d be continuity points of F. Then

$$\left|\int_{\mathbf{R}} f dF_n - \int_{\mathbf{R}} f dF\right| \leq \left|\int_{]c,d]} f dF_n - \int_{]c,d]} f dF\right| + \int_{\mathbf{C}]c,d]} |f| dF_n + \int_{\mathbf{C}]c,d]} |f| dF$$

$$\leq \left|\int_{]c,d]} f dF_n - \int_{]c,d]} f dF\right| + \mathrm{Sup}_{x\in\mathbf{C}]c,d]} |f(x)|.\mathrm{Sup}_n F_n(\mathbf{R}) + \mathrm{Sup}_{x\in\mathbf{C}]c,d]} |f(x)|.F(\mathbf{R}). \quad (G2)$$

$\mathrm{Sup}_n F_n(\mathbf{R})$ and $F(\mathbf{R})$ are finite because the distributions F_n are uniformly bounded. If c is small enough and d large enough, $|f|$ is as small as wanted outside $]c,d]$ because $f(\pm\infty)=0$. Hence, the two last terms of (G2) are less than $\varepsilon>0$ if the interval $]c,d]$ is large enough. Then

$$\left|\int_{\mathbf{R}} f dF_n - \int_{\mathbf{R}} f dF\right| \leq \left|\int_{]c,d]} f dF_n - \int_{]c,d]} f dF_n\right| + 2\varepsilon,$$

and by a,

$$\limsup_{n\uparrow\infty} \left|\int_{\mathbf{R}} f dF_n - \int_{\mathbf{R}} f dF\right| \leq 0 + 2\varepsilon.$$

c. (Case of total mass conservation). $F(\mathbf{C}]c,d])$ is as small as wanted if the interval $]c,d]$ large enough, because $F(\mathbf{R})$ is finite. Hence, continuity points c and d of F exist, such that

$$F(\mathbf{C}]c,d]) \leq \varepsilon.$$

Then n_0 exists such that

$$F_n(\mathbf{C}]c,d]) \leq 2\varepsilon \quad (n \geq n_0),$$

because

$$F_n(\mathbf{C}]c,d]) = F_n(\mathbf{R}) - F_n(]c,d]) = F_n(\mathbf{R}) - [F_n(d)-F_n(c)]$$

$$\to F(\mathbf{R}) - [F(d)-F(c)] = F(\mathbf{R}) - F(]c,d]) = F(\mathbf{C}]c,d]) \text{ as } n\uparrow\infty.$$

Then

$$\left|\int_{\mathbf{R}} f dF_n - \int_{\mathbf{R}} f dF\right| \leq \left|\int_{]c,d]} f dF_n - \int_{]c,d]} f dF\right| + \int_{\mathbf{C}]c,d]} |f| dF_n + \int_{\mathbf{C}]c,d]} |f| dF$$

$$\leq |\int_{]c,d]} fdF_n - \int_{]c,d]} fdF| + \text{Sup}|f|.F_n(\mathbf{C}]c,d]) + \text{Sup}|f|.F(\mathbf{C}]c,d])$$

$$\leq |\int_{]c,d]} fdF_n - \int_{]c,d]} fdF| + 3\varepsilon\, \text{Sup}|f| \quad (n \geq n_0).$$

By part a.,

$$\lim \sup_{n\uparrow\infty} |\int_{\mathbf{R}} fdF_n - \int_{\mathbf{R}} fdF| \leq 0 + 3\varepsilon\, \text{Sup}|f|,$$

where Sup|f| is finite •

G3. Complex Integrals

Let $\alpha(\cdot)$ be a function with complex values defined on the set $S \subseteq \mathbf{R}$. Then α can be displayed as $\alpha = f + gi$ where f and g are real functions on S, and i is the unit of imaginaries. The function α is **F-integrable on S** if f and g are F-integrable on S. Then

$$\int_S \alpha dF := \int_S fdF + i\int_S gdF. \tag{G3}$$

We notice that

$$|f| \leq (f^2+g^2)^{1/2} = |\alpha| \ , \ |g| \leq (f^2+g^2)^{1/2} = |\alpha|. \tag{G4}$$

Hence, **if $|\alpha|$ is F-integrable on S, then α is F-integrable on S.**

Theorem G3

Let the complex function $|\alpha|$ be F-integrable on S. Then

$$|\int_S \alpha dF| \leq \int_S |\alpha| dF. \tag{G5}$$

Proof

We omit S in the notations. Let $\alpha = f + gi$, where f and g are real. Then we must prove that

$$[(\int fdF)^2 + (\int gdF)^2]^{1/2} \leq \int (f^2+g^2)^{1/2}\, dF,$$

i.e.

$$(\int fdF)^2 + (\int gdF)^2 \leq (\int (f^2+g^2)^{1/2}\, dF)^2.$$

This is equivalent to the inequality

$$\int f(s)dF(s).\int f(t)dF(t) + \int g(s)dF(s).\int g(t)dF(t) \leq$$

$$\int (f^2(s)+g^2(s))^{1/2}\, dF(s).\int (f^2(t)+g^2(t))^{1/2}\, dF(t)$$

or

$$\iint [f(s)f(t)+g(s)g(t)]dF(s)dF(t)$$

$$\leq \iint (f^2(s)+g^2(s))^{1/2}\,(f^2(t)+g^2(t))^{1/2}\,dF(s)dF(t),$$

by Fubini. Hence, it is sufficient to verify that

$$f(s)f(t)+g(s)g(t) \leq (f^2(s)+g^2(s))^{1/2}\,(f^2(t)+g^2(t))^{1/2}$$

or

$$[f(s)f(t)+g(s)g(t)]^2 \leq (f^2(s)+g^2(s))\,(f^2(t)+g^2(t)),$$

or

$$f^2(s)f^2(t)+2f(s)f(t)g(s)g(t)+g^2(s)g^2(t)$$

$$\leq f^2(s)f^2(t)+f^2(s)g^2(t)+g^2(s)f^2(t)+g^2(s)g^2(t).$$

This relation is the inequality

$$0 \leq [f(s)g(t)-g(s)f(t)]^2 \quad \bullet$$

G4. Characteristic and Integral Characteristic Functions

Preliminary remarks

Some integration domains are **oriented**: $\int_{[a,b]} := -\int_{[b,a]}$ if $b<a$.

We recall that

$$e^{it} = \cos t + i \sin t,\ \ |e^{it}| = 1\ \ (t\in\mathbf{R}). \tag{G6}$$

a.

$$\int_{]0,\infty[} (\sin t)/t\, dt := \lim_{c\uparrow\infty} \int_{]0,c]} (\sin t)/t\, dt = \pi/2. \tag{G7}$$

This is a classical result easily proved by complex function theory. For reasons of self-containedness, we supply a proof based on real analysis (found in Bauer (1981) p.118).

$$1/t = \int_{[0,\infty[} e^{-st}\, ds\ (t>0)$$

and then by Fubini,

$$\int_{]0,c]} (\sin t)/t\, dt = \int_{[0,\infty[}\Big[\int_{]0,c]} e^{-st} \sin t\, dt\Big]\, ds,$$

where the integral in square brackets in the last member can be calculated by App.K.(K5). The result is

$$\int_{]0,c]} (\sin t)/t\, dt = \int_{[0,\infty[}\big[(1-e^{-cs}\cos c - se^{-cs}\sin c)/(1+s^2)\big]\, ds.$$

By dominated convergence,

$$\lim_{c\uparrow\infty} \int_{]0,c]} (\sin t)/t\, dt = \int_{[0,\infty[} 1/(1+s^2)]ds = [\text{arc tg } s]_0^{\infty} = \pi/2.$$

The relation (G7) implies that

$$\int_{[a,b]} (\sin t)/t \, dt \text{ is a bounded function of } (a,b)\in\mathbf{R}^2. \qquad \text{(G8)}$$

b.

$$|\sin x| \le |x| \quad (x\in\mathbf{R}). \qquad \text{(G9)}$$

Indeed, by Maclaurin,

$$\sin x = \sin 0 + x \cos(\theta x) \quad (0<\theta<1).$$

c.

$$|e^{ib}-e^{ia}| \le |b-a| \quad (a,b\in\mathbf{R}). \qquad \text{(G10)}$$

Indeed,

$$e^{ib}-e^{ia} = e^{i(b+a)/2}[e^{i(b-a)/2} - e^{-i(b-a)/2}] = 2i\, e^{i(b+a)/2} \sin[(b-a)/2]$$

and then (G10) results from (G9) and $|e^{ic}|=1$ $(c\in\mathbf{R})$.

d.

$$\int_{[-c,+c]} (e^{ibt}-e^{iat})/(it)\, dt = 2\int_{[ac,bc]} (\sin t)/t \, dt \quad (c>0;\ a,b\in\mathbf{R}). \qquad \text{(G11)}$$

Indeed, $(\cos at)/t$ and $(\cos bt)/t$ are odd functions of t, and the first member of (G11) equals

$$\lim_{\varepsilon\downarrow 0} \left(\int_{[-c,-\varepsilon]} + \int_{[\varepsilon,c]}\right)(e^{ibt}-e^{iat})/(it)dt$$

$$= \lim_{\varepsilon\downarrow 0} \left(\int_{[-c,-\varepsilon]} + \int_{[\varepsilon,c]}\right)(\sin bt - \sin at)/t \, dt$$

$$= 2\int_{[0,c]} (\sin bt - \sin at)/t \, dt = 2\int_{[0,bc]} (\sin t)/t \, dt - 2\int_{[0,ac]} (\sin t)/t \, dt$$

$$= 2\int_{[ac,bc]} (\sin t)/t \, dt.$$

Definition of characteristic functions

The (usual) **characteristic function** of the bounded distribution F is the function φ with values

$$\varphi_F(t) := \int_{\mathbf{R}} e^{itx} \, dF(x) \quad (t\in\mathbf{R}). \qquad \text{(G12)}$$

The **integral characteristic function** of the bounded distribution F is the function φ° with values

$$\varphi_F{}^\circ(t) = \int_{[0,t]} \varphi_F(\tau)d\tau \quad (t\in\mathbf{R}). \qquad \text{(G13)}$$

The integral characteristic function is only used as a tool in some proofs.

Remarks

a. e^{itx} is an F-integrable function of x because $|e^{itx}|=1$ and F is bounded.

b. $\varphi_F(t)$ is a continuous function of t by dominated convergence. It is a bounded function because

$$|\varphi_F(t)| \leq \int_{\mathbf{R}} |e^{itx}|\, dF(x) = \int_{\mathbf{R}} dF(x) = F(\mathbf{R}) < \infty \quad (t \in \mathbf{R}). \tag{G14}$$

c.

$$\int_{[0,t]} e^{i\tau x}\, d\tau = (e^{itx}-1)/(ix)$$

and then by Fubini,

$$\varphi_F{}^{\circ}(t) = \int_{\mathbf{R}} (e^{itx}-1)/(ix)\, dF(x). \tag{G15}$$

By (G10),

$$|(e^{itx}-1)/(ix)| = |t|.|(e^{itx}-e^{it0})/(itx-it0)| \leq |t|. \tag{G16}$$

A continuity interval of the distribution F is a bounded interval]a,b] of which the extremities a, b are continuity points of F.

Theorem G4 (Inversion formula)

Let]a,b] be a continuity interval of the bounded distribution F. Then

$$\mathbf{F(]a,b]) = 1/(2\pi)\, \lim_{c\uparrow\infty} \int_{[-c,+c]} [(e^{-ita}-e^{-itb})/(it)]\varphi_F(t)dt.} \tag{G17}$$

Proof

We use the definition (G12) of $\varphi(t)$ in the last member of (G17). Then by Fubini and by (G11), the integral of the last member equals

$$\int_{\mathbf{R}} [\int_{[-c,+c]} (e^{it(x-a)}-e^{it(x-b)})/(it)\, dt]dF(x)$$

$$= 2\int_{\mathbf{R}}[\int_{[(x-b)c,(x-a)c]} (\sin t)/t\, dt]dF(x) \tag{G18}$$

$$\rightarrow 2\int_{\mathbf{R}} I_{a,b}(x)dF(x) \text{ as } c\uparrow\infty, \tag{G19}$$

by dominated convergence (the integral in square brackets of (G18) is bounded by (G8)), where

$$I_{a,b}(x) := \lim_{c\uparrow\infty} \int_{[(x-b)c,(x-a)c]} (\sin t)/t\, dt$$

equals π if $a<x<b$ and 0 if $x<a$ or $b<x$ by (G7). The value for $x=a$ or $x=b$ is irrelevant because $a<b$ are continuity points of F •

Only the following Corollary of the inversion formula is used later.

Corollary (Unicity Theorem for Distributions Defined by Characteristic Functions)

a. φ_F **determines F if F(−∞)=0.**

b. $\varphi_F°$ **determines F if F(−∞)=0.**

Proof

a. By (G17) φ_F determines the F-mass in any continuity interval]a,b] of F. Then it determines F(b) if F(−∞)=0 because

$$\lim_{a\downarrow-\infty} F(]a,b]) = F(b)-F(-\infty) = F(b)$$

Then, by right-continuity, it determines F.

b. $\varphi°$ determines φ because φ is the continuous derivative $(\varphi°)'$ of $\varphi°$ by (G13) •

Lemma 1

Let F_n (n=1,2,...) be a probability distribution with characteristic function φ_n and integral characteristic function $\varphi_n°$. Let $F_n \to_w F$ as $n\uparrow\infty$.

a. $\varphi_n° \to \varphi_F°$ **on R.**

b. **If F is a probability distribution, then $\varphi_n \to \varphi_F$ on R.**

Proof

a. Let $$f_t(x) := (e_{itx}-1)/(ix).$$

Then $$\varphi_n°(t) = \int_{\mathbf{R}} f_t(x)dF_n(x) \to \int_{\mathbf{R}} f_t(x)dF(x) = \varphi_F°(t)$$

by (G15) and Helly-Bray (case of integrand vanishing at ±∞) because $f_t(\pm\infty)$ vanishes.

b. Let F be a probability distribution. Then

$$\varphi_n(t) = \int_{\mathbf{R}} e^{itx}dF_n(x) \to \int_{\mathbf{R}} e^{itx}dF(x) = \varphi_F(x)$$

by Helly-Bray (case of total mass conservation) •

Lemma 2

Let F_n (n=1,2,...) be a probability distribution with characteristic function φ_n such that $F_n \to_w F$ as $n\uparrow\infty$. Let f be a function on R, continuous at 0, such that $\varphi_n \to f$ on R. Then F is a probability distribution and $\varphi_F = f$.

Proof

$$\varphi_n^\circ(t) := \int_{[0,t]} \varphi_n(\tau)d\tau \to \int_{[0,t]} f(\tau)d\tau =: f^\circ(t) \quad (t\in\mathbf{R}),$$

by dominated convergence. By Lemma 1.a, $\varphi_n^\circ \to \varphi_F^\circ$. Hence, $\varphi_F^\circ = f^\circ$ and then

$$1/t \int_{[0,t]} \varphi_F(\tau)d\tau = 1/t \int_{[0,t]} f(\tau)d\tau \ (t\neq 0).$$

As $t\downarrow 0$, we obtain $\varphi_F(0)=f(0)$ because φ is continuous (it is a characteristic function) and f is continuous at 0 (assumption). Hence,

$$f(0) = \varphi_F(0) = \int e^{i0x}\, dF(x) = F(\mathbf{R}).$$

But $1=F_n(\mathbf{R})=\varphi_n(0)\to f(0)$. Hence $f(0)=1$. Then $F(\mathbf{R})=1$. This proves that F is a probability distribution function. Then $\varphi_n \to \varphi_F$ by Lemma 1.b. Then $f=\varphi_F$ because $\varphi_n \to f$ •

Theorem G5 (Continuity Theorem for Characteristic Functions)

Let F_n (n=1,2,...) be a probability distribution with characteristic function φ_n.

a. Let $F_n \to_w F$, where F is a probability distribution. Then $\varphi_n \to \varphi_F$.

b. Let $\varphi_n \to f$, where f is continuous at the origin. Then a probability distribution F exists such that $f=\varphi_F$ and $F_n \to_w F$.

Proof

a. By Lemma 2.b.

b. By the general compactness Theorem (App.E.Th.E3), $F_{n'} \to_w F$ for some subsequence $F_{n'}$ of F_n. Then $\varphi_{n'} \to f$ and then F is a probability distribution and $f=\varphi_F$ by Lemma 2. We now apply the subsequence criterion (Th.G1) in order to prove that $F_n \to_w F$. Let $F_{n''}$ be a subsequence of F_n. By the general compactness Theorem, $F_{n'''} \to_w G$ for some subsequence $F_{n'''}$ of $F_{n''}$. Then $\varphi_{n'''} \to f$ and then G is a probability distribution and $f=\varphi_G$ by Lemma 2. Hence, $\varphi_F=\varphi_G$ and then F=G by the Corollary of Th.G4.

Hence any subsequence $F_{n''}$ of F_n has a subsequence $F_{n'''}$ which converges weakly to F •

I.Ch.3.Th.6. results from the foregoing Theorem. The version with discrete n is equivalent to that one with continuous t because $a(t)\to a$ as $t\uparrow\infty$ iff $a(t_n)\to a$ for any sequence t_n (n=1,2,...) such that $\lim_{n\uparrow\infty} t_n=\infty$.

G5. Differentiation Under an Integral

In the following Theorem, S is an interval in **R** and f(x,s) is a function defined for $x\in\mathbf{R}$ and $s\in S$. Accents represent derivatives with respect to s.

Theorem G6 (Differentiation Under the Integral)

We assume that

a. f′(x,s) exists and it is a continuous function of $s\in S$ for all $x\in\mathbf{R}$.

b. The functions f(x,s) ($s\in S$) are F-integrable functions of x on R.

c. The functions f′(x,s) ($s\in S$) of x are dominated by an F-integrable function g(x) on R:

$$|f'(x,s)| \le g(x) \quad (x\in\mathbf{R},\ s\in S). \tag{G20}$$

Then

$$\partial/\partial s \int f(x,s)dF(x) = \int f'(x,s)dF(x). \tag{G21}$$

Proof

Let $s\in S$ and let $h\neq 0$ be such that $s+h\in S$. Then the first member of (G21) equals.

$$\lim_{h\to 0} 1/h \,[\int f(x,s+h)dF(x) - \int f(x,s+h)dF(x)]$$

$$= \lim_{h\to 0} \int 1/h\, [f(x,s+h)-f(x,s)]dF(x) = \lim_{h\to 0} \int f'(x,s+\theta(x)h)\, dF(x)$$

$$= \int \lim_{h\to 0} f'(x,s+\theta(x)h)\, dF(x) = \int f'(x,s)\, dF(x),$$

by dominated convergence, where $0\le\theta(x)\le 1$ •

If we want to apply the Theorem at a fixed point s in the interior of S, we may of course replace S by $]S-\varepsilon,S+\varepsilon[$, where $\varepsilon>0$.

If S=[c,d[for instance, then $f'(x,c)$ must be understood as being the right-sided derivative at the point c. Then we may replace S by [c,c+ε[.

The Theorem has obvious variants in case of integrals on subsets of **R**.

G6. Expansion of Characteristic Function

In this section G6, we consider a random variable X with distribution F on **R**. We represent by μ_k (k=0,1,2,...) the moment EX^k if it exists, i.e. if $E|X|^k<\infty$.

$o(\tau)$ represents a function of τ such that $\lim_{\tau\to 0} o(\tau) = 0$.

Preliminary remarks

a. **If μ_{k+1} exists, then μ_k exists.**

Indeed, the inequality

$$c^k \leq 1 + c^{k+1} \quad (k=0,1,2,...;\ c\geq 0)$$

holds, because $c^k\leq 1$ if $c\leq 1$, and $c^k\leq c^{k+1}$ if $c>1$. Hence $|X|^k\leq 1+|X|^{k+1}$ and then

$$E|X|^k \leq 1 + E|X|^{k+1}.$$

b. **Let $f(\tau)$ be a real function which, in some neighboorhood of τ=0, has n continuous derivatives. Then**

$$\mathbf{f(\tau) = \sum_{0\leq k\leq n} \tfrac{1}{k!}\, f^{(k)}(0)\, \tau^k + o(\tau)\tau^n.} \tag{G22}$$

Indeed, by Mac Laurin

$$f(\tau) = \sum_{0\leq k\leq n} \tfrac{1}{k!}\, f^{(k)}(0)\, \tau^k + R_n(\tau),$$

where

$$R_n(\tau) = \tfrac{1}{n!}\, [f^{(n)}(\theta\tau)-f^{(n)}(0)]\, \tau^n$$

for some θ (depending on τ) in the interval]0,1[. In the last member, the coefficient of τ^n is a function $o(\tau)$ because we suppose $f^{(n)}(\tau)$ continuous in some neighbourhood of τ=0.

The relation (G22) holds even when f is complex, because then it can be applied separately to the real and to the imaginary part of f.

Theorem G7

Let X be a random variable with distribution function F. Let φ be the characteristic function of F, and let the moment μ_n exist (n fixed). Then

$$\varphi(\tau) = \sum_{0\leq k\leq n} 1/_{k!}\, \mu_k(i\tau)^k + o(\tau)\tau^n. \qquad (G23)$$

Proof

By the *preliminary remark* a, the moments $\mu_1,\ldots,\mu_n$ exist. By Theorem G6, we may differentiate

$$\varphi(\tau) = \int e^{i\tau x}\, dF(x)$$

n times with respect to τ, under the integral:

$$\varphi^{(k)}(\tau) = i^k \int x^k e^{i\tau x}\, dF(x) \quad (k=0,1,\ldots,n).$$

The derivatives $\varphi^k(\tau)$ are continuous by dominated convergence. For $\tau=0$,

$$\varphi^{(k)}(0) = i^k \int x^k e^{i0x}\, dF(x) = i^k \mu_k \quad (k=0,1,\ldots,n).$$

Then the Theorem results from the *preliminary remark* b •

G7. Characteristic Function of Normal Distribution

The integration domain is **R** whenever it is not mentioned.

a.

$$\int e^{-x^2} dx = \pi^{1/2}. \qquad (G24)$$

Indeed, $[\int e^{-x^2}dx]^2 = \int e^{-x^2}dx \int e^{-y^2}\, dy = \iint e^{-(x^2+y^2)}dxdy$

$$= \int_{[0,\infty[} \rho e^{-\rho^2}d\rho . \int_{[0,2\pi[} d\theta = -1/_2 \int_{[0,\infty[} de^{-\rho^2} . 2\pi = \pi,$$

where the couple (x,y) of integration variables has been replaced by the couple (ρ,θ) ($\rho\geq 0$, $0\leq\theta<2\pi$) such that $x=\rho\cos\theta$, $y=\rho\sin\theta$.

b. Substituting $xs^{1/2}$ ($s>0$) for x in (G24), we obtain

$$\int e^{-sx^2}\, dx = \pi^{1/2}s^{-1/2}. \qquad (G25)$$

By Theorem G6 it is easily seen that we may differentiate any number of times under the integral with respect to s, so that

$$\int x^{2k}\, e^{-sx^2}dx = \pi^{1/2}\,(2k)!\,(2^{2k}k!)^{-1}s^{-k}s^{-1/2} \quad (s>0;\ k=0,1,2,\ldots). \qquad (G26)$$

c. By (G25),

$$\pi^{-1/2} s^{1/2} e^{-sx^2} \ (x \in \mathbf{R}) \tag{G27}$$

is a probability density on **R**, for any fixed s>0. **The standardized normal density** is the density (G27) with s= 1/2.

d. The characteristic function of the distribution with density (G27) equals

$$\varphi_s(\tau) := \pi^{-1/2} s^{1/2} \int e^{i\tau x} e^{-sx^2} dx = \pi^{-1/2} s^{1/2} \int \sum_{k=0,1,2,...} 1/k!\, (i\tau x)^k e^{-sx^2} dx$$

$$= \pi^{-1/2} s^{1/2} \int \sum_{k=0,1,2,...} k!^{-1} i^k \tau^k x^k e^{-sx^2} dx$$

$$= \pi^{-1/2} s^{1/2} \sum_{k=0,1,2,...} k!^{-1} i^k \tau^k \int x^k e^{-sx^2} dx$$

$$= \pi^{-1/2} s^{1/2} \sum_{k=0,2,4,...} k!^{-1} i^k \tau^k \int x^k e^{-sx^2} dx$$

$$= \pi^{-1/2} s^{1/2} \sum_{k=0,1,2,...} (2k)!^{-1} i^{2k} \tau^{2k} \int x^{2k} e^{-sx^2} dx$$

$$= \pi^{-1/2} s^{1/2} \sum_{k=0,1,2,...} (2k)!^{-1} i^{2k} \tau^{2k} \pi^{1/2} (2k)!\, (2^{2k} k!)^{-1} s^{-k} s^{-1/2}$$

$$= \sum_{k=0,1,2,...} (-1)^k \tau^{2k} (2^{2k} k!)^{-1} s^{-k} = \sum_{k\geq 0} 1/k!\, [-\tau^2/(4s)]^k = e^{-\tau^2/(4s)},$$

by (27) and by the exponential expansion

$$e^z = \sum_{k\geq 0} 1/k!\, z^k \ (z \text{ complex}).$$

The permutation of $\sum$ and $\int$ is justified by Fubini (sums are particular integrals) because

$$\int \sum_{k=0,1,2,...} | k!^{-1} i^k \tau^k x^k e^{-sx^2} | dx = \int \sum_{k=0,1,2,...} k!^{-1} |\tau|^k x^k e^{-sx^2} dx$$

$$= \int e^{|\tau| x} e^{-sx^2} dx < \infty.$$

Hence,

The characteristic function of the standardized normal distribution is

$$\boldsymbol{\varphi(\tau) = \exp(-\tau^2/2)\ (\tau \in \mathbf{R}).} \tag{G28}$$

Appendix H

Generating Functions

H1. Distributions on N_+

In this Appendix H we consider distributions F concentrated on $\mathbf{N}_+$. Here the distribution function F and the measure F are always connected by the relation

$$F(x) = F(]-\infty,x]). \tag{H1}$$

The distribution F on $\mathbf{N}_+$ is completely specified by its masses $F(\{k\})$ at the points k=0,1,2,... The distribution function F of a distribution concentrated on $\mathbf{N}_+$ is characterized by following properties:

$$F=0 \text{ on }]-\infty,0[\text{ , } F \text{ is constant on } [k,k+1[\text{ } (k=0,1,2,...). \tag{H2}$$

Theorem H1

Let F be a distribution on R and F_n (n=1,2,...) distributions on N_+.

a. If $F_n \to_w F$, then F is a distribution on N_+.

b. $F_n \to_w F$ iff

$$\lim_{n\uparrow\infty} F_n(\{k\}) = F(\{k\}) \text{ } (k=0,1,2,...). \tag{H3}$$

Proof

a. Let $F_n \to_w F$. Let $x<0$ and let us assume that $F(x)\neq 0$. Let $x+\varepsilon<0$ ($\varepsilon>0$) be a continuity point of F such that $F(x+\varepsilon)\neq 0$. This is possible by the right-continuity of F and because the number of discontinuities of F is denumerable. Then $0=\lim_{n\uparrow\infty}F_n(x+\varepsilon)=F(x+\varepsilon)\neq 0$. This contradiction shows that $F(x)=0$.

Now we prove that F is constant on [k,k+1[. Let $k\leq c<d<k+1$, $F(c)\neq F(d)$. We consider continuity points $c+\varepsilon$ ($\varepsilon>0$) and $d+\delta$ ($\delta>0$) of F such that

$$k \leq c < c+\varepsilon < d < d+\delta < k+1 \text{ , } F(c+\varepsilon) \neq F(d+\delta).$$

Then $$F_n(c+\varepsilon) = F_n(d+\delta) \quad (n=1,2,...)$$

and as $n\uparrow\infty$, $F(c+\varepsilon)=F(d+\varepsilon)$. This contradiction shows that $F(c)=F(d)$, i.e. that F is constant on $[k,k+1[$.

b. Let $F_n \rightarrow_w F$. By a, the point $k+(1/2)$ is a continuity point of F. Hence

$$F_n(\{0\}) + F_n(\{1\}) + ... + F_n(\{k\}) = F_n(]-\infty,k+(1/2)])$$

$$\rightarrow F(]-\infty,k+(1/2)]) = F(\{0\}) + F(\{1\}) + ... + F(\{k\}).$$

These relations hold for $k-1$ also. Then by substraction, $F_n(\{k\}) \rightarrow F(\{k\})$.

Now we assume (H3) and we prove that $F_n \rightarrow_w F$, i.e. $F_n(x) \rightarrow F(x)$ when x is a continuity point of F. If $x>0$ is not an integer,

$$F_n(x) = \sum_{k<x} F_n(\{k\}) \rightarrow \sum_{k<x} F(\{k\}) = F(x).$$

If $x<0$, $$F_n(x) = 0 \rightarrow 0 = F(x).$$

If $x=k\in\mathbf{N}_+$ is a continuity point of F, then $F(k-\varepsilon)=F(k)=F(k+\varepsilon)=:p$. Then

$$F_n(k-\varepsilon) \leq F_n(k) \leq F_n(k+\varepsilon)$$

and as $n\uparrow\infty$,

$$p \leq \lim_{n\uparrow\infty} F_n(k) \leq p.$$

Hence, $F_n(k) \rightarrow F(k)$ •

H2. Power Series with Positive Coefficients

In this section H2, we consider the function f with values

$$f(s) = \sum_{k\geq 0} a_k s^k \quad (s\geq 0)$$

in $\mathbf{R}_+\cup\{+\infty\}$, where $a_k\geq 0$ $(k=0,1,2,...)$. In the last member $0^0:=1$ (if $s=k=0$).

It is customary to say that **f(s) converges**, at the fixed point $s\geq 0$, if f(s) is finite.

The following Theorem is a very particular case of a general result of the theory of power series. Its proof is almost direct by the great Theorems of modern integration theory.

Theorem H2

a. **Let $c>0$, $f(c)<\infty$. Then f is infinitely differentiable on $[0,c[$ and the successive derivatives can be taken under the $\sum$ symbol:**

$$f^{(m)}(s) = \sum_{k\geq m} a_k k^{[m]} s^{k-m} \quad (0\leq s<c;\ k=0,1,2...).$$

b. **If $f(\varepsilon)<\infty$ for some $\varepsilon>0$, then**

$$a_m = {}^1/_{m!}\, f^{(m)}(0) \quad (m=0,1,...).$$

Proof

Let A be the distribution on $\mathbf{N}_+$ with mass a_k at point $k=0,1,2,...$ Then

$$f(s) = \int_{[0,\infty[} s^x \, dA(x).$$

a. We prove that f is continuous on $[0,c[$. Let s be a fixed point in that interval and let h_n $(n=1,2,...)$ be a sequence of numbers converging to 0, such that $s+h_n$ belongs to $[0,c[$. Let $h:=\sup_n|h_n|$. Then $s+h<c$. Hence $f(s+h)<\infty$. This means that the function $(s+h)^x$ of $x\in[0,\infty[$ is A-integrable. Then

$$(s+h_n)^x \leq (s+h)^x \quad (x\geq 0;\ n=1,2,...)$$

and hence,

$$f(s+h_n) = \int_{[0,\infty[} (s+h_n)^x \, dA(x) \rightarrow \int_{[0,\infty[} s^x \, dA(x) = f(s) \text{ as } n\uparrow\infty$$

by dominated convergence. This proves the continuity of f at s.

Let g be the function with values

$$g(s) := \sum_{k\geq 1} a_k k s^{k-1} = \int_{[1,\infty[} x s^{x-1} dA(x) \quad (s\geq 0).$$

in $\mathbf{R}_+\cup\{\infty\}$. We prove that g is finite on $[0,c[$. By Fubini (case of positive integrand),

$$\int_{[0,c]} g(s)ds = \int_{[1,\infty[} \left[\int_{[0,c]} x s^{x-1} ds\right] dA(x) = \int_{[1,\infty[} c^x \, dA(x) = f(c)-a_0.$$

The last member is finite. If g is not finite on $[0,c[$, then t exists such that $g(t)=\infty$, $0\leq t<c$. Then $g\equiv\infty$ on $[t,c[$ and then the integral of the first member is infinite. This is a contradiction. Hence, g is finite on $[0,c[$ and then g is continuous on that interval by the first part of the proof (applied to g instead of f).

Now we prove the existence of f' on $[0,c[$. Let r and $r+h$ be numbers in $[0,c[$. Then, as above,

$$\int_{[0,r]} g(s)ds = f(r)-a_0 \ , \quad \int_{[0,r+h]} g(s)ds = f(r+h)-a_0.$$

By difference and division by $h\neq0$

$$1/h[f(r+h)-f(r)] = 1/h \int_{[r,r+h]} g(s)ds = g(r+\theta h),$$

where $0\leq\theta\leq1$ by the mean value Theorem. Hence, as $h\to0$, we obtain $f'(r) = g(r)$. By the definition of g, and because r is any point in [0,c[, this proves that the function f is differentiable on [0,c[and that it may be differentiated under the Σ symbol.

Then a. is true by induction. Indeed, $f'(d)$ is finite $(0\leq d<c)$. Hence, f'' exists on [0,d[. This implies that f'' exists on [0,c[because, given any point $s\in[0,c[$, d can be fixed in]s,c[. This argument can be applied to any derivative $f^{(k)}$ (k=2,3,...).

b. Results from a. with $c=\varepsilon$ and s=0 in the expression of the derivative •

H3. Generating Functions

We consider bounded distributions F concentrated on $\mathbf{N}_+$. In this Appendix, **the generating function of F** is the function γ_F on [0,1] with values

$$\gamma_F(s) = \sum_{k\geq0} F(\{k\})s^k = \int_{[0,\infty[} s^x dF(x) \quad (0\leq s\leq1). \tag{H4}$$

Properties of generating function

a. γ_F is an increasing continuous function on [0,1] with

$$\gamma_F(0) = F(0) = F(\{0\}) \ , \ \gamma_F(1) = F(\mathbf{N}_+) < \infty.$$

b. γ_F has derivatives of all orders on [0,1[given by

$$\gamma_F^{(m)}(s) = \sum_{k\geq m} F(\{k\})k^{[m]}s^{k-m} \quad (0\leq s\leq1). \tag{H5}$$

c. F is determined by the restriction of γ_F to $[0,\varepsilon[$, where ε is any fixed number in the interval]0,1]. (This proposition is a **Unicity Theorem for Distributions Defined by a Generating Function**).

These properties result from Theorem H2.

Lemma 1

Let F_n (n=1,2,...) be a probability distribution concentrated on $\mathbf{N}_+$ with generating function γ_n. Let $F_n \to_w F$ as $n\uparrow\infty$.

a. F is a bounded distribution concentrated on $\mathbf{N}_+$ and $\gamma_n \to \gamma_F$ on [0,1[.

b. If F is a probability distribution, then $\gamma_n \to \gamma_F$ on [0,1].

Proof

a. Any weak limit of probability distribution functions is a function with values in the interval [0,1]. Hence F is bounded. F is concentrated on $\mathbf{N}_+$ by Th.H1.a. Let $0 \le s < 1$. Then s^x is a continuous function of $x \in \mathbf{R}_+$ and $s^x \downarrow 0$ as $x\uparrow\infty$. Hence, by Helly-Bray (case of integrand vanishing at $\pm\infty$),

$$\gamma_n(s) = \int_{[0,\infty[} s^x \, dF_n(x) \to \int_{[0,\infty[} s^x \, dF(x) = \gamma(s).$$

(The integrand has a continuous extension to $\mathbf{R}$ vanishing at $\pm\infty$ and the integration domain can be replaced by $\mathbf{R}$).

b. If F is a probability distribution, then $\gamma_n(1)=F_n(\mathbf{N}_+)=1=F(\mathbf{N}_+)=\gamma(1)$ and then, of course, $\gamma_n(1)\to\gamma(1)$ •

Lemma 2

Let F_n (n=1,2,...) be a probability distribution on $\mathbf{N}_+$ with generation function γ_n such that $F_n \to_w F$ as $n\uparrow\infty$. Let f be a function on [0,1], continuous at 1, such that $\gamma_n \to f$ on [0,1]. Then F is a probability distribution on $\mathbf{N}_+$ and $\gamma_F = f$ on [0,1].

Proof

F is concentrated on $\mathbf{N}_+$ and $\gamma_n \to \gamma_F$ on [0,1[by Lemma 1.a. Hence $f=\gamma_F$ on [0,1[. Then $f=\gamma_F$ on [0,1] because f and γ_F are continuous at 1. Hence,

$$f(1) = \gamma_F(1) = F(\mathbf{N}_+).$$

But

$$1 = F_n(\mathbf{N}_+) = \gamma_n(1) \to f(1).$$

Hence, $f(1)=1$ and then $F(\mathbf{N}_+)=1$ •

Theorem H3 **(Continuity Theorem for Generating Functions)**

Let F_n (n=1,2,...) be a probability distribution on N_+ with generating function γ_n.

a. **Let $F_n \to_w F$, where F is a probability distribution. Then F is concentrated on N_+ and $\gamma_n \to \gamma_F$ on [0,1].**

b. **Let $\gamma_n \to f$ on [0,1], where f is continuous at the point 1. Then a probability distribution F exists on N_+ such that $F_n \to_w F$ and $f = \gamma_F$.**

Proof

a. By Lemma 1.

b. The distributions of the following proof are concentrated on $\mathbf{N}_+$ by Th. H1.a. b. By the general compactness Theorem (App.E.Th.E3), $F_{n'} \to_w F$ for some subsequence $F_{n'}$ of F_n. Then $\gamma_{n'} \to f$ on [0,1] and then F is a probability distribution and $f=\gamma_F$ on [0,1] by Lemma 2. We now apply the subsequence criterion (App.G.Th.G1) in order to prove that $F_n \to_w F$. Let $F_{n''}$ be a subsequence of F_n. By the general compactness Theorem, $F_{n'''} \to_w G$ for some subsequence $F_{n'''}$ of $F_{n''}$. Then $\gamma_{n'''} \to f$ on [0,1] and then G is a probability distribution and $f=\varphi_G$ on [0,1] by Lemma 2. Hence, $\gamma_F=\gamma_G$ on [0,1] and then F=G because the generating function determines the distribution. Hence any subsequence $F_{n''}$ of F_n has a subsequence $F_{n'''}$ which converges weakly to F •

H4. Weierstrass's Approximation Theorem

Let X be a square-integrable random variable with distribution function F. Then the well known Tchebycheff inequality is

$$\text{Prob}(|X-EX|\geq\delta) \leq {}^1/_{\delta^2} \text{ Var } X, \tag{H6}$$

i.e.

$$F(\mathbf{C}[EX-\delta, EX+\delta]) \leq {}^1/_{\delta^2} \text{ Var } X. \tag{H7}$$

In the following Lemma, $X_{n,\theta}$ (n=1,2,...; $\theta\in[0,1]$) is a square-integrable random variable with distribution function $F_{n,\theta}$, such that $0\leq X_{n,\theta}\leq 1$,

$$EX_{n,\theta} = \theta, \tag{H8}$$

and

$$\lim_{n\uparrow\infty} \text{Var } X_{n,\theta} = 0 \tag{H9}$$

for all $\theta\in[0,1]$.

Lemma

Let f be a continuous function on [0,1]. Then

$$\lim_{n\uparrow\infty} \int_{[0,1]} f dF_{n,\theta} = f(\theta) \qquad \text{(H10)}$$

for all $\theta\in[0,1]$. If (H9) is true uniformly in $\theta\in[0,1]$, then (H10) is also true uniformly in $\theta\in[0,1]$.

Proof

$$\begin{aligned}
&|\int_{[0,1]} f dF_{n,\theta} - f(\theta)| = |\int_{[0,1]} [f(x)-f(\theta)]dF_{n,\theta}(x)| \le \int_{[0,1]} |f(x)-f(\theta)|dF_{n,\theta}(x) \\
&= \int_{[0,1]\cap[\theta-\delta,\theta+\delta]} |f(x)-f(\theta)|dF_{n,\theta}(x) + \int_{[0,1]\cap C[\theta-\delta,\theta+\delta]} |f(x)-f(\theta)|dF_{n,\theta}(x) \\
&\le \mathrm{Sup}_{x\in[0,1]\cap[\theta-\delta,\theta+\delta]} |f(x)-f(\theta)| + 2\,(\mathrm{Sup}\, f) \int_{[0,1]\cap C[\theta-\delta,\theta+\delta]} dF_{n,\theta}(x) \\
&\le \mathrm{Sup}_{x\in[0,1]\cap[\theta-\delta,\theta+\delta]} |f(x)-f(\theta)| + 2\,(\mathrm{Sup}\, f)\, F_{n,\theta}(C[\theta-\delta,\theta+\delta]) \\
&\le \mathrm{Sup}_{x\in[0,1]\cap[\theta-\delta,\theta+\delta]} |f(x)-f(\theta)| + 2\,(\mathrm{Sup}\, f).\ 1/\delta^2\ \mathrm{Var}\, X_{n,\theta}. \qquad \text{(H11)}
\end{aligned}$$

Let $\varepsilon>0$. If $\delta>0$ is small enough, the first term of (H11) is less than ε, for all $\theta\in[0,1]$ (continuous fonctions are uniformly continuous on compact intervals). Then, for fixed δ, the last term is less than ε (for all $\theta\in[0,1]$ if (H9) holds uniformly in $\theta\in[0,1]$) if n is large enough •

Let f be a function defined on [0,1]. The corresponding **Bernstein polynomials $B_{n,f}(\theta)$** are defined as

$$B_{n,f}(\theta) := \sum_{0\le k\le n} 1/k!\ n^{[k]} f(k/n)\theta^k(1-\theta)^{n-k} \quad (0\le\theta\le1;\ n=1,2,\ldots). \qquad \text{(H12)}$$

Theorem H4

Let f be a continuous function on [0,1]. Then

$$\lim_{n\uparrow\infty} B_{n,f}(\theta) = f(\theta) \text{ uniformly in } \theta\in[0,1].$$

Proof

Let $Y_{n,\theta}$ be the binomial random variable with parameters θ and n, i.e

$$P(Y_{n,\theta}=k) = 1/k!\ n^{[k]}\theta^k(1-\theta)^{n-k} \quad (k=0,1,\ldots,n). \qquad \text{(H13)}$$

Let $X_{n,\theta} := Y_{n,\theta}/n$. Then the Theorem results from the Lemma because

$$0 \le X_{n,\theta} \le 1\ ,\ EX_{n,\theta} = \theta\ ,\ \mathrm{Var}\, X_{n,\theta} = \theta(1-\theta)/n$$ •

Corollary (Weierstrass's Approximation Theorem)

Let f be a continuous function on the compact interval [a,b]. Then f is the uniform limit of a sequence of polynomials on [a,b].

Proof
By a translation and an introduction of a new unit of length, the interval [a,b] can be replaced by [0,1] and then the foregoing Theorem can be applied •

H5. Absolutely Monotone Functions

Let I be one of the intervals]0,1[or [0,1[and let f be a real function defined on I. The function f is **absolutely monotone** on I if it has positive derivatives of all orders on I:

$$f^{(k)}(s) \geq 0 \quad (s \in I,\ k=0,1,2,\ldots).$$

Here $f^{(0)}(s) \equiv f(s)$.

We use the **ascending difference operators** $\Delta_h \equiv \Delta_h^{\ 1}$, $\Delta_h^{\ 2}$, $\Delta_h^{\ 3}$,... defined by the relations

$$\Delta_h f(s) := f(s+h) - f(s)\ ,\ \Delta_h^{\ 2} f(s) := \Delta_h[\Delta_h f(s)]\ ,\ \Delta_h^{\ 3} f(s) := \Delta_h[\Delta_h^{\ 2} f(s)]\ , \ldots$$

The **increment operators** $E_h \equiv E_h^{\ 1}$, $E_h^{\ 2}$, $E_h^{\ 3}$, ... are defined by the relations

$$E_h f(s) := f(s+h)\ ,\ E_h^{\ 2} f(s) = E_h[E_h f(s)]\ ,\ E_h^{\ 3} f(s) := E_h[E_h^{\ 2} f(s)]\ , \ldots$$

The **identity operator** 1 is defined by $1f(s)=f(s)$. The operators $\Delta_h^{\ k}$ and $E_h^{\ k}$ are used for k=0 also. Then $\Delta_h^{\ 0}:=1$, $E_h^{\ 0}:=1$.

Lemme

$$B_{n,f}(\theta) = \sum_{0 \leq k \leq n} {}^{n^{[k]}}\!/_{k!}\ \theta^k \Delta_{1/n}^{\ \ k} f(0) \quad (0 \leq \theta \leq 1;\ n=1,2,\ldots), \qquad \text{(H14)}$$

where $B_{n,f}$ is the Bernstein polynomial defined by (H12).

Proof
In this proof, we use the notation

$$(k,j) := {}^{k^{[j]}}\!/_{j!} = {}^{k!}\!/_{j!(k-j)!} \quad (j,k \in \mathbf{N}_+;\ j \leq k)$$

for the binomial coefficients.

In the last member of (H14) (superscripts can be treated as exponents),

$$\Delta_{1/n}{}^{k} f(0) = (E_{1/n}-1)^{k} f(0) = \sum_{0\le j\le k} (k,j)\, E_{1/n}{}^{j} (-1)^{k-j} f(0)$$

$$= \sum_{0\le j\le k} (k,j)\, (-1)^{k-j} E_{1/n}{}^{j} f(0) = \sum_{0\le j\le k} (k,j)\, (-1)^{k-j} f(j/n).$$

Hence, the last member of (H14) equals

$$\sum_{0\le k\le n} (n,k)\, \theta^{k} \sum_{0\le j\le k} (k,j)\, (-1)^{k-j} f(j/n) = \sum_{0\le j\le n} \sum_{j\le k\le n} (n,k)\, \theta^{k} (k,j)\, (-1)^{k-j} f(j/n)$$

$$= \sum_{0\le j\le n} f(j/n) \sum_{j\le k\le n} (n,j)\, (n-j,k-j)\, (-1)^{k-j}\theta^{k}$$

$$= \sum_{0\le j\le n} f(j/n) \sum_{0\le k\le n-j} (n,j)\, (n-j,k)\, (-1)^{k}\theta^{k+j}$$

$$= \sum_{0\le j\le n} f(j/n)(n,j)\theta^{j}\sum_{0\le k\le n-j}(n-j,k)(-1)^{k}\theta^{k} = \sum_{0\le j\le n} f(j/n)(n,j)\theta^{j}(1-\theta)^{n-j} = B_{n,f}(\theta).$$

Theorem H5

Let f be a continuous function on [0,1], f(1)=1. Then the following propositions a, b and c are equivalent.

a. **f is the generating function of some probability distribution on $\mathbf{N}_+$.**

b. **f is absolutely monotone on [0,1[.**

c. $\Delta_{1/n}{}^{k}f(0) \ge 0 \quad (n=1,2,\ldots;\ k=0,1,2,\ldots,n).$

Proof

a ⇒ b. Let f be the generating function of the probability distribution F on $\mathbf{N}_+$. By (H5),

$$f^{(k)}(s) = \sum_{m\ge k} F(\{k\})m^{[k]}s^{m-k} \ge 0 \ (0\le s\le 1;\ k=0,1,2,\ldots).$$

Hence, f is absolutely monotone.

b ⇒ c. Let f be absolutely monotone. The monotonicity of the derivatives $f^{(k)}$ implies that $\Delta_{1/n}f$ has positive derivatives of all orders (by the mean value Theorem), and so by induction c is true.

c ⇒ a. We assume c. By (H14), $B_{n,f}$ is the generating function of the distribution F_n with mass

$$n^{[k]}/k!\ \Delta_{1/n}{}^{k}f(0) \ge 0$$

at the point $k\in\mathbf{N}_+$. The total mass equals $B_{n,f}(1)=f(1)$ by (H12). Hence F_n is a probability distribution on $\mathbf{N}_+$ because f(1)=1.

By Th. H4, $B_{n,f} \to f$ on [0,1] as $n \to \infty$. By Theorem H3.b, f is the generating function of a probability distribution F on $\mathbf{N}_+$ •

Theorem H6

The function f is absolutely monotone on the interval [0,1[iff it has a convergent power series expansion

$$f(s) = \sum_{k \geq 0} a_k s^k \quad (0 \leq s < 1) \qquad \text{(H15)}$$

with coefficients $a_k \geq 0$ (k=0,1,2,...).

Proof

a. Let us assume that the expansion (H15) exists. Then the last member can be differentiated any number of times under the $\sum$ by Theorem H2.a.

b. Let f be absolutely monotone on [0,1[. Let $g_\theta(s) := f(\theta s)/f(\theta)$ $(0 \leq s \leq 1, 0 < \theta < 1)$. Then g_θ is absolutely monotone on [0,1[, g_θ is continuous on [0,1] and $g_\theta(1) = 1$. By Theorem H5 (part b⇒a), g_θ has a power series expansion on [0,1] with positive coefficients. Replacing s by s/θ, we have that $f(s) = f(\theta) g_\theta(s/\theta)$ has such an expansion on [0,θ] for all θ∈]0,1[. The coefficients do not depend on θ (unicity of potential series expansion). Hence, f has the required expansion on [0,1[•

Theorem H7

Let f be absolutely monotone on]0,1[and let f be extended to [0,1[by the definition f(0):=f(0+). Then f is absolutely monotone on [0,1[.

Proof

f(0+) is finite because f is positive and increasing. The extended function f is continuous on [0,1[, hence on [0,s] (0<s<1). Then $f'(0) = \lim_{s \downarrow 0} f'(s)$ because

$$[f(s) - f(0)]/s = f'(\xi) \quad (0 < \xi < s)$$

by the mean value Theorem (it is valid in case of functions which are continuous on a closed interval and which have a derivative on the interior of that interval). Hence, $f'(0) = f'(0+)$. Then the existence of $f^{(k)}(0) \geq 0$ follows by induction on k •

By this Theorem, results proved for absolutely monotone functions on [0,1[can be extended to absolutely monotone functions on]0,1[.

Appendix I

Moment Functions

I1. Distributions on [a,b]

In this Appendix I we prove a unicity Theorem and a continuity Theorem akin to distributions F concentrated on the compact interval [a,b]. Then F is bounded (unbounded distributions on bounded intervals are never considered in this book, because all distribution functions have finite values on **R**). The distribution function F and the measure F are connected by the relation $F(x)=F(]-\infty,x])$.

I2. Moment Functions

The **moment function** $\mu_F(\cdot)$ of the distribution F concentrated on I=[a,b] or $I=[0,\infty[$ is the function on $\mathbf{N}_+$ with values

$$\mu_F(k) := \int_I x^k dF(x) \quad (k=0,1,2,...).$$

μ_F may have infinite values when $I=[0,\infty[$. The next Theorem I1 shows that F is determined by μ_F if I=[a,b]. The following example, found in Borel (1947), p.122, shows that F is not necessarily determined by a finite μ_F if $I=[0,\infty[$. Let

$$\alpha(x) := 1/4 \exp(-x^{1/4})\sin x^{1/4} \quad (x\geq 0).$$

Then, by substitution and by App.K.K1,

$$\int_{[0,\infty[} x^n\alpha(x)dx = \int_{[0,\infty[} y^{4n+3}e^{-y}\sin y\, dy = [-e^{-y} \textstyle\sum_{0\leq k\leq 4n+3} s_k(y)(4n+3)^{[k]}y^{4n+3-k}]_0^{\infty}$$

$$= e^{-0}\, s_{4n+3}(0)\,(4n+3)!,$$

where $s_{4n+3}(0)$ is the imaginary part of $(1+i)^{4n+3+1}=[(1+i)^4]^n=(-4)^n$, up to a constant factor. Hence, $\int_{[0,\infty[} x^n\alpha(x)dx=0$.

Let φ be the density of a distribution on $\mathbf{R}_+$ with finite moments of all orders, such that $\varphi+\varepsilon\alpha\geq 0$ on $\mathbf{R}_+$ if $\varepsilon>0$ is small enough, say $\varphi(x):=\exp(-x^{1/5})$. Let F_ε be the distribution with density $\varphi+\varepsilon\alpha$. The moments of F_ε do not depend on ε.

Theorem I1 (Unicity Theorem for Distributions on [a,b] Defined by a Moment Function)

The moment function $\mu_F(\cdot)$ of a distribution concentrated on [a,b] determines its distribution function F.

Proof

Here the characteristic function φ_F of the distribution is determined by the moment function because

$$\varphi_F(t) = \int_{[a,b]} e^{itx}dF(x) = \int_{[a,b]}\sum_{k\geq 0} i^k t^k x^k/k!\ dF(x) = \sum_{k\geq 0} \int_{[a,b]} i^k t^k x^k/k!\ dF(x)$$

$$\sum_{k\geq 0} i^k t^k/k! \int_{[a,b]} x^k\ dF(x) = \sum_{k\geq 0} i^k t^k \mu(k)\ /k!,$$

by dominated convergence (or by Fubini because sums are particular integrals). By App.G.Th.G4.Cor.a, φ determines the mesure F. The measure F determines the distribution function F because we assume that $F(x)=F(]-\infty,x])$. •

Theorem I2 (Continuity Theorem for Moment Functions)

Let F_n (n=1,2,...) be a probability distribution on the compact interval [a,b] with moment function $\mu_n(\cdot)$.

a. **Let F be a distribution on [a,b] such that $F_n \to_w F$ as $n\uparrow\infty$. Then F is a probability distribution on [a,b] and $\mu_n(\cdot)\to\mu_F(\cdot)$ on N_+.**

b. **Let $\mu_n(\cdot)\to f(\cdot)$ on N_+ as $n\uparrow\infty$. Then a probability distribution F exists on [a,b] such that $f=\mu_F$ and $F_n\to_w F$ as $n\uparrow\infty$.**

Proof

a. Results from Helly-Bray (case of a bounded integration domain). Obviously, $F(a-)=0$, $F(b+)=1$ and then

$$F_n(a-) = 0 \to 0 = F(a-),$$

$$F_n(b+) = 1 \to 1 = F(b+) \text{ as } n\uparrow\infty.$$

b. The proof is easy by an argument based on the subsequence criterion for weak convergence (App.G.Th.G1). See proof of App.G.Th.G5.b •

Appendix J

Laplace Transforms

J1. Distributions on $\mathbf{R}_+$

In this Appendix J we consider distributions F concentrated on $\mathbf{R}_+$. Here the distribution function F and the measure F are always connected by the relation $F(x)=F(]-\infty,x])$.

The distribution function F of a distribution concentrated on $\mathbf{R}_+$ is characterized by the following property: F=0 on $]-\infty,0[$.

Weak limits of distributions on $\mathbf{R}_+$ are distributions on $\mathbf{R}_+$.

J2. Laplace Transforms

Hereafter, F is a bounded distribution on $\mathbf{R}_+$. **The Laplace transform of F** is the function $\lambda_F(\cdot)$ on $\mathbf{R}_+$ with values

$$\lambda_F(s) := \int_{[0,\infty[} e^{-sx}\, dF(x) \quad (s\geq 0). \tag{J1}$$

Properties of Laplace transforms

a. λ_F is a decreasing continuous function on $\mathbf{R}_+$ (by dominated convergence) and

$$\lambda_F(0) = F(\mathbf{R}_+) \ , \ \lambda_F(\infty) = F(\{0\}). \tag{J2}$$

b. λ_F has derivatives of all orders on $]0,\infty[$. They can be calculated under the integral in the last member of (J1) by App.G.Th.G6. Hence,

$$\lambda_F^{(k)}(s) := \int_{[0,\infty[} (-x)^k e^{-sx}\, dF(x) \quad (s>0). \tag{J3}$$

Theorem J1 (Inversion Formula)

Let c≥0 be a continuity point of the bounded distribution F on $\mathbf{R}_+$. Then

$$F(]c,\infty[) = \lim_{n\uparrow\infty} \sum_{k\geq 0} {(-1)^k}/{k!}\, e^{knc}\, \lambda_F(kn),$$

where the series in the last member converges absolutely.

Proof.

Let $$f(n) := \sum_{k\geq 0} 1/{k!}\, e^{knc}\, \lambda_F(kn)$$

$$= \sum_{k\geq 0} 1/{k!}\, e^{knc} \int_{[0,\infty[} e^{-knx} dF(x) = \int_{[0,\infty[} \sum_{k\geq 0} 1/{k!}\, e^{knc}\, e^{-knx} dF(x)$$

$$= \int_{[0,\infty[} \sum_{k\geq 0} 1/{k!}\, [e^{n(c-x)}]^k dF(x) = \int_{[0,\infty[} \exp[e^{n(c-x)}] dF(x),$$

by Fubini (case of a positive integrand), because sums are particular integrals. The integrand of the latter integral is bounded for fixed n, because its limit as $x\uparrow\infty$ equals 1. Hence, the integral is finite. This proves the absolute convergence. In the same way,

$$g(n) := \sum_{k\geq 0} {(-1)^k}/{k!}\, e^{knc}\, \lambda_F(kn) = \int_{[0,\infty[} \exp[-e^{n(c-x)}] dF(x),$$

by Fubini, because now the case of an integrable integrand can be applied. As $n\uparrow\infty$, the limit of the integrand of the latter integral is 0, e^{-1}, 1 if $x<c$, $x=c$, $x>c$ resp. This integrand is bounded by 1. Hence, by dominated convergence,

$$\lim_{n\uparrow\infty} g(n) = \int_{[0,\infty[} \lim_{n\uparrow\infty} \exp[-e^{n(c-x)}] dF(x) = \int_{]c,\infty[} dF(x) = F(]c,\infty[)$$

because c is a continuity point of F •

Corollary (Unicity Theorem for Distributions Defined by Laplace Transforms)

The bounded distribution F on $\mathbf{R}_+$ is determined by its Laplace transform.

Proof.

By the Theorem, $F(]c,\infty[)=F(\infty)-F(c)$ (c continuity point of F) is determined by λ_F and $F(\infty)=F(\mathbf{R}_+)=\lambda_F(0)$ by (J2). Hence, F is determined by λ_F at its continuity points, and then everywhere by right-continuity •

Lemma

Let F_n (n=1,2,...) be a probability distribution on $\mathbf{R}_+$ with Laplace transform λ_n such that $F_n \to_w F$ as $n\uparrow\infty$. Let f be a function on $[0,\infty[$, continuous at 0, such that $\lambda_n \to f$ on $[0,\infty[$. Then F is a probability distribution on $\mathbf{R}_+$ and $\lambda_F = f$ on $[0,\infty[$.

Proof
F is concentrated on $\mathbf{R}_+$ and $\lambda_n \to \lambda_F$ on $]0,\infty[$ by Helly-Bray (case of integrand vanishing at $\pm\infty$). Hence $f=\lambda_F$ on $]0,\infty[$. Then $f=\lambda_F$ on $[0,\infty[$ because f and λ_F are continuous at 0. Hence, $f(0) = \gamma_F(0) = F(\mathbf{R}_+)$. But $1= F_n(\mathbf{R}_+) = \lambda_n(0) \to f(0)$. Hence, $f(0)=1$ and then $F(\mathbf{R}_+)=1$ •

Theorem J2 (Continuity Theorem for Laplace transforms)

Let F_n (n=1,2,...) be a probability distribution on $\mathbf{R}_+$ with Laplace transform λ_n.

a. **Let $F_n \to_w F$, where F is a probability distribution. Then F is concentrated on $\mathbf{R}_+$ and $\lambda_n \to \lambda_F$ on $[0,\infty[$.**

b. **Let $\lambda_n \to f$ on $[0,\infty[$, where f is continuous at the point 0. Then a probability distribution F exists on $\mathbf{R}_+$ such that $F_n \to_w F$ and $f=\lambda_F$.**

Proof
a. By Helly-Bray (case of total mass conservation).

b. The distributions of the following proof are concentrated on $\mathbf{R}_+$. By the general compactness Theorem (App.E.Th.E3), $F_{n'} \to_w F$ for some subsequence $F_{n'}$ of F_n. Then $\lambda_{n'} \to f$ on $[0,\infty[$ and then F is a probability distribution and $f=\lambda_F$ on $[0,\infty[$ by the Lemma. We now apply the subsequence criterion (App.G. Th.G1) in order to prove that $F_n \to_w F$. Let $F_{n''}$ be a subsequence of F_n. By the general compactness Theorem, $F_{n'''} \to_w G$ for some subsequence $F_{n'''}$ of $F_{n''}$. Then $\lambda_{n'''} \to f$ on $[0,\infty[$ and then G is a probability distribution and $f=\lambda_G$ on $[0,\infty[$ by the Lemma. Hence, $\gamma_F=\gamma_G$ on $[0,\infty[$ and then F=G because the Laplace transform determines the distribution by the Corollary of Theorem J1. Hence any subsequence $F_{n''}$ of F_n has a subsequence $F_{n'''}$ which converges weakly to F •

J3. Completely Monotone Functions

The function f is **completely monotone** on the interval $]0,\infty[$ if it has derivatives of all orders on $]0,\infty[$ satisfying the relations

$$(-1)^k f^{(k)}(s) \geq 0 \quad (s>0;\ k=0,1,2,...). \tag{J4}$$

Let λ_F be the Laplace transform of the bounded distribution F on $\mathbf{R}_+$. Let $F_c(x)=F(cx)$ $(x\in\mathbf{R})$, where $c>0$. Then the Laplace transform of F_c is

$$\lambda_c(s)= \int_{[0,\infty[} e^{-sx}dF_c(x) = \int_{[0,\infty[} e^{-sx}dF(cx) = \int_{[0,\infty[} e^{-(s/c)x}dF(x) = \lambda(s/c) \quad (s\geq 0). \tag{J5}$$

Let F be a distribution on $\mathbf{N}_+$ with Laplace transform λ_F and generating function γ_F. Then

$$\lambda_F(s) = \int_{[0,\infty[} e^{-sx}dF(x) = \int_{[0,\infty[} (e^{-s})^x dF(x) = \gamma_F(e^{-s}) \quad (s\geq 0). \tag{J6}$$

Theorem J3 (Bernstein)

The bounded function f on $]0,\infty[$ is completely monotone on $]0,\infty[$ iff it is the Laplace transform of some bounded distribution concentrated on $\mathbf{R}_+$.

Proof.

a. Laplace transforms are completely monotone functions by (J3).

b. Let f be completely monotone on $]0,\infty[$. Let $f(0):=f(0+)$. This limit exists and it is finite because f is decreasing and bounded on $]0,\infty[$. Let g_n $(n=1,2,...)$ be the function with values $g_n(s):=f(n-ns)$ $(0\leq s\leq 1)$. Then $g_n^{(k)}(s)\geq 0$ $(0<s<1)$. Hence, g_n is absolutely monotone on $]0,1[$. Then g_n is absolutely monotone on $[0,1[$ by App.H.Th.H7. By App.H.Th.H6, g_n has a power series expansion on $[0,1[$ with positive coefficients. We notice that $\lim_{s\uparrow 1} g_n(s)=f(0)<\infty$. Hence, g_n is the generating function of a bounded distribution on $\mathbf{N}_+$. Then $g_n(e^{-s})$ $(s\geq 0)$ is the Laplace transform of this distribution by (J6). Then $\lambda_n(s):=g_n(e^{-s/n})= f(n-ne^{-s/n})$ $(s\geq 0)$ is the Laplace transform of some bounded distribution F_n on $\mathbf{R}_+$ by (J5) and $F_n(\mathbf{R})=\lambda_n(0)=f(0)$, where we may assume that $f(0)>0$ (because otherwise $f\equiv 0$). Then $\lambda_n/f(0)$ is the Laplace transform of a probability distribution on $\mathbf{R}_+$. Let $s>0$. Then

$$n-ne^{-s/n} = n-n[1-s/n+s^2/(2!n^2)-s^3/(3!n^3)\ ...] = s-s^2/(2!n)+... \to s \ \text{ as } n\uparrow\infty$$

and $\lambda_n(s)/f(0)=f(n-ne^{-s/n})/f(0)\to f(s)/f(0)$ as $n\uparrow\infty$, because f is continuous. By Th.J2.b, $f/f(0)$ is the Laplace transform of a probability distribution on $\mathbf{R}_+$ •

Appendix K

Sums, Integrals, Interpolations and Asymptotic Values

K1. Indefinite Integrals

Let P(x) be a complex polynomial and $a \neq 0$ a complex number. Then

$$\int P(x)e^{-ax}dx = -e^{-ax}[P(x)/a + P'(x)/a^2 + P''(x)/a^3 + \ldots], \qquad \text{(K1)}$$

where the number of terms in the sum in square brackets is finite. Indeed, the differentiation of the last member furnishes the integrand of the first member.

Hereafter P(x) is a real polynomial, i is the unit of imaginaries and $a,b \in \mathbf{R}$. By (K1),

$$\int P(x)[\cos(ax)+i\sin(ax)]dx = \int P(x)e^{iax}dx = \int P(x)e^{-(a/i)x}dx$$

$$= -e^{iax}(i\,P(x)/a + i^2P'(x)/a^2 + i^3P''(x)/a^3 + i^4P'''(x)/a^4 + \ldots)$$

$$= -[\cos(ax)+i\sin(ax)][i\,P(x)/a - P'(x)/a^2 - i\,P''(x)/a^3 + P'''(x)/a^4 + \ldots].$$

Hence, identifying the real and the imaginary parts,

$$\int P(x)\sin(ax)dx \qquad \text{(K2)}$$

$$= [-\cos(ax)P(x)/a + \sin(ax)P'(x)/a^2 + \cos(ax)P''(x)/a^3 - \sin(ax)P'''(x)/a^4$$
$$-\cos(ax)P^{(4)}(x)/a^5 + \sin(ax)P^{(5)}(x)/a^6 + \cos(ax)P^{(6)}(x)/a^7 - \sin(ax)P^{(7)}(x)/a^8 \ldots].$$

$$\int P(x)\cos(ax)dx \qquad \text{(K3)}$$

$$= [+\sin(ax)P(x)/a + \cos(ax)P'(x)/a^2 - \sin(ax)P''(x)/a^3 - \cos(ax)P'''(x)/a^4$$
$$+\sin(ax)P^{(4)}(x)/a^5 - \cos(ax)P^{(5)}(x)/a^6 - \sin(ax)P^{(6)}(x)/a^7 - \cos(ax)P^{(7)}(x)/a^8 \ldots].$$

Similarly, the indefinite integral of any simple function (as defined in Ch.8.2.1) can be obtained by (K1). For instance,

$$\int P(x)e^{-ax}[\cos(bx)+i\sin(bx)]dx = \int P(x)e^{-ax}e^{ibx}dx = \int P(x)e^{-(a-ib)x}dx$$

$$= -e^{-(a-ib)x}[(a-ib)^{-1}P(x) + (a-ib)^{-2}P'(x) + (a-ib)^{-3}P''(x) \ldots]$$

$$= -e^{-ax}[\cos(bx)+i\sin(bx)]$$

$$\times[(a+ib)(a^2+b^2)^{-1}P(x) + (a+ib)^2(a^2+b^2)^{-2}P'(x) + (a+ib)^3(a^2+b^2)^{-3}P''(x) \ldots].$$

Hence,

$$\int P(x)e^{-ax}\cos(bx)dx = -e^{-ax}\sum_{k\geq 0} c_k(x)P^{(k)}(x)$$

and

$$\int P(x)e^{-ax}\sin(bx)dx = -e^{-ax}\sum_{k\geq 0} s_k(x)P^{(k)}(x),$$

where $c_k(x)$ and $is_k(x)$ is the real part and the imaginary part resp. of

$$[\cos(bx)+i\sin(bx)](a+ib)^{k+1}/(a^2+b^2)^{k+1}.$$

Explicitly,

$$\int P(x)e^{-ax}\cos(bx)dx \tag{K4}$$

$$= -e^{-ax}[(a\cos(bx) - b\sin(bx))(a^2+b^2)^{-1}P(x)$$
$$+ ((a^2-b^2)\cos(bx)-2ab\sin(bx))(a^2+b^2)^{-2}P'(x)$$
$$+ ((a^3-3ab^2)\cos(bx)-(3a^2b-b^3)\sin(bx))(a^2+b^2)^{-3}P''(x) \ldots],$$

$$\int P(x)e^{-ax}\sin(bx)dx \tag{K5}$$

$$= -e^{-ax}[(a\sin(bx) + b\cos(bx))(a^2+b^2)^{-1}P(x)$$
$$+ ((a^2-b^2)\sin(bx) + 2ab\cos(bx))(a^2+b^2)^{-2}P'(x)$$
$$+ ((a^3-3ab^2)\sin(bx) + (3a^2b\text{-}b^3)\cos(bx))(a^2+b^2)^{-3}P''(x) \ldots].$$

The foregoing formulas are valid for functions P which are not polynomials, if the involved series are convergent and if they can be differentiated termwise.

K2. Definite Integrals

Theorem K1 (Definition and Properties of Gamma Function)

Let

$$\mathbf{\Gamma(a) := \int_{[0,\infty[} x^{a-1}e^{-x}dx \ \ (a>0).} \tag{K6}$$

a.

$$\mathbf{\Gamma(n) = (n-1)!\ \ (n-1 \in N_+).} \tag{K7}$$

b.

$$\mathbf{\Gamma(a+1) = a\Gamma(a)\ \ (a>0).} \tag{K8}$$

c.

$$\mathbf{\Gamma(1/2) = \int_{]-\infty,+\infty[} e^{-x^2}dx = \pi^{1/2}.} \tag{K9}$$

Proof

a. By (K1),

$$\Gamma(n) = \int_{[0,\infty[} x^{n-1}e^{-x}dx$$

$$= [-e^{-x}(x^{n-1}+(n-1)x^{n-2}+\ldots+(n-1)(n-2)\ldots3.2\,x + (n-1)(n-2)\ldots2.1)]_0^{\infty} = (n-1)!.$$

b. By an integration by parts,

$$\Gamma(a+1)= \int_{]0,\infty[} x^a e^{-x}dx = -\int_{]0,\infty[} x^a de^{-x}= \int_{]0,\infty[} e^{-x}dx^a = a \int_{]0,\infty[} x^{a-1}e^{-x}dx = a\Gamma(a).$$

c.

$$\int_{]-\infty,+\infty[} e^{-x^2}dx = 2\int_{[0,\infty[} e^{-x^2}dx = \int_{[0,\infty[} y^{-1/2}e^{-y}dy = \int_{[0,\infty[} y^{(1/2)-1}e^{-y}dy = \Gamma(1/2),$$

by substitution, with the new integration variable $y=x^2$. This proves the first equality (K9). The last equality (K9) results from App.G.(G4) •

The **gamma distribution with parameters a,b>0** is the probability distribution with density

$$c\, x^{a-1}e^{-bx} \quad (x\in \mathbf{R}_+). \tag{K10}$$

Then

$$1 = c \int_{[0,\infty[} x^{a-1}e^{-bx}dx = (c/b^a) \int_{[0,\infty[} (bx)^{a-1}e^{-bx}d(bx)$$

$$= (c/b^a) \int_{[0,\infty[} y^{a-1}e^{-y}dy = c\Gamma(a)/b^a.$$

Hence,

$$c = b^a/\Gamma(a). \tag{K11}$$

The definition of the **standardized normal distribution** is based on (K9). See App.G.G8.c.

Theorem K2 (Definition and Properties of Beta Function)

Let

$$\boldsymbol{\beta(a,b) := \int_{[0,1]} x^{a-1}(1-x)^{b-1}dx \quad (a,b>0).} \tag{K12}$$

a.

$$\boldsymbol{\beta(a,b) = \Gamma(a)\Gamma(b)/\Gamma(a+b) \quad (a,b>0).} \tag{K13}$$

b.

$$\boldsymbol{\int_{[0,\infty[} y^{a-1}(1+y)^{-(a+b)}dy = \beta(a,b) \quad (a,b>0).} \tag{K14}$$

Proof

a.

$$\Gamma(a)\Gamma(b) = \int_{x\in[0,\infty[} \int_{y\in[0,\infty[} x^{a-1}e^{-x}y^{b-1}e^{-y}dxdy.$$

In the inner integral, we replace the integration variable y by z=x+y and then we apply Fubini (case of positive integrands):

$$\Gamma(a)\Gamma(b) = \int_{x\in[0,\infty[}\int_{z\in[x,\infty[} x^{a-1}(z-x)^{b-1}e^{-z}dxdz = \int_{z\in[0,\infty[}\int_{x\in[0,z]} x^{a-1}(z-x)^{b-1}e^{-z}dxdz.$$

In the inner integral of the last member, we replace the integration variable x by y related to x by z−x=zy. Hence,

$$\Gamma(a)\Gamma(b) = \int_{z\in[0,\infty[}\int_{y\in[0,1]} z^{a-1}(1-y)^{a-1}z^{b-1}y^{b-1}e^{-z}zdydz$$

$$= \int_{[0,\infty[} z^{a+b-1}e^{-z}dz.\int_{[0,1]}y^{b-1}(1-y)^{a-1}dy = \Gamma(a+b)\beta(b,a) = \Gamma(a+b)\beta(a,b).$$

b. Results from the substitution x=y/(1+y) in the last member of (K12) •

The **beta distribution with parameters a,b>0** is the probability distribution with density

$$c\, x^{a-1}(1-x)^{b-1} \quad (0\le x\le 1). \tag{K15}$$

Snedecor's distribution with parameters a,b>0 is the probability distribution with density

$$c\, x^{a-1}(1+x)^{-(a+b)} \quad (x\in\mathbf{R}_+). \tag{K16}$$

By (K12) and (K14),

$$c = 1/\beta(a,b) = \Gamma(a+b)/[\Gamma(a)\Gamma(b)] \tag{K17}$$

in (K15) and (K16).

K3. Sums

$$e^{\lambda} = \sum_{k\ge 0} \lambda^k/k! \quad (\lambda\ge 0). \tag{K18}$$

The **Poisson distribution with parameter $\lambda\ge 0$** is the discrete probability distribution with masses

$$c\, \lambda^k/k! \quad (k=0,1,2,\dots). \tag{K19}$$

By (K18), $c=e^{-\lambda}$.

$$(p+q)^n = \sum_{0\le k\le n} n^{[k]}/k!\; p^k q^{n-k}. \tag{K20}$$

The **binomial distribution with parameters $p\in[0,1]$ and $n\in\mathbf{N}_+$** is the discrete probability distribution with masses

$$n^{[k]}/k!\ p^k(1-p)^{n-k} \quad (k=0,1,2,...,n). \qquad \text{(K21)}$$

$$(1-p)^{-(1+a)} = \sum_{k\geq 0} (a+k)^{[k]}/k!\ p^k \ (1+a>0,\ 0\leq p<1). \qquad \text{(K22)}$$

The **negative binomial distribution with parameters $p\in[0,1[$ and $a>-1$** is the discrete probability distribution with masses

$$c\ (a+k)^{[k]}/k!\ p^k \quad (k=0,1,2,...). \qquad \text{(K23)}$$

By (K22),

$$c = (1-p)^{1+a}. \qquad \text{(K24)}$$

$$(1-p)^{-1} = \sum_{k\geq 0} p^k \quad (0\leq p<1). \qquad \text{(K25)}$$

The **geometric distribution with parameter $p\in[0,1[$** is the discrete probability distribution with masses

$$cp^k \quad (k=0,1,2,...) \qquad \text{(K26)}$$

By (K25), $c=1-p$. This geometric distribution is the negative binomial distribution with parameters $p\in[0,1[$ and $a=0$.

K4. Polynomial Interpolation

The **elementary Euler-Maclaurin expansion for polynomials f** is the formula

$$\int_{[0,h]} f(x)dx = b_{-1}hf(0) + b_0h[f]_0^h + b_1h^2[f']_0^h + b_2h^3[f'']_0^h ..., \qquad \text{(K27)}$$

where the number of terms in the last member is finite. By linearity, it is satisfied for all polynomials iff it is satisfied for the particular polynomials 1, x, x^2, ... Hence, the coefficients b_{-1}, b_0, b_1, ..., result from relations

$$\begin{aligned}
1 &= b_{-1},\\
1/2 &= b_0,\\
1/3 &= b_0 + 2b_1,\\
1/4 &= b_0 + 3b_1 + 6b_2,\\
1/5 &= b_0 + 4b_1 + 12b_2 + 24b_3,\\
&\cdots\cdots
\end{aligned}$$

Then

$$\mathbf{b_{-1} = 1\ ,\ b_0 = 1/2\ ,\ b_1 = -1/12\ ,\ b_2 = 0,}$$

$$\mathbf{b_3 = 1/720\ ,\ b_4 = 0\ ,\ b_5 = -1/30240\ ,\ b_6 = 0}\ ,\ ... \qquad \text{(K28)}$$

(K27) and its consequences, are used for functions f which are not polynomials Then the last member of each formula is an approximation of the first one.

By a translation, (K27) implies

$$\int_{[a,a+h]} f(x)dx = hf(a) + 1/2\, h[f]_a^{a+h} + \sum_{s\geq 1} b_s h^{s+1}[f^{(s)}]_a^{a+h} \qquad \text{(K29)}$$

because f(a+x) is a polynomial if f(x) is one. This relation can be displayed as

$$\int_{[a,a+h]} f(x)dx = hf(a+h) - 1/2\, h[f]_a^{a+h} + \sum_{s\geq 1} b_s h^{s+1}[f^{(s)}]_a^{a+h}. \qquad \text{(K30)}$$

Let $\delta := h/n$ ($n\in \mathbf{N}_{++}$) and let us consider the partition of [a,a+h] in n sub-intervals $[a+k\delta, a+(k+1)\delta]$ ($k=0,1,\ldots,n-1$) of same length δ.

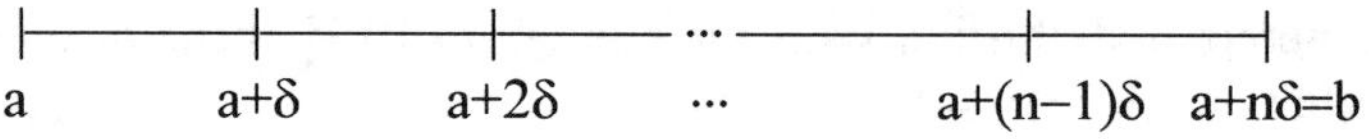

Then (K29) and (K30) imply the following summation formulas:

$$\boldsymbol{\delta \sum_{0\leq k\leq n-1} f(a+k\delta)} \qquad \text{(K31)}$$

$$\boldsymbol{= hf(a) + h(n-1)/(2n)\, [f]_a^{a+h} + \sum_{s\geq 1} b_s h^{s+1}[(n^{s+1}-1)/n^{s+1}]\, [f^{(s)}]_a^{a+h},}$$

$$\boldsymbol{\delta \sum_{1\leq k\leq n} f(a+k\delta)} \qquad \text{(K32)}$$

$$\boldsymbol{= hf(a+h) - h(n-1)/(2n)\, [f]_a^{a+h} + \sum_{s\geq 1} b_s h^{s+1}[(n^{s+1}-1)/n^{s+1}]\, [f^{(s)}]_a^{a+h}.}$$

Indeed,

$$\int_{[a,a+h]} f(x)dx = \sum_{0\leq k\leq n-1} \int_{[a+k\delta,a+(k+1)\delta]} f(x)dx$$

$$= \delta \sum_{0\leq k\leq n-1} f(a+k\delta) + 1/2\, \delta[f]_a^{a+h} + \sum_{s\geq 1} b_s \delta^{s+1}[f^{(s)}]_a^{a+h}, \qquad \text{(K33)}$$

by the application of (K29) to the intervals $[a+k\delta, a+(k+1)\delta]$. Hence, (K33) equals the last member of (K29). This proves (K31). The proof of (K32) is similar.

As an illustration of (K32), we notice the formula

$$\sum_{1\leq k\leq n} k^r = 1/2\, n^r + 1/2\, n^{r+1} + \sum_{1\leq s\leq r-1} r^{[s]} b_s (n^{r+1} - n^{r-s}), \qquad \text{(K34)}$$

used in Part II.Ch.3.8.1, corresponding to the case $f(x)=x^r$, $a=0$, $h=n$, $\delta=1$.

We now consider the partition of an interval [a,b] in m sub-intervals of same length $h:=(b-a)/m$. We apply (K29) to the sub-intervals $[a+jh, a+(j+1)h]$ ($j=0,1,\ldots,m-1$) and then we add up. We obtain

$$\int_{[a,b]} \mathbf{f(x)dx = h[1/2f(a)+\sum_{1\leq j\leq m-1}f(a+jh)+1/2f(b)]+\sum_{s\geq 1}b_s h^{s+1}[f^{(s)}]_a^{\,b}}. \quad (K35)$$

In this relation, f may represent different polynomials on different intervals [a+jh,a+(j+1)h], but we assume that

$$f^{(s)}(a+kh+) = f^{(s)}(a+kh-) \ (k=1,2,...,m-1;\ s=0,1,...,r-1)$$

if the degree of f is r (because we use relations such as $[g]_\alpha^{\beta}+[g]_\beta^{\gamma}=[g]_\alpha^{\gamma}$). (K35) is the **Euler-Maclaurin expansion for functions which are polynomials on the sub-intervals [a+jh,a+(j+1)h]**. The most important case is the linear one, corresponding to polynomials f of degree 1 on the sub-intervals. Then the sum $\sum_s$ disappears in (K35) and this relations is a strict equality if f is continuous on [a,b] and linear on the sub-intervals [a+jh,a+(j+1)h]. It is an approximation if f does not have these properties. Then its meaning is the following in the linear case: f is interpolated linearly on the sub-intervals [a+jh,a+(j+1)h] and the last member results from this interpolation. (K35) is used as **numerical integration formula**. It is the **trapezoid rule** in the linear case.

K5. Exponential Least-Squares Interpolation

Let $f_{abc}(x)=a+be^{c\varphi(x)}$, where a,b,c are unknown parameters and φ a fixed function. We look for the function f_{abc} which graph is closest to the points $(a_1,b_1),...,(a_n,b_n)$ in the usual cartesian plane. More precisely, we want to find the triplet (a,b,c) minimizing

$$Q(a,b,c) = \sum_{1\leq k\leq n} w_k[f_{abc}(a_k)-b_k]^2 = \sum_{1\leq k\leq n} w_k[a+be^{c\varphi(a_k)}-b_k]^2,$$

where $w_1,...,w_n$ are fixed weights. Then (a,b,c) must be such that

$$\partial/\partial a\ Q(a,b,c) = 2\sum w_k[a+be^{c\varphi(a_k)}-b_k] = 0,$$

$$\partial/\partial b\ Q(a,b,c) = 2\sum w_k e^{c\varphi(a_k)}\,[a+be^{c\varphi(a_k)}-b_k] = 0,$$

$$\partial/\partial c\ Q(a,b,c) = 2\sum w_k b\varphi(a_k)e^{c\varphi(a_k)}\,[a+be^{c\varphi(a_k)}-b_k] = 0,$$

where all sums $\sum$ are sums $\sum_{1\leq k\leq n}$. Hence,

$$a\sum w_k + b\sum w_k e^{c\varphi(a_k)} = \sum w_k b_k\ ,\ a\sum w_k e^{c\varphi(a_k)} + b\sum w_k e^{2c\varphi(a_k)} = \sum w_k e^{c\varphi(a_k)}b_k,$$

$$a\sum w_k\varphi(a_k)e^{c\varphi(a_k)} + b\sum w_k\varphi(a_k)e^{2c\varphi(a_k)} = \sum w_k\varphi(a_k)e^{c\varphi(a_k)}b_k,$$

i.e.

$$aS_1 + bS_2 = S_3\ ,\ aS_2+bS_4 = S_5\ ,\ aS_6 + bS_7 = S_8, \qquad \text{(K36)}$$

where $S_1,S_2,\dots,S_8$ are the obvious sums (depending on c). Then

$$a = (S_3S_4-S_2S_5)/(S_1S_4-S_2S_2)\quad ,\quad b = (S_1S_5-S_2S_3)/(S_1S_4-S_2S_2),$$

by the first relations (K36). The substitution of these expressions in the last relation (K36) furnishes an equation for parameter c.

K6. Asymptotic Formulas

We recall that

$$[f(x) \sim g(x) \text{ as } x{\downarrow}p] :\Leftrightarrow [\lim_{x\downarrow p,} f(x)/g(x) = 1],$$

$$[\varphi(n) \sim \gamma(n) \text{ as } n{\uparrow}\infty] :\Leftrightarrow [\lim_{n\uparrow\infty} \varphi(n)/\gamma(n) = 1].$$

Let f be a function on $[p,q[$ where q may be $+\infty$. We say that **p is a strict minimum point of f on [p,q[** if an interval $[p,p+\delta]$ with $\delta>0$ exists in $[p,q[$ so that f is continuous, strictly increasing on $[p,p+\delta]$ and $f(p+\delta)\leq\inf_{x\in[p+\delta,q[} f(x)$. Then $[p,p+\delta]$ is a **regular minimum interval of f**. Of course, if $[p,p+\delta]$ is a regular minimum interval and $0<\delta'<\delta$, then $[p,p+\delta']$ is a regular minimum interval. If p is a strict minimum point, then p is a global minimum point of f.

As a negative example, we consider the function xe^{-x} on $[0,\infty[$. Then 0 is a global minimum point. It is not a strict minimum point because $\lim_{x\uparrow\infty} xe^{-x}$ is not strictly positive: for all $\delta>0$, a large value x_δ exists such that $f(x_\delta)<f(\delta)$.

Theorem K3

Let p be a strict minimum point of the function f on [p,q[and let $f(x)-f(p) \sim a.(x-p)^b$ as $x{\downarrow}p$, where $a,b>0$. Let φ be a function on [p,q[such that $\varphi(x) \sim \alpha.(x-p)^{\beta-1}$ as $x{\downarrow}p$, where $\alpha,\beta>0$. Let the function φe^{-f} be integrable on [p,q[. Then φe^{-nf} (n=1,2,...) is integrable on [p,q[and

$$\int_{[p,q[} \varphi(x)e^{-nf(x)}dx \sim (\alpha/b)\Gamma(\beta/b)(an)^{-\beta/b}e^{-nf(p)} =: \gamma(n) \text{ as } n{\uparrow}\infty. \qquad \text{(K37)}$$

Proof

Let $\varepsilon\in]0,1[$. Let $[p,p+\delta]$ be a regular minimum interval of f such that

$$f(p)+(1-\varepsilon)a(x-p)^b \leq f(x) \leq f(p)+(1+\varepsilon)a(x-p)^b \ \ (p\leq x\leq p+\delta), \qquad \text{(K38)}$$

$$(1-\varepsilon)\alpha(x-p)^{\beta-1} \le \varphi(x) \le (1+\varepsilon)\alpha(x-p)^{\beta-1} \quad (p\le x\le p+\delta). \tag{K39}$$

Then $f(p+\delta)\le f(x)$ $(p+\delta\le x\le q)$ and

$$\int_{[p+\delta,q[} |\varphi(x))|e^{-nf(x)}dx = \int_{[p+\delta,q[} |\varphi(x)|e^{-f(x)}\, e^{-(n-1)f(x)}\, dx$$
$$\le \int_{[p+\delta,q[} |\varphi(x)|e^{-f(x)}\, e^{-(n-1)f(p+\delta)}\, dx \;= c_1\, e^{-(n-1)f(p+\delta)} < \infty. \tag{K40}$$

($c_1,c_2\ldots$ are finite constants). Hence, φe^{-nf} is integrable on $[p+\delta,q[$. By (K39), φ is positive and integrable on $[p,p+\delta]$ Then $\varphi e^{-n[f-f(p)]}$ $(\le\varphi)$ and then also φe^{-nf} are integrable on that interval. Hence, φe^{-nf} is integrable on $[p,q[$.

Let $[p+\delta',q[$ be a regular minimum interval of f with $\delta'<\delta$. Then $f(x)\le f(p+\delta')$ $<f(p+\delta)$, $(p\le x\le p+\delta')$, $\varphi(x)\ge 0$ $(p\le x\le\delta)$ and

$$\int_{[p,p+\delta]} \varphi(x)e^{-nf(x)}dx \ge \int_{[p,p+\delta']} \varphi(x)e^{-nf(x)}dx \ge \int_{[p,p+\delta']} \varphi(x)e^{-nf(p+\delta')}dx = c_2\, e^{-nf(p+\delta')}.$$

Then by (K40),

$$\left|\int_{[p+\delta,q[} \varphi(x)e^{-nf(x)}dx\right| / \left[\int_{[p,p+\delta]} \varphi(x)e^{-nf(x)}dx\right]$$
$$\le \left[\int_{[p+\delta,q[} |\varphi(x)|e^{-nf(x)}dx\right] / \left[\int_{[p,p+\delta]} \varphi(x)e^{-nf(x)}dx\right] \le [c_1\, e^{-(n-1)f(p+\delta)}]/[c_2\, e^{-nf(p+\delta')}]$$
$$= c_3\, e^{-n[f(p+\delta)-f(p+\delta')]} \to 0 \text{ as } n\uparrow\infty$$

and this implies that

$$\left[\int_{[p,q[} \varphi(x)e^{-nf(x)}dx\right] / \left[\int_{[p,p+\delta]} \varphi(x)e^{-nf(x)}dx\right] \to 1 \text{ as } n\uparrow\infty. \tag{K41}$$

By (K38) and (K39) (apply $e^{-n(\cdot)}$ to (K38), multiply by (K39) and integrate),

$$(1-\varepsilon)\alpha\, e^{-nf(p)} \int_{[p,p+\delta]} (x-p)^{\beta-1} \exp[-n(1+\varepsilon)a(x-p)^b]dx \le \int_{[p,p+\delta]} \varphi(x)\, e^{-nf(x)}dx$$
$$\le (1+\varepsilon)\alpha\, e^{-nf(p)} \int_{[p,p+\delta]} (x-p)^{\beta-1} \exp[-n(1-\varepsilon)a(x-p)^b]dx. \tag{K42}$$

The first integral of (K42) equals

$$\int_{[p,p+\delta]} (x-p)^{\beta-1} \exp[-n(1+\varepsilon)a(x-p)^b]dx = \int_{[0,\delta]} x^{\beta-1} \exp[-n(1+\varepsilon)ax^b]dx =$$
$$1/_b\, [n(1+\varepsilon)a]^{-\beta/b} \int_{[0,n(1+\varepsilon)a\delta^b]} y^{(\beta/b)-1}\, e^{-y}\, dy \sim 1/_b\, [n(1+\varepsilon)a]^{-\beta/b}\Gamma(\beta/b)$$
$$= (1+\varepsilon)^{-\beta/b}\, \alpha^{-1}\, e^{nf(p)}\, \gamma(n) \text{ as } n\uparrow\infty$$

by the substitution $y=n(1+\varepsilon)ax^b$. Hence, dividing the first inequality of (K42) by $\gamma(n)$ and taking $\limsup_{n\uparrow\infty}$,

$$(1-\varepsilon)(1+\varepsilon)^{-\beta/b} \le \limsup_{n\uparrow\infty} 1/_{\gamma(n)} \int_{[p,p+\delta]} \varphi(x)e^{-nf(x)}dx. \tag{K43}$$

Similarly, the last inequality of (K42) implies that

$$\limsup_{n\uparrow\infty} 1/\gamma(n) \int_{[p,p+\delta]} \varphi(x)e^{-nf(x)}dx \leq (1+\varepsilon)(1-\varepsilon)^{-\beta/b}. \qquad \text{(K44)}$$

By (K41), relations (K43) and (K44) remain valid if the integration domain [p,p+δ] is replaced by [p,q[. Hence,

$$(1-\varepsilon)(1+\varepsilon)^{-\beta/b} \leq \limsup_{n\uparrow\infty} 1/\gamma(n) \int_{[p,q[} e^{-nf(x)]}dx \leq (1+\varepsilon)(1-\varepsilon)^{-\beta/b}.$$

As $\varepsilon\downarrow 0$:

$$\limsup_{n\uparrow\infty} 1/\gamma(n) \int_{[p,q[} e^{-nf(x)]}dx = 1.$$

In this argument, lim sup may be replaced by lim inf everywhere •

When β and b are integers, Theorem K3 has an obvious version for integrals $\int_{]p,q]} \varphi(x)e^{-nf(x)}dx$ in case the right extremity q of]p,q] is a strict minimum point of f on]p,q] (obvious definition). The latter is called the **right-minimum version of Theorem K3**. Then, by a partition of the integration domain, functions f with strict minimum point (obvious definition) in the interior of that domain can also be treated.

As an illustration, we find an asymptotic expression for n! as $n\uparrow\infty$. By (K6), (K7) and by the replacement of x by nx,

$$n! = \int_{]0,\infty[} x^n e^{-x}dx = n^{n+1} \int_{]0,\infty[} x^n e^{-nx}dx = n^{n+1} \int_{]0,\infty[} e^{-nf(x)}dx = n^{n+1}[I_1(n)+I_2(n)],$$

where

$$f(x) := x-\log x\,,\; I_1(n) := \int_{]0,1]} e^{-nf(x)}dx\,,\; I_2(n) := \int_{]1,\infty[} e^{-nf(x)}dx.$$

f is a concave function on]0,∞[with strict minimum point x=1. Moreover,

$$f(x)-f(1) = x-1-\log[1-(1-x)] = x-1+(1-x)+1/2(1-x)^2+1/3(1-x)^3+\ldots$$

Hence, $f(x)-f(1)\sim 1/2(1-x)^2$ as $x\downarrow 1$. By Theorem K3 with α=β=1, a=1/2, b=2 and by (K9)

$$I_2(n) \sim 1/2\, \Gamma(1/2)(1/2n)^{-1/2}e^{-n} = 1/2\, (2\pi)^{1/2}\, n^{-1/2}e^{-n}.$$

By the right-minimum version of Theorem K3, $I_1(n)$ has the same asymptotic value as $I_2(n)$. Hence

$$\mathbf{n! \sim (2\pi)^{1/2}\, n^{n+(1/2)}e^{-n} \;\; as\; n\uparrow\infty.} \qquad \text{(K45)}$$

This is **Stirling's formula**.

References

Part I

Chapter 1. Basic Analysis, Convolutions and Renewal Equations. Feller (1966), Neveu (1964), Williams (1991), Loève (1955), Bauer (1981).

Chapter 2. Conditional Expectations. Meyer (1966), Williams (1991).

Chapter 3. Risk Models. Gerber (1979), Bühlmann (1970), Seal (1969), Cramér (1958), Taylor (1980), Asmussen (1994).

Chapter 4. Point Processes. De Vylder (1972), De Vylder (1977_2), De Vylder et.al. (1980), Haezendonck et al. (1980), Lundberg (1964), Snyder (1975), Bühlmann (1970), Feller (1960), Feller (1966), Sundt (1991).

Chapter 5. Fixed-Time Ruin Probabilities. Beard et al. (1969), Panjer (1981), Straub (1988). The basic Th. 3 results from a communication (unpublished ?) by the late Prof. J. Haezendonck.

Chapter 6. Finite-Time Ruin Probabilities. De Vylder (1977_3), Gerber (1973), Gerber (1979), De Vylder (1977_4), Takacs (1967).

Chapter 7. Infinite-Time Ruin Probabilies in the Classical Risk Model. Gerber (1979), Bühlmann (1970), Straub (1988), Seal (1969), Sundt (1991), Feller (1966), Taylor (1976), De Vylder et al. (1984), De Vylder (1978_1), Beekman (1974), Bowers et al. (1986), Shiu (1988), Athreya et al. (1972), Chistyakov (1964), Embrechts et al. (1982).

Chapter 8. Explicit Infinite-Time Ruin Probabilities in the Classical Risk Model. De Vylder (1978_2), De Vylder et al. (1995), Segerdahl (1959).

Chapter 9. Infinite-Time Ruin Probabilities in Risk Models with Stochastic Premium Income. Gerber (1979), De Vylder et al. (1994), Harrison (1977), Taylor (1980), Delbaen et al. (1987), Asmussen (1994), Asmussen et al. (to be published).

Chapter 10. Discrete Risk Models. Gerber (1988), De Vylder et al. (1994), De Vylder et al. (Submitted).

Part II

Chapter 1. The Basic Tools. Ioffe et al. (1979), Ekeland et al. (1976), De Vylder et al. (1984).

Chapter 2. General Probability Distribution Spaces. De Vylder (1982), De Vylder (1983_1), De Vylder (1983_2).

Chapter 3. Pure Moment Spaces. Bellman (1960), De Vylder (1982).

Chapter 4. Unimodal Moment Spaces. De Vylder (1982), De Vylder (1983_1), De Vylder (1983_2).

Chapter 5. Linear Programming and Matrix Games. Ioffe et al. (1979), Karlin (1959), Vajda (1956), von Neumann (1928), von Neumann et al. (1953), Vorob'ev (1977).

Chapter 6. Integral Optimization Problems. Taylor (1977), De Vylder (1982_1), De Vylder (1983_1), De Vylder (1983_2), De Vylder et al (1984).

Chapter 7. Duals of Integral Optimization Problems. De Vylder (1982), De Vylder (1983_1), De Vylder (1983_2), De Vylder et al (1984).

Chapter 8. Moment Problems by the Dual Method. Borel (1947), De Vylder (1982), De Vylder (1983_1), De Vylder (1983_2), De Vylder et al (1984), Jansen (1986).

Chapter 9. Stop-Loss Problems by the Dual Method. Bowers (1969), Gagliardi et al. (1974), Bühlmann (1974), Bühlmann et al. (1977), Heilmann (1980), De Vylder et al. (1982_1), De Vylder et al. (1982_2), De Vylder et al. (1983), De Vylder et al. (1983), Mack (1984), Mack (1985), Jansen (1986).

Chapter 10. General Optimization Problems. De Vylder (1996), Ekeland et al. (1976), Ioffe et al. (1979).

Chapter 11. Loaded Premium Problems. Gerber (1979), Goovaerts et al. (1984).

Chapter 12. Ruin Problems. Brockett et al. (1991), Kaas (1991), De Vylder et al. (submitted), De Vylder (1996), De Vylder et al. (1996_1), De Vylder et al. (1996_2), Marceau (1996).

Part III

Chapter 1. Projections in Hilbert Space. Dunford et al. (1957), De Vito (1990), De Vylder (1976).

Chapter 2. Elementary Classical Statistical Models. De Vylder (1976), De Vylder et al. (1992_2), De Vylder et al (1993).

Chapter 3. Time-Homogeneous Credibility Theory. Whitney (1918), Bailey (1945), Bühlmann (1967), Bühlmann (1969), Bühlmann et al. (1970), Bühlmann (1970), Straub (1975), Straub (1988), Taylor (1974), Taylor (1979), Jewell (1974), Jewell (1975_2), Jewell (1976), Jewell (1980), Kahn (1975), Sundt (1979), Sundt (1983_1), Sundt (1983_2), Sundt (1991), Gerber (1979), Gerber (1982), Gerber et al. (1975), Gisler (1980_1), Gisler (1980_2), Dubey et al. (1981), Bichsel et al. (unpublished), Beard et al. (1968), De Vylder (1976_1), De Vylder (1976_2), De Vylder (1977_2), De Vylder et al. (1979), De Vylder (1980), De Vylder et al. (1984), De Vylder et al. (1992_1), De Vylder et al (1992_3), De Vylder et al. (1993), Goovaerts et al (1987).

Chapter 4. Hilbert Spaces of Random Vectors and Random Matrices. De Vylder et al (1992_3).

Chapter 5. Classical Regression Models. Graybill (1961), De Vylder et al. (1992_2).

Chapter 6. Credibility Regression Models. Hachemeister (1975), Jewell (1976), Sundt (1979), De Vylder (1981), De Vylder et al. (1982), De Vylder (1985), De Vylder et al (1992_3).

Chapter 7. Introduction to IBNR-Reserves. De Vylder (1978_3), De Vylder (1982_2), Mack (1990), Goovaerts et al. (1990).

App.A. Continuous Renewal Theorems on $\mathbf{R}_+$. Feller (1966), Prabhu (1965).

App.B. Discrete Renewal Theorems on $\mathbf{N}_+$. Feller (1966), Prabhu (1965).

App.C. Convex Analysis on $\mathbf{R}^n$. Ioffe et al. (1979), Ekeland et al. (1976).

App.D. Matrices. Bellman (1960), Doob (1952).

App.E. Krein-Milman Theorem for Spaces of Distribution Functions. Robertson et al. (1964), Dunford et al. (1957), Karlin (1959).

App.F. Dunford et al. (1957), De Vito (1990).

App.G. Characteristic Functions. Cramér (158), Bauer (1981), Loève (1955), Feller (1966).

App.H. Generating Functions. Feller (1966), Widder (1946).

App.I. Moment Functions. Feller (1966), Widder (1946), Borel (1947).

App.J. Laplace Transforms. Feller (1966), Widder (1946), Mikusinski (1959).

App.K. Sums, Integrals, Interpolations and Asymptotic values. Dieudonné (1968).

Abbreviations

ARAB:	Bulletin de l'Association Royale des Actuaires Belges
ASTIN:	ASTIN Bulletin. A Journal of the International Actuarial Association
Blätter:	Blätter der Deutsche Gesellschaft für Versicherungsmathematiker
IME:	Insurance: Mathematics and Economics (North-Holland)
Mitteilungen:	Mitteilungen der Vereinigung Schweizerischer Versicherungsmathematiker
SAJ:	Scandinavian Actuarial Journal

Books and Articles

1. Abikhalil F. (1986). Finite Time Ruin Problems for Perturbed Experience Rating and Connection with Discounting Risk Models. *ASTIN 16, 1, 33-44*
2. Ajne B., Wide H. (1987). On the Definition of Catastrophe Claims and the Calculation of Their Expected Cost for the Purpose of Long Range Planning and Profit Centre Control. *ASTIN 17, 2, 171-178*
3. Albrecht P. (1983). Parametric Multiple Regression Risk Models: Theory and Statistical Analysis. *IME 2, 1, 49-66*

4. Albrecht P. (1983). Parametric Multiple Regression Risk Models: Some Connection With IBNR. *IME 2, 2, 69-74*
5. Albrecht P. (1983). Parametric Multiple Regression Risk Models: Connection with Tarification, Especially in Motor Insurance. *IME 2, 2, 113-118*
6. Ambagaspitiya R.S., Balakrishnan N. (1994). On the Compound Generalized Poisson Distribution. *ASTIN 24, 2, 255-26*
7. Asmussen S. (1994). *Ruin Probabilities* World Scientific Publ. Co, Singapore
8. Asmussen S., Nielsen H.M. (to be published). Ruin Probabilities via Local adjustment Coefficients
9. Asmussen S., Rolski T. (1992). Computational Methods in Risk Theory: A Matrix-Algorithmic Approach. *IME 10, 4, 259-274*
10. Athreya K.,B., Ney P. (1972). *Branching Processes.* Springer-Verlag
11. Babier J., Chan B. (1992). Approximations of Ruin Probabilities by Di-Atomic or Di-Exponential Claims. *ASTIN 22, 2, 235-246*
12. Bailey A.L. (1945). A Generalized Theory of Credibility. *Proceedings of the Casulaty Actuarial Society 32, 13-20*
13. Bauer H. (1981). *Probability Theory and Elements of Measure Theory.* Academic Press
14. Beard R.E., Pentikaïnen T., Pesonen E.(1968). *Risk Theory.* Methuen
15. Beekman J. (1974). *Two Stochastic Processes.* Halsted Press. New York
16. Beekman J.A. (1985). A Series for Infinite Time Ruin Probabilities. *IME 4, 2, 129-134*
17. Bellman R. (1960). *Introduction to Matrix Analysis.* McGraw-Hill
18. Berliner B. (1977). A Risk Measure Alternative to the Variance. *ASTIN 9, 7, 42-58*
19. Bertram J. (1981). Numerische Berechnung von Gesamtschadenverteilungen. *Blätter, 175-194*
20. Besson J.L., Partrat C. (1992). Trend et Systèmes de Bonus-Malus. *ASTIN 22, 1, 11-32*
21. Beyer D., Riedel M. (1993). Remarks on the Swiss Premium Principle on Positive Risks. *IME* 13, 1, 39-44
22. Bichsel F., Straub E. (unpublished). Erfahrungstarifierung in der Kollektif-Krankenversicherung. *Intern note of the Swiss-Re*
23. Boogaert P., De Waegenaere A. (1990). Simulation of Ruin Probabilities. *IME 9, 2/3, 95-100*
24. Boogaert P., Haezendonck J. (1989). Delay in Claim Settlement. *IME 8, 4, 321-330*
25. Borel E. (1947). *Principes et Formules Classiques du Calcul des Probabilités.* Gauthier-Villars. Paris
26. Bowers N.L. (1969) An Upper Bound on the Stop-loss Net Premium. *Transactions of the Society of Actuaries 21*
27. Bowers N.L., Gerber H.U., Hickman J.C., Jones D.A., Nesbitt C.J. (1986). *Actuarial Mathematics.* Society of Actuaries. Itasca, Illinois
28. Boyle P.P., Mao J. (1982). Optimal Risk Retention Under Partial Insurance. *IME 1, 1, 19-26*
29. Brockett P., Goovaerts M., Taylor G. (1991). The Schmitter's Problem. *ASTIN 21, 1, 129-132*
30. Broeckx F., Goovaerts M., De Vylder F. (1986). Ordering of Risks and Ruin Probabilities. *IME 5, 1, 35-40*
31. Browne S. (1990). Maximizing the Expected Time to Ruin for a Company Operating N Distinct Funds With a 'Superclaim' Process. *IME 9, 1, 33-38*
32. Bühlmann H. (1964). Optimale Prämienstufensysteme. *Mitteilungen 64, 2, 193-214*
33. Bühlmann H. (1967). Experience Rating and Credibility. *ASTIN 4, 3, 199-207*
34. Bühlmann H. (1969). Experience Rating and Credibility. *ASTIN 5, 2, 157-165*

35. Bühlmann H. (1970). *Mathematical Methods in Risk Theory*. Springer-Verlag.
36. Bühlmann H. (1974). Ein Anderer Beweis für die Stop-Loss-Ungleichung in der Arbeit Gagliardi/Straub. *Mitteilungen 74, 2, 284-285*
37. Bühlmann H. (1980). An Economic Premium Principle. *ASTIN 11, 1, 52-60*
38. Bühlmann H., Jewell W.S. (1987). Crédibilité Hiérarchique. *ARAB 81, 43-59*
39. Bühlmann H., Straub E. (1970). Glaubwürdigkeit für Schadensätze. *Mitteilungen, 70, 1, 111-133.*
40. Bühlmann H., Gagliardi B., Gerber H., Straub E. (1977). Some Inequalities for Stop-Loss Premiums. *ASTIN 9, 1, 75-83*
41. Carriere J. (1993). A Semi-Parametric Estimator of a Risk Distribution. *IME 13, 1, 75-82*
42. Centeno de Lourdes M. (1986). Measuring the Effects of Reinsurance by the Adjustment Coefficient. *IME 5, 2, 169-182*
43. Centeno de Lourdes M. (1989). The Bühlmann-Straub Model With Premium Calculated According to the Variance Principle. *IME 8, 1, 3-10*
44. Chan B. (1982). Recursive Formulas for Discrete Distributions. *IME 1, 4, 241-244*
45. Chan L.K., Panjer H. (1983). A Statistical Approach to Graduation by Mathematical Formula. *IME 2, 1, 33-48*
46. Chan F.Y. (1984). On a Family of Aggregate Claims Distributions. *IME 3, 3, 151-156*
47. Chistyakov V.P. (1964). A Theorem on Sums of Independent Random Variables and its Applications to Branching Processes. *Th. Prob. Appl. 9,640-648*
48. Cossette H. (1996). *Dependent Contracts in Credibility Models and Parameter Estimation*. Doct. Thesis I.A.G. Catholic University of Louvain-la-Neuve
49. Covens F., Van Wouwe M., Goovaerts M. (1979). On the Numerical Evaluation of Stop-Loss Premiums. *ASTIN 10, 3, 318-324*
50. Cramér H. (1958). *Mathematical Methods of Statistics*. Princeton University Press.
51. Croux K., Veraverbeke N. (1990). Nonparametric Estimators for the Probability of Ruin. *IME 9, 2/3, 127-130*
52. Dannenburg D. (1994). Some Results on The Estimation of the Credibility Factor in the Classical Bühlmann Model. *IME 14, 1, 39-50*
53. De Groot R. (1979). *Ongelijkheden voor Stop-Loss Premiums Gebaseerd op E.-T. Systemen in het Kader van de Veralgemeende Convexe Analyse*. Doct. Thesis, Fac. Econ. en Toeg. Econ. Wetenschappen. K.U.Leuven
54. De Groot R., Goovaerts M. (1980). On an Extension of Some Stop-Loss Inequalities Based on Convex Analysis. *Transactions of the 21th International Congres of Actuaries. Zurich-Lausanne, 169-177*
55. de Jong P., Zehnwirth B. (1983). Credibility Theory and the Kalman Filter. *IME 2, 4,281-286*
56. Delbaen F. (1990). A Remark on the Moments of Ruin in Classical Risk Theory. *IME 9, 2/3, 121-126*
57. Delbaen F., Haezendonck J (1987). Classical Risk Theory in an Economic Environment. *IME 6, 2, 85-116*
58. De Meerleer D. (1992). *Pratique des Assurances et des Réassurances*. Lecture notes. Catholic University of Louvain-la-Neuve, I.A.G. Départ. Sciences Actuarielles.
59. De Pril N., Goovaerts M. (1983). Bounds for the Optimal Critical Claimsize of a Bonus System. *IME 2, 1, 27-32*
60. De Pril N. (1985). Recursions for the Convolutions of Arithmetic Distributions. *ASTIN 15, 2, 135-139*

61. De Pril N. (1989). The Aggregate Claim Distribution in the Individual Model with Arbitrary Positive Claims. *ASTIN 19, 1, 9-24*
62. De Vito C.L. (1990). *Functional Analysis and Linear Operator Theory*. Addison-Wesley
63. De Vylder F. (1972). Processus Stochastiques Discontinus Elementaires. *ARAB 72, 39-63*
64. De Vylder F. (1976_1). Optimal Semilinear Credibility. *Mitteilungen 76, 1, 27-40*
65. De Vylder F. (1976_2). Geometrical Credibility. *SAJ 76, 121-149*
66. De Vylder F. (1977_1). Iterative Credibility. *Mitteilungen 77, 1, 25-34*
67. De Vylder F. (1977_2). Le Développement Récent de la Théorie de la Crédibilité. *ARAB 72, 54-75*
68. De Vylder F. (1977_3). A new Proof for a known Result in Risk Theory. *Journal of Computational and Applied Math.3, 4, 277-279*
69. De Vylder F. (1977_4). Martingales and Ruin in a Dynamical Risk Process. *SAJ 21. 217-225*
70. De Vylder F. (1978_1). A Practical Solution to the Problem of Ultimate Ruin Probability. *SAJ 114-119*
71. De Vylder F. (1978_2). A Class of Very Regular Distribution Functions and Corresponding Ruin Probabilities. *SAJ 177-181*
72. De Vylder F. (1978_3). Estimation of I.B.N.R. Claims by Least-Squares. *Mitteilungen 78, 2, 249-254*
73. De Vylder F. (1980). Time-Homogeneous Models in Credibility Theory. *Oberwolfach Conference on Risk Theory, October 1980. Not published*
74. De Vylder F. (1981). Regression Model with Scalar Credibility Weights. *Mitteilungen 1, 27-39*
75. De Vylder F. (1982_1). Best Upper Bounds for Integrals with Respect to Measures Allowed to Vary under Conical and Integral Constraints.*IME 1, 2, 109-130*
76. De Vylder F. (1982_2). Estimation of IBNR Claims by Credibility Theory. *IME 1, 1, 35-40*
77. De Vylder F. (1983_1). Maximization, under Equality Constraints, of a Functional of a Probability Distribution. *IME 2, 1, 1-16*
78. De Vylder F. (1983_2). Bounds on Integrals. Elimination of the Dual and Reduction of the Number of Equality Constraints. *IME 2, 3, 139-145*
79. De Vylder F. (1985). Non-Linear Regression in Credibility Theory. *IME 4, 3, 163-172*
80. De Vylder F. (1989). Compound and Mixed Distributions. *IME 8, 1, 57-62*
81. De Vylder F., Marceau E. (1996). The Solution of Schmitter's Simple Problem: Theory. *IME (forthcoming)*
82. De Vylder F, Ballegeer Y. (1979). A Numerical Illustration of Optimal Semilinear Credibility. *ASTIN 10, 2, 131-148*
83. De Vylder F., Cossette H. (1994). Dependent Contracts in Bühlmann's Credibility Model. *Mitteilungen 2, 127-142*
84. De Vylder F., Goovaerts M. (1982_1). Upper and Lower Bounds on Stop-Loss Premiums in Case of Known Expectation and Variance of the Risk Variable. *Mitteilungen 1, 149-164*
85. De Vylder F., Goovaerts M. (1982_2). Analytic Best Upper Bounds for Stop-Loss Premiums. *IME 1, 3, 197-212*
86. De Vylder F., Goovaerts M. (1983). Best Bounds on the Stop-Loss Premium in Case of Known Range, Expectation, Variance and Mode of the Risk. *IME 2, 4, 241-249*

87. De Vylder F., Goovaerts M. (1984) The Structure of the Distribution of a Couple of Observable Random Variables in Credibility Theory. *IME 3, 3, 179-188*
88. De Vylder F., Goovaerts M. (1984). Bounds for Classical Ruin Probabilities. *IME 3, 2, 121-131*
89. De Vylder F., Goovaerts M. (1985). Semilinear Credibility with Several Approximating Functions. *IME 4, 3, 155-162*
90. De Vylder F, Goovaerts M. (1992_1). Estimation of the Heterogeneity Parameter in the Bühlmann-Straub Credibility Theory Model. *IME 10, 4, 233-238*
91. De Vylder F., Goovaerts M. (1992_2). Optimal Parameter Estimation under Zero-Excess Assumptions in a Classical Model. *IME 11, 1, 1-6*
92. De Vylder F., Goovaerts M. (1992_3). A Summary of New Results on Optimal Parameter Estimation under Zero-Excess Assumptions. *IME 11, 2, 153-161*
93. De Vylder F., Goovaerts M. (1993). Estimation de la Variance dans un Modèle Classique, si les Coefficients d'Aplatissement des Variables sont Connus. *Revue de Statistique Appliquée, XLI(3),5-20*
94. De Vylder F., Goovaerts M. (1994). A Note on the Solution of Practical Ruin Problems. *IME 15, 2/3, 181-186*
95. De Vylder F., Haezendonck J. (1980). Explosions in Random Point Processes. *SAJ 195-202*
96. De Vylder F., Marceau E. (1996). Classical Numerical Ruin Probabilities. *SAJ (forthcoming)*
97. De Vylder F., Marceau E. (1995). Explicit Analytic Ruin Probabilities for Bounded Claims. *IME 16, 1, 79-105*
98. De Vylder F., Marceau E. (submitted). Schmitter's Problem: Existence and Atomicity of the Extremals. *ASTIN*
99. De Vylder F., Sundt B. (1982). Constrained Credibility Estimators in the Regression Model. *SAJ 23-37*
100. De Vylder F., Goovaerts M., Marceau E. (1996_1). The Solution of Schmitter's simple problem: Numerical Illustration. *IME (forthcoming)*
101. De Vylder F, Goovaerts M., Marceau E. (1996_2). The Bi-Atomic Uniform Extremal Solution of Schmitter's Problem. *IME (forthcoming)*
102. De Vylder F., Goovaerts M., De Pril N. (1982). Bounds on Modified Stop-Loss Premiums in Case of Known Mean and Variance of the Risk Variable. *ASTIN 13, 1, 25-35*
103. De Vylder F., Goovaerts M., Haezendonck J., Garrido J. (1984). Bornes pour Espérances sous des Contraintes d'Egalité. *ARAB 84, 29-44*
104. Dhaene J., De Pril N. (1994). On a Class of Approximative Computation Methods in the Individual Risk Model. *IME 14, 2, 181-196*
105. Dhaene J., Vandebroek M. (1995). Recursions for the Individual Model. *IME 16, 1, 31-38*
106. Dickson D.C.M. (1993). On the Distribution of the Claim Causing Ruin. *IME 12, 2, 143-154*
107. Dickson D.C.M., dos Reis A.E. (1994). Ruin Problems and Dual Events. *IME 14, 1, 51-60*
108. Dieudonné J. (1968). *Calcul Infinitésimal.* Hermann, Paris
109. Doob J.L. (1952). *Stochastic Processes.* Wiley
110. Dubey A., Gisler A. (1981). On Parameter Estimation in Credibility *Mitteilungen 2, 187-212*

111. Dufresne F., Gerber H.U. (1991). Rational Ruin Problems- A Note for the Teacher. *IME 10, 1, 21-30*
112. Dufresne F., Gerber H.U. (1991). Risk Theory for the Compound Poisson Process That is Perturbed by Diffusion. *IME 10, 1, 51-60*
113. Dufresne F., Gerber H.U. (1993). The Probability of Ruin for the Inverse Gaussian and Related Processes. *IME 12, 1, 9-22*
114. Dunford N., Schwartz J.T. (1957) *Linear Operators*. Part I. Interscience
115. Eichenauer J., Lehn J., Rettig S. (1988). A Gamma-Minimax Result in Credibility Theory. *IME 7, 1, 49-58*
116. Ekeland I., Temam R. (1976). *Convex Analysis and Variational Problems*. North-Holland
117. Embrechts P., Veraverbeke N. (1982). Estimates for the Probability of Ruin with Special Emphasis on the Possibility of large Claims. *IME 1, 1, 55-72*
118. Embrechts P., Mikosch T. (1991). A Bootstrap Procedure for Estimating the Adjustment Coefficient. *IME 10, 3, 181-190*
119. Ettl W. (1983). Recursive Formulas for Compound Distributions by Laplace Transformation Methods. *XVIIth ASTIN Colloquium, Lindau*
120. Feller W. (1960). *An Introduction to Probability Theory and Its Applications*. Vol 1. Wiley
121. Feller W. (1966). *An Introduction to Probability Theory and Its Applications*. Vol 2. Wiley
122. Frees E.W. (1986). Nonparametric Estimation of the Probability of Ruin. *ASTIN 16, S, S81-S90*
123. Gagliardi B, Straub E. (1974). Ein Obere Grenz für Stop-Loss Premie *Mitteilungen 74, 1, 47-58*
124. Garrido J. (1988). Diffusion Premiums for Claim Severities Subject to Inflation. *IME 7, 2, 123-130*
125. Gendron M., Crépeau H. (1989). On the Computation of the Aggregate Claim Distribution When Individual Claims Are Inverse Gaussian. *IME 8, 3, 251-258*
126. Gerber H. (1973). Martingales in Risk Theory. *Mitteilungen, 73, 2. 205-216*
127. Gerber H. (1974_1). On Additive Premium Calculation Principles. *ASTIN 7, 3, 215-222*
128. Gerber H. (1974_2). On Iterative Premium Calculation Principles. *Mitte.lungen 74, 2, 163-172*
129. Gerber H. (1975). The surplus Process as a fair Game-Utilitywise.*ASTIN 8, 3. 307-322*
130. Gerber H.(1979). *An Introduction to Mathematical Risk Theory*. Huebner Foundation. University of Pennsylvania
131. Gerber H. (1982). An Unbayesed Approach to Credibility. *IME 1, 4, 271-276*
132. Gerber H. (1988). Mathematical Fun with Ruin Theory. *IME 7, 1, 15-23*
133. Gerber H. (1992). On the Probability of Ruin for Infinitely Divisible Claim Amount Distributions. *IME 11, 2, 163-166*
134. Gerber H., Goovaerts M. (1981). On the Representation of Additive Principles of Premium Calculation. *SAJ 221-227*
135. Gerber H., Jones D.A. (1975). Credibility Formulas of the Uptading Type. In Kahn (1975). *Credibilty, 89-105*
136. Gilde V., Sundt B. (1989). On Bonus Systems With Credibility Scales. *SAJ 13-22*
137. Gisler A. (1980_1). *Optimales Stutzen von Beobachtungen in Credibility-Modell.* Doctoral Dissertation ETH n° 6556, Zürich

138. Gisler A. (1980_2). Optimum Trimming of Data in the Credibility Model. *Mitteilungen 3, 313-325*
139. Gisler A., Reinhard P. (1993). Robust Credibility. *ASTIN 23, 1, 117-143*
140. Glemser H. (1994). *Credibility-Theorie und Abhängigkeitsannahmen.* Doct. Thesis n° 10868 ETH, Zürich
141. Graybill F.A. (1961). *An Introduction to Linear Statistical Models.* Mc Graw-Hill
142. Grenander U. (Editor) (1959). *The Harald Cramér Volume.* Probability and Statistics. Almqvist & Wiksell, Wiley
143. Gogol D. (1993). Using Expected Loss Ratios in Reserving. *IME 12, 3, 297-300*
144. Goovaerts M., De Vylder F. (1979). A Note on Iterative Premium Calculation Principles. *ASTIN 10, 3, 326-329*
145. Goovaerts M., De Vylder F. (1980_1). Premium Calculation Principles: Some Properties. *Het Verzekeringsarchief 57, 1, 5-13*
146. Goovaerts M., De Vylder F. (1980_2). A Note on Additive Premium Calculation Principles. *ARAB 74, 89-93*
147. Goovaerts M., Hoogstad W. (1987). *Credibility Theory.* Surveys of Actuarial Studies n° 4, Nationale Nederlanden
148. Goovaerts M., De Vylder F., Haezendonck J. (1986). *Insurance Premiums.* North-Holland
149. Goovaerts M., Kaas R., van Heerwaerden A., Bauwelinckx T. (1990). *Effective Actuarial Methods.* North-Holland
150. Hachemeister C.A. (1975). Credibility for Regression Models with Application to Trend. In Kahn (1975), *129-163*
151. Haddi N. (1985). A Note on De Vylder's Method of Estimation of IBNR Claims. *IME 4, 4, 263-266*
152. Haezendonck J., De Vylder F. (1980). A Comparison Criterion for Explosions in Point Processes. *J. Appl. Prob. 17, 1102-1107*
153. Haezendonck J., Goovaerts M. (1982). Premium Calculation Principles and Orlicz Spaces. *IME 1,1,41-54*
154. Haezendonck J., De Vylder F., Delbaen F. (1984). Representation Theorems for Extremal Distributions. *IME 3, 3, 195-200*
155. Hallin M., Ingenbleek J.F. (1981). Etude Statistique de la Probabilbité de Sinistre en Assurance Automobile. *ASTIN 12, 1, 40-56*
156. Heijnen B. (1990). Best Upper and Lower Bounds on Modified Stop-Loss Premiums in Case of Known Range, Mode, Mean and Variance of the Original Risk. *IME 9, 2/3, 207-220*
157. Heilmann W.-R. (1980). Improved Methods for Calculating and Estimating Maximal Stop-Loss Premiums. *Blätter 1980, 21-49*
158. Heilmann W.-R. (1988). *Fundamentals in Risk Theory.* VVW Karlsruhe
159. Heilman W.-R. (1989). Decision Theoretic Foundations of Credibility Theory. *IME 8, 1, 77-96*
160. Hesselager O. (1988). On the Asymptotic Distribution of Weighted Least Squares. *SAJ 69-76*
161. Hipp C. (1985). Approximation of Aggregate Claims Distribution by Compound Poisson Distributions. *IME 4, 4, 227-232*
162. Hogg R.V., Klugman S.A. (1984). *Loss Distributions.* Wiley
163. Hossack I.B., Pollard J.H., Zehnwirth B. (1983). *Introductory Statistics with Applications in General Insurance.* Cambridge University Press

164. Hürlimann W. (1988). Simple Risk Forecasts Using Credibility. *IME 7, 4, 251-260*
165. Ioffe A.D., Tihomirov V.M. (1979). *Theory of Extremal Problems.* North-Holland
166. Jansen K. (1986). Upper Bounds on Stop-Loss Premiums in case of known moments up to the Fourth Order. *Doct. Thesis. Antwerpen. Univ. Instelling*
167. Janssen J. (1982). Détermination de la Valeur de la Probabilité de Ruine avec une Réserve Initiale Nulle pour le Modèle de Risque Semi-Markovien. *Mitteilungen 2, 275-284*
168. Janssen J., De Dominicis R. (1984). Finite Non-Homogeneous Semi-Markov Processes. Theoretical and Computational Aspects. *IME 3, 3,157-166*
169. Janssen J., Reinhard J.M. (1985). Probabilités de Ruine pour une Classe de Modèles de Risque Semi-Markoviens. *ASTIN 15, 2, 123-135*
170. Jewell W.S. (1973). Multidimensional Credibility. *Research Report 73-7. Operations Research Center. Berkeley*
171. Jewell W.S. (1974). Credible Means are exact Bayesian for Expnential Families. *ASTIN 8, 1, 77-90*
172. Jewell W.S. (1975_1). The Use of Collateral Data in Credibility Theory: A Hierarchical Model. *Research Memorandum 75-24. International Institute for Applied Systems Analysis.Laxenburg*
173. Jewell W.S. (1975_2). Model Variations in Credibility Theory. In Kahn (1975). *193-244*
174. Jewell W.S. (1976). A Survey of Credibility Theory. *Research Report 76-31. Operations Resarch Center. Berkeley*
175. Jewell W.S. (1980). Models in Insurance:Paradigms, Puzzles, Communications and Revolutions. *Transactions of the 22nd International Congres of Actuaries. S87-S141*
176. Kremer E. (1982). Exponential Smoothing and Credibility Theory. *IME 1, 3, 213-218*
177. Kaas R. (1991). The Schmitter Problem and a Related Problem: A Partial Solution. *ASTIN 21, 1, 133-146*
178. Kaas R., Goovaerts M., Bauwelinckx T. (1986). Some Elementary Stop-Loss Inequalities. *Mitteilungen 2, 225-229*
179. Kaas R., Van Heerwaerden A., Goovaerts M. (1988_1). On Stop-Loss Premiums for the Individual Model. *ASTIN 18, 1, 91-98*
180. Kaas R., Van Heerwaerden A., Goovaerts M. (1988_2). Between Individual and Collective Model for the Total Claims. *ASTIN 18, 2, 169-174*
181. Kahn P.M. (Editor) (1975). *Credibility. Theory and Applications* Acadmic Press
182. Karlin S. (1959). *Mathematical Methods and Theory in Games, Programming and Economics.* Addison-Westley
183. Klugman S. (1990). Credibility for Increasing Limits. *IME 9, 2/3, 77-80*
184. Klüppelberg C. (1989). Estimation of Ruin Probabilities by Means of Hazard Rates. *IME 8, 4, 279-286*
185. Künsch H.R. (1992). Robust Methods for Credibility. *ASTIN 22, 1, 33-50*
186. Lemaire J. (1985). *Automobile Insurance. Actuarial Models.* Kluwer-Nijhoff Publishing Co
187. Loève M. (1955). *Probability Theory.* Van Nostrand
188. Lundberg O. (1964). *On Random Processes and their Applications to Sickness and Accident Statistics.* Almqvist & Wiksell
189. Mack T. (1984). Calculation of the Maximum Stop-Loss Premium, Given the Three First Moments. *Proc. of the 4 Countires Astin-Symposion 1984*
190. Mack T. (1985). Berechnung der Maximalen Stop-Loss-Prämie wenn die Ersten Drei Momente der Schadenverteilung Gegeben Sind. *Mitteilungen 1, 39-56*

191. Mack T. (1990). Improved Estimation of IBNR Claims by Credibility Theory. *IME 9, 1, 51-58*
192. Mammitzsch V. (1986). A Note on the Adjustment Coefficient in Ruin Theory. *IME 5, 2, 147-150*
193. Marceau E. (1996). *Classical Risk Theory and Schmitter's Problems.* Doct. Thesis I.A.G. Catholic University of Louvain-la-Neuve
194. Meyer P.A. (1966). *Probabilités et Potentiel.* Hermann
195. Meyers G., Beekman J.A. (1987). An Improvement to the Convolution Method of Calculating Ψ(u). *IME 6, 4, 267-274*
196. Michel R. (1989). Representation of Time-Discrete Probability of Eventual Ruin. *IME 8, 2, 149-152*
197. Mikusinski J. (1959). *Operational Calculus.* Pergamon Press
198. Nakamura M., Pérez-Abreu V. (1993). Empirical Probability Generating Function. An Overview. *IME 12, 3, 287-296*
199. Neuhaus W. (1988). A Bonus-Malus System in Automobile Insurance. *IME 7, 2, 103-110*
200. Neveu J. (1964). *Bases Mathématiques du Calcul des Probabilités.* Masson
201. Panjer H. (1981). Recursive Evaluation of a Family of Compound Distributions. *ASTIN, Vol 12, 1, 22-26*
202. Panjer H., Wilmott G.E. (1986). Computational Aspects of Recursive Evaluation of Compound Distributions. *IME 5, 1, 113-116*
203. Partrat C. (1994). Compound Model for Two Dependent Kinds of Claim. *IME 15, 2/3, 219-231*
204. Pellerey F. (1995). On the Preservation of Some Orderings of Risks Under Convolution *IME 16, 1, 23-30*
205. Pentikaïnen T. (1987). Approximative Evaluation of the Distribution Function of Aggregate Claims. *ASTIN 17, 1, 15-40*
206. Picard P. (1994). On Some Measures of the Severity of Ruin in the Classical Poisson Model. *IME 14, 2, 107-116*
207. Picard P., Lefèvre C. (1994). On the Crossing of the Surplus Process with a Given Upper Barrier. *IME 14, 2, 163-180*
208. Pitacco E. (1995). Actuarial Models for Pricing Disability Benefits:Towards a Unifying Approach. *IME 16, 1, 39-62*
209. Prabhu N.U. (1965). *Stochastic Processes.* Macmillan
210. Prémont A. (1993). *Inférence Statistique.* Lecture notes. Université Laval (Québec). Ecole d'Actuariat
211. Pressacco F. (1989). A Managerial Approach to Risk Theory: Some Suggestions From the Theory of Financial Decisions. *IME 8, 1, 47-56*
212. Promislow S.D. (1991). The Probability of Ruin in a Process With Independent Increments. *IME 10, 2, 99-108*
213. Ramsay C.M. (1990). On a Fundamental Identity for Stopping Times and Its Applications to Risk Theory. *IME 9, 2/3, 149-154*
214. Ramsay C.M. (1991). On Blocked Poisson Processes in Risk Theory. *IME 10, 1, 1-8*
215. Rantala J. (Editor) (1982). *Solvency of Insurers and Equalization Reserves. Vol I.* Insurance Publishing Company Ltd., Helsinki
216. Rantala J. (Editor) (1982). *Solvency of Insurers and Equalization Reserves. Vol II.* Insurance Publishing Company Ltd., Helsinki
217. Reich A. (1986). Properties of Premium Calculation Principles. *IME 5, 1, 97-102*

218. Renshaw A.E. (1994). Modelling the Claims Process in the Presence of Covariates. *ASTIN 24, 2, 265-286*
219. Robertson A.P., Robertson W (1964). *Topological Vector Spaces*. Cambridge University Press
220. Runnenburg J.T., Goovaerts M. (1985). Bounds on Compound Distributions and Stop-Loss Premiums. *IME 4, 4, 287-294*
221. Seal H.L.(1969). *Stochastic Theory of a Risk Business*. Wiley
222. Segerdahl C.O. (1959). A Survey of Results in the Collective Risk Theory. In Grenander (1959), *276-299*
223. Shiu E.S.W. (1988). Calculation of the Probability of Eventual Ruin by Beekman's Convolution Series. *IME 7, 1,42-48*
224. Shiu E.S.W. (1985). Moments of Two Distributions in Collective Risk Theory. *SAJ 185-187*
225. Snyder D.L. (1975). *Random Point Processes*. Wiley
226. Stanford D.A., Stroinski K.J. (1994). Recursive Methods for Computing Finite-Time Ruin Probabilities for Phase-Distributed Claim Sizes. *ASTIN 24, 2, 235-254*
227. Steenackers A., Goovaerts M. (1991). Bounds on Stop-Loss Premiums and Ruin Probabilities. *IME 10, 2, 153-160*
228. Stiers D., Goovaerts M., De Vylder F. (1985). Methoden ter Bepaling van Schadereserves. *Tijdschrift voor Economie en Management XXX, 1, 89-106*
229. Straub E. (1975). Credibility in Practice. In Kahn (1975), *347-359*
230. Straub E. (1988). *Non-Life Insurance Mathematics*. Spriger-Verlag
231. Straub E. (1992). Credibility Applications in Switzerland. *IME 11, 2, 109-112*
232. Sundt B. (1979_1). A Hierarchical Credibility Regression Model. *SAJ 25-32*
233. Sundt B. (1979_2). On Choice of Statistics in Credibility Estimation. *SAJ 115-123*
234. Sundt B. (1981). Recursive Credibility Estimation. *SAJ 3-21*
235. Sundt B. (1983_1) Finite Credibility Formulae in Evolutionary Models. *SAJ 106-116*
236. Sundt B (1983_2). Parameter Estimation in Some Credibility Models. *SAJ 239-255*
237. Sundt B. (1991) *An Introduction to Non-Life Insurance Mathematics*. VVW, Karlsruhe
238. Takacs L (1967). *Combinatorial Methods in the Theory of Stochastic Processes*. Wiley
239. Taylor G.C. (1974). Experience Rating with Credibility Adjustment of the Manual Premium. *ASTIN 7, 3, 323-336*
240. Taylor G.C.(1976). Use of differential and integral Inequalities to Bound Ruin and Queuing Probabilities. *SAJ 197-208*
241. Taylor G.C. (1977). Upper Bounds on Stop-Loss Premiums under Constraints on Claim Size Distribution. *SAJ 94-105*
242. Taylor G.C. (1979). Credibility Analysis of a General Hierarchical Model. *SAJ 1-1*
243. Taylor G.C. (1980). Probability of Ruin with Variable Premium Rate. *SAJ 57-76*
244. Taylor G.C. (1985). A Heuristic Review of Some Ruin Theory Results. *ASTIN 15, 2, 73-88*
245. Tremblay L. (1992). Using the Poisson Inverse Gaussian in Bonus-Malus Systems. *ASTIN 22, 1, 97-106*
246. Vajda S. (1956). *The Theory of Games and Linear Programming*. Methuen
247. Valderrama Ospina A., Gerber H.U. (1987). A Simple Proof of Feller's Characterization of the Compound Poisson Distributions. *IME 6, 1, 63-64*

248. Van Goethem P., Goovaerts M. (1977). Approximation Formulae for Compound Processes in Case of Claim Distributions Having Infinite Variance or Infinite Mean. *ARAB 72, 132-143*
249. Van Heerwaerden A., Kaas R., Goovaerts M. (1989). Optimal Reinsurance in Relation to Ordering of Risks. *IME 8, 1, 11-17*
250. Venter G. (1989). A Three-Way Credibility Approach to Loss Reserving. *IME 8, 1, 63-70*
251. Veraverbeke N. (1993). Asymptotic Estimates for the Probability of Ruin in a Poisson Model With Diffusion. *IME 13, 1, 57-62*
252. Verbeek H.G. (1977). A Stop-Loss Inequality for Compound Poisson Process with a Unimodal Claimsize Distribution. *ASTIN 9, 2, 247-256*
253. von Neumann J. (1928). Zur Theory der Gesellschaftsspiele. *Math. Annalen 100, 295-320*
254. von Neumann J., Morgenstern O. (1953). *Theory of Games and Economic Behavior.* Princeton University Press
255. Vorob'ev N.N. (1977). *Game Theory.* Springer-Verlag
256. Wang S. (1995). On Two-Sided Compound Binomial Distributions. *IME 17, 1, 35-42*
257. Wang S., Panjer H. (1993). Critical Starting Points for Stable Evaluation of Mixed Poisson Probabilities. *IME 13, 3, 287-298*
258. Wang S., Panjer H. (1994). Proportional Convergence and Tail-Cutting Techniques in Evaluating Aggregate Claim Distributions. *IME 14, 2, 129-138*
259. Waters H.R., Papatriandafilou A. (1985). Ruin Probabilities Allowing for Delays in Claims Settlement. *IME 4, 2, 113-123*
260. Weba M. (1993). Fitting a Parametric Distribution for Large Claims in Case of Censored or Partitioned Data. *IME 12, 2, 155-166*
261. Whitney A. (1918). *The Theory of Experience Rating.* Prentice-Hall
262. Widder D.V. (1946) *The Laplace Transform.* Princeton University Press
263. Williams D. (1991). *Probability with Martingales.* Cambridge University-Press
264. Wilmot G.E. (1993). Ruin Probabilities in the Compound Binomial Model. *IME 12, 2, 133-142*
265. Witting T. (1987). The Linear Markov Property in Credibility. *ASTIN 17, 1, 17-84*
266. Wolthuis H. (1994). Actuarial Equivalence. *IME 15, 2, 163-180*
267. Zehnwirth B. (1985). Linear Fitting and Recursive Credibility Estimation. *ASTIN 15, 1, 19-36.*

Subject Index